REASON AND CULTURE

An Introduction to Philosophy

Edited by

John Arthur
Amy Shapiro
William Throop

Prentice Hall

Upper Saddle River, New Jersey 07458

Library of Congress Cataloging-in-Publication Data

Reason and culture :   an introduction to philosophy/edited by
John Arthur, Amy Shapiro, William Throop.
    p. cm.
    ISBN 0-13-028566-8
    1. Ethics. 2. Science—Philosophy. 3. Religion—Philosophy.
    4. Philosophy—Introductions. I. Arthur, John (date) II. Shapiro, Amy (date) III. Throop, William.

BJ1012.R37 2001
001—dc 21   00-051502

VP/Editorial Director: Charlyce Jones Owen
Acquisitions Editor: Ross Miller
Assistant Editor: Katie Janssen
Editorial Assistant: Carla Worner
Senior Managing Editor: Jan Stephan
Production Liaison: Fran Russello
Project Manager: Linda B. Pawelchak
Prepress and Manufacturing Buyer: Sherry Lewis
Cover Director: Jayne Conte
Cover Design: Kiwi Design
Cover Image Credit: Frederic Edwin Church, "Rainy Season in the Tropics,"
    1866, oil on canvas, The Granger Collection.
Marketing Manager: Don Allmon

This book was set in 10/11 Janson Text by TSI Graphics, Inc.
and was printed and bound by RR Donnelley & Sons.
The cover was printed by Phoenix Color Corp.

© 2001 by Prentice-Hall, Inc.
A Division of Pearson Education
Upper Saddle River, New Jersey 07458

Printed in the United States of America
10   9   8   7   6   5   4   3   2   1

ISBN 0-13-028566-8

Prentice-Hall International (UK) Limited, *London*
Prentice-Hall of Australia Pty. Limited, *Sydney*
Prentice-Hall Canada Inc., *Toronto*
Prentice-Hall Hispanoamericana, S.A., *Mexico*
Prentice-Hall of India Private Limited, *New Delhi*
Prentice-Hall of Japan, Inc., *Tokyo*
Pearson Education Asia Pte. Ltd., *Singapore*
Editora Prentice-Hall do Brasil, Ltda., *Rio de Janeiro*

Contents

Preface

Philosophy has undergone important shifts in the last few decades. Perhaps the most striking change is that it has come to pay more attention to human practices. Less confident in its ability to offer a priori justifications or substantive critiques of the core beliefs of religion, morality, and science, philosophy now seeks to understand them in the context of human life generally as well as to evaluate their most basic claims.

Sensitive to the richness and detail of human social and cultural life, philosophy has thus become to some extent interpretive, taking human practices as given. Philosophy of religion attends more closely to actual religious practices, rituals, and language, while political philosophy and ethics are more sensitive to the workings of legal and political institutions. Much of this reflects both a new modesty and a new appreciation (following the later Wittgenstein) of the importance of language as used and practices as discovered.

Another implication of this shift is that the boundary between philosophy and other disciplines has become more porous and philosophy itself more interdisciplinary. Philosophers are more attuned to developments in cognate disciplines as well as to culture generally. Philosophy of mind closely follows research in cognitive science, philosophy of science is sensitive to the history of science and to developments in the natural sciences, and moral philosophy is often informed by moral psychology and anthropology.

Finally, some philosophers have embraced a Deweyian ideal of public philosophy. They focus more of their energy on issues of the day, and they explore a richer array of topics. Many areas of applied philosophy are flourishing.

We hope instructors will find this book useful in different contexts, mainly as an introductory text or in courses about values and so-ciety. Texts such as this ordinarily take one of two approaches. Some are primarily historical, while others treat the field as a series of problems or topics. Each of these approaches has its advantages and disadvantages. We believe that we have found a better way to introduce students to the discipline.

We have sought in this book to reflect philosophy's growing interest in practices by directing attention to the three practices of morality, science, and religion, and thus to the fact that they can be studied from the dual perspectives of reason and culture. We integrate historical figures because the history of philosophy is important, and students often enjoy reading major figures in Western thought. We also think that a course should be thematic and coherent, and perhaps most important, it should bring students into the discipline by showing its importance to their interests and concerns.

We chose morality, science, and religion carefully. All are infused with philosophical issues, arguments, and concepts. In our experience, students are interested in all three, often before they have taken any philosophy courses. As instructors we have found that these topics engage our students while also providing a good grounding for future work in the discipline. Indeed, we believe that everyone's life is fashioned in large measure from these three practices and so cannot be disentangled from the philosophical issues found in these readings.

With these objectives in mind, we have tried to provide an introductory text that maintains the critical, rational edge of traditional philosophical writing while at the same time incorporating a more interdisciplinary perspective that broadens the focus to include the interactions among the practices as well as their cultural implications. The book discusses each practice from three perspectives: the nature of the practice, its relation to culture, and the role reason plays in the practice.

The first collection of readings offers a variety of perspectives on the nature of the practice and then turns to the relationship between the practice and the problems of human meaning and purpose. Since students often come to philosophy through questions about how they should live and what their relationships are or should be with morality, religion, and science (in the form of technology or understanding the natural world), we begin discussing each practice by raising those questions.

The second part discusses the practice in relation to culture and explores some of the social issues arising out of the practice. These sections often involve topics that are not ordinarily covered in introductory classes and encourage students to think critically about the cultural and ethical ramifications of developments in ethics, science, and religion.

Finally, the third part, on reason, focuses on truth claims made in the practice. These readings address the nature and limits of such claims, their justification, and specific issues to which these claims give rise. Many traditional philosophical issues appear here, though sometimes in an unusual context. For example, issues in the philosophy of mind are explored in a section on the limits of scientific explanation, while free will is addressed alongside determinism and behavioral science. Problems related to justice and individual rights are discussed in the context of religious practice and the complex interplay among law, politics, and religion. In this way traditional philosophical problems are shown to emerge naturally, out of our participation in the three practices. We believe that by explicitly linking traditional issues to the practices of morality, science, and religion, we can show philosophical reflection to be a natural part of human life and social interaction.

A final note: Introductory philosophy courses often avoid issues in the philosophy of science, fearing that students may lack adequate scientific or philosophical background. We believe that this is a mistake. Science shapes human culture and informs much current philosophical debate. Thus, the impact of science on culture is a dominant theme of this text. Both classical and contemporary problems are woven into this theme: Is religious faith based on a prescientific picture of nature that no contemporary person can sustain? Does a materialistic conception of nature mean moral properties and values are superfluous to a complete understanding of the world? Does anthropology prove that values are relative or subjective? Should we limit scientific research on moral grounds? What are the implications for our lives and our self-understanding of biotechnology, such as human cloning?

We have tried hard to integrate the readings into a coherent whole, so that each of the three parts speaks to the others. The relationships among morality, science, and religion are explored throughout the book, in a variety of contexts. We have also sought to provide instructors with an unusual level of flexibility by enabling them to tailor the readings to their own needs while still maintaining an integrated, thematic course. It is possible, for example, to emphasize only one or two of the three practices, leaving aside the third except perhaps for the introductory sections discussing the nature of the practice itself. Another option is for an instructor to emphasize the "Reason" or the "Culture" sections throughout, using the other only as time and interest permit. More classically oriented instructors may wish to focus on reason; those more interested in culture studies can teach a very different course by emphasizing those sections.

Several people deserve special thanks for helping with the production of this book. Jennifer Oleszkowicz often worked overtime preparing the manuscript; without her efficient research and office work, it would not have been completed on time. Meriel Brooks cheerfully provided essential support for the project. We would like to thank our secretaries Jeanne Constable and Melanie Yawowski, for their tireless work on this and other projects. Thanks also to India Burnett-Holiday. And finally thanks go to Rebecca Haimowitz, for being such a great kid.

PART I

Morality, Science, and Religion

Introduction

We have chosen in this book to focus on three broad areas that deeply influence modern life: religion, science, and morality. Although not everyone, including the three of us, participates actively in each practice, we are all affected by the practices in many different ways. And, of course, the decision not to participate may itself have important implications. Thus, we believe that everyone can benefit from adopting a reasoned, thoughtful stance toward each of these practices, and we hope this book will help you do just that.

WHY THREE PRACTICES?

The discoveries in science and its practical twin, technology, have exploded in recent decades. This startling success, which reaches from biotechnology, medicine, and communication to space exploration and nuclear physics, raises a host of questions. So a central theme developed throughout the book is the challenge science poses to culture in general and religion and morality in particular. Is the scientific worldview compatible with religious faith? Can morality withstand the challenges posed by those who see science and scientific reasoning as the epitome of rational inquiry? What meaning can be assigned to human life in a universe indifferent to human hopes and values and without a larger purpose? Lying behind these questions is, of course, the nature of science itself, whether it is in fact uniquely able to explain the natural world, and whether religious or moral belief must inevitably conflict with science.

In addition to questions about science and its impact on religion and morality, this book explores other relationships among morality, religion, and culture, including the role of religion in politics and in education; the role of morality in markets, law, and art; and the potential dangers and advantages of scientific inquiry. Philosophically exploring these practices will give you a broad and systematic understanding of key forces in modern culture, an understanding that we believe will improve your ability to chart a meaningful and satisfying path in the world as an individual, a member of a community, and a citizen of the world.

Thinking of morality, science, and religion as practices has a number of advantages. First, it forces us to clarify what we are thinking about. We begin the discussion of each practice with a series of readings asking just what, exactly, morality, science, and religion are about and how they work. Practices include systems of beliefs and values, characteristic patterns of activity, and often, social institutions. Thus, by thinking in terms of practices, we enlarge the scope of concern beyond just asking what we should believe or what we should do and also try to understand what we *are* doing when we judge our own or others' actions, seek scientific understanding, or engage in religious ritual. We do not presume that these practices are merely cultural artifacts; indeed, questions of the meaningfulness, the truth, and the justification of claims made in these areas are left open by seeing them as practices. These issues are addressed later on, in the sections on reason.

After discussing the nature of the practices, we then ask how participation in morality, science, and religion is related to leading a good or successful life. Should we participate in the practice at all? Is the practice of value to us individually, or to society? Is it dangerous, as some have said of science? Or foolish, as some have said of religion?

After these initial discussions of the practice and its larger meaning for human life, we then look at the practice from the point of view of its impact on culture. Essays in the culture sections investigate the larger social, economic, and political implications of the practice. For instance, what is the role of morality in popular culture? In markets? In education? What are the practical and cultural implications of science and technology on our understanding of moral responsibility? On human reproduction and our conception of human nature? On our relationship with other creatures and the natural environment? What are the implications of the information age? Is religion socially useful or is it, on balance, harmful? What is religion's proper role in education? Should it be kept out of politics?

These sections introduce you to some of the classic readings in the history of philosophy, although sometimes in a nonstandard fashion. Thus, freedom and determinism are explored in the context of behavioral science; theories of justice and individual rights in the readings on religion and politics; and the nature of art in the context of popular culture and censorship. In each case, we think looking at a traditional text in a new way sheds light on both the subject and the text itself. We also include topics and approaches that are not ordinarily covered in introductory classes, such as work from other disciplines and culture studies. Thus, the book reflects the expanded boundaries of the discipline of philosophy.

After discussing the practice itself and some of its cultural implications, we turn to the role of reason in the practices. Here readings ponder questions such as the following: Are moral, scientific, or religious claims justified? In what sense might they be true or objective? Does truth matter? Are there limits on what each is able to understand about the universe? Should we participate in the practice even if its core claims are not true or able to be shown so? Although the reason sections cover some of the more familiar territory for introductory courses, they frame the material distinctively. We do not just ask disembodied questions about our knowledge of God or of morality; instead, we explore the validity of ways in which pervasive human practices have described their subject matter.

MORALITY

The practice of morality is woven into the fabric of our lives—both personal and social. Every time we react to other people and what they have done or might do with resentment or praise or anger, we are participating in the practice of morality. We also participate as we think about our own behavior. Are we proud of something we did, or do we feel bad and wish we had acted differently? Morality is also present when we think about whether our lives would be genuinely happier or more worthwhile if we continue in school, drop out to take a job, or join the Peace Corps. It also poses such questions as whether government may insist that the rich be taxed to help the poor or whether women may have an abortion, sell their bodies as prostitutes, or bear children for money as surrogates? Thus, voting and other forms of political participation are moral actions and require moral decisions. Indeed, it is hard even to imagine a human life outside of the practice of morality, that is, a life in which a person never evaluates, praises, criticizes, rewards, resents, punishes, blames, or feels guilt. It might be argued that the practice of morality actually constitutes—in an important sense—what we are as persons. Yet for all its pervasiveness and familiarity, our practice of morality raises a series of questions and problems to which philosophers have for centuries sought answers. Indeed those questions are unavoidable once one begins to think critically and step back from one's own cultural rules and inherited attitudes.

It may be helpful in thinking about morality to distinguish between two types of reason. If we think of theoretical reason as concerned with understanding and explaining how the natural world works, then science might be thought to be the place where that form of reason is most at home and most effective. But reasoning seems not to end with explaining nature and discovering its laws; we also reason when deciding about practical questions, asking "What should I do?" Often philosophers think of morality and moral practice as part of what is termed "practical reason."

We can broadly distinguish three areas of practical reason. First is prudential reasoning. Everybody does this. It involves evaluating different courses of action in the light of which one will give us the most effective or efficient means to our end. Suppose you want a sunny vacation that is not very expensive. Practical reasoning involves finding out which of many possible destinations is most likely to achieve your goals. The editors of this book live in upstate New York, and we can assure you that while visiting here would get you half of what you want (living here is relatively easy on a tight budget), it will not get you the rest (sunshine is in short supply during the winter). So practical reason in the prudential sense would counsel looking elsewhere; if you don't you would be irrational.

A second form of practical reason asks not what would be the most efficient means to achieve an objective but rather what we owe to one another. Thus, although pushing an old man down and taking his wallet could be prudent if you would not get caught or feel guilty later, it still seems unreasonable. Whether a thief wants to or not, there is good reason (some think) that he not take the man's wallet.

The third form of practical reason, different from rational prudence and reasonableness toward others, involves ourselves and what kind of life would be most successful for us. Should I pursue a career in law or education? Should I marry this person, whom I do not really respect but have lots of fun being around? If you know what you want and are asking these questions only in the prudential sense, then you are doing practical reasoning in the first sense. But suppose you are asking whether that sort of life is one that is worthy or valuable. Suppose, in other words, that your problem is not how to achieve the goals you have settled on but rather what goals would be worthwhile or valuable. The answer to such questions may be hard to discern and may vary from person to person. It may involve thinking about where your particular talents lie, for instance, as well as your history. Many will think that the best life for them has something to do with who they are in terms of their family, religious, cultural, or national background. Maybe carrying on the tradition of a family of lawyers matters, just as religious background may seem important to one person but not to another.

So the practice of morality seems to have two important features. First, it is pervasive—and importantly so. Human life is infused with decisions and emotions that are broadly moral in character. Second, morality seems to be a form of practical reason, that is, reasoning about what we ought to do. Our treatment of moral practice is divided into three parts. The first is the nature of the practice itself, and whether we have good reason to follow its rules and precepts. The next two consider morality's relationship with culture and with reason.

The Practice of Morality

In this part, the authors consider two questions: What is morality? And why should I (or anybody else) be moral when it is not to my advantage? As it turns out, there is deep disagreement about the nature of morality itself, beyond the obvious point that it involves evaluation of actions and policies. Selections in **"What Is Morality"** present three perspectives. One is that the practice of morality is like other rule-governed human practices, such as games or language. At base, it is a social practice that has its roots in the norms that a society follows and teaches. There is therefore no universal, objective point of view from which we can say that one set of moral attitudes and customs is true and another false. A second perspective, very different from this, believes that the practice of morality tracks an objective moral law, and furthermore that this law shows the underlying truth of theism. The third conception of moral practice, presented by Thomas Hobbes, sees morality as a practical solution arrived at by people who need to advance their own and their collective interests. It is a form of agreement we all make to forgo using force against one another in order that all can benefit.

The next section, **"Why Care About Morality?,"** discusses whether or not morality is a "fool's game" unless it coincides with a person's advantage. To act morally, in this view, is a kind of irrationality, whereas to act in one's own interest is smart, if not always popular. Thus, while it might be in one's interest to *appear* to be moral, it is never rational to *be* moral unless it serves self-interest. Embedded in this discussion is the related issue of whether it is even possible for people to act contrary to their own desires and interests.

Moral Practice and Culture

This part includes four sections, each discussing the role that the practice of morality plays in an important aspect of culture. Though the topics vary from film and painting to the college curriculum, work, and reproduction, two themes recur throughout the various essays. One is whether or not morality has a role to play at all. Some have argued, for example, that there are severe moral limits on what people should publish, produce as an artist, and sell or trade among themselves. Others argue that justice or some other feature of morality demands that people be left free to create, publish, and distribute whatever they want as long as they do not violate the rights of others.

A second, related question is more narrow. Suppose that a piece of popular culture—a film for instance—succeeds in glorifying and making beautiful an evil regime. How would that affect the aesthetic value of the work? **"Values in Popular Culture"** discusses that question. In this section, the authors use examples from *Triumph of the Will*, a brilliant and even beautiful propaganda film intended to glorify Nazism, and *The Man Who Shot Liberty Valance*, John Ford's classic western, which attacks feminine and religious values in favor of values emphasizing courage in the face of death. Among the questions discussed are whether the ideas these films represent undermine the artistic value of the film, whether evil content means viewers ought to refuse to watch them, and whether at its best art presents an argument or claim about how people should live.

This leads into the next section, **"Censorship and the Limits of Liberty,"** in which the focus is again on cultural forms of expression, with particular emphasis on censorship. The first reading is a U.S. Supreme Court opinion in which a majority of the Court held that laws banning obscene material are constitutional, even if only consenting adults are using them. U.S. Representative Henry Hyde next discusses a federally funded art exhibit that included "Piss Christ"—a painting that was deeply offensive to many people. Hyde uses that incident to explore the proper role of governmental funding of the arts, censorship, the responsibility of artists, and the nature of art itself. The last reading in this section is John Stuart Mill's *On Liberty.* A true classic, this work presents a powerful defense of free expression against those who would censor it, along with an account of the limits of governmental authority in general.

Turning from censorship to the college curriculum, **"Values in the Curriculum"** presents two positions on an issue that has been the focus of heated debate on many U.S. college and university campuses. Defending the traditional curriculum, renowned philosopher of mind John Searle offers a critique of those who insist that political, racial, and gender considerations replace merit and truth as the basis for deciding what is to be taught. Laura Purdy takes the opposite view, claiming that Searle has misconstrued the position of feminists and others who, like herself, want the curriculum opened up to include new voices and fresh perspectives.

The last section presents very different perspectives on an important topic debated around the world—capitalism. **"Morality in Markets"** considers the particular virtues and vices of capitalism, the proper role of markets, and the situations in which markets should not be allowed. In the opening essay, Michael Novak argues that far from encouraging greed and selfishness, as is sometimes charged, markets encourage democratic values, promote cooperation, and enhance a sense of community. Libertarians defend capitalism in different terms. Robert Nozick, for instance, argues that market capitalism reflects the basic right of all persons to trade what they legitimately own with others, as long as the exchange is voluntary. "Capitalist relations between consenting adults" is a basic right, as Nozick summarizes his position. Yet surely there are limits to markets, insists Michael Walzer. He argues that far from rewarding hard work, markets do the opposite. The section concludes with an essay by Debra Satz that focuses on another topic of growing importance socially: the sale of women's reproductive labor. Is there anything wrong, she asks, with a woman freely choosing to rent her body as a surrogate?

Moral Practice and Reason

Articles in this part explore the nature and the content of practical reason. The first section, **"Feelings and Reason in Morality,"** focuses on those who have been skeptical about the power of practical reason to motivate action. It begins with an essay by a contemporary philosopher, Jonathan Bennett, who describes the conflict people sometimes experience between feelings for somebody and duty. He uses surprising examples to focus his discussion: Huck Finn, Adolph Eichmann, and Jonathan Edwards. Many philosophers have agreed with eighteenth-century philosopher David Hume that reason can tell us how to achieve only what our feelings incline us to want. Reason, he argues, cannot tell us what to want, whom to condemn or approve, or how to live our own lives without feelings to provide the motivation. Thomas Nagel disagrees with Hume, however, contending that feelings and desires cannot by themselves ever provide adequate reason to act, any more than our desires that a mathematical proof succeed can be a reason to believe it does.

"Classical Theories of Morality" includes selections from what are usually thought to be the three best attempts to give a coherent, attractive, and generally applicable account of moral practice. Aristotle famously argues that morality is best understood by reflecting on the ideal or best life and on the role of reason and of virtue in such a life. Utilitarians such as John Stuart Mill, on the other hand, think of morality in instrumental terms, as a means by which to increase total social utility or happiness. Mill thus considers the nature of happiness, why it is reasonable to suppose that people acting in accord with the requirements of morality would maximize it, and the nature of justice in the context of utilitarian moral theory. The third philosopher, Immanuel Kant, vigorously rejects the Millian idea that morality involves prudential reasoning about maximizing happiness. He argues that moral duty requires us to follow something close to the Golden Rule, that rational agents must act in accord with maxims that they could consistently will everyone acted on or, as he puts it, can be willed to become universal law.

Essays in the concluding section, **"Critical Perspectives on Morality,"** call into question various aspects of these traditional approaches. Virginia Held discusses the moral tradition from a feminist perspective, arguing that it shows within itself a bias in favor of the perspective of men over that of women. Next Robert Nozick discusses happiness, criticizing those who argued that it is the primary component of a worthy life and then giving his own account of what happiness consists in. Friedrich Nietzche offers a very different criticism of the tradition, arguing that moral philosophers have failed to appreciate how the dominant "slave" morality, based on weakness, resentment, sympathy, and the desire for happiness, is incompatible with the virtues of courage, accomplishment, and the natural human will to power. In the final essay, Joshua Cohen argues that rather than opposing and working against the natural order, justice and equality are part of the world. Slavery failed, he claims, not just because it was widely *believed* to be an unjust distribution of power but because it was in fact unjust.

SCIENCE

The practice of science plays such a pervasive role in our culture that its influence and its results are largely taken for granted. As the Catholic Church was to the Middle Ages, so science is to our time. We give science a dominant role in policymaking, we use it to create the technology we crave, and we adopt scientific approaches to solve social problems. As a result, science shapes our culture in myriad ways. But, because it conflicts with other practices, it also creates many problems. Many believe that questions about the meaning of life, the status of ethical claims, and the significance of religion cannot be answered independently of scientific theories, or at least that our answers must be compatible with scientifically established truths. For example: Do our lives have meaning if we are only temporary collections of atoms? Can ethical claims be objectively true if the world consists only of properties describable by science? Is it rational to believe in God or join in religious practices if we accept the scientific worldview?

Many people insist that their religious and moral beliefs are consistent with our best scientific theories, so that what is most important in these practices can be included in a scientific view of the world. Others, however, challenge the dominance of science. Some attempt to show that scientific practice is no more reliable than conflicting practices, either by elevating the claims these other practices make or by questioning the reliability of science. Still others hope to make room for religion and morality by establishing that science is incomplete and must be supplemented with other kinds of knowing. They would argue that beliefs about values, morality, aesthetics or spiritual matters do not conflict with scientific understanding, but rather complement it.

Although most people in postindustrial societies are aware of the tremendous significance of science in shaping their lives, relatively few are trained in science. In this respect, our relation to the practice of science may well differ from our relation to moral practice, and perhaps also religious practice. Even if we construe the practice of science broadly, so that it includes basic science, applied science, and the development of technology, most adults enjoy the results of science without either understanding the practice or participating in it directly. Consequently, attitudes toward science may be based on stereotypes and are often charged with deep ambivalence.

The Practice of Science

Although scientific practice is known for its emphasis on testing and the quest for public consensus, experts differ significantly about how to characterize science. Some emphasize the nature of scientific theories, others look to method, and still others focus on the institutional structures of science and the values they incorporate. The first section, **"What Is Science?,"** examines each of these approaches. Karl Popper asks how scientific theories can be distinguished from pseudoscience, and he replies that scientific theories are falsifiable. John Ziman is interested in ways that science differs from history, philosophy, and law, and he suggests that the aim of achieving rational consensus shapes the behavior of scientists in distinctive ways. Larry Laudan is less concerned with what makes science distinctive. He explores the idea that science is best understood as problem solving, and indeed his view makes it continuous with our everyday knowledge-gathering activities.

Theories of modern science are often thought to generate concern about the meaning of human lives. The authors in **"Alienation and the Scientific Worldview"** critically examine such concerns. If the world lacks any purpose for human life, does that mean lives lack all meaning? Can we feel at home in a world where order is merely a result of either chance or human activity? Kurt Baier maintains that we can create all of the meaning we need without positing any purpose for life beyond our own. Stuart Kauffman thinks that the Newtonian/Darwinian worldview does deprive us of something important, the sacred, but that new developments in science can return this. Neither of these thinkers finds science inevitably alienating.

Scientific Practice and Culture

Readings in **"The Scientific Outlook and Its Critics"** extend and deepen our discussion of the role of science in society. Do we place undue emphasis on science? Has that emphasis limited creative problem solving? Paul Feyerabend says yes to both questions. While science once liberated us from religious dogma, he concludes, it now indoctrinates people into a new dogma. He challenges us to reform education, so that we train truly free individuals who will use whatever method or approach works to solve their cultural problems. Gerald Holton denies that we place undue emphasis on science. Indeed, he worries about the rise of an antiscience movement that threatens the gains of the modern era. Theodore Roszak returns to the theme of alienation, associating science with the monster in Mary Shelley's *Frankenstein*. He argues that science should be augmented by other forms of knowing that address questions about value.

The essays in **"Technology and the Transformation of Culture"** address ways in which science and its products threaten to dramatically alter various aspects of our culture. If we are concerned about the impact of new technologies, we can either restrain the basic research on which they depend or we can restrain the development of the technologies themselves. Each of these options, however, raises serious issues about freedom. Robert Sinsheimer argues that we should avoid pursuing some types of basic research because we are unlikely to be able to control its results. We have already developed the ability to clone a mammal and may soon clone a human. We will need to decide whether to limit new reproductive technologies, such as cloning, that may significantly benefit people but may also threaten deep-seated assumptions about the value of human life, how it should be created, and by whom. The articles on cloning thus raise many of the most vexing questions we face in attempting to assess the moral implications of new technological advances. (These link back to the deep questions about the foundations of morality that were addressed in the **"Moral Practice and Reason"** section.) Kenneth Gergen concludes this section by examining the effect of communications technology on our relationships and our sense of self. He worries that the benefits of enhanced communication bring a tendency to develop one-dimensional relationships and fragmented personal identities. Here we return to issues about the connection between science and alienation.

The next two sections continue our discussion of the cultural implications of science. Essays in **"Evolution and Ecology"** examine morality through the lens of biology, arriving at different though compatible conclusions. Michael Ruse argues that humans have a genetic predisposition to behave altruistically. Using studies on ants, apes, and humans, he suggests that our moral thinking has a biological basis. He does not, however, take the further step of asking whether nonhumans can be moral agents. Frans de Waal makes just that argument, presenting evidence that apes and other animals satisfy many of the requirements for acting morally and holding others morally responsible. While these authors stress our kinship with some nonhumans, Aldo Leopold argues we should extend that kinship to the whole biotic community and that, as a result, we should broaden our moral attitudes to include duties to the land itself. He is led, then, to a radically holistic environmental ethics.

Many philosophers have worried that if science can explain all of our behavior, then it is predictable in principle and we have no free will. In a classic selection from *Walden Two*, B. F. Skinner defends that conclusion, suggesting that a science of behavior can provide us with the knowledge we need to condition people so they will be generally happy. This raises the issue of punishment, however: How can we punish people if they do not act freely? Herbert Morris juxtaposes a therapy model for altering criminal behavior and a punishment model that is based on retribution and argues that we should prefer the latter. His startling conclusion is that we have a right to punishment, which is based on the claim that people deserve punishment out of respect for their capacities as rational agents. Morris assumes people have free will, though he does not defend it; Richard Taylor attempts to fill this gap by providing reasons to believe that the causes for human action are fundamentally different from the causes for other events. These readings in the **"Science of Behavior"** section bring to a close the discussion of the impact of science on culture.

Scientific Practice and Reason

Our attitude toward the role science plays in our culture is likely to depend on our answers to basic questions in the philosophy of science. These include: Should we think of theory choice in science as objective (normally)? Does science progress toward truth? Should we strive toward a complete unified scientific view of the world? What are the relations among the theories of psychology, biology, and physics? In **"Objectivity and Values in Science,"** the authors explore different challenges to objectivity. The first comes from an interpretation of the history of science that reveals that institutions cannot live up to the ideal of objectivity. In contrast to the familiar image of scientists striving to evaluate theories using methods available to all participants, Israel Sheffler notes that disputing scientists often do not share the same data, the same concepts, or the same values. A distinct challenge comes from a feminist analysis of science. Evelyn Fox Keller explores the myth that science is masculine, and therefore biased. Although she does not claim that the myth is reality, she sketches a provocative link between typical male development and the dominant modes of knowing in science. A third critique of scientific objectivity emphasizes the role of values in science. Can science be objective if it presupposes value judgments that cannot be confirmed by science? Doesn't science threaten the objectivity of values? Patrick Grim argues that science does indeed involve value judgments but that this does not compromise objectivity. Indeed, he claims, some value commitments actually explain why science is revered as a source of knowledge.

Worries about objectivity are inevitably connected to issues about the truth of theories. Frequently those who find little objectivity also find little reason to suppose that science progresses toward truth. Thomas Kuhn is the most famous twentieth-century example. **"Truth and Progress in Science"** begins with selections from his widely discussed *The Structure of Scientific Revolutions* that describe the differences between normal science and revolutionary science. On the surface, normal science looks somewhat like the ideal sketched by Sheffler, while revolutionary science reveals significant subjective elements that prevent theory change from being a fully rational affair. Since revolutions characterize most scientific development, Kuhn argues we should abandon the view of scientific progress as the gradual accumulation of information about a mind-independent world. In Larry Laudan's dialogue, four imaginary philosophers, who bear significant resemblance to Kuhn, Popper, Carnap, and Laudan himself, debate the nature of scientific progress. This section ends with a sophisticated discussion of scientific realism—the view that science does approximate the truth. Philip Kitcher defends scientific realism against the inductive argument that because most prior scientific theories have turned out to be false, our current theories are probably false as well.

Selections in **"How Much Can Science Explain?"** ask whether all features of the world can be fully explained by science. Can science explain why there is something rather than nothing, for example? Does it leave room for alternative explanations that emphasize the purpose for events in the world? Some theists make room for God by limiting the range of scientific explanation and demanding alternative explanations of what, they claim, science cannot understand. Kurt Baier examines such arguments and finds them wanting. Another oft-heard claim that scientific explanation is limited involves the nature of the mind. Can science adequately explain all we know about mind? And do we have a soul that is outside the realm that science addresses? After outlining some standard arguments for the belief that the mind is independent of the body, Paul Churchland argues that the evidence strongly indicates that it is not. John Searle closes this section with a puzzle about how we can honor the physical basis for mind (its connection with the brain) while also acknowledging distinctive properties such as conscious experience that differentiate the mind from other entities explained by science—including the brain. Although many philosophies of mind fail to integrate the scientific/physical with the mental, Searle shows one way in which the issue can be resolved without abandoning either science or consciousness.

RELIGION

Of the three practices studied in this text, religion is the most deeply controversial. While some skeptics have rejected morality and science completely, most critical discussion centers not on whether the practices are worthwhile but on what role they should play. Should we rely less on science for answers? Is science a threat to humanity or its potential savior? Similarly, while some would deny that the claims of morality should be taken seriously, most of the disagreement has been over the nature of morality and its scope in human life. With religion the ground has shifted, for here many hold that the entire practice should be abandoned in favor of a naturalistic, rather than supernaturalistic, conception of the universe in which God has no place.

That said, however, it is far from agreed that belief in God is irrational; indeed, many philosophers maintain just the opposite: that on balance the weight of evidence favors belief in God. And even if nothing like a god that we can know exists, whether we should therefore abandon religious practices, prayers, rituals, and creeds is far from settled. Controversy also abounds regarding the role of religious faith in the larger culture—especially in education and politics.

One other interesting feature of religious practice, compared with morality and science, is that while some are inclined to reject it completely, its hold on others seems to be stronger and run deeper than does their commitment to science and even perhaps to morality. Few would say, for instance, that their relationship to science dominates all aspects of their lives, defining who they are, what they value, and how they should live. Religious people, however, may find themselves claiming exactly that. Religious practice is inseparable from how they see themselves and their relationship to the world: Their purpose and their duties as well as their interpretation of the universe itself cannot be disentangled from their religious beliefs. Opinions about religion are therefore deeply divided. While to some religion is in an important sense optional, for others it is as far from optional as it is possible to be. That suggests the first question we address in the following sections: the nature of religion. For it turns out that even those who regard it as fundamentally important may differ profoundly among themselves about why it is important, and about how religion should be interpreted and practiced.

The Practice of Religion

As with morality and science, we begin by asking **"What Is Religion?"** One idea is that it varies widely from culture to culture: Indeed, that may seem obvious as one considers the three readings that begin this section. William James suggests a theistic approach in which belief in God is fundamental; Joseph Soloveitchik emphasizes the importance of law; and Ashok Malhorta describes a Buddhist's religious perspective as neither theistic nor legalistic but instead personal. John Hick next wonders whether there is a common theme and core of belief uniting all major religions, while anthropologist Clifford Geertz proposes a more scientific understanding of religion.

The next three essays, gathered together in **"Religion and the Meaning of Life,"** center on the profoundly important question of whether life has a meaning or purpose or whether human life is absurd. Leo Tolstoy famously defended the claim that religion, and only religion, can give a life real meaning. Using the myth of Sisyphus (in which the gods have condemned Sisyphus to an eternity of rolling a large stone to the top of a hill, watching it roll down, and pushing it up again), the next two articles offer differing perspectives on the significance of that story and on the meaninglessness and absurdity of human existence.

Religious Practice and Culture

The three sections in this part focus on the practice of religion in relation to culture. The first section, **"Social Critiques of Religious Practice,"** discusses religious practice in general. It begins with a discussion of feminist criticisms of Christianity, and how they might be answered by reinterpreting religious practice including especially the conception of God as mother rather than father. Bertrand Russell attacks Christianity on a number of fronts, such as its confused and mistaken moral teachings and its tendency to retard social progress. He concludes with some speculations about why people are drawn to religion. Freud extends and deepens these ideas with a discussion of religion's role in civilization and its status as an "illusion." The next section's readings weigh the role of **"Religion in Education,"** and in particular whether creationism should be taught in public schools along with evolutionary theory. One of the questions at issue involves the law, and how the courts have treated the evolution/creationism controversy. Two court opinions follow. One takes a strong position that teaching evolution and other components of "secular humanism" is tantamount to teaching a religion, in violation of the separation of church and state. The other concludes the Amish people have the right to refuse to send their children to school, based on the claim that doing so would endanger the children's religious faith by exposing them to atheistic, secular culture.

The last group of readings begins where these leave off. Essays in **"Religion and Politics"** look at the twin issues of religious freedom, on one hand, and the demand that public policy be justified without reference to religion, on the other. The first selection is the classic argument for a strict separation of religion from government and defense of freedom of conscience: John Locke's *A Letter Concerning Toleration.* The next selection first presents the core of John Rawls's influential account of justice and fairness, followed by his argument that there is a right enjoyed by all against interference by government in religious matters. Rawls concludes with a brief account of the grounds on which the state may sometimes intervene to limit religious practices.

The last essay on religious practice and culture is a detailed criticism of the position that Rawls defends. Michael Sandel claims that by insisting on governmental neutrality, liberals such as Rawls have undermined respect for religion and weakened democratic politics. Indeed, says Sandel, the very conception of the person on which liberalism is based fails to take seriously the religious and other duties that people have.

Religious Practice and Reason

Is it reasonable to believe in God? Do we have good reason to believe there is no God? Is it reasonable to practice religion in the absence of solid evidence either way? What is religious faith? Is religious truth in some way fundamentally different from more familiar types of truths we discover in science or rely on in common sense? These are some of the key questions in this section.

The first group of essays, gathered together under the heading **"Evidence for the Existence of God,"** includes the three most important philosophical arguments that there is a God, together with the equally important criticisms of those authors. The Design Argument's basic contention is that the lawlike, purposive order of nature gives good reason to suppose there was a mind that created the universe just as we would conclude a mind created a watch we might find in a forest. The Cosmological Argument rests on the different claim that the very existence of the universe, which after all might not have existed, shows that there had to have been a creator who brought it into existence. The last, the Ontological Argument, claims that we can know God exists because we have the concept of God—a being than which nothing greater can be conceived. The next two essays focus on **"Evidence There Is No God."** Atheists have long claimed that the universe we inhabit cannot possibly be the product of an all-powerful, just, and omniscient creator. Such a being simply would not allow the amount of moral evil and innocent suffering that we observe every day. Authors in this section take opposing sides of this issue, which has long been central to the debate over God's existence.

In **"Faith and Reason,"** the discussion shifts from the weight of the evidence to the rationality or irrationality of faith in the absence of evidence. It begins with a famous critique by W. C. Clifford of those who may be tempted to allow wishful thinking to shape beliefs. Indeed, he argues that we have an ethical obligation always to be sure that we believe only what the evidence warrants; without adequate evidence, the only responsible position is to withhold belief altogether. In response, William James claims that under certain specific circumstances, it is not just acceptable to believe without adequate evidence but is in fact irrational *not* to do so. But what then, exactly, is religious faith or belief? The last readings in this section form a discussion among three philosophers who weigh different answers to that question. The first, Anthony Flew, contends that while religious beliefs *seem* to have content, in fact they do not. This is because they are compatible with whatever happens in the world and whatever observations we may make. Religious belief, Flew suggests, is therefore more an expression of feeling about the world than a genuine belief that might be true or false. This claim is disputed by two other philosophers. R. M. Hare defends religious faith by inventing another parable, arguing that while the difference between the way religious and nonreligious people see the world may not be resolvable through a testing procedure, it is nonetheless a fundamentally important question to which the atheist's answer is at best only one of the alternatives. Raeburne Heimbeck focuses on the nature of belief itself, asking why religious beliefs should ever have been thought to belong in a category with normal empirical and factual claims. He describes a variety of other beliefs that, like religious ones, are not empirically testable.

These themes are explored further in the last section, **"Rethinking Religious Practice."** Dewi Z. Phillips first questions whether the god of the "philosophers" is really the same being that religious people pray to and worship. The next two readings go still further, arguing that it is rational to participate in religious practices without believing in any god at all except in the sense that we play a game of "make believe." The section concludes with a famous essay by John Wisdom. Rejecting both the claim that religion is based on argument of an experimental or mathematical sort and the claim that it is merely an expression of attitudes, Wisdom offers a variety of analogies and parables in trying to understand religious practice as it is experienced and practiced by the faithful.

Man Against Darkness: The Challenge of Science to Religion and Morality

W. T. Stace

This opening essay sets the stage for much—though by no means all—of what follows in the rest of the book. W. T. Stace argues that modern science cannot be written off as merely one view among many competing approaches to reality. Partly because of its success, which far outstrips traditional ways of trying to understand nature and human life, science has had a devastating impact on traditional religious and moral thinking. No longer can the religious picture—of a world created with an inherent plan or purpose—be sustained. Our world, rather, is just as it seems: a cold, indifferent place that takes no concern for the values or interests of human beings.

Science also has had an impact on morality, as people have come to see moral strictures not as the orders of a divine being but instead as a merely human construction rooted in human likes and dislikes. Even human freedom, and the related idea that we are morally responsible for our actions, is called into question by scientific advances that assume human actions are no different from other natural events whose causes we can discern. Stace concludes with a brief discussion of the social implications of this change in view and of the possibilities that a different conception of either religious faith or of science itself may hold the solution. The truth, he concludes, is that people must learn to face up to the new reality and find a way to have a decent, happy life without illusions.

Walter Stace was born in London in 1886, educated at Trinity College, Dublin, and then worked for two decades in the British Civil Service in Ceylon. He even served as mayor of Columbo for a period. In 1932, he joined the philosophy faculty at Princeton University in New Jersey, where he wrote numerous books on a wide range of topics, including morality, religion, and time.

As you read through this essay, consider the following:

1. How does Stace understand religious faith? Does he believe that it is compatible with evolutionary theory?
2. What is it about the scientific picture of the world that is incompatible with religious faith?
3. How is morality understood from within the scientific worldview?
4. In what ways does Stace think that science has led to a weakening of morality and of social controls?
5. Why is Stace skeptical that philosophy, religion, or science itself can solve the problems he has described for the modern world?

6. Do you think that faith in God might actually be compatible with science? Explain, indicating where you think Stace may be mistaken.
7. How does Stace understand morality? Is he right in assuming it rests on either a divine lawgiver or on human interests? Explain.
8. Could religious practice be defended without belief either in God or in a world that is designed to serve a larger purpose? Explain.

I

The Catholic bishops of America recently issued a statement in which they said that the chaotic and bewildered state of the modern world is due to man's loss of faith, his abandonment of God and religion. For my part I believe in no religion at all. Yet I entirely agree with the bishops. It is no doubt an oversimplification to speak of *the* cause of so complex a state of affairs as the tortured condition of the world today. Its causes are doubtless multitudinous. Yet allowing for some element of oversimplification, I say that the bishops' assertion is substantially true.

M. Jean-Paul Sartre, the French existentialist philosopher, labels himself an atheist. Yet his views seem to me plainly to support the statement of the bishops. So long as there was believed to be a God in the sky, he says, men could regard him as the source of their moral ideals. The universe, created and governed by a fatherly God, was a friendly habitation for man. We could be sure that, however great the evil in the world, good in the end would triumph and the forces of evil would be routed. With the disappearance of God from the sky all this has changed. Our own ideals, therefore, must proceed only from our own minds; they are our own inventions. Thus the world which surrounds us is nothing but an immense spiritual emptiness. It is a dead universe. We do not live in a universe which is on the side of our values. It is completely indifferent to them.

Years ago Mr. Bertrand Russell, in his essay *A Free Man's Worship*, said much the same thing:

Such in outline, but even more purposeless, more void of meaning, is the world which Science presents for our belief. Amid such a world, if anywhere, our ideals henceforward must find a home. . . . Blind to good and evil, reckless of destruction, omnipotent matter rolls on its relentless way; for man, condemned today to lose his dearest, tomorrow himself to pass through the gate of darkness, it remains only to cherish, ere yet the blow falls, the lofty thoughts that ennoble his little day; . . . to worship at the shrine his own hands have built; . . . to sustain alone, a weary but unyielding Atlas, the world that his own ideals have fashioned despite the trampling march of unconscious power.

It is true that Mr. Russell's personal attitude to the disappearance of religion is quite different from either that of M. Sartre or the bishops or myself. The bishops think it a calamity. So do I. M. Sartre finds it "very distressing." And he berates as shallow the attitude of those who think that without God the world can go on just the same as before, as if nothing had happened. This creates for mankind, he thinks, a terrible crisis. And in this I agree with him. Mr. Russell, on the other hand, seems to believe that religion has done more harm than good in the world, and that its disappearance will be a blessing. But his picture of the world, and of the modern mind, is the same as that of M. Sartre. He stresses the *purposelessness* of the universe, the facts that man's ideals are his own creations, that the universe outside him in no way supports them, that man is alone and friendless in the world.

Mr. Russell notes that it is science which has produced this situation. There is no doubt that this is correct. But the way in which it has come about is not generally understood. There is a popular belief that some particular scientific discoveries or theories, such as the

---

W. T. Stace, "Man Against Darkness," *The Atlantic Monthly* (September 1948), pp. 53–58.

Darwinian theory of evolution or the views of geologists about the age of the earth, or a series of such discoveries, have done the damage. It would be foolish to deny that these discoveries have had a great effect in undermining religious dogmas. But this account does not at all go to the root of the matter. Religion can probably outlive any scientific discoveries which could be made. It can accommodate itself to them. The root cause of the decay of faith has not been any particular discovery of science, but rather the general spirit of science and certain basic assumptions upon which modern science, from the seventeenth century onwards, has proceeded.

II

It was Galileo and Newton—notwithstanding that Newton himself was a deeply religious man—who destroyed the old comfortable picture of a friendly universe governed by spiritual values. And this was effected, not by Newton's discovery of the law of gravitation nor by any of Galileo's brilliant investigations, but by the general picture of the world which these men and others of their time made the basis of science, not only of their own day, but of all succeeding generations down to the present. That is why the century immediately following Newton, the eighteenth century, was notoriously an age of religious skepticism. Skepticism did not have to wait for the discoveries of Darwin and the geologists in the nineteenth century. It flooded the world immediately after the age of the rise of science.

Neither the Copernican hypothesis nor any of Newton's or Galileo's particular discoveries were the real causes. Religious faith might well have accommodated itself to the new astronomy. The real turning point between the medieval age of faith and the modern age of unfaith came when the scientists of the seventeenth century turned their backs upon what used to be called "final causes." The final cause of a thing or event meant the purpose which it was supposed to serve in the universe, its cosmic purpose. What lay back of this was the presupposition that there is a cosmic order or plan and that everything which exists could in the last analysis be explained in terms of its place in this cosmic plan, that is, in terms of its purpose.

Plato and Aristotle believed this, and so did the whole medieval Christian world. For instance, if it were true that the sun and the moon were created and exist for the purpose of giving light to man, then this fact would explain why the sun and the moon exist. We might not be able to discover the purpose of everything, but everything must have a purpose. Belief in final causes thus amounted to a belief that the world is governed by purposes, presumably the purposes of some overruling mind. This belief was not the invention of Christianity. It was basic to the whole of Western civilization, whether in the ancient pagan world or in Christendom, from the time of Socrates to the rise of science in the seventeenth century.

The founders of modern science—for instance, Galileo, Kepler, and Newton—were mostly pious men who did not doubt God's purposes. Nevertheless they took the revolutionary step of consciously and deliberately expelling the idea of purpose as controlling nature from their new science of nature. They did this on the ground that inquiry into purposes is useless for what science aims at; namely the prediction and control of events. To predict an eclipse, what you have to know is not its purpose but its causes. Hence science from the seventeenth century onwards became exclusively an inquiry into causes. The conception of purpose in the world was ignored and frowned on. This, though silent and almost unnoticed, was the greatest revolution in human history, far outweighing in importance any of the political revolutions whose thunder was reverberated through the world.

For it came about in this way that for the past three hundred years there has been growing up in men's minds, dominated as they are by science, a new imaginative picture of the world. The world, according to this new picture, is purposeless, senseless, meaningless.

Nature is nothing but matter in motion. The motions of matter are governed, not by any purpose, but by blind forces and laws. Nature on this view, says Whitehead—to whose writings I am indebted in this part of my paper, is "merely the hurrying of material, endlessly, meaninglessly." You can draw a sharp line across the history of Europe dividing it into two epochs of very unequal length. The line passes through the lifetime of Galileo. European man before Galileo—whether ancient pagan or more recent Christian—thought of the world as controlled by plan and purpose. After Galileo European man thinks of it as utterly purposeless. This is the great revolution of which I spoke.

It is this which has killed religion. Religion could survive the discoveries that the sun, not the earth, is the center; that men are descended from simian ancestors; that the earth is hundreds of millions of years old. These discoveries may render out of date some of the details of older theological dogmas, may force their restatement in new intellectual frameworks. But they do not touch the essence of the religious vision itself, which is the faith that there is plan and purpose in the world, that the world is a moral order, that in the end all things are for the best. This faith may express itself through many different intellectual dogmas, those of Christianity, of Hinduism, of Islam. All and any of these intellectual dogmas may be destroyed without destroying the essential religious spirit. But that spirit cannot survive destruction of belief in a plan and purpose of the world, for that is the very heart of it. Religion can get on with any sort of astronomy, geology, biology, physics. But it cannot get on with a purposeless and meaningless universe.

If the scheme of things is purposeless and meaningless, then the life of man is purposeless and meaningless too. Everything is futile, all effort is in the end worthless. A man may, of course, still pursue disconnected ends, money, fame, art, science, and may gain pleasure from them. But his life is hollow at the center. Hence the dissatisfied, disillusioned, restless, spirit of modern man.

The picture of a meaningless world, and a meaningless human life is, I think, the basic theme of much modern art and literature. Certainly it is the basic theme of modern philosophy. According to the most characteristic philosophies of the modern period from Hume in the eighteenth century to the so-called positivists of today, the world is just what it is, and that is the end of all inquiry. There is no reason for its being what it is. Everything might just as well have been quite different, and there would have been no reason for that either. When you have stated what things are, what things the world contains, there is nothing more which could be said, even by an omniscient being. To ask any question about *why* things are thus, or what purpose their being so serves, is to ask a senseless question, because they serve no purpose at all. For instance, there is for modern philosophy no such thing as the ancient problem of evil. For this once famous question presupposes that pain and misery, though they seem so inexplicable and irrational to us, must ultimately subserve some rational purpose, must have their places in the cosmic plan. But this is nonsense. There is no such overruling rationality in the universe. Belief in the ultimate irrationality of everything is the quintessence of what is called the modern mind.

It is true that, parallel with these philosophies which are typical of the modern mind, preaching the meaninglessness of the world, there has run a line of idealistic philosophies whose contention is that the world is after all spiritual in nature and that moral ideals and values are inherent in its structure. But most of these idealisms were simply philosophical expressions of romanticism, which was itself no more than an unsuccessful counterattack of the religious against the scientific view of things. They perished, along with romanticism in literature and art, about the beginning of the present century, though of course they still have a few adherents.

At the bottom these idealistic systems of thought were rationalizations of man's wishful thinking. They were born of the refusal of men to admit the cosmic darkness. They were comforting illusions within the warm glow of which the more tender-minded intellectuals sought to shelter themselves from the icy winds of the universe. They lasted a little while. But they are shattered now and we return once more to the vision of a purposeless world.

III

Along with the ruin of the religious vision there went the ruin of moral principles and indeed of all values. If there is a cosmic purpose, if there is in the nature of things a drive towards goodness, then our moral systems will derive their validity from this. But if our moral rules do not proceed from something outside us in the nature of the universe—whether we say it is God or simply the universe itself—then they must be our own inventions. Thus it came to be believed that moral rules must be merely an expression of our own likes and dislikes. But likes and dislikes are notoriously variable. What pleases one man, people, or culture displeases another. Therefore morals are wholly relative.

This obvious conclusion from the idea of a purposeless world made its appearance in Europe immediately after the rise of science, for instance in the philosophy of Hobbes. Hobbes saw at once that if there is no purpose in the world there are no values either. "Good and evil," he writes, "are names that signify our appetites and aversions; which in different tempers, customs, and doctrines of men are different. . . . Every man calleth that which pleaseth him, good; and that which displeaseth him, evil."

This doctrine of the relativity of morals, though it has recently received an impetus from the studies of anthropologists, was thus really implicit in the whole scientific mentality. It is disastrous for morals because it destroys their entire traditional foundation. That is why philosophers who see the danger signals, from the time at least of Kant, have been trying to give morals a new foundation, that is, a secular or nonreligious foundation. This attempt may very well be intellectually successful. Such a foundation, independent of the religious view of the world, might well be found, but the question is whether it can ever be a *practical* success, that is, whether apart from its logical validity and its influence with intellectuals, it can ever replace among the masses of men the lost religious foundation. On that question hangs perhaps the future of civilization. But meanwhile disaster is overtaking us.

The widespread belief in "ethical relativity" among philosophers, psychologists, ethnologists, and sociologists is the theoretical counterpart of the repudiation of principle which we see all around us, especially in international affairs, the field in which morals have always had the weakest foothold. No one any longer effectively believes in moral principles except as the private prejudices either of individual men or of nations or cultures. This is the inevitable consequence of the doctrine of ethical relativity, which in turn is the inevitable consequence of believing in a purposeless world.

Another characteristic of our spiritual state is loss of belief in the freedom of the will. This also is a fruit of the scientific spirit, though not of any particular scientific discovery. Science has been built up on the basis of determinism, which is the belief that every event is completely determined by a chain of causes and is therefore theoretically predictable beforehand. It is true that recent physics seems to challenge this. But so far as its practical consequences are concerned, the damage has long ago been done. A man's actions, it was argued, are as much events in the natural world as is an eclipse of the sun. It follows that men's actions are as theoretically predictable as an eclipse. But if it is certain now that John Smith will murder Joseph Jones at 2:15 P.M. on January 1, 1963, what possible meaning can it have to say that when that time comes John Smith will be *free* to choose whether he will commit the murder or not? And if he is not free, how can he be held responsible?

It is true that the whole of this argument can be shown by a competent philosopher to be a tissue of fallacies—or at least I claim that it can. But the point is that the analysis required to show this is much too subtle to be understood by the average entirely unphilosophical man. Because of this, the argument against free will is generally swallowed whole by the unphilosophical. Hence the thought that man is not free, that he is the helpless plaything of forces over which he has no control, has deeply penetrated the modern mind. We hear of economic determinism, cultural determinism, historical determinism. We are not responsible for what we do because our glands control us, or because we are the products of environment or heredity. Not moral self-control, but the doctor, the psychiatrist, the educationist, must save us from doing evil. Pills and injections in the future are to do what Christ and the prophets have failed to do. Of course I do not mean to deny that doctors and educationists can and must help. And I do not mean in any way to belittle their efforts. But I do wish to draw attention to the weakening of moral controls, the greater or less repudiation of personal responsibility which, in the popular thinking of the day, result from these tendencies of thought.

IV

What, then, is to be done? Where are we to look for salvation from the evils of our time? All the remedies I have seen suggested so far are, in my opinion, useless. Let us look at some of them.

Philosophers and intellectuals generally can, I believe, genuinely do something to help. But it is extremely little. What philosophers can do is to show that neither the relativity of morals nor the denial of free will really follows from the grounds which have been supposed to support them. They can also try to discover a genuine secular basis for morals to replace the religious basis which has disappeared. Some of us are trying to do these things. But in the first place philosophers unfortunately are not agreed about these matters, and their disputes are utterly confusing to the non-philosophers. And in the second place their influence is practically negligible because their analyses necessarily take place on a level on which the masses are totally unable to follow them. . . .

. . . It is not merely that particular dogmas, like that of the virgin birth, are unacceptable to the modern mind. That is true, but it constitutes a very superficial diagnosis of the present situation of religion. Modern skepticism is of a wholly different order from that of the intellectuals of the ancient world. It has attacked and destroyed not merely the outward forms of the religious spirit, its particularized dogmas, but the very essence of that spirit itself, belief in a meaningful and purposeful world. For the founding of a new religion a new Jesus Christ or Buddha would have to appear, in itself a most unlikely event and one for which in any case we cannot afford to sit and wait. But even if a new prophet and a new religion did appear, we may predict that they would fail in the modern world. No one for long would believe in them, for modern men have lost the vision, basic to all religion, of an ordered plan and purpose of the world. They have before their minds the picture of a purposeless universe, and such a world-picture must be fatal to any religion at all, not merely to Christianity.

We must not be misled by occasional appearances of a revival of the religious spirit. Men, we are told, in their disgust and disillusionment at the emptiness of their lives, are turning once more to religion, or are searching for a new message. It may be so. We must expect such wistful yearnings of the spirit. We must expect men to wish back again the light that is gone, and to try to bring it back. But however they may wish and try, the light will not shine again—not at least in the civilization to which we belong.

Another remedy commonly proposed is that we should turn to science itself, or the scientific spirit, for our salvation. . . . This seems to me to be utterly naive. It is not likely that science, which is basically the cause of our spiritual troubles, is likely also to produce the cure for them. Also it lies in the nature of science that, though it can teach us the best means for achieving our ends, it can never tell us what ends to pursue. It cannot give us any ideals. And our trouble is about ideals and ends, not about the means for reaching them.

V

No civilization can live without ideals, or to put it in another way, without a firm faith in moral ideas. Our ideals and moral ideas have in the past been rooted in religion. But the religious basis of our ideals has been undermined, and the superstructure of ideals is plainly tottering. None of the commonly suggested remedies on examination seems likely to succeed. It would therefore look as if the early death of our civilization were inevitable.

Of course we know that it is perfectly possible for individual men, very highly educated men, philosophers, scientists, intellectuals in general, to live moral lives without any religious convictions. But the question is whether a whole civilization, a whole family of people, composed almost entirely of relatively uneducated men and women, can do this.

It follows, of course, that if we could make the vast majority of men as highly educated as the very few are now, we might save the situation. And we are already moving slowly in that direction through the techniques of mass education. But the critical question seems to concern the time-lag. Perhaps in a few hundred years most of the population will, at the present rate, be sufficiently highly educated and civilized to combine high ideals with an absence of religion. But long before we reach any such stage, the collapse of our civilization may have come about. How are we to live through the intervening period?

I am sure that the first thing we have to do is to face the truth, however bleak it may be, and then next we have to learn to live with it. Let me say a word about each of these two points. What I am urging as regards the first is complete honesty. Those who wish to resurrect Christian dogmas are not, of course, consciously dishonest. But they have that kind of unconscious dishonesty which consists in lulling oneself with opiates and dreams. Those who talk of a new religion are merely hoping for a new opiate. Both alike refuse to face the truth that there is, in the universe outside man, no spirituality, no regard for values, no friend in the sky, no help or comfort for man of any sort. To be perfectly honest in the admission of this fact, not to seek shelter in new or old illusions, not to indulge in wishful dreams about this matter, this is the first thing we shall have to do.

I do not urge this course out of any special regard for the sanctity of truth in the abstract. It is not self-evident to me that truth is the supreme value to which all else must be sacrificed. Might not the discoverer of a truth which would be fatal to mankind be justified in suppressing it, even in teaching men a falsehood? Is truth more valuable than goodness and beauty and happiness? To think so is to invent yet another absolute, another religious delusion in which Truth with a capital T is substituted for God. The reason why we must now boldly and honestly face the truth that the universe is non-spiritual and indifferent to goodness, beauty, happiness, or truth is not that it would be wicked to suppress it, but simply that it is too late to do so, so that in the end we cannot do anything else but face it. Yet we stand on the brink, dreading the icy plunge. We need courage. We need honesty.

Now about the other point, the necessity of learning to live with the truth. This means learning to live virtuously and happily, or at least contentedly, without illusions. And this is going to be extremely difficult because what we have now begun dimly to perceive is that human life in the past, or at least human happiness, has almost wholly depended upon illusions. It has been said that man lives by truth, and that the truth will make us free. Nearly the opposite seems to me to be the case. Mankind has managed to live only by means of lies, and the truth may very well destroy us.

If one were a Bergsonian one might believe that nature deliberately puts illusions into our souls in order to induce us to go on living.

The illusions by which men have lived seem to be of two kinds. First, there is what one may perhaps call the Great Illusion—I mean the religious illusion that the universe is moral and good, that it follows a wise and noble plan, that it is gradually generating some supreme value, that goodness is bound to triumph in it. Secondly, there is a whole host of minor illusions on which human happiness nourishes itself. How much of human happiness notoriously comes from the illusions of the lover about his beloved? Then again we work and strive because of the illusions connected with fame, glory, power, or money. Banners of all kinds, flags, emblems, insignia, ceremonials, and rituals are invariably symbols of some illusion or other. The British Empire, the connection between mother country and dominions, is partly kept going by illusions surrounding the notion of kingship. Or think of the vast amount of human happiness which is derived from the illusion of supposing that if some nonsense syllable, such as "sir" or "count" or "lord" is pronounced in conjunction with our names, we belong to a superior order of people.

There is plenty of evidence that human happiness is almost wholly based upon illusions of one kind or another. But the scientific spirit, or the spirit of truth, is the enemy of human happiness. That is why it is going to be so difficult to live with the truth.

There is no reason why we should have to give up the host of minor illusions which render life supportable. There is no reason why the lover should be scientific about the loved one. Even the illusions of fame and glory may persist. But without the Great Illusion, the illusion of a good, kindly, and purposeful universe, we shall *have* to learn to live. And to ask this is really no more than to ask

that we become genuinely civilized beings and not merely sham civilized beings.

I can best explain the difference by a reminiscence. I remember a fellow student in my college days, an ardent Christian, who told me that if he did not believe in a future life, in heaven and hell, he would rape, murder, steal, and be a drunkard. That is what I call being a sham civilized being. On the other hand, not only could a Huxley, a John Stuart Mill, a David Hume, live great and fine lives without any religion, but a great many others of us, quite obscure persons, can at least live decent lives without it.

To be genuinely civilized means to be able to walk straightly and to live honorably without the props and crutches of one or another of the childish dreams which have so far supported men. That such a life is likely to be ecstatically happy, I will not claim. But that it can be lived in quiet content, accepting resignedly what cannot be helped, not expecting the impossible, and thankful for small mercies, this I would maintain. That it will be difficult for men in general to learn this lesson I do not deny. But that it will be impossible I would not admit since so many have learned it already.

Man has not yet grown up. He is not adult. Like a child he cries for the moon and lives in a world of fantasies. And the race as a whole has perhaps reached the great crisis of its life. Can it grow up as a race in the same sense as individual men grow up? Can man put away childish things and adolescent dreams? Can he grasp the real world as it actually is, stark and bleak, without its romantic or religious halo, and still retain his ideals, striving for great ends and noble achievements? If he can, all may yet be well. If he cannot, he will probably sink back into the savagery and brutality from which he came, taking a humble place once more among the lower animals.

PART II

The Practice of Morality

What Is Morality?

An Anthropologist's View: Morality as Culturally Approved Habits

Ruth Benedict

In this essay, Ruth Benedict looks at morality and human behavior through the lens of a scientific anthropologist. She seeks a "critical science of ethics" that would enable us to see clearly the real nature of our particular understanding of value, good, and evil. Noted as a pioneer in the field of cultural anthropology, Benedict argues that whatever people and cultures may think about the origins of their moral attitudes, they are in fact a reflection of how a specific culture has defined what is "normal" and what is "abnormal." Phenomena such as trances and homosexuality are regarded as deviant in some cultures but accepted or even admired in others, as are acts of revenge and other culturally approved habits. Just as languages and grammar rules vary, so also do concepts of the good and of value. They all reflect what is taught, and learned, by cultures. Ruth Benedict was a major figure in American anthropology and the author of *Patterns of Culture* (1935).

> *As you read through this essay, consider the following:*
>
> 1. How do different societies understand what is normal and abnormal?
> 2. What lessons does Benedict draw from the differences she discovered among cultural practices and definitions of what is normal?

3. Do you agree or disagree with Benedict's suggestion that morality and value resemble languages?

4. To what degree might it be argued that the differences Benedict describes flow from different beliefs about the world as against different values themselves? Or is that distinction even tenable?

5. Benedict speaks of the need for cultures to "select" from among the different possible behavior traits those that it wishes to encourage and discourage. Do you think it is unimportant what traits are selected? How do you think Benedict might answer that question?

Modern social anthropology has become more and more a study of the varieties and common elements of cultural environment and the consequences of these in human behavior. For such a study of diverse social orders primitive peoples fortunately provide a laboratory not yet entirely vitiated by the spread of a standardized worldwide civilization. Dyaks and Hopis, Fijians and Yakuts are significant for psychological and sociological study because only among these simpler peoples has there been sufficient isolation to give opportunity for the development of localized social forms. In the higher cultures the standardization of custom and belief over a couple of continents has given a false sense of the inevitability of the particular forms that have gained currency, and we need to turn to a wider survey in order to check the conclusions we hastily base upon this near-universality of familiar customs. Most of the simpler cultures did not gain the wide currency of the one which, out of our experience, we identify with human nature, but this was for various historical reasons, and certainly not for any that gives us as its carriers a monopoly of social good or of social sanity. Modern civilization, from this point of view, becomes not a necessary pinnacle of human achievement but one entry in a long series of possible adjustments.

These adjustments, whether they are in mannerisms like the ways of showing anger,

From "Anthropology and the Abnormal," by Ruth Benedict, *The Journal of General Psychology*, 1934, vol. 10, pp. 59–82. Reprinted by permission of Helen Dwight Reid Educational Foundation. Published by Heldref Publications, 1319 Eighteenth St., NW, Washington, D.C. 20036–1802. Copyright © 1934.

or joy, or grief in any society, or in major human drives like those of sex, prove to be far more variable than experience in any one culture would suggest. In certain fields, such as that of religion or of formal marriage arrangements, these wide limits of variability are well known and can be fairly described. In others it is not yet possible to give a generalized account, but that does not absolve us of the task of indicating the significance of the work that has been done and of the problems that have arisen.

One of these problems relates to the customary modern normal-abnormal categories and our conclusions regarding them. In how far are such categories culturally determined, or in how far can we with assurance regard them as absolute? In how far can we regard inability to function socially as diagnostic of abnormality, or in how far is it necessary to regard this as a function of the culture?

As a matter of fact, one of the most striking facts that emerges from a study of widely varying cultures is the ease with which our abnormals function in other cultures. It does not matter what kind of "abnormality" we choose for illustration, those which indicate extreme instability, or those which are more in the nature of character traits like sadism or delusions of grandeur or of persecution, there are well-described cultures in which these abnormals function at ease and with honor, and apparently without danger or difficulty to the society.

The most notorious of these is trance and catalepsy. Even a very mild mystic is aberrant in our culture. But most peoples have regarded even extreme psychic manifestations not only as normal and desirable, but even as characteristic of highly valued and gifted individuals. This was true even in our own cultural background in that period when Catholicism made the ecstatic experience the mark of sainthood. It is hard for us, born and brought up in a culture that makes no use of the experience, to realize how important a role it may play and how many individuals are capable of it, once it has been given an honorable place in any society. . . .

Cataleptic and trance phenomena are, of course, only one illustration of the fact that those whom we regard as abnormals may function adequately in other cultures. Many of our culturally discarded traits are selected for elaboration in different societies. Homosexuality is an excellent example, for in this case our attention is not constantly diverted, as in the consideration of trance, to the interruption of routine activity which it implies. Homosexuality poses the problem very simply. A tendency toward this trait in our culture exposes an individual to all the conflicts to which all aberrants are always exposed, and we tend to identify the consequences of this conflict with homosexuality. But these consequences are obviously local and cultural. Homosexuals in many societies are not incompetent, but they may be such if the culture asks adjustments of them that would strain any man's vitality. Wherever homosexuality has been given an honorable place in any society, those to whom it is congenial have filled adequately the honorable roles society assigns to them. Plato's *Republic* is, of course, the most convincing statement of such a reading of homosexuality. It is presented as one of the major means to the good life, and it was generally so regarded in Greece at that time. . . .

. . . Among the Kwakiutl it did not matter whether a relative had died in bed of disease, or by the hand of an enemy, in either case death was an affront to be wiped out by the death of another person. The fact that one had been caused to mourn was proof that one had been put upon. A chief's sister and her daughter had gone up to Victoria, and either because they drank bad whiskey or because their boat capsized they never came back. The chief called together his warriors, "Now I ask you, tribes, who shall wail? Shall I do it or shall another?" The spokesman answered, of course, "Not you, Chief. Let some other of the tribes." Immediately they set up the war pole to announce their intention of wiping out the injury, and gathered a war party. They set out, and found seven men and two children asleep and killed them. "Then they felt good when they arrived at Sebaa in the evening."

The point which is of interest to us is that in our society those who on that occasion would feel good when they arrived at Sebaa that evening would be the definitely abnormal. There would be some, even in our society, but it is not a recognized and approved mood under the circumstances. On the Northwest Coast those are favored and fortunate to whom that mood under those circumstances is congenial, and those to whom it is repugnant are unlucky. This latter minority can register in their own culture only by doing violence to their congenial responses and acquiring others that are difficult for them. The person, for instance, who, like a Plains Indian whose wife has been taken from him, is too proud to fight, can deal with the Northwest Coast civilization only by ignoring its strongest bents. If he cannot achieve it, he is the deviant in that culture, their instance of abnormality.

This head-hunting that takes place on the Northwest Coast after a death is no matter of blood revenge or of organized vengeance. There is no effort to tie up the subsequent killing with any responsibility on the part of the victim for the death of the person who is being mourned. A chief whose son has died goes visiting wherever his fancy dictates, and he says to his host, "My prince has died today, and you go with him." Then he kills him. In this, according to their interpretation, he acts nobly because he has not been downed. He has thrust back in return. The whole procedure is meaningless without the fundamental paranoid reading of bereavement. Death, like all the other untoward accidents of existence, confounds man's pride and can only be handled in the category of insults.

Behavior honored upon the Northwest Coast is one which is recognized as abnormal in our civilization, and yet it is sufficiently close to the attitudes of our own culture to be intelligible to us and to have a definite vocabulary with which we may discuss it. The megalomaniac paranoid trend is a definite danger in our society. It is encouraged by some of our major preoccupations, and it confronts us with a choice of two possible attitudes. One is to brand it as abnormal and reprehensible, and is the attitude we have chosen in our civilization. The other is to make it an essential attribute of ideal man, and this is the solution in the culture of the Northwest Coast.

These illustrations, which it has been possible to indicate only in the briefest manner, force upon us the fact that normality is culturally defined. An adult shaped to the drives and standards of either of these cultures, if he were transported into our civilization, would fall into our categories of abnormality. He would be faced with the psychic dilemmas of the socially unavailable. In his own culture, however, he is the pillar of society, the end result of socially inculcated mores, and the problem of personal instability in his case simply does not arise.

No one civilization can possibly utilize in its mores the whole potential range of human behavior. Just as there are great numbers of possible phonetic articulations, and the possibility of language depends on a selection and standardization of a few of these in order that speech communication may be possible at all, so the possibility of organized behavior of every sort, from the fashions of local dress and houses to the dicta of a people's ethics and religion, depends upon a similar selection among the possible behavior traits. In the field of recognized economic obligations or sex tabus this selection is as nonrational and subconscious a process as it is in the field of phonetics. It is a process which goes on in the group for long periods of time and is historically conditioned by innumerable accidents of isolation or of contact of peoples. In any com-

prehensive study of psychology, the selection that different cultures have made in the course of history within the great circumference of potential behavior is of great significance.

Every society, beginning with some slight inclination in one direction or another, carries its preference farther and farther, integrating itself more and more completely upon its chosen basis, and discarding those types of behavior that are uncongenial. Most of those organizations of personality that seem to us most incontrovertibly abnormal have been used by different civilizations in the very foundations of their institutional life. Conversely the most valued traits of our normal individuals have been looked on in differently organized cultures as aberrant. Normality, in short, within a very wide range, is culturally defined. . . .

. . . We do not any longer make the mistake of deriving the morality of our locality and decade directly from the inevitable constitution of human nature. We do not elevate it to the dignity of a first principle. We recognize that morality differs in every society, and is a convenient term for socially approved habits. Mankind has always preferred to say, "It is morally good," rather than "It is habitual," and the fact of this preference is matter enough for a critical science of ethics. But historically the two phrases are synonymous.

The concept of the normal is properly a variant of the concept of the good. It is that which society has approved. A normal action is one which falls well within the limits of expected behavior for a particular society. Its variability among different peoples is essentially a function of the variability of the behavior patterns that different societies have created for themselves, and can never be wholly divorced from a consideration of culturally institutionalized types of behavior.

Each culture is a more or less elaborate working-out of the potentialities of the segment it has chosen. In so far as a civilization is well integrated and consistent within itself, it will tend to carry farther and farther, according to its nature, its initial impulse toward a particular type of action, and from the point of view of any other culture those elaborations will include more and more extreme and aberrant traits.

Each of these traits, in proportion as it reinforces the chosen behavior patterns of that culture, is for that culture normal. Those individuals to whom it is congenial either congenitally, or as the result of childhood sets, are accorded prestige in that culture, and are not visited with the social contempt or disapproval which their traits would call down upon them in a society that was differently organized. On the other hand, those individuals whose characteristics are not congenial to the selected type of human behavior in that community are the deviants, no matter how valued their personality traits may be in a contrasted civilization. . . .

I have spoken of individuals as having sets toward certain types of behavior, and of these sets as running sometimes counter to the types of behavior which are institutionalized in the culture to which they belong. From all that we know of contrasting cultures it seems clear that differences of temperament occur in every society. The matter has never been made the subject of investigation, but from the available material it would appear that these temperament types are very likely of universal recurrence. That is, there is an ascertainable range of human behavior that is found wherever a sufficiently large series of individuals is observed. But the proportion in which behavior types stand to one another in different societies is not universal. The vast majority of individuals in any group are shaped to the fashion of that culture. In other words, most individuals are plastic to the moulding force of the society into which they are born. In a society that values trance, as in India, they will have supernormal experience. In a society that institutionalizes homosexuality, they will be homosexual. In a society that sets the gathering of possessions as the chief human objective, they will amass property. . . . The small proportion of the number of the deviants in any culture is not a function of the sure instinct with which that society has built itself upon the fundamental sanities, but of the universal fact that, happily, the majority of mankind quite readily take any shape that is presented to them.

A Religious View: The Reality of the Law of Nature

C. S. Lewis

C. S. Lewis was born in Belfast, Northern Ireland, in 1898. He entered Oxford at nineteen and enjoyed it so much he never left. He wrote widely, in literature and philosophy. Among his best-known works are the *Screwtape Letters, Mere Christianity*, and the seven books known collectively as the *Narnia Chronicles*. He wrote works of poetry, novels, and literary criticism. But he also delivered and later published a series of lectures on BBC Radio. Indeed he was so well known that he appeared on the cover of *Time* magazine. In 1956, he surprised many of his Oxford friends by marrying Joy Gresham, a divorced American woman of Jewish descent who had been a Communist. Joy died of cancer in 1960, after four years of happy marriage.

In this selection, taken from *Mere Christianity*, Lewis first defends the "law of human nature" as the source of objectively valid claims on persons. He discusses various problems with the position of ethical relativists such as Benedict, including the supposed differences in moral codes among cultures, the importance of the distinction between a culture's moral teachings and its beliefs about the world, the question of whether morality can be better or worse if one accepts relativism, and the idea of moral progress. Turning to the *implications* of the existence of the Moral Law, Lewis argues that because we cannot reasonably doubt that the Moral Law exists, there must be something like a mind behind the universe. The purely "scientific" picture is therefore incomplete because it ignores the ordering mind that appears to us in the form of the Moral Law.

As you read through this essay, consider the following:

1. What does Lewis mean by the Law of Nature?
2. Lewis answers those who think the Law of Nature is unsound because different civilizations have different moralities in a variety of different ways. One has to do with the nature of the variations among cultures. What does he mean?
3. On what basis does Lewis reject the idea that the moral law is merely an "instinct"?
4. On what basis does Lewis reject the idea that the moral law is merely a convention that we are taught by our culture?
5. Why does Lewis think that moral progress, and even the ability to criticize another culture's morality, shows that the Moral Law is real and not relative to culture?
6. Some have suggested that we can "explain away" the Law of Nature by saying it is really about what we find convenient. How does Lewis respond?
7. Lewis claims science cannot account for the one thing we know more certainly than anything we observe, and that we therefore have reason to believe in the mind that is the source of the Law of Nature. Explain what he means.
8. Discuss the following claim: Lewis has at most shown that we *believe* there is a Moral Law. He has not shown that it exists. Nor has he shown that there must be a God to explain that law even if it does exist.

THE LAW OF HUMAN NATURE

Every one has heard people quarrelling. Sometimes it sounds funny and sometimes it sounds merely unpleasant; but however it sounds, I believe we can learn something very important from listening to the kind of things they say. They say things like this: "How'd you like it if anyone did the same to you?"— "That's my seat, I was there first"—"Leave him alone, he isn't doing you any harm"— "Why should you shove in first?"—"Give me a bit of your orange, I gave you a bit of mine"—"Come on, you promised." People say things like that every day, educated people as well as uneducated, and children as well as grown-ups.

Now what interests me about all these remarks is that the man who makes them is not merely saying that the other man's behaviour does not happen to please him. He is appealing to some kind of standard of behaviour which he expects the other man to know about. And the other man very seldom replies: "To hell with your standard." Nearly always he tries to make out that what he has been doing does not really go against the standard, or that if it does there is some special excuse. He pretends there is some special reason in this particular case why the person who took the seat first should not keep it, or that things were quite different when he was given the bit of orange, or that something has turned up which lets him off keeping his promise. It looks, in fact, very much as if both parties had in mind some kind of Law or Rule of fair play or decent behaviour or morality or whatever you like to call it, about which they

From C. S. Lewis, *Mere Christianity* (New York: Macmillan, 1943). Reprinted by permission.

really agreed. And they have. If they had not, they might, of course, fight like animals, but they could not *quarrel* in the human sense of the word. Quarrelling means trying to show that the other man is in the wrong. And there would be no sense in trying to do that unless you and he had some sort of agreement as to what Right and Wrong are; just as there would be no sense in saying that a footballer had committed a foul unless there was some agreement about the rules of football.

Now this Law or Rule about Right and Wrong used to be called the Law of Nature. Nowadays, when we talk of the "laws of nature" we usually mean things like gravitation, or heredity, or the laws of chemistry. But when the older thinkers called the Law of Right and Wrong "the Law of Nature," they really meant the Law of *Human* Nature. The idea was that, just as all bodies are governed by the law of gravitation and organisms by biological laws, so the creature called man also had *his* law—with this great difference, that a body could not choose whether it obeyed the law of gravitation or not, but a man could choose either to obey the Law of Human Nature or to disobey it.

We may put this in another way. Each man is at every moment subjected to several different sets of law but there is only one of these which he is free to disobey. As a body, he is subjected to gravitation and cannot disobey it; if you leave him unsupported in midair, he has no more choice about falling than a stone has. As an organism, he is subjected to various biological laws which he cannot disobey any more than an animal can. That is, he cannot disobey those laws which he shares with other things; but the law which is peculiar to his human nature, the law he does not share with animals or vegetables or inorganic things, is the one he can disobey if he chooses.

This law was called the Law of Nature because people thought that every one knew it by nature and did not need to be taught it. They did not mean, of course, that you might not find an odd individual here and there who did not know it, just as you find a

few people who are colour-blind or have no ear for a tune. But taking the race as a whole, they thought that the human idea of decent behaviour was obvious to every one. And I believe they were right. If they were not, then all the things we said about the war were nonsense. What was the sense in saying the enemy were in the wrong unless Right is a real thing which the Nazis at bottom knew as well as we did and ought to have practised? If they had had no notion of what we mean by right, then, though we might still have had to fight them, we could no more have blamed them for that than for the colour of their hair.

I know that some people say the idea of a Law of Nature or decent behaviour known to all men is unsound, because different civilisations and different ages have had quite different moralities.

But this is not true. There have been differences between their moralities, but these have never amounted to anything like a total difference. If anyone will take the trouble to compare the moral teaching of, say, the ancient Egyptians, Babylonians, Hindus, Chinese, Greeks and Romans, what will really strike him will be how very like they are to each other and to our own. Some of the evidence for this I have put together in the appendix of another book called *The Abolition of Man;* but for our present purpose I need only ask the reader to think what a totally different morality would mean. Think of a country where people were admired for running away in battle, or where a man felt proud of double-crossing all the people who had been kindest to him. You might just as well try to imagine a country where two and two made five. Men have differed as regards what people you ought to be unselfish to—whether it was only your own family, or your fellow countrymen, or everyone. But they have always agreed that you ought not to put yourself first. Selfishness has never been admired. Men have differed as to whether you should have one wife or four. But they have always agreed that you must not simply have any woman you liked.

But the most remarkable thing is this. Whenever you find a man who says he does not believe in a real Right and Wrong, you will find the same man going back on this a moment later. He may break his promise to you, but if you try breaking one to him he will be complaining "It's not fair" before you can say Jack Robinson. A nation may say treaties do not matter; but then, next minute, they spoil their case by saying that the particular treaty they want to break was an unfair one. But if treaties do not matter, and if there is no such thing as Right and Wrong—in other words, if there is no Law of Nature—what is the difference between a fair treaty and an unfair one? Have they not let the cat out of the bag and shown that, whatever they say, they really know the Law of Nature just like anyone else?

It seems, then, we are forced to believe in a real Right and Wrong. People may be sometimes mistaken about them, just as people sometimes get their sums wrong; but they are not a matter of mere taste and opinion any more than the multiplication table. Now if we are agreed about that, I go on to my next point, which is this. None of us are really keeping the Law of Nature. If there are any exceptions among you, I apologise to them. They had much better read some other work, for nothing I am going to say concerns them. And now, turning to the ordinary human beings who are left:

I hope you will not misunderstand what I am going to say. I am not preaching, and Heaven knows I do not pretend to be better than anyone else. I am only trying to call attention to a fact; the fact that this year, or this month, or, more likely, this very day, we have failed to practise ourselves the kind of behaviour we expect from other people. There may be all sorts of excuses for us. That time you were so unfair to the children was when you were very tired. That slightly shady business about the money—the one you have almost forgotten—came when you were very hard up. And what you promised to do for old So-and-so and have never done—well, you never would have promised if you had known how frightfully busy you were going to be. . . .

The question at the moment is not whether they are good excuses. The point is that they are one more proof of how deeply, whether we like it or not, we believe in the Law of Nature. If we do not believe in decent behaviour, why should we be so anxious to make excuses for not having behaved decently? . . .

SOME OBJECTIONS

If they are the foundation, I had better stop to make that foundation firm before I go on. Some of the letters I have had show that a good many people find it difficult to understand just what this Law of Human Nature, or Moral Law, or Rule of Decent Behaviour is.

For example, some people wrote to me saying, "Isn't what you call the Moral Law simply our herd instinct and hasn't it been developed just like all our other instincts?" Now I do not deny that we may have a herd instinct: but that is not what I mean by the Moral Law. We all know what it feels like to be prompted by instinct—by mother love, or sexual instinct, or the instinct for food. It means that you feel a strong want or desire to act in a certain way. And, of course, we sometimes do feel just that sort of desire to help another person: and no doubt that desire is due to the herd instinct. But feeling a desire to help is quite different from feeling that you ought to help whether you want to or not. Supposing you hear a cry for help from a man in danger. You will probably feel two desires—one a desire to give help (due to your herd instinct), the other a desire to keep out of danger (due to the instinct for self-preservation). But you will find inside you, in addition to these two impulses, a third thing which tells you that you ought to follow the impulse to help, and suppress the impulse to run away. Now this thing that judges between two instincts, that decides which should be encouraged, cannot itself be either of them. You might as well say that the sheet of music which tells you, at a given moment, to play one note on the piano and not another, is itself one of the notes on the keyboard. The

Moral Law tells us the tune we have to play: our instincts are merely the keys.

Another way of seeing that the Moral Law is not simply one of our instincts is this. If two instincts are in conflict, and there is nothing in a creature's mind except those two instincts, obviously the stronger of the two must win. But at those moments when we are most conscious of the Moral Law, it usually seems to be telling us to side with the weaker of the two impulses. You probably *want* to be safe much more than you want to help the man who is drowning: but the Moral Law tells you to help him all the same. And surely it often tells us to try to make the right impulse stronger than it naturally is? I mean, we often feel it our duty to stimulate the herd instinct, by waking up our imaginations and arousing our pity and so on, so as to get up enough steam for doing the right thing. But clearly we are not acting *from* instinct when we set about making an instinct stronger than it is. The thing that says to you, "Your herd instinct is asleep. Wake it up," cannot itself *be* the herd instinct. The thing that tells you which note on the piano needs to be played louder cannot itself be that note.

Here is a third way of seeing it. If the Moral Law was one of our instincts, we ought to be able to point to some one impulse inside us which was always what we call "good," always in agreement with the rule of right behaviour. But you cannot. There is none of our impulses which the Moral Law may not sometimes tell us to suppress, and none which it may not sometimes tell us to encourage. It is a mistake to think that some of our impulses—say mother love or patriotism— are good, and others, like sex or the fighting instinct, are bad. All we mean is that the occasions on which the fighting instinct or the sexual desire need to be restrained are rather more frequent than those for restraining mother love or patriotism. But there are situations in which it is the duty of a married man to encourage his sexual impulse and of a soldier to encourage the fighting instinct. There are also occasions on which a mother's love for her own children or a man's love for his own country have to be suppressed or they will lead to unfairness towards other people's children or countries. Strictly speaking, there are no such things as good and bad impulses. Think once again of a piano. It has not got two kinds of notes on it, the "right" notes and the "wrong" ones. Every single note is right at one time and wrong at another. The Moral Law is not any one instinct or any set of instincts: it is something which makes a kind of tune (the tune we call goodness or right conduct) by directing the instincts. . . .

Other people wrote to me saying, "Isn't what you call the Moral Law just a social convention, something that is put into us by education?" I think there is a misunderstanding here. The people who ask that question are usually taking it for granted that if we have learned a thing from parents and teachers, then that thing must be merely a human invention. But, of course, that is not so. We all learned the multiplication table at school. A child who grew up alone on a desert island would not know it. But surely it does not follow that the multiplication table is simply a human convention, something human beings have made up for themselves and might have made different if they had liked? I fully agree that we learn the Rule of Decent Behaviour from parents and teachers, and friends and books, as we learn everything else. But some of the things we learn are mere conventions which might have been different—we learn to keep to the left of the road, but it might just as well have been the rule to keep to the right—and others of them, like mathematics, are real truths. The question is to which class the Law of Human Nature belongs.

There are two reasons for saying it belongs to the same class as mathematics. The first . . . is that though there are differences between the moral ideas of one time or country and those of another, the differences are not really very great—not nearly so great as most people imagine—and you can recognise the same law running through them all: whereas mere conventions, like the rule of the road or the kind of clothes people wear, may differ to any extent. The other reason is this.

When you think about these differences between the morality of one people and another, do you think that the morality of one people is ever better or worse than that of another? Have any of the changes been improvements? If not, then of course there could never be any moral progress. Progress means not just changing, but changing for the better. If no set of moral ideas were truer or better than any other, there would be no sense in preferring civilised morality to savage morality, or Christian morality to Nazi morality. In fact, of course, we all do believe that some moralities are better than others. We do believe that some of the people who tried to change the moral ideas of their own age were what we would call Reformers or Pioneers—people who understood morality better than their neighbours did. Very well then. The moment you say that one set of moral ideas can be better than another, you are, in fact, measuring them both by a standard, saying that one of them conforms to that standard more nearly than the other. But the standard that measures two things is something different from either. You are, in fact, comparing them both with some Real Morality, admitting that there is such a thing as a real Right, independent of what people think, and that some people's ideas get nearer to that real Right than others. Or put it this way. If your moral ideas can be truer, and those of the Nazis less true, there must be something—some Real Morality—for them to be true about. The reason why your idea of New York can be truer or less true than mine is that New York is a real place, existing quite apart from what either of us thinks. If when each of us said "New York" each meant merely "The town I am imagining in my own head," how could one of us have truer ideas than the other? There would be no question of truth or falsehood at all. In the same way, if the Rule of Decent Behaviour meant simply "whatever each nation happens to approve," there would be no sense in saying that any one nation had ever been more correct in its approval than any other; no sense in saying that the world could ever grow morally better or morally worse.

I conclude then, that though the differences between people's ideas of Decent Behaviour often make you suspect that there is no real natural Law of Behaviour at all, yet the things we are bound to think about these differences really prove just the opposite. But one word before I end. I have met people who exaggerate the differences, because they have not distinguished between differences of morality and differences of belief about facts. For example, one man said to me, "Three hundred years ago people in England were putting witches to death. Was that what you call the Rule of Human Nature or Right Conduct?" But surely the reason we do not execute witches is that we do not believe there are such things. If we did—if we really thought that there were people going about who had sold themselves to the devil and received supernatural powers from him in return and were using these powers to kill their neighbours or drive them mad or bring bad weather, surely we would all agree that if anyone deserved the death penalty, then these filthy quislings did. There is no difference of moral principle here: the difference is simply about matter of fact. It may be a great advance in knowledge not to believe in witches: there is no moral advance in not executing them when you do not think they are there. You would not call a man humane for ceasing to set mousetraps if he did so because he believed there were no mice in the house.

THE REALITY OF THE LAW

I now go back to what I said at the end of the first chapter, that there were two odd things about the human race. First, that they were haunted by the idea of a sort of behaviour they ought to practise, what you might call fair play, or decency, or morality, or the Law of Nature. Second, that they did not in fact do so. Now some of you may wonder why I called this odd. It may seem to you the most natural thing in the world. In particular, you may have thought I was rather hard on the human race. After all, you may say, what I call breaking the Law of Right and Wrong or of Nature, only means that people are not perfect. And why on earth should I expect them to be? That would be a good answer if what I was trying to do was to fix the exact amount of blame which is due to us for not behaving as we expect others to behave. But that is not my job at all. I am not concerned at present with blame; I am trying to find out truth. And from that point of view the very idea of something being imperfect, of its not being what it ought to be, has certain consequences.

If you take a thing like a stone or a tree, it is what it is and there seems no sense in saying it ought to have been otherwise. Of course you may say a stone is "the wrong shape" if you want to use it for a rockery, or that a tree is a bad tree because it does not give you as much shade as you expected. But all you mean is that the stone or tree does not happen to be convenient for some purpose of your own. You are not, except as a joke, blaming them for that. You really know, that, given the weather and the soil, the tree could not have been any different. What we, from our point of view, call a "bad" tree is obeying the laws of its nature just as much as a "good" one.

Now have you noticed what follows? It follows that what we usually call the laws of nature—the way weather works on a tree for example—may not really be *laws* in the strict sense, but only in a manner of speaking. When you say that falling stones always obey the law of gravitation, is not this much the same as saying that the law only means "what stones always do"? You do not really think that when a stone is let go, it suddenly remembers that it is under orders to fall to the ground. You only mean that, in fact, it does fall. In other words, you cannot be sure that there is anything over and above the facts themselves, any law about what ought to happen, as distinct from what does happen. The laws of nature, as applied to stones or trees, may only mean "what Nature, in fact, does." But if you turn to the Law of Human Nature, the Law of Decent Behaviour, it is a different matter. That law certainly does not mean "what human beings, in fact, do"; for as I said before,

many of them do not obey this law at all, and none of them obey it completely. The law of gravity tells you what stones do if you drop them; but the Law of Human Nature tells you what human beings ought to do and do not. In other words, when you are dealing with humans, something else comes in above and beyond the actual facts. You have the facts (how men do behave) and you also have something else (how they ought to behave). In the rest of the universe there need not be anything but the facts. Electrons and molecules behave in a certain way, and certain results follow, and that may be the whole story.* But men behave in a certain way and that is not the whole story, for all the time you know that they ought to behave differently.

Now this is really so peculiar that one is tempted to try to explain it away. For instance, we might try to make out that when you say a man ought not to act as he does, you only mean the same as when you say that a stone is the wrong shape; namely, that what he is doing happens to be inconvenient to you. But that is simply untrue. A man occupying the corner seat in the train because he got there first, and a man who slipped into it while my back was turned and removed my bag, are both equally inconvenient. But I blame the second man and do not blame the first. . . . If a man asks what is the point of behaving decently, it is no good replying, "in order to benefit society," for trying to benefit society, in other words being unselfish (for "society" after all only means "other people"), is one of the things decent behaviour consists in; all you are really saying is that decent behaviour is decent behaviour. You would have said just as much if you had stopped at the statement, "Men ought to be unselfish."

And that is where I do stop. Men ought to be unselfish, ought to be fair. Not that men are unselfish, nor that they like being unselfish, but that they ought to be. The Moral Law, or Law of Human Nature, is not

---

*I do not think it *is* the whole story, as you will see later. I mean that, as far as the argument has gone up to date, it *may* be.

simply a fact about human behaviour in the same way as the Law of Gravitation is, or may be, simply a fact about how heavy objects behave. On the other hand, it is not a mere fancy, for we cannot get rid of the idea, and most of the things we say and think about men would be reduced to nonsense if we did. And it is not simply a statement about how we should like men to behave for our own convenience; for the behaviour we call bad or unfair is not exactly the same as the behaviour we find inconvenient, and may even be the opposite. Consequently, this Rule of Right and Wrong, or Law of Human Nature, or whatever you call it, must somehow or other be a real thing—a thing that is really there, not made up by ourselves. And yet it is not a fact in the ordinary sense, in the same way as our actual behaviour is a fact. It begins to look as if we shall have to admit that there is more than one kind of reality; that, in this particular case, there is something above and beyond the ordinary facts of men's behaviour, and yet quite definitely real—a real law, which none of us made, but which we find pressing on us.

WHAT LIES BEHIND THE LAW

Let us sum up what we have reached so far. In the case of stones and trees and things of that sort, what we call the Laws of Nature may not be anything except a way of speaking. When you say that nature is governed by certain laws, this may only mean that nature does, in fact, behave in a certain way. The so-called laws may not be anything real—anything above and beyond the actual facts which we observe. But in the case of Man, we saw that this will not do. The Law of Human Nature, or of Right and Wrong, must be something above and beyond the actual facts of human behaviour. In this case, besides the actual facts, you have something else—a real law which we did not invent and which we know we ought to obey.

I now want to consider what this tells us about the universe we live in. Ever since men were able to think, they have been wondering what this universe really is and how it came to be there. And, very roughly, two views have been held. First, there is what is called the materialist view. People who take that view think that matter and space just happen to exist, and always have existed, nobody knows why; and that the matter, behaving in certain fixed ways, has just happened, by a sort of fluke, to produce creatures like ourselves who are able to think. By one chance in a thousand something hit our sun and made it produce the planets; and by another thousandth chance the chemicals necessary for life, and the right temperature, occurred on one of these planets, and so some of the matter on this earth came alive; and then, by a very long series of chances, the living creatures developed into things like us. The other view is the religious view. According to it, what is behind the universe is more like a mind than it is like anything else we know. That is to say, it is conscious, and has purposes, and prefers one thing to another. And on this view it made the universe, partly for purposes we do not know, but partly, at any rate, in order to produce creatures like itself—I mean, like itself to the extent of having minds. Please do not think that one of these views was held a long time ago and that the other has gradually taken its place. Wherever there have been thinking men both views turn up. And note this too. You cannot find out which view is the right one by science in the ordinary sense. Science works by experiments. It watches how things behave. Every scientific statement in the long run, however complicated it looks, really means something like, "I pointed the telescope to such and such a part of the sky at 2:20 A.M. on January 15th and saw so-and-so," or, "I put some of this stuff in a pot and heated it to such-and-such a temperature and it did so-and-so." Do not think I am saying anything against science: I am only saying what its job is. And the more scientific a man is, the more (I believe) he would agree with me that this is the job of science—and a very useful and necessary job it is too. But why anything comes to be there at all, and whether there is anything behind the things science observes—something of a different kind—this is not a scientific question. If there is "Something Behind," then either it will have to remain altogether unknown to men or else make itself known in some different way. The statement that there is any such thing, and the statement that there is no such thing, are neither of them statements that science can make. And real scientists do not usually make them. It is usually the journalists and popular novelists who have picked up a few odds and ends of half-baked science from textbooks who go in for them. After all, it is really a matter of common sense. Supposing science ever became complete so that it knew every single thing in the whole universe. Is it not plain that the questions, "Why is there a universe?" "Why does it go on as it does?" "Has it any meaning?" would remain just as they were?

Now the position would be quite hopeless but for this. There is one thing, and only one, in the whole universe which we know more about than we could learn from external observation. That one thing is Man. We do not merely observe men, we *are* men. In this case we have, so to speak, inside information; we are in the know. And because of that, we know that men find themselves under a moral law, which they did not make, and cannot quite forget even when they try, and which they know they ought to obey. Notice the following point. Anyone studying Man from the outside as we study electricity or cabbages, not knowing our language and consequently not able to get any inside knowledge from us, but merely observing what we did, would never get the slightest evidence that we had this moral law. How could he? for his observations would only show what we did, and the moral law is about what we ought to do. In the same way, if there were anything above or behind the observed facts in the case of stones or the weather, we, by studying them from outside, could never hope to discover it.

The position of the question, then, is like this. We want to know whether the universe simply happens to be what it is for no reason or whether there is a power behind it that makes it what it is. Since that power, if it exists, would be not one of the observed facts but a reality which makes them, no mere observation of the facts can find it. There is only one case in which we can know whether there is anything more, namely our own case. And in that one case we find there is. Or put it the other way round. If there was a controlling power outside the universe, it could not show itself to us as one of the facts inside the universe—no more than the architect of a house could actually be a wall or staircase or fireplace in that house. The only way in which we could expect it to show itself would be inside ourselves as an influence or a command trying to get us to behave in a certain way. And that is just what we do find inside ourselves. Surely this ought to arouse our suspicions? In the only case where you can expect to get an answer, the answer turns out to be Yes; and in the other cases, where you do not get an answer, you see why you do not. Suppose someone asked me, when I see a man in a blue uniform going down the street leaving little paper packets at each house, why I suppose that they contain letters? I should reply, "Because whenever he leaves a similar little packet for me I find it does contain a letter." And if he then objected, "But you've never seen all these letters which you think the other people are getting," I should say, "Of course not, and I shouldn't expect to, because they're not addressed to me. I'm explaining the packets I'm not allowed to open by the ones I am allowed to open." It is the same about this question. The only packet I am allowed to open is Man. When I do, especially when I open that particular man called Myself, I find that I do not exist on my own, that I am under a law; that somebody or something wants me to behave in a certain way. I do not, of course, think that if I could get inside a stone or a tree I should find exactly the same thing, just as I do not think all the other people in the street get the same letters as I do. I should expect, for instance, to find that the stone had to obey the law of gravity—that whereas the sender of the letters merely tells me to obey the law of my human nature, He compels the stone to obey the laws of its stony nature. But I should expect to find that there was, so to speak, a sender of letters in both cases, a Power behind the facts, a Director, a Guide.

Do not think I am going faster than I really am. I am not yet within a hundred miles of the God of Christian theology. All I have got to is a Something which is directing the universe, and which appears in me as a law urging me to do right and making me feel responsible and uncomfortable when I do wrong. I think we have to assume it is more like a mind than it is like anything else we know—because after all the only other thing we know is matter and you can hardly imagine a bit of matter giving instructions.

A Pragmatic View: Morality as Rational Advantage

Thomas Hobbes

Thomas Hobbes was born in 1588 when the approach of the Spanish Armada was threatening Britain. "Fear and I were born twins," he would later say, emphasizing his conviction that the need for security was the foundation of society and the basis of political obligation. He lived during a critical and difficult period of English history, which included struggles over the traditional authority of the church and the emerging role of modern science. He also saw radical political change, including the absolutism of the Stuart monarchy, the English Civil War, the influence of Cromwell, and the restoration of the monarchy. He died just before constitutional government won its final victory. Hobbes served as tutor for Charles II, who gave Hobbes a pension when he was restored to the throne. Hobbes was later sent into exile, condemned in the House of Commons, and even after he died, his books were burned at Oxford. He was suspected of atheism, and, perhaps most important, he rejected the divine basis of political authority. God, he said, is beyond rational understanding; we can only know he exists as the first cause of the universe. Hobbes lived until the age of ninety-one, enjoying a life of travel, study, polemical controversy, and literary and philosophical activity. He was personally temperate, lively, and a loyal friend; he played tennis until the age of seventy-five and attributed his lifelong good health to exercise and singing in bed. He wrote on a variety of subjects, but his most famous work by far is **Leviathan**, published in 1651.

Hobbes was heavily influenced by the new, Galilean scientific method and thought that physical laws could account for human behavior, just as they do all other phenomena. He sought to understand humanity (and politics) in accord with the new scientific methods.

Just before the selection reprinted here, Hobbes argued that the world, including human beings, is comprised of material particles. Minds, he argued, are therefore no different from bodies; human "motion" such as walking, speaking, and other acts are caused by our desires, appetites, and aversions. In this selection, Hobbes discusses how reason and the human condition induce people to leave a "state of nature" and agree to be ruled by a common power strong enough to enforce contracts and ensure peace. Morality is, therefore, a form of convention, agreed to by all in order to avoid the war of all against all. Without an agreement, and the threat of harm imposed by the sovereign, there can be neither morality nor justice. Power and threats are the necessary bases of all obligations.

As you read through this essay, consider the following:

1. Hobbes is often described as a "psychological egoist." What might that mean, given his understanding of human deliberation and motivation?
2. How does Hobbes understand felicity or happiness?
3. What is the state of nature? When does Hobbes think it would arise? What would life be like under it?
4. What are the laws of nature, according to Hobbes?
5. Explain how all of morality, not just politics, may be understood as an agreement for mutual advantage.
6. How does Hobbes respond to the "fool" who claims that justice is contrary to reason and that a rational person would act unjustly?
7. Does Hobbes think morality applies in a state of war where there is no state or society? Explain.
8. Evaluate Hobbes's answer to question 7. Why do you agree or disagree?

THE FIRST PART: OF MAN

Good. Evil. . . . Whatsoever is the object of any man's appetite or desire, that is it which he for his part calleth *good:* and the object of his hate and aversion, *evil;* and of his contempt, *vile* and *inconsiderable.* For these words of good, evil, and contemptible, are ever used with relation to the person that useth them: there being nothing simply and absolutely so. . . .

Deliberation. When in the mind of man, appetites, and aversions, hopes, and fears, concerning one and the same thing, arise alternately; and divers good and evil consequences of the doing, or omitting the thing propounded, come successively into our thoughts; so that sometimes we have an appetite to it; sometimes an aversion from it; sometimes hope to be able to do it; sometimes despair, or fear to attempt it; the whole sum of desires, aversions, hopes and fears continued till the thing be either done, or thought impossible, is that we call DELIBERATION. . . .

The Will. In *deliberation,* the last appetite, or aversion, immediately adhering to the action, or to the omission thereof, is that we call the WILL. . . .

Felicity. Continual success in obtaining those things which a man from time to time desireth, that is to say, continual prospering, is that men call FELICITY; I mean the felicity of this life. For there is no such thing as perpetual tranquility of mind, while we live here; because life itself is but motion, and can never be without desire, nor without fear, no more than without sense. . . .

Of the Natural Condition of Mankind as Concerning Their Felicity and Misery

Men by Nature Equal. Nature hath made men so equal, in the faculties of the body, and mind; as that though there be found one man sometimes manifestly stronger in body, or of quicker mind than another; yet when all is reckoned together, the difference between man, and man, is not so considerable, as that one man can thereupon claim to himself any benefit, to which another may not pretend, as well as he. For as to the strength of body, the weakest has strength enough to kill the strongest, either by secret machination, or by confederacy with others, that are in the same danger with himself.

And as to the faculties of the mind, setting aside the arts grounded upon words, and especially that skill of proceeding upon general, and infallible rules, called science; which very few have, and but in few things; as being not a

---

From Thomas Hobbes, *Leviathan* (1651).

native faculty, born with us: nor attained, as prudence, while we look after somewhat else, I find yet a greater equality amongst men, than that of strength. For prudence, is but experience; which equal time, equally bestows on all men, in those things they equally apply themselves unto. That which may perhaps make such equality incredible, is but a vain conceit of one's own wisdom, which almost all men think they have in a greater degree, than the vulgar; that is, than all men but themselves, and a few others, whom by fame, or for concurring with themselves, they approve.

From Equality Proceeds Diffidence. From this equality of ability, ariseth equality of hope in the attaining of our ends. And therefore if any two men desire the same thing, which nevertheless they cannot both enjoy, they become enemies; and in the way to their end, which is principally their own conservation, and sometimes their delectation only, endeavor to destroy, or subdue one another. And from hence it comes to pass, that where an invader hath no more to fear, than another man's single power; if one plant, sow, build, or possess a convenient seat, others may probably be expected to come prepared with forces united, to dispossess, and deprive him, not only of the fruit of his labour, but also of his life, or liberty. And the invader again is in the like danger of another.

From Diffidence War. And from this diffidence of one another, there is no way for any man to secure himself, so reasonable, as anticipation; that is, by force, or wiles, to master the persons of all men he can, so long, till he sees no other power great enough to endanger him: and this is no more than his own conservation requireth, and is generally allowed. Also because there be some, that taking pleasure in contemplating their own power in the acts of conquest, which they pursue farther than their security requires; if others, that otherwise would be glad to be at ease within modest bounds, should not by invasion increase their power, they would not be able, long time, by standing only on their defence, to subsist. And

by consequence, such augmentation of dominion over men being necessary to a man's conservation, it ought to be allowed him.

Again, men have no pleasure, but on the contrary a great deal of grief, in keeping company, where there is no power able to overawe them all. For every man looketh that his companion should value him, at the same rate he sets upon himself: and upon all signs of contempt, or undervaluing, naturally endeavors, as far as he dares, (which amongst them that have no common power to keep them in quiet, is far enough to make them destroy each other), to extort a greater value from his contemners, by damage; and from others, by the example.

So that in the nature of man, we find three principal causes of quarrel. First, competition; secondly, diffidence; thirdly, glory.

The first, maketh men invade for gain; the second, for safety; and the third, for reputation. The first use violence, to make themselves masters of other men's persons, wives, children, and cattle; the second, to defend them; the third, for trifles, as a word, a smile, a different opinion, and any other sign of undervalue, either direct in their persons, or by reflection in their kindred, their friends, their nation, their profession, or their name.

Out of Civil States, There Is Always War of Every One Against Every One. Hereby it is manifest, that during the time men live without a common power to keep them all in awe, they are in that condition which is called war; and such a war, as is of every man, against every man. For WAR, consisteth not in battle only, or the act of fighting; but in a tract of time, wherein the will to contend by battle is sufficiently known: and therefore the notion of *time*, is to be considered in the nature of war; as it is in the nature of weather. For as the nature of foul weather, lieth not in a shower or two of rain; but in an inclination thereto of many days together: so the nature of war, consisteth not in actual fighting; but in the known disposition thereto, during all the time there is no assurance to the contrary. All other time is PEACE.

The Incommodities of Such a War.
Whatsoever therefore is consequent to a time
of war, where every man is enemy to every
man; the same is consequent to the time,
wherein men live without other security, than
what their own strength, and their own
invention shall furnish them withal. In such
condition, there is no place for industry;
because the fruit thereof is uncertain: and
consequently no culture of the earth; no navigation,
nor use of the commodities that may
be imported by sea; no commodious building;
no instruments of moving, and removing,
such things as require much force; no knowledge
of the face of the earth; no account of
time; no arts; no letters; no society; and which
is worst of all, continual fear, and danger of
violent death; and the life of man, solitary,
poor, nasty, brutish, and short.

It may seem strange to some man, that
has not well weighed these things; that
nature should thus dissociate, and render
men apt to invade, and destroy one another:
and he may therefore, not trusting to this
inference, made from the passions, desire
perhaps to have the same confirmed by experience.
Let him therefore consider with himself,
when taking a journey, he arms himself,
and seeks to go well accompanied; when
going to sleep, he locks his doors; when even
in his house he locks his chests; and this
when he knows there be laws, and public officers,
armed, to revenge all injuries shall be
done him; what opinion he has of his fellow-subjects,
when he rides armed; of his fellow
citizens, when he locks his doors; and of his
children, and servants, when he locks his
chests. Does he not there as much accuse
mankind by his actions, as I do by my words?
But neither of us accuse man's nature in it.
The desires, and other passions of man, are
in themselves no sin. No more are the
actions, that proceed from those passions, till
they know a law that forbids them: which till
laws be made they cannot know: nor can any
law be made, till they have agreed upon the
person that shall make it.

It may peradventure be thought, there
was never such a time, nor condition of war
as this; and I believe it was never generally
so, over all the world; but there are many
places, where they live so now. For the savage
people in many places of America, except the
government of small families, the concord
whereof dependeth on natural lust, have no
government at all; and live at this day in that
brutish manner, as I said before. Howsoever,
it may be perceived what manner of life there
would be, where there were no common
power to fear, by the manner of life, which
men that have formerly lived under a peaceful
government, use to degenerate into, in a
civil war.

But though there had never been any
time, wherein particular men were in a condition
of war one against another; yet in all
times, kings, and persons of sovereign authority,
because of their independency, are in continual
jealousies, and in the state and posture
of gladiators; having their weapons pointing,
and their eyes fixed on one another; that is,
their forts, garrisons, and guns upon the frontiers
of their kingdoms; and continual spies
upon their neighbours; which is a posture of
war. But because they uphold thereby, the
industry of their subjects; there does not follow
from it, that misery, which accompanies
the liberty of particular men.

In Such a War Nothing Is Unjust. To
this war of every man, against every man, this
also is consequent; that nothing can be
unjust. The notions of right and wrong, justice
and injustice have there no place. Where
there is no common power, there is no law:
where no law, no injustice. Force, and fraud,
are in war the two cardinal virtues. Justice,
and injustice are none of the faculties neither
of the body, nor mind. If they were, they
might be in a man that were alone in the
world, as well as his senses, and passions.
They are qualities, that relate to men in society,
not in solitude. It is consequent also to
the same condition, that there be no propriety,
no dominion, no *mine* and *thine* distinct;
but only that to be every man's, that he can
get: and for so long, as he can keep it. And
thus much for the ill condition, which man

by mere nature is actually placed in; though with a possibility to come out of it, consisting partly in the passions, partly in his reason.

The Passions That Incline Men to Peace.

The passions that incline men to peace, are fear of death; desire of such things as are necessary to commodious living; and a hope by their industry to obtain them. And reason suggesteth convenient articles of peace, upon which men may be drawn to agreement. These articles, are they, which otherwise are called the Laws of Nature: whereof I shall speak more particularly [below].

Of the First and Second Natural Laws, and of Contracts

Right of Nature What.

The RIGHT OF NATURE, which writers commonly call *jus naturale*, is the liberty each man hath, to use his own power, as he will himself, for the preservation of his own nature; that is to say, of his own life; and consequently, of doing any thing, which in his own judgment, and reason, he shall conceive to be the aptest means thereunto.

Liberty What.

By LIBERTY, is understood, according to the proper signification of the word, the absence of external impediments: which impediments, may oft take away part of a man's power to do what he would; but cannot hinder him from using the power left him, according as his judgment, and reason shall dictate to him.

A Law of Nature What. Difference of Right and Law.

A LAW OF NATURE, *lex naturalis*, is a precept or general rule, found out by reason, by which a man is forbidden to do that, which is destructive of his life, or taketh away the means of preserving the same; and to omit that, by which he thinketh it may be best preserved. . . .

Naturally Every Man Has Right to Every Thing. The Fundamental Law of Nature.

And because the condition of man, as hath been declared [above], is a condition of war of every one against every one; in which case every one is governed by his own reason; and there is nothing he can make use of, that may not be a help unto him, in preserving his life against his enemies; it followeth, that in such a condition, every man has a right to every thing; even to one another's body. And therefore, as long as this natural right of every man to every thing endureth, there can be no security to any man, how strong or wise soever he be, of living out the time, which nature ordinarily alloweth men to live. And consequently it is a precept, or general rule of reason, *that every man, ought to endeavor peace, as far as he has hope of obtaining it; and when he cannot obtain it, that he may seek, and use, all helps, and advantages of war. . . .*

The Second Law of Nature.

From this fundamental law of nature, by which men are commanded to endeavor peace, is derived this second law; *that a man be willing, when others are so too, as far-forth, as for peace, and defence of himself he shall think it necessary, to lay down this right to all things; and be contented with so much liberty against other men, as he would allow other men against himself.* For as long as every man holdeth this right, of doing any thing he liketh; so long are all men in the condition of war. But if other men will not lay down their right, as well as he; then there is no reason for anyone to divest himself of his: for that wereto expose himself to prey, which no man is bound to rather than to dispose himself to peace. . . .

Not All Rights Are Alienable.

Whensoever a man transferreth his right, or renounceth it; it is either in consideration of some right reciprocally transferred to himself; or for some other good he hopeth for thereby. For it is a voluntary act: and of the voluntary acts of every man, the object is some *good to himself.* And therefore there be some rights, which no man can be understood by any words, or other signs, to have abandoned, or transferred. As first a man cannot lay down the right of resisting them, that assault him by force, to take away his life;

because he cannot be understood to aim thereby, at any good to himself. The same may be said of wounds, and chains, and imprisonment; because there is no benefit consequent to such patience; as there is to the patience of suffering another to be wounded, or imprisoned. . . .

Covenants of Mutual Trust, When Invalid. If a covenant be made, wherein neither of the parties perform presently, but trust one another; in the condition of mere nature, which is a condition of war of every man against every man, upon any reasonable suspicion, it is void; but if there be a common power set over them both, with right and force sufficient to compel performance, it is not void. For he that performeth first, has no assurance the other will perform after; because the bonds of words are too weak to bridle men's ambition, avarice, anger, and other passions, without the fear of some coercive power; which in the condition of mere nature, where all men are equal, and judges of the justness of their own fears, cannot possibly be supposed. And therefore he which performeth first does but betray himself to his enemy; contrary to the right, he can never abandon, of defending his life, and means of living. . . .

Covenants Extorted by Fear Are Valid. Covenants entered into by fear, in the condition of mere nature, are obligatory. For example, if I covenant to pay a ransom, or service for my life, to an enemy; I am bound by it: for it is a contract, wherein one receiveth the benefit of life; the other is to receive money, or service for it; and consequently, where no other law, as in the condition of mere nature, forbiddeth the performance, the covenant is valid. . . .

Of Other Laws of Nature

The Third Law of Nature, Justice. From that law of nature, by which we are obliged to transfer to another, such rights, as being retained, hinder the peace of mankind, there followeth a third; which is this, *that men perform their covenants made:* without which, covenants are in vain, and but empty words; and the right of all men to all things remaining, we are still in the condition of war.

Justice and Injustice What. And in this law of nature, consisteth the fountain and original of JUSTICE. For where no covenant hath preceded, there hath no right been transferred, and every man has right to every thing; and consequently, no action can be unjust. But when a covenant is made, then to break it is unjust: and the definition of INJUSTICE, is no other than *the not performance of covenant.* And whatsoever is not unjust, is *just.*

Justice and Propriety Begin With the Constitution of Commonwealth. But because covenants of mutual trust, where there is a fear of not performance on either part, as hath been said in the former chapter, are invalid; though the original of justice be the making of covenants; yet injustice actually there can be none, till the cause of such fear be taken away; which while men are in the natural condition of war, cannot be done. Therefore before the names of just, and unjust can have place, there must be some coercive power, to compel men equally to the performance of their covenants, by the terror of some punishment, greater than the benefit they expect by the breach of their covenant; and to make good that propriety, which by mutual contract men acquire, in recompense of the universal right they abandon: and such power there is none before the erection of a commonwealth. . . .

Justice Not Contrary to Reason. The fool hath said in his heart, there is no such thing as justice; and sometimes also with his tongue: seriously alleging, that every man's conservation, and contentment, being committed to his own care, there could be no reason, why every man might not do what he thought conduced thereunto. He does not therein deny, that there are covenants; and that they are sometimes broken, sometimes kept; but he questioneth whether injustice, taking away the fear of God, may not sometimes stand with that reason, which dictateth to every man his own good. . . .

[I say that] in a condition of war, wherein every man to every man, for want of a common power to keep them all in awe, is an enemy, there is no man who can hope by his own strength, or wit, to defend himself from destruction without the help of confederates; where every one expects the same defence by the confederation, that any one else does: and therefore he which declares he thinks it reason to decieve those that help him, can in reason expect no other means of safety than what can be had from his own single power. He therefore that breaketh his covenant, and consequently declareth that he thinks he may with reason do so, cannot be received into any society, that unite themselves for peace and defence, but by the error of them that receive him; nor when he is received, be retained in it, without seeing the danger of their error; which errors a man cannot reasonably reckon upon as the means of his security: and therefore if he be left, or cast out of society he perisheth; and if he live in society, it is by the errors of other men, which he could not foresee, nor reckon upon; and consequently against the reason of his preservation. . . .

THE SECOND PART: OF COMMONWEALTH

Of the Causes, Generation, and Definition of a Commonwealth

The End of Commonwealth, Particular Security. The final cause, end, or design of men, who naturally love liberty, and dominion over others, in the introduction of that restraint upon themselves, in which we see them live in commonwealths, is the foresight of their own preservation, and of a more contented life thereby; that is to say, of getting themselves out from that miserable condition of war, which is necessarily consequent, as hath been shown, to the natural passions of men, when there is no visible power to keep

them in awe, and tie them by fear of punishment to the performance of their covenants, and observation of those laws of nature set down [above].

Which Is Not to Be Had from the Law of Nature. For the laws of nature, as *justice, equality, modesty, mercy*, and, in sum, *doing to others, as we would be done to*, of themselves, without the terror of some power, to cause them to be observed, are contrary to our natural passions, that carry us to partiality, pride, revenge, and the like. And covenants, without the sword, are but words, and of no strength to secure a man at all. Therefore notwithstanding the laws of nature (which every one hath then kept, when he has the will to keep them, when he can do it safely) if there be no power erected or not great enough for our security; every man will, and may lawfully rely on his own strength and art, for caution against all other men. . . . For if we could suppose a great multitude of men to consent in the observation of justice, and other laws of nature, without a common power to keep them all in awe; we might as well suppose all mankind to do the same; and then there neither would be, nor need to be any civil government, or commonwealth at all; because there would be peace without subjection. . . .

The Generation of a Commonwealth. The Definition of a Commonwealth. The only way to erect such a common power, as may be able to defend them from the invasion of foreigners, and the injuries of one another, and thereby to secure them in such sort, as that by their own industry, and by the fruits of the earth, they may nourish themselves and live contentedly; is, to confer all their power and strength upon one man, or upon one assembly of men, that may reduce all their wills, by plurality of voices, unto one will: which is as much as to say, to appoint one man, or assembly of men, to bear their person; and every one to own, and acknowledge himself to be author of whatsoever he that so beareth their person, shall act, or cause to be acted, in those things which concern the common peace and safety; and therein to submit their wills, every one to his will, and their judgments, to his judgment. This is more than consent, or concord; it is a real unity of them all, in one and the same person, made by covenant of every man with every man, in such manner, as if every man should say to every man, *I authorize and give up my right of governing myself, to this man, or to this assembly of men, on this condition, that thou give up thy right to him, and authorize all his actions in like manner.* This done, the multitude so united in one person, is called a COMMONWEALTH, in Latin CIVITAS. This is the generation of that great LEVIATHAN, or rather, to speak more reverently, of that *mortal god,* to which we owe under the *immortal God,* our peace and defence. For by this authority, given him by every particular man in the commonwealth, he hath the use of so much power and strength conferred on him, that by terror thereof, he is enabled to form the wills of them all, to peace at home, and mutual aid against their enemies abroad. And in him consisteth the essence of the commonwealth; which, to define it, is *one person, of whose acts a great multitude, by mutual covenants one with another, have made themselves every one the author, to the end he may use the strength and means of them all, as he shall think expedient, for their peace and common defence.*

Why Care About Morality?

Egoism and Self-interest

James Rachels

It is sometimes argued that people act morally *only* when it is in their interests, on the ground that people always act based on their own interests—however altruistic they may appear. Others defend the related claim that, despite appearances, the *right thing to do* is in fact identical to whatever is in a person's genuine, long-term interest. In this selection, James Rachels criticizes both of these claims. He concludes with a discussion of the reasons we have for being moral when it is contrary to our interests and of human motivation generally. James Rachels is professor of philosophy at the University of Alabama at Birmingham.

As you read through this essay, consider the following:

1. What is the story of Gyges's ring? What question does Plato raise with the story?
2. What is psychological egoism, and how does it differ from ethical egoism?
3. What are the two arguments that might be given on behalf of psychological egoism?
4. What is the distinction between selfishness and self-interest? Explain how this distinction is relevant to the argument over psychological egoism.
5. Rachels claims that psychological egoism rests on a "false dichotomy." What does he mean?
6. Some have claimed that ethical egoists are "inconsistent." Why does Rachels think that ethical egoists are not, in fact, inconsistent?
7. Does Rachels think ethical egoism can be refuted? If so, how?
8. Lying behind Rachels's essay is a picture of human action and the reasons we have for doing what we do. How does Rachels understand people's motives for acting?

I

Our ordinary thinking about morality is full of assumptions that we almost never question. We assume, for example, that we have an obligation to consider the welfare of other people when we decide what actions to perform or what rules to obey; we think that we must refrain from acting in ways harmful to others, and that we must respect their rights and interests as well as our own. We also assume that people are in fact capable of being motivated by such considerations, that is, that people are not wholly selfish and that they do sometimes act in the interests of others.

Both of these assumptions have come under attack by moral sceptics as long ago as by Glaucon in Book II of Plato's *Republic.* Glaucon recalls the legend of Gyges, a shepherd who was said to have found a magic ring in a fissure opened by an earthquake. The ring would make its wearer invisible and thus would enable him to go anywhere and do anything undetected. Gyges used the power of the ring to gain entry to the Royal Palace where he seduced the Queen, murdered the King, and subsequently seized the throne. Now Glaucon asks us to determine that there are two such rings, one given to a man of virtue and one given to a rogue. The rogue, of course, will use his ring unscrupulously and do anything necessary to increase his own wealth and power. He will recognize no moral constraints on his conduct, and, since the cloak of invisibility will protect him from discovery, he can do anything he pleases without fear of reprisal. So, there will be no end to the mischief he will do. But how will the so-called virtuous man behave? Glaucon suggests that he will behave no better than the rogue: "No one, it is commonly believed, would have such iron strength of mind as to stand fast in doing right or keep his hands off other men's goods, when he could go to the marketplace and fearlessly help himself to

anything he wanted, enter houses and sleep with any woman he chose, set prisoners free and kill men at his pleasure, and in a word go about among men with the powers of a god. He would behave no better than the other; both would take the same course."[1] Moreover, why shouldn't he? Once he is freed from the fear of reprisal, why shouldn't a man simply do what he pleases, or what he thinks is best for himself? What reason is there for him to continue being "moral" when it is clearly not to his own advantage to do so?

These sceptical views suggested by Glaucon have come to be known as *psychological egoism* and *ethical egoism* respectively. Psychological egoism is the view that all men are selfish in everything that they do, that is, that the only motive from which anyone ever acts is self-interest. On this view, even when men are acting in ways apparently calculated to benefit others, they are actually motivated by the belief that acting in this way is to their own advantage, and if they did not believe this, they would not be doing that action. Ethical egoism is, by contrast, a normative view about how men *ought* to act. It is the view that, regardless of how men do in fact behave, they have no obligation to do anything except what is in their own interests. According to the ethical egoist, a person is always justified in doing whatever is in his own interests, regardless of the effect on others.

Clearly, if either of these views is correct, then "the moral institution of life" (to use Butler's well-turned phrase) is very different than what we normally think. The majority of mankind is grossly deceived about what is, or ought to be, the case, where morals are concerned.

II

Psychological egoism seems to fly in the face of the facts. We are tempted to say: "Of course people act unselfishly all the time. For example, Smith gives up a trip to the country, which he would have enjoyed very much, in order to stay behind and help a friend with

Reprinted from *A New Introduction to Philosophy* by Steven M. Cahn (New York: Harper & Row, 1971), by permission of the author.

his studies, which is a miserable way to pass the time. This is a perfectly clear case of unselfish behavior, and if the psychological egoist thinks that such cases do not occur, then he is just mistaken." Given such obvious instances of "unselfish behavior," what reply can the egoist make? There are two general arguments by which he might try to show that all actions, including those such as the one just outlined, are in fact motivated by self-interest. Let us examine these in turn:

A. The first argument goes as follows. If we describe one person's action as selfish, and another person's action as unselfish, we are overlooking the crucial fact that in both cases, assuming that the action is done voluntarily, *the agent is merely doing what he most wants to do.* If Smith stays behind to help his friend, that only shows that he wanted to help his friend more than he wanted to go to the country. And why should he be praised for his "unselfishness" when he is only doing what he most wants to do? So, since Smith is only doing what he wants to do, he cannot be said to be acting unselfishly.

This argument is so bad that it would not deserve to be taken seriously except for the fact that so many otherwise intelligent people have been taken in by it. First, the argument rests on the premise that people never voluntarily do anything except what they want to do. But this is patently false; there are at least two classes of actions that are exceptions to this generalization. One is the set of actions which we may not want to do, but which we do anyway as a means to an end which we want to achieve; for example, going to the dentist in order to stop a toothache, or going to work every day in order to be able to draw our pay at the end of the month. These cases may be regarded as consistent with the spirit of the egoist argument, however, since the ends mentioned are wanted by the agent. But the other set of actions are those which we do, not because we want to, nor even because there is an end which we want to achieve, but because we feel ourselves *under an obligation* to do them. For example, someone may do something because he has promised to do it, and thus feels obligated, even though he does not want to do it. It is sometimes suggested that in such cases we do the action because, after all, we want to keep our promises; so, even here, we are doing what we want. However, this dodge will not work: if I have promised to do something, and if I do not want to do it, then it is simply false to say that I want to keep my promise. In such cases we feel conflict precisely because we do *not* want to do what we feel obligated to do. It is reasonable to think that Smith's action falls roughly into this second category: he might stay behind, not because he wants to, but because he feels that his friend needs help.

But suppose we were to concede, for the sake of the argument, that all voluntary action is motivated by the agent's wants, or at least that Smith is so motivated. Even if this were granted, it would not follow that Smith is acting selfishly or from self-interest. For if Smith wants to do something that will help his friend, even when it means forgoing his own enjoyments, that is precisely what makes him *un*selfish. What else could unselfishness be, if not wanting to help others? Another way to put the same point is to say that it is the *object* of a want that determines whether it is selfish or not. The mere fact that I am acting on *my* wants does not mean that I am acting selfishly; that depends on *what it is* that I want. If I want only my own good, and care nothing for others, then I am selfish; but if I also want other people to be well-off and happy, and if I act on *that* desire, then my action is not selfish. So much for this argument.

B. The second argument for psychological egoism is this. Since so-called unselfish actions always produce a sense of self-satisfaction in the agent,[2] and since this sense of satisfaction is a pleasant state of consciousness, it follows that the point of the action is really to achieve a pleasant state of consciousness, rather than to bring about any good for others. Therefore, the action is "unselfish" only at a superficial level of analysis. Smith will feel much better with himself for having stayed to help his friend—if he had gone to the country, he would have felt terrible about it—and that is the real point of the action. According to a well-known story, this argument was once expressed by Abraham Lincoln:

> Mr. Lincoln once remarked to a fellow-passenger on an old-time mud-coach that all men were prompted by selfishness in doing good. His fellow-passenger was antagonizing this position when they were passing over a corduroy bridge that spanned a slough. As they crossed this bridge they espied an old razorbacked sow on the bank making a terrible noise because her pigs had got into the slough and were in danger of drowning. As the old coach began to climb the hill, Mr. Lincoln called out, "Driver, can't you stop just a moment?" Then Mr. Lincoln jumped out, ran back, and lifted the little pigs out of the mud and water and placed them on the bank. When he returned, his companion remarked: "Now, Abe, where does selfishness come in on this little episode?" "Why, bless your soul, Ed, that was the very essence of selfishness. I should have had no peace of mind all day had I gone on and left that suffering old sow worrying over those pigs. I did it to get peace of mind, don't you see?"[3]

This argument suffers from defects similar to the previous one. Why should we think that merely because someone derives satisfaction from helping others this makes him selfish? Isn't the unselfish man precisely the one who *does* derive satisfaction from helping others, while the selfish man does not? If Lincoln "got peace of mind" from rescuing the piglets, does this show him to be selfish, or, on the contrary, doesn't it show him to be compassionate and good-hearted? (If a man were truly selfish, why should it bother his conscience that *others* suffer—much less pigs?) Similarly, it is nothing more than shabby sophistry to say, because Smith takes satisfaction in helping his friend, that he is behaving selfishly. If we say this rapidly, while thinking about something else, perhaps it will sound all right; but if we speak slowly, and pay attention to what we are saying, it sounds plain silly.

Moreover, suppose we ask *why* Smith derives satisfaction from helping his friend. The answer will be, it is because Smith cares for him and wants him to succeed. If Smith did not have these concerns, then he would take no pleasure in assisting him; and these concerns, as we have already seen, are the marks of unselfishness, not selfishness. To put the point more generally: if we have a positive attitude toward the attainment of some goal, then we may derive satisfaction from attaining that goal. But the *object* of our attitude is *the attainment of that goal*; and we must want to attain the goal *before* we can find any satisfaction in it. We do not, in other words, desire some sort of "pleasurable consciousness" and then try to figure out how to achieve it; rather, we desire all sorts of different things—money, a new fishing-boat, to be a better chess player, to get a promotion in our work, etc.—and because we desire these things, we derive satisfaction from attaining them. And so, if someone desires the welfare and happiness of another person, he will derive satisfaction from that; but this does not mean that this satisfaction is the object of his desire, or that he is in any way selfish on account of it.

It is a measure of the weakness of psychological egoism that these insupportable arguments are the ones most often advanced in its favor. Why, then, should anyone ever have thought it a true view? Perhaps because of a desire for theoretical simplicity: In thinking about human conduct, it would be nice if there were some simple formula that would unite the diverse phenomena of human behavior under a single explanatory principle, just as simple formulae in physics bring together a great many apparently different phenomena. And since it is obvious that self-regard is an overwhelmingly important factor in motivation, it is only natural to wonder whether all motivation might not be explained in these terms. But the answer is clearly No; while a great many human actions are motivated entirely or in part by self-interest, only by a deliberate distortion of the facts can we say that all conduct is so motivated. This will be clear, I think, if we correct three confusions which are commonplace. The exposure of these confusions will remove the last traces of plausibility from the psychological egoist thesis.

The first is the confusion of selfishness with self-interest. The two are clearly not the same. If I see a physician when I am feeling poorly, I am acting in my own interest but no one would think of calling me "selfish" on account of it. Similarly, brushing my teeth, working hard at my job, and obeying the law are all in my self-interest but none of these are examples of selfish conduct. This is because selfish behavior is behavior that ignores the interests of others, in circumstances in which their interests ought not to be ignored. This concept has a definite evaluative flavor; to call someone "selfish" is not just to describe his action but to condemn it. Thus, you would not call me selfish for eating a normal meal in normal circumstances (although it may surely be in my self-interest); but you would call me selfish for hoarding food while others about are starving.

The second confusion is the assumption that every action is done *either* from self-interest or from other-regarding motives. Thus, the egoist concludes that if there is no such thing as genuine altruism then all actions must be done from self-interest. But this is certainly a false dichotomy. The man who continues to smoke cigarettes, even after learning about the connection between smoking and cancer, is surely not acting from self-interest, not even by his own standards—self-interest would dictate that he quit smoking—and he is not acting altruistically either. He *is*, no doubt, smoking for the pleasure of it, but all that this shows is that undisciplined pleasure-seeking and acting from self-interest are very different. This is what led Butler to remark that "The thing to be lamented is, not that men have so great regard to their own good or interest in the present world, for they have not enough."[4]

The last two paragraphs show (*a*) that it is false that all actions are selfish, and (*b*) that it is false that all actions are done out of self-interest. And it should be noted that these two points can be made, and were, without any appeal to putative examples of altruism.

The third confusion is the common but false assumption that a concern for one's own welfare is incompatible with any genuine concern for the welfare of others. Thus, since it is obvious that everyone (or very nearly everyone) does desire his own well-being, it might be thought that no one can really be concerned with others. But again, this is false. There is no inconsistency in desiring that everyone, including oneself *and* others, be well-off and happy. To be sure, it may happen on occasion that our own interests conflict with the interests of others, and in these cases we will have to make hard choices. But even in these cases we might sometimes opt for the interests of others, especially when the others involved are our family or friends. But more importantly, not all cases are like this: sometimes we are able to promote the welfare of others when our own interests are not involved at all. In these cases not even the strongest self-regard need prevent us from acting considerately toward others.

Once these confusions are cleared away, it seems to me obvious enough that there is no reason whatever to accept psychological egoism. On the contrary, if we simply observe people's behavior with an open mind, we may find that a great deal of it is motivated by self-regard, but by no means all of it; and that there is no reason to deny that "the moral institution of life" can include a place for the virtue of beneficence.[5]

III

The ethical egoist would say at this point, "Of course it is possible for people to act altruistically, and perhaps many people do act that way—but there is no reason why they *should* do so. A person is under no obligation to do anything except what is in his own interests."[6] This is really quite a radical doctrine. Suppose I have an urge to set fire to some public building (say, a department store) just for the fascination of watching the spectacular blaze: according to this view, the fact that several people might be burned to death provides no reason whatever why I should not do it. After all, this only concerns *their* welfare, not my own, and according to the ethical egoist the only person I need think of is myself.

Some [such as Hobbes] might deny that ethical egoism has any such monstrous consequences. They would point out that it is really to my own advantage not to set the fire—for, if I do that I may be caught and put into prison (unlike Gyges, I have no magic ring for protection). Moreover, even if I could avoid being caught it is still to my advantage to respect the rights and interests of others, for it is to my advantage to live in a society in which people's rights and interests are respected. Only in such a society can I live a happy and secure life; so, in acting kindly toward others, I would merely be doing my part to create and maintain the sort of society which it is to my advantage to have.[7] Therefore, it is said, the egoist would not be such a bad man; he would be as kindly and considerate as anyone else, because he would see that it is to his own advantage to be kindly and considerate.

This is a seductive line of thought, but it seems to me mistaken. Certainly it is to everyone's advantage (including the egoist's) to preserve a stable society where people's interests are generally protected. But there is no reason for the egoist to think that merely because *he* will not honor the rules of the social game, decent society will collapse. For the vast majority of people are not egoists, and there is no reason to think that they will be converted by his example—especially if he is discreet and does not unduly flaunt his style of life. What this line of reasoning shows is not that the egoist himself must act benevolently, but that he must encourage *others* to do so. He must take care to conceal from public view his own self-centered method of decision-making, and urge others to act on precepts very different from those on which he is willing to act.

The rational egoist, then, cannot advocate that egoism be universally adopted by everyone. For he wants a world in which his own interests are maximized; and if other people adopted the egoistic policy of pursuing their own interests to the exclusion of his interests, as he pursues his interests to the exclusion of theirs, then such a world would be impossible. So he himself will be an egoist, but he will want others to be altruists.

This brings us to what is perhaps the most popular "refutation" of ethical egoism current among philosophical writers—the argument that ethical egoism is at bottom inconsistent because it cannot be universalized. The argument goes like this:

To say that any action or policy of action is *right* (or that it *ought* to be adopted) entails that it is right for *anyone* in the same sort of circumstances. I cannot, for example, say that it is right for me to lie to you, and yet object when you lie to me (provided, of course, that the circumstances are the same). I cannot hold that it is all right for me to drink your beer and then complain when you drink mine. This is just the requirement that we be consistent in our evaluations: it is a requirement of logic. Now it is said that ethical egoism cannot meet this requirement because, as we have already seen, the egoist would not want others to act in the same way that he acts. Moreover, suppose he *did* advocate the universal adoption of egoistic policies: he would be saying to Peter, "You ought to pursue your own interests even if it means destroying Paul"; and he would be saying to Paul, "You ought to pursue your own interests even if it means destroying Peter." The attitudes expressed in these two recommendations seem clearly inconsistent—he is urging the advancement of Peter's interests at one moment, and countenancing their defeat at the next. Therefore, the argument goes, there is no way to maintain the doctrine of ethical egoism as a consistent view about how we ought to act. We will fall into inconsistency whenever we try.

What are we to make of this argument? Are we to conclude that ethical egoism has been refuted? Such a conclusion, I think, would be unwarranted; for I think that we can show, contrary to this argument, how ethical egoism can be maintained consistently. We need only to interpret the egoist's position in a sympathetic way: we should say that he has in mind a certain kind of world which he would prefer over all others; it would be a world in which his own interests were maximized, regardless of the effects on other people. The egoist's primary policy of action, then, would be to act in such a way as to bring about, as nearly as possible, this sort of world. Regardless of however morally reprehensible we might find it, there is nothing *inconsistent* in someone's adopting this as his ideal and acting in a way calculated to bring it about. And if someone did adopt this as his ideal, then he would not advocate universal egoism; as we have already seen, he would want other people to be altruists. So, if he advocates any principles of conduct for the general public, they will be altruistic principles. This would not be inconsistent; on the contrary, it would be perfectly consistent with his goal of creating a world in which his own interests are maximized. To be sure, he would have to be deceitful; in order to secure the good will of others, and a favorable hearing for his exhortations to altruism, he would have to pretend that he was himself prepared to accept altruistic principles. But again, that would be all right; from the egoist's point of view, this would merely be a matter of adopting the necessary means to the achievement of his goal—and while we might not approve of this, there is nothing inconsistent about it. Again, it might be said: "He advocates one thing, but does another. Surely *that's* inconsistent." But it is not; for what he advocates and what he does are both calculated as means to an end (the *same* end, we might note); and as such, he is doing what is rationally required in each case. Therefore, contrary to the previous argument, there is nothing inconsistent in the ethical egoist's view. He cannot be refuted by the claim that he contradicts himself.

Is there, then, no way to refute the ethical egoist? If by "refute" we mean show that he has made some *logical* error, the answer is that there is not. However, there is something more that can be said. The egoist challenge to our ordinary moral convictions amounts to a demand for an explanation of why we should adopt certain policies of action, namely policies in which the good of others is given importance. We can give an answer to this demand, albeit an indirect one. The reason one ought not to do actions that would hurt other people is: other people would be hurt. The reason one ought to do actions that would benefit other people is: other people would be benefited. This may at first seem like a piece of philosophical sleight-of-hand, but it is not. The point is that the welfare of human beings is something that most of us value *for its own sake*, and not merely for the sake of something else. Therefore, when *further* reasons are demanded for valuing the welfare of human beings, we cannot point to anything further to satisfy this demand. It is not that we have no reason for pursuing these policies, but that our reason *is* that these policies are for the good of human beings.

So: if we are asked "Why shouldn't I set fire to this department store?" one answer would be "Because if you do, people may be burned to death." This is a complete, sufficient reason which does not require qualification or supplementation of any sort. If someone seriously wants to know why this action shouldn't be done, that's the reason. If we are pressed further and asked the skeptical question "But why shouldn't I do actions that will harm others?" we may not know what to say—but this is because the questioner has included in his question the very answer we would like to give: "Why shouldn't you do actions that will harm others? Because, doing those actions would harm others."

The egoist, no doubt, will not be happy with this. He will protest that *we* may accept this as a reason, but *he* does not. And here the argument stops: there are limits to what can be accomplished by argument, and if the egoist really doesn't care about other people—if he honestly doesn't care whether they are helped or hurt by his actions—then we have reached those limits. If we want to persuade him to act decently toward his fellow humans, we will have to make our appeal to such other attitudes as he does possess, by threats, bribes, or other cajolery. That is all that we can do.

Though some may find this situation distressing (we would like to be able to show that the egoist is just *wrong*), it holds no embarrassment for common morality. What we have come up against is simply a fundamental requirement of rational action, namely, that the existence of reasons for action always depends on the prior existence of certain attitudes in the agent. For example, the fact that a certain course of action would make the agent a lot of money is a reason for doing it only if the agent wants to make money; the fact that practicing at chess makes one a better player is a reason for practicing only if one wants to be a better player; and so on. Similarly, the fact that a certain action would help the agent is a reason for doing the action only if the agent cares about his own welfare, and the fact that an action would help others is a reason for doing it only if the agent cares about others. In this respect ethical egoism and what we might call ethical altruism are in exactly the same fix: both require that the agent *care* about himself, or about other people, before they can get started.

So a nonegoist will accept "It would harm another person" as a reason not to do an action simply because he cares about what happens to that other person. When the egoist says that he does *not* accept that as a reason, he is saying something quite extraordinary. He is saying that he has no affection for friends or family, that he never feels pity or compassion, that he is the sort of person who can look on scenes of human misery with complete indifference, so long as he is not the one suffering. Genuine egoists, people who really don't care at all about anyone other than themselves, are rare. It is important to keep this in mind when thinking about ethical egoism; it is easy to forget just how fundamental to human psychological makeup the feeling of sympathy is. Indeed, a man without any sympathy at all would scarcely be recognizable as a man; and that is what makes ethical egoism such a disturbing doctrine in the first place.

IV

There are, of course, many different ways in which the sceptic might challenge the assumptions underlying our moral practice. In this essay I have discussed only two of them, the two put forward by Glaucon in the passage that I cited from Plato's *Republic*. It is important that the assumptions underlying our moral practice should not be confused with particular judgments made within that practice. To defend one is not to defend the other. We may assume—quite properly, if my analysis has been correct—that the virtue of beneficence does, and indeed should, occupy an important place in "the moral institution of life"; and yet we may make constant and miserable errors when it comes to judging when and in what ways this virtue is to be exercised. Even worse, we may often be able to make accurate moral judgments, and know what we ought to do, but not do it. For these ills, philosophy alone is not the cure.

Notes

1. *The Republic of Plato*, translated by F. M. Cornford (Oxford, 1941), p. 45.
2. Or, as it is sometimes said, "It gives him a clear conscience," or "He couldn't sleep at night if he had done otherwise," or "He would have been ashamed of himself for not doing it," and so on.
3. Frank C. Sharp, *Ethics* (New York, 1928), pp. 74–75. Quoted from the Springfield (Ill.) *Monitor in the Outlook*, vol. 56, p. 1059.
4. *The Works of Joseph Butler*, edited by W. E. Gladstone (Oxford, 1896), vol. II, p. 26. It should be noted that most of the points I am making against psychological egoism were first made by Butler. Butler made all the important points; all that is left for us is to remember them.
5. The capacity for altruistic behavior is not unique to human beings. Some interesting experiments with rhesus monkeys have shown that these animals will refrain from operating a device for securing food if this causes other animals to suffer pain. See Masserman, Wechkin, and Terris, "'Altruistic' Behavior in Rhesus Monkeys," *The American Journal of Psychiatry*, vol. 121 (1964), 584–585.
6. I take this to be the view of Ayn Rand, in so far as I understand her confusing doctrine.
7. Thomas Hobbes, *Leviathan* (London, 1651), ch. 17.

Morality, Resentment, and Impartiality

Thomas Nagel

In this essay, Thomas Nagel disputes those who argue that we have no reason to care about morality unless it is to our advantage or we happen to want to be moral. Beginning with an example of a friend who asks another to help smuggle a book out of the library, Nagel goes on to discuss the idea that something's being wrong is a reason for not doing it. But what if a person does not care about doing wrong, he asks. Why *should* he care? One answer, which Nagel rejects, is that God has ordered us, His creation, to behave in accord with His law. Instead, claims Nagel, morality must rest on concern for others. But again, what if a person just does not care? Nagel begins with the fact that when people treat us wrongly we *resent* it, and we also believe we are justified in taking that attitude. This leads, finally, to the conclusion that we have reason to be moral and thus to be impartial, in the sense that we give due consideration not just to our own interests but also to those of others. Just what such impartiality requires in practice, however, he leaves open. Thomas Nagel has written numerous books and articles on a wide array of topics. His books include *The Possibility of Altruism*, *The View from Nowhere*, and *Equality and Partiality*. Thomas Nagel is professor of philosophy at New York University.

As you read through this essay, consider the following:

1. Why does Nagel reject the idea that a person's reason for being motivated to act morally depends on fear of God or even love of God?
2. Why does Nagel think that God's having commanded that we not commit murder cannot be the reason murder is wrong?
3. Nagel says there is one argument against hurting people that can be given to anybody who experiences resentment and that person should find the argument persuasive. Explain what he means.
4. How does Nagel defend the claim that being moral requires impartiality?

Suppose you work in a library, checking people's books as they leave, and a friend asks you to let him smuggle out a hard-to-find reference work that he wants to own.

You might hesitate to agree for various reasons. You might be afraid that he'll be caught, and that both you and he will then get into trouble. You might want the book to stay in the library so that you can consult it yourself.

But you may also think that what he proposes is wrong—that he shouldn't do it and you shouldn't help him. If you think that, what does it mean, and what, if anything, makes it true?

To say it's wrong is not just to say it's against the rules. There can be bad rules which prohibit what isn't wrong—like a law against criticizing the government. A rule can also be bad because it requires something that *is* wrong—like a law that requires racial segregation in hotels and restaurants. The ideas of wrong and right are different from the ideas of what is and is not against the rules. Otherwise they couldn't be used in the evaluation of rules as well as of actions.

From Thomas Nagel, *What Does It All Mean?* (New York: Oxford University Press, 1987). © Thomas Nagel. Reprinted by permission.

If you think it would be wrong to help your friend steal the book, then you will feel uncomfortable about doing it: in some way you won't want to do it, even if you are also reluctant to refuse help to a friend. Where does the desire not to do it come from; what is its motive, the reason behind it?

There are various ways in which something can be wrong, but in this case, if you had to explain it, you'd probably say that it would be unfair to other users of the library who may be just as interested in the book as your friend is, but who consult it in the reference room, where anyone who needs it can find it. You may also feel that to let him take it would betray your employers, who are paying you precisely to keep this sort of thing from happening.

These thoughts have to do with effects on others—not necessarily effects on their feelings, since they may never find out about it, but some kind of damage nevertheless. In general, the thought that something is wrong depends on its impact not just on the person who does it but on other people. They wouldn't like it, and they'd object if they found out.

But suppose you try to explain all this to your friend, and he says, "I know the head librarian wouldn't like it if he found out, and probably some of the other users of the library would be unhappy to find the book gone, but who cares? I want the book; why should I care about them?"

The argument that it would be wrong is supposed to give him a reason not to do it. But if someone just doesn't care about other people, what reason does he have to refrain from doing any of the things usually thought to be wrong, if he can get away with it: what reason does he have not to kill, steal, lie, or hurt others? If he can get what he wants by doing such things, why shouldn't he? And if there's no reason why he shouldn't, in what sense is it wrong?

Of course most people do care about others to some extent. But if someone doesn't care, most of us wouldn't conclude that he's exempt from morality. A person who kills someone just to steal his wallet, without caring about the victim, is not automatically excused.

The fact that he doesn't care doesn't make it all right: He *should* care. But *why* should he care?

There have been many attempts to answer this question. One type of answer tries to identify something else that the person already cares about, and then connect morality to it.

For example, some people believe that even if you can get away with awful crimes on this earth, and are not punished by the law or your fellow men, such acts are forbidden by God, who will punish you after death (and reward you if you didn't do wrong when you were tempted to). So even when it seems to be in your interest to do such a thing, it really isn't. Some people have even believed that if there is no God to back up moral requirements with the threat of punishment and the promise of reward, morality is an illusion: "If God does not exist, everything is permitted."

This is a rather crude version of the religious foundation for morality. A more appealing version might be that the motive for obeying God's commands is not fear but love. He loves you, and you should love Him, and should wish to obey His commands in order not to offend Him.

But however we interpret the religious motivation, there are three objections to this type of answer. First, plenty of people who don't believe in God still make judgments of right and wrong, and think no one should kill another for his wallet even if he can be sure to get away with it. Second, if God exists, and forbids what's wrong, that still isn't what *makes* it wrong. Murder is wrong in itself, and that's *why* God forbids it (if He does). God couldn't make just any old thing wrong—like putting on your left sock before your right—simply by prohibiting it. If God would punish you for doing that it would be inadvisable to do it, but it wouldn't be wrong. Third, fear of punishment and hope of reward, and even love of God, seem not to be the right motives for morality. If you think it's wrong to kill, cheat, or steal, you should want to avoid doing such things because they are bad things to do to the victims, not just because you fear the consequences for yourself, or because you don't want to offend your Creator.

This third objection also applies to other explanations of the force of morality which appeal to the interests of the person who must act. For example, it may be said that you should treat others with consideration so that they'll do the same for you. This may be sound advice, but it is valid only so far as you think what you do will affect how others treat you. It's not a reason for doing the right thing if others won't find out about it, or against doing the wrong thing if you can get away with it (like being a hit and run driver).

There is no substitute for a direct concern for other people as the basis of morality. But morality is supposed to apply to everyone: and can we assume that everyone has such a concern for others? Obviously not: some people are very selfish, and even those who are not selfish may care only about the people they know, and not about everyone. So where will we find a reason that everyone has not to hurt other people, even those they don't know?

Well, there's one general argument against hurting other people which can be given to anybody who understands English (or any other language), and which seems to show that he has *some* reason to care about others, even if in the end his selfish motives are so strong that he persists in treating other people badly anyway. It's an argument that I'm sure you've heard, and it goes like this: "How would you like it if someone did that to you?"

It's not easy to explain how this argument is supposed to work. Suppose you're about to steal someone else's umbrella as you leave a restaurant in a rainstorm, and a bystander says, "How would you like it if someone did that to you?" Why is it supposed to make you hesitate, or feel guilty?

Obviously the direct answer to the question is supposed to be, "I wouldn't like it at all!" But what's the next step? Suppose you were to say, "I wouldn't like it if someone did that to me. But luckily no one *is* doing it to me. I'm doing it to someone else, and I don't mind that at all!"

This answer misses the point of the question. When you are asked how you would like it if someone did that to you, you are sup-posed to think about all the feelings you would have if someone stole your umbrella. And that includes more than just "not liking it"—as you wouldn't "like it" if you stubbed your toe on a rock. If someone stole your umbrella you'd *resent* it. You'd have feelings about the umbrella thief, not just about the loss of the umbrella. You'd think, "Where does he get off, taking my umbrella that I bought with my hard-earned money and that I had the foresight to bring after reading the weather report? Why didn't he bring his own umbrella?" and so forth.

When our own interests are threatened by the inconsiderate behavior of others, most of us find it easy to appreciate that those others have a reason to be more considerate. When you are hurt, you probably feel that other people should care about it: you don't think it's no concern of theirs, and that they have no reason to avoid hurting you. That is the feeling that the "How would you like it?" argument is supposed to arouse.

Because if you admit that you would *resent* it if someone else did to you what you are now doing to him, you are admitting that you think he would have a reason not to do it to you. And if you admit that, you have to consider what that reason is. It couldn't be just that it's *you* that he's hurting, of all the people in the world. There's no special reason for him not to steal *your* umbrella, as opposed to anyone else's. There's nothing so special about you. Whatever the reason is, it's a reason he would have against hurting anyone else in the same way. And it's a reason anyone else would have too, in a similar situation, against hurting you or anyone else.

But if it's a reason anyone would have not to hurt anyone else in this way, then it's a reason *you* have not to hurt someone else in this way (since *anyone* means *everyone*). Therefore it's a reason not to steal the other person's umbrella now.

This is a matter of simple consistency. Once you admit that another person would have a reason not to harm you in similar circumstances, and once you admit that the reason he would have is very general and doesn't apply only to you, or to him, then to be consistent you have to admit that the same reason applies to you now. You shouldn't steal the umbrella, and you ought to feel guilty if you do.

Someone could escape from this argument if, when he was asked, "How would you like it if someone did that to you?" he answered, "I wouldn't resent it at all. I wouldn't *like* it if someone stole my umbrella in a rainstorm, but I wouldn't think there was any reason for him to consider my feelings about it." But how many people could honestly give that answer? I think most people, unless they're crazy, would think that their own interests and harms matter, not only to themselves, but in a way that gives other people a reason to care about them too. We all think that when we suffer it is not just bad *for us*, but *bad, period*.

The basis of morality is a belief that good and harm to particular people (or animals) is good or bad not just from their point of view, but from a more general point of view, which every thinking person can understand. That means that each person has a reason to consider not only his own interests but the interests of others in deciding what to do. And it isn't enough if he is considerate only of some others—his family and friends, those he specially cares about. Of course he will care more about certain people, and also about himself. But he has some reason to consider the effect of what he does on the good or harm of everyone. If he's like most of us, that is what he thinks others should do with regard to him, even if they aren't friends of his.

* * *

Even if this is right, it is only a bare outline of the source of morality. It doesn't tell us in detail how we should consider the interests of others, or how we should weigh them against the special interest we all have in ourselves and the particular people close to us. It doesn't even tell us how much we should care about people in other countries in comparison with our fellow citizens. There are many disagreements among those who accept morality in general, about what in particular is right and what is wrong.

For instance: should you care about every other person as much as you care about yourself? Should you in other words love your neighbor as yourself (even if he isn't your neighbor)? Should you ask yourself, every time you go to a movie, whether the cost of the ticket could provide more happiness if you gave it to someone else, or donated the money to famine relief?

Very few people are so unselfish. And if someone were that impartial between himself and others, he would probably also feel that he should be just as impartial *among* other people. That would rule out caring more about his friends and relatives than he does about strangers. He might have special feelings about certain people who are close to him, but complete impartiality would mean that he won't *favor* them—if for example he has to choose between helping a friend or a stranger to avoid suffering, or between taking his children to a movie and donating the money to famine relief.

This degree of impartiality seems too much to ask of most people: someone who had it would be a kind of terrifying saint. But it's an important question in moral thought, how much impartiality we should try for. You are a particular person, but you are also able to recognize that you're just one person among many others, and no more important than they are, when looked at from outside. How much should that point of view influence you? You do matter somewhat from outside—otherwise you wouldn't think other people had any reason to care about what they did to you. But you don't matter as much from the outside as you matter to yourself, from the inside—since from the outside you don't matter any more than anybody else.

Not only is it unclear how impartial we should be; it's unclear what would make an answer to this question the right one. Is there a single correct way for everyone to strike the balance between what he cares about personally and what matters impartially? Or will the answer vary from person to person depending on the strength of their different motives?

Essay and Paper Topics for "The Practice of Morality"

1. Benedict and Lewis disagree sharply about the nature of morality and specifically about the claim that it is best understood as culturally acquired attitudes and habits. Explain why Lewis rejects that position, and then discuss how Benedict might respond to the strongest of Lewis's arguments against her. Who has the stronger of the two positions? Why?

2. Suppose you were Ruth Benedict. After reading the essay by Hobbes, write an essay in which you explore the ways in which you, as Benedict, would disagree or possibly agree with Hobbes.

3. How might Benedict and Hobbes account for what Lewis terms the "Moral Law"? Is their explanation better than that of Lewis? Why or why not?

4. Thomas Hobbes is described by Rachels as an ethical egoist. Discuss whether or not you agree with that interpretation of Hobbes.

5. Suppose somebody came to you and said "Morality is a fool's game. Truly smart people ignore it unless it is in their self-interest not to do so." How would you respond?

6. "Nobody ever really does anything unless he or she wants to, which proves people are basically selfish." Would Rachels and Nagel agree or disagree? Explain who you think is right, and why. Or is there still another position that nobody has defended, and that you want to put forth?

PART III

Moral Practice and Culture

Section 4

Values in Popular Culture

Beauty and Evil: The Case of Leni Riefenstahl's *Triumph of the Will*

Mary Devereaux

Film and television are dominant cultural forms. In this essay, Mary Devereaux asks whether and in what ways a film's moral content—in this case the fact that it sought to justify Nazism—should influence our assessment of the work as a whole. She begins with a description of the film: first its political message and then its structure, vision, and narrative strategy. All of these, she argues, contribute to its power as a work of propaganda. What is troubling about the film is the way it successfully integrates evil and beauty. Rejecting those who argued that the film's merit is purely aesthetic and nonpolitical (including the director herself), Devereaux claims that what is most troubling is the fact that the film's vision of the German people and Hitler is made to seem beautiful. Content cannot be separated from aesthetics, as "formalists" sometimes claim one should do by taking an "aesthetic distance." She concludes with a discussion of how the film should ultimately be assessed (as a work of art), how an audience should respond to the film's vision of National Socialism, and whether it is possible to see and appreciate such a film without compromising oneself morally.

As you read through this essay, consider the following:

1. How would you summarize the movie *Triumph of the Will* based on Devereaux's description (or on your own experience if you have seen it yourself)?

2. What is the "vision" of the film?
3. What is the formalists' position, and why does Devereaux reject it as a way of understanding *Triumph of the Will*?
4. What finally does Devereaux think of the film, as a work of art?

I

Leni Riefenstahl's documentary of the 1934 Nuremberg rally of the National Socialist German Workers' Party, *Triumph of the Will*, is perhaps the most controversial film ever made. At once masterful and morally repugnant, this deeply troubling film epitomizes a general problem that arises with art. It is both beautiful and evil. I shall argue that it is this conjunction of beauty and evil that explains why the film is so disturbing. My aim in this essay is to explore the relationship of beauty and evil in *Triumph of the Will* and to use this examination of a particular case as a way of investigating the more general problem of beauty and evil in art. Having looked at this case in detail, I want to draw some broader conclusions about the inadequacy of the usual solution to the problem of beauty and evil in art and to suggest the direction we should move in to develop an account of aesthetic value rich enough to handle cases as difficult as *Triumph of the Will*.

My main aim is philosophical, but I shall have to turn to more concrete matters before taking up the philosophical issues. I will briefly describe the historical background of the film and the circumstances in which it was produced (Section II). I will also provide some sense of *Triumph of the Will* itself, that is, of its artistic strategy and how it contributes to the film's overall effect (Section III). I will then be in a position to turn to the problem of beauty and evil in the film and to

the more general problem of beauty and evil in art that is my central concern (Sections IV–VI).

II

The 1934 Nuremberg party rally was one of several mammoth political rallies sponsored by the Nazi Party between 1923 and 1939. It lasted seven days, involved tens of thousands of participants, and was estimated to have drawn as many as 500,000 spectators.

The film of these events was made at Hitler's personal request and with his support. Hitler himself gave the film its title, *Triumph des Willens*. He also went to Nuremberg to help with the preproduction planning, carefully orchestrating the spectacle that would involve thousands of troops, marching bands, and ordinary citizens.

Like the rally, the film's production was a large, well-organized event. Riefenstahl's crew consisted of 172 persons: 36 cameramen and assistants, 9 aerial photographers, 17 newsreel men, 17 lighting technicians, and so on. The crew, uniformed as SA (Sturmabteilung der NSDAP) men so that they would not be noticeable in the crowd, used thirty cameras and worked nonstop for a week. Riefenstahl held daily directorial meetings at which each member of the camera crew received instructions for the next day. Scenes were rehearsed beforehand, and the front ranks of the Labor Service men were trained to speak in unison.

Concerned that the long parades, endless speeches, and days of nearly identical events would bore her audience, Riefenstahl rejected the static format and voice-over commentary of the conventional newsreel. Instead, she adopted and expanded methods of mobile

From *Aesthetics and Ethics*, ed. Jerrold Levinson. Copyright © 1998 by Cambridge University Press. Reprinted by permission of Cambridge University Press.

photography developed by Abel Gance and others for the (fictional) feature film. Wherever possible she had rails and tracks laid throughout the rally site, including a circular track built around the speakers' podium[1] and a lift installed on a 140-foot flagpole. The crew was even instructed to practice roller skating. These devices enabled Riefenstahl to infuse shots of her frequently stationary subjects with action and motion.

Distilled from sixty-one hours of footage, in a process of editing that Riefenstahl worked twelve to eighteen hours a day for five months to complete, the final version of the film ran just over two hours. Its intensely dynamic visual material was set to a score of Wagnerian music, German folk songs, military marches, and party anthems (including the official party anthem, "Das Horst Wessel Lied") intercut with the sound of cheering crowds and party speeches. The result, in both style and effect, was a radical departure from the standard newsreel. An innovation in documentary filmmaking, *Triumph of the Will* was also, as is generally recognized, a major contribution to the history of film.

The film premiered at the Ufa Palast in Berlin in March 1935 before an audience of foreign diplomats, army generals, and top party officials, including Hitler. None of the Nazi officials, not even Hitler, had seen the film in advance—an extremely unusual circumstance at the time, since no film could be screened in private or public until it was passed by the censorship board. Some party members thought the film "too artistic," though whether the objection was to artistic technique itself or to the film's suitability for political use isn't clear. Others, especially members of the army, were angry at Riefenstahl's omission of most of the military exercises (the footage had been shot in bad weather). Hitler, however, was delighted with the film. Although it is difficult to know exactly how widely *Triumph of the Will* was shown or how it was received, it apparently enjoyed some popular success, despite the German public's preference for entertainment films.

In any case, artistically, *Triumph of the Will* immediately established itself, winning recognition not only in Germany (where it was awarded the 1935 National Film Prize), but also abroad, where it won the Gold Medal at the Venice Film Festival. Two years later, it won the Grand Prix at the 1937 Paris Film Festival, where, to their credit, French workers protested Riefenstahl's appearance when she came in person to accept her award.

III

In turning to the film itself, there are three things to note: its structure, its vision, and its narrative strategy. Each of these features contributes to the film's notable effect.

Structurally, *Triumph of the Will* has twelve sections or scenes, each focused on a particular party rally event: Hitler's arrival in Nuremberg, the Hitler Youth rally, the folk parade, Hitler's address to the SA, and so on. The film *appears* to present these events as they unfold. In fact, Riefenstahl ignores chronological order almost entirely, working instead to create a rhythmic structure for the film. Her aim, she states, was "to bring certain elements into the foreground and put others into the background," to create a dramatic succession of highlights and retreats, peaks and valleys.[2] This musical structure was created largely in the editing room, where, working without a script, Riefenstahl used a variety of means—alternating scenes of day and night, moving from solemnity to exuberance, and generally altering the pace of the film from sequence to sequence and within the individual scenes themselves—to give the film a determinate rhythmic structure.

This rhythmic structure is manifest in sequences such as the film's third section, "The City Awakening." The portrait of early-morning Nuremberg begins slowly and lyrically as the camera travels high above the quiet, mist-covered rooftops of the old city. Church bells toll and the film dissolves to a lively shot of morning activity in the tented city used to house rally participants. Here, drums beat and bugles announce the start of day for residents, who emerge jauntily from their tents to wash, shave, and eat breakfast. The tempo and pace of this montage of daily activity increase, climaxing in brightly lit shots of healthy, bare-chested youths, working and singing old German folk songs as they polish shoes, haul wood for the camp stoves, and prepare for the more serious activities of the rally itself.

By building these scenes to a crescendo of dramatic intensity, Riefenstahl means to hold the spectator's attention and generate some of the same enthusiasm and excitement felt by rally participants. These same techniques are used throughout the film, in scenes of Hitler's speeches, troop reviews, and the like. Even the most prosaic subjects, such as the repetitive passages of military marching, are made visually interesting and dramatic by these techniques. Not surprisingly, these tightly organized rhythmic sequences are quite effective.

Much has been written on the formal features of Riefenstahl's art. What has not been generally appreciated is that the film's artistic achievement is not merely structural or formal. Equally important is Riefenstahl's masterful command of traditional narrative means: theme and characterization, the use of symbolism, and the handling of point of view. It is the use of these devices to tell a *story*—the story of the New Germany—that, combined with the structural techniques already surveyed, creates the vision of Hitler and National Socialism that makes *Triumph of the Will* so powerful. . . . Seen from the perspective of the film, Hitler is the hero of a grand narrative. He is both leader and savior, a new Siegfried come to restore a defeated Germany to its ancient splendor.

In establishing this heroic vision, Riefenstahl works with several striking motifs: the swastika, the German eagle, flags, Albert Speer's towering architecture, torches and burning pyres, moon and clouds, the roar of the crowds, Hitler's voice. Her strategy is to use these aural and visual motifs to establish three key ideas, encapsulated in the National Social-

ist slogan *Ein Volk. Ein Führer. Ein Reich* (One People. One Leader. One Empire). These three ideas, introduced by Riefenstahl in slightly different order, are the *Führerprinzip*, leader principle or cult of the leader (the *Führer*), the unity of the people or national community (the *Volk*), and the strength and power of the German nation (the *Reich*). Each has a central role both in the film's vision of Hitler and in its story of the New Germany.

The first and most important idea, the *Führerprinzip*, has obvious roots in messianic Christianity. The idea of a great historical figure or great man who has the will and power to actualize the true will of the German people was frequently dramatized in Nazi cinema. But *Triumph of the Will* is the only Nazi film that directly identifies this mystical leader with Hitler himself. From its very first frames, Riefenstahl's film presents Hitler as the leader long sought by the German people and as "the bearer of the people's will." He is a godlike, mystical figure who descends—literally—from the clouds, his plane flying in over the mist-enshrouded towers and spires of medieval Nuremberg. These shots of the advancing plane are intercut with striking aerial footage of Nuremberg—a city representative of the old Germany and of the glorious Teutonic past, its castle a bulwark against foreign intruders. The shadow of the approaching plane falls over the columns and columns of marching troops who fill the streets below. All this takes place as themes from Wagner's *Die Meistersinger* slowly give way to the Nazi Party anthem, much as the old Germany slowly gives way to the new. The climax of this scene comes several minutes into the film when the plane lands, its door opens, and Hitler appears to a roar of approval from the waiting crowds. By such means, Riefenstahl makes Hitler's arrival at the rally—as well as his every subsequent appearance—resonate with deep historical and national significance for the German people.

In the early sequences of the film, Riefenstahl stresses not only Hitler's messianic leadership, but his humanity. This is a leader who moves among the people, who shakes hands and smiles. Shots of Hitler are intercut with shots not only of enormous crowds but of individuals, especially children, laughing and smiling. Even small details, like Hitler stopping his motorcade to accept flowers from a mother and child along the road, are designed to support the film's vision of Hitler as the much-beloved father of the German people.

The second key idea of *Triumph of the Will* is the unity of the support for Hitler among the German people (*ein Volk*). Within the universe of the film, *everyone* supports Hitler. The crowds that fill scene after scene are staggering in number, their enthusiasm unending. Nowhere do we see anyone—a postman, a traffic cop, or a pedestrian—engaged in ordinary business. Day after day, the narrow Nuremberg streets are filled to overflowing with old and young. People hang from the windows; they throng the stadium. All yearn to catch a glimpse of the *Führer.*

The beauty and sheer exuberance of these scenes celebrate these pro-Nazi sentiments. Indeed, several scenes appear to have been explicitly constructed to demonstrate that Hitler's support knows no class or regional barriers. . . . Hitler's supporters, the film shows us, are a unity—one people—despite their differences; it is Hitler—one leader—who brings them together. The stirring music, the marshaling of flags, and the great German eagle towering over the stadium underscore the importance of the contribution of even the most ordinary laborers to the New Germany—planting forests, building roads "from village to village, from town to town." In the words of the workers themselves: *"Ein Volk. Ein Führer. Ein Reich—Deutschland."* The effect is one of order and national purpose, a national purpose made manifest in the final shot of the sequence: the Labor Services men marching toward the camera, their image superimposed over Hitler's raised fist.

The third and final idea central to *Triumph of the Will,* one *Reich,* is most prominent in the film's final sequences. Here Riefen-stahl's strategy is the visual display of power (*Macht*). Her aim is to show the enormous military forces that stand behind the *Führer* and the solidity of their support. In demonstrating power, the ritual of the mass meeting itself had a central role: the waving swastikas, the uniforms, the legions of marching, chanting followers, the torches against the night sky—all contributed to the spectacle designed to display Hitler's personal and political power.

Triumph of the Will does more than present a set of ideas; it weaves them into a story, makes them part of a grand narrative. . . . Riefenstahl works with the themes of both unity and power, manipulating artistic form not only to create enthusiasm for Hitler and the National Socialists but to evoke fear. As noted, the opening of the film focuses on cheerful scenes emphasizing the spontaneous loyalty or ordinary people. Party and military forces are little in evidence. In contrast, the two final sequences—the military parade with which the Nazis leave Nuremberg and the somewhat anticlimactic final congress—center on Hitler, high-ranking party officials, and regiment after regiment of tightly disciplined troops. There are no smiles or laughing children, no young boys, no women with flowers. These are men—ready to go to war.

Running nearly twenty minutes, the final parade sequence is the longest of the film. Riefenstahl presents a seemingly inexhaustible stream of massed forces. We see the straight-legged, stiff-kneed marching troops from every angle, constantly moving, in a dazzling display of dynamic editing. Riefenstahl cuts back and forth between shots of the men in uniform, party officials, and Hitler. In contrast to the opening scenes, Hitler stands alone, apart from the people: watching, saluting, receiving ovations. The mood is somber. The power of the Nazis is presented as daunting and unquestionable.

To summarize, then, Riefenstahl weaves the narrative and thematic elements of her film around the central National Socialist slogan *Ein Führer. Ein Volk. Ein Reich* as tightly as she weaves the visual elements of eagle and swastika. As she tells it, the tale of Hitler—stalwart and alone, heroic—is the tale of the German people. His will is their will. His power their future. It is all this and more that makes *Triumph of the Will* the powerful film it is.

IV

Clearly, *Triumph of the Will* is a troubling film. My claim is that it is so because of its conjunction of beauty and evil, because it presents as beautiful a vision of Hitler and the New Germany that is morally repugnant. . . .

. . . Riefenstahl and her supporters contend that her concerns in *Triumph of the Will*—as in all her films—were aesthetic, not political: that it was the cult of beauty, not the cult of the *Führer*, that Riefenstahl worshiped. The claim is that stylistic devices like the cloud motif in the film's opening sequence, the rhythmic montage of faces in the Labor Services sequence, and so on were *just* that: stylistic devices meant to avoid newsreel reportage, enrich the film artistically, and nothing more.

Certainly Riefenstahl *was* preoccupied with beauty in *Triumph of the Will*. Her films of the 1936 Berlin Olympics, her photographs of the Nuba, indeed the whole of her artistic corpus, make clear that visual beauty was one of her central artistic preoccupations. But the claim that a concern for beauty and stylistic innovation is the only thing going on in *Triumph of the Will* is undermined by the film itself. As we have seen, the film is aimed not simply at stylistic innovation and formally beautiful images, but at using these means to create a particular vision of Hitler and National Socialism.

The pure-aestheticism defense is also belied by the historical record. Riefenstahl was, as she willingly admits, a great admirer of Hitler. Attending a political rally for the first time in her life in February 1932, she was "paralyzed," "fascinated," "deeply affected" by the appearance of Hitler and the crowd's "bondage to this man."[3] Even at the end of the war, by which point she, like many Nazi sympathizers, claims to have harbored doubts about Hitler's plans for Germany, Riefenstahl, by her own admission, "wept all night" at the news of his suicide.[4] To this day, Riefenstahl has never distanced herself from the political content of *Triumph of the Will* or any of the other films she made for Hitler. Nor, despite years of ostracism and public controversy, has she shown—or even feigned—remorse for her artistic and personal association with many members of the Nazi Party.

It might be added that Riefenstahl agreed to film the 1934 Nuremberg rally only on condition that she be given complete artistic control over the project, a condition to which Hitler apparently agreed. She demanded, and got, final cut. Thus, we can assume that the film Riefenstahl made—the film organized around the ideas of *Ein Führer. Ein Volk. Ein Reich* that presents Hitler as savior to the German people, and that describes the Nazi future as full of promise—is the film she chose to make. . . .

So *Triumph of the Will* is a work of Nazi propaganda. And that is clearly part of what makes the film so troubling. But Riefenstahl is not the first or last artist to make fascist art. Hundreds of propaganda films were made in Germany between 1933 and 1945. Many, like the feature film *Jud Süss*, had much wider popular success. And some, like the virulently anti-Semitic "documentary" *Der ewige Jude* (The Eternal Jew, 1940), had arguably as harmful an effect on German thought and behavior.

Triumph of the Will is distinguished from these and other Nazi propaganda films in two ways. First, it is extremely well made. (And the fact that it is an excellent work of propaganda is part of what makes it so disturbing.) But the film is more than first-class propaganda. It is also a work of art. A work of creative imagination, stylistically and formally innovative, its every detail contributes to its central vision and overall effect. The film is also very, very beautiful. *Triumph of the Will* can be properly called a work of art because it offers a beautiful, sensuous presentation—a vision—of the German people, leader, and empire in a recognized artistic genre (documentary) of a recognized artistic medium (film). It is the fact that *Triumph of the Will* is an excellent work of propaganda *and* a work of art that explains why Riefenstahl's film has more than historical interest and why it has a place in film and not just history classes.

V

As art, *Triumph of the Will* is problematic for reasons other than those associated with its excellence as a work of propaganda (e.g., its capacity to mobilize the German people in the 1930s), and it is as art that *Triumph of the Will* is most disturbing. What makes *Triumph of the Will* problematic and disturbing as art is its artistic vision: its vision of the German people, leader, and empire. Riefenstahl's film portrays National Socialism (something morally evil) as beautiful. To view the film in the way in which it was intended to be seen is to see and be moved by (what Riefenstahl presents as) the beauty of National Socialism.

If this is right, it raises a question about how we are to respond to this film. Its every detail is designed to advance a morally repugnant vision of Hitler, a vision that, as history was to prove, falsified the true character of Hitler and National Socialism. Enjoying *this film*—recognizing that we may be caught up, if only slightly, in its pomp and pageantry or be stirred by its beauty—is likely to make us ask, "What kind of person am I to enjoy or be moved by this film?" Isn't there something wrong with responding in this way to a Nazi film?

This worry arises because *Triumph of the Will* presents National Socialism as attractive and, in so doing, aims to make us think of National Socialism as good. Hitler and what he stood for are commended. This is different from a case like Klaus Mann's novel about Nazism, *Mephisto*, where the evil described is clearly not presented as attractive or as meant to win our allegiance.

Riefenstahl doesn't just ask us to imagine finding the *Führer* and his message appealing, but actually to find them so.

The concern is not only that if I enjoy such a film, I may be led to act badly (e.g., to support neo-Nazi movements), but also that certain kinds of enjoyment, regardless of their effects, may themselves be problematic. Pleasure in this work of art (like pleasure in a work of art that celebrates sadism or pedophilia) might lead one to ask not just about what one may *become*, but about who one is *now*. The point is an Aristotelian one. If virtue consists (in part) in taking pleasure in the right things and not in the wrong things, then what is my character now such that I can take pleasure in these things?

Triumph of the Will also raises pressing questions about the attitude we should adopt toward the film as art. Should we praise it for its widely acclaimed aesthetic qualities despite its celebration of National Socialism? We recognize D. W. Griffith's *Birth of a Nation* as an important film despite its racism, and we admire the Pyramids despite the great human cost paid for their production. Should we similarly bracket questions of good and evil in looking at *Triumph of the Will?* Alternatively, should we insist that the moral implications of Riefenstahl's work undermine its aesthetic value? Or is this formulation of the problem too simple?

These questions merely highlight the long-standing general problem of beauty and evil: that aesthetic and moral considerations may pull in different directions. The problem emerges not only with *Triumph of the Will* and the other cases mentioned earlier but with, for example, the literary works of the Marquis de Sade and T. S. Eliot. The problem posed by the conflict between the demands of art and the demands of morality is familiar. What are we to make of it?

For much of the twentieth century, the standard solution to this conflict has been to recommend that we look at art from an "aesthetic distance." . . .

The basic strategy here is simple: when approaching a work of art that raises moral issues, sever aesthetic evaluation from moral evaluation and evaluate the work in aesthetic (i.e., formal) terms alone. This is the formalist response to the problem of beauty and evil. Formalism treats the aesthetic and the moral as wholly independent domains. It allows us to say that, evaluated morally, *Triumph of the Will* is bad but, evaluated aesthetically, it is good. . . .

But in the case of *Triumph of the Will*, the formalist strategy fails. It won't work here, not because we're too obsessed by the moral issues to assume a properly distanced standpoint, or because when we assume a posture of aesthetic distance we forget about the historical realities associated with the film, or because adopting an attitude of aesthetic distance toward a film like *Triumph of the Will* is itself an immoral position (though some may wish to argue that it is). Nor does adopting an attitude of aesthetic distance require that we literally forget about the historical realities. Aesthetic distance is, after all, only a shift in perspective, and a temporary one at that.

The reason the formalist strategy fails in the case of *Triumph of the Will* is that distancing ourselves from the morally objectionable elements of the film—its deification of Hitler, the story it tells about him, the party, and the German people, and so on—means distancing ourselves from the features that make it the work of art it is. If we distance ourselves from these features of the film, we will not be in a position to understand its artistic value— that is, why this lengthy film of political speeches and endless marching is correctly regarded as a cinematic masterpiece. We will also miss the beauty (horrifying though it is) of its vision of Hitler. . . .

. . . *Triumph of the Will* is a work of artistic mastery—perhaps, I dare say, of genius—not merely because of the film's purely formal features (the beauty of Riefenstahl's cinematography, her skillful editing techniques, etc.) but, perhaps most important, because of its artistic vision, its particular, utterly horrifying vision of Hitler and National Socialism. That vision is the essence of the film.

If taking an attitude of aesthetic distance means paying attention only to the formal aspects of the work (to the image and not to what it means), then aesthetic distance fails in the case of *Triumph of the Will* because it requires us to ignore the essence of the film.

Now, defenders of formalism can opt for a more complex understanding of aesthetic distance, one that does not require us to bracket an artwork's content. According to this view (call it "sophisticated formalism"), understanding a work of art consists in grasping and appreciating the relationship between its form and content, that is, the connection between the message and the means used to convey it. . . .

. . . A work's aesthetic achievement consists in the skill with which it expresses its content. Understood in this way, the aesthetic value of *Triumph of the Will* involves not just its formal accomplishments, but also how these stylistic means are used to convey feelings of awe, admiration, and oneness with Hitler.

Note that sophisticated formalism doesn't require abandoning the distinction between aesthetic and moral evaluation. As with the simpler version, with sophisticated formalism, aesthetic evaluation belongs to one domain, moral evaluation to another. Sophisticated formalism tells us to judge not the message but its expression. . . .

Indeed, according to sophisticated formalism, *Triumph of the Will* and works of art like it shouldn't (from an aesthetic point of view) cause any problem at all. We can distance ourselves from—that is, set aside—the moral dimension of the work's content while still *paying attention to* that content—that is, the way in which the film's content figures in its expressive task.

Is this broader, more inclusive understanding of aesthetic distance satisfactory? The answer, I think, is no. Even sophisticated formalism, with its richer concept of the aesthetic, makes it impossible to talk about the political meaning of *Triumph of the Will*, the truth or falsity of its picture of Hitler, whether it is good or evil, right or wrong—*while doing aesthetics*. These cognitive and moral matters are ones we are meant to distance ourselves from when engaged in the business of aesthetic evaluation. Sophisticated formalism doesn't ignore content, but it does *aestheticize* it. When we follow its recommendations, we adopt an aesthetic attitude toward the Christianity of *The Divine Comedy* and an aesthetic attitude toward the National Socialism of *Triumph of the Will*. Sophisticated formalism is, after all, a kind of formalism. It focuses on the (formal) relation between form and content. From its perspective, the content of the film (its vision) is relevant to evaluation only insofar as it is expressed well or badly. Thus, even on sophisticated varieties of formalism, essential elements of *Triumph of the Will* remain irrelevant to its aesthetic evaluation. Hence, here too, formalism fails to respond fully to the work of art that *Triumph of the Will* is.

Content is not always as important as it is in the case of *Triumph of the Will*, but here, as in the case of much political and religious art, the formalist response makes it difficult or impossible to explain why works like *Triumph of the Will* should be considered problematic in the first place.

At this point there are two ways to go. We can say that there is more to art than aesthetics or that there is more to aesthetics than beauty and form. The first option allows us to keep the historically important, eighteenth-century conception of the aesthetic intact. (It is in effect the conception of the aesthetic introduced by sophisticated formalism.) This conception has the advantage of keeping the boundaries of the aesthetic relatively narrow and clearly defined. And it keeps aesthetic evaluation relatively simple. Questions of political meaning, of truth and falsity, good and evil, right and wrong fall outside the category of the aesthetic. One implication of adopting this option is that, since there are works of art that raise these issues, the category of the artistic outstrips the category of the aesthetic.

The second option broadens the concept of the aesthetic beyond its traditional boundaries. It says that we are responding to a work of art "aesthetically" not only when we respond to its formal elements or to the relationship between its formal elements and its content, but also whenever we respond to a feature that makes a work the work of art it is. (These features may include substantive as well as formal features.) On this second option, the aesthetic is understood in such a way as to track the artistic, however broadly or narrowly that is to be understood.[5]

It is this second route that I recommend. Let me at least briefly say why. The first option remains wedded to a conception of the aesthetic that preserves the eighteenth-century preoccupation with beauty. This is a rich and important tradition, but it focuses—and keeps us focused—on a feature of art that is no longer so important to us. Indeed, one of the significant and widely noted facts about the development of modern art is that beauty is no longer central to art. The price of regarding this conception of the aesthetic as the only legitimate one is to marginalize aesthetics—isolating it from much of the philosophy of art—and, indeed, from much of our experience of art.

Opting for this broader conception of the aesthetic gives us a more inclusive category, one more adequate to what art is in all of its historical and cultural manifestations and to the full range of its values. It sets much of what we humanly care about back into the aesthetic arena and offers a much more complete view of the value of art.

My claim, which employs this richer conception of the aesthetic, is, then, that in order to get things aesthetically right about *Triumph of the Will*, we have to engage with its vision. And this means that we have to engage with the moral issues it raises. This nonformalist notion of the aesthetic rides piggyback on a nonformalist conception of art. It doesn't require wholesale abandonment of the distinction between aesthetic and moral value. We can, for example, still distinguish between the formal beauty of *Triumph of the Will's* stylistic devices and its moral status as a work of National Socialist propaganda. Nor does it require denying that art and morality belong to different domains. But it does require recognizing that there are areas where these domains overlap and that certain works of art, especially works of religious and political art, fall within this overlapping area.

VI

In Section IV, we began by canvassing different explanations for the troubling nature of *Triumph of the Will:* that it is disturbing because of the horrible events it documents, because it is a work of propaganda, because it propagates a highly selective and distorted picture of Hitler and National Socialism. Each of these factors helps to explain why the film is troubling, but none of them gets at what is, I have argued, the most unsettling feature of the film: its conjunction of beauty and evil.

We then, in Section V, considered the standard solution for dealing with the problem of beauty and evil, namely, formalism, which holds that aesthetic evaluation can be severed from moral evaluation and that art *qua* art must be evaluated in formal terms alone. Each of the two versions of formalism we considered, simple and sophisticated, maintained that the problem posed by the juncture of beauty and evil in *Triumph of the Will* (and works like it) is illusory. The simple version attempted to dissolve the problem of the juncture of beauty and evil by focusing on the formal features of the film and relegating the film's content to a domain outside the boundaries of aesthetic evaluation. The sophisticated version attempted to dissolve the problem by focusing on the relation of form and content in the film. It, too, held consideration of the film's morally objectionable content (its vision) to fall outside the domain of aesthetic evaluation. But, as we have seen, formalism fails in the case of *Triumph of the Will* because in bracketing the very components that make the film morally objectionable (i.e., it content), it also brackets the film's essence as a work of art—its vision of National Socialism.

The failure of formalism shows that the problem of beauty and evil is real. Indeed,

each of the candidate explanations for the threatening nature of the film can be recast as accepting and giving different interpretations to this problem. As a documentary, *Triumph of the Will* conjoins beautifully rendered footage and the celebration of horrible historical events; as propaganda, the film conjoins a masterfully constructed political narrative and a distorted picture of Hitler's character and aims; as formal expression, it conjoins masterful cinematography and morally repugnant content. But the most trenchant account of the relation of beauty and evil in *Triumph of the Will* focuses on the fact that the film renders something that is evil, namely National Socialism, beautiful and, in so doing, tempts us to find attractive what is morally repugnant.

The upshot of these reflections is that the question we considered before—How are we to respond to *Triumph of the Will?*—can't be evaded. As we have seen, there are really two questions here, one about us, one about how we are to evaluate the film as art.

First, the question about us. What does it mean about us if we find this film beautiful? Does it show that there is something wrong with our character? That we really approve of or endorse fascism or the doctrines of National Socialism? That we approve of the Final Solution? The answer to the question about us depends on what, in finding the film beautiful, we are responding *to*. As the simple version of formalism showed, some elements of the film are unproblematically beautiful: the film's fine camera work, its rhythmic editing, and so on. Responding to these elements of the film isn't the same as endorsing its National Socialism. One can respond to the formal elements of the film without supporting the work's message. Nor is there anything problematic about responding to the relation between form and content in the film. If we are responding not to the film's content *per se*, but only to how that content is *presented*, then, here too, we are not endorsing the film's message.

My analysis, however, shows that there is another feature of the film that is not so innocuous: its vision. In order to respond fully to the film as a work of art, we must respond to this vision. Indeed, my analysis implies that appreciating the film as a work of art requires responding to the beauty of this vision of National Socialism. But this means that the proper formulation of the question about us is, What kind of people are we if we find this vision beautiful? It is not immediately obvious that we *can* find this vision beautiful without endorsing fascism or the doctrines of National Socialism.

Here it is important to be very clear about what is meant by the film's vision. When I speak of the film's vision, I do not mean something that might be meant by the word "vision," namely the abstract doctrines or ideals of National Socialism, but rather the film's deifying portrait of Hitler as the beloved father of a happy, smiling people and of a national community unified by its desire to labor for the New Germany.

Appreciating the beauty of this vision (seeing the possible appeal of the idea of a benevolent leader, of a unified community, of a sense of national purpose) is not the same thing as finding the doctrines or ideals of National Socialism appealing. I can consistently see this concrete vision as beautiful (or attractive) and reject the doctrines and ideals of the National Socialists, be utterly horrified by what they did, and so on.

There is a step between finding the film's concrete artistic vision beautiful and endorsing the doctrines and ideals of National Socialism. The step is a moral one, a step we need not (and, of course, should not) take. So it is possible to appreciate the beauty of the film's vision without compromising ourselves morally. But, it is important to note, one of the central aims of *Triumph of the Will* is to move its audience to take this step, to find the historical realities and doctrines of National Socialism appealing. Part of the evil of the film consists in the fact that it is designed to move us in this way—in the direction of evil.

That the film aims to move us to find National Socialism appealing is also one of the things that makes responding to it so

problematic. The film *is* potentially corrupting. To appreciate the beauty of its vision—or to acknowledge our appreciation—is to open ourselves to a work that presents us with the temptations of fascism. One reason that the sense that there is something troubling about *Triumph of the Will* will not—and should not—go away is that there *is* something morally dangerous about the film.

I want now to turn to the second question: How should the fact that the film is evil figure in our evaluation of it as a work of art? Having gotten clearer about the real insidiousness of the film, we may be tempted to claim that it is of little or no artistic value. But this response won't do. *Triumph of the Will* clearly is of artistic value. As we have seen, it is an extremely powerful film, perhaps even a work of genius.

Should we then say that *Triumph of the Will* is a terrific work of art, despite its insidiousness? Here I think we should hesitate. For all its accomplishments, *Triumph of the Will* is flawed. It is flawed because its vision is flawed. Its vision is flawed because it misrepresents the character of Hitler and National Socialism and because it presents as beautiful and good things that are evil, namely Hitler and National Socialism. These flaws are relevant to the evaluation of *Triumph of the Will* as art because, as our examination makes clear, the film's vision of National Socialism is part of the work of art that it is. If that vision is flawed, then so is the work of art. . . .

. . . If good art must not only please the senses, but also engage and satisfy us intellectually and emotionally, then we are, I suggest, justified in criticizing *Triumph of the Will* for rendering something evil beautiful.

We are justified in doing so not just as moralists but as critics of art. This is not to say that works of art should only show good people doing good things, or that they are meant to endorse only conventional conceptions of goodness. Nor is it meant to deny that a work of art—even one as morally flawed as *Triumph of the Will*—may nevertheless be of artistic value. But there is reason, I am claiming, to withhold the highest aesthetic praise from works of art that present as beautiful, attractive, and good what, on reflection, can be seen to be evil.

One question remains. If Riefenstahl's film is flawed in the ways I have described, why watch it? Well, we obviously don't sit down to watch *Triumph of the Will* for fun. But it is an important film. It is worth watching because of its historical value as a chronicle of the rise of fascism in Germany and of events leading to the Second World War and as a case study in how propaganda works. It is also worth watching for its formal beauty and expressive power. In addition, we may watch *Triumph of the Will* for much the same reason some feminists examine works of pornography: so that in confronting these works we may learn something about a way of seeing the world we reject.

There are at least two further reasons for watching the film. The more obvious one is that part of preventing a recurrence of fascism involves understanding how fascism came to be thought attractive, how parties like the National Socialist German Worker's Party called upon and met certain underlying human wishes of many Germans in the 1930s (e.g., for a strong leader, for community, for a sense of national purpose). Deciding not to ban (or avoid) materials like *Triumph of the Will* means learning not to deny, but to live

with, the historical reality of the Third Reich. The second, related reason is that confronting the film's vision of National Socialism may allow us to understand more fully ourselves as human beings. Imagining seeing the world as Riefenstahl represents it, however disturbing, may enable us to confront, and come a little closer to comprehending, both the real and potential tendencies that have come to define human evil.

The most important reason, though, for watching *Triumph of the Will* is that it provides the very conjunction of beauty and evil we find so unsettling. It allows us to see that beauty and evil can, and have been, conjoined. And it allows us to see that one of the disturbing things about art is that it can make evil appear beautiful and good. Thus, what we might think is a reason for *not* watching the film is, upon reflection, the very reason we should watch it.

Notes

1. Leni Riefenstahl, *Leni Riefenstahl: A Memoir* (New York: Picador, 1987), 160.
2. Andrew Sarris (ed.), *Interviews with Film Directors* (New York: Avon Books, 1967), 461.
3. Riefenstahl, *A Memoir*, 101.
4. Ibid., 304–5.
5. An example of this general approach can be found in Wayne Booth's *The Company We Keep: An Ethics of Fiction* (Berkeley: University of California Press, 1988).

Ethics and Death in Westerns: John Ford's *The Man Who Shot Liberty Valance*

Peter A. French

Philosophers do not usually write about films, let alone westerns. But in this essay, Peter French explores the moral vision found in western movies much as Mary Devereaux did in *Triumph of the Will*. After first describing what he terms "Christian and feminine" values, French contrasts these with the values of the western. But westerns are not just anti-Christian and anti-women; they also affirm alternative values of courage, especially in the face of death. French describes the lead characters in films such as *The Shootist* and especially *The Man*

Who Shot Liberty Valance as representatives of an "executive" account of virtue and courage. He then links the western and its conception of virtue with Giambattista Vico's understanding of the different ages through which cultures pass and the types of characters that each age creates. *The Man Who Shot Liberty Valance* illustrates this well, he claims, and the film is the perfect vehicle to depict the transition from one age to another. He concludes by contrasting the western's conception of virtue with what is often regarded as the "masculine" approach to morality as opposed to a more "feminist" one. Peter A. French holds the Cole Chair in Ethics and is professor of philosophy at the University of South Florida.

As you read through this essay, consider the following:

1. How does French describe "Christian and feminine" values?
2. What are the values that are expressed in the western, according to French?
3. How does Vico describe the three ages that cultures go through?
4. How does *The Man Who Shot Liberty Valance* illustrate the claim Vico makes about the different ages through which cultures pass?
5. How do westerns differ from contemporary thought about "male" morality?
6. How would Devereaux criticize or defend watching westerns?

1. CHRISTIAN AND FEMININE VALUES IN THE WEST

If my daughter, or the daughter of anyone else, my family or other family, is in trouble, my place is there. . . . Jesus said, "Go out into the highways and hedges." He said this to women, as well as men.

[Carrie] Nation's call was answered [in the nineteenth century] by thousands of women who took up all manner of social causes in the name of Christianity. A rising tide of civilizing and Christianizing not only was led by women, but threatened to wash away the very activities and beliefs that men held to be their special domain, what they cared most about. Women, some men must have feared, were taking over and, to make matters worse, they were doing so under the banner of Christian righteousness. To stand against that would require either a reformation of Christian dogma or a desertion of the religion alto-

From *Cowboy Metaphysics* by Peter A. French (New York: Rowman and Littlefield, 1997). Reprinted by permission of the publisher.

gether. After all, these women were out to convert the frontier and the wilderness, where a man could be a man, into the domain of the two institutions in which femininity dominated: the home and the church. Nation's home had no walls, and her church was founded on doctrines that threatened to emasculate the frontier spirit. A theological assault was, by and large, rejected, perhaps because those capable of taking on the task realized straightaway that the women did, in fact, have God (or at least scripture) on their side. Their speeches and writings positively dripped with supporting quotations from the Sermon on the Mount that were indisputably put to good and fair use. Desertion of the Christian ethic, at least in fiction if not in fact, and the construction of an alternative bastion to house an opposing world view, a radically different collection of cares, was apparently a more appealing endeavor. And in that bundle of cares both of those co-opted institutions, the home and the church, would have to be either rejected or excluded as unsuitable. In that philosophic and literary climate, the westerner that in the twentieth century would fill the silver screen was created. The writers of the frontier—Mark Twain, Owen Wister,

Bret Harte, and Zane Grey—blazed that sagebrush trail for a century of Western film directors and script writers to ride, saddlebags packed with a world view that always is a rejection of, but much more than a rejection of, feminized Christianity.

. . . I want to concentrate on what the westerner (both hero and villain) in the films cares and does not care about and the ethics and meta-ethics that supervene on those cares and, of course, the world view that the films place in opposition to the cares of the westerner: the Christian feminine bundle of cares.

The anti-Christian stance in Westerns appears in a multitude of ways. For example, ordinary men (not the heroes or villains) are generally depicted as embued with Christian values, even living Christian lives. And it is they who are revealed to be incapable of rising to challenges, inadequate to the tasks crucial to surviving and flourishing in the West, in its towns and in its wide open spaces. They are fathers and husbands, storekeepers and farmers who are portrayed as constrained by ethical considerations that are inappropriate for the circumstances. They are emasculated and left defenseless by the civilized Christian ideals they have adopted or that have, more often than not, been forced on them by women. In *The Man Who Shot Liberty Valance*, a film I will discuss in more detail, we first meet Ransom Stoddard, played by James Stewart, as an easterner lawyer who is savagely beaten by the outlaw Liberty Valance. Valance rips up Stoddard's law books and says that what he is doing is giving the dude a lesson in Western law. Stoddard is portrayed as utterly incapable of effective response. In the early scenes of *Pale Rider* the shopkeeper, who is described as and seen to be a good Christian fellow, stands behind his window watching his friend, the independent miner Hull Barrett, being verbally insulted and mercilessly beaten. If the husbands and would-be husbands of the female leads remain in the story at all, in the *Shane*-type stories or ones with significant *Shane*-type elements, of which *Pale Rider*, *Will Penny*, *The Shootist*, *Hondo*, and *The Tall T* are examples, they may

be able occasionally to display residual aggressive masculine traits when inspired by a true westerner, but, by and large, they are . . . dominated by women.

In *Shane*, Marion decries the use of the gun to settle matters, and she opposes the shooting lesson Shane gives to her son, Little Joey. She wants a valley free of guns where families can be raised in peace and love. She will not accept Shane's explanation that a gun is just a tool like any other, only as good or as bad as the person who uses it. Perhaps she sees the gun as a phallic symbol, a powerful and deadly icon of the masculine. Perhaps that is what she wants banned from the valley.

In *Pale Rider*, Megan's mother, Sarah, pleads with her fiancé, Hull, to negotiate with the villain, and even the emasculated Hull recognizes that will be fruitless. Negotiation, mediation, arbitration are the civilized responses to conflict situations. In Westerns they are represented as feminine responses, and as utterly ineffectual.

In *Stagecoach*, the rule of women and their identification with both the Christian church and civilization itself is made manifestly clear when Dallas, the prostitute (with a heart of gold), is driven out of town by a gaggle of self-righteous females spouting Christian platitudes and marching to Christian hymns. *Stagecoach* also defines for us the two types of women who will appear in Westerns. There are the easterners, the crusaders for Christianity and its "civilized" family values, so many incarnations of Carrie Nation, and there are the prostitutes, virtually westerners, at least in attitude, though usually constrained by caring about some of the feminine easterner cares, especially those surrounding the concept of home, and so never fully westernized. It has always struck me as revealing, in some difficult-to-articulate way, that the good Christian easterner women of Westerns seem always to have and are referred to by full names, (or what Philip French calls WASPish names) like Lucy Mallory (the cavalry officer's wife in *Stagecoach*), while the saloon women and the prostitutes bear the names of cities like Dallas (in *Stagecoach*),

Chihuahua (in *My Darling Clementine*), and Vienna (in *Johnny Guitar*). I suppose Mrs. Miller (of *McCabe and Mrs. Miller*) is an exception, and perhaps her name was chosen for that very reason.

The prostitutes typically share more of the westerner's perspective than their Christian easterner sisters. For example, the prostitutes in *Unforgiven*, as a just penalty for the slashing of the face of one of their own, reject civilized ways of settling disputes and throw the town back into the violent days of vengeance. They will accept no form of restitution short of the death of the offenders. Most uncivilized! Most unChristian! And difficult for the recently civilized male population of the town, including the sheriff who is building a house, to understand. "Why would they want to go and do that?" he says.

Although male ministers make appearances (perhaps the most interesting is the ambiguous reverend in *The Searchers* who deftly doffs his clerical garb and leads the Texas Ranger unit, literally, at the drop of a collar), Christianity is almost always the province, domain, and retreat of women in Westerns. Bond Rogers, played by Lauren Bacall, in *The Shootist* is a good case in point. At first she vehemently expresses the desire to throw the notorious gunman J. B. Books, John Wayne's character, out of her boardinghouse. When she learns he is dying of cancer, she recants and begs his forgiveness for the most unChristian way she had acted. It is evident, to us and to her, that she bears the responsibilities of Christian service, even toward a most thoroughly nonChristian "assassin," as she calls him.

Christian rituals, services, and hymn singing in the films are typically organized by women or solely conducted by women and feeble, cowardly men. In *The Outlaw Josey Wales*, for example, only the women know the words and sing the hymn of thanksgiving, a hymn that, as it happens, is interrupted by more important matters, the appearance of a threat to life that calls the westerner into violent, and certainly not Christian, response. In *Will Penny*, Will (played by Charlton Heston)

sheepishly admits to Catherine Allen and her son Horace that he does not know any Christmas carols. They are surprised and somewhat appalled. In *The Cowboys* the way for the young lads to become true cowboys, westerners, is for their mothers to give them up to the hardened training of a westerner, the obsessive Will Anderson (played by John Wayne), who rudely scrapes off their Christian, civilized veneer and turns them into calculating killers who risk death to avenge the savage murder of their surrogate father.

What are the central ethical doctrines and concepts of feminized Christianity? They are the familiar ones: turning the other cheek, loving (the *agape* variety) neighbors and enemies, antiviolence, leaving vengeance to God, the meek shall inherit the earth, showing mercy, being forgiving, humility, caring, kindness, doing onto others as one would have them do unto you. The admonitions of The Sermon on the Mount pretty well cover the territory occupied and defended by women in Westerns. . . .

2. ARISTOTLE CONTEMPLATING THE DYING DUKE

The typical plot of a Western clearly places its main characters in those "situations that bring a sudden death." The showdown—the gun battle—is a standard climax of Westerns, and, by its very nature, the battle is intended to reveal the true characters of the westerners. But are such gunfights noble circumstances? . . .

[Recall] the scene in *The Shootist* in which Books visits Doctor Hostetler. During that scene he is provided with a rather graphic account of how the cancer in his body will advance and how the pain will increase until he is unable to get out of bed. "One morning you're just going to wake up and say 'Here I am in this bed and here I'm going to stay.'" He is given laudanum to ease the pain, but he is told that after awhile that will prove useless. Then the doctor hints to him that he should consider suicide rather than suffer through the excruciating series of events that the disease has in store for him. The doctor, in fact, leads into that suggestion by remarking that he could not do it in his own case because he does not have Books's courage. Books only grunts as he leaves the office.

We, and especially media reporters, tend to throw words like "courage" and "brave" around with as little care as we talk of tragedy. Having recently watched some of the Olympic Games on television, I am satiated with "tragic" and "courageous." I wonder sometimes whether reporters have any other words in their vocabularies. In one three hour period the television audience was told how courageous a diver was because she was to attempt a difficult dive, how tragic was the failure of a runner to finish a race because she pulled a thigh muscle, and how brave a gymnast must have been to attempt a vault when she was in pain. "Hero," of course, got even more overworked, usually accompanied by some sappy music sung by a lead vocalist and a choir of thousands. However, we typically talk about a person showing courage when he or she has to deal with pain and suffering. If we are ready and willing to talk that way about the healthiest of the specimens of the human race among us: Olympic athletes, it is not surprising that we are willing to talk of the courage of a person suffering from a terminal disease. "He showed great courage in the final stages of the illness." That's what we might say to express our admiration for the way he coped with the pain and suffering he must have been experiencing. But would Aristotle be willing to call such a person courageous?

In a way that is much more persuasive than may first appear to us, Aristotle would insist that a person may face the pain of a terminal illness with a certain admirable toughness, but that that person cannot be courageous with respect to it. Aristotle writes, "In disease the brave man is fearless for he has given up hope, he dislikes the thought of death in this shape. . . . We show courage in situations where there is the opportunity of showing prowess or where death is noble; but in the form of death in disease neither of these conditions is fulfilled."

Why would he say this? In part, in situations of terminal illness where the pain ultimately overwhelms the person, there is no real scope for the afflicted to act, no opportunity for prowess. For Aristotle, the scope of the person's actions in the circumstances is always crucial. And, it so happens, this is the central problematic of *The Shootist*. J. B. Books can die the painful death of cancer that the laudanum will not be able to overcome or he can die another death, the death of a gunfighter, a shootist, a death in which he has a genuine opportunity to display his prowess, in which he has a scope of actions in which he can hope to display his virtue. As we are shown in the clips that begin the film, Books has been a courageous person, a town-taming lawman.

What is involved in the expression of the virtue of courage? In the first place and important for Aristotle, courage is an executive virtue. That is, courage is a virtue that is always practiced in the cause of some end that is over and above the expression of courage itself—courage is not practiced only as an end in itself. In effect, unlike some of the other virtues, courage has both an internal and an external goal, to borrow language from David Pears. Its internal goal is the one it shares with other virtues: to be practiced for its own sake. Its external goal will vary from situation to situation, but will be some morally desirable end, or what Aristotle calls "the noble." In the terminal illness case there can be, due to the situation, no external goal, and so courage in such a case cannot serve its executive function. . . .

Being tough with respect to his imminent death is not enough for a character like Books. He has been a personification of courage and his life is being cheapened by a noncourageous death, a death that the local buffoon of a marshal (played by Harry Morgan) cannot help pointing out to him is not only ironic, but downright comic.

Marshal Thibido (to Books): Excuse me if I don't pull a long face. I can't . . . Don't take too long to die. Be a gent and convenience everybody and do it soon . . . The day they lay you away, what I'll do on your grave won't pass for flowers . . . Keeping you alive long enough to die natural is costing us a pretty penny . . . How you feelin'? A little more poorly everyday? Books, this is nineteen ought one, the old days are gone and you don't know it. We got a waterworks, telephones, and lights, and we'll have our streetcar electrified by next year, and we've started to pave the streets. Oh, we've still got some weedin' to do, but once we're rid of people like you, we'll have a goddamn Garden of Eden here. To put it in a nutshell, you've outlived your time . . . When my time comes to die, I won't drag it out. I'll just do it. Why the hell don't you?

A smarmy newspaper reporter, the undertaker, and a golddigging ex-girlfriend provide Books with ample evidence that his life is not coming to an end worthy of the way he has lived, of the virtue he has personified. What he cares most about is being denied him by the disease. Aristotle wrote that "human good turns out to be activity of soul in accordance with virtue . . . 'in a complete life'."[1] Books comes to understand that his plan to die alone in the bed in the boarding house, after he has read the entire newspaper he purchased on arrival in Carson City, does not befit who he is. It offends his character. It does not appropriately conclude his life. To do that he must find a courageous way to die. The lead story in the newspaper is the death of Queen Victoria. Books tells Bond Rogers, the landlady of the boardinghouse:

Books: Well, maybe she outlived her time. Maybe she was a museum piece. But she never lost her dignity, nor sold her guns. She hung onto her pride and went out in style. Now that's the kind of an old gal I'd like to meet.

Of course, he is comparing her to himself, and he does not like the way he looks in the comparison.

For Aristotle, to be truly courageous a person must face the dangers of the deadly activity "for the sake of the noble, the noble being the end of virtue." . . .

3. THE DEATH OF DEATH

The following conversation between Captain Woodrow Call and Pea Eye Parker occurs in *Streets of Laredo* after they come across the old-timer Ben Lilly, whose dogs have been burned by the sadistic Mox Mox.

Call: Damn few left like him.

Pea Eye: Like him how, Captain?

Call: Like him, like Gus, like Hickok, old Kit Carson. They done what they wanted. They went where they wanted. It wasn't always good, but least they lived free lives. You're a farmer yourself, corporal. You're respectable. Charlie Goodnight's got his ranch. It's just the killers and a few like old Ben Lilly that's kept the old ways.

Pea Eye: And you, captain.

Call: What?

Pea Eye: You've kept to the old ways.

Call gives a double take and sighs. Then he stares off to the horizon.

The Man Who Shot Liberty Valance is an especially disturbing film for fans of John Ford. Ford Westerns were typically shot in the broad and spectacular vistas of Monument Valley. The grandeur of the great outdoors virtually swallows up the human stories, gives them perspective against the enormous monoliths of raw nature. In fact, most Westerns, not just those of John Ford, establish their locations and their moods by opening scenes of either the desert or the stark, snow-covered mountains. Think of *Stagecoach*, *Red River*, *The Searchers*, *High Plains Drifter*, *Pale Rider*, and so many more. It never ceases to amaze me when I drive across states like Kansas, as I do at least twice a year on my way to the mountains, that it was in uninspiring prairies where most of the real stories of the West occurred. Dodge City, Abilene, and Wichita are nowhere near mountains or deserts. At least Deadwood is in the Black Hills of South Dakota and Tombstone in Arizona does have some reasonably impressive hills and desert outside of town. . . .

The barren beautiful landscapes are as much characters in the films as any of the humans. The wilderness is the one thing the westerner reveres. J. B. Books tells Mrs. Rogers that he will not accept her invitation to attend church services, because his church has always been the wilderness. He will worship in no other. Joshua Sloan, the ersatz preacher in *The Ballad of Cable Hogue*, remarks in his eulogy for Hogue, "He never went to church. He didn't need to. The whole desert was his cathedral." The wilderness is the one thing with which the westerner seeks identity. And, of course, in the end he generally achieves it.

The landscape also makes clear what the films reject as unworthy: cities, soft people, and soft things, and of course, anything Eastern, anything civilized. As Will Penny tells Catherine Adams, "This is a hard country, double hard." If you want to survive in the West, you must imitate the West itself, its hardness, its bleakness, its unforgiving nature. All of that being true, why in what is his most bitter vision of the death of the West, did John Ford not avail himself of the landscape of death? Why was this typically prevailing character not cast in *The Man Who Shot Liberty Valance*?

The film, like the majority of Westerns, is centrally about death and dying. Unlike most Westerns, it is bleak, interior. It is about a West that is already dead and replaced with flimsy, artificial legend. The film is a funeral, black and gray and dark, all vertical and horizontal planes, shot in deep-focus chiaroscuro. It is also something of a morality play in which the good, as discussed earlier, does something bad in order to do something good. The problem is that what is good and what is bad has gotten twisted and redefined in the process so that there is a genuine ambiguity about what is right and what is wrong and what is left.

The film is set at a funeral, or rather at the undertaker's, as the body of Tom Doniphon is prepared for burial. The highly respected Senator Ransom Stoddard (played by James Stewart) and his wife Hallie (Vera Miles) arrive to pay their last respects. Most of the townsfolk are puzzled as to why the Senator would bother. Doniphon was a drunken bum with no special social or moral standing in the town of Shinbone. Stoddard has been a highly successful politico, rising through the elected ranks to his current position. The local newspaper editor, whose name is Scott, wants the story that explains Stoddard's appearance at the undertaker's and Stoddard, the consummate politician, obliges him. The bulk of the film is a flashback to the early days of Shinbone and the story, as told by Stoddard, of the odd relationship that emerged between Tom Doniphon (played by John Wayne), Stoddard, and Hallie.

Stoddard, an easterner with a law school education, was pulled from the stagecoach that was taking him to Shinbone and severely beaten by the outlaw Liberty Valance. Doniphon finds Stoddard and brings him to his girlfriend Hallie so that she and the Ericsons, who run a restaurant, can nurse him. Throughout most of the flashback Stoddard is shown in light and neutral colors and, importantly, he is almost always in a prone, horizontal, position being looked down upon by Doniphon, Valance, and the other westerners, including Hallie. This is in stark contrast to the opening and closing sequences where he is vertical and straight while it is Doniphon, prone in his pine coffin, who is looked down upon by Stoddard. The film is about that change of positions, from the horizontal to the vertical and vice versa.

Hallie is, arguably, the most interesting character throughout the film. A convincing case can be made that she is the symbol of the West for Ford and that the story is one of her repression, as well as the death of the West, at the hands of the civilizing easterner. At the beginning of the flashback, Hallie is wild, loud-mouthed, and free. She is unafraid to criticize the men. She dresses in light colored dresses, her hair is in pigtails, and she "radiates around the men."[2] As she comes under the influence of Stoddard, however, she is more and more toned down. Her spirit is sapped and when we see her at the end of the film, she is bitter, but resigned. Hallie could not read or write and so she is tutored by Stoddard, but when we see her in his class she already shows signs of the repression of civilization. "Hallie's repression is like that of the West—Ranse's influence 'tames' her, makes her respectable and educated, but takes the fire, freedom, and passion out of her."[3] As Stoddard and his wife are leaving on the train out of Shinbone, their visit completed, Hallie gazes out of the window and, rather laconically but with a distinct edge of bitterness, says to the Senator, "Look at it. It was once a wilderness; now it's a garden. Aren't you proud?" Of course, the sad fact is that he is proud and willing to take the credit. After all, he is a politician. To become that he has, himself, changed. He was once a terrified, inept dude, suited primarily for woman's work, wearing an apron in many of the scenes, including his "shoot-out" with Liberty Valance. Now he has become a heartless, platitude-spouting, superficial politician who cannot even find the right words to say over the coffin to the oldest friends of Doniphon. At his farewell to Pompey, Doniphon's servant who had a great deal to do with getting both Doniphon and Stoddard out of tough situations, all he can do is to slip some money in his hand and say, "pork chop money." Whatever sincerity and verve Stoddard had in the old days, like Hallie's fire, has been extinguished. And so, the West.

The film's title is *The Man Who Shot Liberty Valance*. The legend on which the Senator's career was built is that Stoddard was that man. And for a short while he even believed that he had killed Valance. He learns from Doniphon that, from the shadows of an alley, Doniphon had shot Valance with a rifle. Doniphon, the true westerner, killed Liberty: and he did it in a way that violated all of the principles of the westerner. By letting Stoddard take the credit, credit he would not want anyway, Doniphon propels Stoddard into the political limelight, and more important, he seals his own doom. But who really killed Liberty Valance?

The answer is unambiguous. Stoddard killed Liberty even if the bullet from his gun never entered the body of Liberty Valance. The easterner's conception of civilization and law and order, the very idea that the wilderness could and should be converted into a garden, destroyed the West. And with the demise of the conditions the westerner requires to flourish, what was left for Tom Doniphon? His moral compass was shattered. Everything he cared about was destroyed. And so was he. "Tom's progression, from the respectable, capable moral center of the town to a virtual bum, is inversely related to Ranse's progression and in a strange way parallels that of Hallie. He is kindly and jovial in the beginning of the film, very much in control and respected by everyone. What he loses . . . is his personal center."[4]

Doniphon creates a new hero for a new West (Ransom Stoddard) by destroying the West in which he, Doniphon, can comfortably function. That West contains Liberty Valances, Jack Wilsons, Franks, and various and sundry mean and ornery individuals taking too much advantage of the freedom the wilderness offers. As Marshal Thibido, in *The Shootist*, tells Books, they must be weeded out to make the West a "goddam Garden of Eden." In effect, the westerners must be buried to make things safe for law, order, and civilization.

Doniphon, however, weeds himself out, unknowingly sacrifices himself, thinking he is big enough to bear the responsibility for what he has done. He is not. He cannot be killed off by Stoddard and he has run out of West into which to ride away. All of that monumental scenery in the other Ford Westerns is reduced in *The Man Who Shot Liberty Valance* to a single cactus rose stuck on what is obviously a sound stage, a cactus rose that Stoddard disparages when he tells Hallie that she will have real roses, the cultivated, garden-variety type that are put in glass vases in tea rooms.

My interpretation of *The Man Who Shot Liberty Valance* is guided in some, not insignificant, measure by a conversation I had with German scholar Vittorio Hosle and the reading of an article he and Mark Roche wrote about the film.[5] Hosle and Roche persuasively find a conceptual structure for the film in Giambattista Vico's concept of human history. Vico distinguished three ages in the history of every culture: the age of gods, the age of heroes, and the age of men. Vico writes, "The first nature (in the historical course nations run), by a powerful deceit of imagination . . . was a poetic or creative nature which we may be allowed to call divine, as it ascribed to physical things the being of substances animated by gods, assigning the gods to them according to its idea of each . . . The second was heroic nature . . . They justly regarded their heroism as including the natural nobility in virtue of which they were the princes of the human race . . . The third was human nature, intelligent and hence modest, benign, and reasonable, recognizing for laws conscience, reason, and duty."[6] With regard to the customs of each age he tells us, "The first customs were all tinged with religion and pity . . . The second were choleric and punctilious, like those related to Achilles. The third are dutiful, taught to everyone by his own sense of civil duty."[7] With reference to kinds of governments he says, "The first were divine, or, as the Greeks would say, theocratic . . . The second were heroic or aristocratic governments which is to say governments of the optimates in the sense of the most powerful . . . The third are human governments, in which, in virtue of the equality of the intelligent nature which is the proper nature of man, all are accounted equal under the laws . . ."[8] And the three ages also give rise to three kinds of characters. Vico writes, "The first were divine . . . The second were heroic characters, which were also imaginative universals to which they reduced the various species of heroic things, as to Achilles all deeds of valiant fighters and to Ulysses all devises of clever men . . . Finally, there were

invented (in the age of men) the vulgar characters which went along with the vulgar languages."[9]

The Man Who Shot Liberty Valance is a film about the transition from the heroic to the nonheroic age of men. The same theme, of course, dominates such films as *Butch Cassidy and the Sundance Kid*, *The Ballad of Cable Hogue*, *The Wild Bunch*, *McCabe and Mrs. Miller*, and the "modern" Westerns such as *Rancho Deluxe*, *Kid Blue*, *Hearts of the West*, *The Good Old Boys*, and *Lonely Are the Brave*. Vico's age of heroes is an age without a civil state, rather like Hobbes's state of nature, though Vico rejects Hobbes's account. It is an age in which physical prowess, force, and violence set the rules of human interactions. In the opening segment of the flashback . . . while Liberty Valance is flogging Stoddard, he tears up Stoddard's law books and tells him he is giving him a lesson in Western law.

In Vico's age of heroes the duel between two strong men, strong of will and strong in physical force and prowess, is the defining moment of human action. What happens in the duel between Liberty Valance and Ransom Stoddard is a travesty, a mocking of that primary symbol of the heroic age, a sure sign that the age is ending. Its replacement, for Vico, is an age dominated by the rule of law and reason and not physical prowess or force, the age of modern men and their machinery.

Stoddard is the transition figure in *The Man Who Shot Liberty Valance*, hopefully and confidently he preaches and teaches the virtues of the new age, literacy, representative government, equality. It is an age in which he will thrive, paradoxically, because the general public thinks he is heroic and he knows that he is not. Characteristic of the age of men is the rise of public education, facility with language, and, as Hosle and Roche note, "calculating intellect." They write, "The age of men necessarily culminates in what Vico calls the 'barbarism of reflection,' an empty reasoning that has lost any substantial contents, a strategic attitude toward fellow human beings, a lack of roots and traditions and therefore of emotional richness. One aspect of the barbarism of reflection is the spreading of lying."[10]

As noted earlier, westerners hate liars. Lying is an art of language, and language is the tool of the easterner. The westerner says little, and when he does talk he is direct and honest. Vico's age of men is sustained on language and so lies. "The question will no longer be, who is quicker at shooting, but who is better at speaking."[11] In *The Man Who Shot Liberty Valance* nothing is both clearer and more poignant than the hero's, Tom Doniphon's, willingness to allow a lie to be promulgated, a lie on which not only Stoddard's whole career will be based, but one that will destroy both Doniphon and the age of heroes in which he thrives and has moral authority.

We see one particularly pernicious form of civilized lying, characteristic of the new age, in the contrast between the two newspaper editors in the film. Denton Peabody, the courageous editor of the *Shinbone Star* in the flashback, is a champion of the truth. He prints the truth even though it nearly costs him his life. He is an easterner, sent west by Horace Greeley's advice, but he grasps and adopts the westerner's demand for truth and he honors it. Editor Scott, who interviews Senator Stoddard in the beginning and end of the film, is the epitome of the current journalist. He could care less about the truth. What matters to him is the story, and rather than going out to investigate, he prefers to merely report on what people say, usually in staged press conferences. The neat twist in *The Man Who Shot Liberty Valance* is that even after learning the truth from the Senator's confession about who actually shot Liberty, the editor prefers the legend. "This is the West, sir." he says, "When the legend becomes fact, print the legend." The only reason the legend has become fact, of course, is because that is what people want to believe, and the Senator needed them to believe it to achieve his position of power. Furthermore, the most ironic claim of all is "This is the West, sir." It most certainly is not the West,

the West died with Liberty Valance and Tom Doniphon. It has become the new East, West only in geographic location relative to the old East, or, rather, it is Vico's age of men, where stories are judged on merits quite other than their truth. What sells to the largest audience is what is worthy of print.

There is a moral, an ethical, depth (to borrow a term from Hosle and Roche) to the westerner hero, to Tom Doniphon, that is almost completely lacking in Ransom Stoddard and absent in those who have followed after him in our civilized age. Doniphon is a suffering servant who makes a hero out of Stoddard at the cost of his own virtue. Doniphon could, we are aware, at any time call out Liberty Valance and, face to face, shoot it out with him. He almost does so in Peter Ericson's restaurant when Liberty trips Stoddard causing him to fall, sending Doniphon's steak to the floor. There is also little doubt that in a duel Doniphon would prevail. Why then does he let Stoddard go out into the street on that dark night to face Valance? Is it perhaps that he recognizes that his time is passing? Or does he want to see if Stoddard is brave enough to face what will surely be his death? I suppose it does not matter, but it does concern me because had Doniphon taken Stoddard's place in a face-to-face duel with Valance, he could have preserved his age for at least a short time longer, perhaps through his life. He could have succeeded in doing something J. B. Books does: saving himself from the new age. But the act he chooses to perform is, I suspect, of a greater ethical value.

Doniphon cold-bloodedly shoots Valance. What makes that so important is that by killing Valance that way, by murdering him, he forever deprives himself of the opportunity to publicly claim the deed. His act does not fit the heroic model so he cannot proclaim it. Instead, the only one who can claim the deed is the bumbling dude with the apron on who had at least enough nerve to face Valance out in the open. By killing Valance in what the hero knows is a cowardly fashion, the hero forfeits his claim to the heroic. Doniphon is well aware of that. Still, it makes sense to say that what he did was perhaps more morally admirable than had he stood out in the light and called out Valance for a face-to-face duel. He not only kills off a bullying threat to the civilizing forces in the town, a force of evil from any perspective, he gives the state a leader versed in the new age's arts of rhetoric and representative government, and with the essential ability to sustain a public career built on a lie. A dirty, unshaven, scruffy-looking Doniphon confronts Stoddard at the state-hood convention, when Stoddard is reluctant to accept the nomination to represent the territory in Washington.

> Doniphon: Cold-blooded murder, but I can live with it. Hallie's happy. She wanted you alive.
>
> Stoddard: But you saved my life.
>
> Doniphon: I wish I hadn't. Hallie's your girl now. Go back in there and take that nomination. You taught her to read and write, now give her something to read and write about.

Doniphon senses, as we see him in the bar directly after the shooting of Liberty, that he has killed something essential to his own welfare: the West, the land of heroes and death. "With the introduction of legality and the elimination of Liberty (and the forces he symbolizes), the hero becomes superfluous. Tom's killing Liberty consummates the Western in a very specific sense that it renders the hero unnecessary."[12]

Liberty Valance is virtually a caricature of evil in the film. He is played by Lee Marvin in exaggerated stylistic ways. From his flamboyant dress to his bellowing and swaggering and threatening, he is evil personified. You cannot miss it. He proclaims himself the bad guy by everything he does, every move he makes, every word that he utters. If you want to know what is evil in the old Shinbone, there is an unambiguous ostensive answer: Liberty. But where, or who, is evil after Liberty is killed? The moral clarity of the heroic age is muddied in the age of men. Ironically perhaps, the only character in the nonflashback segments of the film who dresses in anything

like the distinct whites and blacks favored by Liberty Valance and Tom Doniphon is Senator Stoddard. He wears a black suit and sports a white hat. Doniphon usually wears a black shirt and a white hat. But in the new age, evil is rendered into shades of gray and death has lost its sting.

. . . [The] easterner's civilization brings with it the Christian's conception of death. Death is no longer annihilation, and so it is no longer to be greatly feared, in and of itself, as the end of all you are or ever will be. What is to be feared is a tortured afterlife as punishment for a life of sin. Sin avoidance is more important than courageously facing one's death. The death of the West is the death of death. Little wonder that the civilized world ostracizes death. It will not countenance a return of the phantom of the wilderness.

Tom Doniphon's death is not courageous. It is, in fact, pathetic. He died a destitute bum who had sold his guns to buy booze. His figurative death occurred many years before he was finally laid out in the pine coffin in the undertaker's parlor. It occurred on that same night he shot Liberty Valance. He sees Hallie embrace the wounded Stoddard and assumes that means that she is in love with Ranse rather than with him. That he is wrong in that assumption, is, of course, of no consequence for the story. He heads to the bar and gets falling-down drunk. Pompey has to throw him in a buckboard to take him back to his ranch. A little earlier the corpse of Liberty Valance had been thrown into a similar buckboard. The two dominant figures of the heroic age are rendered prone, horizontal, in one evening, and both are unceremoniously carted out of town. The westerner hero takes the same exit as the westerner villain he has banished. Without each other, both are finished. Once they rode horses, now they are carted away in wagons. If they had hung around longer, like Senator Stoddard, they would arrive and depart on a symbol of the age of men, the mechanical age, the train that opens and closes the film. The primitive natural world of the westerner is replaced with machinery.

. . . [The] westerner really fears and so . . . really cares most about . . . the destruction of the domain in which he has a morally significant role to play and in which his death, his annihilation, can amount to something. Cable Hogue says as he is dying, "All my life I've been scared of this livin'. Now I've got to do the other." That women in the stories happen typically to be identified with the world view that annihilates death only indicates that they are, as the Western and the westerner sees it, on the winning side. The Western does not offer hope to men in fear of losing their identities to a society dominated by women. Just the opposite. Tom Doniphon dies a bum whom almost everyone in Shinbone has forgotten. McCabe dies forgotten in a snowdrift. Most of the others ride off into the mountains or the desert with little or no hope and death waiting at every bend of the river.

And further, in *The Man Who Shot Liberty Valance*, it is a man, not a woman, who corrupts the West with civilization. Hallie is herself corrupted and repressed by Stoddard. She sacrifices her relationship with Doniphon, she loved him and never stopped loving him, to marry Stoddard. We have some hints that she regrets her choice. She is cold to the Senator both when they arrive in Shinbone and when they leave. She is responsible for placing the cactus rose on the coffin, and she wants to return to Shinbone and leave the Washington power circle. She has personally undergone the transition of the West, and it is a painful experience. We can only wonder if she is also in on the great lie, the lie that Stoddard feels finally compelled to reveal to the newspaper editor. Would he tell him, and, therefore, likely the whole world, and not have told her? When the conductor at the end of the film says to Stoddard, "Nothing's too good for the man who shot Liberty Valance," Hallie vaguely sighs and turns away from Stoddard. If he did tell her, then she should have realized that the man who really needed her love is the man who has lost everything. And that is not Stoddard.

Stoddard in the beginning of the film appears to be the weakling. As previously noted, he is almost always in a prone position vis-à-vis the other major characters. They all loom over him, including Hallie. But Stoddard's position turns out to be a deception. He would have been strong enough on his own to move up the political ladder. After the early stages of nursing him back to health, he does not really need Hallie. But Doniphon needs her, and, some might say, he has earned her by sacrificing himself by shooting Liberty Valance. She, apparently, does not recognize this at the crucial time and, we see from her actions when she arrives to pay respects to his corpse, that she regrets her failure.

The "transition Westerns" depict the loss of the West, the death of the West, and the ascension to dominance of Vico's modern age of men and machines—the industrial civilization that the westerner associates with the East. . . .

In the transition Westerns like *The Man Who Shot Liberty Valance*, there is little optimism about the new age. There is mostly a deep sense of loss, perpetuated by a vague sort of nostalgia for the former age of heroes. There is no sense that it was paradise lost, but it was a time of clearer moral distinctions, and a time when passion was not sucked out of the system by rules and laws and formal education in reading, writing, and civics. Even Senator Stoddard feels the loss, though probably not as much as does Hallie. In a flat-affected way she tells the Senator, "My roots are here. I guess my heart is here. Yes, let's come back." But it sounds as if she knows that she can't go home again. In her case, home is not there anymore. The train may stop in the new Shinbone, but only a stagecoach that is now a relic in cobwebs once traveled to the Shinbone that was her home. Modernity, the age of men, has changed it all. The heroes are now dead and buried and forgotten. Well, all are dead and buried except the one who is a phony: her husband. When the conductor says that fateful final line to the Stoddards as the train leaves Shinbone, "Nothing's too good for the man who shot Liberty Valance," the cringing inside Stoddard is felt by all of us. "Not only is the Senator disturbed by the fact that the merit of another person is ascribed to him (he cannot, for example, light his pipe), he also finally grasps that not only his existence, but the age of men as a whole is based on a lie."[13]

Josh, in *The Ballad of Cable Hogue*, emphasizes once again the westerner's hatred of the lie in his eulogy for Cable. He says to God:

Josh: Now most funeral orations lie about a man, compare him to the angels, whitewash him with a really wide brush. But you know, Lord, and I know, that it is just not true. Now a man is made out of bad as well as good, all of us. Cable Hogue was born into this world, nobody knows when or where. He came stumbling out of the wilderness like a prophet of old. Out of the barren wastes, he carved himself a one-man kingdom. Some said he was ruthless . . . But you could do worse, Lord, than to take to your bosom Cable Hogue. He wasn't really a good man. He wasn't a bad man. But, Lord, he was a man . . .

Stoddard's eulogy will be dominated by the lie that he was the man who shot Liberty Valance. Doniphon may have thought he could live with having committed cold-blooded murder. He was wrong. But Stoddard has lived the lie, and he has prospered. The age of men has made living the lie far easier than the age of heroes would permit living with cold-blooded murder.

The motion picture is a perfect medium in which to depict the transition between these ages of Vico. Novels and poems fall far short of the film. The reason is that the transition is most evident in the distinction between language-using and action. Those of the heroic age, as noted earlier, are not talkers. Most are not even literate. Pea Eye Parker, in *Streets of Laredo*, is married to Lorena. She is a schoolteacher, but Pea has mastered only two letters, P and Y. Tom Doniphon can barely read; Hallie can neither read nor write until she becomes Stoddard's pupil. Will Penny is not literate. The list could go on. But literacy, or rather the lack of it, is only part of the story. The westerners reject talking in favor of body language and actions. They communicate in gestures, usually very subtle ones: a wink, a grimace, a nod, a scowl, even a smile. A study of Clint Eastwood's "Man With No Name" series of films would undoubtedly provide an adequate primer on the westerner's use of such facial expressions. He runs through most of them in the first five minutes of *A Fistful of Dollars*. In the medium of film the juxtaposition of these two forms of communication, nonverbal and verbal, can be brought out in touching clarity. The film shows what words cannot tell: there can be deep bonds of understanding between people who don't talk to each other very much.

The modern age is the age of the talker, where talking is assimilated to acting and where philosophers have spent the better part of a century analyzing language as if it were the most important part of human life. If only we could understand reference, speech acts, language games, and semantic meaning, we would grasp the essence of relationships between humans and between humans and the world! Doniphon tells Stoddard, "You talk too much, think too much." Sometimes the mere placement of a cactus rose can convey so much more than all of one's attempts to verbalize how much was lost and how inferior the new age might be to the good old days. But such communication only occurs between the worn-out survivors of the former nonverbal age. In *The Man Who Shot Liberty Valance*, Hallie, Link Appleyard, and Pompey grasp the message, but there must remain doubt as to whether the Senator "gets it." On the train, after he does not respond to Hallie's "Aren't you proud?" Stoddard asks, "Hallie, who put the cactus roses on Tom's coffin?" She simply and flatly responds, "I did." He says no more. Why did he ask?

The transition Westerns take us "west of everything." They all end with death. What is of some interest is the types of deaths that are portrayed. The Wild Bunch, J. B. Books, Butch Cassidy and the Sundance Kid go out with their boots on and guns blazing. But all, in different ways, are killed by their inferiors.

Books is shot in the back by the bartender. Pike is shot by a prostitute and a young boy in a soldier suit, reminiscent of the opening shot of the children feeding the scorpions to the killer ants. Butch and Sundance are gunned down by what looks to be a major segment of the nondescript Bolivian army. None of their killers are their equals. Butch and Sundance throughout their getaway fear that they are being tracked by the famous scout LeFors. He would be worthy of them. In their last moments alive in Bolivia, they convince themselves that LeFors is not in the army that surrounds them and so they have hope of survival. Pike should be killed by someone of the stature of Thornton, not by a Mexican whore and a boy playing soldier. But the end of the age does not go out with a bang. Tom Doniphon dies a drunken bum whose boots have been stolen by the undertaker, and Cable Hogue is run over by a driverless automobile. Only Doniphon is killed by someone worthy of his stature. He is killed by himself, but even then he is but a mere shell of the man who shot Liberty Valance. . . .

AFTERWORD

Where does all of this fixation on death as annihilation lead with respect to ethics in Westerns? I think it is of secondary, but still important, interest that the ethics that emerges is *not*, in most respects, the ethics typically identified as masculine in the recent philosophical literature, where a contrast is usually drawn between a masculine ethics of rules and principles focused on contract and justice and a feminine ethics of care and kindness focused on relationships between people. The Western scrambles the categories.

The Western's ethics are not antithetical to caring and kindness for others, but it doles them out only as and when warranted in accord with what comes close to an Aristotelian account of friendship. Of note in the *Nicomachean Ethics* is that the perfect kind of friendship is described as a rare thing that can be extended from a person to a partner only after "each partner has impressed the other that he is worthy of affection, and until each has won the other's confidence."[14] Such perfect friendship is not to be indiscriminately tendered to the meek, the peacemakers, and the other subjects of the Christian Beatitudes. In the Western, a comparable understanding of real friendship is played out in hundreds of plots. The crucial concepts are understood in terms of demonstrable worth and confidence. Recall Josey Wales's "I rode with him; I got no complaints."

The ethics of the Western places very high value on independence, pride, loyalty, friendship or camaraderie, honor, self-reliance, valor, and, most important, vengeance and moral (righteous) hatred. Each of those concepts needs to be explicated in the context of the Western, and I will take up that task in a subsequent work. The westerner is relatively tolerant and is certainly not a social reformer. But circumstances do arise when the Western ethic requires him to take a stand. As Randolph Scott says in *The Tall T*, "There's some things a man can't ride around." What falls in that category defines, in large measure, the ethics of Westerns and the virtues of vengeance.

Notes

1. Aristotle, *Nicomachean Ethics*, bk. 3, 1115a.
2. J. A. Place, *The Westerns of John Ford* (Secaucus, N.J., 1974), 220.
3. Ibid.
4. Ibid., 223–24.
5. Mark W. Roche and Vittorio Hosle, "Vico's Age of Heroes and the Age of Men in John Ford's Film *The Man Who Shot Liberty Valance*," *Clio* 23, no. 2 (1993): 131–47.
6. T. G. Bergin and M. Fisch, *The New Science of Giambattista Vico* (Ithaca, N.Y., 1968), 336.
7. Ibid., 337.
8. Ibid., 339.
9. Ibid., 341.
10. Roche and Hosle, 135.
11. Ibid., 138.
12. Ibid., 143.
13. Ibid., 139.
14. Aristotle, 1156b.

Obscenity

Paris Adult Theatre v. Slaton

Defining obscenity has presented the U.S. Supreme Court with serious problems. This case accompanied another, *Miller v. California* (1973), in which the justices offered a new definition. Revising the basic approach it had followed since its decision in *Roth v. United States* (1957) the Court said in Miller that there are three parts to the definition of obscenity:

> (a) whether the average person, applying contemporary community standards would find that the work, taken as a whole, appeals to the prurient interest; (b) whether the work depicts or describes, in a patently offensive way, sexual conduct specifically defined by the applicable state law; and (c) whether the work, taken as a whole, lacks serious literary, artistic, political, or scientific value.

The Court went on to say that "our nation is simply too big and too diverse" for a single standard to apply in all fifty states and therefore held that each jury should evaluate the material based on the individual "community" where the sale took place. Armed with its new definition, the Court went on in a companion case to explain the reasoning behind its unwillingness to extend constitutional protection to obscenity. That second case, *Paris Adult Theatre V. Slaton*, arose when police prevented two Atlanta movie theaters from showing sexually explicit movies. No sexually explicit material was displayed outside the theater, and a sign at the entrance said "Adult Theatre—You must be 21 and able to prove it. If viewing the nude body offends you, Please Do Not Enter." The local district attorney tried to get two of the films declared obscene because of their graphic depiction of sexual acts. The lower court agreed that the films were obscene but also held that because there was "requisite notice" to the public of their nature and reasonable protection against admittance of minors, the showing of the films was constitutionally protected. The U.S. Supreme Court, however, disagreed.

Chief Justice Warren Burger, speaking for a majority of the justices, delivered the Supreme Court's verdict that the state is permitted to ban the public exhibition of obscene material.

As you read through this essay, consider the following:

1. What is the standard the Supreme Court uses to decide whether or not a film is obscene?
2. On what ground did Chief Justice Burger determine that banning these films is constitutional, even though there was no suggestion that the films were being shown to children or nonconsenting adults?
3. How might Mary Devereaux understand this case? Can obscenity be beautiful and yet evil, as she argued *Triumph of the Will* is?
4. Is there any reason to worry about the effect on people of watching obscenity, as Devereaux worried about the effect of viewing *Triumph of the Will?*

Mr. Chief Justice Burger:

It should be clear from the outset that we do not undertake to tell the States what they must do, rather to define the area in which they may chart their own course in dealing with obscene material. This Court has consistently held that obscene material is not protected by the First Amendment as a limitation on the state police power by virtue of the Fourteenth Amendment. . . .

413 U.S. 49 (1973).

We categorically disapprove the theory, apparently adopted by the trial judge, that obscene, pornographic films acquire constitutional immunity from state regulation simply because they are exhibited for consenting adults only. . . .

In particular, we hold that there are legitimate state interests at stake in stemming the tide of commercialized obscenity, even assuming it is feasible to enforce effective safeguards against exposure to juveniles and to passersby. Rights and interests "other than those of the advocates are involved." These include the interest of the public in the quality of life and the total community environment; the tone of commerce in the great city centers, and, possibly, the public safety itself. The Hill-Lind Minority Report of the Commission on Obscenity and Pornography indicates that there is at least an arguable correlation between obscene material and crime. Quite apart from sex crimes, however, there remains one problem of large proportions aptly described by Professor Bickel: "It concerns the tone of the society, the mode, or to use terms that have perhaps greater currency, the style and quality of life, now and in the future. A man may be entitled to read an obscene book in his room, or expose himself indecently there. . . . We should protect his privacy. But if he demands a right to obtain the books and pictures he wants in the market, and to foregather in public places—discreet, if you will, but accessible to all—with others who share his tastes, *then to grant him his right is to affect the world about the rest of us, and to impinge on other privacies.* Even supposing that each of us can, if he wishes, effectively avert the eye and stop the ear (which, in truth, we cannot), what is commonly read and seen and heard and done intrudes upon us all, want it or not." 22 The Public Interest 25–26 (Winter 1971). (Emphasis added.)

As Mr. Chief Justice [Earl] Warren stated, there is a "right of the Nation and of the States to maintain a decent society. . . ." *Jacobellis v. Ohio.*

But, it is argued, there are no scientific data which conclusively demonstrate that exposure to obscene material adversely affects men and women or their society. It is urged on behalf of the petitioners that, absent such a demonstration, any kind of state regulation is "impermissible." We reject this argument. It is not for us to resolve empirical uncertainties underlying state legislation, save in the exceptional case where that legislation plainly impinges upon rights protected by the Constitution itself. . . .

The sum of experience, including that of the past two decades, affords an ample basis for legislatures to conclude that a sensitive, key relationship of human existence, central to family life, community welfare, and the development of human personality, can be debased and distorted by crass commercial exploitation of sex. Nothing in the Constitution prohibits a State from reaching such a conclusion and acting on it legislatively. . . .

It is also argued that the State has no legitimate interest in "control [of] the moral content of a person's thoughts," and we need not quarrel with this. But we reject the claim that the State of Georgia is here attempting to control the minds or thoughts of those who patronize theaters. Preventing unlimited display or distribution of obscene material, which by definition lacks any serious literary, artistic, political, or scientific value as communication, is distinct from a control of reason and the intellect. . . . Where communication of ideas, protected by the First Amendment, is not involved, or the particular privacy of the home protected by *Stanley* or any of the other "areas or zones" of constitutionally protected privacy, the mere fact that, as a consequence, some human "utterances" or "thoughts" may be incidentally affected does not bar the State from acting to protect legitimate state interests. . . .

The issue in this context goes beyond whether someone, or even the majority, considers the conduct depicted as "wrong" or "sinful." The States have the power to make a morally neutral judgment that public exhibition of obscene material, or commerce in such material, has a tendency to injure the community as a whole, to endanger the public safety, or to jeopardize, in Mr. Chief Justice Warren's words, the States' "right . . . to maintain a decent society." *Jacobellis v. Ohio.* . . .

Section 5

Censorship and the Limits of Liberty

Fighting the Culture War: The Responsibilities of Artists

Henry J. Hyde

Few controversies over popular culture have raised as much controversy as the "Piss Christ" and its sponsorship by the National Endowment for the Arts. Depicting a crucifix in a container of urine, the work raised not only the question of public funding of unpopular and offensive works but also the purpose of art, the limits of censorship, and the nature of culture itself. Henry J. Hyde is a lawyer and member of the United States Congress from Illinois.

> *As you read through this essay, consider the following:*
>
> 1. How does Hyde answer those who think the issue involves censorship?
> 2. In what does he think the purpose of artistic freedom consists?
> 3. What are the three "transcendentals" and how do they relate to the aims of art?
> 4. Does Hyde think art should aspire to the provocative or the evocative? What does he mean?

I'm not quite sure what it says about America that one of the most intense public controversies in the months between the Tiananmen Square massacre and the breaching of the Berlin Wall had to do with homoerotic photographs and a crucifix suspended in a vat of urine.

My formulation is deliberately provocative. While Central and Eastern Europe were giving birth, in joy and pain, to the Revolution of 1989, Americans were transfixed by an argument over, let me say it again, homoerotic photographs and a crucifix suspended in a vat of urine. One might have been tempted to think that Oswald Spengler was right, and Francis Fukuyama wrong: the West was indeed headed down the slippery slope to decadence and irrelevance; but the "end of history" wouldn't be so much boring as appalling.

Whatever else can be said for or against our national media, their attention span is short: and so public life moves on. But we shouldn't be quite so eager to leave the debate over Mapplethorpe and Serrano behind us. For the Great Arts Controversy demonstrated that America is, in truth, involved in a *Kulturkampf*—a culture war, a war between cultures and a war about the very meaning of "culture."

Many people would prefer to deny this. But the conscientious public servant and the thoughtful citizen cannot afford to miss the full truth of our situation, for politics is, at its deepest level, a function of culture. The American *Kulturkampf* may be understood, to paraphrase Clausewitz, as civil war by other means.

It is best to be precise about the terminology here. By "culture war," I don't mean arguments over the relative merits of Mozart and Beethoven, *Henry V* on stage and *Henry V* on screen, Eliot and Auden, Tom Wolfe and E. L. Doctorow, the Chicago Symphony Orchestra and the New York Philharmonic. Nor do I mean the tensions between highbrows and lowbrows, between sports fans and opera buffs, between people who think Bruce Springsteen is the greatest artist alive and people who wouldn't know Bruce Springsteen if he rang their doorbell and asked to use the telephone.

No, by "culture war" I mean the struggle between those who believe that the norms of "bourgeois morality" (which is drawn in the main from classic Jewish and Christian morality) should form the ethical basis of our common life, and those who are determined that those norms will be replaced with a radical and thoroughgoing moral relativism. That the "relativism" in question is as absolutist and as condescendingly self-righteous as any sixteenth-century inquisitor is a nice irony. But that is the division in our house.

WHOSE MONEY?

The public policy issue is, to my mind, not all that difficult to resolve. Public funds, in a democracy, are to be spent for public purposes, not for the satisfaction of individuals' aesthetic impulses. And if the impulse in question produces a work which is palpably offensive to the sensibilities of a significant proportion of the public, then that work ought not to be supported by public funds.

Ideally, the funding agencies would understand this principle and abide by it. Legislatures and courts are ill suited to setting the boundaries in an area such as this, as we should have learned from the days of Anthony Comstock and the Boston Watch and Ward Society. But when the funding agencies do not set the boundaries in a way that maintains public confidence, then the legislature must act.

To do so is not an act of censorship, *pace* President Bush. In announcing his support for continued federal funding of the National Endowment for the Arts, the President stated he didn't "know anybody in the government . . . that should be set up to censor what you write or what you paint or how you express yourself." However, the President went on to say: "I am deeply offended by some of the filth that I see into which federal money has gone, and some of the sacrilegious, blasphemous depictions that are portrayed as art."

Congressman Dana Rohrabacher (R., Calif.), while cheered by the fact that the President doesn't like pornography any better than he likes broccoli, points out that "We're talking about sponsorship, not censorship." If the

Reprinted by permission of Representative Henry J. Hyde.

NEA were prohibited from funding certain types of work, no artist's right to create his work and display it would have been infringed. Censorship and refusal to subsidize are two very different things. All that a legislature would be saying is that the public has no responsibility to pay for a work that would give deep offense to a significant proportion of that public. One would hope that the artist, out of self-respect if nothing else, would agree.

There are those who argue that these kinds of entanglements are unavoidable and that we should therefore extract the Federal Government from the business of funding the arts. It may, over time, come to that. But I would hope not. It would be bad (although certainly not fatal) for the arts. But it would also say something deeply saddening about America: it would tell us that we simply can't reach agreement on a reasonable approach to issues at the intersection of politics and culture. And that is not the situation of choice for the American experiment in ordered liberty.

NEGOTIATING THE KULTURKAMPF

How might we craft an approach to the American *Kulturkampf* that would at least begin a civilized conversation about our differences? How do we argue these issues within the bounds of democratic tolerance: not the false tolerance that glosses over differences, but the true tolerance that engages differences forthrightly but civilly? Here are some themes that may be worth exploring.

1. *On the freedom of the artist:* Artists should, of course, be free from political coercion in their work. Those of us who have celebrated the triumph of Vaclav Havel have no desire to shackle the poet, the composer, the painter, the dramatist, or the photographer.

The key question for the cultural debate, however, is: Freedom *for what?* The artist's purpose is surely not fulfilled in mere self-expression; for if self-expression were all there is to art, then a puppy chasing kittens would be as much an artist as Raphael, Vermeer, or Bach. Rather, as Thomas Aquinas wrote in the *Summa*, "The test of the artist does not lie in the will with which he goes to work, but in the excellence of the work he produces."

So the purpose of the artist's freedom is to help him and us to a fuller apprehension of, and delight in, the three transcendentals—the good, the true, and the beautiful. Lord Acton got it quite right: "Freedom is not the power to do what you want, but rather the right to do what you ought." Art detached from the quest for truth and goodness is, to repeat, simply self-expression and ultimately self-absorption. It is narcissism, and, like Narcissus, it inevitably destroys itself.

I am aware that this understanding of the purpose of artistic freedom can be dismissed as hopelessly provincial. But "art for art's sake" presents a serious problem to legislators who are expected at least to explain, if not justify, their expenditure of tax dollars. We are now told that "great art forces us to abandon our most cherished values," but most people aren't pleased to have their most cherished values challenged, much less to pay for the experience. Franklin W. Robinson, director of a museum attached to the Rhode Island School of Design, has been quoted as saying: "Among the many things that art does for us all is that it challenges us, it demands that we rethink our assumptions about every issue in life, from religion to politics, from love to sex to death and afterlife." Thus the twentieth-century artist has changed the object of art from the three transcendentals to challenge and revolution.

The congressional reaction to what Carol Iannone calls "the insistent and progressive artistic exploration of the forbidden frontiers of human experience" was predictable, but at least has drawn attention to the "works of art" involved and to the difficult issues of artistic freedom and congressional accountability. Censorship, discrimination—these words have unpleasant connotations. But when a limited amount of money must be distributed among a large number of applicants, some form of discrimination is inevitable. I was interested in a case of curatorial discretion written up in the October 1989 *Arts Journal.* Mr. Ted Potter, the director of the Southeastern Center for Contemporary Art, is quoted as explaining why he refused to display a videotape that was "grossly racist" as to both the black and the Jewish populations. Mr. Potter said: "It was just a straightforward case of racial slurs and bigotry, and I'm not interested in that, so we didn't show it."

Justice Potter Stewart once said that he couldn't define pornography, but he knew it when he saw it. I suggest that where racism and bigotry are present, most people, even congressmen, are capable of exercising curatorial discretion.

Modern artists also demean the memory of their predecessors when they suggest that any boundary-setting by public authorities is a threat to art itself. Evelyn Waugh was indulging in characteristic exaggeration when he wrote in 1939 that "most of the greatest art has appeared under systems of political tyranny." But there is something there to think about. Great art may have been created because it enjoyed the financial favor of public authorities at the time (whether the public authority in question was a prince or a president); but it endures because it enables men and women to discern the true and the good in fuller proportion than before.

2. *On democratic civility:* Public opinion cannot be the final touchstone of artistic merit. That, too, should go without saying. While it certainly would not be accurate to suggest that virtually all great artists experienced public rejection before they enjoyed (sometimes posthumous) acceptance—Haydn, Bach, and Brahms, to choose from just one art, were quite comfortably secure in public esteem—it is also true that public opinion can be slow to recognize artistic genius, particularly when that genius is consciously striving to break new aesthetic ground.

But there is a converse truth that is rarely acknowledged. Gratuitous insults to the religious sensibilities of fellow citizens, by artists or anyone else, are damaging to civil comity and democratic tolerance. Whatever the art world may think, Americans remain an incorrigibly religious people. Happily for the Republic, the growth of American religiosity has, over the past two generations, bred an even greater religious tolerance: the overwhelming majority of Americans believe it to be the will of God that we not kill each other over what constitutes the will of God. One wonders, though, if the democratic courtesy of tolerance is always reciprocated.

Let me take the obvious example. Whatever ex-post-facto rationalizations Andres Serrano may have constructed, I cannot believe that his *Piss Christ* was anything other than a deliberate attempt to provoke: in this case, to provoke Christians. Suppose Mr. Serrano's work had involved suspending a Torah scroll in a vat of urine; would any reasonable person have doubted that this was a gross act of anti-Semitism? Or, at an entirely different level, suppose that Mr. Serrano had suspended a peace symbol in a vat of urine and labeled it *Piss Peace?* Can you believe that this would have been defended as legitimate artistic endeavor by the same people who defended the funding of *Piss Christ?* Whatever else it was, *Piss Christ* was a vicious violation of democratic civility.

The artist may well have a gift of insight that transcends the capabilities of less aesthetically endowed citizens. But that insight confers no right to indulge oneself in thoughtless—or, worse, deliberate—trashing of others' deepest convictions.

3. *Provocative or evocative?* Some people, in fact some quite distinguished people, seem to think that any expression issuing from an artist is art. Robert McCormick Adams, secretary of the Smithsonian Institution, has even argued that graffiti are art. Would that include, I'm immediately tempted to ask, graffiti spray-painted onto the East Building of the National Gallery of Art in Washington, of which Mr. Adams is a trustee? After all, the East Building provides a much more inviting canvas for the graffiti-ist than a New York subway car, and

ever so many more people would have the opportunity to see the "artist's" work if it weren't buried underground and whisked away from the viewer within a minute or so.

My argument is not against provocation per se. The first two crashing chords (indeed the entire first movement) of Beethoven's Third Symphony were a deliberate provocation: a challenge to the genteel limits which had characterized earlier uses of the symphonic form. But this was provocation in the service of a larger end. It was not provocation for its own sake.

I am no philosopher of aesthetics, but I would suggest that we ought to consider the possibility that good art is evocative rather than provocative, although the evocative quality can sometimes involve the artist in provocative expressions. Provocation, in short, should be at the service of evocation.

Which immediately raises the question, Evocative of what? Again, with the caution of a philosophical amateur, I would suggest: evocative of man's highest and noblest aspirations, our aspirations for the good, the true, and the beautiful. Put another way, art as evocation is neither art at the service of some political program nor art as an ideological instrument, but art as one means by which man gains a glimpse of the transcendent dimension of the human experience.

BEYOND THE NEURAL ITCH

I suppose this returns me, in a roundabout way, to my first point: that art is not, and must not be, mere self-indulgent self-expression. If we can agree on that—if we can agree that discipline, craftsmanship, and a purpose transcending the mere satisfying of a neural itch are of the essence of the truly artistic act—then we have marked off the ground on which we can intelligibly debate questions of boundary-setting, funding, and all the rest of the public-policy arts agenda.

And that would be no small accomplishment.

On Liberty

John Stuart Mill

John Stuart Mill (1806–1873) had an unusual childhood, by almost any standard. His father, James Mill, was a friend of the economist David Ricardo and the legal theorist John Austin. He developed a plan for the education of his son, John Stuart, that included a rigorous tutoring program and isolation from other children. Young John was a brilliant student. By the age of three, he had begun learning Greek. At eight, he learned Latin and pursued mathematics and history. By the age of twelve, he was studying logic and political economy, and at fifteen, he studied law at University College, London, with John Austin.

At twenty-four, Mill began a lifelong friendship and intellectual collaboration with Mrs. Harriet Taylor. For two decades, they were close companions, until Harriet's husband, John Taylor, died, and she and John Stuart Mill married. The two then withdrew from "insipid society" and the gossip they had endured for years; they lived happily for seven years until her death. Mill served briefly as a member of Parliament and died in France (where he had lived in a house near the cemetery in which Harriet was buried).

Mill's influence has been tremendous; he wrote important books on logic, philosophy of science, and economics, as well as on ethics and political philosophy. None of Mill's works has had a greater impact than *On Liberty*; its ideas are often discussed by academics, politicians, and the general public, even by people who have never heard of him. According to letters and other material from Mill's life, *On Liberty* should be thought of as a joint work authored by Mill and Harriet Taylor. Mill even said in a letter that there was not a sentence in the book that the two did not go over together many times. Mill examines a fundamental question of political philosophy: What are the limits of society's power over the individual? Mill's answer is that society may interfere using the power of law with an individual's speech or actions only on the grounds of society's self-protection. Mill discusses the importance of individuality to a person's overall well-being, and then he considers his famous "harm principle," which provides that government is justified in interfering with a citizen's liberty only if there is the threat of harm to others.

As you read through this essay, consider the following:

1. Mill argues that the good life involves more than mere contentment. Of what else, specifically, does true well-being consist?
2. What "faculties" does Mill believe people living truly worthwhile and valuable lives will employ?
3. Mill admits that many acts may affect others, but he insists that unless they also harm others, government may not intervene. How does Mill define harm?
4. Describe how Mill thinks society may try to influence people whose actions are harmless to others but either immoral or not in their true interest.
5. What reasons does Mill give to support his claim that harming others is necessary to justify punishment?
6. Sometimes, Mill says, society is wise *not* to interfere even though an act is harmful to another. Give an example of such an act; then explain why Mill thinks society should nevertheless not interfere.

INTRODUCTORY

The subject of this essay is . . . civil, or social liberty: the nature and limits of power which can be legitimately exercised by society over the individual.

. . . [In] old times this contest was between subjects, or some classes of subjects, and the government. By liberty, was meant protection against the tyranny of the political rulers. The rulers were conceived (except in some of the popular governments of Greece) as in a necessarily antagonistic position to the people whom they ruled. . . .

A time, however, came, in the progress of human affairs, when men ceased to think it a necessity of nature that their governors should be an independent power, opposed in

From John Stuart Mill, *On Liberty* (1859).

interest to themselves. It appeared to them much better that the various magistrates of the State should be their tenants or delegates, revocable at their pleasure. In that way alone, it seemed, could they have complete security that the powers of government would never be abused to their disadvantage. . . .

But in political and philosophical theories, as well as in persons, success discloses faults and infirmities which failure might have concealed from observation. . . . It was now perceived that such phrases as "self-government," and "the power of the people over themselves," do not express the true state of the case. The "people" who exercise the power are not always the same people with those over whom it is exercised; and the "self-government" spoken of is not the government of each by himself, but of each by all the rest. The will of the people, moreover, practically means the will of the most numerous or the most active *part* of the people—the majority, or those who succeed in making themselves accepted as the majority; the people, consequently, *may* desire to oppress a part of their number, and precautions are as much needed against this as against any other abuse of power. The limitation, therefore, of the power of government over individuals loses none of its importance when the holders of power are regularly accountable to the community, that is, to the strongest party therein. . . .

The object of this essay is to assert one very simple principle, as entitled to govern absolutely the dealings of society with the individual in the way of compulsion and control, whether the means used by physical force in the form of legal penalties or the moral coercion of public opinion. That principle is, that the sole end for which mankind are warranted, individually or collectively, in interfering with the liberty of action of any of their number, is self-protection. That the only purpose for which power can be rightfully exercised over any member of a civilized community, against his will, is to prevent harm to others. His own good, either physical or moral, is not a sufficient warrant. He cannot rightfully be compelled to do or forbear because it will be better for him to do so, because it will make him happier, because, in the opinions of others, to do so would be wise or even right. These are good reasons for remonstrating with him, or reasoning with him, or persuading him, or entreating him, but not for compelling him or visiting him with any evil in case he do otherwise. To justify that, the conduct from which it is desired to deter him must be calculated to produce evil to someone else. The only part of the conduct of anyone, for which he is amenable to society, is that which concerns others. In the part which merely concerns himself, his independence is, of right, absolute. Over himself, over his own body and mind, the individual is sovereign.

It is, perhaps, hardly necessary to say that this doctrine is meant to apply only to human beings in the maturity of their faculties. We are not speaking of children, or of young persons below the age which the law may fix as that of manhood or womanhood. Those who are still in a state to require being taken care of by others, must be protected against their own actions as well as against external injury. . . .

It is proper to state that I forego any advantage which could be derived to my argument from the idea of abstract right, as a thing independent of utility. I regard utility as the ultimate appeal on all ethical questions; but it must be utility in the largest sense, grounded on the permanent interests of a man as a progressive being. These interests, I contend, authorized the subjection of individual spontaneity to external control, only in respect to those actions of each which concern the interest of other people. If anyone does an act hurtful to others, there is a *prima facie* case for punishing him, by law, or, where legal penalties are not safely applicable, by general disapprobation. There are also many positive acts for the benefit of others, which he may rightfully be compelled to perform: such as to give evidence in a court of justice; to bear his fair share in the common defense, or in any other joint work necessary to the interest of the society of which he enjoys the protection; and to perform certain acts of individual beneficence, such as saving a fellow-creature's life, or interposing to protect the defenseless against ill-usage, things which whenever it is obviously a man's duty to do, he may rightfully be made responsible to society for not doing. A person may cause evil to others not only by his actions but by his inaction, and in either case he is justly accountable to them for the injury. The latter case, it is true, requires a much more cautious exercise of compulsion than the former. . . .

This, then is the appropriate region of human liberty. It comprises, *first*, the inward domain of consciousness; demanding liberty of conscience in the most comprehensive sense; liberty of thought and feeling; absolute freedom of opinion and sentiment on all subjects, practical or speculative, scientific, moral or theological. The liberty of expressing and publishing opinions may seem to fall under a different principle, since it belongs to that part of the conduct of an individual which concerns other people; but, being almost of as much importance as the liberty of thought itself, and resting in great part on the same reasons, is practically inseparable from it. *Secondly*, the principle requires liberty of tastes and pursuits; of framing the plan of our life to suit our own character; of doing as we like, subject to such consequences as may follow: without impediment from our fellow-creatures, so long as what we do does not harm them, even though they should think our conduct foolish, perverse, or wrong. *Thirdly*, from this liberty of each individual, follows the liberty, within the same limits, of combinations among individuals; freedom to unite, for any purpose not involving harm to others: the persons combining being supposed to be of full age, and not forced or deceived.

No society in which these liberties are not, on the whole, respected, is free, whatever may be its form of government; and none is completely free in which they do not exist absolute and unqualified. The only freedom which deserves the name, is that of pursuing our own good in our own way, as long as we do not attempt to deprive others of theirs, or impede their efforts to obtain it. Each is the proper guardian of his own health, whether bodily, or mental and spiritual. Mankind are greater gainers by suffering each other to live as seems good to themselves, than by compelling each to live as seems good to the rest. . . .

OF THE LIBERTY OF THOUGHT AND DISCUSSION

. . . Let us suppose . . . that government is entirely at one with the people, and never thinks of exerting any power of coercion unless in agreement with what it conceives to be their voice. But I deny the right of the people to exercise such coercion, either by themselves or by their government. . . .

First, the opinion which it is attempted to suppress by authority may possibly be true. Those who desire to suppress it, of course, deny its truth; but they are not infallible. They have no authority to decide the question for all mankind and exclude every other person from the means of judging. To refuse a hearing to an opinion because they are sure that it is false, is to assume that *their* certainty is the same thing as *absolute* certainty. All silencing of discussion is an assumption of infallibility. . . .

. . . There is the greatest difference between presuming an opinion to be true because, with every opportunity for contesting it, it has not been refuted, and assuming its truth for the purpose of not permitting its refutation. Complete liberty of contradicting and disproving our opinion is the very condition which justifies us in assuming its truth for purposes of action; and on no other terms can a being with human faculties have any rational assurance of being right. . . .

Let us now pass to the second division of the argument, and dismissing the supposition that any of the received opinions may be false, let us assume them to be true and examine into the worth of the manner in which they are likely to be held when their truth is not freely and openly canvassed. . . .

. . . If the cultivation of the understanding consists in one thing more than in another, it is surely in learning the grounds of one's own opinions. Whatever people believe, on subjects on which it is of the first importance to believe rightly, they ought to be able to defend against at least the common objections. . . . Nor is it enough that he should hear the arguments of adversaries from his own teachers, presented as they state them, and accompanied by what they offer as refutations. That is not the way to do justice to the arguments or bring them into real contact with his own mind. He must be able to hear them from persons who actually believe them, who defend them in earnest and do their very utmost for them. He must know them in their most plausible and persuasive form; he must feel the whole force of the difficulty which the true view of the subject has to encounter and dispose of, else he will never really possess himself of the portion of truth which meets and removes that difficulty. . . .

. . . The fact . . . is that not only the grounds of the opinion are forgotten in the absence of discussion, but too often the meaning of the opinion itself. The words which convey it cease to suggest ideas, or suggest only a small portion of those they were originally employed to communicate. Instead of a vivid conception and a living belief, there remain only a few phrases retained by rote; or, if any part, the shell and husk only of the meanings is retained, the finer essence being lost. The great chapter in human history which this fact occupies and fills cannot be too earnestly studied and meditated on. . . .

. . . We have hitherto considered only two possibilities: that the received opinion may be false, and some other opinion, consequently, true; or that, the received opinion being true, a conflict with the opposite error is essential to a clear apprehension and deep feeling of its truth. But there is a commoner case than either of these: when the conflicting doctrines, instead of being one true and the other false, shared the truth between them, and the nonconforming opinion is needed to supply the remainder of the truth of which the received doctrine embodies only a part. Popular opinions, on subjects not palpable to sense, are often true, but seldom or never the whole truth. They are a part of the truth, sometimes a greater, sometimes a smaller part, but exaggerated, distorted, and disjointed from the truths by which they ought to be accompanied and limited. Heretical opinions, on the other hand, are generally some of these suppressed and neglected truths. . . . Even progress, which ought to superadd, for the most part only substitutes one partial and incomplete truth for another. . . .

OF INDIVIDUALITY, AS ONE OF THE ELEMENTS OF WELL-BEING

. . . No one pretends that actions should be as free as opinions. On the contrary, even opinions lose their immunity when the circumstances in which they are expressed are such as to constitute their expression a positive instigation to some mischievous act. An opinion that corn-dealers are starvers of the poor, or that private property is robbery, ought to be unmolested when simply circulated through the press, but may justly incur punishment when delivered orally to an excited mob assembled before the house of a corn-dealer, or when handed about among the same mob in the form of a placard. . . .

. . . Few persons, out of Germany, even comprehend the meaning of the doctrine which Wilhelm von Humboldt, so eminent both as a savant and as a politician, made the text of a treatise—that "the end of man, or that which is prescribed by the eternal or immutable dictates of reason, and not suggested by vague and transient desires, is the highest and most harmonious development of his powers to a complete and consistent whole," that, therefore, the object "towards which every human being must ceaselessly direct his efforts, and on which especially those who design to influence their fellow-men must ever keep their eyes, is the individuality of power and development;" that for this there are two requisites, "freedom, and variety of situations;" and that from the union of these arise "individual vigor and manifold diversity," which combine themselves in "originality." . . .

He who lets the world, or his own portion of it, choose his plan of life for him, has no need of any other faculty than the ape-like one of imitation. He who chooses his plan for himself, employs all his faculties. He must use observation to see, reasoning and judgment to foresee, activity to gather materials for decision, discrimination to decide, and when he has decided, firmness and self-control to hold to his deliberate decision. And these qualities he requires and exercises exactly in proportion as the part of his conduct which he determines according to his own judgment and feelings is a large one. It is possible that he might be guided in some good path, and kept out of harm's way, without any of these things. But what will be his comparative worth as a human being? It really is of importance, not only what men do, but also what manner of men they are that do it. Among the works of man which human life is rightly employed in perfecting and beautifying, the first in importance surely is man himself. . . .

OF THE LIMITS TO THE AUTHORITY OF SOCIETY OVER THE INDIVIDUAL

. . . Though society is not founded on a contract, and though no good purpose is answered by inventing a contract in order to deduce social obligations from it, everyone who receives the protection of society owes a return for the benefit, and the fact of living in society renders it indispensable that each should be bound to observe a certain line of conduct towards the rest. This conduct consists, *first*, in not injuring the interests of one another; or rather certain interests, which either by express legal provision or by tacit understanding, ought to be considered as rights; and *secondly*, in each person's bearing his share (to be fixed on some equitable principle) of the labors and sacrifices incurred for defending the society or its members from injury and molestation. These conditions society is justified in enforcing, at all costs to those who endeavor to withhold fulfillment. Nor is this all that society may do. The acts of an individual may be hurtful to others, or wanting in due consideration for their welfare, without going to the length of violating any of their constituted rights. The offender may then be justly punished by opinion, though not by law. As soon as any part of a person's conduct affects prejudicially the interests of others, society has jurisdiction over it, and the question whether the general welfare will or will not be promoted by interfering with it, becomes open to discussion. But there is no room for entertaining any such question when a person's conduct affects the interests of no persons besides himself, or needs not affect them unless they like (all the persons concerned being of full age, and the

ordinary amount of understanding). In all such cases, there should be perfect freedom, legal and social, to do the action and stand the consequences.

It would be a great misunderstanding of this doctrine to suppose that it is one of selfish indifference, which pretends that human beings have no business with each other's conduct in life, and that they should not concern themselves about the well-doing or well-being of one another, unless their own interest is involved. Instead of any diminution, there is need of a great increase of disinterested exertion to promote the good of others. But disinterested benevolence can find other instruments to persuade people to their good than whips and scourges, either of the literal or the metaphorical sort. I am the last person to undervalue the self-regarding virtues: they are only second in importance, if even second, to the social. It is equally the business of education to cultivate both. But even education works by conviction and persuasion as well as by compulsion, and it is by the former only that, when the period of education is passed, the self-regarding virtues should be inculcated. Human beings owe to each other help to distinguish the better from the worse, and encouragement to choose the former and avoid the latter. They should be forever stimulating each other to increased exercise of their higher faculties, and increased direction of their feelings and aims towards wise instead of foolish, elevating instead of degrading, objects and contemplations. But neither one person, nor any number of persons, is warranted in saying to another human creature of ripe years, that he shall not do with his life for his own benefit what he chooses to do with it. He is the person most interested in his own well-being: the interest which any other person, except in cases of strong personal attachment, can have in it, is trifling, compared with that which he himself has; the interest which society has in him individually (except as to conduct to others) is fractional, and altogether indirect; while with respect to his own feelings and circumstances, the most ordinary man or woman has means of knowledge immeasurably surpassing those that can be possessed by anyone else. The interference of society to overrule his judgment and purposes in what only regards himself must be grounded on general presumptions; which may be altogether wrong, and even if right, are as likely as not to be misapplied to individual cases, by persons no better acquainted with the circumstances of such cases than those are who look at them merely from without. In this department, therefore, of human affairs, individuality has its proper field of action. In the conduct of human beings towards one another it is necessary that general rules should for the most part be observed, in order that people may know what they have to expect; but in each person's own concerns his individual spontaneity is entitled to free exercise. Considerations to aid his judgment, exhortations to strengthen his will, may be offered to him, even obtruded on him, by others: but he himself is the final judge. All errors which he is likely to commit against advice and warning are far outweighed by the evil of allowing others to constrain him to what they deem his good. . . .

Though doing no wrong to anyone, a person may so act as to compel us to judge him, and feel to him, as a fool, or as a being of an inferior order; and since this judgment and feeling are a fact which he would prefer to avoid, it is doing him a service to warn him of it beforehand, as of any other disagreeable consequence to which he exposes himself. . . . We have a right, also, in various ways, to act upon our unfavorable opinion of anyone, not to the oppression of his individuality, but in the exercise of ours. We are not bound, for example, to seek his society; we have a right to avoid it (though not to parade the avoidance), for we have a right to choose the society most acceptable to us. We have a right, and it may be our duty, to caution others against him, if we think his example or conversation likely to have a pernicious effect on those with whom he associates. We may give others a preference over him in optional good offices, except those which tend to his improvement. In these various modes a per-

son may suffer very severe penalties at the hands of others for faults which directly concern only himself; but he suffers these penalties only in so far as they are the natural and, as it were, the spontaneous consequences of the faults themselves, not because they are purposely inflicted on him for the sake of punishment. . . .

What I contend for is, that the inconveniences which are strictly inseparable from the unfavorable judgment of others, are the only ones to which a person should ever be subjected for that portion of his conduct and character which concerns his own good, but which does not affect the interest of others in their relations with him. Acts injurious to others require a totally different treatment. Encroachment on their rights; infliction on them of any loss or damage not justified by his own rights; falsehood or duplicity in dealing with them; unfair or ungenerous use of advantages over them; even selfish abstinence from defending them against injury—these are fit objects of moral reprobation, and, in grave cases, of moral retribution and punishment. And not only these acts, but the dispositions which lead to them, are properly immoral, and fit subjects of disapprobation which may rise to abhorrence. . . .

The distinction here pointed out between the part of a person's life which concerns only himself, and that which concerns others, many persons will refuse to admit. How (it may be asked)—can any part of the conduct of a member of society be a matter of indifference to the other members? No person is an entirely isolated being; . . . No person ought to be punished simply for being drunk; but a soldier or policeman should be punished for being drunk on duty. Whenever, in short, there is a definite damage, or a definite risk of damage, either to an individual or to the public, the case is taken out of the province of liberty and placed in that of morality or law.

But with regard to the merely contingent or, as it may be called, constructive injury which a person causes to society by conduct which neither violates any specific duty to the public, nor occasions perceptible hurt to any assignable individual except himself, the inconvenience is one which society can afford to bear, for the sake of the greater good of human freedom. If grown persons are to be punished for not taking proper care of themselves, I would rather it were for their own sake than under pretense of preventing them from impairing their capacity or rendering to society benefits which society does not pretend it has a right to exact. But I cannot consent to argue the point as if society had no means of bringing its weaker members up to its ordinary standard of rational conduct, except waiting till they do something irrational, and then punishing them, legally or morally, for it. Society has had absolute power over them during all the early portion of their existence; it has had the whole period of childhood and nonage in which to try whether it could make them capable of rational conduct in life. The existing generation is master both of the training and the entire circumstances of the generation to come; it cannot indeed make them perfectly wise and good, because it is itself so lamentably deficient in goodness and wisdom; and its best efforts are not always, in individual cases, its most successful ones; but it is perfectly well able to make the rising generation, as a whole, as good as, and a little better than, itself. If society lets any considerable number of its members grow up mere children, incapable of being acted on by rational consideration of distant motives, society has itself to blame for the consequences. Armed not only with all the powers of education, but with the ascendancy which the authority of a received opinion always exercises over the minds who are least fitted to judge for themselves, and aided by the *natural* penalties which cannot be prevented from falling on those who incur the distaste or the contempt of those who know them—let not society pretend that it needs, besides all this, the power to issue commands and enforce obedience in the personal concerns of individuals in which, on all principles of justice and policy, the decision ought to rest with those who are to abide the

consequences. Nor is there anything which tends more to discredit and frustrate the better means of influencing conduct than a resort to the worse. If there be among those whom it is attempted to coerce into prudence or temperance any of the material of which vigorous and independent characters are made, they will infallibly rebel against the yoke. No such person will ever feel that others have a right to control him in his concerns, such as they have to prevent him from injuring them in theirs; and it easily comes to be considered a mark of spirit and courage to fly in the face of such usurped authority and do with ostentation the exact opposite of what it enjoins, as in the fashion of grossness which succeeded, in the time of Charles II, to the fanatical moral intolerance of the Puritans. With respect to what is said of the necessity of protecting society from the bad example set to others by the vicious or the self-indulgent, it is true that bad example may have a pernicious effect, especially the example of doing wrong to others with impunity to the wrongdoer. But we are now speaking of conduct which, while it does no wrong to others, is supposed to do great harm to the agent himself; and I do not see how those who believe this can think otherwise than that the example, on the whole, must be more salutary than hurtful, since, if it displays the misconduct, it displays also the painful or degrading consequences which, if the conduct is justly censured, must be supposed to be in all or most cases attendant on it.

But the strongest of all the arguments against the interference of the public with purely personal conduct is that, when it does interfere, the odds are that it interferes wrongly and in the wrong place. On questions of social morality, of duty to others, the opinion of the public, that is, of an overruling majority, though often wrong, is likely to be still oftener right, because on such questions they are only required to judge of their own interests, of the manner in which some mode of conduct, if allowed to be practiced, would affect themselves. But the opinion of a similar majority, imposed as a law on the minority, on questions of self-regarding conduct is quite as likely to be wrong as right, for in these cases public opinion means, at the best, some people's opinion of what is good or bad for other people, while very often it does not even mean that—the public, with the most perfect indifference, passing over the pleasure or convenience of those whose conduct they censure and considering only their own preference. There are many who consider as an injury to themselves any conduct which they have a distaste for, and resent it as an outrage to their feelings; as a religious bigot, when charged with disregarding the religious feelings of others, has been known to retort that they disregard his feelings by persisting in their abominable worship or creed. But there is no parity between the feeling of a person for his own opinion and the feeling of another who is offended at his holding it, no more than between the desire of a thief to take a purse and the desire of the right owner to keep it. And a person's taste is as much his own peculiar concern as his opinion or his purse.

Section 6

Values in the Curriculum

The Storm over the University

John Searle

Many colleges and universities have faced deep divisions over the content of their curricula. Critics have attacked what they often term the "canon" on the ground that it is narrow, European centered, and exclusive of women and minorities. Behind these issues are larger ones, involving the purposes of education, the merits of classical works, and the "hierarchical" nature of Western political and educational practices. In this well-known and hotly disputed essay, John Searle discusses the merits of these and other criticisms made by what he terms the "cultural left." He focuses in particular on the charge that the cultural left has destroyed the humanities' traditional commitment to the search for truth. John Searle is professor of philosophy at the University of California at Berkeley. He has written widely in philosophy, especially in the philosophy of mind.

As you read through this essay, consider the following:

1. How would you summarize the various criticisms of university curricula that Searle attributes to the "cultural left"?
2. How does Searle respond to the claim that the curriculum is elitist?
3. Searle disputes the assumptions made by his opponents about the function of teaching in the humanities. What is the issue here, and why does Searle reject their position in favor of a different understanding of the role of the humanities?

98

4. Underlying this debate, Searle argues, is a dispute about "objectivity" and "truth." Explain why he thinks that is an issue, and how he defends metaphysical realism.

1.

I cannot recall a time when American education was not in a "crisis." We have lived through Sputnik (when we were "falling behind the Russians"), through the era of "Johnny can't read," and through the upheavals of the Sixties. Now a good many books are telling us that the university is going to hell in several different directions at once. I believe that, at least in part, the crisis rhetoric has a structural explanation: since we do not have a national consensus on what success in higher education would consist of, no matter what happens, some sizable part of the population is going to regard the situation as a disaster. As with taxation and relations between the sexes, higher education is essentially and continuously contested territory. . . .

I think the best way to enter this discussion is by examining at least briefly the current debate about the status of what is called the "canon" of the best works in our civilization, and what part the canon should play in the education of undergraduates. . . .

Consider what would have been taken to be a platitude a couple of decades ago, and is now regarded in many places as a wildly reactionary view. Here it is: there is a certain Western intellectual tradition that goes from, say, Socrates to Wittgenstein in philosophy, and from Homer to James Joyce in literature, and it is essential to the liberal education of young men and women in the United States that they should receive some exposure to at least some of the great works in this intellectual tradition; they should, in Matthew Arnold's over-quoted words, "know the best that is known and thought in the world." The arguments given for this view—on the rare occasions when it was felt that arguments were even needed—were that knowledge of the tradition was essential to the self-understanding of educated Americans since the country, in an important sense, is the product of that tradition; that many of these works are historically important because of their influence; and that most of them, for example several works by Plato and Shakespeare, are of very high intellectual and artistic quality, to the point of being of universal human interest.

Until recently such views were not controversial. What exactly is the debate about? The question is more complex than one might think because of the variety of different objections to the tradition and the lack of any succinct statement of these objections. For example, many African Americans and Hispanic Americans feel left out of the "canon," and want to be included. Just as a few years ago they were demanding the creation of ethnic studies departments, so now they are demanding some representation of their experiences and their point of view as part of the general education of all undergraduates. This looks like a standard political demand for "representation" of the sort we are familiar with in higher education. If the objection to the "canon" is that it consists almost entirely of works by white males, specifically white males of European (including North American) origin, then there would appear to be an easy and common-sense solution to the problem: simply open the doors to admit the work of talented writers who are not white, or not male, or not European. If, for example, the contribution of women in literature has been neglected, there are plenty of writers of similar stature to Jane Austen, George Eliot, and Virginia Woolf who can be added.

Some of the opponents of the tradition will accept this reform, but [many] would not, and you will have misunderstood the nature of the dispute if you think that it can be resolved so simply. The central objections to the tradition are deeper and more radical, and they go far beyond the mere demand for increased representation. What are these objections?

To approach this question, I have selected the proceedings of the North Carolina conference not because they contain any notable or original ideas—such conferences seldom do—but because they express a mode of literary and political sensibility that has become fairly widespread in some university departments in the humanities and is characterized approvingly by some of the participants at the conference as "the cultural left." I doubt that "the cultural left" is a well-defined notion because it includes so many altogether different points of view. It includes 1960s-style radicals, feminists, deconstructionists, Marxists, people active in "gay studies" and "ethnic studies," and people of left-wing political persuasion who happen to teach in universities. But on certain basic issues of education these groups tend to agree. In describing the North Carolina Conference in his concluding statement Richard Rorty writes:

> Our conference has been in large part a rally of this cultural left. The audience responded readily and favorably to notions like "subversive readings," "hegemonic discourse," "the breaking down of traditional logocentric hierarchies," and so on. It chortled derisively at mentions of William Bennett, Allan Bloom, and E. D. Hirsch, Jr., and nodded respectfully at the names of Nietzsche, Derrida, Gramsci, or Foucault.

Whether or not Rorty is justified in using the label, the views expressed show a remarkable consensus in their opposition to the educational tradition and in their hostility to those who . . . have supported a version of the tradition. Here are some typical passages:

Mary Louise Pratt, a professor of comparative literature at Stanford, writes,

> Bloom, Bennett, Bellow, and the rest (known by now in some quarters as the Killer B's) are advocating [the creation of] a narrowly specific cultural capital that will be the normative *refer-*

ent for everyone, but will remain the *property* of a small and powerful caste that is linguistically and ethnically unified. It is this caste that is referred to by the "we" in Saul Bellow's astoundingly racist remark that "when the Zulus have a Tolstoy, *we* will read him." Few doubt that behind the Bennett-Bloom program is a desire to close not the American mind, but the American university, to all but a narrow and highly uniform elite with no commitment to either multiculturalism or educational democracy. Thus while the Killer B's (plus a C— Lynne Cheney, the Bennett mouthpiece now heading the National Endowment for the Humanities) depict themselves as returning to the orthodoxies of yesteryear, their project must not be reduced to nostalgia or conservatism. Neither of these explain the blanket contempt they express for the country's universities. They are fueled not by reverence for the past, but by an aggressive desire to lay hold of the present and future. The B's act as they do not because they are unaware of the cultural and demographic diversification underway in the country; they are utterly aware. That is what they are trying to shape; that is why they are seeking, and using, national offices and founding national foundations.

Pratt laments "the West's relentless imperial expansion" and the "monumentalist cultural hierarchy that is historically as well as morally distortive." . . .

One of the conferees, Gerald Graff of Northwestern, writes:

> Speaking as a leftist, I too find it tempting to try to turn the curriculum into an instrument of social transformation.

He goes on to resist the temptation with the following (italics mine):

> But I doubt whether the curriculum (*as opposed to my particular course*) can or should become an extension of the politics of the left.

It turns out that he objects to politicizing the entire curriculum not because there must be something immoral about using the classroom to impose a specific ideology on students, but because of the unfortunate fact that universities also contain professors who are not "leftists" and who do not want their courses to become "an extension of the politics of the left"; and there seems to be no answer to the question, "What is to be done with those constituencies which do not happen to agree . . . that social transformation is the primary goal of education." What indeed?

I said earlier that it was difficult to find a succinct statement of the objections to the educational tradition made by the so-called cultural left, but this is largely because the objections are taken for granted. If you read enough material of the sort I have quoted, and, more importantly, if you attend enough of these conferences, it is easy to extract the central objection. It runs something like this: the history of "Western Civilization" is in large part a history of oppression. Internally, Western civilization oppressed women, various slave and serf populations, and ethnic and cultural minorities generally. In foreign affairs, the history of Western civilization is one of imperialism and colonialism. The so-called canon of Western civilization consists in the official publications of this system of oppression, and it is no accident that the authors in the "canon" are almost exclusively Western white males, because the civilization itself is ruled by a caste consisting almost entirely of Western white males. So you cannot reform education by admitting new members to the club, by opening up the canon; the whole idea of "the canon" has to be abolished. It has to be abolished in favor of something that is "multicultural" and "nonhierarchical."

The word "nonhierarchical" in the last sentence is important and I will come back to it. In the meantime I hope I have given enough of the arguments from those who oppose the traditional conceptions of liberal education to make it clear why the dispute cannot be resolved just by opening up the club to new members, and why it seems so intractable. Even if the canon is opened up, even if membership in the club is thrown open to all comers, even after you have admitted every first-rate woman writer from Sappho to Elizabeth Bishop, the various groups that feel that they have been excluded are still going to feel excluded, or marginalized. At present there are still going to be too many Western white males.

The actual arguments given often speak of improving education, but the central presuppositions of each side are seldom explicitly stated. With few exceptions, those who defend the traditional conception of a liberal education with a core curriculum think that Western civilization in general, and the United States in particular, have on the whole been the source of valuable institutions that should be preserved and of traditions that should be transmitted, emphatically including the intellectual tradition of skeptical critical analysis. Those who think that the traditional canon should be abandoned believe that Western civilization in general, and the United States in particular, are in large part oppressive, imperialist, patriarchal, hegemonic, and in need of replacement, or at least of transformation. . . .

There is a certain irony in this in that earlier student generations, my own for example, found the critical tradition that runs from Socrates through the *Federalist Papers*, through the writings of Mill and Marx, down to the twentieth century, to be liberating from the stuffy conventions of traditional American politics and pieties. Precisely by inculcating a critical attitude, the "canon" served to demythologize the conventional pieties of the American bourgeoisie and provided the student with a perspective from which to critically analyze American culture and institutions. Ironically, the same tradition is now regarded as oppressive. The texts once served an unmasking function; now we are told that it is the texts which must be unmasked.

More puzzling than the hatred of Bloom is the hostility shown to E. D. Hirsch, Jr. After all, Hirsch's central idea is that it would be desirable for American schoolchildren to be taught a common body of knowledge, a set of elementary facts and concepts that Hirsch calls "cultural literacy." (Among the texts and ideas he believes should be "explained in depth" are, for example, the Bill of Rights, *Don Quixote*, and ecology.) It is hard to imagine how anybody could object to such an innocuous proposal for improving education in the grade schools and high schools. However, even this is greeted with rage; indeed, only Bloom and Bennett arouse more anger than Hirsch in these polemics. In a savage attack, Barbara Herrnstein Smith quotes Hirsch as saying that his project of cultural literacy will result in

> breaking the cycle of illiteracy for deprived children; raising the living standards of families who have been illiterate; making our country more competitive in international markets; achieving greater social justice; enabling all citizens to participate in the political process; bringing us that much closer to the Ciceronian ideal of universal public discourse—in short, achieving the fundamental goals of the Founders at the birth of the republic.

To this project, she responds:

> Wild applause; fireworks; music—*America the Beautiful;* all together, now: *Calvin Coolidge, Gunga Din, Peter Pan, spontaneous combustion.* Hurrah for America and the national culture! Hurrah!

Why the hysterical tone of opposition? Herrnstein Smith reveals her own preoccupations when she says that Hirsch is "promoting a *deeply conservative view of American society and culture* through a rousing populist rhetoric" (my italics). But of course there is no reason at all why students who become familiar with the range of facts and ideas compiled by Hirsch should not arrive at "radical" or "liberal" or other positions.

But what about the question of intellectual excellence? The very ideal of excellence implied in the canon is itself perceived as a threat. It is considered "elitist" and "hierarchical" to suppose that "intellectual excellence" should take precedence over such considerations as fairness, representativeness, the expression of the experiences of previously underrepresented minorities, etc. Indeed, in the recent debate at Stanford about the course in Western

civilization, one of the arguments against the traditional curriculum (quoted with approval by Pratt) went as follows:

> A course with such readings creates two sets of books, those privileged by being on the list and those not worthy of inclusion. Regardless of the good intentions of those who create such lists, the students have not viewed and will not view these separate categories as equal.

I find this an amazing argument. One obvious difficulty with it is that if it were valid, it would argue against any set of required readings whatever; indeed, any list you care to make about anything automatically creates two categories, those that are on the list and those that are not.

One curious feature of the entire debate about what is "hegemonic," "patriarchal," or "exclusionary" is that it is largely about the study of literature. No one seems to complain that the great ideas in physics, mathematics, chemistry, and biology, for example, also come in large part from dead white European males. Historians of science have been showing how talented women were discouraged throughout modern history from pursuing scientific careers. But I have not heard any complaints from physics departments that the ideas of Newton, Einstein, Rutherford, Bohr, Schrödinger, etc. were deficient because of the scientists' origins or gender. Even in history of philosophy courses—as opposed to general education courses—there is little or no objection to the fact that the great philosophers taught in these courses are mostly white Western males, from Socrates, Plato and Aristotle through Frege, Russell, and Wittgenstein.

No doubt literature articulates the variety of human experience in ways that are unlike those of the sciences, but that is not enough by itself to explain the selective attitude that causes the humanities to be treated so differently from the sciences. To understand this difference you have to understand a second fundamental, but usually unstated, feature of the debate: in addition to having political objections to the United States and

Europe, many members of the cultural left think that the primary function of teaching the humanities is political; they do not really believe that the humanities are valuable in their own right except as a means of achieving "social transformation." They (apparently) accept that in subjects like physics and mathematics there may be objective and socially independent criteria of excellence (though they do not say much about the sciences at all), but where the humanities are concerned they think that the criteria that matter are essentially political. The argument goes: since any policy in the humanities will inevitably have a political dimension, courses in the humanities might as well be explicitly and beneficially political, instead of being disguised vehicles of oppression. . . .

. . . Henry Giroux tells us the following about how we should teach "the canon":

How we read or define a "canonical" work may not be as important as challenging the overall function and social uses the notion of the canon has served. Within this type of discourse, the canon can be analyzed as part of a wider set of relations that connect the academic disciplines, teaching, and power to considerations defined through broader, intersecting political and cultural concerns such as race, class, gender, ethnicity, and nationalism,. What is in question here is not merely a defense of a particular canon, but the issue of struggle and empowerment. In other words, the liberal arts should be defended in the interest of creating critical rather than "good" citizens. The notion of the liberal arts has to be reconstituted around a knowledge-power relationship in which the question of curriculum is seen as a form of cultural and political production grounded in a radical conception of citizenship and public wisdom.

He concludes that this transformation of our attitudes toward the tradition will link the liberal arts to "the imperatives of a critical democracy."

Notwithstanding its opaque prose, Giroux's message should be clear: the aim of a liberal education is to create political radicals, and the main point of reading the "canon" is to demythologize it by showing how it is used as a tool by the existing system of oppression. The traditional argument that the humanities are the core of a liberal education because of the intrinsic intellectual and aesthetic merits and importance of the works of Plato, Shakespeare, or Dante is regarded with scorn. Giroux again:

The liberal arts cannot be defended either as a self-contained discourse legitimating the humanistic goal of broadly improving the so-called "life of the mind" or as a rigorous science that can lead students to indubitable truths.

So the frustrating feature of the recent debate is that the underlying issues seldom come out into the open. Unless you accept two assumptions, that the Western tradition is oppressive, and that the main purpose of teaching the humanities is political transformation, the explicit arguments given against the canon will seem weak: that the canon is unrepresentative, inherently elitist, and, in a disguised form, political. Indeed if these arguments were strong ones, you could apply them against physics, chemistry, or mathematics.

From the point of view of the tradition, the answers to each argument are fairly obvious. First, it is not the aim of education to provide a representation or sample of everything that has been thought and written, but to give students access to works of high quality. Second, for that very reason, education is by its very nature "elitist" and "hierarchical" because it is designed to enable and encourage the student to discriminate between what is good and what is bad, what is intelligent and what is stupid, what is true and what is false. Third, the "tradition" is by no means a unified phenomenon, and, properly taught, it should impart a critical attitude to the student, precisely because of the variety and intellectual independence of the works being taught, and the disagreements among them. Fourth, of course the humanities have a political dimension at least in the sense that they have political consequences; so does everything else. But it does not follow from the fact that there is a political dimension to the humanities—as there is to music, art, gastronomy, and sex, as well as mathematics, philosophy, and physics—that the only, or even the principal, criteria for assessing these efforts should be political ones. . . .

2.

. . . In my experience there never was, in fact, a fixed "canon"; there was rather a certain set of tentative judgments about what had importance and quality. Such judgments are always subject to revision, and in fact they were constantly being revised.

Furthermore both the composition of our student bodies and the relation of the United States to the rest of the world have undergone some enormous changes in the past generation. For example, in my own university more than 50 percent of the freshman class are non-whites. And we are all aware that countries like Japan, China, and those of Latin America play a much larger part in our relations to the rest of the world than they did in the 1950s. It is an interesting question what influence these facts should have on our conception of the education of undergraduates. Perhaps in the end we will say they should have no effect, but it is not obvious.

Worse yet, the debate over college curriculum mainly concerns only a tiny fraction of undergraduate education, usually a single required freshman course in the humanities, together with other courses in literature which the scholars who describe themselves as the "cultural left" may seek to control, and which may (or may not) therefore be vehicles for promoting ideologies of "social transformation." Most undergraduate education—as well as our lack of any coherent theory of what we are trying to achieve in undergraduate education—is largely untouched by this discussion. Neither side has much to say about what actually happens in most college classrooms. . . .

Suppose that one is dissatisfied with the low intellectual level of the "cultural left," but that one feels at the same time that much undergraduate education should be improved. This question was faced in an acute form in the debate at Stanford, concerning the reform of the curriculum in Western culture. Both the debate and its results are instructive. Stanford had a required one-year course in Western culture that had to be taken by all incoming students. This course was given in eight different "tracks," corresponding roughly to different departments and schools. Among the tracks, for example, were history, literature and the arts, philosophy, and Western thought and technology. But all shared a required reading list, containing the Bible, Plato's *Republic*, Homer, several medieval and Renaissance readings, including Augustine, Dante, Thomas More, Machiavelli, Luther, and Galileo, and of the moderns, Voltaire, Marx, Freud, and Darwin. In addition, a list of writers ranging from Thucydides to Nietzsche was "strongly recommended."

Many of the objections made to this course were predictable, reflecting the views of the cultural left I have mentioned, as were the defenses. What emerged appears to have been a kind of compromise arrived at after many months of debate. Unfortunately, the controversy became so fogged by political polemics and by partial and inaccurate reports in the press that the central issues, and what actually occurred, were not made clear to the general public.

The title of the course was changed to "Culture, Ideas, Values," ("CIV" for short, with "Western" left out). The readings required for all tracks now include the Bible, "a Classical Greek philosopher, an early Christian thinker, a Renaissance dramatist, an Enlightenment thinker," and readings from Marx and Freud. At least one non-European work must be studied and at some point in each academic quarter "substantial attention" must be given to "the issues of *race, gender,* and *class.*" . . .

[It] seems to me one can make a fairly strong case for the new course on purely educational grounds. Of eight tracks, it is not necessarily a bad thing to have one optional track where European civilization is taught as simply one civilization among others, and it does not seem to me at all worrying that Aristotle and Tocqueville are taught along with Frantz Fanon. Of course, as with all courses it all depends on how the course is taught. Yet even if we assume that the organizers have political goals, as I suppose they do, one of the most liberating effects of "liberal education" is in coming to see one's own culture as one possible form of life and sensibility among others; and the reading lists for the new course suggest that such an outcome is likely. Also, it is important to keep reminding ourselves that students are not just passive receptacles. In my experience, students are good at arguing back at professors, and indeed that is in large part what professors are for: to argue with. So my general impression from observing events at Stanford is that reports of the demise of "culture," Western or otherwise, in the required freshman course at Stanford are grossly exaggerated. If I were a freshman at Stanford, I might well be tempted to take "Europe and the Americas."

3.

One of the most ominous charges made [against the cultural left] is that the cultural left in the humanities today has lost its traditional commitment to the search for truth. . . . [M]any no longer believe in the enterprise of an objective and disinterested search for truth, because they do not believe that such a thing is even possible. The claim is not that it is difficult and perhaps impossible to attain complete disinterest and objectivity, but rather that the very enterprise of trying to attain such things is misconceived from the beginning, because there is no objective reality for our objectivist methodology to attain. In short, many academics who make up the cultural left . . . reject the "correspondence theory of truth"; they reject the idea that true statements are ever made true by virtue of the fact that there is an independently existing set of objects and features of the world to which such statements correspond.

[A] favorite target is a pamphlet produced by the American Council of Learned Societies, called *Speaking for the Humanities*. It is the product of a committee of six professors, five professors of English, and one professor of French and comparative literature. The pamphlet was explicitly designed to answer such critics as Bloom and Bennett, and it is written in a bland, academic prose. Its central sections, starting with "Ideology and Objectivity," begin somewhat condescendingly with the following: "Perhaps the most difficult aspect of modern thought, even for many humanities professors and certainly for society at large, is its challenge to the positivist ideal of objectivity and disinterest." But we learn after several pages that in fact this "positivist ideal" has been decisively replaced by something they call "theory," and that there are an overwhelming number of—unidentified—authorities who agree about this:

> Over the past two decades, traditional assumptions about ways of studying the humanities have been contested, in large measure because a number of related disciplines—cultural anthropology, linguistics, psychoanalysis, the philosophy of language—were undergoing major changes that inevitably forced humanists to ask basic questions about their methods and the very definition of their fields.

Furthermore,

> The challenge to claims of intellectual authority alluded to in the introduction of this report issues from almost all areas of modern thought—*science, psychology, feminism, linguistics, semiotics,* and *anthropology* [my italics].

And again,

> *As the most powerful modern philosophies* and theories have been demonstrating, claims of disinterest, objectivity, and universality are not to be trusted and themselves tend to reflect local historical conditions [my italics].

As someone who takes more than a passing interest in "the most powerful modern philosophies," I know none of which it could be said that it "demonstrates" that such claims are "not to be trusted." Unfortunately the authors do not tell us exactly what results in these disciplines they have in mind. They also confidently quote "relativity and quantum mechanics" as supporting their new conception of the humanities. One wishes they had told us in some detail how the study of, say, inertial frames in relativity theory or the collapse of the wave function in quantum mechanics support their peculiar conception of the study of literature.

On first reading . . . it may appear that [this] is too hard on this pamphlet, but a close reading of the pamphlet makes it clear that he is not nearly hard enough. I do not here have the space to convey the smugness of its tone, the feebleness of its argument, or the weakness of its constant appeals to authority. Typical passages claim support from, "the most distinguished philosophers of science of our time," or tell us that, "the consensus of most of the dominant theories is. . . ."

One recurring fallacy deserves special mention. There is throughout the pamphlet a persistent confusion between epistemology and ontology; between how we know and what it is that we know when we know. It is an obvious fact that our epistemological efforts are undertaken by historically situated people, subject to all the usual imperfections, not merely of prejudice but of intellect. All investigations are relative to investigators. But it does not follow, nor is it indeed true, that all the matters investigated are relative to investigators. Real human investigators have to discover, e.g., that water is made of hydrogen and oxygen, but the fact that water is made of hydrogen and oxygen is not relative to any investigators. . . .

. . . If you think there is no reality that words could possibly correspond to, then obviously it will be a waste of time to engage in an "objective and disinterested search for truth," because there is no such thing as truth. There are just various forms of discourse engaged in by various groups of people. Philosophers have a name for the view that there exists a reality independent of our

representations of it. It is called "realism" or sometimes "metaphysical realism" or "scientific realism." An immediate difficulty with denials of metaphysical realism is that they remove the rational constraints that are supposed to shape discourse, when that discourse aims at something beyond itself. To paraphrase Dostoevsky, without metaphysical realism, anything is permissible.

Many arguments have been made against metaphysical realism, all of them in my view inadequate. This is not the place to go through each argument, but one can at least cite . . . Thomas Kuhn's *The Structure of Scientific Revolutions.* . . . Kuhn is supposed to have shown that science does not consist in the detached search for the truth, but that scientists instead are an irrational community, who grasp hold of one "paradigm" until they find it dissatisfying; then they have another "scientific revolution" and rush to another paradigm.

I do not for a moment believe that this is the correct interpretation of Kuhn's book, although he could have been clearer about whether he was referring to the sociology of scientific communities or the epistemology of scientific discovery. But whatever Kuhn's intentions, the effect has been to demythologize science in the eyes of people in literary studies, many of whom think that the claim of science to represent any independently existing reality has been discredited. When the authors of *Speaking for the Humanities* refer to "the most distinguished philosophers of science of our time," they clearly have Kuhn in mind. . . .

Are there convincing arguments for metaphysical realism? The demand for a proof of the existence of a reality that is independent of our representations of reality is a puzzling one, because it looks like making the demand itself already presupposes what is demanded to be proved. The situation is a bit like those challenges one used to hear in the 1960s, when students would ask for a proof of rationality, "What is your argument for rationality?" But any demand for an "argument" or "proof" already presupposes standards of rationality, the applicability of which is constitutive of something's being an argument or proof. You cannot in the same breath appeal to argument and proof and deny rationality.

A similar point applies, but even more radically, to metaphysical realism. The person who denies metaphysical realism presupposes the existence of a public language, a language in which he or she communicates with other people. But what are the conditions of possibility of communication in a public language? What do I have to assume when I ask a question or make a claim that is supposed to be understood by others? At least this much: if we are using words to tell about something in a way that we expect to be understood by others, then there must be a least the possibility of something those words can be used to talk about. Consider any claim, from particular statements such as "my dog has fleas," to theoretical claims such as "water is made of hydrogen and oxygen," to grand theories such as evolution or relativity, and you will see that they presuppose for their intelligibility that we are taking metaphysical realism for granted.

I am not claiming that one can prove metaphysical realism to be true from some standpoint that exists apart from our human linguistic practices. What I am arguing, rather, is that those practices themselves presuppose metaphysical realism. So one cannot within those practices intelligibly deny metaphysical realism, because the meaningfulness of our public utterances already presupposes an independently existing reality to which expressions in those utterances can refer. Metaphysical realism is thus not a thesis or a theory; it is rather the condition of having theses or theories or even of denying theses or theories. This is not an epistemic point about how we come to know truth as opposed to falsehood, rather it is a point about the conditions of possibility of communicating intelligibly. Falsehood stands as much in need of the real world as does truth.

Politics and the College Curriculum

Laura M. Purdy

In this essay, Laura Purdy discusses the merits of "traditionalists" and "revolutionaries" in their battles over the college curriculum. Her particular interest is in feminist philosophy's attempts at educational reform. She begins with an account of the history of higher education—the fact that it has changed over time in response to changing social values and that society has refused to see women as the equals of men. She next responds to John Searle and others who charge that advocates of reform are "relativists" who deny the objectivity of value judgments and concludes with a discussion of the politicization of the college curriculum and the ways in which feminists in fact seek to improve the curriculum by making it more thorough and more humane. Laura Purdy teaches at the Joint Center for Bioethics at the University of Toronto.

As you read through this essay, consider the following:

1. How does Purdy describe the history of higher education's curricular changes?
2. What does Purdy have to say to people such as John Searle who claim that radicals are relativists? Is she herself a relativist?

3. Does Purdy think the curriculum cannot avoid being "politicized" or does she think it depends on what is meant by the term?
4. What purpose do you imagine Purdy sees the humanities as serving for students attending colleges and universities?

For us to attempt to reform the education of our brothers at public schools and universities would be to invite a shower of dead cats, rotten eggs and broken gates from which only street scavengers and locksmiths would benefit, while the gentlemen in authority, history assures us, would survey the tumult from their study windows without taking the cigars from their lips or ceasing to sip, slowly, as its bouquet deserves, their admirable claret.

Virginia Woolf, *Three Guineas*

American education has been profoundly compromised in the past two decades. Standards have been eroded, curriculum has been debased, and research trivialized or distorted by ideology.

Statement of Editorial Purpose,
Academic Questions

INTRODUCTION

There is a war on over the curriculum in higher education and the scholarship that supports it. It is an important war because curricular decisions define in large part what educated people will know and think, and that in turn makes a significant difference in how we all live.

Many people (I shall call them "traditionalists") think the curriculum is basically fine the way it is. According to them, it is now in part a neutral representation of truth (or reality) and is, for the rest, composed of works chosen for their excellence according to objective principles. Its content constitutes the canon. Although the curriculum could no doubt be improved in various ways, changes

From Robert L. Simon, ed. *Neutrality and the Academic Ethics* (New York: Rowman and Littlefield, 1994). Reprinted by permission.

ought to be made in accordance with these principles of neutrality and excellence. . . .

The critics (I shall call them "revolutionaries") believe that the picture of the world presented by much of the traditional curriculum, by failing to take into account such categories of analysis as gender, race, and class, is seriously biased. They also maintain that the allegedly objective principles according to which works are judged worthy of inclusion in the curriculum are by no means neutral with respect to these categories, so that many factors apart from excellence play a part in constructing the canon.

. . . My aim in this paper is to see what, if anything, can be said on behalf of feminist philosophy, one kind of revolutionary thought, in response to traditionalist objections to it. . . .

In particular, our examination will explore whether revolutionary contributions necessarily weaken the curriculum and the extent to which revolutionary scholarship is compatible with rigorous critical inquiry, the central element of Simon's conception of institutional neutrality.

HISTORICAL OBSERVATIONS

Ignorance of history leaves us with unrealistic conceptions of both past and present. It is therefore helpful to have some reminders about the history of higher education and about women's place in human society.

It is tempting to imagine a calm and rational Golden Age of higher education. For instance, John Silber writes:

In the past, the belief that there were transcendent principles by which we could guide our lives helped give society a goal and an understanding of the human condition. There was a shared vision, a set of standards which could measure conduct and a motivation to strive for excellence.

Attractive though this image is, we should be asking what principles Silber is referring to, and by whom they were formulated and "shared."

Furthermore, knowing a bit of history undermines the vision he presses upon us. Few scholars are taught that the first colleges were religious institutions geared toward educating a small elite; women were barred from them. . . .

Not only then has higher education changed over time to accommodate social values, but such change has been thought desirable. A cursory look at the history of American higher education shows it adapting—not promptly, and for the most part not very willingly—but nonetheless, in the end, adapting to those changes.

How is all this information relevant to the question at hand? I think it requires us to see college curricula as constantly evolving constellations of courses and programs that are responsive to a variety of influences. Some are internal, including no doubt the same kind of personal ambitions and idiosyncracies that now play a considerable role in academic decision making, and some are external, created by the larger currents within society as a whole. And although the general direction of curricular changes can be judged positively, there is certainly little here to suggest that the curriculum has ever been the coherent and rigorous expression of a wise educational ideal.

Let us now turn to the woman question. Most influential Western thinkers, from Socrates to Nietzsche, have thought women were different from men in ways that go beyond mere biological difference. At best, they have viewed women as complementary to men, playing a perhaps important but basically subsidiary role in society. At worst, and unfortunately most typically, they have asserted women's inferiority, equating us with unthinking nature and unchecked emotion,

unable to reason well or think morally. What little argument buttressed those claims has rested on unfounded assumptions, bad logic, and transparently self-serving moral claims.

The central problem here is, in my opinion, that society has been unwilling to see women as agents, as people with legitimate interests of our own. Hence there has been considerable resistance to the notion that what is good for us could sometimes take precedence over what is good for others. One manifestation of that resistance is the reluctance to take seriously our own conceptions of our interests.

Because of our alleged intellectual and moral inferiority, it has been difficult for women to become educated. In the United States, higher education has been available to women for little more than a hundred years. In fact, it was not until the 1960s that women were admitted to the most prestigious men's institutions.

Given this history, it is not surprising that there are few influential women in academe. It is well known that most women are to be found in the least prestigious institutions, in the lowest ranks, and spend the bulk of their time teaching, not writing or setting academic policy. Because of the power structure of academe, this means that our voices have relatively little weight in discussions about curriculum, and, to the extent that prejudice against women still exists, those voices command even less attention than would otherwise be the case.

Now, higher education is important. Not only does good education help develop mind and character, but it is crucial for social mobility. Yet our system of higher education was shaped largely by men with allegiances to a tradition that has, for the most part, found women intellectually and morally wanting. Given this history, it is surely appropriate for the burden of proof to rest on the shoulders of those who maintain that it nonetheless responds equally well to the interests of women and men, contrary to the . . . assertion that it is "ludicrous" to think that the "liberal arts oppress minorities and women."

The importance of this question is still further underlined by the following consideration. Technical institutes could prepare people for highly skilled jobs, so why do we need colleges and universities at all? The answer, it seems to me, is that they are expected to provide society with wise citizens and leaders, and it is the liberal arts—the humanities in particular—that are to do that.

No wonder, then, that there is such bitterness about the proper content of the humanities when there is so much disagreement about what they should achieve. Wisdom, after all, is not the mere instrumental ability to get to B from A, but much more importantly, knowing which Bs are worth having. Likewise, conceptions of the good society involve a host of judgments about the good life and about what justice requires. None of these claims consist solely of facts that could be established by means of the relevant observations, but rather involve value judgments about what activities and states of affairs are good, worthwhile, and fair. No such judgments are therefore neutral in the sense that the claim "the worm creeping up on my foot is brown" can be neutral. The extent to which value judgments can be neutral (or objective) in some other way is perhaps the central question underlying the curriculum debate.

How, more precisely, do the humanities create wise citizens and leaders? Some traditionalists hold that they tell us what wisdom is. A second major strand of traditionalism defends the humanities not because they have the answers about life, but because they grapple with the right questions.

Revolutionaries are somewhat less forthcoming about the general aims of liberal education. *Speaking for the Humanities*, a revolutionary pamphlet put out in 1989 by the American Council of Learned Societies, suggests that the humanities should be conceived of "as fields of exploration and critique rather than materials for transmission. . . ." Other scholars emphasize their importance for teaching democracy, or for making people's lives better. Still others emphasize the role of the humanities in helping students see new possibilities and making judgments about good lives.

Oddly then, there is surprisingly widespread agreement about the importance of rational examination of the basic question of how we ought to live, as individuals and as a society. So what is the problem? Despite substantial basic agreement about the aim of education, traditionalists object to revolutionary work on a number of grounds, most prominently, relativism and "politicizing" scholarship. But what do these claims mean? And, are they justified?

RELATIVISM

Traditionalists appear to be convinced that revolutionaries are relativists. By this, they mean that revolutionaries either doubt the existence of any objective world about which we can make judgments that are true or false, or else that although such a world does exist, we cannot know enough about it to make these kinds of judgments. Furthermore, traditionalists also attribute to relativists the view that it is impossible to make objective value judgments, either because no acts or states of affairs are better than any others or because we couldn't ever know enough to do so. Therefore, revolutionaries are believed to have given up the search for truth, abdicated from judgments about the quality of literary and artistic work, and to have concluded that power, not reason, is the only possible basis for "moral" action.

What is the evidence for revolutionary relativism? John Searle, in his review of several recent books on higher education, [states] that

. . . the cultural left in the humanities today has lost its traditional commitment to the search for the truth. Indeed, according to Kimball, many no longer believe in the enterprise of an objective and disinterested search for truth, because they do not believe that such a thing is even possible. The claim is not that it is difficult and perhaps impossible to attain disinterest and objectivity, but rather that the very enterprise of trying to attain such things is misconceived from the beginning, because there is no objective reality for our objectivist methodology to attain.

Is this accusation true? Granted, radical revolutionaries have given up on truth and reason. There is also a good deal of wild talk. Liberal revolutionaries who aren't philosophers quite often say things that seem to imply relativism. In my experience, however, when pressed, they back off and reformulate their claims more carefully. Yet in the survey of the literature I did for this paper, there was not a single assertion of relativism.

At the eye of this storm is the ACLS pamphlet *Speaking for the Humanities (SH).* Although it has been attacked on several fronts, the charge of relativism is central to the case against its alleged position. . . .

In his review piece "The Storm Over the University," [John] Searle repeats . . . the revolutionary conception of truth: "they reject the idea that true statements are ever made true by virtue of the fact that there is an independently existing set of objects and feature of the world to which such statements correspond." . . .

. . . His argument for metaphysical realism is right on the mark—but irrelevant, since there is no evidence in *SH* of the confusion between epistemological uncertainty and ontological nihilism at which it aims. That is, *SH* is warning against assumptions of infallibility, not denying that there is a truth to be found through reasoned argument and discussion.

What, precisely, is at issue here? Three different kinds of criticisms can be raised with respect to objectivity:

1. The claim that a particular assertion fails to meet agreed-upon criteria of objectivity.
2. The claim that a particular conception of objectivity is inadequate.
3. The claim that there is no such thing as objectivity.

Searle (and other traditionalists) appear to believe that revolutionaries are arguing for

(3). I believe, however, that despite some language suggestive of (3), liberal revolutionaries are arguing only for (1) and sometimes for (2).

Why is there such serious confusion? It appears to arise from the position in *SH* that "all thought develops from particular standpoints, perspectives, interests." In other words, human thought may be influenced by the views of those who produced them. This position is being interpreted as a claim that it is therefore impossible to attain objectivity: Even widely accepted "truths" are inevitably tainted by irrelevant interests, and conflicting points of view are irreducibly contradictory.

But this interpretation of the position that thought arises from persons is not the only one, and given what we have already seen of *SH*, certainly not the most plausible one. It can instead be taken as a reminder of the importance of scrutinizing the origins of ideas to see where bias is most likely to creep in; disagreements can be taken as evidence that further investigation and argument is needed, not that argument and inquiry are necessarily ineffective.

What *SH* emphasizes is the difficulty of achieving an objective view; never is it asserted that there is nothing to be known or that reason is impotent in helping us find truth or make judgments. *SH* explicitly addresses this issue, recognizing that people will find its position threatening, for they make take it to mean that "it gives license to anything since there would appear to be on this account no objective grounds of argument, only various versions of personal or political interest." But, it says, this inference is mistaken: "At its best, contemporary humanistic thinking does not peddle ideology, but rather attempts to sensitize us to the presence of ideology in our work, and to its capacity to delude us into promoting as universal values that in fact belong to one nation, one social class, one sect."

What is being said here is that claims of objectivity have often been in fact mere partial accounts that have presented only part of the story. *SH* asserts that contemporary theory presses us about the "boundaries and limits of knowledge, about where we stand when we claim to speak with authority," but does not deny the possibility of definite knowledge claims.

In sum, *SH* points out that political judgments are not facts, and that ideas come from human beings. Both of these claims are plausible and widely accepted. They are nonetheless widely interpreted as assertions of relativism, despite a reasonably successful effort on the part of its authors to distinguish their position from relativism. How is it possible to escape the conclusion that either the critics of *SH* are unacceptably sloppy or that they deliberately sought to mislead readers about its position? Skeptics should go look for themselves.

Now, it may well be true that some of the excerpts traditionalists quote would, if followed up, yield expressions of relativism by *radical* revolutionaries. But even if they did, traditionalists would be no closer to making their case, which has to be that revolutionary challenges to the curriculum are *necessarily* relativistic and therefore not worth taking seriously. In other words, in order to avoid dealing with the specific details of revolutionary claims, traditionalists often rely instead on rather general epistemological claims that they believe pull the rug out from under every revolutionary case. Thus, by attributing relativism to revolutionaries, traditionalists suggest that the assertion that gender makes an empirical or moral difference is incoherent. Once the charge of relativism is shown to be untenable, however (by showing that many revolutionaries neither consider themselves to be relativists nor are relativists in fact), the discussion must focus on the plausibility of specific claims. It should be clear by now that a significant segment of the revolutionary camp denies relativism. Nor is it reasonable to construe revolutionary claims relativistically—quite the contrary, for the most part they assume both an objective empirical world that is best understood by using gender as a category of analysis and a moral world that can be made better by doing so. Hence, for example, feminists object to the common

practice of doing biological research on exclusively male samples. In these cases, the possibility that gender makes a difference is ignored, even though it may be, as in the study of the effects of aspirin ingestion on heart attacks, a matter of life or death.

Thus it seems that traditionalist refusal to take revolutionary work seriously on the basis of its relativism is unwarranted. Let us now turn to the second fundamental traditionalist objection to revolutionary work—that it "politicizes" academe.

"POLITICIZATION"

"Politicized" work is work that inappropriately injects political considerations into the scholarly world. But such a claim requires analysis both of "inappropriate" and "political."

"Inappropriate" could mean injecting political considerations where they appear to have no place whatsoever, or raising the wrong issues in value discourse. One possible target of the first claim might be feminist work in epistemology and the philosophy of science. This work is predicated on the assumption that most of our existing theory was created by men, mostly middle- and upper-class white men, and that, although the fields are apparently nonpolitical in nature, they might still incorporate certain political biases common to this group. The traditionalist interpretation of this assumption as the claim that biology somehow determines thought is insensitive to the point that individuals with different experience may well see the world differently and that theory can only benefit from the contribution of diverse perspectives.

Now, I am myself unconvinced of some of the more far-reaching claims by the work I have read so far. However, the idea here that our most fundamental conceptions about knowing are at present marked in unnecessary and perhaps harmful ways by their genesis is interesting, and, if true, would constitute a clear advance in theory. That none of this feminist work has so far been unambiguously successful ought neither to be surprising, given its short history, nor grounds for the contempt now being heaped upon it. How many radical new intellectual perspectives got it right immediately? We cannot, in any case, say *a priori* where politics will turn out to be relevant.

The view that it is possible to raise the "wrong" questions in value discourse will be examined later. Let us now turn to questions about the meaning of "political."

One of the interesting features of the curriculum debate is the glaring absence of definitions of this key word. So we need to start here by looking at the way the word gets used. One clear implication of the claim that a given piece of work is "political" seems to be the view that politics are incompatible with good scholarship. That could mean either that political conviction is incompatible with scholarly integrity or that it is incompatible with appropriate scholarly openness.

That political conviction is incompatible with scholarly integrity is rarely articulated in a straightforward way by traditionalists, but it forms an unmistakable undercurrent in their work. In some cases, it may be an appeal to the clearly false claim that all revolutionaries are relativists, since integrity is irrelevant for scholarship that makes no truth claims. The new charge would have to be that revolutionaries' political convictions override all other values, including honesty. So they are believed to ignore inconvenient evidence, take material out of context, twist their opponents' arguments, gloss over contradictions in their own positions, and indulge in a variety of fallacies such as straw person, hasty generalization, and red herring. . . .

The difficulty in evaluating this matter is obvious: The impact of political beliefs on scholarship is hard to measure, partly because no one is free of political leanings and partly because of the enormous scope of the inquiry. I believe, however, that there are some basic rules of good scholarship and they can help us tell good work from bad. Nobody using those rules could conclude that revolutionaries have a monopoly on bad scholarship. . . .

Let us now go on to consider whether feminism undermines good scholarship by interfering with scholarly openness. Before looking in detail at this question, we need to get clear about what it means to be a feminist. Although I cannot speak for every feminist, it is generally agreed that women's interests are not treated with the same respect as those of men and that justice requires that this state of affairs be remedied.

Narrowing the question now to philosophy, and in particular to ethics and political philosophy, what does feminism mean? Alison Jaggar suggests that feminist philosophers are committed to eliminating male bias in ethics. Many readers are no doubt skeptical that there is any significant male bias in ethics, and hence regard this project with jaundiced eye. Before dismissing it, however, recall that the discipline of ethics has been until lately the creation of men. It is therefore quite possible that despite their attempts to be rational and objective, ethics now bears the marks of distinctively male interests—in both senses of the term. Surely it is better to be alert to this possibility so as to detect bias if it exists than to be so convinced of its absence that it wouldn't be noticed even if it were there.

Jaggar maintains that this project assumes the wrongness of women's subordination and the equal seriousness of women's and men's moral experience. These assumptions in turn require us to use gender as a category of analysis, as it is always possible that women and men are not similarly situated. When they are not, it is important to investigate whether the differences are either a result of or a source of hitherto unnoticed unfairness. They also require us to keep in mind the broad consequences of actions and to extend moral reasoning to the domestic realm.

What, in practical terms, are the consequences of these guidelines? First, because of our conviction that women are as important as men, we notice when women's interests are discounted or ignored, or where issues that are especially important to our lives are not considered worthy of investigation at all. Second, these concerns lead us often to adopt a number of specific strategies. One is an interest in understanding the reasons why people behave as they do. Another is making sure we look at a given situation from the point of view of all the affected parties, and over the long run. Still a third is attempting to come up with solutions to moral conflicts that involve structural rather than purely individual change and to find remedies that spread costs as equally as possible. In short, we try to be quick to understand and sympathize, and slow to condemn.

Apart from these approaches, feminist work is mostly conducted in the usual ways. We try to get a full picture of the problematic situation, consider alternative explanations of how it got that way, and try to envision different possible solutions. We sift through arguments and objections, evaluating claims according to reason, employing principles, logic and evidence. The diversity of feminist viewpoints means that we spend substantial amounts of time criticizing each other in the attempt to come up with solid answers. For example, I often disagree with radical feminist critics of new reproductive practices. In that work I give grounds for rejecting some of their basic premises, argue for the relevance of facts they ignore, and point out bad consequences of their proposed solutions. My arguments—and theirs—can be judged by the usual criteria for scholarship.

Is there anything unscholarly about these interests, strategies, or approaches? On the contrary, I contend that they are an improvement over the less thorough and humane work now quite common in applied ethics. Traditionalists may criticize our overall goal of eliminating male bias in ethics, but it remains to be shown that this goal is any more "political" than the conviction that ethics is fine the way it is. Thus it would be unwarranted to reject feminist ethics on the grounds that they are "politicized" or biased. . . .

Section 7

Morality in Markets

The Inherent Morality of Capitalism

Michael Novak

Capitalism is controversial. It is credited with creating prosperity and wealth that were unimaginable in previous generations, and with encouraging the independence of mind and self-reliance necessary for democratic institutions to flourish and for citizens to lead worthy lives. It is also sometimes blamed for encouraging greed and selfishness, for destroying traditional cultures, and for being incompatible with the ideals of community. Michael Novak disputes these criticisms of capitalism. Beginning with a description of the close link that exists between capitalism and democracy—both spring from the same historical impulses—Novak goes on to defend the economic and political achievements of capitalism. He then turns to the issue of character, arguing that far from encouraging selfishness, capitalism rewards cooperation while at the same time being realistic about human capacities for sin. Rather than fostering aristocratic and elitist values, capitalism encourages diligence, democracy, and practicality. It also encourages self-esteem. Novak concludes with a discussion of the role capitalism plays in creating a sense of community among people.

As you read through this essay, consider the following:

1. What links does Novak see between capitalism and democratic government?
2. What are the historic achievements of democratic capitalism that he identifies?
3. How does he respond to those who say capitalism encourages greed and acquisitiveness?

115

4. What are the "commercial virtues" and how does Novak understand their importance compared to other virtues?
5. How have Americans differed from Europeans in terms of communal ties?
6. What sorts of communal ties does Novak believe are encouraged under American capitalism?

CAPITALISM, SOCIALISM, AND RELIGION—AN INQUIRY INTO THE SPIRITUAL WEALTH OF NATIONS

Of all the systems of political economy which have shaped our history, none has so revolutionized ordinary expectations of human life—lengthened the life span, made the elimination of poverty and famine thinkable, enlarged the range of human choice—as democratic capitalism. Recall the societies of the Roman Empire and Carolingian period. Contemplate the Catholic and Protestant powers of the seventeenth century, colonial and mercantilist. Examine the many forms of socialism in the present day. Each of these systems of political economy has had its theological admirers. Yet no theologian, Christian or Jewish, has yet assessed the theological significance of democratic capitalism. . . .

What do I mean by "democratic capitalism"? I mean three systems in one: a predominantly market economy; a polity respectful of the rights of the individual to life, liberty, and the pursuit of happiness; and a system of cultural institutions moved by ideals of liberty and justice for all. In short, three dynamic and converging systems functioning as one: a democratic polity, an economy based on markets and incentives, and a moral-cultural system which is pluralistic and, in the largest sense, liberal. Social systems like those of the United States, West Germany, and Japan (with perhaps a score of others among the world's nations) illustrate the type.

From Michael Novak, *The Spirit of Democratic Capitalism* (1982). © Michael Novak, 1982, 1991 (2nd ed.). Madison Books: Lanham, Maryland. Reprinted by permission.

The premise of this book may startle some. In the conventional view, the link between a democratic political system and a market economy is merely an accident of history. My argument is that the link is stronger: political democracy is compatible in practice only with a market economy. In turn, both systems nourish and are best nourished by a pluralistic liberal culture. It is important to give attention to all three systems. The full implications of a system which is threefold, rather than unitary, are developed through all the pages of this book.

To begin with, modern democracy and modern capitalism proceed from identical historical impulses. These impulses had moral form before institutions were invented to realize them; they aimed (1) to limit the power of the state, in defense against tyranny and stagnation; and (2) to liberate the energies of individuals and independently organized communities. Such impulses gave birth to modern European cities, whose first citizens took as their battle cry "City air makes men free." Such citizens sought liberation from the crippling taxation, heavy bureaucracy, and dreary regulations of state and church. The moral vision of such citizens demanded forms of self-government in "city republics" and "free cities." It led them to cherish economies based upon free markets, incentives, and contracts. Gradually, such citizens developed polities based upon covenants, suffrage, the separation of powers, and the declaration of individual rights. The two revolutions—political and economic—in practice, but also in theory, nourished each other. Karl Marx recognized this link in his term of contempt: "bourgeois democracy," he called it. Both spring from the same logic, the same moral principles, the same nest of cultural values, institutions, and presuppositions.

While bastard forms of capitalism do seem able for a time to endure without democracy, the natural logic of capitalism leads to democracy. For economic liberties without political liberties are inherently unstable. Citizens economically free soon demand political freedoms. Thus dictatorships or monarchies which permit some freedoms to the market have a tendency to evolve into political democracies, as has happened in recent years in Greece, Portugal, Spain, and other nations. On the other side, the state which does not recognize limits to its power in the economic sphere inevitably destroys liberties in the political sphere. . . .

The Historical Achievements of Democratic Capitalism

Consider the world at the beginning of the democratic capitalist era. The watershed year was 1776. Almost simultaneously, Adam Smith published *An Inquiry into the Nature and Causes of the Wealth of Nations* and the first democratic capitalist republic came into existence in the United States. Until that time, the classical pattern of political economy was mercantilist. Famines ravaged the civilized world on the average once a generation.[1] Plagues seized scores of thousands. In the 1780s, four fifths of French families devoted 90 percent of their incomes simply to buying bread—only bread—to stay alive. Life expectancy in 1795 in France was 27.3 years for women and 23.4 for men. In the year 1800, in the whole of Germany fewer than a thousand people had incomes as high as $1,000.[2] . . .

The invention of the market economy in Great Britain and the United States more profoundly revolutionized the world between 1800 and the present than any other single force. After five millennia of blundering, human beings finally figured out how wealth may be produced in a sustained, systematic way. In Great Britain, real wages doubled between 1800 and 1850, and doubled again between 1850 and 1900. Since the population of Great Britain quadrupled in size, this represented a 1600 percent increase within one century.[3] The gains in liberty of personal choice—in a more varied diet, new beverages, new skills, new vocations—increased accordingly.

The churches did not understand the new economics. Officially and through the theologians, they often regarded "the new spirit of capitalism" as materialistic, secular, and dangerous to religion, as in many respects—being in and of the world—it was. They often protested the rising spirit of individualism. They seldom grasped the new forms of cooperation indispensable to the new economics. They tried to douse the new fire. . . .

In previous generations, taking its spiritual inheritance for granted, democratic capitalism felt no acute need for a theory about itself. It did not seem to need a moral theory, a theory about the life of the spirit, since it—erroneously—relied upon its own moral-cultural leaders to maintain one. The age of such innocence has long since passed. The glaring inadequacies of actual socialist societies do not seem to discourage newborn socialists. Entire nations, like Gadarene herds, cast themselves over the precipice. Within democratic capitalist societies as well, humans do not live by bread alone. Inattention to theory weakens the life of the spirit and injures the capacity of the young to dream of noble purposes. Irving Kristol in *Two Cheers for Capitalism* describes a moral vision "desperately needed by the spiritually impoverished civilization that we have constructed on what once seemed to be sturdy bourgeois foundations." He discerns the loss suffered by "a capitalist, republican community, with shared values and a quite unambiguous claim to the title of a just order" when it does not rethink its spiritual foundations and is thoughtlessly "severed from its moral moorings."[4] . . .

VIRTUOUS SELF-INTEREST

R. H. Tawney described the age of capitalism as the age of acquisitiveness. Marx described it as the reduction of every human relation to the cash nexus. Pamphleteers for generations have denounced its licensing of greed. Yet simple reflection upon one's own life and the life of others, including the lives of those critics who denounce the system from within, suggests that there are enormous reservoirs of high motivation and moral purpose among citizens in democratic capitalist societies. The history of democratic capitalism is alive with potent movements of reform and idealistic purpose. As the world goes, its people do not in fact seem to be more greedy, grasping, selfish, acquisitive, or anarchic than citizens in traditional or in socialist societies. If democratic capitalism is to be blamed for sins it permits to flourish, the virtues it nourishes also deserve some credit.

In practice, the bone of contention seems most often to be the central concept of self-interest. A system committed to the principle that individuals are best placed to judge their real interests for themselves may be accused of institutionalizing selfishness and greed—but only on the premise that individuals are so depraved that they never make any other choice.

The founders of democratic capitalism did not believe that such depravity is universal. Furthermore, they held that the laws of free economic markets are such that the real interests of individuals are best served in the long run by a systematic refusal to take short-term advantage. Apart from internal restraints, the system itself places restraints upon greed and narrowly constructed self-interest. Greed and selfishness, when they occur, are made to have their costs. A firm aware of its long-term fiduciary responsibilities to its shareholders must protect its investments for future generations. It must change with the times. It must maintain a reputation for reliability, integrity, and fairness. In one large family trucking firm, for example, the last generation of owners kept too much in profits and invested too little in new technologies and new procedures, with the result that their heirs received a battered company unable to compete or to solve its cash-flow problems. Thus a firm committed to greed unleashes social forces that will sooner or later destroy it. Spasms of greed will disturb its own inner disciplines, corrupt its executives, anger its patrons, injure the morale of its workers, antagonize its suppliers and purchasers, embolden its competitors, and attract public retribution. In a free society, such spasms must be expected; they must also be opposed.

The real interests of individuals, furthermore, are seldom merely self-regarding. To most persons, their families mean more than their own interests; they frequently subordinate the latter to the former. Their communities are also important to them. In the human breast, commitments to benevolence, fellow-feeling, and sympathy are strong. Moreover, humans have the capacity to see themselves as others see them, and to hold themselves to standards which transcend their own selfish inclinations. Thus the "self" in self-interest is complex, at once familial and communitarian as well as individual, other-regarding as well as self-regarding, cooperative as well as independent, and self-judging as well as self-loving. Understood too narrowly, self-interest destroys firms as surely as it destroys personal lives. Understood broadly enough, as a set of realistic limits, it is a key to all the virtues, as prudence is.

Like prudence in Aristotelian thought, self-interest in democratic capitalist thought has an inferior reputation among moralists. Thus it is necessary to stress again that a *society* may not work well if all its members act always from benevolent intentions. On the other hand, democratic capitalism as a system deliberately enables many persons to do well by doing good (or even purporting to do good). It offers incentives of power, fame, and money to reformers and moralists.

The economic system of democratic capitalism depends to an extraordinary extent upon the social capacities of the human person. Its system of inheritance respects the familial character of motivation. Its corporate pattern reflects the necessity of shared risks and shared rewards. Its divisions both of labor and of specialization reflect the demands of teamwork and association. Its separated churches and autonomous universities reflect the importance of independent moral communities. The ideology of individualism, too much stressed by some proponents and some opponents alike, disguises the essential communitarian character of its system. . . .

In brief, the term "self-interest" encodes a view of human liberty that far exceeds self-regard, selfishness, acquisitiveness, and greed. Adam Smith attempted to suggest this by speaking of *rational* self-interest, by which he meant a specification of human consciousness not only intelligent and judgmental, beyond the sphere of mere desire or self-regard, but also guided by the ideal of objectivity. In *The Theory of Moral Sentiments* (1759), he argued that what is truly rational must be seen to be so not merely from the point of view of the self-interested party but from that of a disinterested rational observer as well. He called the achievement of such realistic judgment "the perfection of human nature." The whole system, as he imagined it, is aimed toward the acquisition of such realism: "We endeavour to examine our own conduct as we imagine any other fair and impartial spectator would examine it." Again: "To feel much for others, and little for ourselves . . . to restrain our selfish, and to indulge our benevolent, affections, constitutes the perfection of human nature."[5]

Democratic capitalism, then, rests on a complex theory of sin. While recognizing ineradicable sinful tendencies in every human, it does not count humans depraved. While recognizing that no system of political economy can escape the ravages of human sinfulness, it has attempted to set in place a system which renders sinful tendencies as productive of good as possible. While basing itself on something less than perfect virtue, reasoned self-interest, it has attempted to draw from self-interest its most creative potential. It is a system designed for sinners, in the hope of achieving as much moral good as individuals and communities can generate under conditions of ample liberty.

Can human society imitate Providence?

PROFIT AND COMMERICAL VALUES

While markets encourage the exercise of choice, they stand accused of corrupting morals. Money, markets, and profits are this worldly, not otherworldly, terms. They seem to symbolize Mammon, and to run against the perfectionist strain in Christianity. As Irving Kristol has pointed out, certain Christian traditions reflect hostility to commerce unknown in Jewish traditions.[6] Just as some forms of Christianity have harbored excessively negative attitudes toward sex, so some also harbor negative attitudes toward monetary commerce. In particular, the long tradition of hostility toward lending money for profit ("usury") seems to have spilled over into moral antipathy toward profit. "Is the profit motive compatible with humane purposes?" is for some a slow-pitch question whose answer is in the resounding negative.

Yet commerce is not without its own moral structure. The inventors of democratic capitalism—Montesquieu, John Adams, Adam Smith, Benjamin Franklin, Benjamin Rush, James Madison, Thomas Jefferson, and others were not themselves primarily men of commerce or manufacturing. . . . In trying to imagine a "new order," the founders of democratic capitalism considered the historical record. They found serious structural difficulties in the civic orders of ancient Greece and Rome, in those of the Holy Roman Empire, and in the various anciens régimes of their experience. In the old regimes, "the king had his glory, the nobles their honor, the Christians their salvation, the citizens of pagan antiquity their ambition."[7] In all such orders, privileges were preserved for too few. Contemplating the historical parade of aristocratic pretension, religious persecution, cults of heroism and glory, and the public presumption of deference to the powerful, the founders of democratic capitalism thought these bred "extravagant rashness and folly," and were at bottom "absurd."[8] Although each of the old orders of political economy appealed to high ideals of disinterestedness, nobility, and honor, these masked much "avidity and injustice" in high places. Based upon human ideals too high for the ordinary mundane business of life, their perfectionism was out of touch with reality. Under their influence, over many centuries, the lot of the ordinary mass of humanity had scarcely advanced at all.

The old orders endowed each man of high birth and inherited status with false notions of "self-sufficiency and absurd conceit of his own superiority."[9] They sold too short the capacities of commoners to direct their own activities, to form their own practical judgments, and to make their own choices. Moreover, they overlooked the tremendous economic potential of practicality, inventiveness, and enterprise on the part of free individuals.

Aristocratic pride produces no wealth, Adam Smith argued. Even from situations of great original wealth, it produces laziness, extravagance, poverty, and ruin. Spain and Portugal did not become rich from the enormous wealth they expropriated from the mines of South America; they were propelled, instead, upon historical decline. Aristocratic taste with its preference for elegance may generate high art, works of beauty, palaces and churches ornately decorated in silver and gold. But, corrupting practical wisdom, it in the end impoverishes.

Thus, the founding fathers rejected aristocratic morals in favor of the common, the useful, the mundane. Favorite words in their new vocabulary were "common sense" and "utility," which they thought to be in tune with the plain teaching of the gospels. In the essay of which I have been making extensive use in this section, Ralph Lerner speaks not of democratic capitalism but of "the commercial republic," a republic which places the moral qualities required for successful commerce at the center of its social life. In such a republic, commerce is by no means the whole of life. Yet in it commerce is given greater freedom, and its prospering is made to be more central to the purposes of the state than in any previous form of civic order.

The ethic of commerce furnishes a school of virtue favorable to democratic governance. This ethic is not pretentious in its conception of reason and human nature. It enhances the cooperative spirit, since economic tasks cannot be accomplished by one person alone. It increases attention to law. It singles out the self-determination of the individual as the main source of social energy. It places limits on the state and other authorities. It incites imagination and industry. It disciplines all to common sense. It teaches respect for "an exact attention to small savings and small gains"[10] which, in turn, are the single most significant engine of sustained economic growth, since progress takes place at the margins and depends upon increments of new investment and new invention. It breaks the grip of those high utopian ideals of earlier civic orders which, while pretending to represent Reason in one or another of its lofty forms, proved in fact to be so impoverishing for real people. It is a system in tune with emergent probability, the limitations of human intelligence, and the unreliability of the human heart. The ethic of commerce is proportioned to man as he is, not as dreams would have him, and plainly appeared to the founders to support "the natural system of liberty and justice."

Early travelers to America observed this "new order" in practice. De Tocqueville noted that everywhere in America citizens were "calculating and weighing and computing."[11] Since practical intelligence yields tangible progress, men and women had an incentive to acquire it, to become savvy, to develop each of their crafts to new heights of inventiveness and effect. In Europe, the code of the gentleman required that one not appear to be too industrious, intent, or sweaty in one's work; everything, it was thought, ought to appear effortless, spontaneous, natural. In America, the market taught men and women to roll up their sleeves, to dirty their hands, and to shrug off "that inconsiderate contempt for practice" typical of aristocrats. European attitudes may have required contempt for crass practicalities and respect for loftiness of station. In America, even the landed gentry took pride in physical labor and attention to practical detail. . . .

A commercial civilization breaks the monopoly of public service enjoyed by the great. Even the humblest person has opportunity both to improve his station and to enrich the republic. Ambition courses through millions who, under other regimes, would seem sullen and inert. Individuals set goals for themselves—to be a master carpenter, or foreman, or linesman, whatever each might rationally aspire to—and enjoy the satisfaction of self-improvement, whereas the aristocrat "shudders with horror at the thought of . . . continued and long exertion of patience, industry, fortitude and application of thought."[12] More romantic social orders stimulate great passions, de Tocqueville observed, but citizens in a commercial republic exhibit love of order, regard for conventional morality, distrust of genius, and preference for the practical over the theoretical. "Violent political passions have little hold on men whose whole thoughts are bent on the pursuit of well being. Their excitement about small matters makes them calm about great ones."[13] But this is not exactly right. For trade and navigation are seen to be surrogates for war. Great deeds and heroic exertions are borne, not solely for the self, but usually for family and often for the pure achievement of the thing. The man of commerce treats all of life "like a game of chance, a time of revolution, or the day of a battle."[14] Building industries where none stood before yields creative satisfactions.

In the new order, ordinary people feel a lift in self-esteem. Their aspirations realistically reach higher than their fathers'. Their efforts, not in every case but in a sufficiently large number of cases, have continued to be rewarded. Their personal goals, if proportional to their abilities, have a good chance of being realized. Self-realization becomes a common aim. Commerce also teaches that no one can be right all the time, since nearly all sometimes experience failure. The market puts a ceiling on ambition, proportional to each. Not all succeed equally. Luck and timing play important roles. The market raises up many who under other regimes were last, and tumbles many who in earlier regimes were first. New cycles of progress and technological development continue this process. The resulting social system is highly mobile and fluid, compared to others.

A market system entails great human losses. For realists, this was a foregone conclusion. Montesquieu counted the cost of old communal ties, which would be replaced by the less effective ties of mutual interests in liberty and order. Adam Smith was even more aware of the human losses to be expected. The new order would narrow and demean the human spirit, such that the "heroic spirit" would be "almost entirely extinguished."[15] The rapacity of some merchants would lead them to try to close open markets through monopolistic practices. Competitive markets are not sustained by magic; they must be maintained through vigilance on the part of the public and the state. The division of labor would force some into tasks that would mutilate their minds, encourage gross ignorance and stupidity, and corrupt "the nobler parts of human character."[16] Society would have to find compensatory means to redress these injustices; the market alone would not do that. Moreover, since every virtue may be corrupted, the commercial virtues may degenerate into avarice, social meanness, cowardice, and hedonism. Since the greater dangers lay in the indolence and extravagance of aristocracy, in the intolerance of the clergy, and in the despotism of the state, these costs can be borne; but they must be seen to be costs. . . .

The commercial virtues are not, then, sufficient to their own defense. A commercial system needs taming and correction by a moral-cultural system independent of commerce. At critical points, it also requires taming and correction by the political system and the state. The founding fathers did not imagine that the institutions of religion, humanism, and the arts would ever lose their indispensable role. They did not imagine that the state would wither away. Each of the three systems needs the other.

Yet they did understand that an economic system without profit is merely spinning its wheels, providing neither for the unmet needs of the poor nor for progress. Even "small gains and small savings" have extraordinary impact. A growth rate averaging just 2 percent a year was sustained in Great Britain from 1780 until 1914,[17] and made that tiny nation the world's leading power. To have invented a system capable of such sustained development was a gain for humanity. For in the wake of economic development came political and moral-cultural developments of great importance, including a great flowering of individual possibility, the arts, and good works (including many not for profit).

Thus, neither commercial virtues nor profits are merely economic in their character or in their effects. On the other hand, they are not sufficient for a full human life. They play an indispensable role in the achievement of the common good, and societies which lack them struggle in swamps of hopelessness unknown to those that possess them. One may believe the commercial virtues to be less than the highest of virtues, but it is not contrary to biblical faith to honor them for their instrumental role.

COMMUNITY IN PRACTICE

Between individualism and collectivism, there is a third way: a rich pattern of association. Just because individuals are not collectivized it does not follow that they are not communal. . . .

For example, my wife and I found a memoir written some ninety years ago by an ancestor of hers. He was Charles E. Brown, the first Baptist missionary in the Iowa Territory, who journeyed westward with his family from Upstate New York in 1842. One of the most stunning features of his memoir is that nearly all the daily activities he reports were cooperative and fraternal. Families helped each other putting up homes and barns. Together, they built churches, schools, and common civic buildings. They collaborated to build roads and bridges. They took pride in being free persons, independent, and self-reliant; but the texture of their lives was cooperative and fraternal.

These pioneer experiences of fraternity were not unlike those of later waves of immigrants, who began coming to America about 1870, notably to the minefields and smaller industrial cities of the northeast. They too lived richly communal lives. They built fraternals, lodges, and associations of many sorts. They too built many of their own homes and common buildings. While it is true that many of them left Europe as individuals, breaking from their own families, their lives in America continued to be intensely familial and associative. Many were active in the labor unions. Virtually all were active in churches, clubs, and many other associations. The experience of my wife's family and mine were not, then, those of "rugged individuals" alone.

It is true that life in America was rather less tribal, less limited to kin, and less homogeneous than in Europe. Neighborhoods and villages tended to be "melting pots" or, as some were later to say, "little leagues of nations." Both the public and the parochial schools tended to unite persons of many diverse backgrounds and linguistic traditions. The idea of fraternity was sharply real. It was not without friction.

The great mobility and patterns of opportunity in America began, however, to change the nature and meaning of community. For many, there still remained many forms of *Gemeinschaft*, that closeness of belonging, kinship, and common memory and faith which their ancestors had known in Europe. Yet every American family has also known the experience of uprooting, often more than once, and virtually all have been aware that their neighbors and friends in the New World belong to kinship networks, cultures, religions, and races different from their own. Pluralism is part of everyday experience. The huge dislocations of World War II, moreover, dramatically introduced even previously distant groups of Americans to one another in military service, in travel, at work. Lads from mining towns and city ghettoes took basic training in the South, visited California, served abroad.

In the years following World War II, mobility and interchange increased. Through these changes, the American people in all their variety continued to manifest loyalties to family, to civic life, and to countless forms of association. Yet in their freedom they have also experienced much rupture of close ties, many separations, and significant loneliness.

One reason problems of community are so acute among Americans is that most of us live between two experiences. More than is commonly thought, a great many of us have known a strong familial, neighborhood, and village life. We are fairly close to the experience of traditional societies known to our grandparents. On the other hand, we know new liberties. This is especially true of those more highly educated professionals whose jobs may carry them anywhere in the nation or the world. Such freedom disciplines the human spirit to the kind of "detachment" which religious superiors used to preach to young priests and religious. The latter's frequent changes of assignment, they were instructed, would oblige them to be uprooted often and to disrupt close human associations many times. They would accept these disciplines for the common good and for their own inner development.

This example shows that "community" is a reality of many kinds. My wife often teases me that I could be happy anywhere, as long as I could have my books and some writing paper. This made me recognize that many of my best friends and kindred spirits—whose books I lug with me from place to place—have been dead for hundreds of years. There are real communities of the spirit, which we carry with us even in solitude. At the Catholic Mass, as in the Jewish sabbath services, one recalls consciously that one is part of a community stretching across thousands of years. Intimate proximity is not essential to community.

In our sentimental age, however, there is a tendency to desire a different sort of community, less a community of the spirit and the inner life than a community of sentiment, emotional support, and often expressed intimacy. Such communities are no doubt precious, but they are also often dubious, cloying, and imprisoning. Community is not a simple reality. The much celebrated "loss of community" is not, correspondingly, all loss.

There is one form of community worth stressing here. It is a community of colleagueship, task-oriented, goal-directed, freely entered into and freely left. Its members have much respect for each other, learn much from each other, come to expect truth from each other, and treat one another fairly. Still, they may not have much emotional attachment to each other, spend much time looking into each other's eyes for moral support, or be particularly intimate with one another. They may enjoy comradeship in fighting the same battles, in enduring together the slings of hostile fortune, and in taking up each other's necessities.

Such community is not like the closeness of medieval villagers, nor does it require having the same faith, worldview, or vision of reality. There are "bands of brothers" who do not occupy the same metaphysical ground. Add to this form of community many years of comradeship, growing mutual esteem, and the competitive urging of each other to new heights of development, and one experiences within it a form of friendship not unknown to the ancients, yet quite distinctively modern. For much modern work requires intense collaboration over long periods of time with skilled and dedicated colleagues. Democratic capitalism is not, I think, inferior in nurturing many such communities. Sports offer an approximation through extended experiences of teamwork. Later life goes far beyond sports.

Thus, in discussing community, I have found it useful to ask: According to which ideal? The sorts of community known to villages and neighborhoods are quite admirable, but they have their own limitations and liabilities. Affective communities which seek to vibrate together on compatible wavelengths also have their attractions and their limits. Collective solidarity seems strong and ennobling; yet it renders dissent and individual difference suspect. Communities of "joy, love and hope"—to cite the words of one contemporary Catholic hymn—inspire gladness but seem superficial. (Psalms of grief, enmity, and despair strike me as truer, deeper, more reliable.)

In order to experience the community of colleagueship, one needs an ethos deeper than individualism and collectivism, an ethos of association, teamwork, and collaboration, oriented by tasks and goals, voluntarily entered into. The ethos of democratic capitalism is rich in such encouragement. This is not the only form of community, but it is a noble one. It is not, however, given. It must be created.

Thus the social life of Americans remains so associative that it is often difficult to get parents and children to sit down together for one meal each day. Eight-year-olds belong to more groups than two parents can supply drivers for. During political campaigns, strangers from all parts of the country converge on states like Iowa and New Hampshire and, without delay, establish patterns of teamwork and swift cooperation. . . .

I do not mean to pen a rhapsody to the social life of America. There is much wrong with it. Yet it would be wrong to be entirely silent about the distinctive forms of community it does build. The experiences America has given to my family, and to many millions of other families, have been so rich in opportunity, in possibility, in dream, that they cannot easily be fathomed. The enormous wealth produced by a free system sometimes masks these social benefits from our sight.

In *Socialism*, Michael Harrington observes that many of the spiritual realities intended by the name "socialism" have been realized under another name, the name "America."[18] Among these are not only political democracy and opportunity, but also marvelously strong traditions of family and association, cooperation and fraternity. A pluralistic society, in particular, draws out in each of us skills in tolerance, collaboration, and mutual respect that are all the more remarkable when compared to the still-bitter antagonisms between groups, religions, and cultures in the lands from which we are derived. . . .

. . . The life of the spirit is far from stifled by democratic capitalism, but in the absence of strong moral guidance, it is often squandered. Our moral-cultural institutions do their job less well than our economic institutions do theirs. The twain are not yet matched. We need a spirituality appropriate for democratic capitalism as it is, and we do not have it.

Some common misperceptions seem to block us from even starting to acquire it. When I think of the many families in America known to me, most of the descriptions of Americans common to sociological and literary conventions do not seem to fit. In particular, descriptions like "the consumer society," "greed," and "materialism" seem very wide of the mark. These are not saintly families, only ordinary human beings. Yet the more one knows about them, the deeper and more worthy of respect they seem to be. If we would help them to become better than they are, we must at least come to know them as they are. Their generosity may be historically unparalleled. It is a generosity not of financial giving only but of an enormous network of volunteer activities. Faced with a problem, Americans almost by instinct form a committee. Their contributions to humanitarian purposes around the world and to their neighbors are not inferior to those of traditional or socialist societies.[19] . . .

It is sometimes said that capitalism introduces a "competitive" system, a "rat race," "dog-eat-dog." One does not notice that athletes from socialist nations are any less competitive than those from democratic capitalist lands. Nor is the competition for political power in socialist states any less fearsome than the competition for the more various forms of power open to the citizens of democratic capitalist societies. Still, most persons in America do *not* seem to want to rise to the top. Many compete mostly with themselves.

They set goals for themselves and try to realize them in their own way and at their own pace. Taking it easy, playing it as it comes, easy does it—these attributes seem to be at least as widely celebrated and realized as the competitive drive. Individuals choose their own roads—even children from one family go in multiple directions.

The ideal of a democratic capitalist society is to guarantee the right of each person to pursue happiness. (Happiness itself is not guaranteed.) Thus the system as a whole must be open to enormous variety. It must afford satisfactions at work as well as in free time. Since it is in the nature of humans to be social, the ideal is also to build decent and even affectionate relations among those who work together. For many Americans, there is almost as much friendship and mutuality with colleagues or buddies on the job as in the family. Indeed, for some, there may be a larger store of shared values with workmates than with the whole extended family at Thanksgiving dinner, at which they must sit down with persons whose politics they abhor, whose religious views they cannot abide, and whose occupational biases, ideas, values, and even social class may be far removed from their own. We may within limits choose our communities.

In short, even the economic system within democratic capitalism has its own internal impulses toward community, though of a different sort than any known before. Concerning these, we need far more careful thought than anywhere is yet in evidence. They have produced a new type of human being, the communitarian individual. Perhaps we have not seen what is around us because we are too close to it—and have learned too many clichés about the bourgeois man and woman, the middle class, ourselves.

Notes

1. Henry Hazlitt, *The Conquest of Poverty* (New Rochelle, N.Y.: Arlington House, 1973), pp. 13–18.
2. See Paul Johnson, "Has Capitalism a Future?" in *Will Capitalism Survive?* ed. Ernest W. Lefever (Washington, D.C.: Ethics and Public Policy Center, 1979), p. 5.
3. Johnson, "Has Capitalism a Future?"
4. Irving Kristol, *Two Cheers for Capitalism* (New York: Basic Books, 1978), pp. 262, 270.
5. Adam Smith, *The Theory of Moral Sentiments* (Indianapolis: Liberty Classics, 1969), pp. 204, 71.
6. See Irving Kristol, "The Spiritual Roots of Capitalism and Socialism," in *Capitalism and Socialism: A Theological Inquiry*, ed. Michael Novak (Washington, D.C.: American Enterprise Institute, 1979), p. 1.
7. Ralph Lerner, "Commerce and Character: The Anglo-American as New-Model Man," *William and Mary Quarterly* 36 (January 1979); 3–26; see p. 5.
8. Smith, *The Theory of Moral Sentiments*, pp. 407, 416.
9. Ibid., p. 416.
10. Ibid., p. 364.
11. See de Tocqueville, *Democracy in America*, pp. 400–07.
12. Smith, *The Theory of Moral Sentiments*, see Lerner, p. 16.
13. De Tocqueville, *Democracy in America*, see Lerner, pp. 16–17.
14. Ibid., p. 404.
15. Smith, *Wealth of Nations*, see Lerner, p. 22. Elsewhere Smith criticizes certain landlords with withering contempt: "All for ourselves, and nothing for other people, seems, in every age of the world, to have been the vile maxim of the masters of mankind." *Wealth of Nations*, pp. 388–89.
16. See Joseph A. Schumpeter, *Capitalism, Socialism and Democracy*, 3d ed. (New York: Harper & Row, 1950), esp. the section entitled "The Sociology of the Intellectual," pp. 145–55.
17. See Johnson, "Has Capitalism a Future?" p. 4.
18. See Michael Harrington, *Socialism* (New York: Saturday Review Press, 1972), p. 118.
19. In 1978 Americans contributed $39.6 billion in private philanthropic funds, including $32.8 billion contributed by individuals, and the remainder by foundations, corporations, and bequests; see U.S. Bureau of the Census, *Statistical Abstract of the United States: 1979*, 100th ed. (Washington, D.C.: 1979), table 582.

A Libertarian Defense of the Market

Robert Nozick

Robert Nozick begins with a strong commitment to prepolitical individual rights—rights that may not be transgressed by others, either as individuals or collectively as the state. Commonly called *negative rights*, they constitute "side constraints" on the actions of others, ensuring a person's freedom from interference in the pursuit of his or her own life. These rights are negative because they require only that others refrain from acting in certain ways, in particular, that they refrain from interfering with people as they pursue their own lives. Beyond this, no one should be forced to do anything positive for us; we have no right, for example, to require others to provide us with satisfying work or with any material goods we might need. Each individual is to be seen as autonomous and responsible and should be left to fashion his or her own life free from the interference of others. Only the acknowledgment of this almost absolute right to be free from coercion, argues Nozick, fully respects the distinctiveness of persons, each with a unique life to lead.

This framework of individual rights and corresponding duties constitutes the basis of what power the government may legitimately have. In Nozick's view, the only morally legitimate state is the so-called *night-watchman state*, one whose functions are restricted to protecting the negative rights of citizens, that is, to protecting them against force, theft, fraud, and so on. In the selection that follows, Nozick is especially concerned with rejecting the claim that a larger state is necessary in order to achieve a just economic distribution.

In contrast to theories he calls "end-state" and "patterned," Nozick proposes the entitlement theory of justice. According to this theory, a distribution is just if it arises from a prior just distribution by just means. Thus, as Locke also argued, unowned resources may be acquired originally by taking something from nature, subject to the proviso that others are not harmed by the taking. And, once legitimately owned, there is only a limited number of ways of legitimately transferring justly acquired objects—gifts and voluntary exchange are among them; theft and blackmail are not. There is, however, no pattern to which a just distribution should conform. In the absence of force and fraud, people may freely do what they wish with their holdings. Taxation for purposes of redistribution, he then argues, is on a par with forced labor. That is because taking the product of a person's labor is doing something very like requiring forced labor. In the final section, "The Tale of a Slave," Nozick creates an imaginary series of events meant to illustrate his argument. Robert Nozick teaches philosophy at Harvard University. He is the author of numerous books including *Philosophical Explanations* and *The Examined Life* (part of which is reprinted later in this text).

As you read through this essay, consider the following:

1. Why does Nozick think that the notion of "distributive justice" is misleading?
2. What are the three topics that, according to Nozick, constitute the subject of justice in holdings?
3. How does Nozick distinguish historical from end-result principles?
4. What is a patterned principle?
5. How does Nozick use the Chamberlain example to explain his argument that no patterned principle is compatible with freedom?
6. In what way does Nozick think taxation is comparable to forced labor?
7. How would you answer the question at the end of Nozick's essay?

The term "distributive justice" is not a neutral one. Hearing the term "distribution," most people presume that some thing or mechanism uses some principle or criterion to give out a supply of things. Into this process of distributing shares some error may have crept. So it is an open question, at least, whether *re*distribution should take place; whether we should do again what has already been done once, though poorly. However, we are not in the position of children who have been given portions of pie by someone who now makes last minute adjustments to rectify careless cutting. There is no *central* distribution, no person or group entitled to control all the resources, jointly deciding how they are to be doled out. What each person gets, he gets from others who give to him in exchange for something, or as a gift. In a free society, diverse persons control different resources, and new holdings arise out of the voluntary exchanges and actions of persons. There is no more a distributing or distribution of shares than there is a distributing of mates in a society in which persons choose whom they shall marry. The total result is the product of many individual decisions which the different individuals involved are entitled to make. . . . We shall speak of people's holdings; a principle of justice in holdings describes (part of) what justice tells us (requires) about holdings. I shall state first what I take to be the correct view about justice in holdings, and then turn to the discussion of alternate views.

THE ENTITLEMENT THEORY

The subject of justice in holdings consists of three major topics. The first is the *original acquisition of holdings*, the appropriation of unheld things. This includes the issues of how

unheld things may come to be held, the process, or processes, by which unheld things may come to be held, the things that may come to be held by these processes, the extent of what comes to be held by a particular process, and so on. We shall refer to the complicated truth about this topic, which we shall not formulate here, as the principle of justice in acquisition. The second topic concerns the *transfer of holdings* from one person to another. By what processes may a person transfer holdings to another? How may a person acquire a holding from another who holds it? Under this topic come general descriptions of voluntary exchange, and gift and (on the other hand) fraud, as well as reference to particular conventional details fixed upon in a given society. The complicated truth about this subject (with placeholders for conventional details) we shall call the principle of justice in transfer. (And we shall suppose it also includes principles governing how a person may divest himself of a holding, passing it into an unheld state.)

If the world were wholly just, the following inductive definition would exhaustively cover the subject of justice in holdings.

1. A person who acquires a holding in accordance with the principle of justice in acquisition is entitled to that holding.
2. A person who acquires a holding in accordance with the principle of justice in transfer, from someone else entitled to the holding, is entitled to the holding.
3. No one is entitled to a holding except by (repeated) applications of 1 and 2.

The complete principle of distributive justice would say simply that a distribution is just if everyone is entitled to the holdings they possess under the distribution.

A distribution is just if it arises from another just distribution by legitimate means. The legitimate means of moving from one distribution to another are specified by the principle of justice in transfer. The legitimate first "moves" are specified by the principle of justice in acquisition. Whatever arises from a just situation by just steps is itself just. The means of change specified by the principle of justice in transfer preserve justice. . . .

Not all actual situations are generated in accordance with the two principles of justice in holdings: the principle of justice in acquisition and the principle of justice in transfer. Some people steal from others, or defraud them, or enslave them, seizing their product and preventing them from living as they choose, or forcibly exclude others from competing in exchanges. None of these are permissible modes of transition from one situation to another. And some persons acquire holdings by means not sanctioned by the principle of justice in acquisition. The existence of past injustice (previous violations of the first two principles of justice in holdings) raises the third major topic under justice in holdings: the rectification of injustice in holdings. If past injustice has shaped present holdings in various ways, some identifiable and some not, what now, if anything, ought to be done to rectify these injustices? What obligations do the performers of injustice have toward those whose position is worse than it would have been had the injustice not been done? Or, than it would have been had compensation been paid promptly? How, if at all, do things change if the beneficiaries and those made worse off are not the direct parties in the act of injustice, but, for example, their descendants? Is an injustice done to someone whose holding was itself based upon an unrectified injustice? How far back must one go in wiping clean the historical slate of injustices? What may victims of injustice permissibly do in order to rectify the injustices being done to them, including the many injustices done by persons acting through their government? I do not know of a thorough or theoretically sophisticated treatment of such issues. Idealizing greatly, let us suppose theoretical investigation will produce a principle of rectification. This principle uses historical information about previous situations and injustices done in them (as defined by the first two principles of justice and rights against interference), and information about the actual course of events that flowed from

these injustices, until the present, and it yields a description (or descriptions) of holdings in the society. The principle of rectification presumably will make use of its best estimate of subjunctive information about what would have occurred (or a probability distribution over what might have occurred, using the expected value) if the injustice had not taken place. If the actual description of holdings turns out not to be one of the descriptions yielded by the principle, then one of the descriptions yielded must be realized.

The general outlines of the theory of justice in holdings are that the holdings of a person are just if he is entitled to them by the principles of justice in acquisition and transfer, or by the principle of rectification of injustice (as specified by the first two principles). If each person's holdings are just, then the total set (distribution) of holdings is just. . . .

HISTORICAL PRINCIPLES AND END-RESULT PRINCIPLES

The general outlines of the entitlement theory illuminate the nature and defects of other conceptions of distributive justice. The entitlement theory of justice in distribution is *historical;* whether a distribution is just depends upon how it came about. In contrast, *current time-slice principles* of justice hold that the justice of a distribution is determined by how things are distributed (who has what) as judged by some *structural* principle(s) of just distribution. A utilitarian who judges between any two distributions by seeing which has the greater sum of utility and, if the sums tie, applies some fixed equality criterion to choose the more equal distribution, would hold a current time-slice principle of justice. . . .

Most persons do not accept current time-slice principles as constituting the whole story about distributive shares. They think it relevant in assessing the justice of a situation to consider not only the distribution it embodies, but also how that distribution came about. If some persons are in prison for murder or war crimes, we do not say that to assess the justice of the distribution in the society we must look only at what this person has, and that person has, and that person has, . . . at the current time. We think it relevant to ask whether someone did something so that he *deserved* to be punished, deserved to have a lower share. Most will agree to the relevance of further information with regard to punishments and penalties. Consider also desired things. One traditional socialist view is that workers are entitled to the product and full fruits of their labor; they have earned it; a distribution is unjust if it does not give the workers what they are entitled to. Such entitlements are based upon some past history. No socialist holding this view would find it comforting to be told that because the actual distribution *A* happens to coincide structurally with the one he desires *D*, *A* therefore is no less just than *D*; it differs only in that the "parasitic" owners of capital receive under *A* what the workers are entitled to under *D*, and the workers receive under *A* what the owners are entitled to under *D*, namely very little. This socialist rightly, in my view, holds onto the notions of earning, producing, entitlement, desert, and so forth, and he rejects current time-slice principles that look only to the structure of the resulting set of holdings. (The set of holdings resulting from what? Isn't it implausible that how holdings are produced and come to exist has no effect at all on who should hold what?) His mistake lies in his view of what entitlements arise out of what sorts of productive processes.

We construe the position we discuss too narrowly by speaking of *current* time-slice principles. Nothing is changed if structural principles operate upon a time sequence of current time-slice profiles and, for example, give someone more now to counterbalance the less he has had earlier. . . . Henceforth, we shall refer to such unhistorical principles of distributive justice, including the current time-slice principles, as *end-result principles* or *end-state principles*.

In contrast to end-result principles of justice, *historical principles* of justice hold that past circumstances or actions of people can create differential entitlements or differential deserts to things. . . .

PATTERNING

The entitlement principles of justice in holdings that we have sketched are historical principles of justice. To better understand their precise character, we shall distinguish them from another subclass of the historical principles. Consider, as an example, the principle of distribution according to moral merit. This principle requires that total distributive shares vary directly with moral merit; no person should have a greater share than anyone whose moral merit is greater. (If moral merit could be not merely ordered but measured on an interval or ratio scale, stronger principles could be formulated.) Or consider the principle that results by substituting "usefulness to society" for "moral merit" in the previous principle. . . . The principle of distribution in accordance with moral merit is a patterned historical principle, which specifies a patterned distribution. "Distribute according to I.Q." is a patterned principle that . . . is not historical, however, in that it does not look to any past actions creating differential entitlements to evaluate a distribution; it requires only distributional matrices whose columns are labeled by I.Q. scores. The distribution in a society, however, may be composed of such simple patterned distributions, without itself being simply patterned. Different sectors may operate different patterns, or some combination of patterns may operate in different proportions across a society. A distribution composed in this manner, from a small number of patterned distributions, we also shall term "patterned." And we extend the use of "pattern" to include the overall designs put forth by combinations of end-state principles.

Almost every suggested principle of distributive justice is patterned: to each according to his moral merit, or needs, or marginal product, or how hard he tries, or the weighted sum of the foregoing, and so on. The principle of entitlement we have sketched is *not* patterned. There is no one natural dimension or weighted sum or combination of a small number of natural dimensions that yields the distributions generated in accordance with the principle of entitlement. The set of holdings that results when some persons receive their marginal products, others win at gambling, others receive a share of their mate's income, others receive gifts from foundations, others receive interest on loans, others receive gifts from admirers, others receive returns on investment, others make for themselves much of what they have, others find things, and so on, will not be patterned. . . .

HOW LIBERTY UPSETS PATTERNS

It is not clear how those holding alternative conceptions of distributive justice can reject the entitlement conception of justice in holdings. For suppose a distribution favored by one of these nonentitlement conceptions is realized. Let us suppose it is your favorite one and let us call this distribution D_1; perhaps everyone has an equal share, perhaps shares vary in accordance with some dimension you treasure. Now suppose that Wilt Chamberlain is greatly in demand by basketball teams, being a great gate attraction. (Also suppose contracts run only for a year, with players being free agents.) He signs the following sort of contract with a team: In each home game, twenty-five cents from the price of each ticket of admission goes to him. (We ignore the question of whether he is "gouging" the owners, letting them look out for themselves.) The season starts, and people cheerfully attend his team's games; they buy their tickets, each time dropping a separate twenty-five cents of their admission price into a special box with Chamberlain's name on it. They are excited about seeing him play; it is worth the total admission price to them. Let us suppose that in one season

one million persons attend his home games, and Wilt Chamberlain winds up with $250,000, a much larger sum than the average income and larger even than anyone else has. Is he entitled to this income? Is this new distribution D_2, unjust? If so, why? There is *no* question about whether each of the people was entitled to the control over the resources they held in D_1; because that was the distribution (your favorite) that (for the purposes of argument) we assumed was acceptable. Each of these persons chose to give twenty-five cents of their money to Chamberlain. They could have spent it on going to the movies, or on candy bars, or on copies of *Dissent* magazine, or of *Monthly Review*. But they all, at least one million of them, converged on giving it to Wilt Chamberlain in exchange for watching him play basketball. If D_1 was a just distribution, and people voluntarily moved from it to D_2, transferring parts of their shares they were given under D_1 (what was it for if not to do something with?), isn't D_2 also just? If the people were entitled to dispose of the resources to which they were entitled (under D_1), didn't this include their being entitled to give it to, or exchange it with, Wilt Chamberlain? Can anyone else complain on grounds of justice? Each other person already has his legitimate share under D_1. Under D_1, there is nothing that anyone has that anyone else has a claim of justice against. After someone transfers something to Wilt Chamberlain, third parties *still* have their legitimate shares; *their* shares are not changed. By what process could such a transfer among two persons give rise to a legitimate claim of distributive justice on a portion of what was transferred, by a third party who had no claim of justice on any holding of the others *before* the transfer? . . .

The general point illustrated by the Wilt Chamberlain example . . . is that no end-state principle or distributional-patterned principle of justice can be continuously realized without continuous interference with people's lives. Any favored pattern would be transformed into one unfavored by the principle, by people choosing to act in various ways; for example, by people exchanging goods and services with other people, or giving things to other people, things the transferrers are entitled to under the favored distributional pattern. To maintain a pattern one must either continually interfere to stop people from transferring resources as they wish to, or continually (or periodically) interfere to take from some persons resources that others for some reason chose to transfer to them. . . .

REDISTRIBUTION AND PROPERTY RIGHTS

Apparently, patterned principles allow people to choose to spend upon themselves, but not upon others, those resources they are entitled to (or rather, receive) under some favored distributional pattern D_1. For if each of several persons chooses to expend some of his D_1 resources upon one other person, then that other person will receive more than his D_1 share, distributing the favored distributional pattern. Maintaining a distributional pattern is individualism with a vengeance! Patterned distributional principles do not give people what entitlement principles do, only better distributed. For they do not give the right to choose what to do with what one has; they do not give the right to choose to pursue an end involving (intrinsically, or as a means) the enhancement of another's position. To such views, families are disturbing; for within a family occur transfers that upset the favored distributional pattern. Either families themselves become units to which distribution takes place, the column occupiers (on what rationale?), or loving behavior is forbidden. We should note in passing the ambivalent position of radicals toward the family. Its loving relationships are seen as a model to be emulated and extended across the whole society, at the same time that it is denounced as a suffocating institution to be broken and condemned as a focus of parochial concerns that interfere with achieving radical goals. Need we say that it is not appropriate to enforce across the wider society the relationships of love and care appropriate within a family, relationships which are voluntarily undertaken? Incidentally, love is an interesting instance of another relationship that is historical, in that (like justice) it depends upon what actually occurred. An adult may come to love another because of the other's characteristics; but it is the other person, and not the characteristics, that is loved. The love is not transferable to someone else with the same characteristics, even to one who "scores" higher for these characteristics. And the love endures through changes of the characteristics that give rise to it. One loves the particular person one actually encountered. Why love is historical, attaching to persons in this way and not to characteristics, is an interesting and puzzling question.

Proponents of patterned principles of distributive justice focus upon criteria for determining who is to receive holdings; they consider the reasons for which someone should have something, and also the total picture of holdings. Whether or not it is better to give than to receive, proponents of patterned principles ignore giving altogether. In considering the distribution of goods, income, and so forth, their theories are theories of recipient justice; they completely ignore any right a person might have to give something to someone. Even in exchanges where each party is simultaneously giver and recipient, patterned principles of justice focus only upon the recipient role and its supposed rights. Thus discussions tend to focus on whether people (should) have a right to inherit, rather than on whether people (should) have a right to bequeath or on whether persons who have a right to hold also have a right to choose that others hold in their place. I lack a good explanation of why the usual theories of distributive justice are so recipient oriented; ignoring givers and transferrers and their rights is of a piece with ignoring producers and their entitlements. But why is it *all* ignored?

Patterned principles of distributive justice necessitate *re*distributive activities. The likelihood is small that any actual freely-arrived-at set of holdings fits a given pattern;

and the likelihood is nil that it will continue to fit the pattern as people exchange and give. From the point of view of an entitlement theory, redistribution is a serious matter indeed, involving, as it does, the violation of people's rights. (An exception is those takings that fall under the principle of the rectification of injustices.) From other points of view, also, it is serious.

Taxation of earnings from labor is on a par with forced labor.* Some persons find this claim obviously true: taking the earnings of *n* hours labor is like taking *n* hours from the person; it is like forcing the person to work *n* hours for another's purpose. Others find the claim absurd. But even these, *if* they object to forced labor, would oppose forcing unemployed hippies to work for the benefit of the needy. And they would also object to forcing each person to work five extra hours each week for the benefit of the needy. But a system that takes five hours' wages in taxes does not seem to them like one that forces someone to work five hours, since it offers the person forced a wider range of choice in activities than does taxation in kind with the particular labor specified. (But we can imagine a gradation of systems of forced labor, from one that specifies a particular activity, to one that gives a choice among two activities, to . . . ; and so on up.) Furthermore, people envisage a system with something like a proportional tax on everything above the amount necessary for basic needs. Some think this does not force someone to work extra hours, since there is no fixed number of extra hours he is forced to work, and since he can avoid the tax entirely by earning only enough to cover his basic needs. This is a very uncharacteristic view of forcing for those who *also* think people are forced to do

something *whenever* the alternatives they face are considerably worse. However, *neither* view is correct. The fact that others intentionally intervene, in violation of a side constraint against aggression, to threaten force to limit the alternatives, in this case to paying taxes or (presumably the worse alternative) bare subsistence, makes the taxation system one of forced labor and distinguishes it from other cases of limited choices which are not forcings.

The man who chooses to work longer to gain an income more than sufficient for his basic needs prefers some extra goods or services to the leisure and activities he could perform during the possible nonworking hours: whereas the man who chooses not to work the extra time prefers the leisure activities to the extra goods or services he could acquire by working more. Given this, if it would be illegitimate for a tax system to seize some of a man's leisure (forced labor) for the purpose of serving the needy, how can it be legitimate for a tax system to seize some of a man's goods for that purpose? Why should we treat the man whose happiness requires certain material goods or services differently from the man whose preferences and desires make such goods unnecessary for his happiness? Why should the man who prefers seeing a movie (and who has to earn money for a ticket) be open to the required call to aid the needy, while the person who prefers looking at a sunset (and hence need earn no extra money) is not? Indeed, isn't it surprising that redistributionists choose to ignore the man whose pleasures are so easily attainable without extra labor, while adding yet another burden to the poor unfortunate who must work for his pleasures? If anything, one would have expected the reverse. Why is the person with the nonmaterial or nonconsumption desire allowed to proceed unimpeded to his most favored feasible alternative, whereas the man whose pleasures or desires involve material things and who must work for extra money (thereby serving whomever considers his activities valuable enough to pay him) is constrained in what he can realize? Perhaps there is no dif-

---

*I am unsure as to whether the arguments I present below show that such taxation merely is forced labor; so that "is on a par with" means "is one kind of." Or alternatively, whether the arguments emphasize the great similarities between such taxation and forced labor, to show it is plausible and illuminating to view such taxation in the light of forced labor.

ference in principle. And perhaps some think the answer concerns merely administrative convenience. (These questions and issues will not disturb those who think that forced labor to serve the needy or to realize some favored end-state pattern is acceptable.) In a fuller discussion we would have (and want) to extend our argument to include interest, entrepreneurial profits, and so on. Those who doubt that this extension can be carried through, and who draw the line here at taxation of income from labor, will have to state rather complicated patterned *historical* principles of distributive justice, since end-state principles would not distinguish *sources* of income in any way. It is enough for now to get away from end-state principles and to make clear how various patterned principles are dependent upon particular views about the sources or the illegitimacy or the lesser legitimacy of profits, interest, and so on; which particular views may well be mistaken.

What sort of right over others does a legally institutionalized end-state pattern give one? The central core of the notion of a property right in X, relative to which other parts of the notion are to be explained, is the right to determine what shall be done with X; the right to choose which of the constrained set of options concerning X shall be realized or attempted. The constraints are set by other principles or laws operating in the society; in our theory, by the Lockean rights people possess (under the minimal state). My property rights in my knife allow me to leave it where I will, but not in your chest. I may choose which of the acceptable options involving the knife is to be realized. This notion of property helps us to understand why earlier theorists spoke of people as having property in themselves and their labor. They viewed each person as having a right to decide what would become of himself and what he would do, and as having a right to reap the benefits of what he did. . . .

When end-result principles of distributive justice are built into the legal structure of a society, they (as do most patterned principles) give each citizen an enforceable claim to some portion of the total social product; that

is, to some portion of the sum total of the individually and jointly made products. This total product is produced by individuals laboring, using means of production others have saved to bring into existence, by people organizing production or creating means to produce new things or things in a new way. It is on this batch of individual activities that patterned distributional principles give each individual an enforceable claim. Each person has a claim to the activities and the products of other persons, independently of whether the other persons enter into particular relationships that give rise to these claims, and independently of whether they voluntarily take these claims upon themselves, in charity or in exchange for something.

Whether it is done through taxation on wages or on wages over a certain amount, or through seizure of profits, or through there being a big *social pot* so that it's not clear what's coming from where and what's going where, patterned principles of distributive justice involve appropriating the actions of other persons. Seizing the results of someone's labor is equivalent to seizing hours from him and directing him to carry on various activities. If people force you to do certain work, or unrewarded work, for a certain period of time, they decide what you are to do and what purposes your work is to serve apart from your decisions. This process whereby they take this decision from you makes them a *part-owner* of you; it gives them a property right in you. Just as having such partial control and power of decision, by right, over an animal or inanimate object would be to have a property right in it.

End-state and most patterned principles of distributive justice institute (partial) ownership by others of people and their actions and labor. These principles involve a shift from the classical liberals' notion of self-ownership to a notion of (partial) property rights in *other* people. . . .

May a person emigrate from a nation that has institutionalized some end-state or patterned distributional principle? . . . Consider a nation having a compulsory scheme of minimal social provision to aid the neediest (or one organized so as to maximize the position of the worst-off group); no one may opt out of participating in it. (None may say, "Don't compel me to contribute to others and don't provide for me via this compulsory mechanism if I am in need.") Everyone above a certain level is forced to contribute to aid the needy. But if emigration from the country were allowed, anyone could choose to move to another country that did not have compulsory social provision but otherwise was (as much as possible) identical. In such a case, the person's *only* motive for leaving would be to avoid participating in the compulsory scheme of social provision. And if he does leave, the needy in his initial country will receive no (compelled) help from him. What rationale yields the result that the person be permitted to emigrate, yet forbidden to stay and opt out of the compulsory scheme of social provision? If providing for the needy is of overriding importance, this does militate against allowing internal opting out; but it also speaks against allowing external emigration. (Would it also support, to some extent, the kidnapping of persons living in a place without compulsory social provision, who could be forced to make a contribution to the needy in your community?) . . .

THE TALE OF THE SLAVE

Consider the following sequence of cases, which we shall call *The Tale of the Slave*, and imagine it is you.

1. There is a slave completely at the mercy of his brutal master's whims. He often is cruelly beaten, called out in the middle of the night, and so on.
2. The master is kindlier and beats the slave only for stated infractions of his rules (not fulfilling the work quota, and so on). He gives the slave some free time.
3. The master has a group of slaves, and he decides how things are to be allocated among them on nice grounds, taking into account their needs, merit, and so on.

4. The master allows his slaves four days on their own and requires them to work only three days a week on his land. The rest of the time is their own.
5. The master allows his slaves to go off and work in the city (or anywhere they wish) for wages. He requires only that they send back to him three-sevenths of their wages. He also retains the power to recall them to the plantation if some emergency threatens his land; and to raise or lower the three-sevenths amount required to be turned over to him. He further retains the right to restrict the slaves from participating in certain dangerous activities that threaten his financial return, for example, mountain climbing, cigarette smoking.
6. The master allows all of his 10,000 slaves, except you, to vote, and the joint decision is made by all of them. There is open discussion, and so forth, among them, and they have the power to determine to what uses to put whatever percentage of your (and their) earnings they decide to take; what activities may legitimately be forbidden to you, and so on.

Let us pause in this sequence of cases to take stock. If the master contracts this transfer of power so that he cannot withdraw it, you have a change of master. You now have 10,000 masters instead of just one; rather you have one 10,000-headed master. Perhaps the 10,000 even will be kindlier than the benevolent master in case 2. Still, they are your master. However, still more can be done. A kindly single master (as in case 2) might allow his slave(s) to speak up and try to persuade him to make a certain decision. The 10,000-headed master can do this too.

7. Though still not having the vote, you are at liberty (and are given the right) to enter into the discussions of the 10,000 to try to persuade them to adopt various policies and to treat you and themselves in a certain way. They then go off to vote to decide upon policies covering the vast range of their powers.
8. In appreciation of your useful contributions to discussion, the 10,000 allow you to vote if they are deadlocked; they commit them-

selves to this procedure. After the discussion you mark your vote on a slip of paper, and they go off and vote. In the eventuality that they divide evenly on some issue, 5,000 for and 5,000 against, they look at your ballot and count it. This has never yet happened; they have never yet had the occasion to open your ballot. (A single master also might commit himself to letting his slave decide

any issue concerning about which he, the master, was absolutely indifferent.)

9. They throw your vote in with theirs. If they are exactly tied your vote carries the issue. Otherwise it makes no difference to the electoral outcome.

The question is: which transition from case 1 to case 9 made it no longer the tale of a slave?

Markets and Desert

Michael Walzer

Sometimes it seems that everything is for sale in a capitalist state, or at least almost everything. Michael Walzer begins by describing the range of "blocked exchanges," that is, the many different types of goods that are not for sale. Turning to the market sphere, where goods and labor are for sale, he discusses the oft-heard claim that the market rewards those who deserve it for their hard, dangerous, or unpleasant work. Walzer disputes this claim, by describing a group of garbage collectors who formed a company that linked hard and unpleasant work with other activities such as self-government and economic reward. He concludes with some suggestions about how the United States might transform hard work in ways that benefit the workers and the community as a whole. Michael Walzer is professor of politics at Harvard University.

As you read through this essay, consider the following:

1. What are the different sorts of "blocked exchanges" that Walzer describes?
2. What is the proper sphere of the market?
3. How does Walzer distinguish hard, dangerous, and dirty work?
4. What is the Sunset Scavenger Company? How does it work?
5. What reforms does Walzer propose in how our society understands and distributes work?

MONEY AND COMMODITIES

Blocked Exchanges

Let me try to suggest the full set of blocked [market] exchanges in the United States today. I will rely in part on the first chapter of

From Michael Walzer, *Spheres of Justice*. Copyright © 1983 by Basic Books, Inc. Reprinted by permission of Basic Books, a member of Perseus Books, L.L.C.

Arthur Okun's *Equality and Efficiency*, where Okun draws a line between the sphere of money and what he calls "the domain of rights."[1] Rights, of course, are proof against sale and purchase, and Okun revealingly recasts the Bill of Rights as a series of blocked exchanges. But it's not only rights that stand outside the cash nexus. Whenever we ban the use of money, we do indeed establish a right—namely, that this particular good be distributed in some other way. But we must argue about the meaning of the good before we can say anything more about its rightful distribution. . . . Blocked exchanges set limits on the dominance of wealth.

1. Human beings cannot be bought and sold. The sale of slaves, even of oneself as a slave, is ruled out. This is an example of what Okun calls "prohibitions on exchanges born of desperation."[2] There are many such prohibitions; but the others merely regulate the labor market, and I will list them separately. This one establishes what is and is not marketable: not persons or the liberty of persons, but only their labor power and the things they make. (Animals are marketable because we conceive them to be without personality, even though liberty is undoubtedly a value for some of them.) Personal liberty is not, however, proof against conscription or imprisonment; it is proof only against sale and purchase.

2. Political power and influence cannot be bought and sold. Citizens cannot sell their votes or officials their decisions. Bribery is an illegal transaction. It hasn't always been so; in many cultures gifts from clients and suitors are a normal part of the remuneration of office holders. But here the gift relationship will only work—that is, fit into a set of more or less coherent meanings—when "office" hasn't fully emerged as an autonomous good, and when the line between public and private is hazy and indistinct. It won't work in a republic, which draws the line sharply: Athens, for example, had an extraordinary set of rules designed to repress bribery; the more offices the citizens shared, the more elaborate the rules became.

3. Criminal justice is not for sale. It is not only that judges and juries cannot be bribed, but that the services of defense attorneys are a matter of communal provision—a necessary form of welfare given the adversary system.

4. Freedom of speech, press, religion, assembly: none of these require money pay-

ments; none of them are available at auction; they are simply guaranteed to every citizen. It's often said that the exercise of these freedoms costs money, but that's not strictly speaking the case: talk and worship are cheap; so is the meeting of citizens; so is publication in many of its forms. Quick access to large audiences is expensive, but that is another matter, not of freedom itself but of influence and power.

5. Marriage and procreation rights are not for sale. Citizens are limited to one spouse and cannot purchase a license for polygamy. And if limits are ever set on the number of children we can have, I assume that these won't take the form [of] licenses to give birth that can be traded on the market.

6. The right to leave the political community is not for sale. The modern state has, to be sure, an investment in every citizen, and it might legitimately require that some part of that investment be repaid, in work or money, before permitting emigration. The Soviet Union has adopted a policy of this sort, chiefly as a mechanism to bar emigration altogether. Used differently, it seems fair enough, even if it then has differential effects on successful and unsuccessful citizens. But the citizens can claim, in their turn, that they never sought the health care and education that they received (as children, say) and owe nothing in return. That claim underestimates the benefits of citizenship, but nicely captures its consensual character. And so it is best to let them go, once they have fulfilled those obligations-in-kind (military service) that are fulfilled in any case by young men and women who aren't yet fully consenting citizens. No one can buy his way out of these.

7. And so, again, exemptions from military service, from jury duty, and from any other form of communally imposed work cannot be sold by the government or bought by citizens—for reasons I have already given.

8. Political offices cannot be bought; to buy them would be a kind of simony, for the political community is like a church in this sense, that its services matter a great deal to its members and wealth is no adequate sign of a capacity to deliver those services. Nor can professional standing be bought, insofar as this is regulated by the community, for doctors and lawyers are our secular priests; we need to be sure about their qualifications.

9. Basic welfare services like police protection or primary and secondary schooling are purchasable only at the margins. A minimum is guaranteed to every citizen and doesn't have to be paid for by individuals. If policemen dun shopkeepers for protection money, they are acting like gangsters, not like policemen. But shopkeepers can hire security guards and nightwatchmen for the sake of a higher level of protection than the political community is willing to pay for. Similarly, parents can hire private tutors for their children or send them to private schools. The market in services is subject to restraint only if it distorts the character, or lowers the value, of communal provision. (I should also note that some goods are partially provided, hence partially insulated from market control. The mechanism here is not the blocked but the subsidized exchange—as in the case of college and university education, many cultural activities, travel generally, and so on.)

10. Desperate exchanges, "trades of last resort," are barred, though the meaning of desperation is always open to dispute. The eight-hour day, minimum wage laws, health and safety regulations: all these set a floor, establish basic standards, below which workers cannot bid against one another for employment. Jobs can be auctioned off, but only within these limits. This is a restraint of market liberty for the sake of some communal conception of personal liberty, a reassertion, at lower levels of loss, of the ban on slavery.

11. Prizes and honors of many sorts, public and private, are not available for purchase. The Congressional Medal of Honor cannot be bought, nor can the Pulitzer Prize or the Most Valuable Player Award, or even the trophy given by a local Chamber of Commerce to the "businessman of the year." Celebrity is certainly for sale, though the price can be high, but a good name is not. Prestige, esteem, and status stand somewhere between these two. Money is implicated in their distribution; but even in our own society, it is only sometimes determinative.

12. Divine grace cannot be bought—and not only because God doesn't need the money. His servants and deputies often do need it. Still, the sale of indulgences is commonly thought to require reform, if not Reformation.

13. Love and friendship cannot be bought, not on our common understanding of what these two mean. Of course, one can buy all sorts of things—clothing, automobiles, gourmet foods, and so on—that make one a better candidate for love and friendship or more self-confident in the pursuit of lovers and friends. Advertisers commonly play on these possibilities, and they are real enough.

. . . But the direct purchase is blocked, not in the law but more deeply, in our shared morality and sensibility. Men and women marry for money, but this is not a "marriage of true minds." Sex is for sale, but the sale does not make for "a meaningful relationship." People who believe that sexual intercourse is morally tied to love and marriage are likely to favor a ban on prostitution—just as, in other cultures, people who believed that intercourse was a sacred ritual would have deplored the behavior of priestesses who tried to make a little money on the side. Sex can be sold only when it is understood in terms of pleasure and not exclusively in terms of married love or religious worship.

14. Finally, a long series of criminal sales are ruled out. Murder, Inc., cannot sell its services; blackmail is illegal; heroin cannot be sold, nor can stolen goods, or goods fraudulently described, or adulterated milk, or information thought vital to the security of the state. And arguments go on about unsafe cars, guns, inflammable shirts, drugs with uncertain side effects, and so on. All these are useful illustrations of the fact that the sphere of money and commodities is subject to continuous redefinition.

I think that this is an exhaustive list, though it is possible that I have omitted some crucial category. In any case, the list is long enough to suggest that if money answereth all things, it does so, as it were, behind the backs of many of the things and in spite of their social meanings. The market where exchanges of these sorts are free is a black market, and the men and women who frequent it are likely to do so sneakily and then to lie about what they are doing.

What Money Can Buy

What is the proper sphere of money? What social goods are rightly marketable? The obvious answer is also the right one; it points us to a range of goods that have probably always been marketable, whatever else has or has not been: all those objects, commodities, products, services, beyond what is communally provided, that individual men and women find useful or pleasing, the common stock of bazaars, emporiums, and trading posts. . . .

The market produces and reproduces inequalities; people end up with more or less, with different numbers and different kinds of possessions. There is no way to ensure that everyone is possessed of whatever set of things marks the "average American," for any such effort will simply raise the average. Here is a sad version of the pursuit of happiness: communal provision endlessly chasing consumer demand. Perhaps there is some point beyond which the fetishism of commodities will lose its grip. Perhaps, more modestly, there is some

lower point at which individuals are safe against any radical loss of status. That last possibility suggests the value of partial redistributions in the sphere of money, even if the result is something well short of simple equality. But it also suggests that we must look outside that sphere and strengthen autonomous distributions elsewhere. There are, after all, activities more central to the meaning of membership than owning and using commodities.

Our purpose is to tame "the inexorable dynamic of a money economy," to make money harmless—or at least, to make sure that the harms experienced in the sphere of money are not mortal, not to life and not to social standing [as equal citizens] either. But the market remains a competitive sphere, where risk is common, where the readiness to take risks is often a virtue, and where people win and lose. An exciting place: for even when money buys only what it should buy, it is still a very good thing to have. It answereth some things that nothing else can answer. And once we have blocked every wrongful exchange and controlled the sheer weight of money itself, we have no reason to worry about the answers the market provides. Individual men and women still have reason to worry, and so they will try to minimize their risks, or to share them or spread them out, or to buy themselves insurance. In the regime of complex equality, certain sorts of risks will regularly be shared, because the power to impose risks on others, to make authoritative decisions in factories and corporations, is not a marketable good. This is only one more example of a blocked exchange; I will take it up in detail later. Given the right blocks, there is no such thing as a maldistribution of consumer goods. It just doesn't matter, from the standpoint of complex equality, that you have a yacht and I don't. . . .

The Marketplace

There is a stronger argument about the sphere of money, the common argument of the defenders of capitalism: that market outcomes matter a great deal because the market, if it is free, gives to each person exactly what he deserves. The market rewards us all in accordance with the contributions we make to one another's well-being. The goods and services we provide are valued by potential consumers in such-and-such a way, and these values are aggregated by the market, which determines the price we receive. And that price is our desert, for it expresses the only worth our goods and services can have, the worth they actually have for other people. But this is to misunderstand the meaning of desert. Unless there are standards of worth independent of what people want (and are willing to buy) at this or that moment in time, there can be no deservingness at all. We would never know what a person deserved until we saw what he had gotten. And that can't be right.

Imagine a novelist who writes what he hopes will be a best seller. He studies his potential audience, designs his book to meet the current fashion. Perhaps he had to violate the canons of his art in order to do that, and perhaps he is a novelist for whom the violation was painful. He has stooped to conquer. Does he now deserve the fruits of his conquest? Does he deserve a conquest that bears fruit? His novel appears, let's say, during a depression when no one has money for books, and very few copies are sold; his reward is small. Has he gotten less than he deserves? (His fellow writers smile at his disappointment; perhaps that's what he deserves.) Years later, in better times, the book is reissued and does well. Has its author become more deserving? Surely desert can't hang on the state of the economy. There is too much luck involved here; talk of desert makes little sense. We would do better to say simply that the writer is entitled to his royalties, large or small. . . .

HARD WORK

Equality and Hardness

It is not a question here of demanding or strenuous work. In that sense of the word, we can work hard in almost any office and at almost any job. I can work hard writing this book, and sometimes do. A task or a cause that seems to us worth the hard work it entails is clearly a good thing. For all our natural laziness, we go looking for it. But *hard* has another sense—as in "hard winter" and "hard heart"—where it means harsh, unpleasant, cruel, difficult to endure. . . .

This kind of work is a negative good, and it commonly carries other negative goods in its train: poverty, insecurity, ill health, physical danger, dishonor and degradation. And yet it is socially necessary work; it needs to be done, and that means that someone must be found to do it.

The conventional solution to this problem has the form of a simple equation: the negative good is matched by the negative status of the people into whose hands it is thrust. Hard work is distributed to degraded people. Citizens are set free; the work is imposed on slaves, resident aliens, "guest workers"—outsiders all. Alternatively, the insiders who do the work are turned into "inside" aliens, like the Indian untouchables or the American blacks after emancipation. In many societies, women have been the most important group of "inside" aliens, doing the work that men disdained and freeing the men not only for more rewarding economic activities but also for citizenship and politics. Indeed, the household work that women traditionally have done—cooking, cleaning, caring for the sick and the old—makes up a substantial part of the hard work of the economy today, for which aliens are recruited (and women prominently among them).

The idea in all these cases is a cruel one: negative people for a negative good. The work should be done by men and women whose qualities it is presumed to fit. Because of their race or sex, or presumed intelligence, or social status, they deserve to do it, or they don't deserve not to do it, or they somehow qualify for it. It's not the work of citizens, free men, white men, and so on. But what sort of desert, what sort of qualification is this? It would be hard to say what the hard workers of this or any other society have done to deserve the danger and degradation their work commonly entails; or how they, and they alone, have qualified for it. What secrets have we learned about their moral character? When convicts do hard labor, we can at least argue that they deserve their punishment. But even they are not state slaves; their degradation is (most often) limited and temporary, and it is by no means clear that the most oppressive sorts of work should be assigned to them. And if not to them, surely to no one else. Indeed, if convicts are driven to hard labor, then ordinary men and women should probably be protected from it, so as to make it clear that they are not convicts and have never been found guilty by a jury of their peers. And if even convicts shouldn't be forced to endure the oppression (imprisonment being oppression enough), then it is *a fortiori* true that no one else should endure it.

Nor can it be imposed on outsiders. . . . [T]he people who do this sort of work are so closely tied into the everyday life of the political community that they can't rightly be denied membership. Hard work is a naturalization process, and it brings membership to those who endure the hardship. At the same time, there is something attractive about a community whose members resist hard work (and whose new members are naturalized into the resistance). They have a certain sense of themselves and their careers that rules out the acceptance of oppression; they refuse to be degraded and have the strength to sustain the refusal. Neither the sense of self nor the personal strength are all that common in human history. They represent a significant achievement of modern democracy, closely connected to economic growth, certainly, but also to the success or the partial success of complex equality in the sphere of welfare. . . .

Dangerous Work

Soldiering is a special kind of hard work. In many societies, in fact, it is not conceived to be hard work at all. It is the normal occupation of young men, their social function, into which they are not so much drafted as ritually

initiated, and where they find the rewards of camaraderie, excitement, and glory. It would be as odd, in these cases, to talk about conscripts as to talk about volunteers; neither category is relevant. . . .

Even when its true character is understood, however, soldiering is not a radically degraded activity. Rank-and-file soldiers are often recruited from the lowest classes, or from outcasts or foreigners, and they are often regarded with contempt by ordinary citizens. But the perceived value of their work is subject to sudden inflation, and there is always the chance that they will one day appear as the saviors of the country they defend. Soldiering is socially necessary, at least sometimes; and when it is, the necessity is visible and dramatic. At those times, soldiering is also dangerous, and it is dangerous in a way that makes a special mark on our imaginations. The danger is not natural but human; the soldier inhabits a world where other people—his enemies and ours, too—are trying to kill him. And he must try to kill them. He runs the risk of killing and being killed. For these reasons, I think, this is the first form of hard work that citizens are required, or require each other, to share. Conscription has other purposes too—above all, to produce the vast numbers of troops needed for modern warfare. But its moral purpose is to universalize or randomize the risks of war over a given generation of young men.

When the risks are of a different sort, however, the same purpose seems less pressing. Consider the case of coal mining. "The rate of accidents among miners is so high," wrote George Orwell in *The Road to Wigan Pier* ". . . that casualties are taken for granted as they would be in a minor war."[3] It isn't easy, however, to imagine this sort of work being shared. Mining may not be highly skilled work, but it is certainly very difficult, and it's best done by men who have done it for a long time. It requires something more than "basic training." "At a pitch," wrote Orwell, "I could be a tolerable road-sweeper, or . . . a tenth-rate farm hand. But by no conceivable amount of effort or training could I become a coal-miner; the work would kill me in a few weeks."[4] Nor does it make much sense to break in upon the solidarity of the miners. Work in the pits breeds a strong bond, a tight community that is not welcoming to transients. That community is the great strength of the miners. A deep sense of place and clan and generations of class struggle have made for staying power. . . .

Dirty Work

In principle, there is no such thing as intrinsically degrading work; degradation is a cultural phenomenon. It is probably true in practice, however, that a set of activities having to do with dirt, waste, and garbage has been the object of disdain and avoidance in just about every human society. The precise list will vary from one time and place to another, but the set is more or less common. In India, for example, it includes the butchering of cows and the tanning of cowhide—jobs that have a rather different standing in Western cultures. . . .

So long as there is a reserve army, a class of degraded men and women driven by their poverty and their impoverished sense of their own value, the market will never be effective. Under such conditions, the hardest work is also the lowest paid, even though nobody wants to do it. But given a certain level of communal provision and a certain level of self-valuation, the work won't be done unless it is very well paid indeed (or unless the working conditions are very good). The citizens will find that if they want to hire their fellows as scavengers and sweepers, the rates will be high—much higher, in fact, than for more prestigious or pleasant work. This is a direct consequence of the fact that they are hiring *fellow* citizens. It is sometimes claimed that under conditions of genuine fellowship, no one would agree to be a scavenger or a sweeper. In that case, the work would have to be shared. But the claim is probably false. "We are so accustomed," as Shaw has written, "to see dirty work done by dirty and poorly paid people that we have come to think that it

is disgraceful to do it, and that unless a dirty and disgraced class existed, it would not be done at all."[5] If sufficient money or leisure were offered, Shaw rightly insisted, people would come forward.

His own preference was for rewards that take the form of leisure or "liberty"—which will always be, he argued, the strongest incentive and the best compensation for work that carries with it little intrinsic satisfaction:

> In a picture gallery you will find a nicely dressed lady sitting at a table with nothing to do but to tell anyone who asks what is the price of any particular picture, and take an order for it if one is given. She has many pleasant chats with journalists and artists; and if she is bored she can read a novel. . . . But the gallery has to be scrubbed and dusted each day; and its windows have to be kept clean. It is clear that the lady's job is a much softer one than the charwoman's. To balance them you must either let them take their turns at the desk and at the scrubbing on alternate days or weeks; or else, as a first-class scrubber and duster and cleaner might make a very bad business lady, and a very attractive business lady might make a very bad scrubber, you must let the charwoman go home and have the rest of the day to herself earlier than the lady at the desk.[6]

The contrast between the "first-rate" charwoman and the "very attractive" business lady nicely combines the prejudices of class and sex. If we set aside those prejudices, the periodic exchange of work is less difficult to imagine. The lady, after all, will have to share in the scrubbing, dusting, and cleaning at home (unless she has, as Shaw probably expected her to have, a charwoman there, too). And what is the charwoman to do with her leisure? Perhaps she will paint pictures or read books about art. But then, though the exchange is easy, it may well be resisted by the charwoman herself. One of the attractions of Shaw's proposal is that it establishes hard work as an opportunity for people who want to protect their time. So they will clean or scrub or collect garbage for the sake of their leisure, and avoid if they can any more engaging, competitive, or time-consuming employment. Under the right conditions, the market provides a kind of sanctuary from the pressures of the market. The price of the sanctuary is so many hours a day of hard work—for some people, at least, a price worth paying.

The major alternative to Shaw's proposal is the reorganization of the work so as to change, not its physical requirements (for I'm assuming that they are not changeable), but its moral character. The history of garbage collecting in the city of San Francisco offers a nice example of this sort of transformation, which I want to dwell on briefly. . . .

The San Francisco Scavengers. For the past sixty years, roughly half of the garbage of the city of San Francisco has been collected and disposed of by the Sunset Scavenger Company, a cooperative owned by its workers, the men who drive the trucks and carry the cans. In 1978 the sociologist Stewart Perry published a study of Sunset, a fine piece of urban ethnography and a valuable speculation on "dirty work and the pride of ownership"—it is my sole source in the paragraphs that follow. The cooperative is democratically run, its officers elected from the ranks and paid no more than the other workers. Forced by the Internal Revenue Service in the 1930s to adopt bylaws in which they are referred to as "stockholders," the members nevertheless insisted that they were, and would remain, faithful to the program of the original organizers "who intended to form and carry on a cooperative . . . where every member was a worker and actually engaged in the common work and where every member did his share of the work and expected every other member to work and do his utmost to increase the collective earnings."[7] Indeed, earnings have increased (more than those of manual workers generally); the company has grown; its elected officers have shown considerable entrepreneurial talent. Perry believes that the cooperative provides better-than-average service to the citizens of San Francisco and, what is more important here, better-than-average working conditions to its own members. That doesn't mean

that the work is physically easier; rather, cooperation has made it more pleasant—has even made it a source of pride.

In one sense, the work is in fact easier: the accident rate among Sunset members is significantly lower than the industry average. Garbage collecting is a dangerous activity. In the United States today, no other occupation has a higher risk of injury (though coal miners are subject to more serious injury). The explanation of these statistics is not clear. Garbage collecting is strenuous work, but no more so than many other jobs that turn out to have better safety records. Perry suggests that there may be a connection between safety and self-valuation. "The 'hidden injuries' of the status system may be linked to the apparent injuries that public health and safety experts can document."[8] The first "accident" of garbage collecting is the internalization of disrespect, and then other accidents follow. Men who don't value themselves don't take proper care of themselves. If this view is right, the better record of Sunset may be connected to the shared decision making and the sense of ownership.

Membership in the Sunset Scavenger Company is distributed by a vote of the current members and then by the purchase of shares (it has generally not been difficult to borrow the necessary money, and the shares have steadily increased in value). The founders of the company were Italian-Americans, and so are the bulk of the members today; about half of them are related to other members; a fair number of sons have followed their fathers into the business. The success of the cooperative may owe something to the easiness of the members with one another. In any case, and whatever one wants to say about the work, they have made membership into a good thing. They don't distribute the good they have created, however, in accordance with "fair equality of opportunity." In New York City, because of a powerful union, garbage collecting is also a widely desired job, and there the job has been turned into an office. Candidates must qualify for the work by taking a civil service exam.[9] It would be interesting to know something about the self-valuation of the men who pass the exam and are hired as public employees. They probably earn more than the members of the Sunset cooperative, but they don't have the same security; they don't own their jobs. And they don't share risks and opportunities; they don't manage their own company. The New Yorkers call themselves "sanitationmen"; the San Franciscans, "scavengers": who has the greater pride? If the advantage lies, as I think it does, with the members of Sunset, then it is closely connected to the character of Sunset: a company of companions, who choose their own fellows. There is no way to qualify for the work except to appeal to the current members of the company. No doubt the members look for men who can do the necessary work and do it well, but they also look, presumably, for good companions.

But I don't want to underestimate the value of unionization, for this can be another form of self-management and another way of making the market work. There can't be any doubt that unions have been effective in winning better wages and working conditions for their members; sometimes they have even succeeded in breaking the link between income differentials and the status hierarchy (the New York garbage collectors are a prime example). Perhaps the general rule should be that wherever work can't be unionized or run cooperatively, it should be shared by the citizens—not symbolically and partially, but generally. Indeed, when union or cooperative work is available to everyone (when there is no reserve army), other work just won't get done unless people do it for themselves. This is clearly the case with domestic cooking and cleaning, an area where jobs are increasingly filled by new immigrants, not by citizens. "Mighty few young black women are doin' domestic work [today]," Studs Terkel was told by a very old black woman, a servant all her life. "And I'm glad. That's why I want my kids to go to school. This one lady told me, 'All you people are gettin' like that.' I said, 'I'm glad.'

There's no more gettin' on their knees.[10] This is the sort of work that is largely dependent on its (degraded) moral character. Change the character, and the work may well become un-doable, not only from the perspective of the worker but from that of the employer, too. "When domestic servants are treated as human beings," wrote Shaw, "it is not worthwhile to keep them. . . ."[11]

What is most attractive in the experience of the Sunset company (as of the Israeli kibbutz) is the way in which hard work is connected to other activities—in this case, the meetings of the "stockholders," the debates over policy, the election of officers and new members. The company has also expanded into land-fill and salvage operations, providing new and diversified employment (including managerial jobs) for some of the members; though all of them, whatever they do now, have spent years riding the trucks and carrying the cans. Throughout most of the economy, the division of labor has developed very differently, continually separating out rather than integrating the hardest sorts of work. This is especially true in the area of the human services, in the care we provide for the sick and the old. Much of that work is still done in the home, where it is connected with a range of other jobs, and its difficulties are relieved by the relationships it sustains. Increasingly, however, it is institutional work; and within the great caretaking institutions—hospitals, mental asylums, old-age homes—the hardest work, the dirty work, the most intimate service and supervision, is relegated to the most subordinate employees. Doctors and nurses, defending their place in the social hierarchy, shift it onto the shoulders of aides, orderlies, and attendants—who do for strangers, day in and day out, what we can only just conceive of doing in emergencies for the people we love.

Perhaps the aides, orderlies, and attendants win the gratitude of their patients or of the families of their patients. That's not a reward I would want to underestimate, but gratitude is most often and most visibly the reward of doctors and nurses, the healers rather than merely the caretakers of the sick. The resentment of the caretakers is well known. W. H. Auden was clearly thinking of the patients, not the hospital staff, when he wrote:

> . . . the hospitals alone remind us of the equality of man.[12]

Orderlies and attendants have to cope for long hours with conditions that their institutional superiors see only intermittently, and that the general public doesn't see at all and doesn't want to see. Often they look after men and women whom the rest of the world has given up on (and when the world gives up, it turns away). Underpaid and overworked, at the bottom of the status system, they are nevertheless the last comforters of humanity—though I suspect that unless they have a calling for the work, they give as little comfort as they get. And sometimes they are guilty of those petty cruelties that make their jobs a little easier, and that their superiors, they firmly believe, would be as quick to commit in their place.

"There is a whole series of problems here," Everett Hughes has written, "which cannot be solved by some miracle of changing the social selection of those who enter the job."[13] In fact, if caretaking were shared—if young men and women from different social backgrounds took their turns as orderlies and attendants—the internal life of hospitals, asylums, and old-age homes would certainly be changed for the better. Perhaps this sort of thing is best organized locally rather than nationally, so as to establish a connection between caretaking and neighborliness; it might even be possible, with a little invention, to reduce somewhat the rigid impersonality of institutional settings. But such efforts will be supplementary at best. Most of the work will have to be done by people who have chosen it as a career, and the choice will not be easy to motivate in a society of equal citizens. Already, we must recruit foreigners to do a great deal of the hard and dirty work of our caretaking institu-

tions. If we wish to avoid that sort of recruitment (and the oppression it commonly entails), we must, again, transform the work. "I have a notion," says Hughes, "that . . . 'dirty work' can be more easily endured when it is part of a good role, a role that is full of rewards to one's self. A nurse might do some things with better grace than a person who is not allowed to call herself a nurse, but is dubbed 'subprofessional' or 'non-professional.'"[14] That is exactly right. National service might be effective because, for a time at least, the role of neighbor or citizen would cover the necessary work. But over a longer period, the work can be covered only by an enhanced sense of institutional or professional place. . . .

We can share (and partially transform) hard work through some sort of national service; we can reward it with money or leisure; we can make it more rewarding by connecting it to other sorts of activity—political, managerial, and professional in character. We can conscript, rotate, cooperate, and compensate; we can reorganize the work and rectify its names. We can do all these things, but we will not have abolished hard work; nor will we have abolished the class of hard workers. The first kind of abolitionism is, as I have already argued, impossible; the second would merely double hardness with coercion. The measures that I have proposed are at best partial and incomplete. They have an end appropriate to a negative good: a distribution of hard work that doesn't corrupt the distributive spheres with which it overlaps, carrying poverty into the sphere of money, degradation into the sphere of honor, weakness and resignation into the sphere of power. To rule out negative dominance: that is the purpose of collective bargaining, cooperative management, professional conflict, the rectification of names—the politics of hard work. The outcomes of this politics are indeterminate, certain to be different in different times and places, conditioned by previously established hierarchies and social understandings. But they will also be conditioned by the solidarity, the skillfulness, and the energy of the workers themselves. . . .

Notes

1. Arthur Okun, *Equality and Efficiency: The Big Tradeoff* (Washington, D.C., 1975), pp. 6ff.

2. Ibid., p. 20.

3. George Orwell, *The Road to Wigan Pier* (New York, 1958), p. 44.

4. Ibid., pp. 32–33.

5. George Bernard Shaw, *The Intelligent Woman's Guide to Socialism, Capitalism, Sovietism, and Fascism* (Hammondsworth, England, 1937).

6. Ibid., p. 109.

7. Stewart E. Perry, *San Francisco Scavengers* (Berkeley, 1978).

8. Ibid., p. 8.

9. Ibid., pp. 188–91.

10. Studs Terkel, *Working* (New York, 1975), p. 168.

11. Bernard Shaw, "Maxims for Revolutionists," *Man and Superman*, in *Seven Plays* (New York, 1951), p. 736.

12. W. H. Auden, "In Time of War" (XXV), in *The English Auden: Poems, Essays, and Dramatic Writings 1927–1939*, ed. Edward Mendelson (New York, 1978), p. 261.

13. Everett Hughes, *The Sociological Eye* (Chicago, 1971), p. 345.

14. Ibid., p. 314.

Markets in Women's Reproductive Labor

Debra Satz

In this essay, Debra Satz discusses another of the vexing issues surrounding the proper role of markets in human life: reproduction. Is there a fundamental difference—an "asymmetry"—between those areas where we do and should allow free exchanges versus women's reproductive labor, that is, producing babies? Satz first criticizes several common arguments that try to prove that reproduction and child-bearing are different and so should be shielded from the marketplace by laws banning contract pregnancy. But how exactly is a contract involving pregnancy different from one to work for another person?

After outlining three arguments in favor of markets, Satz turns to those who argue that reproductive labor is essentially different because it is "degrading"; it is incompatible with parental love and is bad for children. She rejects these, however, but concludes by defending the restrictions on reproductive contracts on grounds of women's equality and control. Debra Satz is professor of philosophy at Stanford University.

As you read through this essay, consider the following:

1. What are the arguments economists use to defend markets?
2. Why does Satz reject claims similar to the one Carole Pateman uses, which relies on the tie between a woman's identity and reproductive labor?
3. What are the major arguments against reproductive labor contracts that are based on the special relationship between a mother and child? Why does Satz reject them?
4. Satz also rejects the claim that such contracts are bad for children. What are her reasons?
5. Despite having found little merit in these arguments, why does Satz nonetheless think reproductive contracts should not be allowed?

Much of the evolution of social policy in the twentieth century has occurred around conflicts over the scope of markets. To what extent, under what conditions, and for what reasons should we limit the use of markets? Recently, American society has begun to experiment with markets in women's reproductive labor. Many people believe that markets in women's reproductive labor, as exemplified by contract pregnancy,[1] are more problematic than other currently accepted labor markets. I will call this the asymmetry thesis because its proponents believe that there ought to be an asymmetry between our treatment of reproductive labor and our treatment of other forms of labor. Advocates of the asymmetry thesis hold that treating reproductive labor as a commodity, as something subject to the supply-and-demand principles that govern economic markets, is worse than treating other types of human labor as commodities. Is the asymmetry thesis true? And, if so, what are the reasons for thinking that it is true?

My aims in this article are to criticize several popular ways of defending the asymmetry thesis and to offer an alternative defense. . . .

Many feminists hold that the asymmetry thesis is true because women's reproductive labor is a special kind of labor that should not be treated according to market norms. They draw a sharp dividing line between women's reproductive labor and human labor in general: while human labor may be bought and sold, women's reproductive labor is intrinsically not a commodity. According to these views, contract pregnancy allows for the extension of the market into the "private" sphere of sexuality and reproduction. . . .

Below, I argue that this is the wrong way to defend the asymmetry thesis. While I agree with the intuition that markets in women's reproductive labor are more troubling than other labor markets, in this article I develop an alternative account of why this should be so. My analysis has four parts. In the first part, I criticize the arguments against the commodification of women's reproductive labor that turn on the assumption that reproductive labor is a special form of labor, part of a separate realm of sexuality. I argue that there is no distinction between women's reproductive labor and human labor generally, which is relevant to the debate about contract pregnancy. Moreover, I argue that the sale of women's reproductive labor is not *ipso facto* degrading. Rather, it becomes "degrading" only in a particular political and social context. In the second part, I criticize arguments in support of the asymmetry thesis that appeal to norms of parental love. Here, the asymmetry between reproductive labor and labor in general is taken to derive from a special bond between mothers and children: the bond between a mother and her child is different from the bond between a worker and his product. In response, I argue that the bond between mothers and children is more complicated than critics of contract pregnancy have assumed and that, moreover, contract pregnancy does not cause parents to view children as commodities. The third part of the article examines an argument that stresses the potential negative consequences of contract pregnancy for children. While this argument has some merit, I argue that it is unpersuasive.

The first three parts of the article argue that the various reasons given in the literature for banning contract pregnancy on the basis of its asymmetry with other forms of labor are inadequate. Nonetheless, most people think that there should be some limits to commodification, and there does seem to be something more problematic about pregnancy contracts than other types of labor contract. The question is, what is the basis for and the significance of these intuitions? And what, apart from its agreement with these particular intuitions, can be said in favor of the asymmetry thesis?

In the fourth part of my article, I argue . . . that the most compelling objection to contract pregnancy concerns the background conditions of gender inequality that characterize our society. Markets in women's reproductive labor are especially troubling because they reinforce gender hierarchies in a way that other accepted labor markets do not. My defense of the asymmetry thesis thus rests on the way that contract pregnancy reinforces asymmetrical social relations of gender domination in American society. . . .

I. THE SPECIAL NATURE OF REPRODUCTIVE LABOR

A wide range of attacks on contract pregnancy turn out to share a single premise, viz., that the intrinsic nature of reproductive labor is different from that of other kinds of labor. Critics claim that reproductive labor is not just another kind of work; they argue that unlike other forms of labor, reproductive labor is not properly regarded as a commodity. I will refer to this thesis as the essentialist thesis, since it holds that reproductive labor is *essentially* something that should not be bought and sold.

In contrast to the essentialist thesis, modern economic theories tend to treat . . . all goods and capacities as exchangeable commodities, at least in principle. Economists generally base their defense of markets as distributive mechanisms on three distinct ideas.

First, there is the idea that markets are good for social welfare. Indeed, the fundamental theorem of welfare economics states that every competitive (market) equilibrium is Pareto optimal. A Pareto optimum is a distribution point at which, given the initial distribution of resources, no individual can become better off (in view of her preferences) without at least one other individual becoming worse off. The so-called converse theorem of welfare economics states that every Pareto optimum is a competitive equilibrium.

Second, there is the idea that markets promote freedom. The agent of economic theory is a free, autonomous chooser. Markets enhance her capacities for choosing by decentralizing decision-making, decentralizing information, and providing opportunities for experimentation. Markets also place limits on the viability of unjust social relationships by providing avenues for individual exit, thereby making the threat of defection a credible bargaining device.

Third, there is the idea that excluding a free exchange of some good, as a matter of principle, is incompatible with liberal neutrality. Liberalism requires state neutrality among conceptions of value. This neutrality constrains liberals from banning free exchanges: liberals cannot mandate that individuals accept certain values as having "intrinsic" or ultimate worth. Liberals can, of course, seek to regulate exchanges so that they fall within the bounds of justice. But any argument prohibiting rather than regulating market activity is claimed to violate liberal neutrality.

If we accept the logic of the economic approach to human behavior, we seem led to endorse a world in which everything is potentially for sale: body parts, reproductive labor, children, even persons. Many people are repulsed by such a world. But what exactly is the problem with it? Defenders of the essentialist thesis provide the starting point for a counterattack: not all human goods are commodities. In particular, human reproductive labor is improperly treated as a commodity. When reproductive labor is purchased on the market, it is inappropriately valued.

The essentialist thesis provides support for the asymmetry thesis. The nature of reproductive labor is taken to be fundamentally different from that of labor in general. In particular, proponents of the essentialist thesis hold that women's reproductive labor should be respected and not used. What is it about women's reproductive labor that singles it out for a type of respect that precludes market use?

Some versions of the essentialist thesis focus on the biological or naturalistic features of women's reproductive labor: (1) Women's reproductive labor has both a genetic and a gestational component. Other forms of labor do not involve a genetic relationship between the worker and her product. (2) While much human labor is voluntary at virtually every step, many of the phases of the reproductive process are involuntary. Ovulation, conception, gestation, and birth occur without the conscious direction of the mother. (3) Reproductive labor extends over a period of approximately nine months; other types of labor do not typically necessitate a long-term commitment. (4) Reproductive labor involves significant restrictions of a woman's behavior during pregnancy; other forms of labor are less invasive with respect to the worker's body.

These characteristics of reproductive labor do not, however, establish the asymmetry thesis: (1) With respect to the genetic relationship between the reproductive worker and her product, most critics object to contract pregnancy even where the "surrogate" is not the genetic mother. In fact, many critics consider "gestational surrogacy"—in which a woman is implanted with a preembryo formed in vitro from donated gametes—more pernicious than those cases in which the "surrogate" is also the genetic mother. In addition, men also have a genetic tie to their offspring, yet many proponents of the asymmetry thesis would not oppose the selling of sperm. (2) With respect to the degree to which reproductive labor is involuntary, there are many forms of work in which workers do not have control over the work process; for example, mass-production workers cannot generally control the speed of the assembly line, and they have no involvement in the overall purpose of their activity. (3) With regard to the length of the contract's duration, some forms of labor involve contracts of even longer duration, for example, book contracts. Like pregnancy contracts, these are not contracts in which one can quit at the end of the day. Yet, presumably, most proponents of the essentialist thesis would not find commercial publishing contracts objectionable. (4) With regard to invasions into the woman's body, nonreproductive labor can also involve incursions into the body of the

worker. To take an obvious example, athletes sign contracts that give team owners considerable control over their diet and behavior, allowing owners to conduct periodic tests for drug use. Yet there is little controversy over the sale of athletic capacities. Sales of blood also run afoul of a noninvasiveness condition. In fact, leaving aside the genetic component of reproductive labor, voluntary military service involves features 2 through 4; do we really want to object to such military service on *essentialist* grounds?

Carole Pateman suggests a different way of defending the asymmetry thesis as the basis for an argument against contract pregnancy. Rather than focusing on the naturalistic, biological properties of reproductive labor, she argues that a woman's reproductive labor is more "integral" to her identity than her other productive capacities. Pateman first sketches this argument with respect to prostitution: "Womanhood, too, is confirmed in sexual activity, and when a prostitute contracts out use of her body she is thus selling herself in a very real sense. Women's selves are involved in prostitution in a different manner from the involvement of the self in other occupations. Workers of all kinds may be more or less 'bound up in their work,' but the integral connection between sexuality and sense of the self means that, for self-protection, a prostitute must distance herself from her sexual use."[2]

Pateman's objection to prostitution rests on a claim about the intimate relation between a woman's sexuality and her identity. It is by virtue of this tie, Pateman believes, that sex should not be treated as an alienable commodity. Is her claim true? How do we decide which of a woman's attributes or capacities are essential to her identity and which are not? In particular, why should we consider sexuality more integral to self than friendship, family, religion, nationality, and work? Yet we allow commodification in each of these spheres. For example, rabbis or priests may view their religion as central to their identity, but they often accept payment for performing religious services, and hardly anyone objects to their doing so. Does Pateman think that *all* activities that fall within these spheres and that bear an intimate relationship to a person's identity should be inalienable?

. . . But this more general argument is implausible. It would not allow individuals to sell their homes or their paintings or their book manuscripts or their copyrights. . . .

. . . We [also] sometimes sell things that we also respect. As Margaret Radin puts it, "we can both know the price of something and know that it is priceless."[3] For example, I think that my teaching talents should be respected, but I don't object to being paid for teaching on such grounds. Giving my teaching a price does not diminish the other ways in which my teaching has value.

This point undermines Pateman's argument as well. For although Pateman would not endorse the idea that sexuality is part of a private realm, she does believe that it bears a special relationship to our identities and that by virtue of that relationship it should be inalienable. But we sometimes sell things intimately tied to our identities, without ceasing to be the people that we are. For example, as I suggested above, a person's home may be intimately tied to her identity, but she can also sell it without losing her sense of self.

Finally, I believe that it is a mistake to focus . . . on maintaining certain cultural values without examining critically the specific social circumstances from which those values emerge. Thus, the view that selling sexual or reproductive capacities is "degrading" may reflect society's attempts to control women and their sexuality. At the very least, the relations between particular views of sexuality and the maintenance of gender inequality must be taken into account. . . .

II. THE SPECIAL BONDS OF MOTHERHOOD

Sometimes what critics of pregnancy contracts have in mind is not the effect of such contracts on the relationship between reproductive labor and a woman's sense of self or her dignity, but its effect on her views (and ours) of the mother-fetus and mother-child bond. On this view, what is wrong with commodifying reproductive labor is that by relying on a mistaken picture of the nature of these relationships, it degrades them. Further, it leads to a view of children as fungible objects. In part 1 of this section I examine arguments against contract pregnancy based on its portrayal of the mother-fetus bond; in part 2 I examine arguments based on contract pregnancy's portrayal of the mother-child bond.

1. Mothers and Fetuses

Some critics of contract pregnancy contend that the relationship between a mother and a fetus is not simply a biochemical relationship or a matter of contingent physical connection. They claim that the relationship between a mother and a fetus is essentially different from that between a worker and her material product. The long months of pregnancy and the experience of childbirth are part of forming a relationship with the child-to-be. . . .

Surely there is truth in the claim that pregnancy contracts may reinforce a vision of women as baby machines or mere "wombs." Recent court rulings with respect to contract pregnancy have tended to acknowledge women's contribution to reproduction only insofar as it is identical to men's: the donation of genetic material. The gestational labor involved in reproduction is explicitly ignored in such rulings. Thus, Mary Beth Whitehead won back her parental rights in the "Baby M" case because the New Jersey Supreme Court acknowledged her genetic contribution.

However, as I will argue in Section IV below, the concern about the discounting of women's reproductive labor is best posed in terms of the principle of equal treatment. By treating women's reproductive labor as identical to men's when it is not, women are not in fact being treated equally. But those who conceptualize the problem with pregnancy contracts in terms of the degradation of the mother-fetus relationship rather than in terms of the equality of men and women tend to interpret the social practice of pregnancy in terms of a maternal "instinct," a sacrosanct bonding that takes place between a mother and her child-to-be. However, not all women "bond" with their fetuses. Some women abort them.

Indeed, there is a dilemma for those who wish to use the mother-fetus bond to condemn pregnancy contracts while endorsing a woman's right to choose abortion. They must hold that it is acceptable to abort a fetus, but not to sell it. . . . One possible response to this objection would be to claim that women do not bond with their fetuses in the first trimester. But the fact remains that some women never bond with their fetuses; some women even fail to bond with their babies after they deliver them. . . .

2. Mothers and Children

A somewhat different argument against contract pregnancy contends that the commodification of women's reproductive labor entails the commodification of children. Once again, the special nature of reproduction is used to support the asymmetry thesis: the special nature of maternal love is held to be incompatible with market relations. Children should be loved by their mothers, yet commercial surrogacy responds to and promotes other motivations. Critics argue that markets in reproductive labor give people the opportunity to "shop" for children. Prospective womb-infertile couples will seek out arrangements that "maximize" the value of their babies: sex, eye color, and race will be assessed in terms of market considerations. Having children on the basis of such preferences reflects an inferior conception of persons. It brings commercial attitudes into a sphere that is thought to be properly governed by love.

What are the reasons that people seek to enter into contract pregnancy arrangements? Most couples or single people who make use

of "surrogates" want simply to have a child that is "theirs," that is, genetically related to them. In fact, given the clogged adoption system, some of them may simply want to have a child. Furthermore, the adoption system itself is responsive to people's individual preferences: it is much easier, for example, to adopt an older black child than a white infant. Such preferences may be objectionable, but no one seriously argues that parents should have no choice in the child they adopt nor that adoption be prohibited because it gives rein to such preferences. Instead, we regulate adoption to forbid the differential payment of fees to agencies on the basis of a child's ascribed characteristics. Why couldn't contract pregnancy be regulated in the same way?

Critics who wish to make an argument for the asymmetry thesis based on the nature of maternal love must defend a strong claim about the relationship between markets and love. In particular, they must claim that even regulated markets in reproductive services will lead parents to love their children for the wrong reasons: love will be conditional on the child's having the "right" set of physical characteristics. While I share the view that there is something wrong with the "shopping" attitude in the sphere of personal relations, I wonder if it has the adverse effects that the critics imagine. Individuals in our society seek partners with attributes ranging from a specified race and height to a musical taste for Chopin. Should such singles' advertisements in magazines be illegal? Should we ban dating services that cater to such preferences? Isn't it true that people who meet on such problematic grounds may grow to love each other? I suspect that most parents who receive their child through a contract pregnancy arrangement will love their child as well.

Even if contract pregnancy does not distort our conception of personhood per se, critics can still associate contract pregnancy with baby-selling. One popular argument runs: In contract pregnancy women not only sell their reproductive services, but also their babies. Because baby-selling is taken to be intrinsically wrong, this type of argument attempts to use an analogy to support the following syllogism: If baby-selling is wrong, and contract pregnancy is a form of baby-selling, then contract pregnancy is wrong. . . .

It is important to keep in mind that pregnancy contracts do not enable fathers (or prospective "mothers," women who are infertile or otherwise unable to conceive) to acquire children as property. Even where there has been a financial motivation for conceiving a child, and whatever the status of the labor that produced it, the *child* cannot be treated as a commodity. The father cannot, for example, destroy, transfer, or abandon the child. He is bound by the same norms and laws that govern the behavior of a child's biological or adoptive parents. Allowing women to contract for their reproductive services does not entail baby-selling, if we mean by that a proxy for slavery.

. . . Like adoption, pregnancy contracts could be regulated to respect a change of mind of the "surrogate" within some specified time period; to accord more with an "open" model in which all the parties to the contract retain contact with the child; or by making pregnancy contracts analogous to contracts that require informed consent, as in the case of medical experiments. Pregnancy contracts could be required to provide detailed information about the emotional risks and costs associated with giving up a child.

Finally, some writers have objected to pregnancy contracts on the ground that they must, by their nature, exploit women. They point to the fact that the compensation is very low, and that many of the women who agree to sell their reproductive labor have altruistic motivations. . . .

Two responses are possible to this line of argument. First, even if it is the case that all or most of the women who sell their reproductive labor are altruistically motivated, it is unfair to argue that the other parties to the contract are motivated solely in accord with market values. The couples who use contract pregnancy are not seeking to make a profit, but to have a child. Some of them might even be willing to maintain an "extended family" relationship with the "surrogate" after the child's birth. Second, even if an asymmetry in motivation is established, it is also present in many types of service work: teaching, health care, and social work are all liable to result in "exploitation" of this sort. In all of these areas, the problem is at least partially addressed by regulating compensation. Why is contract pregnancy different?

III. THE CONSEQUENCES OF CONTRACT PREGNANCY FOR CHILDREN

Susan Okin makes an argument against contract pregnancy that is based on its direct consequences for children, and not on the intrinsic features of reproductive labor or the bonds of motherhood. She argues that the problem with pregnancy contracts is that they do not consider the interests of the child.[4] Okin thus focuses on a different aspect of the concern that contract pregnancy leads us to adopt an inferior understanding of children. She points not to the conception itself, but to its consequences for children. The asymmetry, then, between reproductive labor and other forms of labor is based on the fact that only in the former are the child's interests directly at stake.

Putting aside the difficult question of what actually constitutes the child's best interests, it is not certain that such interests will always be served by the child's remaining with its biological parents. Some children may be better off separated from their biological parents when such parents are abusive. . . .

. . . One of the difficulties with evaluating pregnancy contracts in terms of their effects on children is that we have very little empirical evidence of these effects. . . . We should be wary of prematurely making abstract arguments based on the child's best interests without any empirical evidence. Moreover, in the case of families whose life situation may be disapproved of by their community, we may have moral reasons for overriding the best interests of an individual child. For example, if the child of a single or lesbian mother were to suffer discrimination, I do not think that this would justify removal of the child from the mother. Thus, while pregnancy contracts may threaten the interests of children, this is not yet established; nor is this consideration by itself a sufficient reason for forbidding such contracts.

IV. REPRODUCTIVE LABOR AND EQUALITY

In the preceding three sections I have argued that the asymmetry thesis cannot be defended by claiming that there is something "essential" about reproductive labor that singles it out for different treatment from other forms of labor; nor by arguing that contract pregnancy distorts the nature of the bonds of motherhood; nor by the appeal to the best interests of the child. The arguments I have examined ignore the existing background conditions that underlie pregnancy contracts, many of which are objectionable. . . .

I think that the strongest argument against contract pregnancy that depends upon the asymmetry thesis is derived from considerations of gender equality. It is this consideration that I believe is tacitly driving many of the arguments; for example, it is the background gender inequality that makes the commodification of women's and children's attributes especially objectionable. My criticism of contract pregnancy centers on the hypothesis that in our society such contracts will turn women's labor into something that is used and controlled by others and will reinforce gender stereotypes that have been used to justify the unequal treatment of women.

Contrary to the democratic ideal, gender inequality is pervasive in our society. This inequality includes the unequal distribution of housework and child care that considerably restricts married women's opportunities in the work force; the fact that the ratio between an average full-time working woman's earnings and those of her average male counterpart is 59.3:100,[5] and the fact that divorce is an economically devastating experience for women (during the 1970s, the standard of living of young divorced mothers fell 73%, while men's standard of living following divorce rose 42%).[6] These circumstances constitute the baseline from which women form their preferences and make their "choices." Thus, even a woman's choice to engage in commercial surrogacy must be viewed against a background of unequal opportunity. Most work done by women in our society remains in a "female ghetto": service and clerical work, secretarial work, cleaning, domestic labor, nursing, elementary school teaching, and waitressing.

I assume that there is something deeply objectionable about gender inequality. My argument is that contract pregnancy's reinforcing of this inequality lies at the heart of what is wrong with it. In particular, reproduction is a sphere that historically has been marked by inequality: women and men have not had equal influence over the institutions and practices involved in human reproduction. In its current form and context, contract pregnancy contributes to gender inequality in three ways:

1. Contract pregnancy gives others increased access to and control over women's bodies and sexuality. [But there is] a crucial difference between artificial insemination by donor (AID) and a pregnancy contract. AID does not give anyone control over men's bodies and sexuality. A man who elects AID simply sells a product of his body or his sexuality; he does not sell control over his body itself. The current practices of AID and pregnancy contracts are remarkably different in the scope of intervention and control they allow the "buyer." Pregnancy contracts involve substantial control over women's bodies.[7]

What makes this control objectionable, however, is not the intrinsic features of women's reproductive labor, but rather the ways in which such control reinforces a long history of unequal treatment. Consider an analogous case that has no such consequence: voluntary (paid) military service, where men sell their fighting capacities. Military service, like contract pregnancy, involves significant invasions into the body of the seller; soldiers' bodies are controlled to a large extent by their commanding officers under conditions in which the stakes are often life and death. But military service does not *directly* serve to perpetuate traditional gender inequalities. The fact that pregnancy contracts, like military contracts, give someone control over someone else's body is not the issue. Rather, the issue is that in contract pregnancy the body that is controlled belongs to a woman, in a society that historically has subordinated women's interests to those of men, primarily through its control over her sexuality and reproduction.

Market theorists might retort that contract pregnancy could be regulated to protect women's autonomy, in the same way that we regulate other labor contracts. However, it will be difficult, given the nature of the interests involved, for such contracts not to be very intrusive with respect to women's bodies in spite of formal agreements. The purpose of such contracts is, after all, to produce a healthy child. In order to help guarantee a healthy baby, a woman's behavior must be highly controlled.[8] . . .

2. Contract pregnancy reinforces stereotypes about the proper role of women in the reproductive division of labor. At a time when women have made strides in labor force participation, moving out of the family into other social spheres, pregnancy contracts provide a monetary incentive for women to remain in the home. And, while some women may "prefer" to stay at home, we need to pay attention to the limited range of economic opportunities available to these women, and to the ways in which these opportunities have shaped their preferences. Under present conditions, pregnancy contracts entrench a traditional division of labor—men at work, women in the home—based on gender.

Additionally, pregnancy contracts will affect the way society views women: they will tend to reinforce the view of women as "baby machines." It is also likely that they will affect the way women see themselves. Insofar as the sale of women's reproductive capacities contributes to the social subordination of women, and only of women, there are antidiscrimination grounds for banning it.

3. Contract pregnancy raises the danger, manifested in several recent court rulings, that "motherhood" will be defined in terms of genetic material, in the same way as "fatherhood." Mary Beth Whitehead won back parental rights to Baby M on the basis of her being the genetic "mother." On the other hand, Anna Johnson, a "gestational" surrogate, lost such rights because she bore no genetic relationship to the child. These court rulings establish the principle of motherhood on the basis of genetic contribution. In such cases, women's contribution to reproduction is recognized only insofar as it is identical to that of men. Genes alone are taken to define natural and biological motherhood. By not taking women's actual gestational contributions into account, the courts reinforce an old stereotype of women as merely the incubators of men's seeds. In fact, the court's inattention to women's unique labor contribution is itself a form of unequal treatment. By defining women's rights and contributions in terms of those of men, when they are different, the courts fail to recognize an adequate basis for women's rights and needs. These rulings place an additional burden on women.

Given its consequences for gender inequality, I think that the asymmetry thesis is true, and that pregnancy contracts are especially troubling. Current gender inequality lies at the heart of what is wrong with pregnancy contracts. The problem with commodifying women's reproductive labor is not that it "degrades" the special nature of reproductive labor, or "alienates" women from a core part of their identities, but that it reinforces a traditional gender-hierarchical division of labor. A consequence of my argument is that under very different background conditions, in which men and women had equal power and had an equal range of choices, such contracts would be less objectionable. For example, in a society in which women's work was valued as much as men's and in which child care was shared equally, pregnancy contracts might serve primarily as a way for single persons, disabled persons, and same-sex families to have children. Indeed, pregnancy contracts and similar practices have the potential to transform the nuclear family. We know too little about possible new forms of family life to restrict such experiments on a priori grounds; but in our society, I have argued that there are consequentialist reasons for making this restriction. . . .

V. CONCLUSION: WAGE LABOR, REPRODUCTIVE LABOR, AND EQUALITY

In this article, I have analyzed various grounds for forbidding markets in women's reproductive labor. While I rejected most of these grounds, including the essentialist thesis, the opposing approach of market theorists misses the point that there are noneconomic values that should constrain social policy. Market theorists, in representing all of human behavior as if it were a product of voluntary choice, ignore the fact of unequal power in the family and in the wider society.

While market theorists often defend their approach in terms of the values of liberty, welfare, and neutrality, they abstract away from the inegalitarian social context in which an individual's preferences are formed. But how preferences are formed, and in the light of what range of choices, has a great deal to do with whether or not acting on those preferences is liberty- and welfare-enhancing. Under some circumstances, for example, it could be welfare-enhancing to sell oneself into slavery.

What about liberal neutrality? Market theorists may claim that the asymmetry thesis is a violation of liberal neutrality: it imposes a standard of gender equality on free exchanges. Furthermore, it may seem biased—distinguishing activities that harm women from those that harm everyone. The issue of neutrality is a difficult matter to assess, for there are many interpretations of neutrality. At the very least, however, two considerations seem relevant. First, why should existing distributions serve as the standard against which neutrality is measured? I have argued that it is a mistake to assume that the realm of reproduction and sexuality is "neutral"; it is a product (at least in part) of the unequal social, political, and economic power of men and women. Second, most liberals draw the line at social practices such as slavery, indentured servitude, labor at slave wages, and the selling of votes or political liberties. Each of these practices undermines a framework of free deliberation among equals. If such restrictions violate viewpoint "neutrality," then the mere violation of neutrality does not seem objectionable.

Contract pregnancy places women's bodies under the control of others and serves to perpetuate gender inequality. The asymmetries of gender—the fact of social relations of gender domination—provide the best foundation for the asymmetry thesis. However, not all of the negative consequences of contract pregnancy involve its effects on gender inequality. I have also referred to its possible effects on children, and to the problematic form that such contracts will have to take to be self-enforcing. In addition, a full assessment of the practice would have to consider both its potential for deepening racial inequality and the unequal bargaining power of the parties to the contract. Some of these features of pregnancy contracts are shared with other labor contracts. Indeed, there is an important tradition in social philosophy that argues that it is precisely these shared features that make wage labor itself unacceptable. This tradition emphasizes that wage labor, like contract pregnancy, places the productive capacities of one group of citizens at the service and under the control of another. Unfortunately, there has been little attention in political philosophy to the effects of gender and class inequality on the development of women's and workers' deliberative capacities or on the formation of their preferences. We have to ask: What kinds of work and family relations and environments best promote the development of the deliberative capacities needed to support democratic institutions?

Notes

1. I will use the terms *contract pregnancy* and *pregnancy contract* in place of the misleading term *surrogacy*. The so-called surrogate mother is not a surrogate; she is the biological and/or gestational mother. In this article, I do not make any assumptions about who is and who is not a "real" mother.

2. Carole Pateman, *The Sexual Contract* (Stanford: Stanford University Press, 1988), p. 207.

3. Margaret Jane Radin, "Justice and the Market Domain," in *Markets and Justice*, ed. John W. Chapman and J. R. Pennock (New York: New York University Press, 1989), p. 175.

4. Susan Okin, "A Critique of Pregnancy Contracts: Comments on Articles by Hill, Merrick, Shevory, and Woliver," *Politics and the Life Sciences* 8 (1990):205–10.

5. This figure compares the earnings of white women and white men. In 1980, black and Hispanic women earned, respectively, 55.3% and 40.1% of white men's earnings. See Sara M. Evans and Barbara Nelson,

Wage Justice: Comparable Worth and the Paradox of Technocratic Reform (Chicago: University of Chicago Press, 1989).

6. Lenore J. Weitzman, *The Divorce Revolution: The Unexpected Social and Economic Consequences for Women and Children in America* (New York: The Free Press, 1985), p. 323.

7. A man who buys women's reproductive labor can choose his "surrogate"; he does not legally require his wife's permission; pregnancy contracts include substantial provisions regulating the surrogate's behavior. Such provisions include agreements concerning medical treatment, the conditions under which the surrogate agrees to undergo an abortion, and regulation of the surrogate's emotions. Thus, in the case of Baby M, Mary Beth Whitehead consented to refrain from forming or attempting to form any relationship with the child she would conceive. She agreed not to smoke cigarettes, drink alcoholic beverages, or take medications without written consent from her physician. She also agreed to undergo amniocentesis and to abort the fetus "upon demand of William Stern, natural father" if tests found genetic or congenital defects. See "Appendix: Baby M Contract," *Beyond Baby M*, ed. Dianne Bartels (Clifton, N.J.: Humana Press, 1990).

8. There is already legal precedent for regulating women's behavior in the "best interests" of the fetus. A Massachusetts woman was charged with vehicular homicide when her fetus was delivered stillborn following a car accident. See Eileen McNamara, "Fetal Endangerment Cases on the Rise," *Boston Globe*, 3 October 1989; cited in Lawrence Tribe, *Abortion: The Clash of Absolutes* (New York: Norton, 1990).

Essay and Paper Topics for "Moral Practice and Culture"

1. Using the selections by Devereaux and Hyde, discuss the importance of art in culture.

2. Given the role of art in culture, do you think censorship is justified based on the content of the work? Discuss this question using at least two of the authors in this section.

3. Discuss the debate about the curriculum in light of the readings in this section, focusing in particular on what you think the most important issues are that distinguish the different positions. Which side has the stronger position? Why?

4. Using Mill's *On Liberty* as a starting point, discuss the question of whether government should forbid people to do things that are not harmful to others.

5. Discuss the effects of living in a capitalist economy on the character of people.

6. How would Nozick respond to Walzer and Satz? Are his responses sound, or do you think one of them has, implicitly, a better argument? Explain.

7. How would Mill answer the argument made by Satz concerning markets in reproductive labor? Does Satz's argument indicate a weakness in Mill's harm principle?

8. How much of human life should be controlled by markets, and how much by government?

Part IV

Moral Practice and Reason

Section 8

Feelings and Reason in Morality

The Conscience of Huckleberry Finn

Jonathan Bennett

Sometimes a situation may arise in which a person feels a conflict between doing the right thing and sympathy for those who may be hurt as a result of meeting morality's demands. Here, Jonathan Bennett graphically illustrates this conflict in three surprising and fascinating examples: Huck Finn's conflict over whether to free his slave friend Jim; Nazi commander Heinrich Himmler's feelings for the Jews and the duty he felt to kill them; and Jonathan Edwards's attitudes toward fallen people, who he thought were doomed to live in hell, and the justice of the wrathful God who condemns them. Bennett uses these examples to explore the relations between duty and sympathy as well as the dangers and advantages of relying on our feelings when they conflict with our sense of duty. Jonathan Bennett was professor of philosophy at Syracuse University.

As you read through this essay, consider the following:

1. What are the examples Bennett uses to illustrate how feelings and duty may conflict?
2. How does Bennett characterize the relationship between morality and sympathy? In light of his examples, do you agree with the role he gives to each?
3. Why does Bennett think Edwards's morality was worse than Himmler's?
4. Besides sympathy, what means are available to criticize our own or others' moral decisions?
5. How does Bennett's understanding of the nature of morality compare with that of two of the following: Ruth Benedict, C. S. Lewis, and Thomas Hobbes?

158

In this paper,[1] I shall present not just the conscience of Huckleberry Finn but two others as well. One of them is the conscience of Heinrich Himmler. He became a Nazi in 1923; he served drably and quietly, but well, and was rewarded with increasing responsibility and power. At the peak of his career he held many offices and commands, of which the most powerful was that of leader of the S.S.—the principal police force of the Nazi regime. In this capacity, Himmler commanded the whole concentration-camp system, and was responsible for the execution of the so-called "final solution of the Jewish problem." It is important for my purposes that this piece of social engineering should be though of not abstractly but in concrete terms of Jewish families being marched to what they think are bathhouses, to the accompaniment of loud-speaker renditions of extracts from *The Merry Widow* and *Tales of Hoffman*, there to be choked to death by poisonous gases. Altogether, Himmler succeeded in murdering about four and a half million of them, as well as several million gentiles, mainly Poles and Russians.

The other conscience to be discussed is that of the Calvinist theologian and philosopher Jonathan Edwards. He lived in the first half of the eighteenth century, and has a good claim to be considered America's first serious and considerable philosophical thinker. He was for many years a widely-renowned preacher and Congregationalist minister in New England; in 1748 a dispute with his congregation led him to resign (he couldn't accept their view that unbelievers should be admitted to the Lord's Supper in the hope that it would convert them); for some years after that he worked as a missionary, preaching to Indians through an interpreter; then in 1758 he accepted the presidency of what is now Princeton University, and within two

months died from a small-pox inoculation. Along the way he wrote some first-rate philosophy: his book attacking the notion of free will is still sometimes read. Why I should be interested in Edwards' conscience will be explained in due course.

I shall use Heinrich Himmler, Jonathan Edwards and Huckleberry Finn to illustrate different aspects of a single theme, namely the relationship between *sympathy* on the one hand and *bad morality* on the other.

All that I can mean by a "bad morality" is a morality whose principles I deeply disapprove of. When I call a morality bad, I cannot prove that mine is better; but when I here call any morality bad, I think you will agree with me that it is bad; and that is all I need.

There could be dispute as to whether the springs of someone's actions constitute a *morality*, I think, though, that we must admit that someone who acts in ways which conflict grossly with our morality may nevertheless have a morality of his own—a set of principles of action which he sincerely assents to, so that for him the problem of acting well or rightly or in obedience to conscience is the problem of conforming to those principles. The problem of conscientiousness can arise as acutely for a bad morality as for any other: rotten principles may be as difficult to keep as decent ones.

As for "sympathy": I use this term to cover every sort of fellow-feeling, as when one feels pity over someone's loneliness, or horrified compassion over his pain, or when one feels a shrinking reluctance to act in a way which will bring misfortune to someone else. These feelings must not be confused with *moral judgments*. My sympathy for someone in distress may lead me to help him, or even to think that I ought to help him; but in itself it is not a judgment about what I ought to do but just a feeling for him in his plight. We shall get some light on the difference between feelings and moral judgments when we consider Huckleberry Finn.

Obviously, feelings can impel one to action, and so can moral judgments; and in a particular case sympathy and morality may

Jonathan Bennett, "The Conscience of Huckleberry Finn," *Philosophy*, 49 (April 1974). © 1974 by the Royal Institute of Philosophy. Reprinted with the permission of Cambridge University Press.

pull in opposite directions. This can happen not just with bad moralities, but also with good ones like yours and mine. For example, a small child, sick and miserable, clings tightly to his mother and screams in terror when she tries to pass him over to the doctor to be examined. If the mother gave way to her sympathy, that is to her feeling for the child's misery and fright, she would hold it close and not let the doctor come near; but don't we agree that it might be wrong for her to act on such a feeling? Quite generally, then, anyone's moral principles may apply to a particular situation in a way which runs contrary to the particular thrusts of fellow-feeling that he has in that situation. My immediate concern is with sympathy in relation to bad morality, but not because such conflicts occur only when the morality is bad.

Now, suppose that someone who accepts a bad morality is struggling to make himself act in accordance with it in a particular situation where his sympathies pull him another way. He sees the struggle as one between doing the right, conscientious thing, and acting wrongly and weakly, like the mother who won't let the doctor come near her sick, frightened baby. Since we don't accept this person's morality, we may see the situation very differently, thoroughly disapproving of the action he regards as the right one, and endorsing the action which from his point of view constitutes weakness and backsliding.

Conflicts between sympathy and bad morality won't always be like this, for we won't disagree with every single dictate of a bad morality. Still, it can happen in the way I have described, with the agent's right action being our wrong one, and vice versa. that is just what happens in a certain episode in chapter 16 of *The Adventures of Huckleberry Finn*, an episode which brilliantly illustrates how fiction can be instructive about real life.

Huck Finn has been helping his slave friend Jim to run away from Miss Watson, who is Jim's owner. In their raft-journey down the Mississippi River, they are near to the place at which Jim will become legally free. Now let Huck take over the story:

Jim said it made him all over trembly and feverish to be so close to freedom. Well, I can tell you it made me all over trembly and feverish, too, to hear him, because I begun to get it through my head that he was most free—and who was to blame for it? Why, me. I couldn't get that out of my conscience, no how nor no way. It hadn't ever come home to me, before, what this thing was that I was doing. But now it did; and it stayed with me, and scorched me more and more. I tried to make out to myself that I warn't to blame, because I didn't run Jim off from his rightful owner; but it warn't no use, conscience up and say, every time: "But you knowed he was running for his freedom, and you could a paddled ashore and told somebody." That was so—I couldn't get around that, no way. That was where it pinched. Conscience says to me: "What had poor Miss Watson done to you, that you could see her nigger go off right under your eyes and never say one single word? What did that poor old woman do to you, that you could treat her so mean? . . ." I got to feeling so mean and so miserable I most wished I was dead.

Jim speaks of his plan to save up to buy his wife, and then his children, out of slavery; and he adds that if the children cannot be bought he will arrange to steal them. Huck is horrified:

Thinks I, this is what comes of my not thinking. Here was this nigger which I had as good as helped to run away, coming right out flat-footed and saying he would steal his children—children that belonged to a man I didn't even know; a man that hadn't ever done me no harm.

I was sorry to hear Jim say that, it was such a lowering of him. My conscience got to stirring me up hotter than ever, until at last I says to it: "Let up on me—it ain't too late, yet—I'll paddle ashore at first light, and tell." I felt easy, and happy, and light as a feather, right off. All my troubles was gone.

This is bad morality all right. In his earliest years Huck wasn't taught any principles, and the only ones he has encountered since then are those of rural Missouri, in which slave-owning is just one kind of ownership and is not subject to critical pressure. It hasn't occurred to Huck to question those principles. So the action, to us abhorrent, of turning Jim in to the authorities presents itself clearly to Huck as the right thing to do.

For us, morality and sympathy would both dictate helping Jim to escape. If we felt any conflict, it would have both these on one side and something else on the other—greed for a reward, or fear of punishment. But Huck's morality conflicts with his sympathy, that is, with his unargued, natural feeling for his friend. The conflict starts when Huck sets off in the canoe towards the shore, pretending that he is going to reconnoitre, but really planning to turn Jim in:

> As I shoved off, [Jim] says: "Pooty soon I'll be a-shout'n for joy, en I'll say, it's all on accounts o' Huck I's a free man . . . Jim won't ever forgit you, Huck; you's de bes' fren' Jim's ever had; en you's de only fren' old Jim's got now."
>
> I was padding off, all in a sweat to tell on him; but when he says this, it seemed to kind of take the tuck all out of me. I went along slow then, and I warn't right down certain whether I was glad I started or whether I warn't. When I was fifty yards off, Jim says:
>
> "Dah you goes, de ole true Huck; de on'y white genlman dat ever kep' his promise to ole Jim." Well, I just felt sick. But I says, I *got* to do it—I can't get *out* of it.

In the upshot, sympathy wins over morality. Huck hasn't the strength of will to do what he sincerely thinks he ought to do. Two men hunting for runaway slaves ask him whether the man on his raft is black or white:

> I didn't answer up prompt. I tried to, but the words wouldn't come. I tried, for a second or two, to brace up and out with it, but I warn't man enough—hadn't the spunk of a rabbit. I see I was weakening; so I just give up trying, and up and says: "He's white."

So Huck enables Jim to escape, thus acting weakly and wickedly—he thinks. In this conflict between sympathy and morality, sympathy wins.

One critic has cited this episode in support of the statement that Huck suffers "excruciating moments of wavering between

honesty and respectability." That is hopelessly wrong, and I agree with the perceptive comment on it by another critic, who says:

> The conflict waged in Huck is much more serious: he scarcely cares for respectability and never hesitates to relinquish it, but he does care for honesty and gratitude—and both honesty and gratitude require that he should give Jim up. It is not, in Huck, honesty at war with respectability but love and compassion for Jim struggling against his conscience. His decision is for Jim and hell: a right decision made in the mental chains that Huck never breaks. His concern for Jim is and remains irrational. Huck finds many reasons for giving Jim up and none for stealing him. To the end Huck sees his compassion for Jim as a weak, ignorant, and wicked felony.[2]

That is precisely correct—and it can have that virtue only because Mark Twain wrote the episode with such unerring precision. The crucial point concerns reasons, which all occur on one side of the conflict. On the side of conscience we have principles, arguments, considerations, ways of looking at things:

> "It hadn't ever come home to me before what I was doing"
> "I tried to make out that I warn't to blame"
> "Conscience said 'But you knowed . . .'—I couldn't get around that"
> "What had poor Miss Watson done to you?"
> "This is what comes of my not thinking"
> "children that belonged to a man I didn't even know"

On the other side, the side of feeling, we get nothing like that. When Jim rejoices in Huck, as his only friend, Huck doesn't consider the claims of friendship or have the situation "come home" to him in a different light. All that happens is: "When he says this, it seemed to kind of take the tuck all out of me. I went along slow then, and I warn't right down certain whether I was glad I started or whether I warn't." Again, Jim's words about Huck's "promise" to him don't give Huck any reason for changing his plan: in his morality promises to slaves probably don't count.

Their effect on him is of a different kind: "Well, I just felt sick." And when the moment for final decision comes, Huck doesn't weight up pros and cons: he simply *fails* to do what he believes to be right—he isn't strong enough, hasn't "the spunk of a rabbit." This passage in the novel is notable not just for its finely wrought irony, with Huck's weakness of will leading him to do the right thing, but also for its masterly handling of the difference between general moral principles and particular unreasoned emotional pulls.

Consider now another case of bad morality in conflict with human sympathy, the case of odious Himmler. Here, from a speech he made to some S.S. generals, is an indication of the content of his morality:

> What happens to a Russian, to a Czech, does not interest me in the slightest. What the nations can offer in the way of good blood of our type, we will take, if necessary by kidnapping their children and raising them here with us. Whether nations live in prosperity or starve to death like cattle interests me only in so far as we need them as slaves to our Kultur; otherwise it is of no interest to me. Whether 10,000 Russian females fall down from exhaustion while digging an anti-tank ditch interests me only in so far as the anti-tank ditch for Germany is finished.[3]

But has this a moral basis at all? And if it has, was there in Himmler's own mind any conflict between morality and sympathy? Yes there was. Here is more from the same speech:

> . . . I also want to talk to you quite frankly on a very grave matter . . . I mean . . . the extermination of the Jewish race . . . Most of you must know what it means when 100 corpses are lying side by side, or 500, or 1,000. To have stuck it out and at the same time—apart from exceptions caused by human weakness—to have remained decent fellows, that is what has made us hard. This is a page of glory in our history which has never been written and is never to be written.

Himmler saw his policies as being hard to implement while still retaining one's human sympathies—while still remaining a "decent fellow." He is saying that only the weak take the easy way out and just squelch their sympathies, and is praising the stronger and more glorious course of retaining one's sympathies while acting in violation of them. In the same spirit, he ordered that when executions were carried out in concentration camps, those responsible "are to be influenced in such a way as to suffer no ill effect in their character and mental attitude." A year later he boasted that the S.S. had wiped out the Jews

> without our leaders and their men suffering any damage in their minds and souls. The danger was considerable, for there was only a narrow path between the Scylla of their becoming heartless ruffians unable any longer to treasure life, and the Charybdis of their becoming soft and suffering nervous breakdowns.

And there really can't be any doubt that the basis of Himmler's policies was a set of principles which constituted his morality—a sick, bad, wicked *morality*. He described himself as caught in 'the old tragic conflict between will and obligation.' And when his physician Kersten protested at the intention to destroy the Jews, saying that the suffering involved was "not to be contemplated," Kersten reports that Himmler replied:

> He knew that it would mean much suffering for the Jews. . . . "It is the curse of greatness that it must step over dead bodies to create new life. Yet we must cleanse the soil or it will never bear fruit. It will be a great burden for me to bear."

This, I submit, is the language of morality.

So in this case, tragically, bad morality won out over sympathy. I am sure that many of Himmler's killers did extinguish their sympathies, becoming "heartless ruffians" rather than "decent fellows"; but not Himmler himself. Although his policies ran against the human grain to a horrible degree, he did not sandpaper down his emotional surfaces so that there was no grain there, allowing his actions to slide along smoothly and easily. He did, after all, bear his hideous burden, and even paid a price for it. He suffered a variety of nervous and physical disabilities, including nausea and stomach-convulsions, and Kersten was doubtless right in saying that these were "the expression of a psychic division which extended over his whole life."

This same division must have been present in some of those officials of the Church who ordered heretics to be tortured so as to change their theological opinions. Along with the brutes and the cold careerists, there must have been some who cared, and who suffered from the conflict between their sympathies and their bad morality.

In the conflict between sympathy and bad morality, then, the victory may go to sympathy as in the case of Huck Finn, or to morality as the case of Himmler.

Another possibility is that the conflict may be avoided by giving up, or not ever having, those sympathies which might interfere with one's principles. That seems to have been the case with Jonathan Edwards. I am afraid that I shall be doing an injustice to Edwards' many virtues, and to his great intellectual energy and inventiveness; for my concern is only with the worst thing about him—namely his morality, which was worse than Himmler's.

According to Edwards, God condemns some men to an eternity of unimaginably awful pain, though he arbitrarily spares others—"arbitrarily" because none deserve to be spared:

Natural men are held in the hand of God over the pit of hell . . . ; they have deserved the fiery pit, and are already sentenced to it; and God is dreadfully provoked, his anger is as great towards them as to those that are actually suffering the executions of the fierceness of his wrath in hell; the devil is waiting for them, hell is gaping for them, the flames gather and flash about them, and would fain lay hold on them . . . ; and . . . there are no means within reach that can be any security to them. . . . All that preserves them is the mere arbitrary will, and uncovenanted unobliged forebearance of an incensed God.[4]

Notice that he says "they have deserved the fiery pit." Edwards insists that men *ought* to be condemned to eternal pain; and his posi-

tion isn't that this is right because God wants it, but rather that God wants it because it is right. For him, moral standards exist independently of God, and God can be assessed in the light of them (and of course found to be perfect). For example, he says:

They deserve to be cast into hell; so that . . . justice never stands in the way, it makes no objection against God's using his power at any moment to destroy them. Yea, on the contrary, justice calls aloud for an infinite punishment of their sins.

Elsewhere, he gives elaborate arguments to show that God is acting justly in damning sinners. For example, he argues that a punishment should be exactly as bad as the crime being punished: God is infinitely excellent; so any crime against him is infinitely bad; and so eternal damnation is exactly right as a punishment—it is infinite, but, as Edwards is careful also to say, it is "no more than infinite."

Of course, Edwards himself didn't torment the damned; but the question still arises of whether his sympathies didn't conflict with his approval of eternal torment. Didn't he find it painful to contemplate any fellow-human's being tortured for ever? Apparently not:

The God that holds you over the pit of hell, much as one holds a spider or some loathsome insect over the fire, abhors you, and is dreadfully provided; . . . he is of purer eyes than to bear to have you in his sight; you are ten thousand times so abominable in his eyes as the most hateful venomous serpent is in ours.

When God is presented as being as misanthropic as that, one suspects misanthropy in the theologian. This suspicion is increased when Edwards claims that "the saints in glory will . . . understand how terrible the sufferings of the damned are; yet . . . will not be sorry for [them]."[5] He bases this partly on a view of human nature whose ugliness he seems not to notice:

The seeing of the calamities of others tends to heighten the sense of our own enjoyments. When the saints in glory, therefore, shall see the doleful state of the damned, how will this heighten their sense of the blessedness of their own state. . . . When they shall see how miserable others of their fellow-creatures are . . . ; when they shall see the smoke of their torment, . . . and hear their dolorous shrieks and cries, and consider that they in the mean time are in the most blissful state, and shall surely be in it to all eternity; how they will rejoice!

I hope this is less than the whole truth! His other main point about why the saints will rejoice to see the torments of the damned is that it is *right* that they should do so:

The heavenly inhabitants . . . will have no love nor pity to the damned. . . . [This will not show] a want of a spirit of love in them . . . ; for the heavenly inhabitants will know that it is not fit that they should love [the damned] because they will know then, that God has no love to them, nor pity for them.

The implication that *of course* one can adjust one's feelings of pity so that they conform to the dictates of some authority—doesn't this suggest that ordinary human sympathies played only a small part in Edwards' life?

Huck Finn, whose sympathies are wide and deep, could never avoid the conflict in that way; but he is determined to avoid it, and so he opts for the only other alternative he can see—to give up morality altogether. After he has tricked the slave-hunters, he returns to the raft and undergoes a peculiar crisis:

I got aboard the raft, feeling bad and low, because I knowed very well I had done wrong, and I see it warn't no use for me to try to learn to do right; a body that don't get *started* right when he's little, ain't got no show—when the pinch comes there ain't nothing to back him up and keep him to his work, and so he gets beat. Then I thought a minute, and says to myself, hold on—s'pose you'd a done right and give Jim up; would you feel better than what you do now? No, says I, I'd feel bad—I'd feel just the same way I do now. Well, then, says I, what's the use of you learning to do right, when it's troublesome to do right and ain't no trouble to do wrong, and the wages is just the same? I was stuck. I couldn't answer that. So I reckoned I

wouldn't bother no more about it, but after this always do whichever come handiest at the time.

Huck clearly cannot conceive of having any morality except the one he has learned—too late, he thinks—from his society. He is not entirely a prisoner of that morality, because he does after all reject it; but for him that is a decision to relinquish morality as such; he cannot envisage revising his morality, altering its content in face of the various pressures to which it is subject, including pressures from his sympathies. For example, he does not begin to approach the thought that slavery should be rejected on moral grounds, or the thought that what he is doing is not theft because a person cannot be owned and therefore cannot be stolen.

The basic trouble is that he cannot or will not engage in abstract intellectual operations of any sort. In chapter 33 he finds himself "feeling to blame, somehow" for something he knows he had no hand in; he assumes that this feeling is a deliverance of conscience; and this confirms him in his belief that conscience shouldn't be listened to:

It don't make no difference whether you do right or wrong, a person's conscience ain't got no sense, and just goes for him *anyway*. If I had a yaller dog and didn't know no more than a person's conscience does, I would poison him. It takes up more room than all the rest of a person's insides, and yet ain't no good, nohow.

That brisk, incurious dismissiveness fits well with the comprehensive rejection of morality back on the raft. But this is a digression.

On the raft, Huck decides not to live by principles, but just to do whatever "comes handiest at the time"—always acting according to the mood of the moment. Since the morality he is rejecting is narrow and cruel, and his sympathies are broad and kind, the results will be good. But moral principles are good to have, because they help to protect one from acting badly at moments when one's sympathies happen to be in abeyance. On the highest possible estimate of the role one's sympathies should have, one can still allow for principles as embodiments of one's best feelings, one's broadest and keenest sympathies. On that view, principles can help one across intervals when one's feelings are at less than their best, i.e. through periods of misanthropy or meanness or self-centredness or depression or anger.

What Huck didn't see is that one can live by principles and yet have ultimate control over their content. And one way such control can be exercised is by checking of one's principles in the light of one's sympathies. This is sometimes a pretty straightforward matter. It can happen that a certain moral principle becomes untenable—meaning literally that one cannot hold it any longer—because it conflicts intolerably with the pity or revulsion or whatever that one feels when one sees what the principle leads to. One's experience may play a large part here: experiences evoke feelings, and feelings force one to modify principles. Something like this happened to the English poet Wilfred Owen, whose experiences in the First World War transformed him from an enthusiastic soldier into a virtual pacifist. I can't document his change of conscience in detail; but I want to present something which he wrote about the way experience can put pressure on morality.[6]

The Latin poet Horace wrote that it is sweet and fitting (or right) to die for one's country—*dulce et decorum est pro patria mori*—and Owen wrote a fine poem about how experience could lead one to relinquish that particular moral principle. He describes a man who is too slow donning his gas mask during a gas attack—"As under a green sea, I saw him drowning," Owen says. The poem ends like this:

In all my dreams, before my helpless sight
He plunges at me, guttering, choking, drowning.
If in some smothering dreams you too could pace
Behind the wagon that we flung him in,
And watch the white eyes writhing in his face,
His hanging face, like a devil's sick of sin;
If you could hear, at every jolt, the blood
Come gargling from the froth-corrupted lungs,

Obscene as cancer, bitter as the cud
Of vile, incurable sores on innocent tongues,—
My friend, you would not tell with such high zest
To children ardent for some desperate glory,
The old Lie: Dulce et decorum est
Pro patria mori.

There is a difficulty about drawing from all this a moral for ourselves. I imagine that we agree in our rejection of slavery, eternal damnation, genocide, and uncritical patriotic self-abnegation; so we shall agree that Huck Finn, Jonathan Edwards, Heinrich Himmler, and the poet Horace would have done well to bring certain of their principles under severe pressure from ordinary human sympathies. But then we can say this because we can say that all those are bad moralities, whereas we cannot look at our own moralities and declare them bad. This is not arrogance: it is obviously incoherent for someone to declare the system of moral principles that he accepts to be bad, just as one cannot coherently say of anything that one *believes* it but it is *false*.

Still, although I can't point to any of my beliefs and say "That is false," I don't doubt that some of my beliefs *are* false; and so I should try to remain open to correction. Similarly, I accept every single item in my morality—that is inevitable—but I am sure that my morality could be improved, which is to say that it could undergo changes which I should be glad of once I had made them. So I must try to keep my morality open to revision, exposing it to whatever valid pressures there are—including pressures from my sympathies.

I don't give my sympathies a blank cheque in advance. In a conflict between principle and sympathy, principles ought sometimes to win. For example, I think it was right to take part in the Second World War on the Allied side; there were many ghastly individual incidents which might have led someone to doubt the rightness of his participation in that war; and I think it would have been right for such a person to keep his sympathies in a subordinate place on those occasions, not allowing them to modify his principles in such a way as to make a pacifist of him.

Still, one's sympathies should be kept as sharp and sensitive and aware as possible, and not only because they can sometimes affect one's principles or one's conduct or both. Owen, at any rate, says that feelings and sympathies are vital even when they can do nothing but bring pain and distress. In another poem he speaks of the blessings of being numb in one's feelings: "Happy are the men who yet before they are killed/Can let their veins run cold," he says. These are the ones who do not suffer from any compassion which, as Owen puts it, "makes their feet/Sore on the alleys cobbled with their brother." He contrasts these "happy" ones, who "lose imagination," with himself and others "who with a thought besmirch/Blood over all our soul." Yet the poem's verdict goes against the "happy" ones. Owen does not say that they will act worse than the others whose souls are besmirched with blood because of their keen awareness of human suffering. He merely says that they are the losers because they have cut themselves off from the human condition:

By choice they made themselves immune
To pity and whatever moans in man
Before the last sea and the hapless stars;

Whatever mourns when many leave these
    shores;
Whatever shares
The eternal reciprocity of tears.

Notes

1. This paper began life as the Potter Memorial Lecture, given at Washington State University in Pullman, Washington, in 1972.

2. M. J. Sidnell, "Huck Finn and Jim," *The Cambridge Quarterly*, vol. 2, pp. 205–206.

3. Quoted in William L. Shirer, *The Rise and Fall of the Third Reich* (New York, 1960), pp. 937–938. Next quotation; ibid., p. 966, All further quotations relating to Himmler are from Roger Manwell and Heinrich Fraenkel, *Heinrich Himmler* (London, 1965), pp. 132, 197, 184 (twice), 187.

4. Vergilius Ferm, ed., *Puritan Sage: Collected Writings of Jonathan Edwards* (New York, 1953), p. 370. Next three quotations: ibid., p. 366, p. 294 ("no more than infinite"), p. 372.

5. This and the next two quotations are from "The End of the Wicked Contemplated by the Righteous: or, The Torments of the Wicked in Hell, no Occasion of Grief to the Saints in Heaven," from *The Works of President Edwards* (London, 1817), vol. IV, pp. 507–8, 511–12 and 509, respectively.

6. Extracts from "Dulce et Decorum Est" and "Insensibility" are from *The Collected Poems of Wilfred Owen*, ed. by C. Day Lewis. © Chatto & Windus Ltd. 1946, 1963. Reprinted by permission of The Owen Estate, Chatto & Windus Ltd., and New Directions Publishing Corporation.

Feelings as the Basis of Morality

David Hume

David Hume (1711–1776) was a towering figure of the Scottish Enlightenment. He lived in Edinburgh, where he wrote on a wide array of subjects, including epistemology, history, religion, science, ethics, and politics. Hume attended Edinburgh University until he was about fifteen. By the age of twenty-eight, he had already published his massive, critical study of knowledge and morality titled *A Treatise of Human Nature*. Deeply disappointed by the book's reception, which, he wrote, "fell dead born from the press," Hume rewrote it as *An Enquiry Concerning Human Understanding* (1748) and *An Enquiry Concerning the Principles of Morals* (1751). He subsequently published *Political Discourses* (1752) and *History of England* (1754), which won him wide acclaim.

Hume was an amiable, moderate man whose company was widely sought. His philosophy, however, was radically critical. Taking his lead from modern science, especially Newton,

Hume sought to use the tools of scientific observation and philosophical argument together to understand human knowledge, religion, morality, and politics. As an empiricist, Hume believed that things that can be present to the mind (which he termed "perceptions") are either impressions or ideas. Impressions occur whenever we feel an emotion or have an image of an external object; ideas are present whenever we reflect on impressions we have had. Ideas are therefore weaker than impressions, and all of our ideas are derived from sense impressions. Mathematics concerns itself merely with the relationships among our ideas.

Hume's key claim, then, is that reasoning can never motivate people, since it involves either the pure relations of ideas (mathematics) or the causes and effects of objects on other objects including bodies. What does motivate us then must be our own feelings, which include our own pleasures and pains, of course, but also the sentiments we feel when thinking about the experiences of others. Values and morality are therefore sharply distinct from facts about the world or about mathematical ideas. Moral condemnation and approval arise from feelings alone, which are uniquely capable of motivating us to act. The selection concludes with a brief account of benevolence and its role in morality.

As you read through this essay, consider the following:

1. Hume says it is common to think of reason and passion or sentiments in conflict. Why does he think passion cannot conflict with abstract relations of ideas?
2. Why does Hume think that the impulse to avoid a pain arises not from reason but from passion?
3. In what sense does Hume mean a passion can never be called "unreasonable"?
4. What is the difference between "calm desires and tendencies" and "violent" ones?
5. If neither moral judgment nor actions come from reason, where do they come from?
6. Explain what Hume means in saying that one can never derive an "ought" from an "is."
7. In what sense does Hume think morality rests not on self-love but on benevolence?

1. REASON SUBORDINATE TO EMOTION

Nothing is more usual in philosophy, and even in common life, than to talk of the combat of passion and reason, to give the preference to reason, and assert that men are only so far virtuous as they conform themselves to its dictates. Every rational creature, it is said, is obliged to regulate his actions by reason; and if any other motive or principle challenge the direction of his conduct, he ought to oppose it, till it be entirely subdued, or at least brought to a conformity with that superior principle. On this method of thinking the

greatest part of moral philosophy, ancient and modern, seems to be founded. . . . I shall endeavor to prove *first*, that reason alone can never be a motive to any action of the will; and *secondly*, that it can never oppose passion in the direction of the will.

The understanding exerts itself after two different ways, as it judges from demonstration or probability; as it regards the abstract relations of our [mathematical] ideas, or those relations of objects, of which experience only gives us information. I believe it scarce will be asserted, and the first species of reasoning alone is ever the cause of any action. As its proper province is the world of ideas, and as the will always places us in that of realities, demonstration and volition seem, upon that account, to be totally removed from each other. Mathematics, indeed, are useful in all mechanical operations, and arithmetic in

From David Hume, *A Treatise of Human Nature* (1739–40) and *An Enquiry Concerning the Principles of Morals* (1751).

almost every art and profession: but it is not of themselves they have any influence. Mechanics are the art of regulating the motions of bodies *to some designed end or purpose;* and the reason why we employ arithmetic in fixing the proportions of numbers, is only that we may discover the proportions of their influence and operation. A merchant is desirous of knowing the sum total of his accounts with any person: why? but that he may learn what sum will have the same *effects* in paying his debt, and going to market, as all the particular articles taken together. Abstract or demonstrative reasoning, therefore, never influences any of our actions, but only as it directs our judgment concerning causes and effects; which leads us to the second operation of the understanding.

It is obvious that when we have the prospect of pain or pleasure from any object, we feel a consequent emotion of aversion or propensity, and are carried to avoid or embrace what will give us this uneasiness or satisfaction. It is also obvious that this emotion rests not here, but making us cast our view on every side, comprehends whatever objects are connected with its original one by the relation of cause and effect. Here then reasoning takes place to discover this relation; and according as our reasoning varies, our actions receive a subsequent variation. But it is evident in this case, that the impulse arises not from reason, but is only directed by it. It is from the prospect of pain or pleasure that the aversion or propensity arises towards any object: and these emotions extend themselves to the causes and effects of that object, as they are pointed out to us by reason and experience. It can never in the least concern us to know that such objects are causes, and such others effects, if both the causes and effects be indifferent to us. Where the objects themselves do not affect us, their connection can never give them any influence; and it is plain, that as reason is nothing but the discovery of this connection, it cannot be by its means that the objects are able to affect us.

Since reason alone can never produce any action, or give rise to volition, I infer, that the same faculty is as incapable of preventing volition, or of disputing the preference with any passion or emotion. This consequence is necessary. . . .

A passion is an original existence, or, if you will, modification of existence, and contains not any representative quality, which renders it a copy of any other existence or modification. When I am angry, I am actually possessed with the passion, and in that emotion have no more a reference to any other object, than when I am thirsty, or sick, or more than five foot high. It is impossible, therefore, that this passion can be opposed by, or be contradictory to truth and reason; since this contradiction consists in the disagreement of ideas, considered as copies, with those objects, which they represent. . . .

It is certain, there are certain calm desires and tendencies, which, although they be real passions, produce little emotion in the mind, and are more known by their effects than by the immediate feeling or sensation. These desires are of two kinds; either certain instincts originally implanted in our natures, such as benevolence and resentment, the love of life, and kindness to children; or the general appetite to good, and aversion to evil, considered merely as such. When any of these passions are calm, and cause no disorder in the soul, they are very readily taken for the determinations for reason, and are supposed to proceed from the same faculty, with that, which judges of truth and falsehood. Their nature and principles have been supposed the same, because their sensations are not evidently different.

Beside these calm passions, which often determine the will, there are certain violent emotions of the same kind, which have likewise a great influence on that faculty. When I receive any injury from another, I often feel a violent passion of resentment, which makes me desire his evil and punishment, independent of all considerations of pleasure and advantage to myself. When I am immediately threatened with any grievous ill, my fears, apprehensions, and aversions rise to a great height, and produce a sensible emotion.

The common error of metaphysicians has lain in ascribing the direction of the will entirely to one of these principles, and supposing the other to have no influence. Men often act knowingly against their interest: For which reason the view of the greatest possible good does not always influence them. Men often counteract a violent passion in prosecution of their interests and designs: It is not therefore the present uneasiness alone, which determines them. In general we may observe, that both these principles operate on the will; and where they are contrary, that either of them prevails, according to the *general* character or *present* disposition of the person. What we call strength of mind, implies the prevalence of the calm passions above the violent; although we may easily observe, there is no man so constantly possessed of this virtue, as never on any occasion to yield to the solicitations of passion and desire. . . .

According to this principle, which is so obvious and natural, it is only in two senses, that any affection can be called unreasonable. First, when a passion, such as hope or fear, grief or joy, despair or security, is founded on the supposition of the existence of objects, which really do not exist. Secondly, when in exerting any passion in action, we choose means insufficient for the designed end, and deceive ourselves in our judgment of causes and effects. Where a passion is neither founded on false suppositions, nor chooses means insufficient for the end, the understanding can neither justify nor condemn it. It is not contrary to reason to prefer the destruction of the whole world to the scratching of my finger. It is not contrary to reason for me to choose my total ruin to prevent the least uneasiness of an Indian or person wholly unknown to me. It is as little contrary to reason to prefer even my own acknowledged lesser good to my greater, and have a more ardent affection for the former than the latter. A trivial good may, from certain circumstances, produce a desire superior to what arises from the greatest and most valuable enjoyment; nor is there any thing more extraordinary in this, than in mechanics to see one

pound weight raise up a hundred by the advantage of its situation. In short, a passion must be accompanied with some false judgment, in order to its being unreasonable; and even then it is not the passion, properly speaking, which is unreasonable, but the judgment.

The consequences are evident. Since a passion can never, in any sense, be called unreasonable, but when founded on a false supposition, or when it chooses means insufficient for the designed end, it is impossible, that reason and passion can ever oppose each other, or dispute for the government of the will and actions. The moment we perceive the falsehood of any supposition, or the insufficiency of any means, our passions yield to our reason without any opposition. I may desire any fruit as of an excellent relish; but whenever you convince me of my mistake, my longing ceases. I may will the performance of certain actions as means of obtaining any desired good; but as my willing of these actions is only secondary, and founded on the supposition, that they are causes of the proposed effect; as soon as I discover the falsehood of that supposition, they must become indifferent to me. . . .

2. MORAL DISTINCTIONS NOT DERIVED FROM REASON

It would be tedious to repeat all the arguments, by which I have proved, that reason is perfectly inert, and can never either prevent or produce any action or affection. It will be easy to recollect what has been said upon that subject. I shall only recall on this occasion one of these arguments, which I shall endeavor to render still more conclusive, and more applicable to the present subject.

Reason is the discovery of truth or falsehood. Truth or falsehood consists in an agreement or disagreement either to the *real* relations of ideas, or to *real* existence and matter of fact. Whatever, therefore, is not susceptible of this agreement or disagreement, is incapable of being true or false, and can never be an object of our reason. Now it is evident our passions, volitions, and actions, are not susceptible of any such agreement or disagreement; being original facts and realities, complete in themselves, and implying no reference to other passions, volitions, and actions. It is impossible, therefore, they can be pronounced either true or false, and be either contrary or conformable to reason.

This argument is of double advantage to our present purpose. For it proves *directly*, that actions do not derive their merit from a conformity to reason, nor their blame from a contrariety to it; and it proves the same truth more *indirectly*, by showing us, that as reason can never immediately prevent or produce any action by contradicting or approving of it, it cannot be the source of moral good and evil, which are found to have that influence. Actions may be laudable or blameable; but they cannot be reasonable or unreasonable: laudable or blameable, therefore, are not the same with reasonable or unreasonable. The merit and demerit of actions frequently contradict, and sometimes control our natural propensities. But reason has no such influence. Moral distinctions, therefore, are not the offspring of reason. Reason is wholly inactive, and can never be the source of so active a principle as conscience, or a sense of morals. . . .

. . . Take any action allowed to be vicious: wilful murder, for instance. Examine it in all lights, and see if you can find that matter of fact, or real existence, which you call *vice*. In whichever way you take it, you find only certain passions, motives, volitions and thoughts. There is no other matter of fact in the case. The vice entirely escapes you, as long as you consider the object. You never can find it, till you turn your reflection into your own breast, and find a sentiment of disapprobation, which arises in you, towards this action. Here is a matter of fact; but it is the object of feeling, not of reason. It lies in yourself, not in the object. So that when you pronounce any action or character to be vicious, you mean nothing, but that from the constitution of your nature you have a feeling or sentiment of blame from the contemplation of it. Vice

and virtue, therefore, may be compared to sounds, colours, heat and cold, which, according to modern philosophy, are not qualities in objects, but perceptions in the mind: and this discovery in morals, like that other in physics, is to be regarded as a considerable advancement of the speculative sciences; though, like that too, it has little or no influence on practice. Nothing can be more real, or concern us more, than our own sentiments of pleasure and uneasiness; and if these be favourable to virtue, and unfavourable to vice, no more can be requisite to the regulation of our conduct and behaviour.

I cannot forbear adding to these reasonings an observation, which may, perhaps, be found of some importance. In every system of morality, which I have hitherto met with, I have always remarked, that the author proceeds for some time in the ordinary way of reasoning, and establishes the being of a God, or makes observations concerning human affairs; when of a sudden I am surprised to find, that instead of the usual copulations of propositions, *is*, and *is not*, I meet with no proposition that is not connected with an *ought*, or an *ought not*. This change is imperceptible; but is, however, of the last consequence. For as this *ought*, or *ought not*, expresses some new relation or affirmation, it is necessary that it should be observed and explained; and at the same time that a reason should be given, for what seems altogether inconceivable, how this new relation can be a deduction from others, which are entirely different from it. But as authors do not commonly use this precaution, I shall presume to recommend it to the readers; and am persuaded, that this small attention would subvert all the vulgar systems of morality, and let us see, that the distinction of vice and virtue is not founded merely on the relations of objects, nor is perceived by reason.

3. WHY UTILITY PLEASES

. . . It has often been asserted, that, as every man has a strong connexion with society, and perceives the impossibility of his solitary subsistence, he becomes, on that account, favourable to all those habits or principles, which promote order in society, and insure to him the quiet possession of so inestimable a blessing. As much as we value our own happiness and welfare, as much must we applaud the practice of justice and humanity, by which alone the social confederacy can be maintained, and every man reap the fruits of mutual protection and assistance.

This deduction of morals from self-love, or a regard to private interest, is an obvious thought. . . . [Y]et is not this an affair to be decided by authority, and the voice of nature and experience seems plainly to oppose the selfish theory.

We frequently bestow praise on virtuous actions, performed in very distant ages and remote countries; where the utmost subtilty of imagination would not discover any appearance of self-interest, or find any connexion of our present happiness and security with events so widely separated from us.

A generous, a brave, a noble deed, performed by an adversary, commands our approbation; while in its consequences it may be acknowledged prejudicial to our particular interest. . . .

Usefulness is agreeable, and engages our approbation. This is a matter of fact, confirmed by daily observation. But, useful? For what? For somebody's interest, surely. Whose interest then? Not our own only: For our approbation frequently extends farther. It must, therefore, be the interest of those, who are served by the character of action approved of; and these we may conclude, however remote, are not totally indifferent to us. . . .

. . . The human countenance, says Horace, borrows smiles or tears from the human countenance. Reduce a person to solitude, and he loses all enjoyment, except either of the sensual or speculative kind; and that because the movements of his heart are not forwarded by correspondent movements in his fellow-creatures. The signs of sorrow and mourning, though arbitrary, affect us with melancholy; but the natural symptoms, tears and cries and groans, never fail to infuse com-

passion and uneasiness. And if the effects of misery touch us in so lively a manner; can we be supposed altogether insensible or indifferent towards its causes; when a malicious or treacherous character and behaviour are presented to us? . . .

In general, it is certain, that, wherever we go, whatever we reflect on or converse about, everything still presents us with the view of human happiness or misery, and excites in our breast a sympathetic movement of pleasure or uneasiness. In our serious occupations, in our careless amusements, this principle still exerts its active energy. . . . We surely take into consideration the happiness and misery of others, in weighing the several motives of action, and incline to the former, where no private regards draw us to seek our own promotion or advantage by the injury of our fellow-creatures. And if the principles of humanity are capable, in many instances, of influencing our actions, they must, at all times, have *some* authority over our sentiments, and give us a general approbation of what is useful to society, and blame of what is dangerous or pernicious. The degrees of these sentiments may be the subject of controversy; but the reality of their existence, one should think, must be admitted in every theory or system. . . . Sympathy, we shall allow, is much fainter than our concern for ourselves, and sympathy with persons remote from us much fainter than that with persons near and contiguous; but for this very reason it is necessary for us, in our calm judgments and discourse concerning the characters of men, to neglect all these differences, and render our sentiments more public and social. Besides, that we ourselves often change our situation in this particular, we every day meet with persons who are in a situation different from us, and who could never converse with us were we to remain constantly in that position and point of view, which is peculiar to ourselves. The intercourse of sentiments, therefore, in society and conversation, makes us form some general unalterable standard, by which we may approve or disapprove of characters and manners. . . .

It is sufficient for our present purpose, if it be allowed, what surely, without the greatest absurdity cannot be disputed, that there is some benevolence, however small, infused into our bosom; some spark of friendship for human kind; some particle of the dove kneaded into our frame, along with the elements of the wolf and serpent. Let these generous sentiments be supposed ever so weak; let them be insufficient to move even a hand or finger of our body, they must still direct the determinations of our mind, and where everything else is equal, produce a cool preference of what is useful and serviceable to mankind, above what is pernicious and dangerous. A *moral distinction*, therefore, immediately arises; a general sentiment of blame and approbation; a tendency, however faint, to the objects of the one, and a proportionable aversion to those of the other. . . .

Avarice, ambition, vanity, and all passions vulgarly, though improperly, comprised under the denomination of *self-love*, are here excluded from our theory concerning the origin of morals, not because they are too weak, but because they have not a proper direction for that purpose. The notion of morals implies some sentiment common to all mankind, which recommends the same object to general approbation, and makes every man, or most men, agree in the same opinion or decision concerning it. It also implies some sentiment, so universal and comprehensive as to extend to all mankind, and render the actions and conduct, even of the persons the most remote, an object of applause or censure, according as they agree or disagree with that rule of right which is established. . . .

When a man denominates another his *enemy*, his *rival*, his *antagonist*, his *adversary*, he is understood to speak the language of self-love, and to express sentiments, peculiar to himself, and arising from his particular circumstances and situation. But when he bestows on any man the epithets of *vicious* or *odious* or *depraved*, he then speaks another language and expresses sentiments, in which he expects all his audience to concur with him. He must here, therefore, depart from his private and particular situation, and must choose a point of view, common to him with others; he must move some universal principle of the human frame, and touch a string to which all mankind have an accord and symphony. If he mean, therefore, to express that this man possesses qualities, whose tendency is pernicious to society, he has chosen this common point of view, and has touched the principle of humanity, in which every man, in some degree, concurs. While the human heart is compounded of the same elements as at present, it will never be wholly indifferent to public good, nor entirely unaffected with the tendency of characters and manners. And though this affection of humanity may not generally be esteemed so strong as vanity or ambition, yet, being common to all men, it can alone be the foundation of morals, or of any general system of blame or praise.

Morality and Practical Reason

Thomas Nagel

In this essay (taken from his book titled, interestingly, *The Last Word*), Thomas Nagel discusses a variety of issues and philosophers encountered in previous sections. He begins by looking at the differences between scientific and practical reasoning, the role played by empirical testing in each domain, and the claim that our moral views depend on the culture into which we happen to be born. He then askes whether moral issues can be dissolved by appeals to facts about history, culture, or even our own desires, arguing that they cannot.

Nagel concludes with a discussion of Hume's claim that reason never evaluates sentiments and feelings but instead that reason must treat sentiments simply as givens, as part of the raw material on which reason is to operate. Thomas Nagel is professor of philosophy at New York University.

As you read through this essay, consider the following:

1. What is the difference between scientific and practical reasoning? What is it that makes scientific beliefs true but cannot confirm moral ones, according to Nagel?
2. How does Nagel respond to those who say that we have our moral beliefs *only* because of our society and would not have the ones we do if we had been raised in a radically different society?
3. What does Nagel mean by the suggestion that there is a "slight space" between inclination and decision?
4. How does Nagel respond to Hume's "implausible" skepticism by the suggestion that the issue is one of the "order of explanation" and whether or not the motivational explanation can "displace" the normative or moral one?

Let me now turn to the question of whether moral reasoning is . . . fundamental and inescapable. Unlike logical or arithmetical reasoning, it often fails to produce certainty, justified or unjustified. It is easily subject to distortion by morally irrelevant factors, social and personal, as well as outright error. It resembles empirical reason in not being reducible to a series of self-evident steps.

I take it for granted that the objectivity of moral reasoning does not depend on its having an external reference. There is no moral analogue of the external world—a universe of moral facts that impinge on us causally. Even if such a supposition made sense, it would not support the objectivity of moral reasoning. Science, which this kind of reifying realism takes as its model, doesn't derive its objective validity from the fact that it starts from perception and other causal relations between us and the physical world. The real work comes after that, in the form of active scientific reasoning without which no amount of causal impact on us by the external world would generate a belief in Newton's or Maxwell's or Ein-

stein's theories, or the chemical theory of elements and compounds, or molecular biology.

If we had rested content with the causal impact of the external world on us, we'd still be at the level of sense perception. We can regard our scientific beliefs as objectively true not because the external world causes us to have them but because we are able to arrive at those beliefs by methods that have a good claim to be reliable, by virtue of their success in selecting among rival hypotheses that survive the best criticisms and questions we can throw at them. Empirical confirmation plays a vital role in this process, but it cannot do so without theory.

Moral thought is concerned not with the description and explanation of what happens but with decisions and their justification. It is mainly because we have no comparably uncontroversial and well-developed methods for thinking about morality that a subjectivist position here is more credible than it is with regard to science. But just as there was no guarantee at the beginnings of cosmological and scientific speculation that we humans had the capacity to arrive at objective truth beyond the deliverances of sense-perception—that in pursuing it we were doing anything more than spinning collective fantasies—so there can be no decision in advance as to whether we are or are not talking about a real subject when we reflect and argue about morality. The answer must come from the results themselves. Only the effort to reason about morality can show us whether it is possible—whether, in thinking about what to do and how to live, we can find methods, reasons, and principles whose validity does not have to be subjectively or relativistically qualified.

Since moral reasoning is a species of practical reasoning, its conclusions are desires, intentions, and actions, or feelings and convictions that can motivate desire, intention, and action. We want to know how to live, and why, and we want the answer in general terms, if possible. Hume famously believed that because a 'passion' immune to rational assessment must underlie every motive, there can be no such thing as specifically practical reason, nor specifically moral reason either. That is false, because while 'passions' are the source of some reasons, other passions or desires are themselves motivated and/or justified by reasons that do not depend on still more basic desires. And I would contend that either the question whether one should have a certain desire or the question whether, given that one has that desire, one should act on it, is always open to rational consideration.

The issue is whether the procedures of justification and criticism we employ in such reasoning, moral or merely practical, can be regarded finally as just something we do—a cultural or societal or even more broadly human collective practice, within which reasons come to an end. I believe that if we ask ourselves seriously how to respond to proposals for contextualization and relativistic detachment, they usually fail to convince. Although it is less clear than in some of the other areas we've discussed, attempts to get entirely outside of the object language of practical reasons, good and bad, right and wrong, and to see all such judgments as expressions of a contingent, nonobjective perspective will eventually collapse before the independent force of the first-order judgments themselves.

Suppose someone says, for example, "You only believe in equal opportunity because you are a product of Western liberal society. If you had been brought up in a caste society or one in which the possibilities for men and women were radically unequal, you wouldn't have the moral convictions you have or accept as persuasive the moral arguments you now accept." The second, hypothetical sentence is probably true, but what about the first—specifically the "only"? In general, the fact that I wouldn't believe something if I hadn't learned it proves nothing about the status of the belief or its grounds. It may be impossible to explain the learning without invoking the content of the belief itself, and the reasons for its truth; and it may be clear that what I have learned is such that even if I hadn't learned it, it would still be true. The reason the genetic fallacy is a fallacy is that the explanation of a belief can sometimes confirm it.

To have any content, a subjectivist position must say more than that my moral convictions are my moral convictions. That, after all, is something we can all agree on. A meaningful subjectivism must say that they are just my moral convictions—or those of my moral community. It must qualify ordinary moral judgments in some way, must give them a self-consciously first-person (singular or plural) reading. That is the only type of antiobjectivist view that is worth arguing against or that it is even possible to disagree with.

But I believe it is impossible to come to rest with the observation that a belief in equality of opportunity, and a wish to diminish inherited inequalities, are merely expressions of our cultural tradition. True or false, those beliefs are essentially objective in intent. Perhaps they are wrong, but that too would be a nonrelative judgment. Faced with the fact that such values have gained currency only recently and not universally, one still has to try to decide whether they are right—whether one ought to continue to hold them. That question is not displaced by the information of contingency: The question remains, at the level of moral content, whether I would have been in error if I had accepted as natural, and therefore justified, the inequalities of a caste society, or a fairly rigid class system, or the orthodox subordination of women. It can take in additional facts as material for reflection, but the question of the relevance of those facts is inevitably a moral question: Do these cultural and historical variations and their causes tend to show that I and others have less reason than we had supposed to favor equality of opportunity? Presentation of an array of historically and culturally conditioned attitudes, including my own, does not disarm first-order moral judgment but simply gives it something more to work on—including information about influences on the formation of my convictions that may lead me to change them. But the relevance of such information is itself a matter for moral reasoning—about what are and are not good grounds for moral belief.

When one is faced with these real variations in practice and conviction, the requirement to put oneself in everyone's shoes when assessing social institutions—some version of universalizability—does not lose any of its persuasive force just because it is not universally recognized. It dominates the historical and anthropological data: Presented with the description of a traditional caste society, I have to ask myself whether its hereditary inequalities are justified, and there is no plausible alternative to considering the interests of all in trying to answer the question. If others feel differently, they must say why they find these cultural facts relevant—why they require some qualification to the objective moral claim. On both sides, it is a moral issue, and the only way to defend universalizability or equal opportunity against subjectivist qualification is by continuing the moral argument. It is a matter of understanding exactly what the subjectivist wants us to give up, and then asking whether the grounds for those judgments disappear in light of his observations.

In my opinion, someone who abandons or qualifies his basic methods of moral reasoning on historical or anthropological grounds alone is nearly as irrational as someone who abandons a mathematical belief on other than mathematical grounds. Even with all their uncertainties and liability to controversy and distortion, moral considerations occupy a position in the system of human thought that makes it illegitimate to subordinate them completely to anything else. Particular moral claims are constantly being discredited for all kinds of reasons, but moral considerations per se keep rising again to challenge in their own right any blanket attempt to displace, defuse, or subjectivize them.

This is an instance of the more general truth that the normative cannot be transcended by the descriptive. The question "What should I do?" like the question "What should I believe?" is always in order. It is always possible to think about the question in normative terms, and the process is not rendered pointless by any fact of a different kind—any desire or emotion or feeling, any habit or practice or convention, any contingent cultural or social background. Such things may in fact, guide our actions, but it is always possible to take their relation to action as an object of further normative reflection and ask, "How should I act, given that these things are true of me or of my situation?"

The type of thought that generates answers to this question is practical reason. But, further, it is always possible for the question to take a specifically moral form, since one of the successor questions to which it leads is, "What should anyone in my situation do?"—and consideration of that question leads in turn to questions about what everyone should do, not only in this situation but more generally.

Such universal questions don't always have to be raised, and there is good reason in general to develop a way of living that makes it usually unnecessary to raise them. But if they are raised, as they always can be, they require an answer of the appropriate kind—even though the answer may be that in a case like this one may do as one likes. They cannot be ruled out of order by pointing to something more fundamental—psychological, cultural, or biological—that brings the request for justification to an end. Only a justification can bring the request for justifications to an end. Normative questions in general are not undercut or rendered idle by anything, even though particular normative answers may be. (Even when some putative justification is exposed as a rationalization, that implies that something else could be said about the justifiability or nonjustifiability of what was done.)

The point of view to defeat, in a defense of the reality of practical and moral reason, is in essence the Humean one. Although Hume was wrong to say that reason was fit only to serve as the slave of the passions, it is nevertheless true that there are desires and sentiments prior to reason that it is not appropriate for reason to evaluate—that it must simply treat as part of the raw material on which its judgments operate. The question then arises how pervasive such brute motivational data are, and whether some of them cannot perhaps be identified as the true sources of those grounds of action which are usually described as reasons. Hume's theory of the "calm" passions was designed to make this extension, and resisting it is not a simple matter—even if it is set in the context of a minimal framework of practical rationality stronger than Hume would have admitted.

If there is such a thing as practical reason, it does not simply dictate particular actions but, rather, governs the *relations* among actions, desires, and beliefs—just as theoretical reason governs the relations among beliefs and requires some specific material to work on. Prudential rationality, requiring uniformity in the weight accorded to desires and interests situated at different times in one's life, is an example—and the example about which Hume's skepticism is most implausible, when he says it is not contrary to reason "to prefer even my own acknowledged lesser good to my greater, and have a more ardent affection for the former than the latter." Yet Hume's position always seems a possibility,

because whenever such a consistency requirement or similar pattern has an influence on our decisions, it seems possible to represent this influence as the manifestation of a systematic second-order desire or calm passion, which has such consistency as its object and without which we would not be susceptible to this type of "rational" motivation. Hume need then only claim that while such a desire (for the satisfaction of one's future interests) is quite common, to lack it is not contrary to reason, any more than to lack sexual desire is contrary to reason. The problem is to show how this misrepresents the facts.

The fundamental issue is about the order or explanation, for there is no point in denying that people have such second-order desires: the question is whether they are sources of motivation or simply the manifestation in our motives of the recognition of certain rational requirements. A parallel point could be made about theoretical reason. It is clear that the belief in modus ponens, for example, is not a rationally ungrounded *assumption* underlying our acceptance of deductive arguments that depend on modus ponens: Rather, it is simply a recognition of the validity of that form of argument.

The question is whether something similar can be said of the "desire" for prudential consistency in the treatment of desires and interests located at different times. I think it can be and that if one tries instead to regard prudence as simply a desire among others, a desire one happens to have, the question of its appropriateness inevitably reappears as a normative question, and the answer can only be given in terms of the principle itself. The normative can't be displaced by the psychological.

If I think, for example, "What if I didn't care about what would happen to me in the future?" the appropriate reaction is not like what it would be to the supposition that I might not care about movies. True, I'd be missing something if I didn't care about movies, but there are many forms of art and entertainment, and we don't have to consume them all. Note that even this is a judgment of the *rational acceptability* of such variation—of there being no reason to regret it. The supposition that I might not care about my own future cannot be regarded with similar tolerance: It is the supposition of a real failure—the paradigm of something to be regretted—and my recognition of that failure does not reflect merely the antecedent presence in me of a contingent second-order desire. Rather, it reflects a judgment about what is and what is not relevant to the justification of action against a certain factual background.

Relevance and consistency both get a foothold when we adopt the standpoint of decision, based on the total circumstances, including our own condition. This standpoint introduces a subtle but profound gap between desire and action, into which the free exercise of reason enters. It forces us to the idea of the difference between doing the right thing and doing the wrong thing (here, without any specifically ethical meaning as yet)—given our total situation, *including* our desires. Once I see myself as the subject of certain desires, as well as the occupant of an objective situation, I still have to decide what to do, and that will include deciding what justificatory weight to give to those desires.

This step back, this opening of a slight space between inclination and decision, is the condition that permits the operation of reason with respect to belief as well as with respect to action, and that poses the demand for generalizable justification. The two kinds of reasoning are in this way parallel. It is only when, instead of simply being pushed along by impressions, memories, impulses, desires, or whatever, one stops to ask "What should I do?" or "What should I believe?" that reasoning becomes possible—and, having become possible, becomes necessary. Having stopped the direct operation of impulse by interposing the possibility of decision, one can get one's beliefs and actions into motion again only by thinking about what, in light of the circumstances, one should do.

The controversial but crucial point, here as everywhere in the discussion of this subject, is that the standpoint from which one assesses one's choices after this step back is not just first-personal. One is suddenly in the position of judging what one ought to do, against the background of all one's desires and beliefs, in a way that does not merely flow from those desires and beliefs but *operates* on them—by an assessment that should enable anyone else also to see what is the right thing for you to do against that background.

It is not enough to find some higher order desires that one happens to have, to settle the matter: such desires would have to be placed among the background conditions of decision along with everything else. Rather, even in the case of a purely self-interested choice, one is seeking the right answer. One is trying to decide what, given the inner and outer circumstances, *one should do*—and that means not just what *I* should do but what *this person* should do. The same answer should be given to that question by anyone to whom the data are presented, whether or not he is in your circumstances and shares your desires. That is what gives practical reason its generality.

The objection that has to be answered, here as elsewhere, is that this sense of unconditioned, nonrelative judgment is an illusion—that we cannot, merely by stepping back and taking ourselves as objects of contemplation, find a secure platform from which such judgment is possible. On this view whatever we do, after engaging in such an intellectual ritual, will still inevitably be a manifestation of our individual or social nature, not the deliverance of impersonal reason—for there is no such thing.

But I do not believe that such a conclusion can be established a priori, and there is little reason to believe it could be established empirically. The subjectivist would have to show that all purportedly rational judgments about what people have reason to do are really expressions of rationally unmotivated desires or dispositions of the person making the judgment—desires or dispositions to which normative assessment has no application. The motivational explanation would have to have the effect of *displacing* the normative one—showing it to be superficial and deceptive. It would be necessary to make out the case about many actual judgments of this kind and to offer reasons to believe that something similar was true in all cases. Subjectivism involves a positive claim of empirical psychology.

Is it conceivable that such an argument could succeed? In a sense, it would have to be shown that all our supposed practical reasoning is, at the limit, a form of rationalization.

But the defender of practical reason has a general response to all psychological claims of this type. Even when some of his actual reasonings are convincingly analyzed away as the expression of merely parochial or personal inclinations, it will in general be reasonable for him to add this new information to the body of his beliefs about himself and then step back once more and ask, "What, in light of all this, do I have reason to do?"

Classical Theories of Morality

Nicomachean Ethics

Aristotle

Aristotle (384–322 B.C.) was born in Stagira, a town near Macedonia. He went to Athens when he was seventeen years old and studied with Plato at the Academy for twenty years. When Plato died, Aristotle left Athens and traveled to Macedonia, where he tutored the young heir to the throne—who was later to become known as Alexander the Great. In 334 B.C., Aristotle returned to Athens and founded his own school, the Lyceum. When Alexander died in 323, there was strong anti-Macedonian feeling in Athens, and Aristotle left for Chalcis, where he died the next year at sixty-two.

Aristotle studied and wrote about an astonishing range of subjects. No single person, it is often said, has ever founded and advanced so many fields of learning. Aristotle wrote separate treatises on physics, biology, logic, psychology, ethics, metaphysics, aesthetics, literary criticism, and political science. In the Middle Ages, he was known simply as "The Philosopher."

In this selection, taken from *Nicomachean Ethics*, Aristotle begins with a discussion of the study of ethics and of human nature and then turns to the nature of *eudainomonia*—that is, well-being or happiness. To understand happiness, it is necessary to understand the natural purpose or function of man, which Aristotle describes as activity in accordance with reason. In that sense, happiness is also an excellent, specifically virtuous activity. Virtues, he argues, are those habits and traits that allow people to live well in communities, and true happiness is not, contrary to popular opinion, merely a pleasure. Nor is happiness to be found in economic wealth, although living a virtuous and happy life requires at least some wealth and certainly brings pleasure to the one who is able to achieve it. Turning finally to the nature of the virtues, Aristotle first distinguishes intellectual from moral virtue, arguing that while intellectual virtues can be taught, moral virtues must be acquired through habit and require a certain sort of community if they are to be realized. Using examples such as courage and liberality, he argues that moral virtues can best be understood as a mean between extremes.

As you read through this essay, consider the following:

1. What is the end or function of human beings, according to Aristotle?
2. How does Aristotle understand happiness? Why does he think it is the supreme good?
3. Why does Aristotle reject the pursuit of money or pleasure as the key to happiness?
4. How does Aristotle understand the nature of virtue and its connection with habit?
5. What does Aristotle mean when he says virtues are a mean between extremes? What are some examples of virtues?

BOOK I: HAPPINESS AND THE GOOD OF MAN

Every art and every scientific inquiry, and similarly every action and purpose, may be said to aim at some good. Hence the good has been well defined as that at which all things aim. But it is clear that there is a difference in ends; for the ends are sometimes activities, and sometimes results beyond the mere activities. Where there are ends beyond the action, the results are naturally superior to the action.

As there are various actions, arts, and sciences, it follows that the ends are also various. Thus health is the end of the medical art, a ship of shipbuilding, victory of strategy, and wealth of economics. It often happens that a number of such arts or sciences combine for a single enterprise, as the art of making bridles and all such other arts as furnish the implements of horsemanship combine for horsemanship, and horsemanship and every military action for strategy; and in the same way, other arts or sciences combine for others. In all these cases, the ends of the master arts or sciences, whatever they may be, are more desirable than those of the subordinate arts or

From *Nicomachean Ethics*, trans. James E. C. Weldon (1892). Titles added.

sciences, as it is for the sake of the former that the latter are pursued. It makes no difference to the argument whether the activities themselves are the ends of the action, or something beyond the activities, as in the above-mentioned sciences.

If it is true that in the sphere of action there is some end which we wish for its own sake, and for the sake of which we wish everything else, and if we do not desire everything for the sake of something else (for, if that is so, the process will go on ad infinitum, and our desire will be idle and futile), clearly this end will be good and the supreme good. Does it not follow then that the knowledge of this good is of great importance for the conduct of life? Like archers who have a mark at which to aim, shall we not have a better chance of attaining what we want? If this is so, we must endeavor to comprehend, at least in outline, what this good is, and what science or faculty makes it its object. . . .

As every science and undertaking aims at some good, what is in our view the good at which political science [including morality] aims, and what is the highest of all practical goods? As to its name there is, I may say, a general agreement. The masses and the cultured classes agree in calling it happiness, and conceive that "to live well" or "to do well" is the same thing as "to be happy." But as to what happiness is they do not agree, nor do the masses give the same account of it as the philosophers. The former take it to be something visible and palpable, such as pleasure, wealth, or honor; different people, however, give different definitions of it, and often even the same man gives different definitions at different times. When he is ill, it is health, when he is poor, it is wealth; if he is conscious of his own ignorance, he envies people who use grand language above his own comprehension. Some philosophers, on the other hand, have held that, besides these various goods, there is an absolute good which is the cause of goodness in them all. [These were members of Plato's school of thought.] It would perhaps be a waste of time to examine all these opinions; it will be enough to examine such as are most popular or as seem to be more or less reasonable.

. . . Men's conception of the good or of happiness may be read in the lives they lead. Ordinary or vulgar people conceive it to be a pleasure, and accordingly choose a life of enjoyment. For there are, we may say, three conspicuous types of life, the sensual, the political, and, thirdly, the life of thought. Now the mass of men present an absolutely slavish appearance, choosing the life of brute beasts, but they have ground for so doing because so many persons in authority share the tastes of Sardanapalus. [A half legendary ruler of ancient Assyria, whose name to the Greeks stood for the extreme of Oriental luxury and extravagance.] Cultivated and energetic people, on the other hand, identify happiness with honor, as honor is the general end of political life. But this seems too superficial an idea for our present purpose; for honor depends more upon the people who pay it than upon the person to whom it is paid, and the good we feel is something which is proper to a man himself and cannot be easily taken away from him. Men too appear to seek honor in order to be assured of their own goodness. Accordingly, they seek it at the hands of the sage and of those who know them well, and they seek it on the ground of their virtue; clearly then, in their judgment at

any rate, virtue is better than honor. Perhaps then we might look on virtue rather than honor as the end of political life. Yet even this idea appears not quite complete; for a man may possess virtue and yet be asleep or inactive throughout life, and not only so, but he may experience the greatest calamities and misfortunes. Yet no one would call such a life a life of happiness, unless he were maintaining a paradox. But we need not dwell further on this subject, since it is sufficiently discussed in popular philosophical treatises. The third life is the life of thought. . . .

The life of money making is a life of constraint; and wealth is obviously not the good of which we are in quest; for it is useful merely as a means to something else. It would be more reasonable to take the things mentioned before—sensual pleasure, honor, and virtue—as ends than wealth, since they are things desired on their own account. Yet these too are evidently not ends, although much argument has been employed to show that they are. . . .

But leaving this subject for the present, let us revert to the good of which we are in quest and consider what it may be. For it seems different in different activities or arts; it is one thing in medicine, another in strategy, and so on. What is the good in each of these instances? It is presumably that for the sake of which all else is done. In medicine this is health, in strategy victory, an architecture a house, and so on. In every activity and undertaking it is the end, since it is for the sake of the end that all people do whatever else they do. If then there is an end for all our activity, this will be the good to be accomplished; and if there are several such ends, it will be these.

Our argument has arrived by a different path at the same point as before; but we must endeavor to make it still plainer. Since there are more ends than one, and some of these ends—for example, wealth, flutes, and instruments generally—we desire as means to something else, it is evident that not all are final ends. But the highest good is clearly something final. Hence if there is only one final end, this will be the object of which we are in search; and if there are more than one, it will be the most final. We call that which is sought after for its own sake more final than that which is sought after as a means to something else; we call that which is never desired as a means to something else more final than things that are desired both for themselves and as means to something else. Therefore, we call absolutely final that which is always desired for itself and never as a means to something else. Now happiness more than anything else answers to this description. For happiness we always desire for its own sake and never as a means to something else, whereas honor, pleasure, intelligence, and every virtue we desire partly for their own sakes (for we should desire them independently of what might result from them), but partly also as means to happiness, because we suppose they will prove instruments of happiness. Happiness, on the other hand, nobody desires for the sake of these things, nor indeed as a means to anything else at all. . . .

Perhaps, however, it seems a commonplace to say that happiness is the supreme good; what is wanted is to define its nature a little more clearly. The best way of arriving at such a definition will probably be to ascertain the function of man. For, as with a flute player, a sculptor, or any artist, or in fact anybody who has a special function or activity, his goodness and excellence seem to lie in his function, so it would seem to be with man, if indeed he has a special function. Can it be said that, while a carpenter and a cobbler have special functions and activities, man, unlike them, is naturally functionless? Or, as the eye, the hand, the foot, and similarly each part of the body has a special function, so may man be regarded as having a special function apart from all these? What, then, can this function be? It is not life; for life is apparently something that man shares with plants; and we are looking for something peculiar to him. We must exclude therefore the life of nutrition and growth. There is next what may be called the life of sensation. But this too, apparently, is shared by man with horses, cattle, and all other animals.

There remains what I may call the active life of the rational part of man's being. Now this rational part is twofold; one part is rational in the sense of being obedient to reason, and the other in the sense of possessing and exercising reason and intelligence. . . .

The function of man then is activity of soul in accordance with reason, or not apart from reason. Now, the function of a man of a certain kind, and of a man who is good of that kind—for example, of a harpist and a good harpist—are in our view the same in kind. This is true of all people of all kinds without exception, the superior excellence being only an addition to the function; for it is the function of a harpist to play the harp, and of a good harpist to play the harp well. This being so, if we define the function of man as a kind of life, and this life as an activity of the soul or a course of action in accordance with reason, and if the function of a good man is such activity of a good and noble kind, and if everything is well done when it is done in accordance with its proper excellence, it follows that the good of man is activity of soul in accordance with virtue, or, if there are more virtues than one, in accordance with the best and most complete virtue. But we must add the words "in a complete life." For as one swallow or one day does not make a spring, so one day or a short time does not make a man blessed or happy. . . .

Our account accords too with the view of those who hold that happiness is virtue or excellence of some sort; for activity in accordance with virtue is virtue. But there is plainly a considerable difference between calling the supreme good possession or use, a state of mind, or an activity. For a state of mind may exist without producing anything good—for example, if a person is asleep, or in any other way inert. Not so with an activity, since activity implies acting and acting well. As in the Olympic games it is not the most beautiful and strongest who receive the crown but those who actually enter the combat, for from those come the victors, so it is those who act that win rightly what is noble and good in life.

Their life too is pleasant in itself. For pleasure is a state of mind, and whatever a man is fond of is pleasant to him, as a horse is to a lover of horses, a show to a lover of spectacles, and, similarly, just acts to a lover of justice, and virtuous acts in general to a lover of virtue. Now most men find a sense of discord in their pleasures, because their pleasures are not all naturally pleasant. But the lovers of nobleness take pleasure in what is naturally pleasant, and virtuous acts are naturally pleasant. Such acts then are pleasant both to these persons and in themselves. Nor does the life of such persons need more pleasure attached to it as a sort of charm; it possesses pleasure in itself. For, it may be added, a man who does not delight in noble acts is not good; as nobody would call a man just who did not enjoy just action, or liberal who did not enjoy liberal action, and so on. If this is so, it follows that acts of virtue are pleasant in themselves. They are also good and noble, and good and noble in the highest degree, for the judgment of the virtuous man on them is right, and his judgment is as we have described. Happiness then is the best and noblest and pleasantest thing in the world. . . .

Still it is clear, as we said, that happiness requires the addition of external goods; for it is impossible, or at least difficult, to do noble deeds with no outside means. For many things can be done only through the aid of friends or wealth or political power; and there are some things the lack of which spoils our felicity, such as good birth, wholesome children, and personal beauty. For a man who is extremely ugly in appearance or low born or solitary and childless can hardly be happy; perhaps still less so, if he has exceedingly bad children or friends, or has had good children or friends and lost them by death. As we said, then, happiness seems to need prosperity of this kind in addition to virtue. For this reason some persons identify happiness with good fortune, though others do so with virtue. . . .

It is reasonable then not to call an ox or a horse or any other animal happy; for none of them is capable of sharing in this activity. For the same reason no child can be happy, since the youth of a child keeps him for the time being from such activity; if a child is ever called happy, the ground of felicitation is his promise, rather than his actual performance. For happiness demands, as we said, a complete virtue and a complete life. And there are all sorts of changes and chances in life, and the most prosperous of men may in his old age fall into extreme calamities, as Priam did in the heroic legends. [The disastrous fate of Priam, king of Troy, was part of the well-known Homeric tales.] And a person who has experienced such chances and died a miserable death, nobody calls happy. . . .

Now the events of chance are numerous and of different magnitudes. Small pieces of good fortune or the reverse do not turn the scale of life in any way, but great and numerous events make life happier if they turn out well, since they naturally give it beauty and the use of them may be noble and good. If, on the other hand, they turn out badly, they mar and mutilate happiness by causing pain and hindrances to many activities. Still, even in these circumstances, nobility shines out when a person bears with calmness the weight of accumulated misfortunes, not from insensibility but from dignity and greatness of spirit.

Then if activities determine the quality of life, as we said, no happy man can become miserable; for he will never do what is hateful and mean. For our idea of the truly good and wise man is that he bears all the chances of life with dignity and always does what is best in the circumstances, as a good general makes the best use of the forces at his command in war, or a good cobbler makes the best shoe with the leather given him, and so on through the whole series of the arts. If this is so, the happy man can never become miserable. I do not say that he will be fortunate if he meets such chances of life as Priam. Yet he will not be variable or constantly changing, for he will not be moved from his happiness easily or by ordinary misfortunes, but only be great and numerous ones; nor after them will he quickly regain his happiness. If he regains it at all, it will be only over a long and complete period of time and after great and notable achievement.

We may safely then define a happy man as one who is active in accord with perfect virtue and adequately furnished with external goods, not for some chance period of time but for his whole lifetime. . . .

Inasmuch as happiness is an activity of soul in accordance with complete or perfect virtue, it is necessary to consider virtue, as this will perhaps be the best way of studying happiness. . . .

BOOK II: VIRTUE AND THE MEAN

Virtue is twofold, partly intellectual and partly moral, and intellectual virtue is originated and fostered mainly by teaching; it therefore demands experience and time. Moral virtue on the other hand is the outcome of habit. From this fact it is clear that moral virtue is not implanted in us by nature, for a law of nature cannot be altered by habituation. Thus a stone, that naturally tends to fall downwards, cannot be habituated or trained to rise upwards. It is neither by nature then nor in defiance of nature that virtues are implanted in us. Nature gives us the capacity of receiving them, and that capacity is perfected by habit.

Again, if we take the various natural powers which belong to us, we first possess the proper faculties and afterwards display the activities. It is obviously so with the senses. Not by seeing frequently or hearing frequently do we acquire the sense of seeing or hearing; on the contrary, because we have the senses we make use of them; we do not get them by making use of them. But the virtues we get by first practicing them, as we do in the arts. For it is by doing what we ought to do when we study the arts that we learn the arts themselves; we become builders by building and harpists by playing the harp. Similarly, it is by doing just acts that we become just, by doing temperate acts that we become temperate, by doing brave acts that we become brave. The experience of states confirms this statement, for it is by training in good habits that lawmakers make the citizens good. This is the object all lawmakers have at heart; if they do not succeed in it, they fail of their purpose; and it makes the distinction between a good constitution and a bad one.

Again, the causes and means by which any virtue is produced and destroyed are the same. It is by our actions in dealing between man and man that we become either just or unjust. It is by our actions in the face of danger and by our training ourselves to fear or to courage that we become either cowardly or courageous. It is much the same with our appetites and angry passions. People become temperate and gentle, others licentious and passionate, by behaving in one or the other way in particular circumstances. In a word, moral states are the results of activities like the states themselves. It is our duty therefore to keep a certain character in our activities, since our moral states depend on the differences in our activities. So the difference between one and another training in habits in our childhood is not a light matter, but important, or rather, all-important.

Our present study is not, like other studies, purely theoretical in intention; for the object of our inquiry is not to know what virtue is but how to become good, and that is the sole benefit of it. We must, therefore, consider the right way of performing actions, for it is acts that determine the character of the resulting moral states.

That we should act in accordance with right reason is a common general principle, which may here be taken for granted. . . .

The first point to be observed is that in matters we are now considering deficiency and excess are both fatal. It is so, we see, in questions of health and strength. Too much or too little gymnastic exercise is fatal to strength. Similarly, too much or too little meat and drink is fatal to health, whereas a suitable amount produces, increases, and sustains it. . . .

It is the same with temperance, courage, and other moral virtues. A person who avoids and is afraid of everything and faces nothing becomes a coward; a person who is not afraid of anything but is ready to face everything becomes foolhardy. Similarly, he who enjoys every pleasure and abstains from none is licentious; he who refuses all pleasures, like a boor, is an insensible sort of person. For temperance and courage are destroyed by excess and deficiency but preserved by the mean. . . .

Every art then performs its function well, if it regards the mean and refers the works which it produces to the mean. This is the reason why it is usually said of successful works that it is impossible to take anything from them or to add anything to them, which implies that excess or deficiency is fatal to excellence but that the mean state ensures it. Good artists too, as we say, have an eye to the mean in their works. But virtue, like Nature herself, is more accurate and better than any art; virtue therefore will aim at the mean;—I speak of moral virtue, as it is moral virtue which is concerned with emotions and actions, and it is these which admit of excess and deficiency and the mean. Thus it is possible to go too far, or not to go far enough, in respect of fear, courage, desire, anger, pity, and pleasure and pain generally, and the excess and the deficiency are alike wrong; but to experience these emotions at the right times and on the right occasions and towards the right persons and for the right causes and in the right manner is the mean or the supreme good, which is characteristic of virtue. Similarly there may be excess, deficiency, or the mean, in regard to actions. But virtue is concerned with emotions and actions, and here excess is an error and deficiency a fault, whereas the mean is successful and laudable, and success and merit are both characteristics of virtue.

It appears then that virtue is a mean state, so far at least as it aims at the mean. . . .

Virtue then is a state of deliberate moral purpose consisting in a mean that is relative to ourselves, the mean being determined by reason, or as a prudent man would determine it. . . .

But not every action or every emotion admits of a mean. There are some whose very name implies wickedness, as, for example, malice, shamelessness, and envy among the emotions, and adultery, theft, and murder among the actions. All these and others like them are marked as intrinsically wicked, not merely the excesses or deficiencies of them. It is never possible then to be right in them; they are always sinful. Right or wrong in such acts as adultery does not depend on our committing it with the right woman, at the right time, or in the right manner; on the contrary it is wrong to do it at all. It would be equally false to suppose that there can be a mean or excess of deficiency in unjust, cowardly or licentious conduct. . . .

There are then three dispositions, two being vices, namely, excess and deficiency, and one virtue, which is the mean between them; and they are all in a sense morally opposed. Thus the brave man appears foolhardy compared with the coward, but cowardly compared with the foolhardy. Similarly, the temperate man appears licentious compared with the insensible man but insensible compared with the licentious; and the liberal man appears extravagant compared with the stingy man but stingy compared with the spendthrift. The result is that the extremes each denounce the mean as belonging to the other extreme; the coward calls the brave man foolhardy, and the foolhardy man calls him cowardly; and so on in other cases. . . .

That is why it is so hard to be good; for it is always hard to find the mean in anything; anybody can get angry—that is easy—and anybody can give or spend money, but to give it to the right person, to give the right amount of it, at the right time, for the right cause and in the right way, this is not what anybody can do, or is it easy. That is why goodness is rare, praiseworthy and noble.

Utilitarianism

John Stuart Mill

John Stuart Mill (1806–1873) was among the nineteenth century's most important philosophers. He wrote on a vast range of topics and had an extraordinary personal life. (For further bibliographical information on Mill, take a look at the selection from *On Liberty* reprinted earlier.)

The book from which the following selections are taken is generally regarded as the classic statement of the utilitarian ethical theory. As is evident from the beginning, Mill is concerned to answer critics of utilitarianism. Among the targets of those critics was Jeremy Bentham, whose work influenced Mill and Mill's father tremendously. Bentham was a radical social reformer who contended that laws and moral teaching are sound only if they serve the general welfare by maximizing total "utility." Heretofore, argued these reformers, impartiality has been sacrificed by political and moral systems that served the interests of the few rather than of everyone equally. While Mill shared Bentham's general commitment to utilitarianism, he rejected some of the details of Bentham's position, including his conception of utility. Instead of understanding the goal of human actions and laws as Bentham and other classical hedonists did, that is, as maximizing the amount and intensity of pleasant experiences, Mill gives an account of happiness that includes more than Bentham's simple account of pleasure. Mill then discusses the rational basis of the utilitarian principle and answers various other objections brought against utilitarianism.

> *As you read through this essay, consider the following:*
>
> 1. Bentham and classical hedonists claim that only intensity and duration of a pain or pleasure matter, not its inherent nature. Mill rejects that. What does he mean in claiming that some pleasures are "higher" than others? What argument does Mill give for that conclusion?
> 2. Does Mill think people should specifically consider what would maximize utility when deciding what to do, or should they rely on other standards or attitudes?
> 3. What is Mill's "proof" of the utility principle?
> 4. How does Mill account for the apparent fact that people value and desire virtue for its own sake?
> 5. What is justice, according to Mill?
> 6. How does Mill understand moral rights? Are they universally applicable in all societies?

GENERAL REMARKS

On the present occasion, I shall attempt to contribute something toward the understanding and appreciation of the Utilitarian or Happiness theory, and towards such proof as it is susceptible of. It is evident that this can-

From John Stuart Mill, *Utilitarianism* (1861).

not be proof in the ordinary and popular meaning of the term. Questions of ultimate ends are not amenable to direct proof. We are not, however, to infer that its acceptance or rejection must depend on blind impulse, or arbitrary choice. Considerations may be presented capable of determining the intellect either to give or withhold its assent to the doctrine; and this is equivalent of proof.

WHAT UTILITARIANISM IS

The creed which accepts as the foundation of morals *utility* or the *greatest happiness principle* holds that actions are right in proportion as they tend to promote happiness, wrong as they tend to produce the reverse of happiness. By "happiness" is intended pleasure, and the absence of pain; by "unhappiness," pain, and the privation of pleasure. To give a clear view of the moral standard set up by the theory, much more requires to be said; in particular, what things it includes in the ideas of pain and pleasure, and to what extent this is left an open question. But these supplementary explanations do not affect the theory of life on which this theory of mortality is grounded—namely, that pleasure, and freedom from pain, are the only things desirable as ends; and that all desirable things (which are as numerous in the utilitarian as in any other scheme) are desirable either for the pleasure inherent in themselves, or as means to the promotion of pleasure and the prevention of pain.

Now such a theory of life excites in many minds, and among them in some of the most estimable in feeling and purpose, inveterate dislike. To suppose that life has (as they express it) no higher end than pleasure—no better and nobler object of desire and pursuit—they designate as utterly mean and groveling; as a doctrine worthy only of swine. . . .

[But it] is quite compatible with the principle of utility to recognize the fact, that some *kinds* of pleasure are more desirable and more valuable than others. It would be absurd that while, in estimating all other things, quality is considered as well as quantity, the estimation of pleasures should be supposed to depend on quantity alone.

If I am asked what I mean by difference of quality in pleasures, or what makes one pleasure more valuable than another merely as a pleasure, except its being greater in amount, there is but one possible answer. Of two pleasures, if there be one to which all or almost all who have experience of both give a decided preference, irrespective of any feeling of moral obligation to prefer it, that is the more desirable pleasure. If one of the two is, by those who are competently acquainted with both, placed so far above the other that they prefer it, even though knowing it to be attended with a greater amount of discontent, and would not resign it for any quantity of the other pleasure which their nature is capable of, we are justified in ascribing to the preferred enjoyment a superiority in quality, so far outweighing quantity as to render it, in comparison, of small account.

Now it is an unquestionable fact that those who are equally acquainted with, and equally capable of appreciating and enjoying, both, do give a most marked preference to the manner of existence which employs their higher faculties. Few human creatures would consent to be changed into any of the lower animals, for a promise of the fullest allowance of a beast's pleasures; no intelligent human being would consent to be a fool; no instructed person would be an ignoramus, no person of feeling and conscience would be selfish and base, even though they should be persuaded that the fool, the dunce, or the rascal is better satisfied with his lot than they are with theirs. They would not resign what they possess more than he for the most complete satisfaction of all the desires which they have in common with him. If they ever fancy they would, it is only in cases of unhappiness so extreme, that to escape from it they would exchange their lot for almost any other, however undesirable in their own eyes. A being of higher faculties requires more to make him happy, is capable probably of more acute suffering, and certainly accessible to it at more points, than one of an inferior type; but in spite of these liabilities, he can never really wish to sink into what he feels to be a lower grade of existence. We may give what explanation we please of this unwillingness: we may attribute it to pride, a name which is given indiscriminately to some of the most and to some of the least estimable feelings of which mankind are capable; we may refer it to the love of liberty and personal independence, an appeal to which was with the Stoics one of the most effective means for the inculcation of it; to the love of power, or to the love of excitement, both of which do really enter into and contribute to it: but its most appropriate appellation is a sense of dignity, which all human beings possess in one form or other, and in some, though by no means in exact, proportion to their higher faculties, and which is so essential a part of the happiness of those in whom it is strong, that nothing which conflicts with it could be, otherwise than momentarily, an object of desire to them. . . .

From this verdict of the only competent judges I apprehend there can be no appeal. On a question which is the best worth having of two pleasures, or which of two modes of existence is the most grateful to the feelings, apart from its moral attributes and from its consequences, the judgment of those who are qualified by knowledge of both, or, if they differ, that of the majority among them, must be admitted as final. And there need be the less hesitation to accept this judgment respecting the quality of pleasures, since there is no other tribunal to be referred to even on the question of quantity. What means are there of determining which is the acutest of two pains, or the intensest of two pleasurable sensations, except the general suffrage of those who are familiar with both? Neither pains nor pleasures are homogeneous, and pain is always heterogeneous with pleasure. What is there to decide whether a particular pleasure is worth purchasing at the cost of a particular pain, except the feelings and judgment of the experienced? When, therefore, those feelings and judgment declare the pleasures derived from the higher faculties to be preferable in kind, apart from the question of intensity, to those of which the animal nature, disjoined from the higher faculties, is susceptible, they are entitled on this subject to the same regard. . . .

Though it is only in a very imperfect state of the world's arrangements that anyone can best serve the happiness of others by the absolute sacrifice of his own, yet so long as the world is in that imperfect state, I fully acknowledge that the readiness to make such a sacrifice is the highest virtue which can be found in man. I will add that in this condition of the world, paradoxical as the assertion may be, the conscious ability to do without happiness gives the best prospect of realizing such happiness as is attainable. For nothing except that consciousness can raise a person above the chances of life, by making him feel that, let fate and fortune do their worst, they have not power to subdue him. . . .

The utilitarian morality does recognize in human beings the power of sacrificing their own greatest good for the good of others. It only refuses to admit that the sacrifice is itself a good. A sacrifice which does not increase, or tend to increase, the sum total of happiness, it considers as wasted. . . .

The assailants of utilitarianism seldom have the justice to acknowledge, that the happiness which forms the utilitarian standard of what is right in conduct is not the agent's own happiness but that of all concerned. As between his own happiness and that of others, utilitarianism requires him to be as strictly impartial as a disinterested and benevolent spectator. In the golden rule of Jesus of Nazareth, we read the complete spirit of the ethics of utility. "To do as you would be done by," and "to love your neighbor as yourself," constitute the ideal perfection of utilitarian morality. As the means of making the nearest approach to this ideal, utility would enjoin, first, that laws and social arrangements should place the happiness or (as speaking practically, it may be called) the interest of every individual as nearly as possible in harmony with the interest of the whole; and, secondly, that education and opinion, which have so vast a power over human character, should so use that power as to establish in the mind of every individual an indissoluble association between his own happiness and the good of the whole, especially between his own happiness and the practice of such modes of conduct, negative and positive, as regard for the universal happiness prescribes; so that not only he may be unable to conceive the possibility of happiness to himself, consistent with the conduct opposed to the general good, but also that a direct impulse to promote the general good may be every individual one of the habitual motives of action, and the sentiments connected therewith may fill a large and prominent place in every human being's sentient existence. . . .

We not uncommonly hear the doctrine of utility inveighed against as a *godless* doctrine. If it be necessary to say anything at all against so mere an assumption, we may say that the question depends upon what idea we have formed of the moral character of the Deity. If it be a true belief that God desires, above all things, the happiness of his creatures, and that this was his purpose in their creation, utility is not only not a godless doctrine, but more profoundly religious than any other. If it be meant that utilitarianism does not recognize the revealed will of God as the supreme law of morals, I answer that a utilitarian who believes in the perfect goodness and wisdom of God necessarily believes that whatever God has thought fit to reveal on the subject of morals must fulfill the requirements of utility in a supreme degree. . . .

Again, defenders of utility often find themselves called upon to reply to such objections as this—that there is not time, previous to action, for calculating and weighing the effects of any line of conduct on the general happiness. This is exactly as if anyone were to say that it is impossible to guide our conduct by Christianity because there is not time, on every occasion on which anything has to be done, to read through the Old and New Testaments. The answer to the objection is that there has been ample time, namely, the whole past duration of the human species. During all that time mankind have been learning by experience the tendencies of actions; on which experience all the prudence as well as all the morality of life are dependent. The corollaries from the principle of utility, like the precepts of every practical art, admit of indefinite improvement, and, in a progressive state of the human mind, their improvement is perpetually going on. But to consider the rules of morality as improvable is one thing; to pass over the intermediate generalization entirely and endeavor to test each individual action directly by the first principle is another. It is a strange notion that the acknowledgment of a

first principle is inconsistent with the admission of secondary ones. To inform a traveler respecting the place of his ultimate destination is not to forbid the use of landmarks and direction-posts on the way. . . .

There exists no moral system under which there do not arise unequivocal cases of conflicting obligation. These are real difficulties, the knotty points both in the theory of ethics and in the conscientious guidance of personal conduct. They are overcome practically, with greater or with less success, according to the intellect and virtue of the individual; but it can hardly be pretended that anyone will be the less qualified for dealing with them, from possessing an ultimate standard to which conflicting rights and duties can be referred. If utility is the ultimate source of moral obligations, utility may be invoked to decide between them when their demands are incompatible. Though the application of the [utilitarian] standard may be difficult, it is better than none at all; while in other systems, the moral laws all claiming independent authority, there is no common umpire entitled to interfere between them; their claims to precedence one over another rest on little better than sophistry, and, unless determined, as they generally are, by the unacknowledged influence of consideration of utility, afford a free scope for the action of personal desires and partialities. We must remember that only in these cases of conflict between secondary principles is it requisite that first principles should be appealed to. There is no case of moral obligation in which some secondary principle is not involved; and if only one, there can seldom be any real doubt which one it is, in the mind of any person by whom the principle itself is recognized.

OF WHAT SORT OF PROOF THE PRINCIPLE OF UTILITY IS SUSCEPTIBLE

It has already been remarked that questions of ultimate ends do not admit of proof, in the ordinary acceptation of the term. To be incapable of proof by reasoning is common to all first principles; to the first premises of our knowledge, as well as to those of our conduct. But the former, being matters of fact, may be the subject of a direct appeal to the faculties which judge of fact—namely, our senses, and our internal consciousness. Can an appeal be made to the same faculties on questions of practical ends? Or by what other faculty is cognizance taken of them?

Questions about ends are, in other words, questions about what things are desirable. The utilitarian doctrine is, that happiness is desirable, and the only thing desirable, as an end; all other things being only desirable as means to that end. What ought to be required of this doctrine—what conditions is it requisite that the doctrine should fulfil—to make good its claim to be believed?

The only proof capable of being given that an object is visible, is that people actually see it. The only proof that a sound is audible, is that people hear it: and so of the other sources of our experience. In like manner, I apprehend, the sole evidence it is possible to produce that anything is desirable, is that people do actually desire it. If the end which the utilitarian doctrine proposes to itself were not, in theory and in practice, acknowledged to be an end, nothing could ever convince any person that it was so. No reason can be given why the general happiness is desirable, except that each person, so far as he believes it to be attainable, desires his own happiness. This, however, being a fact, we have not only all the proof which the case admits of, but all which it is possible to require, that happiness is a good: that each person's happiness is a good to that person, and the general happiness, therefore, a good to the aggregate of all persons. Happiness has made out its title as one of the ends of conduct, and consequently one of the criteria of morality.

But it has not, by this alone, proved itself to be the sole criterion. To do that, it would seem, by the same rule, necessary to show, not only that people desire happiness, but that they never desire anything else. Now it is palpable that they do desire things which, in common language, are decidedly distinguished from happiness. They desire, for example, virtue, and the absence of vice, no less really than pleasure and the absence of pain. The desire of virtue is not as universal, but it is as authentic a fact, as the desire of happiness. And hence the opponents of the utilitarian standard deem that they have a right to infer that there are other ends of human action besides happiness, and that happiness is not the standard of approbation and disapprobation.

The ingredients of happiness are very various, and each of them is desirable in itself, and not merely when considered as swelling an aggregate. The principle of utility does not mean that any given pleasure, as music, for instance, or any given exemption from pain, as for example health, is to be looked upon as means to a collective something termed happiness, and to be desired on that account. They are desired and desirable in and for themselves; besides being a means, they are part of the end. Virtue, according to the utilitarian doctrine, is not naturally and originally part of the end, but is capable of becoming so; and in those who live disinterestedly it has become so, and is desired and cherished, not as a means to happiness, but as part of their happiness.

To illustrate this further, we may remember that virtue is not the only thing originally a means, and which if it were not a means to anything else would be and remain indifferent, but which by association with what it is a means to comes to be desired for itself, and that too with the utmost intensity. What, for example, shall we say of the love of money? There is nothing originally more desirable about money than about any heap of glittering pebbles. Its worth is solely that of the things which it will buy; the desires for other things than itself, which it is a means of gratifying. Yet the love of money is not only one of the strongest moving forces of human life, but money is, in many cases, desired in and for itself; the desire to possess it is often stronger than the desire to use it, and goes on increasing when all the desires which point to ends beyond it, to be compassed by it, are falling off. It may, then, be said truly that money is desired not for the sake of an end, but as part of the end. From being a means to happiness, it has come to be itself a principal ingredient of the individual's conception of happiness. The same may be said of the majority of the great objects of human life: power, for example, or fame, except that to each of these there is a certain amount of immediate pleasure annexed, which has at least the semblance of being naturally inherent in them—a thing which cannot be said of money. . . .

It results from the preceding considerations that there is in reality nothing desired except happiness. Whatever is desired otherwise than as a means to some end beyond itself, and ultimately to happiness, is desired as itself a part of happiness, and is not desired for itself until it has become so. . . .

We have now, then, an answer to the question, of what sort of proof the principle of utility is susceptible. If the opinion which I have now stated is psychologically true—if human nature is so constituted as to desire nothing which is not either a part of happiness or a means of happiness—we can have no other proof, and we require no other, that these are the only things desirable. If so, happiness is the sole end of human action, and the promotion of it the test by which to judge of all human conduct; from whence it necessarily follows that it must be the criterion of morality, since a part is included in the whole. . . .

ON THE CONNECTION BETWEEN JUSTICE AND UTILITY

In all ages of speculation, one of the strongest obstacles to the reception of the doctrine that Utility or Happiness is the criterion of right and wrong, has been drawn from the idea of Justice. . . .

To throw light upon this question, it is necessary to attempt to ascertain what is the distinguishing character of justice, or of injustice. . . .

In the first place it is mostly considered unjust to deprive anyone of his personal liberty, his property, or any other thing which belongs to him by law. Here, therefore, is one instance of the application of the terms just and unjust in a perfectly definite sense, namely, that it is just to respect, unjust to violate, the *legal rights* of any one. . . .

Secondly; the legal rights of which he is deprived, may be rights which *ought* not to have belonged to him; in other words, the law which confers on him these rights, may be a bad law. . . . When, however, a law is thought to be unjust, it seems to be regarded as being so in the same way in which a breach of law is unjust, namely, by infringing somebody's right; which, as it cannot in this case be a legal right. . . . is called a moral right. We may say, therefore, that a second case of injustice consists in taking or withholding from any person that to which he has a *moral right.*

Thirdly, it is universally considered just that each person should obtain that (whether good or evil) which he *deserves;* and unjust that he should obtain a good, or be made to undergo an evil, which he does not deserve. . . . Speaking in a general way, a person is understood to deserve good if he does right, evil if he does wrong; and in a more particular sense, to deserve good from those to whom he does or has done good, and evil from those to whom he does or has done evil. . . .

Fourthly, it is confessedly unjust to *break faith* with any one: to violate an engagement, either express or implied, or disappoint expectations raised by our own conduct, at least if we have raised those expectations knowingly and voluntarily. . . .

Fifthly, it is, by universal admission, inconsistent with justice to be *partial*—to show favor or preference to one person over another in matters in which favor and preference do not apply. . . .

Among the many diverse applications of the term "justice" it is a matter of some difficulty to seize the mental link which holds them together. . . . In our survey of the various popular acceptations of justice, the term appeared generally to involve the idea of a personal right—a claim on the part of one or more individuals, like that which the law gives when it confers a proprietary or other legal right. Whether the injustice consists in depriving a person of a possession, or in breaking faith with him, or in treating him worse than he deserves, or worse than other people who have no greater claims—in each case the supposition implies two things: a wrong done, and some assignable person who is wronged. Injustice may also be done by treating a person better than others; but the wrong in this case is to the competitors, who are also assignable persons. It seems to me that this feature in the case—a right in some person, correlative to the moral obligation—constitutes the specific difference between justice and generosity or beneficence. Justice implies something which is not only right to do, and wrong not to do, but which some individual person can claim from us as his moral right. No one has a moral right to our generosity or beneficence because we are not morally bound to practice those virtues toward any given individual. . . .

[T]he idea of justice supposes two things; a rule of conduct, and a sentiment which sanctions the rule. The first must be supposed common to all mankind, and intended for their good. The other (the sentiment) is a desire that punishment may be suffered by those who infringe the rule. There is involved, in addition, the conception of some definite person who suffers by the infringement; whose rights (to use the expression appropriated to the case) are violated by it. And the sentiment of justice appears to me to be, the animal desire to repel or retaliate a hurt or damage to oneself, or to those with whom one sympathizes, widened so as to include all persons, by the human capacity of enlarged sympathy, and the human conception of intelligent self-interest. From the latter elements, the feeling derives its morality; from the former, its peculiar impressiveness, and energy of self-assertion.

I have, throughout, treated the idea of a *right* residing in the injured person, and violated by the injury, not as a separate element in the composition of the idea and sentiment, but as one of the forms in which the other two elements clothe themselves. These elements are, a hurt to some assignable person or persons on the one hand, and a demand for punishment on the other. An examination of our own minds, I think, will show, that these two things include all that we mean when we speak of violation of a right. When we call anything a person's right, we mean that he has a valid claim on society to protect him in the possession of it, either by the force of law, or by that of education and opinion. If he has what we consider a sufficient claim, on whatever account, to have something guaranteed to him by society, we say that he has a right to it. If we desire to prove that anything does not belong to him by right, we think this done as soon as it is admitted that society ought not to take measures for securing it to him, but should leave him to chance, or to his own exertions. Thus, a person is said to have a right to what he can earn in fair professional competition; because society ought not to allow any other person to hinder him from endeavouring to earn in that manner as much as he can. But he has not a right to three hundred a year, though he may happen to be earning it; because society is not called on to provide that he shall earn that sum. On the contrary, if he owns ten thousand pounds three per cent, stock, he *has* a right to three hundred a year; because society has come under an obligation to provide him with an income of that amount.

To have a right, then, is, I conceive, to have something which society ought to defend me in the possession of. If the objector goes on to ask, why it ought? I can give him no other reason than general utility. If that expression does not seem to convey a sufficient feeling of the strength of the obligation, nor to account for the peculiar energy of the feeling, it is because there goes to the composition of the sentiment, not a rational only but also an animal element—the thirst for retaliation; and this thirst derives its intensity, as well as its moral justification, from the extraordinarily important and impressive kind of utility which is concerned. The interest involved is that of security, to everyone's feelings the most vital of all interests. . . .

We are continually informed that utility is an uncertain standard, which every different person interprets differently, and that there is no safety but in the immutable, ineffaceable, and unmistakable dictates of justice, which carry their evidence in themselves. [But] not only have different nations and individuals different notions of justice, but in the mind of one and the same individual, justice is not some one rule, principle, or maxim but many which do not always coincide in their dictates, and, in choosing between which, he is guided either by some extraneous standard or by his own personal predilections.

For instance, there are some who say that it is unjust to punish anyone for the sake of example to others. Others maintain the extreme reverse, contending that to punish persons who have attained years of discretion for their own benefit, is despotism and injustice since, if the matter is solely their own good, no one has a right to control their own judgment of it; but that they may justly be punished to prevent evil to others. . . .

To escape these and other difficulties, a favorite contrivance has been the fiction of a contract whereby at some unknown period all members of society engaged to obey the laws and consented to be punished for any disobedience to them, thereby giving to their legislators the right, which it is assumed they would not otherwise have had, of punishing them, either for their own good or for that of the society. This happy thought was considered to get rid of the whole difficulty and to legitimate the infliction of punishment, in virtue of another received maxim of justice—that is not unjust which is done with the consent of the person who is supposed to be hurt by it. I need hardly remark that, even if consent were not a mere fiction, this maxim is not superior in authority to others which it is brought in to supersede. It is, on the contrary, an instructive specimen of the loose and irregular matter in which supposed principles of justice grow up. . . .

Again, . . . how many conflicting conceptions of justice come to light in discussing the proper apportionment of punishment to offenses. [One is] an eye for an eye, a tooth for a tooth. [Others think] it should be measured by the moral guilt of the culprit, [or] what amount of punishment is necessary to deter the offense. . . . Who shall decide between these appeals to conflicting principles of justice? Each, from his own point of view, is unanswerable; and any choice between them, on grounds of justice, must be perfectly arbitrary. Social utility alone can decide the preference.

The Fundamental Principles of the Metaphysic of Morals

Immanuel Kant

Immanuel Kant lived his entire life within a few miles of Konilgsberg, in East Prussia, where he was born in 1724. Kant never married and was a man of remarkable organization and regularity of habits; it is even said that people would set their clocks based on his afternoon walks. He lived a long and very productive life, dying in 1804 at the age of eighty. Kant's writing has had and continues to have an immense impact on all areas of philosophy from epistemology and ethics to metaphysics and political theory.

Rejecting both Aristotle, who believed it necessary to study human psychology and the nature of human happiness closely in order to understand morality, and utilitarians, who believed sentiment and feeling were at the root of morality, Kant argues that duty is based solely on reason. To be genuinely worthy, Kant argues, one must not just act in accordance with duty; one must also act for duty's sake. To do the right thing out of selfish motives (for fear of getting caught, for example) would not be to act for the sake of duty and therefore would not evidence the kind of value that actions done purely for the sake of duty do.

How then is one to know what duty requires? Reacting against Hume's emphasis on feeling to understanding moral actions and the consequences of actions as a test of morality, Kant argues that reason provides the foundation on which duty rests. An action is right, he claims, if it conforms to a moral rule that any agent must follow if he is to act rationally. That rule, which distinguishes right from wrong, is what Kant calls the *categorical* (that is, exceptionless) imperative, an imperative that Kant expressed as requiring that a person must never perform an act unless he or she can consistently will that the maxim or principle that motivates the action could become a universal law. In this way, Kant argues, the categorical imperative comprises the heart of the distinction between right and wrong—a distinction that any rational being can comprehend and act on.

Kant also speaks of a second formulation of the categorical imperative that he believed was equivalent to the one previously mentioned. The second formulation states that one must act so as to treat people as ends in themselves, never merely as means. That second version, then, looks at actions from the perspective of the victim rather than the agent. Kant concludes with a brief discussion of what he termed the "kingdom of ends" as well as of human dignity and autonomy.

As you read through this essay, consider the following:

1. What distinguishes acting from inclination and acting from duty? Which reflects genuine moral worth? Why?
2. How do hypothetical and categorical imperatives differ?
3. What does Kant mean by a "maxim"?
4. What are the two versions Kant gives of the categorical imperative? How is the categorical imperative applied?
5. What does Kant mean by autonomy? Are all human beings autonomous?

THE GOOD WILL

Nothing can possibly be conceived in the world, or even out of it, which can be called good without qualification, except a *good will*. Intelligence, wit, judgment, and the other talents of the mind, however they may be named, or courage, resolution, perseverance, as qualities of temperament, are undoubtedly good and desirable in many respects; but these gifts of nature may also become extremely bad and mischievous if the will which is to make use of them, and which, therefore, constitutes what is called *character*, is not good. It is the

same with the *gifts of fortune*. Power, riches, honor, even health, and the general well-being and contentment with one's conditions which is called *happiness*, inspire pride, and often presumption, if there is not a good will to correct the influence of these on the mind, and with this also to rectify the whole principle of acting, and adapt it to its end. The sight of a being who is not adorned with a single feature of a pure and good will, enjoying unbroken prosperity, can never give pleasure to an impartial rational spectator. Thus a good will appears to constitute the indispensable condition even of being worthy of happiness.

There are even some qualities which are of service to this good will itself, and may facilitate its action, yet which have no intrinsic uncondi-

From *The Fundamental Principles of the Metaphysic of Morals* (1785), trans. Thomas K. Abbott (1873).

tional value, but always presuppose a good will, and this qualifies the esteem that we justly have for them, and does not permit us to regard them as absolutely good. Moderation in the affections and passions, self-control, and calm deliberation are not only good in many respects, but even seem to constitute part of the intrinsic worth of the person; but they are far from deserving to be called good without qualification, although they have been so unconditionally praised by the ancients. For without the principles of a good will, they may become extremely bad; and the coolness of a villain not only makes him far more dangerous, but also directly makes him more abominable in our eyes than he would have been without it.

A good will is good not because of what it performs or effects, not by its aptness for the attainment of some proposed end, but simply by virtue of the volition—that is, it is good in itself, and considered by itself is to be esteemed much higher than all that can be brought about by it in favor of any inclination, nay, even of the sum-total of all inclinations. Even if it should happen that, owing to special disfavor of fortune, or the niggardly provision of a stepmotherly nature, this will should wholly lack power to accomplish its purpose, if with its greatest efforts it should yet achieve nothing, and there should remain only the good will (not, to be sure, a mere wish, but the summoning of all means in our power), then, like a jewel, it would still shine by its own light, as a thing which has its whole value in itself. Its usefulness of fruitlessness can neither add to nor take away anything from this value. It would be, as it were, only the setting to enable us to handle it the more conveniently in common commerce, or to attract to it the attention of those who are not yet connoisseurs, but not to recommend it to true connoisseurs, or to determine its value. . . .

THE FIRST PROPOSITION OF MORALITY

We have then to develop the notion of a will which deserves to be highly esteemed for itself, and is good without a view to anything further. . . . [Consider] that it is always a matter of duty that a tradesman should not overcharge an inexperienced purchaser; and wherever there is much commerce the prudent tradesman does not overcharge, but keeps a fixed price of everyone, so that a child buys of him as well as any other. Men are thus honestly served, but this is not enough to make us believe that the tradesman acted from duty and from principles of honesty: his own advantage required it. Accordingly the action was done neither from duty nor from direct inclination, but merely with a selfish view. . . .

On the other hand, it is a duty to maintain one's life; and, in addition, everyone also has a direct inclination to do so. But on this account the often anxious care which most men take for it has no intrinsic worth, and their maxim has no moral import. They preserve their life *as duty requires*, no doubt, but not *because duty requires.* On the other hand, if adversity and hopeless sorrow have completely taken away the relish for life; if the unfortunate one, strong in mind, indignant at his fate rather than desponding or dejected, wishes for death, and yet preserves his life without loving it—not from inclination of fear, but from duty—then his maxim has a moral worth. . . .

To be beneficent when we can is a duty; and besides this, there are many minds so sympathetically constituted that, without any other motive of vanity or self-interest, they find a pleasure in spreading joy around them, and can take delight in the satisfaction of others so far as it is their own work. But I maintain that in such a case an action of this kind, however proper, however amiable it may be, has nevertheless no true moral worth, but is on a level with other inclinations, for example, the inclination to honor, which, if it is happily directed to that which is in fact of public utility and accordant with duty, and consequently honorable, deserves praise and encouragement, but not esteem. For the maxim lacks the moral import, namely, that such actions be done *from duty*, not from inclination. Put the case that the mind of that philanthropist was clouded by sorrow of his own, extinguishing all sympathy with the lot of others, and that while he still has the power to benefit others in distress, he is not touched by their trouble because he is absorbed with his own; and now suppose that he tears himself out of this dead insensibility and performs the action without any inclination to it, but simply from duty, then . . . has his action its genuine moral worth. . . . It is just in this that the moral worth of the character is brought out which is incomparably the highest of all, namely, that he is beneficent, not from inclination, but from duty. . . .

It is in this manner, undoubtedly, that we are to understand those passages of Scripture in which we are commanded to love our neighbour, even our enemy. For love, as an affection, cannot be commanded, but beneficence for duty's sake may. This is *practical* love, and not *pathological*—a love that is seated in the will, and not in the propensities of feeling—in principles of action and not of tender sympathy; and it is this love alone which can be commanded.

THE SECOND AND THIRD PROPOSITION OF MORALITY

The second proposition is: That an action done from duty derives its moral worth, *not from the purpose* which is to be attained by it, but from the maxim by which it is determined, and therefore does not depend on the realization of the object of the action, but merely on the *principle of volition* by which the action has taken place, without regard to any object of desire. It is clear from what precedes that the purposes which we may have in view in our actions, or their effects regarded as ends and springs of the will, cannot give to actions any unconditional or moral worth. In what, then, can their worth lie if it is not to consist in the will and in reference to its expected effect? It cannot lie anywhere but in the *principle of the will* without regard to the ends which can be attained by the action. . . .

The third proposition, which is a consequence of the two preceding, I would express thus: *Duty is the necessity of acting from respect for the law*. I may have *inclination* for an object as the effect of my proposed action, but I cannot have *respect* for it just for this reason that it is an effect and not an energy of will. Similarly, I cannot have respect for inclination, whether my own or another's; I can at most, if my own, approve it; if another's, sometimes even love it, that is, look on it as favorable to my own interest. It is only what is connected with my will as a principle, by no means as an effect—what does not subserve my inclination, but overpowers it, or at least in case of choice excludes it from its calculation—in other words, simply the law of itself, which can be an object of respect, and hence a command. Now an action done from duty must wholly exclude the influence of inclination, and with it every object of the will, so that nothing remains which can determine the will except objectively the *law*, and subjectively *pure respect* for this practical law, and consequently the maxim that I should follow this law even to the thwarting of all my inclinations.

Thus the moral worth of an action does not lie in the effect expected from it, nor in any principle of action which requires to borrow its motive from this expected effect. For all these effects—agreeableness of one's condition, and even the promotion of the happiness of others—could have been also brought about by other causes, so that for this there would have been no need of the will of a rational being; whereas it is in this alone that the supreme and unconditional good can be found. The pre-eminent good which we call moral can therefore consist in nothing else than *the conception of law* in itself, *which certainly is only possible in a rational being*, in so far as this conception, and not the expected effect, determines the will. This is a good which is already present in the person who acts accordingly, and we have not to wait for it to appear first in the result.

THE SUPREME PRINCIPLE OF MORALITY: THE CATEGORICAL IMPERATIVE

But what sort of law can that be the conception of which must determine the will, even without paying any regard to the effect expected from it, in order that this will may be called good absolutely and without qualification? As I have deprived the will of every impulse which could arise to it from obedience to any law, there remains nothing but the universal conformity of its actions to law in general, which alone is to serve the will as a principle, that is, I am never to act otherwise than so *that I could also will that my maxim should become a universal law.* Here, now, it is the simple conformity to law in general, without assuming any particular law applicable to certain actions, that serves the will as its principle, and must so serve it if duty is not to be a vain delusion and a chimerical notion. The common reason of men in its practical judgments perfectly coincides with this, and always has in view the principle here suggested. Let the question be, for example: May I when in distress make a promise with the intention not to keep it? I readily distinguish here between the two significations which the question may have: whether it is prudent or whether it is right to make a false promise? The former may undoubtedly often be the case. I see clearly indeed that it is not enough to extricate myself from a present difficulty by means of this subterfuge, but it must be well considered whether there may not hereafter spring from this lie much greater inconvenience than that from which I now free myself, and as, with all my supposed *cunning,* the consequences cannot be so easily foreseen but that credit once lost may be much more injurious to me than any mischief which I seek to avoid at present, it should be considered whether it would not be more *prudent* to act herein according to a universal maxim, and to make it a habit to promise nothing except with the intention of keeping it. But it is soon clear to me that such a maxim will still only be based on the fear of consequences. Now it is a wholly different thing to be truthful from duty, and to be so from apprehension of injurious consequences. In the first case, the very notion of the action already implies a law for me; in the second case, I must first look about elsewhere to see what results may be combined with it which would affect myself. For to deviate from the principle of duty is beyond all doubt wicked; but to be unfaithful to my maxim of prudence may often be very advantageous to me, although to abide by it is certainly safer. The shortest way, however, and an unerring one, to discover the answer to this question whether a lying promise is consistent with duty, is to ask myself, Should I be content that my maxim (to extricate myself from difficulty by a false promise) should hold good as a universal law, for myself as well as for others; and should I be able to say to myself, "Every one may make a deceitful promise when he finds himself in a difficulty from which he cannot otherwise extricate himself"? Then I presently become aware that, while I can will the lie, I can by no means will that lying should be a universal law. For with such a law there would be no promises at all, since it would be in vain to allege my intention in regard to my future actions to those who would not believe this allegation, or if they over-hastily did so, would pay me back in my own coin. Hence my maxim, so soon as it should be made a universal law, would necessarily destroy itself.

I do not, therefore, need any far-reaching penetration to discern what I have to do in order that my will may be morally good. Inexperienced in the course of the world, incapable of being prepared for all its contingencies, I only ask myself: Canst thou also will that thy maxim should be a universal law? If not, then it must be rejected, and that not because of a disadvantage accruing from it to myself or even to others, but because it cannot enter as a principle into a possible universal legislation, and reason extorts from me immediate respect for such legislation. I do not indeed as yet *discern* on what this respect is based (this the philosopher may inquire), but at least I understand this—that it is an estimation of the worth which far outweighs all worth of what is recommended by inclination, and that the necessity of acting from pure respect for the practical law is what constitutes duty, to which every other motive must give place because it is the condition of a will being good *in itself*, and the worth of such a will is above everything.

Thus, then, without quitting the moral knowledge of common human reason, we have arrived at its principle. And although, no doubt, common men do not conceive it in such an abstract and universal form, yet they always have it really before their eyes and use it as the standard of their decision. Here it would be easy to show how, with this compass in hand, men are well able to distinguish, in every case that occurs, what is good, what bad, conformably to duty or inconsistent with it. . . .

IMPERATIVES: HYPOTHETICAL AND CATEGORICAL

Everything in nature works according to laws. Rational beings alone have the faculty of acting according *to the conception of laws*, that is according to principles, *i.e.*, have a *will*. Since the deduction of actions from principles requires *reason*, the will is nothing but practical reason. . . .

The conception of an objective principle, in so far as it is obligatory for a will, is called a command (of reason), and the formula of the command is called an Imperative.

All imperatives are expressed by the word *ought* [or *shall*], and thereby indicate the relation of an objective law of reason to a will, which from its subjective constitution is not necessarily determined by it (an obligation). . . .

Now all *imperatives* command either *hypothetically* or *categorically*. The former represent the practical necessity of a possible action as means to something else that is willed (or at least which one might possibly will). The categorical imperative would be that which represented an action as necessary of itself without reference to another end, that is, as objectively necessary. . . .

If now the action is good only as a means to *something else*, then the imperative is *hypothetical*; if it is conceived as good *in itself* and consequently as being necessarily the principle of a will which of itself conforms to reason, then it is *categorical*. . . .

Accordingly the hypothetical imperative only says that the action is good for some purpose, *possible or actual*. In the first case it is a *problematical*, in the second an *assertorial* practical principle. The categorical imperative which declares an action to be objectively necessary in itself without reference to any purpose, that is, without any other end, is valid as an *apodictic* (practical) principle. . . .

FIRST FORMULATION OF THE CATEGORICAL IMPERATIVE: UNIVERSAL LAW

When I conceive a hypothetical imperative, in general I do not know beforehand what it will contain until I am given the condition. But when I conceive a categorical imperative, I know at once what it contains. For as the imperative contains besides the law only the necessity that the maxims shall conform to this law, while the law contains no conditions restricting it, there remains nothing but the general statement that the maxim of the action should conform to a universal law, and it is this conformity alone that the imperative properly represents as necessary.

There is therefore but one categorical imperative, namely, this: *Act only on that maxim whereby thou canst at the same time will that it should become a universal law.*

Now if all imperatives of duty can be deduced from this one imperative as from their principle, then, although it should remain undecided whether what is called duty is not merely a vain notion, yet at least we shall be able to show what we understand by it and what this notion means. . . .

Four Illustrations

We will now enumerate a few duties, adopting the usual division of them into duties to ourselves and to others, and into perfect and imperfect duties.

1. A man reduced to despair by a series of misfortunes feels wearied of life, but is still so far in possession of his reason that he can ask himself whether it would not be contrary to his duty to himself to take his own life. Now he inquires whether the maxim of his action could become a universal law of nature. His maxim is: From self-love I adopt it as a principle to shorten my life when its longer duration is likely to bring more evil than satisfaction. It is asked then simply whether this principle founded on self-love can become a universal law of nature. Now we see at once that a system of nature of which it should be a law to destroy life by means of the very feeling whose special nature it is to impel to the improvement of life would contradict itself, and therefore could not exist as a system of nature; hence that maxim cannot possibly exist as a universal law of nature, and consequently would be wholly inconsistent with the supreme principle of all duty.

2. Another finds himself forced by necessity to borrow money. He knows that he will not be able to repay it, but sees also that nothing will be lent to him unless he promises stoutly to repay it in a definite time. He desires to make this promise, but he has still so much conscience as to ask himself: Is it not unlawful and inconsistent with duty to get out of a difficulty in this way? Suppose, however, that he resolves to do so, then the maxim of his action would be expressed thus: When I think myself in want of money, I will borrow money and promise to repay it, although I know that I never can do so. Now this principle of self-love or of one's own advantage may perhaps be consistent with my whole future welfare; but the question now is, Is it right? I change then the suggestion of self-love into a universal law, and state the question thus: How would it be if my maxim were a universal law? Then I see at once that it could never hold as a universal law of nature, but would necessarily contradict itself. For supposing it to be a universal law that everyone when he thinks himself in a difficulty should be able to promise whatever he pleases, with the purpose of not keeping his promise, the promise itself would become impossible, as well as the end that one might have in view in it, since no one would consider that anything was promised to him, but would ridicule all such statements as vain pretenses.

3. A third finds in himself a talent which with the help of some culture might make him a useful man in many respects. But he finds himself in comfortable circumstances and prefers to indulge in pleasure rather than to take pains in enlarging and improving his happy natural capacities. He asks, however, whether his maxim of neglect of his natural gifts, besides agreeing with his inclination to indulgence, agrees also with what is called duty. He sees then that a system of nature could indeed subsist with such a universal law, although men (like the South Sea islanders) should let their talents rest and resolve to devote their lives merely to idleness, amusement, and propagation of their species—in a word, to enjoyment; but he cannot possibly will that this should be a universal law of nature, or be implanted in us as such by a natural instinct. For, as a rational being, he necessarily wills that his faculties be developed, since they serve him, and have been given him, for all sorts of possible purposes.

4. A fourth, who is in prosperity, while he sees that others have to contend with great wretchedness and that he could help them, thinks: What concern is it of mine? Let everyone be as happy as Heaven pleases, or as he can make himself; I will take nothing from him nor even envy him, only I do not wish to contribute anything to his welfare or to his assistance in distress! Now no doubt, if such a mode of thinking were a universal law, the human race might very well subsist, and doubtless even better than in a state in which everyone talks of sympathy and good-will, or even takes care occasionally to put it into practice, but, on the other side, also cheats when he can, betrays the rights of men, or otherwise violates them. But although it is possible that a universal law of nature might exist in accordance with that maxim, it is impossible to *will* that such a principle should have the universal validity of a law of nature. For a will which resolved this would contradict itself, inasmuch as many cases might occur in which one would have need of the love and sympathy of others, and in which, by such a law of nature, sprung from his own will, he would deprive himself of all hope of the aid he desires.

These are a few of the many actual duties, or at least what we regard as such, which obviously fall into two classes on the one principle that we have laid down. We must be *able to will* that a maxim of our action should be a universal law. This is the canon of the moral appreciation of the action generally. Some actions are of such a character that their maxim cannot without contradiction be even *conceived* as a universal law of nature, far from it being possible that we should *will* that it *should* be so. In others, this intrinsic impossibility is not found, but still it is impossible to *will* that their maxim should be raised to the universality of a law of nature, since such a will would contradict itself. . . .

SECOND FORMULATION OF THE CATEGORICAL IMPERATIVE: HUMANITY AS END IN ITSELF

The will is conceived as a faculty of determining oneself to action *in accordance with the conception of certain laws*. And such a faculty can be found only in rational beings. The ends which a rational being proposes to himself at pleasure as *effects* of his actions are all only relative, for it is only their relation to the particular desires of the subject that gives them their worth, which therefore cannot furnish principles universal and necessary for all rational beings and every volition, that is to say practical laws. Hence all these relative ends can give only hypothetical imperatives. Supposing, however, that there were something *whose existence* has *in itself* an absolute worth, something which, being *an end in itself*, could be a source of definite laws, then in this and this alone would lie the source of a possible categorical imperative, i.e. a practical law. . . .

Now I say: man and generally any rational being exists as an end in himself, *not merely as a means* to be arbitrarily used by this or that will, but in all his actions, whether they concern himself or other rational beings, must be always regarded at the same time as an end. All objects of the inclinations have only a conditional worth; for if the inclinations and the wants founded on them did not exist, then their object would be without value. Thus the worth of any object which is *to be acquired* by our action is always conditional. Beings whose existence depends not on our will but on nature's, have nevertheless, if they are nonrational beings, only a relative value as means, and are therefore called *things*; rational beings, on the contrary, are called *persons*, because their very nature points them out as ends in themselves, that is, as something which must not be used merely as means, and so far therefore restricts freedom of action (and is an object of respect). These, therefore, are not merely subjective ends whose existence has a worth *for us* as an effect of our action, but *objective ends*, that is, things whose existence is an end in itself—an end, moreover, for which no other can be substituted, which they should subserve *merely* as means, for otherwise nothing whatever would possess *absolute worth*; . . .

If then there is a supreme practical principle or, in respect of the human will, a categorical imperative, it must be one which, being drawn from the conception of that which is necessarily an end for everyone because it is *an end in itself*, constitutes an objective principle of will, and can therefore serve as a universal practical law. The foundation of this principle is: *rational nature exists as an end in itself.* Man necessarily conceives his own existence as being so: so far then this is a *subjective* principle of human actions. But every other rational being regards its existence similarly, just on the same rational principle that holds for me: so that it is at the same time an objective principle, from which as a supreme practical law all laws of the will must be capable of being deduced. Accordingly the practical imperative will be as follows: *So act as to treat humanity, whether in thine own person or in that of any other, in every case as an end withal, never as means only.* We will now inquire whether this can be practically carried out. . . .

THE KINGDOM OF ENDS

The conception of the will of every rational being as one which must consider itself as giving in all the maxims of its will universal laws, so as to judge itself and its actions from this point of view—this conception leads to another which depends on it and is very fruitful, namely that of a *kingdom of ends.*

By a *kingdom* I understand the union of different rational beings in a system by common laws. Now since it is by laws that ends are determined as regards their universal validity, hence, if we abstract from the personal differences of rational beings and likewise from all the content of their private ends, we shall be able to conceive all ends combined in a systematic whole (including both rational beings as ends in themselves, and also the special ends which each may propose to himself), that is to say, we can conceive a kingdom of ends, which on the preceding principles is possible.

For all rational beings come under the *law* that each of them must treat itself and all others *never merely as means*, but in every case *at the same time as ends in themselves.* Hence results a systematic union of rational beings by common objective laws, *i.e.*, a kingdom which may be called a kingdom of ends, since what these laws have in view is just the rela-

tion of these beings to one another as ends and means. It is certainly only an ideal.

A rational being belongs as a *member* to the kingdom of ends when although giving universal laws in it he is also himself subject to these laws. He belongs to it *as sovereign*, when while giving laws he is not subject to the will of any other.

A rational being must always regard himself as giving laws in a kingdom of ends which freedom of the will makes possible, whether it be as member or as sovereign. He cannot, however, maintain the latter position merely by the maxims of his will, but only in case he is a completely independent being without wants and with unrestricted power adequate to his will.

Morality consists then in the reference of all action to the legislation which alone can render a kingdom of ends possible. This legislation must be capable of existing in every rational being, and of emanating from his will, so that the principle of this will, is never to act on any maxim which could not without contradiction be also a universal law, and accordingly always so to act *that the will could at the same time regard itself as giving in its maxims universal laws.* If now the maxims of rational beings are not by their own nature coincident with this objective principle, then the necessity of acting on it is called practical obligation, *i.e.*, *duty.* Duty does not apply to the sovereign in the kingdom of ends, but it does to every member of it and to all in the same degree.

The practical necessity of acting on this principle, i.e. duty, does not rest at all on feelings, impulses, or inclinations, but solely on the relation of rational beings to one another, a relation in which the will of a rational being must always be regarded as *legislative.* . . .

In the kingdom of ends everything has either Value or Dignity. Whatever has a value can be replaced by something else which is *equivalent;* whatever on the other hand is above all value, and therefore admits of no equivalent, has a dignity.

Whatever has reference to the general inclinations and wants of mankind has a *market value;* whatever without presupposing a want, corresponds to a certain taste, that is to a satisfaction in the mere purposeless play of our facilities, has a *fancy value*; but that which constitutes the condition under which alone anything can be an end in itself, this has not merely a relative worth, *i.e.*, value, but an intrinsic worth, that is, *dignity*.

Now morality is the condition under which alone a rational being can be an end in himself, since by this alone is it possible that he should be a legislating member in the kingdom of ends. Thus morality, and humanity as capable of it, is that which alone has dignity. Skill and diligence in labour have a market value; wit, lively imagination, and humour have a fancy value; on the other hand, fidelity to promises, benevolence from principle (not from instinct) have an intrinsic worth. Neither nature nor art contains anything which in default of these it could put in their place, for their worth consists not in the effects which spring from them, not in the use and advantage which they secure, but in the disposition of mind, that is the maxims of the will which are ready to manifest themselves in such actions, even though they should not have the desired effect. These actions also need no recommendation from any subjective taste or sentiment, that they may be looked on with immediate favour and satisfaction: they need no immediate propensities or feeling for them; they exhibit the will that performs them as an object of an immediate respect, and nothing but reason is required to *impose* them on the will; not to *flatter* it into them, which in the case of duties would be a contradiction. This estimation therefore shows that the worth of such a disposition is dignity, and places it infinitely above all value, with which it cannot for a moment be brought into comparison or competition without as it were violating its sanctity.

What then is it which justifies virtue or the morally good disposition, in making such lofty claims? It is nothing less than the privilege it secures to the rational being of participating in the giving of universal laws, by which it qualifies him to be a member of a possible kingdom of ends, a privilege to which he was already destined by his own nature as being an end in himself, and on that account legislating in the kingdom of ends; free as regards all laws of physical nature, and obeying those only which he himself gives, and by which his maxims can belong to a system of universal law, to which at the same time he submits himself. For nothing has any worth except what the law assigns it. Now the legislation itself which assigns the worth of everything, must for that very reason possess dignity, that is an unconditional incomparable worth, and the word *respect* alone supplies a becoming expression for the esteem which a rational being must have for it. *Autonomy* then is the basis of the dignity of human and of every rational nature. . . .

THE AUTONOMY OF THE WILL

Autonomy of the will is the property that the will has of being a law to itself (independently of any property of the objects of volition). The principle of autonomy is this: Always choose in such a way that in the same volition the maxims of the choice are at the same time present as universal law.

If the will seeks the law that is to determine it anywhere but in the fitness of its maxims for its own legislation of universal laws, and if it thus goes outside of itself and seeks this law in the character of any of its objects, then heteronomy always results. The will in that case does not give itself the law, but the object does so because of its relation to the will. This relation, whether it rests on inclination or on representations of reason, admits only of hypothetical imperatives: I ought to do something because I will something else. On the other hand, the moral, and hence categorical, imperative says that I ought to act in this way or that way, even though I did not will something else. . . .

Section 10

Critical Perspectives on Morality

Feminist Transformations of Moral Theory

Virginia Held

In this essay, Virginia Held discusses the history of ethics from the perspective of feminism. That history shows a distinctively male bias, she argues: Its assumptions have reflected not human experience but men's. In particular, Held criticizes the distinction often drawn between reason and emotion, the tendency to equate women with emotions, the way that the public/private distinction has worked to privilege the male perspective, and the gender-biased view ethics presents of the person or self. Virginia Held is professor of philosophy at Hunter College and the Graduate School of the City University of New York.

As you read through this essay, consider the following:

1. How does Held think the tendency in philosophy to distinguish reason from emotion has influenced the development of philosophical thought about ethics?
2. What is the "public/private" distinction, and why does Held think those who employ it privilege the male point of view?
3. In what way, according to Held, was Hobbes's view of human nature misleading from a female point of view? Was Kant any better? Explain.
4. Held thinks women have a different approach to philosophy than do men. Explain what she means. Do you agree?

The history of philosophy, including the history of ethics, has been constructed from male points of view, and has been built on assumptions and concepts that are by no means gender-neutral. Feminists characteristically begin with different concerns and give different emphases to the issues we consider than do non-feminist approaches. And, as Lorraine Code expresses it, "starting points and focal points shape the impact of theoretical discussion."[1] Within philosophy, feminists often start with, and focus on, quite different issues than those found in standard philosophy and ethics, however "standard" is understood. Far from providing mere additional insights which can be incorporated into traditional theory, feminist explorations often require radical transformations of existing fields of inquiry and theory. From a feminist point of view, moral theory along with almost all theory will have to be transformed to take adequate account of the experience of women.

I shall in this paper [examine] how various fundamental aspects of the history of ethics have not been gender-neutral. And I shall discuss three issues where feminist rethinking is transforming moral concepts and theories.

Consider the ideals embodied in the phrase "the man of reason." As Genevieve Lloyd has told the story, what has been taken to characterize the man of reason may have changed from historical period to historical period, but in each, the character ideal of the man of reason has been constructed in conjunction with a rejection of whatever has been taken to be characteristic of the feminine. "Rationality," Lloyd writes, "has been conceived as transcendence of the 'feminine,' and the 'feminine' itself has been partly constituted by its occurrence within this structure."[2]

This has of course fundamentally affected the history of philosophy and of ethics. The split between reason and emotion is one of the most familiar of philosophical conceptions. And the advocacy of reason "controlling" unruly emotion, of rationality guiding responsible human action against the blindness of passion, has a long and highly influential history, almost as familiar to non-philosophers as to philosophers. We should certainly now be alert to the ways in which reason has been associated with male endeavor, emotion with female weakness, and the ways in which this is of course not an accidental association. As Lloyd writes, "From the beginnings of philosophical thought, femaleness was symbolically associated with what Reason supposedly left behind—the dark powers of the earth goddesses, immersion in unknown forces associated with mysterious female powers. The early Greeks saw women's capacity to conceive as connecting them with the fertility of Nature. As Plato later expressed the thought, women 'imitate the earth.'"[3]

Reason, in asserting its claims and winning its status in human history, was thought to have to conquer the female forces of Unreason. Reason and clarity of thought were early associated with maleness, and as Lloyd notes, "what had to be shed in developing culturally prized rationality was, from the start, symbolically associated with femaleness."[4] In later Greek philosophical thought, the form/matter distinction was articulated, and with a similar hierarchical and gendered association. Maleness was aligned with active, determinate, and defining form; femaleness with mere passive, indeterminate, and inferior matter. Plato, in the *Timaeus*, compared the defining aspect of form with the father, and indefinite matter with the mother; Aristotle also compared the form/matter distinction with the male/female distinction. To quote Lloyd again, "This comparison . . . meant that the very nature of knowledge was implicitly associated with the extrusion of what was symbolically associated with the feminine."[5]

The associations, between Reason, form, knowledge, and maleness, have persisted in various guises, and have permeated what has been thought to be moral knowledge as well

From *Philosophy and Phenomenological Research*, Fall 1990 (Supplement). Reprinted by permission. This is the first part of a larger essay. Some footnotes omitted.

as what has been thought to be scientific knowledge, and what has been thought to be the practice of morality. The associations between the philosophical concepts and gender cannot be merely dropped, and the concepts retained regardless of gender, because gender has been built into them in such a way that without it, they will have to be different concepts. As feminists repeatedly show, if the concept of "human" were built on what we think about "woman" rather than what we think about "man," it would be a very different concept. Ethics, thus, has not been a search for universal, or truly human guidance, but a gender-biased enterprise.

Other distinctions and associations have supplemented and reinforced the identification of reason with maleness, and of the irrational with the female; on this and other grounds "man" has been associated with the human, "woman" with the natural. Prominent among distinctions reinforcing the latter view has been that between the public and the private, because of the way they have been interpreted. Again, these provide as familiar and entrenched a framework as do reason and emotion, and they have been as influential for nonphilosophers as for philosophers. It has been supposed that in the public realm, man transcends his animal nature and creates human history. As citizen, he creates government and law; as warrior, he protects society by his willingness to risk death; and as artist or philosopher, he overcomes his human mortality. Here, in the public realm, morality should guide human decision. In the household, in contrast, it has been supposed that women merely "reproduce" life as natural, biological matter. Within the household, the "natural" needs of man for food and shelter are served, and new instances of the biological creature that man is are brought into being. But what is distinctively human, and what transcends any given level of development to create human progress, are thought to occur elsewhere.

This contrast was made highly explicit in Aristotle's conceptions of polis and household; it has continued to affect the basic assumptions of a remarkably broad swath of thought ever since. In ancient Athens, women were confined to the household; the public sphere was literally a male domain. In more recent history, though women have been permitted to venture into public space, the associations of the public, historically male sphere with the distinctively human, and of the household, historically a female sphere, with the merely natural and repetitious, have persisted. These associations have deeply affected moral theory, which has often supposed the transcendent, public domain to be relevant to the foundations of morality in ways that the natural behavior of women in the household could not be. To take some recent and representative examples, David Heyd, in his discussion of supererogation, dismisses a mother's sacrifice for her child as an example of the supererogatory because it belongs, in his view, to "the sphere of natural relationships and instinctive feelings (which lie outside morality)."[6] J. O. Urmson had earlier taken a similar position. In his discussion of supererogation, Urmson said, "Let us be clear that we are now considering cases of natural affection, such as the sacrifice made by a mother for her child; such cases may be said with some justice not to fall under the concept of morality. . . ."[7] And in a recent article called "Distrusting Economics," Alan Ryan argues persuasively about the questionableness of economics and other branches of the social sciences built on the assumption that human beings are rational, self-interested calculators; he discusses various examples of non self-interested behavior, such as of men in wartime, which show the assumption to be false, but nowhere in the article is there any mention of the activity of mothering, which would seem to be a fertile locus for doubts about the usual picture of rational man.[8] Although Ryan does not provide the kind of explicit reason offered by Heyd and Urmson for omitting the context of mothering from consideration as relevant to his discussion, it is difficult to understand the omission without a comparable assumption being implicit here, as it so often is elsewhere. Without feminist insistence on the relevance for morality of the experience in mothering, this context is largely ignored by moral theorists. And yet, from a gender-neutral point of view, how can this vast and fundamental domain of human experience possibly be imagined to lie "outside morality"?

The result of the public/private distinction, as usually formulated, has been to privilege the points of view of men in the public domains of state and law, and later in the marketplace, and to discount the experience of women. Mothering has been conceptualized as a primarily biological activity, even when performed by humans, and virtually no moral theory in the history of ethics has taken mothering, as experienced by women, seriously as a source of moral insight, until feminists in recent years have begun to. Women have been seen as emotional rather than as rational beings, and thus as incapable of full moral personhood. Women's behavior has been interpreted as either "natural" and driven by instinct, and thus as irrelevant to morality and to the construction of moral principles, or it has been interpreted as, at best, in need of instruction and supervision by males better able to know what morality requires and better able to live up to its demands.

The Hobbesian conception of reason is very different from the Platonic or Aristotelian conceptions before it, and from the conceptions of Rousseau or Kant or Hegel later; all have in common that they ignore and disparage the experience of reality of women. Consider Hobbes's account of man in the state of nature contracting with other men to establish society. These men hypothetically come into existence fully formed and independent of one another, and decide on entering or staying outside of civil society. As Christine Di Stefano writes, "What we find in Hobbes's account of human nature and political order is a vital concern with the survival of a self conceived in masculine terms. . . . This masculine dimension of Hobbes's atomistic egoism is powerfully underscored in his state of nature, which is effectively built on the foundation of denied maternity."[9] In *The Citizen*, where Hobbes gave his first systematic exposition of the state

of nature, he asks us to "consider men as if but even now sprung out of the earth, and suddenly, like mushrooms, come to full maturity, without all kinds of engagement with each other."[10] As Di Stefano says, it is a most incredible and problematic feature of Hobbes's state of nature that the men in it "are not born of, much less nurtured by, women, or anyone else."[11] To abstract from the complex web of human reality an abstract man for rational perusal, Hobbes has, Di Stefano continues, "expunged human reproduction and early nurturance, two of the most basic and typically female-identified features of distinctively human life, from his account of basic human nature. Such a strategy ensures that he can present a thoroughly atomistic subject. . . ."[12] From the point of view of women's experience, such a subject or self is unbelievable and misleading, even as a theoretical construct. The Leviathan, Di Stefano writes, "is effectively comprised of a body politic of orphans who have reared themselves, whose desires are situated within and reflect nothing but independently generated movement. . . . These essential elements are natural human beings conceived along masculine lines."[13]

Rousseau, and Kant, and Hegel, paid homage to the emotional power, the aesthetic sensibility, and the familial concerns, respectively, of women. But since in their views morality must be based on rational principle, and women were incapable of full rationality, or a degree or kind of rationality comparable to that of men, women were deemed, in the view of these moralists, to be inherently wanting in morality. For Rousseau, women must be trained from childhood to submit to the will of men lest their sexual power lead both men and women to disaster. For Kant, women were thought incapable of achieving full moral personhood, and women lose all charm if they try to behave like men by engaging in rational pursuits. For Hegel, women's moral concern for their families could be admirable in its proper place, but is a threat to the more universal aims to which men, as members of the state, should aspire.

These images, of the feminine as what must be overcome if knowledge and morality are to be achieved, of female experience as naturally irrelevant to morality, and of women as inherently deficient moral creatures, are built into the history of ethics. Feminists examine these images, and see that they are not the incidental or merely idiosyncratic suppositions of a few philosophers whose views on many topics depart far from the ordinary anyway. Such views are the nearly uniform reflection in philosophical and ethical theory of patriarchal attitudes pervasive throughout human history. Or they are exaggerations even of ordinary male experience, which exaggerations then reinforce rather than temper other patriarchal conceptions and institutions. They distort the actual experience and aspirations of many men as well as of women. Annette Baier recently speculated about why it is that moral philosophy has so seriously overlooked the thrust between human beings that in her view is an utterly central aspect of moral life. She noted that "the great moral theorists in our tradition not only are all men, they are mostly men who had minimal adult dealings with (and so were then minimally influenced by) women."[14] They were for the most part "clerics, misogynists, and puritan bachelors," and thus it is not surprising that they focus their philosophical attention "so singlemindedly on cool, distanced relations between more or less free and equal adult strangers. . . ."[15] As feminists, we deplore the patriarchal attitudes that so much of philosophy and moral theory reflect. But we recognize that the problem is more serious even than changing those attitudes. For moral theory as so far developed is incapable of correcting itself without an almost total transformation. It cannot simply absorb the gender that has been "left behind," even if both genders would want it to. To continue to build morality on rational principles opposed to the emotions and to include women among the rational will leave no one to reflect the promptings of the heart, which promptings can be moral rather than merely instinctive. To simply bring women into the public and male domain of the polis will leave no one to speak for the household. Its values have been hitherto unrecognized, but they are often moral values. Or to continue to seek contractual restraints on the pursuits of self-interest by atomistic individuals, and to have women join men in devotion to these pursuits, will leave no one involved in the nurturance of children and cultivation of social relations, which nurturance and cultivation can be of greatest moral import.

There are very good reasons for women not to want simply to be accorded entry as equals into the enterprise of morality as so far developed. In a recent survey of types of feminist moral theory, Kathryn Morgan notes that "many women who engage in philosophical reflection are acutely aware of the masculine nature of the profession and tradition, and feel their own moral concerns as women silenced or trivialized in virtually all the official settings that define the practice."[16] Women should clearly not agree, as the price of admission to the masculine realm of traditional morality, to abandon our own moral concerns as women. And so we are groping to shape new moral theory. Understandably, we do not yet have fully worked out feminist moral theories to offer. But we can suggest some directions our project of developing such theories is taking. As Kathryn Morgan points out, there is not likely to be a "star" feminist moral theorist on the order of a Rawls or Nozick: "There will be no individual singled out for two reasons. One reason is that vital moral and theoretical conversations are taking place on a large dialectical scale as the feminist community struggles to develop a feminist ethic. The second reason is that this community of feminist theoreticians is calling into question the very model of the individualized autonomous self presupposed by a star-centered male-dominated tradition. . . . We experience it as a common labour, a common task."[17]

The dialogues that are enabling feminist approaches to moral theory to develop are proceeding. As Alison Jaggar makes clear in her useful overview of them, there is no unitary view of ethics that can be identified as "feminist ethics." Feminist approaches to ethics share a commitment to "rethinking ethics with a view to correcting whatever forms of male bias it may contain."[18] While those who develop these approaches are "united by a shared project, they diverge widely in their views as to how this project is to be accomplished."[19]

Not all feminists, by any means, agree that there are distinctive feminist virtues or values. Some are especially skeptical of the attempt to give positive value to such traditional "feminine virtues" as a willingness to nurture, or an affinity with caring, or reluctance to seek independence. They see this approach as playing into the hands of those who would confine women to traditional roles. Other feminists are skeptical of all claims about women as such, emphasizing that women are divided by class and race and sexual orientation in ways that make any conclusions drawn from "women's experience" dubious. Still, it is possible, I think, to discern various important focal points evident in current feminist attempts to transform ethics into a theoretical and practical activity that could be acceptable from a feminist point of view. In the glimpse I have presented of bias in the history of ethics, I focused on what, from a feminist point of view, are three of its most questionable aspects: 1) the split between reason and emotion and the devaluation of emotion; 2) the public/private distinction and the relegation of the private to the natural; and 3) the concept of the self as constructed from a male point of view. . . .

Notes

1. Lorraine Code, "Second Persons," in *Science, Morality and Feminist Theory*, ed. Marsha Hanen and Kai Nielsen (Calgary: University of Calgary Press, 1987), p. 360.

2. Genevieve Lloyd, *The Man of Reason: "Male" and "Female" in Western Philosophy* (Minneapolis: University of Minnesota Press, 1984), p. 104.

3. Ibid., p. 2.

4. Ibid., p. 3.

5. Ibid., p. 4.

6. David Heyd, *Supererogation: Its Status in Ethical Theory* (New York: Cambridge University Press, 1982), p. 134.

7. J. O. Urmson, "Saints and Heroes," in *Essays in Moral Philosophy*, ed. A. I. Melden (Seattle: University of Washington Press, 1958), p. 202. I am indebted to Marcia Baron for pointing out this and the previous example in her "Kantian Ethics and Supererogation," *The Journal of Philosophy* 84 (May, 1987): 237–62.

8. Alan Ryan, "Distrusting Economics," *New York Review of Books* (May 18, 1989): 25–27. For a different treatment, see *Beyond Self-Interest*, ed. Jane Mansbridge (Chicago: University of Chicago Press, 1990).

9. Christine Di Stefano, "Masculinity as Ideology in Political Theory: Hobbesian Man Considered," *Women's Studies International Forum* (Special Issue: *Hypatia*), Vol. 6, No. 6 (1983): 633–44, p. 637.

10. Thomas Hobbes, *The Citizen: Philosophical Rudiments Concerning Government and Society*, ed. B. Gert (Garden City, New York: Doubleday, 1972 [1651]), p. 205.

11. Di Stefano, op. cit., p. 638.

12. Ibid.

13. Ibid., p. 639.

14. Annette Baier, "Trust and Anti-Trust," *Ethics* 96 (1986): 231–60, pp. 247–48.

15. Ibid.

16. Kathryn Pauly Morgan, "Strangers in a Strange Land: Feminists Visit Relativists" in *Perspectives on Relativism*, ed. D. Odegaard and Carole Stewart (Toronto: Agathon Press, 1990).

17. Kathryn Morgan, "Women and Moral Madness," in *Science, Morality and Feminist Theory*, ed. Hanen and Nielsen, p. 223.

18. Alison M. Jaggar, "Feminist Ethics: Some Issues For The Nineties," *Journal of Social Philosophy* 20 (Spring/Fall 1989), p. 91.

19. Ibid.

Happiness

Robert Nozick

What exactly is happiness? Earlier writers, especially Mill, have emphasized its importance and even argued that happiness is the *only* thing that matters in a life. But is that right? In this essay, Robert Nozick undertakes two tasks: to explain what happiness is and to discover whether, in fact, it is the only thing that makes a life go well or succeed from the perspective of the person living it. Using an ingenious example of an experience machine, he discusses what pleasure is and argues that what matters to us is more than happiness understood as pleasant experiences. He concludes with a discussion of what happiness actually is, if not pleasant experiences, and why we care about things other than happiness even if happiness is understood as the feeling of satisfaction with our life as a whole. Robert Nozick is professor of philosophy at Harvard University.

As you read through this essay, consider the following:

1. What does Nozick mean by a life's narrative curve, and what is its significance?
2. What is the experience machine, and what lessons does Nozick draw from our attitude toward it?
3. How does Nozick understand happiness?
4. The third sense of happiness requires that the evaluations on which the emotion is based not be obviously wrong. What does Nozick mean by that?

Some theorists have claimed that happiness is the *only* important thing about life; all that should matter to a person—they say—is being happy; the sole standard for assessing a life is the amount or quantity of happiness it contains. It is ironic that making this exclusive claim for happiness distorts the flavor of what happy moments are like. For in these moments, almost everything seems wonderful: the way the sun shines, the way that person looks, the way water glistens on the river, the way the dogs play (yet not the way the murderer kills). This openness of happiness, its generosity of spirit and width of appreciation, gets warped and constricted by the claim—pretending to be its greatest friend—that only happiness matters, nothing else.

That claim is begrudging, unlike happiness itself. Happiness can be precious, perhaps even preeminent, yet still be one important thing among others.

There are various ways to nibble away at the apparent obviousness of the view that happiness is the one thing that is important. First, even if happiness were the only thing we cared about, we would not care solely about its total amount. (When I use "we" in this way, I am inviting you to examine whether or not you agree. If you do, then I am elaborating and exploring our common view, but if after reflecting on the matter you find you do not agree, then I am traveling alone for a while.) We would care also about how that happiness was distributed within a lifetime. Imagine graphing someone's total happiness through life; the amount of happiness is represented on the vertical axis, time on the horizontal one. (If the phenomenon of happiness is extremely complicated and multidimensional, it is implausible that its amount could be graphed in this way—but in that case too the purported goal of maximizing our happiness becomes unclear.) If only the total amount of happiness mattered, we would be indifferent between a life of constantly increasing happiness and one of constant decrease, between an upward- and a downward-sloping curve, provided that the total amount of happiness, the total area under the curve, was the same in the two cases. Most of us, however, would prefer the upward-sloping line to the downward; we would prefer a life of increasing happiness to one of decrease. Part of the reason, but only a part, may be that since it makes us happy to look forward to greater happiness, doing so makes our current happiness score even higher. (Yet the person on the downward-sloping curve alternatively can have the current Proustian pleasure of remembering past happiness.) Take the pleasure of anticipation into account, though, by building it into the curve whose height is therefore increased at certain places; still most of us would not care merely about the area under *this* enhanced curve, but about the curve's direction also. (Which life would you prefer your children to have, one of decline or of advance?)

We would be willing, moreover, to give up some amount of happiness to get our lives' narratives moving in the right direction, improving in general. Even if a downwardly sloping curve had slightly more area under it, we would prefer our own lives to slope upward. (If it encompassed vastly greater area, the choice might be different.) Therefore, the contour of the happiness has an independent weight, beyond breaking ties among lives whose total amounts of happiness are equal. In order to gain a more desirable narrative direction, we sometimes would choose *not* to maximize our total happiness. And if the factor of narrative direction might justify forgoing some amount of happiness, so other factors might also.

Straight lines are not the only narrative curves. It would be silly, though, to try to pick the best happiness curve; diverse biographies can fit the very same curve, and we care also about the particular content of a life story. That thing we really want to slope upward might be our life's narrative story, not its amount of happiness. With these stories held constant, we might then care only about happiness's amount, not its slope. However, this too would support the general point that something matters—an upward slope, whether to the narrative line or to the happiness curve—besides the quantity of happiness.

We also can show that more matters than pleasure or happiness by considering a life that has these but otherwise is empty, a life of mindless pleasures or bovine contentment or frivolous amusements only, a happy life but a superficial one. "It is better," John Stuart Mill wrote, "to be a human being dissatisfied than a pig satisfied; better to be Socrates dissatisfied than a fool satisfied." And although it might be best of all to be Socrates satisfied, having both happiness and depth, we would give up some happiness in order to gain the depth.

We are not empty containers or buckets to be stuffed with good things, with pleasures or possessions or positive emotions or even with a rich and varied internal life. Such a bucket has no appropriate structure within; how the experiences fit together or are contoured over time is of no importance except insofar as some particular arrangements make further happy moments more probable. The view that only happiness matters ignores the question of what *we*—the very ones to be happy—are like. How could the most important thing about our life be what it *contains*, though? What makes the felt experiences of pleasure or happiness more important than what we ourselves are like?

Freud thought it a fundamental principle of behavior that we seek pleasure and try to avoid pain or unpleasure—he called this the pleasure principle. Sometimes one can more effectively secure pleasure by not proceeding to it directly; one countenances detours and postponements in immediate satisfaction, one even renounces particular sources of pleasure, due to the nature of the outside world. Freud called this acting in accordance with the reality principle. . . .

. . . Notice that there can be two different specifications of the pleasure to be maximized: the net immediate pleasure (that is, the total immediate pleasure minus the total immediate pain or unpleasure), or the total amount of net pleasure over a lifetime. (This latter goal might fully incorporate Freud's reality principle.) Since pleasure alone seemed too much tied to immediate sensation or excitement, some philosophers modulated the pleasure principle by distinguishing some kinds of pleasure as "higher." But even if this distinction between higher and lower pleasures were adequately formulated—something that hasn't yet been done—this would only add complications to the issue of choice: Can some amount of lower pleasure outweigh a higher pleasure? How much higher are the higher pleasures and do they too differ in their height? What is the overarching goal that incorporates this qualitative distinction? The distinction does not say that something different from pleasure also is important, just that the one thing that is important, pleasure, comes in different grades.

We can gain more precision about what pleasure is. By a pleasure or a pleasurable feeling I mean a feeling that is desired (partly) because of its own felt qualities. The feeling is not desired wholly because of what it leads to or enables you to do or because of some injunction it fulfills. If it is pleasurable, it is desired (in part at least) because of the felt qualities it has. I do not claim there is just one felt quality that always is present whenever pleasure occurs. Being pleasurable, as I use this term, is a function of being wanted partly for its own felt qualities, whatever these qualities may be. On this view, a masochist who desires pain for its own felt quality will find pain pleasurable. This is awkward, but no more so than masochism itself. If, however, the masochist desires pain because he (unconsciously) feels he deserves to be punished, hurt, or humiliated, not desiring pain for its own felt qualities but for what that pain

announces, then in that case the pain itself will not count as pleasurable. Someone *enjoys* an activity to the extent he engages in the activity because of its own intrinsic properties, not simply because of what it leads to or produces later. Its intrinsic properties are not limited to felt qualities, though; this leaves open the possibility that something is enjoyed yet not pleasurable. An example might be tennis played very forcefully; lunging for shots, scraping knees and elbows on the ground, you enjoy playing, but it is not exactly—not precisely—pleasurable.

From this definition of pleasure, it does not follow that there actually are any experiences that are wanted because of their own felt qualities; nor does it follow that we want there to be pleasurable experiences, ones we desire because of their felt qualities. What does follow from (my use of) the term is this: *If* experiences are pleasurable to us, then we do want them (to some extent). The term *pleasurable* just indicates that something is wanted because of its felt qualities. How much we want it, though, whether enough to sacrifice other things we hold good, and whether other things also are wanted, and wanted even more than pleasure, is left open. A person who wants to write a poem needn't want (primarily) the felt qualities of writing, or the felt qualities of being known to have written the poem. He may want, primarily, *to write* such a poem—for example, because he thinks *it* is valuable, or the activity of doing so is, with no special focus upon any felt qualities.

We care about things in addition to how our lives *feel* to us from the inside. This is shown by the following thought experiment. Imagine a machine that could give you any experience (or sequence of experiences) you might desire. When connected to this experience machine, you can have the experience of writing a great poem or bringing about world peace or loving someone and being loved in return. You can experience the felt pleasures of these things, how they feel "from the inside." You can program your experiences for tomorrow, or this week, or this year, or even for the rest of your life. If your imagination is impoverished, you can use the library of suggestions extracted from biographies and enhanced by novelists and psychologists. You can live your fondest dreams "from the inside." Would you choose to do this for the rest of your life? If not, why not? (Other people also have the same option of using these machines which, let us suppose, are provided by friendly and trustworthy beings from another galaxy, so you need not refuse connecting in order to help others.) The question is not whether to try the machine temporarily, but whether to enter it for the rest of your life. Upon entering, you will not remember having done this; so no pleasures will get ruined by realizing they are machine-produced. Uncertainty too might be programmed by using the machine's optional random device (upon which various preselected alternatives can depend).

The question of whether to plug in to this experience machine is a question of value. (It differs from two related questions: an epistemological one—Can you know you are not already plugged in?—and a metaphysical one—Don't the machine experiences themselves constitute a real world?) The question is not whether plugging in is preferable to extremely dire alternatives—lives of torture, for instance—but whether plugging in would constitute the very best life, or tie for being best, because all that matters about a life is how it feels from the inside.

Notice that this is a *thought* experiment, designed to isolate one question: Do only our internal feelings matter to us? It would miss the point, then, to focus upon whether such a machine is technologically feasible. Also, the machine example must be looked at on its own; to answer the question by filtering it through a fixed view that internal experiences are the only things that *can* matter (so of course it would be all right to plug into the machine) would lose the opportunity to test that view independently. One way to determine if a view is inadequate is to check its consequences in particular cases, sometimes extreme ones, but if someone always decided what the result should be in any case by *apply-*

ing the given view itself, this would preclude discovering it did not correctly fit the case. Readers who hold they *would* plug in to the machine should notice whether their first impulse was *not* to do so, followed later by the thought that since only experiences could matter, the machine would be all right after all.

Few of us really think that only a person's experiences matter. We would not wish for our children a life of great satisfactions that all depended upon deceptions they would never detect: although they take pride in artistic accomplishments, the critics and their friends too are just pretending to admire their work yet snicker behind their backs; the apparently faithful mate carries on secret love affairs; their apparently loving children really detest them; and so on. Few of us upon hearing this description would exclaim, "What a wonderful life! It feels so happy and pleasurable from the inside." That person is living in a dream world, taking pleasure in things that aren't so. What he wants, though, is not merely to take pleasure in them; he wants *them to be so*. He values their being that way, and he takes pleasure in them because he thinks they *are* that way. He doesn't take pleasure merely in *thinking* they are.

We care about more than just how things feel to us from the inside; there is more to life than feeling happy. We care about what is actually the case. We want certain situations we value, prize, and think important to actually hold and be so. We want our beliefs, or certain of them, to be true and accurate; we want our emotions, or certain important ones, to be based upon facts that hold and to be fitting. We want to be importantly connected to reality, not to live in a delusion. We desire this not simply in order to more reliably acquire pleasures or other experiences, as Freud's reality principle dictates. Nor do we merely want the added pleasurable feeling of being connected to reality. Such an inner feeling, an illusory one, also can be provided by the experience machine.

What we want and value is an actual connection with reality. Call this the second reality principle (the first was Freud's): To focus on external reality, with your beliefs, evaluations, and emotions, is valuable *in itself*, not just as a means to more pleasure or happiness. And it is this connecting that is valuable, not simply having within ourselves true beliefs. Favoring truth introduces, in a subterranean fashion, the value of the connecting anyway—why else would true beliefs be (intrinsically) more valuable within us than false ones? And if we want to connect to reality by knowing it, and not simply to have true beliefs, then if knowledge involves tracking the facts—a view I have developed elsewhere—this involves a direct and explicit external connection. We do not, of course, simply want contact with reality; we want contact of certain kinds: exploring reality and responding, altering it and creating new actuality ourselves. Notice that I am not saying simply that since we desire connection to actuality the experience machine is defective because it does not give us whatever we desire—though the example is useful to show we *do* desire some things in addition to experiences—for that would make "getting whatever you desire" the primary standard. Rather, I am saying that the connection to actuality is important whether or not we desire it—that is *why* we desire it—and the experience machine is inadequate because it doesn't give us *that*.

No doubt, too, we want a connection to actuality that we also share with other people. One of the distressing things about the experience machine, as described, is that you are alone in your particular illusion. (Is it more distressing that the others do not share your "world" or that you are cut off from the one they do share?) However, we can imagine that the experience machine provides the very same illusion to everyone (or to everyone you care about), giving each person a coordinate piece of it. When all are floating in the *same* tank, the experience machine may not be *as* objectionable, but it is objectionable nevertheless. Sharing coordinate perspectives might be one criterion of actuality, yet it does not guarantee that; and it is *both* that we want, the actuality *and* the sharing.

Notice that we have not said one should never plug in to such a machine, even temporarily. It might teach you things, or transform you in a way beneficial for your actual life later. It also might give pleasures that would be quite acceptable in limited doses. This is all quite different from spending the rest of your life on the machine; the internal contents of *that* life would be unconnected to actuality. It seems too that once on the machine a person would not make any choices, and certainly would not choose anything *freely*. One portion of what we want to be actual is our actually (and freely) choosing, not merely the appearance of that.

My reflections about happiness thus far have been about the *limits* of its role in life. What *is* its proper role, though, and what exactly is happiness; why has its role so often been exaggerated? A number of distinct emotions travel under the label of *happiness*, along with one thing that is more properly called a *mood* rather than an emotion. I want to consider three types of happiness emotion here: first, being happy that something or other is the case (or that many things are); second, feeling that your life is good now; and third, being satisfied with your life as a whole. Each of these three related happiness emotions will exhibit the general threefold structure that emotions have . . . : a belief, a positive evaluation, and a feeling based upon these. Where these three related emotions differ is in the object of the belief and evaluation, and perhaps also in the felt character of the associated feeling.

The first type of happiness, being happy that some particular thing is the case, is reasonably familiar and clear, a straightforward instance. . . . The second type—feeling that your life is good now—is more intricate. Recall those particular moments when you thought and felt, blissfully, that there was nothing else you wanted, your life was good then. Perhaps this occurred while walking alone in nature, or being with someone you loved. What marks these times is their completeness. There is something you have that you want, and no other wants come crowding in; there is nothing else that you think of wanting right then. . . .

One might worry that being happy all the time, in this second sense of the emotion of happiness, wanting nothing else, would eliminate all motivation for further activity or accomplishment. However, if what we want nothing other than is to be engaged in a process of living of a certain kind, for example, one involving exploring, responding, relating and creating—to be sure, we may want and expect this process also to include many moments of complete satisfaction of the first (nonprocess) type—then further activities and endeavors will be components of that very process.

When someone thinks, "My life now is good" the extent of time denoted by "now" is not fixed in advance. Hence, one can change its reference according to need. Even in a generally miserable period, you might narrow your gaze to a very particular moment, and want nothing else right then; alternatively, during a miserable moment you can recall that over a wider time period, one you also can call "now," your life is not miserable, and you might want nothing other than to be engaged in that life process, miserable moment and all. On the other hand, during moments of intense happiness we sometimes want to recall other kinds. For instance, within the Jewish tradition, at weddings one recalls and acknowledges the most bitter event, the destruction of the Temple; during school class reunions, one might pause in the celebrations to remember those who have died. We have not forgotten these events or people and even in our most intense happiness we pause to give them continuing due weight.

The third form taken by the emotion of happiness—satisfaction with one's life as a whole—has been explored by the Polish philosopher Wladyslaw Tatarkiewicz [*Analysis of Happiness*, 1976]. According to his account, happiness involves a complete, enduring, deep, and full satisfaction with the whole of one's life, a satisfaction whose component evaluation is true and justified.

Tatarkiewicz builds so much into this notion—complete and total satisfaction, etc.—because he wants nothing to be superior to a happy life. But this makes it difficult for there to be two happy lives, one happier than the other. Here, we can be more relaxed about the fullness of the satisfaction, and about how high a degree of positiveness the evaluation involves. A happy life will be evaluated as good enough on the whole. A life can be a happy one in another sense, too, by containing many events of feeling happy about one thing or another—that was the first type of happiness emotion. Such a life might frequently feel happy, yet that person need not positively evaluate his life as a whole, even unconsciously. Indeed, he might make the opposite evaluation if he focused upon his life as a whole, perhaps because he thinks the constituent happy feelings not very important. Despite his frequent happy moments, then, he would not be happy in the third sense of being satisfied with his life as a whole.

We would be reluctant to term someone happy at a particular moment or in life in general if we thought the evaluations upon which his emotion was based were wildly wrong. Yet it would be too stringent simply to require that the evaluations be correct. Looking back upon earlier historical times, we may see people making evaluations which (by our lights) are incorrect yet which were understandable and not egregiously unjustified at that time; the incorrectness of the evaluation should not be an automatic bar to its composing happiness. (After all, we hope that recent gains in moral sensitivity to issues such as women's equality, homosexual rights, racial equality, and minority relations will not be the last.) Simply to substitute "justified" (or "not unjustified") for "correct" would misclassify the person whose emotion is based upon correct but at that time, in that context, unjustified evaluations. Perhaps what serves is the weaker disjunction: true or at any rate justified (or not completely unjustified). Someone whose emotion is based upon completely and egregiously unjustified and false evaluations we will be reluctant to term happy, however he feels. He should have known better.*

This third sense of happiness—satisfaction with one's life as a whole—makes it extremely easy to understand why we would want to be happy or to have a happy life. First, there is simply the pleasure of having that emotion. Feeling happy or satisfied about one's life as a whole is pleasurable in itself; it is something we want for its own felt qualities. (This feeling generally will not be as intense, though, as the joy which accompanies the second notion of happiness, wanting nothing else.) However, other emotions also can involve equally intense pleasurable feelings; why, then, has happiness loomed so central? We also want this emotion of happiness to be *fitting*. If the emotion does fit our life, then the component beliefs about our life as a whole will be true and the component positive evaluation will be correct. Hence, we *will* have a life that *is* valuable, one it is correct to evaluate positively.

The object of this third form of the emotion of happiness is one's life as a whole. That object—life as a whole—also is precisely what we are trying to evaluate when we try to discover what a very good life is, in order to decide how to live. What could be simpler than to focus upon an emotion that does the evaluating for us? Add that the emotion is fit-

ting, and we therefore can be sure the life is a good one. (Add only that the evaluation was justified or not egregiously false, and it has a decent chance of being a good one.) However, for all we yet know, the reason a happy life must be a good one is not necessarily because of any feelings it contains but merely because if that evaluation was correct, the life has to be good. To think, because happiness certifies that a life is desirable, that happiness is supremely important in life is like thinking an accountant's positive statement is itself the most important fact in the operation of a firm. (Each statement, though, might produce further effects of its own.)

Another way to make this point: A life cannot just be happy while having nothing else valuable in it. Happiness rides piggyback on other things that are positively evaluated correctly. Without these, the happiness doesn't get started.

Happiness can occur at the metalevel as an evaluation *of* one's life, and at the object level as a feeling *within* the life; it can be in both places at once. No wonder happiness can seem to be the most important constituent of a life. For it *is* extremely important at the metalevel and it does occur (and can have some importance) at the object level too. The central importance of (this third notion of) happiness lies at the metalevel, though, as an evaluation of a life as a whole; hence, the crucial question is what in particular makes a life best. What characteristics must it have to be (correctly) evaluated in an extremely positive way? It is not very illuminating at this point simply to mention emotions of happiness once again.

This conclusion is reinforced if we ask what particular evaluation enters into this third emotion of happiness. Precisely which of the many different possible positive evaluations does happiness make of a life as a whole? Not that the life is a *moral* one, for that needn't make one happy; not that it is a happy one—that circle would not help; not simply that it is valuable that the life exist, that the universe is a better place for it, for someone might make that evaluation without

---

*Notice that an evaluation made now about your life during an earlier time period can differ from the evaluation you made then. The fact that different evaluations can be produced of that period of life—yours then, yours now, and also the evaluation that we, the observers, make—complicates the question of whether that period counts as happy. We are reluctant simply to treat its proper evaluation, for these purposes, as the one the person actually made then. For example, if you then evaluated your life positively and felt accordingly, but now in looking back you evaluate your overall life then in a negative way, were you happy then or not? At that earlier time you *felt* happy about your life then, but now you do not feel happy about your life then. Because of your current negative evaluation (especially if it is one we endorse), we would be reluctant to say, simply, that you were happy then. . . .

being happy; not simply that the life is good, for you might grudgingly recognize that without thinking it fulfilled your major goals or that it was very good. Perhaps the evaluation of the life must be something like the following: that it is very good, also *for* the person living it, in whatever dimensions he considers most important and whatever dimensions *are* most important. This clearly leaves us with the question of which dimensions of a life *are* the important ones. What does make a life a good one?

Master and Slave Morality

Friedrich Nietzsche

Friedrich Nietzsche was born in a small village in Saxony, Prussia, in 1844. His father died when Nietzsche was six. Nietzsche attended the University of Bonn, and later the University of Leipzig. He served during the war with Austria but was injured when thrown from a horse and was unable to complete his tour of duty. His health was poor, yet he was able to produce a large and important body of work. He spent years writing and trying to return to health. He became friends with Wagner. But, in 1889, Nietzsche became increasingly ill and soon went insane; the cause of his insanity is disputed. After spending time in a sanitarium, Nietzsche died in 1890.

Nietzsche's work has had a large impact, especially on the European continent. Nietzsche was impressed with classical Greek and Roman civilization and was deeply opposed to religion in general and to Christianity in particular. It is, he said, "the most fatal and seductive lie that has ever existed" and teaches a "morality of the paltry people." Nietzsche tirelessly attacked what he saw as the decadence of Europe at that time.

In this essay, Nietzsche discusses the nature of morality now that "God is dead" as he famously stated. He offers a view of human nature, and of the role of morality in society, that is radically at odds with ones that have gone before. After a brief discussion of aristocratic societies and corruption, he goes on to distinguish the morality of the slave and the master-morality. The former, he contends, is based on values of sympathy and utility, the latter on courage and accomplishment.

As you read through this essay, consider the following:

1. How does Nietzsche understand human nature and the "will to power"?
2. What is the morality of the slave? What does it value?
3. What does Nietzsche mean by the master-morality?
4. Many philosophers have argued that morality rests on feeling or sentiment. Does Nietzsche agree or disagree with that?
5. How might the idea of a slave-morality be thought to rest on the emotion of resentment?

Every elevation of the type "man," has hitherto been the work of an aristocratic society and so it will always be—a society believing in a long scale of gradations of rank and differences of worth among human beings, and requiring slavery in some form or other. Without the *pathos of distance*, such as grows out of the incarnated difference of classes, out of the constant outlooking and downlooking of the ruling caste on subordinates and instruments, and out of their equally constant practice of obeying and commanding, of keeping down and keeping at a distance—that other more mysterious pathos could never have arisen, the longing for an ever new widening of distance within the soul itself, the formation of ever higher, rarer, further, more extended, more comprehensive states, in short, just the elevation of the type "man," the continued "self-surmounting of man," to use a moral formula in a supermoral sense. To be sure, one must not resign oneself to any humanitarian illusions about the history of the origin of an aristocratic society (that is to say, of the preliminary condition for the elevation of the type "man"): the truth is hard. Let us acknowledge unprejudicedly how ever higher civilisation hitherto has *originated!* Men with a still natural nature, barbarians in every terrible sense of the word, men of prey, still in possession of unbroken strength of will and desire for power, threw themselves upon weaker, more moral, more peaceful races (perhaps trading or cattle-rearing communities), or upon old mellow civilisations in which the final vital force was flickering out in brilliant fireworks of wit and depravity. At the commencement, the noble caste was always the barbarian caste: their superiority did not consist first of all in their physical, but in their psychical power—they were more *complete* men (which at every point also implies the same as "more complete beasts").

Corruption—as the indication that anarchy threatens to break out among the instincts, and

that the foundation of the emotions, called "life," is convulsed—is something radically different according to the organisation in which it manifests itself. When, for instance, an aristocracy like that of France at the beginning of the Revolution, flung away its privileges with sublime disgust and sacrificed itself to an excess of its moral sentiments, it was corruption:—it was really only the closing act of the corruption which had existed for centuries, by virtue of which that aristocracy had abdicated step by step its lordly prerogatives and lowered itself to a *function* of royalty (in the end even to its decoration and parade-dress). The essential thing, however, in a good and healthy aristocracy is that it should *not* regard itself as a function either of the kingship or the commonwealth, but as the *significance* and highest justification thereof—that it should therefore accept with a good conscience the sacrifice of a legion of individuals, who, *for its sake*, must be suppressed and reduced to imperfect men, to slaves and instruments. Its fundamental belief must be precisely that society is *not* allowed to exist for its own sake, but only as a foundation and scaffolding, by means of which a select class of beings may be able to elevate themselves to their higher duties, and in general to a higher *existence*. . . .

To refrain mutually from injury, from violence, from exploitation, and put one's will on a par with that of others: this may result in a certain rough sense in good conduct among individuals when the necessary conditions are given (namely, the actual similarity of the individuals in amount of force and degree of worth, and their co-relation within one organisation). As soon, however, as one wished to take this principle more generally, and if possible even as *the fundamental principle of society*, it would immediately disclose what it really is—namely, a Will to the *denial* of life, a principle of dissolution and decay. Here one must think profoundly to the very basis and resist all sentimental weakness: life itself is *essentially* appropriation, injury, conquest of the strange and weak, suppression, severity, obtrusion of peculiar forms, incorporation, and at the least, putting it mildest, exploitation;—but why should one for ever use precisely these words on which for ages a disparaging

From *Friedrich Nietzsche, Beyond Good and Evil* in *The Complete Works of Nietzsche*, ed. Oscar Levy (1910).

purpose has been stamped? Even the organisation within which, as was previously supposed, the individuals treat each other as equal—it takes place in every healthy aristocracy—must itself, if it be a living and not a dying organisation, do all that towards other bodies, which the individuals within it refrain from doing to each other: it will have to be the incarnated Will to Power, it will endeavour to grow, to gain ground, attract to itself and acquire ascendency—not owing to any morality or immorality, but because it *lives*, and because life *is* precisely Will to Power. On no point, however, is the ordinary consciousness of Europeans more unwilling to be corrected than on this matter; people now rave everywhere, even under the guise of science, about coming conditions of society in which "the exploiting character" is to be absent:—that sounds to my ears as if they promised to invent a mode of life which should refrain from all organic functions. "Exploitation" does not belong to a depraved, or imperfect and primitive society: it belongs to the *nature* of the living being as a primary organic function; it is a consequence of the intrinsic Will to Power, which is precisely the Will to Life.—Granting that as a theory this is a novelty—as a reality it is the *fundamental fact* of all history: let us be so far honest towards ourselves!

In a tour through the many finer and coarser moralities which have hitherto prevailed or still prevail on the earth, I found certain traits recurring regularly together, and connected with one another, until finally two primary types revealed themselves to me, and a radical distinction was brought to light. There is *master-morality* and *slave-morality;*—I would at once add, however, that in all higher and mixed civilisations, there are also attempts at the reconciliation of the two moralities; but one finds still oftener the confusion and mutual misunderstanding of them, indeed, sometimes their close juxtaposition—even in the same man, within one soul. The distinctions of moral values have either originated in a ruling caste, pleasantly conscious of being different from the ruled—or among the ruled class, the slaves and dependents of all sorts. In the first case, when it is the rulers who determine the conception "good," it is the exalted, proud disposition which is regarded as the distinguishing feature, and that which determines the order of rank. The noble type of man separates from himself the beings in whom the opposite of this exalted, proud disposition displays itself: he despises them. Let it at once be noted that in this first kind of morality the antithesis "good" and "bad" means practically the same as "noble" and "despicable";—the antithesis "good" and "*evil*" is of a different origin. The cowardly, the timid, the insignificant, and those thinking merely of narrow utility are despised; moreover, also, the distrustful, with their constrained glances, the self-abasing, the dog-like kind of men who let themselves be abused, the mendicant flatterers, and above all the liars:— it is a fundamental belief of all aristocrats that the common people are untruthful. "We truthful ones"—the nobility in ancient Greece called themselves. It is obvious that everywhere the designations of moral value were at first applied to *men*, and were only derivatively and at a later period applied to *actions*; it is a gross mistake, therefore, when historians of morals start with questions like, "Why have sympathetic actions been praised?" The noble type of man regards *himself* as a determiner of values; he does not require to be approved of; he passes the judgment: "What is injurious to me is injurious in itself"; he knows that it is he himself only who confers honour on things; he is a *creator of values*. He honours whatever he recognises in himself: such morality is self-glorification. In the foreground there is the feeling of plenitude, of power, which seeks to overflow, the happiness of high tension, the consciousness of a wealth which would fain give and bestow:—the noble man also helps the unfortunate, but not—or scarcely—out of pity, but rather from an impulse generated by the super-abundance of power. The noble man honours in himself the powerful one, him also who has power over himself, who knows how to speak and how to keep silence, who takes pleasure in subjecting himself to severity and hardness, and has reverence for all that is severe and hard. "Wotan placed a hard heart in my breast," says an old Scandinavian Saga: it is thus rightly expressed from the soul of a proud Viking. Such a type of man is even proud of *not* being made for sympathy; the hero of the Saga therefore adds warningly: "He who has not a hard heart when young, will never have one." The noble and brave who think thus are the furthest removed from the morality which sees precisely in sympathy, or in acting for the good of others, or in *désintéressement*, the characteristic of the moral; faith in oneself, pride in oneself, a radical enmity and irony towards "selflessness," belong as definitely to noble morality, as do a careless scorn and precaution in presence of sympathy and the "warm heart."—It is the powerful who *know* how to honour, it is their art, their domain for invention. The profound reverence for age and for tradition—all law rests on this double reverence,—the belief and prejudice in favour of ancestors and unfavourable to newcomers, is typical in the morality of the powerful; and if, reversely, men of "modern ideas" believe almost instinctively in "progress" and the "future," and are more and more lacking in respect for old age, the ignoble origin of these "ideas" has complacently betrayed itself thereby. A morality of the ruling class, however, is more especially foreign and irritating to present-day taste in the sternness of its principle that one has duties only to one's equals; that one may act towards beings of a lower rank, towards all that is foreign, just as seems good to one, or "as the heart desires," and in any case "beyond good and evil": it is here that sympathy and similar sentiments can have a place. The ability and obligation to exercise prolonged gratitude and prolonged revenge—both only within the circle of equals,—artfulness in retaliation, *raffinement* of the idea in friendship, a certain necessity to have enemies (as outlets for the emotions of envy, quarrelsomeness, arrogance—in fact, in order to be a good *friend*): all these are typical characteristics of the noble morality, which, as has been pointed out, is not the morality of "modern ideas," and is therefore at present difficult to realise and also to unearth and disclose.—It is

otherwise with the second type of morality, *slave-morality*. Supposing that the abused, the oppressed, the suffering, the unemancipated, the weary, and those uncertain of themselves, should moralise, what will be the common element in their moral estimates? Probably a pessimistic suspicion with regard to the entire situation of man will find expression, perhaps a condemnation of man, together with his situation. The slave has an unfavourable eye for the virtues of the powerful; he has a scepticism and distrust, a *refinement* of distrust of everything "good" that is there honoured—he would fain persuade himself that the very happiness there is not genuine. On the other hand, *those* qualities which serve to alleviate the existence of sufferers are brought into prominence and flooded with light; it is here that sympathy, the kind, helping hand, the warm heart, patience, diligence, humility, and friendliness attain to honour; for here these are the most useful qualities, and almost the only means of supporting the burden of existence. Slave-morality is essentially the morality of utility. Here is the seat of the origin of the famous antithesis "good" and "evil":— power and dangerousness are assumed to reside in the evil, a certain dreadfulness, subtlety, and strength, which do not admit of being despised. According to slave-morality, therefore, the "evil" man arouses fear; according to master-morality, it is precisely the "good" man who arouses fear and seeks to arouse it, while the bad man is regarded as the despicable being. The contrast attains its maximum when, in accordance with the logical consequences of slave-morality, a shade of depreciation—it may be slight and well-intentioned—at last attaches itself to the "good" man of this morality; because, according to the servile mode of thought, the good man must in any case be the *safe* man: he is good-natured, easily deceived, perhaps a little stupid, *un bonhomme*. Everywhere that slave-morality gains the ascendency, language shows a tendency to approximate the significations of the words "good" and "stupid."—A last fundamental difference: the desire for *freedom*, the instinct for happiness and the refinements of the feeling of liberty belong as necessarily to slave-morals and morality, as artifice and enthusiasm in reverence and devotion are the regular symptoms of an aristocratic mode of thinking and estimating.—Hence we can understand without further detail why love *as a passion*—it is our European specialty—must absolutely be of noble origin; as is well known, its invention is due to the Provençal poet-cavaliers, those brilliant, ingenious men of the *"gai saber,"* to whom Europe owes so much, and almost owes itself.

Vanity is one of the things which are perhaps most difficult for a noble man to understand: he will be tempted to deny it, where another kind of man thinks he sees it self-evidently. The problem for him is to represent to his mind beings who seek to arouse a good opinion of themselves which they themselves do not possess—and consequently also do not "deserve,"—and who yet *believe* in this good opinion afterwards. This seems to him on the one hand such bad taste and so self-disrespectful, and on the other hand so grotesquely unreasonable, that he would like to consider vanity an exception, and is doubtful about it in most cases when it is spoken of. He will say, for instance: "I may be mistaken about my value, and on the other hand may nevertheless demand that my value should be acknowledged by others precisely as I rate it:—that, however, is not vanity (but self-conceit, or, in most cases, that which is called 'humility,' and also 'modesty')." Or he will even say: "For many reasons I can delight in the good opinion of others, perhaps because I love and honour them, and rejoice in all their joys, perhaps also because their good opinion endorses and strengthens my belief in my own good opinion, perhaps because the good opinion of others, even in cases where I do not share it, is useful to me, or gives promise of usefulness:—all this, however, is not vanity." The man of noble character must first bring it home forcibly to his mind, especially with the aid of history, that, from time immemorial, in all social strata in any way dependent, the ordinary man *was* only that which he *passed for:*—not being at all accustomed to fix values, he did

not assign even to himself any other value than that which his master assigned to him (it is the peculiar *right of masters* to create values). It may be looked upon as the result of an extraordinary atavism, that the ordinary man, even at present, is still always *waiting* for an opinion about himself, and then instinctively submitting himself to it; yet by no means only to a "good" opinion, but also to a bad and unjust one (think, for instance, of the greater part of the self-appreciations and self-depreciations which believing women learn from their confessors, and which in general the believing Christian learns from his Church). In fact, conformably to the slow rise of the democratic social order (and its cause, the blending of the blood of masters and slaves), the originally noble and rare impulse of the masters to assign a value to themselves and to "think well" of themselves, will now be more and more encouraged and extended; but it has at all times an older, ampler, and more radically ingrained propensity opposed to it—and in the phenomenon of "vanity" this older propensity overmasters the younger. The vain person rejoices over *every* good opinion which he hears about himself (quite apart from the point of view of its usefulness, and equally regardless of its truth or falsehood), just as he suffers from every bad opinion: for he subjects himself to both, he *feels* himself subjected to both, by that oldest instinct of subjection which breaks forth in him.—It is "the slave" in the vain man's blood, the remains of the slave's craftiness—and how much of the "slave" is still left in woman, for instance!—which seeks to *seduce* to good opinions of itself; it is the slave, too, who immediately afterwards falls prostrate himself before these opinions, as though he had not called them forth.—And to repeat it again: vanity is an atavism.

A *species* originates, and a type becomes established and strong in the long struggle with essentially constant *unfavourable* conditions. On the other hand, it is known by the experience of breeders that species which receive superabundant nourishment, and in general a surplus of protection and care, immediately tend in the most marked way to develop variations, and are fertile in prodigies and monstrosities (also in monstrous vices). Now look at an aristocratic commonwealth, say an ancient Greek *polis*, or Venice, as a voluntary or involuntary contrivance for the purpose of *rearing* human beings; there are there men beside one another, thrown upon their own resources, who want to make their species prevail, chiefly because they *must* prevail, or else run the terrible danger of being exterminated. The favour, the superabundance, the protection are there lacking under which variations are fostered; the species needs itself as species, as something which, precisely by virtue of its hardness, its uniformity, and simplicity of structure, can in general prevail and make itself permanent in constant struggle with its neighbours, or with rebellious or rebellion-threatening vassals. The most varied experience teaches it what are the qualities to which it principally owes the fact that it still exists, in spite of all Gods and men, and has hitherto been victorious: these qualities it calls virtues, and these virtues alone it develops to maturity. It does so with severity, indeed it desires severity; every aristocratic morality is intolerant in the education of youth, in the control of women, in the marriage customs, in the relations of old and young, in the penal laws (which have an eye only for the degenerating): it counts intolerance itself among the virtues, under the name of "justice." A type with few, but very marked features, a species of severe, warlike, wisely silent, reserved and reticent men (and as such, with the most delicate sensibility for the charm and *nuances* of society) is thus established, unaffected by the vicissitudes of generations; the constant struggle with uniform *unfavourable* conditions is, as already remarked, the cause of a type becoming stable and hard. Finally, however, a happy state of things results, the enormous tension is relaxed; there are perhaps no more enemies among the neighbouring peoples, and the means of life, even of the enjoyment of life, are present in superabundance. With one stroke the bond and constraint of the old discipline severs: it is no longer regarded as necessary, as a condition of existence—if it would continue, it can only do so as a form of *luxury*, as an archaising *taste*. Variations, whether they be deviations (into the higher, finer, and rarer), or deteriorations and monstrosities, appear suddenly on the scene in the greatest exuberance and splendour; the individual dares to be individual and detach himself. At this turning-point of history there manifest themselves, side by side, and often mixed and entangled together, a magnificent, manifold, virgin-forest-like up-growth and up-striving, a kind of *tropical tempo* in the rivalry of growth, and an extraordinary decay and self-destruction, owing to the savagely opposing and seemingly exploding egoisms, which strive with one another, "for sun and light," and can no longer assign any limit, restraint, or forbearance for themselves by means of the hitherto existing morality. It was this morality itself which piled up the strength so enormously, which bent the bow in so threatening a manner:—it is now "out of date," it is getting "out of date." The dangerous and disquieting point has been reached when the greater, more manifold, more comprehensive life *is lived beyond* the old morality; the "individual" stands out, and is obliged to have recourse to his own law-giving, his own arts and artifices for self-preservation, self-elevation, and self-deliverance. Nothing but new "Whys," nothing but new "Hows," no common formulas any longer, misunderstanding and disregard in league with each other, decay, deterioration, and the loftiest desires frightfully entangled, the genius of the race overflowing from all the cornucopias of good and bad, a portentous simultaneousness of Spring and Autumn, full of new charms and mysteries peculiar to the fresh, still inexhausted, still unwearied corruption. Danger is again present, the mother of morality, great danger; this time shifted into the individual, into the neighbour and friend, into the street, into their own child, into their own heart, into all the most personal and secret recesses of their desires and volitions. What will the moral philosophers who appear at this time have to preach? They discover, these sharp onlookers and loafers, that the end is quickly approaching, that everything around them decays and produces decay, that nothing will endure until the day after tomorrow, except one species of man, the incurably *mediocre*. The mediocre alone have a prospect of continuing and propagating themselves—they will be the men of the future, the sole survivors; "be like them! become mediocre!" is now the only morality which has still a significance, which still obtains a hearing.—But it is difficult to preach this morality of mediocrity! it can never avow what it is and what it desires! it has to talk of moderation and dignity and duty and brotherly love—it will have difficulty *in concealing its irony!*

The Arc of the Moral Universe

Joshua Cohen

In this essay, Joshua Cohen considers the nature of morality and its place in the larger human world. Is it reasonable, Cohen asks, to fear or hate the world for its indifference and even hostility toward morality and justice? Cohen's particular focus is on slavery—in what sense it was unjust, and whether the fact of its being unjust contributed to its destruction. He argues that the full explanation of slavery's demise goes beyond such historical facts as political and military power or the attitudes of people who opposed slavery. The institution's failure is also, says Cohen, explained in part by the fact that slavery *was* unjust.

Cohen argues that slave laws and practices were based on power, and that the nature of the institutions of slavery reflected the fact that slaves had certain legitimate interests. Because of the conflict between these interests and the practice of slavery, it is unjust in the sense that slavery would not be the outcome of an agreement among free and independent equals. And because slavery could not be the object of agreement among people pursuing their legitimate interests, he argues, it was difficult for slavery to survive. The fact that slavery was unjust, in that sense, is part of the explanation of people's hatred of it and therefore, ultimately, of its demise. The universe, he concludes, is more friendly to justice than to injustice. It has a moral "arc," as Martin Luther King used to say, that bends toward justice. Joshua Cohen is professor of philosophy and Arthur and Ruth Sloan Professor of Political Science at Massachusetts Institute of Technology.

As you read through this essay, consider the following:

1. What are the three legitimate interests slaves had that slavery largely ignored? What does Cohen mean in saying they are "legitimate"?
2. How does he argue that in fact slaves had those interests?
3. In what sense was slavery unjust?
4. Why was the conflict of interests slavery created a source of weakness and limited viability for the system?
5. What are two ways that slavery's injustice (in Cohen's sense) is relevant to the explanation of its destruction?
6. Cohen thinks his argument makes a difference for how people should view the universe, even if they are not religious. Why do you think he says that?
7. Can Cohen's argument be applied to another type of injustice, for instance, religious oppression or oppression of women? Is the argument as strong in those cases?

I. ETHICAL EXPLANATION

William Williams was born into slavery in Salisbury, North Carolina. He escaped to Canada in 1849, where he was later interviewed by the American abolitionist Samuel Gridley Howe. It was two years into the American Civil War, and Williams said: "I think the North will whip the South, because I believe they are in the right."[1]

Williams's remark provides a striking example of an *ethical explanation*. Generally speaking, ethical explanations cite ethical norms—for example, norms of justice—in explaining why some specified social facts obtain, or, as in Williams's case, can be expected to obtain. The norms are offered in explanations of social facts, not only in appraisals of them: Williams expects the North to win because they are right. Similarly, the great abolitionist minister Theodore Parker predicted defeat for the "slave power" because it was wrong: Speaking to the New England Anti-Slavery Convention in 1858, he said of the slave power: "Its Nature of wickedness is its manifest Destiny of Ruin."[2]

Philosophers, historians, and social scientists often recoil from ethical explanations: How *could* the injustice of slavery contribute to explaining its demise? Or the justice of sexual subordination to explaining the instability of systems that subordinate women? Or the injustice of exclusion from the suffrage to explaining twentieth-century suffrage extension? Such explanations seem both too relaxed about distinctions between fact and value and too Panglossian: Does right really make might? Still, ethical explanations play an important role in certain common-sense schemes of social and historical understanding: they are elements of certain folk moralities, so to speak. Martin Luther King said that "the arc of the moral universe is long but it bends toward justice."[3] If

there is an arc, King is right about its length. But is there one that bends toward justice? . . .

I think that some ethical explanations—for example, about slavery, sexual subordination, and suffrage extension—have force. That force derives from the general claim that the injustice of a social arrangement limits its viability. This general claim rests in turn on the role played by the notion of a voluntary system of social cooperation in plausible accounts of both justice and the long-term viability of social forms. Social arrangements better able to elicit voluntary cooperation have both moral and practical advantages over their more coercive counterparts.

This theme lies at the basis of Enlightenment theories of history: Adam Smith's account of the pressures that encourage the emergence of a system of natural liberty, Hegel's account of the instabilities of social systems that enable only incomplete forms of human self-consciousness, and Marx's thesis that exploitative social relations ultimately give way because of the constraints they impose on the free development of human powers. . . .

[I will argue] that the injustice of slavery contributed to its demise. I will defend this claim by arguing for the following four:

Thesis One: The basic structure of slavery as a system of power stands in sharp conflict with fundamental slave interests in material well-being, autonomy, and dignity.

Thesis Two: Slavery is unjust because the relative powerlessness of slaves, reflected in the conflict between slavery and slave interests, implies that it could not be the object of a free, reasonable, and informed agreement.

Thesis Three: The conflict between slavery and the interests of slaves is an important source of the limited viability of slavery.

Thesis Four: Characterizing slavery as unjust conveys information relevant to explaining the demise of slavery that is not conveyed simply by noting that slavery conflicts with the interests of slaves.

. . . First, my focus here is on the role (if any) played by the injustice of slavery in explaining the ultimate demise of slavery. Slavery is unjust—as Lincoln said, "If slavery

From Joshua Cohen, "The Arc of the Moral Universe," *Philosophy and Public Affairs*, Vol. 26, No. 2 (1998), 91–134. Copyright © 1998 by Princeton University Press. Reprinted by permission of Princeton University Press.

is not wrong, then nothing is wrong"[4]—and it has been abolished. But did its wrongness contribute to its demise? Historians continue to debate the role of moral convictions about the injustice of slavery—held, for example, by Quakers—in accounting for the abolition of slavery. I do not doubt the causal importance of these convictions, much less their sincerity. Indeed, I will eventually make them part of the story about *how* the injustice of slavery contributed to its demise. But my topic is different. I am not concerned principally with the causal importance of moral convictions in the decline of slavery but the importance of the *injustice itself* in accounting for that demise. In short, I am concerned with the consequences of slavery's injustice—whether "Its Nature of wickedness is its manifest Destiny of Ruin"—and not simply the consequences of the fact that some people came to think of it as wrong. . . .

What is at stake is not the appropriate moral attitude toward slavery or philosophical outlook on morality, but the appropriate attitude toward the social world. How accommodating is the social world to injustice? Is it reasonable, from a moral point of view, to hate the world? . . .

II. SLAVERY

My argument that the injustice of slavery contributed to its demise depends on several background ideas about slavery and slave interests. Briefly summarized, I propose that slavery is a distinctive distribution of *de facto power*; that this distribution was reproduced through both force and "consent," and that patterns in the use of force and strategies for inducing consent provide a basis for attributing to slaves basic interests in material well-being, autonomy, and dignity. . . .

Power

Slavery is best understood, I suggest, in terms of the notion of *de facto power*, rather than, for example, in terms of familiar cultural or legal representations of slaves—as extensions of the will of masters, or as property. To be specific: a slave is, in the first instance, someone largely lacking the power to dispose of his/her physical and mental powers, including both the capacity to produce and control of the body generally (extending to sexuality and reproduction); the power to dispose of the means of production; the power to select a place of residence; the power to associate with others and establish stable bonds; the power to decide on the manner in which one's children will be raised; and the (political) power to fix the rules governing the affairs of the states in which one resides. . . .

But slaves were not entirely powerless—mere extensions and instruments of another's will. To be sure, their power was highly confined, dangerous to exercise, and nearly always insufficient to overturn slavery itself. But slaves did not, as a general matter, lack all forms of power, and sometimes asserted it to improve their conditions and shape the terms of order within the framework of slavery. As an ex-slave and blacksmith named J. W. Lindsay put it in an 1863 interview with the Freedman's Inquiry Commission, "Of course, they treated me pretty well, for the reason that I would not allow them to treat me in any other way. If they attempted to use any barbarity, I would walk off before their faces."[5] Though Lindsay's remark is almost certainly an exaggeration, and certainly not a plausible generalization, it captures a truth put more subtly by Harriet Jacobs, who said, "My master had power and law on his side; I had a determined will. There is might in each."[6]

The power of slaves was most clearly in evidence in the range of activities commonly grouped together as "slave resistance."

First, a variety of forms of resistance could be pursued individually and were not threatening to slavery, including: "Taking" from masters (what slaves called "taking" the masters called "stealing"), lying, feigning illness, slowing down the pace of work, damaging tools and animals, self-mutilation, suicide, infanticide, abortion, arson, murdering the master, and running away. . . .

A second form of resistance—less frequent, but also more collective and threatening—was the widespread phenomenon of "maroon" communities. Established by runaway slaves, some maroon communities were quite small. . . . Others were large-scale and long-standing. . . .

Finally, most dramatically, there are slave revolts. . . .

These examples underscore the limits of the extension-of-will and ownership conceptions of slavery: To appreciate the power of slaves we must distinguish real from legal disabilities, and from the public interpretation of those disabilities. Slaves of course suffered from legal disabilities, which both codified and contributed to their lack of power. But their general lack of legally codified or publicly acknowledged rights also exaggerated their real situation. Thus slaves were commonly able to do what the law denied them the right to do.

For example, slave "marriages" were not recognized at law, but more or less stable unions were part of the practice of virtually all slave societies. And while slaves had no legal right to control the pace of their work, they had, as a general matter, some power—highly qualified, limited, and always dangerous to exercise—to help to shape it through various forms of resistance and threats of resistance. While, then, the actual terms of association among slaves themselves and between slaves and masters reflected the need to find a stable accommodation between agents with vastly different powers, the legal and moral representation of those relations denied that need, emphasizing instead the unilateral dictation of terms and conditions by masters, and the absence of a capacity for independent action on the part of slaves.

Force and Consent

Premising this conception of slavery as distinctive form of power, we come now to the question: How was this form reproduced? . . .

. . . Limited in their power, slaves drew limited benefits from social cooperation, and, since they did not have to sell their labor to gain their subsistence, such benefits as they did get were importantly independent from their activity. So masters faced problems in motivating slaves to work. Force was one solution (we will come to the others). As Adam Smith put it, "A person who can acquire no property, can have no other interest but to eat as much, and to labor as little as possible. Whatever work he does beyond what is sufficient to purchase his own maintenance, can be squeezed out of him by violence only, and not by any interest of his own."[7] Smith's contention about "violence only" is overstated, in ways that will become clear when I discuss the use of positive incentives. But it does capture an important problem for masters, and provides a good characterization of the basis of the productive use of force.

Appreciating the scope and limits of the productive use of force requires attention to the costs (to masters) of using force as distinct from other incentives. It might require a staff of overseers, or some other diversion of resources from more productive uses, and might damage the human beings one is seeking to "motivate." . . .

The maintenance of slavery could not, then, proceed through force alone. Masters wanted to elicit greater effort, slaves typically faced impossible odds if they sought their own emancipation, and the result was superficially more consensual forms of servitude. Abstracting from endless varieties of compromise and accommodation, varying across time and place, we can distinguish two broad ways to make servitude (superficially) more voluntary: First, masters deployed positive incentives . . . including material reward, authority, autonomy, family security, and manumission. The importance of the strategic use of incentives is a common theme in ancient and modern treatises on slave management. Genovese quotes an overseer making the strategic case for permitting slaves to pursue private cultivation: "Every means are used to encourage them, and impress on their minds the advantage of holding property, and the disgrace attached to idleness. Surely, if industrious for themselves, they will be so for their masters, and no Negro, with a well-stocked poultry house, a small crop advancing, a canoe partly finished, or a few tubs unsold, all of which he calculates soon to enjoy, will ever run away. In ten years I have lost by absconding, forty-seven days, out of nearly six hundred Negroes."[8] . . .

A majority of slave systems relied as well on practices of manumission through which slaves were individually emancipated by their masters, though rates of manumission varied greatly across different slave systems. The practice might take the form of self-purchase, with the slave using his or her *peculium* to pay for freedom (the Cuban *coartacion* and Islamic *murgu* both involved gradual self-purchase). Other standard processes included the freeing of concubines, the emancipation of the children of concubines, and the manumission of slaves as displays of piety in Islamic societies. . . .

Alongside force and positive incentives, cultural representations of slavery as reasonable—religious and ethical representations justifying slavery—also figure in explaining compliance.

Rousseau's *Social Contract* emphasizes what has come to be a commonplace of modern social theory: that the "strongest is never strong enough to be master all the time, unless he transforms force into right and obedience into duty."[9] The thought is that existing power is made more powerful by public ideas that represent it as a necessity, make a virtue of such necessity, and thereby suggest that the terms of order are an object of common consent and that subjects willingly comply. . . . But three qualifications are equally important.

First, slaves typically did not simply embrace the dominant religious and ethical interpretations of their nature and their condition. . . .

American Afro-Baptism, for example, rejected doctrines of original sin and predestination, and emphasized Old Testament themes of earthly deliverance, comparing the situation and prospects of slaves with the deliverance of the Jews from bondage in Egypt. Thus, the Freedman's Hymn: "Shout the glad tidings o'er Egypt's Dark Sea; Jehovah has triumphed, his people are free." Similarly, the religious views characteristic of East African coastal slaves blended hinterland beliefs and practices with a distinctive form of Islam, which rejected the dominant conception of sharp divisions within God's creation in favor of an emphasis on the importance of love for the Prophet and the possibility of attaining religious purity through that love.

Second, even when slave understandings served as a basis for an accommodation to slavery, the fact that they were not fully accommodations turned them into potential sources of "internal normative criticism" and resistance. By "internal normative criticism" (sometimes called "restorationist" or "traditionalist" criticism) I mean the criticism of practices by appeal to understandings, norms, and values that are, at some level of generality, widely shared. . . .

Finally, no sharp and useful distinction can be drawn between the use of internal norms to criticize practices and more radical forms of criticism that reject those norms in favor of other norms. And the views of some slaves—how many we will never know—seem most plausibly characterized as continuing internal normative criticism to the point where it passes into external criticism. . . .

But if we are to understand better the critical uses of norms, the development of alternative interpretations of norms, the uses slaves made of their power, and the importance and prevalence of positive incentives, we need an account of the interests of slaves.

Interests

Slaves had interests in material well-being, autonomy, and dignity. Perhaps that goes without saying. But the enterprise of attributing interests to people seems to some arbitrary, and attributions of these interests to slaves may strike others as anachronistic, romantic, ideologically blinded, or simply ignorant. These interests, however, play two roles in my argument: the case for both the injustice of slavery and its limited viability turns on the claim that slavery conflicts with the legitimate interests of slaves in material well-being, autonomy, and dignity. So I need to say enough about them to explain why that later appeal to them is plausible.

As a general matter, then, a course of action or state of affairs is in a person's interest just in case that course or state is the best way to realize an end that he or she would affirm on reflection. . . .

First, then, the phenomena of resistance and revolt support the view that at least some slaves cared greatly about autonomy—enough to accept significant risks, e.g., the risks taken by the 6,000 crucified slaves who lined the road from Capua to Rome after the defeat of the rebellion led by Spartacus (100,000 slaves were killed in this revolt). This willingness to accept risks for autonomy is clearest in the case of individual runaways, maroons, and rebels. . . .

Second, the provision of material incentives and manumission, and the various other paraphernalia of voluntary servitude, indicate that slaves wanted material improvement and autonomy, and that masters, aware of those wants, sought to elicit more cooperative behavior by promising to reward such behavior by satisfying those wants. . . .

Third, evidence for the desire for autonomy is provided by American slave narratives, and the interviews conducted by both the Freedman's Inquiry Commission and the WPA. They provide substantial testimony on the aspiration to autonomy; indeed the slave narratives are organized around that aspiration. And they commonly return to the theme suggested by the phenomenon of manumission: that the desire for autonomy is not simply in service of material improvement. . . .

Fourth, the central role of force in establishing and sustaining slave systems also argues for the presence of interests in material well-being and autonomy. The fact that slave "recruitment" typically involved force indicates that slavery was rarely chosen by slaves—and then only under difficult circumstances—and that observing the conditions of others who had been enslaved did not encourage self-enslavement. . . .

Coming now to dignity: the central feature of dignity for our purposes is its social aspect—that it involves a desire for public recognition of one's worth. . . .

Several considerations support the attribution to slaves of an interest in conditions that support and are appropriate to a sense of dignity. First, when we consider the few oral and written records left by slaves, from the fables collected by Phaédrus to American slave narratives, what we find is repeated assertions of their sense of self-worth, and the ways that their conditions violate that sense.[10]

Second, as I already indicated, the normative understandings of slavery held by slaves press the worth of the slaves into focus. . . . A particularly striking statement of this is provided by an ex-slave named Benjamin Miller. In a Freedman's Inquiry Commission interview, Miller says: "I was in bondage in Missouri, too. I can't say that my treatment was bad. In one respect I say it was not bad, but in another I consider it was as bad as could be. I was a slave. That covers it all. I had not the rights of a man."[11]

Taking these remarks about the different interests together, I will hereafter use the term "fundamental interests" as shorthand for the three interests I have just discussed.

III. INJUSTICE AND THE LIMITS OF SLAVERY

Slavery, I have proposed, is best understood as a particular form of power; that form was reproduced through force, strategic incentives, and moral-religious norms; and slave interests in material improvement, autonomy, and dignity are revealed in the practices that reproduce slavery. With these claims as background, I come to the main argument about the injustice of slavery and its viability, which I will pursue by taking up, in turn, the four theses stated earlier.

Slavery and Slave Interests

Thesis One: The basic structure of slavery as a system of power stands in sharp conflict with fundamental slave interests in material well-being, autonomy, and dignity.

Consider, first, the interest in material well-being. The intuitive argument for this aspect of Thesis One is that being a slave is materially undesirable because slaves are relatively powerless. Limited power means limited capacity to protect basic material interests in nourishment and health. So it seems plausible that it is materially better not to be a slave, even if one is a serf or poor peasant. Given the breadth and depth of the limits that define the condition of slave, one can expect to have more power if one is not a slave and to be able to turn that power to material advantage. . . .

Autonomy is a matter of being able to set and pursue one's aspirations. To be in the relatively powerless position of slave is on the whole to lack just such power, or to have it as a result of conditions that are more fortuitous in the lives of slaves than they are even in the lives of other socially subordinate groups. This is clear not just in the arena of work, but (particularly for women slaves) with respect to sexuality as well.

The case of dignity seems equally clear. A characteristic feature of slave systems is that both the organization of power and the symbolic understandings of that organization—especially the pervasive symbolism of social death—deny that slave interests command public respect. Thus the organization of power largely deprived slaves of the powers required for advancing their interests; and the symbolic expression of that organization represented slaves as extensions of the wills of their masters or as their property, as having no legitimate social place, and as legitimately denied the powers required for protecting and advancing their interests. . . .

Injustice

Thesis Two: Slavery is unjust because the relative powerlessness of slaves, reflected in the conflict between slavery and slave interests, implies that it could not be the object of a free, reasonable, and informed agreement.

In stating this second thesis, I introduce a particular account of justice, based on an idealized notion of consensus—a free, reasonable, and informed agreement.[12] I will not defend this account of justice here, nor does the argument depend on its details. What does matter are the intuitive ideas that the ideal consensus view articulates: that a just arrangement gives due consideration to the interests of all its members, and that we give due consideration when we treat people as equals, taking their good fully into account in our social arrangements. The ideal consensus view articulates this requirement of treating people as equals by asking what arrangements people themselves would agree to, if they looked for arrangements acceptable to all, understood as equals. By a *free* agreement, then, I mean an agreement reached under conditions in which there are no bargaining advantages. An agreement is *reasonable* only if it is reached on the basis of interests that can be advanced consistent with the aim of arriving at a free agreement. I will hereafter call such interests "legitimate interests." An *informed* agreement is one in which the parties correctly understand the consequences of the agreement.

According to this ideal consensus view of justice, then, slavery is unjust because it could not be the object of a free and reasonable agreement. Why not? What features of slavery preclude it from being the object of such an agreement? Given the relative powerlessness that defines the condition of slavery, the force essential to sustaining it, and the public interpretation of slaves that is encouraged by that distribution of power, it is reasonable for slaves to have very low expectations about the satisfaction of their fundamental interests, lower even than in alternative systems of direct social subordination. Given this low expectation, slaves could only "consent" to their condition if the relations of power between masters and slaves determined the rational course of their conduct. But such power is excluded by the requirement of a free agreement.

This rejection is reasonable because the fundamental slave interests that lie at its foundation are legitimate. Advancing them was consistent with acknowledging that everyone has the fundamental interests, and that the structure of the social order ought to accommodate those interests. . . . The rejection of slavery would have been reasonable, then, because the elimination of slavery would have improved the conditions of slaves with respect to their fundamental interests; but that improvement need not have imposed on any group a burden at all comparable to that borne by slaves under slavery.

Consider, by contrast, the interest in having slaves—which I suppose at least some masters to have had. This was not a morally legitimate interest, since it could not be advanced as a basis for an agreement consistent with the aim of reaching a free agreement on terms of cooperation. Slavery was in the sharpest conflict with the fundamental interests of slaves. Given that slaves had these interests, masters could only propose slavery if they were not aiming to find mutually acceptable terms of social order, but instead seeking to advance their particular interests. And masters could not reasonably expect slaves to agree to terms that conflict with their interests simply because such an agreement would be advantageous to masters—not as part of a free agreement.

This rejection of slavery would have been an *informed* rejection in that it turns on the general features of slavery that I sketched earlier: that slaves are relatively powerless; because they are relatively powerless their legitimate interests in material well-being and autonomy are at best marginally and insecurely protected; such protection as they in fact receive results either from the whims of masters or from a precarious and shifting balance of power between masters and slaves; and since their interests are typically not recognized as significant either in the organization of power or in the dominant conceptions of slaves and their social standing, slavery is an insult to their dignity. This argument does not turn on identifying slavery with its most murderous forms or slaves as utterly powerless. . . .

Limited Viability

Thesis Three: The conflict between slavery and the interests of slaves is an important source of the limited viability of slavery.

Slavery is unjust, then, because it conflicts with certain interests of slaves—interests that are identified as morally legitimate by the ideal consensus view (and no doubt by other views). Does this injustice-making conflict help to account for the demise of slavery? And where, if at all, does the injustice itself enter in? As a first step to answering these questions, I defend the third thesis by sketching two sources of the limited viability of slavery—two lines of argument that figure as important strands in plausible accounts of abolition.

The first source emphasizes the *recognition of injustice*. The idea is that slavery is undermined in part because it was unjust, because that injustice was recognized, and that recognition motivated opposition. Here the injustice of slavery plays an explanatory role, roughly, by virtue of its being cognized and then serving to motivate moral opposition.

Let's separate the contention that recognition of injustice is relevant to explaining the demise of slavery into three components: some consequential opposition to slavery was motivated by moral conviction; the content of those moral convictions can plausibly be represented by the ideal consensus conception of justice that I have presented here; and those moral convictions are themselves explained in part by the injustice of slavery. Without this third point, it would not be the injustice itself that helps to explain the demise, but only the belief that slavery is wrong. I will consider the first two points here, and return later to the third.

First, then, it seems clear that moral opposition motivated at least some eighteenth- and nineteenth-century abolitionist opponents of slavery who fought against the slave trade and for the abolition of slavery, who objected to slavery on grounds of principle, whose interests are not sufficient to explain their opposition—Quakers being only the most familiar case—and whose opposition was important to abolition. Fogel, who emphasizes the economic success and viability of American slavery, puts the case especially strongly: "[Slavery's] death was an act of 'econocide,' a political execution of an immoral system at its peak of economic success, incited by men ablaze with moral fervor."[13] Moral conviction also provides an explanation of some of the motivations of slaves, particularly those who were animated by external moral criticisms of slavery.

Concerning the second point: Slaves, I have suggested, were motivated to oppose slavery in part by indignation and outrage, and not only by their interests. But this does not suffice to show that they were motivated by a recognition of the injustice of slavery as I have characterized the notion of injustice here. Sometimes—in the case of internal moral criticism—their indignation could be explained by the fact that masters had violated traditional norms and customary understandings. But . . . not all slave opposition can be explained in those terms. Among the forms of opposition that cannot be are the views advanced in the course of the Haitian Revolution, in slave petitions in the United States, in Jamaica's 1831 Christmas rebellion, and in the views that animated the participation of ex-slaves in the fight against the Confederacy. In all these cases, opposition was shaped in part by the notions of due consideration and treating people as equals that provide the intuitive foundation of the ideal consensus conception.

More generally, the conception of slavery—and not merely their own individual enslavement or the violations by masters of customary expectations—as unjust helps explain the late eighteenth century shift that Genovese has described from restorationist rebellions to revolutionary opposition to slavery. Furthermore, this opposition (particularly the revolution in Ste. Dominque) was conse-

quential, and contributed to the end of slavery by, among other things, helping to limit the expansion of slavery and contributing strength to movements to end the slave trade.

The case for the first two aspects of the recognition-of-injustice view seems plausible. Still, we have not yet arrived fully at the recognition of injustice; for that we must also vindicate the claim that there is an explanatory connection between the injustice of slavery and moral beliefs about it. I will discuss the issue later on, and respond in particular to the objection that all that matters here are *beliefs* about injustice, and that talk about "recognition" is misplaced.

The second view is what I call the *conflicting interests* account. This view locates viability problems in slavery directly in the conflict between slavery and the fundamental slave interests, without the mediation of moral beliefs. The contention is that these conflicts are a key source of pressure to move from slave to nonslave systems, because they are a source of conflict within slave systems and of disadvantages that slave systems face when they compete economically and conflict militarily with nonslave systems.

To bring out the content of this view, I want to note that it helps to explain the force and limits of classical economic arguments about the limits of slavery. Those arguments emphasize the costliness of slave labor, deriving from high enforcement costs, constrained productivity, and difficulties of securing a biologically reproductive slave population. Adam Smith, for example, thought that slave labor was the most costly, and was imposed because of false pride and a desire to dominate, not for sound economic reasons. The conflicting interests view argues that these liabilities of slavery result principally from difficulties in inducing the willing cooperation of slaves, and that those problems of motivation in turn reflect the underlying conflict of interests.

If that explanation is right then we should expect problems deriving from the conflicting interests to have noneconomic manifestations as well—for example, relative military weakness, overt slave resistance, and a loss of political confidence by owners.

Consider the military issue. Wars present two problems for slave systems. First, in a wide range of systems, slaves were either not trusted to fight, or otherwise excluded from fighting. With a segment of the population thus excluded, military potential is diminished. . . .

In general, then, the conflicting-interests view contends that the demise of slavery results in part from the *practical advantages* in competition and conflict available to systems less sharply in conflict with the interests of their members than slavery is—advantages expressed through mechanisms akin to natural selection.

A problem for the conflicting interests theory is that it may appear to explain "too much." Although conflicts between slavery and slave interests may have been fundamental and persistent, slavery was not in permanent crisis. But the conflicting interests account does not imply that it would be. That account is not intended to provide a comprehensive explanation of the evolution and demise of slavery, but rather to characterize one important, destabilizing determinant of that evolution. . . .

Justice and Viability

Thesis Four: Characterizing slavery as unjust conveys information relevant to explaining the demise of slavery that is not conveyed simply by noting that slavery conflicts with the interests of slaves.

Suppose, then, that the conflict between slave interests and slavery limits the viability of slavery. What, then, does injustice have to do with limited viability? Why would the same limits not exist even if slave interests were not legitimate? What force is added to the explanation by noting that slave interests are morally weighty?

I suggest two ways that our understanding of the limits of slavery is aided by noting that moral weight. The first is provided by considerations about the recognition of injustice. Recall where we left the discussion

of that recognition: I indicated that moral convictions motivated some consequential opposition to slavery, and that the content of those convictions could reasonably be characterized by the ideal consensus conception of justice. Still, the injustice of slavery is not perhaps evident in this argument: How does the injustice itself shape the moral motivations of opponents? It might be said that simple beliefs on the part of abolitionists and slaves that slavery is unjust suffice to motivate opposition, quite apart from the actual injustice of slavery.

The objection seems to me not to have much force since it is natural to want an explanation of the moral beliefs as well. And part of the explanation for the moral belief is that slaves have interests in material well-being, autonomy, and dignity, and are recognized as having them; that slavery sharply conflicts with those interests, and is recognized as so conflicting; and that those interests are legitimate, and recognized as such. And why is this sequence of points not naturally captured by saying that people believe slavery to be unjust in part because it is unjust? To see why this rendering is appropriate, consider the force of the "because" in "because it is unjust." We can interpret it as follows: Suppose people reason morally about the rightness or wrongness of slavery, and pursue that reasoning in light of an understanding of certain facts about slave interests and the conflict between slavery and those interests. Because the reasoning is moral, it is guided by the thought that the interests of slaves need to be given due consideration, as they are, for example, in the requirement of free agreement. Pursuing that reasoning, they will be driven to the conclusion that slavery is wrong: they do not see how slavery could result from a free agreement. (It is not that difficult to see how this might go: after all, we do something like this now when we ask whether slavery is wrong.) What is essential is to acknowledge that slaves have legitimate interests. And the key to that is to see that slaves have properties—for example, the interest and capacity to deliberate—that others have in virtue of which people are prepared to attribute legitimate interests to those others. . . .

But this recognition is available to anyone who reflects on the practices that help to sustain slavery, in particular on the practice of providing the incentives that I mentioned earlier. For those incentives are in effect the homage paid by a scheme of domination to fundamental human aspirations; to provide them is in effect to acknowledge that slaves have the relevant interests and capacities. . . .

To say, then, that the wrongness of slavery explains the moral belief is to note the following: that moral reasoning mandates the conclusion that slavery is unjust; and that the moral belief is produced in part by that kind of reasoning. And once the injustice is recognized, it is reasonable to expect that that recognition plays some role in motivation, that it contributes to the antagonism of slaves to slavery, that it adds nonslave opponents to the slave opponents, and that, once slavery is abolished, it helps to explain why there are not strong movements to bring it back.

The moral weight also figures implicitly in the conflicting interests view. To see how, keep in mind that an explanation of the demise of slavery is not simply an account of opposition to slavery, or of shifts away from slavery—an account of the evolution of institutional variation—but also an account of the eventual retention of nonslave arrangements, of the absence of "wandering" from slave to nonslave and then back. The competitive disadvantages of slave systems are important to understanding this retention. The conflict of slavery with legitimate slave interests, and the fact that masters' interests in preserving slavery are not legitimate, plausibly helps to "tip the balance" in favor of stable departures from slavery.

To see how, consider a remark from a nineteen-year-old black soldier and ex-slave, who, after the Battle of Nashville, used his furlough to pay a visit to his former mistress. She asked him: "You remember when you were sick and I had to bring you to the house and nurse you." When he replied that he did

remember, she responded: "And now you are fighting me." To which the soldier said: "No'm, I ain't fighting you. I'm fighting to get free."[14] To appreciate the bearing of this remark on the issue here, recall that the rejection of slavery was reasonable and slave interests legitimate because the fundamental interests of slaves could be advanced consistent with the aim of reaching a free agreement. The fundamental interests that provide the basis for a reasonable rejection of slavery are shared by masters, and slavery imposes great hardship on slaves while alternatives to slavery do not impose a hardship on any other group comparable to the hardship imposed on slaves by slavery. Alternatives to slavery accommodate the interests of subordinate groups better than slavery does. Moreover, they provide substantial protections of the fundamental interests at the superordinate positions. By contrast, the slaveowner interest in maintaining slavery was not shared by slaves. Because slaves and masters shared the fundamental interests, slaves could reject slavery consistent with extending to masters the same standing that they desired for themselves. But masters could not have advanced their interest in maintaining slavery except by failing to extend to slaves the same recognition masters desired for themselves. These facts about common and conflicting interests are the basis for the moral condemnation of slavery.

Suppose slave interests were not legitimate. Slaves might still have resisted just as much. But the economic and military disadvantages of slavery, the abolition of slavery, and the apparent stability of that abolition, would be more surprising. Suppose in particular that the fundamental interests were not capable of mutual satisfaction. Then we would expect dissatisfaction with abolition leading to struggles for its reimposition. We would also not expect any particular practical advantage to be conferred by the absence of slavery if those other systems conflicted with the interests of some of their members as sharply as slavery does with some of its members. For if the conflicts were as sharp, then they would have the same difficulties as slavery in eliciting cooperation. Of course, other systems of social subordination are also unjust. But slavery is on the extreme end of powerlessness; alternatives to it permit greater space for material improvement, increased scope for autonomy, and do not rest on an enslaving denial of dignity. So the sources of conflict and instability in the alternatives to slavery do not tend to produce returns to slavery. And the fact that those replacements are improvements with respect to justice makes the stability of the shift away from slavery less surprising.

Thus the fact that there is not wandering back and forth between slavery and abolition reflects the fact that the fundamental slave interests were shared and so could serve as the basis of an agreement. Stating that slavery is unjust and that slave interests are legitimate interests conveys all these relevant facts about the conflict between slavery and the interests of slaves. It represents a second, distinct reason for citing the injustice in an explanation of the end of slavery. We cite the injustice itself, first, then, to indicate that moral reasoning mandates a certain conclusion, that people arrived at the conclusion because they reasoned, and were motivated to act. And we cite it, second, to convey information about the features of the system and of the alternatives to it in virtue of which the moral reasoning condemns it as unjust, and to claim that those very features are a source of instability. . . .

In sum, then, we have no reason to correct William Williams or Theodore Parker. Ethical explanations have some force, given certain plausible background beliefs about the connections between the satisfaction of fundamental interests and the justice of social forms, the tendency of people to act on their interests, and the relationship between the satisfaction of those interests and the viability of social arrangements (especially when those arrangements operate under conditions of competition and conflict). . . .

IV. SCAFFOLD AND THRONE

Appeals to the injustice of slavery can play a role in explaining the demise of slavery. But that role is limited, no greater than the advantages conferred by moral improvements. Those limits in turn underscore the length of the arc of the moral universe. King often coupled his reference to that arc with a stanza from James Russell Lowell:

> Truth forever on the scaffold,
>   Wrong forever on the throne;
> Yet that scaffold sways the future,
>   And behind the dim unknown
> Standeth God within the shadow
>   Keeping watch above His own.

Many of us do not share Lowell's faith—or King's—in a God who keeps watch above His own. But even if we do not, we can find some support for the hopefulness of Lowell, King, and William Williams in the human aspirations and powers that shape the arc of our part of the moral universe.

Notes

1. Cited in John W. Blassingame, ed., *Slave Testimony* (Baton Rouge: Louisiana State University Press, 1977), p. 437.
2. Theodore Parker, *The Relation of Slavery to a Republican Form of Government* (Boston: William Kent and Company, 1858), p. 20. Strictly speaking, Williams and Parker make ethical predictions: they predict a change in a world, and base the predictions on norms of rightness. No doubt they would have embraced the claim that the North won because it was in the right.
3. The phrase "arc of the moral universe" or variants on it occur throughout King's writing and speeches. See Martin Luther King, *A Testament of Hope: The Essential Writings of Martin Luther King, Jr.*, ed. James Washington (San Francisco: Harper and Row, 1986), pp. 141, 207, 230, 277, 438.
4. Quoted in David M. Potter, *The Impending Crisis: 1848–1861*, completed and edited by Don E. Fehrenbacher (New York: Harper and Row, 1976), p. 342. The passage comes from Lincoln's letter to Albert G. Hodges (April 4, 1864).
5. Blassingame, *Slave Testimony*, p. 397.
6. Cited in Elizabeth Fox-Genovese, *Within the Plantation Household: Black and White Women of the Old*

South (Chapel Hill: University of North Carolina Press, 1988), p. 290.

7. Smith, *Wealth of Nations* (New York: Random House, 1965), p. 365.

8. Genovese, *Roll, Jordan, Roll* (New York: Pantheon, 1974), p. 539.

9. Jean-Jacques Rousseau, *Social Contract*, ed. Roger D. Masters, trans. Judith R. Masters (New York: St. Martin's Press, 1978), p. 48.

10. "There is," according to Patterson, "absolutely no evidence from the long and dismal annals of slavery to suggest that any group of slaves ever internalized the conception of degradation held by their masters." Patterson, *Slavery and Social Death*, p. 97.

11. Blassingame, *Slave Testimony* (Baton Rouge: Louisiana State University Press, 1977), p. 439.

12. I draw, as will be evident, on Rawls, *Theory of Justice*; T. M. Scanlon, "Contractualism and Utilitarianism," in Amartya Sen and Bernard Williams, eds., *Utilitarianism and Beyond* (Cambridge: Cambridge University Press, 1982).

13. Fogel, *Without Consent on Contract* (New York: Norton, 1989), p. 410.

14. Cited in Litwack, *Been in the Storm So Long* (New York: Vintage, 1979), p. 97.

Essay and Paper Topics for "Moral Practice and Reason"

1. Using the various authors you have read in this section, write a brief essay on the nature of morality and its relationship with feelings.

2. Suppose you were Jonathan Bennett. Based on his article, how would you respond to the positions developed in this section by Hume and Nagel? Which one, if either, do you agree with? Why?

3. "Impartiality is critical to understanding morality, though impartiality is understood in very different terms by different philosophers." Discuss this claim using at least two of the writers in this section.

4. Compare the different ways that Aristotle, Mill, and Nozick understand human happiness or well-being. Which view seems closest to the truth? Explain.

5. It could be argued that Hobbes and Kant see morality in a similar way, since each thinks in terms of what people reasonably agree to. Describe the two theories, indicating the extent to which you think they agree and disagree about the nature of morality.

6. Discuss the following claim: Utilitarians such as Hume and Mill emphasize the role of sympathy in thinking about morality, while Kant emphasizes reason. In fact, however, we need both.

7. Describe whether or not you think morality is objective or subjective, being careful to define what you mean by those terms.

8. Assess the merits of Held's feminist criticisms of traditional moral theory in light of the works you have read in this section.

9. Suppose you were Joshua Cohen. Write an essay in which you analyze critically Nietzsche's discussion of slave morality.

PART V

The Practice of Science

What Is Science?

Science as Conjectures and Refutations

Karl Popper

Sir Karl Popper (1902–1994) was a key figure in twentieth-century philosophy of science. One of the most pressing problems of his day was the demarcation problem: How can we distinguish science from pseudoscience? More precisely, what features distinguish a scientific theory from other kinds of theories? Popper's solution is that a theory is scientific if it is falsifiable, that is, if we can clearly identify the kinds of experiences that would show the theory to be false. This solution has been tremendously influential, and it continues to be advocated by many working scientists.

Popper's view of the nature of the scientific method mirrors his falsifiability criterion of scientific theories. Scientists proceed by making bold conjectures and subjecting these to the most severe tests. Any conjecture that survives rigorous testing can be accepted until it fails some later test or it is replaced by some more powerful conjecture.

In this essay, Popper outlines the demarcation problem and defends the falsificationist solution. He maintains that the theories of Marx and Freud fail to meet the criterion and hence are not scientific. After juxtaposing his method of conjecture and refutation with the method of induction, he argues that his method solves the problem of induction.

As you read through this essay, consider the following:

1. Why might it be important to demarcate science from pseudoscience? What are some current examples of pseudoscientific theories?

2. Why does Popper prefer the falsification criterion for scientific theories to a criterion that focuses on our ability to confirm a theory?
3. How does Popper argue that induction is not the proper method of science?
4. What is the logical problem of induction and how does Popper think that it can be solved?
5. Why does Popper think that scientists should not seek highly probable hypotheses?
6. Do you think that the method of conjectures and refutations could adequately describe the way we ordinarily reason about the world? Could we replace ordinary inductive reasoning with it?
7. Do you think that it is ever reasonable to believe a theory that is not falsifiable? Why or why not?

Mr. Turnbull had predicted evil consequences, . . . and was now doing the best in his power to bring about the verification of his own prophecies.

Anthony Trollope

I

When I received the list of participants in this course and realized that I had been asked to speak to philosophical colleagues I thought, after some hesitation and consultation, that you would probably prefer me to speak about those problems which interest me most, and about those developments with which I am most intimately acquainted. I therefore decided to do what I have never done before: to give you a report on my own work in the philosophy of science, since the autumn of 1919 when I first began to grapple with the problem, "*When should a theory be ranked as scientific?*" or "*Is there a criterion for the scientific character or status of a theory?*"

The problem which troubled me at the time was neither, "When is a theory true?" nor, "When is a theory acceptable?" My problem was different. I *wished to distinguish between science and pseudo-science;* knowing very well that science often errs, and that pseudo-science may happen to stumble on the truth.

I knew, of course, the most widely accepted answer to my problem: that science is distinguished from pseudo-science—or from

From Sir Karl Popper, *Conjectures and Refutations* (New York: Harper & Row, 1963). © 1963 Karl Popper. Reprinted by permission of The Karl Popper Charitable Trust.

"metaphysics"—by its *empirical method*, which is essentially *inductive*, proceeding from observation or experiment. But this did not satisfy me. On the contrary, I often formulated my problem as one of distinguishing between a genuinely empirical method and a non-empirical or even a pseudo-empirical method—that is to say, a method which, although it appeals to observation and experiment, nevertheless does not come up to scientific standards. The latter method may be exemplified by astrology, with its stupendous mass of empirical evidence based on observation—on horoscopes and on biographies.

But as it was not the example of astrology which led me to my problem I should perhaps briefly describe the atmosphere in which my problem arose and the examples by which it was stimulated. After the collapse of the Austrian Empire there had been a revolution in Austria: the air was full of revolutionary slogans and ideas, and new and often wild theories. Among the theories which interested me Einstein's theory of relativity was no doubt by far the most important. Three others were Marx's theory of history, Freud's psychoanalysis, and Alfred Adler's so-called "individual psychology."

There was a lot of popular nonsense talked about these theories, and especially about relativity (as still happens even today), but I was fortunate in those who introduced me to the study of this theory. We all—the small circle of students to which I belonged—were thrilled with the result of Eddington's eclipse observations which in 1919 brought the first important confirmation of Einstein's theory of gravitation. It was a great experience for us, and one which had a lasting influence on my intellectual development.

The three other theories I have mentioned were also widely discussed among students at that time. I myself happened to come into personal contact with Alfred Adler, and even to co-operate with him in his social work among the children and young people in the working-class districts of Vienna where he had established social guidance clinics.

It was during the summer of 1919 that I began to feel more and more dissatisfied with these three theories—the Marxist theory of history, psycho-analysis, and individual psychology; and I began to feel dubious about their claims to scientific status. My problem perhaps first took the simple form, "What is wrong with Marxism, psycho-analysis, and individual psychology? Why are they so different from physical theories, from Newton's theory, and especially from the theory of relativity?"

To make this contrast clear I should explain that few of us at the time would have said that we believed in the *truth* of Einstein's theory of gravitation. This shows that it was not my doubting the *truth* of those other three theories which bothered me, but something else. Yet neither was it that I merely felt mathematical physics to be more *exact* than the sociological or psychological type of theory. Thus what worried me was neither the problem of truth, at that stage at least, nor the problem of exactness or measurability. It was rather that I felt that these other three theories, though posing as sciences, had in fact more in common with primitive myths than with science; that they resembled astrology rather than astronomy.

I found that those of my friends who were admirers of Marx, Freud, and Adler, were impressed by a number of points common to these theories, and especially by their apparent *explanatory power.* These theories appeared to be able to explain practically everything that happened within the fields to which they referred. The study of any of them seemed to have the effect of an intellectual conversion or revelation, opening your eyes to a new truth hidden from those not yet initiated. Once your eyes were thus opened you saw confirming instances everywhere: the world was full of *verifications* of the theory. Whatever happened always confirmed it. Thus its truth appeared manifest; and unbelievers were clearly people who did not want to see the manifest truth; who refused to see it, either because it was against their class interest, or because of their repressions which were still "un-analysed" and crying aloud for treatment.

The most characteristic element in this situation seemed to me the incessant stream of confirmations, of observations which "verified" the theories in question; and this point was constantly emphasized by their adherents. A Marxist could not open a newspaper without finding on every page confirming evidence for his interpretation of history; not only in the news, but also in its presentation—which revealed the class bias of the paper—and especially of course in what the paper did *not* say. The Freudian analysts emphasized that their theories were constantly verified by their "clinical observations." As for Adler, I was much impressed by a personal experience. Once, in 1919, I reported to him a case which to me did not seem particularly Adlerian, but which he found no difficulty in analysing in terms of his theory of inferiority feelings, although he had not even seen the child. Slightly shocked, I asked him how he could be so sure. "Because of my thousandfold experience," he replied; whereupon I could not help saying: "And with this new case, I suppose, your experience has become thousand-and-one-fold."

What I had in mind was that his previous observations may not have been much sounder than this new one; that each in its turn had been interpreted in the light of "previous experience," and at the same time counted as additional confirmation. What, I asked myself, did it confirm? No more than that a case could be interpreted in the light of the theory. But this meant very little, I reflected, since every conceivable case could be interpreted in the light of Adler's theory, or equally of Freud's. I may illustrate this by two very different examples of human behaviour: that of a man who pushes a child into the water with the intention of drowning it; and that of a man who sacrifices his life in an attempt to save the child. Each of these two cases can be explained with equal ease in Freudian and in Adlerian terms. According to Freud the first man suffered from repression (say, of some component of his Oedipus complex), while the second man had achieved sublimation. According to Adler the first man suffered from feelings of inferiority (producing perhaps the need to prove to himself that he dared to commit some crime), and so did the second man (whose need was to prove to himself that he dared to rescue the child). I could not think of any human behaviour which could not be interpreted in terms of either theory. It was precisely this fact—that they always fitted, that they were always confirmed—which in the eyes of their admirers constituted the strongest argument in favour of these theories. It began to dawn on me that this apparent strength was in fact their weakness.

With Einstein's theory the situation was strikingly different. Take one typical instance—Einstein's prediction, just then confirmed by the findings of Eddington's expedition. Einstein's gravitational theory had led to the result that light must be attracted by heavy bodies (such as the sun), precisely as material bodies were attracted. As a consequence it could be calculated that light from a distant fixed star whose apparent position was close to the sun would reach the earth from such a direction that the star would seem to be slightly shifted away from the sun; or, in other words, that stars close to the sun would look as if they had moved a little away from the sun, and from one another. This is a thing which cannot normally be observed since such stars are rendered invisible in daytime by the sun's overwhelming brightness; but during an eclipse it is possible to take photographs of them. If the same constellation is photographed at night one can measure the distances on the two photographs, and check the predicted effect.

Now the impressive thing about this case is the *risk* involved in a prediction of this kind. If observation shows that the predicted effect is definitely absent, then the theory is simply refuted. The theory is *incompatible with certain possible results of observation*—in fact with results which everybody before Einstein would have expected.[1] This is quite different from the situation I have previously described, when it turned out that the theories in question were compatible with the most divergent human behaviour, so that it was practically impossible to describe any human behaviour that might not be claimed to be a verification of these theories.

These considerations led me in the winter of 1919–20 to conclusions which I may now reformulate as follows:

1. It is easy to obtain confirmations, or verifications, for nearly every theory—if we look for confirmations.

2. Confirmations should count only if they are the result of *risky predictions*; that is to say, if, unenlightened by the theory in question, we should have expected an event which was incompatible with the theory—an event which would have refuted the theory.

3. Every "good" scientific theory is a prohibition: it forbids certain things to happen. The more a theory forbids, the better it is.

4. A theory which is not refutable by any conceivable event is non-scientific. Irrefutability is not a virtue of a theory (as people often think) but a vice.

5. Every genuine *test* of a theory is an attempt to falsify it, or to refute it. Testability is falsifiability; but there are degrees of testability: some theories are more testable, more exposed to refutation, than others; they take, as it were, greater risks.

6. Confirming evidence should not count *except when it is the result of a genuine test of the theory*; and this means that it can be presented as a serious but unsuccessful attempt to falsify the theory. (I now speak in such cases of "corroborating evidence.")

7. Some genuinely testable theories, when found to be false, are still upheld by their admirers—for example by introducing *ad hoc* some auxiliary assumption, or by re-interpreting the

theory *ad hoc* in such a way that it escapes refutation. Such a procedure is always possible, but it rescues the theory from refutation only at the price of destroying, or at least lowering, its scientific status. (I later described such a rescuing operation as a *"conventionalist twist"* or a *"conventionalist stratagem."*)

One can sum up all this by saying that *the criterion of the scientific status of a theory is its falsifiability, or refutability, or testability.*

II

I may perhaps exemplify this with the help of the various theories so far mentioned. Einstein's theory of gravitation clearly satisfied the criterion of falsifiability. Even if our measuring instruments at the time did not allow us to pronounce on the results of the tests with complete assurance, there was clearly a possibility of refuting the theory.

Astrology did not pass the test. Astrologers were greatly impressed, and misled, by what they believed to be confirming evidence—so much so that they were quite unimpressed by any unfavourable evidence. Moreover, by making their interpretations and prophecies sufficiently vague they were able to explain away anything that might have been a refutation of the theory had the theory and the prophecies been more precise. In order to escape falsification they destroyed the testability of their theory. It is a typical soothsayer's trick to predict things so vaguely that the predictions can hardly fail: that they become irrefutable.

The Marxist theory of history, in spite of the serious efforts of some of its founders and followers, ultimately adopted this soothsaying practice. In some of its earlier formulations (for example in Marx's analysis of the character of the "coming social revolution") their predictions were testable, and in fact falsified.[2] Yet instead of accepting the refutations the followers of Marx re-interpreted both the theory and the evidence in order to make them agree. In this way they rescued the theory from refutation; but they did so at the price of adopting a device which made it

irrefutable. They thus gave a "conventionalist twist" to the theory; and by this stratagem they destroyed its much advertised claim to scientific status.

The two psycho-analytic theories were in a different class. They were simply non-testable, irrefutable. There was no conceivable human behaviour which could contradict them. This does not mean that Freud and Adler were not seeing certain things correctly: I personally do not doubt that much of what they say is of considerable importance, and may well play its part one day in a psychological science which is testable. But it does mean that those "clinical observations" which analysts naïvely believe confirm their theory cannot do this any more than the daily confirmations which astrologers find in their practice.[3] And as for Freud's epic of the Ego, the Super-ego, and the Id, no substantially stronger claim to scientific status can be made for it than for Homer's collected stories from Olympus. These theories describe some facts, but in the manner of myths. They contain most interesting psychological suggestions, but not in a testable form.

At the same time I realized that such myths may be developed, and become testable; that historically speaking all—or very nearly all—scientific theories originate from myths, and that a myth may contain important anticipations of scientific theories. Examples are Empedocles' theory of evolution by trial and error, or Parmenides' myth of the unchanging block universe in which nothing ever happens and which, if we add another dimension, becomes Einstein's block universe (in which, too, nothing ever happens, since everything is, four-dimensionally speaking, determined and laid down from the beginning). I thus felt that if a theory is found to be non-scientific, or "metaphysical" (as we might say), it is not thereby found to be unimportant, or insignificant, or "meaningless," or "nonsensical."[4] But it cannot claim to be backed by empirical evidence in the scientific sense—although it may easily be, in some genetic sense, the "result of observation."

(There were a great many other theories of this pre-scientific or pseudo-scientific character, some of them, unfortunately, as influential as the Marxist interpretation of history; for example, the racialist interpretation of history—another of those impressive and all-explanatory theories which act upon weak minds like revelations.)

Thus the problem which I tried to solve by proposing the criterion of falsifiability was neither a problem of meaningfulness or significance, nor a problem of truth or acceptability. It was the problem of drawing a line (as well as this can be done) between the statements, or systems of statements, of the empirical sciences, and all other statements—whether they are of a religious or of a metaphysical character, or simply pseudo-scientific. Years later—it must have been in 1928 or 1929—I called this first problem of mine the *"problem of demarcation."* The criterion of falsifiability is a solution to this problem of demarcation, for it says that statements or systems of statements, in order to be ranked as scientific, must be capable of conflicting with possible, or conceivable, observations. . . .

VIII

Let us now turn from our logical criticism of the *psychology of experience* to our real problem—the problem of *the logic of science.* Although some of the things I have said may help us here, in so far as they may have eliminated certain psychological prejudices in favour of induction, my treatment of the *logical problem of induction* is completely independent of this criticism, and of all psychological considerations. Provided you do not dogmatically believe in the alleged psychological fact that we make inductions, you may now forget my whole story with the exception of two logical points: my logical remarks on testability or falsifiability as the criterion of demarcation; and Hume's logical criticism of induction.

From what I have said it is obvious that there was a close link between the two problems which interested me at that time: demarcation, and induction or scientific method. It was easy to see that the method of science is

criticism, i.e. attempted falsifications. Yet it took me a few years to notice that the two problems—of demarcation and of induction—were in a sense one.

Why, I asked, do so many scientists believe in induction? I found they did so because they believed natural science to be characterized by the inductive method—by a method starting from, and relying upon, long sequences of observations and experiments. They believed that the difference between genuine science and metaphysical or pseudo-scientific speculation depended solely upon whether or not the inductive method was employed. They believed (to put it in my own terminology) that only the inductive method could provide a satisfactory *criterion of demarcation.*

I recently came across an interesting formulation of this belief in a remarkable philosophical book by a great physicist—Max Born's *Natural Philosophy of Cause and Chance.*[5] He writes: "Induction allows us to generalize a number of observations into a general rule: that night follows day and day follows night . . . But while everyday life has no definite criterion for the validity of an induction, . . . science has worked out a code, or rule of craft, for its application." Born nowhere reveals the contents of this inductive code (which, as his wording shows, contains a "definite criterion for the validity of an induction"); but he stresses that "there is no logical argument" for its acceptance: "it is a question of faith"; and he is therefore "willing to call induction a metaphysical principle." But why does he believe that such a code of valid inductive rules must exist? This becomes clear when he speaks of the "vast communities of people ignorant of, or rejecting, the rule of science, among them the members of anti-vaccination societies and believers in astrology. It is useless to argue with them; I cannot compel them to accept the same criteria of valid induction in which I believe: the code of scientific rules." This makes it quite clear that *"valid induction" was here meant to serve as a criterion of demarcation between science and pseudo-science.*

But it is obvious that this rule or craft of "valid induction" is not even metaphysical: it simply does not exist. No rule can ever guarantee that a generalization inferred from true observations, however often repeated, is true. (Born himself does not believe in the truth of Newtonian physics, in spite of its success, although he believes that it is based on induction.) And the success of science is not based upon rules of induction, but depends upon luck, ingenuity, and the purely deductive rules of critical argument.

I may summarize some of my conclusions as follows:

1. Induction, i.e. inference based on many observations, is a myth. It is neither a psychological fact, nor a fact of ordinary life, nor one of scientific procedure.

2. The actual procedure of science is to operate with conjectures: to jump to conclusions—often after one single observation. . . .

3. Repeated observations and experiments function in science as *tests* of our conjectures or hypotheses, i.e. as attempted refutations.

4. The mistaken belief in induction is fortified by the need for a criterion of demarcation which, it is traditionally but wrongly believed, only the inductive method can provide.

5. The conception of such an inductive method, like the criterion of verifiability, implies a faulty demarcation.

6. None of this is altered in the least if we say that induction makes theories only probable rather than certain. . . .

IX

If, as I have suggested, the problem of induction is only an instance or facet of the problem of demarcation, then the solution to the problem of demarcation must provide us with a solution to the problem of induction. This is indeed the case, I believe, although it is perhaps not immediately obvious.

For a brief formulation of the problem of induction we can turn again to Born, who writes: ". . . no observation or experiment, however extended, can give more than a finite number of repetitions"; therefore, "the statement of a law—B depends on A—always transcends experience. Yet this kind of statement is made everywhere and all the time, and sometimes from scanty material."[6]

In other words, the logical problem of induction arises from (*a*) Hume's discovery (so well expressed by Born) that it is impossible to justify a law by observation or experiment, since it "transcends experience"; (*b*) the fact that science proposes and uses laws "everywhere and all the time." (Like Hume, Born is struck by the "scanty material," i.e. the few observed instances upon which the law may be based.) To this we have to add (*c*) *the principle of empiricism* which asserts that in science, only observation and experiment may decide upon the *acceptance or rejection* of scientific statements, including laws and theories.

These three principles, (*a*), (*b*), and (*c*), appear at first sight to clash; and this apparent clash constitutes the *logical problem of induction*.

Faced with this clash, Born gives up (*c*), the principle of empiricism (as Kant and many others, including Bertrand Russell, have done before him), in favour of what he calls a "metaphysical principle"; a metaphysical principle which he does not even attempt to formulate; which he vaguely describes as a "code or rule of craft"; and of which I have never seen any formulation which even looked promising and was not clearly untenable.

But in fact the principles (*a*) to (*c*) do not clash. We can see this the moment we realize that the acceptance by science of a law or of a theory is *tentative only;* which is to say that all laws and theories are conjectures, or tentative *hypotheses* (a position which I have sometimes called "hypotheticism"); and that we may reject a law or theory on the basis of new evidence, without necessarily discarding the old evidence which originally led us to accept it.[7]

The principle of empiricism (*c*) can be fully preserved, since the fate of a theory, its acceptance or rejection, is decided by observation and experiment—by the result of tests.

So long as a theory stands up to the severest tests we can design, it is accepted; if it does not, it is rejected. But it is never inferred, in any sense, from the empirical evidence. There is neither a psychological nor a logical induction. *Only the falsity of the theory can be inferred from empirical evidence, and this inference is a purely deductive one.*

Hume showed that it is not possible to infer a theory from observation statements; but this does not affect the possibility of refuting a theory by observation statements. The full appreciation of this possibility makes the relation between theories and observations perfectly clear.

This solves the problem of the alleged clash between the principles (*a*), (*b*), and (*c*), and with it Hume's problem of induction.

X

Thus the problem of induction is solved. But nothing seems less wanted than a simple solution to an age-old philosophical problem. Wittgenstein and his school hold that genuine philosophical problems do not exist; from which it clearly follows that they cannot be solved. Others among my contemporaries do believe that there are philosophical problems, and respect them; but they seem to respect them too much; they seem to believe that they are insoluble, if not taboo; and they are shocked and horrified by the claim that there is a simple, neat, and lucid, solution to any of them. If there is a solution it must be deep, they feel, or at least complicated.

However this may be, I am still waiting for a simple, neat and lucid criticism of the solution which I published first in 1933 in my letter to the Editor of *Erkenntnis*, and later in *The Logic of Scientific Discovery*.

Of course, one can invent new problems of induction, different from the one I have formulated and solved. (Its formulation was half its solution.) But I have yet to see any reformulation of the problem whose solution cannot be easily obtained from my old solu-

tion. I am now going to discuss some of these re-formulations.

One question which may be asked is this: how do we really jump from an observation statement to a theory?

Although this question appears to be psychological rather than philosophical, one can say something positive about it without invoking psychology. One can say first that the jump is not from an observation statement, but from a problem-situation, and that the theory must allow us *to explain* the observations which created the problem (that is, *to deduce* them from the theory strengthened by other accepted theories and by other observation statements, the so-called initial conditions). This leaves, of course, an immense number of possible theories, good and bad; and it thus appears that our question has not been answered.

But this makes it fairly clear that when we asked our question we had more in mind than, "How do we jump from an observation statement to a theory?" The question we had in mind was, it now appears, "How do we jump from an observation statement to a *good* theory?" But to this the answer is: by jumping first to *any* theory and then testing it, to find whether it is good or not; i.e. by repeatedly applying the critical method, eliminating many bad theories, and inventing many new ones. Not everybody is able to do this; but there is no other way.

Other questions have sometimes been asked. The original problem of induction, it was said, is the problem of *justifying* induction, i.e., of justifying inductive inference. If you answer this problem by saying that what is called an "inductive inference" is always invalid and therefore clearly not justifiable, the following new problem must arise: how do you justify your method of trial and error? Reply: the method of trial and error is a *method of eliminating false theories* by observation statements; and the justification for this is the purely logical relationship of deducibility which allows us to assert the falsity of universal statements if we accept the truth of singular ones.

Another question sometimes asked is this: why is it reasonable to prefer non-falsified statements to falsified ones? To this question some involved answers have been produced, for example pragmatic answers. But from a pragmatic point of view the question does not arise, since false theories often serve well enough: most formulae used in engineering or navigation are known to be false, although they may be excellent approximations and easy to handle; and they are used with confidence by people who know them to be false.

The only correct answer is the straightforward one: because we search for truth (even though we can never be sure we have found it), and because the falsified theories are known or believed to be false, while the non-falsified theories may still be true. Besides, we do not prefer *every* non-falsified theory—only one which, in the light of criticism, appears to be better than its competitors: which solves our problems, which is well tested, and of which we think, or rather conjecture or hope (considering other provisionally accepted theories), that it will stand up to further tests.

It has also been said that the problem of induction is, "Why is it *reasonable* to believe that the future will be like the past?," and that a satisfactory answer to this question should make it plain that such a belief is, in fact, reasonable. My reply is that it is reasonable to believe that the future will be very different from the past in many vitally important respects. Admittedly it is perfectly reasonable to *act* on the assumption that it will, in many respects, be like the past, and that well-tested laws will continue to hold (since we can have no better assumption to act upon); but it is also reasonable to believe that such a course of action will lead us at times into severe trouble, since some of the laws upon which we now heavily rely may easily prove unreliable. (Remember the midnight sun!) One might even say that to judge from past experience, and from our general scientific knowledge, the future will *not* be like the past, in perhaps most of the ways which those have in mind who say that it will. Water will sometimes not quench thirst, and air will choke those who breathe it. An apparent way out is to say that the future will be like the past *in the sense that the laws of nature will not change*, but this is begging the question. We speak of a "law of nature" only if we think that we have before us a regularity which does not change; and if we find that it changes then we shall not continue to call it a "law of nature." Of course our search for natural laws indicates that we hope to find them, and that we believe that there are natural laws; but our belief in any particular natural law cannot have a safer basis than our unsuccessful critical attempts to refute it.

I think that those who put the problem of induction in terms of the *reasonableness* of our beliefs are perfectly right if they are dissatisfied with a Humean, or post-Humean, sceptical despair of reason. We must indeed reject the view that a belief in science is as irrational as a belief in primitive magical practices—that both are a matter of accepting a "total ideology," a convention or a tradition based on faith. But we must be cautious if we formulate our problem, with Hume, as one of the reasonableness of our *beliefs*. We should split this problem into three—our old problem of demarcation, or of how to *distinguish* between science and primitive magic; the problem of the rationality of the scientific or critical *procedure*, and of the role of observation within it; and lastly the problem of the rationality of our *acceptance* of theories for scientific and for practical purposes. To all these three problems solutions have been offered here.

One should also be careful not to confuse the problem of the reasonableness of the scientific procedure and the (tentative) acceptance of the results of this procedure—i.e. the scientific theories—with the problem of the rationality or otherwise *of the belief that this procedure will succeed*. In practice, in practical scientific research, this belief is no doubt unavoidable and reasonable, there being no better alternative. But the belief is certainly unjustifiable in a theoretical sense, as I have argued. . . . Moreover, if we could show, on general logical grounds, that the scientific quest is likely to succeed, one could not understand why anything like success has been so rare in the long history of human endeavours to know more about our world.

Yet another way of putting the problem of induction is in terms of probability. Let *t* be the theory and *e* the evidence: we can ask for *P(t,e)*, that is to say, the probability of *t*, given *e*. The problem of induction, it is often believed, can then be put thus: construct a *calculus of probability* which allows us to work out for any theory *t* what its probability is, relative to any given empirical evidence *e*; and show that *P(t,e)* increases with the accumulation of supporting evidence, and reaches high values—at any rate values greater than ½.

In *The Logic of Scientific Discovery* I explained why I think that this approach to the problem is fundamentally mistaken. To make this clear, I introduced there the distinction between *probability* and *degree of corroboration or confirmation*. (The term "confirmation" has lately been so much used and misused that I have decided to surrender it to the verificationists and to use for my own purposes "corroboration" only. The term "probability" is best used in some of the many senses which satisfy the well-known calculus of probability, axiomatized, for example, by Keynes, Jeffreys, and myself; but nothing of course depends on the choice of words, as long as we do not *assume*, uncritically, that degree of corroboration must also be a probability—that is to say, that it must satisfy the calculus of probability.)

I explained in my book why we are interested in theories with a *high degree of corroboration*. And I explained why it is a mistake to conclude from this that we are interested in *highly probable* theories. I pointed out that the probability of a statement (or set of statements) is always the greater the less the statement says: it is inverse to the content or the deductive power of the statement, and thus to its explanatory power. Accordingly every interesting and powerful statement must have a low probability; and *vice versa*: a statement with a high probability will be scientifically uninteresting, because it says little and has no explanatory power. Although we seek theories with a high degree of corroboration, *as scientists we do not seek highly probable theories but explanations; that is to say, powerful and improbable theories*. The opposite view—that science aims at high probability—is a characteristic development of verificationism: if you find that you cannot verify a theory, or make it certain by induction, you may turn to probability as a kind of "*Ersatz*" for certainty, in the hope that induction may yield at least that much.

Notes

1. This is a slight oversimplification, for about half of the Einstein effect may be derived from the classical theory, provided we assume a ballistic theory of light.

2. See, for example, my *Open Society and Its Enemies*, ch. 15, section iii, and notes 13–14.

3. "Clinical observations," like all other observations, are *interpretations in the light of theories* . . .; and for this reason alone they are apt to seem to support those theories in the light of which they were interpreted. But real support can be obtained only from observations undertaken as tests (by "attempted refutations"); and for this purpose *criteria of refutation* have to be laid down beforehand: it must be agreed which observable situations, if actually observed, mean that the theory is refuted. But what kind of clinical responses would refute to the satisfaction of the analyst not merely a particular analytic diagnosis but psycho-analysis itself? And have such criteria ever been discussed or agreed upon by analysts? Is there not, on the contrary, a whole family of analytic concepts, such as "ambivalence" (I do not suggest that there is no such thing as ambivalence), which would make it difficult, if not impossible, to agree upon such criteria? Moreover, how much headway has been made in investigating the question of the extent to which the (conscious or unconscious) expectations and theories held by the analyst influence the "clinical responses" of the patient? (To say nothing about the conscious attempts to influence the patient by proposing interpretations to him, etc.) Years ago I introduced the term "*Oedipus effect*" to describe the influence of a theory or expectation or prediction *upon the event which it predicts* or describes: it will be remembered that the causal chain leading to Oedipus' parricide was started by the oracle's prediction of this event. This is a characteristic and

recurrent theme of such myths, but one which seems to have failed to attract the interest of the analysts, perhaps not accidentally. (The problem of confirmatory dreams suggested by the analyst is discussed by Freud, for example in *Gesammelte Schriften*, III, 1925, where he says on p. 314: "If anybody asserts that most of the dreams which can be utilized in an analysis . . . owe their origin to [the analyst's] suggestion, then no objection can be made from the point of view of analytic theory. Yet there is nothing in this fact," he surprisingly adds, "which would detract from the reliability of our results.")

4. The case of astrology, nowadays a typical pseudo-science, may illustrate this point. It was attacked, by Aristotelians and other rationalists, down to Newton's day, for the wrong reason—for its now accepted assertion that the planets had an "influence" upon terrestrial ("sublunar")

events. In fact Newton's theory of gravity, and especially the lunar theory of the tides, was historically speaking an offspring of astrological lore. Newton, it seems, was most reluctant to adopt a theory which came from the same stable as for example the theory that "influenza" epidemics are due to an astral "influence." And Galileo, no doubt for the same reason, actually rejected the lunar theory of the tides; and his misgivings about Kepler may easily be explained by his misgivings about astrology.

5. Max Born, *Natural Philosophy of Cause and Chance*, Oxford, 1949, p. 7.

6. *Natural Philosophy of Cause and Chance*, p. 6.

7. I do not doubt that Born and many others would agree that theories are accepted only tentatively. But the widespread belief in induction shows that the far-reaching implications of this view are rarely seen.

Science as Public Knowledge

John Ziman

Like Popper in the previous essay, John Ziman rejects the common definitions of science that focus on the inductive method. He argues that good scientists often accept theories that are not well confirmed inductively. Moreover, they do not learn how to do good science by acquiring expertise in the use of the inductive method. Instead, they learn the practical art of scientific research in their chosen fields by imitating senior scientists. What unifies scientific disciplines, according to Ziman, is the goal of achieving rational consensus or "public knowledge." Ziman illustrates what he means by public knowledge by showing how practitioners in law, history, religion, and philosophy pursue somewhat different goals and how their results characteristically differ from those of science.

As you read through this essay, consider the following:

1. What are the four definitions of science that Ziman rejects and why does he think that they are unsatisfactory?
2. What does Ziman mean by saying that science is public knowledge?
3. According to Ziman, how does science differ from each of the following: law, history, religion, and philosophy?
4. How does Ziman think that we should understand the relation between science and technology? Why is it difficult to distinguish the two?
5. Do you think that science is necessarily a social activity? Could a good scientist refuse to care about a "consensus of rational opinion over the widest possible field"?
6. Is Ziman's demarcation criterion for science superior to Popper's? Why or why not?
7. In Ziman's view, could astrology and psychoanalysis be made scientific?

To answer the question "What is Science?" is almost as presumptuous as to try to state the meaning of Life itself. Science has become a major part of the stock of our minds; its products are the furniture of our surroundings. We must accept it, as the good lady of the fable is said to have agreed to accept the Universe.

Yet the question is puzzling rather than mysterious. Science is very clearly a conscious artifact of mankind, with well-documented historical origins, with a definable scope and content, and with recognizable professional practitioners and exponents. The task of defining Poetry, say, whose subject matter is by common consent ineffable, must be self-defeating. Poetry has no rules, no method, no graduate schools, no logic: the bards are self-anointed and their spirit bloweth where it listeth. Science, by contrast, is rigorous, methodical, academic, logical and practical. The very facility that it gives us, of clear understanding, of seeing things sharply in focus, makes us feel that the instrument itself is very real and hard and definite. Surely we can state, in a few words, its essential nature.

It is not difficult to state the order of being to which Science belongs. It is one of the categories of the intellectual commentary that Man makes on his World. Amongst its kith and kin we would put Religion, Art, Poetry, Law, Philosophy, Technology, etc.— the familiar divisions or "Faculties" of the Academy or the Multiversity.

At this stage I do not mean to analyse the precise relationship that exists between Science and each of these cognate modes of thought; I am merely asserting that they are on all fours with one another. It makes some sort of sense (though it may not always be stating a truth) to substitute these words for one another, in phrases like "Science teaches us . . ." or "The Spirit of *Law* is . . ." or "*Tech-*

nology* benefits mankind by . . ." or "He is a student of *Philosophy*." The famous "conflict between Science and Religion" was truly a battle between combatants of the same species—between David and Goliath if you will—and not, say, between the Philistine army and a Dryad, or between a point of order and a postage stamp.

Science is obviously like Religion, Law, Philosophy, etc. in being a more or less coherent set of ideas. In its own technical language, Science is information; it does not act directly on the body; it speaks to the mind. Religion and Poetry, we may concede, speak also to the emotions, and the statements of Art can seldom be written or expressed verbally—but they all belong in the nonmaterial realm.

But in what ways are these forms of knowledge *unlike* one another? What are the special attributes of Science? What is the criterion for drawing lines of demarcation about it, to distinguish it from Philosophy, or from Technology, or from Poetry?

This question has long been debated. Famous books have been devoted to it. It has been the theme of whole schools of philosophy. To give an account of all the answers, with all their variations, would require a history of Western thought. It is a daunting subject. Nevertheless, the types of definition with which we are familiar can be stated crudely.

Science Is the Mastery of Man's Environment. This is, I think, the vulgar conception. It identifies Science with its products. It points to penicillin or to an artificial satellite and tells us of all the wonderful further powers that man will soon acquire by the same agency.

This definition enshrines two separate errors. In the first place it confounds Science with Technology. It puts all its emphasis on the applications of scientific knowledge and gives no hint as to the intellectual procedures by which that knowledge may be successfully obtained. It does not really discriminate between Science and Magic, and gives us no

From John Ziman, *Public Knowledge* (New York: Cambridge University Press, 1968). © Cambridge University Press. Reprinted by permission of Cambridge University Press.

reason for studies such as Cosmology and Pure Mathematics, which seem entirely remote from practical use.

It also confuses ideas with things. Penicillin is not Science, any more than a cathedral is Religion or a witness box is Law. The material manifestations and powers of Science, however beneficial, awe-inspiring, monstrous, or beautiful, are not even symbolic; they belong in a different logical realm, just as a building is not equivalent to or symbolic of the architect's blueprints. A meal is not the same as a recipe.

Science Is the Study of the Material World. This sort of definition is also very familiar in popular thought. It derives, I guess, from the great debate between Science and Religion, whose outcome was a treaty of partition in which Religion was left with the realm of the Spirit whilst Science was allowed full sway in the territory of Matter.

Now it is true that one of the aims of Science is to provide us with a Philosophy of Nature, and it is also true that many questions of a moral or spiritual kind cannot be answered at all within a scientific framework. But the dichotomy between Matter and Spirit is an obsolete philosophical notion which does not stand up very well to careful critical analysis. If we stick to this definition we may end up in a circular argument in which Matter is only recognizable as the subject matter of Science. Even then, we shall have stretched the meaning of words a long way in order to accommodate Psychology, or Sociology, within the Scientific stable.

This definition would also exclude Pure Mathematics. Surely this is wrong. Mathematical thinking is so deeply entangled with the physical sciences that one cannot draw a line between them. Modern mathematicians think of themselves as exploring the logical consequences (the "theorems") of different sets of hypotheses or "axioms," and do not claim absolute truth, in a material sense, for their results. Theoretical physicists and applied mathematicians try to confine their explorations to systems of hypotheses that

they believe to reflect properties of the "real" world, but they often have no license for this belief. It would be absurd to have to say that Newton's *Principia*, and all the work that was built upon it, was not now Science, just because we now suppose that the inverse square law of gravitation is not perfectly true in an Einsteinian universe. I suspect that the exclusion of the "Queen of the Sciences" from her throne is a relic of some ancient academic arrangement, such as the combination of classical literary studies with mathematics in the Cambridge Tripos, and has no better justification than that Euclid and Archimedes wrote in Greek.

Science Is the Experimental Method. The recognition of the importance of experiment was the key event in the history of Science. The Baconian thesis was sound; we can often do no better today than to follow it.

Yet this definition is incomplete in several respects. It arbitrarily excludes Pure Mathematics, and needs to be supplemented to take cognizance of those perfectly respectable sciences such as Astronomy or Geology where we can only observe the consequences of events and circumstances over which we have no control. It also fails to give due credit to the strong theoretical and logical sinews that are needed to hold the results of experiments and observations together and give them force. Scientists do not in fact work in the way that operationalists suggest; they tend to look for, and find, in Nature little more than they believe to be there, and yet they construct airier theoretical systems than their actual observations warrant. Experiment distinguishes Science from the older, more speculative ways to knowledge but it does not fully characterize the scientific method.

Science Arrives at Truth by Logical Inferences from Empirical Observations. This is the standard type of definition favoured by most serious philosophers. It is usually based upon the principle of induction—that what has been seen to happen a great many times is almost sure to happen invariably and may be treated as a basic fact or Law upon which a firm structure of theory can be erected.

There is no doubt that this is the official philosophy by which most practical scientists work. From it one can deduce a number of practical procedures, such as the testing of theory by "predictions" of the results of future observations, and their subsequent confirmation. The importance of speculative thinking is recognized, provided that it is curbed by conformity to facts. There is no restriction of a metaphysical kind upon the subject matter of Science, except that it must be amenable to observations and inference.

But the attempt to make these principles logically watertight does not seem to have succeeded. What may be called the positivist programme, which would assign the label "True" to statements that satisfy these criteria, is plausible but not finally compelling. Many philosophers have now sadly come to the conclusion that there is no ultimate procedure which will wring the last drops of uncertainty from what scientists call their knowledge.

And although working scientists would probably state that this is the Rule of Their Order, and the only safe principle upon which their discoveries may be based, they do not always obey it in practice. We often find complex theories—quite good theories—that really depend on very few observations. It is extraordinary, for example, how long and complicated the chains of inference are in the physics of elementary particles; a few clicks per month in an enormous assembly of glass tubes, magnet fields, scintillator fluids and electronic circuits becomes a new "particle," which in its turn provokes a flurry of theoretical papers and ingenious interpretations. I do not mean to say that the physicists are not correct; but no one can say that all the possible alternative schemes of explanation are carefully checked by innumerable experiments before the discovery is acclaimed and becomes part of the scientific canon. There is far more faith, and reliance upon personal experience and intellectual authority, than the official doctrine will allow.

A simple way of putting it is that the logico-inductive scheme does not leave enough room for genuine scientific error. It is too black and white. Our experience, both as individual scientists and historically, is that we only arrive at partial and incomplete truths; we never achieve the precision and finality that seem required by the definition. Thus, nothing we do in the laboratory or study is "really" scientific, however honestly we may aspire to the ideal. Surely, it is going too far to have to say, for example, that it was "unscientific" to continue to believe in Newtonian dynamics as soon as it had been observed and calculated that the rotation of the perihelion of Mercury did not conform to its predictions.

This summary of the various conceptions of science obviously fails to do justice to the vast and subtle literature on the subject. If I have emphasized the objections to each point of view, this is merely to indicate that none of the definitions is entirely satisfactory. Most practicing scientists, and most people generally, take up one or other of the attitudes that I have sketched, according to the degree of their intellectual sophistication—but without fervour. One can be zealous for Science, and a splendidly successful research worker, without pretending to a clear and certain notion of what Science really is. In practice it does not seem to matter. . . .

The fact is that scientific investigation, as distinct from the theoretical *content* of any given branch of science, is a practical art. It is not learnt out of books, but by imitation and experience. Research workers are trained by apprenticeship, by working for their Ph.D.'s under the supervision of more experienced scholars, not by attending courses in the metaphysics of physics. The graduate student is given his "problem": "You might have a look at the effect of pressure on the band structure of the III-V compounds; I don't think it has been done yet, and it would be interesting to see whether it fits into the pseudopotential theory." Then, with considerable help, encouragement and criticism, he sets up his apparatus, makes his measurements, performs his calculations, etc. and in due course writes a thesis and is accounted a qualified professional. But notice that he will not at any time have been made to study formal logic, nor will he be expected to defend his thesis in a step by step deductive procedure. His examiners may ask him why he had made some particular assertion in the course of his argument, or they may enquire as to the reliability of some particular measurement. They may even ask him to assess the value of the "contribution" he has made to the subject as a whole. But they will not ask him to give any opinion as to whether Physics is ultimately *true*, or whether he is justified now in believing in an external world, or in what sense a theory is verified by the observation of favourable instances. The examiners will assume that the candidate shares with them the common language and principles of their discipline. No scientist really doubts that theories are verified by observation, any more than a Common Law judge hesitates to rule that hearsay evidence is inadmissible.

What one finds in practice is that scientific argument, written or spoken, is not very complex or logically precise. The terms and concepts that are used may be extremely subtle and technical, but they are put together in quite simple logical forms, with expressed or implied relations as the machinery of deduction. It is very seldom that one uses the more sophisticated types of proof used in Mathematics, such as asserting a proposition by proving that its negation implies a contradiction. Of course actual mathematical or numerical analysis of data may carry the deduction through many steps, but the symbolic machinery of algebra and the electronic circuits of the computer are then relied on to keep the argument straight.[1] In my own experience, one more often detects elementary *non sequiturs* in the verbal reasoning than actual mathematical mistakes in the calculations that accompany them. This is not said to disparage the intellectual powers of scientists; I mean simply that the reasoning used in scientific papers is not very different from what we should use in an everyday careful discussion of an everyday problem.

. . . [This point] is made to emphasize the inadequacy of the "logico-inductive" metaphysic of Science. How can this be correct, when few scientists are interested in or understand it, and none ever uses it explicitly in his work? But then if Science is distinguished from other intellectual disciplines neither by a particular style or argument nor by a definable subject matter, what is it?

The answer proposed in this essay is suggested by its title: *Science Is Public Knowledge*. This is, of course, a very cryptic definition, with almost the suggestion of a play upon words. What I mean is something along the following lines. Science is not merely *published* knowledge or information. Anyone may make an observation, or conceive a hypothesis, and, if he has the financial means, get it printed and distributed for other persons to read. Scientific knowledge is more than this. Its facts and theories must survive a period of critical study and testing by other competent and disinterested individuals, and must have been found so persuasive that they are almost universally accepted. The objective of Science is not just to acquire information nor to utter all noncontradictory notions; its goal is a *consensus* of rational opinion over the widest possible field.

In a sense, this is so obvious and well-known that it scarcely needs saying. Most educated and informed people agree that Science is true, and therefore impossible to gainsay. But I assert my definition much more positively; this is the basic principle upon which Science is founded. It is not a subsidiary consequence of the "Scientific Method"; it *is* the scientific method itself.

The defect of the conventional philosophical approach to Science is that it considers only two terms in the equation. The scientist is seen as an individual, pursuing a somewhat one-sided dialogue with taciturn Nature. *He* observes phenomena, notices regularities, arrives at generalizations, deduces consequences, etc. and eventually, Hey Presto! a law of Nature springs into being. But it is not like that at all. The scientific enterprise is corporate. It is not merely, in Newton's incomparable phrase, that one stands on the shoulders of giants, and hence can see a little farther. Every scientist sees through his own eyes—and also through the eyes of his predecessors and colleagues. It is never one individual that goes through all the steps in the logico-inductive chain; it is a group of individuals, dividing their labour but continuously and jealously checking each other's contributions. The cliché of scientific prose betrays itself "Hence we arrive at the conclusion that . . ." The audience to which scientific publications are addressed is not passive; by its cheering or booing, its bouquets or brickbats, it actively controls the substance of the communications that it receives.

In other words, scientific research is a social activity. Technology, Art and Religion are perhaps possible for Robinson Crusoe, but Law and Science are not. To understand the nature of Science, we must look at the way in which scientists behave towards one another, how they are organized and how information passes between them. The young scientist does not study formal logic, but he learns by imitation and experience a number of conventions that embody strong social relationships. In the language of Sociology, he learns to play his *role* in a system by which knowledge is acquired, sifted and eventually made public property. . . .

It has been put to me that one should in fact distinguish carefully between Science as a body of knowledge, Science as what scientists do, and Science as a social institution. This is precisely the sort of distinction that one must *not* make; in the language of geometry, a solid object cannot be reconstructed from its projections upon the separate cartesian planes. By assigning the intellectual aspects of Science to the professional philosophers we make of it an arid exercise in logic; by allowing the psychologists to take possession of the personal dimension we overemphasize the mysteries of "creativity" at the expense of rationality and the critical power of well-ordered argument; if the social aspects are handed over to the sociologists, we get a description of research as an N-person game, with prestige points for stakes and priority

claims as trumps. The problem has been to discover a unifying principle for Science in all its aspects. The recognition that scientific knowledge must be public and *consensible* (to coin a necessary word) allows one to trace out the complex inner relationships between its various facets. Before one can distinguish and discuss separately the philosophical, psychological or sociological dimensions of Science, one must somehow have succeeded in characterizing it as a whole.[2] . . .

SCIENCE AND NON-SCIENCE

In this chapter Science will be considered mainly in its intellectual aspects, as a system of ideas, as a compilation of abstract knowledge. The first question to be answered has already been posed in the introductory chapter: what distinguishes Science from its sister "Faculties"—Law, Philosophy, Technology, etc.? The argument is that Science is unique in striving for, and insisting on, a consensus.

Take Law, for example. We all feel that legal thought is quite different from scientific thought—but what is the basis of this intuition? There are many ways in which legal argument is very close to Science. There is undoubtedly an attempt to make every judgement follow logically on statutes and precedents. Every lawyer seeks to clarify a path of implications through successive stages to validate his case. The judge reasons it out, on the basis of universal principles of equity, in the effort to arrive at a decision that will command the assent of all just and learned men.

The kinship of Law with the mathematical sciences is emphasized by the interesting suggestion that legal decisions might be arrived at automatically by a computer, into which all the conditions and precedents of the case would be fed and a purely mechanical process of logical reduction would produce exactly the correct judgement.[3] Although perhaps the idea is somewhat fanciful, if this procedure were technically feasible it would provide decisions that could not but command the assent of all lawyers—just as a table of values of a mathematical function printed out by a computer commands the assent of all mathematicians. To the extent, therefore, that the Law is strictly logical, it can be made "scientific."

Again, in the concept of "evidence" there is close similarity. This is too primary and basic an idea to be defined readily, but, roughly speaking, it means "any information that is relevant to a disputed hypothesis." In Science, as in Law, we are almost always dealing with theories that are disputable, and that can only be challenged by an appeal to evidence for and against them. It is the duty of scientists, as of lawyers, to bring out this evidence, on both sides, to the full.

In the end, the case may hang upon some very minor item of information—was the man who got off the 3:57 at Little Puddlecome on Monday, 27 May, wearing a black hat? A scientific theory also may be validated by some tiny fact—for example, the almost imperceptible changes in the orbit of the planet Mercury. The question of the *credibility* of evidence can become very important. We may find everyone in full agreement that, if a fact is as stated by a witness, it has vital logical implications for the hypothesis under consideration; yet the court may be completely undecided as to whether this evidence is true or not. The existence of honest error has to be allowed for. This sort of thing happens in Science too, though it does not usually get remembered in the conventional histories. For example, many scientists will recall the interest that was aroused by the publication of evidence for organic compounds in meteorites—probably an erroneous interpretation of a complex observation, but of the most profound significance if it proved to be true. In such cases there may even be questions about the relative reliability, in general, of two different observers—an assessment, perhaps, based upon their scientific standing and expert authority—just as the relative veracity of conflicting witnesses may become the key issue in a legal case.

But, of course, in Science, when the evidence is conflicting, we withhold our assent or dissent, and do the experiment again. This cannot be done in legal disputes, which must be terminated yea or nay. If we are forced to a premature opinion on a scientific question, we are bound to give the Scottish verdict *Not Proven*, or say that the jury have disagreed, and a new trial is needed. In Criminal Law, where the case for the prosecution must be proved up to the hilt, or the accused acquitted, this is well enough; but Civil Law demands a decision, however difficult the case.

The Law is thus unscientific because it *must* decide upon matters which are not at all amenable to a consensus of opinion. Indeed, legal argument is concerned with the conflict between various principles, statutes, precedents, etc.; if there were not an area of uncertainty and contradiction, then there would be no need to go to law about it and get the verdict of the learned judge. In Science, too, we are necessarily interested in those questions that are not automatically resolved by the known "Laws of Nature" (the analogy here with man-made Laws is only of historical interest) but we agree to work and wait until we can arrive at an interpretation or explanation that is satisfactory to all parties.

There are other elements in the Law that are quite outside science—normative principles and moral issues that underlie any notion of justice. As is so often said, Science cannot tell us what *ought* to be done; it can only chart the consequences of what *might* be done.

Normative and moral principles cannot, by definition, be embraced in a consensus; to assert that one *ought* to do so and so is to admit that some people, at least, will not freely recognize the absolute necessity of not doing otherwise. Legal principles and norms are neither eternal nor universal; they are attached to the local, ephemeral situation of this country here and now; their arbitrariness can never be mended by any amount of further logical manipulation. Thus, there are components of legal argument that are necessarily refractory to the achievement of free and general agreement and these quite clearly discriminate between Law and Science as academic Faculties.

To the ordinary Natural Scientist this discussion may perhaps have seemed quite unnecessary—Law, he would say, is a man-made set of social conventions, whilst Science deals with material, objective, eternal verities. But to the Social Scientist this distinction is by no means so clear. He may, for example, find it impossible to disentangle such legal concepts as personal responsibility from his scientific understanding of the power of social determination in a pattern of delinquency. The criterion of consensibility might temper some of the scientific arrogance of the expert witness—"Would *every* criminologist agree with you on this point, Dr. X?"—whilst at the same time throwing the full weight of personal decision and responsibility upon the judge, who should never be allowed to shelter behind the cruel and mechanical absolutes of "Legal Science." The intellectual authority of Science is such that it must not be wielded incautiously or irresponsibly.

At first sight, one would not suppose that much need be said about what distinguishes Science from those disciplines and activities that belong to the Arts and Humanities—Literature, Music, Fine Arts, etc. Our modern view of Poetry, say, is that it is an expression of a private personal opinion. By his skill the poet may strike unsuspected chords of emotion in a vast number of other men, but this is not necessarily his major intention. A poem that is immediately acceptable and agreeable to everyone must be banal in the extreme.

But, of course Arts dons do not write Poetry: they write about it. Literary and artistic critics do sometimes pretend that their judgements are so convincing that it is wilful to oppose them. An imperious temper demands that we accept their every utterance of interpretation and valuation. Fortunately, we have the right of dissent and if our heart and mind carry us along a different path we have no need to be frightened by their shrill cries of contempt.

The point here is that there are genuine differences of taste and feeling, just as there are genuine differences of moral principle. At the back of our definition of Science itself is the assumption that men are free to express their true feelings; without this condition, the notion of a consensus loses meaning. Under a dictatorship we might be constrained to pay lip service to a uniform standard of style or taste, but this is the death of criticism.

There are, of course, periods of "classicism" and "academicism" when some style of technique is overwhelmingly praised and practised, but no one supposes that this is in obedience to the commands of absolute necessity. The attempts of the stupider sort of academic critic to rationalize the taste of his age by rules of "harmony" or "dramatic unity" are invariably by-products of the fashion whose dominance he is seeking to justify, not its determining factors. No sooner are such rules formulated than a great artist cannot resist the temptation to break them, and a new fashion sweeps the land. By their very nature, the Arts are not consensible, and hence are quite distinct from Science as I conceive it.

Science is not immune from fashion—a sure sign of its socio-psychological nature. . . . But what, abstractly, *is* fashion? It means doing what other people do for no better reason than that that is what is done. If everyone were to follow only fashionable lines of thought, there would be a false impression of a consensus; the inhibition of the critical imagination by such a conformist sentiment is the antithesis of the scientific attitude. It is also, of course, another way of death for true Poetry and Art.

But the products and producers of Literature, Art and Music may be studied in more factual aspects than for their emotional or spiritual message. For example, they are the outcome of, or participants in, historical events.

The place of *History* in this analysis is very significant; it seems to be truly one of the borderlands marching between scientific and non-scientific pursuits. Suppose that we are investigating such a problem as the date and place of birth of a writer or statesman. We search in libraries and other collections of material documents for written evidence. From various oblique references we might build up an argument in favour of some particular hypothesis—an argument to persuade our colleagues by its invincible logic that no other interpretation is tenable. This procedure seems quite as scientific as the research of a palaeontologist, who might reconstruct the anatomy of an extinct animal by piecing together fragments of fossil bone. Our aim is the same—to make a thoroughly convincing case which no reasonable person can refute. If, unfortunately, we cannot find sufficient evidence to clinch the case, we do not cling to our hypothesis and abuse our opponents for not accepting it; we quietly concede that the matter is uncertain, and return once more to the search. On such material points, the mood of historical scholarship is perfectly scientific.

The other mood in History is much more akin to Literature or Theology; it is the attempt to understand human history imaginatively and to "explain" it. Having ascertained the "facts," the historian tries to uncover the hidden motives and forces at work, just as the scientist goes behind the phenomena to the laws of their being.

The trouble is that the complex events of history can seldom be explained convincingly in the language of elementary cause and effect. To ascribe the English Civil War, for example, to the "Rise of the Gentry" may be a brilliant and fruitful hypothesis, but it is almost impossible to prove. Even though one may feel that this is the essence of the matter, and though one may marshal factual evidence forcefully in its favour, the case can be no more than circumstantial and hedged with vagueness and provisos. It will go into the canon of interesting historical theories, but experience tells us that it will not, as would a valid scientific theory, be so generally acceptable as to eliminate all competitors.

The rule in Science is not to attempt explanations of such complex phenomena at all, or at least to postpone this enterprise until answers are capable of being agreed upon. Imagination in the search for such problems is essential, but speculation is always kept rigidly under control. Even in such disciplines as Cosmology, where it sometimes seems as if a new theory of the Universe is promulgated each week, the range of discussion is limited quite narrowly to model systems whose mathematical properties are calculable and can be critically assessed by other scholars.

History does not impose such restrictions upon its pronouncements. It is felt, quite naturally, that the larger questions, although more difficult, are very important and must be discussed, even if they cannot be answered with precision. To restrict oneself to decidable propositions would be to miss the lessons that the strange sad story has for mankind. A history of "facts," of dates and kings and queens, although acceptable to the consensus, would be banal and trivial. In other words, History also has to provide other spiritual values, and to satisfy other normative principles, than scientific accuracy.

There are, of course, historians who have claimed universal "scientific" validity for their larger schemes and "Laws." It is not inconceivable that historical events do follow discernible patterns, and that there are, indeed, hidden forces—the class struggle, say, or the Protestant ethic—which largely determine the outcome of human affairs. It would not be necessary for such a theory to be absolute and mathematically rigorous for it to acquire scientific validity, any more than the proof that smoking causes lung cancer requires every smoker to die at the age of 50. It is not inherently absurd to search for historical laws, any more than it was absurd, 200 years ago, to search for the laws governing smallpox. Seemingly haphazard events often turn out to have their pattern, and to be capable of rational explanation.

All I am saying is that no substantial general principles of historical explanation have yet won universal acceptance. There have been fashionable doctrines, and dogmas backed by naked force, but never the sort of consensus of free and well-informed scholars that we ordinarily find in the Natural Sciences. Many historians assert that historical events are the outcome of such a variety of chance causes that they could never be subsumed to simpler, more general laws. Others say that the number of instances of exactly similar situations is always too small to provide sufficient statistical evidence to support an abstract theoretical analysis.

Whatever their reasons, historians do not agree on the general theoretical foundations or methodology of their studies. Instead of establishing, by mutual criticism and tacit cooperation, a limited common basis of acceptable theory, from which to build upwards and outwards, they often feel bound to set up antagonistic "schools" of interpretation, like so many independent walled cities.

They are not to be blamed for such behaviour; it only shows that this is a field where a scientific consensus is not the main objective. If you insisted that historians should work more closely together, they would object that the knowledge that they have in common is too dull, too trivial, too distant from the interesting problems of History, to circumscribe the thought of a serious scholar. To write about the Civil War without asking why the whole extraordinary thing happened is to compose a mere chronicle. For that reason, much of historical scholarship is not essentially scientific.

It would be wrong, on the other hand, to give the approving label "Science" only to the new techniques of historical research derived from the physical and biological sciences and technologies—carbon dating, aerial photography, demographic statistics, chemical analysis of ink and parchment. Such techniques are often powerful, but they are not more "scientific" than the traditional scholarly exercises of editing texts, verifying references and making rational deductions from the written words of documents. There is no reason at all why marks on paper in comprehensible language should be treated as inherently less evidential than the pointer readings of instruments or the print-out from a computer. In

German the word *Wissenschaft*, which we translate as *Science*, includes quite generally all the branches of scholarship, including literary and historical studies.

To maintain, therefore, an impassable divide between Science and the Humanities is to perpetrate a gross misunderstanding that springs in the British case solely from a peculiarity of educational curricula. The Story, the Arts, the Poetry of Mankind are worthy both of spiritual contemplation and scholarly study, whether by laymen in general education or by experts as their life career. In many aspects this study is perfectly akin to the scientific study of electrons, molecules, cells, organisms or social systems: consensible knowledge may be acquired whether as isolated facts or as generally valid explanations. But to confine oneself, in education as in scholarship, to such aspects would impoverish the imagination, and even restrict the scope of possible further advance. Without general concepts as a guide—however uncertain, personal and provisional—we simply could not see any larger patterns in the picture. Historical and literary scholarship cannot therefore pretend to be scientific through and through, but that does not prevent their making progress towards a close definition of the truth. In the end, bold speculative generalization and unverifiable psychological insight may go further in establishing a convincing narrative than a rigid insistence on precise minutiae.

It scarcely needs to be said that *Religion*, as we nowadays study and practise it, is also quite distinct from Science. This seems so obvious in our enlightened age that one wonders how there could have been any conflict and confusion between them. But was not Religion primitive Science—the corpus of generally accepted public knowledge? Should we not see Science as growing out of, and eventually severing itself from, this parent body—or perhaps as a process of differentiation and specialization within the unity of the medieval *Summum*? Just because many religious beliefs are now seen to be wrong, it does not follow that they were not seriously, freely and rationally accepted in their time. Conventional science too can be wrong at times.

Let me give an example. In the late eighteenth and early nineteenth centuries, prehistoric remains were found that we now see as pointing to the great antiquity of Man. But many scholars stood out against this interpretation because it did not square with the Biblical chronology of the past. Is it fair to treat this as a conflict between scientific rationality and religious prejudice? Would it not be more just to say that a widely accepted theory was being ousted by a better one as new evidence came to light?

The point is that this debate was open and free. The participants on one side may have been blinkered by their upbringing, but their beliefs were honestly held and rationally maintained. They may often have used poor arguments to defend their case—but they did not call in the secular arm or the secret police. In the end, they lost; and since then the appeal to Divine Scripture has ceased to be an acceptable element in scientific discussion.

What I am arguing is that there is a progressive improvement in the techniques and criteria of such discussion, and that the use of abstract theological principles was once respectable but is now discredited, just as the absolute justification of Euclidean geometry from the Parallelism Axiom is now discredited. The "Scientific Revolution" of the seventeenth century is not a complete break with the past. The idea of presenting a rational noncontradictory account of the universe is perhaps a legacy of Greece, but it is very strong in medieval Philosophy and Theology. It may be that the very existence of a dogmatic system of metaphysics, implying a rational order of things and fiercely debated in detail, was the prerequisite for the development of an alternative system, using some of the same logical techniques but based upon different principles and more extensive evidence.[4] The doctrinaire consensus of the Church may have been prolonged beyond its acceptability to free men by the power of the

Holy Office, but it had originally provided an example of a generally agreed picture of the world. These are subtle and deep questions which I am not competent to discuss, but I wonder whether the failure of Science to grow in China and India was due as much to the general doctrinal permissiveness of their religious systems as to any other cause. Toleration of deviation, and the lack of a very sharp tradition of logical debate may have made the very idea of a consensus of opinion on the Philosophy of Nature as absurd to them as the idea of absolute agreement on ethical principles would be to us.

The relationship between Science and *Philosophy* is altogether more complex and confused. In a sense, all of modern science is the Philosophy of Nature, as distinct from, say, Moral or Political Philosophy. But this terminology is somewhat old-fashioned, and we try to make a distinction between Physics and Metaphysics, between the Philosophy *of* Science and Philosophy *as* Science. Some philosophers attempt to limit themselves to statements as precise and verifiable as those of scientists, and confine their arguments to the rigid categories of symbolic logic. The consensus criterion would be acceptable to them, for they would hold that by a continuous process of analysis and criticism they would make progress towards creating a generally agreed upon set of principles governing the use of words and the establishment of valid truths. Others hold that such a hope can never be realized and that by limiting philosophical discourse in this way they would only allow themselves to make trivial statements, however unexceptionable. For this school of Philosophy it is important to be free to comment on grander topics, even though such comments will only reveal the variety and contradictory character of the views of different philosophers.

As with History we can only say that if Philosophy is what academic philosophers write in their books, then some of it is not very different from Science. But generally the motivation is nonscientific, by our definition, and the multiplicity of viewpoints indicates that there is no dominant urge to find maximum regions of agreement. Whatever their claims, the proponents of "scientific" philosophical systems do not convince the majority of their colleagues that theirs is the only way to truth.

Let us now consider *Technology*—Engineering, Medicine, etc. For the multitude, Science is almost synonymous with its applications, whereas scientists themselves are very careful to stress the distinction between "pure" knowledge, studied "for its own sake," and technological knowledge applied to human ends.

The trouble is that this distinction is very difficult to make in practice. Suppose, for example, that we are researching on the phenomenon of "fatigue" in metals. We are almost forced into the position of saying that on Monday, Wednesday and Friday we are just honest seekers after truth, adding to our understanding of the natural world, etc., whilst on Tuesday, Thursday and Saturday we are practical chaps trying to stop aeroplanes from falling to pieces, advancing the material welfare of mankind and so on. Or we may have to make snobbish distinctions between Box, a pure scientist working in a University, and Cox, a technologist, doing the same research but employed by an aircraft manufacturer. There was once a time when Science was academic and useless and Technology was a practical art, but now they are so interfused that one is not surprised that the multitude cannot tell them apart.

Here again, a definition in terms of the scientific consensus can be really effective. The technologist has to fulfil a need; he must provide the means to do a definite job—bridge this river, cure this disease, make better beer. He must do the best he can with the knowledge available. That knowledge is almost always inadequate for him to calculate the ideal solution to his problem—and he cannot wait while all the research is done to obtain it. The bridge must be built this year; the patient must be saved today; the brewery will go bankrupt if its product is not improved.

So there will be a large element of the incalculable, of sheer art, in what he does. A different engineer would come out with quite a different design; a different doctor would prescribe quite different treatment. These might be better or worse, in their results—but nobody quite knows. Each situation is so complex, and has so many unassessable factors, that the only sensible policy for the client is to choose his engineer or doctor carefully and then rely upon his skill and experience. To look for a solution acceptable to all the professional experts is a familiar recipe for disaster—"Design by Committee."

The technologist's prime responsibility is towards his employer, his customer or his patient, not to his professional peers. His task is to solve the problem in hand, not to address himself to the opinions of the other experts. If his proposed solution is successful, then it may well establish a lead, and eventually add to the "Science" of his Technology; but that should not be in his mind at the outset.

What we find, of course, is that a corpus of generally accepted principles develops in every technical field. Modern Technology is deliberately scientific, in that there is continuous formal study and empirical investigation of aspects of technique, in addition to the mere accumulation of experience from successfully accomplished tasks. The aim of such research is not to solve immediate specific problems, but to acquire knowledge for the use of the experts in their professional work. It is directed, therefore, at the mind of the profession, as a potential contribution to the consensus opinion. This sort of work is thus genuinely scientific, however trivial and limited its scope may be.

The abstract distinction here being made between a "scientific Technology" and "technological Science" has its psychological counterpart. It is a commonplace in the literature on the Management of Industrial Research that applied scientists often suffer from divided loyalties. On the one hand, they owe their living to the company that employs them, and that expects its return in the profitable solution of immediate problems. On the other hand, they give their intellectual allegiance to their scientific profession—to Colloid Chemistry, or Applied Mathematics, or whatever it is—where they look for scholarly recognition. Although the rewards for "technological" work are greater and more direct, they very often prefer to stick to their "scientific" research.

This preference seems almost incomprehensible to management experts, because they fail to see that the scientific loyalty is not just towards a prestigious professional group but to an ideology. The young scientist is trained to make contributions to public knowledge. All the habits and practices of his years of apprenticeship emphasize the importance of making them convincing, and thus making them part of the common pool. Being a successful scientist is not just winning prizes; it is having other scientists cite your work. To give this up is worse than losing caste; it is to give up one's faith and be made to worship foreign idols.

Nevertheless, one must agree that Science and Technology are now so intimately mingled that the distinction can become rather pedantic. Take, for example, a typical Consumers Association report on a motor car. Some of the tests, such as the measure of petrol consumption, may be perfectly scientific in that their validity would be universally acceptable. Other tests, such as whether the springing was comfortable, would not satisfy this criterion, although it would be one of the important skills of the designer to attend to just such "subjective" and "qualitative" features. For this reason, to say that a car has been "scientifically designed" is merely to assert that it has been well designed by competent engineers. Yet an account, by the designer, of the rationale behind various technical features of the model could rank as a serious contribution to the Science of Automobile Engineering by adding to the body of agreed principles at the basis of that mysterious art.

All that I can claim is that these distinctions, although subtle and perhaps pedantic, are not entirely arbitrary or unreal. We do not need to look far ahead to some conceivable remote application of the knowledge in question, nor do we need to examine the hidden, perhaps unconscious, motives of those who produce it. We do not need to decide whether some particular laboratory is "technological" or "scientific," and then attach the appropriate label to its products. The criterion is in the work itself, in the form in which it is presented, and in the audience to which it is addressed. . . .

This survey of the Faculties has necessarily been brief and schematic. Why should we even want to decide whether a particular discipline is scientific or not? The answer is, simply, that, *when it is available*, scientific knowledge is more reliable, on the whole, than non-scientific. When there are conflicts of authority, when Sociology tells us to go one way and History another, we need to weigh their respective claims to validity. Our general argument here is that in a discipline where there is a scientific consensus the amount of *certain* knowledge may be limited, but it will be honestly labelled: "Trust your neck to this," or "This ladder was built by a famous scholar, but no one else has been able to climb it."

In the end, the best way to decide whether a particular body of knowledge is scientific or not is often to study the attitudes of its professional practitioners to one another's work. A sure symptom of non-science is personal abuse and intolerance of the views of one scholar by another. The existence of irreconcilable "schools" of thought is familiar in such academic realms as Theology, Philosophy, Literature and History. When we find them in a "scientific" discipline, we should be on our guard.

This is the reason why for example we should be very suspicious of the claims of Psychoanalysis. The history of this subject is a continuous series of bitter conflicts between persons, schools and theories. Freud himself had the most honest and sincere desire to create a thoroughly respectable scientific discipline, but for some reason he failed to understand this key point—the need to move slowly forward, step by step, from a basis of generally accepted ideas. Perhaps the struggle to get anyone to listen at all was too bitter, or perhaps his mind was too active and impatient to endure continuous critical assessment of each new theory or interpretation. Whatever the reason, the mood of Psychoanalysis in its formative period was antagonistic to the covert cooperative spirit of true Science. Its clinical successes were only of technological significance, and did not scientifically validate the theories on which they were said to be based.

I have given this example, not out of prejudice against psychoanalytic ideas (one or other of the contending schools may well be right: we shall see) but to show that the principle of the consensus is a powerful criterion, with something definite to say on this vexed topic. To some people the words "scientific" and "unscientific" have come to mean no more than "true" and "false," or "rational" and "irrational." In this chapter I have tried to show, by reference to other organized bodies of knowledge, that this usage is quite improper, and grossly unfair to those scholars who seek rationality and truth in bolder ways than by microscopic dissection of minutiae.

Notes

1. This point I owe to Professor Körner.
2. "Hence a true philosophy of science must be a philosophy of scientists and laboratories as well as one of waves, particles and symbols." Patrick Meredith in *Instruments of Communication*, p. 40.
3. I am indebted to Professor Julius Stone for sending me his fascinating critical essay on this subject.
4. This point is made in *Science in the Modern World* by A. N. Whitehead (New York: Macmillan, 1931).

Science as Problem Solving

Larry Laudan

In this essay, Larry Laudan explores some implications of viewing science as essentially a problem-solving activity. He maintains that theories should be evaluated on the basis of whether they provide "satisfactory solutions to important problems," and he sharply differentiates this approach from evaluating theories in terms of the facts that they explain. After identifying the range of situations that can create empirical problems, Laudan distinguishes between solved problems, unsolved problems, and anomalous problems. An unsolved problem is a genuine, important problem that suggests a line for future research. A problem is an anomaly for a theory if it is an unsolved problem that is solved by some competitor theory. Progress in science occurs when unsolved problems or anomalies become solved problems. Problem solutions can be approximate; a theory need not exactly predict some data in order for the theory to solve a problem constituted by the data. Moreover, truth need not play any role in a problem solution. Further implications of this pragmatist view of science are explored in Laudan's dialogue on progress in science, which is included in the later **"Scientific Practice and Reason"** section. Larry Laudan was a professor of philosophy at the University of Hawaii.

As you read through this essay, consider the following:

1. According to Laudan, how does solving problems differ from explaining facts?
2. What does Laudan mean when he says "science is essentially a problem-solving activity"?

3. When is an inquiry situation an empirical problem, according to Laudan?
4. Should all scientists be able to agree on what counts as a problem according to Laudan's view? Why or why not?
5. Does conceiving of science as problem solving require that science be public in Ziman's sense?
6. Can we fruitfully see most intellectual inquiry as problem solving? What might we gain and what might we lose if we adopted such a view?
7. Can we distinguish scientific problem solving from other kinds of problem solving?

Science is essentially a problem-solving activity. This anodine bromide, more a cliché than a philosophy of science, has been espoused by generations of science textbook writers and self-professed specialists on "*the* scientific method." But for all the lip service which has been paid to the view that science is fundamentally the solving of problems, scant attention has been paid, either by philosophers of science or historians of science, to the ramifications of such an approach for understanding science. Philosophers of science, by and large, have imagined that they can lay bare the rationality of science by ignoring, in their analyses, the fact that scientific theories are usually attempts to solve specific empirical problems about the natural world. Similarly, historians of science, for their part, have usually imagined that the chronology of scientific theories possesses an intrinsic intelligibility which requires little or no cognizance of the particular problems which prominent theories in the past were designed to solve.

It is the purpose of this [essay] to sketch what seem to be the implications, for both the history of science and its philosophy, of a view of scientific inquiry which perceives science as being—above all else—a problem-solving activity.

The approach taken here is not meant to imply that science is "nothing but" a problem-solving activity. Science has as wide a variety of aims as individual scientists have a multitude of motivations: science aims to explain and control the natural world; scientists seek (among other things) truth, influence, social utility, and prestige. Each of these goals could be (and has been) used to provide a framework within which one might try to explain the development and nature of science. My approach, however, contends that a view of science as a problem-solving system holds out more hope of capturing what is most characteristic about science than any alternative framework has.

As it becomes clear that many of the classic problems of philosophy of science, and many of the standard issues of the history of science, take on a very different perspective when we look at science as a problem-solving and problem-oriented activity, it will be argued that an attentive analysis of science from this perspective generates new insights which run counter to much of the "conventional wisdom" which historians and philosophers of science have taken for granted.

There is nothing modest about the claims this study makes. In brief, I shall be suggesting that a sophisticated theory of science qua problem-solving activity *must* alter the way we perceive both the central issues in the historiography of science and the central problems in the philosophy or methodology of science. I shall argue that if we take seriously the doctrine that the aim of science (and of all intellectual inquiry, for that matter) is the resolution or clarification of problems, then we shall have a very different picture of the historical evolution and the cognitive evaluation of science.

Before I contrast the problem-solving view of science with certain better known philosophies and histories of science, I must indicate specifically what I mean by a "problem-oriented theory of science." . . .

THE NATURE OF SCIENTIFIC PROBLEMS

Throughout this essay, I shall be talking about what I call *scientific problems*. I should stress at the outset that I do not believe that "scientific" problems are fundamentally different from other kinds of problems (though they often are different in degree). . . .

If problems are the focal point of scientific thought, theories are its end result. Theories matter, they are *cognitively* important, insofar as—and only insofar as—they provide adequate solutions to problems. If problems constitute the questions of science, it is theories which constitute the answers. The function of a theory is to resolve ambiguity, to reduce irregularity to uniformity, to show that what happens is somehow intelligible and predictable; it is this complex of functions to which I refer when I speak of theories as solutions to problems.

Thesis 1: *The first and essential acid test for any theory is whether it provides acceptable answers to interesting questions: whether, in other words, it provides satisfactory solutions to important problems.*

At one level, this might appear completely noncontroversial. Most writers who have dealt with the nature of science would probably claim to subscribe to such a view. Unfortunately, as we shall see, most philosophies of science manifestly fail to go so far as to justify even that seemingly harmless and obvious sentiment, let alone to explore its many ramifications.

The literature of the methodology of science offers us neither a taxonomy of the types of scientific problems, nor any acceptable method of grading their relative importance. It is noticeably silent about what the criteria are for an adequate solution to a problem. It does not recognize there are degrees of adequacy in problem solution, some solutions being better and richer than others. Insofar as contemporary philosophy of science says anything at all about these matters, it tends to

regard all solutions on a par, and to assign all problems equal weight. In assessing the adequacy of any theory, the philosopher of science will usually ask how many facts confirm it, not how important those facts are. He will ask how many problems the theory solves, not about the significance of those problems. To this extent, contemporary philosophy of science has not captured the sense of thesis (1) above. It is for reasons such as these that I propose:

Thesis 2: *In appraising the merits of theories, it is more important to ask whether they constitute adequate solutions to significant problems than it is to ask whether they are "true," "corroborated," "well-confirmed" or otherwise justifiable within the framework of contemporary epistemology.*

But if it is plausible to think that the counterpoint between challenging problems and adequate theories is the basic dialectic of science, we must get a great deal clearer than we now are about what problems are and how they work, about how problems are weighted, and about the nature of theories and their precise relation to the problems which generate them (and which, as we shall see, they sometimes generate).

EMPIRICAL PROBLEMS

There are two very *different* kinds of problems which scientific theories are designed to solve. For now, I want to focus on the first, more familiar and archetypal, sense of the concept, which I shall call an *empirical* problem. Empirical problems are easier to illustrate than to define. We observe that heavy bodies fall toward the earth with amazing regularity. To ask how and why they so fall is to pose such a problem. We observe that alcohol left standing in a glass soon disappears. To seek an explanation for that phenomenon is, again, to raise an empirical problem. We may observe that the offspring of plants and animals bear striking resemblances to their parents. To inquire into the mechanism of trait transmission is also to raise an empirical problem. More generally, anything about the natural world which strikes us as odd, or otherwise in need of explanation, constitutes an empirical problem.

In calling such inquiry situations "empirical" problems, I do not mean to suggest they are directly given by the world as veridical bits of unambiguous data. Both historical examples and recent philosophical analysis have made it clear that the world is always perceived through the "lenses" of some conceptual network or other and that such networks and the languages in which they are embedded may, for all we know, provide an ineliminable "tint" to what we perceive. More to the point, *problems* of all sorts (including empirical ones) *arise within a certain context of inquiry* and are partly defined by that context. Our theoretical presuppositions about the natural order tell us what to expect and what seems peculiar or "problematic" or questionable (in the literal sense of that term). Situations which pose problems within one inquiry context will not necessarily do so within others. Hence, whether something is regarded as an empirical problem will depend, in part, on the theories we possess.

Why, then, call them "empirical" problems at all? I do so because, even granting that they arise only in certain contexts of theoretical inquiry, even granting that their formulation will be influenced by our theoretical commitments, it is nonetheless the case that we *treat* empirical problems as if they were problems about the world. If we ask, "How fast do bodies fall near the earth?," we are assuming there are objects akin to our conceptions of body and earth which move towards one another according to some regular rule. That assumption, of course, is a theory-laden one, but we nonetheless assert it to be about the physical world. Empirical problems are thus *first order problems;* they are substantive questions about the objects which constitute the domain of any given science. Unlike other, higher order problems . . ., we judge the adequacy of solutions to empirical problems by studying the objects in the domain.

We have already noted that there is an apparent functional similarity between talk of problems and problem solving and the more familiar rhetoric about facts and the explanation of facts. Given that similarity, one might be inclined to translate the claims I shall make about the nature and logic of problem solving into assertions about the logic of explanation. To do so, however, would be to misconstrue the enterprise, for problems are very different from "facts" (even "theory-laden facts") and solving a problem can not be reduced to "explaining a fact." Full discussion of the disanalogies must wait until later, but some of the discrepancies can be seen by considering a few of the differences between facts or states of affairs on the one hand, and empirical problems on the other.

Certain presumed states of affairs regarded as posing empirical problems are actually *counterfactual.* A problem need not accurately describe a real state of affairs to be a problem: all that is required is that it be *thought to be* an actual state of affairs by some agent. For instance, early members of the Royal Society of London, convinced by mariners' tales of the existence of sea serpents, regarded the properties and behavior of such serpents as an empirical problem to be solved. Medieval natural philosophers such as Oresme, took it to be the case that hot goat's blood could split diamonds and developed theories to explain this counterfactual empirical "occurrence." Similarly, early nineteenth century biologists, convinced of the existence of spontaneous generation, took it to be an empirical problem to show how meat left in the sun could transmute into maggots or how stomach juices could turn into tapeworms. For centuries, medical theory sought to explain the "fact" that bloodletting cured certain diseases. If factuality were a necessary condition for something to count as an empirical problem, then such situations could not count as problems. So long as we insist that theories are designed only to explain "facts" (i.e., true statements about the world), we shall find ourselves unable to explain most of the theoretical activity which has taken place in science.

There are many facts about the world which do not pose empirical problems simply because they are *unknown*. It is, for instance, presumably a fact (and always has been) that the sun is composed chiefly of hydrogen; but until the fact was discovered (or invented), it could not have generated a problem. In sum, a fact only becomes a problem when it is treated and recognized as such; facts, on the other hand, are facts, whether they are ever recognized. The only kind of facts which can possibly count as problems are *known* facts.

But even many known facts do not necessarily constitute empirical problems. To regard something as an empirical problem, we must feel that *there is a premium on solving it*. At any given moment in the history of science, many things will be well-known phenomena, but will not be felt to be in need of explanation or clarification. It was known since the earliest times, for instance, that most trees have green leaves. But that "fact" only became an "empirical problem" when someone decided it was sufficiently interesting and important to deserve explanation. Again, early societies knew certain drugs could produce hallucinations, but that widely known fact only became a recognized problem for physiological theories relatively recently.

Finally, problems recognized as such at one time can, for perfectly rational reasons, *cease* to be problems at later times. Facts could never undergo that sort of transformation. Early geological theorists, for instance, regarded one of the central problems of their discipline to be that of explaining how the earth took its shape within the last 6,000 to 8,000 years. With the elongation of the geological time scale, that staggering issue no longer remained a problem to be solved.

TYPES OF EMPIRICAL PROBLEMS

Having seen some of the differences between facts and empirical problems and the need for clearly separating the two, we can now turn to the role which such problems play in the process of scientific analysis. Although a fuller taxonomy will be developed later, we can roughly divide empirical problems into three types, relative to the function they have in theory evaluation: (1) *unsolved problems*—those empirical problems which have not yet been adequately solved by *any* theory; (2) *solved problems*—those empirical problems which have been adequately solved by a theory; (3) *anomalous problems*—those empirical problems which a *particular* theory has not solved, but which one or more of its competitors have.

Clearly, solved problems count in favor of a theory, anomalous ones constitute evidence *against* a theory, and unsolved ones simply indicate lines for future theoretical inquiry. Using this terminology, we can argue that *one of the hallmarks of scientific progress is the transformation of anomalous and unsolved empirical problems into solved ones*. Of any and every theory, we must ask how many problems it has solved and how many anomalies confront it. This question, in a slightly more complex form, becomes one of the primary tools for the comparative evaluation of scientific theories.

THE STATUS OF UNSOLVED PROBLEMS

It is part of the conventional wisdom that unsolved problems provide the stimulus for scientific growth and progress; and there can be no doubt that transforming unsolved into solved problems is one (though by no means the only) way in which progressive theories establish their scientific credentials. But it is too often assumed that the body of unsolved problems at any given time is clear cut and well defined, that scientists have a definite sense of which unsolved problems should be solved by their theories, and that a theory's failure to digest its unsolved problems is a clear liability.

A careful examination of many historical cases reveals, however, that the status of unsolved problems is a great deal more ambiguous than is often imagined. Whether a given "phenomenon" is a genuine problem, how important it is, how heavily it counts against a theory if it fails to solve it; these are all very complex questions, but a good first approximation to an answer is this: *unsolved problems generally count as genuine problems only when they are no longer unsolved.* Until solved by some theory in a domain they are generally only "potential" problems rather than actual ones. There are two factors chiefly responsible for this: one, which we have already discussed, arises when we are unsure an empirical effect is genuine. Because many experimental results are difficult to reproduce, because physical systems are impossible to isolate, because measuring instruments are often unreliable, because the theory of error even leads us to expect "freak" results, it often takes a considerable time before a phenomenon is sufficiently authenticated to be taken seriously as a well-established effect. Second, it is often the case that even when an effect has been well authenticated, *it is very unclear to which domain of science it belongs* and, therefore, which theories should seek, or be expected, to solve it. Is the fact that the moon seems larger near the horizon a problem for astronomical theories, for optical theories, or for psychological ones? Is the formation of crystals and crystalline growth a problem for chemistry or biology or geology? Are "shooting stars" a problem for astronomy or for upper-atmosphere physics? Is the twitching of an electrified frog leg a problem for biology, chemistry, or electrical theory? We now have answers to all these questions and feel confident about assigning these problems to one domain or another. The chief reason for our confidence is that we have *solved* these problems. But for long periods in the history of science, these problems were unsolved and it was very unclear within what domain they should fall. As a result of that uncertainty, it did not count seriously against any theory in a given domain if it failed to solve these unsolved problems; for no one could show convincingly that theories in any particular domain should be expected to solve such problems. . . .

Cases in which there is doubt about the appropriate domain for some unsolved problem have frequently been of decisive historical importance. The vicissitudes of comets provide a neat example. During antiquity and the Middle Ages, comets were classified as sublunary phenomena and thus fell within the domain of meteorology. Astronomers, whose concern was exclusively with problems in the celestial regions, felt no need to offer theories about comets, nor even to plot their courses. By the sixteenth century, however, it had become customary to classify comets as celestial phenomena. This domain transition was crucial for the Copernican theory, since the motion of comets came to constitute one of the decisive anomalies for geocentric astronomy and one of the solved problems for the heliocentric theory.

One ought not conclude from their ambiguity that unsolved problems are unimportant for science, for transforming unsolved problems into solved ones is one of the means by which theories make empirical progress. But it must be stressed at the same time that a theory's failure to solve some unsolved problem generally will not weigh heavily against that theory, because we usually cannot know *a priori* that the problem in question should be soluble by that sort of theory. *The only reliable guide to the problems relevant to a particular theory is an examination of the problems which predecessor—and competing—theories in that domain (including the theory itself) have already solved.* Hence, in appraising the relative merits of theories, the class of unsolved problems is altogether irrelevant. What matters for purposes of theory evaluation are only those problems which have been solved, not necessarily by the theory in question, but by *some* known theory. (Here, as elsewhere, the evaluation of a theory is closely linked to a knowledge of its competitors.)

THE NATURE OF SOLVED PROBLEMS

We have already indicated that "the solving of problems" ought not be confused with "the explaining of facts," and have discussed at some length the disanalogies between facts and empirical problems. What requires further elaboration is the difference between the logic and pragmatics of problem solution, and the logic and pragmatics of scientific explanation.

Most of the major differences emerge clearly if we begin by exploring the criteria for something to count as a solved problem. In very rough form, we can say that an empirical problem is solved when, within a particular context of inquiry, scientists properly no longer regard it as an unanswered question, i.e., when they believe they understand why the situation propounded by the problem is the way it is. Now clearly, it is theories which are meant to provide such understanding and any reference to a solved problem presupposes the existence of a theory which purportedly solves the problem in question. So when we ask whether a problem has been solved, we are really asking whether it stands in a certain relationship to some theory or other.

What does that relationship amount to? If we ask a logician of science the analogous question (to wit: what is the relation between an explanans and its explanandum?), he will generally tell us: the explaining theory must (along with certain initial conditions) entail an *exact* statement of fact to be explained; the theory must be either *true* or highly *probable*; whatever counts as an adequate explanation of any fact must be regarded as always having been such (so long as the epistemic appraisal of the explanans does not change). By way of contrast, I shall claim that: a theory may solve a problem so long as it entails even an *approximate* statement of the problem; in determining if a theory solves a problem, *it is irrelevant whether the theory is true or false, well or poorly confirmed*; what counts as a solution to a problem at one time will not necessarily be regarded as such at all times. Each of these differences demands further clarification.

The Approximative Character of Problem Solution. Although rare, it sometimes happens that a theory exactly predicts an experimental outcome. When that desirable result is achieved, there is cause for general rejoicing. It is far more common for the predictions deduced from a theory to come close to reproducing the data which constitute a specific problem, but with no exact coincidence of results. Newton was not able to explain exactly the motion of the planets; Einstein's theory did not exactly entail Eddington's telescopic observations; modern chemical bonding theory does not predict with exactitude the orbital distance of electrons in a molecule; thermodynamics does not precisely fit heat transfer data for any known steam engine. There are many reasons one could suggest (e.g., the use of "ideal cases," the non-isolation of real systems, imperfections in our measuring instruments) to explain the frequent small discrepancies between "theoretical results" and "laboratory results," but they are not of primary concern here. What is relevant is that facts are very rarely if ever explained (if we take our sense of explanation from the classical deductive model), because there is usually a discordance between what a theory entails and our laboratory data. By contrast, empirical problems are frequently solved because for problem solving purposes we do not require an exact, but only an approximate, resemblance between theoretical results and experimental ones. Newton did solve, and was widely regarded as having solved, the problem of the curvature of the earth—even though his results were not identical with observational findings. The thermodynamic theories of Carnot and Clausius were correctly perceived in the nineteenth century as adequate solutions to various problems of heat transfer, in spite of the fact that they applied exactly only to ideal (i.e., nonexistent) heat engines.

As should be clear, the notion of solution is highly relative and comparative in a way that the notion of explanation is not. We can have two different theories which solve the same problem, and yet say one is a better solution (i.e., a closer approximation) than the other. Comparable locutions and comparisons within the rhetoric of explanation are disallowed by many philosophers of science;

on the standard model of explanation, something either is or definitely is not an explanation—degrees of explanatory adequacy are not countenanced. For instance, philosophers of science have been very troubled by the relationship of Galileo's and Newton's theories of fall and the data. Unable to say that both theories "explained" the phenomena of fall (because the two are formally inconsistent), they invented a variety of devices for excluding the title "explanatory" from one or the other of the theories. Yet it is surely more natural historically, and more sensible conceptually, to say that *both* theories (Galileo's and Newton's) solved the problem of free fall, one perhaps with more precision than the other (although even that is dubious). It redounds to the credit of both that, as Newton himself perceived, each provided an adequate solution to the problem at hand. We are, however, precluded from taking this natural way of describing the situation if we accept many of the current doctrines about the nature of explanation.

The Irrelevance of Truth and the Falsity to Solving a Problem. The suggestion that questions of truth and probability are irrelevant when determining whether a theory solves a particular problem probably seems heretical, if only because one is so conditioned to considering the search for true understanding as one of the core aims of science. But whatever role questions of truth have in the scientific enterprise . . . , one need not, and scientists generally do not, consider matters of truth and falsity when determining whether a theory does or does not solve a particular empirical problem. . . .

The Frequent Nonpermanence of Solutions. One of the richest and healthiest dimensions of science is the growth through time of the standards it demands for something to count as a solution to a problem. What one generation of scientists will accept as a perfectly adequate solution will often be viewed by the next generation as a hopelessly inadequate one. The history of science is replete with cases where solutions whose precision and specificity were perfectly adequate for one epoch are totally inadequate for another. Consider a few examples:

In his *Physics,* Aristotle cites the problem of fall as a central phenomenon for any theory of terrestrial mechanics. Aristotle himself sought to understand both why bodies fall downwards and why they accelerate in fall. Aristotelian physics provided answers to these questions which were taken seriously for over two millenia. For Galileo, Descartes, Huygens, and Newton, however, Aristotle's views were not really solutions to the problem of fall at all, for they failed utterly to explain the "uniform difform" (i.e., uniformly accelerated) character of the fall of a body. One might want to say that the later thinkers were simply working with a very different problem than Aristotle was; I would be more inclined to see this as a case where, through the course of time, the criteria for what counts as solving a problem have evolved so much that what was once regarded as an adequate solution ceases to be regarded as such. . . .

In the history of many disciplines, humanistic as well as scientific, one can perceive a gradual tightening and strengthening of the threshold at which a theory will be conceded to be a solution to the relevant problem. Unless we acknowledge that the criteria for acceptable problem solutions do themselves evolve through time, the history of thought will seem enigmatic indeed.

THE SPECIAL ROLE OF ANOMALOUS PROBLEMS

Many historians and philosophers of science have attached special significance to the place of anomalies in science. Thinkers from Bacon through Mill, Popper, Grünbaum and Lakatos have stressed the importance of refuting or falsifying experiments in the appraisal of scientific theories. Indeed, certain philosophies of science (especially those of Bacon and Popper) make the search for, and resolution of, anomalies the *raison d'être* of the scientific enterprise, and the absence of anomalies the hallmark of scientific virtue. While sharing the view that anomalous instances have been, and should be, among the most important components of scientific rationality, I find myself seriously at odds with the conventional wisdom about what anomalies are and about the interpretation of their undoubted significance.

On the traditional view, anomalies have two chief characteristics:

(a) the occurrence of even one anomaly for a theory should force the rational scientist to abandon it;

(b) the only empirical data which can count as anomalies are those which are *logically inconsistent* with the theory for which they are anomalies.

I find these characteristics factually misleading as to actual scientific practice (both past and present), and a conceptual hindrance in understanding the role of anomalies in theory appraisal. I want to claim, by contrast, that:

(a´) the occurrence of an anomaly raises doubts about, but need *not* compel the abandonment of, the theory exhibiting the anomaly;

(b´) anomalies need *not* be inconsistent with the theories to which they are anomalies.

The first of these two contentions (a´) is the less controversial, if only because numerous critics of the classical view have already offered cogent arguments for it; as a result, here I shall only briefly rehearse the reasons for it. The second thesis (b´), however, is not a familiar one, and I shall elaborate on it at some length.

Taking (a´) first, several philosophers (particularly Pierre Duhem, Otto Neurath, and W. Quine) have argued that we cannot rationally decide whether a particular theory which generates an anomaly should be abandoned because of certain ineliminable *ambiguities* about the testing situation. The principal ambiguities are two:

1. In any empirical test, it is *an entire network of theories* which is required for deriving any experimental prediction. If the prediction turns out to be erroneous, we do not know where to locate the error within the network. The decision that one particular theory within the network is false is, these critics argue, completely arbitrary.

2. To abandon a theory because it is incompatible with the data assumes that our knowledge of the data is infallible and veridical. Once we realize that the data themselves are only probable, the occurrence of an anomaly does not necessarily require the abandonment of a theory (we might rationally choose, for instance, to "abandon" the data).

Still other critics of (a) have stressed not the ambiguity, but the *pragmatics*, of theory testing and theory choice. They point out that almost every theory in history has had some anomalities or refuting instances; indeed, no one has ever been able to point to a single major theory which did not exhibit some anomalies. Accordingly, if we were to take (a) seriously, then we should find ourselves abandoning our entire theoretical repertoire in wholesale fashion, and thereby totally unable to say anything whatever about most domains of nature. For these reasons, there seem strong grounds for replacing (a) by the weaker, but more realistic, view (a´).

However, almost all writers on the subject of anomalies, whether defenders or critics of the classical view (a), seem to subscribe to (b), and to hold that an anomaly is only generated when there is a *logical* inconsistency between our "theoretical" predictions and our "experimental" observations. They have argued, in other words, that the only time data can be epistemically threatening for a theory is when such data contradict the claims of the theory. This strikes me as a far too restrictive notion of an anomalous problem. It is true, of course, that a genuine inconsistency between theory and observation may, under certain circumstances, constitute a particularly vivid example of anomaly. But such inconsistencies are far from being the only form of anomalous problem.

If, as I think we must, we take (a´) seriously, it is reasonable to characterize an anomaly as an empirical situation which, while perhaps not offering definitive grounds for abandoning a theory, does raise rational doubts about the empirical credentials of the theory. Proponents of (a´), in criticizing (a), are not claiming that we should ignore anomalies; rather, they are simply stressing that *anomalies constitute important, but not necessarily decisive, objections to any theory which exhibits them*. If we regard anomalies in this light (i.e., *as empirical problems which raise reasonable doubts about the empirical adequacy of a theory*), then we should abandon (b) for (b´), since by parity of reasoning, there are many empirical problems which, although consistent with a theory, can cast doubt upon its empirical foundations. Putting the point another way, there are occasions when scientists have *rationally* treated certain problems (which were consistent with a theory) in the same way that they would treat anomalies which were clearly inconsistent with the theory. Such situations arise when a theory in some field or domain fails to say anything about a kind of problem which other theories in the same domain have already solved.

Whether we treat such cases as anomalous depends, in part, of course, on our views about the aims of science. If one takes the narrow view that the object of science is simply to avoid making mistakes (i.e., false statements), then unsolved problems will not necessarily count seriously against a theory. But if one takes the broader view that science aims to maximize its problem-solving capacity (or, in more conventional language, its "explanatory content") then the failure of a theory to solve some well-recognized problem, which has been solved by a competitor theory, is a very serious mark against it. Ironically, most philosophers of science have paid lip service to the broader view, yet they have refused to recognize what that view entails—*the existence of a class of nonrefuting anomalies*. . . .

One of the most cognitively significant activities in which any scientist can engage is the successful transformation of a presumed empirical anomaly for a theory into a confirming instance for that theory. Unlike the solution of some new problem, the conversion of anomalies into problem-solving successes does double service: it not only exhibits the problem solving capacities of a theory (which the solution of any problem will do) but it simultaneously eliminates one of the major cognitive liabilities confronting the theory. . . .

Section 12

Alienation and the Scientific Worldview

Modern Science and the Loss of Purpose

Kurt Baier

Modern science seems to leave little room for purposes in nature; it presents a special challenge for those who seek an ultimate purpose for their lives. According to the scientific worldview, we are a relatively recent species that inhabits an insignificant planet in an apparently purposeless universe. If we accept this view, then our struggles to live a decent life are threatened with meaninglessness. Why should we bother to carry on with difficult projects, or to try to do the right thing, when there is no purpose behind anything that happens and all our efforts will come to nothing in the long run? For such reasons, some believe that the scientific worldview is alienating. Kurt Baier disagrees.

After briefly sketching the impact of science on the medieval worldview, Baier argues that science does not deprive life of meaning. He distinguishes between two kinds of purposes, those that persons have and those that objects have. The former are determined by someone's intentions; for example, one can have a variety of purposes for taking a philosophy course. According to Baier, the scientific worldview is fully compatible with our having purposes in this sense. Objects, such as this book, have purposes because someone has purposes for them. Science is incompatible with our lives having purposes in the second sense; there are no supernatural beings that have purposes for us. Baier argues that we should not want the latter kind of purpose and that the former provides all the meaning in life that we need. Kurt Baier is professor of philosophy emeritus at the University of Pittsburgh.

As you read through this essay, consider the following:

1. According to Baier, why is the acceptance of the scientific worldview often accompanied with the feeling that life is purposeless?
2. How is confusion about two different kinds of purpose responsible for the view that science deprives life of meaning?
3. What are some problems with the view that God has given our lives purpose?
4. According to Baier, what might make a life worthwhile?
5. Do you think that we judge whether a life has been worthwhile? How might we defend such judgments?
6. Has Baier effectively shown how life can have meaning even if there is no ultimate purpose for life? How might one object to his line of argument?

Tolstoy, in his autobiographical work, "A Confession," reports how, when he was fifty and at the height of his literary success, he came be obsessed by the fear that life was meaningless.

> At first I experienced moments of perplexity and arrest of life, as though I did not know what to do or how to live; and I felt lost and became dejected. But this passed, and I went on living as before. Then these moments of perplexity began to recur oftener and oftener, and always in the same form. They were always expressed by the questions: What is it for? What does it lead to? At first it seemed to me that these were aimless and irrelevant questions. I thought that it was all well known, and that if I should ever wish to deal with the solution it would not cost me much effort; just at present I had no time for it, but when I wanted to, I should be able to find the answer. The questions however began to repeat themselves frequently, and to demand replies more and more insistently; and like drops of ink always falling on one place they ran together into one black blot.[1]

A Christian living in the Middle Ages would not have felt any serious doubts about Tolstoy's questions. To him it would have seemed quite certain that life had a meaning and quite clear what it was. The medieval Christian world picture assigned to man a

highly significant, indeed the central part in the grand scheme of things. The universe was made for the express purpose of providing a stage on which to enact a drama starring Man in the title role.

To be exact, the world was created by God in the year 4004 B.C. Man was the last and the crown of this creation, made in the likeness of God, placed in the Garden of Eden on earth, the fixed centre of the universe, round which revolved the nine heavens of the sun, the moon, the planets and the fixed stars, producing as they revolved in their orbits the heavenly harmony of the spheres. And this gigantic universe was created for the enjoyment of man, who was originally put in control of it. Pain and death were unknown in paradise. But this state of bliss was not to last. Adam and Eve ate of the forbidden tree of knowledge, and life on this earth turned into a death-march through a vale of tears. Then, with the birth of Jesus, new hope came into the world. After He had died on the cross, it became at least possible to wash away with the purifying water of baptism some of the effects of Original Sin and to achieve salvation. That is to say, on condition of obedience to the law of God, man could now enter heaven and regain the state of everlasting, deathless bliss, from which he had been excluded because of the sin of Adam and Eve.

To the medieval Christian the meaning of human life was therefore perfectly clear. The stretch on earth is only a short interlude, a temporary incarceration of the soul in the

From Kurt Baier, "The Meaning of Life." Inaugural Lecture delivered at the Canberra University College, 1957. © Kurt Baier. Reprinted by permission.

prison of the body, a brief trial and test, fated to end in death, the release from pain and suffering. What really matters, is the life after the death of the body. One's existence acquires meaning not by gaining what this life can offer but by saving one's immortal soul from death and eternal torture, by gaining eternal life and everlasting bliss.

The scientific world picture which has found ever more general acceptance from the beginning of the modern era onwards is in profound conflict with all this. At first, the Christian conception of the world was discovered to be erroneous in various important details. The Copernican theory showed up the earth as merely one of several planets revolving round the sun, and the sun itself was later seen to be merely one of many fixed stars each of which is itself the nucleus of a solar system similar to our own. Man, instead of occupying the centre of creation, proved to be merely the inhabitant of a celestial body no different from millions of others. Furthermore, geological investigations revealed that the universe was not created a few thousand years ago, but was probably millions of years old.

Disagreements over details of the world picture, however, are only superficial aspects of a much deeper conflict. The appropriateness of the whole Christian outlook is at issue. For Christianity, the world must be regarded as the "creation" of a kind of Superman, a person possessing all the human excellences to an infinite degree and none of the human weaknesses, Who has made man in His image, a feeble, mortal, foolish copy of Himself. In creating the universe, God acts as a sort of playwright-cum-legislator-cum-judge-cum-executioner. In the capacity of playwright, He creates the historical world process, including man. He erects the stage and writes, in outline, the plot. He creates the *dramatis personae* and watches over them with the eye partly of a father, partly of the law. While on stage, the actors are free to extemporise, but if they infringe the divine commandments, they are later dealt with by their creator in His capacity of judge and executioner.

Within such a framework, the Christian attitudes towards the world are natural and sound: it is natural and sound to think that all is arranged for the best even if appearances belie it; to resign oneself cheerfully to one's lot; to be filled with awe and veneration in regard to anything and everything that happens; to want to fall on one's knees and worship and praise the Lord. These are wholly fitting attitudes within the framework of the world view just outlined. And this world view must have seemed wholly sound and acceptable because it offered the best explanation which was then available of all the observed phenomena of nature.

As the natural sciences developed, however, more and more things in the universe came to be explained without the assumption of a supernatural creator. Science, moreover, could explain them better, that is, more accurately and more reliably. The Christian hypothesis of a supernatural maker, whatever other needs it was capable of satisfying, was at any rate no longer indispensable for the purpose of explaining the existence or occurrence of anything. In fact, scientific explanations do not seem to leave any room for this hypothesis. . . .

It might be argued that the more clearly we understand the explanations given by science, the more we are driven to the conclusion that human life has no purpose and therefore no meaning. The science of astronomy teaches us that our earth was not specially created about 6,000 years ago, but evolved out of hot nebulae which previously had whirled aimlessly through space for countless ages. As they cooled, the sun and the planets formed. On one of these planets at a certain time the circumstances were propitious and life developed. But conditions will not remain favourable to life. When our solar system grows old, the sun will cool, our planet will be covered with ice, and all living creatures will eventually perish. Another theory has it that the sun will explode and that the heat generated will be so great that all organic life on earth will be destroyed. That is the comparatively short history and prospect of life on earth. Altogether it amounts to very little when compared with the endless history of the inanimate universe.

Biology teaches us that the species man was not specially created but is merely, in a long chain of evolutionary changes of forms of life, the last link, made in the likeness not of God but of nothing so much as an ape. The rest of the universe, whether animate or inanimate, instead of serving the ends of man, is at best indifferent, at worst savagely hostile. Evolution to whose operation the emergence of man is due is a ceaseless battle among members of different species, one species being gobbled up by another, only the fittest surviving. Far from being the gentlest and most highly moral, man is simply the creature best fitted to survive, the most efficient if not the most rapacious and insatiable killer. And in this unplanned, fortuitous, monstrous, savage world man is madly trying to snatch a few brief moments of joy, in the short intervals during which he is free from pain, sickness, persecution, war or famine until, finally, his life is snuffed out in death. Science has helped us to know and understand this world, but what purpose or meaning can it find in it?

Complaints such as these do not mean quite the same to everybody, but one thing, I think, they mean to most people: science shows life to be meaningless, because life is without purpose. The medieval world picture provided life with a purpose, hence medieval Christians could believe that life had a meaning. The scientific account of the world takes away life's purpose and with it its meaning.

There are, however, two quite different senses of "purpose." Which one is meant? Has science deprived human life of purpose in both senses? And if not, is it a harmless sense, in which human existence has been robbed of purpose? Could human existence still have meaning if it did not have a purpose in that sense?

What are the two senses? In the first and basic sense, purpose is normally attributed only to persons or their behaviour as in "Did you have a purpose in leaving the ignition on?" In the second sense, purpose is normally attributed only to things, as in "What is the purpose of that gadget you installed in the workshop?" The two uses are intimately connected. We cannot attribute a purpose to a thing without implying that someone did something, in the doing of which he had some purpose, namely, to bring about the thing with the purpose. Of course, *his* purpose is not identical with *its* purpose. In hiring labourers and engineers and buying materials and a site for a factory and the like, the entrepreneur's purpose, let us say, is to manufacture cars, but the purpose of cars is to serve as a means of transportation.

There are many things that a man may do, such as buying and selling, hiring labourers, ploughing, felling trees, and the like, which it is foolish, pointless, silly, perhaps crazy, to do if one has no purpose in doing them. A man who does these things without a purpose is engaging in inane, futile pursuits. Lives crammed full with such activities devoid of purpose are pointless, futile, worthless. Such lives may indeed be dismissed as meaningless. But it should also be perfectly clear that acceptance of the scientific world picture does not force us to regard our lives as being without a purpose in this sense. Science has not only not robbed us of any purpose which we had before, but it has furnished us with enormously greater power to achieve these purposes. Instead of praying for rain or a good harvest or offspring, we now use ice pellets, artificial manure, or artificial insemination.

By contrast, having or not having a purpose, in the other sense, is value neutral. We do not think more or less highly of a thing for having or not having a purpose. "Having a purpose," in this sense, confers no kudos, "being purposeless" carries no stigma. A row of trees growing near a farm may or may not have a purpose: it may or may not be a windbreak, may or may not have been planted or deliberately left standing there in order to prevent the wind from sweeping across the fields. We do not in any way disparage the trees if we say they have no purpose, but have just grown that way. They are as beautiful, made of as good wood, as valuable, as if they had a purpose. And, of course, they break the wind just as well. The same is true of living creatures. We do not disparage a dog when we say that it has no purpose, is not a sheep dog or a watch dog or a rabbiting dog, but just a dog that hangs around the house and is fed by us.

Man is in a different category, however. To attribute to a human being a purpose in that sense is not neutral, let alone complimentary: it is offensive. It is degrading for a man to be regarded as merely serving a purpose. If, at a garden party, I ask a man in livery, "What is your purpose?" I am insulting him. I might as well have asked, "What are you *for?*" Such questions reduce him to the level of a gadget, a domestic animal, or perhaps a slave. I imply that *we* allot to *him* the tasks, the goals, the aims which he is to pursue; that *his* wishes and desires and aspirations and purposes are to count for little or nothing. We are treating him, in Kant's phrase, merely as a means to our ends, not as an end in himself.

The Christian and the scientific world pictures do indeed differ fundamentally on this point. The latter robs man of a purpose in this sense. It sees him as a being with no purpose allotted to him by anyone but himself. It robs him of any goal, purpose, or destiny appointed for him by any outside agency. The Christian world picture, on the other hand, sees man as a creature, a divine artefact, something halfway between a robot (manufactured) and an animal (alive), a homunculus, or perhaps Frankenstein, made in God's laboratory, with a purpose or task assigned him by his Maker.

However, lack of purpose in this sense does not in any way detract from the meaningfulness of life. I suspect that many who reject the scientific outlook because it involves the loss of purpose of life, and therefore meaning, are guilty of a confusion between the two senses of "purpose" just distinguished. They confusedly think that if the scientific world picture is true, then their lives

must be futile because that picture implies that man has no purpose given him from without. But this is muddled thinking, for, as has already been shown, pointlessness, is implied only by purposelessness in the other sense, which is not at all implied by the scientific picture of the world. These people mistakenly conclude that there can be no purpose *in* life because there is no purpose *of* life; that *men* cannot themselves adopt and achieve purposes because *man*, unlike a robot or a watch dog, is not a creature with a purpose.[2]

However, not all people taking this view are guilty of the above confusion. Some really hanker after a purpose of life in this sense. To some people the greatest attraction of the medieval world picture is the belief in an omnipotent, omniscient, and all-good Father, the view of themselves as His children who worship Him, of their proper attitude to what befalls them as submission, humility, resignation in His will, and what is often described as the "creaturely feeling."[3] All these are attitudes and feelings appropriate to a being that stands to another in the same sort of relation, though of course on a higher plane, in which a helpless child stands to his progenitor. Many regard the scientific picture of the world as cold, unsympathetic, unhomely, frightening, because it does not provide for any appropriate object of this creaturely attitude. There is nothing and no one in the world, as science depicts it, in which we can have faith or trust, on whose guidance we can rely, to whom we can turn for consolation, whom we can worship or submit to—except other human beings. This may be felt as a keen disappointment, because it shows that the meaning of life cannot lie in submission to His will, in acceptance of whatever may come, and in worship. But it does not imply that life can have *no* meaning. It merely implies that it must have a different meaning from that which it was thought to have. Just as it is a great shock for a child to find that he must stand on his own feet, that his father and mother no longer provide for him, so a person who has lost his faith in God must reconcile himself to the idea that he has to stand on his own feet, alone in the world except for whatever friends he may succeed in making.

But is not this to miss the point of the Christian teaching? Surely, Christianity can tell us the meaning of life because it tells us the grand and noble end for which God has created the universe and man. No human life, however pointless it may seem, is meaningless because in being part of God's plan, every life is assured of significance.

This point is well taken. It brings to light a distinction of some importance: we call a person's life meaningful not only if it is worthwhile, but also if he has helped in the realization of some plan or purpose transcending his own concerns. A person who knows he must soon die a painful death, can give significance to the remainder of his doomed life by, say, allowing certain experiments to be performed on him which will be useful in the fight against cancer. In a similar way, only on a much more elevated plane, every man, however humble or plagued by suffering, is guaranteed significance by the knowledge that he is participating in God's purpose.

What, then, on the Christian view, is the grand and noble end for which God has created the world and man in it? We can immediately dismiss that still popular opinion that the smallness of our intellect prevents us from stating meaningfully God's design in all its imposing grandeur.[4] This view cannot possibly be a satisfactory answer to our question about the purpose of life. It is, rather, a confession of the impossibility of giving one. If anyone thinks that this "answer" can remove the sting from the impression of meaninglessness and insignificance in our lives, he cannot have been stung very hard.

If, then, we turn to those who are willing to state God's purpose in so many words, we encounter two insuperable difficulties. The first is to find a purpose grand and noble enough to explain and justify the great amount of undeserved suffering in this world. We are inevitably filled by a sense of bathos when we read statements such as this: ". . . history is the scene of a divine purpose, in which the whole history is included, and Jesus

of Nazareth is the centre of that purpose, both as revelation and as achievement, as the fulfillment of all that was past, and the promise of all that was to come. . . . If God is God, and if He made all these things, why did He do it? . . . God created a universe, bounded by the categories of time, space, matter, and causality, because He desired to enjoy for ever the society of a fellowship of finite and redeemed spirits which have made to His love the response of free and voluntary love and service?[5] Surely this cannot be right? Could a God be called omniscient, omnipotent, *and* all-good who, for the sake of satisfying his desire to be loved and served, imposes (or has to impose) on his creatures the amount of undeserved suffering we find in the world?

There is, however, a much more serious difficulty still: God's purpose in making the universe must be stated in terms of a dramatic story many of whose key incidents symbolize religious conceptions and practices which we no longer find morally acceptable: the imposition of a taboo on the fruits of a certain tree, the sin and guilt incurred by Adam and Eve by violating the taboo, the wrath of God,[6] the curse of Adam and Eve and all their progeny, the expulsion from Paradise, the Atonement by Christ's bloody sacrifice on the cross which makes available by way of the sacraments God's Grace by which alone men can be saved (thereby, incidentally, establishing the valuable power of priests to forgive sins and thus alone make possible a man's entry to heaven,[7]) Judgment Day on which the sheep are separated from the goats and the latter condemned to eternal torment in hell-fire.

Obviously it is much more difficult to formulate a purpose for creating the universe and man that will justify the enormous amount of undeserved suffering which we find around us, if that story has to be fitted in as well. For now we have to explain not only why an omnipotent, omniscient, and all-good God should create such a universe and such a man, but also why, foreseeing every move of the feeble, weak-willed, ignorant, and covetous creature to be created, He should nevertheless have created him and, having done so, should be incensed and outraged by man's sin, and why He should deem it necessary to sacrifice His own son on the cross to atone for this sin which was, after all, only a disobedience of one of his commands, and why this atonement and consequent redemption could not have been followed by man's return to Paradise—particularly of those innocent children who had not yet sinned—and why, on Judgment Day, this merciful God should condemn some to eternal torment.[8] It is not surprising that in the face of these and other difficulties, we find, again and again, a return to the first view: that God's purpose cannot meaningfully be stated.

It will perhaps be objected that no Christian to-day believes in the dramatic history of the world as I have presented it. But this is not so. It is the official doctrine of the Roman Catholic, the Greek Orthodox, and a large section of the Anglican Church.[9] Nor does Protestantism substantially alter this picture. In fact, by insisting on "Justification by Faith Alone" and by rejecting the ritualistic, magical character of the medieval Catholic interpretation of certain elements in the Christian religion, such as indulgences, the sacraments, and prayer, while at the same time insisting on the necessity of grace, Protestantism undermined the moral element in medieval Christianity expressed in the Catholics' emphasis on personal merit.[10] Protestantism, by harking back to St. Augustine, who clearly realized the incompatibility of grace and personal merit,[11] opened the way for Calvin's doctrine of Predestination (the intellectual parent of that form of rigid determinism which is usually blamed on science) and Salvation or Condemnation from all eternity.[12] Since Roman Catholics, Lutherans, Calvinists, Presbyterians and Baptists officially subscribe to the views just outlined, one can justifiably claim that the overwhelming majority of professing Christians hold or ought to hold them.

It might still be objected that the best and most modern views are wholly different. I have not the necessary knowledge to pronounce on the accuracy of this claim. It may

well be true that the best and most modern views are such as Professor Braithwaite's who maintains that Christianity is, roughly speaking, "morality plus stories," where the stories are intended merely to make the strict moral teaching both more easily understandable and more palatable.[13] Or it may be that one or the other of the modern views on the nature and importance of the dramatic story told in the sacred Scriptures is the best. My reply is that even if it is true, it does not prove what I wish to disprove, that one can extract a sensible answer to our question, "What is the meaning of life?" from the kind of story subscribed to by the overwhelming majority of Christians, who would, moreover, reject any such modernist interpretation at least as indignantly as the scientific account. Moreover, though such views can perhaps avoid some of the worst absurdities of the traditional story, they are hardly in a much better position to state the purpose for which God has created the universe and man in it, because they cannot overcome the difficulty of finding a purpose grand and noble enough to justify the enormous amount of undeserved suffering in the world.

Let us, however, for argument's sake, waive all these objections. There remains one fundamental hurdle which no form of Christianity can overcome: the fact that it demands of man a morally repugnant attitude towards the universe. It is now very widely held[14] that the basic element of the Christian religion is an attitude of worship towards a being supremely worthy of being worshipped and that it is religious feelings and experiences which apprise their owner of such a being and which inspire in him the knowledge or the feeling of complete dependence, awe, worship, mystery, and self-abasement. There is, in other words, a bi-polarity (the famous "I-Thou relationship") in which the object, "the wholly-other," is exalted whereas the subject is abased to the limit. Rudolf Otto has called this the "creature-feeling"[15] and he quotes as an expression of it, Abraham's words when venturing to plead for the men of Sodom: "Behold now, I have taken upon me to speak

unto the Lord, which am but dust and ashes."
(Gen. XVIII.27). Christianity thus demands
of men an attitude inconsistent with one of
the presuppositions of morality: that man is
not wholly dependent on something else, that
man has free will, that man is in principle
capable of responsibility. We have seen that
the concept of grace is the Christian attempt
to reconcile the claim of total dependence
and the claim of individual responsibility
(partial independence), and it is obvious that
such attempts must fail. We may dismiss certain doctrines, such as the doctrine of original
sin or the doctrine of eternal hellfire or the
doctrine that there can be no salvation outside the Church as extravagant and peripheral, but we cannot reject the doctrine of total
dependence without rejecting the characteristically Christian attitude as such.

Perhaps some of you will have felt that I have
been shirking the real problem. To many people the crux of the matter seems as follows.
How can there be any meaning in our life if it
ends in death? What meaning can there be in
it that our inevitable death does not destroy?
How can our existence be meaningful if there
is no after-life in which perfect justice is
meted out? How can life have any meaning if
all it holds out to us are a few miserable
earthly pleasures and even these to be enjoyed
only rarely and for such a piteously short
time?

I believe this is the point which exercises
most people most deeply. Kirilov, in Dostoevsky's novel, *The Possessed*, claims, just before
committing suicide, that as soon as we realize
that there is no God, we cannot live any
longer, we must put an end to our lives. One
of the reasons which he gives is that when we
discover that there is no paradise, we have
nothing to live for.

". . . there was a day on earth, and in the
middle of the earth were three crosses. One
on the cross had such faith that He said to
another, 'To-day thou shalt be with me in
paradise.' The day came to an end, both died,
and they went, but they found neither paradise nor resurrection. The saying did not

come true. Listen: that man was the highest
of all on earth. . . . There has never been any
one like Him before or since, and never will
be. . . . And if that is so, if the laws of Nature
did not spare even *Him*, and made even Him
live in the midst of lies and die for a lie, then
the whole planet is a lie and is based on a lie
and a stupid mockery. So the very laws of the
planet are a lie and a farce of the devil. What,
then, is there to live for?"[16] And Tolstoy, too,
was nearly driven to suicide when he came to
doubt the existence of God and an after-
life.[17] And this is true of many.

What, then, is it that inclines us to think
that if life is to have a meaning, there would
be an after-life? It is this. The Christian
world view contains the following three
propositions. The first is that since the Fall,
God's curse of Adam and Eve, and the expulsion from Paradise, life on earth for mankind
has not been worth while, but a vale of tears,
one long chain of misery, suffering, unhappiness, and injustice. The second is that a perfect after-life is awaiting us after the death of
the body. The third is that we can enter this
perfect life only on certain conditions, among
which is also the condition of enduring our
earthly existence to its bitter end. In this way,
our earthly existence which, in itself, would
not (at least for many people if not all) be
worth living, acquires meaning and significance: only if we endure it, can we gain
admission to the realm of the blessed.

It might be doubted whether this view is
still held to-day. However, there can be no
doubt that even to-day we all imbibe a good
deal of this view with our earliest education.
In sermons, the contrast between the perfect
life of the blessed and our life of sorrow and
drudgery is frequently driven home and we
hear it again and again that Christianity has a
message of hope and consolation for all those
"who are weary and heavy laden."[18]

It is not surprising, then, that when the
implications of the scientific world picture
begin to sink in, when we come to have
doubts about the existence of God and
another life, we are bitterly disappointed. For
if there is no afterlife, then all we are left is

our earthly life which we have come to regard as a necessary evil, the painful fee of admission to the land of eternal bliss. But if there is no eternal bliss to come and if this hell on earth is all, why hang on till the horrible end?

Our disappointment therefore arises out of these two propositions, that the earthly life is not worth living, and that there is another perfect life of eternal happiness and joy which we may enter upon if we satisfy certain conditions. We can regard our lives as meaningful, if we believe both. We cannot regard them as meaningful if we believe merely the first and not the second. It seems to me inevitable that people who are taught something of the history of science, will have serious doubts about the second. If they cannot overcome these, as many will be unable to do, then they must either accept the sad view that their life is meaningless or they must abandon the first proposition: that this earthly life is not worth living. They must find the meaning of their life in this earthly existence. But is this possible?

A moment's examination will show us that the Christian evaluation of our earthly life as worthless, which we accept in our moments of pessimism and dissatisfaction, is not one that we normally accept. Consider only the question of murder and suicide. On the Christian view, other things being equal, the most kindly thing to do would be for every one of us to kill as many of our friends and dear ones as still have the misfortune to be alive, and then to commit suicide without delay, for every moment spent in this life is wasted. On the Christian view, God has not made it that easy for us. He has forbidden us to hasten others or ourselves into the next life. Our bodies are his private property and must be allowed to wear themselves out in the way decided by Him, however painful and horrible that may be. We are, as it were, driving a burning car. There is only one way out, to jump clear and let it hurtle to destruction. But the owner of the car has forbidden it on pain of eternal tortures worse than burning. And so we do better to burn to death inside.

On this view, murder is a less serious wrong than suicide. For murder can always be confessed and repented and therefore forgiven, suicide cannot—unless we allow the ingenious way out chosen by the heroine of Graham Greene's play, *The Living Room*, who swallows a slow but deadly poison and, while awaiting its taking effect, repents having taken it. Murder, on the other hand, is not so serious because, in the first place, it need not rob the victim of anything but the last lap of his march in the vale of tears, and, in the second place, it can always be forgiven. Hamlet, it will be remembered, refrains from killing his uncle during the latter's prayers because, as a true Christian, he believes that killing his uncle at that point, when the latter has purified his soul by repentance, would merely be doing him a good turn, for murder at such a time would simply despatch him to undeserved and everlasting happiness.

These views strike us as odd, to say the least. They are the logical consequence of the official medieval evaluation of this our earthly existence. If this life is not worth living, then taking it is not robbing the person concerned of much. The only thing wrong with it is the damage to God's property, which is the same both in the case of murder and suicide. We do not take this view at all. Our view, on the contrary, is that murder is the most serious wrong because it consists in taking away from some one else against his will his most precious possession, his life. For this reason, when a person suffering from an incurable disease asks to be killed, the mercy killing of such a person is regarded as a much less serious crime than murder because, in such a case, the killer is not robbing the other of a good against his will. Suicide is not regarded as a real crime at all, for we take the view that a person can do with his own possessions what he likes.

However, from the fact that these are our normal opinions, we can infer nothing about their truth. After all, we could easily be mistaken. Whether life is or is not worthwhile, is a value judgment. Perhaps all this is merely a matter of opinion or taste. Perhaps no objective answer can be given. Fortunately, we need not enter deeply into these difficult and controversial questions. It is quite easy to show that the medieval evaluation of earthly life is based on a misguided procedure.

Let us remind ourselves briefly of how we arrive at our value judgments. When we determine the merits of students, meals, tennis players, bulls, or bathing belles, we do so on the basis of some criteria and some standard or norm. Criteria and standards notoriously vary from field to field and even from case to case. But that does not mean that we have *no* idea about what are the appropriate criteria or standards to use. It would not be fitting to apply the criteria for judging bulls to the judgment of students or bathing belles. They score on quite different points. And even where the same criteria are appropriate as in the judgment of students enrolled in different schools and universities, the standards will vary from one institution to another. Pupils who would only just pass in one, would perhaps obtain honours in another. The higher the standard applied, the lower the marks, that is, the merit conceded to the candidate.

The same procedure is applicable also in the evaluation of a life. We examine it on the basis of certain criteria and standards. The medieval Christian view uses the criteria of the ordinary man: a life is judged by what the person concerned can get out of it: the balance of happiness over unhappiness, pleasure over pain, bliss over suffering. Our earthly life is judged not worthwhile because it contains much unhappiness, pain, and suffering, little happiness, pleasure, and bliss. The next life is judged worthwhile because it provides eternal bliss and no suffering.

Armed with these criteria, we can compare the life of this man and that, and judge which is more worthwhile, which has a greater balance of bliss over suffering. But criteria alone enable us merely to make comparative judgments of value, not absolute ones. We can say which is more and which is less worthwhile, but we cannot say which is worthwhile and which is not. In order to determine the latter, we must introduce a standard. But what standard ought we to choose?

Ordinarily, the standard we employ is the average of the kind. We call a man and a tree tall if they are well above the average of their kind. We do not say that Jones is a short man because he is shorter than a tree. We do not judge a boy a bad student because his answer to a question in the Leaving Examination is much worse than that given in reply to the same question by a young man sitting for his finals for the Bachelor's degree.

The same principles must apply to judging lives. When we ask whether a given life was or was not worthwhile, then we must take into consideration the range of worthwhileness which ordinary lives normally cover. Our end poles of the scale must be the best possible and the worst possible life that one finds. A good and worthwhile life is one that is well above average. A bad one is one well below.

The Christian evaluation of earthly lives is misguided because it adopts quite unjustifiably high standard. Christianity singles out the major shortcomings of our earthly existence: there is not enough happiness; there is too much suffering; the good and bad points are quite unequally and unfairly distributed; the underprivileged and underendowed do not get adequate compensation; it last only a short time. It then quite accurately depicts the perfect or ideal life as that which does not have any of these shortcomings. Its next step is to promise the believer that he will be able to enjoy this perfect life later on. And then it adopts as its standard of judgment the perfect life, dismissing as inadequate anything that falls short of it. Having dismissed earthly life as miserable, it further damns it by characterizing most of the pleasures of which earthly existence allows as bestial, gross, vile, and sinful, or alternatively as not really pleasurable.

This procedure is as illegitimate as if I were to refuse to call anything tall unless it is infinitely tall, or anything beautiful unless it is perfectly flawless, or any one strong unless he is omnipotent. Even if it were true that there is available to us an after-life which is flawless and perfect, it would still not be legitimate to judge earthly lives by this standard. We do not fail every candidate who is not an Einstein.

And if we do not believe in an after-life, we must of course use ordinary earthly standards.

I have so far only spoken of the worth-whileness, only of what a person can get out of a life. There are other kinds of appraisal. Clearly, we evaluate people's lives not merely from the point of view of what they yield to the persons that lead them, but also from that of other men on whom these lives have impinged. We judge a life more significant if the person has contributed to the happiness of others, whether directly by what he did for others, or by the plans, discoveries, inventions, and work he performed. Many lives that hold little in the way of pleasure or happiness for its owner are highly significant and valuable, deserve admiration and respect on account of the contributions made.

It is now quite clear that death is simply irrelevant. If life can be worthwhile at all, then it can be so even though it be short. And if it is not worthwhile at all, then an eternity of it is simply a nightmare. It may be sad that we have to leave this beautiful world, but it is so only if and because it is beautiful. And it is no less beautiful for coming to an end. I rather suspect that an eternity of it might make us less appreciative, and in the end it would be tedious.

It will perhaps be objected now that I have not really demonstrated that life has a meaning, but merely that it can be worthwhile or have value. It must be admitted that there is a perfectly natural interpretation of the question, "What is the meaning of life?" on which my view actually proves that life has no meaning. I mean the interpretation discussed [earlier] in . . . this lecture, where I attempted to show that, if we accept the explanations of natural science, we cannot believe that living organisms have appeared on earth in accordance with the deliberate plan of some intelligent being. Hence, on this view, life cannot be said to have a purpose, in the sense in which man-made things have a purpose. Hence it cannot be said to have a meaning or significance in that sense.

However, this conclusion is innocuous. People are disconcerted by the thought that *life as such* has no meaning in that sense only because they very naturally think it entails that no individual life can have meaning either. They naturally assume that *this* life or *that* can have meaning only if *life as such* has meaning. But it should by now be clear that your life and mine may or may not have meaning (in one sense) even if life as such has none (in the other). Of course, it follows from this that your life may have meaning while mine has not. The Christian view guarantees a meaning (in one sense) to every life, the scientific view does not (in any sense). By relating the question of meaningfulness of life to the particular circumstances of an individual's existence, the scientific view leaves it an open question whether an individual's life has meaning or not. It is, however, clear that the latter is the important sense of "having a meaning." Christians, too, must feel that their life is wasted and meaningless if they have not achieved salvation. To know that even such lost lives have a meaning in another sense is no consolation to them. What matters is not that life should have a guaranteed meaning, whatever happens here or hereafter, but that, by luck (Grace) or the right temperament and attitude (Faith) or a judicious life (Works) a person should make the most of his life.

"But here lies the rub," it will be said. "Surely, it makes all the difference whether there is an after-life. This is where morality comes in." It would be a mistake to believe that. Morality is not the meting out of punishment and reward. To be moral is to refrain from doing to others what, if they followed reason, they would not do to themselves, and to do for others what, if they followed reason, they would want to have done. It is, roughly speaking, to recognize that others, too, have a right to a worthwhile life. Being moral does not make one's own life worthwhile, it helps others to make theirs so.

. . . I have attempted to explain why so many people come to the conclusion that human existence is meaningless and to show that this conclusion is false. In my opinion, this pessimism rests on a combination of two beliefs, both partly true and partly false: the belief that the meaningfulness of life depends on the satisfaction of at least three conditions, and the belief that this universe satisfies none of them. The conditions are, first, that the universe is intelligible, second, that life has a purpose, and third, that all men's hopes and desires can ultimately be satisfied. It seemed to medieval Christians and it seems to many Christians to-day that Christianity offers a picture of the world which can meet these conditions. To many Christians and non-Christians alike it seems that the scientific world picture is incompatible with that of Christianity, therefore with the view that these three conditions are met, therefore with the view that life has a meaning. Hence they feel that they are confronted by the dilemma of accepting either a world picture incompatible with the discoveries of science or the view that life is meaningless.

I have attempted to show that the dilemma is unreal because life can be meaningful even if not all of these conditions are met. My main conclusion, therefore, is that acceptance of the scientific world picture provides no reason for saying that life is meaningless, but on the contrary every reason for saying that there are many lives which are meaningful and significant. My subsidiary conclusion is that one of the reasons frequently offered for retaining the Christian world picture, namely, that its acceptance gives us a guarantee of a meaning for human existence, is unsound. We can see that our lives can have a meaning even if we abandon it and adopt the scientific world picture instead.

Notes

1. Count Leo Tolstoy, "A Confession," reprinted in *A Confession, The Gospel in Brief, and What I Believe*, No. 229, The World's Classics (London: Geoffrey Cumberlege, 1940).

2. See e.g. "Is Life Worth Living?" B.B.C. Talk by the Rev. John Sutherland Bonnell in *Asking Them Questions*, Third Series, ed. by R. S. Wright (London: Geoffrey Cumberlege, 1950).

3. See e.g. Rudolf Otto, *The Idea of the Holy*, pp. 9–11. See also C. A. Campbell, *On Selfhood and Godhood*

(London: George Allen & Unwin Ltd., 1957) p. 246, and H. J. Paton, *The Modern Predicament*, pp. 69–71.

4. For a discussion of this issue, see the eighteenth century controversy between Deists and Theists, for instance, in Sir Leslie Stephen's *History of English Thought in the Eighteenth Century* (London: Smith, Elder & Co., 1902) pp. 112–119 and pp. 134–163. See also the attacks by Toland and Tindal on "the mysterious" in *Christianity not Mysterious* and *Christianity as Old as the Creation, or the Gospel a Republication of the Religion of Nature*, resp., parts of which are reprinted in Henry Bettenson's *Doctrines of the Christian Church*, pp. 426–431. For modern views maintaining that mysteriousness is an essential element in religion, see Rudolf Otto, *The Idea of the Holy*, esp. pp. 25–40, and most recently M. B. Foster, *Mystery and Philosophy* (London: S.C.M. Press, 1957) esp. Chs. IV. and VI. For the view that statements about God must be nonsensical or absurd, see e.g. H. J. Paton, op. cit. pp. 119–120, 367–369. See also "Theology and Falsification" in *New Essays in Philosophical Theology*, ed. by A. Flew and A. MacIntyre (London: S.C.M. Press, 1955) pp. 96–131; also N. McPherson, "Religion as the Inexpressible," ibid., esp. pp. 137–143.

5. Stephen Neill, *Christian Faith To-day* (London: Penguin Books, 1955) pp. 240–241.

6. It is difficult to feel the magnitude of this first sin unless one takes seriously the words "Behold, the man has eaten of the fruit of the tree of knowledge of good and evil, and is become as one of us; and now, may he not put forth his hand, and take also of the tree of life, and eat, and live for ever?" Genesis iii, 22.

7. See in this connection the pastoral letter of 2nd February, 1905, by Johannes Katschtaler, Prince Bishop of Salzburg on the honour due to priests, contained in *Quellen zur Geschichte des Papsttums*, by Mirbt pp. 497–499, translated and reprinted in *The Protestant Tradition*, by J. S. Whale (Cambridge: University Press, 1955) pp. 259–262.

8. How impossible it is to make sense of this story has been demonstrated beyond any doubt by Tolstoy in his famous "Conclusion of A Criticism of Dogmatic Theology," reprinted in *A Confession, The Gospel in Brief, and What I Believe*.

9. See "The Nicene Creed," "The Tridentine Profession of Faith," "The Syllabus of Errors," reprinted in *Documents of the Christian Church*, pp. 34, 373 and 380 resp.

10. See e.g. J. S. Whale, *The Protestant Tradition*, Ch. IV., esp. pp. 48–56.

11. See ibid., pp. 61 ff.

12. See "The Confession of Augsburg" esp. Articles II., IV., XVIII., XIX., XX.; "Christianae Religionis Institutio," "The Westminster Confession of Faith," esp. Articles III., VI., IX., X., XI., XVI., XVII.; "The Baptist Confession of Faith," esp. Articles III., XXI., XXIII., reprinted in *Documents of the Christian Church*, pp. 294 ff., 298 ff., 344 ff., 349 ff.

13. See e.g. his *An Empiricist's View of the Nature of Religious Belief* (Eddington Memorial Lecture).

14. See e.g. the two series of Gifford Lectures most

recently published: *The Modern Predicament* by H. J. Paton (London: George Allen & Unwin Ltd., 1955) pp. 69 ff., and *On Selfhood and Godhood* by C. A. Campbell (London: George Allen & Unwin Ltd., 1957) pp. 231–250.

15. Rudolf Otto, *The Idea of the Holy*, p. 9.

16. Fyodor Dostoyevsky, *The Devils* (London: The Penguin Classics, 1953) pp. 613–614.

17. Leo Tolstoy, *A Confession, The Gospel in Brief, and What I Believe*, The World's Classics, p. 24.

18. See for instance J. S. Whale, *Christian Doctrine*, pp. 171, 176–178, etc. See also Stephen Neill, *Christian Faith To-day*, p. 241.

At Home in the Universe

Stuart Kauffman

Stuart Kauffman begins this essay with a reminder of the story of paradise lost through the progress of modern science. He emphasizes the role that Darwin plays in this story. According to the standard version of the theory of evolution, all life seems to arise from blind natural selection operating on chance mutations. He suggests that we do not feel at home in such a universe.

In contrast to this picture, Kauffman argues that the order we see in organisms is a function of laws of self-organization that provide the raw material on which natural selection works. He defends a theory of emergence in which order arises naturally out of systems that exist "at the edge of chaos." Several evocative examples suggest that when some systems enter a transition to a chaotic state, they become organized in novel ways. Kauffman sees self-organization at the edge of chaos as a promising new paradigm for understanding complex systems. He also sees it as an opportunity to regain our sense of being at home in the world. If science gives us a worldview in which life mysteriously arises out of complex and unpredictable processes, then it also provides us with a source of the sacred. The problem of how we can see our lives to be meaningful arises not out of science per se, but out of a particular view about the universe that science may abandon. Stuart Kauffman was professor of biochemistry at the University of Pennsylvania, and he is now external professor at the Santa Fe Institute.

As you read through this essay, consider the following:

1. Why does Kauffman think that we must reinvent the sacred?
2. According to Kauffman, how does Darwin contribute to a worldview in which we do not feel at home?
3. What does Kauffman mean by a theory of emergence?
4. What is "the edge of chaos" and how does it affect our ability to predict what will happen?
5. According to Kauffman, why is it easier for us to feel at home in a world characterized by the laws of self-organization?
6. In what kind of a worldview would you feel at home? Is such a worldview compatible with science?

What stories we tell ourselves, of origins and endings, of form and transformation, of gods, the word, and law. All people, at all times, must have created myths and stories to sketch a picture of our place under the sun. Cro-Magnon man, whose paintings of animals seem to exhibit a respect and awe, let alone line and form, that equals or surpasses those of later millennia, must have spun answers to these questions: Who are we? Where did we come from? Why are we here? Did Neanderthal, *Homo habilis*, or *Homo erectus* ask? Around which fire in the past 3 million years of hominid evolution did these questions first arise? Who knows.

Somewhere along our path, paradise has been lost, lost to the Western mind, and in the spreading world civilization, lost to our collective mind. John Milton must have been the last superb poet of Western civilization who could have sought to justify the ways of God to man in those early years foreshadowing the modern era. Paradise has been lost, not to sin, but to science. Once, a scant few centuries ago, we of the West believed ourselves the chosen of God, made in his image, keeping his word in a creation wrought by his love for us. Now, only 400 years later, we find ourselves on a tiny planet, on the edge of a humdrum galaxy among billions like it scattered across vast megaparsecs, around the curvature of space-time back to the Big Bang. We are but accidents, we're told. Purpose and value are ours alone to make. Without Satan and God, the universe now appears the neutral home of matter, dark and light, and is utterly indifferent. We bustle, but are no longer at home in the ancient sense.

We accept, of course, that the rise of science and the consequent technological explosion has driven us to our secular worldview. Yet a spiritual hunger remains. I recently met N. Scott Momaday, a Native American author, winner of the Pulitzer Prize, at a small meeting in northern New Mexico intended to try to articulate the fundamental issues facing humanity. (As if a small group of thinkers could possibly succeed.) Momaday told us that the central issue we confront is to reinvent the sacred. He told of a sacred shield of the Kiowa, sanctified by the sacrifices and suffering of the warriors who had been honored to hold it in battle. The shield had been stolen following a battle with U.S. cavalry forces after the Civil War. He told us of the recent discovery and return of the shield from the family home of the post–Civil War general who had taken it. Momaday's deep voice fell gently over us as he described the welcome set forth for that shield and the place it holds, quiet, somber, still, revered for the passion and suffering distilled within its arc.

Momaday's search for the sacred settled deep on me, for I hold the hope that what some are calling the new sciences of complexity may help us find anew our place in the universe, that through this new science, we may recover our sense of worth, our sense of the sacred, just as the Kiowa ultimately recovered that sacred shield. At the same meeting, I suggested that the most important problem confronting humanity was the emergence of a world civilization, its profound promise, and the cultural dislocations this transformation will cause. To undergird the pluralistic global community that is aborning, we shall need, I think, an expanded intellectual basis—a new way to think about origins, evolution, and the profound naturalness of life and its myriad patterns of unfolding. This book is an effort to contribute to that new view, for the emerging sciences of complexity, as we shall see, offer fresh support for the idea of a pluralistic democratic society, providing evidence that it is not merely a human creation but part of the natural order of things. One is always wary of deducing from first principles the political order of one's own society. The nineteenth-century philosopher James Mill once succeeded in deducing from first principles that a constitutional monarchy, remarkably like that in England early in the last century, was the highest natural form of governance. But, as I hope to show, the very laws of complexity my colleagues and I are seeking suggest that democracy has evolved as perhaps the optimal mechanism to achieve the best attainable compromises among conflicting practical, political, and moral interests. Momaday must be right as well. We shall also need to reinvent the sacred—this sense of our own deep worth—and reinvest it at the core of the new civilization.

The story of our loss of paradise is familiar but worth retelling. Until Copernicus, we believed ourselves to be at the center of the universe. Nowadays, in our proclaimed sophistication, we look askance at a church that sought to suppress a heliocentric view. Knowledge for knowledge's sake, we say. Yes, of course. But was the church's concern with the disruption of a moral order really no more than a narrow vanity? To pre-Copernican Christian civilization, the geocentric view was no mere matter of science. Rather, it was the cornerstone evidence that the entire universe revolved around us. With God, angels, man, the beasts, and fertile plants made for our benefit, with the sun and stars wheeling overhead, we knew our place: at the center of God's creation. The church feared rightly that the Copernican views would ultimately dismantle the unity of a thousand-year-old tradition of duty and rights, of obligations and roles, of moral fabric.

Copernicus blew his society open. Galileo and Kepler did not help much either, particularly Kepler, with his demonstration that planets orbit in ellipses rather than in the rational perfect circles envisioned by Aristotle. Kepler is such a wonderful transitional figure, a descendant of the tradition of the magus, or great magi a century earlier. He had not sought ellipses, but rather harmonic orbits corresponding to the five perfect solids, from which Plato himself tried to build the world.

Then Newton, hero to us all, escaped the plague and wrenched Everyman into a universe even farther from paradise. What a giant step he took. Just imagine what it must have felt like to Newton as his new laws of mechanics took form in his mind. What wonder he must have felt. With a mere three laws of motion and a universal law of gravitation in hand, Newton not only derived tides and orbits, but unleashed on the Western mind a clockwork universe. Before Newton, a scholastic philosopher, certain that an arrow arced toward its target because, as Aristotle taught, it was constantly acted on by a mysterious force, or impetus, could easily believe in a God who also moved things along by according them his sustained attention. Such a God might look after one if properly addressed. Such a God might return one to paradise. But after Newton, the laws alone sufficed. The universe could be wound up by God and released, thereafter left to tick inevitably toward eternity under the unfolding of his law, without further intervention. If the stars and tides moved without divine intervention, thinking people began to find it more difficult to hope for such intervention in their own affairs.

But there was some consolation. If the planets and all of inanimate matter obey eternal laws, then surely living things, with man at their summit, sitting at the top of the great chain of being, must reflect God's intention. Adam himself had named them all: insects, fish, reptiles, birds, mammals, man. Like the hierarchy of the church itself—laity, priest, bishop, archbishop, pope, saints, angels—the great chain of being stretched from the lowliest to the Almighty.

How Darwin and his theory of evolution by natural selection devastated all this! We, who are heritors of Darwin, who see the living world through the categories he taught us more than a century ago, even we have trouble with the implications: man as the result of a chain of accidental mutations, sifted by a law no more noble than survival of the fittest. Creation science is no accident in late-twentieth-century America. Its proponents adhere to it in an ardent effort to forestall the feared moral implications of humans as descendants of a haphazard lineage branching from some last common ancestor more remote in time than the Cambrian explosion some 500 million years ago. The science in creation science is no science at all, but is the moral anguish so foolish? Or should creationism be viewed rather more sympathetically—misguided, to be sure, but part of a broader quest to reinvent the sacred in our secular world? . . .

Darwin devastated this world. Species are not fixed by the squares of the Linnean chart; they evolve from one another. Natural selection acting on random variation, not God or some principle of Rational Morphology, accounted for the similarity of limb and fin, for creatures so marvelously attuned to their environments. The implications of these ideas, as understood by biologists today, have transformed humans, along with all other living forms, from works of a creator into ultimately historical accidents wrought by the opportunism of evolution. "Evolution is chance caught on the wing," wrote the biologist Jacques Monod. Evolution tinkers together contraptions, agreed François Jacob, the French geneticist who shared the Nobel with Monod. In the Judeo-Christian tradition, we had become used to thinking of ourselves as fallen angels. At least fallen angels have some hope of redemption and grace, of climbing back up the ecclesiastical ladder. Evolution left us stuck on the earth with no ladder to climb, contemplating our fate as nature's Rube Goldberg machines.

Random variation, selection sifting. Here is the core, the root. Here lies the brooding sense of accident, of historical contingency, of design by elimination. At least physics, cold in its calculus, implied a deep order, an inevitability. Biology has come to seem a science of the accidental, the ad hoc, and we just one of the fruits of this ad hocery. Were the tape played over, we like to say, the forms of organisms would surely differ dramatically. We humans, a trumped-up, tricked-out, horn-blowing, self-important presence on the globe, need never have occurred. So much for our pretensions; we are lucky to have our hour. So much, too, for paradise.

Where, then, does this order come from, this teeming life I see from my window: urgent spider making her living with her pre-nylon web, coyote crafty across the ridgetop, muddy Rio Grande aswarm with no-see-ems (an invisible insect peculiar to early evenings)? Since Darwin, we turn to a single, singular force, Natural Selection, which we might as well capitalize as though it were the new deity. Random variation, selection-sifting. Without it, we reason, there would be nothing but incoherent disorder.

I shall argue . . . that this idea is wrong. For, as we shall see, the emerging sciences of complexity begin to suggest that the order is not all accidental, that vast veins of spontaneous order lie at hand. Laws of complexity spontaneously generate much of the order of the natural world. It is only then that selection comes into play, further molding and refining. Such veins of spontaneous order have not been entirely unknown, yet they are just beginning to emerge as powerful new clues to the origins and evolution of life. We have all known that simple physical systems exhibit spontaneous order: an oil droplet in water forms a sphere; snowflakes exhibit their evanescent sixfold symmetry. What is new is that the range of spontaneous order is enormously greater than we have supposed. Profound order is being discovered in large, complex, and apparently random systems. I believe that this emergent order underlies not only the origin of life itself, but much of the order seen in organisms today. So, too, do many of my colleagues, who are starting to find overlapping evidence of such emergent order in all different kinds of complex systems.

The existence of spontaneous order is a stunning challenge to our settled ideas in biology since Darwin. Most biologists have believed for over a century that selection is the sole source of order in biology, that selection alone is the "tinkerer" that crafts the forms. But if the forms selection chooses among were generated by laws of complexity, then selection has always had a handmaiden. It is not, after all, the sole source of order, and organisms are not just tinkered-together contraptions, but expressions of deeper natural laws. If all this is true, what a revision of the Darwinian worldview will lie before us! Not we the accidental, but we the expected.

The revision of the Darwinian worldview will not be easy. Biologists have, as yet, no conceptual framework in which to study an evolutionary process that commingles both self-organization and selection. How does selection work on systems that already generate spontaneous order? Physics has its profound spontaneous order, but no need of selection. Biologists, subliminally aware of such spontaneous order, have nevertheless ignored it and focused almost entirely on selection. Without a framework to embrace both self-organization and selection, self-organization has been rendered almost invisible, like the background in a gestalt picture. With a sudden visual shift, the background can become the foreground, and the former foreground, selection, can become the background. Neither alone suffices. Life and its evolution have always depended on the mutual embrace of spontaneous order and selection's crafting of that order. We need to paint a new picture. . . .

. . . The past 550 million years have witnessed well-fossilized life-forms emerging onto and then ebbing from the stage. Speciation and extinction go roughly hand in hand. Indeed, recent evidence suggests that the highest rate of extinction, as well as speciation, occurred in the Cambrian itself. Over the next 100 million years, the average diversity of species increased to a kind of rough steady state. But that level was, and persistently is, perturbed by small and large avalanches of extinctions that wipe out modest numbers or large numbers of species, genera, or families. Many of these catastrophes may have been caused by small and large meteors. Indeed, the extinction at the end of the Cretaceous, which coincided with the denouement of the dinosaurs, was probably caused by a massive misfortune that landed near the Yucatán.

. . . It does not always take a meteor or some outside cataclysm to wipe out whole species. Rather, speciation and extinction seem very likely to reflect the spontaneous dynamics of a community of species. The very struggle to survive, to adapt to the small and large changes of one's coevolutionary partners, may ultimately drive some species to extinction while creating novel niches for others. Life, then, unrolls in an unending procession of change, with small and large bursts of speciations, and small and large bursts of extinctions, ringing out the old, ringing in the new. If this view is correct, then the patterns of life's bursts and burials are caused by internal processes, endogenous and natural. These patterns of speciations and extinctions, avalanching across ecosystems and time, are somehow self-organized, somehow collective emergent phenomena, somehow natural expressions of the laws of complexity we seek. And somehow, when understood, such patterns must afford us a deeper understanding of the game we have all joined, for we are all part of the same pageant.

No small matter these small and large avalanches of creativity and destruction, for the natural history of life for the past 550 million years has echoes of the same phenomena at all levels: from ecosystems to economic systems undergoing technological evolution, in which avalanches of new goods and technologies emerge and drive old ones extinct. Similar small and large avalanches even occur in evolving cultural systems. The natural history of life may harbor a new and unifying intellectual underpinning for our economic, cultural, and social life. . . . I suspect that the fate of all complex adapting systems in the biosphere—from single cells to economies— is to evolve to a natural state between order and chaos, a grand compromise between structure and surprise. Here, at this poised state, small and large avalanches of coevolutionary change propagate through the system as a consequence of the small, best choices of the actors themselves, competing and cooperating to survive. I will suggest that, on small and large scales, we all do the best we can but will eventually be hustled offstage by some unanticipated consequences of our own best efforts. We will find a place in the sun, poised on the edge of chaos, sustained for a time in that sun's radiance, but only for a moment before we slip from sight. Untold many actors come and go, each, as a fine playwright once said, strutting and fretting its hour upon the stage. A smiling irony is our fate.

We all make our livings—frog, fern, bracken, bird, seafarer, or landed gentry. From the metabolic mutualisms of legume root and nitrogen-fixing bacteria, by which each makes a nutrient needed by the other, to the latest research partnership between drug giant and small biotech firm, we are all selling and trading our stuff to one another to get our daily bread. And somehow, the burgeoning diversity of the Cambrian—where each new species offers a novel niche or two to the others that feed on it, flee from it, or share with it—looks rather like the burgeoning diversity of an economic system in which each new good or service affords a niche or two for other goods or services, whose providers thereby make a living. We are all trading our stuff to one another. We all must make our living. Might general laws govern all this activity? Might general laws govern phenomena ranging from the Cambrian explosion to our postmodern technological era, in which the exploding rate of innovation brings the time horizon of future shock ever closer? . . .

ORDER FOR FREE

The vast mystery of biology is that life should have emerged at all, that the order we see should have come to pass. A theory of emergence would account for the creation of the stunning order out our windows as a natural expression of some underlying laws. It would tell us if we are at home in the universe, expected in it, rather than present despite overwhelming odds.

Some words or phrases are evocative, even provocative. So it is with the word *emergent*. Commonly, we express this idea with the sentence, The whole is greater than the sum of its parts. The sentence is provocative, for what extra can be in the whole that is not in the parts? I believe that life itself is an emergent phenomenon, but I mean nothing mystical by this. . . . Sufficiently complex mixes of chemicals can spontaneously crystallize into systems with the ability to collectively catalyze the network of chemical reactions by which the molecules themselves are formed. Such collectively autocatalytic sets sustain themselves and reproduce. This is no less than what we call a living metabolism, the tangle of chemical reactions that power every one of our cells. Life, in this view, is an emergent phenomenon arising as the molecular diversity of a prebiotic chemical system increases beyond a threshold of complexity. If true, then life is not located in the property of any single molecule—in the details—but is a collective property of systems of interacting molecules. Life, in this view, emerged whole and has always remained whole. Life, in this view, is not to be located in its parts, but in the collective emergent properties of the whole they create. Although life as an emergent phenomenon may be profound, its fundamental holism and emergence are not at all mysterious. A set of molecules either does or does not have the property that it is able to catalyze its own formation and reproduction from some simple food molecules. No vital force or extra substance is present in the emergent, self-reproducing whole. But the collective system does possess a stunning property not possessed by any of its parts. It is able to reproduce itself and to evolve. The collective system is alive. Its parts are just chemicals.

One of the most awesome aspects of biological order in ontogeny, the development of an adult organism. In humans, this process starts with a single cell, the fertilized egg, or zygote. The zygote undergoes about 50 cell divisions to create about 1 quadrillion cells that form the newborn infant. At the same time, the single cell type of the zygote differentiates to form the roughly 260 cell types of the adult—liver parenchymal cells, nerve cells, red blood cells, muscle cells, and so forth. The genetic instructions controlling development lie in the DNA within the nucleus of each cell. This genetic system harbors about 100,000 different genes, each encoding a different protein. Remarkably, the set of genes in all cell types is virtually identical. Cells differ because different subsets of genes are active within them, producing various enzymes and other proteins. Red blood cells have hemoglobin, muscle cells abound in the actin and myosin that form muscle fibers, and so forth. The magic of ontogeny lies in the fact that genes and their RNA and protein products form a complex network, switching one another on and off in a wondrously precise manner.

We can think of this genomic system as a complex chemical computer, but this computer differs from familiar serial-processing computers, which carry out one action at a time. In the genomic computer system, many genes and their products are active at the same time; hence the system is a parallel-processing chemical computer of some kind. The different cell types of the developing embryo and its trajectory of development are, in some sense, expressions of the behavior of this complex genomic network. The network within each cell of any contemporary organism is the result of at least 1 billion years of evolution. Most biologists, heritors of the Darwinian tradition, suppose that the order of ontogeny is due to the grinding away of a molecular Rube Goldberg machine, slapped together piece by piece by evolution. I present a countering thesis: most of the beautiful order seen in ontogeny is spontaneous, a natural expression of the stunning self-organization that abounds in very complex regulatory networks. We appear to have been profoundly wrong. Order, vast and generative, arises naturally.

The emergent order seen in genomic networks foretells a conceptual struggle, perhaps even a conceptual revolution, in evolutionary theory. . . . I propose that much of the order in organisms may not be the result of selection at all, but of the spontaneous order of self-organized systems. Order, vast and generative, not fought for against the entropic tides but freely available, undergirds all subsequent biological evolution. The order of organisms is natural, not merely the unexpected triumph of natural selection. For example, I shall later give strong grounds to think that the homeostatic stability of cells (the biological inertia that keeps a liver cell, say, from turning into a muscle cell), the number of cell types in an organism compared with the number of its genes, and other features are not chance results of Darwinian selection but part of the order for free afforded by the self-organization in genomic regulatory networks. If this idea is true, then we must rethink evolutionary theory, for the sources of order in the biosphere will now include both selection *and* self-organization.

This is a massive and difficult theme. We are just beginning to embrace it. In this new view of life, organisms are not merely tinkered-together contraptions, bricolage, in Jacob's phrase. Evolution is not merely "chance caught on the wing," in Monod's evocative image. The history of life captures the natural order, on which selection is privileged to act. If this idea is true, many features of organisms are not merely historical accidents, but also reflections of the profound order that evolution has further molded. If true, we are at home in the universe in ways not imagined since Darwin stood natural theology on its head with his blind watchmaker.

Yet more is presaged by self-organization. I said we must encompass the roles of both self-organization *and* Darwinian selection in evolution. But these sources of order may meld in complex ways that we hardly begin to understand. No theory in physics, chemistry, biology, or elsewhere has yet brokered this marriage. We must think anew. Among the progeny of this mating of self-organization and selection may be new universal laws.

It is perhaps astonishing, perhaps hopeful and wonderful, that we might even now begin to frame possible universal laws governing this proposed union. For what can the teeming molecules that hustled themselves into self-reproducing metabolisms, the cells coordinating their behaviors to form multicelled organisms, the ecosystems, and even economic and political systems have in common? The wonderful possibility, to be held as a working hypothesis, bold but fragile, is that on many fronts, life evolves toward a regime that is poised between order and chaos. The evocative phrase that points to this working hypothesis is this: life exists at the edge of chaos. Borrowing a metaphor from physics, life may exist near a kind of phase transition. Water exists in three phases: solid ice, liquid water, and gaseous steam. It now begins to appear that similar ideas might apply to complex adapting systems. For example, we will see that the genomic networks that control development from zygote to adult can exist in three major regimes: a frozen ordered regime, a gaseous chaotic regime, and a kind of liquid regime located in the region between order and chaos. It is a lovely hypothesis, with considerable supporting data, that genomic systems lie in the ordered regime near the phase transition to chaos. Were such systems too deeply into the frozen ordered regime, they would be too rigid to coordinate the complex sequences of genetic activities necessary for development. Were they too far into the gaseous chaotic regime, they would not be orderly enough. Networks in the regime near the edge of chaos—this compromise between order and surprise—appear best able to coordinate complex activities and best able to evolve as well. It is a very attractive hypothesis that natural selection achieves genetic regulatory networks that lie near the edge of chaos.

Evolution is a story of organisms adapting by genetic changes, seeking to improve their fitness. Biologists have long harbored images of fitness landscapes, where the peaks represent high fitness, and populations wander under the drives of mutation, selection, and random drift across the landscape seeking peaks, but perhaps never achieving them. The idea of fitness peaks applies at many levels. For example, it can refer to the capacity of a protein molecule to catalyze a given chemical reaction. Then peaks of the landscape correspond to enzymes that are better catalysts for this reaction than all their neighboring proteins—those in the foothills and, worst of all, those in the valleys. Fitness peaks can also refer to the fitness of whole organisms. In that more complex case, an organism with a given set of traits is fitter—higher on the landscape—than all its near variants if, roughly speaking, it is more likely to have offspring.

We will find . . . that whether we are talking about organisms or economies, surprisingly general laws govern adaptive processes on multipeaked fitness landscapes. These general laws may account for phenomena ranging from the burst of the Cambrian explosion in biological evolution, where taxa fill in from the top down, to technological evolution, where striking variations arise early and dwindle to minor improvements. The edge-of-chaos theme also arises as a potential general law. In scaling the top of the fitness peaks, adapting populations that are too methodical and timid in their explorations are likely to get stuck in the foothills, thinking they have reached as high as they can go; but a search that is too wide ranging is also likely to fail. The best exploration of an evolutionary space occurs at a kind of phase transition between order and disorder, when populations begin to melt off the local peaks they have become fixated on and flow along ridges toward distant regions of higher fitness.

The edge-of-chaos image arises in coevolution as well, for as we evolve, so do our competitors; to remain fit, we must adapt to their adaptations. In coevolving systems, each partner clambers up its fitness landscape toward fitness peaks, even as that landscape is constantly deformed by the adaptive moves of its coevolutionary partners. Strikingly, such coevolving systems also behave in an ordered regime, a chaotic regime, and a transition regime. It is almost spooky that such systems seem to coevolve to the regime at the edge of chaos. As if by an invisible hand, each adapting species acts according to its own selfish advantage, yet the entire system appears magically to evolve to a poised state where, on average, each does as best as can be expected. Yet, as in many of the dynamical systems . . . , each is eventually driven to extinction, despite its own best efforts, by the collective behavior of the system as a whole.

. . . Technological evolution may be governed by laws similar to those governing pre-biotic chemical evolution and adaptive coevolution. The origin of life at a threshold of chemical diversity follows the same logic as a theory of economic takeoff at a threshold of diversity of goods and services. Above that critical diversity, new species of molecules, or goods and services, afford niches for yet further new species, which are awakened into existence in an explosion of possibilities. Like coevolutionary systems, economic systems link the selfish activities of more or less myopic agents. Adaptive moves in biological evolution and technological evolution drive avalanches of speciation and extinction. In both cases, as if by an invisible hand, the system may tune itself to the poised edge of chaos where all players fare as well as possible, but ultimately exit the stage.

The edge of chaos may even provide a deep new understanding of the logic of democracy. We have enshrined democracy as our secular religion; we argue its moral and rational foundations, and base our lives on it. We hope that our heritage of democracy will spill out its abundance of freedom over the globe. And in the following chapters we will find surprising new grounds for the secular wisdom of democracy in its capacity to solve extremely hard problems characterized by intertwining webs of conflicting interests. People organize into communities, each of which acts for its own benefit, jockeying to seek compromises among conflicting interests. This seemingly haphazard process also shows an ordered regime where poor compromises are found quickly, a chaotic regime where no compromise is ever settled on, and a phase transition where compromises are achieved, but not quickly. The best compromises appear to occur at the phase transition between order and chaos. Thus we will see

hints of an apologia for a pluralistic society as the natural design for adaptive compromise. Democracy may be far and away the best process to solve the complex problems of a complex evolving society, to find the peaks on the coevolutionary landscape where, on average, all have a chance to prosper.

WISDOM, NOT POWER

I suggest in the ensuing chapters how life may have formed as a natural consequence of physics and chemistry, how the molecular complexity of the biosphere burgeoned along a boundary between order and chaos, how the order of ontogeny may be natural, and how general laws about the edge of chaos may govern coevolving communities of species, of technologies, and even of ideologies.

This poised edge of chaos is a remarkable place. It is a close cousin of recent remarkable findings in a theory physicists Per Bak, Chao Tang and Kurt Wiesenfeld called self-organized critically. The central image here is of a sand-pile on a table onto which sand is added at a constant slow rate. Eventually, the sand piles up and avalanches begin. What one finds are lots of small avalanches and few large ones. If the size of the avalanche is plotted on the familiar x-axis of a Cartesian coordinate system, and the number of avalanches at that size are plotted on the y-axis, a curve is obtained. The result is a relationship called a power law. The particular shape of this curve, to which we shall return in later chapters, has the stunning implication that the same-sized grain of sand can unleash small or large avalanches. Although we can say that in general there will be more tiny avalanches and only a few big landslides (that is the nature of a power-law distribution), there is no way to tell whether a particular one will be insignificant or catastrophic.

Sandpiles, self-organized criticality, and the edge of chaos. If I am right, the very nature of coevolution is to attain this edge of chaos, a web of compromises where each species prospers as well as possible but where none can be sure if its best next step will set off a trickle or a landslide. In this precarious world, avalanches, small and large, sweep the system relentlessly. One's own footsteps shed small and large avalanches, which sweep up or by the other hikers on the slopes below. One may even be carried off in the avalanche started by his or her own footsteps. This image may capture the essential features of the new theory of emergence we seek. At this poised state between order and chaos, the players cannot foretell the unfolding consequences of their actions. While there is law in the distribution of avalanche sizes that arise in the poised state, there is unpredictability in each individual case. If one can never know if the next footstep is the one that will unleash the landslide of the century, then it pays to tread carefully.

In such a poised world, we must give up the pretense of long-term prediction. We cannot know the true consequences of our own best actions. All we players can do is be locally wise, not globally wise. All we can do, all anyone can do, is hitch up our pants, put on our galoshes, and get on with it the best

we can. Only God has the wisdom to understand the final law, the throws of the quantum dice. Only God can foretell the future. We, myopic after 3.45 billion years of design, cannot. We, with all the others, cannot foretell the avalanches and their intertwinings that we jointly generate. We can do only our local, level best. We can get on with it.

Since the time of Bacon our Western tradition has regarded knowledge as power. But as the scale of our activities in space and time has increased, we are being driven to understand the limited scope of our understanding and even our potential understanding. If we find general laws, and if those laws entail that the biosphere and all within it coevolve to some analogue of the sandpile, poised on the edge of chaos, it would be wise to be wise. We enter a new millennium. It is best to do so with gentle reverence for the ever-changing and unpredictable places in the sun that we craft ever anew for one another. We are all at home in the universe, poised to sanctify by our best, brief, only stay.

Essay and Paper Topics for "The Practice of Science"

1. Compare and contrast the accounts of science given by Popper, Ziman, and Laudan. Which of these seems to capture what is most distinctive about science?

2. Describe a theory that most people believe to be pseudoscientific and outline the advice that Popper and/or Ziman might give about how a research community could make it a respectable scientific theory.

3. Develop and defend your view about whether the worldview of modern science is alienating. What key features of that view do people find alienating, according to Baier and Stace (in the introductory essay, p. 13)? Are such reactions appropriate?

4. Explore options for living a meaningful life within the context of the scientific worldview. Which options for meaning are compatible with that view and which are not? What do you think is necessary for us to live a truly meaningful life?

5. Evaluate Kauffman's claims that modern science tends to eliminate the sacred, and that his new paradigm can avoid this result. Do you think our lives are impoverished without a sense of the sacred? Why or why not?

PART VI

Scientific Practice and Culture

The Scientific Outlook and Its Critics

How to Defend Society Against Science

Paul Feyerabend

Paul Feyerabend (1924–1994) was a philosophical gadfly who excelled at providing powerful arguments against widely accepted views. His most well-known book, *Against Method*, attempted to show that there should be no generally accepted method in science. In the lecture that follows, Feyerabend argues that society should be defended against all ideologies, including science. He claims that while science once liberated people from religious dogma, it now limits free thought.

The key role science plays in our society as an arbiter of truth is often justified by claims that it has found the correct method for discovering truth and that this is evident from the many results that it has achieved. Feyerabend argues that each of these claims is highly suspect. No one has been able to provide a substantive account of scientific method that reflects the practice of scientists. Moreover, the results of science are not clearly superior to the results of some nonscientific ideologies; indeed, many great scientific achievements had sources outside science. Feyerabend concludes that education should be altered so that it does not indoctrinate students into science. He maintains that the goal of education should be to produce critical thinkers who use whatever approaches best suit their ends, including, of course, scientific approaches. Paul Feyerabend was professor of philosophy at the University of California, Berkeley.

As you read through this essay, consider the following:

1. Why does Feyerabend believe that science is an ideology today?
2. How does Feyerabend criticize Popper's falsifiability criterion of science?
3. What is Feyerabend's argument against the view that science is guided by a clear method?
4. Why does he think that the results of science do not justify us in wholly trusting science as a guide in practical affairs?
5. How does Feyerabend think that education should be transformed?
6. Do you think that science unduly constrains our freedom of thought?

Practitioners of a strange trade, friends, enemies, ladies, and gentlemen: Before starting with my talk, let me explain to you, how it came into existence.

About a year ago I was short of funds. So I accepted an invitation to contribute to a book dealing with the relation between science and religion. To make the book sell I thought I should make my contribution a provocative one and the most provocative statement one can make about the relation between science and religion is that science is a religion. Having made the statement the core of my article I discovered that lots of reasons, lots of excellent reasons, could be found for it. I enumerated the reasons, finished my article, and got paid. That was stage one.

Next I was invited to a Conference for the Defense of Culture. I accepted the invitation because it paid for my flight to Europe. I also must admit that I was rather curious. When I arrived in Nice I had no idea what I would say. Then while the conference was taking its course I discovered that everyone thought very highly of science and that everyone was very serious. So I decided to explain how one could defend culture from science. All the reasons collected in my article would apply here as well and there was no need to invent new things. I gave my talk, was

rewarded with an outcry about my "dangerous and ill-considered ideas," collected my ticket and went on to Vienna. That was stage number two.

Now I am supposed to address you. I have a hunch that in some respect you are very different from my audience in Nice. For one, you look much younger. My audience in Nice was full of professors, businessmen, and television executives, and the average age was about 58½. Then I am quite sure that most of you are considerably to the left of some of the people in Nice. As a matter of fact, speaking somewhat superficially I might say that you are a leftist audience while my audience in Nice was a rightist audience. Yet despite all these differences you have some things in common. Both of you, I assume, respect science and knowledge. Science, of course, must be reformed and must be made less authoritarian. But once the reforms are carried out, it is a valuable source of knowledge that must not be contaminated by ideologies of a different kind. Secondly, both of you are serious people. Knowledge is a serious matter, for the Right as well as for the Left, and it must be pursued in a serious spirit. Frivolity is out, dedication and earnest application to the task at hand is in. These similarities are all I need for repeating my Nice talk to you with hardly any change. So, here it is.

FAIRYTALES

I want to defend society and its inhabitants from all ideologies, science included. All ideologies must be seen in perspective. One must not take them too seriously. One must

[This] article is a revised version of a talk given to the Philosophy Society at Sussex University in November 1974.

From Paul Feyerabend, "How to Defend Society Against Science," *Radical Philosophy* 11 (1975): 3–8. Copyright © 1975 by Paul Feyerabend. Reprinted by permission.

read them like fairytales which have lots of interesting things to say but which also contain wicked lies, or like ethical prescriptions which may be useful rules of thumb but which are deadly when followed to the letter.

Now, is this not a strange and ridiculous attitude? Science, surely, was always in the forefront of the fight against authoritarianism and superstition. It is to science that we owe our increased intellectual freedom vis-à-vis religious beliefs; it is to science that we owe the liberation of mankind from ancient and rigid forms of thought. Today these forms of thought are nothing but bad dreams—and this we learned from science. Science and enlightenment are one and the same thing—even the most radical critics of society believe this. Kropotkin wants to overthrow all traditional institutions and forms of belief, with the exception of science. Ibsen criticizes the most intimate ramifications of nineteenth-century bourgeois ideology, but he leaves science untouched. Levi-Strauss has made us realize that Western Thought is not the lonely peak of human achievement it was once believed to be, but he excludes science from his relativization of ideologies. Marx and Engels were convinced that science would aid the workers in their quest for mental and social liberation. Are all these people deceived? Are they all mistaken about the role of science? Are they all the victims of a chimera?

To these questions my answer is a firm *Yes and No.*

Now, let me explain my answer.

My explanation consists of two parts, one more general, one more specific.

The general explanation is simple. Any ideology that breaks the hold a comprehensive system of thought has on the minds of men contributes to the liberation of man. Any ideology that makes man question inherited beliefs is an aid to enlightenment. A truth that reigns without checks and balances is a tyrant who must be overthrown, and any falsehood that can aid us in the overthrow of this tyrant is to be welcomed. It follows that seventeenth- and eighteenth-century science indeed *was* an instrument of liberation and enlightenment. It

does not follow that science is bound to *remain* such an instrument. There is nothing inherent in science or in any other ideology that makes it *essentially* liberating. Ideologies can deteriorate and become stupid religions. Look at Marxism. And that the science of today is very different from the science of 1650 is evident at the most superficial glance.

For example, consider the role science now plays in education. Scientific "facts" are taught at a very early age and in the very same manner in which religious "facts" were taught only a century ago. There is no attempt to waken the critical abilities of the pupil so that he may be able to see things in perspective. At the universities the situation is even worse, for indoctrination is here carried out in a much more systematic manner. Criticism is not entirely absent. Society, for example, and its institutions, are criticized most severely and often most unfairly and this already at the elementary school level. But science is excepted from the criticism. In society at large the judgement of the scientist is received with the same reverence as the judgement of bishops and cardinals was accepted not too long ago. The move towards "demythologization," for example, is largely motivated by the wish to avoid any clash between Christianity and scientific ideas. If such a clash occurs, then science is certainly right and Christianity wrong. Pursue this investigation further and you will see that science has now become as oppressive as the ideologies it had once to fight. Do not be misled by the fact that today hardly anyone gets killed for joining a scientific heresy. This has nothing to do with science. It has something to do with the general quality of our civilization. Heretics in science are still made to suffer from the *most severe* sanctions this relatively tolerant civilization has to offer.

But—is this description not utterly unfair? Have I not presented the matter in a very distorted light by using tendentious and distorting terminology? Must we not describe the situation in a very different way? I have said that science has become rigid, that it has ceased to be an instrument of *change* and *liber-*

ation, without adding that it has found the *truth*, or a large part thereof. Considering this additional fact we realize, so the objection goes, that the rigidity of science is not due to human wilfulness. It lies in the nature of things. For once we have discovered the truth —what else can we do but follow it?

This trite reply is anything but original. It is used whenever an ideology wants to reinforce the faith of its followers. "Truth" is such a nicely neutral word. Nobody would deny that it is commendable to speak the truth and wicked to tell lies. Nobody would deny that —and yet nobody knows what such an attitude amounts to. So it is easy to twist matters and to change allegiance to truth in one's everyday affairs into allegiance to the Truth of an ideology which is nothing but the dogmatic defense of that ideology. And it is of course *not* true that we *have* to follow the truth. Human life is guided by many ideas. Truth is one of them. Freedom and mental independence are others. If Truth, as conceived by some ideologists, conflicts with freedom, then we have a *choice*. We may abandon freedom. But we may also abandon Truth. (Alternatively, we may adopt a more sophisticated idea of truth that no longer contradicts freedom; that was Hegel's solution.) My criticism of modern science is that it inhibits freedom of thought. If the reason is that it has found the truth and now follows it, then I would say that there are better things than first finding, and then following such a monster.

This finishes the general part of my explanation.

There exists a more specific argument to defend the exceptional position science has in society today. Put in a nutshell the argument says (1) that science has finally found the correct *method* for achieving results and (2) that there are many *results* to prove the excellence of the method. The argument is mistaken—but most attempts to show this lead into a dead end. Methodology has by now become so crowded with empty sophistication that it is extremely difficult to perceive the simple errors at the basis. It is like fighting the hydra—cut off one ugly head, and eight formalizations take its place. In this situation the only answer is superficiality: when sophistication loses content then the only way of keeping in touch with reality is to be crude and superficial. This is what I intend to be.

AGAINST METHOD

There is a method, says part (1) of the argument. What is it? How does it work?

One answer which is no longer as popular as it used to be is that science works by collecting facts and inferring theories from them. The answer is unsatisfactory as theories never *follow from* facts in the strict logical sense. To say that they may yet be *supported* from facts assumes a notion of support that (a) does not show this defect and (b) is sufficiently sophisticated to permit us to say to what extent, say, the theory of relativity is supported by the facts. No such notion exists today, nor is it likely that it will ever be found (one of the problems is that we need a notion of support in which grey ravens can be said to support "all ravens are black"). This was realized by conventionalists and transcendental idealists who pointed out that theories *shape* and *order* facts and can therefore be retained come what may. They can be retained because the human mind either consciously or unconsciously carries out its ordering function. The trouble with these views is that they assume for the mind what they want to explain for the world, viz., that it works in a regular fashion. There is only one view which overcomes all these difficulties. It was invented twice in the nineteenth century, by Mill, in his immortal essay *On Liberty*, and by some Darwinists who extended Darwinism to the battle of ideas. This view takes the bull by the horns: theories cannot be justified and their excellence cannot be shown without reference to other theories. We may explain the *success* of a theory by reference to a more comprehensive theory (we may explain the success of Newton's theory by using the general theory of relativity); and we may explain our *preference* for it by comparing it with other theories.

Such a comparison does not establish the intrinsic excellence of the theory we have chosen. As a matter of fact, the theory we have chosen may be pretty lousy. It may contain contradictions, it may conflict with well-known facts, it may be cumbersome, unclear, ad hoc in decisive places, and so on. But it may still be better than any other theory that is available at the time. It may in fact be the best lousy theory there is. Nor are the standards of judgment chosen in an absolute manner. Our sophistication increases with every choice we make, and so do our standards. Standards compete just as theories compete and we choose the standards most appropriate to the historical situation in which the choice occurs. The rejected alternatives (theories; standards; "facts") are not eliminated. They serve as correctives (after all, we may have made the wrong choice) and they also explain the content of the preferred views (we understand relativity better when we understand the structure of its competitors; we know the full meaning of freedom only when we have an idea of life in a totalitarian state, of its advantages—and there are many advantages—as well as of its disadvantages). Knowledge so conceived is an ocean of alternatives channeled and subdivided by an ocean of standards. It forces our mind to make imaginative choices and thus makes it grow. It makes our mind capable of choosing, imagining, criticizing.

Today this view is often connected with the name of Karl Popper. But there are some very decisive differences between Popper and Mill. To start with, Popper developed his view to solve a special problem of epistemology—he wanted to solve "Hume's problem." Mill, on the other hand, is interested in conditions favorable to human growth. His epistemology is the result of a certain theory of man, and not the other way around. Also Popper, being influenced by the Vienna Circle, improves on the logical form of a theory before discussing it, while Mill uses every

theory in the form in which it occurs in science. Thirdly, Popper's standards of comparison are rigid and fixed, while Mill's standards are permitted to change with the historical situation. Finally, Popper's standards eliminate competitors once and for all: theories that are either not falsifiable or falsifiable and falsified have no place in science. Popper's criteria are clear, unambiguous, precisely formulated; Mill's criteria are not. This would be an advantage if science itself were clear, unambiguous, and precisely formulated. Fortunately, it is not.

To start with, no new and revolutionary scientific theory is ever formulated in a manner that permits us to say under what circumstances we must regard it as endangered: many revolutionary theories are unfalsifiable. Falsifiable versions do exist, but they are hardly ever in agreement with accepted basic statements: every moderately interesting theory is falsified. Moreover, theories have formal flaws, many of them contain contradictions, ad hoc adjustments, and so on and so forth. Applied resolutely, Popperian criteria would eliminate science without replacing it by anything comparable. They are useless as an aid to science. In the past decade this has been realized by various thinkers, Kuhn and Lakatos among them. Kuhn's ideas are interesting but, alas, they are much too vague to give rise to anything but lots of hot air. If you don't believe me, look at the literature. Never before has the literature on the philosophy of science been invaded by so many creeps and incompetents. Kuhn encourages people who have no idea why a stone falls to the ground to talk with assurance about scientific method. Now I have no objection to incompetence but I do object when incompetence is accompanied by boredom and self-righteousness. And this is exactly what happens. We do not get interesting false ideas, we get boring ideas or words connected with no ideas at all. Secondly, wherever one tries to make Kuhn's ideas more definite one finds that they are *false*. Was there ever a period of normal science in the history of thought? No—and I challenge anyone to prove the contrary.

Lakatos is immeasurably more sophisticated than Kuhn. Instead of theories he considers research programs which are sequences of theories connected by methods of modification, so-called heuristics. Each theory in the sequence may be full of faults. It may be beset by anomalies, contradictions, ambiguities. What counts is not the shape of the single theories, but the tendency exhibited by the sequence. We judge historical developments and achievements over a period of time, rather than the situation at a particular time. History and methodology are combined into a single enterprise. A research program is said to progress if the sequence of theories leads to novel predictions. It is said to degenerate if it is reduced to absorbing facts that have been discovered without its help. A decisive feature of Lakatos's methodology is that such evaluations are no longer tied to methodological rules which tell the scientist either to retain or to abandon a research program. Scientists may stick to a degenerating program; they may even succeed in making the program overtake its rivals and they therefore proceed rationally whatever they are doing (provided they continue calling degenerating programs degenerating and progressive programs progressive). This means that Lakatos offers *words* which *sound* like the elements of a methodology; he does not offer a methodology. There is no method according to the most advanced and sophisticated methodology in existence today. This finishes my reply to part (1) of the specific argument.

AGAINST RESULTS

According to part (2), science deserves a special position because it has produced *results*. This is an argument only if it can be taken for granted that nothing else has ever produced results. Now it may be admitted that almost everyone who discusses the matter makes such an assumption. It may also be admitted that it is not easy to show that the assumption is false. Forms of life different from science

either have disappeared or have degenerated to an extent that makes a fair comparison impossible. Still, the situation is not as hopeless as it was only a decade ago. We have become acquainted with methods of medical diagnosis and therapy which are effective (and perhaps even more effective than the corresponding parts of Western medicine) and which are yet based on an ideology that is radically different from the ideology of Western science. We have learned that there are phenomena such as telepathy and telekinesis which are obliterated by a scientific approach and which could be used to do research in an entirely novel way (earlier thinkers such as Agrippa of Nettesheim, John Dee, and even Bacon were aware of these phenomena). And then—is it not the case that the Church saved souls while science often does the very opposite? Of course, nobody now believes in the ontology that underlies this judgment. Why? Because of ideological pressures identical with those which today make us listen to science to the exclusion of everything else. It is also true that phenomena such as telekinesis and acupuncture may eventually be absorbed into the body of science and may therefore be called "scientific." But note that this happens only after a long period of resistance during which a science *not yet* containing the phenomena wants to get the upper hand over forms of life that contain them. And this leads to a further objection against part (2) of the specific argument. The fact that science has results counts in its favor only if these results were achieved by science alone, and without any outside help. A look at history shows that science hardly ever gets its results in this way. When Copernicus introduced a new view of the universe, he did not consult *scientific* predecessors, he consulted a crazy Pythagorean such as Philolaos. He adopted his ideas and he maintained them in the face of all sound rules of scientific method. Mechanics and optics owe a lot to artisans, medicine to midwives and witches. And in our own day we have seen how the interference of the state can advance science: when the Chinese communists refused to be intimidated by the judgment of experts and ordered traditional medicine back into universities and hospitals there was an outcry all over the world that science would now be ruined in China. The very opposite occurred: Chinese science advanced and Western science learned from it. Wherever we look we see that great scientific advances are due to outside interference which is made to prevail in the face of the most basic and most "rational" methodological rules. The lesson is plain: there does not exist a single argument that could be used to support the exceptional role which science today plays in society. Science has done many things, but so have other ideologies. Science often proceeds systematically, but so do other ideologies (just consult the records of the many doctrinal debates that took place in the Church) and, besides, there are no overriding rules which are adhered to under any circumstances; there is no "scientific methodology" that can be used to separate science from the rest. *Science is just one of the many ideologies that propel society and it should be treated as such* (this statement applies even to the most progressive and most dialectical sections of science). What consequences can we draw from this result?

The most important consequence is that there must be a *formal separation between state and science* just as there is now a formal separation between state and church. Science may influence society but only to the extent to which any political or other pressure group is permitted to influence society. Scientists may be consulted on important projects but the final judgement must be left to the democratically elected consulting bodies. These bodies will consist mainly of laymen. Will the laymen be able to come to a correct judgment? Most certainly, for the competence, the complications and the successes of science are vastly exaggerated. One of the most exhilarating experiences is to see how a lawyer, who is a layman, can find holes in the testimony, the technical testimony, of the most advanced expert and thus prepare the jury for its verdict. Science is not a closed book that is understood only after years of training. It is

an intellectual discipline that can be examined and criticized by anyone who is interested and that looks difficult and profound only because of a systematic campaign of obfuscation carried out by many scientists (though, I am happy to say, not by all). Organs of the state should never hesitate to reject the judgment of scientists when they have reason for doing so. Such rejection will educate the general public, will make it more confident, and it may even lead to improvement. Considering the sizeable chauvinism of the scientific establishment we can say: the more Lysenko affairs, the better (it is not the *interference* of the state that is objectionable in the case of Lysenko, but the *totalitarian* interference which kills the opponent rather than just neglecting his advice). Three cheers to the fundamentalists in California who succeeded in having a dogmatic formulation of the theory of evolution removed from the textbooks and an account of Genesis included. (But I know that they would become as chauvinistic and totalitarian as scientists are today when given the chance to run society all by themselves. Ideologies are marvelous when used in the companies of other ideologies. They become boring and doctrinaire as soon as their merits lead to the removal of their opponents.) The most important change, however, will have to occur in the field of *education.*

EDUCATION AND MYTH

The purpose of education, so one would think, is to introduce the young into life, and that means: into the *society* where they are born and into the *physical* universe that surrounds the society. The method of education often consists in the teaching of some *basic myth.* The myth is available in various versions. More advanced versions may be taught by initiation rites which firmly implant them into the mind. Knowing the myth, the grownup can explain almost everything (or else he can turn to experts for more detailed information). He is the master of Nature and of Society. He understands them both and he knows how to interact with them. However, *he is not the master of the myth that guides his understanding.*

Such further mastery was aimed at, and was partly achieved, by the Presocratics. The Presocratics not only tried to understand the *world.* They also tried to understand, and thus to become the masters of, the *means of understanding the world.* Instead of being content with a single myth they developed many and so diminished the power which a well-told story has over the minds of men. The sophists introduced still further methods for reducing the debilitating effect of interesting, coherent, "empirically adequate," et cetera, et cetera tales. The achievements of these thinkers were not appreciated and they certainly are not understood today. When teaching a myth we want to increase the chance that it will be understood (i.e., no puzzlement about any feature of the myth), believed, *and accepted.* This does not do any harm when the myth is counterbalanced by other myths: even the most dedicated (i.e., totalitarian) instructor in a certain version of Christianity cannot prevent his pupils from getting in touch with Buddhists, Jews, and other disreputable people. It is very different in the case of science, or of rationalism where the field is almost completely dominated by the believers. In this case it is of paramount importance to strengthen the minds of the young, and "strengthening the minds of the young" means strengthening them *against* any easy acceptance of comprehensive views. What we need here is an education that makes people *contrary, countersuggestive,* without making them incapable of devoting themselves to the elaboration of any single view. How can this aim be achieved?

It can be achieved by protecting the tremendous imagination which children possess and by developing to the full the spirit of contradiction that exists in them. On the whole children are much more intelligent than their teachers. They succumb, and give up their intelligence because they are bullied, or because their teachers get the better of

them by emotional means. Children can learn, understand, and keep separate two to three different languages ("children" and by this I mean three- to five-year-olds, *not* eight-year-olds who were experimented upon quite recently and did not come out too well; why? because they were already loused up by incompetent teaching at an earlier age). Of course, the languages must be introduced in a more interesting way than is usually done. There are marvelous writers in all languages who have told marvelous stories—let us begin our language teaching with *them* and not with "der Hund hat einen Schwanz" and similar inanities. Using stories we may of course also introduce "scientific" accounts, say, of the origin of the world and thus make the children acquainted with science as well. But science must not be given any special position except for pointing out that there are lots of people who believe in it. Later on the stories which have been told will be supplemented with "reasons," where by reasons I mean further accounts of the kind found in the tradition to which the story belongs. And, of course, there will also be contrary reasons. Both reasons and contrary reasons will be told by the experts in the fields and so the young generation becomes acquainted with all kinds of sermons and all types of wayfarers. It becomes acquainted with them, it becomes acquainted with their stories, and every individual can make up his mind which way to go. By now everyone knows that you can earn a lot of money and respect and perhaps even a Nobel Prize by becoming a scientist, so many will become scientists. They will *become* scientists *without having been taken in by the ideology of science,* they will *be* scientists *because they have made a free choice.* But has not much time been wasted on unscientific subjects and will this not detract from their competence once they have become scientists? Not at all! The progress of science, of good science depends on novel ideas and on intellectual freedom: science has very often been advanced by outsiders (remember that Bohr and Einstein regarded themselves as outsiders). Will not many people make the wrong choice and end up in a dead end? Well, that depends on what you mean by a "dead end." Most scientists today are devoid of ideas, full of fear, intent on producing some paltry result so that they can add to the flood of inane papers that now constitutes "scientific progress" in many areas. And, besides, what is more important? To lead a life which one has chosen with open eyes, or to spend one's time in the nervous attempt of avoiding what some not so intelligent people call "dead ends"? Will not the number of scientists decrease so that in the end there is nobody to run our precious laboratories? I do not think so. Given a choice many people may choose science, for a science that is run by free agents looks much more attractive than the science of today which is run by slaves, slaves of institutions and slaves of "reason." And if there is a temporary shortage of scientists the situation may always be remedied by various kinds of incentives. Of course, scientists will not play any predominant role in the society I envisage. They will be more than balanced by magicians, or priests, or astrologers. Such a situation is unbearable for many people, old and young, right and left. Almost all of you have the firm belief that at least some kind of truth has been found, that it must be preserved, and that the method of teaching I advocate and the form of society I defend will dilute it and make it finally disappear. You have this firm belief; many of you may even have reasons. *But what you have to consider is that the absence of good contrary reasons is due to a historical accident;* it does *not* lie in the nature of things. Build up the kind of society I recommend and the views you now despise (without knowing them, to be sure) will return in such splendor that you will have to work hard to maintain your own position and will perhaps be entirely unable to do so. You do not believe me? Then look at history. Scientific astronomy was firmly founded on Ptolemy and Aristotle, two of the greatest minds in the history of Western Thought. Who upset their well-argued, empirically adequate, and precisely formulated system? Philolaos the mad

and antediluvian Pythagorean. How was it that Philolaos could stage such a comeback? Because he found an able defender: Copernicus. Of course, you may follow your intuitions as I am following mine. But remember that your intuitions are the result of your "scientific" training where by science I also mean the science of Karl Marx. My training, or, rather, my nontraining, is that of a journalist who is interested in strange and bizarre events. Finally, is it not utterly irresponsible, in the present world situation, with millions of people starving, others enslaved, downtrodden, in abject misery of body and mind, to think luxurious thoughts such as these? Is not freedom of choice a luxury under such circumstances? Is not the flippancy and the humor I want to see combined with the freedom of choice a luxury under such circumstances? Must we not give up all self-indulgence and *act?* Join together, and *act?* This is the most important objection which today is raised against an approach such as the one recommended by me. It has tremendous appeal, it has the appeal of unselfish dedication. Unselfish dedication—to what? Let us see!

We are supposed to give up our selfish inclinations and dedicate ourselves to the liberation of the oppressed. And selfish inclinations are what? They are our wish for maximum liberty of thought in the society in which we live *now,* maximum liberty not only of an abstract kind, but expressed in appropriate institutions and methods of teaching. This wish for concrete intellectual and physical liberty in our own surroundings is to be put aside, for the time being. This assumes, first, that we do not need this liberty for our task. It assumes that we can carry out our task with a mind that is firmly closed to some alternatives. It assumes that the correct way of liberating others *has always been found* and that all that is needed is to carry it out. I am sorry, I cannot accept such doctrinaire self-assurance in such extremely important matters. Does this mean that we cannot act at all? It does not. But it means that *while acting we have to try to realize as much of the freedom I have recommended so that our actions may be corrected in the light of the ideas we get while increasing our freedom.* This will slow us down, no doubt, but are we supposed to charge ahead simply because some people tell us that they have found an explanation for all the misery and an excellent way out of it? Also we want to liberate people not to make them succumb to a new kind of slavery, *but to make them realize their own wishes,* however different these wishes may be from our own. Self-righteous and narrow-minded liberators cannot do this. As a rule they soon impose a slavery that is worse, because more systematic, than the very sloppy slavery they have removed. And as regards humor and flippancy the answer

should be obvious. Why would anyone want to liberate anyone else? Surely not because of some *abstract* advantage of liberty but because liberty is the best way to free development *and thus to happiness.* We want to liberate people so that *they can smile.* Shall we be able to do this if we ourselves have forgotten how to smile and are frowning on those who still remember? Shall we then not spread another disease, comparable to the one we want to remove, the disease of puritanical self-righteousness? Do not object that dedication and humor do not go together—Socrates is an excellent example to the contrary. *The hardest task needs the lightest hand or else its completion will not lead to freedom but to a tyranny much worse than the one it replaces.*

The Anti-Science Phenomenon

Gerald Holton

Just as some observers are concerned that science is too powerful in our culture, others such as Gerald Holton believe that our culture is threatened by growing antiscience movements. Charlatans peddle their pseudoscientific theories to an unsuspecting public for profits and political gains. Although much pseudoscience may be harmless, some of it may fuel dangerous political movements. Holton suggests that the current rise of antiscience movements reflects a deep historical rivalry between rational and nonrational approaches to knowing. Since the fates of a culture are often affected by which side in this rivalry has the upper hand, we should be wary of those who would trivialize concerns about antiscience. Gerald Holton is Mallinckrodt Professor of Physics and professor of history of science at Harvard University.

As you read through this essay, consider the following:

1. According to Holton, what kind of antiscience is particularly malignant?
2. What evidence does Holton provide for the growth of the antiscience movement?
3. What reasons does he give for thinking that the antiscience movement is alarming? How do you think Feyerabend might respond to Holton's concerns?
4. What are some of the sources of discontent with science that Holton outlines?
5. Should we try to strengthen the hold of the scientific worldview on our society? Why or why not?

Opposition to science as conventionally defined can take a great variety of forms, from interest in astrology to attacks on relativity theory, from false beliefs based on scientific illiteracy to support of Lysenkoism or Creationism. Which of these attacks are relatively negligible, and which are dangerous? What do these symptoms of disaffection with the Enlightenment-based tradition portend for science and culture in our time? Once we have a framework to deal with the belief in anti-science (or "alternative science," "para-science"), we shall recognize that such belief is grounded in a person's functional world view; it is one symptom of a long-standing struggle over the legitimacy of the authority of conventional science, as well as of the concept of modernity within which science claims to be embedded. An analysis of anti-scientific beliefs might lead finally to the identification of a set of strategies for dealing with the countervisions that periodically attempt to raise themselves from the level of apparent harmlessness to that of politically ambitious success. . . .

Recently, a conference was called to help scholars in the republics of the former Soviet Union to understand and deal with the Glasnost-released flowering in their lands of publications promoting "other ways of knowing," mystics, clairvoyants, astrologers, extraterrestrial visitors, faith healers, and the rest of the—to us—familiar cast of characters. Just as there has been a downturn of interest in pursuing science and engineering as a profession in the West, a similar attitude has become prominent in those countries. So it appears that an alarm bell is sounding on both continents, one that calls us to contemplate "how superstition won and science lost," to use the title of John C. Burnham's useful book.[1] We seem to be urged to share any knowledge that can be expected to help cure

the body politic of its disease and return it to the healthy state to which we, as children of the Enlightenment, think our fellow-citizens have the right and duty to aspire at the end of this blood-drenched century: a state that is rational, progressive, anti-superstitious, pro-science, and free of the medieval curses of folk magic, miracle, mystery, false authority, and mindless iconoclasm.

However, conscience demands that I declare at the outset that I shall not try to provide a map to this paradise. First the category *anti-* will have to be reformulated if we are to grasp the problem correctly. Indeed, I see my main task to outline how to think about anti-science at the proper level. The term *anti-science* can lump together too many, quite different things that have in common only that they tend to annoy or threaten those who regard themselves as more enlightened. We must disaggregate from the disparate jumble that which is the truly worrisome part of anti-science, so that we can discriminate between "real" science (good, bad, and indifferent; old, new or just emerging); pathological science (as in Irving Langmuir's essay on people who thought they were doing real science but were misled);[2] pseudoscience (astrology and the "science" of the paranormal); blatant silliness and superstition ("pyramid power"); scientism (the over-enthusiastic importation of "scientific" models into nonscientific fields; or the vastly exaggerated claims of technocrats for scientific and technological powers, such as the "Star Wars" projects); and other forms.

Thereby we shall be able to focus on the single most malignant part of the phenomenon: the type of pseudo-scientific nonsense that manages to pass itself off as an "alternative science," *and does so in the service of political ambition.* Here our Russian colleagues may be able to instruct us because of their unhappy experience in past decades with Lysenkoism, attacks on the relativity theory and quantum mechanics, and on cosmologists who were thought to have offended against the doctrines of Engels' *Anti-Dühring*. That is the general area which will call for careful atten-

The Anti-Science Phenomenon ☞ **303**

tion. We must not become preoccupied with surface phenomena. For example, much of tabloid sensationalism involving UFOs is merely hucksterism feeding on primitive ignorance (unless, as with the reputed recent inauguration of a section on "UFO-logy" in the Russian Academy of Science, the craze gets official backing).

Yet, if our aim is to filter out, name, and analyze the really dangerous segment of what some call the "anti-science movement," we shall not find much help in the literature. There exists no adequate, serious treatment of it, nor even of the modern outlook that feels threatened by anti-science. All of us enter this study equally in need of a better understanding. Nor do we really comprehend the causes of one of the preconditions of false ideas, namely the rampant scientific illiteracy in the United States. There is an extensive literature on this topic; here we need only refer to a report conveyed to the Congress by the President's Science Adviser.[3] Public scientific literacy in the United States is now at a level where "half the adults questioned did not know that it took one year for the Earth to orbit the Sun" (p. 8). (As we know from other surveys,[4] less than 7 percent of U.S. adults can be called scientifically literate by the most generous definition, only 13 percent have at least a minimum level of understanding of the process of science, and 40 percent disagree with the statement "astrology is not at all scientific.") In particular, "Teaching is a profession in crisis. . . . We are currently losing thirteen mathematics and science teachers for each one entering the profession" (p. 5). Only the following percentages of teachers meet the minimum established standards for course work preparation at the high school level: 29 percent in biology, 31 percent in chemistry, 12 percent in physics (p. 6). Typically, in nearly 30 percent of U.S. high schools, physics courses are not even offered (p. 5), and only 20 percent of the high school graduates have taken physics courses of any kind. "In the most recent international science assessments, in comparison with students in 12 other countries, our high school students finished 9th in physics, 11th in chemistry, and last in biology. . . . In mathematics, our top 13 percent generally fell into the bottom 25 percent in comparison with other countries" (p. 25).[5]

WHY DOES THE ANTI-SCIENCE PHENOMENON CONCERN US?

That such a small fraction of U.S. adults can be called scientifically literate at a time when the accomplishments of modern science, the feats of technology, and the effects of both on our lives are more spectacular than ever is not merely ironic but profoundly in need of explanation. To this intellectually important point is joined a political one: in a democracy, no matter how poorly informed the citizens are, they do properly demand a place at the table where decisions are made, even when those decisions have a large scientific/technical component. In that lies the potential for erroneous policy and eventual social instability. . . . History has shown repeatedly that a disaffection with science and its view of the world can turn into a rage that links up with far more sinister movements.

It is thoughts of this kind which the phenomenon of anti-science raises in the minds of many intellectuals, West and East. By themselves, all the astrologers, anti-evolutionists, spiritualists, psychics, and peddlers of New Age thinking could otherwise be merely a target of our condescension or a source of amusement. We seem to discern behind these multi-faceted phenomena—and the related illiteracy in history, geography, etc., which we shall cover for now with the delicacy of embarrassed silence—something perilous, a potentially fatal flaw in the self-conception of the people today. . . . Soon after the start of this century, Oswald Spengler taught a fascinated public that the ideas of modern science themselves contained the poison leading to the inevitable Decline of the West, by what he called "metaphysical exhaustion"; and Max Weber announced that the method of natural science was a systematic "process of disenchantment" of the world, with its resulting loss of "any meaning that goes beyond the purely practical and technical . . . [a] question raised in the most principled form in the works of Leo Tolstoy."[6] Could it be that, on having reached the end of the twentieth century, we will find that the widespread lack of a proper understanding of science itself might be either a source, or a tell-tale sign, of our culture's decline?

It would be a vast oversimplification to think this alone is an explanation of a complex social development; but one must not dismiss it as one component for our consideration. And it is not an unfamiliar position. One of the most eloquent analyses of the exhaustion or abandonment thesis, and its parallel in early history, is to be found in the last chapter, entitled "The Fear of Freedom," in E. R. Dodds's book, *The Greeks and the Irrational.*[7] The rise of the Greek Enlightenment in the sixth century B.C., following the Homeric Age, was characterized by a "progressive replacement of the mythological by rational thinking among the Greeks." But by the end of the reign of Pericles, the tide had turned again, and teaching astronomy or expressing doubts about the supernatural became dangerous. Cults, astrology, magical healing, and other familiar practices were symptoms of the onset of a long decline, which Dodds terms the "Return of the Irrational." And, Dodds asks, have we similarly entered now on the end phase of that second great experiment with rationalism, generally identified with the Scientific Revolution and the Era of Enlightenment? Is there not even a parallel here to one of the reasons for the opening of the abyss in antiquity—that "as the intellectuals withdrew further into a world of their own [from the late period of Plato on], the popular mind was left increasingly defenseless . . . and, left without guidance, a growing number relapsed with a sigh of relief into the pleasures and comforts of the primitive"?

By the late fifth century, "the growing rationalism of the intellectuals was matched by regressive symptoms in popular belief," as the gap widened "into something approach-ing a complete divorce." Intellectually abandoned during a sort of Decline of the Mandarins, the masses were prey to the spread of astrology and the like, in good part because of the "political conditions: in the troubled half-century that preceded the Roman conquest of Greece it was particularly important to know what was going to happen. . . . For a century or more the individual had been face to face with his own intellectual freedom, and now he turned tail and bolted from the horrid prospect—better the rigid determinism of the astrological Fate than that terrifying burden of daily responsibility," that freedom which did not lead to certainty and safety.

Who does not hear in this the thundering voice of the Grand Inquisitor of Dostoevsky's *Brothers Karamazov?*

> No science will give the masses bread so long as they remain free. In the end they will lay their freedom at our feet and say to us: "Make us slaves, but feed us." . . . There are three powers, three powers alone, able to conquer and to hold captive forever the conscience of these impotent rebels for their happiness—those forces are miracle, mystery, and authority.

One may try to shrug off such dark thoughts by pointing to the bright side, not least the practically universal popular enchantment with high-tech. One may seek comfort in the fact that even though only less than half of the U.S. adult population believes in the evolutionary descent of human beings from earlier species, and even though half has trouble finding one side of a square when given one of the other sides, the U.S. public at large reports to pollsters a greater level of belief in the potential of science and technology as a force for the good (at least in the abstract) than equivalent tests have shown for other major industrial countries, such as France and Japan.

This uninformed assertion of interest is not troubled by the well-documented, contradictory feeling about scientists, which is far less positive. In America today it is not science but religion which, as in the days of the seventeenth-century Pilgrims, is perhaps the strongest force in private and national life—

just as Tocqueville had noticed in the 1830s. About one-third of our adults, and a large fraction of these from evangelical sects, now say they are "born-again" believers; over half believe in the possibility of the daily occurrence of miracles through prayer; 60 percent say they believe in the literal existence of Hell for the eternally damned. And the financial support given annually as private donations to religious organizations now amounts to well over $75 billion. But here again, there is little consciousness of any contradiction, despite the fact that the modern, science-based world view evolved in good part from a reaction to just such a contradiction, and indeed suffers still from the inability to find a way to bridge the chasm between these two undeniable imperatives, science and faith. By contrast, the large majority of average Americans reports experiencing no conflict at all between these different forces.[8]

Similarly, while ideas that one commonly takes to be anti-scientific are widespread in the U.S., there is important evidence that this, too, is not a simple or monolithic attitude. Rather, there is a coexistence of potentially opposing kinds of consciousness. And that, as we shall see, lends itself to strategies for change. Like the different tectonic plates in the Earth's crust that tend to move in opposite directions, with occasionally disastrous results, the various elements making up the mind-set of the average person today do not form a harmonious whole. As Dostoevsky's Grand Inquisitor knew, the liberal, Enlightenment-based view deludes itself if it assumes it has been victorious. Indeed, the "pro-science"–imbued world picture of the late twentieth century is a rather vulnerable and fragile minority position, the more so as scientists and other intellectuals as a group have not managed to create sufficient effective institutional or other intellectual forums for even discussing among themselves, and with others, what the powers and limits of science in these respects are. (The uneasy toehold of Science–Technology–Society studies in most major universities is just one evidence of this lack of attention.)

ANTI-SCIENCE AS COUNTERVISION: FORCES OF DELEGITIMATION

The evidence of internal contradictions is a signal that we must submit the anti-science phenomenon to another level of analysis. To understand in more satisfactory terms what in fact is meant by anti-science, and what it may imply for the future of our culture, we must start with the recognition that no culture can be truly anti-scientific, in the sense of opposing the activity "science" (science as defined, for example, in the *American Heritage Dictionary of the English Language:* "The observation, identification, description, experimental investigation, and theoretical explanation of natural phenomena"). Although some philosophers of science will have trouble with aspects of such a definition, I do not find even the most Dionysian "anti-scientists" calling for opposition to that activity as such.

Moreover, the anti-science phenomenon is not at all just an incomplete or ignorant or damaged form of the "proper" world view that many believe should characterize our civilization at this time in history. Instead— and leaving aside the banal, relatively harmless, or ignorant varieties—what the more sophisticated so-called anti-scientists offer is, to put it bluntly, an articulated and functional, and potentially powerful, countervision of the world, within which there exists an allegiance to a "science" very different from conventional science. And that countervision has as its historic function nothing less than the delegitimation of (conventional) science in its widest sense: a delegitimation which extends to science's ontological and epistemological claims, and above all to its classic, inherently expansionist ambition to define the meaning and direction of human progress. In short, we are watching here an ancient, persistent, obstinate, and hardly ameliorating combat.

Many scientists, busily at work at their bench, will be surprised to hear this. But throughout history every great society has been subject to the dispute of competing parties under three headings: power, production, and belief. Science, far from merely being a joyous activity within the walls of the laboratory, has been more deeply involved in all three than almost any other pursuit. Since the early seventeenth century, the sciences have more and more aggressively asserted their primacy under each of these headings, at the cost of the previous occupants. Since Francis Bacon and Isaac Newton, who respectively promised omnipotence and omniscience, and whose followers have continued to brandish these hopes, science and science-driven technology have worked hard to penetrate into and transform this whole triad of power, production, and belief. It was not on the better calculation of planetary orbits or cannon ball trajectories that scientists in the seventeenth century based their chief claim to attention, but on their role in replacing the whole pre-scientific belief system. For over three centuries since then, they have pointed to their grand program of fashioning an irresistible, overarching, well-integrated world conception based on rational science. Of course such an imperious project scandalized the previous chief cultural dominators of Western society, and they have resisted being nudged aside.

During the nineteenth century, the claim of science became secularized, but otherwise only increased in its ambitions. James Frazer, author of the *Golden Bough*, taught that Western civilization has passed successively in stages from myth to religion to science. Of course he was wrong—we exist today still in a boiling mixture of these three systems, and the mutual challenges and attempts to delegitimate one another as the foundation of our culture have continued. Thus the nineteenth-century Romantics wanted to put what they called their Visionary Physics in place of the mechanistic one of their day, holding with the poet Blake that Newton, Locke, and Bacon were the "infernal Trinity" that had satanic influences on humanity. Parallel to these beliefs, that century saw a flourishing of mesmerism, phrenology, table-raising spiritualism, and the electrical creation of life forms.

Today there exist a number of different groups which from their various perspectives oppose what they conceive of as the hegemony of science-as-done-today in our culture. These groups do not form a coherent movement, and indeed have little interest in one another; some focus on the epistemological claims of science, others on its effects via technology, others still long for a return to a romanticized pre-modern version of science. But what they do have in common is that each, in its own way, advocates nothing less than the end of science as we know it. That is what makes these disparate assemblages operationally members of a loose consortium.

The most prominent portions of this current counter-constituency, this cohort of delegitimators, are four in number. Starting from the intellectually most serious end, there is a type of modern philosopher who asserts that science can now claim no more than the status of one of the "social myths"—the term used by Mary Hesse[9]—not to speak of a new wing of sociologists of science who wish, in Bruno Latour's words, to "abolish the distinction between science and fiction."[10]

Next, there is a group, small but very influential, of alienated intellectuals, of whom Arthur Koestler served as prominent exemplar. For them to be doomed to ignorance is the worst wound. But the fantastic growth rate of new knowledge and our spotty record as educators have left them impotent, and, as Lionel Trilling honorably confessed, inflict on them a devastating "humiliation."[11] In this way, powerful intellectuals who in previous centuries would have been among the friends and most useful critics of science (as the more thoughtful cultural critics still are) find themselves abandoned—and in exasperation write attacks on science such as are to be found in Koestler's later books.

Third, there is a resurgence among what I have called the Dionysians, with their dedication ranging from New Age thinking to wishful parallelism with Eastern mysticism.[12] Some have their roots in nineteenth-century Romanticism, some in the 1960s' countercultures; but all agree that one of the worst sins of modern thought is the concept of objectively reachable data.

A fourth group, again very different, is a radical wing of the movement represented by such writers as Sandra Harding, who claims that physics today "is a poor model [even] for physics itself."[13] For her, science now has the fatal flaw of "androcentrism"; that, together with faith in the progressiveness of scientific rationality, has brought us to the point where, she writes, "a more radical intellectual, moral, social, and political revolution [is called for] than the founders of modern Western cultures could have imagined."[14] One of her like-minded colleagues goes even further, into the fantasy that science is the projection of Oedipal obsessions with such notions as force, energy, power, or conflict.

That these groups have been able to gain considerable attention is due in part to the fact that the ground for dismay with modern science and technology has been prepared by three different factors, all operating in the same direction. Two are international in character, the third is local to the United States, and all of them play into the hands of the intentional delegitimators.

First, with science and engineering now central components of modern life, from birth to death, it is not surprising that concern is widespread over some real or imagined consequences of science-driven technology, nor that some of these have in fact been first examined and made public by scientists and engineers. Interestingly, we hear less now about a feared displacement of human labor by machines, which agitated the United States during the Great Depression. The concern today is closer to that expressed by Franklin D. Roosevelt in his second inaugural address and again later in 1937 in a letter to President K. T. Compton of the Massachusetts Institute of Technology, where Roosevelt wrote that the engineer's responsibility should include considering "social processes," "more perfect adjustment to environment," and designing mechanisms "to absorb the shocks of the impact of science."[15] Today's interrogators of engineering tend to go much further, fearing that technological devices, if mismanaged, can lead to the technologization of barbarism or curtail the life-sustaining capacity of this globe. The ordinary "man in the street" who harbors such fears is not convinced that the bulk of the community of scientists and engineers is sufficiently dedicated to the containment of these threats or that its protests are taken seriously at high policy levels.

This leads us to the second factor, of which the now international ecology movement is an indicator. Earlier than even most scientists, some critics intuited the fragility and delicacy of the interconnections that govern the well-being of all species on Earth. Their methodology and their rhetoric may not always have been sound, but their motivation has been a Darwinian one.

The need for ecological-systems thinking, both for its benign significance and because of the evident threats, is rather new, having emerged into global thought only in the last third of the twentieth century, and is bound to become a chief preoccupation of the twenty-first. There were of course very significant pioneers earlier, such as John Muir and Patrick Geddes, who prepared our minds in terms of their local or localizable concerns. Even Rachel Carson was focusing only on the threats to the ecosystem from certain chemicals. We now treasure these pioneers even more, because they prepared us to understand better the global meaning that had to be extrapolated from their messages. We now know that a relatively local insult to the ecosystem can and often does produce effects far "downwind." One thinks here of the discovery of dangerous radioactive fallout from A-bomb tests; the disaster for Indian farmers traceable to deforestation in Nepal; the effect on people and agriculture owing to the Chernobyl disaster; the tragedy of the decimation of the Amazonian rain forest; the widespread pollution at the Hanford Engineer Works, along the Rhine, at Love Canal, and many other sites; the linkage of droughts and floods to poor land management far away; and of course, insistently—as if the globe as a whole were rousing itself to shout for our attention—ozone depletion and the greenhouse effect. Once again, citizens who are reaching out for a new ethos of global stewardship find that they have relatively few visible and vocal allies among the academic scientists and engineers, even fewer among their brethren in industry.

Last but not least, with the rise of many scientists to prominence in our own nation's life, something was triggered in the American response which is perhaps idiosyncratic for this country but in fact is fundamentally healthy—namely, skepticism against this, as against any, form of strong, organized authority. As the astute political scientist Don K. Price has pointed out, Americans tend to have a special response to science, one that has roots in our ingrained political philosophy. From the beginning, the predominant attitude toward any large-scale organized authority in the United States has been essentially negative, and our political institutions are set up with the purpose of impeding the assertion of centralized authority as far as possible. In the first century and a half of the Republic, scientists and engineers were seen as outsiders, even as a force against established authority, as challengers of all dogma and successors of the religious dissenters who founded this country. When Joseph Priestley, equally unorthodox as a chemist, political writer, and theologian, fled England and the mob that destroyed his house, library, and laboratory, Thomas Jefferson embraced him on his arrival to America as a fellow dissident against the King and his Church. Scientists became the inheritors of the belief in progress.

But, Price says, "during the past generation there has been a sharp break with this tradition."[16] As scientists have become far more numerous and their work, directly or indirectly, has begun to change our daily lives, they have come to be identified not with dissent but with authority. Thus, although science itself is still seen as a positive force by a majority of Americans, scientists—who have been slow to understand this reaction—have become increasingly targets of suspicion. . . .

We began by asking the question whether the multi-faceted anti-science phenomenon, even if widespread, is at bottom only a more or less harmless diversion, or whether it signals an important cultural challenge and must therefore be taken seriously.

The answer is now clear. If we leave aside as comparatively unimportant the passing fads, ignorance, banalizations, and their commercial exploitation, we can focus on pseudo- or parascientific schemes that arise from deep conviction. These are grounded in a fairly stable and functional, motivating world view. It is these that can be directed at the core of contemporary culture (as would, for example, an analogous anti-literature phenomenon: in fact, some of the new cultural movements in the United States have just that purpose). Even though the counter-constructs embodying parascience are a minority view today in the United States, their entrenchment is a living reminder of an old, worldwide struggle of mutual delegitimation of rival cultural claimants. How alarming this is felt to be depends of course on one's degree of satisfaction with or allegiance to the modern world picture. And what the likely trend of this conflict may be in the near future will depend to some degree on whether earnest and successful interventions are undertaken in opposition to the counter-construct, or whether intellectuals and policy makers on the whole will continue to give only lip service to this problem, as they have done with scientific and general cultural illiteracy. . . .

Among examples that help us derive guidelines from this analysis are two in particular. One is the rise of the machine-breaking Luddites in Britain from 1811 to 1816. It was a movement first spawned by economic grievances, but it eventually became a violent explosion against the technological symbols of a suffocating and unyielding factory system.[17] Here we need only refer to it, because it has a certain overlap with the other example, which took place in the 1920s and early 1930s. In the early phase of the growth of Nazism in Germany, there arose, in the words of Fritz Stern, the "cultural Luddites, who in their resentment of modernity sought to smash the whole machinery of culture."[18]

In that case, the discontent with industrial civilization joined with the reaction against aspects of the program of modernity identifiable with "the growing power of liberalism and secularism." The gathering fury did not fail to include prominently science itself. One of the German ideologues most widely read in the 1920s was Julius Langbehn, who taught that there is an opposition between the scientific and the creative and who decried science, especially its tendency to splinter into specialization. In Stern's words: "Hatred of science dominated all of Langbehn's thought. . . . To Langbehn, science signified positivism, rationalism, empiricism, mechanistic materialism, technology, scepticism, dogmatism, and specialization . . ." (p. 122).

Thus it was not an accident that conventional science came under siege in Germany well before the Nazis assumed governmental power—with some German scientists demanding an "Aryan" science that was based on intuitive concepts, on the ether (as a residence of "Geist," or "Spirit"), on experimental rather than formalistic or abstract conceptions, and above all on advances "made by Germans." Spengler's conceptions seemed tailor-made to be incorporated in the Nazi ideology, and it was to his great credit that he courageously repelled all efforts to draw him into that net. But once allowed to take over the government, the Nazis put their weight behind a whole panoply of officially backed countersciences, from astrology to Himmler's "World Ice Theory," from versions of quantum mechanics that served their ideology to heinous schemes for "race purification." The readiness with which large numbers of physicians, jurists, scientists, and other academics lent themselves to the abominations committed under the last of these show that scientific literacy by itself provides no immunization; it also attests to the pliability of even so-called intellectuals when there is a cultural upheaval in which politics and parascience join. Indeed, as J. D. Bernal noted in his seminal book *The Social Function of Science*, the rise of Nazism had been prepared by irrational movements, including elements of the anti-science phenomenon in Germany at that time.[19]

In looking back on such historic cases, we can draw two important lessons. The first is that alternative sciences or parasciences by themselves may be harmless enough except as one of the opiates of the masses, but that when they are incorporated into political movements they can become a time bomb waiting to explode. We have recently been watching just such a possibility in the United States. Among the relevant documentation is an important essay by James Moore, released by the American Academy of Arts and Sciences, entitled "The Creationist Cosmos of Protestant Fundamentalism."[20] It chronicles the recent rise and political power of the anti-evolution movement in the United States. While opposition to evolutionist teachings has a long history in America, Moore notes that "today, Fundamentalists may have a fair claim that up to a quarter of the population of the U.S., and a rapidly increasing number of converts worldwide, live in a universe created miraculously [in six days] only a few thousand years ago, and on an earth tenanted only by those fixed organic kinds that survived a global Flood. . . . The creationist cosmos of Protestant Fundamentalism has acquired an authority rivaling that of the established sciences" (p. 46).

Far from being led by old-fashioned and anti-scientist theologians of the sort familiar from the nineteenth century, the intellectual agenda of the current creationist movement has been propelled chiefly by a small but dedicated group trained in science and engineering, many with doctorates and research positions and capable of living with glaring contradictions within their total world picture. Their motivation was initially a joining of a belief in the literal truth of the Bible with a Cold War opposition to the perceived Soviet threat. They are well financed and well organized, highly productive of eloquent publications in their own journals, books, films, radio and TV programs, and educational institutes. Above all they are well connected to the most conservative political segments and church groups. Much of their activism has centered on gaining access to the minds of the young—the introduction of what they call "Scientific Creationism" into the school science curriculum through pressure exerted on local school boards—as an alternative to evolution, which they speak of as Satanically inspired and antithetical to Christianity. Beyond that, there is now indication that the movement is going to deal with Copernicus as it has with Darwin, by embarking on geocentrism.

The most noteworthy point is the joining of "Creationism" with the agenda of politically ambitious evangelists such as Jerry Falwell, Pat Robertson, Jimmy Swaggart, Jim Bakker, D. James Kennedy, and many others. "Already the shapers of opinion in churchgoing America . . . [despite the temporary disgrace of some] have become the most visible and influential defenders of the creationist cosmos." This movement is part of an attack on secular humanism, which they also see as part of a Satanic ideology (p. 61). As the proponents' published view shows, the stakes are much higher for them than merely displacing current biology texts. They focus on the traditional Fundamentalist task: how to prepare this world for the coming of the next.

On the way to that goal, they have encountered surprisingly little vocal opposition from the world of scholarship, science, or theology. On the contrary, they have acquired powerful allies in high places. Their sympathizers included a President of the United States in the 1980s; he is on record as holding to a world view that has open arms not only for astrology but also for UFOs, for creationism, and for a form of premillenialist Fundamentalism that concerns itself with the inevitable approach in the near future of an apocalyptic Ending. While the United States will have to live with the after-effects of many of his ideological positions, it was perhaps a lucky chance that his genial lack of deep commitment on many matters extended also to these alternative-science views and their religio-political connections; for it is sobering to think how different it might have been if he had had a driving passion for them. It may of course go the other way with some future incumbent—here or in some other country vulnerable to the same combination of forces. Moore's essay ends on the ominous note that today's *fin-de-siècle* Fundamentalism and "the reigning assumptions of liberal, evolutionary enlightenment" may yet confront each other in a *Kulturkampf*, in which they will "clash, violently perhaps, to mobilize consent and enforce political order" (p. 64).

The other lesson to draw from our historic cases is simply this. History records an important and revealing asymmetry: the original machine Luddites of the nineteenth century were soon brutally crushed; but the Cultural Luddites have often, at least for some time, been the winners, although at great cost to their civilization. It is sobering that in every case there were intellectuals who tried to stand up to the Cultural Luddites—but they rose too late, were far too small in number, received little encouragement from their peers, and had less commitment and staying power than did their opponents.

As we have seen, history records that the serious and dedicated portion of the anti-science phenomenon, when married to political power, does signal a major cultural challenge. At its current level, this challenge may not be an irreparable threat to the modern world view as such. But it cannot be dismissed as just a distasteful annoyance either, nor only as a reminder of the failure of educators. On the contrary, the record from Ancient Greece to Fascist Germany and Stalin's U.S.S.R. to our day shows that movements to delegitimate conventional science are ever present and ready to put themselves at the service of other forces that wish to bend the course of civilization their way—for example, by the glorification of populism, folk belief, and violence, by mystification, and by an ideology that arouses rabid ethnic and nationalistic passions.

In short, it is prudent to regard the committed and politically ambitious parts of the anti-science phenomenon as a reminder of the Beast that slumbers below. When it awakens, as it has again and again over the past few centuries, and as it undoubtedly will again some day, it will make its true power known.

Notes

1. A rare example of a full-length treatment of anti-science is J. C. Burnham, *How Superstition Won and Science Lost* (New Brunswick, N.J.: Rutgers University Press, 1987). For specific facets of anti-science, see the essays by Helga Nowotny, Gernot Bohme, Otto Ullrich, and Hilary Rose in Helga Nowotny and H. Rose, *Counter-Movements in the Sciences* (Dordrecht: Reidel, 1979); and essays by Leo Marx, Lynn White, Jr., and Robert S. Morison in Gerald Holton and R. S. Morison, *Limits of Scientific Inquiry* (New York: W. W. Norton, 1979).

2. Irving Langmuir, "Pathological Science," *Physics Today*, 42 (1989): 36.

3. D. A. Bromley, "By the Year 2000: First in the World," *Report of the Federal Coordinating Council for Science, Engineering & Technology (FCCSET), Committee on Education and Human Resources* (Washington, D.C.: FCCSET, 1991).

4. J. Miller, "The Public Understanding of Science and Technology in the U.S., 1990," Draft Report to the National Science Foundation, 1 February 1991.

5. These findings are little different from those in National Commission on Excellence in Education, *A Nation at Risk: The Imperative for Educational Reform* (Washington, D.C.: National Commission on Excellence in Education, 1983). For surveys see National Science Board, *Science and Engineering Indicators* (Washington, D.C.: U.S. Government Printing Office, 1989), chap. 8; and R. G. Niemi, J. Mueller, and T. W. Smith, *Trends in Public Opinion: A Compendium of Survey Data* (New York: Greenwood Press, 1989).

6. M. Weber, "Science as a Vocation" (1918), reprinted in *Daedalus* (Winter 1958): 117 (this inaugural issue was devoted to the topic "science and the modern world view").

7. E. R. Dodds, *The Greeks and the Irrational* (Boston: Beacon Press, 1957); originally published by the University of California Press in 1951. For a more extensive discussion of it, see Gerald Holton, *The Advancement of Science, and Its Burdens* (New York: Cambridge University Press, 1986), chap. 10.

8. Niemi, Mueller, and Smith, *Trends in Public Opinion*.

9. In Richard Q. Elvee, ed., *The End of Science? Attack and Defense* (Lanham, Md.: University Press of America, 1992), p. 57.

10. S. Woolgar, ed., *Knowledge and Reflexivity: New Frontiers in the Sociology of Knowledge* (London: Sage Publications, 1988), p. 166.

11. Lionel Trilling, *Mind in the Modern World: The 1972 Jefferson Lecture in the Humanities* (New York: Viking, 1972).

12. I have treated this phenomenon in G. Holton, "Dionysians, Apollonians, and the Scientific Imagination," in *The Advancement of Science*, chap. 3. A carefully supported analysis of the fashionable attempts to link modern science and Eastern lore is S. Restivo, "Parallels and Paradoxes in Modern Physics and Eastern Mysticism," *Social Studies of Science*, 8, Part I (1978): 143–181, and 12, Part II (1982): 37–71.

13. Sandra Harding, "Why Physics Is a Bad Model for Physics," in Elvee, ed., *The End of Science?*

14. Sandra Harding, *The Science Question in Feminism* (Ithaca: Cornell University Press, 1986), p. 10; see the trenchant reviews of this issue in M. Levin, *American Scholar*, 57 (1988): 100–106, and in Clifford Geertz, "A Lab of One's Own," *New York Review of Books*, 37 (8 November 1990): 19–23.

15. Carroll W. Purcell, in M. C. La Follette and J. K. Stine, eds., *Technology and Choice* (Chicago: University of Chicago Press, 1991), p. 169.

16. Don K. Price, *America's Unwritten Constitution* (Baton Rouge: Louisiana State University Press, 1983).

17. See, for example, M. I. Thomis, *The Luddites: Machine-Breaking in Regency England* (Hamden, Conn.: M. Archon Books, 1970); F. O. Darvall, *Popular Disturbances and Public Order in Regency England* (London: Oxford University Press, 1934); and G. Pearson, "Resistance to the Machine," in *Counter-Movements in the Sciences*, ed. Helga Nowotny and H. Rose (Dordrecht: Reidel, 1979).

18. Fritz Stern, *The Politics of Cultural Despair: A Study of the Rise of German Ideology* (Berkeley: University of California Press, 1961), p. xvii. See also the important book: Alan Beyerchen, *Scientists under Hitler: Politics in the Third Reich* (New Haven, Conn.: Yale University Press, 1977). A review of more recent scholarship is provided in Alan Beyerchen, "What We Now Know about Nazism and Science," *Social Research*, 59 (1992): 616–641.

19. J. D. Bernal, *The Social Function of Science* (London: Routledge, 1946), p. 3.

20. In M. E. Marty and R. S. Appleby, *Fundamentalisms and Society: Reclaiming the Sciences, the Family, and Education*, vol. 2 (Chicago, Ill.: University of Chicago Press, 1992).

The Monster and the Titan

Theodore Roszak

Dissatisfaction with science comes in many forms. Theodore Roszak is particularly concerned about the effect modern science has on the spirit. He claims that because our best current scientific theories tell us that the world is meaningless, we are led to despair (if we are sufficiently thoughtful). Despair injures the spirit, but it is not inevitable if we recognize that there are different styles of knowing. Science provides us with reductive knowledge; it strips away the significance of the objects under scrutiny. By contrast, an "augmentive" style of knowing focuses on the significance of objects—their personal implications, their beauty, and their religious significance. Roszak argues that we should be seeking "gnosis," a traditional style of knowing that emphasizes both "hard facts" and an array of meanings we find in these facts. Since in our culture, science has tended to eliminate other styles of knowing and leave us with incomplete understanding, it becomes a monster. This result is not necessary, however, and Roszak urges us to reinforce all of the styles of knowing that make up gnosis. Theodore Roszak is professor of history at California State University, Hayward.

As you read through this essay, consider the following:

1. Why does Roszak associate science with "the monster"?
2. What is augmentive knowledge? Do you think this deserves to be called knowledge?
3. What does Roszak mean by gnosis? Why does he think it is important?
4. How has science led to the suppression of gnosis? Was this result inevitable?
5. Do you think that we should expand our appreciation of gnosis? If so, how might our culture encourage this?

The title of the book was *Frankenstein*. The subtitle was *The Modern Prometheus*.

An inspired moment when Mary Shelley decided that a maker of monsters could nonetheless be a Titan of discovery—one whose research might, in our time, win him the laurels of Nobel. She claimed the story broke upon her in a "waking dream." It may well have been by benefit of some privileged awareness that one so young fused into a single dramatic image the warring qualities that made Victor Frankenstein both mad doctor

and demigod. A girl of only nineteen, but by virtue of that one, rare insight, she joined the ranks of history's great myth makers. What else but a myth could tell the truth so shrewdly, capturing definitively the full moral tension of this strange intellectual passion we call science? And how darkly prophetic that science, the fairest child of the Enlightenment, should find the classic statement of its myth in a Gothic tale of charnel houses and graveyards, nightmares and bloody murder.

Asked to nominate a worthy successor to Victor Frankenstein's macabre brainchild, what should we choose from our contemporary inventory of terrors? The bomb? The cyborg? The genetically synthesized android? The behavioral brain washer? The despot computer? Modern science provides us with a surfeit of monsters, does it not?

From Theodore Roszak, "The Monster and the Titan: Science, Knowledge, and Gnosis." Reprinted by permission of *Daedalus*, Journal of the American Academy of Arts and Sciences, from the issue entitled, "Science and Its Public: The Changing Relationship," Summer 1974, vol. 103, no. 3.

I realize there are many scientists—perhaps the majority of them—who believe that these and a thousand other perversions of their genius have been laid unjustly at their doorstep. These monsters, they would insist, are the bastards of technology: sins of applied, not pure science. Perhaps it comforts their conscience somewhat to invoke this much muddled division of labor, though I must confess that the line which segregates research from development within the industrial process these days looks to me like one of gossamer fineness, hardly like a moral *condon sanitaire*.

I realize, too, that there are some—those who champion a "science for the people"— who believe that mad doctors are an aberration of science that can be wholly charged to the account of military desperados and corporate profiteers. Their enemies are also mine; I write in full recognition of how the wrongheaded power elites of the world corrupt the promise of science. But I fear there are more unholy curiosities at work in their colleagues' laboratories than capitalism, its war lords, and hucksters can be made the culprits for. Certainly they must share my troubled concern to see the worst excesses of behavioral psychology and reductionist materialism become unquestionable orthodoxies in the socialist societies.

I will grant to both these views some measure of validity (less to the first, much more to the second). But here and now I have no wish to pursue the issues they raise, because I have another monster in mind that troubles me as much as all the others—one who is nobody's child but the scientist's own and whose taming is no political task. I mean an invisible demon who works by subtle poison, not upon the flesh and bone, but upon the spirit. I refer to the monster of meaninglessness. The psychic malaise. The existential void where modern man searches in vain for his soul.

Of course there are few scientists who will readily accept this unlovely charge upon their paternity. The creature I name wears the face of despair; its lineaments are those of spiritual desperation; in its bleak features scientists will see none of their own exhilaration and buoyant morale. They forget with what high hopes and dizzy fascination Victor Frankenstein pursued his research. He too undertook the adventure of discovery with feverish delight, intending to invent a new and superior race of beings, creatures of majesty and angelic beauty. It was only when his work was done and he stepped back to view it as a whole that its true—and terrifying—character appeared.

The pride of science has always been its great-hearted humanism. What place, one may wonder, is there in the humanist's philosophy for despair? But there is more than one species of humanism, though the fact is too often brushed over. In the modern West, we have, during the past three centuries, run a dark, downhill course from an early morning humanism to a midnight humanism; from a humanism of celebration to a humanism of resignation. The humanism of celebration— the humanism of Pico and Michelangelo, of Bacon and Newton—stems from an experience of man's congruency with the divine. But for the humanism of resignation, there is no experience of the divine, only the experience of man's infinite aloneness. And from that is born a desperate and anxious humanism, one that clings to the human as if it were a raft adrift in an uncharted sea. In that condition of forsakenness, we are not humanists by choice, but by default—humanists because there is nothing else we have the conviction to be, humanists because the only alternative is the nihilist abyss.

If I say it is science that has led us from the one humanism to the other, that it is science which has made our universe an unbounded theater of the absurd . . . does that sound like an accusation? Perhaps. But I intend no condemnation, because I believe that, at every step, the intentions of the scientists have been wholly honest and honorable. They have pursued the truth and followed bravely where it took them, even when its destination became the inhuman void. In any case, I say no more than thoughtful scientists have themselves recognized to be true—in some cases with no little pride. Thus, Jacques Monod:

> By a single stroke [science] claimed to sweep away the tradition of a hundred thousand years, which had become one with human nature itself. It wrote an end to the ancient animist covenant between man and nature, leaving nothing in place of that precious bond but an anxious quest in a frozen universe of solitude.[1]

Or, as Steven Weinberg puts it elsewhere in this volume [*Daedalus*, vol. 103 (1974)]:

> The laws of nature are as impersonal and free of human values as the rules of arithmetic. We didn't want it to come out this way, but it did. . . . The whole system of the visible stars stands revealed as only a small part of the spiral arm of one of a huge number of galaxies, extending away from us in all directions. Nowhere do we see human value or human meaning.[2]

Our universe. The only universe science can comprehend and endorse. "A universe," Julian Huxley has called it, "of appalling vastness, appalling age, appalling meaninglessness." But not for that reason, an uninteresting universe. On the contrary, it is immensely, inexhaustibly *interesting*. There is no reason, after all, why what is wholly alien to us should not be wholly absorbing. Nor is there any reason why, in such a universe, we should not make up meanings for ourselves—whatever meanings we please and as many as we can imagine. Is this not the favorite preoccupation of modern culture, the intellectual challenge that adds the spice of variety to our lifestyle? We may even decide to regard science itself as the most meaningful way of all to pass the time. All we need remember—if we are to remain scientifically accountable—is that none of these meanings resides in nature. They simply express a subjective peculiarity of our species. They are arbitrary constructions having no point of reference "Out There." Which is to say: the universe we inhabit—insofar as we let it be the universe science tells us we inhabit—is an *inhuman* universe. We share some minute portion

of its dead matter, but it shares no portion of our living mind. It is (again to quote Jacques Monod) an "unfeeling immensity, out of which [man] emerged only by chance . . ." and where "like a gypsy, he lives on the boundary of an alien world, a world that is deaf to his music, just as indifferent to his hopes as it is to his suffering or his crimes."

Perhaps not every reader agrees with me that meaninglessness is a monster. If not, then our sensibilities are of a radically different order and we may have to part company from this point forward, for this is not the place to try closing the gap between us. But I believe more than a few scientists have looked out at times upon the "unfeeling immensity" of their universe with some unease. Note Weinberg's phrase, "We didn't want it to come out this way. . . ."

Perhaps not every reader regards the degradation of meaning in nature as a *moral* issue. But I do. Because meaninglessness breeds despair, and despair, I think, is a secret destroyer of the human spirit, as real and as deadly a menace to our cultural sanity as the misused power of the atoms is to our physical survival. By my lights at least, to kill old gods is as terrible a transgression of conscience as to concoct new babies in a test tube.

But even if scientists should agree that their discipline buys its progress at a dear price in existential meaning, what are they to do? Steven Weinberg faces the question squarely in his essay and offers an answer which would, I suspect, be endorsed by many of his colleagues. He tells us that "other modes of knowledge" (the example he gives is aesthetic perception) might be accommodated alongside science in a position of coexistence, but they cannot be given a place *within* science as part of a radical shift of sensibilities.

> . . . science cannot change in this way without destroying itself, because however much human values are involved in the scientific process or are affected by the results of scientific research, there is an essential element in science that is cold, objective, and nonhuman. . . . Having committed ourselves to the scientific standard of truth, we have thus been forced, not by our

own choosing, away from the rhapsodic sensibility . . . In the end, the choice is a moral, or even a religious, one. Having once committed ourselves to look at nature on its own terms, it is something like a point of honor not to flinch at what we see.

"The universe," Weinberg insists, "is what it is." And science, as the definitive natural philosophy, can have no choice but to tell it like it is, and "not to flinch."

One cannot help admiring the candor of such an answer—and grieving a little for the pathos of its resignation. But it is, in any case, a Promethean answer, one that reminds us that the free pursuit of knowledge *is*, after all, a supreme value, a need of the mind as urgent as the body's need for our food. However much one may upbraid science for having disenchanted our lives, sooner or later one must come to grips with the animating spirit of the discipline, the myth that touches it with an epic grandeur. Call up the monster, and the scientist calls up the Titan. Press the claims of spiritual need, and the scientist presses the claims of mind as, in their own right, a sovereign good.

Any critique of science that challenges the paramount good of knowledge risks becoming a crucifixion of the intellect. If Prometheus is to stop producing monsters, it must not be at the sacrifice of his Titanic virtues. The search for knowledge must be a free adventure; yet it must not choose, in its freedom, to do us harm in body, mind, or spirit. One no sooner states the matter in this way than it seems like an impossible dilemma. We are asking that the mind in search of knowledge should be left wholly free and yet be morally disciplined at the same time. Is this possible?

I believe it is, but only if we recognize that there are *styles* of knowledge as well as *bodies* of knowledge. Besides *what* we know, there is *how* we know it—how wisely, how gracefully, how life-enhancingly. The life of the mind is a constant dialogue between knowing and being, each shaping the other. This is what makes it possible to raise a question which, at first sight, is apt to appear odd in the extreme. *Can we be sure that what science gives us is indeed knowledge?*

PLATO, DON JUAN, AND GNOSIS

For most Western intellectuals that might seem a preposterous question, since for the better part of three centuries now science has served as the measure of knowledge in our society. But to raise it is only to recall the Platonic tradition, within which our science would have been regarded as an intellectual transaction distinctly beneath the level of knowledge. There is no telling for sure how highly Plato might have rated the spectacular theoretical work of the modern world's best scientific brains, but I suspect he would have respected it as "information"—a coherent, factually related account of the physical structure and function of things: a clever scheme for "saving the appearances," as Plato liked to characterize the astronomy of his day. Here we have a demanding and creditable labor of the intellect; but on Plato's well-known four-step ladder of the mind, science would be placed somewhere between the second and third levels of the hierarchy—above mere uninformed "opinion," but distinctly below "knowledge."

Easy enough to dismiss Plato as backward or plain perverse for refusing to rate science any higher on the scale. But how much more interesting to let the mind follow where his gesture takes it when he invites us to look beyond experiment, theory, and mathematical formulation to a higher object of knowledge which he calls "the essential nature of the Good . . . from which everything that is good and right derives its value for us."

Significantly, when Plato tried to put this object of knowledge into words, his habit, like that of many another mystic, was to enlist the services of myth and allegory, or to warn how much must be left unsaid. "There is no writing of mine about these matters," he tells us in the Seventh Epistle in a passage that might be a description of the Zen Buddhist Satori, "nor will there ever be one. For this knowledge is not something that can be put into words like other sciences; but after long-continued intercourse between teacher and pupil, in joint pursuit of the subject, suddenly, like light flashing forth when a fire is kindled, it is born in the soil and straightaway nourishes itself." No doubt, at first glance, such an elusive conception of knowledge is bound to seem objectionable to many scientists. But in light of all that Michael Polanyi has written about the "personal knowledge" and the "tacit dimension" involved in science, Plato's remarks should not seem wholly alien. Plato is reminding us of those subtleties that can only be conveyed between person and person at some nonverbal level; to force such insights into words or into a formal pedagogy would be to destroy them. If we are to learn them at all, there is no way around intimate association with a guru who can alone make sure that each realization is sensibly adapted to the time, and the place, and the person. So too in science, as in every craft and art. Is not much that is essential to the study left to be learned from one's master by way of nuance and hint, personal taste and emotional texture? And does this not include the most important matters of all: the spirit of the enterprise, the choice of a problem deemed worth studying, the instinctive sense of what is and what is not a reputable scientific approach to any subject, the decision as to when a hypothesis has been sufficiently demonstrated to merit publication? How much of all this is taught by the glint in the eye or the inflection in the voice, by subtle ridicule or the merest gesture of approval? Even the exact sciences could not do without their elements of taste and intuitive judgment, talents which students learn by doing or from the living example before them.

Plato is, of course, pushing the uses of reticence much further. He contends that, if only the tacit dimension of instruction between guru and student is exploited to its fullest, we can find our way to a knowledge, properly so-called, which grasps the nature and *the value* of things as a whole, and so raises us to a level at which intellect and conscience become one and inseparable in the act of knowing. "Without that knowledge," he insists, "to know everything else, however

well, would be of no value to us, just as it is of no use to possess anything without getting the good of it."

Again, I suspect that Plato is not so far removed in his pursuit from a familiar scientific experience, one which comes in the wake of any significant discovery. It is the sense that, over and above what the particular discovery in question has shown to be factually so, this activity of the mind has proved itself *good*; it has, as a human project, elevated us to a level of supremely satisfying existence. One has not only found out something correct (perhaps that is the least of it, in the long run) but one has *been* something worth being. It is an experience many people have known, at least fleetingly, in their work as artists, craftsmen, teachers, athletes, doctors, etc. We might call it "an experience of excellence," and let it go at that. But what Plato wished to do was to isolate that experience as an object of knowledge, and to treat it, not as the by-product of some other, lesser activity, but as a goal in its own right. He wished to know the Good in itself which we only seem to brush against now and again in passing as we move from one occasional task to another. Nothing in modern science would have appalled Plato more than the way in which a professional scientific paper seeks, in the name of objectivity, to depersonalize itself to the point of leaving out all reference to that "experience of excellence"—that fleeting glimpse of the higher Good. For, I believe Plato would have objected, if no such experience was there, then the work was not worth doing; and if it was, then why leave it out, since it must surely be the whole meaning and value of science? Once you omit *that*, you have nothing left except . . . information.

If I invoke Plato here, it is not because I wish to endorse his theory of knowledge, but only to use him as a convenient point of departure. I recognize the logical blemishes that have dogged his epistemology through the centuries—and regard many of them as unanswerable within the framework Plato erected for his work. He is, however, the most renowned philosophical spokesman for a style of knowledge which is far older than formal philosophy; in his work we confront a visionary tradition which runs through nearly every culture, civilized and primitive. The prime value of Plato—so it has always seemed to me—lies not so much in the intellectual territory he occupied and surveyed, as in his stubborn determination to keep open a passage through which the mind might cross over from philosophy to ecstasy; from intellect to illumination. His dialogues stand on the border of a transrational sensibility whose charm seems a constant feature of human culture—a sensibility perhaps as old as the mind itself, and yet as contemporary as the latest best-seller list. Recall what the Yaqui Indian shaman Don Juan calls himself in Carlos Castaneda's recent popular reports: "a man of *knowledge*." And, for all the differences of personal style and lore that part the two men, the old sorcerer means knowledge in exactly the way Plato meant it, as an ecstatic insight into the purpose and place of human existence in the universe, a glimpse of the eternal.

What both Plato the philosopher and Don Juan the sorcerer seek as knowledge is precisely that *meaningfulness* of things which science has been unable to find as an "objective" feature of nature. To follow where such a conception of knowledge takes us is not to denigrate the value or fascination of information. It is to be neither antiscientific nor antirational. It leads us not to an either/or choice, but to a recognition of priorities within an integrated philosophical context. Information can be exciting to collect; it can be urgently useful: a tool for our survival. But it is not the same as the knowledge we take with us into the crises of life. Where ethical decision, death, suffering, failure confront us, or in those moments when the awesome vastness of nature presses in upon us, making us seem frail and transient, what the mind cries out for is the meaning of things, the purpose they teach, the enduring significance they give our existence. And that, I take it, is Plato's knowledge of the Good.

To call this *another kind* of knowledge may seem a convenient compromise or a generous concession. But I submit that either as compromise or concession, this policy of Cartesian apartheid is treacherous. At best, it asks for the sort of schizophrenic coexistence that divides the personality cruelly between fact and feeling. At worst, it is the first step toward denying the "other knowledge" any status as knowledge at all—toward considering it a sort of irrational spasm devoid of any claim to truth or reality, perhaps an infantile weakness of the ego that is only forgiveable because it is so universally human. At that point we are not far from treating the need for meaning as a purely subjective question for which there is no objective answer—as an unfortunate behavioral trait which we leave psychologists or brain physiologists to stake out for investigation. Once it ceases to be the basis for knowledge, it may finish as an occasion for therapy.

My purpose here is to call back to mind the traditional style of knowledge for which the nature of things was as much a reservoir of meanings as of facts—a style of knowledge which science is now aggressively replacing in every society on earth. Let us call this knowledge "gnosis," borrowing the word not to designate a second and separate kind of knowledge, but an *older* and *larger* kind of knowledge from which our style of knowledge derives by way of a sudden and startling transformation of the sensibilities over the past three centuries. My contention is that this process of derivation has been spiritually impoverishing and psychically distorting. It has resulted in a narrowing of our full human potentialities and has left us—especially in science—with a diminished Titanism that falsely borrows upon the myth it champions. When the modern Prometheus reaches for knowledge, it is not the torch of gnosis he brings back or even searches for, but the many candles of information. Yet not a million of those candles will equal the light of that torch, for these are fires of a different order.

AUGMENTATIVE KNOWLEDGE

I will not try to characterize gnosis here as an "alternative cognitive system" in any programmatic way—as if to offer a new methodology or curriculum. Rather, I want to speak of gnosis as a different sense of what knowledge is than science provides. When we search for knowledge, it is a certain texture of intelligibility we first and most decisively seek, a *feeling* in the mind that tells us, "Yes, here is what we are looking for. This has meaning and significance to it." Though it may work well below the level of deliberate awareness, this touchstone of the mind is what makes the persuasive difference in our thinking. Indeed, science itself arose in just this way, when men of Galileo's generation came to feel, with an uncanny spontaneity, that to know was to measure, that all else was subjective and unreal, a realm of "secondary qualities."

In the broadest sense, gnosis is *augmentative* knowledge, in contrast to the *reductive* knowledge characteristic of the sciences. It is a hospitality of the mind that allows the object of study to expand itself and become as much as it might become, with no attempt to restrict or delimit. Gnosis invites every object to swell with personal implications, to become special, wondrous, perhaps a turning point in one's life, "a moment of truth." Paul Tillich has called gnosis "knowledge by participation . . . as intimate as the relation between husband and wife." Gnosis, he tells us, "is not the knowledge resulting from analytic and synthetic research. It is the knowledge of union and salvation, existential knowledge in contrast to scientific knowledge."

It is the guiding principle of gnosis that only augmentative knowledge is adequate to its object. As long as we, at our most open and sensitive, feel there is something left over or left out of any account we give of any object, we have fallen short of gnosis. Gnosis is that nagging whisper at the edge of the mind which tells us, whenever we seek completeness of understanding or pretend to premature comprehension, "not yet . . . not quite." It is our immediate awareness, often at a level deeper than intellect, that we seem not to have done justice to the object—not because there remains quantitatively more of the object to be investigated, but because its essential *quality* still eludes us.

I speak here of the experience many people have known when faced with some brutally reductionist explanation of human conduct. We feel the explanation "reduces" precisely because it leaves out so much of what we spontaneously know about humanness from inside our own experience. We look at the behaviorist's model and we know—as immediately as our eye would know that a circle is not a square—that this is not *us*. It may not even be an important part or piece of us, but only a degraded figment. Even if such knowledge "worked"—in the sense that it allowed others to manipulate our conduct as precisely as an engineer can manipulate mechanical and electrical forms of energy—would we not still protest that *knowing how* to dangle us like a puppet on a string is not *knowing* us at all? Might we not insist that such "knowledge" works in the very opposite direction—that it is an ignorant, insulting violation of our nature? As Abraham Maslow once observed of his own experience in behavioral psychology: "When I can predict what a person will do under certain circumstances, this person tends to resent it. . . . He tends to feel dominated, controlled, outwitted."[3] Between "knowing" and "knowing how" there can be a fearful discord—like Bach being played on skillets and soup kettles: more mockery than music.

That discord shows up readily enough when we ourselves are the specimens under study. In that case, the standard of adequacy is provided by the object of investigation. We can speak for ourselves and fend off the assault upon our dignity. But what about the nonhuman objects of the world? Does it make any sense to say that our scientific knowledge of them may be *qualitatively* inadequate?

To answer that question, let us begin with a familiar comparison: that between art and science. The coincidence of the two fields has been observed many times, especially in so far as they share a common fascination for form and structure in nature. Yet, while there is an overlap, it is, from the scientist's point of view, an overlap of interest only, not of intellectual competence. Both art and science find an aesthetic aspect in nature (though of course many scientists have done significant research without pausing over that aspect). But for the scientist, the aesthetic appearance is a *surface;* knowledge stands behind that surface in some underlying mechanism or activity requiring analysis. What the artist sees is not regarded by science as knowledge of what is *in* the object as one of its constituent properties. Instead, what preoccupies the artist is called "beauty" (though often it would better be understood as awe, conceivably mixed with fear, anxiety, dread). Beauty is, for science, a sort of subjective supplement to knowledge, a decoration the mind supplies before or after the act of cognition, and which can or even ought to be omitted from professional publication. Aesthetic fascination may attract us to the object; it may later help flavor popularized accounts of research. From the scientist's viewpoint, however, only further study (dissection, deep analysis, comparison, experiment, measurement) allows us to find out something about the object, something demonstrable, predictive, useful. Compared to such hard fact, the artist's perception is merely dumb wonder, which, apparently, artists have not the intellectual rigor to go beyond. Jacob Bronowski has, for example, referred to the artist's response to nature as "a strangled, unformed and unfounded experience." But, he goes on, "science is a base for [that experience] which constantly renews the experience and gives it a coherent meaning."[4]

If this were not the supposition, we might imagine an entire specialization in science devoted to studying the nature poets and painters: biologists sprinkling their research with quotations from Wordsworth or Goethe . . . neophyte botanists taking required courses in landscape painting . . . astronomers drawing hypotheses from Van Gogh's "Starry Night" . . . theoretical physicists pondering the bizarre conceptions of time and space one finds in the serial tone row, cubism, constructivism, or Joyce's *Finnegans Wake.* Of course, nothing forbids scientists from wandering into these exotic realms, but what curriculum *requires* that they do so?

From the viewpoint of gnosis, however, what artists find in nature is decidedly knowledge of the object, indeed knowledge of a uniquely valuable kind. It is not repeatable or quantitative, nor is it open to experimentation or utilitarian application. It is usually not logically articulable; that is why special languages of sound, color, line, texture, metaphor and symbol have been invented to carry the message, in much the same way that mathematics has been developed as the special language of objective consciousness. But that message is as much knowledge as when, in addition to knowing your chemical composition, I discern that you are noble or base, lovable or vicious. So artists discover the communicative mood and quality that attach to form, color, sound, image. They teach us those qualities, and these become an inseparable part of our total response to the world.

Of course, these qualities can be screened out if our interest is directed to something less than the whole, but this does not mean the sensuous and aesthetic qualities are not really there as a constituent property of the world—a property that is being artfully *displayed* to us. Would it not, in fact, be truer to our experience to conceive of the world about us as a *theater,* rather than as a mechanism or a randomized aggregation of events? It is surely striking how often science quite naturally presents its discoveries as if it were unfolding a spectacle before us, thus borrowing heavily on sensibilities that have been educated by the dramatists and story-tellers. All cosmology is talked about in this way, and even a good deal of high energy physics and molecular biology. Everything we have lately discovered about the evolution of stars is, quite spontaneously, cast in the mode of biography: birth, youth, maturity, senility, death, and at last the mysterious transformation into an afterlife called "the black hole." Or, take the classic example of aesthetic perception in science. Can there be any doubt that much of the cogency of Darwin's theory of natural selection stemmed from the pure drama of the idea? Natural selection was presented as a billion-year-old epic of struggle, tragic disasters, lucky escapes, triumph, ingenious survival. Behind the sensibility to which Darwin's theory appealed lay three generations of Romantic art which had pioneered the perception of strife, dynamism, and unfolding process in nature. Behind Darwin stand Byron's Manfred, Goethe's Faust, Constable's cloud-swept landscapes, Beethoven's tempestuous quartets and sonatas. All this became an integral part of the Darwinian insight. I doubt there is anyone who does not still bring to the study of evolution this Romantic taste for effortful growth, conflict, and self-realization. The qualities are not only in the idea, but also in the phenomenon. It is not that these dramatic qualities have been "read" into nature by us, but rather that *nature* has read them into *us* and now summons them forth by the spectacle of evolution we find displayed around us.

We should by now be well aware of the price we pay for regarding aesthetic quality as arbitrary and purely subjective rather than as a real property of the object. Such a view opens the way to that brutishness which feels licensed to devastate the environment on the grounds that beauty is only "a matter of taste." And since one person's taste is as good as another's, who is to say—as a matter of *fact*—that the hard cash of a strip mine counts for less than the grandeur of an untouched mountain? Is such barbarism to be "blamed" on science? Obviously not in any direct way. But it is deeply rooted in a scientized reality principle that treats quantities as objective knowledge and qualities as a matter of subjective preference.

THE SPECTRUM OF GNOSIS

Now to push the point a little further. If art overlaps science at one wing, it overlaps visionary religion at the other. If artists have

found the cool beauty of orderly structure in nature, they have also found there the burning presence of the sacred. For some artists, as for the Deist scientists of Newton's day, God's imprint has appeared in the rhythmic cycles and stately regularities of nature. For other artists—Trahern, Blake, Keats, Hopkins—the divine grandeur of the world appears all at once, in an ecstatic flash, a jolt, a "high." Here we find the artist becoming seer and prophet. For such sensibilities, a burning bush, a storm-battered mountaintop can be, by the sheer awesomeness of the event, an immediate encounter with the divine.

To know God from the order of things is a deduction, a shaky one perhaps in the eyes of skeptical logicians, but at least remotely scientific in character. To know God from the power of the moment is an epiphany, a knowledge that takes us a long way from scientific respectability. Yet here is where gnosis mounts to its heights, becoming knowledge willingly obedient to the discipline of the sacred. It does not close itself to the epiphanies life offers by regarding them as "merely subjective." Rather, it allows, it *invites* experience to expand and become all that it can. After all, if Galileo was right to call those men fools who refused to view the moon through a telescope, what shall we say of those who refuse Blake's invitation to see eternity in a grain of sand? Gnosis seeks to integrate these moments of ecstatic wonder; it regards them as an advance upon reality, and by far the most exciting advance the mind has undertaken. For here is the reality that gives transcendent meaning to our lives.

Perhaps the best way to summarize what I have said so far is to conceive of the mind as a spectrum of possibilities, all of which properly blend into one another—unless we insist on erecting barriers across the natural flow of our experience. At one end, we have the hard, bright lights of science; here we find information. In the center we have the sensuous hues of art; here we find the aesthetic shape of the world. At the far end, we have the dark, shadowy tones of religious experience, shading off into wave lengths beyond all perception; here we find meaning. Science is properly part of this spectrum. *But gnosis is the whole spectrum.*

If, in the past, gnosis has been more heavily weighted on the side of meaning than information, it should not be difficult to understand why. Our ancestors saw fit to put first things first. Before they felt the need to know how fire burns or how seeds germinate, they needed to know the place and purpose of their own strange existence in the universe. And this they found generously offered to them in the nature of things. Yet, I know of no visionary tradition that has ever refused to agree that natural objects possess a structure and function worthy of study. Certainly none of these traditions has been as adamantly closed to the technical level of knowledge as our science has been closed to gnosis. Plato may have wanted the mind to rise to a level of ecstatic illumination, but he never said there was no such thing as information or that its pursuit was a sign of madness or intellectual incompetence. Similarly, the alchemists may have sought their spiritual regeneration in natural phenomena, but they never refused to examine the way nature works. Undeniably, where gnosis becomes our standard of knowledge, science and technology proceed at a much slower rate than the wild pace we accept (or suffer with) as normal. This is not to say, however, that gnosis is without its practical aspect, but rather that its sense of practicality embraces spirit as well as body, the need for psychic as much as for physical sustenance.

The most familiar examples we have of culture dominated by gnosis are in the world's primitive and pagan societies. Many of these societies have been capable of investing agrarian and hunting technologies every bit as ingenious as the machine technics of modern times. But, in stark contrast to the culture of urban-industrialism, their technology blended at every step with poetic insight and the worship of the elements. The tools and routines of daily life normally participated in the religious sensibility of the society, functioning as symbols of life's higher significance. From the viewpoint of the modern West, such a culture may look like a hodge-podge of wholly unre-

lated factors. In reality, it is an ideal expression of gnosis, for it expresses a unitary vision bringing together art, religion, science, and technics. Our habit, in dealing with such cultures, is to interpret their technics as lucky accidents and their aesthetic-religious context as an encumbrance. But by at least one critical standard, these "underdeveloped" cultures have proved more technically successful than our own may. They have *endured*, in some cases a hundred times longer than urban industrialism may yet endure. Surely that is some measure of how well a culture understands its place in nature.

Most of the world's mystic and occult traditions have been worked up from the gnosis of primitive and pagan cultures. At bottom, these traditions are sophisticated, speculative adaptations of the old folk religions, which preserve in some form their antique wisdom and modes of experience. Behind the Cabbala and Hermeticism, we can still see the shadowy forms of ritual magic and fertility rites, symbols of a sacred continuum binding man to nature and prescribing value. In all these mystic traditions, to know the real is to know the good, the beautiful, and the sacred at the same time.

This is not to say that all who followed these traditions achieved gnosis. The human mind goes wrong in many ways. It can go mad with ecstasies as well as with logic. Discriminating among the levels and directives of transrational experience is a project in its own right—one I do not even touch upon here, for the discussion would be far too premature at this point. There are disciplines of the visionary mind as well as of the rational intellect, as anyone will know who has done more than scratch the surface of the great mystic traditions. All I stress here is the difference between a taste for gnosis and a taste for knowledge whose visionary overtones have been systematically stilled as a supposed "distortion" of reality. . . .

This much of the problem stands out prominently enough: the mystic disciplines, on which gnosis depends, have never been as highly refined and widely practiced in the West as in the oriental cultures. In large part, they have suffered neglect because they cut across the doctrinal grain of conventional Christianity with its insistent emphasis on historicity and dogmatic theology. (I often think that few positivists realize how great a debt they owe to the peculiarly one-dimensional religious psychology of mainstream Christianity; its literalism and verbal rigidities paved the way for the secular skepticism of the religion's deadliest critics.) Still, in the Hermetic, Cabbalistic, Neo-Platonic, and alchemical schools of the Renaissance, at least a promising foundation existed for the building of a true gnosis. In these currents of thought we find an appreciation of myth, symbol, meditative stillness, and rhapsodic intellect that might, with maturity, have matched the finest flights of Tantric or Taoist mysticism.

But if these elements were mixed with early science in many exotic combinations, they were soon enough filtered out as violations of that strict objectivity which is the distinguishing feature of the Western scientific sensibility. It was Galileo's quantitative austerity and Descartes' dualism that carried the day with science, casting out of nature everything that was not matter in motion mathematically expressed. Here was the crucial point at which scientific knowledge ceased to be gnosis. Value, quality, soul, spirit, animist communion were all ruthlessly cut away from scientific thought like so much excess fat. What remained was the world-machine—sleek, dead, and alien. However much physics has, in our time, modified the mechanistic imagery of its classical period, the impersonality of the Newtonian world view continues to dominate the scientist's vision of nature. The models and metaphors of science may alter, but the sensibility of the discipline remains what it was. Since the quantum revolution, modern physics has ceased to be mechanistic, but it has scarcely become in any sense "mystical." The telling fact is that both in style and content it serves today as an ideal foundation for molecular biology and behavioral psychology,

sciences which have of late become as mechanistic as the crudest reductionism of the seventeenth century. Almost universally these days, biologists regard the cell as a "chemical factory" run by "information-transfer" technology. And, at the same time, the arch-behaviorist B. F. Skinner suggests that since physics only began to make progress when it "stopped personifying things," psychology is not apt to gain a firm scientific footing until it likewise purges itself of "careless references to purpose" and ceases "to trace behavior to states of mind, feelings, traits of character, human nature, and so on"[6]—meaning, one gathers, that the way forward for psychology is to stop personifying people . . . and to begin mechanizing them.

THE SUPPRESSION OF GNOSIS

Why has science taken this course toward even more aggressive depersonalization? Perhaps the myth of Dr. Frankenstein suggests an answer—a tragic answer. Where did the doctor's great project go wrong? Not in his intentions, which were beneficent, but in the dangerous haste and egotistic myopia with which he pursued his goal. It is both a beautiful and a terrible aspect of our humanity, this capacity to be carried away by an idea. For all the best reasons, Victor Frankenstein wished to create a new and improved human type. What he knew was the secret of his creature's physical assemblage; he knew how to manipulate the material parts of nature to achieve an astonishing result. What he did not know was the secret of personality in nature. Yet he raced ahead, eager to play God, without knowing God's most divine mystery. So he created something that was soulless. And when that monstrous thing appealed to him for the one gift that might redeem it from monstrosity, Frankenstein discovered to his horror that, for all his genius, it was not within him to provide that gift. Nothing in his science comprehended it. The gift was love. The doctor knew everything there was to know about his creature—except how to love it as a person.

To find the cultural meaning of modern science, for "*Frankenstein's monster*," read "nature-at-large" as we in the modern West experience it.

In the early days of the scientific revolution, Robert Boyle, convinced of the "excellency" of the new "mechanical hypothesis," insisted that nature, if it was to be mastered, must be treated like an "engine" or an "admirably contrived automaton." His argument prophetically relegated to the dustbin every lingering effort to personify nature, even by remote metaphor.

> The veneration, wherewith men are imbued for what they call nature, has been a discouraging impediment to the empire of man over the inferior creatures of God. For many have not only looked upon it as an impossible thing to compass, but as something impious to attempt, the removing of those boundaries which nature seems to have put and settled among her productions; and whilst they look upon her as such a venerable thing, some make a kind of scruple of conscience to endeavor so to emulate her works as to excel them.[7]

Here was a deliberate effort—and by a devout Christian believer—to cut science off from every trace of Hermetic or alchemical influence, from every connection with animist sympathy and visionary tradition. Boyle—like Bacon, Descartes, Galileo, and Hobbes—realized that herein lay the promise of material power. From that point on, it became permissible for the scientist to admire the mechanical intricacy of nature, but not to love it as a living presence endowed with soul and reflecting a higher order of reality. A machine can be studied zealously, but it cannot be loved. By virtue of that change of sensibilities—which may of course have transpired at a subliminal level of consciousness—the New Philosophy could lay claim to power (at least short-term manipulative power) but it had lost the *anima mundi*, which, as an object of love, belongs only to gnosis.

Still, from time to time, something of the spirit of gnosis intrudes itself into scientific thought, if only as a passing reflection upon some aspect of design in nature which hints that there is indeed *something* more to be known than conventional research can reveal. Science is not without such moments. But they appear only as autobiographical minutiae along the margins of "knowledge," modest confessions of faith, personal eccentricities, a bit of subprofessional self-indulgence on the part of established great names. These ethical, aesthetic, and visionary aspects have long since become human interest sideshows of science, the sort of anecdotal material that never makes it into the textbooks or the standard curriculum, except perhaps as a whimsical footnote.

And yet, have scientists never noticed how the lay public hangs upon these professions of wonder and ultimate belief, seemingly drawn to them with even more fascination than to the great discoveries? If people want more from science than fact and theory, it is because there lingers on in all of us the need for gnosis. We want to know the meaning of our existence, and we want that meaning to ennoble our lives in a way that makes an enduring difference in the universe. We want that meaning not out of childish weakness of mind, but because we sense in the depths of us that it is *there*, a truth that belongs to us and completes our condition. And we know that others have found it, and that it has seized them with an intoxication we envy.

It is precisely at this point—where we turn to our scientists for a clue to our destiny—that they have indeed a Promethean role to perform, as has every artist, sage, and seer. If people license the scientist's unrestricted pursuit of knowledge as a good in its own right, it is because they hope to see the scientists yet discharge that role; they hope to find gnosis in the scientist's knowledge. To the extent that scientists refuse that role, to the extent that their conception of what science is prevents them from seeking to join knowledge to wisdom, they are confessing that science is not gnosis, but something far less. And to that extent they forfeit—deservedly—the trust and allegiance of their society.

Dr. Faustus, Dr. Frankenstein, Dr. Moreau, Dr. Jekyll, Dr. Cyclops, Dr. Caligari, Dr. Strangelove. The scientist who does not face up to the warning in this persistent folklore of mad doctors is himself the worst enemy of science. In these images of our popular culture resides a legitimate public fear of the scientist's stripped-down, depersonalized conception of knowledge—a fear that our scientists, well-intentioned and decent men and women all, will go on being titans who create monsters.

What is a monster? The child of knowledge without gnosis, of power without spiritual intelligence.

The reason one despairs of discussing "alternative cognitive systems" with scientists is that scientists inevitably want an alternative system to do exactly what science already does—to produce predictive, manipulative information about the structure and function of nature—only perhaps to do so more prolifically and more rapidly. What they fail to understand is that no amount of information on earth would have taught Victor Frankenstein how to redeem his flawed creation from monstrosity.

But there is, in the Hermetic tradition we have left far behind us, a myth which teaches how nature may, by meditation, prayer, and sacrifice, be magically transmuted into the living presence of the divine. That was the object of the alchemist's Great Work, a labor of the spirit undertaken in love whose purpose was the mutual perfection of the macrocosm, which is the universe, and the microcosm, which is the human soul.

> And what if all of animated nature
> Be but organic Harps diversely fram'd
> That tremble into thought, as o'er them
> sweeps
> Plastic and vast, one intellectual breeze
> At once the Soul of each and God of all?
>   Samuel Taylor Coleridge

Notes

1. Jacques Monod, *Chance and Necessity* (New York: Knopf, 1971), p. 172.

2. Steven Weinberg, "Reflections of a Working Scientist." *Daedalus*, vol. 103 (1974), p. 43.

3. Abraham Maslow, *The Psychology of Science* (New York: Harper and Row, 1966), p. 42.

4. J. Bronowsky, *Science and Human Values* (New York: Harper Torchbooks, 1965), p. 95.

5. Frances Yates, *Rosicrucian Enlightenment* (London: Routledge, 1972). See also P. M. Rattansi, "The Social Interpretation of Science in the Seventeenth Century." *Science and Society 1600–1900* (Cambridge: Cambridge University Press, 1972).

6. B. F. Skinner, *Beyond Freedom and Dignity* (New York: Knopf, 1971), pp. 5–7.

7. Robert Boyle, "A Free Inquiry into the Received Notion of Nature," *Works* (1744), Ch. IV, p. 363.

Technology and the Transformation of Culture

The Presumptions of Science

Robert L. Sinsheimer

Throughout the twentieth century, society has benefited tremendously from technologies developed as a result of increases in scientific knowledge. With the enhanced power to transform culture in positive ways comes significant risks; we can destroy as easily as we create. The risks have led many people to wonder whether we should restrict the development of certain technologies; fewer seriously contemplate restraining the growth of scientific knowledge itself. Robert Sinsheimer, professor of biochemistry at California Institute of Technology, falls into the latter category. He argues that scientists have a duty to evaluate research in part on the basis of the consequences of our having the resulting knowledge. He identifies three areas of research that are of dubious merit—research on the separation of uranium isotopes, the search for extraterrestrial intelligence, and research into the aging process. In each case, he suggests that the potential for negative consequences outweighs the value of the knowledge. Once we take into account the range of human values that are affected by science, we see that some powerful arguments against restraining the pursuit of knowledge are more than balanced by strong reasons for limiting science.

As you read through this essay, consider the following:

1. What does Sinsheimer mean by the resilience of nature and why does he doubt that our faith in the resilience of nature is justified today?

2. According to Sinsheimer, why do scientists frequently ignore the impact of their research on human welfare?
3. What are Sinsheimer's reasons for thinking restraint of science is both possible and appropriate?
4. Is knowledge always good as long as we are careful how we use it?
5. What areas of scientific research, if any, do you think we might wisely restrain?

Can there be "forbidden"—or, as I prefer, "inopportune" knowledge? Could there be knowledge, the possession of which, at a given time and stage of social development, would be inimical to human welfare—and even fatal to the further accumulation of knowledge? Could it be that just as the information latent in the genome of a developing organism must be revealed in an orderly pattern, else disaster ensue, so must our knowledge of the universe be acquired in a measured order, else disaster ensue?

Biological organisms are equipped with many sensors essential to their survival, sensors for heat, cold, pain, thirst, hunger. Social organisms similarly need sensors of peril, particularly as they evolve into new domains—and for these we must use our intelligence, limited as it may be.

Discussion of the possible restraint of inquiry touches a most sensitive nerve in the academic community. If one believes that the highest purpose available to humanity is the acquisition of knowledge (and in particular of scientific knowledge, knowledge of the natural universe), then one will regard any attempt to limit or direct the search for knowledge as deplorable—or worse.

If, however, one believes that there may be other values to be held even higher than the acquisition of knowledge—for instance, general human welfare—and that science and possible other modes of knowledge acquisition should subserve these higher values, then one is willing to (indeed, one must) consider

such issues as: the possible restriction of the rate of acquisition of scientific knowledge to an "optimal" level relative to the social context into which it is brought; the selection of certain areas of scientific research as more or less appropriate for that social context; the relative priorities at a given time of the acquisition of scientific knowledge or of other knowledge such as the effectiveness of modes of social integration, or of systems of justice, or of educational patterns.

In short, if one does not regard the acquisition of scientific knowledge as an unquestioned ultimate good, one is willing to consider its disciplined direction. One may, of course, still have grave doubt as to whether mankind can know enough to be able intelligently to guide the rate or direction of the scientific endeavor, but at least one will then accept that we have a responsibility to seek answers—if there be any—to such questions.

THE IMPACT OF SCIENCE

In 1930 Robert A. Millikan, Nobel Prize winner, founder and long-time leader of Caltech, wrote in an article entitled "The Alleged Sins of Science" that one may "sleep in peace with the consciousness that the Creator has put some foolproof elements into his handiwork, and that man is powerless to do it any titanic physical damage."[1]

To what was Millikan referring? Stimulated by the recombinant DNA controversy, I have looked back to see if there were any similar admonitions or premonitions with respect to the possible consequences of nuclear energy. And there were. Millikan, in 1930, was responding to an earlier writing of Frederick

From "The Presumption of Science," reprinted by permission of *Daedalus*, Journal of the American Academy of Arts and Sciences, from the issue entitled, "Limits of Scientific Inquiry," Spring 1978, Vol. 107, No. 2.

Soddy. In a book entitled *Science and Life* Soddy, who had been a collaborator of Rutherford, had written:

> Let us suppose that it became possible to extract the energy which now oozes out, so to speak, from radioactive material over a period of thousands of millions of years, in as short a time as we pleased. From a pound weight of such substance one could get about as much energy as would be obtained by burning 150 tons of coal. How splendid. Or a pound weight could be made to do the work of 150 tons of dynamite. Ah, there's the rub. . . . It is a discovery that conceivably might be made tomorrow in time for its development and perfection, for the use or destruction, let us say, of the next generations, and, which it is pretty certain, will be made by science sooner or later. Surely it will not need this actual demonstration to convince the world that it is doomed if it fools with the achievements of science as it has fooled too long in the past.
>
> War, unless in the meantime man has found a better use for the gifts of science, would not be the lingering agony it is today. Any selected section of the world, or the whole of it if necessary, could be depopulated with a swiftness and dispatch that would leave nothing to be desired.[2]

Millikan commented, just prior to his statement quoted above, "Since Mr. Soddy raised the hobgoblin of dangerous quantities of available subatomic energy [science] has brought to light good evidence that this particular hobgoblin—like most of the hobgoblins that crowd in on the mind of ignorance—was a myth. . . . The new evidence born of further scientific study is to the effect that it is highly improbable that there is any appreciable amount of available subatomic energy to tap."[3]

So much for scientific prophecy. But it is indeed instructive and also troubling to recognize that our scientific endeavor truly does rest upon unspoken, even unrecognized, faith—a faith in the resilience, even the benevolence, of nature as we have probed it, dissected it, rearranged its components in novel configurations, bent its forms and diverted its forces to human purpose. Scientific endeavor rests upon the faith that our scientific probing and our technological ventures will not displace some key element of our protective environment and thereby collapse our ecological niche. It is a faith that nature does not set booby traps for unwary species.

Our bold scientific thrusts into *new* territories uncharted by experiment and unencompassed by theory must rely wholly upon our faith in the resilience of nature. In the past that faith has been justified and rewarded, but will it always be so? The faith of one era is not always appropriate to the next, and an unexamined faith is unworthy of science. Ought we step more cautiously as we explore the deeper levels of matter and life?

Most states of nature are quasiequilibria, the outcome of competing forces. Small deviations from equilibrium, the result of natural processes or human intervention, are most often countered by an opposing force and the equilibrium restored, at some rate dependent upon the kinetics of the processes, the sizes of the relevant natural pools of components, and other factors. Although we may therefore speak of the resilience of nature, this restorative capacity is finite and is limited in rate.

For example, if the ozone layer of the atmosphere is lightly and transiently depleted by a nuclear explosion or the atmospheric release of fluorocarbons, the natural processes which generate the ozone layer can restore it to the original level within a brief period. However, should the ozone layer be massively depleted—as by extended, large-scale release of fluorocarbons—many decades would be required for its renewal by natural processes, even if the release of fluorocarbons ceased.

Similarly, the populations of most living creatures can achieve an equilibrium level dependent upon birth rates and upon death rates from various causes. Most species have an excess capacity for reproduction, so that minor additions to the process of their removal (as by the harvesting of fish) cannot appreciably influence the equilibrium population. Patently however, excessive harvesting removing numbers beyond the reproductive capacity of the species will in time bring about its extinction.

In a similar manner lakes and rivers and air basins can absorb and dispose of limited amounts of pollutant but can be overwhelmed by masses beyond their capacity. Once overwhelmed the very agents responsible for disposal of pollution in small quantities may be destroyed, leaving a "dead" sea.

The concept of resilience extends to the planet as a whole and to the impact upon the manifold equilibria upon which the network of life forms depends as we continue to expand our intensive monoculture agriculture, as we continue to increase the total of human energy consumption (the man-made release of energy in the Los Angeles basin is now estimated at about 5 percent of the solar input), as we continue to raise the atmospheric level of CO_2 by combustion of fossil fuel, and so forth.

Because human beings (and most creatures) are adapted by evolution to the near equilibrium states, the resilience provided by the restorative forces of nature has appeared to us to be not only benevolent, but unalterable. Less overt than our faith in the resilience of nature is the faith with which we have relied upon the resilience of our social institutions and their capacity to contain the stress of change and to adapt the knowledge gained by science—and the power inherent in that knowledge—to the benefit of society, more than to its detriment. The fragility of the equilibria underlying social institutions is even more apparent than of the equilibria of nature. Political, economic, and cultural balances have shifted drastically in human history under the impact of new technologies, or new ideologies or religions, of invading peoples, of resource exhaustion, and other changes. Our faith in the resilience of both natural and man-made phenomena is increasingly strained by the acceleration of technical change and the magnitude of the powers deployed.

Physics and chemistry have given us the power to reshape the physical nature of the planet. We wield forces comparable to, even greater than those of, natural catastrophes. And now biology is bringing to us a comparable power over the world of life. The recombinant DNA technology, while significant and potentially a grievous hazard in itself (through the conceivable production, by design or by inadvertance, of new human, animal, or plant pathogens or of novel forms capable of disrupting important biological equilibria), must be seen as a portent of things to come.

The present recombinant DNA technology, which permits the addition or replacement of a few genes in living cells, is but the first prototype of genetic engineering. More powerful means involving cell fusion or chromosome transfer are already close to hand; even more sophisticated future developments appear assured. Since genes determine the basic structures and biological potentials of all living forms, the ultimate potential of genetic engineering for the modification and redesign of plants and animals to meet human needs and desires seems virtually unlimited.

Such capabilities will pose major questions as to the extent to which mankind will want to assume the responsibility for the life forms of the planet. Further, there is no reason to believe the same technology will not be applicable to mankind as well; the capability of human genetic engineering will raise profound questions of values and judgment for human societies.

It seems paradoxical that a living organism emergent from the evolutionary process after billions of years of blind circumstance should undertake to determine its own future evolution. The process is perhaps analogous to that of the mind seeking to understand itself. In both cases it is uncertain whether the attempt can possibly be successful. Nonetheless, at this point perhaps we had best step back and reconsider what it is we are about.

For four centuries science has progressively expanded our knowledge and reshaped our perception of the world. In that same time technology has correspondingly reshaped the pattern of our lives and the world in which we live.

Most people would agree that the net consequence of these activities has been benign. But it may be that the conditions which fostered such a benign outcome of scientific advance and technological innovation are changing to a less favorable set. Changes in the nature of science or technology or in the external society—in either the scale of events or their temporal order—can affect the preconditions, the presumptions, of scientific activity, and can thus alter the future consequences of such activities.

Both quantitative and qualitative changes have surely affected the impact of science and technology upon society. Quantitatively, the exponential growth of scientific activity and the unprecedented magnitude of modern industrial ventures permit the introduction of new technologies (e.g., fluorocarbon sprays) on a massive scale within very brief periods often with unforeseen consequence. Qualitatively, science and technology have been directed increasingly to synthesis—to the formulation of new substances designed for specific human purpose. Thus we have synthetic atoms (plutonium, strontium-90), synthetic molecules (dioxin, kepone, DDT) and now synthetic microorganisms (recombinant DNA). In these activities we introduce wholly novel substances into the planetary environment, substances with which our evolution has not always prepared us to cope.

Can we continue to rely upon the past four centuries as a guide for scientific activity given these changes? Other human activities of this same era are now increasingly seen in a different hue. The same period witnessed exponential increases in population and in the exploitation of natural resources for material wealth. Few would argue continuance of such trends will be benign.[4] The same era has witnessed the constant acceleration of the rate of change, the increasing dominance of technology in the affairs of men.

The constantly accelerating accretion of knowledge, therefore, may not always be counted as a good. Can circumstances change so as to devalue the net worth of new knowledge? Might a pause or slowdown for consolidation and reflection then be more in order? Indeed, could it be that some knowledge could, at this time, be positively malign? Hard questions, perhaps not answerable, perhaps not the right questions, but they are not answered for 1977 by invoking Galileo or Darwin or Freud. I believe they demand our thought.

I would advance for consideration some propositions that frankly I'm not at all sure I entirely believe. I think that in order to find out what one does believe it is necessary to go beyond what one can readily accept—to explore honestly more extreme and more remote positions so that one's position is based upon intelligent choice, not simple ignorance.

The domain I propose to explore can be indicated by a question. The question is one I have actually raised within the administration at Caltech (and it could as well be raised elsewhere). Institutions such as Caltech and others devote much energy and effort and talent to the advancement of science. We raise funds, we provide laboratories, we train students, and so on. In so doing we apply essentially only one criterion—that it be good science as science—that the work be imaginative, skillfully done, in the forefront of the field. Is that, as we approach the end of the twentieth century, enough? As social institutions, do Caltech and others have an obligation to be concerned about the likely *consequences* of the research they foster? And if so, how might they implement such a responsibility?

For reasons which probably need no elaboration Caltech has been more than reluctant to come to grips with this question. And, indeed, it just may be—and I say this with real sorrow—that scientists are simply not the people qualified to cope with such a question. The basic tactic of natural science is analysis: fragment a phenomenon into its components, analyze each part and process in isolation, and thereby derive an understanding of the subject. In physics, chemistry, even biology, this tactic has worked splendidly.

To answer my question, however, the focus must not be inward but outward, not narrowed but broadened. The focus must be on all the ties of the sciences to society and culture and on the impact of scientific knowledge and technological advancement on all human, indeed all planetary, life.

Consider as an instance the recombinant DNA issue. The natural tendency of the scientist, if he will admit this a problem, is to break it down, to decompose it into individually analyzable situations. If there is a danger, quantitate it: what is the numerical chance of the organisms escaping, of their colonizing the gut, of their penetrating the intestinal epithelium, of their causing disease (what disease)? If you point out that there is a nearly infinite set of possible scenarios of misfortune—that accidents do happen and in unpredictable ways, that humans do err, that bacterial or viral cultures do become contaminated, that indeed aspects of this technology involve inherently unpredictable consequence and hence are not susceptible to quantitative analysis—you are regarded as unscientific.

The consequences of the interaction of known but foreign gene products with the complex contents of a bacterial cell would be difficult enough to predict, much less the consequences of the interactions of unknown gene products, as produced in "shotgun" experiments. Some of these consequences may well modify, in unpredictable ways, the likelihood of the organism's survival or persistence in various environments, its potential toxicity for a host or nearby life forms. It may alter, for instance, an organism's survival in an animal intestine, contrary to our expectations, for we have presumed that we know all factors important for survival there and that no new successful adaptations could emerge.

For complex reasons, consideration of the potential hazards from organisms with recombinant DNA has focused upon immediate medical concerns. That these organisms with unpredictable properties might have impact upon any of the numerous microbiological processes which are important components of our life support systems is simply dismissed as improbable. The fact that these organisms are evolutionary innovations and have within themselves, as do all living forms, the capacity (if they survive) for their own unpredictable future evolutionary development is ignored, or dismissed as mystical.

If you point out that the recombinant DNA issue simply cannot be effectively considered in isolation but must be viewed in perspective and in a larger context as a possible precursor to future technologies available to many elements of society (including totalitarian governments, the military, and terrorist factions) your remarks are regarded as irrelevant to science.

There is an intensity of focus in the scientific perspective which is both its immediate strength and its ultimate weakness. The scientific approach focuses rigorously upon the problem at hand, ignoring as irrelevant the antecedents of motive and the prospectives of consequence.

Viewed objectively such an approach can only make sense if either (1) the consequences are always trivial, which is patently untrue, or (2) the consequences are always benign, that is, if the acquisition of knowledge, of any knowledge at any time, is always good, a proposition one might find hard to defend, or (3) the dangers and difficulties inherent in any attempt to restrict the acquisition of knowledge are so great as to make the unhindered pursuit of science the lesser evil.

In thinking about the impacts of science, we should, perhaps, reflect upon the inverse of the uncertainty principle. Perhaps it might be called the certainty principle. The uncertainty principle is concerned with the inevitable impact of the observer upon the observed, which thereby alters the observed. Conversely, there is an effect of the observed upon the observer. The discovery of new knowledge, the addition of new certainty, which correspondingly diminishes the domain of uncertainty and mystery, inevitably alters the perspective of the observer. We do not see the world with the same eyes as a Newton or a Descartes, or even a Faraday or a Rutherford.

The acquisition of a discipline sharpens our vision in its domain, but too frequently it seems also to blind us to other concerns. Thus immersion in the world of science, with its store of accumulated and substantiated fact, can make the participant intolerant of, and impatient with the uncertainties and non-reproducibilities of the human world. Engrossed in the search for knowledge, scientists tend to adopt the position that more knowledge is the key to the solution to human problems. They may not see that the uses we make of knowledge or the ways in which we organize to use knowledge can, as well, be the limiting factors to the human condition, and they forget that even within science our knowledge and our theories are always human constructs. Moreover, we should always remember (lest we become too secure and even smug) that our knowledge and our theories are ever incomplete.

OF DUBIOUS MERIT

To make this discussion more specific let me consider three examples of research that I personally consider to be, on balance, of dubious merit. One is in an area of rather applied research, the second in a very speculative but surely basic area, and the third in the domain of biomedical research, which we most often conceive to be wholly benign.

The first I would cite is current research upon improved means for isotope fractionation. In one technique, one attempts to use sophisticated lasers[5] to activate selectively one isotope of a set. I do not wish to discuss the technology but rather the likely consequences of its success. To be sure, there are benign experiments that would be facilitated by the availability of less expensive, pure isotopes. For some years I wanted to do an experiment with oxygen 18 but was always deterred by the cost.

But does anyone doubt that the most immediate application of isotope fractionation techniques would be the separation of uranium isotopes? This country has recently chosen to defer, at least, if not in fact to abandon, the plutonium economy and the breeder reactor because of well-founded concern that plutonium would inevitably find its way into weapons. We are thus left with uranium-fueled reactors. But uranium 235 can also be made into a bomb. Its use for power is safer only because of the difficulty in the separation of uranium 235 from the more abundant uranium 238. If we supersede the complex technology of Oak Ridge, if we devise quick and ingenious means for isotope separation, then one of the last defenses against nuclear terror will be breached. Is the advantage worth the price?

A second instance I would cite of research of dubious merit, and one probably even more tendentious than the first, relates to the proposal to search for and contact extraterrestrial intelligence.[6] Recent proposals suggest that, using advanced electronic and computer technology, we could monitor a million "channels" in a likely region of the electromagnetic spectrum, "listening" over several years for signals with an "unnatural" regularity or complexity.

I am concerned about the psychological impact upon humanity of such contact. We have had the technical capacity to search for such postulated intelligence for less than two decades, an instant in cosmic terms. If such intelligent societies exist and if we can "hear" them, we are almost certain to be technologically less advanced and thus distinctly inferior in our development to theirs. What would be the impact of such knowledge upon human values?

Copernicus was a deep cultural shock to man. The universe did not revolve about us. But God works in mysterious ways and we could still be at the center of importance in His universe. Darwin was a deep cultural shock to man. But we were still number one. If we are closer to the animals than we thought before, and through them to the rocks and the sea, it does not really devalue man to revalue matter. To really be number two, or number 37, or in truth to be wholly outclassed, an inferior species, inferior on our own turf of intellect and creativity and imagination, would, I think, be very hard for humanity.

The impact of more advanced cultures upon less advanced has almost invariably been disastrous to the latter. We are well acquainted with such impacts as the Spanish upon the Aztecs and Incas or the British and French upon the Polynesians and Hawaiians. These instances were, however, compounded by physical interventions (warfare) and the introduction of novel diseases. I want to emphasize the purely cultural shock. Hard learned skills determinant of social usefulness and positions become quickly obsolete. Less advanced cultures quickly become derivative, seeking technological handouts. What would happen to *our* essential tradition of self-reliance? Would we be reduced to seekers of cosmic handouts?

The distance of the contacted society might, to some degree, mitigate its consequent impact. A contact with a round trip communication time of ten years would have much more effect than one with a thousand years. The likelihood of either is, however, a priori, unknown. Nor is it inconceivable that an advanced society could devise means for communication faster than light.

The proponents of such interactions have considered the consequences briefly. In a 427-page book *Communication with Extraterrestrial Intelligence*[7] sixteen pages comprise a chapter entitled "Consequences of Contact." Opinion therein ranges from "Our obligation is, I feel, to stress that in any sensible way this problem has no danger for human society. I believe we can give a full guarantee of this" to "If we come in contact with some superior civilization this would mean the end of our civilization, although that might take a while. Our period of culture would be finished."

How and by whom should such a momentous decision[8] be made—one that will clearly, if successful, have an impact upon all humanity? Somehow I cannot believe it should be left to a small group of enthusiastic radioastronomers.

My concern here does not extend so far that I would abolish the science of astronomy. If the astronomers in the course of their science come across phenomena that can only be understood as the product of intelligent activity, so be it. But I do not believe that is the same as deliberately setting out to look for such activity with overt pretensions of social benefit.

The third example of research I consider of dubious merit concerns the aging process. I would suggest this subject exemplifies in supreme degree the eternal conflict between the welfare of the individual and the welfare of society and, indeed, the species. Obviously, as individuals, we would prefer youth and continued life. Equally obviously, on a finite planet, extended individual life must restrict the production of new individuals and that renewal which provides the vitality of our species.

The logic is inexorable. In a finite world the end of death means the end of birth. Who will be the last born?

If we propose such research we must take seriously the possibility of its success. The impact of a major extension of the human life span upon our entire social order, upon the life styles, mores, and adaptations associated with "three score and ten," upon the carrying capacity of a planet already facing overpopulation would be devastating. At this time we hardly need such enormous additional problems. Research on aging seems to me to exemplify the wrong research on the wrong problem in the wrong era. We need that talent elsewhere.

IS RESTRAINT FEASIBLE?

If one concedes, however reluctantly, that restraint of some directions of scientific inquiry is desirable, it is appropriate to ask if it is feasible and, if so, at what cost.

Some of my colleagues, not only in biology but in other fields of science as well, have indicated to me that they too increasingly sense that our curiosity, our exploration of nature, may unwittingly lead us into an irretrievable disaster. But they argue we have no alternative.[9] Such a position is, of course, a self-fulfilling prophecy.

I would differentiate among what might be called physical feasibility, logical feasibility, and political feasibility.

I believe that actual physical restraint is in principle feasible. There are two evident avenues of control: the power of the purse and access to instruments. Control of funding is indeed already a powerful means for control of the directions of inquiry for better or worse. To the extent that there exists a multiplicity of sources of support, such control is porous and incomplete, but it is clearly a first line of restraint.

Research today cannot be done with household tools. It is difficult to imagine, for instance, any serious research on aging that would not require the use of radioisotopes or an ultracentrifuge or an electron microscope. The use of isotopes is already regulated for other reasons. Access to electron microscopes could, in principle, be regulated, albeit at very real cost to our current concepts of intellectual freedom.

An immediately related, important aspect of any policy of restraint concerns the distinctions to be made about the nature of research. Can we logically differentiate research on aging from general basic biologic studies? I expect we cannot in any simple, absolute sense. Yet obviously the people who established the National Institute of Aging must have believed that there is a class of studies which deserves specific support under that rubric. Indeed, distinctions of this sort are made all the time by the various institutes of National Institutes of Health in deciding which grant applications are potentially eligible for their particular support. Pragmatically, and with some considerable margin of error, such distinctions can be and are made.

It is frequently claimed that the "unpredictability" of the outcome of research makes its restraint, for social or other purpose, illogical and indeed futile. However, the unpredictability of a research outcome is not an absolute but is both quantitatively and qualitatively variable.

In more applied research within a field with well-defined principles, the range of possible outcomes is surely circumscribed. In more fundamental research, in wholly new fields remote from prior human experience—as in the cosmos, or the subatomic world, or the core of the planet—wholly novel phenomena may be discovered. But, for instance, even in a fundamental science such as biology, most of the overt phenomena of life have been long known.

The basic principles of heredity were discovered by Mendel a century ago and were elaborated by Morgan and others early in this century. The understanding of genetic mechanism, the reduction of genetics to chemistry, had to await the advent of molecular biology. This understanding of mechanism has now provided the potential for human interventions, for genetic engineering, but it has not significantly modified our comprehension of the genetic basis of biological process.[10]

The path of modern biology will surely lead to further understanding of biological mechanism, with subsequent application to medicine and agriculture (and accompanying social impact). But it would seem likely that only within the central nervous system may there be the potential for wholly novel—and correspondingly wholly unpredictable—process. Even there, the facts of human psychology and the subjective realities of human consciousness have long been familiar to us, albeit the underlying mechanisms are indeed obscure.

Political feasibility is, of course, another question. The constituency most immediately affected is, of course, the scientific. And despite our protestations and alarms this community does have real political influence. It would seem unlikely to me that a policy of scientific restraint could be adopted in any sector unless a major portion of the scientific community came to believe it desirable.

For this to happen, that community will clearly have to become far more alert to, and aware of, and responsible for the consequences of their activities. The best discipline is self-discipline. Scientists are keenly sensitive to the evaluations of their peers. The scientific community and the leaders of our scientific and technical institutions will have to develop a collective conscience; they will have to let it be known certain types of research are looked upon askance, much as biological warfare research is today; it needs to be understood that such research will not be weighed in considerations of tenure and promotion; societies need to agree not to sponsor symposia on such topics. All of these and similar measures short of law could indeed be very effective.

I am well aware of the dangers implicit in such forms of cultural restraint. But I think we really must look at the dangers we face in the absence of self-restraint. Do we accept only the restraint of catastrophe?

If we are to consider this position, we must do so in a forthright manner. We must be willing to explore the vistas exposed if we lower conventional taboos and sanctions. We may not at first enjoy what we see, but at least we will have a better perception of the available alternatives. Any attempt to limit the freedom of scientific inquiry will surely involve what will appear, at least at first, to be quite arbitrary distinctions—judgmental decisions, the establishment of boundaries in gray and amorphous terrain. These are, however, familiar processes in our society, in the courts, in the legislatures. Indeed, most of us are familiar with such problems in our educational activities. The selection of new faculty, the award of tenure, the assignment of grades are clearly judgmental decisions.

In science we try with some success to elude the necessity for such very human judgments. Indeed, one suspects that many persons go into science precisely to avoid the necessity for such complex decisions—in search of a domain of unique and unequivocal answers of enduring validity. And it is painful to see the sanctuary invaded.

Admittedly it is difficult to achieve consensus on the criteria for judgmental decisions. Such consensus is all the more difficult in the sphere of international activities such as science which involve participants from diverse cultures and traditions.

Conversely there are many persons who prefer the more common, perhaps the more human world of ambiguity and compromise and temporally valid judgments and who resist the seemingly brutal, life and death, cataclysmic types of decision increasingly imposed upon society by the works of science. And science and scientists cannot stand wholly aloof from these latter dilemmas—for science is a human activity and scientists live in the human society. We cannot expect the adaptation to be wholly one-sided.

Even if, at best, we can only slow the rate of acquisition of certain areas of knowledge, such a tactic would give us more time to prepare for social adaptation—if we mobilize ourselves to use that time.

THE CASE FOR RESTRAINT

The view one exposes by lifting that sanction we label freedom of inquiry is frankly gloomy. It would seem that we are asked to make thorny decisions and delicate differentiations, to relinquish long-cherished rights of free inquiry, to forego clear prospects of technological progress. And it would seem that all these concessions stem ultimately from recognition of human frailty and from recognition of the limitations of human rationality and foresight, of human adaptability and even good will. Just such recognitions have already spawned many of our institutions and professions—religions, the law, government, United Nations—yet all of these are as imperfect as the world they are designed to restrain and improve.

At each level of human activity, whether individual, group, or national, we continually struggle to find acceptable compromises between the freedom to pursue varied courses and goals and the conflicts that arise when one person's actions run contrary to another's. In a crude sense the greater the power available to an entity, the more limitations must be imposed upon its freedom if conflict is to be averted. Ideally such limits are internalized through education and conscience, but we all understand the inadequacy of that process.

In short, we must pay a price for freedom, for the toleration of diversity, even eccentricity. That price may require that we forego certain technologies, even certain lines of inquiry where the likely application is incompatible with the maintenance of other freedoms. If this is so and if we can recognize and understand this, perhaps we can, as scientists, be more accepting.

Some will argue that knowledge simply provides us with more options and thus that the decision point should not be at the acquisition of knowledge but at its application.

Such a view, however ideal, overlooks the difficulty inherent in the restriction of application of new knowledge, once that knowledge has become available in a free society. Does anyone really believe, for instance, that knowledge permitting an extension of the human life span would not be applied once it were available?

One must also recognize again that the very acquisition of knowledge can change both the perceptions and the values of the acquirer. Could, for instance, deeper knowledge of the realities of human genetics affect our commitment to democracy?

It may be argued that the cost, however it may be measured, of impeding research would be greater to a society than the cost of impeding application. Perhaps so. This issue could be debated, but it must be debated in realistic terms with regard for the nature of real people and real society and with full understanding that knowledge is indeed power.

Although the nature of the measures necessary to restrict the application of knowledge has seldom been analyzed, the measures needed would surely be dependent upon the size of investment required to apply the knowledge, as well as on the form of and the need for the potential benefits of the knowledge, among other things. The compatibility of such restrictive measures with the principles of a democratic society would need to be considered. Restriction of nuclear power may be a case in point.

Alvin Weinberg has developed the concept of the technological fix as the simple solution to cut the Gordian knot of complex social problems. However, we seem to be discovering that the application of one technological fix seems to lead us into another technological fix. For example, the development of antibiotics and other triumphs of modern medicine has led to the tyranny of overpopulation. In efforts to cope with overpopulation by more intensive agriculture, we develop pesticides, herbicides and other chemicals which increase the level of environmental carcinogenesis. And so on.

The moral is that we cannot ignore the social and cultural context within which the technology is deployed. In retrospect we can see that in the cultural and social context of the seventeenth, eighteenth, and nineteenth centuries the consequences of technological innovation were most often benign. Whether because of change in the society and culture or change in the nature and effectiveness of technology, at some time in the twentieth century the balance began to shift and by now our addiction to technology begins to assume an unpleasant cast.

We are indeed addicted to technology. We rely ever more upon it and thus become its servant as well as its master. It has led to human populations insupportable without its aid. Further, new technologies shape our perceptions; they spawn expectations of change or stir deep fears of disaster. They dissociate us from the past and becloud the shape of the future. Even the oldest boundary conditions of humanity fall as we leave the planet and as we plan to reshape our genes.

Our academic institutions and our professional societies foster and promote science. To some degree they also have concern for its consequences, but it is a minor aspect. The principle that one should separate agencies which promote and agencies which regulate may apply here.

But where then is the balance, the necessary check to the force of scientific progress? Is the accumulation of knowledge unique among human activities—an unmitigated good that needs no counterweight? Perhaps that was true when science was young and impotent, but hardly now. Yet we lack the institutional mechanisms for regulation.

Our experience with constraint upon science has hardly been encouraging. From the Inquisition to Lysenko such constraint has been the work of bigots and charlatans. Obviously, if it is to be done to a good purpose, any restraint must be informed, both as to science and as to the larger society on which science impacts.

The acquisition of knowledge is a human, a social, enterprise. If we, through the relentless, single-minded pursuit of new knowledge so destabilize society as to render it incapable—or unwilling—to continue to support the scientific enterprise, then we will have, through our obsession, defeated ourselves.

At Caltech and the many other academic institutions, we have now, *culturally*, cloned Galileo a millionfold. We have nurtured this Galilean clone well; we award prizes and honors to those most like the original. No doubt this clone has been most beneficial for humanity, but perhaps there is a time for Galileos. Perhaps we need in this time to start another clone.

References

1. R. A. Millikan, "Alleged Sins of Science," *Scribners Magazine*, 87 (2) (1930): 119–130.

2. Frederick Soddy, *Science and Life* (London: John Murray, 1920).

3. Precisely what evidence Dr. Millikan had in mind is uncertain. However, it was generally appreciated that the efficiency of nuclear transformation by the charged particles then in use was so low that there was no significant prospect of a net release of energy. No practical chain reaction could yet be envisaged.

4. A. V. Hill in his presidential address to the British Association for the Advancement of Science in 1952, referring to the population problem, said, "If ethical principles deny our right to do evil in order that good may come, are we justified in doing good when the foreseeable consequence is evil?"

5. See A. S. Krass, "Laser Enrichment of Uranium: The Proliferation Connection," *Science*, 196 (1977): 721–731; also B. M. Casper, "Laser Enrichment: A New Path to Proliferation?" *Bulletin of Atomic Scientists*, 33 (1) (1977): 28–41.

6. See T. B. H. Kuiper and M. Morris, "Searching for Extraterrestrial Civilizations," *Science*, 196 (1977): 616–621; also B. Murray, S. Gulkis, and R. E. Edelson, "Extraterrestrial Intelligence: An Observational Approach," *Science*, in press.

7. C. Sagan (ed.), *Communication with Extraterrestrial Intelligence (EETC)* (Cambridge, Mass.: MIT Press, 1973).

8. Conceivably, we might not be given this choice if an advanced civilization were determined to contact us. At present however, it would seem to be our option.

9. This is not a new perception. "The world is now faced with a self-evolving system which it cannot stop. There are dangers and advantages in this situation. . . . Modern science has imposed upon humanity the necessity for wandering. Its progressive thought and its progressive technology make the transition through time, from generation to generation, a true migration into uncharted seas of adventure. The very benefit of wandering is that it is dangerous and needs skill to avert evils. We must expect, therefore, that the future will disclose dangers. It is the business of the future to be dangerous; and it is the merit of science that it equips the future for its duties," wrote A. W. Whitehead in *Science and the Modern World*.

10. Indeed the failure to discover a new class of phenomena underlying genetics has been most disappointing to some. See Gunther S. Stent, "That Was the Molecular Biology That Was," *Science*, 160 (1968): 390–395.

Can Science Go Too Far?: The Debate About Cloning Humans

The Case Against Cloning: Leon Kass

In Defense of Cloning: Gregory Pence

One of the most symbolically significant recent incursions into a realm of "forbidden knowledge" occurred in 1996 when scientists in Scotland successfully cloned a sheep. In the cloning process, the nucleus of an adult cell was transferred to an egg whose nucleus had been removed; the egg was then transplanted into a ewe. Although the process is far from reliable, it immediately raised the specter of cloning humans. While prior advances in human reproductive technologies, such as in vitro fertilization, have been challenged on religious and ethical grounds, they have not aroused widespread public concern. The prospect of cloning humans, with its potential for creating numerous genetically identical copies of an individual, has already led to broad resistance. The U.S. National Bioethics Advisory Board, charged by President Bill Clinton to address human cloning, recommended that Congress pass a law prohibiting the cloning of a human.

Is the negative reaction to human cloning another instance of irrational resistance to the progress of science, or is it a realization that cloning compromises deep human values, such as the value of individuality? Leon Kass, Addie Clark Harding Professor in the College and the Committee on Social Thought at the University of Chicago, argues that we should ban the cloning of humans on ethical grounds. He attributes moral significance to the revulsion that many feel at a nonnatural means of procreation that diminishes the genetic uniqueness of individuals. Gregory Pence, a bioethicist at the University of Alabama, argues that emphasizing such revulsion creates a self-fulfilling prophecy; it increases the chances that cloned children will be harmed by negative stereotypes. If we simply look rationally at the facts, he believes we will see that the risks involved in cloning are not appreciably greater than many other risks we willingly accept.

The approaches to cloning taken by Kass and Pence can be applied to a wide range of new technologies that are transforming our culture. Developments in agricultural biotechnology threaten deep-seated views about how nature should function, and advances in computer technology shift the structure of interpersonal interactions. If we give credence to current views about what is natural and emphasize risks, we will tend to believe that science has gone too far. On the other hand, if we generalize from the history of similar fears about technological advances—fears that now appear unfounded—we will tend toward more optimistic assessments of the new worlds that science promises.

> *As you read through these essays, consider the following:*
>
> 1. According to Kass, how have changes in the last twenty-five years made it difficult for us to seriously consider moral arguments against cloning? Do you think that advances in science and social changes have numbed us to certain moral concerns?
> 2. Why does Kass believe that many people's revulsion at the cloning of a human being has moral significance?
> 3. What are Kass's arguments that we should ban the cloning of humans? Would these arguments be relevant to other areas of applied scientific research?

4. How does Pence try to show that fears about cloning are irrational?
5. What are Pence's arguments that cloning is unlikely to harm humans?
6. Do you think cloning is a case of "science going too far"?

The Case Against Cloning: Leon Kass

Our habit of delighting in news of scientific and technological breakthroughs has been sorely challenged by the birth announcement of a sheep named Dolly. Though Dolly shares with previous sheep the "softest clothing, woolly, bright," William Blake's question, "Little Lamb, who made thee?" has for her a radically different answer: Dolly was, quite literally, made. She is the work not of nature or nature's God but of man, an Englishman, Ian Wilmut, and his fellow scientists. What's more, Dolly came into being not only asexually—ironically, just like "He [who] calls Himself a Lamb"—but also as the genetically identical copy (and the perfect incarnation of the form or blueprint) of a mature ewe, of whom she is a clone. This long-awaited yet not quite expected success in cloning a mammal raised immediately the prospect—and the specter—of cloning human beings: "I a child and Thou a lamb," despite our differences, have always been equal candidates for creative making, only now, by means of cloning, we may both spring from the hand of man playing at being God. . . .

TAKING CLONING SERIOUSLY, THEN AND NOW

Cloning first came to public attention roughly thirty years ago, following the successful asexual production, in England, of a clutch of tad-

From Leon Kass, "The Wisdom of Repugnance," *The New Republic*, 2 June 1997. © The New Republic, Inc. Reprinted by permission.

From Gregory Pence, *Flesh of My Flesh: The Ethics of Cloning Humans* (New York: Rowman & Littlefield Publishers, Inc., 1998). Copyright © 1998 Rowman & Littlefield Publishers, Inc. Reprinted by permission.

pole clones by the technique of nuclear transplantation. The individual largely responsible for bringing the prospect and promise of human cloning to public notice was Joshua Lederberg, a Nobel Laureate geneticist and a man of large vision. In 1966, Lederberg wrote a remarkable article in *The American Naturalist* detailing the eugenic advantages of human cloning and other forms of genetic engineering, and the following year he devoted a column in *The Washington Post*, where he wrote regularly on science and society, to the prospect of human cloning. He suggested that cloning could help us overcome the unpredictable variety that still rules human reproduction, and allow us to benefit from perpetuating superior genetic endowments. These writings sparked a small public debate in which I became a participant. At the time a young researcher in molecular biology at the National Institutes of Health (NIH), I wrote a reply to the *Post*, arguing against Lederberg's amoral treatment of this morally weighty subject and insisting on the urgency of confronting a series of questions and objections, culminating in the suggestion that "the programmed reproduction of man will, in fact, dehumanize him."

Much has happened in the intervening years. It has become harder, not easier, to discern the true meaning of human cloning. We have in some sense been softened up to the idea—through movies, cartoons, jokes and intermittent commentary in the mass media, some serious, most lighthearted. We have become accustomed to new practices in human reproduction: not just in vitro fertilization, but also embryo manipulation, embryo donation and surrogate pregnancy. Animal biotechnology has yielded transgenic animals and a burgeoning science of genetic engineering, easily and soon to be transferable to humans.

Even more important, changes in the broader culture make it now vastly more difficult to express a common and respectful understanding of sexuality, procreation, nascent life, family, and the meaning of motherhood, fatherhood and the links between the generations. Twenty-five years ago, abortion was still largely illegal and thought to be immoral, the sexual revolution (made possible by the extramarital use of the pill) was still in its infancy, and few had yet heard about the reproductive rights of single women, homosexual men and lesbians. (Never mind shameless memoirs about one's own incest!) Then one could argue, without embarrassment, that the new technologies of human reproduction—babies without sex—and their confounding of normal kin relations—who's the mother: the egg donor, the surrogate who carries and delivers, or the one who rears?—would "undermine the justification and support that biological parenthood gives to the monogamous marriage." Today, defenders of stable, monogamous marriage risk charges of giving offense to those adults who are living in "new family forms" or to those children who, even without the benefit of assisted reproduction, have acquired either three or four parents or one or none at all. Today, one must even apologize for voicing opinions that twenty-five years ago were nearly universally regarded as the core of our culture's wisdom on these matters. In a world whose once-given natural boundaries are blurred by technological change and whose moral boundaries are seemingly up for grabs, it is much more difficult to make persuasive the still compelling case against cloning human beings. As Raskolnikov put it, "man gets used to everything—the beast!"

Indeed, perhaps the most depressing feature of the discussions that immediately followed the news about Dolly was their ironical tone, their genial cynicism, their moral fatigue: "AN UDDER WAY OF MAKING LAMBS" (*Nature*), "WHO WILL CASH IN ON BREAKTHROUGH IN CLONING?" (*The Wall Street Journal*), "IS CLONING BAAAAAAAAD?" (*The Chicago Tribune*). Gone from the scene are the wise and courageous voices of Theodosius Dobzhansky (genetics), Hans Jonas (philosophy) and Paul Ramsey (theology) who, only twenty-five years ago, all made powerful moral arguments against ever cloning a human being. We are now too sophisticated for such argumentation; we wouldn't be caught in public with a strong moral stance, never mind an absolutist one. We are all, or almost all, postmodernists now.

Cloning turns out to be the perfect embodiment of the ruling opinions of our new age. Thanks to the sexual revolution, we are able to deny in practice, and increasingly in thought, the inherent procreative teleology of sexuality itself. But, if sex has no intrinsic connection to generating babies, babies need have no necessary connection to sex. Thanks to feminism and the gay rights movement, we are increasingly encouraged to treat the natural heterosexual difference and its preeminence as a matter of "cultural construction." But if male and female are not normatively complementary and generatively significant, babies need not come from male and female complementarity. Thanks to the prominence and the acceptability of divorce and out-of-wedlock births, stable, monogamous marriage as the ideal home for procreation is no longer the agreed-upon cultural norm. For this new dispensation, the clone is the ideal emblem: the ultimate "single-parent child."

Thanks to our belief that all children should be *wanted* children (the more high-minded principle we use to justify contraception and abortion), sooner or later only those children who fulfill our wants will be fully acceptable. Through cloning, we can work our wants and wills on the very identity of our children, exercising control as never before. Thanks to modern notions of individualism and the rate of cultural change, we see ourselves not as linked to ancestors and defined by traditions, but as projects for our own self-creation, not only as self-made men but also man-made selves; and self-cloning is simply an extension of such rootless and narcissistic self-re-creation.

Unwilling to acknowledge our debt to the past and unwilling to embrace the uncertainties and the limitations of the future, we have a false relation to both: cloning personifies our desire fully to control the future, while being subject to no controls ourselves. Enchanted and enslaved by the glamour of technology, we have lost our awe and wonder before the deep mysteries of nature and of life. We cheerfully take our own beginnings in our hands and, like the last man, we blink.

Part of the blame for our complacency lies, sadly, with the field of bioethics itself and its claim to expertise in these moral matters. Bioethics was founded by people who understood that the new biology touched and threatened the deepest matters of our humanity: bodily integrity, identity and individuality, lineage and kinship, freedom and self-command, eros and aspiration, and the relations and strivings of body and soul. With its capture by analytic philosophy, however, and its inevitable routinization and professionalization, the field has by and large come to content itself with analyzing moral arguments, reacting to new technological developments and taking on emerging issues of public policy, all performed with a naïve faith that the evils we fear can all be avoided by compassion, regulation and a respect for autonomy. Bioethics has made some major contributions in the protection of human subjects and in other areas where personal freedom is threatened; but its practitioners, with few exceptions, have turned the big human questions into pretty thin gruel. . . .

. . . Human cloning, though it is in some respects continuous with previous reproductive technologies, also represents something radically new, in itself and in its easily foreseeable consequences. The stakes are very high indeed. I exaggerate, but in the direction of the truth, when I insist that we are faced with having to decide nothing less than whether human procreation is going to remain human, whether children are going to be made rather than begotten, whether it is a good thing, humanly speaking, to say yes in principle to the road which leads (at best) to the dehumanized rationality of *Brave New World.* This is not business as usual, to be fretted about for a while but finally to be given our seal of approval. We must rise to the occasion and make our judgments as if the future of our humanity hangs in the balance. For so it does.

THE STATE OF THE ART

If we should not underestimate the significance of human cloning, neither should we exaggerate its imminence or misunderstand just what is involved. The procedure is conceptually simple. The nucleus of a mature but unfertilized egg is removed and replaced with a nucleus obtained from a specialized cell of an adult (or fetal) organism (in Dolly's case, the donor nucleus came from mammary gland epithelium). Since almost all the hereditary material of a cell is contained within its nucleus, the renucleated egg and the individual into which this egg develops are genetically identical to the organism that was the source of the transferred nucleus. An unlimited number of genetically identical individuals—clones—could be produced by nuclear transfer. In principle, any person, male or female, newborn or adult, could be cloned, and in any quantity. With laboratory cultivation and storage of tissues, cells outliving their sources make it possible even to clone the dead.

The technical stumbling block, overcome by Wilmut and his colleagues, was to find a means of reprogramming the state of the DNA in the donor cells, reversing its differentiated expression and restoring its full totipotency, so that it could again direct the entire process of producing a mature organism. Now that this problem has been solved, we should expect a rush to develop cloning for other animals, especially livestock, in order to propagate in perpetuity the champion meat or milk producers. Though exactly how soon someone will succeed in cloning a human being is anybody's guess, Wilmut's technique, almost certainly applicable to humans, makes *attempting* the feat an imminent possibility.

Yet some cautions are in order and some possible misconceptions need correcting. For a start, cloning is not Xeroxing. As has been reassuringly reiterated, the clone of Mel Gibson, though his genetic double, would enter the world hairless, toothless and peeing in his diapers, just like any other human infant. Moreover, the success rate, at least at first, will probably not be very high: the British transferred 277 adult nuclei into enucleated sheep eggs, and implanted twenty-nine clonal embryos, but they achieved the birth of only one live lamb clone. For this reason, among others, it is unlikely that, at least for now, the practice would be very popular, and there is no immediate worry of mass-scale production of multicopies. The need of repeated surgery to obtain eggs and, more crucially, of numerous borrowed wombs for implantation will surely limit use, as will the expense; besides, almost everyone who is able will doubtless prefer nature's sexier way of conceiving.

Still, for the tens of thousands of people already sustaining over 200 assisted reproduction clinics in the United States and already availing themselves of in vitro fertilization, intracytoplasmic sperm injection and other techniques of assisted reproduction, cloning would be an option with virtually no added fuss (especially when the success rate improves). . . .

In anticipation of human cloning, apologists and proponents have already made clear possible uses of the perfected technology, ranging from the sentimental and compassionate to the grandiose. They include: providing a child for an infertile couple; "replacing" a beloved spouse or child who is dying or has died; avoiding the risk of genetic disease; permitting reproduction for homosexual men and lesbians who want nothing sexual to do with the opposite sex; securing a genetically identical source of organs or tissues perfectly suitable for transplantation; getting a child with a genotype of one's own choosing, not excluding oneself; replicating individuals of great genius, talent or beauty—having a child who really could "be like Mike"; and creating large sets of genetically identical humans suitable for research on, for instance, the question of nature versus nurture, or for special missions in peace and war (not excluding espionage), in which using identical humans would be an advantage. Most people who envision the cloning of human beings, of course, want none of these scenarios. That they cannot say why is not surprising. What is surprising, and welcome, is that, in our cynical age, they are saying anything at all.

THE WISDOM OF REPUGNANCE

"Offensive." "Grotesque." "Revolting." "Repugnant." "Repulsive." These are the words most commonly heard regarding the prospect of human cloning. Such reactions come both from the man or woman in the street and from the intellectuals, from believers and atheists, from humanists and scientists. Even Dolly's creator has said he "would find it offensive" to clone a human being.

People are repelled by many aspects of human cloning. They recoil from the prospect of mass production of human beings, with large clones of lookalikes, compromised in their individuality; the idea of father-son or mother-daughter twins; the bizarre prospects of a woman giving birth to and rearing a genetic copy of herself, her spouse or even her deceased father or mother; the grotesqueness of conceiving a child as an exact replacement for another who has died; the utilitarian creation of embryonic genetic duplicates of oneself, to be frozen away or created when necessary, in case of need for homologous tissues or organs for transplantation; the narcissism of those who would clone themselves and the arrogance of others who think they know who deserves to be cloned or which genotype any child-to-be should be thrilled to receive; the Frankensteinian hubris to create human life and increasingly to control its destiny; man playing God. Almost no one finds any of the suggested reasons for human cloning compelling; almost everyone anticipates its possible misuses and abuses. Moreover, many people feel oppressed by the sense that there is probably nothing we can do to prevent it from happening. This makes the prospect all the more revolting.

Revulsion is not an argument; and some of yesterday's repugnances are today calmly accepted—though, one must add, not always for the better. In crucial cases, however, repugnance is the emotional expression of deep wisdom, beyond reason's power fully to articulate it. Can anyone really give an argument fully adequate to the horror which is father-daughter incest (even with consent), or having sex with animals, or mutilating a corpse, or eating human flesh, or even just (just!) raping or murdering another human being? Would anybody's failure to give full rational justification for his or her revulsion at these practices make that revulsion ethically suspect? Not at all. On the contrary, we are suspicious of those who think that they can rationalize away our horror, say, by trying to explain the enormity of incest with arguments only about the genetic risks of inbreeding.

The repugnance at human cloning belongs in this category. We are repelled by the prospect of cloning human beings not because of the strangeness or novelty of the undertaking, but because we intuit and feel, immediately and without argument, the violation of things that we rightfully hold dear. Repugnance, here as elsewhere, revolts against the excesses of human willfulness, warning us not to transgress what is unspeakably profound. Indeed, in this age in which everything is held to be permissible so long as it is freely done, in which our given human nature no longer commands respect, in which our bodies are regarded as mere instruments of our autonomous rational wills, repugnance may be the only voice left that speaks up to defend the central core of our humanity. Shallow are the souls that have forgotten how to shudder.

The goods protected by repugnance are generally overlooked by our customary ways of approaching all new biomedical technologies. The way we evaluate cloning ethically will in fact be shaped by how we characterize it descriptively, by the context into which we place it, and by the perspective from which we view it. The first task for ethics is proper description. And here is where our failure begins.

Typically, cloning is discussed in one or more of three familiar contexts, which one might call the technological, the liberal and the meliorist. Under the first, cloning will be seen as an extension of existing techniques for assisting reproduction and determining the genetic makeup of children. Like them, cloning is to be regarded as a neutral technique, with no inherent meaning or goodness, but subject to multiple uses, some good, some bad. The morality of cloning thus depends absolutely on the goodness or badness of the motives and intentions of the cloners: as one bioethicist defender of cloning puts it, "the ethics must be judged [only] by the way the parents nurture and rear their resulting child and whether they bestow the same love and affection on a child brought into existence by a technique of assisted reproduction as they would on a child born in the usual way."

The liberal (or libertarian or liberationist) perspective sets cloning in the context of rights, freedoms and personal empowerment. Cloning is just a new option for exercising an individual's right to reproduce or to have the kind of child that he or she wants. Alternatively, cloning enhances our liberation (especially women's liberation) from the confines of nature, the vagaries of chance, or the necessity for sexual mating. Indeed, it liberates women from the need for men altogether, for the process requires only eggs, nuclei and (for the time being) uteri—plus, of course, a healthy dose of our (allegedly "masculine") manipulative science that likes to do all these things to mother nature and nature's mothers. For those who hold this outlook, the only moral restraints on cloning are adequately informed consent and the avoidance of bodily harm. If no one is cloned without her consent, and if the clonant is not physically damaged, then the liberal conditions for licit, hence moral, conduct are met. Worries that go beyond violating the will or maiming the body are dismissed as "symbolic"—which is to say, unreal.

The meliorist perspective embraces valetudinarians and also eugenicists. The latter were formerly more vocal in these discussions, but they are now generally happy to see their goals advanced under the less threatening banners of freedom and technological growth. These people see in cloning a new prospect for improving human beings—minimally, by ensuring the perpetuation of healthy individuals by avoiding the risks of genetic disease inherent in the lottery of sex, and maximally, by producing "optimum babies," preserving outstanding genetic material, and (with the help of soon-to-come techniques for precise genetic engineering) enhancing inborn human capacities on many fronts. Here the morality of cloning as a means is justified solely by the excellence of the end, that is, by the outstanding traits or individuals cloned—beauty, or brawn, or brains.

These three approaches, all quintessentially American and all perfectly fine in their places, are sorely wanting as approaches to human procreation. It is, to say the least, grossly distorting to view the wondrous mysteries of birth, renewal and individuality, and the deep meaning of parent-child relations, largely through the lens of our reductive science and its potent technologies. Similarly, considering the reproduction (and the intimate relations of family life!) primarily under the political-legal, adversarial and individualistic notion of rights can only undermine the private yet fundamentally social, cooperative and duty-laden character of child-bearing, child-rearing and their bond to the covenant of marriage. Seeking to escape entirely from nature (in order to satisfy a natural desire or a natural right to reproduce!) is self-contradictory in theory and self-alienating in practice. For we are erotic beings only because we are embodied beings, and not merely intellects and wills unfortunately imprisoned in our bodies. And, though health and fitness are clearly great goods, there is something deeply disquieting in looking on our prospective children as artful products perfectible by genetic engineering, increasingly held to our willfully imposed designs, specifications and margins of tolerable error.

The technical, liberal and meliorist approaches all ignore the deeper anthropological, social and, indeed, ontological meanings of bringing forth new life. To this more fitting and profound point of view, cloning shows itself to be a major alteration, indeed, a major violation, of our given nature as embodied, gendered and engendering beings—and of the social relations built on this natural ground. Once this perspective is recognized, the ethical judgment on cloning can no longer be reduced to a matter of motives and intentions, rights and freedoms, benefits and harms, or even means and ends. It must be regarded primarily as a matter of meaning: Is cloning a fulfillment of human begetting and belonging? Or is cloning rather, as I contend, their pollution and perversion? To pollution and perversion, the fitting response can only be horror and revulsion; and conversely, generalized horror and revulsion are prima facie evidence of foulness and violation. The burden of moral argument must fall entirely on those who want to declare the widespread repugnances of humankind to be mere timidity or superstition.

Yet repugnance need not stand naked before the bar of reason. The wisdom of our horror at human cloning can be partially articulated, even if this is finally one of those instances about which the heart has its reasons that reason cannot entirely know.

THE PROFUNDITY OF SEX

To see cloning in its proper context, we must begin not, as I did before, with laboratory technique, but with the anthropology—natural and social—of sexual reproduction.

Sexual reproduction—by which I mean the generation of new life from (exactly) two complementary elements, one female, one male, (usually) through coitus—is established (if that is the right term) not by human decision, culture or tradition, but by nature; it is the natural way of all mammalian reproduction. By nature, each child has two complementary biological progenitors. Each child thus stems from and unites exactly two lineages. In natural generation, moreover, the precise genetic constitution of the resulting offspring is determined by a combination of nature and chance, not by human design: each human child shares the common natural human species genotype, each child is genetically (equally) kin to each (both) parent(s), yet each child is also genetically unique.

These biological truths about our origins foretell deep truths about our identity and about our human condition altogether. Every one of us is at once equally human, equally enmeshed in a particular familial nexus of origin, and equally individuated in our trajectory from birth to death—and, if all goes well, equally capable (despite our morality) of participating, with a complementary other, in the very same renewal of such human possibility through procreation. Though less momentous than our common humanity, our genetic individuality is not humanly trivial. It shows itself forth in our distinctive appearance through which we are everywhere recognized; it is revealed in our "signature" marks of fingerprints and our self-recognizing immune system; it symbolizes and foreshadows exactly the unique, never-to-be-repeated character of each human life.

Human societies virtually everywhere have structured child-rearing responsibilities and systems of identity and relationship on the bases of these deep natural facts of begetting. The mysterious yet ubiquitous "love of one's own" is everywhere culturally exploited, to make sure that children are not just produced but well cared for and to create for everyone clear ties of meaning, belonging and obligation. But it is wrong to treat such naturally rooted social practices as mere cultural constructs (like left- or right-driving, or like burying or cremating the dead) that we can alter with little human cost. What would kinship be without its clear natural grounding? And what would identity be without kinship? We must resist those who have begun to refer to sexual reproduction as the "traditional method of reproduction," who would have us regard as merely traditional, and by implication arbitrary, what is in truth not only natural but most certainly profound.

Asexual reproduction, which produces "single-parent" offspring, is a radical departure from the natural human way, confounding all normal understandings of father, mother, sibling, grandparent, etc., and all moral relations tied thereto. It becomes even more of a radical departure when the resulting offspring is a clone derived not from an embryo, but from a mature adult to whom the clone would be an identical twin; and when the process occurs not by natural accident (as in natural twinning), but by deliberate human design and manipulation; and when the child's (or children's) genetic constitution is preselected by the parent(s) (or scientists). Accordingly, as we will see, cloning is vulnerable to three kinds of concerns and objections, related to these three points: cloning threatens confusion of identity and individuality, even in small-scale cloning; cloning represents a giant step (though not the first one) toward transforming procreation into manufacture, that is, toward the increasing depersonalization of the process of generation and, increasingly, toward the "production" of human children as artifacts, products of human will and design (what others have called the problem of "commodification" of new life); and cloning—like other forms of eugenic engineering of the next generation—represents a form of despotism of the cloners over the cloned, and thus (even in benevolent cases) represents a blatant violation of the inner meaning of parent-child relations, of what it means to have a child, of what it means to say "yes" to our own demise and "replacement." . . .

We are now ready for the more specific objections to cloning.

THE PERVERSITIES OF CLONING

First, an important if formal objection: any attempt to clone a human being would constitute an unethical experiment upon the resulting child-to-be. As the animal experiments (frog and sheep) indicate, there are grave risks of mishaps and deformities. Moreover, because of what cloning means, one cannot presume a future cloned child's consent to be a clone, even a healthy one. Thus, ethically speaking, we cannot even get to know whether or not human cloning is feasible.

I understand, of course, the philosophical difficulty of trying to compare a life with defects against nonexistence. Several bioethicists, proud of their philosophical cleverness, use this conundrum to embarrass claims that once can injure a child in its conception, precisely because it is only thanks to that complained-of conception that the child is alive to complain. But common sense tells us that we have no reason to fear such philosophisms. For we surely know that people can harm and even main children in the very act of conceiving them, say, by paternal transmission of the AIDS virus, maternal transmission of heroin dependence or, arguably, even by bringing them into being as bastards or with no capacity or willingness to look after them properly. And we believe that to do this intentionally, or even negligently, is inexcusable and clearly unethical.

The objection about the impossibility of presuming consent may even go beyond the obvious and sufficient point that a clonant, were he subsequently to be asked, could rightly resent having been made a clone. At issue are not just benefits and harms, but doubts about the very independence needed to give proper (even retroactive) consent, that is, not just the capacity to choose but the disposition and ability to choose freely and well. It is not at all clear to what extent a clone will truly be a moral agent. For, as we shall see, in the very fact of cloning, and of rearing him as a clone, his makers subvert the cloned child's independence, beginning with that aspect

that comes from knowing that one was an unbidden surprise, a gift, to the world, rather than the designed result of someone's artful project.

Cloning creates serious issues of identity and individuality. The cloned person may experience concerns about his distinctive identity not only because he will be in genotype and appearance identical to another human being, but, in this case, because he may also be twin to the person who is his "father" or "mother"—if one can still call them that. What would be the psychic burdens of being the "child" or "parent" of your twin? The cloned individual, moreover, will be saddled with a genotype that has already lived. He will not be fully a surprise to the world. People are likely always to compare his performances in life with that of his alter ego. True, his nurture and his circumstance in life will be different; genotype is not exactly destiny. Still, one must also expect parental and other efforts to shape this new life after the original—or at least to view the child with the original version always firmly in mind. Why else did they clone from the star basketball player, mathematician and beauty queen—or even dear old dad—in the first place?

Since the birth of Dolly, there has been a fair amount of doublespeak on this matter of genetic identity. Experts have rushed in to reassure the public that the clone would in no way be the same person, or have any confusions about his or her identity: as previously noted, they are pleased to point out that the clone of Mel Gibson would not be Mel Gibson. Fair enough. But one is shortchanging the truth by emphasizing the additional importance of the intrauterine environment, rearing and social setting: genotype obviously matters plenty. That, after all, is the only reason to clone, whether human beings or sheep. The odds that clones of Wilt Chamberlain will play in the NBA are, I submit, infinitely greater than they are for clones of Robert Reich.

Curiously, this conclusion is supported, inadvertently, by the one ethical sticking point insisted on by friends of cloning: no cloning without the donor's consent. Though an orthodox liberal objection, it is in fact quite puzzling when it comes from people (such as Ruth Macklin) who also insist that genotype is not identity or individuality, and who deny that a child could reasonably complain about being made a genetic copy. If the clone of Mel Gibson would not be Mel Gibson, why should Mel Gibson have grounds to object that someone had been made his clone? We already allow researchers to use blood and tissue samples for research purposes of no benefit to their sources: my falling hair, my expectorations, my urine and even my biopsied tissues are "not me" and not mine. Courts have held that the profit gained from uses to which scientists put my discarded tissues do not legally belong to me. Why, then, no cloning without consent—including, I assume, no cloning from the body of someone who just died? What harm is done the donor, if genotype is "not me"? Turth to tell, the only powerful justification for objecting is that genotype really does have something to do with identity, and everybody knows it. If not, on what basis could Michael Jordan object that someone cloned "him," say, from cells taken from a "lost" scraped-off piece of his skin? The insistence on donor consent unwittingly reveals the problem of identity in all cloning.

Genetic distinctiveness not only symbolizes the uniqueness of each human life and the independence of its parents that each human child rightfully attains. It can also be an important support for living a worthy and dignified life. Such arguments apply with great force to any large-scale replication of human individuals. But they are sufficient, in my view, to rebut even the first attempts to clone a human being. One must never forget that these are human beings upon whom our eugenic or merely playful fantasies are to be enacted.

Troubled psychic identity (distinctiveness), based on all-too-evident genetic identity (sameness), will be made much worse by the utter confusion of social identity and kinship ties. For, as already noted, cloning radically confounds lineage and social relations, for "offspring" as for "parents." As bioethicist James Nelson has pointed out, a female child cloned from her "mother" might develop a desire for a relationship to her "father," and might understandably seek out the father of her "mother," who is after all also her biological twin sister. Would "grandpa," who thought his paternal duties concluded, be pleased to discover that the clonant looked to him for paternal attention and support?

Social identity and social ties of relationship and responsibility are widely connected to, and supported by, biological kinship. Social taboos on incest (and adultery) everywhere serve to keep clear who is related to whom (and especially which child belongs to which parents), as well as to avoid confounding the social identity of parent-and-child (or brother-and-sister) with the social identity of lovers, spouses and co-parents. True, social identity is altered by adoption (but as a matter of the best interest of already living children: we do not deliberately produce children for adoption). True, artificial insemination and in vitro fertilization with donor sperm, or whole embryo donation, are in some way forms of "prenatal adoption"—a not altogether unproblematic practice. Even here, though, there is in each case (as in all sexual reproduction) a known male source of sperm and a known single female source of egg—a genetic father and a genetic mother—should anyone care to know (as adopted children often do) who is genetically related to whom.

In the case of cloning, however, there is but one "parent." The usually sad situation of the "single-parent child" is here deliberately planned, and with a vengeance. In the case of self-cloning, the "offspring" is, in addition, one's twin; and so the dreaded result of incest—to be parent to one's sibling—is here brought about deliberately, albeit without any act of coitus. Moreover, all other relationships will be confounded. What will father, grandfather, aunt, cousin, sister mean? Who will bear what ties and what burdens? What sort of social identity will someone have with one whole side—"father's" or "mother's"—necessarily excluded? It is no answer to say that our society, with its high incidence of divorce, remarriage, adoption, extramarital childbearing and the rest, already confounds lineage and confuses kinship and responsibility for children (and everyone else), unless one also wants to argue that this is, for children, a preferable state of affairs.

Human cloning would also represent a giant step toward turning begetting into making, procreation into manufacture (literally, something "handmade"), a process already begun with in vitro fertilization and genetic testing of embryos. With cloning, not only is the process in hand, but the total genetic blueprint of the cloned individual is selected and determined by the human artisans. To be sure, subsequent development will take place according to natural processes; and the resulting children will still be recognizably human. But we here would be taking a major step into making man himself simply another one of the man-made things. Human nature becomes merely the last part of nature to succumb to the technological project, which turns all of nature into raw material at human disposal, to be homogenized by our rationalized technique according to the subjective prejudices of the day.

How does begetting differ from making? In natural procreation, human beings come together, complementarily male and female, to give existence to another being who is formed, exactly as we were, *by what we are:* living, hence perishable, hence aspiringly erotic, human beings. In clonal reproduction, by contrast, and in the more advanced forms of manufacture to which it leads, we give existence to a being not by what we are but by what we intend and design. As with any product of our making, no matter how excellent, the artificer stands above it, not as an equal but as a superior, transcending it by his will and creative prowess. Scientists who clone

animals make it perfectly clear that they are engaged in instrumental making; the animals are, from the start, designed as means to serve rational human purposes. In human cloning, scientists and prospective "parents" would be adopting the same technocratic mentality to human children: human children would be their artifacts.

Such an arrangement is profoundly dehumanizing, no matter how good the product. Mass-scale cloning of the same individual makes the point vividly; but the violation of human equality, freedom and dignity are present even in a single planned clone. And procreation dehumanized into manufacture is further degraded by commodification, a virtually inescapable result of allowing baby-making to proceed under the banner of commerce. Genetic and reproductive biotechnology companies are already growth industries, but they will go into commercial orbit once the Human Genome Project nears completion. Supply will create enormous demand. Even before the capacity for human cloning arrives, established companies will have invested in the harvesting of eggs from ovaries obtained at autopsy or through ovarian surgery, practiced embryonic genetic alteration, and initiated the stockpiling of prospective donor tissues. Through the rental of surrogate-womb services, and through the buying and selling of tissues and embryos, priced according to the merit of the donor, the commodification of nascent human life will be unstoppable.

Finally, and perhaps most important, the practice of human cloning by nuclear transfer—like other anticipated forms of genetic engineering of the next generation—would enshrine and aggravate a profound and mischievous misunderstanding of the meaning of having children and of the parent-child relationship. When a couple now chooses to procreate, the partners are saying yes to the emergence of new life in its novelty, saying yes not only to having a child but also, tacitly, to having whatever child this child turns out to be. In accepting our finitude and opening ourselves to our replacement, we are tacitly confessing the limits of our control. In this ubiquitous way of nature, embracing the future by procreating means precisely that we are relinquishing our grip, in the very activity of taking up our own share in what we hope will be the immortality of human life and the human species. This means that our children are not *our* children: they are not our property, not our possessions. Neither are they supposed to live our lives for us, or anyone else's life but their own. To be sure, we seek to guide them on their way, imparting to them not just life but nurturing, love, and a way of life; to be sure, they bear our hopes that they will live fine and flourishing lives, enabling us in small measure to transcend our own limitations. Still, their genetic distinctiveness and independence are the natural foreshadowing of the deep truth that they have their own and never-before-enacted life to live. They are sprung from a past, but they take an uncharted course into the future.

Much harm is already done by parents who try to live vicariously through their children. Children are sometimes compelled to fulfill the broken dreams of unhappy parents; John Doe Jr. or the III is under the burden of having to live up to his forebear's name. Still, if most parents have hopes for their children, cloning parents will have expectations. In cloning, such overbearing parents take at the start a decisive step which contradicts the entire meaning of the open and forward-looking nature of parent-child relations. The child is given a genotype that has already lived, with full expectation that this blueprint of a past life ought to be controlling of the life that is to come. Cloning is inherently despotic, for it seeks to make one's children (or someone else's children) after one's own image (or an image of one's choosing) and their future according to one's will. In some cases, the despotism may be mild and benevolent. In other cases, it will be mischievous and downright tyrannical. But despotism—the control of another through one's will—it inevitably will be. . . .

BAN THE CLONING OF HUMANS

What, then, should we do? We should declare that human cloning is unethical in itself and dangerous in its likely consequences. In so doing, we shall have the backing of the overwhelming majority of our fellow Americans, and of the human race, and (I believe) of most practicing scientists. Next, we should do all that we can to prevent the cloning of human beings. We should do this by means of an international legal ban if possible, and by a unilateral national ban, at a minimum. Scientists may secretly undertake to violate such a law, but they will be deterred by not being able to stand up proudly to claim the credit for their technological bravado and success. Such a ban on clonal baby-making, moreover, will not harm the progress of basic genetic science and technology. On the contrary, it will reassure the public that scientists are happy to proceed without violating the deep ethical norms and intuitions of the human community.

This still leaves the vexed question about laboratory research using early embryonic human clones specially created only for such research purposes with no intention to implant them into a uterus. There is no question that such research holds great promise for gaining fundamental knowledge about normal (and abnormal) differentiation, and for developing tissue lines for transplantation that might be used, say, in treating leukemia or in repairing brain or spinal cord injuries—to mention just a few of the conceivable benefits. Still, unrestricted clonal embryo research will surely make the production of living human clones much more likely. Once the genies put the cloned embryos into the bottles, who can strictly control where they go (especially in the absence of legal prohibitions against implanting them to produce a child)?

I appreciate the potentially great gains in scientific knowledge and medical treatment available from embryo research, especially with cloned embryos. At the same time, I have serious reservations about creating human embryos for the sole purpose of experimentation. There is something deeply repugnant and fundamentally transgressive about such a utilitarian treatment of prospective human life. This total, shameless exploitation is worse, in my opinion, than the "mere" destruction of nascent life. But I see no added objections, as a matter of principle, to creating and using *cloned* early embryos for research purposes, beyond the objections that I might raise to doing so with embryos produced sexually.

And yet, as a matter of policy and prudence, any opponent of the manufacture of cloned humans must, I think, in the end oppose also the creating of cloned human embryos. Frozen embryonic clones (belonging to whom?) can be shuttled around without detection. Commercial ventures in human cloning will be developed without adequate oversight. In order to build a fence around the law, prudence dictates that one oppose—for this reason alone—all production of cloned human embryos, even for research purposes. We should allow for all cloning research on animals to go forward, but the only safe trench that we can dig across the slippery slope, I suspect, is to insist on the inviolable distinction between animal and human cloning. . . .

In Defense of Cloning: *Gregory Pence*

The most important moral objection to originating a human by cloning is the claim that the resulting person may be unnecessarily harmed, either by something in the process of cloning or by the unique expectations placed upon the resulting child. This essay considers this kind of objection.

By now the word "cloning" has so many bad associations from science fiction and political demagoguery that there is no longer any good reason to continue to use it. A more neutral phrase, meaning the same thing, is "somatic cell nuclear transfer" (SCNT), which refers to the process by which the genotype of an adult, differentiated cell can be used to create a new human embryo by transferring its nucleus to an enucleated human egg. The resulting embryo can then be gestated to create a baby who will be a delayed twin of its genetic ancestor.

For purposes of clarity and focus, I will only discuss the simple case where a couple wants to originate a single child by SCNT and not the cases of multiple origination of the same genotype. I will also not discuss questions of who would regulate reproduction of genotypes and processes of getting consent to reproduce genotypes.

PARALLELS WITH IN VITRO FERTILIZATION: REPEATING HISTORY?

Any time a new method of human reproduction may occur, critics try to prevent it by citing possible harm to children. The implicit premise: before it is allowed, any new method must prove that only healthy children will be created. Without such proof, the new method amounts to "unconsented to" experimentation on the unborn. So argued the late conservative, Christian bioethicist Paul Ramsey in the early 1970s about in vitro fertilization (IVF).[1]

Of course, ordinary sexual reproduction does not guarantee healthy children every time. Nor can a person consent until he is born. Nor can he really consent until he is old enough to understand consent. The requirement of "consent to be born" is silly.

Jeremy Rifkin, another critic of IVF in the early 1970s, seemed to demand that new forms of human reproduction be risk-free.[2] Twenty years later, Rifkin predictably bolted out the gate to condemn human cloning, demanding its world-wide ban, with penalties for transgressions as severe as those for rape and murder: "It's a horrendous crime to make a Xerox of someone," he declared ominously. "You're putting a human into a genetic straitjacket. For the first time, we've taken the principles of industrial design—quality control, predictability—and applied them to a human being."[3]

Daniel Callahan, a philosopher who had worked in the Catholic tradition and who founded the Hastings Center for research in medical ethics, argued in 1978 that the first case of IVF was "probably unethical" because there was no possible guarantee that Louise Brown would be normal.[4] Callahan added that many medical breakthroughs are unethical because we cannot know (using the philosopher's strong sense of "know") that the first patient will not be harmed. Two decades later, he implied that human cloning would also be unethical: "We live in a culture that likes science and technology very much. If someone wants something, and the rest of us can't prove they are going to do devastating harm, they are going to do it."[5]

Leon Kass, a social conservative and biologist-turned-bioethicist, argued strenuously in 1971 that babies created by artificial fertilization might be deformed: "It doesn't matter how many times the baby is tested while in the mother's womb," he averred, "they will never be certain the baby won't be born without defect."[6]

What these critics overlooked is that no reasonable approach to life avoids all risks. Nothing in life is risk-free, including having children. Even if babies are born healthy, they do not always turn out as hoped. Taking such chances is part of becoming a parent.

Without some risk, there is no progress, no advance. Without risk, pioneers don't cross prairies, astronauts don't walk on the moon, and Freedom Riders don't take buses to integrate the South. The past critics of assisted reproduction demonstrated a psychologically normal but nevertheless unreasonable tendency to magnify the risk of a harmful but unlikely result. Such a result—even if very bad—still represents a very small risk. A baby born with a lethal genetic disease is an extremely bad but unlikely result; nevertheless, the risk shouldn't deter people from having children.

HUMANITY WILL NOT BE HARMED

Human SCNT is even more new and strange-sounding than in vitro fertilization

(IVF). All that means is that it will take longer to get used to. Scare-mongers have predicted terrible harm if children are born by SCNT, but in fact very little will change. Why is that?

First, to create a child by SCNT, a couple must use IVF, which is an expensive process, costing about $8,000 per attempt. Most American states do not require insurance companies to cover IVF, so IVF is mostly a cash-and-carry operation. Second, most IVF attempts are unsuccessful. The chances of any couple taking home a baby is quite low—only about 15%.

Only about 40,000 IVF babies have been born in America since the early 1980s. Suppose 50,000 such babies are born over the next decade. How many of these couples would want to originate a child by SCNT? Very few—at most, perhaps, a few hundred.

These figures are important because they tamp down fears. As things now stand, originating humans by SCNT will never be common. Neither evolution nor old-fashioned human sex is in any way threatened. Nor is the family or human society. Most fears about human cloning stem from ignorance.

Similar fears linking cloning to dictatorship or the subjugation of women are equally ignorant. There are no artificial wombs (predictions, yes; realities, no—otherwise we could save premature babies born before 20 weeks). A healthy woman must agree to gestate any SCNT baby and such a woman will retain her right to abort. Women's rights to abortion are checks on evil uses of any new reproductive technology.

NEW THINGS MAKE US FEAR HARMS IRRATIONALLY

SCNT isn't really so new or different. Consider some cases on a continuum. In the first, the human embryo naturally splits in the process of twinning and produces two genetically-identical twins. Mothers have been conceiving and gestating human twins for all of human history. Call the children who result from this process Rebecca and Susan.

In the second case a technique is used where a human embryo is deliberately twinned in order to create more embryos for implantation in a woman who has been infertile with her mate. Instead of a random quirk in the uterus, now a physician and an infertile couple use a tiny electric current to split the embryo. Two identical embryos are created. All embryos are implanted and, as sometimes happens, rather than no embryo implanting successfully or only one, both embryos implant. Again, Rebecca and Susan are born.

In the third case, one of the twinned embryos is frozen (Susan) along with other embryos from the couple and the other embryo is implanted. In this case, although several embryos were implanted, only the one destined to be Rebecca is successful. Again, Rebecca is born.

Two years pass, and the couple desires another child. Some of their frozen embryos are thawed and implanted in the mother. The couple knows that one of the implanted embryos is the twin of Rebecca. In this second round of reproductive assistance, the embryo destined to be Susan successfully implants and a twin is born. Now Susan and Rebecca exist as twins, but born two years apart. Susan is the delayed twin of Rebecca. (Rumors abound that such births have already occurred in American infertility clinics.)

Suppose now that the "embryo that could become Susan" was twinned, and the "non-Susan" embryo is frozen. The rest of the details are then the same as the last scenario, but now two more years pass and the previously-frozen embryo is now implanted, gestated, and born. Susan and Rebecca now have another identical sister, Samantha. They would be identical triplets, born two and four years apart. In contrast to SCNT, where the mother's contribution of mitochondrial genes introduces small variations in nearly-identical genotypes, these embryos would have identical genomes.

Next, suppose that the embryo that could have been Rebecca miscarried and never

became a child. The twinned embryo that could become Susan still exists. So the parents implant this embryo and Susan is born. Query to National Bioethics Advisory Commission: have the parents done something illegal? A child has been born who was originated by reproducing an embryo with a unique genotype. Remember, the embryo-that-could-become Rebecca existed first. So Susan only exists as a "clone" of the non-existent Rebecca.

Now, as bioethicist Leroy Walters emphasizes, let us consider an even thornier but more probable scenario.[7] Suppose we took the embryo-that-could-become Susan and transferred its nucleus to an enucleated egg of Susan's mother. Call the person who will emerge from this embryo "Suzette," because she is like Susan but different, because of her new mitochondrial DNA. Although the "Susan" embryo was created sexually, Suzette's origins are through somatic cell nuclear transfer. It is not clear that this process is illegal. The NBAC *Report* avoids taking a stand on this kind of case.[8]

Now compare all the above cases to originating Susan asexually by SCNT from the genotype of the adult Rebecca. Susan would again have a nearly-identical genome with Rebecca (identical except for mitochondrial DNA contributed by the gestating woman). Here we have nearly identical female genotypes, separated in time, created by choice. But how is this so different from choosing to have a delayed twin-child? Originating a child by SCNT is not a breakthrough in kind but a matter of degree along a continuum involving twins and a special kind of reproductive choice.

COMPARING THE HARMS OF HUMAN REPRODUCTION

The question of multiple copies of one genome and its special issues of harm are ones that will not be discussed in this essay, but one asymmetry in our moral intuitions should be noticed.

The increasing use of fertility drugs has expanded many times the number of humans born who are twins, triplets, quadruplets, quintuplets, sextuplets, and even (in November of 1997 to the McCaugheys of Iowa) septuplets. If an entire country can rejoice about seven humans who are gestated in the same womb, raised by the same parents, and simultaneously created randomly from the same two sets of chromosomes, why should the same country fear deliberately originating copies of the same genome, either at once or over time? Our intuitions are even more skewed when we rejoice in the statistically-unlikely case of the seven healthy McCaughey children and ignore the far more likely cases where several of the multiply-gestated fetuses are disabled or dead.

People exaggerate the fears of the unknown and downplay the very real dangers of the familiar. In a very important sense, driving a car each day is far more dangerous to children than the new form of human reproduction under discussion here. Many, many people are hurt and killed every day in automobile wrecks, yet few people consider not driving.

In SCNT, there are possible dangers of telomere shortening, inheritance of environmental effects on adult cells passed to embryonic cells, and possible unknown dangers. Mammalian animal studies must determine if such dangers will occur in human SCNT origination. Once such studies prove that there are no special dangers of SCNT, the crucial question will arise: how safe must we expect human SCNT to be before we allow it?

In answering this question, it is very important to ask about the baseline of comparison. How safe is ordinary, human sexual reproduction? How safe is assisted reproduction? Who or what counts as a subject of a safety calculation about SCNT?

At least 40% of human embryos fail to implant in normal sexual reproduction.[9] Although this fact is not widely known, it is important because some discussions tend to assume that every human embryo becomes a human baby unless some extraordinary event occurs such as abortion. But this is not true. Nature seems to have a genetic filter, such that malformed embryos do not implant. About 50% of the rejected embryos are chromosomally abnormal, meaning that if they were somehow brought to term, the resulting children would be mutants or suffer genetic dysfunction.

A widely-reported but misleading aspect of Ian Wilmut's work was that it took 277 embryos to produce one live lamb. In fact, Wilmut started with 277 eggs, fused nuclei with them to create embryos, and then allowed them to become the best 29 embryos, which were allowed to gestate further. He had three lambs almost live, with one true success, Dolly. Subsequent work may easily bring the efficiency rate to 25%. When the calves "Charlie" and "George" were born in 1998, four live-born calves were created from an initial batch of only 50 embryos.[10]

Wilmut's embryo-to-birth ratio only seems inefficient or unsafe because the real inefficiency fate of accepted forms of human assisted reproduction is so little known. In in vitro fertilization, a woman is given drugs to stimulate superovulation so that physicians can remove as many eggs as possible. At each cycle of attempted in vitro fertilization, three or four embryos are implanted. Most couples make several attempts, so as many as nine to twelve embryos are involved for each couple. As noted, only about 15–20% of couples undergoing such attempts ever take home a baby.

Consider what these numbers mean when writ large. Take a hundred couples attempting assisted reproduction, each undergoing (on average) three attempts. Suppose there are unusually good results and that 20% of these couples eventually take home a baby. Because more than one embryo may implant, assume that among these 20 couples, half have non-identical twins. But what is the efficiency rate here? Assuming a low number of three embryos implanted each time for the 300 attempts, it will take 900 embryos to produce 30 babies, for an efficiency rate of 1 in 30.

Nor is it true that all the loss of human potential occurred at the embryonic stage.

Unfortunately, some of these pregnancies will end in miscarriages of fetuses, some well along in the second trimester.

Nevertheless, such loss of embryos and fetuses is almost universally accepted as morally permissible. Why is that? Because the infertile parents are trying to conceive their own children, because everyone thinks that is a good motive, and because few people object to the loss of embryos and fetuses *in this context of trying to conceive babies.* Seen in this light, what Wilmut did, starting out with a large number of embryos to get one successful lamb at birth, is not so novel or different from what now occurs in human assisted reproduction.

SUBJECTS AND NONSUBJECTS OF HARM

One premise that seems to figure in discussions of the safety of SCNT and other forms of assisted reproduction is that loss of human embryos morally matters. That premise should be rejected.

As the above discussion shows, loss of human embryos is a normal part of human conception and, without this process, humanity might suffer much more genetic disease. This process essentially involves the loss of human embryos as part of the natural state of things. Indeed, some researchers believe that for every human baby successfully born, there has been at least one human embryo lost along the way.

In vitro fertilization is widely-accepted as a great success in modern medicine. As said, over 40,000 American babies have been born this way. But calculations indicate that as many as a million human embryos may have been used in creating such successes.

Researchers often create embryos for subsequent cycles of implantation, only to learn that a pregnancy has been achieved and that such stored embryos are no longer needed. Thousands of such embryos can be stored indefinitely in liquid nitrogen. No one feels any great urgency about them and,

indeed, many couples decline to pay fees to preserve their embryos.

The above considerations point to the obvious philosophical point that embryos are not persons with rights to life. Like an acorn, their value is all potential, little actual. Faced with a choice between paying a thousand dollars to keep two thousand embryos alive for a year in storage, or paying for an operation to keep a family pet alive for another year, no one will choose to pay for the embryos. How people actually act says much about their real values.

Thus an embryo cannot be harmed by being brought into existence and then being taken out of existence. An embryo is generally considered such until nine weeks after conception, when it is called a "fetus" (when it is born, it is called a "baby"). Embryos are not sentient and cannot experience pain. They are thus not the kind of subjects that can be harmed or benefitted.

As such, whether it takes one embryo to create a human baby or a hundred does not matter morally. It may matter aesthetically; financially, emotionally, or in time spent trying to reproduce, but it does not matter morally. As such, new forms of human reproduction such as IVF and SCNT that involve significant loss of embryos cannot be morally criticized on this charge.

Finally, because embryos don't count morally, they could be tested in various ways to eliminate defects in development or genetic mishaps. Certainly, if four or five SCNT embryos were implanted, only the healthiest one should be brought to term. As such, the risk of abnormal SCNT babies could be minimized.

SETTING THE STANDARD ABOUT THE RISK OF HARM

Animal tests have not yet shown that SCNT is safe enough to try in humans, and extensive animal testing should be done over the next few years. That means that, before we attempt SCNT in humans, we will need to be able to routinely produce healthy offspring by SCNT in lambs, cattle, and especially, non-human primates. After this testing is done, the time will come when a crucial question must be answered: how safe must human SCNT be before it is allowed? This is probably the most important, practical question before us now.

Should we have a very high standard, such that we take virtually no risk with a SCNT child? Daniel Callahan and Paul Ramsey, past critics of IVF, implied that unless a healthy baby could be guaranteed the first time, it was unethical to try to produce babies in a new way. At the other extreme, a low standard would allow great risks.

What is the appropriate standard? How high should be the bar over which scientists must be made to jump before they are allowed to try to originate a SCNT child? In my opinion, the standard of Callahan and Ramsey is too high. In reality, only God can meet that Olympian standard. It is also too high for those physicians trying to help infertile couples. If this high standard had been imposed on these people in the past, no form of assisted reproduction—including in vitro fertilization—would ever have been allowed.

On the other end of the scale, one could look at the very worst conditions for human gestation, where mothers are drug-dependent during pregnancy or exposed to dangerous chemicals. Such worst-case conditions include parents with a 50% chance of passing on a lethal genetic disease. The lowest standard of harm allows human reproduction even if there is such a high risk of harm ("harm" in the sense that the child would likely have a sub-normal future). One could argue that since society allows such mothers and couples to reproduce sexually, it could do no worse by allowing a child to be originated by SCNT.

I believe that the low standard is inappropriate to use with human SCNT. There is no reason to justify down to the very worst conditions under which society now tolerates humans being born. If the best we can do by

SCNT is to produce children as good as those born with fetal-maternal alcohol syndrome, we shouldn't originate children this way.

Between these standards, there is the normal range of risk that is accepted by ordinary people in sexual reproduction. Human SCNT should be allowed when the predicted risk from animal studies falls within this range. "Ordinary people" refers to those who are neither alcoholic nor dependent on an illegal drug and where neither member of the couple knowingly passes on a high risk for a serious genetic disease.

This standard seems reasonable. It does not require a guarantee of a perfect baby, but it also rejects the "anything goes" view. For example, if the rate of serious deformities in normal human reproduction is 1%, and if the rate of chimpanzee SCNT reproduction were brought down to this rate, and if there were no reason to think that SCNT in human primates would be any higher, it should be permissible to attempt human SCNT.

WE ALREADY ALLOW MORE DANGEROUS FORMS OF FAMILIAR THINGS

Consider the case of an infertility researcher trying to increase the chances of older women successfully giving birth by using eggs of younger women. The practice of using an egg of a younger woman increases the chances of a 44-year-old woman giving birth from the 3.5% chance of IVF to 50%.[11] The problem with this practice is that the gestating, older woman does not have a genetic connection to the resulting child.

But there is a new, possible way to solve this problem. Researcher James Grifo, chief of New York University's infertility clinic, proposes to enucleate an egg of a younger woman and insert the sexually-mixed chromosomes into it from an embryo of an older couple.[12] The older woman will gestate the new SCNT-created embryo, an embryo that may successfully implant because it has the outer cytoplasm and mitochondria of a younger woman's egg. Creating an embryo by such a SCNT process is not "cloning," not asexual reproduction, because the chromosomes randomly mixed when sperm met egg. Nevertheless, the process of creating a human embryo (created sexually) by SCNT here is obviously very close to the process of creating a human embryo by *asexual* SCNT.

This new, nucleus-transferring procedure is controversial but permitted under existing law. It undoubtedly is experimental and risks possible harm to any resulting child, but because this procedure does not have the emotional associations of "cloning," it will probably pass unnoticed in the general world. This is exactly what happened with intracytoplasmic sperm injection—where only one sperm is used to fertilize an egg—despite its unknown safety record when first attempted.[13] Such new procedures, and the possible harm of doing them, are very close to those of SCNT. We say the sky will fall if we try SCNT while we ignore the fact that very similar risks are being taken all around us.

Finally, we are already doing things far more radical than human SCNT. Putting human genes in pigs to create possible organ transplants from such altered pigs is far more radical than human SCNT. Transplants from such pig organs open up the possibility of a two-way travel of porcine viruses to humans and vice-versa (of concern to those who think that AIDS came from simian-human contact). In 1987, we allowed Harvard University to patent its oncomouse (aka the "Harvard oncomouse"). Since then over a thousand applications for such patents have been filed and over 50 patents on genetically-altered or genetically-created animals have been issued by the U.S. Patent Office.[14] Overall, from genetically-altered tomatoes to pig-grown livers for transplanting into humans, we are doing radically new things to save human lives, crossing natural barriers all the time, and hardly blinking an eye about it. Why, then, are we so concerned about SCNT?

PSYCHOLOGICAL HARM TO THE CHILD

Another concern is about psychological harm to a child originated by SCNT. According to this objection, choosing to have a child is not like choosing a car or house. It is a moral decision because another being is affected. Having a child should be a careful, responsible choice and focused on what's best for the child. Having a child originated by SCNT is not morally permissible because it is not best for the child.

The problem with this argument is the last six words of the last sentence, which assumes bad motives on the part of parents. Unfortunately, SCNT is associated with bad motives in science fiction, but until we have evidence that it will be used this way, why assume the worst about people?

Certainly, if someone deliberately brought a child into the world with the intention of causing him harm, that would be immoral. Unfortunately, the concept of harm is a continuum and some people have very high standards, such that not providing a child a stay-at-home parent constitutes harming the child. But there is nothing about SCNT per se that is necessarily linked to bad motives. True, people would have certain expectations of a child created by SCNT, but parents-to-be already have certain expectations about children.

Too many parents are fatalistic and just accept whatever life throws at them. The very fact of being a parent for many people is something they must accept (because abortion was not a real option). Part of this acceptance is to just accept whatever genetic combination comes at birth from the random assortment of genes.

But why is such acceptance a good thing? It is a defeatist attitude in medicine against disease; it is a defeatist attitude toward survival when one's culture or country is under attack; and it is a defeatist attitude toward life in general. "The expectations of parents will be too high!" critics repeat. "Better to leave parents in ignorance and to leave their children as randomness decrees." The silliness of that view is apparent as soon as it is made explicit.

If we are thinking about harm to the child, an objection that comes up repeatedly might be called the argument for an open future. "In the case of cloning," it is objected, "the expectations are very specifically tied to the life of another person. So in a sense, the child's future is denied to him because he will be expected to be like his ancestor. But part of the wonder of having children is surprise at how they turn out. As such, some indeterminacy should remain a part of childhood. Human SCNT deprives a person of an open future because when we know how his previous twin lived, we will know how the new child will live."

It is true that the adults choosing this genotype rather than that one must have some expectations. There has to be some reason for choosing one genotype over another. But these expectations are only half based in fact. As we know, no person originated by SCNT will be identical to his ancestor because of mitochondrial DNA, because of his different gestation, because of his different parents, because of his different time in history, and perhaps, because of his different country and culture. Several famous pairs of conjoined twins, such as Eng and Chang, with both identical genotypes and identical uterine/childhood environments, have still had different personalities.[15] To assume that a SCNT child's future is not open is to assume genetic reductionism.

Moreover, insofar as parents have specific expectations about children created by SCNT, such expectations will likely be no better or worse than the normal expectations by parents of children created sexually. As said, there is nothing about SCNT per se that necessitates bad motives on the part of parents.

Notice that most of the expected harm to the child stems *from the predicted, prejudicial attitudes of other people to the SCNT child.* ("Would you want to be a cloned child? Can you imagine being called a freak and having only one genetic parent?") As such, it is important to remember that social expectations are *merely* social expectations. They are malleable and can change quickly. True, parents might initially have expectations that are too high and other people might regard such children with prejudice. But just as such inappropriate attitudes faded after the first cases of in vitro fertilization, they will fade here too.

Ron James, the Scottish millionaire who funded much of Ian Wilmut's research, points out that social attitudes change fast. Before the announcement of Dolly, polls showed that people thought that cloning animals and gene transfer to animals were "morally problematic," whereas germ-line gene therapy fell in the category of "just wrong." Two months after the announcement of Dolly, and after much discussion of human cloning, people's attitudes had shifted to accepting animal cloning and gene transfer to humans as "morally permissible," whereas germ-line gene therapy had shifted to being merely "morally problematic."[16]

James Watson, the co-discoverer of the double helix, once opposed in vitro fertilization by claiming that prejudicial attitudes of other people would harm children created this way. . . . [17] In that piece, the prejudice was really in Watson, because the way that he was stirring up fear was doing more to create the prejudice than any normal human reaction. Similarly, Leon Kass's recent long essay in *The New Republic* . . . , where he calls human asexual reproduction "repugnant" and a "horror," creates exactly the kind of prejudiced reaction that he predicts.[18] Rather than make a priori, self-fulfilling prophecies, wouldn't it be better to be empirical about such matters? To be more optimistic about the reactions of ordinary parents?

Children created by SCNT would not *look* any different from other children. Nobody at age two looks like he does at age 45 and, except for his parents, nobody knows what the 45-year-old man looked like at age two. And since ordinary children often look like their parents, no one would be able to tell a SCNT child from others until he had lived a decade.

Kass claims that a child originated by SCNT will have "a troubled psychic identity" because he or she will be "utterly" confused about his social, genetic, and kinship ties.[19] At worst, this child will be like a child of "incest" and may, if originated as a male from the father, have the same sexual feelings towards the wife as the father. An older male might in turn have strong sexual feelings toward a young female with his wife's genome.

Yet if this were so, any husband of any married twin might have an equally troubled psychic identity because he might have the same sexual feelings toward the twin as his wife. Instead, those in relationships with twins claim that the individuals are very different.

Much of the above line of criticism simply begs the question and assumes that humans created by SCNT will be greeted by stigma or experience confusion. It is hard to understand why, once one gets beyond the novelty, because a child created asexually would know *exactly* who his ancestor was. No confusion there. True, prejudicial expectations could damage children, but why make public policy based on that?

Besides, isn't this kind of argument hypocritical in our present society? Where no one is making any serious effort to ban divorce, despite the overwhelming evidence that divorce seriously damages children, even teenage children. It is always far easier to concentrate on the dramatic, far-off harm than the ones close-at-hand. When we are really concerned about minimizing harm to children, we will pass laws requiring all parents wanting to divorce to go through counseling sessions or to wait a year. We will pass a federal law compelling child-support from fathers who flee to other states, and make it impossible to renew a professional license or get paid in a public institution in another state until all child-support is paid. After that is done, then we can non-hypocritically talk about how much our society cares about not harming children who may be originated in new ways.

In conclusion, the predicted harms of SCNT to humans are wildly exaggerated,

lack a comparative baseline, stem from irrational fears of the unknown, overlook greater dangers of familiar things, and are often based on the armchair psychological speculation of amateurs. Once studies prove SCNT as safe as normal sexual reproduction in non-human mammals, the harm objection will disappear. Given other arguments that SCNT could substantially benefit many children, the argument that SCNT would harm children is a weak one that needs to be weighed against its many potential benefits.[20]

Notes

1. Paul Ramsey, *Fabricated Man: The Ethics of Genetic Control* (New Haven, Conn.: Yale University Press, 1970).

2. "What are the psychological implications of growing up as a specimen, sheltered not by a warm womb but by steel and glass, belonging to no one but the lab technician who joined together sperm and egg? In a world already populated with people with identity crises, what's the personal identity of a test-tube baby?" J. Rifkin and T. Howard, *Who Shall Play God?* (New York: Dell, 1977), 15.

3. Ehsan Massod, "Cloning Technique 'Reveals Legal Loophole'," *Nature* 38, 27 February 1987.

4. *New York Times*, 27 July 1978, A16.

5. Knight-Ridder newspapers, 10 March 1997.

6. Leon Kass, "The New Biology: What Price Relieving Man's Estate?" *Journal of the American Medical Association*, vol. 174, 19 November 1971, 779–788.

7. Leroy Walters, "Biomedical Ethics and Their Role in Mammalian Cloning," Conference on Mammalian Cloning: Implications for Science and Society, 27 June 1997, Crystal City Marriott, Crystal City, Virginia.

8. National Bioethics Advisory Commission (NBAC), *Cloning Human Beings: Report and Recommendations of the National Bioethics Advisory Commission*, Rockville, Md., June 1997.

9. A. Wilcox et al., "Incidence of Early Loss of Pregnancy," *New England Journal of Medicine* 319, no. 4, 28 July 1988, 189–194. See also J. Grudzinskas and A. Nysenbaum, "Failure of Human Pregnancy after Implantation," *Annals of New York Academy of Sciences* 442, 1985, 39–44; J. Muller et al., "Fetal Loss after Implantation," *Lancet* 2, 1980, 554–556.

10. Rick Weiss, "Genetically Engineered Calves Cloned," 21 January 1998, *Washington Post*, A3.

11. Lisa Belkin, "Pregnant with Complications," *New York Times Magazine*, October 26, 1997, 38.

12. ABC News report, October 27, 1997.

13. Axel Kahn, "Clone Animals . . . Clone Man?" specially-commissioned article to accompany articles from *Nature* on cloning on the web site of *Nature*.

14. See the web site of a leading law firm in this area, Elman & Associates, at http://www.elman.com/elman.

15. David R. Collins, *Eng and Chang: The Original Siamese Twins* (New York: Dillon Press, 1994). Elaine Landau, *Joined at Birth: The Lives of Conjoined Twins* (New York: Grolier Publishing, 1997). See also Geoffrey A. Machin, "Conjoined Twins: Implications for Blastogenesis," *Birth Defects: Original Articles Series* 20, no. 1, 1993, March of Dimes Foundation, 142.

16. Ron James, Managing Director, PPL Therapeutics, "Industry Perspective: The Promise and Practi-

cal Applications," Conference on Mammalian Cloning: Implications for Science and Society, 27 June 1997, Crystal City Marriott, Crystal City, Virginia.

17. James D. Watson, "Moving Towards the Clonal Man," *Atlantic*, May 1971, 50–53.

18. Leon Kass, "The Wisdom of Repugnance," *The New Republic*, 2 June 1997.

19. Kass, "The Wisdom of Repugnance," 22–23.

20. Thanks to Mary Litch for comments on this essay.

Persons and Relationships in the Information Age

Kenneth Gergen

We often focus on the advantages of new technologies. We want the newest computers, the fastest Internet access, the greatest number of cable TV channels, and the cheapest cell phones; all of these have obvious benefits. Advances in applied science have made these technologies available at prices that many can afford, so their use is widespread. We tend to be less aware of the costs that accompany the cultural transformations resulting from such technologies. Kenneth Gergen develops an impressionistic account of the effects of communications technologies on social relations and personal identity. When personal relations are mediated electronically, we are able to experience many more individuals and to maintain more friendships. At the same time, our knowledge of others becomes more fragmented, and our relationships become thinner. He suggests that while TV, e-mail, and other communication technologies enhance our knowledge about relationships, they also expand our desires and our obligations. Increasingly, we are drawn in different directions and experience what he calls "multiphrenia," a new pattern of divided self-consciousness. Gergen takes an equivocal stance toward these changes. The reader is left to form a summative evaluation of the costs and benefits of the Information Age that he identifies. Kenneth Gergen is professor of psychology at Swarthmore College.

As you read through this essay, consider the following:

1. According to Gergen, how have our social relationships been transformed by recent technological advances?
2. How does Gergen think social saturation affects our lives? On balance do you think the effects are beneficial?
3. What features of "multiphrenia" does Gergen highlight?
4. Why does he think that modern communications technologies increase our sense of obligation and threaten our capacity for rationality?
5. Do you think that the benefits of the Information Age outweigh its costs? If not, can we avoid these costs or prevent the transformation of our culture?

A century ago, social relationships were largely confined to the distance of an easy walk. Most were conducted in person, within small communities: family, neighbors, towns-people. Yes, the horse and carriage made longer trips possible, but even a trip of thirty miles could take all day. The railroad could speed one away, but cost and availability limited such travel. If one moved from the community, relationships were likely to end. From birth to death one could depend on relatively even-textured social surroundings. Words, faces, gestures, and possibilities were relatively consistent, coherent, and slow to change.

For much of the world's population, especially the industrialized West, the small, face-to-face community is vanishing into the pages of history. We go to country inns for weekend outings, we decorate condominium interiors with clapboards and brass beds, and we dream of old age in a rural cottage. But as a result of the technological developments just described, contemporary life is a swirling sea of social relations. Words thunder in by radio, television, newspaper, mail, telephone, fax, wire service, electronic mail, billboards, Federal Express, and more. Waves of new faces are everywhere—in town for a day, visiting for the weekend, at the Rotary lunch, at the church social—and incessantly and incandescently on television. Long weeks in a single community are unusual; a full day within a single neighborhood is becoming rare. We travel casually across town, into the countryside, to neighboring towns, cities, states; one might go thirty miles for coffee and conversation.

Through the technologies of the century, the number and variety of relationships in which we are engaged, potential frequency of contact, expressed intensity of relationship, and endurance through time all are steadily increasing. As this increase becomes extreme we reach a state of social saturation. Let us consider this state in greater detail.

In the face-to-face community the cast of others remained relatively stable.[1] There were changes by virtue of births and deaths, but moving from one town—much less state or country—to another was difficult. The number of relationships commonly maintained in today's world stands in stark contrast. Counting one's family, the morning television news, the car radio, colleagues on the train, and the local newspaper, the typical commuter may confront as many different persons (in terms of views or images) in the first two hours of a day as the community-based predecessor did in a month. The morning calls in a business office may connect one to a dozen different locales in a given city, often across the continent, and very possibly across national boundaries. A single hour of prime-time melodrama immerses one in the lives of a score of individuals. In an evening of television, hundreds of engaging faces insinuate themselves into our lives. It is not only the immediate community that occupies our thoughts and feelings, but a constantly changing cast of characters spread across the globe.

Two aspects of this expansion are particularly noteworthy. First there is what may be termed the *perseverance of the past*. Formerly, increases in time and distance between persons typically meant loss. When someone moved away, the relationship would languish. Long-distance visits were arduous, and the mails slow. Thus, as one grew older, many active participants would fade from one's life. Today, time and distance are no longer such serious threats to a relationship. One may sustain an intimacy over thousands of miles by frequent telephone raptures punctuated by occasional visits. One may similarly retain relationships with high-school chums, college roommates, old military cronies, or friends from a Caribbean vacation five years earlier. Birthday books have become a standard household item; one's memory is inadequate to record the festivities for which one is responsible. In effect, as we move through life, the cast of relevant characters is ever expanding. For some this means an ever-increasing sense of stress: "How can we make friends with them? We don't even have time for the friends we already have!" For others there is a sense of comfort, for the social caravan in which we travel through life remains always full.

Yet at the same time that the past is preserved, continuously poised to insert itself into the present, there is an *acceleration of the future*. The pace of relationships is hurried, and processes of unfolding that once required months or years may be accomplished in days or weeks. A century ago, for example, courtships were often carried out on foot or horseback, or through occasional letters. Hours of interchange might be punctuated by long periods of silence, making the path from acquaintanceship to intimacy lengthy. With today's technologies, however, it is possible for a couple to maintain almost continuous connection. Not only do transportation technologies chip away at the barrier of geographic distance, but through telephone (both stable and cordless), overnight mail, cassette recordings, home videos, photographs, and electronic mail, the other may be "present" at almost any moment. Courtships may thus move from excitement to exhaustion within a short time. The single person may experience not a handful of courtship relationships in a lifetime but dozens. In the same way, the process of friendship is often accelerated. Through the existing technologies, a sense of affinity may blossom into a lively sense of interdependence within a brief space of time. As the future opens, the number of friendships expands as never before. . . .

New patterns of relationship also take shape. In the face-to-face community one participated in a limited set of relationships—with family, friends, storekeepers, clerics, and the like. Now the next telephone call can thrust us suddenly into a new relationship—with a Wall Street broker, a charity solicitor, an alumni campaigner from the old school, a childhood friend at a nearby convention, a relative from across the country, a child of a friend, or even a sex pervert. One may live in a suburb with well-clipped neighbors, but commute to a city for frequent confrontation with street people, scam merchants, panhandlers, prostitutes, and threatening bands of juveniles. One may reside in Houston, but establish bonds—through business or leisure travel—with a Norwegian banker, a wine merchant from the Rhine Pfalz, or an architect from Rome.

Of course, it is television that most dramatically increases the variety of relationships in which one participates—even if vicariously. One can identify with heroes from a thousand tales, carry on imaginary conversations with talk-show guests from all walks of life, or empathize with athletes from around the globe. One of the most interesting results of this electronic expansion of relationships occurs in the domain of parent-child relationships. As Joshua Meyrowitz proposes in *No Sense of Place*, children of the preceding century were largely insulated from information about the private lives of adults.[2] Parents, teachers, and police could shield children from their adult proceedings by simply conducting them in private places. Further, books dealing with the misgivings, failings, deceits, and conflicts of the adult world were generally unavailable to children. Children remained children. Television has changed all that. Programming systematically reveals the full panoply of "backstage" trials and tribulations to the child. As a result the child no longer interacts with one-dimensional, idealized adults, but with persons possessing complex private lives, doubt-filled and vulnerable. In turn, parents no longer confront the comfortably naive child of yesteryear, but one whose awe is diminished and whose insights may be acute.

The technology of the age both expands the variety of human relationships and modifies the form of older ones. When relationships move from the face-to-face to the electronic mode, they are often altered. Relationships that were confined to specific situations—to offices, living rooms, bedrooms—become "unglued." They are no longer geographically confined, but can take place anywhere. Unlike face-to-face relationships, electronic relationships also conceal visual information (eye movement, expressive movements of the mouth), so a telephone speaker cannot read the facial cues of the listener for signs of approval or disapproval. As a result, there is a greater tendency to create an imaginary other with whom to relate. One can fantasize that the other is feeling warm and enthusiastic or cold and angry, and act accordingly. An acquaintance told me that he believed his first marriage to be a product of the heavy phoning necessary for a long-distance courtship. By phone she seemed the most desirable woman in the world; it was only months after the wedding that he realized that he had married a mirage.

Many organizations are now installing electronic-mail systems, which enable employees to carry out their business with each other by computer terminals rather than by traditional, face-to-face means. Researchers find that employee relations have subtly changed as a result. Status differences begin to crumble as lower-ranking employees feel freer to express their feelings and question their superiors electronically than in person. Harvard Business School's Shoshana Zuboff suggests that the introduction of "smart machines" into businesses is blurring the distinctions between managers and workers. Managers are no longer the "thinkers" while the workers are consigned to the "doing."[3] Rather, out of necessity the workers now become managers of information, and as a result, they considerably augment their power. . . .

Consider the moments:

- Over lunch with friends you discuss Northern Ireland. Although you have never spoken a word on the subject, you find yourself heatedly defending British policies.
- You work as an executive in the investments department of a bank. In the evenings you smoke marijuana and listen to the Grateful Dead.
- You sit in a café and wonder what it would be like to have an intimate relationship with various strangers walking past.

- You are a lawyer in a prestigious midtown firm. On the weekends you work on a novel about romance with a terrorist.
- You go to a Moroccan restaurant and afterward take in the latest show at a country-and-western bar.

In each case individuals harbor a sense of coherent identity or self-sameness, only to find themselves suddenly propelled by alternative impulses. They seem securely to be one sort of person, but yet another comes bursting to the surface—in a suddenly voiced opinion, a fantasy, a turn of interests, or a private activity. Such experiences with variation and self-contradiction may be viewed as preliminary effects of social saturation. They may signal a *populating of the self*, the acquisition of multiple and disparate potentials for being. It is this process of self-population that begins to undermine the traditional commitments to both romanticist and modernist forms of being. It is of pivotal importance in setting the stage for the postmodern turn. Let us explore.

The technologies of social saturation expose us to an enormous range of persons, new forms of relationship, unique circumstances and opportunities, and special intensities of feeling. One can scarcely remain unaffected by such exposure. As child-development specialists now agree, the process of socialization is lifelong. We continue to incorporate information from the environment throughout our lives. When exposed to other persons, we change in two major ways. We increase our capacities for *knowing that* and for *knowing how*. In the first case, through exposure to others we learn myriad details about their words, actions, dress, mannerisms, and so on. We ingest enormous amounts of information about patterns of interchange. Thus, for example, from an hour on a city street, we are informed of the clothing styles of blacks, whites, upper class, lower class, and more. We may learn the ways of Japanese businessmen, bag ladies, Sikhs, Hare Krishnas, or flute players from Chile. We see how relationships are carried out between mothers and daughters, business executives, teenage friends, and construction workers. An hour in a business office may expose us to the political views of a Texas oilman, a Chicago lawyer, and a gay activist from San Francisco. Radio commentators espouse views on boxing, pollution, and child abuse; pop music may advocate machoism, racial bigotry, and suicide. Paperback books cause hearts to race over the unjustly treated, those who strive against impossible odds, those who are brave or brilliant. And this is to say nothing of television input. Via television, myriad figures are allowed into the home who would never otherwise trespass. Millions watch as talk-show guests—murderers, rapists, women prisoners, child abusers, members of the KKK, mental patients, and others often discredited—attempt to make their lives intelligible. There are few six-year-olds who cannot furnish at least a rudimentary account of life in an African village, the concerns of divorcing parents, or drug-pushing in the ghetto. Hourly our storehouse of social knowledge expands in range and sophistication.

This massive increase in knowledge of the social world lays the groundwork for a second kind of learning, a *knowing how*. We learn how to place such knowledge into action, to shape it for social consumption, to act so that social life can proceed effectively. And the possibilities for placing this supply of information into effective action are constantly expanding. The Japanese businessman glimpsed on the street today, and on the television tomorrow, may be well confronted in one's office the following week. On these occasions the rudiments of appropriate behavior are already in place. If a mate announces that he or she is thinking about divorce, the other's reaction is not likely to be dumb dismay. The drama has so often been played out on television and movie screens that one is already prepared with multiple options. If one wins a wonderful prize, suffers a humiliating loss, faces temptation to cheat, or learns of a sudden death in the family, the reactions are hardly random. One more or less knows how it goes, is more or less ready for action. Having seen it all before, one approaches a state of ennui.

In an important sense, as social saturation proceeds we become pastiches, imitative assemblages of each other. In memory we carry others' patterns of being with us. If the conditions are favorable, we can place these patterns into action. Each of us becomes the other, a representative, or a replacement. To put it more broadly, as the century has progressed selves have become increasingly populated with the character of others.[4] We are not one, or a few, but like Walt Whitman, we "contain multitudes." We appear to each other as single identities, unified, of whole cloth. However, with social saturation, each of us comes to harbor a vast population of hidden potentials—to be a blues singer, a gypsy, an aristocrat, a criminal. All the selves lie latent, and under the right conditions may spring to life.

The populating of the self not only opens relationships to new ranges of possibility, but one's subjective life also becomes more fully laminated. Each of the selves we acquire from others can contribute to inner dialogues, private discussions we have with ourselves about all manner of persons, events, and issues. These internal voices, these vestiges of relationships both real and imagined, have been given different names: *invisible guests* by Mary Watkins, *social imagery* by Eric Klinger, and *social ghosts* by Mary Gergen, who found in her research that virtually all the young people she sampled could discuss many such experiences with ease.[5] Most of these ghosts were close friends, often from earlier periods of their lives. Family members were also frequent, with the father's voice predominating, but grandparents, uncles, aunts, and other relatives figured prominently. Relevant to the earlier discussion of relations with media figures, almost a quarter of the ghosts mentioned were individuals with whom the young people had never had any direct interchange. Most were entertainers: rock stars, actors and actresses, singers, and the like. Others were religious figures such as Jesus and Mary, fictitious characters such as James Bond and Sherlock Holmes, and celebrities such as Chris Evert, Joe Montana, Barbara Walters, and the president.

The respondents also spoke of the many ways the social ghosts functioned in their lives. It was not simply that they were there for conversation or contemplation; they also served as models for action. They set standards for behavior; they were admired and were emulated. As one wrote, "Connie Chung was constantly being used as a role model for me and I found myself responding to a question about what I planned to do after graduation by saying that I wanted to go into journalism just because I had been thinking of her." Or, as another wrote of her grandmother, "She showed me how to be tolerant of all people and to show respect to everyone regardless of their state in life." Ghosts also voiced opinions on various matters. Most frequently they were used to bolster one's beliefs. At times such opinions were extremely important. As one wrote of the memory of an early friend, "She is the last link I have to Christianity at this point in my life when I am trying to determine my religious inclinations." Still other respondents spoke of the way their ghosts supported their self-esteem: "I think my father and I know that he would be proud of what I have accomplished." Many mentioned the sense of emotional support furnished by their ghosts: "My grandmother seems to be watching me and showing that she loves me even if I am not doing so well."

In closely related work, the psychologists Hazel Markus and Paula Nurius speak of *possible selves*, the multiple conceptions people harbor of what they might become, would like to become, or are afraid to become.[6] In each case, these possible selves function as private surrogates for others to whom one has been exposed—either directly or via the media. The family relations specialists Paul Rosenblatt and Sara Wright speak similarly of the *shadow realities* that exist in close relationships.[7] In addition to the reality that a couple shares together, each will harbor alternative interpretations of their lives together—interpretations that might appear unacceptable and threatening if revealed to the partner. These shadow realities are typically generated and supported by persons outside the relationship—possibly members of the extended family, but also figures from the media. Finally, the British psychologist Michael Billig and his colleagues have studied the values, goals, and ideals to which people are committed in their everyday lives.[8] They found the typical condition of the individual to be internal conflict: for each belief there exists a strong countertendency. People feel their prejudices are justified, yet it is wrong to be intolerant; that there should be equality but hierarchies are also good; and that we are all basically the same, but we must hold on to our individuality. For every value, goal, or ideal, one holds to the converse as well. Billig proposes that the capacity for contradiction is essential to the practical demands of life in contemporary society.

This virtual cacophony of potentials is of no small consequence for either romanticist or modernist visions of the self. For as new and disparate voices are added to one's being, committed identity becomes an increasingly arduous achievement. How difficult for the romantic to keep a firm grasp on the helm of an idealistic undertaking when a chorus of internal voices sing the praises of realism, skepticism, hedonism, and nihilism. And can the committed realist, who believes in the powers of rationality and observation, remain arrogant in the face of inner urges toward emotional indulgence, moral sentiment, spiritual sensitivity, or aesthetic fulfillment? Thus, as social saturation adds incrementally to the population of self, each impulse toward well-formed identity is cast into increasing doubt; each is found absurd, shallow, limited, or flawed by the onlooking audience of the interior. . . .

It is sunny Saturday morning and he finishes breakfast in high spirits. It is a rare day in which he is free to do as he pleases. With relish he contemplates his options. The back door needs fixing, which calls for a trip to the hardware store. This would allow a much-needed haircut; and while in town he could get a birthday card for his brother, leave off his shoes for repair, and pick up shirts at the cleaners. But, he ponders, he really should get some exercise; is there time for jogging in the afternoon? That reminds him of a championship game he wanted to see at the same time. To be taken more seriously was his ex-wife's repeated request for a luncheon talk. And shouldn't he also settle his vacation plans before all the best locations are taken? Slowly his optimism gives way to a sense of defeat. The free day has become a chaos of competing opportunities and necessities.

If such a scene is vaguely familiar, it attests only further to the pervasive effects of social saturation and the populating of the self. More important, one detects amid the hurly-burly of contemporary life a new constellation of feelings or sensibilities, a new pattern of self-consciousness. This syndrome may be termed *multiphrenia*, generally referring to the splitting of the individual into a multiplicity of self-investments. This condition is partly an outcome of self-population, but partly a result of the populated self's efforts to exploit the potentials of the technologies of relationship. In this sense, there is a cyclical spiraling toward a state of multiphrenia. As one's potentials are expanded by the technologies, so one increasingly employs the technologies for self-expression; yet, as the technologies are further utilized, so do they add to the repertoire of potentials. It would be a mistake to view this multiphrenic condition as a form of illness, for it is often suffused with a sense of expansiveness and adventure. Someday there may indeed be nothing to distinguish multiphrenia from simply "normal living."

However, before we pass into this oceanic state, let us pause to consider some prominent features of the condition.[9] Three of these are especially noteworthy.

With the technology of social saturation, two of the major factors traditionally impeding relationships—namely time and space—are both removed. The past can be continuously renewed—via voice, video, and visits, for example—and distance poses no substantial barriers to ongoing interchange. Yet this same freedom ironically leads to a form of enslavement. For each person, passion, or potential incorporated into oneself exacts a penalty—a penalty both of *being* and of *being with*. In the former case, as others are incorporated into the self, their tastes, goals, and values also insinuate themselves into one's being. Through continued interchange, one acquires, for example, a yen for Thai cooking, the desire for retirement security, or an investment in wildlife preservation. Through others one comes to value whole-grain breads, novels from Chile, or community politics. Yet as Buddhists have long been aware, to desire is simultaneously to become a slave of the desirable. To "want" reduces one's choice to "want not." Thus, as others are incorporated into the self, and their desires become one's own, there is an expansion of goals—of "musts," wants, and needs. Attention is necessitated, effort is exerted, frustrations are encountered. Each new desire places its demands and reduces one's liberties.

There is also the penalty of being with. As relationships develop, their participants acquire local definitions—friend, lover, teacher, supporter, and so on. To sustain the relationship requires an honoring of the definitions—both of self and other. If two persons become close friends, for example, each acquires certain rights, duties, and privileges. Most relationships of any significance carry with them a range of obligations—for communication, joint activities, preparing for the other's pleasure, rendering appropriate congratulations, and so on. Thus, as relations accumulate and expand over time, there is a steadily increasing range of phone calls to make and answer, greeting cards to address, visits or activities to arrange, meals to prepare, preparations to be made, clothes to buy, makeup to apply. . . . And with each new opportunity—for skiing together in the Alps, touring Australia, camping in the Adirondacks, or snorkling in the Bahamas—there are "opportunity costs." One must unearth information, buy equipment, reserve hotels, arrange travel, work long hours to clear one's desk, locate babysitters, dogsitters, homesitters. . . . Liberation becomes a swirling vertigo of demands.

In the professional world this expansion of "musts" is strikingly evident. In the university of the 1950s, for example, one's departmental colleagues were often vital to one's work. One could walk but a short distance for advice, information, support, and so on. Departments were often close-knit and highly interdependent; travels to other departments or professional meetings were notable events. Today, however, the energetic academic will be linked by post, long-distance phone, fax, and electronic mail to like-minded scholars around the globe. The number of interactions possible in a day is limited only by the constraints of time. The technologies have also stimulated the development of hundreds of new organizations, international conferences, and professional meetings. A colleague recently informed me that if funds were available he could spend his entire sabbatical traveling from one professional gathering to another. A similar condition pervades the business world. One's scope of business opportunities is no longer so limited by geography; the technologies of the age enable projects to be pursued around the world. (Colgate Tartar Control toothpaste is now sold in over forty countries.) In effect, the potential for new connection and new opportunities is practically unlimited. Daily life has become a sea of drowning demands, and there is no shore in sight. . . .

It is not simply the expansion of self through relationships that hounds one with the continued sense of "ought." There is also the seeping of self-doubt into everyday consciousness, a subtle feeling of inadequacy that smothers one's activities with an uneasy sense of impending emptiness. In important respects this sense of inadequacy is a by-product of the populating of self and the presence of social ghosts. For as we incorporate others into ourselves, so does the range of proprieties expand—that is, the range of what we feel a "good," "proper," or "exemplary" person should be. Many of us carry with us the "ghost of a father," reminding us of the values of honesty and hard work, or a mother challenging

us to be nurturing and understanding. We may also absorb from a friend the values of maintaining a healthy body, from a lover the goal of self-sacrifice, from a teacher the ideal of worldly knowledge, and so on. Normal development leaves most people with a rich range of "goals for a good life," and with sufficient resources to achieve a sense of personal well-being by fulfilling these goals.

But now consider the effects of social saturation. The range of one's friends and associates expands exponentially; one's past life continues to be vivid; and the mass media expose one to an enormous array of new criteria for self-evaluation. A friend from California reminds one to relax and enjoy life; in Ohio an associate is getting ahead by working eleven hours a day. A relative from Boston stresses the importance of cultural sophistication, while a Washington colleague belittles one's lack of political savvy. A relative's return from Paris reminds one to pay more attention to personal appearance, while a ruddy companion from Colorado suggests that one grows soft.

Meanwhile newspapers, magazines, and television provide a barrage of new criteria of self-evaluation. Is one sufficiently adventurous, clean, well traveled, well read, low in cholesterol, slim, skilled in cooking, friendly, odor-free, coiffed, frugal, burglarproof, family-oriented? The list is unending. More than once I have heard the lament of a subscriber to the Sunday *New York Times*. Each page of this weighty tome will be read by millions. Thus each page remaining undevoured by day's end will leave one precariously disadvantaged—a potential idiot in a thousand unpredictable circumstances.

Yet the threat of inadequacy is hardly limited to the immediate confrontation with mates and media. Because many of these criteria for self-evaluation are incorporated into the self—existing within the cadre of social ghosts—they are free to speak at any moment. The problem with values is that they are sufficient unto themselves. To value justice, for example, is to say nothing of the value of love; investing in duty will blind one to the value of spontaneity. No one value in itself recognizes the importance of any alternative value. And so it is with the chorus of social ghosts. Each voice of value stands to discredit all that does not meet its standard. All the voices at odds with one's current conduct thus stand as internal critics, scolding, ridiculing, and robbing action of its potential for fulfillment. One settles in front of the television for enjoyment, and the chorus begins: "twelve-year-old," "couch potato," "lazy," "irresponsible." . . . One sits down with a good book, and again, "sedentary," "antisocial," "inefficient," "fantasist." . . . Join friends for a game of tennis and "skin cancer," "shirker of household duties," "underexercised," "overly competitive" come up. Work late and it is "workaholic," "heart attack-prone," "overly ambitious," "irresponsible family member." Each moment is enveloped in the guilt born of all that was possible but now foreclosed. . . .

A third dimension of multiphrenia is closely related to the others. The focus here is on the rationality of everyday decision making—instances in which one tries to be a "reasonable person." Why, one asks, is it important for one's children to attend college? The rational reply is that a college education increases one's job opportunities, earnings, and likely sense of personal fulfillment. Why should I stop smoking? one asks, and the answer is clear that smoking causes cancer, so to smoke is simply to invite a short life. Yet these "obvious" lines of reasoning are obvious only so long as one's identity remains fixed within a particular group.

The rationality of these replies depends altogether on the sharing of opinions—of each incorporating the views of others. To achieve identity in other cultural enclaves turns these "good reasons" into "rationalizations," "false consciousness," or "ignorance." Within some subcultures a college education is a one-way ticket to bourgeois conventionality—a white-collar job, picket fence in the suburbs, and chronic boredom. For many,

smoking is an integral part of a risky lifestyle; it furnishes a sense of intensity, offbeatness, rugged individualism. In the same way, saving money for old age is "sensible" in one family, and "oblivious to the erosions of inflation" in another. For most Westerners, marrying for love is the only reasonable (if not conceivable) thing to do. But many Japanese will point to statistics demonstrating greater longevity and happiness in arranged marriages. Rationality is a vital by-product of social participation.

Yet as the range of our relationships is expanded, the validity of each localized rationality is threatened. What is rational in one relationship is questionable or absurd from the standpoint of another. The "obvious choice" while talking with a colleague lapses into absurdity when speaking with a spouse, and into irrelevance when an old friend calls that evening. Further, because each relationship increases one's capacities for discernment, one carries with oneself a multiplicity of competing expectations, values, and beliefs about "the obvious solution." Thus, if the options are carefully evaluated, every decision becomes a leap into gray vapors. Hamlet's bifurcated decision becomes all too simple, for it is no longer being or nonbeing that is in question, but to which of multifarious beings one can be committed. T. S. Eliot began to sense the problem when Prufrock found "time yet for a hundred indecisions / And for a hundred visions and revision, / Before taking of a toast and tea."[10]

The otherwise simple task of casting a presidential vote provides a useful illustration. As one relates (either directly or vicariously) to various men and women, in various walks of life, and various sectors of the nation or abroad, one's capacities for discernment are multiplied. Where one might have once employed a handful of rational standards, or seen the issues in only limited ways, one can now employ a variety of criteria and see many sides of many issues. One may thus favor candidate *A* because he strives for cuts in the defense budget, but also worry about the loss of military capability in an unsteady world climate. Candidate *B*'s plans for stimulating the growth of private enterprise may be rational from one standpoint, but the resulting tax changes seem unduly to penalize the middle-class family. At the same time, there is good reason to believe that *A*'s cuts in defense spending will favor *B*'s aims for a stimulated economy, and that *B*'s shifts in the tax structure will make *A*'s reductions in the military budget unnecessary. To use one criterion, candidate *A* is desirable because of his seeming intelligence, but from another, his complex ideas seem both cumbersome and remote from reality. Candidate *B* has a pleasing personality, useful for him to garner popular support for his programs, but in another sense his pleasant ways suggest he cannot take a firm stand. And so on.

Increasing the criteria of rationality does not, then, move one to a clear and univocal judgment of the candidates. Rather, the degree of complexity is increased until a rationally coherent stand is impossible. In effect, as social saturation steadily expands the population of the self, a choice of candidates approaches the arbitrary. A toss of a coin becomes equivalent to the diligently sought solution. We approach a condition in which the very idea of "rational choice" becomes meaningless.

So we find a profound sea change taking place in the character of social life during the twentieth century. Through an array of newly emerging technologies the world of relationships becomes increasingly saturated. We engage in greater numbers of relationships, in a greater variety of forms, and with greater intensities than ever before. With the multiplication of relationships also comes a transformation in the social capacities of the individual—both in knowing how and knowing that. The relatively coherent and unified sense of self inherent in a traditional culture gives way to manifold and competing potentials. A multiphrenic condition emerges in which one swims in ever-shifting, concatenating, and contentious currents of being. One bears the burden of an increasing array of oughts, of self-doubts and irrationalities. The possibility for committed romanticism or strong and single-minded modernism recedes, and the way is opened for the postmodern being.

Notes

1. A useful description of communication in the traditional or "monocultural" community is furnished by W. Barnett Pearce in *Communication and the Human Condition* (Carbondale: University of Northern Illinois Press, 1989).

2. Joshua Meyrowitz, *No Sense of Place* (New York: Oxford University Press, 1985). A similar thesis is developed by Neil Postman in *The Disappearance of Childhood* (New York: Delacorte, 1982).

3. Shoshana Zuboff, *In the Age of the Smart Machine* (New York: Basic Books, 1988).

4. Bruce Wilshire describes the process by which humans come to imitate each other as *mimetic engulfment*. See his "Mimetic Engulfment and Self-Deception," in Amelie Rorty, ed., *Self-Deception* (Berkeley: University of California Press, 1988). Many social scientists believe that such tendencies are innate, appearing as early as the first two weeks of life.

5. Mary Watkins, *Invisible Guests: The Development of Imaginal Dialogues* (Hillsdale, N.J.: Analytic Press, 1986); Eric Klinger, "The Central Place of Imagery in Human Functioning," in Eric Klinger, ed., *Imagery, Volume 2: Concepts, Results, and Applications* (New York: Plenum, 1981); Mary Gergen, "Social Ghosts, Our Imaginal Dialogues with Others" (paper presented at American Psychological Association Meetings, New York, August 1987). See also Mark W. Baldwin and John G. Holmes, "Private Audiences and Awareness of the Self," *Journal of Personality and Social Psychology* 52 (1987): 1087–198.

6. Hazel Markus and Paula Nurius, "Possible Selves," *American Psychologist* 41 (1986): 954–69. Closely related is Barbara König's fascinating novel, *Personen-Person* (Frankfurt: Carl Hanser Verlag, 1981). The narrator realizes that she may be soon meeting an attractive man. The entire volume is then composed of a dialogue among her many inner voices—the residuals of all her past relations.

7. Paul C. Rosenblatt and Sara E. Wright, "Shadow Realities in Close Relationships," *American Journal of Family Therapy* 12 (1984): 45–54.

8. Michael Billig et al., *Ideological Dilemmas* (London: Sage, 1988).

9. See Peter Berger, Brigitte Berger, and Hansfried Kellner, *The Homeless Mind* (New York: Random House, 1973), for a precursor to the present discussion.

10. T. S. Eliot, "The Love Song of J. Alfred Prufrock," in *The Waste Land and Other Poems* (New York: Harvest, 1930).

Evolution and Ecology: Expanding the Scope of Morality

Darwinian Ethics

Michael Ruse

Many philosophers have tried to justify claims that we ought to act in certain ways by arguing that such actions are natural. Others have resisted this approach, either because they see it as illicitly deriving an "ought" from an "is" or because they believe that morality frequently tells us to resist our natural urges. Since Darwin, appeals to natural selection—the survival of the fittest—have often driven the debate between these camps. At the heart of this dispute is the question of whether biology can help us understand morality or whether morality operates in a sphere largely independent of biological explanations.

Michael Ruse argues that human morality is rooted in genetic predispositions to behave altruistically. He describes how behavior that helps others can arise from natural selection through the mechanisms of kin selection and reciprocal altruism. In humans, the tendency to behave altruistically is supported through characteristic forms of moral thinking, such as classifying some acts as wrong. Ruse maintains that there are "epigenetic rules" that describe the links between genetic structures and their cultural manifestations. He aims to provide reasons for thinking that morality has a significant biological component, but he is careful to avoid any suggestion that human behavior is genetically determined. These reasons come from research into altruistic behavior in animals and "primitive" human societies. Michael Ruse is professor of philosophy and zoology at the University of Guelph, Ontario.

As you read through this essay, consider the following:

1. According to Ruse, how can evolutionary theory explain altruism?
2. What is the difference between biological altruism and moral altruism? How does the latter arise out of the former?
3. What is Ruse's evidence that kin selection and reciprocal altruism exist in the animal kingdom?
4. How does he argue that human behavior reveals significant biological determinants?
5. Do you find plausible Ruse's arguments that natural selection favors cooperation as much as it does selfishness?
6. Would the existence of a biological basis for morality reduce our free will or limit our responsibility for actions?

THE EVOLUTION OF MORALITY

. . . At the substantival level, endorsements or facilitations of the process of natural selection seems so often to be so immoral. If morality means anything, it means being prepared to hold out a helping hand to others. Christians, utilitarians, Kantians, and everyone else come together on this. (Duties to oneself are a different, more complex matter; but they need not detain us here.)

The problem, raised by Huxley and a host of others, is that natural selection and its products are prima facie the very antithesis of help and cooperation. We start with a struggle for existence, and go on to find that winning alone counts from an evolutionary perspective. Because of this, virtually all of our features, physical and mental, are directed to personal success. Selfishness personified! No wonder that Huxley wrote: "Let us understand, once for all, that the ethical progress of society depends not on imitating the cosmic process, still less in running away from it, but in combating it" (Huxley and Huxley, 1947, p. 82). There is nothing moral in the process of evolution, and there is no morality in its effects.

However, as Charles Darwin . . . himself and many followers down to and (especially) including Edward O. Wilson . . . have pointed

out, to assume that matters rest here is naïvety personified. Supporters of evolutionary ethics, like Sumner, and opponents like Huxley, have been sharing false empirical premises. Natural selection does indeed promote features that rebound to self-benefit, but to conclude that we all spend our days like characters in a Spaghetti Western, forever grinding opponents into the dust, is to show a farcically incomplete grasp of the evolutionary process. You can frequently further your own ends much more successfully by subtle alternative strategies. In particular, you can often get a lot more for yourself by aiding and working with others. In other words, selection can be expected to promote what biologists call *altruism*. (For the moment, let us understand this as a technical, metaphorically derived term of Darwinian science, meaning no more than co-operation which furthers the individual participant's reproductive interests. Whether it ever is or can lead to genuine altruism will be discussed shortly.)

It is necessary to tread carefully here. A good number of evolutionists, thinking they were working in the true spirit of Darwinism, have argued that humans (and other animals) help each other as a natural consequence of that inevitable spirit of friendship which binds members of the same species. This friendship supposedly evolves because it is of benefit to the whole group. Zebras working together against predators thus keep up the species. This was the refrain of natural selection's co-discoverer, Alfred Russel Wallace . . ., and . . . was stressed in most detail by the late nineteenth-century Russian anarchist, Prince Peter Kropotkin. . . . However, as we know, this approach was explicitly rejected by Darwin, as well as by his modern-day supporters. Any "group selection" analysis of behaviour, including human behaviour, falls before strong counter-evidence. . . .

The Darwinian insists that we stay with the individual. All help given must rebound ultimately to the individual's benefit. Any benefits which others receive should be seen as incidental, and might well be selected against. Nevertheless, even within these constraints, help and co-operation can evolve. We all know of the principle of enlightened self-interest, where I help others because I thereby get help in return. And we all know that frequently I am much better off because of the help received (or potential of such help being received), despite any payments in help that I might have to make. Buying insurance is a classic case in point. Most of the time my premiums go to pay other people's debts. But, against this, I have the security of knowing that should I ever be faced with a large bill, I need not bankrupt myself to pay it. I speak with some feeling as the owner of a parked car that was recently smashed up, by a drunken lout driving without insurance.

How might selection work through such a business or bargaining process, thus promoting features and behaviours of help or altruism? Remember that evolution is not interested in mere survival for survival's sake. It is reproduction that counts. Or, more accurately, success in evolution lies in increasing the percentage of one's own genes in future generations, at the expense of others. Hence, any co-operative or helpful behaviour promoted by selection must be such that one's own genes' reproductive chances are improved. Behaviour without such a pay-off is going to be at a selective disadvantage.

Against this background, Darwinians who study social behaviour ("sociobiologists") strongly favour two primary mechanisms supposedly capable of producing help and co-operation between humans. . . . The first is the relatively obvious process whereby

humans develop innate tendencies to work together, because the cost of co-operation is (on average) significantly less than the hope of return. Suppose we all stand in risk of drowning. I help you from drowning, because of my biological urges to do so. Although this puts me at a 1 in 20 risk of drowning myself, I in turn avoid the 1 in 2 risk of drowning were you never to respond to my sometime cry for help. I may not need such help now, but we were all young once, we will all grow old someday, we all fall sick on occasion. We all have a share of bad luck during our lives, and the same goes for our children, the most immediate bearers of our genes.

This mechanism for promoting co-operative interactions between humans is called a "reciprocal altruism." . . . It can occur between genetic strangers, although in real life these could and may well be good friends. In theory, it can even occur between humans and members of other species (the shepherd and his dog). The important distinguishing feature is that, although help is given, returns are in some way anticipated. Pushing the insurance model, one does not necessarily expect immediate repayment for every kind act. Rather, one throws one's help into the general pool, as it were, and expects to be able to draw on the pool as needed. (Why not cheat? Why not take without giving? Because, if everyone behaved this way, the system would collapse. Nevertheless, because evolution is always looking for ways to get ahead, you expect a certain amount of cheating. Also, you expect the evolution of techniques for spotting and preventing cheating.)

Darwin himself proposed reciprocal altruism as a possible causal factor behind the help that we humans give to each other: "as the reasoning powers and foresight of the members became improved, each man would soon learn from experience that if he aided his fellow-men, he would commonly receive aid in return" (Darwin, 1871, 1, p. 163). . . .

The second supposed mechanism of (biological) altruism is much more recent, and indeed could not have been developed without a proper knowledge of the principles of heredity. The key to evolutionary success lies in improving your gene ratios. This means passing on your genes at a higher rate than do others. But not that, literally, you do not pass on your genes. If successful, you leave behind *copies* of your genes. My children do not have my actual genes. They each have a half-set, which are exact replicas of mine. But this possession of genes exactly like mine holds true of people other than my children—parents, siblings, nephews, nieces, grandchildren, and more. All of one's blood relatives have, to greater or lesser extent, copies of the same genes as oneself. Therefore, inasmuch as relatives reproduce, copies of one's own genes are being passed on. Reproduction by proxy, as it were.

What this all means is that help given to relatives in itself rebounds to the favour of one's own reproductive interests, even though these relatives may themselves reciprocate with little or no help. As a consequence, what you expect through this process, known as 'kin selection', is the evolution of help-giving attributes, without necessarily having the parallel evolution of attributes, expecting or enforcing tangible returns. Any return comes indirectly, via the genes. . . .

As I am sure you can see, this simple conclusion readily lends itself to higher levels of refinement. You are more closely related to some relatives than to others. To children, siblings, and parents, first. Then to half-siblings, grandchildren, uncles and aunts. Eventually, to cousins, at various degrees of remove. The Darwinian, therefore, expects stronger acts and sentiments of altruism towards one's own children, rather than (say) to one's siblings' children. And likewise, as the circle of relatedness widens. There will be some help given toward lesser relatives, but not as much as towards greater relatives.

Also, one expects evolution to have taken time and age into consideration. For fairly obvious reasons, there are diminishingly small returns on promoting the well-being of grandparents. In general, there will be a predisposition towards youth. Most obviously, your own children will be the focus of attention. Then, in lesser degrees, siblings and

their children, grandchildren, and so forth. You are more closely related to your siblings than to your grandchildren. But your siblings normally will be past need of help by the time you can offer it, and when your own children are launched, your grandchildren will be next in need of help.

Summing up, Wilson labels the results of the mechanisms of help as "hard-core" and "soft-core" altruism. The former is the result of kin selection. It occurs between relatives, and there is no expectation of direct return. The latter is the result of reciprocal altruism. It occurs between non-relatives, and there is expectation of return, or at least of the potential for such return:

> Individual behaviour, including seemingly altruistic acts bestowed on tribe and nation, are directed, sometimes very circuitously, toward the Darwinian advantage of the solitary human being and his closest relatives. The most elaborate forms of social organization, despite their outward appearance, serve ultimately as the vehicles of individual welfare. Human altruism appears to be substantially hard-core when directed at closest relatives, although still to a much lesser degree than in the case of the social insects and the colonial invertebrates. The remainder of our altruism is essentially soft. The predicted result is a melange of ambivalence, deceit, and guilt that continuously troubles the individual mind. (Wilson, 1978, pp. 158-9).

All that remains is an interpretation of these ideas in the language of epigenetic rules, those intermediaries between the genes and human thought and action. And, in theory, this is readily done. . . . The Darwinian's claim is that we have genetically based dispositions to approve of certain courses of action and to disapprove of other courses of action. But they are more than mere likes and dislikes. Here we start to move towards genuine morality and its evolution—from "altruism" (in the biological sense of working harmoniously together, thus promoting reproductive ends), to altruism (in the literal sense, demanding genuine sentiments about right and wrong).

Logically, there is no demand by Darwinism that we be moral. "Altruism" could have been effected, as with the ants, by firm genetic control. But then we would have had to waste the virtues of our brain power, and the flexibility which it gives us. Conversely, "altruism" could have been effected by purely rational, consciously self-directed decisions. But this would have required massive brain power to calculate probabilities and the like. And pure rationality might not have been sufficiently rapid for real life. (Even computers have not the time to explore every option, when playing chess.) Thus selection has taken a middle-road option, setting within us epigenetic rules that will incline us towards actions that are (unbeknownst to us) "altruistic" in the biological sense.

The key move in this middle-road option is morality. It is absolutely fundamental to the Darwinian case that, in order to spur us into action—perhaps indeed to go against other self-directed emotions—we have rules incorporating that prescriptive force which is distinctly characteristic of morality. As in the case of sibling incest, our feelings are backed by a (likewise innate) sense that approved actions are "right" and that disapproved actions are "wrong."

It is not just that we do not want to go to bed with our siblings. We feel that we *ought* not have to intercourse with them. We have such a strong drive to copulate, particularly with any member of the opposite sex who is almost literally thrown at us, that (biologically) we need something really strong to steer us away. Morality does the trick. Similarly, in the face of our general inclination to serve ourselves, because it is biologically advantageous to us to help and co-operate, morality (as mediated through the epigenetic rules) has evolved to guide and stiffen our will. We are moved by genuine, non-metaphorical altruism. To get "altruism," we humans are altruistic.

Thus, in the light of our current biological understanding, we expect the epigenetic rules to influence our thought and behaviour towards relatives. We will feel that we *should* love and care for our children and others (biologically) close to us. Moreover, our obligations will be particularly strong towards these people—if someone is carrying (copies of) your genes, that surely measures well against any possible help from others. "Blood is thicker than water." And we will feel that our obligations to these people persist, even though no returns come or are expected. "All I ask of my children is that they do for their children what I did for them." Then we expect the rules to influence our thought and behaviour towards other people, especially those with whom we come into close and/or ongoing contact. Here we look for a sense of the need to help and work together with our fellow humans. But again, note, we are talking of more than a mere feeling that we want to help others. It will be an innately based sense of obligation towards others. We have a duty to help. However, in this case it will be a balanced sense of obligation. Because we are helpers, we expect help in return. If no such help is forthcoming, then the reciprocity breaks down and tensions arise.

I must add at once, however, that this expectation (of which, more later) has, within its content, nothing to do with the biological facts of the case. Neither regarding human sentiments caused by kin selection, nor regarding human sentiments caused by reciprocal altruism, is the Darwinian claim that we humans know wherein lie our biological ends. The person who helped another, consciously intending to promote his own biological advantage, would not be moral. He would be crazy. The Darwinian's point is that our moral sense is a biological adaptation, just like hands and feet. We think in terms of right and wrong. It so happens that the overall effects are biological.

This is the (empirical) Darwinian case for morality, and for its biological underpinnings. Epigenetic rules giving us a sense of obligation have been put in place by selection, because of their adaptive value. Of course, as with scientific knowledge, no one is claiming that every last moral twitch is tightly controlled by the genes. In science, the claim was that human reason has certain rough or broad constraints, as manifested through the epigenetic rules. The application of these leads to the finished product, which in many respects soars into the cultural realm, transcending its biological origin. In the case of ethics, the Darwinian urges a similar position. Human moral thought has constraints, as manifested through the epigenetic rules, and the application of these leads to moral codes, soaring from biology into culture. . . .

THE EMPIRICAL EVIDENCE: SOCIAL ANIMALS

As we begin this too brief review of the underlying empirical support for the Darwinian account of the evolution of morality, I must first restress an important point made earlier. By this stage in our enquiry, we are not starting out in total ignorance, as though the very idea that evolution might have some connection with *Homo sapiens* requires a totally fresh, comprehensive, supporting brief. We know that evolution occurred, that it was Darwinian in nature, and that humans are part of the natural order. Therefore, in something as important to us as our morality, there is a strong presumption that natural selection will have had a causal influence. Such a presumption may ultimately prove wrong. I doubt anyone expects a definitive case. Nevertheless, we go into our enquiry with a great deal of positive background knowledge.

Turning to the task at hand, let us begin with the animal world considered as a whole. At the most general level, the past two decades have seen the accumulation of a simply colossal body of data attesting to the tight control exercised on animal behaviour by the genes. . . . Furthermore, every sign is that such behaviour is directed to the betterment of the individual's reproductive chances. I emphasize that in speaking of "behaviour" here, I refer not simply to those actions where the individual obviously benefits—as when the predator chases the prey and the prey runs to escape. I am speaking of social behaviour, within the same species, where individuals interact in such ways as will improve their own biological fitness.

To illustrate, I will mention but one elegant study, drawn from literally hundreds. A group of researchers from Cambridge University has recently shown, with much detail and subtlety, that the behaviour of red deer (living on an island of Scotland) is just as much a function of natural selection as are the animals' various body-sizes and shapes (Clutton-Brock, Guinness and Albon, 1982). Males, for instance, gather the females into harems. Females, conversely, let themselves be so gathered. The actions of both sexes can and must be seen in the light of selection for individual success, and strong quantitative evidence supports the conclusion that to the victor goes the prize. More prosaically, those animals which do most successfully and efficiently precisely what everybody seems to be trying to do—gathering and being gathered—are those very animals which leave the highest representation of genes in the next generation. Red deer behaviour is not random, or a function of causes beyond biology. It is as much a result of natural selection, working at the individual level, as is any other feature of the animals. . . .

What of co-operation and (biological) "altruism"? In particular, does the animal world taken as a whole support the case for the effective operation of kin selection and reciprocal altruism? Few workers today, within the field of animal social behaviour, would doubt the importance of either mechanism. Kin selection, in particular, is one of the great triumphs of twentieth-century biology. From before the time of Darwin, naturalists were troubled by the self-sacrificing behaviour shown by workers in the social insects, particularly the Hymenoptera (the ants, the bees and the wasps). Why does one find females, who are themselves sterile, spending all of their lives in toil, raising the offspring of their fertile mothers? Such "nobility" seems the very antithesis of a life of Darwinian struggle for reproduction.

Thanks to the brilliant insight of William Hamilton . . . , we now know that the family lives of social insects owe much to kin selection. Because of a rather odd reproductive system, females are more closely related to sisters than they are to daughters. Thus, biologically, they are better occupied raising fertile sisters than fertile daughters. In other words, ultimately, there is nothing paradoxical about the behaviour of workers. They are simply reproducing vicariously, as one expects when kin selection is at work. Males have no such unusual relationships with siblings and offspring. Significantly, there are no worker males. Kin selection did not operate. . . .

Reciprocal altruism likewise finds confirming instances throughout the animal world. Some of the most interesting cases involve animals from different species. For instance, members of some species of fish are cleaned by members of other species—the former being thereby freed of parasites and the latter gaining a nutritious lunch. . . . That such behaviour is not accidental, but tightly controlled by selection, is shown by a number of factors. Most pertinently, the cleaning fish are often of a type that would normally at once be eaten by the other (larger) fish. They have, however, developed behavioural signals that simply shut down the aggressive impulses of the cleaned fish. Interestingly, one now gets mimics which take advantage of the situation. Members of yet a third species show the aggression-reducing behaviours, but fail to reciprocate with cleaning. Rather, they are liable to bite big chunks out of the now passive, unsuspecting monsters.

In many branches of the animal world, reciprocation has been found to operate within the same species—in birds, in fish, and in mammals, to name but three such branches. For instance, in one bird species from Africa, the white-fronted bee-eater, there is much help given and received in nest-building, food-gathering, and nesting care. This is most probably a direct function of the fact that the birds' nests are extremely vulnerable to flash-flooding. A high level of reciprocity is an effective way of dealing with irregular yet ongoing calamities. . . .

Let us be quite clear what all of this means. Humans are not white-fronted bee-eaters. Even less are they the bee-eaters' prey. No one would pretend that the way in which humans work together is the exact way in which ants work together, any more than does the fact that humans and ants have each developed organs of sight prove that their principles of perceptual functioning are identical. Nevertheless, reference to social behaviour in the animal world taken as a whole does show that such behaviour—including co-operation and "altruism"—can be produced and promoted by natural selection, working at the level of the individual. It can be done, and is in fact done time and again through the animal world. If humans are part of this world, possibilities and expectations are obviously raised.

How can expectations be raised beyond the point of intriguing prospect to that of plausible hypothesis? What, in the study of the animal world, would lead us to suspect that there really is something in the Darwinian case for the nature and foundations of morality? Going again down a path taken earlier, what we must do is move closer to our own species. If indeed we have an innate predisposition to work with and help our fellow humans, and if this was truly brought about by selective demands, then we might reasonably expect to find something akin to moral behaviour in our closest relatives, the higher primates. They cannot tell us whether they heed the urgings of the Categorical Imperative; nor is there reason to think that they do this in any explicit fashion. However, if the Darwinian is right in claiming that morality is rooted in epigenetic rules, then, as in the case of logical and mathematical reasoning, we may properly look for suggestive behaviour in chimpanzees and gorillas. (The "higher" primates are closer to us. Neither they nor we are higher in some biologically absolute sense.)

Darwinism insists that features evolve gradually, and something as important as morality should have been present in our (very recent) shared ancestors. Furthermore, if morality is as important biologically to humans as is being claimed, it would be odd indeed had all traces now been eliminated from the social interactions of other high-level primates. Conversely, if human morality does not have a biological base, and is for instance a cultural invention of humans some few thousand years ago then there would be no reason to find it present in our ape relatives.

Recent, extended studies of the apes, particularly of chimpanzees, must shake all but the most dogmatic defender of the uniqueness of the human moral capacity. . . . I emphasize that these studies are recent. Anecdotal reports of apes showing friendliness and concern are obviously of limited worth. Apart from anything else, if an ape is reared close to humans, you expect it to learn human-like behaviours, including those simulating morality. . . . The question is whether the brutes show moral-type behaviour innately, without human intervention, in situations which are clearly directly or indirectly of biological value. And to answer such a question, you need long-term studies of apes in natural (or virtually natural) situations, seeing whether or not such behaviour appears. At last, such studies are being performed, and the answer is strong and clear. Apes interact in remarkably human-like fashions, including fashions which, were we to believe them true of humans (rather than apes), we would unhesitatingly label "moral."

I draw your attention to perhaps the most remarkable of all the studies, that of the Utrecht primate ethology group. . . . For over a decade, its members have been observing the dynamics of some fifty semi-wild chimpanzees at the nearby Arnhem Zoo, recording almost every move. Time and again, the primatologists have seen behaviour which differs not at all from human moral behaviour. This is particularly true of the older females. Although it is the mature males who are the physically dominant members of the group, the older females have great authority. For instance, the males seek their aid in forming alliances, younger females look to them for protection, youngsters are wary of them and set them up as models. In a human group, these females would have an important stabilizing effect, helping to mediate disputes and to avoid quarrels. The same is precisely true of the Arnhem chimpanzees.

Consider the following vignette:

> On a hot day two mothers, Jimmie and Tepel, are sitting in the shadow of an oak tree while their two children play in the sand at their feet (playfaces, wrestling, throwing sand). Between the two mothers the oldest female, Mama, lies asleep. Suddenly the children start screaming, hitting and pulling each other's hair. Jimmie admonishes them with a soft, threatening grunt and Tepel anxiously shifts her position. The children go on quarrelling and eventually Tepel wakes Mama by poking her in the ribs several times. As Mama gets up Tepel points to the two quarrelling children. As soon as Mama takes one threatening step forward, waves her arm in the air and barks loudly the children stop quarrelling. Mama then lies down again and continues her siesta. (de Waal, 1982, p. 47)

One should not underestimate the importance of Mama's role here. Conflicts between children regularly escalate into conflicts between adults, leading to fighting and physical damage. In acting as a quietening influence, Mama has brought benefits to all. If this is not to act as a moral force—or, let me say cautiously, a proto-moral force—I do not know what is. "Blessed are the Peace-makers: for they shall be called the Children of God" (Matthew, 5, 9).

It must be stressed that behaviour like Mama's is not isolated or aberrant. Again and again, you see one ape aiding another, materially or (even more impressively), as in the above instance, in resolving conflict or promoting harmony. Chimpanzee groups are forever on the edge of exploding into conflict, primarily because of tensions between alpha males. Group members are, accordingly, forever smoothing over differences, reconciling rivals, and binding psychic wounds. . . .

We come now to our own species. The claim is that human moral thought has constraints, as manifested through the epigenetic rules, and the application of these leads to moral codes, soaring from biology into culture. The question is not whether every last act of Western man or woman is governed by kin selection or reciprocal altruism or some such thing. I am quite sure it is not. Rather, the question is whether we have innate tendencies or dispositions inclining us to social thoughts and actions, which latter would improve our reproductive chances. And, if there be such tendencies, is there reason to think that the proposed causal models for promoting social interactions had any significant input?

Of one thing we can be fairly certain. In the quest for such tendencies, our own society is not the best place to start. Who can doubt that Western technology has distorted and otherwise changed traditional social and moral patterns, making more difficult the discerning of any possible underlying biological factors. Think of the coming of cheap, efficient contraception, and of the changes in sexual mores in the past two decades. We need to focus our attention on societies where science and its after-effects have not yet been fully felt. (I am *not* implying that pre-industrial societies show only the forces of biology. Nor am I implying that biology is now irrelevant to the interactions of the Western human. The Pill may have changed sexual practices. It has hardly eliminated the biology from sex.)

With the scene thus set, we have first the general question about whether (pre-industrial) human societies function in a way suggesting that a prime formative factor is reproductive success, regardless of whether this be explicitly acknowledged. Were one to look at our own species as one might look at a species of ant or monkey, would the reasonable conclusion be that social behaviour is a product of the genes as selected in the struggle for reproduction? And is the corollary that particular behavioural adaptations are directed towards the increase of one's future genetic representation?

These are queries which have sparked much controversy in the past decade. Debate continues almost unabated. . . . I shall here state simply that there is growing evidence that Darwinian factors are important in a full causal understanding of human society. The explicit goals sought by humans tend to be power and status and material riches and the like. Also actively pursued are peace and security, freedom from war and want, and from other humanly caused disasters and disturbances. Virtually all of these things translate readily into reproductive success, and their absence spells reproductive failure. Powerful and rich men and women in societies do not simply contemplate their power and riches. They cash them, in terms of bigger families or, relatedly, in aid to their kin.

A dramatic illustration of this is proved by Napoleon Chagnon's (1980) studies on the Yanomamo Indians from Venezuela and Brazil. These people are almost always at war with each other, with the victors gaining power, land and, ultimately, breeding opportunities. Within the groups, . . . the effects of success—becoming the leaders—is shown in the extent to which headmen out reproduce the others. Note also that this is not a one-sided affair, with males alone striving to pursue the best reproductive strategies. The wives of headmen have significantly more children than do other women.

Many more examples could be given showing that "success" in human societies bears strongly on the number of offspring, and that attitudes and behaviours are directed to reproductive ends. But then, what of the second, more specific question? Is there evidence of kin selection and reciprocal altruism? Is it reasonable to invoke these Darwinian models in explanation of the help which people give to each other, and the co-operation which exists between individuals and groups?

A convincing example of the importance of kin selection has been stressed by Richard D. Alexander. . . . Theoretically, one would expect parents to show most concern of all to their own children. After all, there is a 50 per cent genetic relationship binding parent and child. This compares (say) with the 25 per cent relationship you have with the children of your siblings. (Note that strictly, in making evaluations of comparative relatedness, one is speaking only of those genes that vary within the overall group.) In fact, however, in many societies the adult male responsible for child-care is not the father, but the mother's brother. Maternal uncles have the duty and obligation to provide sustenance, education, and other care needed to achieve full adulthood. How can this be? Alexander points out that the independent evidence is that, in societies where mother's brother's care is common (and only in such societies), there is considerable doubt as to paternity. Because of the looseness of sexual bonds between married couples, biological fatherhood frequently does not equal social fatherhood. However, the mother-child connection is securely known, as is the identity of siblings.

In other words, in such societies where this kind of care occurs, although the mother's brother substitutes a 25 per cent relationship for a 50 per cent relationship, he also substitutes a genuine blood tie for a dubious blood tie—just what one would expect were kin selection at work. Interestingly and surely significantly, we do not have an exactly analogous mother's sister's phenomenon. We do, however, get some expected-according-to-kin-selection interactions where sisters marry the same man. . . .

Note that what the Darwinian would extract from a case like this is more than that we simply do things, or even merely that we want to do things—whether this be for biological or other reasons. The claim is that we want to do things because they are right. Mother's brother's care involves a sense of duty and obligation. Why otherwise should one care about someone else's brats? In short, the Darwinian's claim is that here kin selection achieves its (biological) "altruistic" ends by filling adult males full of (moral) altruistic sentiments.

There is also much evidence in human societies of the kinds of interactions one would expect were non-relatives influenced by reciprocal altruistic causal mechanisms. What is significant is the extent to which

these social encounters can be distinguished from those between kin. The outsider notes at once that social intercourse between non-relatives is balanced. Help and co-operation is given; but, equally, help and co-operation is reciprocated and expected. People form social relationships and alliances for their mutual benefits; but, when one side fails in a relationship, things tend to break down and partners pull out from the pact.

That we do relate differently towards relatives and acquaintances (and yet differently again towards strangers and enemies) is a fact long noted by anthropologists, including those who have been most hostile towards suggestions that biology might play a significant causal role in human thought and behaviour. Marshall Sahlins . . . , no friend of Darwinism, has identified three levels of social interaction between peoples in pre-literate societies. Between relatives, we get what he calls "generalized reciprocity," which involves giving without hope of return. Between non-relatives who have day-to-day social intercourse, we get "balanced reciprocity," which involves giving with expectations of return in some form. And with strangers, especially with threatening strangers, we get "negative reciprocity," where there is tension, suspicion, and the ever present possibility of violent conflict.

This analysis is precisely that forecast by the Darwinian. Generalized reciprocity is what we expect from kin selection. Balanced reciprocity is what we expect from reciprocal altruism. And negative reciprocity is what we expect from people who find each other threatening, and who have not yet found reason to co-operate. In these matters, humans are paradigmatically the products of natural selection. . . .

These are but a few straws in the wind; yet they must suffice for now. Summing up: there is strong, and growing, evidence through the animal world that members of the same species interact socially to their mutual reproductive benefits. The nature of these interactions fits well with the claim that kin selection and reciprocal altruism are important causal mechanisms. Our closest relatives, the chimpanzees, have complex social lives, and behave in precisely the ways one would expect were morality a legacy of our simian past, and were that legacy also inherited by other primates. We humans, especially in our pre-industrial state, show that biology is a crucial causal factor affecting our social nature, and the ways we behave are precisely those expected if selection acts to maximize the reproductive potential of the individual.

Combine all of this with what we know already, particularly about human biological nature and the importance of the epigenetic rules in moulding human conscious thought and action. What do we have? Certainly not a finished case for the evolution for the human moral capacity, even when it is agreed (as it must be) that we talk now only of the basic moral inclinations, leaving the full development to culture. We are going beyond the evidence as we argue that (in the human case) the way in which selection spurs us into biologically advantageous social action is by infusing our pertinent innate dispositions, our epige-

netic rules, with a sense of moral obligation. However, we do now have a strong hypothesis—an hypothesis made yet more plausible when we recollect that the incest barrier, undoubtedly of biological value, can be backed by a forceful sense of right and wrong. It is not just that you do not want to sleep with your sister/brother, but that you feel you should not.

References

Alexander, R. D. 1977. *Evolution, Human Behavior, and Determinism.* Edited by F. Suppe and P. Asquith. East Lansing, Mich.: Philosophy of Science Association, 3–21.

———. 1979. *Darwinism and Human Affairs.* Seattle: University of Washington Press.

Clutton-Brock, T. H., F. E. Guiness, and S. D. Abon, 1982. *Red Deer: Behavior and Ecology of Two Sexes.* Chicago: University of Chicago Press.

Darwin, C. 1871. *The Descent of Man.* London: John Murray.

De Waal, F. 1982. *Chimpanzee Politics: Power and Sex Among Apes.* London: Cape.

Huxley, T. H., and J. S. Huxley. 1947. *Evolution and Ethics.* London: Pilot Press.

Wilson, E. O. 1978. *On Human Nature.* Cambridge, Mass.: Harvard University Press.

Morality in the Great Apes

Frans de Waal

Few of those who believe that morality has a biological basis take the further step of claiming that animals can be moral agents. Morality is often associated with the ability to reason and to choose whether to act in accord with some rule. Since animals do not appear to be able to articulate rules and to freely choose whether to abide by them, we usually think that animals are not morally responsible for their behavior.

On the basis of twenty years of observing apes, Frans de Waal argues against the "prejudice" that morality is uniquely human. He draws a common distinction between descriptive rules and prescriptive rules; the former describe some regularity whereas the latter involve a sense of obligation, often one that has been inculcated by training. While most people believe animals "obey" descriptive rules, they would deny that they obey prescriptive rules. In contrast, de Waal describes numerous examples in which apes, dogs, and other animals are trained by their peers to follow prescriptive rules. Although most philosophical accounts of morality require more than following prescriptive rules, they do so at the expense of excluding much human behavior from the moral sphere. Instead of limiting the moral to its most advanced manifestations, de Waal recommends seeing it as a broad practice characterized by differing degrees of sophistication. Seen in this light, animals do partake in the practice of morality, and the study of animal behavior can reveal much about that practice. Frans de Waal is C. H. Candler Professor of Primate Behavior at Emory University and director of the Living Links Center at the Yerkes Regional Primate Research Center.

As you read through this essay, consider the following:

1. How does de Waal show that animals follow prescriptive rules? How persuasive are his examples?
2. Do de Waal's examples indicate whether animals *choose* to follow the rules? Why or why not?
3. How does de Waal try to expand our concept of morality so that it will include animals? Does he succeed in avoiding semantic questions about what we mean by "morality"?
4. In this selection, de Waal does not emphasize the genetic basis of behavior. Does this make his account of morality in animals more compelling than Ruse's view in the prior essay? Why or why not?
5. How might looking through the lens of biology shape our view of morality?

The overall picture of group organization in these animals [baboons] is of a sensitive balancing of forces, the balance being achieved by the social learning of individuals in the group from the time of birth to adulthood, so that infringements of the group norm are rare. When they do occur, they may be severely punished if the victim is caught.

Ronald Hall

One balmy evening, when the keeper called the chimpanzees inside, two adolescent females refused to enter the building. The rule at Arnhem Zoo being that *none* of the apes will receive food until *all* of them have moved from the island into their sleeping quarters, the chimpanzees actively assist with the rule's enforcement: latecomers meet with a great deal of hostility from the hungry colony.

When the obstinate teenagers finally entered, more than two hours late, they were given a separate bedroom so as to prevent reprisals. This protected them only temporarily, however. The next morning, out on

the island, the entire colony vented its frustration about the delayed meal by a mass pursuit ending in a physical beating of the culprits. Needless to say, they were the first to come in that evening.

A SENSE OF SOCIAL REGULARITY

That animals follow rules has been known for a long time. Female mammals, for example, threaten almost anyone or anything that approaches their young uninvited. They may do so in different ways or to different degrees, but maternal protection is widespread and highly predictable. So much so that we may declare it a rule—a *descriptive rule*, to be precise. Because this kind of rule describes typical behavior, it can be applied not only to animate objects, but to inanimate ones as well. For example, we can say that as a rule stones fall when released, whereas helium balloons do not.

Descriptive rules are not particularly interesting from a moral perspective, as they lack the crucial "ought" quality. Stones do not fall to avoid getting into trouble. Only animals and humans follow *prescriptive rules*, rules actively upheld through reward and

From Frans de Waal, *Good Natured: The Origins of Right and Wrong in Humans and Other Animals* (Cambridge: Harvard University Press, 1996). Copyright © 1996 by Frans B. M. de Waal. Reprinted by permission.

punishment. With regard to other animals we notice this most readily if the rules are of our own design, such as those that we apply to pets and work animals. Yet the remarkable trainability of certain species, such as sheepdogs and Indian elephants, hints at the possibility of a rule-based order among these animals themselves.

To return to maternal protection, it is easy to see how it would affect the way others approach and treat the young of the species. In a chimpanzee colony, any individual deviating from the mother's standards will either meet with her wrath or find it more difficult in the future to obtain the infant from her. A prescriptive rule is born when members of the group learn to recognize the contingencies between their own behavior and that of the mother and act so as to minimize negative consequences. They learn how to handle the infant without making it scream; to bring it back of their own accord; not to climb to dangerous spots with the infant desperately hanging on, and so on. Such heedfulness is not well developed in juveniles, who still have much to learn about infant behavior and maternal reactions. Thus, when a juvenile carries an infant around, the mother is never far behind. When juveniles reach adolescence, most of them have learned the rules well enough that mothers trust them as baby-sitters.

In the stump-tailed macaque all group members, even the largest males, commonly avoid very young infants who wander about unattended. It is as if they are afraid of getting into trouble. This is also the only species of macaque in which infants have a distinct coat color—much lighter than that of older individuals. It makes them hard to miss in a monkey melee. As soon as a baby is near or on its mother, it attracts extraordinary attention. Mothers are typically surrounded by others who utter special vocalizations, known as staccato grunts, while trying to look closely at the infant's face or inspect its genitals. Do these grunts express endearment? Probably something other than that, because if love and affection were the main motivations we would expect mothers to grunt the most, yet

this is not at all the case. For her dissertation research, Kim Bauers recorded hundreds of vocalizations in the stump-tail group at the Wisconsin Primate Center and found that whereas females commonly grunt at each other's babies, they *never* do so at their own offspring.

Bauers found that the shorter the distance between mother and infant, the more likely others will grunt when trying to contact the little one. Even though aimed at the infant, staccato grunts seem intended for the mother as well. Perhaps it is the way members of this species "ask permission" to approach an infant. The fact that mothers themselves do not need such permission would explain the absence of their grunts.

This interpretation is further supported by the appeasing effect of staccato grunts: silent interest in infants is far more often rebuffed by maternal threats and slaps than interest announced by a series of grunts. In other words, directing friendly sounds to an infant forestalls problems with its mother. This may be an acquired social convention; most silent approaches, hence most rebuffs, involve juveniles, who may still be in the process of learning how to overcome maternal protectiveness.

Of even greater interest than rules enforced by individual mothers are rules sanctioned by the community. In the case of the two latecomers in Arnhem, we saw a group response, but the regulation in question was of course put in place by people. Chimpanzees also seem to develop their own rules, however.

Jimoh, the current alpha male of the Yerkes Field Station group, once detected a secret mating between Socko, an adolescent male, and one of Jimoh's favorite females. Socko and the female had wisely disappeared from view, but Jimoh had gone looking for them. Normally, the old male would merely chase off the culprit, but for some reason—perhaps because the female had repeatedly refused to mate with Jimoh himself that day—he this time went full speed after Socko and did not give up. He chased him all around the enclosure—Socko screaming and defecating in fear, Jimoh intent on catching him.

Before he could accomplish his aim, several females close to the scene began to "woaow" bark. This indignant sound is used in protest against aggressors and intruders. At first the callers looked around to see how the rest of the group was reacting; but when others joined in, particularly the top-ranking female, the intensity of their calls quickly increased until literally everyone's voice was part of a deafening chorus. The scattered beginning almost gave the impression that the group was taking a vote. Once the protest had swelled to a chorus, Jimoh broke off his attack with a nervous grin on his face: he got the message. Had he failed to respond, there would no doubt have been concerted female action to end the disturbance.

These are the sorts of moments when we human observers feel most profoundly that there is some moral order upheld by the community. We cannot help but identify with a group that we watch day in and day out, and our own values of order and harmony are so similar that we would have barked along with the chimpanzees if we thought it would have mattered! Whereas some of us are inclined to explain the group's reaction to Jimoh in moral terms, such as "He just went too far," other observers might prefer a more neutral account along the lines of "Chimpanzees sometimes bark in response to aggression." There is one problem with the latter view, however: one never hears woaow barks when a mother punishes her own offspring, or when an adult male controls a tiff among juveniles—even if he uses force in the process. Not every fight triggers these calls. It is a reaction to a very particular kind of disturbance, one that seriously endangers relationships or lives. Thinking in terms of rules and violations may help us come to grips with its relevant features.

Undoubtedly, prescriptive rules and a sense of order derive from a hierarchical organization, one in which the subordinate pays close attention to the dominant. Not that every social rule is necessarily established through coercion and dominance, but prototype rule enforcement comes from above. Without agreement on rank and a certain respect for authority there can be no great sensitivity to social rules, as anyone who has tried to teach simple house rules to a cat will agree. Even if cat lovers fail to see a nonhierarchical nature as a shortcoming—on the contrary!—it does place their pets firmly outside the human moral realm. Evolved as solitary hunters, cats go their own way, indifferent to what the rest of the world thinks of them.

Respect for rules and norms can develop only when the opinions and reactions of others matter. Fear of punishment is important, but not the whole story: the desire to belong to a group, and to fit in, is also involved. According to Lawrence Kohlberg, who pioneered research in this field, these elements are recognizable in the first stages of human moral growth. Development begins with obedience and a wish to stay out of trouble, followed by an orientation toward approval and pleasing others. For the child, it is the adult's approval that is sought; for the adult, it may be that of an omnipotent God infused with absolute moral knowledge. There is obviously more to morality—Kohlberg's scheme counts six stages up to and including an autonomous conscience—yet submission to a higher authority is fundamental. This feature is also less peculiarly human than some of the abilities involved in the later stages: submission to authority is part of a primordial orientation found not only in our fellow primates, but in a host of other animals as well.

It cannot be accidental that obedience and a desire to please are conspicuous traits of man's best friend. That dogs provide almost a caricature of humanity's early moral stages may explain our species' love affair with the canine soul. Most of the time dogs are "good," otherwise we punish them for being "bad" in the hope of changing their behavior. At the same time that dogs are highly sensitive to praise and blame, however, the more advanced stages of human moral development, which emphasize rights and equality, are beyond their comprehension. They think in terms of vertical, not horizontal, arrangements. These animals do not take kindly, for example, to an antiauthoritarian upbringing. Unresolved status disputes provide much of the business of dog therapists. Owners who hate to be masters deprive their pets of the element they need most for psychological stability: a clearly defined social position. Many a dog who cannot be under his owner in the family pack will try to be on top—which, in turn, is bound to undermine the owner's psychological stability!

Dogs inherited their law-and-order mentality from pack-hunting ancestors. In much the way we teach a puppy behavioral rules, dogs and wolves seem to teach their young. . . . A hierarchical orientation is by no means limited to the Canidae, however. It is also widespread in the primates, although in their case it is mitigated by a strong tendency to form alliances, that is, a tendency for two or more parties to band together against a third. Alliances usually bolster the position of dominants, but sometimes subordinates jointly stand against higher-ups. The resulting balancing of power, combined with a tendency for reciprocal exchange, produces the beginnings of an orientation to equity, particularly in the chimpanzee.

We can see this orientation when a group is faced with an attractive resource. Will the bosses claim everything for themselves, or will they share? In chimpanzees begging for food is common, and a beggar who is ignored may express frustration by throwing a fit. Temper tantrums are high drama, capable of inducing possessors to relinquish part of their food. The rhesus macaque, in contrast, lives in a society with rather intolerant dominants. From a safe distance the subordinate silently watches the dominant's food consumption. Sharing is absent in this species, as is begging and protest against monopolization. The contrast can be summarized by saying that rhesus monkeys have different *expectations* than chimpanzees about the distribution of resources. Chimpanzees count on a share; rhesus monkeys do not.

In analogy with the human sense of justice, we may call this a *sense of social regularity*, which I define as follows:

A set of expectations about the way in which oneself (or others) ought to be treated and how resources ought to be divided. Whenever reality deviates from these expectations to one's (or the other's) disadvantage, a negative reaction ensues, most commonly protest by subordinate individuals and punishment by dominant individuals.

The sense of how others should or should not behave is essentially egocentric, although the interests of individuals close to the actor, especially kin, may be taken into account (hence the parenthetical inclusion of others). Note that the expectations have not been specified: they are species typical. Because the expectation, or at least the ideal, of equality is so pronounced in our own species, we perceive the rules among rhesus monkeys as less "fair" than those in our closest relative, the chimpanzee. More important than this human bias, however, is the fact that all species seem to act according to what they can (or have come to) expect from others, thus creating a stable and predictable modus vivendi among themselves.

An obvious problem for the ethologist—and one reason why these issues have not received the attention they deserve—is that expectations are not directly observable. Do animals even have them? We may empirically define an expectation as familiarity with a particular outcome to the degree that a different outcome has an unsettling effect, as reflected in confusion, surprise, or distress. Since O. L. Tinklepaugh's research in the 1920s, we know that a monkey who has learned to find a banana hidden in a particular location will act nonplussed if the banana has been secretly replaced by a mere leaf of lettuce. At first she will leave the lettuce untouched, look around, and inspect the location over and over. She may even turn to the experimenter and shriek at him. Only after a long delay will she "content" herself with the lettuce. How to explain such behavior except as the product of a mismatch between reality and expectation?

A second, even more intractable problem is that of intentionality. I speak without hesitation of social rules from the rule-follower's perspective. When a monkey learns that certain acts always provoke a negative reaction, he will begin to suppress these acts or show them with great circumspection; the monkey can then be said to have submitted to a socially enforced rule. But can we speak of rules from the implementer's perspective? Do animals deliberately teach one another how to behave, or do they just respond to particular situations with frustration, protest, and sometimes violence? I certainly do not wish to exclude the possibility that they purposely impose limits on the behavior of others and carefully monitor the slightest transgression in order to strengthen the rule (the . . . boxed examples hint at this possibility in canids [see pages 384–385]), yet I cannot say that the evidence is overwhelming. We do not know if the rules that we recognize in animal behavior, and that we see being enforced, exist *as rules* in the animals' heads. Without experimentation this thesis will be hard to prove. For the moment, I qualify terms such as social "rule" and "norm" by adding that they refer to behavioral modification by others regardless of the intentionality of the process.

The only way to estimate a species' sense of social regularity is by paying as much attention to spontaneous social acts as to how these acts are *received* by others. We need to determine which kinds of behavior are accepted and which meet with resistance, protest, or punishment. Here is a brand-new research agenda, one that will reveal differences not only between species, but perhaps also between different groups of the same species.

It will be easy enough to find rules imposed from above, according to which dominants constrain the behavior of subordinates. From the perspective of morality, however, the exciting rules will be those that constrain the behavior of everyone, and emphasize sharing and reciprocity. Before exploring the various possibilities in greater depth, let me give a final example of a negative reaction to another individual's behavior. The incident, first reported in *Chimpanzee Politics*, suggests that the chim-

panzee's sense of social regularity is not concerned solely with hierarchical issues, but also with more advanced social arrangements, such as the familiar *One good turn deserves another*.

A high-ranking female, Puist, took the trouble and risk to help her male friend, Luit, chase off a rival, Nikkie. Nikkie, however, had a habit after major confrontations of singling out and cornering allies of his rivals, to punish them. This time Nikkie displayed at Puist shortly after he had been attacked. Puist turned to Luit, stretching out her hand in search of support. But Luit did not lift a finger to protect her. Immediately after Nikkie had left the scene, Puist turned on Luit, barking furiously. She chased him across the enclosure and even pummeled him.

If Puist's fury was in fact the result of Luit's failure to help her after she had helped him, the incident suggests that reciprocity in chimpanzees may be governed by obligations and expectations similar to those in humans. . . .

Even if animals other than ourselves act in ways tantamount to moral behavior, their behavior does not necessarily rest on deliberations of the kind we engage in. It is hard to believe that animals weigh their own interests against the rights of others, that they develop a vision of the greater good of society, or that they feel lifelong guilt about something they should not have done.

WHAT DOES IT TAKE TO BE MORAL?

Members of some species may reach tacit consensus about what kind of behavior to tolerate or inhibit in their midst, but without language the principles behind such decisions cannot be conceptualized, let alone debated. To communicate intentions and feelings is one thing; to clarify what is right, and why, and what is wrong, and why, is quite something else. Animals are no moral philosophers.

But then, how many *people* are? We have a tendency to compare animal behavior with the most dizzying accomplishments of our

Canids have an excellent sense of social rules, which allows for order within the hunting pack and explains their trainability for human purposes. They not only follow rules, they may actively inculcate them in others. Below are examples in which dominant wolves or dogs seem to deliberately wait for or even induce a transgression in order to penalize it.

Example 1. Eberhard Trumler describes how a father dog instills obedience, once his offspring have outgrown their puppy license.

"[One day] he 'declares' an old-bone taboo. First, the pups try to get hold of it. Immediately they are severely punished by the father, who grabs the violator by the scruff of his neck, shaking him vigorously. Naturally the victim yelps and, once released, throws himself submissively on his back. Shortly thereafter, however, when the father appears to be busy with something else, the disciplined pup circumspectly sneaks up to the forbidden bone again—only to receive another castigation. This may be repeated several times, and one gets the impression that the pups want to know exactly what kind of response they can expect from the old one. Anyone with a puppy at home will be familiar with such probing of the educator."

Example 2. Behavioral modification by a mother wolf is reported in *Of Wolves and Men*, by Barry Lopez.

"A female wolf left four or five pups alone in a rendezvous area in the Brooks Range one morning and set off down a trail away from them. When she was well out of sight, she turned around and lay flat in the path, watching her back trail. After a few moments, a pup who had left the rendezvous area trotted briskly over a rise in the trail and came face to face with her. She gave a low bark. He stopped short, looked about as though preoccupied with something else, then, with a dissembling air, began to edge back the way he had come. His mother escorted him to the rendezvous site and departed again. This time she didn't bother watching her back trail. Apparently the lesson had taken, for all the pups stayed put until she returned that evening."

Example 3. The American anthropologist and primatologist Barbara Smuts related another example of apparent rule-teaching seen in her dog, Safi, a mixed sheepherding breed. Safi is older than and dominant over a neighbor dog, an Airedale named Andy, with whom she plays every day in the yard of Smuts's house.

"I threw the ball for them repeatedly. Normally Safi always gets the ball; Andy defers to her even if the ball lands nearest to him. On this occasion the ball bounced in an odd way and landed right at Andy's feet while Safi stood at a distance. He grabbed the ball and brought it back to me. Safi followed with no sign of distress.

"I threw it again, and as usual Safi got it. But instead of returning it to me, as she normally does, she now brought the ball to Andy and dropped it right in front of him, backed off, and waited. Naturally Andy picked it up, at which point Safi pounced on him, pinned him to the ground, and held him with his neck in her mouth, growling softly. Andy immediately dropped the ball and was appropriately submissive. Safi released him and the game continued amicably—except that Andy hasn't been seen since going for the ball. It was as if Safi had intentionally communicated to him 'Thou shalt not pick up my ball!'"

Example 4. Early this century, Captain Max von Stephanitz, the greatest authority on the German shepherd dog, explained that there is a lot more to the learning of rules than fear of punishment. Note the distinctly moral perspective von Stephanitz takes when outlining the objectives of training this breed.

"If the dog is too keenly educated without love, then the young dog will be distressed of soul, and his capabilities will not be developed, because the foundation of confidence, which is cheerful trust, has failed. A healthy education will not make a shy broken slave without a will, or a machine working only when asked, but will make him submerge his own wishes to a higher judgment, and become a creature who works freely, and is pleased to be able to work. The education must awaken and develop dormant qualities and abilities, and moderate all excesses, strengthen all weaknesses, and guide all faults in the right direction."

race, and to be smugly satisfied when a thousand monkeys with a thousand typewriters do not come close to William Shakespeare. Is this a reason to classify ourselves as smart, and animals as stupid? Are we not much of the time considerably less rational than advertised? People seem far better at explaining their behavior after the fact than at considering the consequences beforehand. There is no denying that we are creatures of intellect; it is also evident that we are born with powerful inclinations and emotions that bias our thinking and behavior.

A chimpanzee stroking and patting a victim of attack or sharing her food with a hungry companion shows attitudes that are hard to distinguish from those of a person picking up a crying child, or doing volunteer work in a soup kitchen. To classify the chimpanzee's behavior as based on instinct and the person's behavior as proof of moral decency is misleading, and probably incorrect. First of all, it is uneconomic in that it assumes different processes for similar behavior in two closely related species. Second, it ignores the growing body of evidence for mental complexity in the chimpanzee, including the possibility of empathy. I hesitate to call the members of any species other than our own "moral beings," yet I also believe that many of the sentiments and cognitive abilities underlying human morality antedate the appearance of our species on this planet.

The question of whether animals have morality is a bit like the question of whether they have culture, politics, or language. If we take the full-blown human phenomenon as a yardstick, they most definitely do not. On the other hand, if we break the relevant human abilities into their component parts, some are recognizable in other animals. . . .

Culture: Field primatologists have noticed differences in tool use and communication among populations of the same species. Thus, in one chimpanzee community all adults may crack nuts with stones, whereas another community totally lacks this technology. Group-specific signals and habits have been documented in bonobos as well as chimpanzees. Increasingly, primatologists explain these differences as learned traditions handed down from one generation to the next.

Language: For decades apes have been taught vocabularies of hand signals (such as American Sign Language) and computerized symbols. Koko, Kanzi, Washoe, and several other anthropoids have learned to effectively communicate their needs and desires through this medium.

Politics: Tendencies basic to human political systems have been observed in other primates, such as alliances that challenge the status quo, and tit-for-tat deals between a leader and his supporters. As a result, status struggles are as much popularity contests as physical battles.

It is hard to imagine human morality without the following tendencies and capacities found also in other species.

Sympathy-Related Traits

Attachment, succorance, and emotional contagion.
Learned adjustment to and special treatment of the disabled and injured.
Ability to trade places mentally with others: cognitive empathy.[*]

Norm-Related Characteristics

Prescriptive social rules.
Internalization of rules and anticipation of punishment.[*]

Reciprocity

A concept of giving, trading, and revenge.
Moralistic aggression against violators of reciprocity rules.

Getting Along

Peacemaking and avoidance of conflict.
Community concern and maintenance of good relationships.[*]
Accommodation of conflicting interests through negotiation.

[*]It is particularly in these areas—empathy, internalization of rules and sense of justice, and community concern—that humans seem to have gone considerably further than most other animals.

In each of these domains, nonhuman primates show impressive intelligence yet do not integrate information quite the way we do. The utterances of language-trained apes, for example, show little if any evidence of grammar. The transmission of knowledge from one generation to the next is rarely, if ever, achieved through active teaching. And it is still ambiguous how much planning and foresight, if any, go into the social careers of monkeys and apes.

Despite these limitations, I see no reason to avoid labels such as "primate culture," "ape language," or "chimpanzee politics" as long as it is understood that this terminology points out fundamental similarities without in any way claiming *identity* between ape and human behavior. Such terms serve to stimulate debate about how much or little animals share with us. To focus attention on those aspects in which we differ—a favorite tactic of the detractors of the evolutionary perspective—overlooks the critical importance of what we have in common. Inasmuch as shared characteristics most likely derive from the common ancestor, they probably laid the groundwork for much that followed, including whatever we claim as uniquely ours. To disparage this common ground is a bit like arriving at the top of a tower only to declare that the rest of the building is irrelevant, that the precious concept of "tower" ought to be reserved for the summit.

While making for good academic fights, semantics are mostly a waste of time. Are animals moral? Let us simply conclude that they occupy a number of floors of the tower of morality. Rejection of even this modest proposal can only result in an impoverished view of the structure as a whole.

The Land Ethic

Aldo Leopold

Aldo Leopold (1887–1948) is often called the father of environmental ethics. A forester and wildlife biologist by training, he developed a deep understanding of the dynamics of natural systems through a lifetime of land-use management. Late in his life, he came to the conclusion that we could not avoid degrading the environment unless we changed our ethical outlook regarding the land. He used ecology to understand ethics; in his view, ethics arises out of an instinctual attachment to members of one's community that restrains one's pursuit of immediate self-interest. Our community instinct has historically been limited to other humans and perhaps to a few domestic animals, but Leopold argues that we can, and must, expand our sense of community to include the land itself.

For Leopold, the land is not just soil and rock, but the "fountain of energy" that moves through food webs. Each organism is connected to other organisms by the process of eating, eliminating, and being eaten. These connections establish a community, which also includes earth and water. Leopold believes that we can come to identify ourselves as members of this community and thereby extend our ethical instincts to include all of its members. The community can be damaged if we disrupt the energy flows too drastically. The land ethic urges us to preserve the integrity and stability of this community. Unlike de Waal in the previous essay, Leopold is not concerned about whether members of the land community *have* morality; his expansion of morality is designed to broaden the scope of beings and things that are addressed by our morality.

As you read through this essay, consider the following:

1. What difference does it make if we understand ethics ecologically rather than philosophically?
2. How does Leopold argue that an extension of ethics to the land community is an evolutionary possibility?
3. Why does Leopold think that expanding ethics to include land is an ecological necessity? Why will other approaches to conservation fail?
4. What does Leopold mean by "land"? What is the land ethic?
5. Should we follow Leopold's advice and see ourselves as "plain members of the biotic community"? What would this involve?
6. Is it always right to preserve the integrity and stability of ecosystems? Can you think of cases in which this might be wrong?

When god-like Odysseus returned from the wars in Troy, he hanged all on one rope a dozen slave-girls of his household whom he suspected of misbehavior during his absence.

This hanging involved no question of propriety. The girls were property. The disposal of property was then, as now, a matter of expediency, not of right and wrong.

Concepts of right and wrong were not lacking from Odysseus' Greece: witness the fidelity of his wife through the long years before at last his black-prowed galleys clove the wine-dark seas for home. The ethical structure of that day covered wives, but had not yet been extended to human chattels. During the three thousand years which have since elapsed, ethical criteria have been extended to many fields of conduct, with corresponding shrinkages in those judged by expediency only.

THE ETHICAL SEQUENCE

This extension of ethics, so far studied only by philosophers, is actually a process in ecological evolution. Its sequences may be described in ecological as well as in philosophical terms. An ethic, ecologically, is a limitation on freedom of action in the struggle for existence. An ethic, philosophically, is a differentiation of social from anti-social conduct. These are two definitions of one thing. The thing has its origin in the tendency of interdependent individuals or groups to evolve modes of cooperation. The ecologist calls these symbioses. Politics and economics are advanced symbioses in which the original free-for-all competition has been replaced, in part, by cooperative mechanisms with an ethical content.

The complexity of cooperative mechanisms has increased with population density, and with the efficiency of tools. It was simpler, for example, to define the anti-social uses of sticks and stones in the days of the mastodons than of bullets and billboards in the age of motors.

The first ethics dealt with the relation between individuals; the Mosaic Decalogue is an example. Later accretions dealt with the relation between the individual and society. The Golden Rule tries to integrate the individual to society; democracy to integrate social organization to the individual.

There is as yet no ethic dealing with man's relation to land and to the animals and plants which grow upon it. Land, like Odysseus' slave-girls, is still property. The land-relation is still strictly economic, entailing privileges but not obligations.

The extension of ethics to this third element in human environment is, if I read the evidence correctly, an evolutionary possibility and an ecological necessity. It is the third step in a sequence. The first two have already been taken. Individual thinkers since the days of Ezekiel and Isaiah have asserted that the despoliation of land is not only inexpedient but wrong. Society, however, has not yet affirmed their belief. I regard the present conservation movement as the embryo of such an affirmation.

An ethic may be regarded as a mode of guidance for meeting ecological situations so new or intricate, or involving such deferred reactions, that the path of social expediency is not discernible to the average individual. Animal instincts are modes of guidance for the individual in meeting such situations. Ethics are possibly a kind of community instinct in-the-making.

THE COMMUNITY CONCEPT

All ethics so far evolved rest upon a single premise: that the individual is a member of a community of interdependent parts. His instincts prompt him to compete for his place in the community, but his ethics prompt him also to cooperate (perhaps in order that there may be a place to compete for).

The land ethic simply enlarges the boundaries of the community to include soils, waters, plants, and animals, or collectively: the land.

This sounds simple: do we not already sing our love for and obligation to the land of the free and the home of the brave? Yes, but just what and whom do we love? Certainly not the soil, which we are sending helter-skelter downriver. Certainly not the waters, which we assume have no function except to turn turbines, float barges, and carry off sewage. Certainly not the plants, of which we exterminate whole communities without batting an eye. Certainly not the animals, of which we have already extirpated many of the largest and most beautiful species. A land ethic of course cannot prevent the alteration, management, and use of these "resources," but it does affirm their right to continued existence, and, at least in spots, their continued existence in a natural state.

In short, a land ethic changes the role of *Homo sapiens* from conqueror of the land-community to plain member and citizen of it. It implies respect for his fellow-members, and also respect for the community as such.

In human history, we have learned (I hope) that the conqueror role is eventually self-defeating. Why? Because it is implicit in such a role that the conqueror knows, *ex cathedra*, just what makes the community clock tick, and just what and who is valuable, and what and who is worthless, in community life. It always turns out that he knows neither, and this is why his conquests eventually defeat themselves.

In the biotic community, a parallel situation exists. Abraham knew exactly what the land was for: it was to drip milk and honey into Abraham's mouth. At the present moment, the assurance with which we regard this assumption is inverse to the degree of our education.

The ordinary citizen today assumes that science knows what makes the community clock tick; the scientist is equally sure that he does not. He knows that the biotic mechanism is so complex that its workings may never be fully understood. . . .

THE ECOLOGICAL CONSCIENCE

Conservation is a state of harmony between men and land. Despite nearly a century of propaganda, conservation still proceeds at a snail's pace; progress still consists largely of letterhead pieties and convention oratory. On the back forty we still slip two steps backward for each forward stride.

The usual answer to this dilemma is "more conservation education." No one will debate this, but is it certain that only the *volume* of education needs stepping up? Is something lacking in the *content* as well?

It is difficult to give a fair summary of its content in brief form, but, as I understand it, the content is substantially this: obey the law, vote right, join some organizations, and practice what conservation is profitable on your own land; the government will do the rest.

Is not this formula too easy to accomplish anything worthwhile? It defines no right or wrong, assigns no obligation, calls for no sacrifice, implies no change in the current philosophy of values. In respect of land-use, it urges only enlightened self-interest. Just how far will such education take us? An example will perhaps yield a partial answer.

By 1930 it had become clear to all except the ecologically blind that southwestern Wisconsin's topsoil was slipping seaward. In 1933 the farmers were told that if they would adopt certain remedial practices for five years, the public would donate CCC labor to install them, plus the necessary machinery and materials. The offer was widely accepted, but the practices were widely forgotten when the five-year contract period was up. The farmers continued only those practices that yielded an immediate and visible economic gain for themselves.

This led to the idea that maybe farmers would learn more quickly if they themselves wrote the rules. Accordingly the Wisconsin Legislature in 1937 passed the Soil Conservation District Law. This said to farmers, in effect: *We, the public, will furnish you free technical service and loan you specialized machinery, if you will write your own rules for land-use. Each county may write its own rules, and these will have the force of law.* Nearly all the counties promptly organized to accept the proffered help, but after a decade of operation, *no county has yet written a single rule.* There has been visible progress in such practices as strip-cropping, pasture renovation, and soil liming, but none in fencing woodlots against grazing, and none in excluding plow and cow from steep slopes. The farmers, in short, have selected those remedial practices which were profitable anyhow, and ignored those which were profitable to the community, but not clearly profitable to themselves.

When one asks why no rules have been written, one is told that the community is not yet ready to support them; education must precede rules. But the education actually in progress makes no mention of obligations to land over and above those dictated by self-interest. The net result is that we have more education but less soil, fewer healthy woods, and as many floods as in 1937.

The puzzling aspect of such situations is that the existence of obligations over and above self-interest is taken for granted in such rural community enterprises as the betterment of roads, schools, churches, and baseball teams. Their existence is not taken for granted, nor as yet seriously discussed, in bettering the behavior of the water that falls on the land, or in the preserving of the beauty or diversity of the farm landscape. Land-use ethics are still governed wholly by economic self-interest, just as social ethics were a century ago.

To sum up: we asked the farmer to do what he conveniently could to save his soil, and he has done just that, and only that. The farmer who clears the woods off a 75 per cent slope, turns his cows into the clearing, and dumps its rainfall, rocks, and soil into the community creek, is still (if otherwise decent) a respected member of society. If he puts lime on his fields and plants his crops on contour, he is still entitled to all the privileges and emoluments of his Soil Conservation District. The District is a beautiful piece of social machinery, but it is coughing along on two cylinders because we have been too timid, and too anxious for quick success, to tell the farmer the true magnitude of his obligations. Obligations have no meaning without conscience, and the problem we face is the extension of the social conscience from people to land.

No important change in ethics was ever accomplished without an internal change in our intellectual emphasis, loyalties, affections, and convictions. The proof that conservation has not yet touched these foundations of conduct lies in the fact that philosophy and religion have not yet heard of it. In our attempt to make conservation easy, we have made it trivial.

SUBSTITUTES FOR A LAND ETHIC

When the logic of history hungers for bread and we hand out a stone, we are at pains to explain how much the stone resembles bread. I now describe some of the stones which serve in lieu of a land ethic.

One basic weakness in a conservation system based wholly on economic motives is that most members of the land community have no economic value. Wildflowers and songbirds are examples. Of the 22,000 higher plants and animals native to Wisconsin, it is doubtful whether more than 5 per cent can be sold, fed, eaten, or otherwise put to economic use. Yet these creatures are members of the biotic community, and if (as I believe) its stability depends on its integrity, they are entitled to continuance. . . .

Lack of economic value is sometimes a character not only of species or groups, but of entire biotic communities: marshes, bogs, dunes, and "deserts" are examples. Our formula in such cases is to relegate their conservation to government as refuges, monuments, or parks. The difficulty is that these communities are usually interspersed with more valuable private lands; the government cannot possibly own or control such scattered parcels. The net effect is that we have relegated some of them to ultimate extinction over large areas. If the private owner were ecologically minded, he would be proud to be the custodian of a reasonable proportion of such areas, which add diversity and beauty to his farm and to his community.

In some instances, the assumed lack of profit in these "waste" areas has proved to be wrong, but only after most of them had been done away with. The present scramble to reflood muskrat marshes is a case in point.

There is a clear tendency in American conservation to relegate to government all necessary jobs that private landowners fail to perform. Government ownership, operation, subsidy, or regulation is now widely prevalent in forestry, range management, soil and watershed management, park and wilderness conservation, fisheries management, and migratory bird management, with more to come. Most of this growth in governmental conservation is proper and logical, some of it is inevitable. That I imply no disapproval of it is implicit in the fact that I have spent most of my life working for it. Nevertheless the question arises: What is the ultimate magnitude of the enterprise? Will the tax base carry its eventual ramifications? At what point will governmental conservation, like the mastodon, become handicapped by its own dimensions? The answer, if there is any, seems to be in a land ethic, or some other force which assigns more obligation to the private landowner.

Industrial landowners and users, especially lumbermen and stockmen, are inclined to wail long and loudly about the extension of government ownership and regulation to land, but (with notable exceptions) they show little disposition to develop the only visible alternative: the voluntary practice of conservation on their own lands.

When the private landowner is asked to perform some unprofitable act for the good of the community, he today assents only with outstretched palm. If the act costs him cash this is fair and proper, but when it costs only forethought, open-mindedness, or time, the issue is at least debatable. The overwhelming growth of land-uses subsidies in recent years must be ascribed, in large part, to the government's own agencies for conservation education: the land bureaus, the agricultural colleges, and the extension services. As far as I can detect, no ethical obligation toward land is taught in these institutions.

To sum up: a system of conservation based solely on economic self-interest is hopelessly lopsided. It tends to ignore, and thus eventually to eliminate, many elements in the land community that lack commercial value, but that are (as far as we know) essential to its healthy functioning. It assumes, falsely, I think, that the economic parts of the biotic clock will function without the uneconomic parts. It tends to relegate to government many functions eventually too large, too complex, or too widely dispersed to be performed by government.

An ethical obligation on the part of the private owner is the only visible remedy for these situations.

THE LAND PYRAMID

An ethic to supplement and guide the economic relation to land presupposes the existence of some mental image of land as a biotic mechanism. We can be ethical only in relation to something we can see, feel, understand, love, or otherwise have faith in.

The image commonly employed in conservation education is "the balance of nature." For reasons too lengthy to detail here, this figure of speech fails to describe accurately what little we know about the land mechanism. A much truer image is the one employed in ecology: the biotic pyramid. I shall first sketch the pyramid as a symbol of land, and later develop some of its implications in terms of land-use.

Plants absorb energy from the sun. This energy flows through a circuit called the biota, which may be represented by a pyramid consisting of layers. The bottom layer is the soil. A plant layer rests on the soil, an insect layer on the plants, a bird and rodent layer on the insects, and so on up through various animal groups to the apex layer, which consists of the larger carnivores.

The species of a layer are alike not in where they came from, or in what they look like, but rather in what they eat. Each successive layer depends on those below it for food and often for other services, and each in turn furnishes food and services to those above. Proceeding upward, each successive layer decreases in numerical abundance. Thus, for every carnivore there are hundreds of his prey, thousands of their prey, millions of insects, uncountable plants. The pyramidal form of the system reflects this numerical progression from apex to base. Man shares an intermediate layer with the bears, raccoons, and squirrels which eat both meat and vegetables.

The lines of dependency for food and other services are called food chains. Thus soil-oak-deer-Indian is a chain that has now been largely converted to soil-corn-cow-farmer. Each species, including ourselves, is a link in many chains. The deer eats a hundred plants other than oak, and the cow a hundred plants other than corn. Both, then, are links in a hundred chains. The pyramid is a tangle of chains so complex as to seem disorderly, yet the stability of the system proves it to be a highly organized structure. Its functioning depends on the cooperation and competition of its diverse parts.

In the beginning, the pyramid of life was low and squat; the food chains short and simple. Evolution has added layer after layer, link after link. Man is one of thousands of accretions to the height and complexity of the pyramid. Science has given us many doubts, but it has given us at least one certainty: the trend of evolution is to elaborate and diversify the biota.

Land, then, is not merely soil; it is a fountain of energy flowing through a circuit of soils, plants, and animals. Food chains are the living channels which conduct energy upward; death and decay return it to the soil. The circuit is not closed; some energy is dissipated in decay, some is added by absorption from the air, some is stored in soils, peats, and long-lived forests; but it is a sustained circuit, like a slowly augmented revolving fund of life. There is always a net loss by downhill wash, but this is normally small and offset by the decay of rocks. It is deposited in the ocean and, in the course of geological time, raised to form new lands and new pyramids.

The velocity and character of the upward flow of energy depend on the complex structure of the plant and animal community, much as the upward flow of sap in a tree depends on its complex cellular organization. Without this complexity, normal circulation would presumably not occur. Structure means the characteristic numbers, as well as the characteristic kinds and functions, of the component species. This interdependence between the complex structure of the land and its smooth functioning as an energy unit is one of its basic attributes.

When a change occurs in one part of the circuit, many other parts must adjust themselves to it. Change does not necessarily obstruct or divert the flow of energy; evolution is a long series of self-induced changes, the net result of which has been to elaborate the flow mechanism and to lengthen the circuit. Evolutionary changes, however, are usually slow and local. Man's invention of tools has enabled him to make changes of unprecedented violence, rapidity, and scope. . . .

This thumbnail sketch of land as an energy circuit conveys three basic ideas:

1. That land is not merely soil.
2. That the native plants and animals kept the energy circuit open; others may or may not.
3. That man-made changes are of a different order than evolutionary changes, and have effects more comprehensive than is intended or foreseen.

These ideas, collectively, raise two basic issues: Can the land adjust itself to the new order? Can the desired alterations be accomplished with less violence?

Biotas seem to differ in their capacity to sustain violent conversion. Western Europe, for example, carries a far different pyramid than Caesar found there. Some large animals are lost; swampy forests have become meadows or plowland; many new plants and animals are introduced, some of which escape as pests; the remaining natives are greatly changed in distribution and abundance. Yet the soil is still there and, with the help of imported nutrients, still fertile; and waters flow normally; the new structure seems to function and to persist. There is no visible stoppage or derangement of the circuit.

Western Europe, then, has a resistant biota. Its inner processes are tough, elastic, resistant to strain. No matter how violent the alterations, the pyramid, so far, has developed some new *modus vivendi* which preserves its habitability for man, and for most of the other natives.

Japan seems to present another instance of radical conversion without disorganization.

Most other civilized regions, and some as yet barely touched by civilization, display various stages of disorganization, varying from initial symptoms to advanced wastage. In Asia Minor and North Africa diagnosis is confused by climatic changes, which may have been either the cause or the effect of advanced wastage. In the United States the degree of disorganization varies locally; it is worst in the Southwest, the Ozarks, and parts of the South, and least in New England and the Northwest. Better land-uses may still arrest it in the less advanced regions. In parts of Mexico, South America, South Africa, and Australia a violent and accelerating wastage is in progress, but I cannot assess the prospects.

This almost world-wide display of disorganization in the land seems to be similar to disease in an animal, except that it never culminates in complete disorganization or death. The land recovers, but at some reduced level of complexity, and with a reduced carrying capacity for people, plants, and animals. Many biotas currently regarded as "lands of opportunity" are in fact already subsisting on exploitative agriculture, i.e. they have already exceeded their sustained carrying capacity. Most of South America is overpopulated in this sense.

In arid regions we attempt to offset the process of wastage by reclamation, but it is only too evident that the prospective longevity of reclamation projects is often short. In our own West, the best of them may not last a century.

The combined evidence of history and ecology seems to support one general deduction: the less violent the man-made changes, the greater the probability of successful readjustment in the pyramid. Violence, in turn, varies with human population density; a dense population requires a more violent conversion. In this respect, North America has a better chance for permanence than Europe, if she can contrive to limit her density.

This deduction runs counter to our current philosophy, which assumes that because a small increase in density enriched human life, that an indefinite increase will enrich it indefinitely. Ecology knows of no density relationship that holds for indefinitely wide limits. All gains from density are subject to a law of diminishing returns.

Whatever may be the equation for men and land, it is improbable that we as yet know all its terms. Recent discoveries in mineral and vitamin nutrition reveal unsuspected dependencies in the up-circuit: incredibly minute quantities of certain substances determine the value of soils to plants, of plants to animals. What of the down-circuit? What of the vanishing species, the preservation of which we now regard as an esthetic luxury? They helped build the soil; in what unsuspected ways may they be essential to its maintenance? Professor Weaver proposes that we use prairie flowers to refloculate the wasting soils of the dust bowl; who knows for what purpose cranes and condors, otters and grizzlies may some day be used?

LAND HEALTH AND THE A-B CLEAVAGE

A land ethic, then, reflects the existence of an ecological conscience, and this in turn reflects a conviction of individual responsibility for the health of the land. Health is the capacity of the land for self-renewal. Conservation is our effort to understand and preserve this capacity.

Conservationists are notorious for their dissensions. Superficially these seem to add up to mere confusion, but a more careful scrutiny reveals a single plane of cleavage common to many specialized fields. In each field one group (A) regards the land as soil, and its function as commodity-production; another group (B) regards the land as a biota, and its function as something broader. How much broader is admittedly in a state of doubt and confusion.

In my own field, forestry, group A is quite content to grow trees like cabbages, with cellulose as the basic forest commodity. It feels no inhibition against violence; its ideology is agronomic. Group B, on the other hand, sees forestry as fundamentally different from agronomy because it employs natural species, and manages a natural environment rather than creating an artificial one. Group B prefers natural reproduction on principle. It worries on biotic as well as economic grounds about the loss of species like chestnut, and the threatened loss of the white pines. It worries about a whole series of secondary forest functions: wildlife, recreation, watersheds, wilderness areas. To my mind, Group B feels the stirrings of an ecological conscience.

In the wildlife field, a parallel cleavage exists. For Group A the basic commodities are sport and meat; the yardsticks of production are ciphers of take in pheasants and trout. Artificial propagation is acceptable as a permanent as well as a temporary recourse—if its unit costs permit. Group B, on the other hand, worries about a whole series of biotic side-issues. What is the cost in predators of producing a game crop? Should we have further recourse to exotics? How can management restore the shrinking species, like prairie grouse, already hopeless as shootable game? How can management restore the threatened rarities, like trumpeter swan and whooping crane? Can management principles be extended to wildflowers? Here again it is clear to me that we have the same A-B cleavage as in forestry.

In the larger field of agriculture I am less competent to speak, but there seem to be somewhat parallel cleavages. Scientific agriculture was actively developing before ecology was born, hence a slower penetration of ecological concepts might be expected. Moreover the farmer, by the very nature of his techniques, must modify the biota more radically than the forester or the wildlife manager. Nevertheless, there are many discontents in agriculture which seem to add up to a new vision of "biotic farming."

Perhaps the most important of these is the new evidence that poundage or tonnage is no measure of the food-value of farm crops; the products of fertile soil may be qualitatively as well as quantitatively superior. We can bolster poundage from depleted soils by pouring on imported fertility, but we are not necessarily bolstering food-value. The possible ultimate ramifications of this idea are so immense that I must leave their exposition to abler pens.

The discontent that labels itself "organic farming," while bearing some of the earmarks of a cult, is nevertheless biotic in its direction, particularly in its insistence on the importance of soil flora and fauna.

The ecological fundamentals of agriculture are just as poorly known to the public as in other fields of land-use. For example, few educated people realize that the marvelous advances in technique made during recent decades are improvements in the pump, rather than the well. Acre for acre, they have barely sufficed to offset the sinking level of fertility.

In all of these cleavages, we see repeated the same basic paradoxes: man the conqueror *versus* man the biotic citizen; science the sharpener of his sword *versus* science the searchlight on his universe; land the slave and servant *versus* land the collective organism. Robinson's injunction to Tristram may well be applied, at this juncture, to *Homo sapiens* as a species in geological time:

> Whether you will or not
> You are a King, Tristram, for you are one
> Of the time-tested few that leave the world,
> When they are gone, not the same place it was.
> Mark what you leave.

THE OUTLOOK

It is inconceivable to me that an ethical relation to land can exist without love, respect, and admiration for land, and a high regard for its value. By value, I of course mean something far broader than mere economic value; I mean value in the philosophical sense.

Perhaps the most serious obstacle impeding the evolution of a land ethic is the fact that our educational and economic system is headed away from, rather than toward, an intense consciousness of land. Your true modern is separated from the land by many middlemen, and by innumerable physical gadgets. He has not vital relation to it; to him it is the space between cities on which crops grow. Turn him loose for a day on the land, and if the spot does not happen to be a golf links or a "scenic" area, he is bored stiff. If crops could be raised by hydroponics instead of farming, it would suit him very well. Synthetic substitutes for wood, leather, wool, and other natural land products suit him better than the originals. In short, land is something he has "outgrown."

Almost equally serious as an obstacle to a land ethic is the attitude of the farmer for whom the land is still an adversary, or a taskmaster that keeps him in slavery. Theoretically, the mechanization of farming ought to cut the farmer's chains, but whether it really does is debatable.

One of the requisites for an ecological comprehension of land is an understanding of ecology, and this is by no means co-extensive with "education"; in fact, much higher education seems deliberately to avoid ecological concepts. An understanding of ecology does not necessarily originate in courses bearing ecological labels; it is quite as likely to be labeled geography, botany, agronomy, history, or economics. This is as it should be, but whatever the label, ecological training is scarce.

The case for a land ethic would appear hopeless but for the minority which is in obvious revolt against these "modern" trends.

The "key-log" which must be moved to release the evolutionary process for an ethic is simply this: quit thinking about decent land-use as solely an economic problem. Examine each question in terms of what is ethically and esthetically right, as well as what is economically expedient. A thing is right when it tends to preserve the integrity, stability, and beauty of the biotic community. It is wrong when it tends otherwise.

It of course goes without saying that economic feasibility limits the tether of what can or cannot be done for land. It always has and it always will. The fallacy the economic determinists have tied around our collective neck, and which we now need to cast off, is the belief that economics determines *all* land-use. This is simply not true. An innumerable host of actions and attitudes, comprising perhaps the bulk of all land relations, is determined by the land-users' tastes and predilections, rather than by his purse. The bulk of all land relations hinges on investments of time, forethought, skill, and faith rather than on investments of cash. As a land-user thinketh, so is he.

I have purposely presented the land ethic as a product of social evolution because nothing so important as an ethic is ever "written." Only the most superficial student of history supposes that Moses "wrote" the Decalogue; it evolved in the minds of a thinking community, and Moses wrote a tentative summary of it for a "seminar." I say tentative because evolution never stops.

The evolution of a land ethic is an intellectual as well as emotional process. Conservation is paved with good intentions which prove to be futile, or even dangerous, because they are devoid of critical understanding either of the land, or of economic land-use. I think it is a truism that as the ethical frontier advances from the individual to the community, its intellectual content increases.

The mechanism of operation is the same for any ethic: social approbation for right actions, social disapproval for wrong actions.

By and large, our present problem is one of attitudes and implements. We are remodeling the Alhambra with a steamshovel, and we are proud of our yardage. We shall hardly relinquish the shovel, which after all has many good points, but we are in need of gentler and more objective criteria for its successful use.

The Science of Behavior: Determinism and Moral Responsibility

Freedom and the Science of Behavior

B. F. Skinner

In 1948, B. F. Skinner, a renowned psychologist from Harvard University, published a utopian novel called *Walden Two*. This novel described a planned community in which people were systematically conditioned through positive reinforcement so that they led (mostly) happy lives. The principles used in the conditioning were to be discovered by a scientific "behaviorist" psychology, which Skinner advocated throughout his life.

In the following selection from *Walden Two*, three characters discuss the possibility of a science of behavior and the potential benefits and harms that it might bring. Frazier, the founder of *Walden Two*, defends the use of such a science and argues that it is incompatible with freedom, though not with the feeling of freedom. Castle, a philosopher, argues against Frazier, while Burris, the narrator, attempts to mediate between the two. Skinner's defense of the science of behavior presupposes that all human behavior is causally determined by prior events. If this "determinism" is true, then we have the potential to control the actions of humans for their own and others' good.

As you read through this essay, consider the following:

1. How does Skinner distinguish between real freedom and the experience of freedom one would have in Walden Two?
2. Why does Frazier think that the experience of free choice does not imply that we have free choice?

3. According to Frazier, why is the use of positive reinforcement preferable to punishment?
4. Do you think a science of behavior is possible?
5. What would you do if you had the knowledge provided by a thorough science of behavior? Would you use it to make peoples' lives better? Why or why not?

"Mr. Castle," said Frazier very earnestly, "let me ask you a question. I warn you, it will be the most terrifying question of your life. *What would you do if you found yourself in possession of an effective science of behavior?* Suppose you suddenly found it possible to control the behavior of men as you wished. What would you do?"

"That's an assumption?"

"Take it as one if you like. *I* take it as a fact. And apparently you accept it as a fact too. I can hardly be as despotic as you claim unless I hold the key to an extensive practical control."

"What would I do?" said Castle thoughtfully. "I think I would dump your science of behavior in the ocean."

"And deny men all the help you could otherwise give them?"

"And give them the freedom they would otherwise lose forever!"

"How could you give them freedom?"

"By refusing to control them!"

"But you would only be leaving the control in other hands."

"Whose?"

"The charlatan, the demagogue, the salesman, the ward heeler, the bully, the cheat, the educator, the priest—all who are now in possession of the techniques of behavioral engineering."

"A pretty good share of the control would remain in the hands of the individual himself."

"That's an assumption, too, and it's your only hope. It's your only possible chance to avoid the implications of a science of behvior. If man is free, then a technology of behavior is impossible. But I'm asking you to consider the other case."

"Then my answer is that your assumption is contrary to fact and any further consideration idle."

"And your accusations—?"

"—were in terms of intention, not of possible achievement."

Frazier sighed dramatically.

"It's a little late to be proving that a behavioral technology is well advanced. How can you deny it? Many of its methods and techniques are really as old as the hills. Look at their frightful misuse in the hands of the Nazis! And what about the techniques of the psychological clinic? What about education? Or religion? Or practical politics? Or advertising and salesmanship? Bring them all together and you have a sort of rule-of-thumb technology of vast power. No, Mr. Castle, the science is there for the asking. But its techniques and methods are in the wrong hands—they are used for personal aggrandizement in a competitive world or, in the case of psychologist and educator, for futilely corrective purposes. My question is, have you the courage to take up and wield the science of behavior for the good of mankind? You answer that you would dump it in the ocean!"

"I'd want to take it out of the hands of the politicians and advertisers and salesmen, too."

"And the psychologists and educators? You see, Mr. Castle, you can't have that kind of cake. The fact is, we not only *can* control human behavior, we *must*. But who's to do it, and what's to be done?"

"So long as a trace of personal freedom survives, I'll stick to my position," said Castle, very much out of countenance.

"Isn't it time we talked about freedom?" I said. "We parted a day or so ago on an agreement to let the question of freedom ring. It's time to answer, don't you think?"

"My answer is simple enough," said Frazier. "I deny that freedom exists at all. I must deny it—or my program would be absurd. You can't have a science about a subject matter which hops capriciously about. Perhaps we can never *prove* that man isn't free; it's an assumption. But the increasing success of a science of behavior makes it more and more plausible."

"On the contrary, a simple personal experience makes it untenable," said Castle. "The experience of freedom. I *know* that I'm free."

"It must be quite consoling," said Frazier.

"And what's more—you do, too," said Castle hotly. "When you deny your own freedom for the sake of playing with a science of behavior, you're acting in plain bad faith. That's the only way I can explain it." He tried to recover himself and shrugged his shoulders. "At least you'll grant that you *feel* free."

"The 'feeling of freedom' should deceive no one," said Frazier. "Give me a concrete case."

"Well, right now," Castle said. He picked up a book of matches. "I'm free to hold or drop these matches."

"You will, of course, do one or the other," said Frazier. "Linguistically or logically there seem to be two possibilities, but I submit that there's only one in fact. The determining forces may be subtle but they are inexorable. I suggest that as an orderly person you will probably hold—ah! you drop them! Well, you see, that's all part of your behavior with respect to me. You couldn't resist the temptation to prove me wrong. It was all lawful. You had no choice. The deciding factor entered rather late, and naturally you couldn't foresee the result when you first held them up. There was no strong likelihood that you would act in either direction, and so you said you were free."

"That's entirely too glib," said Castle. "It's easy to argue lawfulness after the fact. But let's see you predict what I will do in advance. Then I'll agree there's law."

"I didn't say that behavior is always predictable, any more than the weather is always predictable. There are often too many factors to be taken into account. We can't measure them all accurately, and we couldn't perform the mathematical operations needed to make a prediction if we had the measurements. The legality is usually an assumption—but none the less important in judging the issue at hand."

"Take a case where there's no choice, then," said Castle. "Certainly a man in jail isn't free in the sense in which I am free now."

"Good! That's an excellent start. Let us classify the kinds of determiners of human behavior. One class, as you suggest, is physical restraint—handcuffs, iron bars, forcible coercion. These are ways in which we shape human behavior according to our wishes. They're crude, and they sacrifice the affection of the controllee, but they often work. Now, what other ways are there of limiting freedom?"

Frazier had adopted a professorial tone and Castle refused to answer.

"The threat of force would be one," I said.

"Right. And here again we shan't encourage any loyalty on the part of the controllee. He has perhaps a shade more of the feeling of freedom, since he can always 'chose to act and accept the consequences,' but he doesn't feel exactly free. He knows his behavior is being coerced. Now what else?"

I had no answer.

"Force or the threat of force—I see no other possibility," said Castle after a moment.

"Precisely," said Frazier.

"But certainly a large part of my behavior has no connection with force at all. There's my freedom!" said Castle.

"I wasn't agreeing that there was no other possibility—merely that *you* could see no other. Not being a good behaviorist—or a good Christian, for that matter—you have no feeling for a tremendous power of a different sort."

"What's that?"

"I shall have to be technical," said Frazier. "But only for a moment. It's what the science of behavior calls 'reinforcement theory.' The things that can happen to us fall into three classes. To some things we are indifferent. Other things we like—we want them to happen, and we take steps to make them happen again. Still other things we don't like—we don't want them to happen and we take steps to get rid of them or keep them from happening again.

"*Now*," Frazier continued earnestly, "if it's in our power to create any of the situations which a person likes or to remove any situation he doesn't like, we can control his behavior. When he behaves as we want him to behave, we simply create a situation he likes, or remove one he doesn't like. As a result, the probability that he will behave that way again goes up, which is what we want. Technically it's called 'positive reinforcement.'

"The old school made the amazing mistake of supposing that the reverse was true, that by removing a situation a person likes or setting up one he doesn't like—in other words by punishing him—it was possible to *reduce* the probability that he would behave in a given way again. That simply doesn't hold. It has been established beyond question. What is emerging at this critical stage in the evolution of society is a behavioral and cultural technology based on positive reinforcement alone. We are gradually discovering—at an untold cost in human suffering—that in the long run punishment doesn't reduce the probability that an act will occur. We have been so preoccupied with the contrary that we always take 'force' to mean punishment. We don't say we're using force when we send shiploads of food into a starving country, though we're displaying quite as much *power* as if we were sending troops and guns."

"I'm certainly not an advocate of force," said Castle. "But I can't agree that it's not effective."

"It's *temporarily* effective, that's the worst of it. That explains several thousand years of bloodshed. Even nature has been fooled. We 'instinctively' punish a person who doesn't behave as we like—we spank him if he's a child or strike him if he's a man. A nice distinction! The immediate effect of the blow teaches us to strike again. Retribution and revenge are the most natural things on earth.

But in the long run the man we strike is no less likely to repeat his act."

"But he won't repeat it if we hit him hard enough," said Castle.

"He'll still *tend* to repeat it. He'll *want* to repeat it. We haven't really altered his potential behavior at all. That's the pity of it. If he doesn't repeat it in our presence, he will in the presence of someone else. Or it will be repeated in the disguise of a neurotic symptom. If we hit hard enough, we clear a little place for ourselves in the wilderness of civilization, but we make the rest of the wilderness still more terrible.

"Now, early forms of government are naturally based on punishment. It's the obvious technique when the physically strong control the weak. But we're in the throes of a great change to positive reinforcement—from a competitive society in which one man's reward is another man's punishment, to a cooperative society in which no one gains at the expense of anyone else.

"The change is slow and painful because the immediate, temporary effect of punishment overshadows the eventual advantage of positive reinforcement. We've all seen countless instances of the temporary effect of force, but clear evidence of the effect of not using force is rare. That's why I insist that Jesus, who was apparently the first to discover the power of refusing to punish, must have hit upon the principle by accident. He certainly had none of the experimental evidence which is available to us today, and I can't conceive that it was possible, no matter what the man's genius, to have discovered the principle from casual observation."

"A touch of revelation, perhaps?" said Castle.

"No, accident. Jesus discovered one principle because it had immediate consequences, and he got another thrown in for good measure."

I began to see light.

"You mean the principle of 'love your enemies'?" I said.

"Exactly! To 'do good to those who despitefully use you' has two unrelated consequences. You gain the peace of mind we talked about the other day. Let the stronger man push you around—at least you avoid the torture of your own rage. *That's* the immediate consequence. What an astonishing discovery it must have been to find that in the long run you could *control the stronger man* in the same way!"

"It's generous of you to give so much credit to your early colleague," said Castle, "but why are we still in the throes of so much misery? Twenty centuries should have been enough for one piece of behavioral engineering."

"The conditions which made the principle difficult to discover made it difficult to teach. The history of the Christian Church doesn't reveal many cases of doing good to one's enemies. To inoffensive heathens, perhaps, but not enemies. One must look outside the field of organized religion to find the principle in practice at all. Church governments are devotees of *power*, both temporal and bogus."

"But what has all this got to do with freedom?" I said hastily.

Frazier took time to reorganize his behavior. He looked steadily toward the window, against which the rain was beating heavily.

"Now that we *know* how positive reinforcement works and why negative doesn't," he said at last, "we can be more deliberate, and hence more successful, in our cultural design. We can achieve a sort of control under which the controlled, though they are following a code much more scrupulously than was ever the case under the old system, nevertheless *feel free*. They are doing what they want to do, not what they are forced to do. That's the source of the tremendous power of positive reinforcement—there's no restraint and no revolt. By a careful cultural design, we control not the final behavior, but the *inclination* to behave—the motives, the desires, the wishes.

"The curious thing is that in that case *the question of freedom never arises*. Mr. Castle was free to drop the matchbook in the sense that nothing was preventing him. If it had been securely bound to his hand he wouldn't have been free. Nor would he have been quite free if I'd covered him with a gun and threatened to shoot him if he let it fall. The question of freedom arises when there is restraint—either physical or psychological.

"But restraint is only one sort of control, and absence of restraint isn't freedom. It's not control that's lacking when one feels 'free,' but the objectionable control of force. Mr. Castle felt free to hold or drop the matches in the sense that he felt no restraint—no threat of punishment in taking either course of action. He neglected to examine his positive reasons for holding or letting go, in spite of the fact that these were more compelling in this instance than any threat of force.

"We have no vocabulary of freedom in dealing with what we want to do," Frazier went on. "The question never arises. When men strike for freedom, they strike against jails and the police, or the threat of them—against oppression. They never strike against forces which make them want to act the way they do. Yet, it seems to be understood that governments will operate only through force or the threat of force, and that all other principles of control will be left to education, religion, and commerce. If this continues to be the case, we may as well give up. A government can never create a free people with the techniques now allotted to it.

"The question is: Can men live in freedom and peace? And the answer is: Yes, if we can build a social structure which will satisfy the needs of everyone and in which everyone will want to observe the supporting code. But so far this has been achieved only in *Walden Two*. Your ruthless accusations to the contrary, Mr. Castle, this is the freest place on earth. And it is free precisely because we make no use of force or the threat of force. Every bit of our research, from the nursery through the psychological management of our adult membership, is directed toward that end—to exploit every alternative to forcible control. By skillful planning, by a wise choice of techniques we *increase* the feeling of freedom.

"It's not planning which infringes upon freedom, but planning which uses force. A sense of freedom was practically unknown in the planned society of Nazi Germany, because the planners made a fantastic use of force and the threat of force.

"No, Mr. Castle, when a science of behavior has once been achieved, there's no alternative to a planned society. We can't leave mankind to an accidental or biased control. But by using the principle of positive reinforcement—carefully avoiding force or the threat of force—we can preserve a personal sense of freedom."

Punishment, Not Therapy

Herbert Morris

Societies have a strong interest in altering the behavior of their members to avoid social disharmony. How they do this depends in large part on their vision of human behavior. A society that emphasizes the role of free human choice in human affairs will tend toward a very different system of social control than one that emphasizes the role of causes for which actors cannot be responsible. Most scientific approaches to human behavior, especially ones that emphasize causal determinism, favor the latter. In this essay, Herbert Morris outlines two systems of social control that might be used to constrain criminals. The first is a system of just punishment. Where rules are designed to benefit everyone, punishment prevents those who violate the rules from gaining an unfair advantage over those who adhere to them. The offender can be seen as owing a debt to society. The second system is one that views criminal behavior as a kind of disease and sees the criminal as in need of therapy. Because Morris finds such a therapy system morally objectionable, he concludes that we have a right not just to a system of punishment (rather than therapy), but once such a system is in place, a right to be punished.

As you read through this essay, consider the following:

1. What are the features of a just system of punishment as Morris describes it?
2. What are the basic features of a disease-and-therapy model?
3. How do the two models differ in the way they view human behavior?
4. How does Morris argue that we have a right to a system of just punishment? Does he provide good evidence for the view of human behavior implicit in this model?
5. Do you agree with Morris that there is something deeply objectionable about the therapy model? Why or why not?
6. How might Skinner respond to Morris's concerns?

They acted and looked . . . at us, and around in our house, in a way that had about it the feeling—at least for me—that we were not people. In their eyesight we were just things, that was all.
— Malcolm X

We have no right to treat a man like a dog.
— Governor Maddox of Georgia

Alfredo Traps in Dürrenmatt's tale discovers that he has brought off, all by himself, a murder involving considerable ingenuity. The mock prosecutor in the tale demands the death penalty "as reward for a crime that

From Herbert Morris, "Persons and Punishment," *The Monist* 52, no. 4. © *The Monist.* Copyright © 1968, *The Monist*, La Salle, Illinois 61301. Reprinted by permission.

merits admiration, astonishment, and respect."
Traps is deeply moved; indeed, he is exhila-
rated, and the whole of his life becomes more
heroic, and, ironically, more precious. His
defense attorney proceeds to argue that Traps
was not only innocent but incapable of guilt,
"a victim of the age." This defense Traps dis-
avows with indignation and anger. He makes
claim to the murder as his and demands the
prescribed punishment—death.

The themes to be found in this macabre
tale do not often find their way into philosophical discussions of punishment. These
discussions deal with large and significant
questions of whether or not we ever have the
right to punish, and if we do, under what conditions, to what degree, and in what manner.
There is a tradition, of course, not notable for
its present vitality, that is closely linked with
motifs in Dürrenmatt's tale of crime and punishment. Its adherents have urged that justice
requires a person be punished if he is guilty.
Sometimes—though rarely—these philosophers have expressed themselves in terms of
the criminals' *right to be punished*. Reaction to
the claim that there is such a right has been
astonishment combined, perhaps, with a
touch of contempt for the perversity of the
suggestion. A strange right that no one would
ever wish to claim! With that flourish the
subject is buried and the right disposed of. In
this paper the subject is resurrected.

My aim is to argue . . . that we have a
right to punishment. . . .

When someone claims that there is a
right to be free, we can easily imagine situations in which the right is infringed and easily
imagine situations in which there is a point to
asserting or claiming the right. With the right
to be punished, matters are otherwise. The
immediate reaction to the claim that there is
such a right is puzzlement. And the reasons
for this are apparent. People do not normally
value pain and suffering. Punishment is associated with pain and suffering. When we
think about punishment we naturally think of
the strong desire most persons have to avoid
it, to accept, for example, acquittal of a criminal charge with relief and eagerly, if con-

victed, to hope for pardon or probation.
Adding, of course, to the paradoxical character of the claim of such a right is difficulty in
imagining circumstances in which it would be
denied one. When would one rightly demand
punishment and meet with any threat of the
claim being denied?

So our first task is to see when the claim
of such a right would have a point. I want to
approach this task by setting out two complex
types of institutions both of which are
designed to maintain some degree of social
control. In the one a central concept is punishment for wrongdoing and in the other the
central concepts are control of dangerous
individuals and treatment of disease.

Let us first turn attention to the institutions in which punishment is involved. The
institutions I describe will resemble those we
ordinarily think of as institutions of punishment; they will have, however, additional
features we associate with a system of just
punishment.

Let us suppose that men are constituted
roughly as they now are, with a rough equivalence in strength and abilities, a capacity to be
injured by each other and to make judgments
that such injury is undesirable, a limited
strength of will, and a capacity to reason and
to conform conduct to rules. Applying to the
conduct of these men are a group of rules,
ones I shall label "primary," which closely
resemble the core rules of our criminal law,
rules that prohibit violence and deception and
compliance with which provides benefits for
all persons. These benefits consist in noninterference by others with what each person
values, such matters as continuance of life and
bodily security. The rules define a sphere for
each person, then, which is immune from
interference by others. Making possible this
mutual benefit is the assumption by individuals of a burden. The burden consists in the
exercise of self-restraint by individuals over
inclinations that would, if satisfied, directly
interfere or create a substantial risk of interference with others in proscribed ways. If a
person fails to exercise self-restraint even
though he might have and gives in to such

inclinations, he renounces a burden which others have voluntarily assumed and thus gains an advantage which others, who have restrained themselves, do not possess. This system, then, is one in which the rules establish a mutuality of benefit and burden and in which the benefits of noninterference are conditional upon the assumption of burdens.

Connecting punishment with the violation of these primary rules, and making public the provision for punishment, is both reasonable and just. First, it is only reasonable that those who voluntarily comply with the rules be provided some assurance that they will not be assuming burdens which others are unprepared to assume. Their disposition to comply voluntarily will diminish as they learn that others are with impunity renouncing burdens they are assuming. Second, fairness dictates that a system in which benefits and burdens are equally distributed have a mechanism designed to prevent a maldistribution in the benefits and burdens. Thus, sanctions are attached to noncompliance with the primary rules so as to induce compliance with the primary rules among those who may be disinclined to obey. In this way the likelihood of an unfair distribution is diminished.

Third, it is just to punish those who have violated the rules and caused the unfair distribution of benefits and burdens. A person who violates the rules has something others have—the benefits of the system—but by renouncing what others have assumed, the burdens of self-restraint, he has acquired an unfair advantage. Matters are not even until this advantage is in some way erased. Another way of putting it is that he owes something to others, for he has something that does not rightfully belong to him. Justice—that is punishing such individuals—restores the equilibrium of benefits and burdens by taking from the individual what he owes, that is, exacting the debt. It is important to see that the equilibrium may be restored in another way. Forgiveness—with its legal analogue of a pardon—while not the righting of an unfair distribution by making one pay his debt is, nevertheless, a restoring of the equilibrium by forgiving the debt. Forgiveness may be viewed, at least in some types of cases, as a gift after the fact, erasing a debt, which had the gift been given before the fact, would not have created a debt. But the practice of pardoning has to proceed sensitively, for it may endanger in a way the practice of justice does not, the maintenance of an equilibrium of benefits and burdens. If all are indiscriminately pardoned less incentive is provided individuals to restrain their inclinations, thus increasing the incidence of persons taking what they do not deserve.

There are also in this system we are considering a variety of operative principles compliance with which provides some guarantee that the system of punishment does not itself promote an unfair distribution of benefits and burdens. For one thing, provision is made for a variety of defenses, each one of which can be said to have as its object diminishing the chances of forcibly depriving a person of benefits others have if that person has not derived an unfair advantage. A person has not derived an unfair advantage if he could not have restrained himself or if it is unreasonable to expect him to behave otherwise than he did. Sometimes the rules preclude punishment of classes of persons such as children. Sometimes they provide a defense if on a particular occasion a person lacked the capacity to conform his conduct to the rules. Thus, someone who in an epileptic seizure strikes another is excused. Punishment in these cases would be punishment of the innocent, punishment of those who do not voluntarily renounce a burden others have assumed. Punishment in such cases, then, would not equalize but rather cause an unfair distribution in benefits and burdens. . . .

Finally, because the primary rules are designed to benefit all and because the punishments prescribed for their violation are publicized and the defenses respected, there is some plausibility in the exaggerated claim that in choosing to do an act violative of the rules an individual has chosen to be punished. This way of putting matters brings to our attention the extent to which, when the system is as I have described it, the criminal "has brought the punishment upon himself" in contrast to those cases where it would be misleading to say "he has brought it upon himself," cases, for example, where one does not know the rules or is punished in the absence of fault.

To summarize, then: first, there is a group of rules guiding the behavior of individuals in the community which establish spheres of interest immune from interference by others; second, provision is made for what is generally regarded as a deprivation of something of value if the rules are violated; third, the deprivations visited upon any person are justified by that person's having violated the rules; fourth, the deprivation, in this just system of punishment, is linked to rules that fairly distribute benefits and burdens and to procedures that strike some balance between not punishing the guilty and punishing the innocent, a class defined as those who have not voluntarily done acts violative of the law, in which it is evident that the evil of punishing the innocent is regarded as greater than the nonpunishment of the guilty.

At the core of many actual legal systems one finds, of course, rules and procedures of the kind I have sketched. It is obvious, though, that any ongoing legal system differs in significant respects from what I have presented here, containing "pockets of injustice."

I want now to sketch an extreme version of a set of institutions of a fundamentally different kind, institutions proceeding on a conception of man which appears to be basically at odds with that operative within a system of punishment.

Rules are promulgated in this system that prohibit certain types of injuries and harms.

In this world we are now to imagine when an individual harms another his conduct is to be regarded as a symptom of some pathological condition in the way a running nose is a symptom of a cold. Actions diverging from some conception of the normal are viewed as manifestations of a disease in the way in which we might today regard the arm and leg movements of an epileptic during a seizure. Actions con-

forming to what is normal are assimilated to the normal and healthy functioning of bodily organs. What a person does, then, is assimilated, on this conception, to what we believe today, or at least most of us believe today, a person undergoes. We draw a distinction between the operation of the kidney and raising an arm on request. This distincrion between mere events or happenings and human actions is erased in our imagined system.[1] . . .

Let us elaborate on this assimilation of conduct of a certain kind to symptoms of a disease. First, there is something abnormal in both the case of conduct, such as killing another, and a symptom of a disease such as an irregular heart beat. Second, there are causes for this abnormality in action such that once we know of them we can explain the abnormality as we now can explain the symptoms of many physical diseases. The abnormality is looked upon as a happening with a causal explanation rather than an action for which there were reasons. Third, the causes that account for the abnormality interfere with the normal functioning of the body, or, in the case of killing with what is regarded as a normal functioning of an individual. . . .

With this view of man the institutions of social control respond, not with punishment, but with either preventive detention, in case of "carriers," or therapy in the case of those manifesting pathological symptoms. The logic of sickness implies the logic of therapy. . . . I am concerned now . . . with what the implications would be were the world indeed one of therapy . . . for I want to suggest tendencies of thought that arise when one is immersed in the ideology of disease and therapy.

First, punishment is the imposition upon a person who is believed to be at fault of something commonly believed to be a deprivation where that deprivation is justified by the person's guilty behavior. It is associated with resentment, for the guilty are those who have done what they had no right to do by failing to exercise restraint when they might have and where others have. Therapy is not a response to a person who is at fault. We respond to an individual, not because of what he has done, but because of some condition from which he is suffering. If he is no longer suffering from the condition, treatment no longer has a point. Punishment, then, focuses on the past; therapy on the present. Therapy is normally associated with compassion for what one undergoes, not resentment for what one has illegitimately done.

Second, with therapy, unlike punishment, we do not seek to deprive the person of something acknowledged as a good, but seek rather to help and to benefit the individual who is suffering by ministering to his illness in the hope that the person can be cured. The good we attempt to do is not a reward for desert. The individual suffering has not merited by his disease the good we seek to bestow upon him but has, because he is a creature that has the capacity to feel pain, a claim upon our sympathies and help.

Third, we saw with punishment that its justification was related to maintaining and restoring a fair distribution of benefits and burdens. Infliction of the prescribed punishment carries the implication, then, that one has "paid one's debt" to society, for the punishment is the taking from the person of something commonly recognized as valuable. It is this conception of "a debt owed" that may permit, as I suggested earlier, under certain conditions, the nonpunishment of the guilty, for operative within a system of punishment may be a concept analogous to forgiveness, namely pardoning. . . .What is clear is that the conceptions of "paying a debt" or "have a debt forgiven" or pardoning have no place in a system of therapy.

Fourth, with punishment there is an attempt at some equivalence between the advantage gained by the wrongdoer—partly based upon the seriousness of the interest invaded, partly on the state of mind with which the wrongful act was performed—and the punishment meted out. Thus, we can understand a prohibition on "cruel and unusual punishments" so that disproportionate pain and suffering are avoided. With therapy attempts at proportionality make no sense. It is perfectly plausible giving someone who kills a pill and treating for a lifetime

within an institution one who has broken a dish and manifested accident proneness. We have the concept of "painful treatment." We do not have the concept of "cruel treatment." Because treatment is regarded as a benefit, though it may involve pain, it is natural that less restraint is exercised in bestowing it, than in inflicting punishment. Further, protests with respect to treatment are likely to be assimilated to the complaints of one whose leg must be amputated in order for him to live, and, thus, largely disregarded. To be sure, there is operative in the therapy world some conception of the "cure being worse than the disease," but if the disease is manifested in conduct harmful to others, and if being a normal operating human being is valued highly, there will naturally be considerable pressure to find the cure acceptable.

Fifth, the rules in our system of punishment governing conduct of individuals were rules violation of which involved either direct interference with others or the creation of a substantial risk of such interference. . . . Though we are interested in diminishing violations of the primary rules, we are not prepared to punish too many individuals who would never have violated the rules in order to achieve this aim. In a system motivated solely by a preventive and curative ideology there would be less reason to wait until symptoms manifest themselves in socially harmful conduct. It is understandable that we should wish at the earliest possible stage to arrest the development of the disease. In the punishment system, because we are dealing with deprivations, it is understandable that we should forbear from imposing them until we are quite sure of guilt. In the therapy system, dealing as it does with benefits, there is less reason for forbearance from treatment at an early stage. . . .

In our system of punishment an attempt was made to maximize each individual's freedom of choice by first of all delimiting by rules certain spheres of conduct immune from interference by others. The punishment associated with these primary rules paid deference to an individual's free choice by connecting punishment to a freely chosen act violative of the rules, thus giving some plausibility to the claim, as we saw, that what a person received by way of punishment he himself had chosen. With the world of disease and therapy all this changes and the individual's free choice ceases to be a determinative factor in how others respond to him. All those principles of our own legal system that minimize the chances of punishment of those who have not chosen to do acts violative of the rules tend to lose their point in the therapy system, for how we respond in a therapy system to a person is not conditioned upon what he has chosen but rather on what symptoms he has manifested or may manifest and what the best therapy for the disease is that is suggested by the symptoms.

Now, it is clear I think, that were we confronted with the alternatives I have sketched, between a system of just punishment and a thoroughgoing system of treatment, a system, that is, that did not reintroduce concepts appropriate to punishment, we could see the point in claiming that a person has a right to be punished, meaning by this that a person had a right to all those institutions and practices linked to punishment. For these would provide him with, among other things, a far greater ability to predict what would happen to him on the occurrence of certain events than the therapy system. There is the inestimable value to each of us of having the responses of others to us determined over a wide range of our lives by what we choose rather than what they choose. A person has a right to institutions that respect his choices. Our punishment system does; our therapy systems does not.

Apart from those aspects of our therapy model which would relate to serious limitations on personal liberty, there are clearly objections of a more profound kind to the mode of thinking I have associated with the therapy model.

First, human beings pride themselves in having capacities that animals do not. A common way, for example, of arousing shame in a child is to compare the child's conduct to that of an animal. In a system where all actions are assimilated to happenings we are assimilated to creatures—indeed, it is more extreme than this—whom we have always thought possessed of less than we. Fundamental to our practice of praise and order of attainment is that one who can do more—one who is capable of more and one who does more is more worthy of respect and admiration. And we have thought of ourselves as capable where animals are not of making, of creating, among other things, ourselves. The conception of man I have outlined would provide us with a status that today, when our conduct is assimilated to it in moral criticism, we consider properly evocative of shame.

Second, if all human conduct is viewed as something men undergo, thrown into question would be the appropriateness of that extensive range of peculiarly human satisfactions that derive from a sense of achievement. For these satisfactions we shall have to substitute those mild satisfactions attendant upon a healthy well-functioning body. Contentment is our lot if we are fortunate; intense satisfaction at achievement is entirely inappropriate.

Third, in the therapy world nothing is earned and what we receive comes to us through compassion, or through a desire to control us. Resentment is out of place. We can take credit for nothing but must always regard ourselves—if there are selves left to regard once actions disappear—as fortunate recipients of benefits or unfortunate carriers of disease who must be controlled. We know that within our own world human beings who have been so regarded and who come to accept this view of themselves come to look upon themselves as worthless. When what we do is met with resentment, we are indirectly paid something of a compliment.

Fourth, attention should also be drawn to a peculiar evil that may be attendant upon regarding a man's actions as symptoms of disease. The logic of cure will push us toward forms of therapy that inevitably involve changes in the person made against his will. The evil in this would be most apparent in those cases where the agent, whose action is determined to be a manifestation of some disease, does not regard his action in this way.

He believes that what he has done is, in fact, "right" but his conception of "normality" is not the therapeutically accepted one. When we treat an illness we normally treat a condition that the person is not responsible for. He is "suffering" from some disease and we treat the condition, relieving the person of something preventing his normal functioning. When we begin treating persons for actions that have been chosen, we do not lift from the person something that is interfering with his normal functioning but we change the person so that he functions in a way regarded as normal by the current therapeutic community. We have to change him and his judgments of value. In doing this we display a lack of respect for the moral status of individuals, that is, a lack of respect for the reasoning and choices of individuals. They are but animals who must be conditioned. I think we can understand and, indeed, sympathize with a man's preferring death to being forcibly turned into what he is not.

Finally, perhaps most frightening of all would be the derogation in status of all protests to treatment. If someone believes that he has done something right, and if he protests being treated and changed, the protest will itself be regarded as a sign of some pathological condition, for who would not wish to be cured of an affliction? What this leads to are questions of an important kind about the effect of this conception of man upon what we now understand by reasoning. Here what a person takes to be a reasoned defense of an act is treated, as the action was, on the model of a happening of a pathological kind. Not just a person's acts are taken from him but also his attempt at a reasoned justification for the acts. In a system of punishment a person who has committed a crime may argue that what he did was right. We make him pay the price and we respect his right to retain the judgment he has made. A conception of pathology precludes this form of respect. . . .

I want also to make clear in concluding . . . that I have argued, though very indirectly, not just for a right to a system of punishment, but for a right to be punished once there is in existence such a system. Thus, a man has the right to be punished rather than treated if he is guilty of some offense. And, indeed, one can imagine a case in which, even in the face of an offer of a pardon, a man claims and ought to have acknowledged his right to be punished.

Note

1. "When a man is suffering from an infectious disease, he is a danger to the community, and it is necessary to restrict his liberty of movement. But no one associates any idea of guilt with such a situation. On the contrary, he is an object of commiseration to his friends. Such steps as science recommends are taken to cure him of his disease, and he submits as a rule without reluctance to the curtailment of liberty involved meanwhile. The same method in spirit ought to be shown in the treatment of what is called 'crime.'"
Bertrand Russell, *Roads to Freedom* (London: George Allen and Unwin Ltd., 1918), p. 135.
"We do not hold people responsible for their reflexes—for example, for coughing in church. We hold them responsible for their operant behavior—for example, for whispering in church or remaining in church while coughing. But there are variables which are responsible for whispering as well as coughing, and these may be just as inexorable. When we recognize this, we are likely to drop the notion of responsibility altogether and with it the doctrine of free will as an inner causal agent."
B. F. Skinner, *Science and Human Behavior* (1953), pp. 115–6.
"Basically, criminality is but a symptom of insanity, using the term in its widest generic sense to express unacceptable social behavior based on unconscious motivation flowing from a disturbed instinctive and emotional life, whether this appears in frank psychoses, or in less obvious form in neuroses and unrecognized psychoses. . . . If criminals are products of early environmental influences in the same sense that psychotics and neurotics are, then it should be possible to reach them psychotherapeutically."
Benjamin Karpman, "Criminal Psychodynamics," *Journal of Criminal Law and Criminology*, 47 (1956), p. 9.
"We, the agents of society, must move to end the game of tit-for-tat and blow-for-blow in which the offender has foolishly and futilely engaged himself and us. We are not driven, as he is, to wild and impulsive actions. With knowledge comes power, and with power there is no need for the frightened vengeance of the old penology. In its place should go a quiet, dignified, therapeutic program for the rehabilitation of the disorganized one, if possible, the protection of society during the treatment period, and his guided return to useful citizenship, as soon as this can be effected."
Karl Menninger, "Therapy, Not Punishment," *Harper's Magazine* (August 1959), pp. 63–64.

Deliberation and Freedom

Richard Taylor

At bottom, questions about how we should understand freedom and moral responsibility depend on whether our actions are causally determined. If humans are to fit nicely within the world of medium-sized objects, as described by science, then it seems that human behaviors must have causes like any other events. And these causes must be sufficient to bring about the effects that follow them. If this is correct, however, then how can we reasonably deliberate about what to do, and how can we believe that what we do is "up to us"? Richard Taylor argues that because deliberation seems reasonable, and because it is incompatible with both determinism and indeterminism, we must assume that humans can cause their behaviors in a distinctive way that is compatible with (real) freedom. Humans are self-determining. This vision of human action differentiates it from other natural events and raises deep questions about the limits of a science of behavior.

As you read through this essay, consider the following:

1. How does Taylor characterize determinism? Why does he think that it appeals to us?
2. What are the implications of deliberation? What follows from the belief that certain things are "up to us"?
3. Why does indeterminism fail to provide an adequate explanation of deliberation and free action?
4. What is the theory of agency and why does Taylor think we should take it seriously?
5. Is Taylor's closing reference to the mysteriousness of the world intellectually satisfying? Can a scientifically minded person accept mysterious agent causation?
6. What views about freedom and determinism do you find most reasonable? Why?

From Richard Taylor, *Metaphysics*, 4th ed. © 1974. Reprinted by permission of Prentice-Hall, Inc., Upper Saddle River, NJ.

If I consider the world or any part of it at any particular moment, it seems certain that it is perfectly determinate in every detail. There is no vagueness, looseness, or ambiguity. There is, indeed, vagueness and even error, in my conceptions of reality, but not in reality itself. A lilac bush, which surely has a certain exact number of blossoms, appears to me only to have many blossoms, and I do not know how many. Things seen in the distance appear of indefinite form, and often of a color and size that in fact they are not. Things near the border of my visual field seem to me vague and amorphous, and I can never even say exactly where that border itself is, it is so indefinite and vague. But all such indeterminateness resides solely in my conceptions and ideas; the world itself shares none of it. The sea, at any exact time and place, has exactly a certain salinity and temperature, and every grain of sand on its shore is exactly disposed with respect to all the others. The wind at any point in space has at any moment a certain direction and force, not more nor less. It matters not whether these properties and relations are known to anyone. A field of wheat at any moment contains just an exact number of ripening grains, each having reached just the ripeness it exhibits, each presenting a determinate color and shade, an exact shape and mass. A person, too, at any given point in his life, is perfectly determinate to the minutest cells of his body. My own brain, nerves—even my thoughts, intentions, and feelings—are at any moment just what they then specifically are. These thoughts might, to be sure, be vague and even false as representations, but as thoughts they are not, and even a false idea is no less an exact and determinate idea than a true one.

Nothing seems more obvious. But if I now ask *why* the world and all its larger or smaller parts are this moment just what they are, the answer comes to mind: because the world, the moment before, was precisely what it then was. Given exactly what went before, the world, it seems, could now be none other than it is. And what it was a moment before, in all its larger and minuter parts, was the consequence of what had gone just before then, and so on, back to the very beginning of the world, if it had a beginning, or through an infinite past time, in case it had not. In any case, the world as it now is, and every part of it, and every detail of every part, would seem to be the only world that now could be, given just what it has been.

DETERMINISM

Reflections such as these suggest that, in the case of everything that exists, there are antecedent conditions, known or unknown, given which that thing could not be other than it is. That is an exact statement of the metaphysical thesis of determinism. More loosely, it says that everything, including every cause, is the effect of some cause or causes; or that everything is not only determinate but causally determined. The statement, moreover, makes no allowance for time, for past, or for future. Hence, if true, it holds not only for all things that have existed but for all things that do or ever will exist.

Of course people rarely think of such a principle, and hardly one in a thousand will ever formulate it to himself in words. Yet all do seem to assume it in their daily affairs, so much so that some philosophers have declared it an *a priori* principle of the understanding, that is, something that is known independently of experience, while others have deemed it to be at least a part of the common sense of mankind. Thus, when I hear a noise I look up to see where it came from. I never suppose that it was just a noise that came from nowhere and had no cause. Everyone does the same—even animals, though they have never once thought about metaphysics or the principle of universal determinism. People believe, or at least act as though they believed, that things have causes, without exception. When a child or animal touches a hot stove for the first time, it unhesitatingly believes that the pain then felt was caused by that stove, and so firm and immediate is that belief that hot stoves are avoided ever after. We all use our metaphysical principles, whether we think of them or not, or are even capable of thinking of them. If I have a bodily or other disorder—a rash, for instance, or a fever or a phobia—I consult a physician for a diagnosis and explanation in the hope that the cause of it might be found and removed or moderated. I am never tempted to suppose that such things just have no causes, arising from nowhere, else I would take no steps to remove the causes. The principle of determinism is here, as in everything else, simply assumed, without being thought about.

DETERMINISM AND HUMAN BEHAVIOR

I am a part of the world. So is each of the cells and minute parts of which I am composed. The principle of determinism, then, in case it is true, applies to me and to each of those minute parts, no less than to the sand, wheat, winds, and waters of which we have spoken. There is no particular difficulty in thinking so, as long as I consider only what are sometimes called the "purely physiological" changes of my body, like growth, the pulse, glandular secretions, and the like. But what of my thoughts and ideas? And what of my behavior that is supposed to be deliberate, purposeful, and perhaps morally significant? These are all changes of my own being, changes that I undergo, and if these are all but the consequences of the conditions under which they occur, and these conditions are the only ones that could have obtained, given the state of the world just before and when they arose, what now becomes of my responsibility for my behavior and of the control over my conduct that I fancy myself to possess? What am I but a helpless product of nature, destined by her to do whatever I do and to become whatever I become?

There is no moral blame nor merit in anyone who cannot help what he does. It matters not whether the explanation for his behavior is found within him or without, whether it is expressed in terms of ordinary physical causes or allegedly "mental" ones, or whether the causes be proximate or remote. I am not responsible for being a man rather than a woman, nor for having the temperament and desires characteristic of that sex. I was never asked whether these should be given to me. The kleptomaniac, similarly, steals from compulsion, the alcoholic drinks from compulsion, and sometimes even the hero dies from compulsive courage. Though these causes are within them, they compel no less for that, and their victims never chose to have them inflicted upon themselves. To say they are compulsions is to say only that they compel. But to say that they compel is only to say that they cause; for the cause of a thing being given, the effect cannot fail to follow. By the thesis of determinism, however, everything whatever is caused, and not one single thing could ever be other than exactly what it is. Perhaps one thinks that the kleptomaniac and the drunkard did not have to become what they are, that they could have done better at another time and thereby ended up better than they are now, or that the hero could have done worse and then ended up a coward. But this shows only an unwillingness to understand what made them become as they are. Having found that their behavior is caused from within them, we can hardly avoid asking what caused these inner springs of action, and then asking what were the causes of these causes, and so on through the infinite past. We shall not, certainly, with our small understanding and our fragmentary knowledge of the past ever know why the world

should at just this time and place have produced just this thief, this drunkard, and this hero, but the vagueness and smattered nature of our knowledge should not tempt us to imagine a similar vagueness in nature herself. Everything in nature is and always has been determinate, with no loose edges at all, and she was forever destined to bring forth just what she has produced, however slight may be our understanding of the origins of these works. Ultimate responsibility for anything that exists, and hence for any person and his deeds, can thus rest only with the first cause of all things, if there is such a cause, or nowhere at all, in case there is not. Such at least seems to be the unavoidable implication of determinism.

DETERMINISM AND MORALS

Some philosophers, faced with all this, which seems quite clear to the ordinary understanding, have tried to cling to determinism while modifying traditional conceptions of morals. They continue to *use* such words as *merit*, *blame*, *praise*, and *desert*, but they so divest them of their meanings as to finish by talking about things entirely different, sometimes without themselves realizing that they are no longer on the subject. An ordinary person will hardly understand that anyone can possess merit or vice and be deserving of moral praise or blame, as a result of traits that he has or of behavior arising from those traits, once it is well understood that he could never have avoided being just what he is and doing just what he does.

We are happily spared going into all this, however, for the question whether determinism is true of human nature is not a question of ethics at all but of metaphysics. There is accordingly no hope of answering it within the context of ethics. One can, to be sure, simply *assume* an answer to it—assume that determinism is true, for instance—and then see what are the implications of this answer for ethics; but that does not answer the question. Or one can *assume* some theory or other of ethics—

assume some version of "the greatest happiness" principle, for instance—and then see whether that theory is consistent with determinism. But such confrontations of theories with theories likewise make us no wiser, so far as any fundamental question is concerned. We can suppose at once that determinism is consistent with some conceptions of morals, and inconsistent with others, and that the same holds for indeterminism. We shall still not know what theories are true; we shall only know which are consistent with one another.

We shall, then, eschew all considerations of ethics as having no real bearing on our problem. We want to learn, if we can, whether determinism is true, and this is a question of metaphysics. It can, like all good questions of philosophy, be answered only on the basis of certain data; that is, by seeing whether or not it squares with certain things that everyone knows, or believes himself to know, or things of which everyone is at least more sure than the answer to the question at issue.

Now I could, of course, simply affirm that I am a morally responsible being, in the sense in which my responsibility for my behavior implies that I could have avoided that behavior. But this would take us into the nebulous realm of ethics, and it is, in fact, far from obvious that I am responsible in that sense. Many have doubted that they are responsible in that sense, and it is in any case not difficult to doubt it, however strongly one might feel about it.

There are, however, two things about myself of which I feel quite certain and that have no necessary connection with morals. The first is that I sometimes deliberate, with the view to making a decision; a decision, namely, to do this thing or that. And the second is that whether or not I deliberate about what to do, it is sometimes up to me what I do. This might all be an illusion, of course; but so also any philosophical theory, such as the theory of determinism, might be false. The point remains that it is far more difficult for me to doubt that I sometimes deliberate, and that it is sometimes up to me what to do, than to doubt any philosophical theory what-

ever, including the theory of determinism. We must, accordingly, if we ever hope to be wiser, adjust our theories to our data and not try to adjust our data to our theories.

Let us, then, get these two data quite clearly before us so we can see what they are, what they presuppose, and what they do and do not entail.

DELIBERATION

Deliberation is an activity, or at least a kind of experience, that cannot be defined, or even described, without metaphors. We speak of weighing this and that in our minds, of trying to anticipate consequences of various possible courses of action, and so on, but such descriptions do not convey to us what deliberation is unless we already know.

Whenever I deliberate, however, I find that I make certain presuppositions, whether I actually think of them or not. That is, I assume that certain things are true, certain things which are such that, if I thought they were not true, it would be impossible for me to deliberate at all. Some of these can be listed as follows:

First, I find that I can deliberate only about my own behavior and never about the behavior of another. I can try to guess, speculate, or figure out what another person is going to do; I can read certain signs and sometimes infer what he will do; but I cannot deliberate about it. When I deliberate I try to decide something, to make up my mind, and this is as remote as anything could be from speculating, trying to guess, or inferring from signs. Sometimes one *does* speculate on what he is going to do, by trying to draw conclusions from certain signs or omens—he might infer that he is going to sneeze, for instance, or speculate that he is going to become a grandfather—but he is not then deliberating whether to do these things or not. One does, to be sure, sometimes deliberate about whether another person will do a certain act, when that other person is subject to his command or otherwise under his control; but then he is not really deliberating about another person's acts at all, but about his own—namely, whether or not to have that other person carry out the order.

Second, I find that I can deliberate only about future things, never things past or present. I may not know what I did at a certain time in the past, in case I have forgotten, but I can no longer deliberate whether to do it then or not. I can, again, only speculate, guess, try to infer, or perhaps try to remember. Similarly, I cannot deliberate whether nor not to be doing something now; I can only ascertain whether or not I am in fact doing it. If I am sitting I cannot deliberate about whether or not to be sitting. I can only deliberate about whether to remain sitting—and this has to do with the future.

Third, I cannot deliberate about what I shall do if I already know what I am going to do. If I were to say, for example, "I know that I am going to be married tomorrow and in the meantime I am going to deliberate about whether to get married," I would contradict myself. There are only two ways that I could know now what I am going to do tomorrow; namely, either by inferring this from certain signs and omens or by having already decided what I am going to do. But if I have inferred from signs and omens what I am going to do, I cannot deliberate about it—there is just nothing for me to decide; and similarly, if I have already decided. If, on the other hand, I can still deliberate about what I am going to do, to that extent I must regard the signs and omens as unreliable, and the inference uncertain, and I therefore do not know what I am going to do after all.

And finally, I cannot deliberate about what to do, even though I may not know what I am going to do, unless I believe that it is up to me what I am going to do. If I am within the power of another person, or at the mercy of circumstances over which I have no control, then, although I may have no idea what I am going to do, I cannot deliberate about it. I can only wait and see. If, for instance, I am a serviceman, and regulations regarding uniforms are posted each day by my commanding officer and are strictly enforced by him, then I shall not know what uniforms I shall be wearing from time to time, but I cannot deliberate about it. I can only wait and see what regulations are posted; it is not up to me. Similarly, a woman who is about to give birth to a child cannot deliberate whether to have a boy or a girl, even though she may not know. She can only wait and see; it is not up to her. Such examples can be generalized to cover any case wherein one does not know what he is going to do but believes that it is not up to him, and hence no matter for his decision and hence none for his deliberation.

"IT IS UP TO ME"

I sometimes feel certain that it is, at least to some extent, up to me what I am going to do; indeed, I must believe this if I am to deliberate about what to do. But what does this mean? It is, again, hard to say, but the idea can be illustrated, and we can fairly easily see what it does *not* mean.

Let us consider the simplest possible sort of situation in which this belief might be involved. At this moment, for instance, it seems quite certain to me that, holding my finger before me, I can move it either to the left or to the right, that each of these motions is possible for me. This does not mean merely that my finger can move either way, although it entails that, for this would be true in case nothing obstructed it, even if I had no control over it at all. I can say of a distant, fluttering leaf that it can move either way, but not that I can move it, since I have no control over it. How it moves is not up to me. Nor does it mean merely that my finger can be moved either way, although it entails this too. If the motions of my finger are under the control of some other person or of some machine, then it might be true that the finger can be moved either way, by that person or machine, though false that I can move it at all.

If I say, then, that it is up to me how I move my finger, I mean that I can move it in this way and I can move it in that way, and not merely that it can move or be moved in this way and that. I mean that the motion of my finger is within my direct control. If someone were to ask me to move it to the right, I could do that, and if he were to ask me to move it to the left, I could do that too. Further, I could do these simple acts without being asked at all, and having been asked, I could move it in a manner the exact opposite of what was requested, since I can ignore the request. There are, to be sure, some motions of my finger that I cannot make, so it is not *entirely* up to me how it moves. I cannot bend it backward, for instance, or bend it into a knot, for these motions are obstructed by the very anatomical construction of the finger itself; and to say that I can move my finger at all means at least that nothing obstructs such a motion, though it does not mean merely this. There is, however, at this moment, no obstruction, anatomical or otherwise, to my moving it to the right, and none to my moving it to the left.

This datum, it should be noted, is properly expressed as a conjunction and not as a disjunction. That is, my belief is that I can move my finger in one way *and* that I can also move it another way; and it does not do justice to this belief to say that I can move it one way *or* the other. It is fairly easy to see the truth of this, for the latter claim, that I can move it one way *or* the other, would be satisfied in case there were only one way I could move it, and *that* is not what I believe. Suppose, for instance, that my hand were strapped to a device in such a fashion that I could move my finger to the right but not to the left. Then it would still be entirely true that I could move it either to the left *or* to the right—since it would be true that I could move it to the right. But that is not what I now believe. My finger is not strapped to anything, and nothing obstructs its motion in either direction. And what I believe, in this situation, is that I can move it to the right *and* I can move it to the left.

We must note further that the belief expressed in our datum is not a belief in what is logically impossible. It is the belief that I now *can* move my finger in different ways but not that I can move it in different ways at

once. What I believe is that I am now able to move my finger one way and that I am now equally able to move it another way, but I do not claim to be able now or at any other time to move it both ways simultaneously. The situation here is analogous to one in which I might, for instance, be offered a choice of either of two apples but forbidden to take both. Each apple is such that I may select it, but neither is such that I may select it together with the other.

Now, are these two data—the belief that I do sometimes deliberate, and the belief that it is sometimes up to me what I do—consistent with the metaphysical theory of determinism? We do not know yet. We intend to find out. It is fairly clear, however, that they are going to present difficulties to that theory. But let us not, in any case, try to avoid those difficulties by just denying the data themselves. If we eventually deny the data, we shall do so for better reasons than this. Virtually everyone is convinced that beliefs such as are expressed in our data are sometimes true. They cannot be simply dismissed as false just because they might appear to conflict with a metaphysical theory that hardly anyone has ever really thought much about at all. Almost anyone, unless his fingers are paralyzed, bound, or otherwise incapable of movement, believes sometimes that the motions of his fingers are within his control, in exactly the sense expressed by our data. If consequences of considerable importance to him depend on how he moves his fingers, he sometimes deliberates before moving them, or at least he is convinced that he does or that he can. Philosophers might have different notions of just what things are implied by such data, but there is in any case no more, and in fact considerably less, reasons for denying the data than for denying some philosophical theory. . . .

FREEDOM

To say that it is, in a given instance, up to me what I do is to say that I am in that instance *free* with respect to what I then do. Thus, I am sometimes free to move my finger this way and that, but not, certainly, to bend it backward or into a knot. But what does this mean?

It means, first, that there is no *obstacle* or *impediment* to my activity. Thus, there is sometimes no obstacle to my moving my finger this way and that, though there are obvious obstacles to my moving it backward or into a knot. Those things, accordingly, that pose obstacles to my motions limit my freedom. If my hand were strapped in such a way as to permit only a leftward motion of my finger, I would not then be free to move it to the right. If it were encased in a tight cast that permitted no motion, I would not be free to move it at all. Freedom of motion, then, is limited by obstacles.

Further, to say that it is, in a given instance, up to me what I do, means that nothing *constrains* or *forces* me to do one thing rather than another. Constraints are like obstacles, except that while the latter prevent, the former enforce. Thus, if my finger is being forcibly bent to the left—by a machine, for instance, or by another person, or by any force that I cannot overcome—then I am not free to move it this way and that. I cannot, in fact, move it at all; I can only watch to see how it is moved, and perhaps vainly resist: Its motions are not up to me, or within my control, but in the control of some other thing or person.

Obstacles and constraints, then, both obviously limit my freedom. To say that I am free to perform some action thus means at least that there is no obstacle to my doing it, and that nothing constrains me to do otherwise.

Now if we rest content with this observation, as many have, and construe free activity simply as activity that is unimpeded and unconstrained, there is evidently no inconsistency between affirming both the thesis of determinism and the claim that I am sometimes free. For to say that some action of mine is neither impeded nor constrained does not by itself imply that it is not causally determined. The absence of obstacles and constraints is a mere negative condition, and does not by itself rule out the presence of positive causes. It might seem, then, that we can say of some of my actions that there are conditions antecedent to their performance so that no other actions were possible, and also that these actions were unobstructed and unconstrained. And to say that would logically entail that such actions were both causally determined, and free.

SOFT DETERMINISM

It is this kind of consideration that has led many philosophers to embrace what is sometimes called "soft determinism." All versions of this theory have in common three claims, by means of which, it is naïvely supposed, a reconciliation is achieved between determinism and freedom. Freedom being, furthermore, a condition of moral responsibility and the only condition that metaphysics seriously questions, it is supposed by the partisans of this view that determinism is perfectly compatible with such responsibility. This, no doubt, accounts for its great appeal and wide acceptance, even by some people of considerable learning.

The three claims of soft determinism are (1) that the thesis of determinism is true, and that accordingly all human behavior, voluntary or other, like the behavior of all other things, arises from antecedent conditions, given which no other behavior is possible—in short, that all human behavior is caused and determined; (2) that voluntary behavior is nonetheless free to the extent that it is not externally constrained or impeded; and (3) that, in the absence of such obstacles and constraints, the causes of voluntary behavior are certain states, events, or conditions within the agent himself; namely, his own acts of will or volitions, choices, decisions, desires, and so on.

Thus, on this view, I am free, and therefore sometimes responsible for what I do, provided nothing prevents me from acting according to my own choice, desire, or volition, or constrains me to act otherwise. There may, to be sure, be other conditions for my responsibility—such as, for example, an understanding of the probable consequences of my behavior, and that sort of thing—but absence of constraint or impediment is, at least, one such condition. And, it is claimed, it is a condition that is compatible with the supposition that my behavior is caused—for it is, by hypothesis, caused by my own inner choices, desires, and volitions.

THE REFUTATION OF THIS

The theory of soft determinism looks good at first—so good that it has for generations been solemnly taught from innumerable philosophical chairs and implanted in the minds of students as sound philosophy—but no great acumen is needed to discover that far from solving any problem, it only camouflages it.

My free actions are those unimpeded and unconstrained motions that arise from my own inner desires, choices, and volitions; let us grant this provisionally. But now, whence arise those inner states that determine what my body shall do? Are they within my control or not? Having made my choice or decision and acted upon it, could I have chosen otherwise or not?

Here the determinist, hoping to surrender nothing and yet to avoid the problem implied in that question, bids us not to ask it; the question itself, he announces, is without meaning. For to say that I could have done otherwise, he says, means only that I *would* have done otherwise *if* those inner states that determined my action had been different; if, that is, I had decided or chosen differently. To ask, accordingly, whether I could have chosen or decided differently is only to ask whether, had I decided to decide differently or chosen to choose differently, or willed to will differently, I would have decided or chosen or willed differently. And this of course, *is* unintelligible nonsense.

But it is not nonsense to ask whether the causes of my actions—my own inner choices, decisions, and desires—are themselves caused.

And of course they are, if determinism is true, for on that thesis everything is caused and determined. And if they are, then we cannot avoid concluding that, given the causal conditions of those inner states, I could not have decided, willed, chosen, or desired other than I in fact did, for this is a logical consequence of the very definition of determinism. Of course we can still say that, *if* the causes of those inner states, whatever they were, had been different, then their effects, those inner states themselves, would have been different, and that in this hypothetical sense I could have decided, chosen, willed, or desired differently—but that only pushes our problem back still another step. For we will then want to know whether the causes of those inner states were within my control, and so on *ad infinitum*. We are, at each step, permitted to say "could have been otherwise" only in a provisional sense—provided, that is, that something else had been different—but must then retract it and replace it with "could not have been otherwise" as soon as we discover, as we must at each step, that whatever would have to have been different could not have been different. . . .

SIMPLE INDETERMINISM

We might at first now seem warranted in simply denying determinism, and saying that, insofar as they are free, my actions are not caused; or that, if they are caused by my own inner states—my own desires, impulses, choices, volitions, and whatnot—then these, in any case, are not caused. This is a perfectly clear sense in which a person's action, assuming that it was free, could have been otherwise. If it was uncaused, then, even given the conditions under which it occurred and all that preceded, some other act was nonetheless possible, and he did not have to do what he did. Or if his action was the inevitable consequence of his own inner states, and could not have been otherwise, given these, we can nevertheless say that these inner states, being uncaused, could have been otherwise, and could thereby have produced different actions.

Only the slightest consideration will show, however, that this simple denial of determinism has not the slightest plausibility. For let us suppose it is true, and that some of my bodily motions—namely, those that I regard as my free acts—are not caused at all or, if caused by my own inner states, that these are not caused. We shall thereby avoid picturing a puppet, to be sure—but only by substituting something even less like a human being; for the conception that now emerges is not that of a free person, but of an erratic and jerking phantom, without any rhyme or reason at all.

Suppose that my right arm is free, according to this conception; that is, that its motions are uncaused. It moves this way and that from time to time, but nothing causes these motions. Sometimes it moves forth vigorously, sometimes up, sometimes down, sometimes it just drifts vaguely about—these motions all being wholly free and uncaused. Manifestly I have nothing to do with them at all; they just happen, and neither I nor anyone can ever tell what this arm will be doing next. It might seize a club and lay it on the head of the nearest bystander, no less to my astonishment than his. There will never be any point in asking why these motions occur, or in seeking any explanation of them, for under the conditions assumed there is no explanation. They just happen, from no causes at all.

This is no description of free, voluntary, or responsible behavior. Indeed, so far as the motions of my body or its parts are entirely uncaused, such motions cannot even be ascribed to me as my behavior in the first place, since I have nothing to do with them. The behavior of my arm is just the random motion of a foreign object. Behavior that is mine must be behavior that is within my control, but motions that occur from no causes are beyond the control of anyone. I can have no more to do with, and no more control over, the uncaused motions of my limbs than a gambler has over the motions of an honest roulette wheel. I can only, like him, idly wait to see what happens.

Nor does it improve things to suppose that my bodily motions are caused by my own inner states, so long as we suppose these to be wholly uncaused. The result will be the same as before. My arm, for example, will move this way and that, sometimes up and sometimes down, sometimes vigorously and sometimes just drifting about, always in response to certain inner states, to be sure. But since these are supposed to be wholly uncaused, it follows that I have no control over them and hence none over their effects. If my hand lays a club forcefully on the nearest bystander, we can indeed say that this motion resulted from an inner club-wielding desire of mine; but we must add that I had nothing to do with that desire, and that it arose, to be followed by its inevitable effect, no less to my astonishment than to his. Things like this do, alas, sometimes happen. We are all sometimes seized by compulsive impulses that arise we know not whence, and we do sometimes act upon these. But because they are far from being examples of free, voluntary, and responsible behavior, we need only to learn that behavior was of this sort to conclude that it was not free, voluntary, or responsible. It was erratic, impulsive, and irresponsible.

DETERMINISM AND SIMPLE INDETERMINISM AS THEORIES

Both determinism and simple indeterminism are loaded with difficulties, and no one who has thought much on them can affirm either of them without some embarrassment. Simple indeterminism has nothing whatever to be said for it, except that it appears to remove the grossest difficulties of determinism, only, however, to imply perfect absurdities of its own. Determinism, on the other hand, is at least initially plausible. People seem to have a natural inclination to believe in it; it is, indeed, almost required for the very exercise of practical intelligence. And beyond this, our experience appears always to confirm it, so long as we are dealing with everyday facts of common experience, as distinguished from the esoteric researches of theoretical physics.

But determinism, as applied to human behavior, has implications that few can casually accept, and they appear to be implications that no modification of the theory can efface.

Both theories, moreover, appear logically irreconcilable to the two items of data that we set forth at the outset; namely, (1) that my behavior is sometimes the outcome of my deliberation, and (2) that in these and other cases it is sometimes up to me what I do. . . .

THE THEORY OF AGENCY

The only conception of action that accords with our data is one according to which people—and perhaps some other things too—are sometimes, but of course not always, self-determining beings; that is, beings that are sometimes the causes of their own behavior. In the case of an action that is free, it must be such that it is caused by the agent who performs it, but such that no antecedent conditions were sufficient for his performing just that action. In the case of an action that is both free and rational, it must be such that the agent who performed it did so for some reason, but this reason cannot have been the cause of it.

Now, this conception fits what people take themselves to be; namely, beings who act, or who are agents, rather than things that are merely acted upon, and whose behavior is simply the causal consequence of conditions that they have not wrought. When I believe that I have done something, I do believe that it was I who caused it to be done, I who made something happen, and not merely something within me, such as one of my own subjective states, which is not identical with myself. If I believe that something not identical with myself was the cause of my behavior—some event wholly external to myself, for instance, or even one internal to myself, such as a nerve impulse, volition, or whatnot—then I cannot regard that behavior as being an act of mine, unless I further believe that I was the cause of that external or internal event. My pulse, for example, is caused and regulated by certain conditions existing within me, and not by myself. I do not, accordingly, regard this activity of my body as my action, and would be no more tempted to do so if I became suddenly conscious within myself of those conditions or impulses that produce it. This is behavior with which I have nothing to do, behavior that is not within my immediate control, behavior that is not only not free activity, but not even the activity of an agent to begin with; it is nothing but a mechanical reflex. Had I never learned that my very life depends on this pulse beat, I would regard it with complete indifference, as something foreign to me, like the oscillations of a clock pendulum that I idly contemplate.

Now this conception of activity, and of an agent who is the cause of it, involves two rather strange metaphysical notions that are never applied elsewhere in nature. The first is that of a *self* or *person*—for example, a man—who is not merely a collection of things or events, but a self-moving being. For on this view it is a person, and not merely some part of him or something within him, that is the cause of his own activity. Now, we certainly do not know that a human being is anything more than an assemblage of physical things and processes that act in accordance with those laws that describe the behavior of all other physical things and processes. Even though he is a living being, of enormous complexity, there is nothing, apart from the requirements of this theory, to suggest that his behavior is so radically different in its origin from that of other physical objects, or that an understanding of it must be sought in some metaphysical realm wholly different from that appropriate to the understanding of nonliving things.

Second, this conception of activity involves an extraordinary conception of causation according to which an agent, which is a substance and not an event, can nevertheless be the cause of an event. Indeed, if he is a free agent then he can, on this conception, cause an event to occur—namely, some act of his own—without anything else causing him to do so. This means that an agent is sometimes a cause, without being an antecedent sufficient condition;

for if I affirm that I am the cause of some act of mine, then I am plainly not saying that my very existence is sufficient for its occurrence, which would be absurd. If I say that my hand causes my pencil to move, than I am saying that the motion of my hand is, under the other conditions then prevailing, sufficient for the motion of the pencil. But if I then say that I cause my hand to move, I am not saying anything remotely like this, and surely not that the motion of my self is sufficient for the motion of my arm and hand, since these are the only things about me that are moving.

This conception of the causation of events by things that are not events is, in fact, so different from the usual philosophical conception of a cause that it should not even bear the same name, for "being a cause" ordinarily just means "being an antecedent sufficient condition or set of conditions." Instead, then, of speaking of agents as *causing* their own acts, it would perhaps be better to use another word entirely, and say, for instance, that they *originate* them, *initiate* them, or simply that they *perform* them.

Now this is, on the face of it, a dubious conception of what a person is. Yet it is consistent with our data, reflecting the presuppositions of deliberation, and appears to be the only conception that is consistent with them, as determinism and simple indeterminism are not. The theory of agency avoids the absurdities of simple indeterminism by conceding that human behavior is caused, while at the same time avoiding the difficulties of determinism by denying that every chain of causes and effects is infinite. Some such causal chains, on this view, have beginnings, and they begin with agents themselves. Moreover, if we are to suppose that it is sometimes up to me what I do, and understand this in a sense that is not consistent with determinism, we must suppose that I am an agent or a being who initiates his own actions, sometimes under conditions that do not determine what action I shall perform. Deliberation becomes, on this view, something that is not only possible but quite rational, for it does make sense to deliberate about activity that is truly my own and that depends in its outcome upon

me as its author, and not merely upon something more or less esoteric that is supposed to be intimately associated with me, such as my thoughts, volitions, choices, or whatnot.

One can hardly affirm such a theory of agency with complete comfort, however, and wholly without embarrassment, for the conception of agents and their powers which is involved in it is strange indeed, if not positively mysterious. In fact, one can hardly be blamed here for simply denying our data outright, rather than embracing this theory to which they do most certainly point. Our data—to the effect that we do sometimes deliberate before acting, and that when we do, we presuppose among other things that it is up to us what we are going to do—rest upon nothing more than fairly common consent. These data might simply be illusions. It might in fact be that no one ever deliberates but only imagines that he does, that from pure conceit he supposes himself to be the master of his behavior and the author of his acts. Spinoza has suggested that if a stone, having been thrown into the air, were suddenly to become conscious, it would suppose itself to be the source of its own motion, being then conscious of what it was doing but not aware of the real cause of its behavior. Certainly we are *sometimes* mistaken in believing that we are behaving as a result of choice deliberately arrived at. A man might, for example, easily imagine that his embarking upon matrimony is the result of the most careful and rational deliberation, when in fact the causes, perfectly sufficient for that behavior, might be of an entirely physiological, unconscious origin. If it is sometimes false that we deliberate and then act as the result of a decision deliberately arrived at, even when we suppose it to be true, it might always be false. No one seems able, as we have noted, to describe deliberation without metaphors, and the conception of a thing's being "within one's power" or "up to him" seems to defy analysis or definition altogether, if taken in a sense that the theory of agency appears to require.

These are, then, dubitable conceptions, despite their being so well implanted in common sense. Indeed, when we turn to the theory of fatalism, we shall find formidable metaphysical considerations that appear to rule them out altogether. Perhaps here, as elsewhere in metaphysics, we should be content with discovering difficulties, with seeing what is and what is not consistent with such convictions as we happen to have, and then drawing such satisfaction as we can from the realization that, no matter where we begin, the world is mysterious and that we who try to understand it are even more so. This realization can, with some justification, make one feel wise, even in the full realization of his ignorance.

Essay and Paper Topics for "Scientific Practice and Culture"

1. Using examples from authors you have read in this part, develop and defend your view about how much authority should be given to the scientific worldview in our culture. Are we threatened by too much antiscience or too much science?

2. Write an essay comparing the views of Roszak and Holton about nonscientific ways of knowing. Do these threaten us with a rising tide of irrationality, or do they open us to other important aspects of the world?

3. Outline some of the cultural transformations that you think are being produced by contemporary science and technology. Evaluate these changes and decide whether your evaluations justify altering the path of science or technology. If you think that restraining science is justified, indicate how we should do it.

4. Describe the different approaches that Kass and Pence take toward morally evaluating cloning. Show how these approaches relate to the perspectives defended in the earlier section "Feelings and Reason in Morality."

5. Considering arguments from Ruse, de Waal, and Leopold, defend your view about the extent to which biology can help us understand morality. Do evolution and ecology provide us with good reasons to expand the scope of morality?

6. Explain your view about whether the scientific image of humans eliminates important kinds of freedom and leaves us without moral responsibility for our actions. Indicate how we should understand punishment given your view of freedom.

7. Compare Morris's account of the difference between humans and other animals with de Waal's account of the moral behavior of animals. Can we hold humans morally responsible for their actions without doing the same for apes?

Part VII

Scientific Practice and Reason

Section 17

Objectivity and Values
in Science

Objectivity and Its Critics

Israel Scheffler

Is scientific method objective? What do we mean by "objectivity"? Science provides the preferred methods for arriving at knowledge in our culture partly because of its claim to objectivity. This claim has been criticized by some historians and sociologists of science, who do not find much objectivity in the ordinary practice of science. Naturally, some scientists will fall short of the ideal of impartial assessment of their theories, but the critics argue that objectivity is not even reasonable as an ideal. Indeed, they claim that objectivity is impossible.

In this essay, Israel Scheffler describes the standard "objectivist" view of science and vividly formulates several key criticisms of it. According to the standard view, science attempts to arrive at true general laws of nature through public appeals to logic and empirical facts. Its ideal of objectivity embodies a moral impulse to acquire one's beliefs in responsible ways. This ideal is threatened if scientists who accept conflicting theories do not share a common language in which to express their theories and common observations that they can use to decide which theory is better justified. After outlining some reasons for thinking no such common language and observations exist, Scheffler sketches a view of science without objectivity. Although Scheffler does not defend the standard view against its attackers in this selection, he believes that the critics have vastly overstated their case. Israel Scheffler is professor emeritus of philosophy and education at Harvard University.

422

As you read through this essay, consider the following:

1. How does Scheffler describe the scientific attitude? How is that attitude related to the pursuit of knowledge in other areas, such as philosophy and history?
2. Why does Scheffler think objectivity is important? How is it connected to responsibility?
3. How does the paradox of categorization create problems for the objectivity of observation?
4. How do the paradoxes of shared observation and common language alter the standard view?
5. If the critics of objectivity are right, how should we understand the goals of science and the nature of theory change in science?
6. Do you think that the attacks on objectivity create serious problems for the standard view?

A fundamental feature of science is its ideal of objectivity, an ideal that subjects all scientific statements to the test of independent and impartial criteria, recognizing no authority of persons in the realm of cognition. The claimant to scientific knowledge is responsible for what he says, acknowledging the relevance of considerations beyond his wish or advocacy to the judgment of his assertions. In assertion he is not simply expressing himself but making a claim; he is trying to meet independent standards, to satisfy factual requirements whose fulfillment cannot be guaranteed in advance.

To propound one's beliefs in a scientific spirit is to acknowledge that they may turn out wrong under continued examination, that they may fail to sustain themselves critically in an enlarged experience. It is, in effect, to conceive one's self of the here and now as linked through potential converse with a community of others, whose differences of location or opinion yet allow a common discourse and access to a shared world. It is accordingly to lay oneself open to criticism from any quarter and to acquire an impersonal regard for the judgments of others; for what matters is not who they are, but whether they properly voice the import of controlling standards. Assertions that purport to be scientific are, in sum, held subject to control by reference to independent checks.

Commitment to fair controls over assertion is the basis of the scientific attitude of impartiality and detachment; indeed, one might say that it constitutes this attitude. For impartiality and detachment are not to be thought of as substantive qualities of the scientist's personality or the style of his thought; scientists are as variegated in these respects as any other group of people. Scientific habits of mind are compatible with passionate advocacy, strong faith, intuitive conjecture, and imaginative speculation. What is central is the acknowledgment of general controls to which one's dearest beliefs are ultimately subject. These controls, embodied in and transmitted by the institutions of science, represent the fundamental rules of its game. To devise fair controls for new ranges of assertion, and to guarantee the fairness of existing controls in the old, constitute the rationale of these rules. The cold and aloof scientist is, then, a myth.

It must be emphasized that the function of scientific controls is to channel critique and facilitate evaluation rather than to generate discoveries by routine. Control provides, in short, no mechanical substitute for ideas; there *are* no substitutes for ideas. The late Hans Reichenbach drew a sharp distinction in his philosophy of science between the "context of discovery" and the "context of justification,"[1] and he was right to do so. For the mechanical scientist is also a myth.

Now, the ideal of objectivity, as thus far described, characterizes not only the scientist, but also the historian, the philosopher, the mathematician, the man of affairs—insofar as all make cognitive claims in a rational spirit.

A parallel ideal is relevant for the moral person as well. The ideal of objectivity is, indeed, closely tied to the general notion of rationality, which is theoretically applicable to both the cognitive and the moral spheres. In both spheres, we honor demands for relevant reasons and acknowledge control by principle. In both, we suppose a commitment to general rules capable of running against one's own wishes in any particular case. In neither sphere is personal authority decisive; as S. I. Benn and R. S. Peters have put it,

> The procedural rules of science lay it down . . . that hypotheses must be decided on by looking at the evidence, not by appealing to a man. There are also, and can be, no rules to decide who will be the originators of scientific theories.
>
> In a similar way . . . a rule cannot be a moral one if it is to be accepted just because someone has laid it down or made a decision between competing alternatives. Reasons must be given for it, not originators or umpires produced. Of course, in both enterprises provisional authorities can be consulted. But there are usually good reasons for this choice and their pronouncements are never to be regarded as final just because they have made them. In science and morality there are no appointed judges or policemen.[2]

There is thus no ground for restricting the applicability of the *ideal* of objectivity to *de facto* science, as contrasted, for example, with history, philosophy, or human affairs.

Nevertheless, *de facto* science articulates, in a self-conscious and methodologically explicit manner, the demands of objectivity over a staggering range of issues of natural fact, subjecting these issues continuously to the joint tests of theoretical coherence and observational fidelity. "It takes its starting points outside the mind in nature," writes C. C. Gillispie, "and winnows observations of events which it gathers under concepts, to be expressed mathematically if possible and tested experimentally by their success in predicting new events and suggesting new concepts."[3] This it does in a logically deliberate and progressively more general manner, thereby providing us with a comprehensive model of the ideal of objectivity itself, stretching our earlier conceptions of its potentialities, and pointing the way to new and as yet undreamed of embodiments in a variety of realms.

What I am saying may be put summarily as follows: Current science is continuous with other areas of life, and shares with them the distinctive features of the rational quest. However, in institutionalizing this quest so as to subject an ever wider domain of claims to refined and systematic test, science has given us a new appreciation of reason itself. Since reason is, moreover, a moral as well as an intellectual notion, we have thereby been given also a new and enlarged vision of the moral standpoint—of responsibility in belief, embodied not only in a firm commitment to impartial principles by which one's own assertions are to be measured, but in a further commitment to making those principles ever more comprehensive and rigorous. Thus, though science has certainly provided us with new and critically important knowledge of man's surroundings and capacities, such enlightenment far from exhausts its human significance. A major aspect of such significance has been the moral import of science: its dynamic articulation of the impulse to responsible belief, and its suggestion of the hope of an increased rationality and responsibility in all realms of conduct and thought. . . .

The insistence on independent and controlling conditions which define standards of responsibility for the "knowing act" unifies, indeed, the main scientifically oriented philosophies of the present century. Despite their individual variations, these philosophies have been inspired by the moral example of science in the realm of belief; in their several ways they have exalted the ideal of responsible control over assertion. In so doing, they have fed into and strengthened a common philosophy of science with independent roots as well, a philosophy which has attained the status of a standard view, largely shared by reflective scientists, technical philosophers, and the educated public alike, and laying great emphasis upon the objective features of scientific thought. It is to the prospects of this standard view that I wish mainly to address myself, for I believe that it is coming increasingly under fundamental attack.

The philosophical scene is, in this respect, undergoing a radical change indeed. For the standard view has not only been widely entrenched and long taken for granted; it has also, as we have seen, enjoyed the staunch support of the dominant scientifically oriented philosophies of our day. The current attacks thus challenge not only a firm set of habitual attitudes, but also the very opposition between science and speculative idealism, from which the scientifically minded philosophies have sprung. The attacks threaten further the underlying moral motivation of these philosophies, their upholding of the ideal of responsibility in the sphere of belief as against willfulness, authoritarianism, and inertia. The issues are fundamental, indeed more fundamental than is generally realized, precisely because a powerful moral vision has implicitly been called into question. Nor is there any reasonable alternative to a critical confrontation of these issues, in the knowledge that enormously much is at stake. We must now seriously ask ourselves whether scientific objectivity is not, after all, an illusion, whether we have not, after all, been fundamentally mistaken in supposing empirical conceptions capable of responsible control by logic and experience. The question before us becomes, in short: How, if at all, is scientific objectivity possible?

In approaching this question, we shall begin by elaborating what has above been described as the "standard view" of science. Fundamentally, as we have seen, this view affirms the objectivity of science; more specifically, it understands science to be a systematic public enterprise, controlled by logic and by empirical fact, whose purpose it is to formulate the truth about the natural world. The truth primarily sought is general, expressed in laws of nature, which tell us what is always and everywhere the case. Observation, however, supplies the particular empirical facts, the hard phenomenal data which our lawlike hypotheses strive to encompass, and for which it is the ultimate purpose of such hypotheses to account.

Laws or general hypotheses may be ordered in a hierarchy of increasing generality of scope, but a basic distinction is, in any event, to be drawn between observational or experimental laws on the one hand, and theoretical laws on the other. Generalizing upon the data accessible to the senses, observational laws are couched in the language of observation and make reference to perceived things and processes. Theoretical laws, by contrast, are expressed in a more abstract idiom and typically postulate unobservable elements and functions; unlike observational laws, they cannot be subjected to the test of direct inspection or experiment. Their function is not to generalize observed phenomena, but rather to explain the laws which themselves generalize the phenomena. This they do by yielding such laws as deductive consequences of their own abstract postulations. They are, of course, indirectly testable by observation, for should one of their lawlike consequences break down on the level of experiment, such failure would count against them. However, they serve primarily to help relate diverse observational laws suitably within a comprehensive deductive scheme, and they are evaluated not only by their empirical yield but also by their simplicity, their intellectual familiarity, their accessibility to preferred models, and their manageability. They are, to be sure, also applied in the explanation of particular occurrences and in the solution of problems of prediction and control.

Any two theories of the same domain of phenomena may be compared to see if either is superior in accounting for the relevant empirical facts or, if equivalent on this score, if either surpasses the other in simplicity or convenience, etc. A hypothesis that does not itself clash with experience may yet be given up in favor of an alternative hypothesis that explains more facts or is simpler, or easier to handle. A given law may be absorbed into another, more general law by a process of reduction, through which it is shown to follow deductively from the more general law under plausible auxiliary assumptions.

When one hypothesis is superseded by another, the genuine facts it had purported to account for are not inevitably lost; they are typically passed on to its successor, which conserves them as it reaches out to embrace additional facts. Thus it is that science can be cumulative at the observational or experimental level, despite its lack of cumulativeness at the theoretical level; it strives always, and through varying theories, to save the phenomena while adding to them. And in the case of reduction, a reduced law is itself conserved, *in toto*, as a special consequence of its more general successor. Throughout the apparent flux of changing scientific beliefs, then, there is a solid growth of knowledge which represents progress in empirical understanding. Underlying historical changes of theory, there is, moreover, a constancy of logic and method, which unifies each scientific age with that which preceded it and with that which is yet to follow.

Such constancy comprises not merely the canons of formal deduction, but also those criteria by which hypotheses are confronted with the test of experience and subjected to comparative evaluation. We do not, surely, have explicit and general formulations of such criteria at the present time. But they are embodied clearly enough in scientific practice to enable communication and agreement in a wide variety of specific cases. Such communication and consensus indicate that there is a codifiable methodology underlying the conduct of the scientific enterprise. It is a methodology by which beliefs are objectively evaluated and exchanged, rather than an organon of discovery or theoretical invention. Yet it is this methodology which makes possible the cumulative growth of tested scientific knowledge as a public possession.

Now the public character of scientific procedure is not simply a matter of the free interchange of ideas. It is intimately related to the critical testing of beliefs, in the following way: If I put forward a hypothesis in scientific spirit, I suppose from the outset that I may be wrong, by independent tests to which I am prepared to submit my proposal. I suppose, in other words, that my present hypothesis is not to be prejudged as correct during the process of testing; I thus acknowledge that disagreement with

respect to my proposal is no bar to further communication, nor indeed to agreement on the test itself. Indeed, from the latter sort of communication and agreement, consensus on my proposal may eventually grow. Further, insofar as testing involves an appeal to facts disclosed in common observation of things, I suppose that the same things can be observed from different perspectives, and consensus on observation reached without presupposing agreement on relevant theory. In sum, I acknowledge the possibility of common discourse with those who may differ with me in opinion, and assume shared access to an observed world with others who may be differently located or otherwise constituted than I. The methodological publicity of science involves the assumption that differing persons may yet talk intelligibly to one another, that they may observe together the phenomena bearing critically on issues which divide them, and that they may thus join in the testing of disputed conceptions in an effort to seek resolution.

And, indeed, it seems undeniable that resolution often occurs. In the free community of scientific discourse, untrammeled by doctrinal bounds, convergence of opinion yet takes place. It seems, in fact, often to be conserved and progressively expanded, at least on the experimental level, if not on the higher level of theoretical ideas. With no attempt to shape opinion to advance specifications, with free access to evidence and no prior limitation on the community of discourse, opinion nevertheless forms and crystallizes. Does this not provide reasonable grounds for assuming that reality itself, that is to say, a world independent of human wish and will, progressively constrains our scientific beliefs? An interpretation of this sort has been colorfully expressed by Charles Peirce:

> Different minds may set out with the most antagonistic views, but the progress of investigation carries them by a force outside of themselves to one and the same conclusion. This activity of thought by which we are carried, not where we wish, but to a foreordained goal, is like the operation of destiny. No modification of the point of view taken, no selection of other

facts for study, no natural bent of mind even, can enable a man to escape the predestinate opinion. This great law is embodied in the conception of truth and reality. The opinion which is fated to be ultimately agreed to by all who investigate is what we mean by the truth, and the object represented in this opinion is the real. That is the way I would explain reality.[4]

The reality thus revealed under the methodological publicity of scientific method is, moreover, a reality in which we are ourselves but limited natural elements. Our wishes and perceptions have not made this reality, but have sprung up within it as functions of organic development in a small corner of the universe of nature. Objectivity is not only, as we have seen, a fundamental feature of scientific method; the ontological vision in which it culminates is the vision of a universe of objects with independent existences and careers, within which scientific inquiry represents but one region of connected happening and striving. In short, for the standard view I have been describing, objectivity is the end, as well as the beginning, of wisdom.

Recent attacks against this standard view have been launched from various directions. They have varied also in scope and precision, and their larger strategic import has not always been evident, even to the combatants themselves. Yet, taken together, these attacks add up, in my opinion, to a massive threat to the very possibility of objective science. Uncoordinated as they are, they have already subtly altered the balance of philosophical forces, exposing to danger the strongest positions of the objectivist viewpoint.

In dealing with this general situation, I shall divide the field into three main sectors, embracing, respectively, issues of observation, of meaning, and of scientific change. . . .

Consider then, first, the idea that observation supplies us with hard data independent of our conceptions and assertions, data by which, indeed, our conceptions and assertions are controlled. C. I. Lewis has expressed the point in terms of "the given," but the underlying notion is quite widespread and is embedded in the standard view. "The given," he writes, ". . . is what remains unaltered, no matter what our interests, no matter how we think or conceive."[5] Conception, thought, and interest may produce varying interpretations of the given, but they cannot create or change it. Strip away all interpretation contributed by the mind and you will find underneath a somewhat which is what it is as presented to sense, and which must be accepted as such, though estimates of its import may differ. Interpretation must, in short, be interpretation of something, and that something must itself be independent of interpretation if the interpretive process is not to collapse into arbitrariness.

Now it is clear that such a view promises the advantage of providing an external standard for the testing and evaluation of our thought, but is it a tenable view, and can it fulfill the promise? Can we, to begin with, accept the supposition that an unalterable observable somewhat underlies all conceptualization, interpretation, and valuation in experience? Can we even begin to imagine what it would be like to de-categorize our thought and strip away all interpretation, so as to enable the critical confrontation with a pure given, if there be such a thing? There seems to be good psychological reason to suppose that observation is not at all a bare apprehension of pure sense content, but rather an active process in which we anticipate, interpret, and structure in advance what is to be seen. There are, indeed, things right in front of our eyes that we fail to see, and things we see of which we have only the faintest clues in context—guided by expectation, we even see what is not there at all, as any proofreader knows. But if observation is never conceptually neutral, if it cannot occur without expectation and schematization, then stripping away all interpretation leaves nothing at all. And if nothing at all remains, what is there to provide an independent check on such interpretation?

A related line of thought may be developed, which presupposes no special psychological notions concerning the nature of observation, but yields what appears to be a paradox from the vantage point of the standard view. We may call it the *paradox of categorization* and explain it as follows: If my categories of thought determine what I observe, then what I observe provides no independent control over my thought. On the other hand, if my categories of thought do not determine what I observe, then what I observe must be uncategorized, that is to say, formless and nondescript—hence again incapable of providing any test of my thought. So in neither case is it possible for observation, be it what it may, to provide any independent control over thought. Nor does it help to suggest that my thought categories determine only in part, or in certain respects, what I observe. For any part or aspect thus determined can obviously provide no independent control over my thought, while every part or aspect not thus determined must remain for me formless and ineffable, hence, in particular, incapable of categorization in its bearing on my thought. Again the possibility of control over thought by observation seems to have vanished. Observation contaminated by thought yields circular tests; observation uncontaminated by thought yields no tests at all.

Now consider that, on the standard view, people with different theoretical beliefs may observe the same things; shared access to a common world is taken for granted. Yet, unless this common world is to be construed as pure formless given, hence too fluid to yield shareable objects, it must be conceived, on the contrary, as structured by particular categories of thought. It seems to follow, then, that a difference in categories destroys the common character of the world—implying, in fact, a difference in things observed. A small child, for example, sees a hard, table-shaped object resistant to his push, and capable of supporting small items placed on it, whereas a physicist sees a peculiar swarm of electrons obeying complex physical laws. More importantly, scientists with different theories categorize the objects of their observation in correspondingly different ways, and must therefore, in a critical sense, be said to see different things.

N. R. Hanson has suggested a view of this sort in certain passages of his *Patterns of Discovery*, in which he stresses the dependence of seeing upon theory, and argues against the notion that theoretical differences in a given domain must be attributed simply to differing interpretations of the same observational data. "There is a sense, then," he writes, "in which seeing is a 'theory-laden' undertaking. Observation of x is shaped by prior knowledge of x."[6] The visitor to the physicist's laboratory "must learn some physics before he can see what the physicist sees. . . . The infant and the layman can see: they are not blind. But they cannot see what the physicist sees; they are blind to what he sees."[7] To suppose "that Kepler and Tycho see the same thing at dawn just because their eyes are similarly affected is an elementary mistake. There is a difference between a physical state and a visual experience."[8] Controversy in scientific research is too deep-seated, argues Hanson, to be explained simply by appeal to differing interpretations of the same data; divisions at the theoretical level cut down through the level of data as well. "It is the sense in which Tycho and Kepler do not observe the same thing," he writes, "which must be grasped if one is to understand disagreements within microphysics."[9]

Such a line of thought seems again, however, from the perspective of the standard view, to lead to paradox. For if seeing is indeed theory-laden in the sense described, then proponents of two different theories cannot observe the same things in an effort to resolve their differences; they share no neutral observations capable of deciding between them. To judge one theory as superior to the other by appeal to observation is always doomed, therefore, to beg the very question at issue. We may call this the *paradox of common observation*. It has the effect of isolating each scientist within an observed world consonant with his theoretical beliefs.

It cannot be denied, of course, that scientists who differ theoretically may yet share a common observational or experimental vocabulary. This is indeed the basis for the differentiation made, in the standard view, between observational and theoretical levels of scientific discourse. It might thus be argued that even if theoretical differences prevent observation of common things, yet such differences allow for a shared discourse, based on the communication of common meanings. But can this be so? To adopt a new theory is, after all, to employ it not only in rethinking the phenomena, but also in reassigning the roles of relevant descriptive terms and in recasting familiar definitions and explanations. Even where there is no explicit revision of the latter sorts, a newly adopted theory alters the background of assumptions by reference to which every relevant term must be located. A new theory thus, in effect, provides new senses for old observational terms by incorporating them within a new framework of assumptions and meanings. . . .

Such conceptual displacement, if it is conceived as affecting observational as well as theoretical notions, means that the ostensible sharing of observational terms by theoretical opponents is really a delusion. There are perhaps common sounds but no common meanings. There can thus be no intelligible converse between scientists of differing theoretical persuasions. To understand another's apparently observational or experimental references, we must first enter into his theoretical thought-world.

It seems to follow, further, that we cannot literally speak of alternative theories *of the same domain*, nor of comparing these theories to see which gives a better account of the empirical facts within this domain. For there is not, and there cannot be, a neutral account of the domain in question, since the observational derivations of each theory differ in meaning from those of the other, no matter how similar they are simply as sound patterns. Nor can one law really be absorbed into another through a process of reduction, nor observational content passed on from one theory to its successor, for crucial meaning changes have occurred in the process of transfer. We have here another paradox, the *paradox of common language*, and its upshot is that there can be no real community of sci-

ence in any sense approximating that of the standard view, no comparison of theories with respect to their observational content, no reduction of one theory to another, and no cumulative growth of knowledge, at least in the standard sense. The scientist is now effectively isolated within his own system of meanings as well as within his own universe of observed things.

The breakdown of observational community and of the community of meaning, and the consequent rejection of cumulativeness seem to remove all sense from the notion of a rational progression of scientific viewpoints from age to age. If contemporary theoretical alternatives cannot be compared and evaluated with respect to their factual accuracy and comprehensiveness, neither can succeeding theoretical alternatives be thus compared and evaluated. The genesis of a new theory cannot be backed up by an established methodology of justification, such as is presupposed by the standard view; indeed, the very distinction between justification and discovery breaks down as well.

Supplementary arguments of a historical sort are, furthermore, available, to the effect that appeals to evidence are not generally decisive in the process of theoretical transition. Kuhn thus argues, on the basis of historical examples, that before the proponents of differing scientific paradigms "can hope to communicate fully, one group or the other must experience the conversion that we have been calling a paradigm shift. Just because it is a transition between incommensurables, the transition between competing paradigms cannot be made a step at a time, forced by logic and neutral experience."[10] He further writes, "No process yet disclosed by the historical study of scientific development at all resembles the methodological stereotype of falsification by direct comparison with nature."[11] And Michael Polanyi, emphasizing the "intuition of rationality in nature,"[12] argues, on the basis of his interpretation of scientific history, that knowledge in science is personal, committing us "passionately and far beyond our comprehension, to a vision of reality. Of this responsibility we cannot divest ourselves by setting up objective criteria of verifiability—or falsifiability, or testability, or what you will."[13] The general conclusion to which we appear to be driven is that adoption of a new scientific theory is an intuitive or mystical affair, a matter for psychological description primarily, rather than for logical and methodological codification.

The categories of logic and methodology indeed do give way to those of psychology, and even of politics and religion, in certain recent historical accounts of science. Kuhn thus speaks of the "gestalt switch"[14] and Polanyi of "passionate, personal, human appraisals of theories."[15] Kuhn has also employed a political vocabulary in his descriptions: he speaks of crises and revolutions, and of the victory which results in a rewriting of history so as to make progress seem inevitable. And we have already noted the reference to conversion; we now learn that converts to a new theory are made through persuasion, that the light is eventually seen, or, if not, that the new theory gains ascendancy when the opposing generation dies in the wilderness. In Planck's words, cited by Kuhn, "A new scientific truth does not triumph by convincing its opponents and making them see the light, but rather because its opponents eventually die, and a new generation grows up that is familiar with it."[16]

Finally, with cumulativeness gone, the concept of convergence of belief fails, and with it the Peircean notion of reality as progressively revealed through scientific advance. For there is no scientific advance by standard criteria, only the rivalry of theoretical viewpoints and the replacement of some by others. Reality is gone as an independent factor; each viewpoint creates its own reality. Paradigms, for Kuhn, are not only "constitutive of science"; there is a sense, he argues, "in which they are constitutive of nature as well."[17]

But now see how far we have come from the standard view. Independent and public controls are no more, communication has failed, the common universe of things is a delusion, reality itself is made by the scientist

rather than discovered by him. In place of a community of rational men following objective procedures in the pursuit of truth, we have a set of isolated monads, within each of which belief forms without systematic constraints.

I cannot, myself, believe that this bleak picture, representing an extravagant idealism, is true. In fact, it seems to me a *reductio ad absurdum* of the reasonings from which it flows. But it is easier, of course, to say this than to pinpoint the places at which these reasonings go astray.

Notes

1. Hans Reichenbach, *Experience and Prediction* (Chicago: The University of Chicago Press, 1938), chapter 1, sec. 1.

2. S. I. Benn and R. S. Peters, *Social Principles and the Democratic State* (London: George Allen and Unwin, Ltd., 1959), p. 22.

3. C. C. Gillispie, *The Edge of Objectivity* (Princeton: Princeton University Press, 1960), p. 10.

4. Charles S. Peirce, "How to Make Our Ideas Clear," *Popular Science Monthly*, XII (1878), 286–302. Reprinted in Charles S. Peirce, *Essays in the Philosophy of Science*, ed. Vincent Tomas, "The American Heritage Series" no. 17 (Indianapolis: The Bobbs-Merrill Co., Inc., 1957) pp. 31–56; for the passage cited, see Tomas, pp. 53–54.

5. Clarence Irving Lewis, *Mind and the World Order*, republication of first edition with corrections by the author (New York: Dover Publications, Inc., 1956), p. 52. First published, New York: Charles Scribner's Sons, 1929. By permission of Andrew K. Lewis.

6. Norwood Russell Hanson, *Patterns of Discovery* (Cambridge at the University Press, 1958), p. 19.

7. *Ibid.*, p. 17.

8. *Ibid.*, p. 8.

9. *Ibid.*, p. 18.

10. *The Structure of Scientific Revolutions*, p. 149.

11. *Ibid.*, p. 77.

12. Michael Polanyi, *Personal Knowledge* (Chicago: The University of Chicago Press, and London: Routledge & Kegan Paul, Ltd., 1958; revised edition, 1962), p. 16. Reprinted by permission of the publisher. Reissued, Harper Torchbook edition (New York and Evanston: Harper & Bros., 1964).

13. *Ibid.*, p. 64.

14. *The Structure of Scientific Revolutions*, p. 149.

15. *Personal Knowledge*, p. 15.

16. Max Planck, *Scientific Autobiography and Other Papers*, tr. Frank Gaynor (New York: Philosophical Library, 1949), pp. 33–34, cited in Kuhn, p. 150.

17. *The Structure of Scientific Revolutions*, p. 109.

Gender and Science

Evelyn Fox Keller

Feminist critiques of science challenge its objectivity for rather different reasons from those discussed in the previous essay. Evelyn Fox Keller explores the myth that science is masculine. She notes that this myth might partially explain the use of science and technology to dominate nature. It is also consistent with accounts of the development of objectivity in children. Early in their development, males tend to separate more completely from their mothers than do females, and as a result they tend to emphasize their separateness from objects in the world. The assumption that reality consists of independent objects to be studied dispassionately is one of the hallmarks of the masculine myth about science. Keller suggests that this myth leads to sexist and patriarchal biases in science and thus threatens objectivity. Once we become aware of the myth, however, we see the potential for a science that is not masculine. Evelyn Fox Keller is professor of the history and philosophy of science in the Science, Technology, and Society Program at MIT.

As you read through this essay, consider the following:

1. How does Keller support her claims about the "genderization of science"?
2. What does Keller mean by "objectivity"? Does she mean the same thing that Scheffler did in the previous essay?
3. According to Keller, how do we develop our capacity for objectivity? How does the process differ for males and females?
4. How does Keller suggest that the genderization of science affects its objectivity? How might it affect the status of women?
5. Do you find evidence in your experience that science is associated with the masculine?

The requirements of . . . correctness in practical judgments and objectivity in theoretical knowledge . . . belong as it were in their form and their claims to humanity in general, but in their actual historical configuration they are masculine throughout. Supposing that we describe these things, viewed as absolute ideas, by the single word "objective," we then find that in the history of our race the equation objective = masculine is a valid one.
—Simmel, quoted by Horney (1926, p. 200)

In articulating the commonplace, Simmel steps outside the convention of academic discourse. The historically pervasive association

From Evelyn Fox Keller, *Reflections on Gender and Science* (New Haven: Yale University Press, 1985). Copyright © 1985 Yale University. Reprinted by permission.

between masculine and objective, more specifically between masculine and scientific, is a topic that academic critics resist taking seriously. Why is that? Is it not odd that an association so familiar and so deeply entrenched is a topic only for informal discourse, literary allusion, and popular criticism? How is it that formal criticism in the philosophy and sociology of science has failed to see here a topic requiring analysis? The virtual silence of at least the nonfeminist academic community on this subject suggests that the association of masculinity with scientific thought has the status of a myth which either cannot or should not be examined seriously. It has simultaneously the air of being "self-evident" and "nonsensical"—the former by virtue of existing in the realm of common knowledge (that is, everyone knows it), and the latter by virtue of lying outside the realm of formal knowledge, indeed conflicting with our image of science as emotionally and sexually neutral. Taken seriously, it would suggest that, were more women to engage in science, a different science might emerge. Such an idea, although sometimes expressed by nonscientists, clashes openly with the formal view of science as being uniquely determined by its own logical and empirical methodology.

The survival of mythlike beliefs in our thinking about science, the very archetype of antimyth, ought, it would seem, to invite our curiosity and demand investigation. Unexamined myths, wherever they survive, have a subterranean potency; they affect our thinking in ways we are not aware of, and to the extent that we lack awareness, our capacity to resist their influence is undermined. The presence of the mythical in science seems particularly inappropriate. What is it doing there? From where does it come? And how does it influence our conceptions of science, of objectivity, or, for that matter, of gender?

These are the questions I wish to address, but before doing so it is necessary to clarify and elaborate the system of beliefs in which science acquires a gender—a system that amounts to a "genderization" of science. Let me make clear at the outset that the issue that requires discussion is *not*, or at least not simply, the relative absence of women in science. Although it is true that most scientists have been, and continue to be, men, the makeup of the scientific population hardly accounts, by itself, for the attribution of masculinity to science as an intellectual domain. Most culturally validated intellectual and creative endeavors have, after all, historically been the domain of men. Few of these endeavors, however, bear so unmistakably the connotation of masculine in the very nature of the activity. To both scientists and their public, scientific thought is male thought, in ways that painting and writing—also performed largely by men—have never been. As Simmel observed, objectivity itself is an ideal that has a long history of identification with masculinity. The fact that the scientific population is,

even now, a population that is overwhelmingly male, is itself a consequence rather than a cause of the attribution of masculinity to scientific thought.[1] What requires discussion is a *belief* rather than a reality, although the ways in which reality is shaped by our beliefs are manifold and also need articulating.

How does this belief manifest itself? It used to be commonplace to hear scientists, teachers, and parents assert quite baldly that women cannot, should not, be scientists, that they lack the strength, rigor, and clarity of mind for an occupation that properly belongs to men. Now that the women's movement has made such naked assertions offensive, open acknowledgment of the continuing belief in the intrinsic masculinity of scientific thought has become less fashionable. It continues, however, to find daily expression in the language and metaphors we use to describe science. When we dub the objective sciences "hard" as opposed to the softer (that is, more subjective) branches of knowledge, we implicitly invoke a sexual metaphor, in which "hard" is of course masculine and "soft" feminine. Quite generally, facts are "hard," feelings "soft." "Feminization" has become synonymous with sentimentalization. A woman thinking scientifically or objectively is thinking "like a man"; conversely, a man pursuing a nonrational, nonscientific argument is arguing "like a woman."

The linguistic rooting of this stereotype is not lost among children, who remain perhaps the most outspoken and least selfconscious about its expression. From strikingly early ages, even in the presence of astereotypic role models, children learn to identify mathematics and science as male. "Science," my five-year-old son declared, confidently bypassing the fact that his mother was a scientist, "is for men!" The identification between scientific thought and masculinity is so deeply embedded in the culture at large that children have little difficulty internalizing it. They grow up not only expecting scientists to be men but also perceiving scientists as more "masculine" than other male professionals—for example, those in the arts.

Numerous studies of masculinity and femininity in the professions confirm this observation, with the "harder" sciences as well as the "harder" branches of any profession consistently characterized as more masculine.

In one particularly interesting study of attitudes prevalent among English schoolboys, a somewhat different but critically related dimension of the cultural stereotype emerges. Hudson (1972) observes that scientists are perceived as not only more masculine than artists but simultaneously as less sexual. He writes:

> The arts are associated with sexual pleasure, the sciences with sexual restraint. The arts man is seen as having a good-looking, well-dressed wife with whom he enjoys a warm sexual relation; the scientist as having a wife who is dowdy and dull, and in whom he has no physical interest. Yet the scientist is seen as masculine, the arts specialist as slightly feminine. (p. 83)

In this passage we see the genderization of science linked with another, also widely perceived, image of science as antithetical to Eros. These images are not unrelated, and it is important to bear their juxtaposition in mind as we attempt to understand their sources and functions. What is at issue here is the kind of images and metaphors with which science is surrounded. If we can take the use of metaphor seriously, while managing to keep clearly in mind that it is metaphor and language which are being discussed, then we can attempt to understand the influences they might exert—how the use of language and metaphor can become hardened into a kind of reality.

Much attention has been given recently to the technological abuses of modern science, and in many of these discussions blame is directed toward the distortions of the scientific program intrinsic in its ambition to dominate nature without, however, offering an adequate explanation of how that ambition comes to be intrinsic to science. Generally such distortions are attributed to technology, or applied science, which is presumed to be clearly distinguishable from pure science. In

the latter the ambition is supposed to be pure knowledge, uncontaminated by fantasies of control. Although it is probably true that the domination of nature is a more central feature of technology, it is impossible to draw a clear line between pure and applied science. History reveals a most complex relation between the two, as complex perhaps as the interrelation between the dual constitutive motives for knowledge: transcendence and power. It would be naive to suppose that the connotations of masculinity and conquest affect only the uses to which science is put and leave its structure untouched.

Science bears the imprint of its genderization not only in the ways it is used but in the description of reality it offers—even in the relation of the scientist to that description. To see this, it is necessary to examine more fully the implications of attributing masculinity to the very nature of scientific thought.

Having divided the world into two parts—the knower (mind) and the knowable (nature)—scientific ideology goes on to prescribe a very specific relation between the two. It prescribes the interactions which can consummate this union, that is, which can lead to knowledge. Not only are mind and nature assigned gender, but in characterizing scientific and objective thought as masculine, the very activity by which the knower can acquire knowledge is also genderized. The relation specified between knower and known is one of distance and separation. It is that between a subject and an object radically divided, which is to say, no worldly relation. Simply put, nature is objectified. Bacon's "chaste and lawful marriage" is consummated through reason rather than feeling, through "observation" rather than "immediate" sensory experience. The modes of intercourse are defined so as to ensure emotional and physical inviolability for the subject. Concurrent with the division of the world into subject and object is, accordingly, a division of the forms of knowledge into "subjective" and "objective." The scientific mind is set apart from what is to be known, that is, from nature, and its autonomy—and hence the reciprocal autonomy of the object—is guaranteed (or so it had traditionally been assumed) by setting apart its modes of knowing from those in which that dichotomy is threatened. In this process, the characterization of both the scientific mind and its modes of access to knowledge as masculine is indeed significant. Masculine here connotes, as it so often does, autonomy, separation, and distance. It connotes a radical rejection of any commingling of subject and object, which are, it now appears, quite consistently identified as male and female.

What is the real significance of this system of beliefs, whose structure now reveals an intricate admixture of metaphysics, cognitive style, and sexual metaphor? If we reject the position, as I believe we must, that the associations between scientific and masculine are simply "true"—that they reflect a biological difference between male and female brains—then how are we to account for our adherence to them? Whatever intellectual or personality characteristics may be affected by sexual hormones, it has become abundantly clear that our ideas about the differences between the sexes far exceed what can be traced to mere biology; that, once formed, these ideas take on a life of their own—a life sustained by powerful cultural and psychological forces. Even the brief discussion offered above makes it evident that, in attributing gender to an intellectual posture, in sexualizing a thought process, we inevitably invoke the large world of affect. The task of explaining the associations between masculine and scientific thus becomes, short of reverting to an untenable biological reductionism, the task of understanding the emotional substructure that links our experience of gender with our cognitive experience.

The nature of the problem suggests that, in seeking an explanation of the origins and endurance of this mythology, we look to the processes by which the capacity for scientific thought develops, and the ways in which those processes are intertwined with emo-

tional and sexual development. Doing this makes it possible to acquire deeper insight into the structure and perhaps even the functions of the mythology we seek to elucidate. The route I wish to take proceeds along ground laid by psychoanalysts and cognitive psychologists, along a course shaped by the particular questions I have posed. What emerges is a scenario supported by the insights these workers have attained, and held together, it is to be hoped, by its own logical and intuitive coherence.

THE DEVELOPMENT OF OBJECTIVITY

The crucial insight that underlies much of this discussion—an insight for which we are indebted to both Freud and Piaget—is that the capacity for objectivity, for delineating subject from object, is *not* inborn, although the potential for it no doubt is. Rather, the ability to perceive reality "objectively" is acquired as an inextricable part of the long and painful process by which the child's sense of self is formed. In the deepest sense, it is a function of the child's capacity for distinguishing self from not-self, "me" from "not-me." The consolidation of this capacity is perhaps the major achievement of childhood development.

After half a century's clinical observations of children and adults the developmental picture that has emerged is as follows. In the early world of the infant, experiences of thoughts, feelings, events, images, and perceptions are continuous. Boundaries have not yet been drawn to distinguish the child's internal from external environment; nor has order or structure been imposed on either.[2] The external environment, for most children consisting primarily of the mother during this early period, is experienced as an extension of the child. It is only through the assimilation of cumulative experiences of pleasure and pain, of gratification and disappointment, that the child slowly learns to distinguish between self and other, between image and percept, between subject and object. The growing ability to distinguish his or her self from the environment allows for the recognition of an external reality to which the child can relate—at first magically, and ultimately objectively. In the course of time, the inanimate becomes released from the animate, objects from their perspective, and events from wishes; the child becomes capable of objective thought and perception. The process by which this development occurs proceeds through sequential and characteristic stages of cognitive growth, stages that have been extensively documented and described by Piaget and his co-workers.

The background of this development is fraught with intense emotional conflict. The primary object that the infant carves out of the matrix of his/her experiences is an emotional "object," namely, the mother. And along with the emergence of the mother as a separate being comes the child's painful recognition of his/her own separate existence. Anxiety is unleashed, and longing is born. The child (infant) discovers dependency and need—and a primitive form of love. Out of the demarcation between self and mother arises a longing to undo that differentiation, an urge to reestablish the original unity. At the same time, there is also growing pleasure in autonomy, which itself comes to feel threatened by the lure of an earlier state. The process of emotional delineation proceeds in fits and starts, propelled and inhibited by conflicting impulses, desires, and fears. The parallel process of cognitive delineation must be negotiated against the background of these conflicts. As objects acquire a separate identity, they remain for a long time tied to the self by a network of magical ties. The disentanglement of self from world, and of thoughts from things, requires relinquishing the magical bonds that have kept them connected. It requires giving up the belief in the omnipotence—now of the child, now of the mother—that perpetuates those bonds and learning to tolerate the limits and separateness of both. It requires enduring the loss of a wish-dominated existence in exchange for the rewards of living "in reality." In doing so, the child moves from the egocentricity of a self-dominated contiguous world to the recognition of a world outside and independent of him/herself: a world in which objects can take on a "life" of their own.

Thus far my description has followed the standard developmental account. The recognition of the independent reality of both self and other is a necessary precondition both for science and for love. It may not, however, be sufficient—for either. Certainly the capacity for love, for empathy, for artistic creativity requires more than a simple dichotomy between subject and object. Autonomy too sharply defined, reality too rigidly defined, cannot encompass the emotional and creative experiences that give life its fullest and richest depth. Autonomy must be conceived of more dynamically and reality more flexibly if they are to allow for the ebb and flow of love and play. Emotional growth does not end with the mere acceptance of one's own separateness; perhaps it is fair to say that it begins there. Out of a condition of emotional and cognitive union with the mother, the child gradually gains enough confidence in the enduring reality of both him/herself and the environment to tolerate their separateness and mutual independence. A sense of self becomes delineated, in opposition, as it were, to the mother. Ultimately, however, both sense of self and of other become sufficiently secure to permit momentary relaxation of the boundary between—without, that is, threatening the loss of either. One has acquired confidence in the enduring survival of both self and other as vitally autonomous. Out of this recognition and acceptance of one's aloneness in the world, it becomes possible to transcend one's isolation, to truly love another.[3] The final step—of reintroducing ambiguity into one's relation to the world—is a difficult one. It evokes deep anxieties and fears stemming from old conflicts and older desire. The ground of one's selfhood was not easily won, and experiences that appear to threaten the loss of that ground can be seen as acutely dangerous. Milner (1957), in seeking to understand the essence of what makes a drawing "alive," and conversely, the inhibitions that impede artistic expression, has written with rare perspicacity and eloquence about the dangers and anxieties attendant upon opening ourselves to the creative perception so critical for a successful drawing. But unless we can, the world of art is foreclosed to us. Neither love nor art can survive the exclusion of a dialogue between dream and reality, between inside and outside, between subject and object. . . .

. . . It is important to recognize that, although children of both sexes must learn equally to distinguish self from other and have essentially the same need for autonomy, to the extent that boys rest their sexual identity on an opposition to what is both experienced and defined as feminine, the development of their gender identity is likely to accentuate the process of separation. As boys, they must undergo a twofold "disidentification from mother" (Greenson 1968): first for the establishment of a self-identity, and second for the consolidation of a male gender identity. Further impetus is added to this process by the external cultural pressure on the young boy to establish a stereotypic masculinity, now culturally as well as privately connoting independence and autonomy. The traditional cultural definitions of masculine as what can never appear feminine and of autonomy as what can never be relaxed conspire to reinforce the child's earliest associations of female with the pleasures and dangers of merging, and male with both the comfort and the loneliness of separateness. The boy's internal anxiety about both self and gender is here echoed by the cultural anxiety; together they can lead to postures of exaggerated and rigidified autonomy and masculinity that can—indeed that may be designed to—defend against the anxiety and the longing that generates it. Many psychoanalysts have come to believe that, because of the boy's need to switch his identification from the mother to the father, his sense of gender identity tends always to be more fragile than the girl's. On the other hand, her sense of self-identity may be comparatively more vulnerable. It has been suggested that

the girl's development of a sense of separateness may be to some degree hampered by her ongoing identification with her mother. Although she too must disentangle her "self" from the early experience of oneness, she continues to look toward her mother as a model for her gender identity. Whatever vicissitudes her relation to her mother may suffer during subsequent development, a strong identification based on common gender is likely to persist—her need for "disidentification" is not so radical. Cultural forces may further complicate her development of autonomy by stressing dependency and subjectivity as feminine characteristics. To the extent that such traits become internalized, they can be passed on through the generations by leading to an accentuation of the symbiotic bond between mother and daughter. . . .

Thus it seems appropriate to suggest that one possible outcome of these processes is that boys may be more inclined toward excessive and girls toward inadequate delineation: growing into men who have difficulty loving and women who retreat from science. What I am suggesting, and indeed trying to describe, is a network of interactions between gender development, a belief system that equates objectivity with masculinity, and a set of cultural values that simultaneously (and conjointly) elevates what is defined as scientific and what is defined as masculine. The structure of this network is such as to perpetuate and exacerbate distortions in *any* of its parts—including the acquisition of gender identity.

THE DEVELOPMENT OF SCIENTISTS

Whatever differences between the sexes such a network might generate (and, as I have said earlier, the existence of such differences remains ultimately an empirical question), they are in any case certain to be overshadowed by the inevitably large variations that exist within both the male and female populations. Not all men become scientists. A science that advertises itself as revealing a reality in which subject and object are unmistakably distinct may perhaps offer special comfort to those who, as individuals (be they male or female), retain particular anxiety about the loss of autonomy. In short, if we can take the argument presented thus far seriously, then we must follow it through yet another step. Would not a characterization of science which appears to gratify particular emotional needs give rise to a self-selection of scientists—a self-selection that would, in turn, lead to a perpetuation of that same characterization? Without attempting a detailed discussion of either the appropriateness of the imagery with which science is advertised or of the personality characteristics such imagery might select for, it seems reasonable to suggest that such a selection mechanism ought inevitably to operate. The persistence of the characterization of science as masculine, as objectivist, as autonomous of psychological as well as of social and political forces, would then be encouraged, through such selection, by the kinds of emotional satisfaction it provides.

If so, the question that then arises is whether, statistically, scientists do indeed tend to be more anxious about their affective as well as cognitive autonomy than nonscientists. Although it is certainly part of the popular image of scientists that they do, the actual measurement of personality differences between scientists and nonscientists has proven to be extremely difficult; it is as difficult, and subject to as much disagreement, as the measurement of personality differences between the sexes. One obvious difficulty arises out of the term *scientist*, and the enormous heterogeneity of the scientific population. Apart from the vast differences among individuals, characteristics vary across time, nationality, discipline, and, even, with degree of eminence. The Einsteins of history fail, virtually by definition, to conform to more general patterns either of personality or of intellect. Nevertheless, certain themes, however difficult they may be to pin down, continually reemerge with enough prominence to warrant consideration. These are the themes, or stereotypes, on which I have concentrated throughout this essay, and though they can nei-

ther exhaustively nor accurately describe science or scientists as a whole—as stereotypes never can—they do acquire a degree of corroboration from the literature on the "scientific personality." It seems worth noting, therefore, several features that emerge from a number of efforts to describe the personality characteristics which tend to distinguish scientists from nonscientists.

I have already referred to the fact that scientists, particularly physical scientists, score unusually high on "masculinity" tests, meaning only that, on the average, their responses differ greatly from those of women. At the same time, studies (for example, Roe 1953, 1956) report that they tend overwhelmingly to have been loners as children, to be low in social interests and skills, indeed to avoid interpersonal contact. McClelland's subsequent studies confirm these impressions. He writes: "And it is a fact, as Anne Roe reports, that young scientists are typically not very interested in girls, date for the first time late in college, marry the first girl they date, and thereafter appear to show a rather low level of heterosexual drive" (1962, p. 321). One of McClelland's especially interesting findings was that 90 percent of a group of eminent scientists see, in the "mother–son" picture routinely given as part of the Thematic Apperception Test, "the mother and son going their separate ways" (p. 323), a relatively infrequent response to this picture in the general population. It conforms, however, with the more general observation (emerging from biographical material) of a distant relation to the mother,[4] frequently coupled with "open or covert attitudes of derogation" (Roe 1956, p. 215).

Though these remarks are admittedly sketchy and by no means constitute a review of the field, they do suggest a personality profile that seems admirably suited to an occupation seen as simultaneously masculine and asexual. The Baconian image of a "chaste and lawful marriage" becomes remarkably apt insofar as it allows the scientist both autonomy and mastery in his marriage to a bride kept at safe, "objectified" remove.[5]

CONCLUSION

It is impossible to conclude a discussion of the genderization of science without making some brief comments on its social implications. The linking of scientific and objective with masculine brings in its wake a host of secondary consequences that, however self-evident, may nevertheless need articulating. Not only does our characterization of science thereby become colored by the biases of patriarchy and sexism, but simultaneously our evaluation of masculine and feminine becomes affected by the prestige of science. A circular process of mutual reinforcement is established in which what is called scientific receives extra validation from the cultural preference for what is called masculine, and, conversely, what is called feminine—be it a branch of knowledge, a way of thinking, or woman herself—becomes further devalued by its exclusion from the special social and intellectual value placed on science and the model science provides for all intellectual endeavors. This circularity not only operates on the level of ideology but is assisted by the ways in which the developmental processes, both for science and for the child, internalize ideological influences. For each, pressures from the other operate, in the ways I have attempted to describe, to effect biases and perpetuate caricatures.

Neither in emphasizing the self-sustaining nature of these beliefs, nor in relating them to early childhood experience do I wish to suggest that they are inevitable. On the contrary, by examining their dynamics I mean to emphasize the existence of alternative possibilities. The disengagement of our thinking about science from our notions of what is masculine could lead to a freeing of both from some of the rigidities to which they have been bound, with profound ramifications for both. Not only, for example, might science become more accessible to women, but, far more importantly, our very conception of "objective" could be freed from inappropriate constraints. As we begin to understand the ways in which science itself has been influenced by its unconscious mythology, we can begin to perceive the possibilities for a science not bound by such mythology.

Notes

1. For a further elaboration of this theme, see "Women in Science: A Social Analysis" (Keller 1974).

2. Since this article was first published, new research in infant studies has produced increasing evidence challenging the sweep of these assumptions (see Stern 1983). Although this evidence does not alter the essential structure of my own argument, it will undoubtedly give rise to future modifications in our understanding of developmental dynamics. . . .

3. See, e.g., Kernberg (1977) for a psychoanalytic discussion of love.

4. These studies are, as is evident, of male scientists. It is noteworthy, however, that studies of the relatively small number of female scientists reveal a similar, perhaps even more marked, pattern of distance in relations to the mother. For most, the father proved to be the parent of primary emotional and intellectual importance (see, e.g., Plank and Plank 1954).

5. Earlier I pointed out how Bacon's marital imagery constitutes an invitation to the "domination of nature." A fuller discussion of this posture would also require consideration of the role of aggression in the development of object relations and symbolic thought processes (an aspect that has been omitted from the present discussion). It has been suggested by Winnicott that the act of severing subject from object is experienced by the child as an act of violence, and that it carries with it forever, on some level, the feeling tone of aggression. Winnicott observes that "it is the destructive drive that creates the quality of externality" (p. 93), that, in the creation and recognition of the object there is always, and inevitably, an implicit act of destruction. Indeed, he says, "It is the destruction of the object that places the object outside the area of the subject's omnipotent control" (p. 90). Its ultimate survival is, of course, crucial for the child's development. "In other words, because of the survival of the object, the subject may now have started to live in the world of objects, and so the subject stands to gain immeasurably; but the price has to be paid in acceptance of the ongoing destruction in unconscious fantasy relative to object-relating" (p. 90). It seems likely that the aggressive force implicit in this act of objectification must make its subsequent appearance in the relation between the scientist and his object, that is, between science and nature.

References

Greeson, R. 1968. "Disidentifying from Mother: Its Special Importance for the Boy." *Explorations in Psychoanalysis*. New York: International Universities Press.

Horney, Karen. 1926. "The Flight from Womanhood." In *Women and Analysis*, ed. J. Strouse. New York: Dell, 1975.

Hudson, L. 1927. *The Cult of the Fact*. New York: Harper & Row.

Keller, Evelyn Fox. 1974. "Women in Science: A Social Analysis." *Harvard Magazine*, October, pp. 14–19.

Kernberg, O. 1977. "Boundaries and Structure in Love Relations." *Journal of the American Psychoanalytic Association* 25, pp. 81–114.

McClelland, D. C. 1962. "On the Dynamics of Creative Physical Scientists." In *The Ecology of Human Intelligence*, ed. L. Hudson. Harmondsworth: Penguin Books.

Milner, Marion. 1957. *On Not Being Able to Paint*. New York: International Universities Press.

Plank, E. N., and R. Plank. 1954. "Emotional Components in Arithmetic Learning as Seen Through Auto-

biographies." *The Psychoanalytic Study of the Child 9*. New York: International Universities Press.

Roe, A. 1953. *The Making of a Scientist*. New York: Dodd, Mead.

———. 1956. *The Psychology of Occupations*. New York: Wiley.

Stern, Daniel. 1983. "The Early Development of Schemas of Self, Other, and 'Self with Other.'" *Reflections of Self Psychology*, ed. J. D. Lichtenberg and S. Kaplan. New York: International Universities Press.

Winnicott, D. W. 1971. *Playing and Reality*. New York: Basic Books.

Science and Values

Patrick Grim

Because many believe that values are subjective, they think that science is either objective and value-free or value-laden and consequently no better than other subjective world-views. In this essay, Patrick Grim argues that neither of these views is justified. Science must operate against a background of values that determines when risks are acceptable and when evidence is sufficient for belief. Science also essentially involves certain core values; it pursues truth and demands that belief be demonstrated. Although the background values may shift and thereby alter the theories that are justified, Grim maintains that this does not imply that nonscientific approaches to belief are on a par with science. Indeed, he thinks that the core values of science recommend it as a way of acquiring belief. Patrick Grim is professor of philosophy at the State University of New York, Stonybrook.

As you read through this essay, consider the following:

1. How does Grim argue that science is not value-free? What does he mean by saying that science is "shaped by background values"?
2. Why does Grim believe that changes in a culture's ethical values can legitimately affect its scientific claims?
3. How does Grim distinguish between essential and nonessential values in science? What values are essential to science?
4. Why does Grim reject the claim that the choice between science and its "rivals" is a choice between different arbitrary value systems?
5. Do you agree with Grim that the essential scientific values provide reasons for accepting scientific ways of acquiring beliefs?
6. Does the presence of values in science reduce its claim to objectivity?

In that vague realm known as the popular imagination, science is quite frequently conceived of as something that stands apart from values. Science is thought of as value-free, and this supposed freedom from values is thought to be one of its prime virtues. On one side of a fact-value gap lies the quarrelsome morass of bickering values; arbitrary, indefinite, and perhaps merely subjective. On the other side of the gap, pristine and pure, untainted by mere values, stands the imposing edifice of science.

In what follows I hope to challenge this popular image of science and values. The claim that science is or even could be value-free, I shall argue, is simply false.

But at this point it is tempting to replace the first image of science and values with a second image, an image that itself boasts no small measure of current popularity. If science does not stand apart from the morass of values, it seems, it must be but one among many rival "value systems" bogged down in that morass. There is then nothing special to be said for science that could not be said with equal justice for any of its rivals. Any favoring of science over rival "systems" becomes a matter of personal and idiosyncratic taste, ultimately as arbitrary and subjective as any other choice of values.

This second image of science and values, I shall argue, is as wrong as the first. Science is shaped by and is essentially committed to certain values. But I hope to show that because of the *ways* in which science is shaped by values and because of the *particular* values to which it is committed, it does not follow that science is on all fours with any other "system" of values. Nor does it follow that the choice becomes arbitrary between science and Edward Conze's Buddhism, or William James's mysticism, or Carlos Castaneda's Yaqui sorcery.[1]

In order to answer this question we need some sketch or outline or indication, however rough, of what we are to take as "science." But any attempt to define "science" with accuracy, or to offer necessary and sufficient conditions for properly scientific procedure, is bound to embroil us immediately in the devastating difficulties of demarcation. So let us settle, at least initially, for something less: a rough and ready characterization of science in terms of lists of claims.

We are all familiar with a large number of scientific claims; claims such as the following:

(1) Water freezes at 32° F.
(2) Most calico cats are female.
(3) Hydrogen is composed of one proton and one electron.
(4) Syphilis is caused by a spirochete.

(1) through (4) are claims currently accepted, on grounds of scientific study and research, within the scientific community. And at least one way to characterize the science of our times would be in terms of a list, indefinitely large or infinite, of all such scientific claims.

Let us thus envisage such a list of scientific claims. We need not hold that any science at any time will share these claims; it is enough that our current science can be so represented, whatever inevitable discoveries or refutations the future will bring.

With this rough and ready characterization of current science we have at least one way of trying to determine whether science is value-free. Are there any value judgments in the list we have envisaged? If so, it would appear, we have good grounds for concluding that at least *our* science is not value-free. If there are no value judgments in the list, we have at least some basis for claiming that science *is* value-free.

Consider in this regard (1) through (4) above. None of these, I think, is a very promising candidate for a "value judgment." And if our complete list of current scientific claims were composed entirely of claims like (1) through (4), we would have at least some grounds for maintaining that science *is* value-free.

But (1) through (4) are only some of the claims on our list. (5) and (6), for example, would appear to have an equal right to be included among current scientific claims:

(5) Smoking is hazardous to your health.
(6) Contemporary handling of nuclear wastes is unsafe.[2]

We can also expect to find on our list claims concerning other claims, such as (7) and (8):

(7) We have compelling evidence that smoking causes cancer.

(8) It has not yet been satisfactorily established that the use of high-sulfur coal poses a significant environmental risk.

Any list of currently accepted scientific claims that did not include claims such as (5) through (8), I think, would clearly be an inadequate and incomplete list. But it can at least be argued that claims such as (5) through (8) embody value judgments, and thus that at least our current science is not value-free.

Consider claims (5), (6), and (8). (5) invokes a notion of health and of hazards to health. But health, some have argued, is itself a term to which values are crucial. A healthy organism is one that is as it *should* be, and a hazard to health is a *threat*—something that at least prima facie ought to be avoided for the sake of *proper* functioning.[3] Consider also the notions of safety and of risk that appear in (6) and (8). To claim that a situation is unsafe is surely to claim that it jeopardizes something of *value*, and to speak of risk is to speak of probabilities of *loss*. The notions of safety and risk, then, like that of health, appear to assume a particular background of values. Were human lives held to be of no more value than lives of wood lice, we would not speak scientifically of risk and safety in the ways we do. Many of our scientific claims *do* concern risk and safety, and thus assume a background of values.

Consider also a slightly different argument. Claims (7) and (8) invoke notions of compelling evidence and of the satisfactory establishment of claims. And surely any science worth its salt will include claims of this sort concerning the establishment of other claims. But "compelling evidence" and "satisfactory establishment," it can be argued, assume the same sort of background of values as indicated above for "safety" and "risk." Richard Rudner has put this point quite elegantly:

since no scientific hypothesis is ever completely verified, in accepting the hypothesis the scientist must make the decision that the evidence is *sufficiently* strong or that the probability is *suffi-ciently* high to warrant the acceptance of the hypothesis. Obviously our decision regarding the evidence and respecting how strong is "strong enough," is going to be a function of the *importance*, in the typically ethical sense, of making a mistake in accepting or rejecting the hypothesis. Thus, to take a crude but easily manageable example, if the hypothesis under consideration were to the effect that a toxic ingredient of a drug was not present in lethal quantity, we would require a relatively high degree of confirmation or confidence before accepting the hypothesis—for the consequences of making a mistake here are exceedingly grave by our moral standards. On the other hand, if, say, our hypothesis stated that, on the basis of a sample, a certain lot of machine stamped belt buckles was not defective, the degree of confidence we should require would be relatively not so high. *How sure we need to be before we accept a hypothesis will depend on how serious a mistake would be.*[4]

It thus appears, on several grounds, that science is not value-free.[5] Let us state our conclusions here in as strong a form as possible. Some scientific claims concern health, safety, hazard, and risk, and each of these seems to make sense only against a general background of values. Some scientific claims concern compelling evidence, adequate establishment, and sufficiently high probability for the acceptance of other claims. These claims, on Rudner's argument, rely on a similar background of values. But here we can also say more. The envisaged list of claims we have appealed to throughout is a list of claims currently accepted within the scientific community. If so, each claim is presumably on the list because it has been accepted on grounds of "compelling evidence," "adequate establishment," or "sufficiently high probability." Thus the inclusion of *each* item on the list, even of items as apparently dispassionate as (1) through (4), will reflect the general background of values that Rudner indicates. *Some* claims on the list will invoke values in virtue of their content; for example, those that address issues of health, risk, or sufficient establishment. But regardless of its content, the presence of *each* claim on the list will reflect its acceptability in terms of background values.

In Rudner's sense, then, *all* science is shaped by values. We might also note that in principle almost any background value might do the shaping. The scientific acceptability of a claim will depend on the prospects of accepting it or not, and on the relative values we place on those prospects. Almost any value concerns the relative merit of alternative prospects, and almost any value will rank alternatives in some way. Thus in principle almost any value might be of importance for the scientific acceptability of some claim, and in that sense almost any value could be of significance in shaping science.

We have presented in some detail an argument to the effect that science is not value-free. If this argument is adequate, it appears that the first popular image of science and values presented in our introduction is drastically misconceived.

What replies to the argument above might be made in behalf of a notion of "value-free" science? Let us briefly consider two possible replies.

First, it must be noted that the list of claims with which we have been working is merely a list of *current* scientific claims. But no argument on this basis alone, it might be argued, will suffice to show that science *could* not be value-free.

This reply does seem telling, as far as it goes, against the first part of the argument presented above. A science that did not address questions of health, hazard, safety, or risk would to that extent avoid certain questions of value. Thus science *could* escape values to some extent by confining its claims to those such as (1) through (4) and avoiding claims such as (5) through (8).[6]

But this reply does not seem adequate against the full force of Rudner's argument. Surely *any* science must accept and reject claims on the basis of adequate warrant, compelling evidence, sufficiently high probability, and the like. If any such acceptance and rejection of claims demands a background of values, then any science must

assume some such background of values. In that respect, although we have been working with a rough characterization of *current* science, our conclusions would appear to apply as well to any science at any time.

Consider also a second possible reply. What we have taken as "science," it might be argued, is not science *proper* or science *per se* but instead the everyday management, administration, and application of science. The management of science, it might be conceded, is shaped by background values. But science per se is nevertheless value-free. The scientist qua scientist neither accepts nor rejects hypotheses; he merely assigns probabilities to various hypotheses at issue.[7]

By carefully gerrymandering a distinction between "science per se" and the mere "management" of science one could, I think, carve out as "science per se" something that was value-free. But I seriously question the point of any stipulative linguistic exercise of this type. That which one would end up idolizing as "pure science" would be a barely recognizable amputation from current practice, consisting of little more than the mindless manipulation of test tubes and the mechanical marking of charts. It would not be what we think of as science and would not be science as we know it. It would fit best the work of those technicians who know least what they are doing, if it would fit the practice of any working scientist at all, and would relegate to a category of "mere management" the most important work of every Nobel Prize winner we have. If that is the cost of maintaining that science is value-free, we had better simply concede that it is not.

TWO TYPES OF SCIENTIFIC VALUES

Rudner's argument shows that standard scientific notions of "adequate establishment," "compelling evidence," and "sufficiently high probability" assume a background of values. In that sense we might conclude that science is "value-laden." But here it is important to consider precisely *what* values are at issue and precisely *how* science is "laden."

Rudner's argument shows that science is shaped by a background of values. But the argument does not show that any particular set of values must do the shaping. Our current science, perhaps, relies on a particular background of values. And all science, perhaps, must rely on *some* such background. But science *could* nevertheless assume a quite different background of values.

Because we value human life to the extent that we do, and because we do not value chimpanzee life more than we do, we are more wary of accepting claims regarding lethal quantities of food additives as "adequately established" where human lives, and not merely chimpanzees, are at stake. If we valued human life less, or chimpanzee life more, our list of "adequately established" claims could be expected to shift. Similarly, if we ranked Rudner's machine-stamped belt buckles as on a par with original Rembrandts, we could expect our list of acceptable claims to change. Different values would then bear on what establishment we took to be adequate establishment, and as a result different claims would be accepted as adequately established.

But would a science shaped by different values in this way be any less a science? I think not. Although *some* set of values must in this way serve as background for notions of sufficient evidence and adequate establishment, it need not be any particular set of values.[8] Were our values regarding human lives and chimpanzee lives to change tomorrow, which claims we found scientifically acceptable or sufficiently warranted might change as well. But that would not render our current work with either humans or chimpanzees unscientific.

One moral to draw from this is that changes in the ethical values of a society can change its science in subtle but important ways. We might also draw another moral: the fact that a particular set of values shapes scientific practice at any particular time is not necessarily any vindication of that set of values. Nazi science, for example, might well rely on Nazi values. Claims regarding lethal quantities of food additives might be differently treated where Aryans and non-Aryans are at stake much as we treat such claims differently where humans and chimpanzees are at stake. If some sets of values can be twisted or perverse, some forms of science—those forms of science that rely on such values—can be equally perverse.

The background of values that Rudner points out in science is a background that may shift. In that sense the background values that have so far been indicated for our science are what I will term *nonessential* values; science would still be science were these values to be replaced by others.

Are there also *essential* values within science; values such that any "science" that abandoned or replaced those values would no longer be science?[9] Here I want to consider first some values that might be proposed as essential to science, in order to reject them. I then hope to propose some central values that I think *are* genuinely essential to science.

. . . Edward Conze portrays science as a naked manifestation of a mere will to power. He blasts "science-bound philosophers" for their "ruthless will for boundless power," and says of science that "all that it does is to increase 'man's' power to control his 'material environment,' and that is something the yogic method never even attempted." Conze concedes to science its success in this regard, but "to judge all human techniques by the amount of bare 'control' or 'power' they produce is patently unfair."

But must science be committed to a lust for this type of power, or is it always so committed? Does Conze's "ruthless will for boundless power" indicate a value *essential* to science? Certainly not. Science can be pursued, and often has been pursued, for its own sake and for the sake of mere knowledge. Paleontology and archaeology are dubious pursuits for any who lust for power, and not every form of scientific endeavor promises some high-powered technological application. It must be conceded that science *has* often been pursued with technological goals, and it is quite likely that our science would not have the shape it does today were that not the case. But it is also the case that religion has often been used for petty political ends. It no more follows that power is essential to science than that petty politics is essential to religion.

Consider also a second feature that is occasionally suggested as essential to science. It is sometimes proposed that science is in some way committed to, or is an elaborate apologetic for, an "everyday common-sense world of sense experience."[10] In this regard Conze speaks scathingly of the "narrow provincialism" of "sense-bound consciousness."

Is science essentially committed to "the everyday common-sense world of sense experience"? I am not sure what power this would have as a condemnation of science even if true. But in fact nothing could be much farther from the truth. Anyone who delves into contemporary physics expecting to find a familiar universe neatly expansive in absolute space and punctually sequential in time, filled with comfortably solid middle-size objects, will be very much surprised. From the perspective of common sense and everyday experience the claims of contemporary physics will seem among the most bizarre imaginable. The contemporary physicist seems as willing as any yogi to reject "the everyday common-sense world of sense experience" as illusion, and seems as insistent as any yogi that the more fundamental reality lies beyond it.

Neither a lust for power nor a commitment to an "everyday common-sense world of sense experience," then, appears to be essential to science. But there are, I think, values that *are* essential to science; values without which no pursuit could properly be considered science.

The first of these essential values involves an almost obsessive emphasis on truth. The aim of science is not to ennoble or to edify, to satisfy or sanctify or save. The aim of science is simply to sort claims on the basis of their truth or falsity. Within science no other criterion for sorting claims—on the basis, say, of accordance with religious tradition or political appeal—is even a close second. This is not, of course, to say that no claim has ever

been accepted within a scientific community for baser motives than a sincere search for truth. But it is to say that any adoption of claims for other motives is to that extent *un*scientific, and that a "science" that abandoned this central emphasis on truth would no longer be science.[11]

Tied to this first essential characteristic is a second: science *demands* demonstration.[12] If a claim is to be adopted on truly scientific grounds, it must be openly *demonstrable*, and no other appeal—to venerated authority or to the dicta of the properly initiated—will do.

This emphasis on demonstration has sometimes been ridiculed as a myopic devotion to phenomena that fit neatly within the confines of a laboratory. That, I think, is a mistake; science, though essentially committed to demonstration, is committed to no particular type of demonstration. Field studies, expeditions, and the appearances of comets have played a major role in the history of science. Contemporary reliance on mathematics reflects a willingness to accept a priori deductive as well as inductive demonstration. And there are times when the course of science quite properly shifts on the basis of what appear to be almost purely philosophical arguments.[13]

It does not appear, then, that science is confined to any particular type of demonstration. Nevertheless commitment to demonstration, of one type or another, seems essential; a "science" that abandoned or even significantly weakened the demand for demonstration would no longer be recognizable as science.

Here, as with regard to the emphasis on truth, we must concede that the demand for demonstration is an ideal of scientific practice, not always fulfilled. Science has at times been swayed by misplaced authority and has settled too quickly for claims without demanding sufficient demonstration. But that an obsession with truth and a demand for demonstration are *ideals* of scientific practice does not mean that they can be waved cynically aside. That these *are* the ideals of scientific practice, even if "merely" ideals, is crucial; anything that did not value these as ideals would no longer be science.

It appears, then, that science is "value-laden" in two importantly different ways. As noted in the previous section, standard scientific judgments of "compelling evidence," "sufficiently high probability," and "adequate establishment" demand a background of values. These values, I have argued, can shift and hence are not *essential* values; though some set of background values is required by science in this regard, no *particular* set of values is demanded.

But there are also particular values within science that are essential. A purported lust for technological power and a supposed slavery to an "everyday common-sense world of sense experience" are not among these. But an obsession with truth and a commitment to demonstration are; each of these is a value essential to science in the sense that a "science" without them would not be science at all.

SCIENCE AND ITS RIVALS

It appears that we must reject, then, the first image of science and values presented above. Science is far from value-free; it is both shaped by a general background of values and essentially committed to some particular values.

But at this point it is tempting to replace the first image of science and values with a second. It is quite often claimed, at least within some circles, that there are equally worthy alternatives to science. The general claim is that there are bodies of knowledge or types of pursuit that in some way conflict with science but that have an equal or greater claim to our serious attention. Conze appears to hold that forms of Buddhism are the equal or the superior of science, Alan Watts makes similar claims for similar religious traditions, Colin Wilson and Philip Slater hold that the occult somehow embodies a respectable rival to science, and Carlos Castaneda portrays the "world" of a fictitious Yaqui sorcerer as an equally acceptable alternative to the "world" of science.[14]

In the general spirit of this general claim, however, quite different particular claims have been made by different authors, or even by the same author at different times.[15] A complete treatment of all such claims would involve carefully disentangling and clarifying each claim, seeing what support can be offered in its behalf and what can be said against it. That complete task is well beyond us here. Instead I shall concentrate on only a sampling of such claims; those that rely on the "value-ladenness" of science.

If science is "value-laden," as we have argued that it is, is it not then on all fours with any other value system? Does not devotion to science then amount to dogmatic adherence to but one value system among many? Is not then the choice of those values allied with science as ultimately arbitrary as the choice of any alternative set of values?

These are, of course, rhetorical questions; those who pose them expect us to answer "yes" and to concede that science can claim no special status over rival values; that the adoption of scientific values is on a par with the adoption of those values evident in Christianity or Buddhism or Hinduism, or for that matter in Nazism or the fantasies of Carlos Castaneda.

The force of such an attack should not be underestimated. In this regard it may help to use a distinction hinted at above: a distinction between the current practice of what we think of as our scientific community on the one hand, and what we might call *truly* scientific practice on the other. The actual practice of those who staff our laboratories and conduct our various research programs may not always be fully or genuinely scientific. As you read this someone somewhere may be fudging a result, or misrecording an observation so as to support a pet theory, or doctoring the data. There may also be claims applauded by our current scientific community that are not genuinely scientific claims, backed by truly scientific evidence and subjected to genuinely scientific scrutiny. Current practice has its share (although I doubt that it has more than its share) of frauds and foibles and human frailties. And current practice may be *un*scientific to a greater or lesser degree because of such things.

But those who press the type of attack at issue are not merely criticizing "science," in the sense of current practice, for the extent to which it is *un*scientific. We would not need them for that, and they are out for bigger game. To the extent that current practice is *un*scientific, we hardly need an appeal to "rivals" or even a concentrated examination of values to condemn it. And to the extent that claims applauded by the scientific community are not genuinely scientific claims, we hardly need an appeal to "rivals" or a concentrated examination of values to condemn them. *Un*scientific aspects of current practice and claims currently accepted without genuinely scientific warrant are clearly to be condemned on purely scientific grounds, and would be whether or not science had any "rivals" in the sense at issue.

Those who press such an attack are instead questioning current practice precisely to the extent that it *is* scientific. Were it *perfectly* scientific they would still urge Buddhism and the occult and Yaqui sorcery as equivalent rivals or alternatives. Thus the full force of the attack is against science itself, in no matter how pure a form, rather than merely against the variously corrupted forms of current practice.

How good is the attack? *Does* it follow from the fact that science is "value-laden" that it is on all fours with any rival set of values?

As noted, science is "value-laden" in two importantly different ways: it is shaped by a background of inessential values, and it is also committed to some particular values. Consider first, then, those values that function as background to our science, and that shape our notions of "compelling evidence," "sufficiently high probability," and the like. To these values—the relative values we place on human and animal lives, for instance—there are clearly alternatives. Instead of *these* values we might adopt others, and if some religious tradition emphasizes importantly different values, we might come to adopt those values instead. We might decide that all life is as precious as human life, or that Brahmin life is of greater value than the life of lower castes.

But are these rivals to the background values of our science really rivals to *science*? I think not. As we have seen, science demands *some* background of values of the sort Rudner indicates. But it does not demand any *particular* set of values. A form of science shaped in this way by other values than those that shape our science would nevertheless be a form of *science*. So the choice here is not between science and those other values; it is merely a choice between a science shaped by the values by which our science is shaped and a science shaped by other values. If we are to set up a genuine conflict between science and its supposed rivals, then, it must be a conflict regarding something other than merely the background of non-essential scientific values.

Consider then the essential values we have claimed for science, which would seem much more likely candidates for a genuine clash between scientific and other values. If science is *essentially* committed to certain values, is it not *then* on all fours with its alternatives? Have we not *then* shown that the choice between science and its rivals is simply a choice of values?

In order to answer this question carefully we must pay closer attention to the different *types* of things that may be at issue as "rivals" or "alternatives" to science. The term "science" is itself used ambiguously enough that what is meant is sometimes the *activity* of science and sometimes a set of *claims* accepted on scientific grounds. Hence science is sometimes contrasted with other activities or pursuits, and in considering rivals or alternatives we are considering rival or alternative activities or pursuits. But science is also sometimes contrasted with rival sets of claims—the claims of science versus the claims of Genesis, for example.

Let us take these one at a time. Does science, with its essential values, clash with other activities? Not, I think, in the sense that objectors to science commonly have in mind. Essential to the activity of science is an obsession with truth and a commitment to demonstration. And clearly this is not the case with all activities; art, music, and poetry, as well as certain forms of asceticism and meditation, are quite different. Does that mean that one must pursue science, devote oneself to truth and demonstration, and abandon these other activities? Not at all. There are other ways to live one's life, and in some respects—or for some people—these other ways may be infinitely preferable. But that there are other activities that are rivals to science in *this* sense is surely no condemnation of science, any more than one's choice to pursue a career in business is any condemnation of poetry (or vice versa). If this is what objectors to science have meant by portraying science as on all fours with other endeavors, they are certainly right; there is nothing in science or its essential values that absolutely compels us to do science or to emphasize those values. But it would seem odd to characterize this as in any significant respect a *challenge* to science.

So far, then, we have not found a genuine clash between science and its supposed rivals, and thus have not found the clash between science and "equally worthy rivals" suggested by its critics. Alternatives to the inessential background values of science are not alternatives to *science*, because science could assume any of various sets of background values. And alternatives to the activity of science, despite its essential values, are merely other worthy pursuits rather than "rivals" in any more threatening sense.

Finally, however, science is often set in contrast to other sets of claims. And here, unlike in the previous two cases, we do seem to have a genuine conflict. It must be remembered that we are dealing with *genuinely* scientific claims, and not all and only claims accepted by those who staff our laboratories may qualify as genuinely scientific. But even so, there are undoubtedly some claims current within some religious traditions, and some claims accepted within some cultural groups, that will simply contradict genuinely scientific claims. On pain of contradiction, one cannot accept both.

Does it follow from this, together with the fact that science is essentially "value-laden" in the ways specified, that the claims of science are on no firmer ground than any of a number of rival sets of claims, or that each is equally worthy or unworthy of our attention? Certainly not. The mere fact that two sets of claims conflict in no way forces us to throw up our hands, or to suspend judgment, or to pick a set at random. There may be much that can be said for one set rather than another. And the particular values essential to science, far from relegating it to the level of any of various alternatives, may offer a significant argument in its behalf.

At least the following can be said for the claims of science. Science is essentially committed to truth and demonstration, and genuinely scientific claims will reflect those values. They will have been selected with an obsessive ideal of truth and through the patient toil of dogged demonstration. This does not, of course, guarantee their truth; genuinely scientific claims may nevertheless be false and claims adopted without scientific warrant may nevertheless be true. But it does mean that scientific claims will be backed by a wealth of demonstration, evidence, and argument. Only further demonstration, better evidence, and stronger argument can rationally force us to abandon them; and then, of course, we will be replacing some scientific claims with other scientific claims. None of this can be said for most sets of claims that appear as religious or cultural tradition.

The essential values of science, then, are scientific *virtues*, and as genuine virtues are not to be flippantly waved aside. Science *is* essentially committed to particular values, but the values at issue are ideals of truth and demonstration. Those are ideals that are not to be taken lightly and are not to be lightly put aside.

On what basis, then, might one choose to abandon scientific claims and to adopt some other set of claims instead? One might do so by abandoning the essential values of science, or by relegating them to a secondary position. One might take something else as more important than truth, and choose claims contradictory to those of science on the basis of some other value; aesthetic or (broadly) political or personal appeal, perhaps. Or one might take something to have precedence over demonstration; the words of sacred authority or of sacred texts, perhaps, or the counsels of some form of mystical experience. But here other claims will have been accepted on the basis of *other* values, not on the basis merely of truth and demonstration. One will be able to appeal for one's chosen claims on the basis of whatever values they embody. But if they are to be chosen on grounds other than merely ideals of truth and demonstration, one cannot expect to be able to defend them solely with an eye to truth and solely on the basis of demonstration.[16]

One might also, of course, choose to adopt some set of claims—however unpopular—and to demonstrate their truth. This is a very different case. If science can adopt any form of demonstration, as argued above, one will not then have abandoned science. One will be defending one's claims as rival scientific claims, rather than as rivals to scientific claims, and will be contributing to the scientific project rather than renouncing it. One may, indeed, be contesting the accepted claims of current practice. But that is how science proceeds.

None of the arguments considered above, then, shows that science has equal rivals in the sense sometimes proposed by its opponents. Science *does* rely on a background of values, and there are rival values to those on which our current science relies. But this does not mean that those rival values are rivals to science itself. Science *is* one activity among many, and others may for various reasons be rightly pursued instead of science. But these other activities are not *rivals* in the threatening sense that critics of science generally have in mind. Finally, scientific claims will be contradicted by other sets of claims. But it does not follow that these need be *equal* rivals. Genuinely scientific claims, *because* of the essential values of science, have ideals of truth and demonstration on their side.

We have, then, found reason to question each of the images of science and values with which we began. Science is not value-free, and is moreover essentially committed to some particular values. At least with an eye to the arguments considered, however, it need not follow that science, because "value-laden," is on all fours with any of various "rivals" or "alternatives." The essential values of science, far from indicating a fatal weakness, may be its greatest strength.

Notes

1. It is perhaps appropriate to mention also two general topics that I will not attempt to deal with in their entirety. The first is value-relativism. Implicit in both images of science and values above is an assumption that all values corrupt, or that any introduction of values must represent capricious dogmatism, or that all "systems" of value are equally worthy—and hence equally unworthy—of our allegiance. I do not think any of these relativistic assumptions is true, but I will not here be able to argue fully against any of them. Second, it must be said that arguments based on the premise that science is value-laden are only some among the many arguments, not usually distinguished, that attempt to show science to be no better than various rivals. I do not think any of the other arguments are any better than those explicitly addressed here, but in what follows I will concentrate only on arguments that in one way or another turn on the issue of values.

Some of the claims of this essay—particularly those in the final section—are posed in a slightly stronger form than I might choose in another context. For present purposes, and because my intent is to offer a corrective to exaggerated views on the other side, I think this is relatively harmless. . . .

2. That (6) is perhaps controversial is of no importance to the argument here; "Contemporary handling of nuclear wastes is perfectly safe" or "It has not yet been clearly determined whether or not contemporary handling of nuclear wastes is unsafe" would serve our purposes equally well. The same applies to (8).

3. It has become quite widely accepted that the notion of health is value-laden. See Joel Feinberg, *Doing and Deserving* (Princeton: Princeton University Press, 1970), pp. 253–255; and H. Tristram Engelhardt, Jr., "Human Well-Being and Medicine: Some Basic Value-Judgments in the Biomedical Sciences," in *Science, Ethics, and Medicine*, ed. H. Tristram Engelhardt and Daniel Callahan (Hastings, N.Y.: Institute of Society, Ethics, and the Life Sciences, 1976). Both of these are reprinted in Thomas A. Mappes and Jane S. Zembaty, *Biomedical Ethics* (New York: McGraw-Hill, 1981).

4. Richard Rudner, "The Scientist *qua* Scientist Makes Value Judgments," *Philosophy of Science* 20 (1953):

1–6; reprinted in Baruch Brody, ed., *Readings in the Philosophy of Science* (Englewood Cliffs, N.J.: Prentice-Hall, 1970).

5. For the sake of simplicity I have not dealt here with a complex argument to the effect that "the 'softness' of social facts may affect the 'hard' notions of truth and reference" (p. 46), which appears in Hilary Putnam's *Meaning and the Moral Sciences* (Boston: Routledge & Kegan Paul, 1978).

6. A science that scrupulously avoided values in this way, of course, would be a science that was itself of little value.

7. This view appears in Richard C. Jeffrey, "Valuation and Acceptance of Scientific Hypotheses," *Philosophy of Science* 23 (1956): 237–246; reprinted in Brody. But Jeffrey concedes, in the spirit of the following paragraph, that "this account bears no resemblance to our ordinary conception of science."

8. To choose to value human and chimpanzee lives equally, or Rembrandts and belt buckles equally, would of course not be to abandon a background of values but to choose a particular background. As Rudner notes, science could attempt to escape *any* background of values only by abandoning notions of "adequate establishment," "sufficient evidence," and the like.

9. This is all too brief as an introduction of essential properties, let alone of essential values. I hope that it will nevertheless prove adequate for the task at hand.

10. This phrase appears in scare quotes because I am not sure precisely what a "world" is here supposed to include, nor am I sure—even when most sympathetic—that there is only one such "world."

11. This claim does not, I think, conflict with Rudner's conclusion, appealed to above. The fact that various values may be crucial to what we accept as "adequate evidence" for the truth of a claim does not mean that we are ultimately concerned with anything less than the *truth* of the claim.

It might also be noted that even claims that have slipped into currency by illegitimate means may later be offered proper scientific support. I am indebted to David Pomerantz for discussion on this point.

12. The tie between an emphasis on truth and a demand for demonstration is as subtle as it is intimate. The more sincerely one is concerned with truth, the more emphatically one will demand demonstration. And the more one demands demonstration, the better our reason to believe that one is committed to truth. Both of these claims hold only ceteris paribus. But the ceteris-paribus status of each need not indicate that the tie between truth and demonstration is therefore a weak one.

13. Many of the arguments for behaviorism of some forms, against evolutionary "emergence" in biology, for important claims regarding quantum mechanics, and regarding tachyons traveling backward in time seem to be fully "philosophical" arguments.

14. [Edward Conze, "Tacit Assumptions," from *Buddhist Thought in India*; *Three Phases of Buddhist Philosophy* (Ann Arbor, Mich.: University of Michigan Press,

1967). Reprinted in Patrick Grim, ed. *Philosophy of Science and the Occult* (Albany: State University of New York Press, 1982); page references to the reprinted version.] For other authors mentioned, see Carlos Castaneda, *The Teachings of Don Juan: A Yaqui Way of Knowledge* (Berkeley: University of California Press, 1968), *A Separate Reality: Further Conversations with Don Juan* (New York: Simon & Schuster, 1971), *Journey to Ixtlan: The Lessons of Don Juan* (New York: Simon & Schuster, 1972), *Tales of Power* (New York: Simon & Schuster, 1974), and *The Second Ring of Power* (New York: Simon & Schuster, 1977); Colin Wilson, *The Occult* (New York: Random House, 1971), quoted in the general introduction; Philip Slater, *The Wayward Gate* (Boston: Beacon Press, 1977); and Alan Watts, especially *Psychotherapy East and West* (New York: Vintage Books, 1975).

15. Here Conze might serve as a convenient example. At one point Conze criticizes science for ignoring the accounts of yogis: "There is ultimately only one way open to those who do not believe the accounts of the yogins. They will have to repeat the experiment . . . they will have to do what the yogins say should be done and see what happens" (p. 300). If this is an attack on science at all, it is a pretty weak attack. What Conze calls for here is *more* science—a scientific investigation of the claims of yogis—rather than for some alternative to science. Yet a few pages later Conze claims that the world of the yogi is one incapable of scientific exploration; within the magical world "the phenomenon vanishes when the full light is turned on" (p. 304), and within the spiritual world "it is quite impossible to ever establish any fact beyond the possibility of doubt" (p. 304). Here Conze changes his tune and presses a quite different attack: "The methods of science, mighty and effective though they may be, are useless for the exploration of two-thirds of the universe, and the psychic and spiritual worlds are quite beyond them" (p. 304). This is a quite different claim from that proposed earlier, and calls for quite different argumentative support. Can it be *demonstrated* that "two-thirds of the universe" is beyond the reach of science, and that claims made by Conze or anyone else about this major portion of the universe are true? If claims about this portion *can* be demonstrated, and if—as argued in the previous section—science can adopt any form of demonstration, then these claims are within the potential grasp of science after all. If these claims *cannot* be demonstrated, of course, we lose at least one good ground for believing that they are true at all, or for believing Conze's claim that we have overlooked a major portion of the universe.

16. Here it might be claimed that yogic meditation, for example, involves its own unique form of demonstration. I do not think that is true; what is at issue seems to me entirely unlike anything we normally consider "demonstration." But if there *is* a legitimate form of demonstration buried here, then, as argued above, it is grist for the mills of science. What remains to be demonstrated (and this is by no means a unique matter in the history of science) is that there *is* a form of demonstration at issue.

Truth and Progress in Science

Normal and Revolutionary Science

Thomas Kuhn

In 1962, Thomas Kuhn (1922–1996) published one of the most influential books on science of the twentieth century. His *The Structure of Scientific Revolutions* described a vision of science that was strikingly different from the received view of the time. Using detailed studies from the history of science, Kuhn disputed the view that scientific progress occurs through gradual accumulation of facts and rational debate among objective scientists. He argued that progress does not consist of scientists approximating objective truths ever more closely. His history reveals a pattern of normal science punctuated by theoretical revolutions. In normal science, researchers solve the puzzles set by a generally accepted scientific paradigm—a shared exemplar that shows how problems in an area should be solved. In revolutions, some scientists abandon the dominant paradigm and adopt a new one, often based on their somewhat subjective assessments of the promise of the new paradigm. Since scientists who have different paradigms speak different languages, see different data, and adopt different norms for evaluating theories, they cannot rationally convince one another about the virtues of their theories. As a result, a paradigm shift is more like a religious conversion than an objective decision, according to Kuhn. In some of the most radical passages of this book, Kuhn alleges that scientists who accept different paradigms live in different worlds and that what is true in one world is not true in another.

Kuhn was trained as a physicist and then as a historian of science. He later believed that the philosophical implications that he drew from his historical studies could be described less provocatively, and he did this in his 1970 postscript to the second edition of his book. Nonetheless, a generation of scholars in fields ranging from anthropology and sociology to art history and religious studies continued to debate the merits of the more radical versions of his views.

In the following selections from *The Structure of Scientific Revolutions*, Kuhn briefly identifies changes in the history of science that led to his startling conclusions. He outlines his reasons for thinking that science does not progress by accumulating facts and theories. After distinguishing between normal and revolutionary science, he describes ways in which paradigms shape a research program. A discussion of the similarities between paradigm shifts and political revolutions is followed by an argument that a scientist's world changes during a paradigm shift.

As you read through this essay, consider the following:

1. According to Kuhn, why do textbooks produce a skewed picture of science?
2. How does he think that the history of science is changing and how do those changes affect our view of science?
3. How does normal science differ from revolutionary science?
4. What does Kuhn mean by a paradigm and how are paradigms related to normal science?
5. How are scientific revolutions similar to political revolutions, according to Kuhn?
6. How do you think Kuhn's view of science should affect our attitude toward current scientific results?

I. INTRODUCTION: A ROLE FOR HISTORY

History, if viewed as a repository for more than anecdote or chronology, could produce a decisive transformation in the image of science by which we are now possessed. That image has previously been drawn, even by scientists themselves, mainly from the study of finished scientific achievements as these are recorded in the classics and, more recently, in the textbooks from which each new scientific generation learns to practice its trade. Inevitably, however, the aim of such books is persuasive and pedagogic; a concept of science drawn from them is no more likely to fit the enterprise that produced them than an image of a national culture drawn from a tourist brochure or a language

From Thomas S. Kuhn, *The Structure of Scientific Revolutions* (Chicago: The University of Chicago Press, 1962, 1970). Copyright © 1970, 1962 The University of Chicago Press. Reprinted by permission. Notes deleted.

test. This essay attempts to show that we have been misled by them in fundamental ways. Its aim is a sketch of the quite different concept of science that can emerge from the historical record of the research activity itself.

Even from history, however, that new concept will not be forthcoming if historical data continue to be sought and scrutinized mainly to answer questions posed by the unhistorical stereotype drawn from science texts. Those texts have, for example, often seemed to imply that the content of science is uniquely exemplified by the observations, laws, and theories described in their pages. Almost as regularly, the same books have been read as saying that scientific methods are simply the ones illustrated by the manipulative techniques used in gathering textbook data, together with the logical operations employed when relating those data to the textbook's theoretical generalizations. The result has been a concept of science with profound implications about its nature and development.

If science is the constellation of facts, theories, and methods collected in current texts, then scientists are the men who, successfully or not, have striven to contribute one or another element to that particular constellation. Scientific development becomes the piecemeal process by which these items have been added, singly and in combination, to the ever growing stockpile that constitutes scientific technique and knowledge. And history of science becomes the discipline that chronicles both these successive increments and the obstacles that have inhibited their accumulation. Concerned with scientific development, the historian then appears to have two main tasks. On the one hand, he must determine by what man and at what point in time each contemporary scientific fact, law, and theory was discovered or invented. On the other, he must describe and explain the congeries of error, myth, and superstition that have inhibited the more rapid accumulation of the constituents of the modern science text. Much research has been directed to these ends, and some still is.

In recent years, however, a few historians of science have been finding it more and more difficult to fulfil the functions that the concept of development-by-accumulation assigns to them. As chroniclers of an incremental process, they discover that additional research makes it harder, not easier, to answer questions like: When was oxygen discovered? Who first conceived of energy conservation? Increasingly, a few of them suspect that these are simply the wrong sorts of questions to ask. Perhaps science does not develop by the accumulation of individual discoveries and inventions. Simultaneously, these same historians confront growing difficulties in distinguishing the "scientific" component of past observation and belief from what their predecessors had readily labeled "error" and "superstition." The more carefully they study, say, Aristotelian dynamics, phlogistic chemistry, or caloric thermodynamics, the more certain they feel that those once current views of nature were, as a whole, neither less scientific nor more the product of human idiosyncrasy than those current today. If these out-of-date

beliefs are to be called myths, then myths can be produced by the same sorts of methods and held for the same sorts of reasons that now lead to scientific knowledge. If, on the other hand, they are to be called science, then science has included bodies of belief quite incompatible with the ones we hold today. Given these alternatives, the historian must choose the latter. Out-of-date theories are not in principle unscientific because they have been discarded. That choice, however, makes it difficult to see scientific development as a process of accretion. The same historical research that displays the difficulties in isolating individual inventions and discoveries gives ground for profound doubts about the cumulative process through which these individual contributions to science were thought to have been compounded.

The result of all these doubts and difficulties is a historiographic revolution in the study of science, though one that is still in its early stages. Gradually, and often without entirely realizing they are doing so, historians of science have begun to ask new sorts of questions and to trace different, and often less than cumulative, developmental lines for the sciences. Rather than seeking the permanent contributions of an older science to our present vantage, they attempt to display the historical integrity of that science in its own time. They ask, for example, not about the relation of Galileo's views to those of modern science, but rather about the relationship between his views and those of his group, i.e., his teachers, contemporaries, and immediate successors in the sciences. Furthermore, they insist upon studying the opinions of that group and other similar ones from the viewpoint—usually very different from that of modern science—that gives those opinions the maximum internal coherence and the closest possible fit to nature. Seen through the works that result, works perhaps best exemplified in the writings of Alexandre Koyré, science does not seem altogether the same enterprise as the one discussed by writers in the older historiographic tradition. By implication, at least, these historical studies suggest the possibility of a new image of science. This essay aims to delineate that image by making explicit some of the new historiography's implications.

What aspects of science will emerge to prominence in the course of this effort? First, at least in order of presentation, is the insufficiency of methodological directives, by themselves, to dictate a unique substantive conclusion to many sorts of scientific questions. Instructed to examine electrical or chemical phenomena, the man who is ignorant of these fields but who knows what it is to be scientific may legitimately reach any one of a number of incompatible conclusions. Among those legitimate possibilities, the particular conclusions he does arrive at are probably determined by his prior experience in other fields, by the accidents of his investigation, and by his own individual makeup. What beliefs about the stars, for example, does he bring to the study of chemistry or electricity? Which of the many conceivable experiments relevant to the new field does he elect to perform first? And what aspects of the complex phenomenon that then results strike him as particularly relevant to an elucidation of the nature of chemical change or of electrical affinity? For the individual, at least, and sometimes for the scientific community as well, answers to questions like these are often essential determinants of scientific development. We shall note, for example, . . . that the early developmental stages of most sciences have been characterized by continual competition between a number of distinct views of nature, each partially derived from, and all roughly compatible with, the dictates of scientific observation and method. What differentiated these various schools was not one or another failure of method—they were all "scientific"—but what we shall come to call their incommensurable ways of seeing the world and of practicing science in it. Observation and experience can and must drastically restrict the range of admissible scientific belief, else there would be no science. But they cannot alone determine a particular body of such belief. An apparently arbitrary element, compounded of personal and historical accident, is always a formative ingredient of the beliefs espoused by a given scientific community at a given time.

That element of arbitrariness does not, however, indicate that any scientific group could practice its trade without some set of received beliefs. Nor does it make less consequential the particular constellation to which the group, at a given time, is in fact committed. Effective research scarcely begins before a scientific community thinks it has acquired firm answers to questions like the following: What are the fundamental entities of which the universe is composed? How do these interact with each other and with the senses? What questions may legitimately be asked about such entities and what techniques employed in seeking solutions? At least in the mature sciences, answers (or full substitutes for answers) to questions like these are firmly embedded in the educational initiation that prepares and licenses the student for professional practice. Because that education is both rigorous and rigid, these answers come to exert a deep hold on the scientific mind. That they can do so does much to account both for the peculiar efficiency of the normal research activity and for the direction in which it proceeds at any given time. When examining normal science . . . we shall want finally to describe that research as a strenuous and devoted attempt to force nature into the conceptual boxes supplied by professional education. Simultaneously, we shall wonder whether research could proceed without such boxes, whatever the element of arbitrariness in their historic origins and, occasionally, in their subsequent development.

Yet that element of arbitrariness is present, and it too has an important effect on scientific development. . . . Normal science, the activity in which most scientists inevitably spend almost all their time, is predicated on the assumption that the scientific community knows what the world is like. Much of the success of the enterprise derives from the community's willingness to defend that assumption, if necessary at considerable cost. Normal science, for example, often suppresses fundamental novelties because they are necessarily subversive of its basic commitments. Nevertheless, so long as those commitments retain an element of the arbitrary, the very nature of normal research ensures that novelty shall not be suppressed for very long. Sometimes a normal problem, one that ought to be solvable by known rules and procedures, resists the reiterated onslaught of the ablest members of the group within whose competence it falls. On other occasions a piece of equipment designed and constructed for the purpose of normal research fails to perform in the anticipated manner, revealing an anomaly that cannot, despite repeated effort, be aligned with professional expectation. In these and other ways besides, normal science repeatedly goes astray. And when it does—when, that is, the profession can no longer evade anomalies that subvert the existing tradition of scientific practice—then begin the extraordinary investigations that lead the profession at last to a new set of commitments, a new basis for the practice of science. The extraordinary episodes in which that shift of professional commitments occurs are the ones known in this essay as scientific revolutions. They are the tradition-shattering complements to the tradition-bound activity of normal science.

The most obvious examples of scientific revolutions are those famous episodes in scientific development that have often been labeled revolutions before. Therefore . . . where the nature of scientific revolutions is first directly scrutinized, we shall deal repeatedly with the major turning points in scientific development associated with the names of Copernicus, Newton, Lavoisier, and Einstein. More clearly than most other episodes in the history of at least the physical sciences, these display what all scientific revolutions are about. Each of them necessitated the community's rejection of one time-honored scientific theory in favor of another incompatible with it. Each produced a consequent shift in the problems available for scientific scrutiny and in the standards by which the profession determined what should count as an admissible problem or as a legiti-

mate problem-solution. And each transformed the scientific imagination in ways that we shall ultimately need to describe as a transformation of the world within which scientific work was done. Such changes, together with the controversies that almost always accompany them, are the defining characteristics of scientific revolutions.

These characteristics emerge with particular clarity from a study of, say, the Newtonian or the chemical revolution. It is, however, a fundamental thesis of this essay that they can also be retrieved from the study of many other episodes that were not so obviously revolutionary. For the far smaller professional group affected by them, Maxwell's equations were as revolutionary as Einstein's, and they were resisted accordingly. The invention of other new theories regularly, and appropriately, evokes the same response from some of the specialists on whose area of special competence they impinge. For these men the new theory implies a change in the rules governing the prior practice of normal science. Inevitably, therefore, it reflects upon much scientific work they have already successfully completed. That is why a new theory, however special its range of application, is seldom or never just an increment to what is already known. Its assimilation requires the reconstruction of prior theory and the re-evaluation of prior fact, an intrinsically revolutionary process that is seldom completed by a single man and never overnight. No wonder historians have had difficulty in dating precisely this extended process that their vocabulary impels them to view as an isolated event.

Nor are new inventions of theory the only scientific events that have revolutionary impact upon the specialists in whose domain they occur. The commitments that govern normal science specify not only what sorts of entities the universe does contain, but also, by implication, those that it does not. It follows, though the point will require extended discussion, that a discovery like that of oxygen or X-rays does not simply add one more item to the population of the scientist's world. Ultimately it has that effect, but not until the professional community has re-evaluated traditional experimental procedures, altered its conception of entities with which it has long been familiar, and, in the process, shifted the network of theory through which it deals with the world. Scientific fact and theory are not categorically separable, except perhaps within a single tradition of normal-scientific practice. That is why the unexpected discovery is not simply factual in its import and why the scientist's world is qualitatively transformed as well as quantitatively enriched by fundamental novelties of either fact or theory. . . .

In this essay, "normal science" means research firmly based upon one or more past scientific achievements, achievements that some particular scientific community acknowledges for a time as supplying the foundation for its further practice. Today such achievements are recounted, though seldom in their original form, by science textbooks, elementary and advanced. These textbooks expound the body of accepted theory, illustrate many or all of its successful applications, and compare these applications with exemplary observations and experiments. Before such books became popular early in the nineteenth century (and until even more recently in the newly matured sciences), many of the famous classics of science fulfilled a similar function. Aristotle's *Physica*, Ptolemy's *Almagest*, Newton's *Principia* and *Opticks*, Franklin's *Electricity*, Lavoisier's *Chemistry*, and Lyell's *Geology*—these and many other works served for a time implicitly to define the legitimate problems and methods of a research field for succeeding generations of practitioners. They were able to do so because they shared two essential characteristics. Their achievement was sufficiently unprecedented to attract an enduring group of adherents away from competing modes of scientific activity. Simultaneously, it was sufficiently open-ended to leave all sorts of problems for the redefined group of practitioners to resolve.

Achievements that share these two characteristics I shall henceforth refer to as "paradigms," a term that relates closely to "normal science." By choosing it, I mean to suggest

that some accepted examples of actual scientific practice—examples which include law, theory, application, and instrumentation together—provide models from which spring particular coherent traditions of scientific research. These are the traditions which the historian describes under such rubrics as "Ptolemaic astronomy" (or "Copernican"), "Aristotelian dynamics" (or "Newtonian"), "corpuscular optics" (or "wave optics"), and so on. The study of paradigms, including many that are far more specialized than those named illustratively above, is what mainly prepares the student for membership in the particular scientific community with which he will later practice. Because he there joins men who learned the bases of their field from the same concrete models, his subsequent practice will seldom evoke overt disagreement over fundamentals. Men whose research is based on shared paradigms are committed to the same rules and standards for scientific practice. That commitment and the apparent consensus it produces are prerequisites for normal science, i.e., for the genesis and continuation of a particular research tradition. . . .

If the historian traces the scientific knowledge of any selected group of related phenomena backward in time, he is likely to encounter some minor variant of a pattern here illustrated from the history of physical optics. Today's physics textbooks tell the student that light is photons, i.e., quantum-mechanical entities that exhibit some characteristics of waves and some of particles. Research proceeds accordingly, or rather according to the more elaborate and mathematical characterization from which this usual verbalization is derived. That characterization of light is, however, scarcely half a century old. Before it was developed by Planck, Einstein, and others early in this century, physics texts taught that light was transverse wave motion, a conception rooted in a paradigm that derived ultimately from the optical writings of Young and Fresnel in the early nineteenth century. Nor was the wave theory the first to be embraced by almost all practitioners of optical science. During the eighteenth century the paradigm for this field was provided by Newton's *Opticks*, which taught that light was material corpuscles. At that time physicists sought evidence, as the early wave theorists had not, of the pressure exerted by light particles impinging on solid bodies.

These transformations of the paradigms of physical optics are scientific revolutions, and the successive transition from one paradigm to another via revolution is the usual developmental pattern of mature science. It is not, however, the pattern characteristic of the period before Newton's work, and that is the contrast that concerns us here. No period between remote antiquity and the end of the seventeenth century exhibited a single generally accepted view about the nature of light. Instead there were a number of competing schools and sub-schools, most of them espousing one variant or another of Epicurean, Aristotelian, or Platonic theory. One group took light to be particles emanating from material bodies; for another it was a modification of the medium that intervened between the body and the eye; still another explained light in terms of an interaction of the medium with an emanation from the eye; and there were other combinations and modifications besides. Each of the corresponding schools derived strength from its relation to some particular metaphysic, and each emphasized, as paradigmatic observations, the particular cluster of optical phenomena that its own theory could do most to explain. Other observations were dealt with by *ad hoc* elaborations, or they remained as outstanding problems for further research.

At various times all these schools made significant contributions to the body of concepts, phenomena, and techniques from which Newton drew the first nearly uniformly accepted paradigm for physical optics. Any definition of the scientist that excludes at least the more creative members of these various schools will exclude their modern successors as well. Those men were scientists. Yet anyone examining a survey of physical optics before Newton may well conclude that, though the field's practitioners were scientists, the net result of their activity was something less than science. Being able to take no common body of belief for granted, each writer on physical optics felt forced to build his field anew from its foundations. In doing so, his choice of supporting observation and experiment was relatively free, for there was no standard set of methods or of phenomena that every optical writer felt forced to employ and explain. Under these circumstances, the dialogue of the resulting books was often directed as much to the members of other schools as it was to nature. That pattern is not unfamiliar in a number of creative fields today, nor is it incompatible with significant discovery and invention. It is not, however, the pattern of development that physical optics acquired after Newton and that other natural sciences make familiar today. . . .

. . . The preceding discussion has indicated that scientific revolutions are here taken to be those non-cumulative developmental episodes in which an older paradigm is replaced in whole or in part by an incompatible new one. There is more to be said, however, and an essential part of it can be introduced by asking one further question. Why should a change of paradigm be called a revolution? In the face of the vast and essential differences between political and scientific development, what parallelism can justify the metaphor that finds revolutions in both?

One aspect of the parallelism must already be apparent. Political revolutions are inaugurated by a growing sense, often restricted to a segment of the political community, that existing institutions have ceased adequately to meet the problems posed by an environment that they have in part created. In much the same way, scientific revolutions are inaugurated by a growing sense, again often restricted to a narrow subdivision of the scientific community, that an existing paradigm has ceased to function adequately in the exploration of an aspect of nature to which that paradigm itself had previously led the way. In both political and scientific development the sense of malfunction that can lead to crisis is prerequisite to revolution. Furthermore, though it admittedly strains the metaphor, that parallelism holds not only for the major paradigm changes, like those attributable to Copernicus and Lavoisier, but also for the far smaller ones associated with the assimilation of a new sort of phenomenon, like oxygen or X-rays. . . .

. . . This essay aims to demonstrate that the historical study of paradigm change reveals very similar characteristics in the evolution of the sciences. Like the choice between competing political institutions, that between competing paradigms proves to be a choice between incompatible modes of community life. Because it has that character, the choice is not and cannot be determined merely by the evaluative procedures characteristic of normal science, for these depend in part upon a particular paradigm, and that paradigm is at issue. When paradigms enter, as they must, into a debate about paradigm choice, their role is necessarily circular. Each group uses its own paradigm to argue in that paradigm's defense.

The resulting circularity does not, of course, make the arguments wrong or even ineffectual. The man who premises a paradigm when arguing in its defense can nonetheless provide a clear exhibit of what scientific practice will be like for those who adopt the new view of nature. That exhibit can be immensely persuasive, often compellingly so. Yet, whatever its force, the status of the circular argument is only that of persuasion. It cannot be made logically or even probabilistically compelling for those who refuse to step into the circle. The premises and values shared by the two parties to a debate over paradigms are not sufficiently extensive for that. As in political revolutions, so in paradigm choice—there is no standard higher than the assent of the relevant community. . . .

Examining the record of past research from the vantage of contemporary historiog-

raphy, the historian of science may be tempted to exclaim that when paradigms change, the world itself changes with them. Led by a new paradigm, scientists adopt new instruments and look in new places. Even more important, during revolutions scientists see new and different things when looking with familiar instruments in places they have looked before. It is rather as if the professional community had been suddenly transported to another planet where familiar objects are seen in a different light and are joined by unfamiliar ones as well. Of course, nothing of quite that sort does occur: there is no geographical transplantation; outside the laboratory everyday affairs usually continue as before. Nevertheless, paradigm changes do cause scientists to see the world of their research-engagement differently. In so far as their only recourse to that world is through what they see and do, we may want to say that after a revolution scientists are responding to a different world.

It is as elementary prototypes for these transformations of the scientist's world that the familiar demonstrations of a switch in visual gestalt prove so suggestive. What were ducks in the scientist's world before the revolution are rabbits afterwards. The man who first saw the exterior of the box from above later sees its interior from below. Transformations like these, though usually more gradual and almost always irreversible, are common concomitants of scientific training. Looking at a contour map, the student sees lines on paper, the cartographer a picture of a terrain. Looking at a bubble-chamber photograph, the student sees confused and broken lines, the physicist a record of familiar subnuclear events. Only after a number of such transformations of vision does the student become an inhabitant of the scientist's world, seeing what the scientist sees and responding as the scientist does. The world that the student then enters is not, however, fixed once and for all by the nature of the environment, on the one hand, and of science, on the other. Rather, it is determined jointly by the environment and the particular normal-scientific tradition that the student has been trained to pursue. Therefore, at times of revolution, when the normal-scientific tradition changes, the scientist's perception of his environment must be re-educated—in some familiar situations he must learn to see a new gestalt. After he has done so the world of his research will seem, here and there, incommensurable with the one he had inhabited before. That is another reason why schools guided by different paradigms are always slightly at cross-purposes.

Progress in Science: A Dialogue

Larry Laudan

Since Plato in the fifth century B.C.E., philosophers have used dialogues to examine the merits of opposing views. The dialogue form reveals standard moves in a debate and allows the author to adopt an apparently neutral standpoint with regard to the issues. Inevitably, one of the characters in the dialogue defends the author's own view, and, in the end, his or her arguments seem to carry the day.

In this dialogue, Larry Laudan explores the issue of what kind of progress characterizes science. A relativist, Quincy Rortabender, argues that science does not reveal objective progress. Later theories are not objectively better than earlier theories; they certainly do not get closer to the truth. Most of Quincy's arguments are designed to show that realist and positivist accounts of progress fail. Rudy Reichfeigl, the positivist, maintains that science progresses when later theories explain and predict more facts than do earlier theories, but Quincy worries that we cannot compare the number of facts different theories predict. Where Quincy, who sounds much like Kuhn in the prior essay, finds many scientific revolutions in the historical record, Karl Selnam, the realist, finds a great deal of continuity. He claims that in mature sciences, later theories typically include earlier theories as limiting cases. In other words, later theories imply that earlier theories are approximately correct in some restricted domain. This permits him to argue that science does approximate an objective truth. In the end, Percy Lauwey, the pragmatist, shows that progress can be best understood in terms of the increasing capacity of later theories to solve problems. Students who recall Laudan's essay in Section 11, "What Is Science?," will not be surprised by this result.

As you read through this essay, consider the following:

1. Why does the positivist focus on the ability of theories to predict and explain data?
2. What are some problems with comparing the testability of different theories?
3. Why does the positivist think that the realist view of science contributes to the success of relativism?
4. What is the pragmatist's notion of progress and how can it be applied outside science?
5. How does pragmatism avoid the relativist objections to the cumulativity of science?
6. Which theory of scientific progress do you find most promising?

DAY 1, MORNING

Pragmatist: Gentlemen, I think we should begin, since we are already a bit behind schedule. Having been named chair of this committee, I should say that I interpret my charge to be that of seeing to it that our discussions remain focused on our central tasks and that we do not chase after too many wild hares. We already know one another, having crossed swords on several previous occasions, so I think that no preliminaries of that sort are called for. But we probably should give some thought to selecting the key topics that will form our agenda.

Relativist: Since our brief is relativism, especially as regards scientific knowledge, and since I am the only card-carrying relativist here, I have some suggestions to make about what the salient issues should be. Above all, I think that we should start with the collapse of positivism and foundationalism and move from there . . .

Realist: Forgive me for interrupting, Quincy, but the fact that you are keen on relativism gives you no special claim to set our agenda. All of us here have thought about relativism for a long while; the fact that we have rejected it, and that you have accepted it, is neither here nor there.

Positivist: I wonder if, rather than attempting to legislate our full agenda here and now, we couldn't avoid this procedural wrangling by simply agreeing to start somewhere and then take up the topics as they flow naturally from the exchange?

Pragmatist: I wholeheartedly concur, Rudy, Why don't you suggest a place for us to begin.

Positivist: Well, as we all know, one of the key issues in the epistemology of science

has concerned the question of the *growth* of scientific knowledge; thinkers from Peirce to Popper have insisted on the centrality of that problem to scientific epistemology. Nor is it philosophers alone who are preoccupied by it. Scientists and laymen similarly agree that one of the striking features of the diachronic development of science is the *progress* that it exhibits. The philosophical challenge is to find ways to characterize that "progress" as clearly and as unambiguously as we can. Perhaps therefore this would be an appropriate place for us to begin our explorations. And since our brief is to examine the status of contemporary relativism, maybe we could ask Quincy to kick off the discussion with a characterization of the relativist view of cognitive progress.

Relativist: I have no objections to our starting there, if you like, since I share your view that people have an abiding faith in the progress of science. Equally, however, I want to go on record straightaway as having grave reservations as to whether there is any robust, objective notion of the growth of knowledge. I happily grant you that our theoretical understandings and representations of the natural world change dramatically through time, though whether those changes represent "progress" or simply change is unclear. But I think that it would be reversing the natural logic of this subject for me to start things off. Most of us relativists reject the notion of progress because the two well-known accounts of scientific progress—associated with positivism and realism respectively—have been dismal failures. Accordingly, and I can assure you not out of any shyness on my part, I would urge Rudy or Karl to tell us whether they have a coherent theory of scientific progress to put forward. I will fill out my position in response to what they have to tell us.

Pragmatist: That's certainly agreeable as far as I'm concerned. Perhaps we can call on

From Larry Laudan, *Science and Relativism: Some Key Controversies in Philosophy of Science* (Chicago: The University of Chicago Press, 1990). Copyright © 1990 The University of Chicago Press. Reprinted by permission.

Rudy to outline the problem of progress or theory change as he sees it, since the positivist account of scientific progress probably remains the best known.

Positivist: Gladly. In a nutshell: science is the attempt to codify and anticipate experience. The raw materials of science are observational data or measurements. We develop theories and laws to correlate, explain, and predict those data. A science *progresses* just to the extent that later theories in a domain can predict and explain more phenomena than their predecessors did. Since the seventeenth century, the sciences—at least the natural sciences—have done just that.

Relativist: Hang on a minute. When you talk about what a theory "can" predict and explain, are you referring to what it *has* explained and predicted or are you talking about everything that it might be able to predict and explain?

Positivist: You can take it in either sense since science exhibits impressive credentials of both sorts.

Relativist: Well, if we focus on the first sense, what one might call demonstrated progress, I will grant you that some theories have managed to predict and explain some things not guessed at by their rivals. But I'm not sure that this difference gives us a sound basis for maintaining that one theory is really better or truer than another. After all, the fact that one theory has more proven predictive successes to its credit than a rival might be just an artifact of how long each has been around, how assiduously their applications have been explored, how many scientists have worked on them, etc. You surely don't want to argue that the goodness of a theory is a matter of such accidental circumstances as these?

Positivist: Well, as I said earlier, genuinely progressive theories are those which have the capacity to explain and predict a larger range of facts than their rivals. That is, in part, a *prospective* mat-

ter. I accept your point that one theory's known successes might have more to do with these accidents of history than with anything about the theory itself.

Relativist: But if you're saying that, in deciding whether one theory represents progress over another, we have to compare their *prospective* explanatory and predictive ranges, then I don't see how we could ever settle that issue since—as you just noted—we can never know all the consequences of any theory, infinite as that set is. You face a dilemma, Rudy: comparing the known achievements of rival theories can be done but is indecisive since those achievements will be in part a function of various accidents of the distribution of labor in the scientific community; yet it is impossible to compare the *potential* but unknown capacities of rival theories.

Positivist: Quincy is right, up to a point. A theory, any theory, has an infinite range of consequences only some of which will have been examined at any chosen stage of inquiry. But we are nonetheless often in a position to make dependable judgments about the prospective scope of rival theories, even when (as will always be the case) we have actually tested only some of those theories' consequences. Indeed, I can describe for you a procedure which will allow us to make such judgments *even if we have never tested any of the rivals*. Let us suppose that we have two theories under consideration, call them T_1 and T_2. Suppose further that we can show that T_2 *entails* T_1. Under such circumstances, we know that T_2 must have all the consequences of T_1, as well as some additional consequences besides (provided that T_1 does not entail T_2). Hence if a later theory entails an earlier one, but is not entailed by it, then we know that the later theory must be more general than the earlier.

Relativist: I'm not sure I see the point . . .

Positivist: It's simply this: A few moments ago, you said that the comparison of the prospective successes of rival theories was impossible, suggesting thereby that we positivists have no viable theory of scientific progress. What my latest example shows is that we can often demonstrate, even prior to *any* testing, that one theory is more general than another.

Pragmatist: But surely generality alone, in the sense of a maximally large class of entailments, is not scientific progress. If it were, then the adumbration of tautologies—which imply all true statements—and contradictions, which entail everything, would represent the ideal end point of science.

Positivist: What's wrong with tautologies and contradictions alike is not their lack of generality but their nonamenability to empirical test and thus their low information content. When I say that one theory represents progress over another as long as the former entails the latter (but not vice versa), I mean to refer only to theories per se, i.e., to sets of universal statements which are genuinely empirical by virtue of their prohibiting certain states of affairs. Tautologies and contradictions prohibit nothing and are thus not in the class of theories.

Relativist: What you appear to be saying is that scientific progress can occur only if (a) one *testable* theory succeeds another and if (b) the later theory entails the earlier. But Duhem, Quine, and a host of others have shown that scientific theories are not falsifiable and hence not testable.[1] They showed specifically that any theory whatever can be retained in the face of recalcitrant evidence, provided we are prepared to make drastic enough changes elsewhere in our framework of beliefs.

Pragmatist: I think, Quincy, we should tackle one issue at a time. We all know you believe theories are nonfalsifiable in principle, and I for one am prepared to set aside one of our later sessions to deal specifically with that issue. But I wonder if for now we shouldn't allow Rudy to finish setting out his position on scientific change and progress.

Positivist: Thanks for the intervention, Percy. Our relativist friend was overhasty, for I should be the last to claim that greater generality in our theories is a *sufficient* condition for scientific progress. My claim thus far was simply that greater generality was a *necessary* condition for making a well-founded claim of progress.

Pragmatist: Well, what more is required? . . .

Positivist: Well, above all, we expect the more progressive theory to be *better confirmed* than its predecessor. We expect it to have enabled us to explain and predict phenomena which its predecessor either couldn't explain at all or which its predecessor predicted incorrectly.

Realist: But if the earlier theory made an incorrect prediction and the later theory—by virtue of entailing its predecessor—and I believe you called that a necessary condition for progress—exhibits all the consequences of its predecessor, then any false prediction made by an earlier theory is also going to be made by its successor. Hence how could a later theory possibly *both* entail its predecessor *and* predict something correctly which "its predecessor predicted incorrectly"?

Pragmatist: Are you suggesting, Karl, that the old Baconian ideal that later theories should "contain" their predecessors is bankrupt because it would require later theories to incorporate all the failures of earlier ones?

Realist: Exactly. Once we realize that most theories in science are given up precisely because we have found them to be false, then it follows that the last thing we want to insist on is that their successors must capture all their empirical consequences! Perhaps I can put my challenge to the positivists most concisely in this form: I can see that a later and more general theory might well make some predictions—including correct predictions—concerning matters about which its predecessor was wholly silent; but how could the later theory manage to avoid the incorrect predictions made by its predecessor if it entails that predecessor?

Positivist: You have a point, Karl. Answering it will require me to be a bit more precise and detailed than I have been thus far. Let us distinguish, within the context of what I have been loosely calling a theory, between two elements; the theory per se and the associated experimental laws. Laws coordinate observations, and theories coordinate laws. Now, when we discover that a theory has broken down, that it has some false consequences, what we are really discovering is that some of the lawlike generalizations coordinated by that theory are false, i.e., they are not laws at all. Of course, as Karl says, we don't want to demand that a later theory must replicate the known failures of its predecessors.

Relativist: So now what is your story about the relation between successive theories in a progressive science?

Positivist: I suggest that what we expect a progressive theory change to do is to produce a successor theory which (a) retains all the *nondiscredited*, lawlike statements associated with the earlier theory, (b) drops out those pseudo-laws which have already been refuted, and (c) introduces some new lawlike regularities not previously encompassed within the predecessor theory. Things are even clearer if (d) some of the lawlike statements associated with the later theory, and not embraced by its predecessor, correctly predict hitherto unexplained and unpredicted phenomena. When all these conditions obtain, then we have a paradigmatic case of progressive theory change.

Realist: Although my positivist friend and I disagree about many matters, I find myself almost wholly in agreement with the characterization he has just offered.

Perhaps consensus on these issues is within our reach.

Pragmatist: Let's not be too hasty. Rudy's definition of theoretical progress in science does beg a few questions. For one thing it requires us to accept a distinction between a theory per se and the lawlike statements associated with it. As I understand it, that distinction is to be drawn chiefly in light of a distinction between observational terms—which is what occurs in the "laws"—and nonobservational terms which occur in the theory per se. Have I got that right?

Positivist: Or course.

Pragmatist: In that case, I cannot accept your distinction, since I doubt that there is a sharp line between theoretical terms and observational terms; and I suspect that Quincy will find it equally objectionable. And so should Karl, despite his initial willingness to accept Rudy's account of progress, since Karl's realism about science hinges crucially—if I understand it—on the repudiation of any sharp observational/theoretical dichotomy.[2] But even if I were to grant you, Rudy, that there is a viable distinction between what is observational and what is not, I would still have problems with your characterization of scientific progress.

Positivist: And what would those be?

Pragmatist: You originally told us that a sine qua non for progress was that later theories must entail their predecessors. When some of us noted that such a policy would involve retaining all the failures as well as the successes of earlier theories, you backed off and conceded that entailment between theories was too strong a condition. Now you are telling us that one theory is better than another if, among other things, the later theory retains all the nondiscredited lawlike statements of its predecessor.

Positivist: Quite.

Pragmatist: But how does one tell what those are? Since no one believes that we are fully aware of all the empirical or observational consequences of any theory, how can we ever be reasonably confident that a later theory has retained all the (correct) observational consequences of its predecessor?

Relativist: That sounds a bit like my earlier worry about how we can possibly compare the unknown, prospective features of different theories.

Pragmatist: Indeed it does. For all we know, a new theory might have ignored or dropped out many of the correct but unknown laws associated with an earlier theory. Thus, giving up the earlier theory, because of certain *known* failures, and replacing it by a theory which incorporates the earlier theory's *known* successes and avoids its *known* failures—if we could manage to do that—offers us no assurance that the new theory will generally work better than the old one might have.

Positivist: Your point is well taken, but there is an answer to your worries. Specifically, I require that, for progress to occur, successor theories must capture their predecessors as "limiting cases." This requirement enables us both to retain the successes of the earlier theory and to correct for its mistakes. Indeed, this is precisely what happened in physics at the turn of the century when Einstein was able to show that classical mechanics was a limiting case of relativity theory and when Planck and Bohr were able to show that classical electrodynamics was a limiting case of quantum theory.

Realist: Rudy, there is some sleight of hand going on here. You were originally trying to convince us that successive theories in a progressive science *entailed* their predecessors, while going beyond them. You have now shifted to telling us that progressive successor theories must capture their predecessors as "limiting cases." But am I not right in thinking that if one theory, T_1, is a limiting case of another, T_2, then

T_1 may have some consequences not exhibited by T_2?

Positivist: Naturally, and that's a virtue of this analysis; it allows a later theory to capture the relevant successes of its predecessors while avoiding some or all of its failures.

Realist: But what you gain on the swings you lose on the roundabouts. For if T_2 does not entail T_1 but merely captures some of its associated laws as limiting cases, then how can we be confident that all of T_1's *true but unknown* consequences are captured by T_2? Isn't it at least conceivable that classical mechanics, say, had some true consequences which are not explained or predicted by relativity theory?

Positivist: What you say has some surface plausibility, I suppose. But if we are prepared to think, following Hertz, that a theory is just a system of equations, then provided we can show that the equations constituting an earlier theory are derivable—at least as limiting cases—from the equations of a later theory, then we surely have strong grounds for arguing that the later theory will enjoy all the successes of the earlier.

Realist: Even if I were to grant that the equations of classical mechanics are limiting cases of the equations of relativity theory, I can scarcely go along with your naive identification of a theory with the equations with which we represent some of its most fundamental laws. Theories are, after all, much more than sets of equations; they typically involve claims about the basic causal processes and fundamental entities in a domain. Thus, Newton's mechanics is not only his three laws of motion, plus the law of gravity; equally, Newtonian "theory" is a complex set of concepts about absolute space and time, about the nature of matter, forces, and the like. I'm afraid, Rudy, that you cannot begin to grasp what scientific change is about until you realize that successive scientific theories are complex networks of assumptions about the basic building blocks of the world and about how they interact.

Positivist: I'm not sure I see what you're driving at.

Realist: What I'm saying is that even if you establish that the equations associated with successive theories are homologous (and that, at best, is what limiting-case relations exhibit) you are still far from having established that successive theories approximate to one another in the terms that really matter, i.e., in their underlying mechanisms and theoretical entities. No one has ever shown that Newton's mechanics—as opposed to a few mathematical laws associated with it—is a limiting case of either the special or the general theory of relativity.

Positivist: The fact that no one has shown this in its full generality does not mean that it is not so.

Realist: That much is true. But I can give you a perfectly general proof that Newton's theory in the full-bodied sense could never be a limiting case of the general theory of relativity—or of any other theory for that matter.

Positivist: I'm not clear how relevant that would be to the issues at hand, but I'd nonetheless like to hear the argument.

Realist: It's quite simple. By definition, limiting-case relations can be established only between sets of equations. That means that any theoretical claims which are strictly "qualitative" rather than "quantitative" in character can never be a limiting-case of other claims. Newton's physics is full of such qualitative claims. For instance, he asserts that light is corpuscular in character; that, indeed, is the core assumption of his optical theory. But what is the equational representation of that hypothesis? Again, he asserts that repulsive forces of some sort are responsible for the phenomenon of surface tension. Notoriously, Newton holds that space and time are absolute. How, without more detail

than Newton provides, is one to represent that in a form which would lend itself to limiting-case relations?

Positivist: I don't think that you and I, Karl, will ever agree on the nature of theories and their logical structure. Those assertions to which you are referring are not part of what I mean by Newtonian mechanics. They are perhaps a part of Newton's speculative philosophy of nature but not of his physics. Yet I daresay that to defend my views on this topic would take us too far afield. After all, we're supposed to be exploring the status of relativism, and instead positivism is becoming everyone's target.

Pragmatist: The issue, I think, is whether positivism provides a coherent picture of scientific progress. If it doesn't, then we must at least concede that the relativist is right about this much: the philosophy of science that has long been dominant offers no coherent account of scientific progress. And this is important because I seem to remember that Quincy earlier claimed that much of the rationale for his position derives from the collapse of the position which you have been attempting to defend.

Positivist: I am willing to entertain objections from relativists like Quincy, but I get irritated when realists like Karl suggest that I have no coherent account of scientific change. After all, it is the realist's construal of theories, seeing them as bloated ontological instruments, that sets up the grounds for the relativist's critique of scientific knowledge.

Realist: How can you say that? Realism is the only epistemology of science that provides a cogent alternative to relativism about science.

Positivist: What I mean is that the realist view of scientific theories—a view which sees them as making a range of claims about the world which go far beyond anything which can possibly be observed or directly tested—invites the relativist riposte that theories, if construed in that fashion, are articles of metaphysical faith rather than claims closely tied to the evidence. Indeed, if we accept the realist picture of scientific theories, then we are quickly led down the garden path to incommensurability, to the indeterminacy of translation, and ultimately to the inscrutability of reference.

Realist: That's absurd!

Positivist: Has it never occurred to you, Karl, that Feyerabend and Kuhn, two of the best known contemporary relativists, became relativists precisely because they construed rival theories as metaphysically pregnant "worldviews," which made a host of claims about matters beyond any conceivable empirical adjudication?

Pragmatist: You may be right, Rudy, about the realist analysis of science providing ammunition for relativism; but in this context your attack on realism is purely diversionary, for you have yet to show that positivism has a theory of scientific growth or progress which insures that later theories are really better than earlier ones. And without that, you've set the stage for relativism yourself. So, if I may, I'd like to bring you back to focus on that point.

Positivist: I'll give it one more try. As I reflect on the various worries that you three have been raising, the central one seems to be this: most of my characterizations of scientific progress have been concerned to give us ways to compare the thus-far unexplored potential of rival theories. In various ways, you have repeatedly argued that there is a problem about comparing the prospective features of rival theories. I am persuaded by the arguments raised that a theory of scientific progress which involves a priori projections about the prospective success of rival theories is not manageable. Accordingly, I shall propose that we conceive of scientific progress entirely in terms of the *demonstrated successes* of rival theories.

Realist: Can you be more precise?

Positivist: I was about to be! Let me reformulate my demands for progress in this fashion: for scientific progress to occur, (a) a successor theory must embrace all the *confirmed* true consequences of its predecessors. . . . A second condition for scientific progress is (b) that the successor theory must also exhibit some empirical strengths not shown by its predecessor.[3] Of course, this is no ironclad guarantee that the new theory will always hold up better than its predecessor would have, since we can conceive of circumstances in which the untested consequences of the older theory might stand up better than the untested consequences of the newer theory. But there *are* no guarantees where empirical research is concerned, and it is a skeptic's fallacy to demand them. We can judge the future only by the past. If we can show that one theory enjoys all the known strengths of its predecessors, that it avoids some of its predecessor's mistakes, and that, besides, it can explain some things not explained by its predecessor, then we have very powerful reasons for regarding the new theory as an improvement over the old. That is what scientific progress amounts to. And, having offered you that definition, I will go on to make the claim that the natural sciences—and only the natural sciences—exhibit progress of that sort.

Realist: I'm curious why you don't add an obvious third condition: (c) that the later, more progressive theory must avoid some of the false consequences of its predecessor.

Positivist: When that occurs, we have yet further evidence for the progressiveness of the successor theory. But I did not want to make your third condition (c) a necessary one for progress since that would force us to say that one theory could never be progressive over another unless the latter was known to have some false consequences.

Realist: And what's wrong with that?

Positivist: Simply this: I want to leave open the possibility that we may judge one theory to be an improvement over another, even when neither has *yet* been falsified.

Realist: That seems reasonable enough.

Relativist: So far, I have been content to let others do my work for me, but I must strenuously object to this latest redaction of your position, Rudy. I object because it—like every one of your other formulations—depends upon a degree of *cumulativity* during theory change which is wholly belied by the historical record. You began by telling us that later theories must entail their predecessors. They don't. . . . Historical research of the last three decades makes clear that this condition is rarely, if ever, satisfied. Finally, you now tell us that later theories in a progressive science must preserve all the known empirical successes of their predecessors. Again, they don't.

Positivist: Why do you say that?

Relativist: Kuhn and Feyerabend showed repeatedly that there are explanatory losses as well as gains in most theory transitions; because that is so, an account of progress which requires—as yours does—the cumulative retention of known empirical successes from one theory to another is simply demanding too much. If progress is understood as you just defined it, then we have no grounds whatever for holding natural science to be a generally progressive activity. I'll go further than that. In my view, there is no viable notion of cognitive progress which does not require a high degree of cumulativity between earlier and later theories in a science. Rudy was surely right to look for some such explication of progress. The unhappy fact of the matter, however, is that successive theories in the sciences—including the most mature and well-developed sciences like physics—fail to exhibit the requisite degree of cumulativity. That is one rea-

son why a theory of scientific progress is an absolute nonstarter. In a word: no cumulativity, no progress.

Positivist: All this twaddle about recurrent losses of established empirical successes is just hogwash. I defy you to give me an example of a major theory change in the mature sciences which involved such losses.

Relativist: What counts for you as a mature science? Physics since Galileo?

Positivist: Fine. You have my prejudices down pat!

Relativist: Well, what about a case like this: The vortex physics of Descartes explained why the planets moved in the same direction and the same plane, namely, because they were all carried around the sun by a vortex.

Relativist: Well, Newton nowhere in the *Principia* explains those salient facts about planetary motion.

Realist: But Newtonian mechanics does not forbid that the planets might move in the same direction and in the same plane.

Relativist: Right. But my point is that Newton had no explanation for these phenomena. Compatibly with Newtonian celestial mechanics, the alternate planets could have moved in opposite directions and in planes perpendicular to one another. Newton was forced to *assume*, as an initial condition of the solar system, that the planets moved in these ways; whereas Descartes could *explain* these same phenomena. What was an empirical success for the earlier theory was an unexplained fact for the successor. That's what I mean by loss in the history of science; and there are loads of other cases.

Positivist: I think you're being altogether too hasty here, Quincy. After all, Kant and Laplace both showed how—on Newtonian principles—one could get the solar system configured as it is. The nebular hypothesis offers a Newtonian explanation for these facts.

Relativist: So it does; but need I remind you that the nebular hypothesis emerged a century *later* than Newton's *Principia*—and long after virtually all physicists had become Newtonians? If you want to show that the history of science is rational, you must show that there were good reasons at the time for the acceptance of Newtonian mechanics. On your view, we should have to say that it was reasonable to believe that Newtonian mechanics was an improvement on Cartesian physics only by the end of the eighteenth century, fully five decades after everyone doing physics had accepted Newton.

Positivist: I still think my general point is right; for here we have a situation where the later theory had the resources to capture all the known successes of its predecessor, even if physicists at the time didn't know it. The fact remains that the later theory did cumulatively retain all the known successes of the earlier one.

Pragmatist: You and Rudy have reached a bit of an impasse on that issue, so—by way of keeping the conversation moving—I would like to challenge an assumption that you both brought to the discussion. Specifically, you have supposed that cumulative theory change in some sense or other is a precondition for making judgments of scientific progress. I see no reason why the only sorts of changes we call progressive or contributory to the growth of knowledge need be transitions which retain cumulativity. I suspect that this claim will make me odd man out in this discussion, since our realist friend Karl, every bit as much as Rudy and Quincy, takes cumulative retention of empirical success to be a sine qua non for scientific progress. Am I right?

Realist: Of course I do, despite my quibbles with Rudy about whether limiting-case talk is the best way to capture what those retentions are. As such realists as Boyd and Putnam have argued, in any mature and well-developed science later theories entail at least approximations to their predecessors.[4] As a realist, I hold that science through time is moving closer and closer to a correct characterization of the natural world. Because that is so, later theories need to preserve the known successes of their predecessors. If they did not, there would be no coherent sense that we could attach to the notion of science progressively approximating to a true account of the world. Rudy and I are of one mind on this issue, even if we disagree about the nature of theories.

Pragmatist: I'm afraid that I stand with Quincy where the historical record is concerned. Typically, later theories do not entail their predecessors, nor capture them as limiting cases, nor retain in wholesale fashion all their known empirical consequences.[5] But unlike the rest of you, including Quincy, I do not see, in that failing, any grounds for pessimism about the possibility of developing a theory of scientific progress.

Relativist: But scientific progress without the cumulative retention of our successes is no progress at all. I think it was Kuhn who pointed out that, if there are losses as well as gains associated with theory transitions, then there can be no objective way of telling whether the gains outweigh the losses.[6] You have conceded, Percy, that such losses occur yet you continue to hold that science is progressive. It just won't wash.

Pragmatist: Our notion of progress carries with it a lot of baggage, I'll grant you. But neither in science nor elsewhere need we make progress dependent on some sort of total cumulativity. What, after all, is progress—whether scientific or otherwise? We judge an activity to be making progress when it is further along toward the realization of its ends now than it formerly was. Progress is thus a diachronic notion that involves reference to an aim, or set of aims, and an empirically based ranking of the degree to which various efforts at the realization of those aims have in fact furthered them.

Positivist: Are you suggesting that scientific progress is no different from progress in any other area?

Pragmatist: Yes and no. "Progress" is a perfectly general notion of successive movement towards the realization of an end; to that extent progress in science is like progress in, say, bank robbing or arms-control talks. But to the extent that science has a unique set of aims (and I suspect that we will eventually have to fight out that issue in these conversations), then progress towards the realization of scientific ends may be different from other forms of progress just because the ends are different. But in all these cases, progress is movement towards the realization of one's ends.

Realist: I have no objection, Percy, to your defining progress in science instrumentally, as a matter of attempting to realize certain ends, but I can't see how that circumvents the cumulativity issues we were discussing before. Whatever else the ends of science might be, they surely include things like "explaining and predicting everything that happens in the natural world." If so, and if losses of the sort that you and Quincy are so insistent about actually occur, then we are in no position to say that later theories do more to further our ends than earlier ones did.

Pragmatist: I see it rather differently, Karl. Suppose we were to say that one of the central aims of science—perhaps *the* central aim—is to produce theories which are increasingly reliable. Suppose, further, that we unpack that notion of reliability in terms of the ability of theories to stand up to more and more demanding empirical tests. Suppose, finally, that we make certain plausible assumptions about what counts as demanding tests. We might say, for instance, as realists like you are prone to, that theories which make surprising predictions successfully have been more robustly tested than those which do not. Equally, we might say that theories which pass tests by means of controlled experiments have been more convincingly tested than those which are merely tested against haphazardly collected observations. Again, we might say that a theory which has been tested in several domains of its application has been better tested than one which has been tested in only one. Now, to a crude first-order of approximation, my theory of empirical progress simply says that one theory represents progress over another provided that the one has passed tests of a sort that the other has failed to pass (whereas the latter has passed no sorts of tests which the former has failed). As long as our knowledge is becoming more reliable, progress is being made. . . .

Positivist: I can see where you're headed, Percy. You're going to claim that, by virtue of the fact that T_2 has passed more demanding tests than T_1, T_2 represents progress over T_1—even if T_1 manages to have passed certain tests that T_2 was not subjected to.

Pragmatist: Precisely. One theory need not have passed all the tests of a rival for us to judge that it is better tested than, and thus represents progress over, its rival. If a later theory passes more robust tests than its predecessors, then we have good grounds for believing that the later theory will be more reliable than its predecessor, *even if* the earlier theory passed some tests which its successor did not.

Relativist: But what grounds have you for thinking that typical cases of explanatory loss in the history of science are always of this sort? Surely it sometimes happens that a later theory passes tests which are no more robust than those passed by its predecessor.

Pragmatist: To be honest, Quincy, I'm not sure how frequently either case occurs. The point I am trying to make, however, doesn't depend on relative frequencies of the sort you have in mind. What I am trying to show is simply this: the fact that earlier theories sometimes explain some phenomena not explained by their successors—and I do take that to be a fact—is by itself insufficient grounds for us to make the claim that science fails to progress in such episodes. If you want to deny that scientific progress occurs—and I think you do—then you must show (a) that the losses in question concern phenomena which were genuine tests of the earlier theories and (b) that the earlier tests were at least as robust as the tests passed by the later theories. I do not believe that you and your fellow relativists have undertaken either task.

Relativist: I grant you as much, but you are still missing the central philosophical moral of noncumulativity. The fact is that earlier theories generally solve problems not solved by their successors. Since, to paraphrase you pragmatists, the aim of science is to solve problems, and if two rival theories solve different problems, then it is a subjective matter to decide which theory is best, depending on our preferences as to which problems are more important to solve.[7] Progress in such matters is entirely in the eye of the beholder.

Pragmatist: Ever since Kuhn's *Structure of Scientific Revolutions*, you relativists have been making hay out of the fact that earlier theories sometimes solve problems not solved by their successors. But the point I have been trying to make for the last few minutes is that we do not judge theories primarily in terms of whether they solve some problems which we would like to have solutions for, problems to which we may even have assigned a high initial importance.

Realist: I find it a little rich, Percy, that you, as a self-avowed pragmatist, are trying to persuade us that solving

important problems is unimportant in the appraisal of theories.

Pragmatist: I'm saying nothing of the sort. We develop theories because we find ourselves in problematic situations, where certain questions about the natural world forcibly impress themselves on us. Science, in my view, is entirely a problem-solving activity. But as an epistemologist, I am perfectly capable of distinguishing between those problems which arise out of salient practical concerns and those solved problems which constitute especially probative tests of a theory in question. Obviously, we want a theory to solve certain problems, but it would be a very naïve pragmatist indeed who ignored the fact that the ability of a theory to solve the very problems it was devised to solve is usually not a very strenuous *test* of the theory in question, nor a very good indicator of how reliable the theory is, or how likely it is to hold up to further extensions and applications of it. The pragmatist is chiefly interested in whether a theory will be a reliable guide to the future. For that reason, he's apt to attach greater weight to theories that have passed robust tests than to theories which, while perhaps solving many problems, have passed few genuine tests.

Relativist: But if a theory fails to solve some problems we regard as important, we will surely reject the theory, regardless of how well-tested it appears to be.

Pragmatist: Wrong! If a theory fails to provide a solution to problems which we deem especially urgent or compelling, then we will, of course, cast around for some theory which does solve those problems. You are right to that extent. But the failure of a well-tested theory to solve problems that we want solved is no reason to reject the theory in question. If a theory is the best-tested among its rivals, that is, among the known contraries to it, then that must be the theory of choice among the rivals. Of course, if one can develop an equally well-tested, or better tested, theory which also solves one's preferred problems, all the better. But faced with a Hobson's choice between an ill-tested theory which solves a preferred problem and a well-tested theory which does not, the theory of evidence makes it very clear how one's choice should go.

Relativist: That is patently absurd. Are you trying to tell me that if, say, a chemist is interested in developing a theory about how colloidal suspensions work, and that if the best-tested theory of chemistry happens to be one which has nothing to say about colloidal suspensions, then he has no grounds for rejecting that theory, however well tested it is, because it fails to address what he regards as the central problems of chemistry?

Pragmatist: What I am saying is that there are two quite distinct issues which you are running together. One issue concerns the problems to which a theory offers an answer or solution. The other deals with the evidence we have that a theory is well-founded, or is likely to offer adequate solutions to the problems it addresses. Sometimes, theories fail on both counts: they neither address interesting problems nor do they have a successful track record vis-à-vis the tests to which they have been subjected. Both of us, I suspect, can agree that such theories should be rejected.

Relativist: Well, Percy, you know that I have doubts about whether one can ever make an objective decision to reject *any* theory.

Notes

1. For most of the classic texts on this problem, see Harding (1974).

2. Most realists (e.g., Maxwell, Sellars, Popper, and Putnam) hold that the collapse of the theory/observation dichotomy undermines instrumentalism and paves the way for realism about theoretical entities. It should be noted that this way of putting the point smacks of the paradoxical since a realism "about theoretical entities" would seem to presuppose the very distinction whose avowed demise it celebrates.

3. This position has been developed by Post (1971), among others.

4. See Boyd (1973) and Putnam (1978).

5. For a detailed development of this argument, see Laudan (1984, chap. 6).

6. Kuhn makes this point at several places in his work. See, especially, Kuhn (1970, pp. 101–2, 108, 110, 111, 118–19).

7. Kuhn: "Since no paradigm ever solves all the problems it defines and since no two paradigms leave all the same problems unsolved, paradigm debates always involve the question: which problem is it more significant to have solved?" (1970, p. 110).

References

Boyd, Richard. 1973. "Reason, Underdetermination and a Casual Theory of Evidence." *Nous,* 7:1–12.

Harding, Sandra. 1976. *Can Theories Be Refuted?* Dordrecht: Reidel.

Kuhn, Thomas. 1970. *Structure of Scientific Revolutions,* 2d ed. Chicago: University of Chicago Press.

Kuhn, Thomas. 1977. *The Essential Tension.* Chicago: University of Chicago Press.

Laudan, Larry. 1981. *Science and Hypothesis.* Dordrecht: Reidel.

Laudan, Larry. 1984. *Science and Values.* Berkeley: University of California Press.

Post, Heinz. 1971. "Correspondence, Invariance and Heuristics." *Studies in History and Philosophy of Science,* 2:213–55.

Putnam, Hilary. 1978. *Meaning and the Moral Sciences.* London: Routledge.

Realism and Scientific Progress

Philip Kitcher

In this challenging essay, Philip Kitcher defends the realist view that science approximates truths about the world. Antirealists, like Kuhn, claim we cannot make sense of "truth" when it is applied to scientific theories. Moreover, they claim the history of science reveals that theories once believed to be true are rejected at later times. Reasoning inductively, they suggest that our current theories are likely to be rejected by future scientists. This "pessimistic induction" strongly suggests that we should now believe our current theories are false. Kitcher responds, first, by sketching a correspondence theory of truth. Words refer to items in the world, and our sentences are true when those items are related as the sentences say they are. He suggests that the truth of ordinary assertions does not differ significantly from truth in science in that both assume that there is a fixed nature that we try to approximate. Second, he argues that the history of science does not justify the kind of pessimism that the antirealist requires. An optimistic induction is just as reasonable, at least in some areas of science. Furthermore, in some areas, theoretical posits (the entities that a theory claims exist) show sufficient stability over time that it is reasonable to conclude that the theory is approximately true. Philip Kitcher is Presidential Professor of Philosophy at the University of California, San Diego.

As you read through this essay, consider the following:

1. How does Kitcher distinguish global antirealism from local antirealism?
2. How does Kitcher try to show that truth is less mysterious than antirealists think?
3. What is the pessimistic induction? How is it supposed to show that scientific theories are not true?
4. What three responses to the pessimistic induction does Kitcher consider? Which of these does he take to be the most persuasive?
5. Do you find the optimistic induction to be more plausible than the pessimistic induction, at least in some areas of science?
6. In this selection, Kitcher addresses only a few of the arguments used by antirealists. Can you think of other reasons to believe that science does not reach truth? On balance, do you think that some modern scientific theories are close to the truth?

1. FACING THE MUSIC

The account of scientific progress that I [defend] promises old-fashioned virtues. It offers a broadly realist view of science: scientists find out things about a world that is inde-

From Philip Kitcher, *The Advancement of Science: Science Without Legend, Objectivity Without Illusions.* Copyright © 1993 by Oxford University Press, Inc. Reprinted by permission of Oxford University Press, Inc.

pendent of human cognition; they advance true statements, use concepts that conform to natural divisions, develop schemata that capture objective dependencies. Realism is suspect in many quarters, not only among those who are skeptical about the progressiveness of science but also for champions of alternative accounts of scientific progress.[1] . . .

. . . The aim of this [essay] is to investigate lines of criticism that have been developed against other broadly realist proposals, and to show that we can enjoy the old-fashioned virtues of my account of progress without abandoning important recent insights about the growth of science. . . .

The challenges I shall consider can be distilled into a sequence of questions. (1) Is it coherent to suppose that the sciences aim at and attain the truth? (2) How can we know that we are making progress in any of the senses that I have delineated? (3) Doesn't induction on the past history of the sciences reveal to us that our current beliefs are overwhelmingly likely to be wrong? . . . I shall take up these objections in turn.

2. REHABILITATING TRUTH

Truth can seem commonplace, or utterly mysterious, depending on perspective. . . . It is well to start by reminding ourselves of humbler uses of the idea.

Semantic facts concern the relation between language users and nature. In virtue of the state of the language user and the state of the rest of the world, there is sometimes a relation—the relation of reference—between the words spoken or written and items in the world. In consequence, the statement represents the world as being some particular way. The statement is true just in case the way in which the world is represented is the way it really is.

Philosophical concerns about truth, about the coherence of the notion of truth and of supposing that the sciences aim at truth, arise from this picture. Kuhn's own, highly influential, suspicions about talk of truth touch on some venerable questions:

> One often hears that successive theories grow ever closer to, or approximate more and more closely to, the truth. Apparently generalizations like that refer not to the puzzle-solutions and the concrete predictions derived from a theory but rather to its ontology, to the match, that is, between the entities with which the theory populates nature and what is "really there."
>
> Perhaps there is some other way of salvaging the notion of "truth" for application to whole theories, but this one will not do. There is, I think, no theory-independent way to reconstruct phrases like "really there"; the notion of a match between the ontology of a theory and its "real" counterpart in nature now seems to me illusive in principle. Besides, as a historian, I am impressed with the implausibility of the view. I do not doubt, for example, that Newton's mechanics improves on Aristotle's and that Einstein's improves on Newton's as instruments for puzzle-solving. But I can see in their succession no coherent direction of ontological development. On the contrary, in some important respects, though by no means in all, Einstein's general theory of relativity is closer to Aristotle's than either of them is to Newton's. (1962/1970 206–207)

This passage is both highly suggestive, and, I shall argue, deeply puzzling in certain respects.

Kuhn contends that a certain philosophical project, the project of "salvaging the notion of 'truth' for application to whole theories," is doomed. That project is abandoned in the account of scientific progress that I have given. But I do demand things that Kuhn seems disinclined to concede, to wit the conceptions of successful reference, adequate reference potentials, correct explanatory schemata, true statements, and improved false statements. All of these rely on the notion of a match between the scientist's representation of the world and what is "really there," a match Kuhn takes to be "illusive." Thus the first big issue, the one that will occupy us for this section, is whether we can make sense of the idea that conceptual/linguistic items (words, statements, schemata) match elements of reality.

Kuhn continues by offering a different type of objection, one that tries to undercut our practice of claiming a match between our representations of nature and nature itself by pointing to large transitions in the history of science. As I shall try to show, the alleged instability of our conceptions of nature, supported by the invocation of Aristotle, Newton, and Einstein, leads into questions about the proper degree of pessimism we should have concerning our apparent achievements . . . and about the problem of losses in the history of science. . . .

The correspondence theory of truth is often held to involve extravagant metaphysics, but, I claim, its roots lie in our everyday practices. We explain and predict the behavior of our fellows by attributing to them states with propositional content. . . . We explain and predict the differential success of our fellows in coping with the world by supposing that there are relations between the elements of their representations and independent objects. Those with correct beliefs about spatial relations can navigate their way more successfully than those who have faulty beliefs, and they can do so because their beliefs correspond to the ways in which the constituents of the local environment are arranged. Simple psychological ideas form part of the explanation of everyday behavior. Simple semantical ideas, added to those simply psychological ideas, explain the consequences of behavior.

Correspondence truth, I suggest, begins at home. Few are born antirealists, and those who achieve antirealism typically do so because it is thrust upon them by arguments they feel unable to answer. In the present instance, the arguments derive from the denial of the theory-independent perspective.

Kuhn's sympathy for this line of criticism is suggested in his phraseology: "There is no theory-independent way to reconstruct phrases like 'really there'; the notion of a match between the ontology of a theory and its 'real' counterpart in nature now seems to me illusive in principle." . . . Now it is, of course, right to insist that any *description* of what is "really there," however abstract we try to make our formulation, will presuppose some language, some conceptualization of nature. Equally, if one thinks of a match between cognitive/linguistic items and independent nature as requiring some possible process of *matching*, then, because there is no Archimedean point from which both sides can be viewed, the notion of match will come to seem "illusive." The common root of both ideas is that we have no access to nature which does not involve some elements of some scientific practice—a point which is

uncontroversial once one has recognized that the categories and beliefs of common sense are themselves parts of primitive scientific practices. But why should this doom the idea that there is something independent of us to which we have access through processes that are dependent on the state of current science/common sense?

The move from the theory dependence of our *perception* of nature to the theory-dependence of *nature* is apparent in Kuhn's discussion of Priestley and Lavoisier.

> At the very least, as a result of discovering oxygen, Lavoisier saw nature differently. And in the absence of some recourse to that hypothetical fixed nature that he "saw differently," the principle of economy will urge us to say that after discovering oxygen Lavoisier worked in a different world. (Kuhn 1962/70 118)

Realists have their preferred picture of what happened to Lavoisier. There was a constant fixed nature. As a result of a series of interactions with this nature, Lavoisier's cognitive system underwent some changes (the changes we describe by saying that he acquired the concept of oxygen, came to believe that combustion involved the absorption of oxygen, and so forth). In consequence, his subsequent interactions with nature activated new propensities and induced . . . beliefs which would not have been induced in his former self (or in his friend Priestley). Realists add that Lavoisier's new beliefs are better than his old ones because, in some instances, they match the way nature is. Kuhn's challenge to this story seems to be that its postulation of a fixed theory-independent nature is otiose. Since we have no independent access to nature, we are just making up an unnecessary story about the episode. How could we ever now that this is the way to view what occurs? How could we ever tell that Lavoisier's new beliefs match nature more closely than his old ones (the beliefs Priestley stubbornly retains)?

Kuhn's suggested economy is false economy. One way to recognize the work that the idea of a fixed nature does is to see how we are impoverished by giving it up. One difficulty is that it becomes troublesome to understand the improvements in "concrete predictions" and "puzzle solving." We believe that such improvements occur, for example in the transition from young Lavoisier to mature Lavoisier, because we recognize that there is increased harmony within our cognitive system: . . . beliefs that are now induced in scientists can be accommodated more easily within the total set of beliefs. Realism provides a picture of the genesis of perceptual belief that attributes a causal role to something beyond our cognitive systems. That picture has the advantages that it offers an explanation of the apparent fact that some of our beliefs come to us unbidden, it allows for the contents of our perceptual beliefs to be partly determined by our prior cognitive state, and it enables us to understand our seeming ability to achieve greater cognitive harmony in terms of increased match between our representations and an independent reality. To demonstrate that the "hypothetical fixed nature" is unnecessary, antirealists must provide a rival picture that has similar virtues.

Serious epistemological questions remain. How do we know that the statements of the mature Lavoisier match reality more closely than those defended by his younger self? Obviously not by engaging in some out-of-theory experience that reveals to us both our own representations and the aspects of nature to which they are supposed to correspond. Our belief that Lavoisier made progress rests partly on the evidence for Lavoisier's chemistry, partly on our scientific understanding of the relationships between human cognitive systems and the world. . . .

3. PITFALLS OF PESSIMISM

Contemporary biologists agree that human beings and chimpanzees had a common ancestor no more than a few million years ago. I claim that their assertion is true. Critics object. They demand to know why I think that what the biologists say is true. How should they be answered?

I shall start by distinguishing two forms of antirealism. *Global* critiques of realist epistemology contend that we have no basis for claiming that *any* statement is true (when truth is understood in the realist's preferred way). So the global antirealist would be skeptical about the truth of the biologists' claim as a consequence of a sweeping generalization. By contrast, *local* critiques of realist epistemology allow that we are entitled to maintain that some statements are true (in the realist sense) but they complain that statements which realists take to be true, statements with some special feature *U*, outrun this entitlement. So, one kind of local antirealist would deny our justification for accepting as true statements about entities in the remote past and would base skepticism about the biologists' thesis on this denial. The most famous form of local antirealism—one that has flourished in our century—identifies the special feature *U* as that of making reference to unobservables. . . .

Imagine, then, that we face an antirealist who doubts that what the biologists say about our ancestry is true. An obvious first response is to elaborate the evidence that has convinced people about the recency of human-chimp common ancestry. So one can explain the general idea of a molecular clock, show how molecular clocks can be calibrated and how they give an estimate of about five million years for separation of the human and the chimpanzee lineages, and, as the coup de grace, rehearse the details of the fossil record. This will not satisfy a global antirealist. For beyond the issue of demarcating statements like this, which are accepted, from others (such as, Human beings were directly created along with all other animal kinds about 10,000 years ago) which are rejected, global antirealism's prime concern is how *any* statement might earn the title of truth, when truth is conceived as in the realist picture.

But there is an answer to this question. We have scientific views about the relations between ourselves and the rest of nature. In the light of these scientific views we can evaluate the likelihood that we are right about various kinds of things. So we examine the procedures that are involved in accepting the hypothesis about human-chimp separation and show, by appealing to background ideas about reliable detection of aspects of nature, that such procedures would regularly deliver truth (understood in the realist way). Other procedures, such as those underlying the creationist claims that are rejected, would not.

Thoughtful antirealists will not be entirely convinced. A first worry will focus on the appearance of circularity. The envisaged defense of the truth of the claim about human-chimp separation requires acceptance of certain parts of contemporary science. Someone suspicious about molecular clocks or about the fossil findings will not be persuaded. Nor, by the same token, can we expect to satisfy those who think that our current physical-physiological-psychological conceptions of the relationship between human cognitive systems and the environment are mistaken. Skeptics who insist that we begin from *no* assumptions are inviting us to play a mug's game. Descartes's lack of success in generating an account of nature that would survive all possible doubt was in no way the result of deficiencies of intellect or imagination.

The global antirealist aims to challenge the status that is conferred on accepted science as a whole. To respond it is necessary to show how our *scientific* conception of the physical-physiological-psychological relationships between human cognitive systems and nature supports theses to the effect that certain types of processes and procedures yield true beliefs—representations that match nature—and to demonstrate that it is processes and procedures of these privileged kinds that are involved in the generation of accepted science. By hypothesis the skeptic accepts our current science, and that will include the conception of the relations between our cognitive systems and nature. Hence the strategy seems entirely appropriate, for it starts with premises that are accepted by those we intend to address. Moreover, even though science is being used to defend itself, there is no guarantee of success

in our project. Application of our conception of the relation between human cognitive systems and nature might convince us that some procedures crucial to various parts of accepted science are unreliable: suppose, for example, that we were able to show that large parts of contemporary genetics rest upon experiments in which people are required to discriminate mutants in ways that can be shown to outrun the abilities manifested in the test situations of perceptual psychology. . . .

Clever antirealists see that the issue is whether all or some of our accepted beliefs have a particular status, and they use the fact of scientific change to play reason against itself. Their best strategy is the so-called pessimistic induction on the history of science. Here one surveys the discarded theories of the past; points out that these were once accepted on the basis of the same kinds of evidence that we now employ to support our own accepted theories, notes that those theories are, nevertheless, now regarded as false; and concludes that our own accepted theories are very probably false.[2] It should be apparent from my continued emphasis on practices rather than on theories that I shall want to reformulate this pessimistic induction before replying to it. But, even before doing so, I want to suggest that the history of science provides grounds for optimism as well as pessimism.

There are a number of ways to present an optimistic view of the history of science. One . . . is to suggest that we look at the track record of successful uses of theoretical terms. Perhaps most of the posits introduced by our remote predecessors are entities we no longer countenance, but, as time goes on, we find that more and more of the posits of theoretical science endure within contemporary science. We attribute this increased success to improved abilities of scientists to learn about investigating the world. Hence, as Michael Devitt points out, the pessimistic observation that a lot of past theoretical science has been discarded is not enough. The skeptic needs to show that "the history of unobservable posits has been thoroughly *erratic*." . . .

Although this line of argument is suggestive, and although it makes the important point that confidence in the posits of contemporary science could be justified, even if our first efforts were discredited, provided that our practice of positing improved with time, it is vulnerable to some important challenges. Antirealists will deny that they have to show that "the history of unobservable posits has been thoroughly erratic," noting that confidence would be undermined if there were a relatively constant tendency, at all epochs in the history of science, to introduce posits which, roughly as often as not, had to be subsequently abandoned. They will also point out that if endurance simply amounts to temporal persistence, then there were many entities introduced within ancient science—epicycles, humors, and so forth—that survived for a very long time before being discarded. To develop Devitt's argument, one needs to capture the idea that the stability of modern references to molecules, genes, and extinct organisms throughout periods of great theoretical proliferation somehow redounds more to their credit than the persistence of Aristotelian and Galenic conceptions through the Middle Ages. Finally, anti-realists will, quite legitimately, demand careful specifications of the careers of various kinds of posits that have been introduced in the history of science. . . .

For the reasons rehearsed in the last paragraph, I do not think that Devitt's insight furnishes a complete reply to the antirealist. Another line of response is to focus on comparative judgments about the merits of past theories (or components of practice). Consider the following optimistic induction:

> Whenever in the history of science there has been within a field a sequence of theories $T_1, \ldots, T_n$ (or explanatory schemata, statements, terms, instruments, . . .) such that, for each i, T_{i+1} has been accepted as superior to T_i, then for every j greater than $i + 1$, T_{i+1} appears closer to the truth than T_i from the perspective of T_j (more correct or complete in the case of explanatory schemata, equipped with a more adequate reference potential in the case of terms, and so forth).

So, we can expect that our theories will appear to our successors to be closer to the truth than those of our predecessors.

The intuitive idea behind the optimistic induction is a very straightforward one. We believe that Priestley was wrong, Lavoisier was wrong, Dalton was wrong, Avogadro was wrong, and so on. But we also think that Lavoisier improved on Priestley, Dalton on Lavoisier, Avogadro on Dalton. So while we do not endorse the claims of our predecessors we do support their sense of themselves as making progress. In consequence, we expect that our successors will support our sense that we have made further progress.

Antirealists might reply that they too can endorse the progessiveness of the sequence of chemists mentioned, although they would try to explain this in different terms. But this misses the point of the optimistic induction. That induction is intended as a counter to pessimism. The structure of the pessimist's argument is as follows: "Suppose that we assign to the theoretical claims of contemporary science the status that the realist suggests. Notice, then, that our predecessors might have done the same. But the realist doesn't want to confer the privileged status on *their* claims, most of which are now discredited. So how do we justify treating the theoretical claims of contemporary science differently?" To this, the optimistic induction replies as follows: "Sensible realists should abandon the idea that contemporary theoretical claims are literally true in favor of the notion that there has been convergence to the truth. So we accept the pessimist's point. Notice however that this leaves untouched the idea that the historical development can be seen in terms of convergence on the truth, understood in the realist's preferred way. Using the realist's conceptions of increasing truthlikeness of statements (improved false statements, more adequate reference potentials, more complete or more correct schemata) we can take the very same examples that the pessimist uses to undermine our confidence in the literal truth of contemporary theoretical claims and show that they do not invalidate reformed realism's contentions that our theoretical statements are improving, our schemata becoming more complete, our concepts more adequate, when all these are understood in the realist's preferred way. So the pessimistic induction has no force against a properly formulated realism." The optimistic induction, then, is not an attempt to show that the history of science *must* be interpreted in terms of the realist's conception of progress (although it is worth asking the antirealist to explain a rival account of progress in detail and to show that it does not make surreptitious appeals to truth) but to blunt an apparently damaging challenge to explain the difference between the science of the past and the science of the present.

Suggestive as they are, these observations strike me as altogether too weak. The pessimistic induction relies critically on the gross analysis of science as a constellation of theories which are supposed to be true and which are, historically, failures. I oppose to it a simple point. The history of science does not reveal to us that we are fallible in some undifferentiated way. Some kinds of claims endure, other kinds are likely to be discarded as inaccurate. *Furthermore this is exactly what we would have expected given our conception of the relationship between human cognitive systems and nature.* According to that conception we are relatively good at finding out some things, and discover others only with relative difficulty. We would expect that, in the latter sorts of endeavors, history would be peppered with false starts and plausible, but misleading, conclusions. With respect to the former projects we would anticipate doing better.

Instead of a blanket pronouncement to the effect that our current theories are probably wrong, it would be far more instructive to investigate the stability of various components of practice in various fields. *Perhaps* this investigation would pose a challenge to parts of contemporary science, by revealing that processes that we take to be reliable and that are critically involved in supporting those parts of contemporary science have, in the past, given rise to large numbers of erroneous or inadequate ideas. But this needs to be shown. . . .

In the rest of this section, I want to take up the most sweeping use of the pessimistic induction, the global antirealist contention that the past history of science shows that we should not count *any* statement as true (in the realist sense). To defend antirealism about observational claims—either those based on unaided observation or those made with the assistance of instruments—it would be necessary to show how history of science reveals the presence of unanticipated sources of pervasive error in arriving at particular kinds of beliefs in particular kinds of ways. Now there are instances in which projects of measurement encounter difficulty after difficulty, others in which we seem to go from success to success. Microscopes, telescopes, electron microscopes, spectrometers all seem to have delivered a body of claims with high and increasing rates of stability. Define the success rate of an instrument or technique at a time to be the percentage of statements generated by users of the instrument or the technique at the time (judged as competent by the standards of the time) that have endured into the present . . . Optimism about our current instruments and techniques is fostered if we discover that they stand at the end of a sequence of such techniques, whose initial members had high rates of success and whose subsequent members have exhibited successively higher success. For that discovery fosters the idea that we have learned about nature and, as Devitt suggests, learned ever more about learning about nature.

Further historical research could cast a pall over our optimism. We might find out, for example, that long sequences of apparent successes were punctuated by embarrassing reversals, prompted by recognition that what we took to be observational/instrumental/technical improvements were based on quite faulty understanding of the relationship between ourselves and nature, so that an instrument or experimental technique had misled us across the board. If this were to occur frequently in the history of science it would challenge our complacency about current instruments and techniques by raising the probability that there are unanticipated sources of error even for long sequences of high and improving success rates. Yet, as I have indicated before, the pessimist has to do considerable historical work to show that this is the case.

Even more work is required to demonstrate that the use of unaided observation to arrive at claims about the macroscopic properties of medium-sized objects is unreliable. For our descriptive lore about substances and organisms seems remarkably stable, enduring from antiquity into the present with, occasionally, episodes of reconceptualization. . . . We can thus defend against the suggestion that history reveals that we should not claim truth for our ordinary judgments about ordinary things.

Quite plainly we are more likely to be wrong when we advance general conclusions, when we make claims about things that are causally remote from us, and when we attempt precise specifications of magnitude. Our scientific picture of nature provides us with ideas of the limits of our accuracy (at least in some cases). The world may be such that our ability to achieve true generalizations

about it may vary significantly from field to field—and we may use what knowledge we do acquire to differentiate those instances in which pessimism is warranted from those in which we are, justifiably, optimistic.

Notes

1. Thus many contemporary sociologists of science, Bloor, Barnes, Collins, Shapin, Latour, Pickering, and others, will surely find my account of progress incredible, and see this as just another inevitable failure in the sequence of attempts to understand progress in science. Others, such as Laudan, Kuhn, and van Fraassen, will object to my realism but will suppose that an account of scientific progress can be given if it is framed in different terms. In some cases, members of both groups will offer the same criticisms, but it is always good to recall that the conclusions that they draw from the criticisms are not the same.

2. At this point there appear to be two options. One *local* antirealist conclusion is to claim that this shows only that our claims about unobservables are suspect. Global antirealists, perhaps impressed by the theory-ladenness of all our beliefs, draw the more ambitious conclusion that all our current claims about nature are dubious.

References

Devitt, Michael. 1984. *Realism and Truth*. Princeton: Princeton University Press.
Kuhn, Thomas S. 1962/70. *The Structure of Scientific Revolutions*. Chicago: University of Chicago Press.

How Much Can Science Explain?

The Explanation of the Universe

Kurt Baier

As science has increased its influence on the modern world, many thinkers have tried to identify areas that are outside the domain of science. They have done so because long-cherished views seem to conflict with science, and scientific understanding threatens to prevail in the conflict. For example, a potential conflict between religion and science has led some to seek a domain for religion that is distinct from that which science seeks to explain. Kurt Baier critically evaluates a version of this view, one that claims science is limited to answering "How?" questions, whereas religion answers ultimate "Why?" questions. Science does not appear to explain the purposes behind events, so if there are such purposes, then science cannot explain the whole universe, and religion has one subject matter that is outside the domain of science.

Baier argues that science's explanation of the universe is not incomplete. Some explanations create understanding by providing a model for some phenomena. We do not *need* any further explanations of the models provided by science, though we may discover general models that explain more specific models. When something is incompatible with a model, we do *need* a further explanation, what he calls an "unvexing explanation." Baier argues that neither a model explanation nor an unvexing explanation is required for the existence of the universe as a whole, so there is no need for an explanation in terms of the purposes of a supernatural being. Scientific explanations are, in principle, complete.

As you read through this essay, consider the following:

1. What is the difference between a causal explanation and a teleological explanation? Provide an example of each. According to Baier, where are teleological explanations appropriate?
2. Why do some explanations seem to generate an infinite regress?
3. How does Baier argue that scientific explanations do not generate a vicious infinite regress?
4. What is the difference between model-understanding and unvexing-understanding? How does the example of chess help us see the difference between the two?
5. Do you agree that model-explanations do not themselves require further explanations? Why or why not?
6. Is there a deep mystery about why there is something rather than nothing? Would positing the existence of a God who created the universe reduce this mystery or make it more acceptable?

. . . The scientific approach demands that we look for a natural explanation of anything and everything. The scientific way of looking at and explaining things has yielded an immensely greater measure of understanding of, and control over, the universe than any other way. And when one looks at the world in this scientific way, there seems to be no room for a personal relationship between human beings and a supernatural perfect being ruling and guiding men. Hence many scientists and educated men have come to feel that the Christian attitudes towards the world and human existence are inappropriate. They have become convinced that the universe and human existence in it are without a purpose and therefore devoid of meaning.

Such beliefs are disheartening and unplausible. It is natural to keep looking for the error that must have crept into our arguments. And if an error has crept in, then it is most likely to have crept in with science. For before the rise of science, people did not entertain such melancholy beliefs, while the scientific world picture seems literally to force them on us.

There is one argument which seems to offer the desired way out. It runs somewhat as follows. Science and religion are not really in conflict. They are, on the contrary, mutually complementary, each doing an entirely differ-

ent job. Science gives provisional, if precise, explanations of small parts of the universe, religion gives final and over-all, if comparatively vague, explanations of the universe as a whole. The objectionable conclusion, that human existence is devoid of meaning, follows only if we use scientific explanations where they do not apply, namely, where total explanations of the whole universe are concerned.

After all, the argument continues, the scientific world picture is the inevitable outcome of rigid adherence to scientific method and explanation, but scientific, that is, causal explanations from their very nature are incapable of producing real illumination. They can at best tell us *how* things are or have come about, but never *why*. They are incapable of making the universe intelligible, comprehensible, meaningful to us. They represent the universe as meaningless, not because it *is* meaningless, but because scientific explanations are not designed to yield answers to investigations into the why and wherefore, into the meaning, purpose, or point of things. Scientific explanations (this argument continues) began, harmlessly enough, as partial and provisional explanations of the movement of material bodies, in particular the planets, within the general framework of the medieval world picture. Newton thought of the universe as a clock made, originally wound up, and occasionally set right by God. His laws of motion only revealed the ways in which the heavenly machinery worked. Explaining the movement of the planets by these laws was

From Kurt Baier, "The Meaning of Life." Inaugural Lecture delivered at the Canberra University College, Australia, 1957. © Kurt Baier. Reprinted by permission.

analogous to explaining the machinery of a watch. Such explanations showed *how* the thing worked, but not *what it was for* or *why* it existed. Just as the explanation of how a watch works can help our understanding of the watch only if, in addition, we assume that there is a watchmaker who has designed it for a purpose, made it, and wound it up, so the Newtonian explanation of the solar system helps our understanding of it only on the similar assumption that there is some divine artificer who has designed and made this heavenly clockwork for some purpose, has wound it up, and perhaps even occasionally sets it right, when it is out of order.

Socrates, in the Phaedo complained that only explanations of a thing showing the good or purpose for which it existed could offer a *real* explanation of it. He rejected the kind of explanation we now call "causal" as no more than mentioning "that without which a cause could not be a cause," that is, as merely a necessary condition, but not the *real* cause, the real explanation.[1] In other words, Socrates held that *all* things can be explained in two different ways: either by mentioning merely a necessary condition, or by giving the *real* cause. The former is not an elucidation of the explicandum, not really a help in understanding it, in grasping its "why" and "wherefore."

This Socratic view, however, is wrong. It is not the case that there are two kinds of explanation for everything, one partial, preliminary, and not really clarifying, the other full, final, and illuminating. The truth is that these two kinds of explanation are equally explanatory, equally illuminating, and equally full and final, but that they are appropriate for different kinds of explicanda.

When in an uninhabited forest we find what looks like houses, paved streets, temples, cooking utensils, and the like, it is no great risk to say that these things are the ruins of a deserted city, that is to say, of something man-made. In such a case, the appropriate explanation is teleological, that is, in terms of the purposes of the builders of that city. On the other hand, when a comet approaches the earth, it is similarly a safe bet that, unlike the

city in the forest, it was not manufactured by intelligent creatures and that, therefore, a teleological explanation would be out of place, whereas a causal one is suitable.

It is easy to see that in some cases causal, and in others teleological explanations are appropriate. A small satellite circling the earth may or may not have been made by man. We may never know which is the true explanation, but either hypothesis is equally explanatory. It would be wrong to say that only a teleological explanation can *really* explain it. Either explanation would yield complete clarity although, of course, only one can be true. Teleological explanation is only one of several that are possible.

It may indeed be strictly correct to say that the question "*Why* is there a satellite circling the earth?" can only be answered by a teleological explanation. It may be true that "Why?"-questions can really be used properly only in order to elicit *someone's reasons for* doing something. If this is so, it would explain our dissatisfaction with causal answers to "Why?"-questions. But even if it is so, it does not show that "Why is the satellite there?" *must be answered by a teleological explanation*. It shows only that either it must be so answered or it must not be asked. The question "Why have you stopped beating your wife?" can be answered only by a teleological explanation, but if you have never beaten her, it is an improper question. Similarly, if the satellite is not man-made, "Why is there a satellite?" is improper since it implies an origin it did not have. Natural science can indeed only tell us *how* things in nature have come about and not *why*, but this is so not because something else can tell us the *why* and *wherefore*, but because there is none.

There is, however, another point which has not yet been answered. The objection just stated was that causal explanations did not even set out to answer the crucial question. We ask the question "Why?" but science returns an answer to the question "How?" It might now be conceded that this is no ground for a complaint, but perhaps it will instead be said that causal explanations do not give complete or full answers even to that latter question. In causal explanations, it will be objected, the existence of one thing is explained by reference to its cause, but this involves asking for the cause of that cause, and so on, ad infinitum. There is no resting place which is not as much in need of explanation as what has already been explained. Nothing at all is ever fully and completely explained by this sort of explanation.

Leibniz has made this point very persuasively. "Let us suppose a book of the elements of geometry to have been eternal, one copy always having been taken down from an earlier one; it is evident that, even though a reason can be given for the present book out of a past one, nevertheless, out of any number of books, taken in order, going backwards, we shall never come upon *a full* reason; though we might well always wonder why there should have been such books from all time—why there were books at all, and why they were written in this manner. What is true of books is true also of the different states of the world; for what follows is in some way copied from what precedes. . . . And so, however far you go back to earlier states, you will never find in those states *a full reason* why there should be any world rather than none, and why it should be such as it is."[2]

However, a moment's reflection will show that if any type of explanation is merely preliminary and provisional, it is teleological explanation, since it presupposes a background which itself stands in need of explanation. If I account for the existence of the man-made satellite by saying that it was made by some scientists for a certain purpose, then such an explanation can clarify the existence of the satellite only if I assume that there existed materials out of which the satellite was made, and scientists who made it for some purpose. It therefore does not matter what type of explanation we give, whether causal or teleological: either type, any type of explanation, will imply the existence of something by reference to which the explicandum can be explained. And this in turn must be accounted for in the same way, and so on for ever.

But is not God a necessary being? Do we not escape the infinite regress as soon as we reach God? It is often maintained that, unlike ordinary intelligent beings, God is eternal and necessary; hence His existence, unlike theirs, is not in need of explanation. For what is it that creates the vicious regress just mentioned? It is that, if we accept the principle of sufficient reason (that there must be an explanation for the existence of anything and everything the existence of which is not logically necessary, but merely contingent[3]), the existence of all the things referred to in any explanation requires itself to be explained. If, however, God is a logically necessary being, then His existence requires no explanation. Hence the vicious regress comes to an end with God.

Now, it need not be denied that God is a necessary being in some sense of that expression. In one of these senses, I, for instance, am a necessary being: it is impossible that I should not exist, because it is self-refuting to say "I do not exist." The same is true of the English language and of the universe. It is self-refuting to say "There is no such thing as the English language" because this sentence is in the English language, or "There is no such thing as the universe" because whatever there is, *is* the universe. It is impossible that these things should not in fact exist since it is impossible that we should be mistaken in thinking that they exist. For what possible occurrence could even throw doubt on our being right on these matters, let alone show that we are wrong? I, the English language, and the universe, are necessary beings, simply in the sense in which all is necessarily true which has been *proved* to be true. The occurrence of utterances such as "I exist," "The English language exists" and "The universe exists" is in itself sufficient proof of their truth. These remarks are therefore necessarily true, hence the things asserted to exist are necessary things.

But this sort of necessity will not satisfy the principle of sufficient reason, because it is only hypothetical or consequential necessity.[4] *Given that* someone says "I exist," then it is logically impossible that *he* should not exist. Given the evidence we have, the English language and the universe most certainly do exist. But there is no necessity about the evidence. On the principle of sufficient reason, we must explain the existence of the evidence, for its existence is not logically necessary.

In other words, the only sense of "necessary being" capable of terminating the vicious regress is "logically necessary being," but it is no longer seriously in dispute that the notion of a logically necessary being is self-contradictory.[5] Whatever can be conceived of as existing can equally be conceived of as not existing.

However, even if per impossible, there were such a thing as a logically necessary being, we could still not make out a case for the superiority of teleological over causal explanation. The existence of the universe cannot be explained in accordance with the familiar model of manufacture by a craftsman. For that model presupposes the existence of materials out of which the product is fashioned. God, on the other hand, must create the materials as well. Moreover, although we have a simple model of "creation out of nothing," for composers create tunes out of nothing, yet this is a great difference between creating *something to be sung*, and making the sounds which are a singing of it, or producing the piano on which to play it. Let us, however, waive all these objections and admit, for argument's sake, that creation out of nothing is conceivable. Surely, even so, no one can claim that it is the kind of explanation which yields the clearest and fullest understanding. Surely, to round off scientific explanations of the origin of the universe with creation out of nothing, does not add anything to our *understanding*. There may be merit of some sort in this way of speaking, but whatever it is, it is not greater clarity or explanatory power.[6]

What then, does all this amount to? Merely to the claim that scientific explanations are no worse than any other. All that has been shown is that all explanations suffer from the same defect: all involve a vicious infinite regress. In other words, no type of human explanation can help us to unravel the ultimate, unanswerable mystery. Christian ways of looking at things may not be able to render the world any more lucid than science can, but at least they do not pretend that there are no impenetrable mysteries. On the contrary, they point out untiringly that the claims of science to be able to elucidate everything are hollow. They remind us that science is not merely limited to the exploration of a tiny corner of the universe but that, however far out probing instruments may eventually reach, we can never even approach the answers to the last questions: "Why is there a world at all rather than nothing?" and "Why is the world such as it is and not different?" Here our finite human intellect bumps against its own boundary walls.

Is it true that scientific explanations involve an infinite vicious regress? Are scientific explanations really only provisional and incomplete? The crucial point will be this. Do *all* contingent truths call for explanation? Is the principle of sufficient reason sound? Can scientific explanations never come to a definite end? It will be seen that with a clear grasp of the nature and purpose of explanation we can answer these questions.[7]

Explaining something to someone is making him understand it. This involves bringing together in his mind two things, a model which is accepted as already simple and clear, and that which is to be explained, the explicandum, which is not so. Understanding the explicandum is seeing that it belongs to a range of things which could legitimately have been expected by anyone familiar with the model and with certain facts.

There are, however, two fundamentally different positions which a person may occupy relative to some explicandum. He may not be familiar with any model capable of leading him to expect the phenomenon to be explained. Most of us, for instance, are in that position in relation to the phenomena occurring in a good seance. With regard to other things people will differ. Someone who can play chess, already understands chess, already has such a model. Someone who has never seen a game of chess has not. He sees the moves on the board but he cannot understand, cannot follow, cannot make sense of what is happening. Explaining the game to him is giving him an explanation, is making him understand. He can understand or follow chess moves only if he can see them as conforming to a model of a chess game. In order to acquire such a model, he will, of course, need to know the constitutive rules of chess, that is, the permissible moves. But that is not all. He must know that a normal game of chess is a competition (not all games are) between two people, each trying to win, and he must know what it is to win at chess: to manoeuvre the opponent's king into a position of check-mate. Finally, he must acquire some knowledge of what is and what is not conducive to winning: the tactical rules or canons of the game.

A person who has been given such an explanation and who has mastered it—which may take quite a long time—has now reached understanding, in the sense of the ability to follow each move. A person cannot in that sense understand merely one single move of chess and no other. If he does not understand any other moves, we must say that he has not yet mastered the explanation, that he does not really understand the single move either. If he has mastered the explanation, then he understands all those moves which he can see as being in accordance with the model of the game inculcated in him during the explanation.

However, even though a person who has mastered such an explanation will understand many, perhaps most, moves of any game of chess he cares to watch, he will not necessarily understand them all, as some moves of a player may not be in accordance with his model of the game. White, let us say, at his fifteenth move, exposes his queen to capture by Black's knight. Though in accordance with the constitutive rules of the game, this move is nevertheless perplexing and calls for explanation, because it is not conducive to the achievement by White of what must be assumed to be his aim: to win the game. The queen is a much more valuable piece than the knight against which he is offering to exchange.

An onlooker who has mastered chess may fail to understand this move, be perplexed by it, and wish for an explanation. Of course he may fail to be perplexed, for if he is a very inexperienced player he may not *see* the disadvantageousness of the move. But there is such a need whether anyone sees it or not. The move *calls for* explanation because to anyone who knows the game it must appear to be incompatible with the model which we have learnt during the explanation of the game, and by reference to which we all explain and understand normal games.

However, the required explanation of White's fifteenth move is of a very different kind. What is needed now is not the acquisition of an explanatory model, but the removal of the real or apparent incompatibility between the player's move and the model of explanation he has already acquired. In such a case the perplexity can be removed only on the assumption that the incompatibility between the model and the game is merely apparent. As our model includes a presumed aim of both players, there are the following three possibilities: (a) White has made a mistake: he has overlooked the threat to his queen. In that case, the explanation is that White thought his move conducive to his end, but it was not. (b) Black has made a mistake: White set a trap for him. In that case, the explanation is that Black thought White's move was not conducive to White's end, but it was. (c) White is not pursuing the end which any chess player may be presumed to pursue: he is not trying to win his game. In that case, the explanation is that White has made a move which he knows is not conducive to the end of winning his game because, let us say, he wishes to please Black who is his boss.

Let us now set out the differences and similarities between the two types of understanding involved in these two kinds of explanation. I shall call the first kind "model"—understanding and explaining, respectively, because both involve the use of a model by reference to which understanding and explaining is effected. The second kind I shall call "unvexing," because the need for this type of explanation and understanding arises only when there is a perplexity arising out of the incompatibility of the model and the facts to be explained.

The first point is that unvexing presupposes model-understanding, but not vice versa. A person can neither have nor fail to have unvexing-understanding of White's fifteenth move at chess, if he does not already have model-understanding of chess. Obviously, if I don't know how to play chess, I shall fail to have model-understanding of White's fifteenth move. But I can't neither fail to have nor, of course, can I have unvexing-understanding of it, for I cannot be perplexed by it. I merely fail to have model-understanding of this move as, indeed, of any other move of chess. On the other hand, I may well have model-understanding of chess without having unvexing-understanding of every move. That is to say, I may well know how to play chess without understanding White's fifteenth move. A person cannot fail to have unvexing-understanding of the move unless he is vexed or perplexed by it, hence he cannot even fail to have unvexing-understanding unless he already has model-understanding. It is not true that one either understands or fails to understand. On certain occasions, one neither understands nor fails to understand.

The second point is that there are certain things which cannot call for unvexing-explanations. No one can for instance call for an unvexing-explanation of White's first move, which is Pawn to King's Four. For no one can be perplexed or vexed by this move. Either a person knows how to play chess or he does not. If he does, then he must understand this move, for if he does not understand it, he has not yet mastered the game. And if he does not know how to play chess, then he cannot yet have, or fail to have, unvexing-understanding, he cannot therefore need an unvexing-explanation. Intellectual problems do not arise out of ignorance, but out of insufficient knowledge. An ignoramus is puzzled by very little. Once a student can see problems, he is already well into the subject.

The third point is that model-understanding implies being able, without further thought, to have model-understanding of a good many other things, unvexing-understanding does not. A person who knows chess and therefore has model-understanding of it, must understand a good many chess moves, in fact all except those that call for unvexing-explanations. If he claims that he can understand White's first move, but no others, then he is either lying or deceiving himself or he really does not understand any move. On the other hand, a person who, after an unvexing-explanation, understands White's fifteenth move, need not be able, without further explanation, to understand Black's or any other further move which calls for unvexing-explanation.

What is true of explaining deliberate and highly stylized human behaviour such as playing a game of chess is also true of explaining natural phenomena. For what is characteristic of natural phenomena, that they recur in essentially the same way, that they are, so to speak, repeatable, is also true of chess games, as it is not of games of tennis or cricket. There is only one important difference: man himself has invented and laid down the rules of chess, as he has not invented or laid down the "rules or laws governing the behaviour of things." This difference between chess and phenomena is important, for it adds another way to the three already mentioned, in which a perplexity can be removed by an unvexing-explanation, namely, by abandoning the original explanatory model. This is, of course, not possible in the case of games of chess, because the model for chess is not a "construction" on the basis of the already existing phenomena of chess, but an invention. The person who first thought up the model of chess could not have been mistaken. The person who first thought of a model explaining some phenomenon could have been mistaken.

Consider an example. We may think that the following phenomena belong together: the horizon seems to recede however far we walk towards it; we seem to be able to see further the higher the mountain we climb; the sun and moon seem every day to fall into the sea on one side but to come back from behind the mountains on the other side without being any the worse for it. We may explain these phenomena by two alternative models: (a) that the earth is a large disc; (b) that it is a large sphere. However, to a believer in the first theory there arises the following perplexity: how is it that when we travel long enough towards the horizon in any one direction, we do eventually come back to our starting point without ever coming to the edge of the earth? We may at first attempt to "save" the model by saying that there is only an apparent contradiction. We may say either that the model does not require us to come to an edge, for it may be possible only to walk round and round on the flat surface. Or we may say that the person must have walked over the edge without noticing it, or perhaps that the travellers are all lying. Alternatively, the fact that our model is "constructed" and not invented or laid down enables us to say, what we could not do in the case of chess, that the model is inadequate or unsuitable. We can choose another model which fits all the facts, for instance, that the earth is round. Of course, then we have to give an unvexing-explanation for why it *looks* flat, but we are able to do that.

We can now return to our original question, "Are scientific explanations true and full explanations or do they involve an infinite regress, leaving them for ever incomplete?"

Our distinction between model- and unvexing-explanations will help here. It is obvious that only those things which are perplexing *call for* and *can be given* unvexing-explanations. We have already seen that in disposing of one perplexity, we do not necessarily raise another. On the contrary, unvexing-explanations truly and completely explain what they set out to explain, namely, how something is possible which on our explanatory model, seemed to be impossible. There can therefore be no infinite regress here. Unvexing-explanations are real and complete explanations.

Can there be an infinite regress, then, in the case of model-explanations? Take the following example. European children are puz-

zled by the fact that their antipodean counterparts do not drop into empty space. This perplexity can be removed by substituting for their explanatory model another one. The European children imagine that throughout space there is an all-pervasive force operating in the same direction as the force that pulls them to the ground. We must, in our revised model, substitute for this force another acting everywhere in the direction of the centre of the earth. Having thus removed their perplexity by giving them an adequate model, we can, however, go on to ask *why* there should be such a force as the force of gravity, why bodies should "naturally," in the absence of forces acting on them, behave in the way stated in Newton's laws. And we might be able to give such an explanation. We might for instance construct a model of space which would exhibit as derivable from it what in Newton's theory are "brute facts." Here we would have a case of the brute facts of one theory being explained within the framework of another, more general theory. And it is a sound methodological principle that we should continue to look for more and more general theories.

Note two points, however. The first is that we must distinguish, as we have seen, between *the possibility* and *the necessity* of giving an explanation. Particular occurrences can be explained by being exhibited as instances of regularities, and regularities can be explained by being exhibited as instances of more general regularities. Such explanations make things clearer. They organize the material before us. They introduce order where previously there was disorder. But absence of this sort of explanation (model-explanation) does not leave us with a puzzle or perplexity, an intellectual restlessness or cramp. The unexplained things are not unintelligible, incomprehensible, or irrational. Some things, on the other hand, call for, require, demand an explanation. As long as we are without such an explanation, we are perplexed, puzzled, intellectually perturbed. We need an unvexing-explanation.

Now, it must be admitted that we may be

able to construct a more general theory, from which, let us say, Newton's theory can be derived. This would further clarify the phenomena of motion and would be intellectually satisfying. But failure to do so would not leave us with an intellectual cramp. The facts stated in Newton's theory do not require, or stand in need of, unvexing-explanations. They could do so only if we already had another theory or model with which Newton's theory was incompatible. They could not do so, by themselves, prior to the establishment of such another model.

The second point is that there is an objective limit to which such explanations tend, and beyond which they are pointless. There is a very good reason for wishing to explain a less general by a more general theory. Usually, such a unification goes hand in hand with greater precision in measuring the phenomena which both theories explain. Moreover, the more general theory, because of its greater generality, can explain a wider range of phenomena including not only phenomena already explained by some other theories but also newly discovered phenomena, which the less general theory cannot explain. Now, the ideal limit to which such expansions of theories tend is an all-embracing theory which unifies all theories and explains all phenomena. Of course, such a limit can never be reached, since new phenomena are constantly discovered. Nevertheless, theories may be tending towards it. It will be remembered that the contention made against scientific theories was that there is no such limit because they involve an infinite regress. On that view, which I reject, there is no conceivable point at which scientific theories could be said to have explained the whole universe. On the view I am defending, there is such a limit, and it is the limit towards which scientific theories are actually tending. I claim that the nearer we come to this limit, the closer we are to a full and complete explanation of everything. For if we were to reach the limit, then though we could, of course, be left with a model which is itself unexplained and could be yet further explained by derivation from

another model, there would be no need for, and no point in, such a further explanation. There would be no need for it, because any clearly defined model permitting us to expect the phenomena it is designed to explain offers full and complete explanations of these phenomena, however narrow the range. And while, at lower levels of generality, there is a good reason for providing more general models, since they further simplify, systematize, and organize the phenomena, this, which is the only reason for building more general theories, no longer applies once we reach the ideal limit of an all-embracing explanation.

It might be said that there is another reason for using different models: that they might enable us to discover new phenomena. Theories are not only instruments of explanation, but also of discovery. With this I agree, but it is irrelevant to my point: that *the needs of explanation* do not require us to go on for ever deriving one explanatory model from another.

It must be admitted, then, that in the case of model-explanations there is a regress, but it is neither vicious nor infinite. It is not vicious because, in order to explain a group of explicanda, a model-explanation *need* not itself be derived from another more general one. It gives a perfectly full and consistent explanation by itself. And the regress is not infinite, for there is a natural limit, an all-embracing model, which can explain all phenomena, beyond which it would be pointless to derive model-explanations from yet others.

What about our most serious question, "Why is there anything at all?" Sometimes, when we think about how one thing has developed out of another and that one out of a third, and so on back throughout all time, we are driven to ask the same question about the universe as a whole. We want to add up all things and refer to them by the name, "the world," and we want to know why the world exists and why there is not nothing instead. In such moments, the world seems to us a kind of bubble floating on an ocean of nothingness. Why should such flotsam be adrift in empty space? Surely, its emergence from the hyaline billows of nothingness is more mysterious even than Aphrodite's emergence from the sea. Wittgenstein expressed in these words the mystification we all feel: "Not *how* the world is, is the mystical, but *that* it is. The contemplation of the world *sub specie aeterni* is the contemplation of it as a limited whole. The feeling of the world as a limited whole is the mystical feeling."[8]

Professor J. J. C. Smart expresses his own mystification in these moving words:

"That anything should exist at all does seem to me a matter for the deepest awe. But whether other people feel this sort of awe, and whether they or I ought to is another question. I think we ought to. If so, the question arises: If 'Why should anything exist at all?' cannot be interpreted after the manner of the cosmological argument, that is, as an absurd request for the non-sensical postulation of a logically necessary being, what sort of question is it? What sort of question is this question 'Why should anything exist at all?' All I can say is that I do not yet know."[9]

It is undeniable that the magnitude and perhaps the very existence of the universe is awe-inspiring. It is probably true that it gives many people "the mystical feeling." It is also undeniable that our awe, our mystical feeling, aroused by contemplating the vastness of the world, is justified, in the same sense in which our fear is justified when we realize we are in danger. There is no more appropriate object for our awe or for the mystical feeling than the magnitude and perhaps the existence of the universe, just as there is no more appropriate object for our fear than a situation of personal peril. However, it does not follow from this that it is a good thing to cultivate, or indulge in, awe or mystical feelings, any more than it is necessarily a good thing to cultivate, or indulge in, fear in the presence of danger.

In any case, whether or not we ought to have or are justified in having a mystical feeling or a feeling of awe when contemplating the universe, having such a feeling is not the same as asking a meaningful question, although having it may well *incline us* to utter certain forms of words. Our question "Why is there anything at all?" may be no more than the expression of our feeling of awe or mystification, and not a meaningful question at all. Just as the feeling of fear may naturally but illegitimately give rise to the question "What sin have I committed?" so the feeling of awe or mystification may naturally but illegitimately lead to the question "Why is there anything at all?" What we have to discover, then, is whether this question makes sense or is meaningless.

Yes, of course, it will be said, it makes perfectly good sense. There is an undeniable fact and it calls for explanation. The fact is that the universe exists. In the light of our experience, there can be no possible doubt that something or other exists, and the claim that the universe exists commits us to no more than that. And surely this calls for explanation, because the universe must have originated somehow. Everything has an origin and the universe is no exception. Since the universe is the totality of things, it must have originated out of nothing. If it had originated out of something, even something as small as one single hydrogen atom, what has so originated could not be the whole universe, but only the universe minus the atom. And then the atom itself would call for explanation, for it too must have had an origin, and it must be *an origin out of nothing*. And how can anything originate out of nothing? Surely that calls for explanation.

However, let us be quite clear what is to be explained. There are two facts here, not one. The first is that the universe exists, which is undeniable. The second is that the universe must have originated out of nothing, and that is not undeniable. It is true that, *if it has originated at all*, then it must have originated out of nothing, or else it is not the universe that has originated. But need it have originated? Could it not have existed for ever?[10] It might be argued that nothing exists for ever, that everything has originated out of something else. That may well be true, but it is perfectly compatible with the fact that the universe is everlasting. We may well be able to trace the origin of any thing to the time when, by some transformation, it has developed out of some other thing, and yet it may be the case that no thing has its origin in nothing, and the universe has existed for ever. For even if every *thing* has a beginning and an end, the total of mass and energy may well remain constant.

Moreover, the hypothesis that the universe originated out of nothing is, empirically speaking, completely empty. Suppose, for argument's sake, that the annihilation of an object without remainder is conceivable. It would still not be possible for any hypothetical observer to ascertain whether space was empty or not. Let us suppose that *within the range of observation of our observer* one object after another is annihilated without remainder and that only one is left. Our observer could not then tell whether in remote parts of the universe, beyond his range of observation, objects are coming into being or passing out of existence. What, moreover, are we to say of the observer himself? Is he to count for nothing? Must we not postulate him away as well, if the universe is to have arisen out of nothing?

Let us, however, ignore all these difficulties and assume that the universe really has originated out of nothing. Even that does not prove that the universe has not existed for ever. If the universe can conceivably develop out of nothing, then it can conceivably vanish without remainder. And it can arise out of nothing again and subside into nothingness once more, and so on ad infinitum. Of course, "again" and "once more" are not quite the right words. The concept of time hardly applies to such universes. It does not make sense to ask whether one of them is earlier or later than, or perhaps simultaneous with, the other because we cannot ask whether they occupy the same or different spaces. Being separated from one another by "nothing," they are not separated from one another by "anything." We cannot therefore make any statements about their mutual spatio-temporal relations. It is impossible to distinguish between one long continuous universe and two universes separated by nothing. How, for instance, can we tell whether the universe

including ourselves is not frequently annihilated and "again" reconstituted just as it was?

Let us now waive these difficulties as well. Let us suppose for a moment that we understand what is meant by saying that the universe originated out of nothing and that this has happened only once. Let us accept this as a fact. Does this fact call for explanation?

It does not call for an unvexing-explanation. That would be called for only if there were a perplexity due to the incompatibility of an accepted model with some fact. In our case, the fact to be explained is the origination of the universe out of nothing, hence there could not be such a perplexity, for we need not employ a model incompatible with this. If we had a model incompatible with our "fact," then that would be the wrong model and we would simply have to substitute another for it. The model we employ to explain the origin of the universe out of nothing could not be based on the similar origins of other things for, of course, there is nothing else with a similar origin.

All the same, it seems very surprising that something should have come out of nothing. It is contrary to the principle that every thing has an origin, that is, has developed out of something else. It must be admitted that there is this incompatibility. However, it does not arise because a well-established model does not square with an undeniable fact; it arises because a well-established model does not square with *an assumption* of which it is hard even to make sense and for which there is no evidence whatsoever. In fact, the only reason we have for making this assumption, is a simple logical howler: that because every thing has an origin, the universe must have an origin, too, except, that, being the universe, it must have originated out of nothing. This is a howler, because it conceives of the universe as a big thing, whereas in fact it is the totality of things, that is, not a thing. That every thing has an origin does not entail that the totality of things has an origin. On the contrary, it strongly suggests that it has not. For to say that every thing has an origin implies that any given thing must have developed out of something else which in turn, being a thing, must have developed out of something else, and so forth. If we assume that every thing has an origin, we need not, indeed it is hard to see how we can, assume that the totality of things has an origin as well. There is therefore no perplexity, because we need not and should not assume that the universe has originated out of nothing.

If, however, in spite of all that has been said just now, someone still wishes to assume, contrary to all reason, that the universe has originated out of nothing, there would still be no perplexity, for then he would simply have to give up the principle which is incompatible with this assumption, namely, that no thing can originate out of nothing. After all, this principle *could* allow for exceptions. We have no proof that it does not. Again, there is no perplexity, because no incompatibility between our assumption and an inescapable principle.

But, it might be asked, do we not need a model-explanation of our supposed fact? The answer is No. We do not need such an explanation, for there could not possibly be a model for this origin other than this origin itself. We cannot say that origination out of nothing is like birth, or emergence, or evolution, or anything else we know for it is not like anything we know. In all these cases, there is *something* out of which the new thing has originated.

To sum up. The question, "Why is there anything at all?" looks like a perfectly sensible question modelled on "Why does *this* exist?" or "How has *this* originated?" It looks like a question about the origin of a thing. However, it is not such a question, for the universe is not a thing, but the totality of things. There is therefore no reason to assume that the universe has an origin. The very assumption that it has is fraught with contradictions and absurdities. If, nevertheless, it were true that the universe has originated out of nothing, then this would not call either for an unvexing- or a model-explanation. It would not call for the latter, because there could be no model of it taken from another part of our experience, since there is nothing analogous in our experience to origination out of nothing. It would

not call for the former, because there can be no perplexity due to the incompatibility of a well-established model and an undeniable fact, since there is no undeniable fact and no well-established model. If, on the other hand, as is more probable, the universe has not originated at all, but is eternal, then the question why or how it has originated simply does not arise. There can then be no question about why anything at all exists, for it could not mean how or why the universe had originated, since ex hypothesi it has no origin. And what else could it mean?

Lastly, we must bear in mind that the hypothesis that the universe was made by God out of nothing only brings us back to the question who made God or how God originated. And if we do not find it repugnant to say that God is eternal, we cannot find it repugnant to say that the universe is eternal. The only difference is that we know for certain that the universe exists, while we have the greatest difficulty in even making sense of the claim that God exists.

To sum up. According to the argument examined, we must reject the scientific world picture because it is the outcome of scientific types of explanation which do not really and fully explain the world around us, but only tell us *how* things have come about, not *why*, and can give no answer to the ultimate question, why there is anything at all rather than nothing. Against this, I have argued that scientific explanations are real and full, just like the explanations of everyday life and of the traditional religions. They differ from those latter only in that they are more precise and more easily disprovable by the observation of facts.

My main points dealt with the question why scientific explanations were thought to be merely provisional and partial. The first main reason is the misunderstanding of the difference between teleological and causal explanations. It is first, and rightly, maintained that teleological explanations are answers to "Why?"-questions, while causal explanations are answers to "How?"-questions. It is further, and wrongly, maintained that, in order to obtain real and full explanations of anything, one must answer both "Why?" and "How?" questions. In other words, it is thought that all matters can and must be explained by both teleological and causal types of explanation. Causal explanations, it is believed, are merely provisional and partial, waiting to be completed by teleological explanations. Until a teleological explanation has been given, so the story goes, we have not *really* understood the explicandum. However, I have shown that both types are equally real and full explanations. The difference between them is merely that they are appropriate to different types of explicanda.

It should, moreover, be borne in mind that teleological explanations are not, in any sense, unscientific. They are rightly rejected in the natural sciences, not however because they are unscientific, but because no intelligences or purposes are found to be involved there. On the other hand, teleological explanations are very much in place in psychology, for we find intelligence and purpose involved in a good deal of human behaviour. It is not only not unscientific to give teleological explanations of deliberate human behaviour, but it would be quite unscientific to exclude them.

The second reason why scientific explanations are thought to be merely provisional and partial, is that they are believed to involve a vicious infinite regress. Two misconceptions have led to this important error. The first is the general misunderstanding of the nature of explanation, and in particular the failure to distinguish between the two types which I have called model- and unvexing-explanations, respectively. If one does not draw this distinction, it is natural to conclude that scientific explanations lead to a vicious infinite regress. For while it is true of those perplexing matters which are elucidated by unvexing-explanations that they are incomprehensible and cry out for explanation, it is not true that after an unvexing-explanation has been given, this itself is again capable, let alone in need of, a yet further explanation of the same kind. Conversely, while it is true that model-explanations of regularities can themselves

be further explained by more general model-explanations, it is not true that, in the absence of such more general explanations, the less general are incomplete, hang in the air, so to speak, leaving the explicandum incomprehensible and crying out for explanation. The distinction between the two types of explanation shows us that an explicandum is either perplexing and incomprehensible, in which case an explanation of it *is necessary* for clarification and, when given, *complete*, or it is a regularity capable of being subsumed under a model, in which case a further explanation *is possible* and often profitable, but *not necessary* for clarification.

The second misconception responsible for the belief in a vicious infinite regress is the misrepresentation of scientific explanation *as essentially causal*. It has generally been held that, in a scientific explanation, the explicandum is the effect of some event, the cause, temporally prior to the explicandum. Combined with the principle of sufficient reason (the principle that anything is in need of explanation which might conceivably have been different from what it is), this error generates the nightmare of determinism. Since any event might have been different from what it was, acceptance of this principle has the consequence that *every* event must have a reason or explanation. But if the reason is itself an event *prior in time*, then every reason must have a reason preceding it, and so the infinite regress of explanation is necessarily tied to the time scale stretching infinitely back into the endless past. It is, however, obvious from our account that science is not primarily concerned with the forging of such causal chains. The primary object of the natural sciences is not historical at all. Natural science claims to reveal, not the beginnings of things, but their underlying reality. It does not dig up the past, it digs down into the structure of things existing here and now. Some scientists do allow themselves to speculate, and rather precariously at that, about origins. But their hard work is done on the structure of what exists now. In particular those explanations which are themselves further explained are not explanations linking event to event in a gapless chain reaching back to creation day, but generalisations of theories tending towards a unified theory.

Notes

1. See "Phaedo" (*Five Dialogues* by Plato, Everyman's Library No. 456) para. 99, p. 189.

2. "On the Ultimate Origination of Things" (*The Philosophical Writings of Leibniz*, Everyman's Library No. 905) p. 32.

3. See "Monadology" (*The Philosophical Writings of Leibniz*, Everyman's Library No. 905) para. 32–38, pp. 8–10.

4. To borrow the useful term coined by Professor D. A. T. Gasking of Melbourne University.

5. See e.g. J. J. C. Smart, "The Existence of God," reprinted in *New Essays in Philosophical Theology*, ed. by A. Flew and A. MacIntyre (London: S.C.M. Press, 1957) pp. 35–39.

6. That creation out of nothing is not a clarificatory notion becomes obvious when we learn that "in the philosophical sense" it does not imply creation at a particular time. The universe could be regarded as a creation out of nothing even if it had no beginning. See e.g. E. Gilson, *The Christian Philosophy of St. Thomas Aquinas* (London: Victor Gollancz Ltd., 1957) pp. 147–155 and E. L. Mascall, *Via Media* (London: Longmans, Green & Co., 1956) pp. 28 ff.

7. In what follows I have drawn heavily on the work of Ryle and Toulmin. See for instance G. Ryle, *The Concept of Mind* (London: Hutchinson's University Library, 1949) pp. 56–60 etc. and his article, "If, So, and Because," in *Philosophical Analysis* by Max Black, and S. E. Toulmin, *Introduction to the Philosophy of Science* (London: Hutchinson's University Library, 1953).

8. L. Wittgenstein, *Tractatus Logico-Philosophicus* (London: Routledge & Kegan Paul Ltd., 1922), Sect. 6.44–6.45.

9. Op. cit. p. 46. See also Rudolf Otto, *The Idea of the Holy* (London: Geoffrey Cumberlege, 1952) esp. pp. 9–29.

10. Contemporary theologians would admit that it cannot be proved that the universe must have had a beginning. They would admit that we know it only through revelation. . . . I take it more or less for granted that Kant's attempted proof of the Thesis in his First Antinomy of Reason [Immanuel Kant's *Critique of Pure Reason*, trans. by Norman Kemp Smith (London: Macmillan and Co. Ltd., 1950) pp. 396–402] is invalid. It rests on a premise which is false: that the completion of the infinite series of succession of states, which must have preceded the present state if the world has had no beginning, is logically impossible. We can persuade ourselves to think that this infinite series is logically impossible if we insist that it is a series which must, literally, be *completed*. For the verb "to complete," as normally used, implies an activity which, in turn, implies an agent who must have *begun* the activity at some time. If an infinite series is a whole that must be *completed* then, indeed, the world must have had a beginning. But that is precisely the question at issue. If we say, as Kant does at first, "that an eternity has elapsed," we do not feel the same impossibility. It is only when we take seriously the words "synthesis" and "completion," both of which suggest or imply "work" or "activity" and therefore "beginning," that it seems necessary that an infinity of successive states cannot have elapsed. [See also R. Crawshay-Williams, *Methods and Criteria of Reasoning* (London: Routledge & Kegan Paul, 1957) App. iv.]

The Explanation of Mind

Paul Churchland

One of the outstanding unanswered questions for the practice of science is: Can science give an adequate account of mind? The mind seems to have features that are fundamentally different from the properties of the brain. Mental states are subjective, and brain states are objective. Mental states seem to have the property of intentionality, that is, they are directed upon objects, whereas brain states do not. The mind-body problem, as it is typically called, is the puzzle about how minds and bodies (or brains) are related. Dualists solve this problem by arguing that mind is distinct from brain. Materialists or physicalists maintain that ultimately talk of mind is about the brain and its functions. Most people think that science can give an adequate account of how the brain works, so materialists believe that science can also explain mind. Some dualists also accept this view, but others think that their view is incompatible with a scientific understanding of mind.

In this essay, Paul Churchland distinguishes among several forms of dualism before assessing the arguments for and against dualism. In his view, the balance of arguments strongly favors the materialist. Paul Churchland is professor of philosophy at University of California, San Diego.

As you read through this essay, consider the following:

1. Explain the distinction Churchland draws between substance dualism and property dualism. What further distinctions does he draw within these categories?
2. What are the primary arguments in favor of dualism?
3. According to Churchland, why are the arguments in favor of dualism not convincing?
4. What reasons does Churchland provide for thinking that we should reject dualism?
5. Do you agree with Churchland's assessment that the balance of the argument favors materialism? Why or why not?
6. What more would you need to know to help you decide whether science can explain mind?

What is the real nature of mental states and processes? In what medium do they take place, and how are they related to the physical world? Will my consciousness survive the disintegration of my physical body? Or will it disappear forever as my brain ceases to function? Is it possible that a purely physical system such as a computer could be constructed so as to enjoy real conscious intelligence? Where do minds come from? What are they?

These are some of the questions we shall confront. . . . Which answers we should give to them depends on which theory of mind proves to be the most reasonable theory on the evidence, to have the greatest explanatory power, predictive power, coherence, and simplicity. Let us examine the available theories, and the considerations that weigh for and against each.

The dualistic approach to mind encompasses several quite different theories, but they are all agreed that the essential nature of conscious intelligence resides in something *nonphysical*, in something forever beyond the

scope of sciences like physics, neurophysiology, and computer science. Dualism is not the most widely held view in the current philosophical and scientific community, but it is the most common theory of mind in the public at large, it is deeply entrenched in most of the world's popular religions, and it has been the dominant theory of mind for most of Western history. It is thus an appropriate place to begin our discussion.

SUBSTANCE DUALISM

The distinguishing claim of this view is that each mind is a distinct nonphysical thing, an individual "package" of nonphysical substance, a thing whose identity is independent of any physical body to which it may be temporarily "attached." Mental states and activities derive their special character, on this view, from their being states and activities of this unique, nonphysical substance.

This leaves us wanting to ask for more in the way of a *positive* characterization of the proposed mind-stuff. It is a frequent complaint with the substance dualist's approach that his characterization of it is so far almost entirely negative. This need not be a fatal flaw, however, since we no doubt have much

From Paul Churchland, *Matter and Consciousness*, revised edition (Cambridge, Mass.: The MIT Press, 1988). Copyright © 1988 Massachusetts Institute of Technology. Reprinted by permission.

to learn about the underlying nature of mind, and perhaps the deficit here can eventually be made good. On this score, the philosopher René Descartes (1596–1650) has done as much as anyone to provide a positive account of the nature of the proposed mind-stuff, and his views are worthy of examination.

Descartes theorized that reality divides into two basic kinds of substance. The first is ordinary matter, and the essential feature of this kind of substance is that it is extended in space: any instance of it has length, breadth, height, and occupies a determinate position in space. Descartes did not attempt to play down the importance of this type of matter. On the contrary, he was one of the most imaginative physicists of his time, and he was an enthusiastic advocate of what was then called "the mechanical philosophy." But there was one isolated corner of reality he thought could not be accounted for in terms of the mechanics of matter: the conscious reason of Man. This was his motive for proposing a second and radically different kind of substance, a substance that has no spatial extension or spatial position whatever, a substance whose essential feature is the activity of *thinking*. This view is known as *Cartesian dualism*.

As Descartes saw it, the real *you* is not your material body, but rather a nonspatial thinking substance, an individual unit of mind-stuff quite distinct from your material body. This nonphysical mind is in systematic causal interaction with your body. The physical state of your body's sense organs, for example, causes visual/auditory/tactile experiences in your mind. And the desires and decisions of your nonphysical mind cause your body to behave in purposeful ways. Its causal connections to your mind are what make your body yours, and not someone else's.

The main reasons offered in support of this view were straightforward enough. First, Descartes thought that he could determine, by direct introspection alone, that he was essentially a thinking substance and nothing else. And second, he could not imagine how a purely physical system could ever use *language* in a relevant way, or engage in mathe-matical *reasoning*, as any normal human can. Whether these are good reasons, we shall discuss presently. Let us first notice a difficulty that even Descartes regarded as a problem.

If "mind-stuff" is so utterly different from "matter-stuff" in its nature—different to the point that it has no mass whatever, no shape whatever, and no position anywhere in space— then how is it possible for my mind to have any causal influence on my body at all? As Descartes himself was aware (he was one of the first to for-mulate the law of the conservation of momen-tum), ordinary matter in space behaves accord-ing to rigid laws, and one cannot get bodily movement (= momentum) from nothing. How is this utterly insubstantial "thinking substance" to have any influence on ponderous matter? How can two such different things be in any sort of causal contact? Descartes proposed a very subtle material substance—"animal spir-its"—to convey the mind's influence to the body in general. But this does not provide us with a solution, since it leaves us with the same prob-lem with which we started: how something ponderous and spatial (even "animal spirits") can interact with something entirely nonspatial.

In any case, the basic principle of division used by Descartes is no longer as plausible as it was in his day. It is now neither useful nor accurate to characterize ordinary matter as that-which-has-extension-in-space. Electrons, for example, are bits of matter, but our best current theories describe the electron as a point-particle with no extension whatever (it even lacks a determinate spatial position). And according to Einstein's theory of gravity, an entire star can achieve this same status, if it undergoes a complete gravitational collapse. If there truly is a division between mind and body, it appears that Descartes did not put his finger on the dividing line.

Such difficulties with Cartesian dualism provide a motive for considering a less radical form of substance dualism, and that is what we find in a view I shall call *popular dualism*. This is the theory that a person is literally a "ghost in a machine," where the machine is the human body, and the ghost is a spiritual sub-stance, quite unlike physical matter in its internal constitution, but fully possessed of spatial properties even so. In particular, minds are commonly held to be *inside* the bodies they control: inside the head, on most views, in intimate contact with the brain.

This view need not have the difficulties of Descartes'. The mind is right there in contact with the brain, and their interaction can perhaps be understood in terms of their exchanging energy of a form that our science has not yet recognized or understood. Ordinary matter, you may recall, is just a form or manifestation of energy. (You may think of a grain of sand as a great deal of energy condensed or frozen into a small package, according to Einstein's relation, $E = mc^2$.) Perhaps mind-stuff is a well-behaved form or manifestation of energy also, but a different form of it. It is thus *possible* that a dualism of this alternative sort be consistent with familiar laws concerning the conservation of momentum and energy. This is fortunate for dualism, since those particular laws are very well established indeed.

This view will appeal to many for the further reason that it at least holds out the possibility (though it certainly does not guarantee) that the mind might survive the death of the body. It does not guarantee the mind's survival because it remains possible that the peculiar form of energy here supposed to constitute a mind can be produced and sustained only in conjunction with the highly intricate form of matter we call the brain, and must disintegrate when the brain disintegrates. So the prospects for surviving death are quite unclear even on the assumption that popular dualism is true. But even if survival were a clear consequence of the theory, there is a pitfall to be avoided here. Its promise of survival might be a reason for *wishing* dualism to be true, but it does not constitute a reason for *believing* that it *is* true. For that, we would need independent empirical evidence that minds do indeed survive the permanent death of the body. Regrettably, and despite the exploitative blatherings of the supermarket tabloids (TOP DOCS PROVE LIFE AFTER DEATH!!!), we possess no such evidence.

As we shall see later in this section, when we turn to evaluation, positive evidence for the existence of this novel, nonmaterial, thinking *substance* is in general on the slim side. This has moved many dualists to articulate still less extreme forms of dualism, in hopes of narrowing further the gap between theory and available evidence.

PROPERTY DUALISM

The basic idea of the theories under this heading is that while there is no *substance* to be dealt with here beyond the physical brain, the brain has a special set of *properties* possessed by no other kind of physical object. It is these special properties that are nonphysical: hence the term *property dualism*. The properties in question are the ones you would expect: the property of having a pain, of having a sensation of red, of thinking that *P*, of desiring that *Q*, and so forth. These are the properties that are characteristic of conscious intelligence. They are held to be nonphysical in the sense that they cannot ever be reduced to or explained solely in terms of the concepts of the familiar physical sciences. They will require a wholly new and autonomous science—the "science of mental phenomena"—if they are ever to be adequately understood.

From here, important differences among the positions emerge. Let us begin with what is perhaps the oldest version of property dualism: *epiphenomenalism*. This term is rather a mouthful, but its meaning is simple. The Greek prefix "epi-" means "above," and the position at issue holds that mental phenomena are not a part of the physical phenomena in the brain that ultimately determine our actions and behavior, but rather ride "above the fray." Mental phenomena are thus *epi*phenomena. They are held to just appear or emerge when the growing brain passes a certain level of complexity.

But there is more. The epiphenomenalist holds that while mental phenomena are caused to occur by the various activities of the brain, *they do not have any causal effects in turn*.

They are entirely impotent with respect to causal effects on the physical world. They are *mere* epiphenomena. (To fix our ideas, a vague metaphor may be helpful here. Think of our conscious mental states as little sparkles of shimmering light that occur on the wrinkled surface of the brain, sparkles which are caused to occur by physical activity in the brain, but which have no causal effects on the brain in return.) This means that the universal conviction that one's actions are determined by one's desires, decisions, and volitions is false! One's actions are exhaustively determined by physical events in the brain, which events *also* cause the epiphenomena we call desires, decisions, and volitions. There is therefore a constant conjunction between volitions and actions. But according to the epiphenomenalist, it is mere illusion that the former cause the latter.

What could motivate such a strange view? In fact, it is not too difficult to understand why someone might take it seriously. Put yourself in the shoes of a neuroscientist who is concerned to trace the origins of behavior back up the motor nerves to the active cells in the motor cortex of the cerebrum, and to trace in turn their activity into inputs from other parts of the brain, and from the various sensory nerves. She finds a thoroughly physical system of awesome structure and delicacy, and much intricate activity, all of it unambiguously chemical or electrical in nature, and she finds no hint at all of any nonphysical inputs of the kind that substance dualism proposes. What is she to think? From the standpoint of her researches, human behavior is exhaustively a function of the activity of the physical brain. And this opinion is further supported by her confidence that the brain has the behavior-controlling features it does exactly because those features have been ruthlessly selected for during the brain's long evolutionary history. In sum, the seat of human behavior appears entirely physical in its constitution, in its origins, and in its internal activities.

On the other hand, our neuroscientist has the testimony of her own introspection to account for as well. She can hardly deny that she has experiences, beliefs, and desires, nor that they are connected in some way with her behavior. One bargain that can be struck here is to admit the *reality* of mental properties, as nonphysical properties, but demote them to the status of impotent epiphenomena that have nothing to do with the scientific explanation of human and animal behavior. This is the position the epiphenomenalist takes, and the reader can now perceive the rationale behind it. It is a bargain struck between the desire to respect a rigorously scientific approach to the explanation of behavior, and the desire to respect the testimony of introspection.

The epiphenomenalist's "demotion" of mental properties—to causally impotent by-products of brain activity—has seemed too extreme for most property dualists, and a theory closer to the convictions of common sense has enjoyed somewhat greater popularity. This view, which we may call *interactionist property dualism*, differs from the previous view in only one essential respect: the interactionist asserts that mental properties do indeed have causal effects on the brain, and thereby, on behavior. The mental properties of the brain are an integrated part of the general causal fray, in systematic interaction with the brain's physical properties. One's actions, therefore, are held to be caused by one's desires and volitions after all.

As before, mental properties are here said to be *emergent* properties, properties that do not appear at all until ordinary physical matter has managed to organize itself, through the evolutionary process, into a system of sufficient complexity. Examples of properties that are emergent in this sense would be the property of being *solid*, the property of being *colored*, and the property of being *alive*. All of these require matter to be suitably organized before they can be displayed. With this much, any materialist will agree. But any property dualist makes the further claim that mental states and properties are *irreducible*, in the sense that they are not just organizational features of physical matter, as are the examples cited. They are said to be novel properties beyond prediction or explanation by physical science.

This last condition—the irreducibility of mental properties—is an important one, since this is what makes the position a dualist position. But it sits poorly with the joint claim that mental properties emerge from nothing more than the organizational achievements of physical matter. If that is how mental properties are produced, then one would expect a physical account of them to be possible. The simultaneous claim of evolutionary emergence *and* physical irreducibility is prima facie puzzling.

A property dualist is not absolutely bound to insist on both claims. He could let go the thesis of evolutionary emergence, and claim that mental properties are *fundamental* properties of reality, properties that have been here from the universe's inception, properties on a par with length, mass, electric charge, and other fundamental properties. There is even an historical precedent for a position of this kind. At the turn of this century it was still widely believed that electromagnetic phenomena (such as electric charge and magnetic attraction) were just an unusually subtle manifestation of purely *mechanical* phenomena. Some scientists thought that a reduction of electromagnetics to mechanics was more or less in the bag. They thought that radio waves, for example, would turn out to be just travelling oscillations in a very subtle but jellylike aether that fills space everywhere. But the aether turned out not to exist. So electromagnetic properties turned out to be fundamental properties in their own right, and we were forced to add electric charge to the existing list of fundamental properties (mass, length, and duration).

Perhaps mental properties enjoy a status like that of electromagnetic properties: irreducible, but not emergent. Such a view may be called *elemental-property dualism*, and it has the advantage of clarity over the previous view. Unfortunately, the parallel with electromagnetic phenomena has one very obvious failure. Unlike electromagnetic properties, which are displayed at all levels of reality from the sub-atomic level on up, mental properties are displayed only in large physical systems that have evolved a very complex internal organization. The case for the evolutionary emergence of mental properties through the organization of matter is extremely strong. They do not appear to be basic or elemental at all. This returns us, therefore, to the issue of their irreducibility. Why should we accept this most basic of the dualist's claims? Why be a dualist?

ARGUMENTS FOR DUALISM

Here we shall examine some of the main considerations commonly offered in support of dualism. Criticism will be postponed for a moment so that we may appreciate the collective force of these supporting considerations.

A major source of dualistic convictions is the religious belief many of us bring to these issues. Each of the major religions is in its way a theory about the cause or purpose of the universe, and Man's place within it, and many of them are committed to the notion of an immortal soul—that is, to some form of substance dualism. Supposing that one is consistent, to consider disbelieving dualism is to consider disbelieving one's religious heritage, and some of us find that difficult to do. Call this the *argument from religion*.

A more universal consideration is the *argument from introspection*. The fact is, when you center your attention on the contents of your consciousness, you do not clearly apprehend a neural network pulsing with electrochemical activity: you apprehend a flux of thoughts, sensations, desires, and emotions. It seems that mental states and properties, as revealed in introspection, could hardly be more different from physical states and properties if they tried. The verdict of introspection, therefore, seems strongly on the side of some form of dualism—on the side of property dualism, at a minimum.

A cluster of important considerations can be collected under the *argument from irreducibility*. Here one points to a variety of mental phenomena where it seems clear that no purely physical explanation could possibly account for what is going on. Descartes has already cited our ability to use language in a way that is relevant to our changing circumstances, and he was impressed also with our faculty of Reason, particularly as it is displayed in our capacity for mathematical reasoning. These abilities, he thought, must surely be beyond the capacity of any physical system. More recently, the introspectible qualities of our sensations (sensory "qualia"), and the meaningful content of our thoughts and beliefs, have also been cited as phenomena that will forever resist reduction to the physical. Consider, for example, seeing the color or smelling the fragrance of a rose. A physicist or chemist might know everything about the molecular structure of the rose, and of the human brain, argues the dualist, but that knowledge would not enable him to predict or anticipate the quality of these inexpressible experiences.

Finally, parapsychological phenomena are occasionally cited in favor of dualism. Telepathy (mind reading), precognition (seeing the future), telekinesis (thought control of material objects), and clairvoyance (knowledge of distant objects) are all awkward to explain within the normal confines of psychology and physics. If these phenomena are real, they might well be reflecting the superphysical nature that the dualist ascribes to the mind. Trivially they are *mental* phenomena, and if they are also forever beyond physical explanation, then at least some mental phenomena must be irreducibly nonphysical.

Collectively, these considerations may seem compelling. But there are serious criticisms of each, and we must examine them as well. Consider first the argument from religion. There is certainly nothing wrong in principle with appealing to a more general theory that bears on the case at issue, which is what the appeal to religion amounts to. But the appeal can only be as good as the scientific credentials of the religion(s) being appealed to, and here the appeals tend to fall down rather badly. In general, attempts to decide scientific questions by appeal to religious orthodoxy have a very sorry history. That the

stars are other suns, that the earth is not the center of the universe, that diseases are caused by microorganisms, that the earth is billions of years old, that life is a physicochemical phenomenon; all of these crucial insights were strongly and sometimes viciously resisted, because the dominant religion of the time happened to think otherwise. Giordano Bruno was burned at the stake for urging the first view; Galileo was forced by threat of torture in the Vatican's basement to recant the second view; the firm belief that disease was a punishment visited by the Devil allowed public health practices that brought chronic plagues to most of the cities of Europe; and the age of the earth and the evolution of life were forced to fight an uphill battle against religious prejudice even in an age of supposed enlightenment.

History aside, the almost universal opinion that one's own religious convictions are the reasoned outcome of a dispassionate evaluation of all of the major alternatives is almost demonstrably false for humanity in general. If that really were the genesis of most people's convictions, then one would expect the major faiths to be distributed more or less randomly or evenly over the globe. But in fact they show a very strong tendency to cluster: Christianity is centered in Europe and the Americas, Islam in Africa and the Middle East, Hinduism in India, and Buddhism in the Orient. Which illustrates what we all suspected anyway: that *social forces* are the primary determinants of religious belief for people in general. To decide scientific questions by appeal to religious orthodoxy would therefore be to put social forces in place of empirical evidence. For all of these reasons, professional scientists and philosophers concerned with the nature of mind generally do their best to keep religious appeals out of the discussion entirely.

The argument from introspection is a much more interesting argument, since it tries to appeal to the direct experience of everyman. But the argument is deeply suspect, in that it assumes that our faculty of inner observation or introspection reveals things as they really are in their innermost nature. This assumption is suspect because we already know that our other forms of observation—sight, hearing, touch, and so on—do no such thing. The red surface of an apple does not *look* like a matrix of molecules reflecting photons at certain critical wavelengths, but that is what it is. The sound of a flute does not *sound* like a sinusoidal compression wave train in the atmosphere, but that is what it is. The warmth of the summer air does not *feel* like the mean kinetic energy of millions of tiny molecules, but that is what it is. If one's pains and hopes and beliefs do not *introspectively* seem like electrochemical states in a neural network, that may be only because our faculty of introspection, like our other senses, is not sufficiently penetrating to reveal such hidden details. Which is just what one would expect anyway. The argument from introspection is therefore entirely without force, unless we can somehow argue that the faculty of introspection is quite different from all other forms of observation.

The argument from irreducibility presents a more serious challenge, but here also its force is less than first impression suggests. Consider first our capacity for mathematical reasoning which so impressed Descartes. The last ten years have made available, to anyone with fifty dollars to spend, electronic calculators whose capacity for mathematical reasoning—the calculational part, at least—far surpasses that of any normal human. The fact is, in the centuries since Descartes' writings, philosophers, logicians, mathematicians, and computer scientists have managed to isolate the general principles of mathematical reasoning, and electronics engineers have created machines that compute in accord with those principles. The result is a hand-held object that would have astonished Descartes. This outcome is impressive not just because machines have proved capable of some of the capacities boasted by human reason, but because some of those achievements invade areas of human reason that past dualistic philosophers have held up as forever closed to mere physical devices.

Although debate on the matter remains open, Descartes' argument from language use is equally dubious. The notion of a *computer language* is by now a commonplace: consider BASIC, PASCAL, FORTRAN, APL, LISP, and so on. Granted, these artificial "languages" are much simpler in structure and content than human natural language, but the differences may be differences only of degree, and not of kind. As well, the theoretical work of Noam Chomsky and the generative grammar approach to linguistics have done a great deal to explain the human capacity for language use in terms that invite simulation by computers, I do not mean to suggest that truly conversational computers are just around the corner. We have a great deal yet to learn, and fundamental problems yet to solve (mostly having to do with our capacity for inductive or theoretical reasoning). But recent progress here does nothing to support the claim that language use must be forever impossible for a purely physical system. On the contrary, such a claim now appears rather arbitrary and dogmatic. . . .

The next issue is also a live problem: How can we possibly hope to explain or to predict the intrinsic qualities of our sensations, or the meaningful content of our beliefs and desires, in purely physical terms? This is a major challenge to the materialist. But as we shall see in later sections, active research programs are already under way on both problems, and positive suggestions are being explored. It is in fact not impossible to imagine how such explanations might go, though the materialist cannot yet pretend to have solved either problem. Until he does, the dualist will retain a bargaining chip here, but that is about all. What the dualists need in order to establish their case is the conclusion that a physical reduction is outright impossible, and that is a conclusion they have failed to establish. Rhetorical questions, like the one that opens this paragraph, do not constitute arguments. And it is equally difficult, note, to imagine how the relevant phenomena could be explained or predicted solely in terms of the substance dualist's nonphysical mind-stuff.

The explanatory problem here is a major challenge to everybody, not just to the materialist. On this issue then, we have a rough standoff.

The final argument in support of dualism urged the existence of parapsychological phenomena such as telepathy and telekinesis, the point being that such mental phenomena are (a) real, and (b) beyond purely physical explanation. This argument is really another instance of the argument from irreducibility discussed above, and as before, it is not entirely clear that such phenomena, even if real, must forever escape a purely physical explanation. The materialist can already suggest a possible mechanism for telepathy, for example. On his view, thinking is an electrical activity within the brain. But according to electromagnetic theory, such changing motions of electric charges must produce electromagnetic waves radiating at the speed of light in all directions, waves that will contain information about the electrical activity that produced them. Such waves can subsequently have effects on the electrical activity of other brains, that is, on their thinking. Call this the "radio transmitter receiver" theory of telepathy.

I do not for a moment suggest that this theory is true: the electromagnetic waves emitted by the brain are fantastically weak (billions of times weaker than the ever present background electromagnetic flux produced by commercial radio stations), and they are almost certain to be hopelessly jumbled together as well. This is one reason why, in the absence of systematic, compelling, and repeatable evidence for the existence of telepathy, one must doubt its possibility. But it is significant that the materialist has the theoretical resources to suggest a detailed possible explanation of telepathy, if it were real, which is more than any dualist has so far done. It is not at all clear, then, that the materialist *must* be at an explanatory disadvantage in these matters. Quite the reverse.

Put the preceding aside, if you wish, for the main difficulty with the argument from parapsychological phenomena is much, much simpler. Despite the endless pronouncements

and anecdotes in the popular press, and despite a steady trickle of serious research on such things, there is no significant or trustworthy evidence that such phenomena even exist. The wide gap between popular conviction on this matter, and the actual evidence, is something that itself calls for research. For there is not a single parapsychological effect that can be repeatedly or reliably produced in any laboratory suitably equipped to perform and control the experiment. Not one. Honest researchers have been repeatedly hoodwinked by "psychic" charlatans with skills derived from the magician's trade, and the history of the subject is largely a history of gullibility, selection of evidence, poor experimental controls, and outright fraud by the occasional researcher as well. If someone really does discover a repeatable parapsychological effect, then we shall have to reevaluate the situation, but as things stand, there is nothing here to support a dualist theory of mind.

Upon critical examination, the arguments in support of dualism lose much of their force. But we are not yet done: there are arguments against dualism, and these also require examination.

ARGUMENTS AGAINST DUALISM

The first argument against dualism urged by the materialists appeals to the greater *simplicity* of their view. It is a principle of rational methodology that, if all else is equal, the simpler of two competing hypotheses should be preferred. This principle is sometimes called "Ockham's Razor"—after William of Ockham, the medieval philosopher who first enunciated it—and it can also be expressed as follows: "Do not multiply entities beyond what is strictly necessary to explain the phenomena." The materialist postulates only one kind of substance (physical matter), and one class of properties (physical properties), whereas the dualist postulates two kinds of matter and/or two classes of properties. And to no explanatory advantage, charges the materialist.

This is not yet a decisive point against dualism, since neither dualism nor materialism can yet explain all of the phenomena to be explained. But the objection does have some force, especially since there is no doubt at all that physical matter exists, while spiritual matter remains a tenuous hypothesis.

If this latter hypothesis brought us some definite explanatory advantage obtainable in no other way, then we would happily violate the demand for simplicity, and we would be right to do so. But it does not, claims the materialist. In fact, the advantage is just the other way around, he argues, and this brings us to the second objection to dualism: the relative *explanatory impotence* of dualism as compared to materialism.

Consider, very briefly, the explanatory resources already available to the neurosciences. We know that the brain exists and what it is made of. We know much of its microstructure: how the neurons are organized into systems and how distinct systems are connected to one another, to the motor nerves going out to the muscles, and to the sensory nerves coming in from the sense organs. We know much of their microchemistry: how the nerve cells fire tiny electrochemical pulses along their various fibers, and how they make other cells fire also, or cease firing. We know some of how such activity processes sensory information, selecting salient or subtle bits to be sent on to higher systems. And we know some of how such activity initiates and coordinates bodily behavior. Thanks mainly to neurology (the branch of medicine concerned with brain pathology), we know a great deal about the correlations between damage to various parts of the human brain, and various behavioral and cognitive deficits from which the victims suffer. There are a great many isolated deficits—some gross, some subtle—that are familiar to neurologists (inability to speak, or to read, or to understand speech, or to recognize faces, or to add/subtract, or to move a certain limb, or to put information into long-term memory, and so on), and their appearance is closely tied to the occurrence of damage to very specific parts of the brain.

Nor are we limited to cataloguing traumas. The growth and development of the brain's microstructure is also something that neuroscience has explored, and such development appears to be the basis of various kinds of learning by the organism. Learning, that is, involves lasting chemical and physical changes in the brain. In sum, the neuroscientist can tell us a great deal about the brain, about its constitution and the physical laws that govern it; he can already explain much of our behavior in terms of the physical, chemical, and electrical properties of the brain; and he has the theoretical resources available to explain a good deal more as our explorations continue. . . .

Compare now what the neuroscientist can tell us about the brain, and what he can do with that knowledge, with what the dualist can tell us about spiritual substance, and what he can do with those assumptions. Can the dualist tell us anything about the internal constitution of mind-stuff? Of the nonmaterial elements that make it up? Of the laws that govern their behavior? Of the mind's structural connections with the body? Of the manner of its operations? Can he explain human capacities and pathologies in terms of its structures and its defects? The fact is, the dualist can do none of these things, because no detailed theory of mind-stuff has ever been formulated. Compared to the rich resources and explanatory successes of current materialism, dualism is less a theory of mind than it is an empty space waiting for a genuine theory of mind to be put in it.

Thus argues the materialist. But again, this is not a completely decisive point against dualism. The dualist can admit that the brain plays a major role in the administration of both perception and behavior—on his view the brain is the *mediator* between the mind and the body—but he may attempt to argue that the materialist's current successes and future explanatory prospects concern only the mediative functions of the brain, not the *central* capacities of the nonphysical mind, capacities such as reason, emotion, and consciousness itself. On these latter topics, he may argue, both dualism *and* materialism currently draw a blank.

But this reply is not a very good one. So far as the capacity for reasoning is concerned, machines already exist that execute in minutes sophisticated deductive and mathematical calculations that would take a human a lifetime to execute. And so far as the other two mental capacities are concerned, studies of such things as depression, motivation, attention, and sleep have revealed many interesting and puzzling facts about the neurochemical and neurodynamical basis of both emotion and consciousness. The *central* capacities, no less than the peripheral, have been addressed with profit by various materialist research programs.

In any case, the (substance) dualist's attempt to draw a sharp distinction between the unique "mental" capacities proper to the nonmaterial mind, and the merely mediative capacities of the brain, prompts an argument that comes close to being an outright refutation of (substance) dualism. If there really is a distinct entity in which reasoning, emotion, and consciousness take place, and if that entity is dependent on the brain for nothing more than sensory experiences as input and volitional executions as output, *then one would expect reason, emotion, and consciousness to be relatively invulnerable to direct control or pathology by manipulation or damage to the brain.* But in fact the exact opposite is true. Alcohol, narcotics, or senile degeneration of nerve tissue will impair, cripple, or even destroy one's capacity for rational thought. Psychiatry knows of hundreds of emotion-controlling chemicals (lithium, chlorpromazine, amphetamine, cocaine, and so on) that do their work when vectored into the brain. And the vulnerability of consciousness to the anesthetics, to caffeine, and to something as simple as a sharp blow to the head, shows its very close dependence on neural activity in the brain. All of this makes perfect sense if reason, emotion, and consciousness are activities of the brain itself. But it makes very little sense if they are activities of something else entirely.

We may call this the argument from the *neural dependence* of all known mental phenomena. Property dualism, note, is not threatened by this argument, since, like materialism, property dualism reckons the brain as the seat of all mental activity. We shall conclude this section, however, with an argument that cuts against both varieties of dualism: the argument from *evolutionary history.*

What is the origin of a complex and sophisticated species such as ours? What, for that matter, is the origin of the dolphin, the mouse, or the housefly? Thanks to the fossil record, comparative anatomy, and the biochemistry of proteins and nucleic acids, there is no longer any significant doubt on this matter. Each existing species is a surviving type from a number of variations on an earlier type of organism; each earlier type is in turn a surviving type from a number of variations on a still earlier type of organism; and so on down the branches of the evolutionary tree until, some three billion years ago, we find a trunk of just one or a handful of very simple organisms. These organisms, like their more complex offspring, are just self-repairing, self-replicating, energy-driven molecular structures. (That evolutionary trunk has its own roots in an earlier era of purely chemical evolution, in which the molecular elements of life were themselves pieced together.) The mechanism of development that has structured this tree has two main elements: (1) the occasional blind variation in types of reproducing creature, and (2) the selective survival of some of these types due to the relative reproductive advantage enjoyed by individuals of those types. Over periods of geological time, such a process can produce an enormous variety of organisms, some of them very complex indeed.

For purposes of our discussion, the important point about the standard evolutionary story is that the human species and all of its features are the wholly physical outcome of a purely physical process. Like all but the simplest of organisms, we have a nervous system. And for the same reason: a nervous system permits the discriminative guidance of behavior. But a nervous system is just an active matrix of cells, and a cell is just an active matrix of molecules. We are notable only in that our nervous system is more complex and powerful than those of our fellow creatures.

Our inner nature differs from that of simpler creatures in degree, but not in kind.

If this is the correct account of our origins, then there seems neither need, nor room, to fit any nonphysical substances or properties into our theoretical account of ourselves. We are creatures of matter. And we should learn to live with that fact.

Arguments like these have moved most (but not all) of the professional community to embrace some form of materialism. This has not produced much unanimity, however, since the differences between the several materialist positions are even wider than the differences that divide dualism.

Minds, Brains, and Science

John Searle

In this essay, John Searle outlines the challenge of fitting the mind into the modern scientific worldview. Because mind seems so different from brain, standard solutions to the mind-body problem seem either antiscientific or antimind. Some dualisms explicitly reject key features of the scientific worldview, and many forms of physicalism reject key features of the mind. Searle argues that key claims of both dualists and physicalists can be combined into a consistent theory. He suggests that the relation of the mind to the body is like the relation of solidity to the molecular structure of an object. In each case, the former is a property of the latter and the latter causes the former. John Searle is professor of philosophy at the University of California, Berkeley.

As you read through this essay, consider the following:

1. What features of the mind create the challenge for scientific explanations of mind? Does Searle effectively explain how minds can be part of a world made of atoms?
2. How can "brains cause minds" if "minds just are features of brains"?
3. What is Searle's attitude toward the mystery of consciousness?
4. Does Searle succeed in showing how mentalism is consistent with physicalism?
5. Are there any serious disanalogies between the relation of solidity to molecular structure and the relation of minds to brains?

For thousands of years, people have been trying to understand their relationship to the rest of the universe. For a variety of reasons many philosophers today are reluctant to tackle such big problems. Nonetheless, the problems remain, and in this book I am going to attack some of them.

At the moment, the biggest problem is this: We have a certain commonsense picture of ourselves as human beings which is very hard to square with our overall "scientific" conception of the physical world. We think of ourselves as *conscious, free, mindful, rational* agents in a world that science tells us consists entirely of mindless, meaningless physical particles. Now, how can we square these two conceptions? How, for example, can it be the case that the world contains nothing but unconscious physical particles, and yet that it also contains

From John Searle, *Minds, Brains and Science* (Cambridge, Mass.: Harvard University Press, 1984). © John R. Searle. Reprinted by permission.

consciousness? How can a mechanical universe contain intentionalistic human beings—that is, human beings that can represent the world to themselves? How, in short, can an essentially meaningless world contain meanings?

Such problems spill over into other more contemporary-sounding issues: How should we interpret recent work in computer science and artificial intelligence—work aimed at making intelligent machines? Specifically, does the digital computer give us the right picture of the human mind? And why is it that the social sciences in general have not given us insights into ourselves comparable to the insights that the natural sciences have given us into the rest of nature? What is the relation between the ordinary, commonsense explanations we accept of the way people behave and scientific modes of explanation?

. . . I want to plunge right into what many philosophers think of as the hardest problem of all: What is the relation of our minds to the rest of the universe? This, I am sure you will recognise, is the traditional mind-body or mind-brain problem. In its contemporary version it usually takes the form: how does the mind relate to the brain?

I believe that the mind-body problem has a rather simple solution, one that is consistent both with what we know about neurophysiology and with our commonsense conception of the nature of mental states—pains, beliefs, desires and so on. But before presenting that solution, I want to ask why the mind-body problem seems so intractable. Why do we still have in philosophy and psychology after all these centuries a "mind-body problem" in a way that we do not have, say, a "digestion-stomach problem"? Why does the mind seem more mysterious than other biological phenomena?

I am convinced that part of the difficulty is that we persist in talking about a twentieth-century problem in an outmoded seventeenth-century vocabulary. When I was an undergraduate, I remember being dissatisfied with the choices that were apparently available in the philosophy of mind: you could be either a monist or a dualist. If you were a

monist, you could be either a materialist or an idealist. If you were a materialist, you could be either a behaviourist or a physicalist. And so on. One of my aims in what follows is to try to break out of these tired old categories. Notice that nobody feels he has to choose between monism and dualism where the "digestion-stomach problem" is concerned. Why should it be any different with the "mind-body problem"?

But, vocabulary apart, there is still a problem or family of problems. Since Descartes, the mind-body problem has taken the following form: how can we account for the relationships between two apparently completely different kinds of things? On the one hand, there are mental things, such as our thoughts and feelings; we think of them as subjective, conscious, and immaterial. On the other hand, there are physical things; we think of them as having mass, as extended in space, and as causally interacting with other physical things. Most attempted solutions to the mind-body problem wind up by denying the existence of, or in some way downgrading the status of, one or the other of these types of things. Given the successes of the physical sciences, it is not surprising that in our stage of intellectual development the temptation is to downgrade the status of mental entities. So, most of the recently fashionable materialist conceptions of the mind—such as behaviourism, functionalism, and physicalism—end up by denying, implicitly or explicitly, that there are any such things as minds as we ordinarily think of them. That is, they deny that we do really *intrinsically* have subjective, conscious, mental states and that they are as real and as irreducible as anything else in the universe.

Now, why do they do that? Why is it that so many theorists end up denying the intrinsically mental character of mental phenomena? If we can answer that question, I believe that we will understand why the mind-body problem has seemed so intractable for so long.

There are four features of mental phenomena which have made them seem impossible to fit into our "scientific" conception of the world as made up of material things. And it is these four features that have made the mind-body problem really difficult. They are so embarrassing that they have led many thinkers in philosophy, psychology, and artificial intelligence to say strange and implausible things about the mind.

The most important of these features is consciousness. I, at the moment of writing this, and you, at the moment of reading it, are both conscious. It is just a plain fact about the world that it contains such conscious mental states and events, but it is hard to see how mere physical systems could have consciousness. How could such a thing occur? How, for example, could this grey and white gook inside my skull be conscious?

I think the existence of consciousness ought to seem amazing to us. It is easy enough to imagine a universe without it, but if you do, you will see that you have imagined a universe that is truly meaningless. Consciousness is the central fact of specifically human existence because without it all of the other specifically human aspects of our existence—language, love, humour, and so on—would be impossible. I believe it is, by the way, something of a scandal that contemporary discussions in philosophy and psychology have so little of interest to tell us about consciousness.

The second intractable feature of the mind is what philosophers and psychologists call "intentionality," the feature by which our mental states are directed at, or about, or refer to, or are of objects and states of affairs in the world other than themselves. "Intentionality," by the way, doesn't just refer to intentions, but also to beliefs, desires, hopes, fears, love, hate, lust, disgust, shame, pride, irritation, amusement, and all of those mental states (whether conscious or unconscious) that refer to, or are about, the world apart from the mind. Now the question about intentionality is much like the question about consciousness. How can this stuff inside my head be *about* anything? How can it *refer* to anything? After all, this stuff in the skull consists of "atoms in the void," just as all of the

rest of material reality consists of atoms in the void. Now how, to put it crudely, can atoms in the void represent anything?

The third feature of the mind that seems difficult to accommodate within a scientific conception of reality is the subjectivity of mental states. This subjectivity is marked by such facts as that I can feel my pains, and you can't. I see the world from my point of view; you see it from your point of view. I am aware of myself and my internal mental states, as quite distinct from the selves and mental states of other people. Since the seventeenth century we have come to think of reality as something which must be equally accessible to all competent observers—that is, we think it must be objective. Now, how are we to accommodate the reality of *subjective* mental phenomena with the scientific conception of reality as totally *objective?*

Finally, there is a fourth problem, the problem of mental causation. We all suppose, as part of common sense, that our thoughts and feelings make a real difference to the way we behave, that they actually have some *causal* effect on the physical world. I decide, for example, to raise my arm and—lo and behold—my arm goes up. But if our thoughts and feelings are truly mental, how can they affect anything physical? How could something mental make a physical difference? Are we supposed to think that our thoughts and feelings can somehow produce chemical effects on our brains and the rest of our nervous system? How could such a thing occur? Are we supposed to think that thoughts can wrap themselves around the axons or shake the dendrites or sneak inside the cell wall and attack the cell nucleus?

But unless some such connection takes place between the mind and the brain, aren't we just left with the view that the mind doesn't matter, that it is as unimportant causally as the froth on the wave is to the movement of the wave? I suppose if the froth were conscious, it might think to itself: "What a tough job it is pulling these waves up on the beach and then pulling them out again, all day long!" But we know the froth doesn't make any important difference. Why do we suppose our mental life is any more important than a froth on the wave of physical reality?

These four features, consciousness, intentionality, subjectivity, and mental causation are what make the mind-body problem seem so difficult. Yet, I want to say, they are all real features of our mental lives. Not every mental state has all of them. But any satisfactory account of the mind and of mind-body relations must take account of all four features. If your theory ends up by denying any one of them, you know you must have made a mistake somewhere.

The first thesis I want to advance toward "solving the mind-body problem" is this:

> *Mental phenomena, all mental phenomena whether conscious or unconscious, visual or auditory, pains, tickles, itches, thoughts, indeed, all of our mental life, are caused by processes going on in the brain.*

To get a feel for how this works, let's try to describe the causal processes in some detail for at least one kind of mental state. For example, let's consider pains. Of course, anything we say now may seem wonderfully quaint in a generation, as our knowledge of how the brain works increases. Still, the *form* of the explanation can remain valid even though the *details* are altered. On current views, pain signals are transmitted from sensory nerve endings to the spinal cord by at least two types of fibres—there are Delta A fibres, which are specialised for prickling sensations, and C fibres, which are specialised for burning and aching sensations. In the spinal cord, they pass through a region called the tract of Lissauer and terminate on the neurons of the cord. As the signals go up the spine, they enter the brain by two separate pathways: the prickling pain pathway and the burning pain pathway. Both pathways go through the thalamus, but the prickling pain is more localised afterwards in the somato-sensory cortex, whereas the burning pain pathway transmits signals, not only upwards into the cortex, but also laterally into the hypothalamus and other regions at the base of the brain. Because of these differences, it is much easier for us to localise a prickling sen-

sation—we can tell fairly accurately where someone is sticking a pin into our skin, for example—whereas burning and aching pains can be more distressing because they activate more of the nervous system. The actual sensation of pain appears to be caused both by the stimulation of the basal regions of the brain, especially the thalamus, and the stimulation of the somato-sensory cortex.

Now for the purpose of this discussion, the point we need to hammer home is this: our sensations of pains are caused by a series of events that begin at free nerve endings and end in the thalamus and in other regions of the brain. Indeed, as far as the actual sensations are concerned, the events inside the central nervous system are quite sufficient to cause pains—we know this both from the phantom-limb pains felt by amputees and the pains caused by artificially stimulating relevant portions of the brain. I want to suggest that what is true of pain is true of mental phenomena generally. To put it crudely, and counting all of the central nervous system as part of the brain for our present discussion, everything that matters for our mental life, all of our thoughts and feelings, are caused by processes inside the brain. As far as causing mental states is concerned, the crucial step is the one that goes on inside the head, not the external or peripheral stimulus. And the argument for this is simple. If the events outside the central nervous system occurred, but nothing happened in the brain, there would be no mental events. But if the right things happened in the brain, the mental events would occur even if there was no outside stimulus. (And that, by the way, is the principle on which surgical anaesthesia works: the outside stimulus is prevented from having the relevant effects on the central nervous system.)

But if pains and other mental phenomena are caused by processes in the brain, one wants to know: what are pains? What are they really? Well, in the case of pains, the obvious answer is that they are unpleasant sorts of sensations. But that answer leaves us unsatisfied because it doesn't tell us how pains fit into our overall conception of the world.

Once again, I think the answer to the question is obvious, but it will take some spelling out. To our first claim—that pains and other mental phenomena are caused by brain processes, we need to add a second claim:

Pains and other mental phenomena just are features of the brain (and perhaps the rest of the central nervous system).

One of the primary aims of this chapter is to show how *both* of these propositions can be true together. How can it be both the case that brains cause minds and yet minds just are features of brains? I believe it is the failure to see how both these propositions can be true together that has blocked a solution to the mind-body problem for so long. There are different levels of confusion that such a pair of ideas can generate. If mental and physical phenomena have cause and effect relationships, how can one be a feature of the other? Wouldn't that imply that the mind caused itself—the dreaded doctrine of *causa sui*? But at the bottom of our puzzlement is a misunderstanding of causation. It is tempting to think that whenever A causes B there must be two discrete events, one identified as the cause, the other identified as the effect; that all causation functions in the same way as billiard balls hitting each other. This crude model of the causal relationships between the brain and the mind inclines us to accept some kind of dualism; we are inclined to think that events in one material realm, the "physical," cause events in another insubstantial realm, the "mental." But that seems to me a mistake. And the way to remove the mistake is to get a more sophisticated concept of causation. To do this, I will turn away from the relations between mind and brain for a moment to observe some other sorts of causal relationships in nature.

A common distinction in physics is between micro- and macro-properties of systems—the small and large scales. Consider, for example, the desk at which I am now sitting, or the glass of water in front of me. Each object is composed of micro-particles. The micro-particles have features at the level of molecules and atoms as well as at the deeper level of subatomic particles. But each object also has certain properties such as the solidity of the table, the liquidity of the water, and the transparency of the glass, which are surface or global features of the physical systems. Many such surface or global properties can be causally explained by the behaviour of elements at the micro-level. For example, the solidity of the table in front of me is explained by the lattice structure occupied by the molecules of which the table is composed. Similarly, the liquidity of the water is explained by the nature of the interactions between the H_2O molecules. Those macro-features are causally explained by the behaviour of elements at the micro-level.

I want to suggest that this provides a perfectly ordinary model for explaining the puzzling relationships between the mind and the brain. In the case of liquidity, solidity, and transparency, we have no difficulty at all in supposing that the surface features are *caused by* the behaviour of elements at the micro-level, and at the same time we accept that the surface phenomena *just are* features of the very systems in question. I think the clearest way of stating this point is to say that the surface feature is both *caused by* the behaviour of micro-elements, and at the same time is *realised in* the system that is made up of the micro-elements. There is a cause and effect relationship, but at the same time the surface features are just higher level features of the very system whose behaviour at the micro-level causes those features.

In objecting to this someone might say that liquidity, solidity, and so on are identical with features of the micro-structure. So, for example, we might just define solidity as the lattice structure of the molecular arrangement, just as heat often is identified with the mean kinetic energy of molecule movements. This point seems to me correct but not really an objection to the analysis that I am proposing. It is a characteristic of the progress of science that an expression that is originally defined in terms of surface features, features accessible to the senses, is subsequently defined in terms of the micro-structure that causes the surface features. Thus, to take the example of solidity, the table in front of me is solid in the ordinary sense that it is rigid, it resists pressure, it supports books, it is not easily penetrable by most other objects such as other tables, and so on. Such is the commonsense notion of solidity. And in a scientific vein one can define solidity as whatever micro-structure causes these gross observable features. So one can then say either that solidity just is the lattice structure of the system of molecules and that solidity so defined causes, for example, resistance to touch and pressure. Or one can say that solidity consists of such high level features as rigidity and resistance to touch and pressure and that it is caused by the behaviour of elements at the micro-level.

If we apply these lessons to the study of the mind, it seems to me that there is no difficulty in accounting for the relations of the mind to the brain in terms of the brain's functioning to cause mental states. Just as the liquidity of the water is caused by the behaviour of elements at the micro-level, and yet at the same time it is a feature realised in the system of micro-elements, so in exactly that sense of "caused by" and "realised in" mental phenomena are caused by processes going on in the brain at the neuronal or modular level, and at the same time they are realised in the very system that consists of neurons. And just as we need the micro/macro distinction for any physical system, so for the same reasons we need the micro/macro distinction for the brain. And though we can say of a system of particles that it is 10°C or it is solid or it is liquid, we cannot say of any given particle that this particle is solid, this particle is liquid, this particle is 10°C. I can't for example reach into this glass of water, pull out a molecule and say: "This one's wet."

In exactly the same way, as far as we know anything at all about it, though we can say of a particular brain: "This brain is conscious," or: "This brain is experiencing thirst or pain," we can't say of any particular neuron in the brain: "This neuron is in pain, this neuron is experiencing thirst." To repeat this point, though there are enormous empirical mysteries about how the brain works in detail, there are no logical or philosophical or metaphysical obstacles to accounting for the relation between the mind and the brain in terms that are quite familiar to us from the rest of nature. Nothing is more common in nature than for surface features of a phenomenon to be both caused by and realised in a micro-structure, and those are exactly the relationships that are exhibited by the relation of mind to brain.

Let us now return to the four problems that I said faced any attempt to solve the mind-brain problem.

First, how is consciousness possible?

The best way to show how something is possible is to show how it actually exists. We have already given a sketch of how pains are actually caused by neurophysiological processes going on in the thalamus and the sensory cortex. Why is it then that many people feel dissatisfied with this sort of answer? I think that by pursuing an analogy with an earlier problem in the history of science we can dispel this sense of puzzlement. For a long time many biologists and philosophers thought it was impossible, in principle, to account for the existence of *life* on purely biological grounds. They thought that in addition to the biological processes some other element must be necessary, some *élan vital* must be postulated in order to lend life to what was otherwise dead and inert matter. It is hard today to realise how intense the dispute was between vitalism and mechanism even a generation ago, but today these issues are no longer taken seriously. Why not? I think it is not so much because mechanism won and vitalism lost, but because we have come to understand better the biological character of the processes that are characteristic of living organisms. Once we understand how the features that are characteristic of living beings have a biological explanation, it no longer seems mysterious to us that matter should be alive. I think that exactly similar considerations should apply to our discussions of consciousness. It should seem no more mysterious, in principle, that this hunk of matter, this grey and white oatmeal-textured substance of the brain, should be conscious than it seems mysterious that this other hunk of matter, this collection of nucleo-protein molecules stuck onto a calcium frame, should be alive. The way, in short, to dispel the mystery is to understand the processes. We do not yet fully understand the processes, but we understand their general *character*; we understand that there are certain specific electrochemical activities going on among neurons or neuron-modules and perhaps other features of the brain and these processes cause consciousness.

Our second problem was, how can atoms in the void have intentionality? How can they be about something?

As with our first question, the best way to show how something is possible is to show how it actually exists. So let's consider thirst. As far as we know anything about it, at least certain kinds of thirst are caused in the hypothalamus by sequences of nerve firings. These firings are in turn caused by the action of angiotensin in the hypothalamus, and angiotensin, in turn, is synthesised by renin, which is secreted by the kidneys. Thirst, at least of these kinds, is caused by a series of events in the central nervous system, principally the hypothalamus, and it is realised in the hypothalamus. To be thirsty is to have, among other things, the desire to drink. Thirst is therefore an intentional state: it has content; its content determines under what conditions it is satisfied, and it has all the rest of the features that are common to intentional states.

As with the "mysteries" of life and consciousness, the way to master the mystery of intentionality is to describe in as much detail as we can how the phenomena are caused by biological processes while being at the same time realised in biological systems. Visual and auditory experiences, tactile sensations, hunger, thirst, and sexual desire, are all caused by brain processes and they are realised in the structure of the brain, and they are all intentional phenomena.

I am not saying we should lose our sense of the mysteries of nature. On the contrary, the examples I have cited are all in a sense astounding. But I am saying that they are neither more nor less mysterious than other astounding features of the world, such as the existence of gravitational attraction, the process of photosynthesis, or the size of the Milky Way.

Our third problem: how do we accommodate the subjectivity of mental states within an objective conception of the real world?

It seems to me a mistake to suppose that the definition of reality should exclude subjectivity. If "science" is the name of the collection of objective and systematic truths we can state about the world, then the existence of subjectivity is an objective scientific fact like any other. If a scientific account of the world attempts to describe how things are, then one of the features of the account will be the subjectivity of mental states, since it is just a plain fact about biological evolution that it has produced certain sorts of biological systems, namely human and certain animal brains, that have subjective features. My present state of consciousness is a feature of my brain, but its conscious aspects are accessible to me in a way that they are not accessible to you. And your present state of consciousness is a feature of your brain and its conscious aspects are accessible to you in a way that they are not accessible to me. Thus the existence of subjectivity is an objective fact of biology. It is a persistent mistake to try to define "science" in terms of certain features of existing scientific theories. But once this provincialism is perceived to be the prejudice it is, then any domain of facts whatever is a subject of systematic investigation. So, for example, if God existed, then that fact would be a fact like any other. I do not know whether God exists, but I have no doubt at all that subjective mental states exist, because I am now in one and so are you. If the fact of subjectivity runs counter to a certain definition of "science," then it is the definition and not the fact which we will have to abandon.

Fourth, the problem of mental causation for our present purpose is to explain how mental events can cause physical events. How, for example, could anything as "weightless" and "ethereal" as a thought give rise to an action?

The answer is that thoughts are not weightless and ethereal. When you have a thought, brain activity is actually going on. Brain activity causes bodily movements by physiological processes. Now, because mental states are features of the brain, they have two levels of description—a higher level in mental terms, and a lower level in physiological terms. The very same causal powers of the system can be described at either level.

Once again, we can use an analogy from physics to illustrate these relationships. Consider hammering a nail with a hammer. Both hammer and nail have a certain kind of solidity. Hammers made of cottonwool or butter will be quite useless, and hammers made of water or steam are not hammers at all. Solidity is a real causal property of the hammer. But the solidity itself is caused by the behaviour of particles at the micro-level and it is realised in the system which consists of micro-elements. The existence of two causally real levels of description in the brain, one a macro-level of mental processes and the other a micro-level of neuronal processes is exactly analogous to the existence of two causally real levels of description of the hammer. Consciousness, for example, is a real property of the brain that can cause things to happen. My conscious attempt to perform an action such as raising my arm causes the movement of the arm. At the higher level of description, the intention to raise my arm causes the movement of the arm. But at the lower level of description, a series of neuron firings starts a chain of events that results in the contraction of the muscles. As with the case of hammering a nail, the same sequence of events has two levels of description. Both of them are causally real, and the higher level causal features are both caused by and realised in the structure of the lower level elements.

To summarise: on my view, the mind and the body interact, but they are not two different things, since mental phenomena just are features of the brain. One way to characterise this position is to see it as an assertion of both physicalism and mentalism. Suppose we define "naive physicalism" to be the view that all that exists in the world are physical particles with their properties and relations. The power of the physical model of reality is so great that it is hard to see how we can seriously challenge naive physicalism. And let us define "naive mentalism" to be the view that mental phenomena really exist. There really are mental states; some of them are conscious; many have intentionality; they all have subjectivity; and many of them function causally in determining physical events in the world. The thesis of this first chapter can now be stated quite simply. Naive mentalism and naive physicalism are perfectly consistent with each other. Indeed, as far as we know anything about how the world works, they are not only consistent, they are both true.

Essay and Paper Topics for "Scientific Practice and Reason"

1. Compare and contrast the different forms of objectivity discussed in Scheffler, Keller, and Grim. Which kinds of objectivity seem most important for science?

2. Describe the various roles that values play in the visions of science described by Keller, Kuhn, and Grim. Under what conditions do values compromise objectivity? How might they enhance objectivity?

3. Using Scheffler and Keller, explain why many people believe that science has a special claim to objectivity. How do the readings in Section 11, "What Is Science?," contribute to this perception? Is this perception warranted?

4. Evaluate the arguments presented by Kuhn, Laudan, and Kitcher on the issue of whether scientific progress is best understood in terms of increasing approximations to truth.

5. Discuss different answers to the question of whether there is anything that science cannot explain. What would it mean to explain every-thing? Even if science can provide an explanation for everything, does it follow that scientific ways of knowing are the only ways of knowing?

6. Explain the challenges to purely material-ist or physicalist accounts of human being that Churchland and Searle discuss. Evaluate their responses to these challenges.

Part VIII

The Practice of Religion

Three Conceptions of Religion

Theism

William James

William James (1842–1910) is among the best known and most widely read American philosophers. Along with John Dewey and C. S. Peirce, James was a founder of what has come to be known as philosophical pragmatism. In addition to his work as a philosopher, James was also a psychologist and wrote important books in that field as well as in the fields of religion, science, ethics, and other areas of philosophy. William James's brother was Henry James, the novelist. William James was interested in the nature and justification of religious faith (see "The Will to Believe," reprinted in Section 27) as well as in psychological phenomena of mysticism and mystical experience. In one of his most important books, *The Varieties of Religious Experience*, James describes the wide array of experiences people have that might be termed religious or mystical. This reading is taken from two of James's essays on religion. In it, he discusses the difference between the scientific and religious worldview and the core of theistic religious faith.

As you read through this essay, consider the following:

1. What does James mean when he says pessimism is a religious disease?
2. Why does James think worshiping the "God of nature" is mere superstition?
3. What is the "supernaturalist" sense of religion?
4. Which characteristics must God have, according to James, if God is to be worthy of worship?
5. What would one have to believe in order to belong to the religious tradition you know best? Does that require belief in more or less than "theism" as James understands the term?

514

. . . Pessimism [is] an essentially religious disease. The nightmare view of life has plenty of organic sources; but its great reflective source has at all times been the contradiction between the phenomena of nature and the craving of the heart to believe that behind nature there is a spirit whose expression nature is. What philosophers call "natural theology" has been one way of appeasing this craving; that poetry of nature in which our English literature is so rich has been another way. Now, suppose a mind of the latter of our two classes, whose imagination is pent in consequently, and who take its facts "hard"; suppose it, moreover, to feel strongly the craving for communion, and yet to realize how desperately difficult it is to construe the scientific order of nature either theologically or poetically,—and what result *can* there be but inner discord and contradiction? Now, this inner discord (merely as discord) can be relieved in either of two ways: The longing to read the facts religiously may cease, and leave the bare facts by themselves; or, supplementary facts may be discovered or believed-in, which permit the religious reading to go on. These two ways of relief are the two stages of recovery, the two levels of escape from pessimism, to which I made allusion a moment ago, and which the sequel will, I trust, make more clear.

Starting then with nature, we naturally tend, if we have the religious craving, to say with Marcus Aurelius, "O Universe! what thou wishest I wish." Our sacred books and traditions tell us of one God who made heaven and earth, and, looking on them, saw that they were good. Yet, on more intimate acquaintance, the visible surfaces of heaven and earth refuse to be brought by us into any intelligible unity at all. Every phenomenon that we would praise there exists cheek by jowl with some contrary phenomenon that cancels all its religious effect upon the mind. Beauty and hideousness, love and cruelty, life and death keep house together in indissolu-

ble partnership; and there gradually steals over us, instead of the old warm notion of a man-loving Deity, that of an awful power that neither hates nor loves, but rolls all things together meaninglessly to a common doom. This is an uncanny, a sinister, a nightmare view of life. . . .

This is the first stage of speculative melancholy. No brute can have this sort of melancholy; no man who is irreligious can become its prey. It is the sick shudder of the frustrated religious demand, and not the mere necessary outcome of animal experience. . . .

And now, in turning to what religion may have to say to the question, I come to what is the soul of my discourse. Religion has meant many things in human history; but when from now onward I use the word I mean to use it in the supernaturalist sense, as declaring that the so-called order of nature, which constitutes this world's experience, is only one portion of the total universe, and that there stretches beyond this visible world an unseen world of which we now know nothing positive, but in its relation to which the true significance of our present mundane life consists. A man's religious faith (whatever more special items of doctrine it may involve) means for me essentially his faith in the existence of an unseen order of some kind in which the riddles of the natural order may be found explained. In the more developed religions the natural world has always been regarded as the mere scaffolding or vestibule of a truer, more eternal world, and affirmed to be a sphere of education, trial, or redemption. In these religions, one must in some fashion die to the natural life before one can enter into life eternal. The notion that this physical world of wind and water, where the sun rises and the moon sets, is absolutely and ultimately the divinely aimed-at and established thing, is one which we find only in very early religions, such as that of the most primitive Jews. It is this natural religion (primitive still, in spite of the fact that poets and men of science whose good-will exceeds their perspicacity keep publishing it in new editions tuned to our contemporary ears) that, as I said a while ago, has suffered definitive bankruptcy in the opinion of a circle of persons,

From William James, "Is Life Worth Living?" and "Reflex Action and Theism," *The Will to Believe and Other Essays in Popular Philosophy* (1896).

among whom I must count myself, and who are growing more numerous every day. For such persons the physical order of nature, taken simply as science knows it, cannot be held to reveal any one harmonious spiritual intent. It is mere *weather*, as Chauncey Wright called it, doing and undoing without end. . . .

There is included in human nature an ingrained naturalism and materialism of mind which can only admit facts that are actually tangible. Of this sort of mind the entity called "science" is the idol. Fondness for the word "scientist" is one of the notes by which you may know its votaries; and its short way of killing any opinion that it disbelieves in is to call it "unscientific." It must be granted that there is no slight excuse for this. Science has made such glorious leaps in the last three hundred years, and extended our knowledge of nature so enormously both in general and in detail; men of science, moreover, have as a class displayed such admirable virtues,—that it is no wonder if the worshippers of science lose their head. In this very University, accordingly, I have heard more than one teacher say that all the fundamental conceptions of truth have already been found by science, and that the future has only the details of the picture to fill in. But the slightest reflection on the real conditions will suffice to show how barbaric such notions are. They show such a lack of scientific imagination, that it is hard to see how one who is actively advancing any part of science can make a mistake so crude. . . .

. . . God, whether existent or not, is at all events the kind of being which, if he did exist, would form *the most adequate possible object* for minds framed like our own to conceive as lying at the root of the universe. My thesis, in other words, is this: that *some* outward reality of a nature defined as God's nature must be defined, is the only ultimate object that is at the same time rational and possible for the human mind's contemplation. *Anything short of God is not rational, anything more than God is not possible.* . . .

. . . What kind of a being would God be if he did exist? The word "God" has come to mean many things in the history of human thought, from Venus and Jupiter to the "Idee" which figures in the pages of Hegel. Even the laws of physical nature have, in these positivistic times, been held worthy of divine honor and presented as the only fitting object of our reverence. Of course, if our discussion is to bear any fruit, we must mean something more definite than this. We must not call any object of our loyalty a "God" without more ado, simply because to awaken our loyalty happens to be one of God's functions. He must have some intrinsic characteristics of his own besides; and theism must mean the faith of that man who believes that the object of *his* loyalty has those other attributes, negative or positive, as the case may be. . . .

Now, what are these essential features? First, it is essential that God be conceived as the deepest power in the universe; and, second, he must be conceived under the form of a mental personality. The personality need not be determined intrinsically any further than is involved in the holding of certain things dear, and in the recognition of our dispositions toward those things, the things themselves being all good and righteous things. But, extrinsically considered, so to speak, God's personality is to be regarded, like any other personality, as something lying outside of my own and other than me, and whose existence I simply come upon and find. A power not ourselves, then, which not only makes for righteousness, but means it, and which recognizes us,—such is the definition which I think nobody will be inclined to dispute. Various are the attempts to shadow forth the other lineaments of so supreme a personality to our human imagination; various the ways of conceiving in what mode the recognition, the hearkening to our cry, can come. Some are gross and idolatrous; some are the most sustained efforts man's intellect has ever made to keep still living on that subtle edge of things where speech and thought expire. But, with all these differences, the essence remains unchanged. In whatever other respects the divine personality may differ from ours or may resemble it, the two are consanguineous at least in this,—that both have purposes for which they care, and each can hear the other's call.

The Man of the Law

Rabbi Joseph Soloveitchik

Rabbi Joseph Soloveitchik presents a Jewish view of the religious life that rests primarily on the law. But living according to the law means far more than following rules: Halakhic man approaches reality with an already fixed relationship to what he sees, a relationship that is defined by Jewish law. Soloveitchik begins by contrasting this with a "cognitive" person, who approaches the world as a scientist might, seeking to understand its structure with mathematics and theories. Halakhic man, the man of the law, approaches reality not with his theoretical construct tested by his observations but with fixed principles and judgments. Using his own preexisting understandings, he then comprehends not only his responsibilities and duties but also the world itself.

As you read through this essay, consider the following:

1. How does Soloveitchik understand the cognitive approach to reality?
2. When halakhic man looks at a spring, what does he see?
3. Why does Soloveitchik say that the approach of the man of the law involves orienting one's self to "all of reality"?
4. Are the cognitive and halakhic approaches both a priori, that is, prior to observation, experience, and testing? In the same sense? Explain.

1. THE APPROACH OF COGNITIVE MAN TO REALITY

Halakhic man's approach to reality is, at the outset, devoid of any element of transcendence. Indeed, his entire attitude to the world stands out by virtue of its originality and uniqueness. All of the frames of reference constructed by the philosophers and psychologists of religion for explaining the varieties of religious experience cannot accommodate halakhic man as far as his reaction to empirical reality is concerned. Halakhic man studies reality not because he is motivated by plain curiosity the way theoretical man is; nor is he driven to explore the world by any fear of being or anxiety of nonbeing. Nor, for that matter, does halakhic man orient himself to

the world in terms of a nebulous feeling of absolute dependence, or yearnings for the redemption of man, or visions of a great, revealed ethical ideal. Halakhic man orients himself to reality through a priori images of the world which he bears in the deep recesses of his personality. We may, if we so desire, call this a cognitive-normative approach, but it is not to be identified with the cognitive and ethical orientation of which the philosophers, the cognitive men par excellence, speak. . . .

. . . When cognitive man scrutinizes God's world and seeks, through critical probing, to determine its nature (I am not concerned here with the nature of the cause that precipitates cognition), he arrives at two differing decisions: (1) To plunge into the very midst of reality and to contemplate its appearance in order to understand its essence and structure. Cognitive man, in this instance, approaches the world without preconceived programs, without any elaborate preparations. He gropes in the darkness, is astonished and amazed by the

From Rabbi Joseph Soloveitchik, *Halakhic Man* (Philadelphia: The Jewish Publication Society, 1983). Reprinted by permission.

plethora of phenomena and by the "chaos and void" which prevail in the realm of reality, until he stumbles across a repetition of events in a certain order, which he had dimly sensed to begin with, as a result of which he can construct rules and establish laws that can serve as a beacon illuminating the road on which he travels through the cosmos. (2) In order to overcome the mystery in existence, he constructs an ideal, ordered, and fixed world, one that is perfectly clear and lucid; he fashions an a priori [i.e., prior to any experience or observation of the world], ideal creation with which he is greatly pleased. This creation does not cause him any anxiety. It does not attempt to elude him; it can not conceal itself from him. He knows it full well and delights in the knowledge. Whenever he wishes to orient himself to reality and to superimpose his a priori ideal system upon the realm of concrete empirical existence, he comes with his teaching in hand—his a priori teaching. He has no wish to passively cognize reality as it is in itself. Rather, first he creates the ideal a priori image, the ideal structure, and then compares it with the real world. His approach to reality consists solely in establishing the correspondence in effect between his ideal, a priori creation and concrete reality. . . .

2. HALAKHIC REALITY

When halakhic man approaches reality, he comes with his Torah, given to him from Sinai, in hand. He orients himself to the world by means of fixed statutes and firm principles. An entire corpus of precepts and laws guides him along the path leading to existence. Halakhic man, well furnished with rules, judgments, and fundamental principles, draws near the world with an a priori relation. His approach begins with an ideal creation and concludes with a real one. To whom may he be compared? To a mathematician who fashions an ideal world and then uses it for the purpose of establishing a relationship between it and the real world, as was explained above. The essence of the Halakhah, which was received from God, con-

sists in creating an ideal world and cognizing the relationship between that ideal world and our concrete environment in all its visible manifestations and underlying structures. There is no phenomenon, entity, or object in this concrete world which the a priori Halakhah does not approach with its ideal standard. When halakhic man comes across a spring bubbling quietly, he already possesses a fixed, a priori relationship with this real phenomenon: the complex of laws regarding the halakhic construct of a spring. The spring is fit for the immersion of a *zav* (a man with a discharge); it may serve as *mei hatat* (waters of expiation); it purifies with flowing water; it does not require a fixed quantity of forty se'ahs; etc. [See Maimonides, *Laws of Immersion Pools*, 9:8.] When halakhic man approaches a real spring, he gazes at it and carefully examines its nature. He possesses, a priori, ideal principles and precepts which establish the character of the spring as a halakhic construct, and he uses the statutes for the purpose of determining normative law: does the real spring correspond to the requirements of the ideal Halakhah or not?

Halakhic man is not overly curious, and he is not particularly concerned with cognizing the spring as it is in itself. Rather, he desires to coordinate the a priori concept with the a posteriori phenomenon.

When halakhic man looks to the western horizon and sees the fading rays of the setting sun or to the eastern horizon and sees the first light of dawn and the glowing rays of the rising sun, he knows that this sunset or sunrise imposes upon him anew obligations and commandments. Dawn and sunrise obligate him to fulfill those commandments that are performed during the day: the recitation of the morning *Shema*, *tzitzit*, *tefillin*, the morning prayer, *etrog*, *shofar*, *Hallel*, and the like. They make the time fit for the carrying out of certain halakhic practices: Temple service, acceptance of testimony, conversion, *halitzah*, etc., etc. Sunset imposes upon him those obligations and commandments that are performed during the night: the recitation of the evening *Shema*, *matzah*, the counting of the *omer*, etc. The sunset on Sabbath and holiday eves sanctifies the day: the profane and the holy are dependent upon a natural cosmic phenomenon—the sun sinking below the horizon. It is not anything transcendent that creates holiness but rather the visible reality—the regular cycle of the natural order. Halakhic man examines the sunrise and sunset, the dawn and the appearance of the stars; he gazes into the horizon—Is the upper horizon pale and the same as the lower?—and looks at the sun's shadows—Has afternoon already arrived? When he goes out on a clear, moonlit night (until the deficiency of the moon is replenished) he makes a blessing upon it. He knows that it is the moon that determines the times of the months and thus of all the Jewish seasons and festivals, and this determination must rely upon astronomical calculations. . . .

. . . He approaches existential space with an a priori yardstick, with fixed laws and principles, precepts that were revealed to Moses on Mount Sinai: the imaginary bridging of a spatial gap less than three handbreadths; the imaginary vertical extension, upward or downward, of a partition; the imaginary vertical extension of the edge of a roof downward to the ground; the bent wall; the measurements of four square cubits, ten handbreadths, etc., etc. He perceives space by means of these laws just like the mathematician who gazes at existential space by means of the ideal geometric space.

Halakhic man explores every nook and cranny of physical-biological existence. He determines the character of all of the animal functions of man—eating, sex, and all the bodily necessities—by means of halakhic principles and standards: the bulk of an olive (*ke-zayit*), the bulk of a date (*ke-kotevet*), the time required to eat a half-loaf meal (*kedai akhilat peras*), the time required to drink a quarter log (*revi'it*), eating in a normal or nonnormal manner, the beginning of intercourse, the conclusion of intercourse, normal intercourse and unnatural intercourse, etc., etc. Halakhah concerns itself with the normal as well as abnormal functioning of the organism, with the total biological functioning of the organism: the laws of menstruation, the man or woman suffering from a discharge, the mode of determining the onset of menstruation, virginal blood, pregnancy, the various stages in the birth process, the various physical signs that make animals or birds fit or unfit for consumption, etc., etc.

There is no real phenomenon to which halakhic man does not possess a fixed relationship from the outset and a clear, definitive, a priori orientation. He is interested in sociological creations: the state, society, and the relationship of individuals within a communal context. The Halakhah encompasses laws of business, torts, neighbors, plaintiff and defendant, creditor and debtor, partners, agents, workers, artisans, bailees, etc. Family life—marriage, divorce, *halitzah*, *sotah*, conjugal refusal (*mi'un*), the respective rights, obligations, and duties of a husband and a wife—is clarified and elucidated by it. War, the high court, courts and the penalties they impose—all are just a few of the multitude of halakhic subjects. The halakhist is involved with psychological problems—for example, sanity and insanity, the possibility or impossibility of a happy marriage, *miggo* [i.e., the principle that a party's plea gains credibility when a more advantageous plea is available], and assumptions as to the intention behind a specific act (*umdana*), the presumption that a particular individual is a liar or a sinner, the discretion of the judges, etc., etc. "The measure thereof is longer than the earth and broader than the sea" (Job 11:9).

Halakhah has a fixed a priori relationship to the whole of reality in all of its fine and detailed particulars. Halakhic man orients himself to the entire cosmos and tries to understand it by utilizing an ideal world which he bears in his halakhic consciousness. All halakhic concepts are a priori, and it is through them that halakhic man looks at the world. As we said above, his world view is similar to that of the mathematician: a priori and ideal. Both the mathematician and the halakhist gaze at the concrete world from an a priori, ideal standpoint and use a priori categories and concepts which determine from the outset their relationship to the qualitative phenomena they encounter. Both examine empirical reality from the vantage point of an ideal reality.

The Buddhist Way of Compassion

Ashok K. Malhotra

This essay describes yet another understanding of religion and religious faith. Rejecting mysticism, theism, law, and ritual, Buddhism emphasizes this world, self-realization, and salvation through enlightenment. Malhotra conveys a sense of this conception of religion by describing the life of Buddha, the Four Noble Truths, and the pathway toward enlightenment. Ashok K. Malhotra teaches philosophy at the State University of New York, Oneonta.

As you read through this essay, consider the following:

1. What important events does Malhotra describe in the life of the Buddha?
2. How did those events lead to enlightenment for the Buddha?
3. What are the Four Noble Truths?
4. How can people learn to be compassionate? How does the story of the student monk and the dog teach compassion?
5. What is the Eightfold Path?

Buddhism arose as a protest against Hinduism. The Buddha, who was a Hindu prince, found some of the key beliefs and practices of Hinduism to be restrictive, impractical, and outdated. He openly challenged the polytheism and the ritualism of the *Vedas*, the esoteric mysticism of the *Upanishads*, the caste system and belief in the Hindu trinity of the *Bhagavad Gītā*, and the emphasis on self-mortification and restrictive meditative practices of yoga. In its place, the Buddha offered his own unique brand of religion, which was devoid of god, soul, creation, permanence, ritual, external authority, last judgment, and caste distinctions.

Buddha constructed a religion that emphasized human life here and now. For him, the present world was the arena where the drama of life's problems and their solutions was to be enacted. If there was any salvation, it was to be obtained during the course of this existence. Salvation was possible only through one's own efforts. It was a

personal achievement within the reach of each human being.

Buddha rejected discussion of esoteric and metaphysical subjects such as the nature of absolute reality, life after death, and the nature of enlightenment. He regarded such talk as futile and meaningless. Since the uniqueness of the Buddha's religion is interwoven with his personal realization, we can gain access to the basic ideas of Buddhism by presenting the story of his life. This tale can be told in three parts: first, in terms of the Buddha's life leading toward enlightenment; second, the Buddha's description of this enlightenment through the Four Noble Truths; and third, the imparting of enlightenment to others through the Eightfold Path.

THE LIFE OF BUDDHA

The story of the Buddha's life has all the ingredients of a great drama. His original name was "Siddhartha Gautama." He was born in 563 B.C., the son of a king who ruled a small principality in the northern part of India. When a son was born to a Hindu king,

From Ashok K. Malhotra, "Buddhism," in *Pathways to Philosophy*, ed. Douglas W. Schrader and Ashok K. Malhotra, © 1996. Reprinted by permission of Prentice-Hall, Inc., Upper Saddle River, NJ.

it was customary to ask astrologers to predict the child's future. Their prediction was that Siddhartha would either become the greatest king India ever had, or renounce the world to become a great sage. The astrologers warned the king that Siddhartha would choose the second path if faced with suffering associated with disease, decay, and death.

To shield his son from the miseries of life and to nourish in him the earthly pleasures, the king provided the prince with beautiful palaces, exotic gardens, dancing girls, and entertainers. To further ground Siddhartha to this earth, the king arranged his son's marriage to a beautiful princess, Yasodhara. Siddhartha enjoyed a number of years of conjugal love with Yasodhara, who bore him a handsome son, Rahula.

The life of pleasure and leisure did offer a temporary escape from the sorrows of the world. But one day Siddhartha visited the city that lay outside the walls of the palaces and its pleasure gardens. On his first outing, Siddhartha saw an old man, enfeebled by age. On Siddhartha's inquiry, his charioteer explained that this man had been born, lived, and now was near his death. This is the fate of each person. Siddhartha, who had no experience of old age, was deeply touched by this sight.

On his second outing, Siddhartha encountered a man who was seriously ill. Weakened by his disease, he showed signs of helplessness and agony. When Siddhartha asked his charioteer about this man, he was told that the man had an incurable disease and was near death. Again Siddhartha was deeply touched by this man's suffering.

On his third outing, Siddhartha witnessed the cremation of a corpse. Siddhartha, who had never before seen death, inquired about the state of this man. The charioteer replied that everyone who was born was subject to aging, disease, and eventually death. Death takes its toll indiscriminately. It spares neither the rich nor the poor. King and pauper equally fall prey to it. Death is the fate of every creature. After observing the three sights of old age, sickness, and death, Siddhartha's own suffering became unbearable. He decided to look for a way out of this agony.

On his fourth outing, Siddhartha met ascetics in ocher robes. Their way of walking, talking, and looking revealed that they were at peace with themselves and the world. On his inquiry, the charioteer told Siddhartha that these ascetics had conquered their existential agony by renouncing this world. This indicated to Siddhartha a way out of suffering. He decided to abandon the world to join these ascetics. At age twenty-nine he left his kingdom, his wife, and his child to become a recluse. He spent the next six years of his life seeking enlightenment by following the path of asceticism. He put himself on a strict routine of fasting, yogic exercises, and meditation. He mastered all these arts during this short span of six years. After living a life of intense self-mortification, Siddhartha realized that he was no closer to enlightenment than when he started. While sitting under a tree, Siddhartha decided to abandon the path of the ascetic as well as his quest for enlightenment. As he did this, he was enlightened. From that moment onward he was called "the Buddha," which means "the awakened one." The tree became known as the *Bodhi* tree (tree of enlightenment).

During his enlightenment, the Buddha not only experienced the state of sorrowlessness, but also gained wisdom about the reasons for suffering and the method of eliminating the same. He spent the next forty-five years of his life teaching masses of people in India the truths experienced during his enlightenment. He conveyed these insights through the doctrines of the Four Noble Truths and the Eightfold Path.

THE FOUR NOBLE TRUTHS

After the Buddha was enlightened, he formulated his discoveries into four simple principles called the Four Noble Truths. These principles can be outlined as follows:

First, all life is suffering (*dukkha*).

Second, suffering is caused by selfish craving (*tanha*).

Third, suffering can be removed by replacing selfish craving with compassion (*karuna*).

Finally, compassion can be inculcated by practicing the Eightfold Path.

According to the Buddha, if we look closely we will find that all life is marked by pain and misery. Though there are some pleasant moments in one's life, they are evanescent, fleeting, and rare. In contrast, suffering and agony permeate all aspects of human existence. If we reflect on birth, sickness, old age, death, our coming in contact with unpleasant things, our separation from pleasant things, and our unsatisfied cravings, we will see clearly the pervasiveness of suffering (*dukkha*) in all these aspects of life. Suffering, then, is a universal principle that defines human existence on this earth.

The Second Noble Truth deals with the cause of suffering. Why do human beings suffer? What is the reason for this pain and agony, which color human existence from birth to death? According to the Buddha, people suffer because their lives are guided by "selfish craving" (*tanha*). People are conditioned by the society to believe that they possess an ego. We are taught that we can enhance ourselves only through private fulfillment or by increasing our possessions. When the focus is on self-inflation we get trapped by the expanding walls of the ego. This personal aggrandizement separates us from others. The more our egos expand, the more we crave everything for ourselves exclusive of others, and the more our misery increases.

According to the Buddha, this selfish craving is based upon one fundamental mistake. The person who wants everything for her/himself is duped into thinking that the world hides the secret of a stable, immutable being that could be possessed. Furthermore, the individual believes that an aspect of this being in the form of an unchanging self resides in each person. According to the Buddha, the world is in constant motion. Nothing remains the same for more than a moment. Since everything is transitory, there is no stable self in the world or in us. Thus, there is nothing to possess because nothing can be possessed. Once this realization takes place, one is awakened to the futility of one's selfish craving. As one stops these desires, one's isolation from others disappears and one's suffering is lessened.

The Third Noble Truth offers a way out of this ignorance and misery. Through compassion (*karuna*), one can puncture the walls of the ego. These walls come down when genuine compassion, kindness, care, and generosity are shown to others. Compassion for others consists in the forgetting of one's ego, the "going forth" toward the other, and the helping of others as oneself. As one inculcates compassion, one's selfish craving is dissolved and suffering disappears.

How can one learn to be compassionate? What kind of training is needed? The Buddha suggests two ways to develop compassion within oneself. First, one can learn compassion by following the Eightfold Path. Second, one can be educated into compassion by listening to the stories of people who performed deeds that involved care, concern, and generosity.

Buddha and his disciples used parables and stories to teach people the nature of compassion. Buddha believed that morality could be taught by discussion, practice, and listening to examples of those who embodied it. The Buddhist literature is teeming with such stories. Consider the following example.

A student listened to a lecture given by a senior monk about the possibility of experiencing the Buddha in his physical form by practicing egolessness and meditation. The student decided to accomplish this goal for himself. He practiced meditation devotedly and flawlessly for twelve years. He hoped that on the completion of this arduous journey he would have a vision of the Buddha. To the utter surprise and anguish of the student, no Buddha showed up at the conclusion of his meditation.

The student monk was furious, hurt, and resentful. He felt deceived and lied to. He had wasted twelve years of his life foolishly following this path. Angry and frustrated by this futile quest, he left his hermitage to walk toward a nearby village. As he walked, his mind was filled with all the negative emotions of dejection, deception, anger, agitation, and restlessness. His ego was badly injured.

It happened that his glance fell upon a dog standing under a tree. The student monk looked at the gentle face of the dog and observed two beautiful black eyes that showed intense sadness. He looked at the dog's body: The front half appeared to be in good shape, but the hind legs and tail were severely infested with maggots. In his sympathy for the suffering dog, the monk forgot his own mental anguish. Overwhelmed by compassion, he wanted to relieve the dog of the maggots. As he was about to move them, another thought crossed his mind: "By removing the maggots I will be relieving the dog of its misery, but I will also be depriving the maggots of their food."

Driven by concern for both the dog and the maggots, the student monk cut a piece of flesh from his own thigh. He tried to lure the maggots away from the dog's body to this fresh piece of meat, but they refused to move. He thought of moving the maggots with his finger but did not want to injure them. Concerned with both the misery of the dog and the well-being of the maggots, the monk totally forgot himself. It occurred to him that he might be able to use his tongue to gently move the maggots away from the dog's infected body. But when he bent to take the maggots onto his tongue, the dog miraculously transformed into the smiling Buddha.

The astonished monk asked the Buddha why he did not show up at the completion of his meditation. The Buddha, still smiling, replied that the monk was too wrapped up in ego aggrandizement during and after his meditation. It was only when he saw the suffering of the dog and felt compassion for the maggots that he discarded his ego completely. It is only then that he expressed genuine care and concern. Since his compassion toward those two creatures was selfless, he was able to see the Buddha in the dog. As a selfish act

separates us from others, an egoless act unifies us with all existence. Through the performance of a compassionate act, one gets rid of misery and suffering.

Through parables and stories, one can become sensitive to the way others express compassion, care, love, and generosity. As a Buddhist monk, one needs to follow the step-by-step procedure suggested by the Buddha. This method is called the Eightfold Path. It contains eight principles of right knowledge, right inspiration, right speech, right action, right livelihood, right effort, right mindfulness, and right concentration. The first two steps of right knowledge and right inspiration are concerned with adopting a proper mental attitude. The student needs the right views and the correct drive to conduct him/herself wisely and devotedly. This wisdom is required as a guide to the performance of the next three steps (right speech, right action, and right livelihood). These three constitute the ethical disciplines. They instruct the student to behave nonviolently and compassionately when s/he uses language, performs an action, or chooses a profession. Wisdom and moral conduct are the preparatory steps for the right effort, right mindfulness, and right concentration. These last three steps of the path help one develop mental control, which in turn is essential for contemplation and enlightenment. When an individual follows the Eightfold Path devotedly and continuously for a long period of time, s/he is assured of enlightenment.

This stage of enlightenment is called *Nirvāna*. It has been understood in both negative and positive ways. In the negative sense, Nirvāna depicts the highest stage of existence where all the fires of selfish cravings are extinguished, the belief in the existence of a stable self is annihilated, and all attachments to people and things are eliminated. In the positive sense, Nirvāna depicts a stage of existence where the enlightened person has gained serenity, peace, and contentment. All Buddhists aspire to this state, believing it to be the highest accomplishment for any mortal being.

Many Faiths, One Reality

John Hick

John Hick begins with the thought that the existence of so many different religions, all of which claim to be true, might undercut the idea that any of them is, in fact, uniquely true. This in turn leads him to consider what, exactly, constitutes the core or essence of religion and whether or not the disagreements among different religions are fundamental and mutually exclusive or whether there might be a common core of truth that all religions express in different ways. It is possible, he argues, that there is a common divine reality that each religious tradition has confronted and elaborated in its own way. He concludes with a brief discussion of how that common core shared by all religions might be understood in light of Kant's distinction between the world as it is, in itself, and as it is experienced and appears to human consciousness. John Hick is professor of world religions and cultures at Claremont Graduate School.

As you read through this essay, consider the following:

1. Why do differences among religions seem to contribute to doubt?
2. What is Smith's critique of the notion of "a religion"? Why might it be wrong to speak of a religion as being true or false?
3. What picture of religion and its relationship to different cultural forms does Hick suggest?
4. Hick distinguishes three aspects of the question of whether in future we will come to see different religious traditions like people now see different denominations of Christianity. What are the three? Does he think that all the differences among religions can be made compatible?
5. What role does Kant's idea of a thing in itself play in Hick's thinking about the nature of religion?
6. How might the authors in the last selections respond to Hick?

MANY FAITHS, ALL CLAIMING TO BE TRUE

Until comparatively recently each of the different religions of the world had developed in substantial ignorance of the others. There have been, it is true, great movements of expansion which have brought two faiths into contact: above all, the expansion of Buddhism during the last three centuries B.C. and the early centuries of the Christian era, carrying its message throughout India and Southeast Asia and into China, Tibet, and Japan, and

From John Hick, *Philosophy of Religion*, 3d ed. © 1965. Reprinted by permission of Prentice-Hall, Inc., Upper Saddle River, NJ.

then, the resurgence of the Hindu religion at the expense of Buddhism, with the result that today Buddhism is rarely to be found on the Indian subcontinent; next, the first Christian expansion into the Roman Empire; then the expansion of Islam in the seventh and eighth centuries C.E. into the Middle East, Europe, and later India; and finally, the second expansion of Christianity in the missionary movement of the nineteenth century. These interactions, however, were for the most part conflicts rather than dialogues; they did not engender any deep or sympathetic understanding of one faith by the adherents of another. It is only during the last hundred years or so that the scholarly study of world religions has made possible an accurate appreciation of the faiths of other people and so has brought home to an increasing number of us the problem of the conflicting truth claims made by different religious traditions. This issue now emerges as a major topic demanding a prominent place on the agenda of the philosopher of religion.

The problem can be posed very concretely in this way. If I had been born in India, I would probably be a Hindu; if in Egypt, probably a Muslim; if in Sri Lanka, probably a Buddhist; but I was born in England and am, predictably, a Christian. These different religions seem to say different and incompatible things about the nature of ultimate reality, about the modes of divine activity, and about the nature and destiny of the human race. Is the divine nature personal or nonpersonal? Does deity become incarnate in the world? Are human beings reborn again and again on earth? Is the empirical self the real self, destined for eternal life in fellowship with God, or is it only a temporary and illusory manifestation of an eternal higher self? Is the Bible, or the Qur'an, or the *Bhagavad Gita* the Word of God? If what Christianity says in answer to such questions is true, must not what Hinduism says be to a large extent false? If what Buddhism says is true, must not what Islam says be largely false?

The skeptical thrust of these questions goes very deep; for it is a short step from the thought that the different religions cannot all be true, although they each claim to be, to the thought that in all probability none of them is true. . . .

CRITIQUE OF THE CONCEPT OF "A RELIGION"

In his important book *The Meaning and End of Religion*,[1] Wilfred Cantwell Smith challenges the familiar concept of "a religion," upon which much of the traditional problem of conflicting religious truth claims rests. He emphasizes that what we call a religion—an empirical entity that can be traced historically and mapped geographically—is a human phenomenon. Christianity, Hinduism, Judaism, Buddhism, Islam, and so on are human creations whose history is part of the wider history of human culture. Cantwell Smith traces the development of the concept of a religion as a clear and bounded historical phenomenon and shows that the notion, far from being universal and self-evident, is a distinctively Western invention which has been exported to the rest of the world. "It is," he says, summarizing the outcome of his detailed historical argument, "a surprisingly modern aberration for anyone to think that Christianity is true or that Islam is—since the Enlightenment, basically, when Europe began to postulate religions as intellectualistic systems, patterns of doctrine, so that they could for the first time be labeled 'Christianity' and 'Buddhism,' and could be called true or false."[2] The names by which we know the various "religions" today were in fact (with the exception of "Islam") invented in the eighteenth century, and before they were imposed by the influence of the West upon the peoples of the world no one had thought of himself or herself as belonging to one of a set of competing systems of belief concerning which it is possible to ask, "Which of these systems is the true one?" This notion of religions as mutually exclusive entities with their own characteristics and histories—although it now tends to operate as a habitual category of our thinking—may well be an example of the illicit reification, the turning of good adjectives into bad substantives, to which the western mind is prone and against which contemporary philosophy has warned us. In this case a powerful but distorting conceptuality has helped to create phenomena answering to it, namely the religions of the world seeing themselves and each other as rival ideological communities.

Perhaps, however, instead of thinking of religion as existing in mutually exclusive systems, we should see the religious life of mankind as a dynamic continuum within which certain major disturbances have from time to time set up new fields of force, of greater or lesser power, displaying complex relationships of attraction and repulsion, absorption, resistance, and reinforcement. These major disturbances are the great creative religious moments of human history from which the distinguishable religious traditions have stemmed. Theologically, such moments are seen as intersections of divine grace, divine initiative, divine truth, with human faith, human response, human enlightenment. They have made their impact upon the stream of human life so as to affect the development of cultures; and what we call Christianity, Islam, Hinduism, Buddhism, are among the resulting historical-cultural phenomena. It is clear, for example, that Christianity has developed through a complex interaction between religious and non-religious factors. Christian ideas have been formed within the intellectual framework provided by Greek philosophy; the Christian church was molded as an institution by the Roman Empire and its system of laws; the Catholic mind reflects something of the Latin Mediterranean temperament, whereas the Protestant mind reflects something of the northern Germanic temperament, and so on. It is not hard to appreciate the connections between historical Christianity and the continuing life of humanity in the western hemisphere, and of course the same is true, in their own ways, of all the other religions of the world.

This means that it is not appropriate to speak of a religion as being true or false, any more than it is to speak of a civilization as being true or false. For the religions, in the sense of distinguishable religiocultural streams within human history, are expressions of the diversities of human types and temperaments and thought forms. The same differences between the eastern and western mentality that are revealed in characteristically different conceptual and linguistic, social, political, and artistic forms presumably also underlie the contrasts between eastern and western religion.

In *The Meaning and End of Religion* Cantwell Smith examines the development from the original religious event or idea—whether it be the insight of the Buddha, the life of Christ, or the career of Mohammed—to a religion in the sense of a vast living organism with its own credal backbone and its institutional skin. He shows in each case that this development stands in a questionable relationship to that original event or idea. Religions as institutions, with the theological doctrines and the codes of behavior that form their boundaries, did not come about because the religious reality required this, but because such a development was historically inevitable in the days of undeveloped communication between the different cultural groups. Now that the world has become a communicational unity, we are moving into a new situation in which it becomes both possible and appropriate for religious thinking to transcend these cultural-historical boundaries. But what form might such new thinking take, and how would it affect the problem of conflicting truth claims?

TOWARD A POSSIBLE SOLUTION

To see the historical inevitability of the plurality of religions in the past and its non-inevitability in the future, we must note the broad course that has been taken by the religious life of mankind. The human being has been described as a naturally religious animal, displaying an innate tendency to experience the environment as religiously as well as naturally significant and to feel required to live in it as such. This tendency is universally expressed in the cultures of primitive people, with their belief in sacred objects, endowed with *mana*, and in a multitude of spirits needing to be carefully propitiated. The divine reality is here crudely apprehended as a plurality of quasi-animal forces. The next stage seems to have come with the coalescence of tribes into larger groups. The tribal gods were then ranked in hierarchies (some being lost by amalgamation in the process) dominated, in the Middle East, by great national gods such as the Sumerian Ishtar, Amon of Thebes, Jahweh of Israel, Marduk of Babylon, the Greek Zeus, and in India by the

Vedic high gods such as Dyaus (the sky god), Varuna (god of heaven), and Agni (the fire god). The world of such national and nature gods, often martial and cruel and sometimes requiring human sacrifices, reflected the state of humanity's awareness of the divine at the dawn of documentary history, some three thousand years ago.

So far, the whole development can be described as the growth of natural religion. That is to say, primitive spirit worship expressing man's fears of the unknown forces of nature, and later the worship of regional deities—depicting either aspects of nature (sun, sky, etc.) or the collective personality of a nation—represent the extent of humanity's religious life prior to any special intrusions of divine revelation or illumination.

But sometime after 1000 B.C. a golden age of religious creativity, named by Jaspers the Axial Period,[3] dawned. This consisted of a series of revelatory experiences occurring in different parts of the world that deepened and purified people's conceptions of the divine, and that religious faith can only attribute to the pressure of the divine reality upon the human spirit. To quote A. C. Bouquet, "It is a commonplace with specialists in the history of religion that somewhere within the region of 800 B.C. there passed over the populations of this planet a stirring of the mind, which, while it left large tracts of humanity comparatively uninfluenced, produced in a number of different spots on the earth's surface prophetic individuals who created a series of new starting points for human living and thinking."[4] At the threshold of this period some of the great Hebrew prophets appeared (Elijah in the ninth century; Amos, Hosea, and the first Isaiah in the eighth century; and then Jeremiah in the seventh), declaring that they had heard the word of the Lord claiming their obedience and demanding a new level of righteousness and justice in the life of Israel. During the next five centuries, between about 800 and 300 B.C., the prophet Zoroaster appeared in Persia; Greece produced Pythagoras, and then Socrates and Plato, and Aristotle; in China there was Confucius, and

the author or authors of the Taoist scriptures; and in India this creative period saw the formation of the Upanishads and the lives of Gotama the Buddha, and Mahavira, founder of the Jain religion, and around the end of this period, the writing of the *Bhagavad Gita*. Even Christianity, beginning later, and then Islam, both have their roots in the Hebrew religion of the Axial Age, and can hardly be understood except in relation to it.

It is important to observe the situation within which all these revelatory moments occurred. Communication between the different groups of humanity was then so limited that for all practical purposes human beings inhabited a series of different worlds. For the most part people living in China, in India, in Arabia, in Persia, were unaware of the others' existence. There was thus, inevitably, a multiplicity of local religions that were also local civilizations. Accordingly the great creative moments of revelation and illumination occurred separately within the different cultures and influenced their development, giving them the coherence and confidence to expand into larger units, thus producing the vast religiocultural entities that we now call the world religions. So it is that until recently the different streams of religious experience and belief have flowed through different cultures, each forming and being formed by its own separate environment. There has, of course, been contact between different religions at certain points in history, and an influence—sometimes an important influence—of one upon another; nevertheless, the broad picture is one of religions developing separately within their different historical and cultural settings.

In addition to noting these historical circumstances, we need to make use of the important distinction between, on the one hand, human encounters with the divine reality in the various forms of religious experience, and on the other hand, theological theories or doctrines that men and women have developed to conceptualize the meaning of these encounters. These two components of religion, although distinguishable, are not separable. It is as hard to say which came first, as in the celebrated case of the hen and the egg; they continually react upon one another in a joint process of development, experience providing the ground of our beliefs, but these in turn influencing the forms taken by our experience. The different religions are different streams of religious experience, each having started at a different point within human history and each having formed its own conceptual self-consciousness within a different cultural milieu.

In the light of this it is possible to consider the hypothesis that the great religions are all, at their experiential roots, in contact with the same ultimate divine reality but that their differing experiences of that reality, interacting over the centuries with the differing thought forms, of differing cultures, have led to increasing differentiation and contrasting elaboration—so that Hinduism, for example, is a very different phenomenon from Christianity, and very different ways of experiencing and conceiving the divine occur within them. However, now that in the "one world" of today the religious traditions are consciously interacting with each other in mutual observation and dialogue, it is possible that their future developments may move on gradually converging courses. During the next centuries each group will presumably continue to change, and it may be that they will grow closer together, so that one day such names as "Christianity," "Buddhism," "Islam," and "Hinduism" will no longer adequately describe the then current configurations of man's religious experience and belief. I am not thinking here of the extinction of human religiousness in a universal secularization. That is of course a possible future, and indeed many think it the most likely future to come about. But if the human creature is an indelibly religious animal he or she will always, even amidst secularization, experience a sense of the transcendent by which to be both troubled and uplifted. The future I am envisaging is accordingly one in which the presently existing religions will constitute the past history of different emphases and variations, which will then appear more like, for example, the different denominations of Christianity in North America or Europe today than like radically exclusive totalities.

If the nature of religion, and the history of religion, is indeed such that a development of this kind begins to take place . . . what would this imply concerning the problem of the conflicting truth claims of the different religions in their present forms?

We may distinguish three aspects of this question: differences in modes of experiencing the divine reality; differences of philosophical and theological theory concerning that reality or concerning the implications of religious experience; and differences in the key or revelatory experiences that unify a stream of religious experience and thought.

The most prominent and important example of the first kind of difference is probably that between the experience of the divine as personal and as nonpersonal. In Judaism, Christianity, Islam, and the important strand of Hinduism which is focused by the *Bhagavad Gita*, the Ultimate is apprehended as personal goodness, will, and purpose under the different names of Jahweh, God, Allah, Krishna, Shira. Whereas in Hinduism as interpreted by the Advaita Vedānta school, and in Theravada Buddhism, ultimate reality is apprehended as nonpersonal. Mahayana Buddhism, on the other hand, is a more complex tradition, including, for example, both nontheistic Zen and quasi-theistic Pure Land Buddhism. There is, perhaps, in principle no difficulty in holding that these personal and nonpersonal experiences of the Ultimate can be understood as complementary rather than as incompatible. For if, as every profound form of religion has affirmed, the Ultimate reality is infinite and therefore exceeds the scope of our finite human categories, that reality may be both personal Lord and nonpersonal Ground of being. At any rate, there is a program for thought in the exploration of what Aurobindo called "the logic of the infinite"[5] and the question of the extent to which predicates that are incompatible when attributed to a finite reality may no longer be incompatible when referred to infinite reality.

The second type of difference is in philosophical and theological theory or doctrine. Such differences, and indeed conflicts, are not merely apparent, but they are part of the still developing history of human thought; it may be that in time they will be transcended, for they belong to the historical, culturally conditioned aspect of religion, which is subject to change. When one considers, for example, the immense changes that have come about within Christian thought during the last hundred years, in response to the development of modern biblical scholarship and the modern physical and biological sciences, one can set no limit to the further developments that may take place in the future. A book of contemporary Christian theology (post-Darwin, post-Einstein, post-Freud), using modern biblical source criticism and taking for granted a considerable demythologization of the New Testament world view, would have been quite unrecognizable as Christian theology two centuries ago. Comparable responses to modern science are yet to occur in many of the other religions of the world, but they must inevitably come, sooner or later. When all the main religious traditions have been through their own encounter with modern science, they will probably have undergone as considerable an internal development as has Christianity. Besides, there will be an increasing influence of each faith upon every other as they meet and interact more and more freely within the "one world" of today. In the light of all this, the future that I have speculatively projected does not seem impossible.

However, it is the third kind of difference that constitutes the largest difficulty in the way of religious agreement. Each religion has its holy founder or scripture, or both, in which the divine reality has been revealed—the Vedas, the Torah, the Buddha, Christ and the Bible, the Qur'an. Wherever the Holy is revealed, it claims an absolute response of faith and worship, which thus seems incompatible with a like response to any other claimed disclosure of the Holy. Within Christianity, for example, this absoluteness and exclusiveness of response has been strongly developed in the doctrine that Christ was uniquely divine, the only Son of God, of one substance with the Father, the only mediator between God and man. But this traditional doctrine, formed in an age of substantial ignorance of the wider religious life of mankind, gives rise today to an acute tension. On the one hand, Christianity traditionally teaches that God is the Creator and Lord of all mankind and seeks mankind's final good and salvation; and on the other hand that only by responding in faith to God in Christ can we be saved. This means that infinite love has ordained that human beings can be saved only in a way that in fact excludes the large majority of them; for the greater part of all the human beings who have been born have lived either before Christ or outside the borders of Christendom. In an attempt to meet this glaring paradox, Christian theology has developed a doctrine according to which those outside the circle of Christian faith may nevertheless be saved. For example, the Second Vatican Council of the Roman Catholic Church, 1963–1965, declared that "Those who through no fault of theirs are still ignorant of the Gospel of Christ and of his Church yet sincerely seek God and, with the help of divine grace, strive to do his will as known to them through the voice of their conscience, those men can attain to eternal salvation."[6] This represents a real movement in response to a real problem; nevertheless it is only an epicycle of theory, complicating the existing dogmatic system rather than going to the heart of the problem. The epicycle is designed to cover theists ("those who sincerely seek God") who have had no contact with the Christian gospel. But what of the nontheistic Buddhists and the nonethistic Hindus? And what of those Muslims, Jews, Buddhists, Hindus, Jains, Parsees, etc., both theists and nontheists, who have heard the Christian gospel but have preferred to adhere to the faith of their fathers?

Thus it seems that if the tension at the heart of the traditional Christian attitude to non-Christian faiths is to be resolved, Christian thinkers must give even more radical thought to the problem than they have as yet done. It is, however, not within the scope of this book to suggest a plan for the reconstruction of Christian or other religious doctrines.

A PHILOSOPHICAL FRAMEWORK FOR RELIGIOUS PLURALISM

Among the great religious traditions, and particularly within their more mystical strands, a distinction is widely recognized between the Real or Ultimate or Divine *an sich* (in him/her/its-self) and the Real as conceptualized and experienced by human beings. The widespread assumption is that the Ultimate Reality is infinite and as such exceeds the grasp of human thought and language, so that the describable and experienceable objects of worship and contemplation are not the Ultimate in its limitless reality but the Ultimate in its relationship to finite perceivers. One form of this distinction is that between *nirguna* Brahman, Brahman without attributes, beyond the scope of human thought, and *saguna* Brahman, Brahman with attributes, encountered within human experience as Ishvara, the personal creator and governor of the universe. In the west the Christian mystic Meister Eckhart drew a parallel distinction between the Godhead (*Deitas*) and God (*Deus*). The Taoist scripture, the *Tao Te Ching*, begins by affirming that "The Tao that can be expressed is not the eternal Tao." The Jewish Kabbalist mystics distinguished between En Soph, the absolute divine reality beyond all human description, and the God of the Bible; and among the Muslim Sufis, Al Haqq, the Real, seems to be a similar concept to En Soph, as the abyss of Godhead underlying the self-revealing Allah. More recently Paul Tillich has spoken of "the God above the God of theism."[7] A. N. Whitehead, and the process theologians who follow him, distinguish between the primordial and consequent natures of God; and Gordon Kaufman has recently distinguished between the "real God" and the "available God."[8] These all seem to be

somewhat similar (though not identical) distinctions. If we suppose that the Real is one but that our human perceptions of the Real are plural and various, we have a basis for hypothesis, suggested tentatively in the previous section, that the different streams of religious experience represent diverse awarenesses of the same limitless transcendent reality, which is perceived in characteristically different ways by different human mentalities, forming and formed by different cultural histories.

Immanuel Kant has provided (without intending to do so) a philosophical framework within which such a hypothesis can be developed. He distinguished between the world as it is *an sich*, which he called the noumenal world, and the world as it appears to human consciousness, which he called the phenomenal world. His writings can be interpreted in various ways, but according to one interpretation the phenomenal world *is* the noumenal world as humanly experienced. The innumerable diverse sensory clues are brought together in human consciousness, according to Kant, by means of a system of relational concepts or categories (such as "thing" and "cause") in terms of which we are aware of our environment. Thus our environment as we perceive it is a joint product of the world itself and the selecting, interpreting, and unifying activity of the perceiver. Kant was concerned mainly with the psychological contribution to our awareness of the world, but the basic principle can also be seen at work on the physiological level. Our sensory equipment is capable of responding to only a minute proportion of the full range of sound and electromagnetic waves—light, radio, infrared, ultraviolet, X, and gamma—which are impinging upon us all the time. Consequently, the world as we experience it represents a particular selection—a distinctively human selection—from the immense complexity and richness of the world as it is *an sich*. We experience at a certain macro/micro level. What we experience and use as the solid, enduring table would be, to a micro-observer, a swirling universe of discharging energy, consisting of electrons, neutrons, and quarks in continuous rapid activity. We perceive the world as it appears to beings with our particular physical and psychological equipment. Indeed, the way the world *appears* to us is the way the world *is for us* as we inhabit and interact with it. As Thomas Aquinas said long ago, "The thing known is in the knower according to the mode of the knower.[9]

Is it possible to adopt the broad Kantian distinction between the world as it is in itself and the world as it appears to us with our particular cognitive machinery, and apply it to the relation between the Ultimate Reality and our different human awarenesses of that Reality? If so, we shall think in terms of a single divine noumenon and perhaps many diverse divine phenomena. We may form the hypothesis that the Real *an sich* is experienced by human beings in terms of one of two basic religious concepts. One is the concept of God, or of the Real experienced as personal, which presides over the theistic forms of religion. The other is the concept of the Absolute, or of the Real experienced as non-personal, which presides over the various nontheistic forms of religion. Each of these basic concepts is, however, made more concrete (in Kantian terminology, schematized) as a range of particular images of God or particular concepts of the Absolute. These images of God are formed within the different religious histories. Thus the Jahweh of the Hebrew Scriptures exists in interaction with the Jewish people. He is a part of their history and they are a part of his; he cannot be abstracted from this particular concrete historical nexus. On the other hand, Krishna is a quite different divine figure, existing in relation to a different faith-community, with its own different and distinctive religious ethos. Given the basic hypothesis of the reality of the Divine, we may say that Jahweh and Krishna (and likewise, Shiva, and Allah, and the Father of Jesus Christ) are different *personae* in terms of which the divine Reality is experienced and thought within different streams of religious life. These different *per-sonae* are thus partly projections of the divine Reality into human consciousness, and partly projections of the human consciousness itself as it has been formed by particular historical cultures. From the human end they are our different images of God; from the divine end they are God's *personae* in relation to the different human histories of faith.

A similar account will have to be given of the forms of nonpersonal Absolute, or *impersonae*, experienced within the different strands of nontheistic religion—Brahman, Nirvana, Sunyata, the Dharma, the Dharmakaya, the Tao. Here, according to our hypothesis, the same limitless ultimate Reality is being experienced and thought through different forms of the concept of the Real as non-personal.

It is characteristic of the more mystical forms of awareness of the Real that they seem to be direct, and not mediated—or therefore distorted—by the perceptual machinery of the human mind. However, our hypothesis will have to hold that even the apparently direct and unmediated awareness of the Real in the Hindu *moksha*, in the Buddhist *satori*, and in the unitive mysticism of the West, is still the conscious experience of a human subject and as such is influenced by the interpretative set of the cognizing mind. All human beings have been influenced by the culture of which they are a part and have received, or have developed in their appropriation of it, certain deep interpretative tendencies which help to form their experience and are thus continually confirmed within it. We see evidence of such deep "sets" at work when we observe that mystics formed by Hindu, Buddhist, Christian, Muslim, and Jewish religious cultures report distinctively different forms of experience. Thus, far from it being the case that they all undergo an identical experience but report it in different religious languages, it seems more probable that they undergo characteristically different unitive experiences (even though with important common features), the differences being due to the conceptual frameworks and meditational disciplines supplied by the religious traditions in which they participate.

Thus it is a possible, and indeed an attractive, hypothesis—as an alternative to total skepticism—that the great religious traditions of the world represent different human perceptions of and response to the same infinite divine Reality.

Notes

1. Wilfred Cantwell Smith, *The Meaning and End of Religion*, 1962 (New York: Harper & Row, and London: Sheldon Press, 1978).

2. Wilfred Cantwell Smith, *Questions of Religious Truth* (London: Victor Gollancz Ltd., 1967), p. 73.

3. Karl Jaspers, *The Origin and Goal of History*, 1949 (New Haven: Yale University Press, 1953), Chap. 1.

4. A. C. Bouquet, *Comparative Religion* (Harmondsworth, Middlesex: Penguin Books Ltd., 1941), pp. 77–78.

5. Sri Aurobindo, *The Life Divine* (Pondicherry: Sri Aurobindo Ashram, 1949 and Mt. Tremper, N.Y.: Matagiri Sri Aurobindo Center, Inc., 1980), Book II, Chap. 2.

6. *Dogmatic Constitution on the Church*, Art. 16.

7. *The Courage to Be* (New Haven: Yale Univeristy Press, 1952), p. 190.

8. *God the Problem* (Cambridge, Mass.: Harvard University Press, 1972), p. 86.

9. *Summa Theologica*, II/II, Q. 1, art. 2.

Religion as a Cultural System

Clifford Geertz

This essay looks at religion and religious faith from the perspective of a cultural anthropologist. Clifford Geertz argues that religious faith and symbols provide the means whereby people interpret the world. Religion constitutes their worldview by shaping their mood, motivations, and conceptions of order in ways that make them seem factual and realistic. Clifford Geertz was professor of anthropology at the University of Chicago during the 1960s and then went on to the Institute for Advanced Study at Princeton and to Oxford before retiring. He maintained that anthropologists should be interpretive as they approach another culture, much as a literary critic might interpret a novel.

As you read through this essay, consider the following:

1. What does Geertz mean when he says religious symbols produce moods and motivations? How do they do that?
2. Why is evil important?
3. How does Geertz explain the movement from belief in disorder to the religious belief in order?
4. How does the religious perspective differ from the common sense and other perspectives?
5. What might Geertz say to somebody who claimed that his or her religious faith is not just an interpretation, but that it is, in fact, true?

Any attempt to speak without speaking any particular language is not more hopeless than the attempt to have a religion that shall be no religion in particular. . . . Thus every living and healthy religion has a marked idiosyncrasy. Its power consists in its special and surprising message and in the bias which that revelation gives to life. The vistas it opens and the mysteries it propounds are another world to live in; and another world to live in—whether we expect ever to pass wholly over into it or no—is what we mean by having a religion.

—Santayana, *Reason in Religion* (1906)

From *Anthropological Approaches to the Study of Religion*, ed. Michael Banton (London: Tavistock Publications). Reprinted by permission.

As we are to deal with meaning, let us begin with a paradigm: *viz.*, that sacred symbols function to synthesize a people's ethos—the tone, character and quality of their life, its moral and aesthetic style and mood—and their world-view—the picture they have of the way things in sheer actuality are, their most comprehensive ideas of order. In religious belief and practice a group's ethos is rendered intellectually reasonable by being shown to represent a way of life ideally adapted to the actual state of affairs the world-view describes, while the world-view is rendered emotionally convincing by being presented as an image of an actual state of affairs peculiarly well-arranged to accommodate such a way of life. This confrontation and mutual confirmation has two fundamental effects. On the one hand, it objectifies moral and aesthetic preferences by depicting them as the imposed conditions of life implicit in a world with a particular structure, as mere common sense given the unalterable shape of reality. On the other, it supports these received beliefs about the world's body by invoking deeply felt moral and aesthetic sentiments as experiential evidence for their truth. Religious symbols formulate a basic congruence between a particular style of life and a specific (if, most often, implicit) metaphysic, and in so doing sustain each with the borrowed authority of the other.

Phrasing aside, this much may perhaps be granted. The notion that religion tunes human actions to an envisaged cosmic order and projects images of cosmic order onto the plane of human experience is hardly novel. But it is hardly investigated either, so that we have very little idea of how, in empirical terms, this particular miracle is accomplished. We just know that it is done, annually, weekly, daily, for some people almost hourly; and we have an enormous ethnographic literature to demonstrate it. But the theoretical framework which would enable us to provide an analytic account of it, an account of the sort we can provide for lineage segmentation, political succession, labor exchange or the socialization of the child, does not exist.

Let us, therefore, reduce our paradigm to a definition, for although it is notorious that definitions establish nothing in themselves they do, if they are carefully enough constructed, provide a useful orientation, or reorientation, of thought, such that an extended unpacking of them can be an effective way of developing and controlling a novel line of inquiry. They have the useful virtue of explicitness: they commit themselves in a way discursive prose, which, in this field [anthropology] especially, is always liable to substitute rhetoric for argument, does not. Without ado, then, a *religion* is:

(1) a system of symbols which acts to (2) establish powerful, pervasive and long-lasting moods and motivations in men by (3) formulating conceptions of a general order of existence and (4) clothing these conceptions with such an aura of factuality that (5) the moods and motivations seem uniquely realistic.

1. . . . A SYSTEM OF SYMBOLS WHICH ACTS TO . . .

Symbols [e.g., the cross and the number "6" are] any object, act, event, quality or relation which serves as a vehicle for a conception—the conception is the symbol's 'meaning' . . . Symbols are tangible formulations of notions, abstractions from experience fixed in perceptible forms, concrete embodiments of ideas, attitudes, judgements, longings or beliefs . . . [Symbolism is the] content of cultural activity.

So far as culture patterns, i.e., systems or complexes of symbols, are concerned, the genetic trait which is of first importance for us here is that they are extrinsic sources of information. By "extrinsic," I mean only that—unlike genes, for example—they lie outside the boundaries of the individual organism as such in that intersubjective world of common understandings into which all human individuals are born, pursue their separate careers, and leave persisting behind them after they die. By "sources of information," I mean only that—like genes—they provide a blueprint or template in terms of which processes external to themselves can be given a definite form. . . . . To build a dam a beaver needs only an appropriate site and the proper materials—his mode of procedure is shaped by his physiology. But man, whose genes are silent on the building trades, needs also a conception of what it is to build a dam, a conception he can get only from some symbolic source—a blueprint, a textbook or a string of speech by someone who already knows how dams are built, or, of course, from manipulating graphic or linguistic elements in such a way as to attain for himself a conception of what dams are and how they are built.

This point is sometimes put in the form of an argument that cultural patterns are "models," that they are sets of symbols whose relations to one another "model" relations among entities, processes or what-have-you in physical, organic, social or psychological systems by "paralleling," "imitating" or "simulating" them. . . .

2. . . . TO ESTABLISH POWERFUL, PERVASIVE AND LONG-LASTING MOODS AND MOTIVATIONS IN MEN BY . . .

So far as religious activities are concerned . . . two somewhat different sorts of dispositions are induced by them: moods and motivations.

The major difference between moods and motivations is that where the latter are, so to speak, vectorial qualities, the former are merely scalar. Motives have a directional cast, they describe a certain overall course, gravitate toward certain, usually temporary, consummations. But moods vary only as to intensity: they go nowhere. They spring from certain circumstances but they are responsive to no ends. Like fogs, they just settle and lift; like scents, suffuse and evaporate. When present they are totalistic: if one is sad everything and everybody seems dreary; if one is gay, everything and everybody seems splendid. Thus, though a man can be vain, brave, willful and independent at the same time, he can't

very well be playful and listless, or exultant and melancholy at the same time. Further, where motives persist for more or less extended periods of time, moods merely recur with greater or lesser frequency, coming and going for what are often quite unfathomable reasons. But perhaps the most important difference, so far as we are concerned, between moods and motivations is that motivations are "made meaningful" with reference to the ends toward which they are conceived to conduce, while moods are "made meaningful" with reference to the conditions from which they are conceived to spring. We interpret motives in terms of their consummations, but we interpret moods in terms of their sources. We say that a person is industrious because he wishes to succeed, we say that a person is worried because he is conscious of the hanging threat of nuclear holocaust. And this is no less the case when the interpretations invoked are ultimate. Charity becomes Christian charity when it is enclosed in a conception of God's purposes; optimism is Christian optimism when it is grounded in a particular conception of God's nature. The assiduity of the Navaho finds its rationale in a belief that, as "reality" operates mechanically, it is coercible; their chronic fearfulness finds its rationale in a conviction that, however "reality" operates, it is both enormously powerful and terribly dangerous.

3. . . . BY FORMULATING CONCEPTIONS OF A GENERAL ORDER OF EXISTENCE AND . . .

That the symbols or symbol systems which induce and define dispositions we set off as religious and those which place those dispositions in a cosmic framework are the same symbols ought to occasion no surprise. For what else do we mean by saying that a particular mood of awe is religious and not secular except that it springs from entertaining a conception of all-pervading vitality like mana and not from a visit to the Grand Canyon? Or that a particular case of asceticism is an example of a religious motivation except that it is directed toward the achievement of an unconditioned end like nirvana and not a conditioned one like weight-reduction? If sacred symbols did not at one and the same time, induce dispositions in human beings and formulate, however obliquely, inarticulately or unsystematically, general ideas of order, then the empirical differentia of religious activity or religious experience would not exist. A man can indeed be said to be "religious" about golf, but not merely if he pursues it with passion and plays it on Sundays: he must also see it as symbolic of some transcendent truths. And the pubescent boy gazing soulfully into the eyes of the pubescent girl in a William Steig cartoon and murmuring, "There is something about you, Ethel, which gives me a sort of religious feeling," is, like most adolescents, confused. What any particular religion affirms about the fundamental nature of reality may be obscure, shallow or, all too often, perverse, but it must, if it is not to consist of the mere collection of received practices and conventional sentiments we usually refer to as moralism, affirm something. . . .

. . . The extreme generality, diffuseness and variability of man's innate (i.e., genetically programmed) response capacities means that without the assistance of cultural patterns he would be functionally incomplete, not merely a talented ape who had, like some under-privileged child, unfortunately been prevented from realizing his full potentialities, but a kind of formless monster with neither sense of direction nor power of self-control, a chaos of spasmodic impulses and vague emotions. Man depends upon symbols and symbol systems with a dependence so great as to be decisive for his creatural viability and, as a result, his sensitivity to even the remotest indication that they may prove unable to cope with one or another aspect of experience raises within him the gravest sort of anxiety.

There are at least three points where chaos—a tumult of events which lack not just interpretations but *interpretability*—threatens to break in upon man: at the limits of his analytic capacities, at the limits of his powers of endurance, and at the limits of his moral insight. Bafflement, suffering and a sense of intractable ethical paradox are all, if they become intense enough or are sustained long enough, radical challenges to the proposition that life is comprehensible and that we can, by taking thought, orient ourselves effectively within it—challenges with which any religion, however "primitive," which hopes to persist must attempt somehow to cope.

. . . But it does appear to be a fact that at least some men—in all probability, most men—are unable to leave unclarified problems of analysis merely unclarified, just to look at the stranger features of the world's landscape in dumb astonishment or bland apathy without trying to develop, however fantastic, inconsistent or simpleminded, some notions as to how such features might be reconciled with the more ordinary deliverances of experience. Any chronic failure of one's explanatory apparatus, the complex of received culture patterns (common sense, science, philosophical speculation, myth) one has for mapping the empirical world, to explain things which cry out for explanation, tends to lead to a deep disquiet—a tendency rather more widespread and a disquiet rather deeper than we have sometimes supposed since the pseudo-science view of religious belief was, quite rightfully, deposed. After all, even that high priest of heroic atheism, Lord Russell, once remarked that although the problem of the existence of God had never bothered him, the ambiguity of certain mathematical axioms had threatened to unhinge his mind. And Einstein's profound dissatisfaction with quantum mechanics was based on a—surely religious—inability to believe that, as he put it, God plays dice with the universe. . . .

The second experiential challenge in whose face the meaningfulness of a particular pattern of life threatens to dissolve into a chaos of thingless names and nameless things—the problem of suffering—has been rather more investigated, or at least described, mainly because of the great amount of attention given in works on tribal religion to what are perhaps its two main loci: illness and mourning. . . . The inadequacy of this "theology of optimism," as Nadel rather drily called it, is, of course, radical. Over its career religion has probably disturbed men as much as it has cheered them; forced them into a head-on, unblinking confrontation of the fact that they are born to trouble as often as it has enabled them to avoid such a confrontation by projecting them into a sort of infantile fairy-tale world where—Malinowski again—"hope cannot fail nor desire deceive." With the possible exception of Christian Science, there are few if any religious traditions, "great" or "little," in which the proposition that life hurts is not strenuously affirmed and in some it is virtually glorified.

As a religious problem, the problem of suffering is, paradoxically, not how to avoid suffering but how to suffer, how to make of physical pain, personal loss, worldly defeat or the helpless contemplation of others' agony something bearable, supportable—something, as we say, sufferable.

The problem of suffering passes easily into the problem of evil, for if suffering is severe enough it usually, though not always, seems morally undeserved as well, at least to the sufferer. . . .

The problem of evil, or perhaps one should say the problem *about* evil, is in essence the same sort of problem of or about bafflement and the problem of or about suffering. The strange opacity of certain empirical events, the dumb senselessness of intense or inexorable pain, and the enigmatic unaccountability of gross iniquity all raise the uncomfortable suspicion that perhaps the world, and hence man's life in the world, has no genuine order at all—no empirical regularity, no emotional form, no moral coherence. And the religious response to this suspicion is in each case the same: the formulation, by means of symbols, of an image of such a genuine order of the world which will account for, and even celebrate, the perceived ambiguities, puzzles and paradoxes in human experience. The effort is not to deny the undeniable—that there are unexplained events, that life hurts or

that rain falls upon the just—but to deny that there are inexplicable events, that life is unendurable and that justice is a mirage. The principles which constitute the moral order may indeed often elude men in the same way as fully satisfactory explanations of anomalous events or effective forms for the expression of feeling often elude them. What is important, to a religious man at least, is that this elusiveness be accounted for, that it be not the result of the fact that there are no such principles, explanations or forms, that life is absurd and the attempt to make moral, intellectual or emotional sense out of experience is bootless.

The Problem of Meaning . . . is a matter of affirming, or at least recognizing, the inescapability of ignorance, pain and injustice on the human plane while simultaneously denying that these irrationalities are characteristic of the world as a whole. And it is in terms of religious symbolism, a symbolism relating man's sphere of existence to a wider sphere within which it is conceived to rest, that both the affirmation and the denial are made.

4. . . . CLOTHING THESE CONCEPTIONS WITH SUCH AN AURA OF FACTUALITY THAT . . .

There arises here, however, a profounder question: how is it that this denial comes to be believed? how is it that the religious man moves from a troubled perception of experienced disorder to a more or less settled conviction of fundamental order? just what does "belief" mean in a religious context? Of all the problems surrounding attempts to conduct anthropological analysis of religion this is the one that has perhaps been most troublesome and therefore the most often avoided, usually by relegating it to psychology, that raffish outcast discipline to which social anthropologists are forever consigning phenomena they are unable to deal with. . . . But the problem will not go away, it is not "merely" psychological (nothing social is), and no anthropological theory of religion which fails to attack it is worthy of the name. We have been trying to stage Hamlet without the Prince quite long enough.

It seems to me that it is best to begin any approach to this issue with frank recognition that religious belief involves not a Baconian induction from everyday experience—for then we should all be agnostics—but rather a prior acceptance of authority which transforms that experience. The existence of bafflement, pain and moral paradox—of The Problem of Meaning—is one of the things that drive men toward belief in gods, devils, spirits, totemic principles or the spiritual efficacy of cannibalism (an enfolding sense of beauty or a dazzling perception of power are others), but it is not the basis upon which those beliefs rest, but rather their most important field of application.

In tribal religions authority lies in the persuasive power of traditional imagery; in mystical ones in the apodictic force of supersensible experience; in charismatic ones in the hypnotic attraction of an extraordinary personality. But the priority of the acceptance of an authoritative criterion in religious matters over the revelation which is conceived to flow from that acceptance is not less complete than in scriptural or hieratic ones. The basic axiom underlying what we may perhaps call "the religious perspective" is everywhere the same: he who would know must first believe.

But to speak of "the religious perspective" is, by implication, to speak of one perspective among others. A perspective is a mode of seeing, in that extended sense of "see" in which it means "discern," "apprehend," "understand" or "grasp." It is a particular way of looking at life, a particular manner of construing the world, as when we speak of an historical perspective, a scientific perspective, an aesthetic perspective, a common-sense perspective, or even the bizarre perspective embodied in dreams and in hallucinations. The question then comes down to, first, what is "the religious perspective" generically considered, as differentiated from other perspectives; and second, how do men come to adopt it.

If we place the religious perspective against the background of three of the other major

perspectives in terms of which men construe the world—the common-sensical, the scientific and the aesthetic—its special character emerges more sharply. What distinguishes common-sense as a mode of "seeing" is . . . a simple acceptance of the world, its objects and its processes as being just what they seem to be—what is sometimes called naive realism—and the pragmatic motive, the wish to act upon that world so as to bend it to one's practical purposes, to master it, or so far as that proves impossible, to adjust to it. The world of everyday life, itself, of course, a cultural product, for it is framed in terms of the symbolic conceptions of "stubborn fact" handed down from generation to generation, is the established scene and given object of our actions. Like Mt. Everest it is just there and the thing to do with it, if one feels the need to do anything with it at all, is to climb it. In the scientific perspective it is precisely this givenness which disappears. . . . Deliberate doubt and systematic inquiry, the suspension of the pragmatic motive in favor of disinterested observation, the attempt to analyze the world in terms of formal concepts whose relationship to the informal conceptions of common-sense become increasingly problematic—there are the hallmarks of the attempt to grasp the world scientifically. And as for the aesthetic perspective, which under the rubric of "the aesthetic attitude" has been perhaps most exquisitely examined, it involves a different sort of suspension of naive realism and practical interest, in that instead of questioning the credentials of everyday experience that exeperience is merely ignored in favor of an eager dwelling upon appearances, an engrossment in surfaces, an absorption in things, as we say, "in themselves": "The function of artistic illusion is not 'make-believe' . . . but the very opposite, disengagement from belief—the contemplation of sensory qualities without their usual meanings of 'here's that chair,' 'That's my telephone' . . . etc. The knowledge that what is before us has no practical significance in the world is what enables us to give attention to its appearance as such. . . ." And like the common-sensical and the scientific (or the historical, the philosophical and the autistic), this perspective, this "way of seeing" is . . . induced, mediated, and in fact created by means of symbols. It is the artist's skill which can produce those curious quasi-objects—poems, dramas, sculptures, symphonies—which, dissociating themselves from the solid world of common-sense, take on the special sort of eloquence only sheer appearances can achieve.

The religious perspective differs from the common-sensical in that, as already pointed out, it moves beyond the realities of everyday life to wider ones which correct and complete them, and its defining concern is not action upon those wider realities but acceptance of them, faith in them. It differs from the scientific perspective in that it questions the realities of everyday life not out of an institutionalized scepticism which dissolves the world's givenness into a swirl of probabilistic, hypotheses, but in terms of what it takes to be wider, non-hypothetical truths. Rather than detachment, its watchword is commitment; rather than analysis, encounter. And it differs from art in that instead of effecting a disengagement from the whole question of factuality, deliberately manufacturing an air of semblance and illusion, it deepens the concern with fact and seeks to create an aura of utter actuality. It is this sense of the "really real" upon which the religious perspective rests and which the symbolic activities of religion as a cultural system are devoted to producing, intensifying, and, so far as possible, rendering inviolable by the discordant revelations of secular experience. It is, again, the imbuing of a certain specific complex of symbols—of the metaphysic they formulate and the style of life they recommend—with a persuasive authority which, from an analytic point of view, is the essence of religious action. . . .

5. . . . THAT THE MOODS AND MOTIVATIONS SEEM UNIQUELY REALISTIC

But no one, not even a saint, lives in the world religious symbols formulate all of the time, and the majority of men live in it only at moments. The everyday world of common-sense objects and practical acts is . . . the paramount reality in human experience—paramount in the sense that it is the world in which we are most solidly rooted, whose inherent actuality we can hardly question (however much we may question certain portions of it), and from whose pressures and requirements we can least escape. A man, even large groups of men, may be aesthetically insensitive, religiously unconcerned and unequipped to pursue formal scientific analysis, but he cannot be completely lacking in common-sense and survive. The dispositions which religious rituals induce thus have their most important impact—from a human point of view—outside the boundaries of the ritual itself as they reflect back to color the individual's conception of the established world of bare fact. The peculiar tone that marks the Plains vision quest, the Manus confession or the Javanese mystical exercise pervades areas of the life of these peoples far beyond the immediately religious, impressing upon them a distinctive style in the sense both of a dominant mood and a characteristic movement. Religion is sociologically interesting not because, as vulgar positivism would have it, it describes the social order (which, insofar as it does, it does not only very obliquely but very incompletely), but because, like environment, political power, wealth, jural obligation, personal affection, and a sense of beauty, it shapes it.

The movement back and forth between the religious perspective and the common-sense perspective is actually one of the more obvious empirical occurrences on the social scene, though, again, one of the most neglected by social anthropologists, virtually all of whom have seen it happen countless times. Religious belief has usually been presented as an homogeneous characteristic of an individual, like his place of residence, his occupational role, his kinship position, and so on. But religious belief in the midst of ritual, where it engulfs the total person, transporting him, so far as he is concerned, into another mode of existence, and religious belief as the pale, remembered reflection of that experience in the midst of everyday life are not precisely the same thing, and the failure to realize this has led to some confusion. . . .

For an anthropologist, the importance of religion lies in its capacity to serve, for an individual or for a group, as a source of general, yet distinctive conceptions of the world, the self and the relations between them on the one hand—its model *of* aspect—and of rooted, no less distinctive "mental" dispositions—its model *for* aspect—on the other. From these cultural functions flow, in turn, its social and psychological ones.

Religious concepts spread beyond their specifically metaphysical contexts to provide a framework of general ideas in terms of which a wide range of experience—intellectual, emotional, moral—can be given meaningful form. The Christian sees the Nazi movement against the background of The Fall which, though it does not, in a casual sense, explain it, places it in a moral, a cognitive, even an affective sense. A Zande sees the collapse of a granary upon a friend or relative against the background of a concrete and rather special notion of witchcraft and thus avoids the philosophical dilemmas as well as the psychological stress of indeterminism. . . . A synopsis of cosmic order, a set of religious beliefs is also a gloss upon the mundane world of social relationships and psychological events. It renders them graspable.

But more than gloss, such beliefs are also a template. They do not merely interpret social and psychological processes in cosmic terms—in which case they would be philosophical, not religious—but they shape them. In the doctrine of original sin is embedded also a recommended attitude toward life, a recurring mood and a persisting set of motivations. The Zande learns from witchcraft conceptions not just to understand apparent "accidents" as not accidents at all, but to react to these spurious accidents with hatred for the agent who caused them and to proceed against him with appropriate resolution. . . . The moods and motivations a religious orientation produces cast a derivative, lunar light over the solid features of a peoples' secular life.

The tracing of the social and psychological role of religion is thus not so much a matter of finding correlations between specific ritual acts and specific secular social ties—though these correlations do, of course, exist and are very worth continued investigation, especially if we can contrive something novel to say about them. More, it is a matter of understanding how it is that men's notions, however implicit, of the "really real" and the dispositions these notions induce in them, color their sense of the reasonable, the practical, the humane and the moral.

Section 21

Religion and the Meaning of Life

Religion as the Source of Meaning

Leo Tolstoy

In this famous passage from his autobiography, *My Confession*, Leo Tolstoy first describes a period in his life when everything came crashing down and he wanted to kill himself. He describes how he seeks various remedies to his mental state, all of which fail, and how he found a solution only after he turned to religion. Leo Tolstoy (1828–1910) was a towering figure in Russian literature. Author of two classic novels, *Anna Karenina* and *War and Peace*, he was also an influential social critic and reformer.

As you read through this essay, consider the following:

1. How does Tolstoy describe the experience that led to his wanting to kill himself?
2. What solutions did he initially consider? Why did they not help?
3. What are ignorance, as Tolstoy depicts it here, and Epicureanism, and why were they not successful?
4. Which did he think was the worthiest of the four ways "out" he initially considered? Why do you think he thought it worthy?
5. What way did he find? How does he describe the way it worked?
6. How does Tolstoy describe God? Compare Tolstoy's view with the religious views of one or two of the authors in the previous section.

My life came to a standstill. I could breathe, eat, drink, and sleep, and could not help breathing, eating, drinking, and sleeping; but there was no life, because there were no desires the gratification of which I might find reasonable. If I wished for anything, I knew in advance that, whether I gratified my desire or not, nothing would come of it. If a fairy had come and had offered to carry out my wish, I should not have known what to say. If in moments of intoxication I had, not wishes, but habits of former desires, I knew in sober moments that that was a deception, that there was nothing to wish for. I could not even wish to find out the truth, because I guessed what it consisted in. The truth was that life was meaningless. It was as though I had just been living and walking along, and had come to an abyss, where I saw clearly that there was nothing ahead but perdition. And it was impossible to stop and go back, and impossible to shut my eyes, in order that I might not see that there was nothing ahead but suffering and imminent death,—complete annihilation.

What happened to me was that I, a healthy, happy man, felt that I could not go on living,—an insurmountable force drew me on to find release from life. I cannot say that I *wanted* to kill myself.

The force which drew me away from life was stronger, fuller, more general than wishing. It was a force like the former striving after life, only in an inverse sense. I tended with all my strength away from life. The thought of suicide came as naturally to me as had come before the ideas of improving life. That thought was so seductive that I had to use cunning against myself, lest I should rashly execute it. I did not want to be in a hurry, because I wanted to use every effort to disentangle myself: if I should not succeed in disentangling myself, there would always be time for that. And at such times I, a happy man, hid a rope from myself so that I should not hang myself on a cross-beam between

two safes in my room, where I was by myself in the evening, while taking off my clothes, and did not go out hunting with a gun, in order not to be tempted by an easy way of doing away with myself. I did not know myself what it was I wanted: I was afraid of life, strove to get away from it, and, at the same time, expected something from it.

All that happened with me when I was on every side surrounded by what is considered to be complete happiness. I had a good, loving, and beloved wife, good children, and a large estate, which grew and increased without any labour on my part. I was respected by my neighbours and friends, more than ever before, was praised by strangers, and, without any self-deception, could consider my name famous. With all that, I was not deranged or mentally unsound,—on the contrary, I was in full command of my mental and physical powers, such as I had rarely met with in people of my age: physically I could work in a field, mowing, without falling behind a peasant; mentally I could work from eight to ten hours in succession, without experiencing any consequences from the strain. And while in such condition I arrived at the conclusion that I could not live, and, fearing death, I had to use cunning against myself, in order that I might not take my life.

This mental condition expressed itself to me in this form: my life is a stupid, mean trick played on me by somebody. Although I did not recognize that "somebody" as having created me, the form of the conception that some one had played a mean, stupid trick on me by bringing me into the world was the most natural one that presented itself to me.

Involuntarily I imagined that there, somewhere, there was somebody who was now having fun as he looked down upon me and saw me, who had lived for thirty or forty years, learning, developing, growing in body and mind, now that I had become strengthened in mind and had reached that summit of life from which it lay all before me, standing as a complete fool on that summit and seeing clearly that there was nothing in life and never would be. And that was fun to him—

Reprinted from *The Complete Works of Count Tolstoy*, Vol. 13, translated by Leo Wiener, (1904).

But whether there was or was not that somebody who made fun of me, did not make it easier for me. I could not ascribe any sensible meaning to a single act, or to my whole life. I was only surprised that I had not understood that from the start. All that had long ago been known to everybody. Sooner or later there would come diseases and death (they had come already) to my dear ones and to me, and there would be nothing left but stench and worms. All my affairs, no matter what they might be, would sooner or later be forgotten, and I myself should not exist. So why should I worry about all these things? How could a man fail to see that and live,— that was surprising! A person could live only so long as he was drunk; but the moment he sobered up, he could not help seeing that all that was only a deception, and a stupid deception at that! Really, there was nothing funny and ingenious about it, but only something cruel and stupid.

Long ago has been told the Eastern story about the traveller who in the steppe is overtaken by an infuriated beast. Trying to save himself from the animal, the traveller jumps into a waterless well, but at its bottom he sees a dragon who opens his jaws in order to swallow him. And the unfortunate man does not dare climb out, lest he perish from the infuriated beast, and does not dare jump down to the bottom of the well, lest he be devoured by the dragon, and so clutches the twig of a wild bush growing in a cleft of the well and holds on to it. His hands grow weak and he feels that soon he shall have to surrender to the peril which awaits him at either side; but he still holds on and sees two mice, one white, the other black, in even measure making a circle around the main trunk of the bush to which he is clinging, and nibbling at it on all sides. Now, at any moment, the bush will break and tear off, and he will fall into the dragon's jaws. The traveller sees that and knows that he will inevitably perish; but while he is still clinging, he sees some drops of honey hanging on the leaves of the bush, and so reaches out for them with his tongue and licks the leaves. Just so I hold on to the branch of life, knowing that the dragon of death is waiting inevitably for me, ready to tear me to pieces, and I cannot understand why I have fallen on such suffering. And I try to lick that honey which used to give me pleasure; but now it no longer gives me joy, and the white and the black mouse day and night nibble at the branch to which I am holding on. I clearly see the dragon, and the honey is no longer sweet to me. I see only the inevitable dragon and the mice, and am unable to turn my glance away from them. That is not a fable, but a veritable, indisputable, comprehensible truth.

The former deception of the pleasures of life, which stifled the terror of the dragon, no longer deceives me. No matter how much one should say to me, "You cannot understand the meaning of life, do not think, live!" I am unable to do so, because I have been doing it too long before. Now I cannot help seeing day and night, which run and lead me up to death. I see that alone, because that alone is the truth. Everything else is a lie.

The two drops of honey that have longest turned my eyes away from the cruel truth, the love of family and of authorship, which I have called an art, are no longer sweet to me.

"My family—" I said to myself, "but my family, my wife and children, they are also human beings. They are in precisely the same condition that I am in: they must either live in the lie or see the terrible truth. Why should they live? Why should I love them, why guard, raise, and watch them? Is it for the same despair which is in me, or for fullness of perception? Since I love them, I cannot conceal truth from them,—every step in cognition leads them up to this truth. And the truth is death."

"Art, poetry?" For a long time, under the influence of the success of human praise, I tried to persuade myself that that was a thing which could be done, even though death should come and destroy everything, my deeds, as well as my memory of them; but soon I came to see that that, too, was a deception. It was clear to me that art was an adornment of life, a decoy of life. But life lost all its attractiveness for me. How, then, could I entrap others? So long as I did not live my own life, and a strange life bore me on its waves; so long as I believed that life had some sense, although I was not able to express it,—the reflections of life of every description in poetry and in the arts afforded me pleasure, and I was delighted to look at life through this little mirror of art; but when I began to look for the meaning of life, when I experienced the necessity of living myself, that little mirror became either useless, superfluous, and ridiculous, or painful to me. I could no longer console myself with what I saw in the mirror, namely, that my situation was stupid and desperate. It was all right for me to rejoice so long as I believed in the depth of my soul that life had some sense. At that time the play of lights—of the comical, the tragical, the touching, the beautiful, the terrible in life— afforded me amusement. But when I knew that life was meaningless and terrible, the play in the little mirror could no longer amuse me. No sweetness of honey could be sweet to me, when I saw the dragon and the mice that were nibbling down my support.

That was not all. If I had simply comprehended that life had no meaning, I might have known that calmly,—I might have known that that was my fate. But I could not be soothed by that. If I had been like a man living in a forest from which he knew there was no way out, I might have lived; but I was like a man who had lost his way in the forest, who was overcome by terror because he had lost his way, who kept tossing about in his desire to come out on the road, knowing that every step got him only more entangled, and who could not help tossing.

That was terrible. And, in order to free myself from that terror, I wanted to kill myself. I experienced terror before what was awaiting me,—I knew that that terror was more terrible than the situation itself, but I could not patiently wait for the end. No matter how convincing the reflection was that it was the same whether a vessel in the heart should break or something should burst, and

all should be ended, I could not wait patiently for the end. The terror of the darkness was too great, and I wanted as quickly as possible to free myself from it by means of a noose or a bullet. It was this feeling that more than anything else drew me on toward suicide. . . .

Having found no elucidation in science, I began to look for it in life, hoping to find it in the men who surrounded me. I began to observe the people such as I, to see how they lived about me and what attitude they assumed to the question that had brought me to the point of despair.

This is what I found in people who were in the same position as myself through their education and manner of life.

I found that for people of my circle there were four ways out from the terrible condition in which we all are.

The first way out is through ignorance. It consists in not knowing, not understanding that life is evil and meaningless. People of this category—mostly women or very young or very dull persons—have not yet come to understand that question of life which presented itself to Schopenhauer, Solomon, and Buddha. They see neither the dragon that awaits them, nor the mice that are nibbling at the roots of the bushes to which they are holding on, and continue to lick the honey. But they lick the honey only till a certain time: something will direct their attention to the dragon and the mice, and there will be an end to their licking. From them I can learn nothing,—it is impossible to stop knowing what you know.

The second way out is through Epicureanism. It consists in this, that, knowing the hopelessness of life, one should in the meantime enjoy such good as there is, without looking either at the dragon or the mice, but licking the honey in the best manner possible, especially if there is a lot of it in one spot. Solomon expresses this way out like this:

"Go thy way, eat thy bread with joy, and drink thy wine. Live joyfully with the wife whom thou lovest all the days of the life of thy vanity, which he hath given thee under the sun, all the days of thy vanity: for that is thy portion in this life, and in thy labour which thou takest under the sun. Whatsoever thy hand findeth to do, do it with thy might; for there is no work, nor device, nor knowledge, nor wisdom, in the grave, whither thou goest."

Thus the majority of the people of our circle support the possibility of life in themselves. The conditions in which they are give them more good than evil, and their moral dullness makes it possible for them to forget that the advantage of their situation is a casual one; that not everybody can have a thousand wives and palaces, like Solomon; that to every man with a thousand wives there are a thousand men without wives, and for every palace there are a thousand people who built it in the sweat of their brows; and that the accident which had made me a Solomon today, will tomorrow make me a slave of Solomon. The dullness of the imagination of these people makes it possible for them to forget that which gave no rest to Buddha,—the inevitableness of sickness, old age, and death, which sooner or later will destroy all those pleasures.

Thus think and feel the majority of men of our time and our manner of life. The fact that some of these people assert that the dullness of their comprehension and imagination is philosophy, which they call positive, in my opinion does not take them out of the category of those who, in order not to see the question, lick the honey. Such people I could not imitate: as I did not possess their dullness of comprehension, I could not artificially reproduce it in myself. Just like any live man, I could not tear my eyes away from the mice and the dragon, having once seen them.

The third way out is through force and energy. It consists in this, that, having comprehended that life is evil and meaningless, one should set out to destroy it. Thus now and then act strong, consistent people. Having comprehended all the stupidity of the joke which has been played upon them, and seeing that the good of the dead is better than that of the living, and that it is better not to

be at all, they go and carry this out and at once put an end to that stupid joke, so long as there are means for it: a noose about the neck, the water, a knife to pierce the heart with, railway trains. The number of people of our circle who do so is growing larger and larger. These people commit the act generally at the best period of life, when the mental powers are in full bloom and few habits have been acquired that lower human reason.

I saw that that was the worthiest way out, and I wanted to act in that way.

The fourth way out is through weakness. It consists in this, that, comprehending the evil and the meaninglessness of life, one continues to drag it out, knowing in advance that nothing can come of it. People of this calibre know that death is better than life, but, not having the strength to act reasonably, to make an end to the deception, and to kill themselves, they seem to be waiting for something. This is the way of weakness, for if I know that which is better, which is in my power, why not abandon myself to that which is better? I belonged to that category.

Thus people of my calibre have four ways of saving themselves from the terrible contradiction. No matter how much I strained my mental attention, I saw no other way out but those four. The one way out was not to understand that life was meaningless, vanity, and an evil, and that it was better not to live. I could not help knowing it and, having once learned it, I could not shut my eyes to it. The second way out was to make use of life such as it is, without thinking of the future. I could not do that either. Like Sakya-Muni, I could not go out hunting, when I knew that there was old age, suffering, death. My imagination was too vivid. Besides, I could not enjoy the accident of the moment, which for a twinkling threw enjoyment in my path. The third way out was, having come to see that life was an evil and a foolishness, to make an end of it and kill myself. I comprehended that, but for some reason did not kill myself. The fourth way out was to live in the condition of Solomon, of Schopenhauer,—to know that life was a stupid joke played on me, and yet to live, wash and dress myself, dine, speak, and even write books. That was repulsive and painful for me, but still I persisted in that situation. . . .

I remember, it was early in the spring, I was by myself in the forest, listening to the sounds of the woods. I listened and thought all the time of one and the same thing that had formed the subject of my thoughts for the last three years. I was again searching after God.

"All right, there is no God," I said to myself, "there is not such a being as would be, not my concept, but reality, just like my whole life,—there is no such being. And nothing, no miracles, can prove him to me, because the miracles would be my concept, and an irrational one at that.

"But my idea about God, about the one I am searching after?" I asked myself. "Where did that idea come from?" And with this thought the joyous waves of life again rose in me. Everything about me revived, received a meaning; but my joy did not last long,—the mind continued its work.

"The concept of God is not God," I said to myself. "A concept is what takes place within me; the concept of God is what I can evoke or can not evoke in myself. It is not that which I am searching after. I am trying to find that without which life could not be." And again everything began to die around and within me, and I wanted again to kill myself.

Then I looked at myself, at what was going on within me, and I recalled those deaths and revivals which had taken place within me hundreds of times. I remembered that I lived only when I believed in God. As it had been before, so it was even now: I needed only to know about God, and I lived; I needed to forget and not believe in him, and I died.

What, then, are these revivals and deaths? Certainly I do not live when I lose my faith in the existence of God; I should have killed myself long ago, if I had not had the dim hope of finding him. "So what else am I looking for?" a voice called out within me. "Here he is. He is that without which one cannot live. To know God and live is one and the same thing. God is life."

"Live searching after God and then there will be no life without God." And stronger than ever all was lighted up within me and about me, and that light no longer abandoned me.

Thus I was saved from suicide. When and how this transformation took place in me I could not say. Just as imperceptibly and by degrees as my force of life had waned, and I had arrived at the impossibility of living, at the arrest of life, at the necessity of suicide, just so by degrees and imperceptibly did that force of life return to me. Strange to say, the force of life which returned to me was not a new, but the same old force which had drawn me on in the first period of my life.

I returned in everything to the most remote, the childish and the youthful. I returned to the belief in that will which had produced me and which wanted something of me; I returned to this, that the chief and only purpose of my life was to be better, that is, to live more in accord with that will; I returned to this, that the expression of this will I could find in that which all humanity had worked out for its guidance in the vanishing past, that is, I returned to the faith in God, in moral perfection, and in the tradition which had handed down the meaning of life. There was only this difference, that formerly it had been assumed unconsciously, while now I knew that I could not live without it.

This is what seemed to have happened with me: I do not remember when I was put in a boat, was pushed off from some unknown shore, had pointed out to me the direction toward another shore, had a pair of oars given into my inexperienced hands, and was left alone. I plied my oars as well as I could, and moved on; but the farther I rowed toward the middle, the swifter did the current become which bore me away from my goal, and the more frequently did I come across oarsmen like myself, who were carried away by the current. There were lonely oarsmen, who continued to row; there were large boats, immense ships, full of people; some struggled against the current, others submitted to it. The farther I rowed, the more did I look down the current, whither all those boats were carried, and forget the direction which had been pointed out to me. In the middle of the current, in the crush of the boats and ships which bore me down, I lost my direction completely and threw down the oars. On every side of me sailing vessels and rowboats were borne down the current with merriment and rejoicing, and the people in them assured me and each other that there could not even be any other direction, and I believed them and went down the stream with them. I was carried away, so far away, that I heard the noise of the rapids where I should be wrecked, and saw boats that had already been wrecked there. I regained my senses. For a long time I could not understand what had happened with me. I saw before me nothing but ruin toward which I was rushing and of which I was afraid; nowhere did I see any salvation, and I did not know what to do; but, on looking back, I saw an endless number of boats that without cessation stubbornly crossed the current, and I thought of the shore, the oars, and the direction, and began to make my way back, up the current and toward the shore.

That shore was God, the direction was tradition, the oars were the freedom given me to row toward the shore,—to unite myself with God. Thus the force of life was renewed in me, and I began to live once more.

The Meaning of Life

Richard Taylor

Many people have believed that life is meaningless, often without even having a very clear sense of what that might mean. Richard Taylor begins by pointing out that although meaningfulness itself may be difficult to understand, we do have what seems a clearer sense of what meaninglessness involves. It is captured, he suggests, in the myth of Sisyphus. What is it, he asks, about Sisyphus's condemnation to eternally roll a rock up a hill only to have it roll back down that has for centuries captured people's imagination as the essence of meaninglessness? By imagining different variations on the story, Taylor shows that though an existence may be meaningless, it can nonetheless acquire a meaning for the person who is living it. Turning to the question of whether human life is meaningless, he first considers the lives of insects and other animals. He concludes by asking if it would matter if Sisyphus possessed an insatiable desire to roll the rock or if he succeeded in building a beautiful temple as a result of his efforts. Richard Taylor teaches philosophy at the University of Rochester.

As you read through this essay, consider the following:

1. What is the myth of Sisyphus?
2. What is it about Sisyphus's life that makes it meaningless?
3. What is the point about the lives of insects and other animals?
4. Would it matter, according to Taylor, if Sisyphus built a temple through his effort? Why or why not?
5. Does Taylor think human life is without meaning? Explain.

The question whether life has any meaning is difficult to interpret, and the more one concentrates his critical faculty on it the more it seems to elude him, or to evaporate as any intelligible question. . . .

If the idea of meaningfulness is difficult to grasp in this context, so that we are unsure what sort of thing would amount to answering the question, the idea of meaninglessness is perhaps less so. If, then, we can bring before our minds a clear image of meaningless existence, then perhaps we can take a step toward coping with our original question by seeing to what extent our lives, as we actually find them, resemble that image, and draw such lessons as we are able to from the comparison.

MEANINGLESS EXISTENCE

A perfect image of meaninglessness, of the kind we are seeking, is found in the ancient myth of Sisyphus. Sisyphus, it will be remembered, betrayed divine secrets to mortals, and for this he was condemned by the gods to roll a stone to the top of a hill, the stone then immediately to roll back down, again to be pushed to the top by Sisyphus, to roll down once more, and so on again and again, *forever*. Now in this we have the picture of meaningless, pointless toil, of a meaningless existence that is absolutely *never* redeemed. It is not even redeemed by a death that, if it were to accomplish nothing more, would at least bring this idiotic cycle to a close. If we were invited to imagine Sisyphus struggling for awhile and accomplishing nothing, perhaps eventually falling from exhaustion, so that we might suppose him then eventually turning to something having some sort of promise, then the meaninglessness of that chapter of his life would not be so stark. It would be a dark and dreadful dream, from which he eventually awakens to sunlight and reality. But he does not awaken, for there is nothing for him to awaken to. His repetitive toil is his life and reality, and it goes on forever, and it is without any meaning whatever. Nothing ever comes of what he is doing, except simply, more of the same. Not by one step, nor by a thousand, nor by ten thousand does he even expiate by the smallest token the sin against the gods that led him into his fate. Nothing comes of it, nothing at all.

This ancient myth has always enchanted men, for countless meanings can be read into it. Some of the ancients apparently thought it symbolized the perpetual rising and setting of the sun, and others the repetitious crashing of the waves upon the shore. Probably the commonest interpretation is that it symbolizes man's eternal struggle and unquenchable spirit, his determination always to try once more in the face of overwhelming discouragement. This interpretation is further supported by that version of the myth according to which Sisyphus was commanded to roll the stone *over* the hill, so that it would finally roll down the other side, but was never quite able to make it.

I am not concerned with rendering or defending any interpretation of this myth, however. I have cited it only for the one element it does unmistakably contain, namely, that of a repetitious, cyclic activity that never comes to anything. We could contrive other images of this that would serve just as well, and no myth-makers are needed to supply the materials of it. Thus, we can imagine two persons transporting a stone—or even a precious gem, it does not matter—back and forth, relay style. One carries it to a near or distant point where it is received by the other; it is returned to its starting point, there to be recovered by the first, and the process is repeated over and over. Except in this relay nothing counts as winning, and nothing brings the contest to any close, each step only leads to a repetition of itself. Or we can imagine two groups of prisoners, one of them engaged in digging a prodigious hole in the ground that is no sooner finished than it is filled in again by the other group, the latter then digging a new

From Richard Taylor, *Good and Evil* (New York: Macmillan Publishing Co., 1970). © 1970 by Richard Taylor. Reprinted by permission.

hole that is at once filled in by the first group, and so on and on endlessly.

Now what stands out in all such pictures as oppressive and dejecting is not that the beings who enact these roles suffer any torture or pain, for it need not be assumed that they do. Nor is it that their labors are great, for they are no greater than the labors commonly undertaken by most men most of the time. According to the original myth, the stone is so large that Sisyphus never quite gets it to the top and must groan under every step, so that his enormous labor is all for nought. But this is not what appalls. It is not that his great struggle comes to nothing, but that his existence itself is without meaning. Even if we suppose, for example, that the stone is but a pebble that can be carried effortlessly, or that the holes dug by the prisoners are but small ones, not the slightest meaning is introduced into their lives. The stone that Sisyphus moves to the top of the hill, whether we think of it as large or small, still rolls back every time, and the process is repeated forever. Nothing comes of it, and the work is simply pointless. That is the element of the myth that I wish to capture.

Again, it is not the fact that the labors of Sisyphus continue forever that deprives them of meaning. It is, rather, the implication of this: that they come to nothing. The image would not be changed by our supposing him to push a different stone up every time, each to roll down again. But if we supposed that these stones, instead of rolling back to their places as if they had never been moved, were assembled at the top of the hill and there incorporated, say, in a beautiful and enduring temple, then the aspect of meaninglessness would disappear. His labors would then have a point, something would come of them all, and although one could perhaps still say it was not worth it, one could not say that the life of Sisyphus was devoid of meaning altogether. Meaningfulness would at least have made an appearance, and we could see what it was.

That point will need remembering. But in the meantime, let us note another way in which the image of meaninglessness can be altered by making only a very slight change. Let us suppose that the gods, while condemning Sisyphus to the fate just described, at the same time, as an afterthought, waxed perversely merciful by implanting in him a strange and irrational impulse; namely, a compulsive impulse to roll stones. We may if we like, to make this more graphic, suppose they accomplish this by implanting in him some substance that has this effect on his character and drives. I call this perverse, because from our point of view there is clearly no reason why anyone should have a persistent and insatiable desire to do something so pointless as that. Nevertheless, suppose that is Sisyphus' condition. He has but one obsession, which is to roll stones, and it is an obsession that is only for the moment appeased by his rolling them—he no sooner gets a stone rolled to the top of the hill than he is restless to roll up another.

Now it can be seen why this little afterthought of the gods, which I called perverse, was also in fact merciful. For they have by this device managed to give Sisyphus precisely what he wants—by making him want precisely what they inflict on him. However it may appear to us, Sisyphus' fate now does not appear to him as a condemnation, but the very reverse. His one desire in life is to roll stones, and he is absolutely guaranteed its endless fulfillment. Where otherwise he might profoundly have wished surcease, and even welcomed the quiet of death to release him from endless boredom and meaninglessness, his life is now filled with mission and meaning, and he seems to himself to have been given an entry to heaven. Nor need he even fear death, for the gods have promised him an endless opportunity to indulge his single purpose, without concern or frustration. He will be able to roll stones *forever*.

What we need to mark most carefully at this point is that the picture with which we began has not really been changed in the least by adding this supposition. Exactly the same things happen as before. The only change is in Sisyphus' view of them. The picture before was the image of meaningless activity and existence. It was created precisely to be an image of that. It has not lost that meaninglessness, it has now gained not the least shred of meaningfulness. The stones still roll back as before, each phase of Sisyphus' life still exactly resembles all the others, the task is never completed, nothing comes of it, no temple ever begins to rise, and all this cycle of the same pointless thing over and over goes on forever in this picture as in the other. The *only* thing that has happened is this: Sisyphus has been reconciled to it, and indeed more, he has been led to embrace it. Not, however, by reason or persuasion, but by nothing more rational than the potency of a new substance in his veins.

THE MEANINGLESSNESS OF LIFE

I believe the foregoing provides a fairly clear content to the idea of meaninglessness and, through it, some hint of what meaningfulness, in this sense, might be. Meaninglessness is essentially endless pointlessness, and meaningfulness is therefore the opposite. Activity, and even long, drawn-out and repetitive activity, has a meaning if it has some significant culmination, some more or less lasting end that can be considered to have been the direction and purpose of the activity. But the descriptions so far also provide something else; namely, the suggestion of how an existence that is objectively meaningless, in this sense, can nevertheless acquire a meaning for him whose existence it is.

Now let us ask: Which of these pictures does life in fact resemble? And let us not begin with our own lives, for here both our prejudices and wishes are great, but with the life in general that we share with the rest of creation. We shall find, I think, that it all has a certain pattern, and that this pattern is by now easily recognized.

We can begin anywhere, only saving human existence for our last consideration. We can, for example, begin with any animal. It does not matter where we begin, because the result is going to be exactly the same.

Thus, for example, there are caves in New Zealand, deep and dark, whose floors are quiet pools and whose walls and ceilings are covered with soft light. As one gazes in wonder in the stillness of these caves it seems that the Creator has reproduced there in microcosm the heavens themselves, until one scarcely remembers the enclosing presence of the walls. As one looks more closely, however, the scene is explained. Each dot of light identifies an ugly worm, whose luminous tail is meant to attract insects from the surrounding darkness. As from time to time one of these insects draws near it becomes entangled in a sticky thread lowered by the worm, and is eaten. This goes on month after month, the blind worm lying there in the barren stillness waiting to entrap an occasional bit of nourishment that will only sustain it to another bit of nourishment until. . . . Until what? What great thing awaits all this long and repetitious effort and makes it worthwhile? Really nothing. The larva just transforms itself finally to a tiny winged adult that lacks even mouth parts to feed and lives only a day or two. These adults, as soon as they have mated and laid eggs, are themselves caught in the threads and are devoured by the cannibalist worms, often without having ventured into the day, the only point to their existence having now been fulfilled. This has been going on for millions of years, and to no end other than that the same meaningless cycle may continue for another millions of years.

All living things present essentially the same spectacle. The larva of a certain cicada burrows in the darkness of the earth for seventeen years, through season after season, to emerge finally into the daylight for a brief flight, lay its eggs, and die—this all to repeat itself during the next seventeen years, and so on to eternity. We have already noted, in another connection, the struggles of fish, made only that others may do the same after them and that this cycle, having no other point than itself, may never cease. Some birds span an entire side of the globe each year and then return, only to insure that others may follow the same incredibly long path again and again. One is led to wonder what the point of it all is, with what great triumph this ceaseless effort, repeating itself through millions of years, might finally culminate, and why it should go on and on for so long, accomplishing nothing, getting nowhere. But then one realizes that there is no point to it at all, that it really culminates in nothing, that each of these cycles, so filled with toil, is to be followed only by more of the same. The point of any living thing's life is, evidently, nothing but life itself.

This life of the world thus presents itself to our eyes as a vast machine, feeding on itself, running on and on forever to nothing. And we are part of that life. To be sure, we are not just the same, but the differences are not so great as we like to think; many are merely invented, and none really cancels the kind of meaninglessness that we found in Sisyphus and that we find all around, wherever anything lives. We are conscious of our activity. Our goals, whether in any significant sense we choose them or not, are things of which we are at least partly aware and can therefore in some sense appraise. More significantly, perhaps, men have a history, as other animals do not, such that each generation does not precisely resemble all those before. Still, if we can in imagination disengage our wills from our lives and disregard the deep interest each man has in his own existence, we shall find that they do not so little resemble the existence of Sisyphus. We toil after goals, most of them—indeed every single one of them—of transitory significance and, having gained one of them, we immediately set forth for the next, as if that one had never been, with this next one being essentially more of the same. Look at a busy street any day, and observe the throng going hither and thither. To what? Some office or shop, where the same things will be done today as were done yesterday, and are done now so they may be repeated tomorrow. And if we think that, unlike Sisyphus, these labors do have a point, that they culminate in something lasting and, independently of our own deep interests in them, very worthwhile, then we simply have not consid-

ered the thing closely enough. Most such effort is directed only to the establishment and perpetuation of home and family; that is, to the begetting of others who will follow in our steps to do more of the same. Each man's life thus resembles one of Sisyphus' climbs to the summit of his hill, and each day of it one of his steps; the difference is that whereas Sisyphus himself returns to push the stone up again, we leave this to our children. We at one point imagined that the labors of Sisyphus finally culminated in the creation of a temple, but for this to make any difference it had to be a temple that would at least endure, adding beauty to the world for the remainder of time. Our achievements, even though they are often beautiful, are mostly bubbles; and those that do last, like the sand-swept pyramids, soon becomes mere curiosities while around them the rest of mankind continues its perpetual toting of rocks, only to see them roll down. Nations are built upon the bones of their founders and pioneers, but only to decay and crumble before long, their rubble then becoming the foundation for others directed to exactly the same fate. The picture of Sisyphus is the picture of existence of the individual man, great or unknown, of nations, of the race of men, and of the very life of the world.

On a country road one sometimes comes upon the ruined hulks of a house and once extensive buildings, all in collapse and spread over with weeds, A curious eye can in imagination reconstruct from what is left a once warm and thriving life, filled with purpose. There was the hearth, where a family once talked, sang, and made plans; there were the rooms, where people loved, and babes were born to a rejoicing mother; there are the musty remains of a sofa, infested with bugs, once bought at a dear price to enhance an ever-growing comfort, beauty, and warmth. Every small piece of junk fills the mind with what once, not long ago, was utterly real, with children's voices, plans made, and enterprises embarked upon. That is how these stones of Sisyphus were rolled up, and that is how they became incorporated into a beautiful temple, and that temple is what now lies before you. Meanwhile other buildings, institutions, nations, and civilizations spring up all around, only to share the same fate before long. And if the question "What for?" is now asked, the answer is clear: so that just this may go on forever. . . .

THE MEANING OF LIFE

We noted that Sisyphus' existence would have meaning if there were some point to his labors, if his efforts ever culminated in something that was not just an occasion for fresh labors of the same kind. But that is precisely the meaning it lacks. And human existence resembles his in that respect. Men do achieve things—they scale their towers and raise their stones to their hilltops—but every such accomplishment fades, providing only an occasion for renewed labors of the same kind.

But here we need to note something else that has been mentioned, but its significance not explored, and that is the state of mind and feeling with which such labors are undertaken. We noted that if Sisyphus had a keen and unappeasable desire to be doing just what he found himself doing, then, although his life would in no way be changed, it would nevertheless have a meaning for him. It would be an irrational one, no doubt, because the desire itself would be only the product of the substance in his veins, and not any that reason could discover, but a meaning nevertheless.

And would it not, in fact, be a meaning incomparably better than the other? For let us examine again the first kind of meaning it could have. Let us suppose that, without having any interest in rolling stones, as such, and finding this, in fact, a galling toil, Sisyphus did nevertheless have a deep interest in raising a temple, one that would be beautiful and lasting. And let us suppose he succeeded in this, that after ages of dreadful toil, all directed at this final result, he did at last complete his temple, such that now he could say his work was done, and he could rest and for-

ever enjoy the result. Now what? What picture now presents itself to our minds? It is precisely the picture of infinite boredom! Of Sisyphus doing nothing ever again, but contemplating what he has already wrought and can no longer add anything to, and contemplating it for an eternity! Now in this picture we have a meaning for Sisyphus' existence, a point for his prodigious labor, because we have put it there; yet, at the same time, that which is really worthwhile seems to have slipped away entirely. Where before we were presented with the nightmare of eternal and pointless activity, we are now confronted with the hell of its eternal absence.

Our second picture, then, wherein we imagined Sisyphus to have had inflicted on him the irrational desire to be doing just what he found himself doing, should not have been dismissed so abruptly. The meaning that picture lacked was no meaning that he or anyone could crave, and the strange meaning it had was perhaps just what we were seeking.

At this point, then, we can reintroduce what has been until now, it is hoped, resolutely pushed aside in an effort to view our lives and human existence with objectivity; namely, our own wills, our deep interest in what we find ourselves doing. If we do this we find that our lives do indeed still resemble that of Sisyphus, but that the meaningfulness they thus lack is precisely the meaningfulness of infinite boredom. At the same time, the strange meaningfulness they possess is that of the inner compulsion to be doing just what we were put here to do, and to go on doing it forever. This is the nearest we may hope to get to heaven, but the redeeming side of that fact is that we do thereby avoid a genuine hell.

If the builders of a great and flourishing ancient civilization could somehow return now to see archaeologists unearthing the trivial remnants of what they had once accomplished with such effort—see the fragments of pots and vases, a few broken statues, and such tokens of another age and greatness—they could indeed ask themselves what the point of it all was, if this is all it finally came to. Yet, it did not seem so to them then, for it was just the building, and not what was finally built, that gave their life meaning. Similarly, if the builders of the ruined home and farm that I described a short while ago could be brought back to see what is left, they would have the same feelings. What we construct in our imaginations as we look over these decayed and rusting pieces would reconstruct itself in their very memories, and certainly with unspeakable sadness. The piece of a sled at our feet would revive in them a warm Christmas. And what rich memories would there be in the broken crib? And the weed-covered remains of a fence would reproduce the scene of a great herd of livestock, so laboriously built up over so many years. What was it all worth, if this is the final result? Yet, again, it did not seem so to them through those many years of struggle and toil, and they did not imagine they were building a Gibraltar. The things to which they bent their backs day after day, realizing one by one their ephemeral plans, were precisely the things in which their wills were deeply involved, precisely the things in which their interests lay, and there was no need then to ask questions. There is no more need of them now—the day was sufficient to itself, and so was the life.

This is surely the way to look at all of life—at one's own life, and each day and moment it contains; of the life of a nation; of the species; of the life of the world; and of everything that breathes. Even the glow worms I described, whose cycles of existence over the millions of years seem so pointless when looked at by us, will seem entirely different to us if we can somehow try to view their existence from within. Their endless activity, which gets nowhere, is just what it is their will to pursue. This is its whole justification and meaning. Nor would it be any salva-

tion to the birds who span the globe every year, back and forth, to have a home made for them in a cage with plenty of food and protection, so that they would not have to migrate any more. It would be their condemnation, for it is the doing that counts for them, and not what they hope to win by it. Flying these prodigious distances, never ending, is what it is in their veins to do, exactly as it was in Sisyphus' veins to roll stones, without end, after the gods had waxed merciful and implanted this in him.

A human being no sooner draws his first breath than he responds to the will that is in him to live. He no more asks whether it will be worthwhile, or whether anything of significance will come of it, than the worms and the birds. The point of his living is simply to be living, in the manner that it is his nature to be living. He goes through his life building his castles, each of these beginning to fade into time as the next is begun; yet, it would be no salvation to rest from all this. It would be a condemnation, and one that would in no way be redeemed were he able to gaze upon the things he has done, even if these were beautiful and absolutely permanent, as they never are. What counts is that one should be able to begin a new task, a new castle, a new bubble. It counts only because it is there to be done and he has the will to do it. The same will be the life of his children, and of theirs; and if the philosopher is apt to see in this a pattern similar to the unending cycles of the existence of Sisyphus, and to despair, then it is indeed because the meaning and point he is seeking is not there—but mercifully so. The meaning of life is from within us, it is not bestowed from without, and it far exceeds in both its beauty and permanence any heaven of which men have ever dreamed or yearned for.

The Absurd

Thomas Nagel

Thomas Nagel also discusses Sisyphus. But instead of focusing on the *meaning* of life, Nagel discusses a close cousin: its absurdity. He begins by criticizing some of the popular, though mistaken, reasons people have suggested life is absurd. He then defends the absurdity of life on other grounds. Nagel first asks what it is about any particular situation that makes it absurd. He then turns to our lives as a whole, asking whether they are absurd. Unlike animals, whose lives he thinks are not absurd, our lives are because of our capacities as rational beings to take a kind of outsiders' perspective—what Nagel has elsewhere termed a "view from nowhere." Thomas Nagel is professor of philosophy at New York University.

As you read through this essay, consider the following:

1. What are the standard arguments that life is absurd? Why does Nagel reject them?
2. When in ordinary life do we say that a situation or action is absurd? What is the point of saying that in those contexts?
3. Nagel thinks absurdity arises because we can avoid neither seriousness nor doubt. What does he mean?
4. What is the special capacity we humans have that makes our lives absurd?
5. Can we escape the absurdity of our lives? Why or why not?
6. How is the absurd similar to philosophical skepticism about our system of beliefs, evidence, and so on?
7. Why is a mouse's life not absurd?

Most people feel on occasion that life is absurd, and some feel it vividly and continually. Yet the reasons usually offered in defense of this conviction are patently inadequate: they *could* not really explain why life is absurd. Why then do they provide a natural expression for the sense that it is?

I

Consider some examples. It is often remarked that nothing we do now will matter in a million years. But if that is true, then by the same token, nothing that will be the case in a million years matters now. In particular, it does not matter now that in a million years nothing we

do now will matter. Moreover, even if what we did now *were* going to matter in a million years, how could that keep our present concerns from being absurd? If their mattering now is not enough to accomplish that, how would it help if they mattered a million years from now?

Whether what we do now will matter in a million years could make the crucial difference only if its mattering in a million years depended on its mattering, period. But then to deny that whatever happens now will matter in a million years is to beg the question against its mattering, period; for in that sense one cannot know that it will not matter in a million years whether (for example) someone now is happy or miserable, without knowing that it does not matter, period.

What we say to convey the absurdity of our lives often has to do with space or time: we are tiny specks in the infinite vastness of the universe; our lives are mere instants even on a geological time scale, let alone a cosmic one; we will all be dead any minute. But of course none of these evident facts can be what *makes* life absurd, if it is absurd. For suppose we lived forever; would not a life that is absurd if it lasts seventy years be infinitely absurd if it lasted through eternity? And if our lives are absurd given our present size, why would they be any less absurd if we filled the universe (either because we were larger or because the universe was smaller)? Reflection on our minuteness and brevity appears to be intimately connected with the sense that life is meaningless; but it is not clear what the connection is.

Another inadequate argument is that because we are going to die, all chains of justification must leave off in mid-air: one studies and works to earn money to pay for clothing, housing, entertainment, food, to sustain oneself from year to year, perhaps to support a family and pursue a career—but to what final end? All of it is an elaborate journey leading nowhere. (One will also have some effect on other people's lives, but that simply reproduces the problem, for they will die too.)

There are several replies to this argument. First, life does not consist of a sequence of activities each of which has as its purpose some later member of the sequence. Chains of justification come repeatedly to an end within life, and whether the process as a whole can be justified has no bearing on the finality of these end-points. No further justification is needed to make it reasonable to take aspirin for a headache, attend an exhibition of the work of a painter one admires, or stop a child from putting his hand on a hot stove. No larger context or further purpose is needed to prevent these acts from being pointless.

Even if someone wished to supply a further justification for pursuing all the things in life that are commonly regarded as self-justifying, that justification would have to end somewhere too. If *nothing* can justify unless it is justified in terms of something outside itself, which is also justified, then an infinite regress results, and no chain of justification can be complete. Moreover, if a finite chain of reasons cannot justify anything, what could be accomplished by an infinite chain, each link of which must be justified by something outside itself?

Since justifications must come to an end somewhere, nothing is gained by denying that they end where they appear to, within life—or by trying to subsume the multiple, often trivial ordinary justifications of action under a single, controlling life scheme. We can be satisfied more easily than that. In fact, through its misrepresentation of the process of justification, the argument makes a vacuous demand. It insists that the reasons available within life are incomplete, but suggests thereby that all reasons that come to an end are incomplete. This makes it impossible to supply any reasons at all.

The standard arguments for absurdity appear therefore to fail as arguments. Yet I believe they attempt to express something that is difficult to state, but fundamentally correct.

II

In ordinary life a situation is absurd when it includes a conspicuous discrepancy between pretension or aspiration and reality: someone gives a complicated speech in support of a motion that has already been passed; a notorious criminal is made president of a major philanthropic foundation; you declare your love over the telephone to a recorded announcement; as you are being knighted, your pants fall down.

When a person finds himself in an absurd situation, he will usually attempt to change it, by modifying his aspirations, or by trying to bring reality into better accord with them, or by removing himself from the situation entirely. We are not always willing or able to extricate ourselves from a position whose absurdity has become clear to us. Nevertheless, it is usually possible to imagine some change that would remove the absurdity—whether or not we can or will implement it.

The sense that life as a whole is absurd arises when we perceive, perhaps dimly, an inflated pretension or aspiration which is inseparable from the continuation of human life and which makes its absurdity inescapable, short of escape from life itself.

Many people's lives are absurd, temporarily or permanently, for conventional reasons having to do with their particular ambitions, circumstances, and personal relations. If there is a philosophical sense of absurdity, however, it must arise from the perception of something universal—some respect in which pretension and reality inevitably clash for us all. This condition is supplied, I shall argue, by the collision between the seriousness with which we take our lives and the perpetual possibility of regarding everything about which we are serious as arbitrary, or open to doubt.

We cannot live human lives without energy and attention, nor without making choices which show that we take some things more seriously than others. Yet we have always available a point of view outside the particular form of our lives, from which the seriousness appears gratuitous. These two inescapable viewpoints collide in us, and that is what makes life absurd. It is absurd because we ignore the doubts that we know cannot be settled, continuing to live with nearly undiminished seriousness in spite of them.

This analysis requires defense in two respects: first as regards the unavoidability of seriousness; second as regards the inescapability of doubt.

We take ourselves seriously whether we lead serious lives or not and whether we are concerned primarily with fame, pleasure, virtues, luxury, triumph, beauty, justice, knowledge, salvation, or mere survival. If we take other people seriously and devote ourselves to them, that only multiplies the problem. Human life is full of effort, plans, calculation, success and failure: we *pursue* our lives, with varying degrees of sloth and energy.

It would be different if we could not step back and reflect on the process, but were merely led from impulse to impulse without self-consciousness. But human beings do not act solely on impulse. They are prudent, they reflect, they weigh consequences; they ask whether what they are doing is worthwhile. Not only are their lives full of particular choices that hang together in larger activities with temporal structure: they also decide in the broadest terms what to pursue and what to avoid, what the priorities among their various aims should be, and what kind of people they want to be or become. Some men are faced with such choices by the large decisions they make from time to time; some merely by reflection on the course their lives are taking as the product of countless small decisions. They decide whom to marry, what profession to follow, whether to join the Country Club, or the Resistance; or they may just wonder why they go on being salesmen or academics or taxi drivers, and then stop thinking about it after a certain period of inconclusive reflection.

Although they may be motivated from act to act by those immediate needs with which life presents them, they allow the process to continue by adhering to the general system of habits and the form of life in which such motives have their place—or perhaps only by clinging to life itself. They spend enormous quantities of energy, risk, and calculation of the details. Think of how an ordinary individual sweats over his appearance, his health, his sex life, his emotional honesty, his social utility, his self-knowledge, the quality of his ties with family, colleagues, and friends, how well he does his job, whether he understands the world and what is going on in it. Leading a human life is a full-time occupation, to which everyone devotes decades of intense concern.

This fact is so obvious that it is hard to find it extraordinary and important. Each of us lives his own life—lives with himself twenty-four hours a day. What else is he supposed to do—live someone else's life? Yet humans have the special capacity to step back and survey themselves, and the lives to which they are committed, with that detached amazement which comes from watching an ant struggle up a heap of sand. Without developing the illusion that they are able to escape from their highly specific and idiosyncratic position, they can view it *sub specie aeternitatis*—and the view is at once sobering and comical.

The crucial backward step is not taken by asking for still another justification in the chain, and failing to get it. The objections to that line of attack have already been stated; justifications come to an end. But this is precisely what provides universal doubt with its object. We step back to find that the whole system of justification and criticism, which controls our choices and supports our claims to rationality, rests on responses and habits that we never question, that we should not know how to defend without circularity, and to which we shall continue to adhere even after they are called into question.

The things we do or want without reasons, and without requiring reasons—the things that define what is a reason for us and what is not—are the starting points of our skepticism. We see ourselves from outside, and all the contingency and specificity of our aims and pursuits become clear. Yet when we take this view and recognize what we do as arbitrary, it does not disengage us from life, and there lies our absurdity: not in the fact that such an external view can be taken of us, but in the fact that we ourselves can take it, without ceasing to be the persons whose ultimate concerns are so coolly regarded.

III

One may try to escape the position by seeking broader ultimate concerns, from which it is impossible to step back—the idea being that absurdity results because what we take seriously is something small and insignificant and individual. Those seeking to supply their lives with meaning usually envision a role or function in something larger than themselves. They therefore seek fulfillment in service to society, the state, the revolution, the progress of history, the advance of science, or religion and the glory of God.

But a role in some larger enterprise cannot confer significance unless that enterprise is itself significant. And its significance must come back to what we can understand, or it will not even appear to give us what we are seeking. If we learned that we were being raised to provide food for other creatures fond of human flesh, who planned to turn us into cutlets before we got too stringy—even if we learned that the human race had been developed by animal breeders precisely for this purpose—that would still not give our lives meaning, for two reasons. First, we would still be in the dark as to the significance of the lives of those other beings; second, although we might acknowledge that this culinary role would make our lives meaningful to them, it is not clear how it would make them meaningful to us.

Admittedly, the usual form of service to a higher being is different from this. One is supposed to behold and partake of the glory of God, for example, in a way in which chickens do not share in the glory of coq au vin. The same is true of service to a state, a movement, or a revolution. People can come to feel, when they are part of something bigger, that it is part of them too. They worry less about what is peculiar to themselves, but identify enough with the larger enterprise to find their role in it fulfilling.

However, any such larger purpose can be put in doubt in the same way that the aims of an individual life can be, and for the same reasons. It is as legitimate to find ultimate justification there as to find it earlier, among the details of individual life. But this does not alter the fact that justifications come to an end when we are content to have them end—when we do not find it necessary to look any further. If we can step back from the purposes of individual life and doubt their point, we can step back also from the progress of human history, or of science, or the success of a society, or the kingdom, power, and glory of God, and put all these things into question in the same way. What seems to us to confer meaning, justification, significance, does so in virtue of the fact that we need no more reasons after a certain point.

What makes doubt inescapable with regard to the limited aims of individual life also makes it inescapable with regard to any larger purpose that encourages the sense that life is meaningful. Once the fundamental doubt has begun, it cannot be laid to rest.

Camus maintains in *The Myth of Sisyphus* that the absurd arises because the world fails to meet our demands for meaning. This suggests that the world might satisfy those demands if it were different. But now we can see that this is not the case. There does not appear to be any conceivable world (containing us) about which unsettlable doubts could not arise. Consequently the absurdity of our situation derives not from a collision between our expectations and the world, but from a collision within ourselves.

IV

It may be objected that the standpoint from which these doubts are supposed to be felt does not exist—that if we take the recommended backward step we will land on thin air, without any basis for judgment about the natural responses we are supposed to be surveying. If we retain our usual standards of what is important, then questions about the significance of what we are doing with our lives will be answerable in the usual way. But if we do not, then those questions can mean nothing to us, since there is no longer any content to the idea of what matters, and hence no content to the idea that nothing does.

But this objection misconceives the nature of the backward step. It is not supposed to give us an understanding of what is *really* important, so that we see by contrast that our lives are insignificant. We never, in the course of these reflections, abandon the ordinary standards that guide our lives. We merely observe them in operation, and recognize that if they are called into question we can justify them only by reference to themselves, uselessly. We adhere to them because of the way we are put together; what seems to us important or serious or valuable would not seem so if we were differently constituted.

In ordinary life, to be sure, we do not judge a situation absurd unless we have in mind some standards of seriousness, significance, or harmony with which the absurd can be contrasted. This contrast is not implied by the philosophical judgment of absurdity, and that might be thought to make the concept unsuitable for the expression of such judgments. This is not so, however, for the philosophical judgment depends on another contrast which makes it a natural extension from more ordinary cases. It departs from them only in contrasting the pretensions of life with a larger context in which *no* standards can be discovered, rather than with a context from which alternative, overriding standards may be applied.

V

In this respect, as in others, philosophical perception of the absurd resembles epistemological skepticism. In both cases the final, philosophical doubt is not contrasted with any unchallenged certainties, though it is arrived at by extrapolation from examples of doubt within the system of evidence or justification, where a contrast with other certainties *is* implied. In both cases our limitedness joins with a capacity to transcend those limitations in thought (thus seeing them as limitations, and as inescapable).

Skepticism begins when we include ourselves in the world about which we claim knowledge. We notice that certain types of evidence convince us, that we are content to allow justifications of belief to come to an end at certain points, that we feel we know many things even without knowing or having grounds for believing the denial of others which, if true, would make what we claim to know false.

For example, I know that I am looking at a piece of paper, although I have no adequate grounds for claiming I know that I am not dreaming; and if I am dreaming then I am not looking at a piece of paper. Here an ordinary conception of how appearance may diverge from reality is employed to show that we take our world largely for granted; the certainty that we are not dreaming cannot be justified except circularly, in terms of those very appearances which are being put in doubt. It is somewhat far-fetched to suggest I may be dreaming; but the possibility is only illustrative. It reveals that our claims to knowledge depend on our not feeling it necessary to exclude certain incompatible alternatives, and the dreaming possibility or the total-hallucination possibility are just representatives for limitless possibilities most of which we cannot even conceive.[1]

Once we have taken the backward step to an abstract view of our whole system of beliefs, evidence, and justification, and seen that it works only, despite its pretensions, by taking the world largely for granted, we are *not* in a position to contrast all these appearances with an alternative reality. We cannot shed our ordinary responses, and if we could it would leave us with no means of conceiving reality of any kind.

It is the same in the practical domain. We do not step outside our lives to a new vantage point from which we see what is really, objectively significant. We continue to take life largely for granted while seeing that all our decisions and certainties are possible only because there is a great deal we do not bother to rule out.

Both epistemological skepticism and a sense of the absurd can be reached via initial doubts posed within systems of evidence and justification that we accept, and can be stated without violence to our ordinary concepts. We can ask not only why we should believe there is a floor under us, but also why we should believe the evidence of our senses at all—and at some point the framable questions will have outlasted the answers. Similarly, we can ask not only why we should take aspirin, but why we should take trouble over our own comfort at all. The fact that we shall take the aspirin without waiting for an answer to this last question does not show that it is an unreal question. We shall also continue to believe there is a floor under us without waiting for an answer to the other question. In both cases it is this unsupported natural confidence that

generates skeptical doubts; so it cannot be used to settle them.

Philosophical skepticism does not cause us to abandon our ordinary beliefs, but it lends them a peculiar flavor. After acknowledging that their truth is incompatible with possibilities that we have no grounds for believing do not obtain—apart from grounds in those very beliefs which we have called into question—we return to our familiar convictions with a certain irony and resignation. Unable to abandon the natural responses on which they depend, we take them back, like a spouse who has run off with someone else and then decided to return; but we regard them differently (not that the new attitude is necessarily inferior to the old, in either case).

The same situation obtains after we have put in question the seriousness with which we take our lives and human life in general and have looked at ourselves without presuppositions. We then return to our lives, as we must, but our seriousness is laced with irony. Not that irony enables us to escape the absurd. It is useless to mutter: "Life is meaningless; life is meaningless . . ." as an accompaniment to everything we do. In continuing to live and work and strive, we take ourselves seriously in action no matter what we say.

What sustains us, in belief as in action, is not reason for justification, but something more basic than these—for we go on in the same way even after we are convinced that the reasons have given out.[2] If we tried to rely entirely on reason, and pressed it hard, our lives and beliefs would collapse—a form of madness that may actually occur if the inertial force of taking the world and life for granted is somehow lost. If we lose our grip on that, reason will not give it back to us.

VI

In viewing ourselves from a perspective broader than we can occupy in the flesh, we become spectators of our own lives. We cannot do very much as pure spectators of our own lives, so we continue to lead them, and devote ourselves to what we are able at the same time to view as no more than a curiosity, like the ritual of an alien religion.

This explains why the sense of absurdity finds its natural expression in those bad arguments with which the discussion began. References to our small size and short life-span and to the fact that all of mankind will eventually vanish without a trace are metaphors for the backward step which permits us to regard ourselves from without and to find the particular form of our lives curious and slightly surprising. By feigning a nebula's-eye view, we illustrate the capacity to see ourselves without presuppositions, as arbitrary, idiosyncratic, highly specific occupants of the world, one of countless possible forms of life.

Before turning to the question whether the absurdity of our lives is something to be regretted and if possible escaped, let me consider what would have to be given up in order to avoid it.

Why is the life of a mouse not absurd? The orbit of the moon is not absurd either, but that involves no strivings or aims at all. A mouse, however, has to work to stay alive. Yet he is not absurd, because he lacks the capacities for self-consciousness and self-transcendence that would enable him to see that he is only a mouse. If that *did* happen, his life would become absurd, since self-awareness would not make him cease to be a mouse and would not enable him to rise above his mousely strivings. Bringing his new-found self-consciousness with him, he would have to return to his meager yet frantic life, full of doubts that he was unable to answer, but also full of purposes that he was unable to abandon.

Given that the transcendental step is natural to us humans, can we avoid absurdity by refusing to take that step and remaining entirely within our sublunar lives? Well, we cannot refuse consciously, for to do that we would have to be aware of the viewpoint we were refusing to adopt. The only way to avoid the relevant self-consciousness would be either never to attain it or to forget it—neither of which can be achieved by the will.

On the other hand, it is possible to expend effort on an attempt to destroy the other component of the absurd—abandoning one's earthly, individual, human life in order to identify as completely as possible with that universal viewpoint from which human life seems arbitrary and trivial. (This appears to be the ideal of certain Oriental religions.) If one succeeds, then one will not have to drag the superior awareness through a strenuous mundane life, and absurdity will be diminished.

However, insofar as this self-etiolation is the result of effort, will-power, aceticism, and so forth, it requires that one take oneself seriously as an individual—that one be willing to take considerable trouble to avoid being creaturely and absurd. Thus one may undermine the aim of unworldliness by pursuing it too vigorously. Still, if someone simply allowed his individual, animal nature to drift and respond to impulse, without making the pursuit of its needs a central conscious aim, then he might, at considerable dissociative cost, achieve a life that was less absurd than most. It would not be a meaningful life either, of course; but it would not involve the engagement of a transcendent awareness in the assiduous pursuit of mundane goals. And that is the main condition of absurdity—the dragooning of an unconvinced transcendent consciousness into the service of an immanent, limited enterprise like a human life.

The final escape is suicide; but before adopting any hasty solutions, it would be wise to consider carefully whether the absurdity of our existence truly presents us with a *problem*, to which some solution must be found—a way of dealing with prima facie disaster. That is certainly the attitude with which Camus approaches the issue, and it gains support from the fact that we are all eager to escape from absurd situations on a smaller scale.

Camus—not on uniformly good grounds—rejects suicide and the other solutions he regards as escapist. What he recommends is defiance or scorn. We can salvage our dignity, he appears to believe, by shaking a fist at the world which is deaf to our pleas, and continuing to live in spite of it. This will not make our lives un-absurd, but it will lend them a certain nobility.[3]

This seems to me romantic and slightly self-pitying. Our absurdity warrants neither that much distress nor that much defiance. At the risk of falling into romanticism by a different route, I would argue that absurdity is one of the most human things about us: a manifestation of our most advanced and interesting characteristics. Like skepticism in epistemology, it is possible only because we possess a certain kind of insight—the capacity to transcend ourselves in thought.

If a sense of the absurd is a way of perceiving our true situation (even though the situation is not absurd until the perception arises), then what reason can we have to resent or escape it? Like the capacity for epistemological skepticism, it results from the ability to understand our human limitations. It need not be a matter for agony unless we make it so. Nor need it evoke a defiant contempt of fate that allows us to feel brave or proud. Such dramatics, even if carried on in private, betray a failure to appreciate the cosmic unimportance of the situation. If *sub specie aeternitatis* there is no reason to believe that anything matters, then that does not matter either, and we can approach our absurd lives with irony instead of heroism or despair.

Notes

1. I am aware that skepticism about the external world is widely thought to have been refuted, but I have remained convinced of its irrefutability since being exposed at Berkeley to Thompson Clarke's largely unpublished ideas on the subject.

2. As Hume says in a famous passage of the *Treatise:* "Most fortunately it happens, that since reason is incapable of dispelling these clouds, nature herself suffices to that purpose, and cures me of this philosophical melancholy and delirium, either by relaxing this bent of mind, or by some avocation, and lively impression of my senses, which obliterate all these chimeras. I dine, I play a game of backgammon, I converse, and am merry with my friends; and when after three or four hours' amusement, I would return to these speculations, they appear so cold, and strain'd, and ridiculous, that I cannot find in my heart to enter into them any farther" (bk. 1, pt. iv, sect. 7; Selby-Bigge edition, p. 269).

3. "Sisyphus, proletarian of the gods, powerless and rebellious, knows the whole extent of his wretched condition: it is what he thinks of during his descent. The lucidity that was to constitute his torture at the same time crowns his victory. There is no fate that cannot be surmounted by scorn" (*The Myth of Sisyphus*, trans. Justin O'Brien [New York: Vintage, 1959], p. 90; first published, Paris: Gallimard, 1942).

Essay and Paper Topics for "The Practice of Religion"

1. Write an essay in which you compare the views of religion presented in "Three Conceptions of Religion." What role does religion play in human life, according to the three writers?

2. Hick suggests that he has described the central feature of religion. So does Geertz. Write an essay in which you compare and contrast those two essays, indicating whether you think one, both, or neither is correct and why.

3. "Religion is uniquely able to provide meaning for a human life." Write an essay in which you assess this claim in light of the essays you have read in this section.

4. Compare the positions of Taylor and Nagel on the meaning of life and absurdity.

5. Discuss the significance of the myth of Sisyphus, from your own perspective as well as those of Taylor and Nagel.

6. Discuss the following claim: "Ultimately, all religions share a common core even if they differ in many ways." Do you agree or disagree?

Part IX

Religious Practice and Culture

Social Critiques
of Religious Practice

A Feminist Interpretation of Christianity

Patricia Altenbernd Johnson

Many feminists as well as others have argued that traditional religious beliefs and practices are inherently sexist, treating women not as equals but rather as the subordinate inferiors of males. This is said to occur in many different contexts, ranging from the roles assigned to women inside and outside churches, synagogues, and mosques to the very conception of God itself. In this essay, Patricia Altenbernd Johnson suggests a "hermeneutic" or interpretive approach to the Christian faith that seeks to avoid the sexist ideas inherent in its conception of God. Rather than thinking of God as a male, father figure, she argues, one should understand God in terms of mother and female. Patricia Altenbernd Johnson is professor of philosophy at the University of Dayton.

As you read through this essay, consider the following:

1. What is the challenge that Plantinga poses to Christian philosophers?
2. What is the "hermeneutical process"? What does Johnson mean by our "fundamental interpretive stances"?
3. In what ways does Johnson believe women are silenced and treated as less than equals by traditional interpretations of Christianity?
4. How does Johnson use Sara Ruddick's work on mothering to reinterpret Christianity? How are the three demands mothers face relevant to how we should understand God?
5. What does Johnson mean in speaking of religion as a practice that can be reinterpreted?
6. To what extent do her thoughts about Christianity apply to other religions?

ADVICE TO CHRISTIAN PHILOSOPHERS

Seven years ago Alvin Plantinga offered some Advice to Christian Philosophers.[1] He suggested that, within the philosophical community in which we, as Christians, find ourselves, we need to display more autonomy, more integrity, and more boldness. My aim is to offer some further, but related advice. Christian philosophers would do well to heed the voices of feminist philosophers both within and outside of the Christian community. If our philosophy is an "expression of deep and fundamental perspectives, ways of viewing ourselves and the world and God" (Plantinga, p. 271), then we must constantly examine those perspectives in order better to articulate them and to understand how those perspectives relate to our thought and our action. In this paper, I will set out the hermeneutical structure of the task that Plantinga recommends for Christian philosophers and show how the voices of feminism contribute to this task. . . .

THE HERMENEUTICLAL STANCE OF THE CHRISTIAN PHILOSOPHER

Plantinga's advice helps us understand our stance as Christian philosophers in relation to the wider philosophical community. He tells us the story of a young woman (Christian in her religious commitments) who goes to college and discovers that "philosophy is the subject for her" (p. 254). As an undergraduate she learns how philosophy is currently practiced. She goes to grad-school and learns even more fully the standards and assumptions that guide contemporary philosophical thought. She learns these parameters well. She respects her mentors, and she is inclined to think that departure from these parameters is "at best

Patricia Altenbernd Johnson, "Feminist Christian Philosophy." *Faith and Philosophy* 9:3 (July 1992). Used by permission of the editor of *Faith and Philosophy*.

marginally respectable" (p. 255). Plantinga suggests that as time goes on this young philosopher—now a professional—may "note certain tensions between her Christian belief and her way of practicing philosophy" (p. 256). She may become so concerned about these tensions that she tries to put the two together, "to harmonize them" (p. 256). Plantinga's advice to her is that she is misdirected in doing this. What she should do instead is allow her sense of tension to help her critique the presuppositions of current philosophy. Moreover, she should listen to her own voice and be emboldened to set aside the philosophical parameters of her mentors, to reject their presuppositions and begin from within her own context. She must recognize that all philosophy is engaged, is committed to a definite presuppositional stance, and she must have the Christian courage to follow through on her own engagement.

I find this story compelling for a number of reasons. It describes the hermeneutical [i.e., interpretive–Eds.] process of my own philosophical development in a simple and direct manner. It speaks to me as a religious person who loves philosophy and who is schooled within contemporary philosophical parameters. Moreover, it recognizes the philosophical voice of women.

The hermeneutical process depicted by this story is one that can be called a "hermeneutic of transformation." . . . It is a [hermeneutical] process that uncovers and critiques the presuppositions of our fundamental interpretive stances. It then provides us with a transformed framework for further interpreting our basic experiences and texts. This hermeneutical process involves four steps or stages.

(1) Contemporary philosophical hermeneutics has shown us that all understanding is engaged and has a presuppositional structure. Entering into any specific discipline or role requires that we take on certain presuppositions, that we become engaged in certain ways.

Usually we do not reflect on those presuppositions. We learn them as part of standing within a particular role or discipline. We do this from at least the time we begin to learn language. We learn to speak and conceptualize in a particular language long before we ever reflect on the implications of the structure of that language. Indeed, a person can speak a language for all of her or his life and never reflect on the structure of the language.

(2) Sometimes, as was the case with the young philosopher in Plantinga's account, something from our experience leads us to sense a tension between the commitments in one area of our life and those in another area, . . . for example in our religious life, make us suspicious of our commitments in another area, for example in our philosophical activity. Often it is the experience of exclusion or of trivialization of something that our experience tells us is important that leads us to our suspicions. . . . This has certainly been the case for the Christian in contemporary philosophy. The experience of the importance of spiritual life or religious community has led us to be suspicious of any philosophy that excludes these.

(3) The first response to our suspicions is usually to try to harmonize the commitments that we experience in tension. Our understanding changes and we ask for changes in the discipline or role, but we try not to abandon the presuppositions, the engagements, of the areas that are in tension. . . .

(4) While in some cases it may be possible to retain two sets of presuppositions, harmonizing them to eliminate the tensions, in many cases the suspicion raised leads us to reject certain presuppositions and so to transform a discipline or role. Plantinga advises us to listen to our experience as Christians and to be bold enough to philosophize out of that experience rather than to try to accommodate our thought to the parameters of others. Indeed, he advises us that we need not be concerned with trying to convince these others of the legitimacy or importance of our presuppositional structure. We are to do philosophy as Christians. We might say that he suggests that transformation takes place through action. . . .

If we recognize this hermeneutical process as one that we have gone through in our experience as Christians and as philosophers, then we must also recognize the importance of examining the presuppositional structure of our present philosophical engagement. We must listen to the voices of those who, while sharing our Christian commitments, raise suspicions about the nature of our presuppositional structure. It is the voices of women I would urge us to hear today: women who stand commitedly within the Christian community and within the philosophical community, women who raise suspicions out of the experience of lack of agency (exclusion) and silencing (trivialization), and women who speak out of their own experiences of what it means to be bold.

Their suspicion is that patriarchy is deeply embedded in the presuppositional structure of Christianity and so also of any philosophy that accepts unquestioningly this presuppositional structure. Their task, if they are to take Plantinga seriously, is to do Christian philosophy while rejecting patriarchy—to do feminist Christian philosophy. Those who make this attempt are cautioned as to its impossibility by two groups, both claiming that Christianity cannot abandon the presupposition of patriarchy. One group shares the experience of being a woman in a Christian society. They say: Abandon the Christian community. As long as you stay within it you are subject to tyranny and will succumb to patriarchy. This is like the advice that most of us have probably received that we should abandon philosophy so as not to destroy our faith. Others, who share the commitment to Christianity, say that God has ordained patriarchal presuppositions. To be Christian requires the acceptance of those presuppositions. This is not unlike the advice to leave our faith behind when we do philosophy. I would like to repeat Plantinga's advice and suggest that we have integrity and be bold. Let us do feminist Christian philosophy.

I want to suggest some of what this may mean for how we, as Christians, are to view ourselves, name and symbolize the sacred, and conceptualize the work of God in the world.

VISIBILITY, VOICE, AND THE DISCIPLESHIP OF EQUALS

We are aware of gendered language and the way that such language has served to render women invisible. Since experience is so important to the hermeneutic process that I am following, it is still important to remind us of that experience. I grew up speaking the language "properly" using "man" and "he" as generic words. Like most women in our society, I became quite competent at hermeneutics, the art of interpretation, before I had any idea as to what the art was. I learned when these words meant male only and when they included me, and I became quite skilled in these interpretive moves. Like the young philosopher, I was so involved in the joy of what I was learning that I did not experience tensions. An awareness of those tensions came upon me slowly. But I still remember the day that I really understood how this language rendered women invisible. I was with colleagues (all male—and all reasonable people) and we were discussing our curriculum in relation to students' future needs. The pronouns were all male, and the word "guy" occurred frequently. As I listened to my colleagues, it hit me that even though half of their students were women, they really saw only the men. Their language revealed women as invisible.

Women also experience themselves as silenced. In the history of the Christian church, women have been told that their role is to be silent, at least about issues of any theological or social importance. If they do have something to say, it is better to have it spoken by a man. The male voice lends authority. While we may dismiss these ideas as part of the distant past, the experience of women today is often one of being silenced. Recent studies still indicate that women are often not heard. When an idea, already voiced by a

woman, is put forward by a male voice, it becomes viewed as significant.

Other studies confirm this experience.[2] They show that children learn parameters from the language of their culture. Girls quickly come to exclude certain possibilities from their futures when the words and images they have for these possibilities are males. . . . Women [often] experience themselves as silent beings. And so I would urge you to listen to the voices of women who reflect on their experience of invisibility and silence and who develop in their Christian faith a critique of patriarchy that challenges us to rethink our anthropology. Elizabeth Schüssler Fiorenza is one of these voices.[3]

Fiorenza recognizes that women experience invisibility and silence within Christianity, but she also maintains that women find positive experiences within biblical religion; there is a source of strength and boldness. . . . In order to do the reconceptualization necessary to address this oppression, she sets out a feminist critical hermeneutics that stresses the importance of identifying, acknowledging, and taking responsibility for our theoretical presuppositions. This activity is particularly important as we reflect on the Jesus tradition and scriptures. While her work is primarily theological, it is important to our work as philosophers because it examines and critiques the biblical and theological presuppositions that often go unexamined in our work. . . .

One presupposition that many readings of the Jesus movement perpetuate is that women were excluded from the new community that Jesus formed. The image of the disciples is of a band of itinerant men who had left family (including wives) and home behind them to live a radical ethos . . . that those left at home did not live. This radical ethos is identified especially by the abandonment of traditional family relations. . . . Fiorenza concludes that it is clear that Jesus did not respect patriarchal family bonds. Moreover, it would be a misreading "to claim that such a radical a-familial ethos is asked only of the male wandering charismatics" (p. 146) and not also of female disciples.

Fiorenza takes a further step in the interpretation that Jesus advocated a community of equal discipleship by looking at those texts where Jesus discusses the constitution of his true family. These texts (Mark 10:29–30 and 3:31–35) mention brothers, sisters, and mothers, but no fathers. . . . She concludes: "The discipleship community abolishes the claims of the patriarchal family and constitutes a new familial community, one that does not include fathers in its circle" (p. 147).

Certainly this does not mean that men who participated in the procreation of children were not part of the community. But that the word "father" is not used is significant. . . . The term "father" is not to be used to justify patriarchal relationships in the community. Reserving the term for God is intended "precisely to reject all such claims, powers, and structures" (p. 150). "Thus liberation from patriarchal structures is not only explicitly articulated by Jesus but is in fact at the heart of proclamation" (p. 151).

From her work Fiorenza proposes to draw strength for women in overcoming sexism and prejudice, especially that encountered within religion. But there are equally important implications to be drawn for Christian philosophy. If we acknowledge our roots in biblical tradition as important presuppositions to our work, then we must also acknowledge as part of our anthropological and political commitments the community of equality and the overcoming of patriarchy. More particularly, we must be committed to the visibility of women as women and be bold enough to follow out the implications of that commitment. If the name "Father" was to be reserved for God, but has been usurped by men within the family and within the church to perpetuate patriarchal structure, then how do we name God? . . .

MATERNAL WORK, MATERNAL THINKING, AND MOTHER-GOD

In the context of this paper, I can neither set out nor develop all of the implications of incorporating the image of Mother-God into Christian symbolism and thus into the presuppositions of Christian philosophy arising out of the image of Mother-God. Since most of those working in Christian philosophy are men, many of whom identify with the name "father," I wish to stress that these suggestions are not intended to set mother against father. They are intended to lead to further reflection on the implications of including the image of mother.

There are many feminist philosophers who are reflecting on the epistemological and ethical implications of the work of mothering. These reflections come from a wide range of feminist perspectives. Sara Ruddick's recent book, *Maternal Thinking*,[4] is not particularly aimed at the Christian community and does not discuss the issue of God language. I will, however, present aspects of her work showing how these contribute to the discussion of what it means to speak of Mother-God.

Ruddick begins her analysis from the perspective that she terms "practicalism." She explains: "From the practicalist view, thinking arises from and is tested against practices. Practices are collective human activities distinguished by the aims that identify them and by the consequent demands made on practitioners committed to those aims" (pp. 13–14). It is from within the context of our practice that we raise questions, judge these questions to be sensible, determine criteria of truth and falsity, and determine what will count as evidence. In other words, practice and thinking are radically interconnected. Her contention is that the maternal practice gives rise to maternal thinking. She acknowledges that mothers as individuals are diverse and shaped by many practices. She focuses on the demands that all mothers must face and the disciplined reflection that arises out of the attempts to meet those demands. She . . . does not restrict the activity of mothering to women. Men also perform maternal labor. She does think that mothering is far more often the work of women than of men [and] that we should be careful not to gloss over the labor of carrying and giving birth which only women do. In order not to conceal women's role she emphasizes the importance of retaining the word "maternal" rather than using "parental."

I find her work helpful to the task of thinking about the image of Mother-God. If God is our mother, then we are imaging Mother-God as carrying out certain practices and as thinking in ways similar to humans who carry out these practices.

She suggests that maternal practice is founded on giving birth. . . . Ruddick identifies three demands that all mothers face that are correlated with three sorts of maternal practice. The demands are for preservation, growth, and social acceptability. The work required is that of preservative love, nurturance, and training. Ruddick does not idealize the role of mother in her analysis. She uses stories that emphasize that the practice of mothering is a struggle, sometimes even a struggle against our own violence. Yet, she believes that out of this practice and struggle certain cognitive capacities can and do arise. Reflecting on these helps us better to understand what it means to be a mother.

The first demand, that for preservation, requires the mother to develop "cognitive capacities and virtues of protective control" (p. 71). One capacity that mothers often develop is what Ruddick calls the scrutinizing gaze. Children must be watched, but not watched too closely. It is not that mothers relinquish control. They come to think about it differently. Often because of desire to resort either to domination or passivity, mothers can come to recognize the patience required in order to exhibit appropriate control. If children are to survive they must be protected, and yet they must learn to deal with their world, both social and natural. The practice of mothering tends to lead to the development of an ability to identify danger and to deal with it, not always by eliminating that danger, but by helping the child to deal with the danger. Sometimes that means helping the child to die.

Christian philosophers may be able to use this notion of the scrutinizing gaze of Mother-God in reflections on theodicy [i.e., the religious understanding of evil and suffering—Eds.]. If the preservative love of Mother-God is of this sort, then we should not be expected to be protected from all evil. On the other hand, we should expect a hopeful and supportive presence to help us face and cope with our lives. If God's power is not so much that of total control as of helping us deal with the real dangers of our existence, then the concern of theodicy may be to show how a caring Mother-God helps us to confront and cope with the real dangers and griefs of our lives. The expectation is not that Mother-God will prevent all evil. Rather, the power of Mother-God is to help us preserve ourselves so that we may grow and flourish. I am not suggesting that this image will solve the problems of reconciling a good God with the existence of evil. Like human mothers, Mother-God may be experienced as destructive rather than preservative. That the image contributes to the complexity of the issue should not count against its significance.

The second demand that Ruddick identifies is for growth. This demand results in the development of ways of thinking that help the mother and child grow and change. Ruddick identifies storytelling as one of these cognitive practices. . . . To tell a child a story is to help that child incorporate change into an ongoing unity. It is to help the child and the mother to share a history.

Thinking of Mother-God as storyteller seems very compatible with the image of God as presented in Christian scriptures and traditions. The stories presented there tell of a *Heilsgeschichte*, a history of the presence and activity of the divine in and with human history. The notion of Mother-God can augment this tradition. The contribution of this aspect of maternal work to Christian philosophy may be to direct us to focus more on narrative and the use of narrative in legitimating philosophical as well as religious presuppositions.

The third demand, that for social acceptance, requires the work of training. Ruddick describes training as a work of conscience. The work of training is to help "a child to be the kind of person whom others can accept and whom the mothers themselves can actively appreciate" (p. 104). Again, mothers must struggle against the tendency to dominate. There are many pressures placed on mothers, many of whom are quite young, to have well-behaved children. I remember well the pressure on me to toilet train my son. One person claimed that all of her children were trained by nine months—so mine should be too. A mother is pushed to examine her own conscience as she tries to give guidance to her children. Perhaps the child could be trained at nine months, but what sort of power would that require and what sort of relation would it establish? The work of training requires the mother to trust herself and to be sensitive to the spirit of her child. Ruddick suggests that when this practice is developed at its best, mother becomes more trustworthy so that the child can be trustworthy. Moreover, the child comes to recognize that when trust breaks down, as it inevitably does, it is proper to protest.

If Mother-God is our trainer, our guide in coming to conscience, then she is one who is our help in the ongoing struggle to develop our human goodness and trust. We look to her not as a source of all answers or as a dominating rule to be obeyed. She is a help, a guide, a refuge. She recognizes that the work of conscience is a struggle, ongoing and often difficult. . . .

. . . Reflecting on how human parents change when they both trust and are trusted by their children could contribute to the process claim that God is, at least in one respect, changing. Such reflection could also provide a way of understanding God as both changing and unchanging. The mothering person may be very trustworthy to begin with, but in concretely exhibiting that characteristic, by being self-reflective about trustworthiness, and by being trusted by a child, may be said to be more trustworthy. So also, Mother-God might be said to be trustworthy and yet to become more trustworthy in the process of divine-human rela-

tionships. Indeed, the image of Mother-God may be better received by process theology than by other forms of Christian theology because process thought is already inclined to be open to changing images of God as well as to a changing God.

CONCLUSION

There is much more work going on in feminist religious and philosophical thought. Most of it remains to be incorporated into the work of Christian philosophy. What I have touched on in this paper only gives some suggestions for a beginning. In Alvin Plantinga's advice, with which I began, he warned us to be "wary about assimilating or accepting presently popular philosophical ideas and procedures" (p. 271). Some of you may be wary of developing feminist Christian philosophy, thinking that you are assimilating that which comes from outside the tradition. I have chosen to look primarily at thinkers who show us the basis of feminist work from within the Christian tradition. Reflecting on their work leads me to conclude that the autonomy, integrity, and boldness that Plantinga called for is advanced by the work of feminists. In particular, the integration of the name "Mother" for the sacred may help us relate to God in ways that enable us to develop these very virtues and thereby strengthen Christian philosophy.

Notes

1. Plantinga, Alvin. "Advice to Christian Philosophers," *Faith and Philosophy*, volume 1, number 3 (1984), pp. 253–271.
2. Vetterling-Braggin, Mary. *Sexist Language* (New York: Littlefield, Adams, 1981); and Baron, Dennis. *Grammar and Gender* (New Haven: Yale University Press, 1986).
3. Fiorenza, Elizabeth Schüssler. *In Memory of Her. A Feminist Theological Reconstruction of Christian Origins* (New York: Crossroad, 1989).
4. Ruddick, Sara. *Maternal Thinking: Toward a Politics of Peace* (Boston: Beacon, 1989).

The Evils of Christianity

Bertrand Russell

Bertrand Russell (1872–1970) was among the twentieth century's most influential philosophers. His grandfather served twice as prime minister of Britain, and he and his family were close friends of John Stuart Mill, who served as a sort of godparent to Russell. He studied and later taught at Trinity College, Cambridge. One of his students was another of the century's greatest philosophers, Ludwig Wittgenstein. World War I had a huge impact on Russell's thinking. His objection to the war and his pacifism resulted in his losing his job and being fined by the government. When he refused to pay the fine, the government confiscated and sold his books. Russell had no teaching position from 1916 until the late 1930s, when he came to the United States to teach. He then taught at the University of Chicago and UCLA but was refused a position at the City University of New York for his views on religion, sex, and marriage. He was later given another position at Cambridge and in 1942 won the Nobel Prize for Literature. Russell pressed for social change throughout his life, becoming active in the antinuclear and anti–Vietnam War movements. Russell had a profound faith in reason. With A. N. Whitehead he did groundbreaking work in the foundation of mathematics and logic in *Principia Mathematica* (3 volumes, 1910–1913).

Besides his free thinking about sex and marriage, Russell also actively opposed religion and especially Christianity. In this essay, Russell explains the defects in the moral teaching of Jesus, the disastrous effect the Christian religion has had historically, and the psychological weakness that leads people to want to be religious in the first place.

As you read through this essay, consider the following:

1. What is it about Christ's character that Russell approves?
2. Which of Christ's teachings does Russell reject, and why?
3. What is the real reason people are religious, according to Russell?
4. In what ways has the Christian Church retarded progress?

THE CHARACTER OF CHRIST

I now want to say a few words upon a topic which I often think is not quite sufficiently dealt with by Rationalists, and that is the question whether Christ was the best and the wisest of men. It is generally taken for granted that we should all agree that that was so. I do not myself. I think that there are a good many points upon which I agree with

Christ a great deal more than the professing Christians do. I do not know that I could go with Him all the way, but I could go with Him much further than most professing Christians can. You will remember that He said, "Resist not evil: but whosoever shall smite thee on thy right cheek, turn to him the other also." That is not a new precept or a new principle. It was used by Lao-tse and Buddha some 500 or 600 years before Christ, but it is not a principle which as a matter of fact Christians accept. I have no doubt that the present Prime Minister,* for instance, is a

*Stanley Baldwin.

most sincere Christian, but I should not advise any of you to go and smite him on one cheek. I think you might find that he thought this text was intended in a figurative sense.

Then there is another point which I consider excellent. You will remember that Christ said, "Judge not lest ye be judged." That principle I do not think you would find was popular in the law courts of Christian countries. I have known in my time quite a number of judges who were very earnest Christians, and none of them felt that they were acting contrary to Christian principles in what they did. Then Christ says, "Give to him that asketh of thee, and from him that would borrow of thee turn not thou away." That is a very good principle. Your Chairman has reminded you that we are not here to talk politics, but I cannot help observing that the last general election was fought on the question of how desirable it was to turn away from him that would borrow of thee, so that one must assume that the Liberals and Conservatives of this country are composed of people who do not agree with the teaching of Christ, because they certainly did very emphatically turn away on that occasion.

Then there is one other maxim of Christ which I think has a great deal in it, but I do not find that it is very popular among some of our Christian friends. He says, "If thou wilt be perfect, go and sell that which thou hast, and give to the poor." That is a very excellent maxim, but as I say, it is not much practiced. All these, I think, are good maxims, although they are a little difficult to live up to. I do not profess to live up to them myself; but then, after all, it is not quite the same thing as for a Christian.

DEFECTS IN CHRIST'S TEACHING

Having granted the excellence of these maxims, I come to certain points in which I do not believe that one can grant either the superlative wisdom or the superlative goodness of Christ as depicted in the Gospels; and here I may say that one is not concerned with the historical question. Historically it is quite doubtful whether Christ ever existed at all, and if He did we do not know anything about Him, so that I am not concerned with the historical question, which is a very difficult one. I am concerned with Christ as He appears in the Gospels, taking the Gospel narrative as it stands, and there one does find some things that do not seem to be very wise. For one thing, He certainly thought that His second coming would occur in clouds of glory before the death of all the people who were living at that time. There are a great many texts that prove that. He says, for instance, "Ye shall not have gone over the cities of Israel till the Son of Man be come." Then He says, "There are some standing here which shall not taste death till the Son of Man comes into His Kingdom"; and there are a lot of places where it is quite clear that He believed that His second coming would happen during the lifetime of many then living. That was the belief of His earlier followers, and it was the basis of a good deal of His moral teaching. When He said, "Take no thought for the morrow," and things of that sort, it was very largely because He thought that the second coming was going to be very soon, and that all ordinary mundane affairs did not count. I have, as a matter of fact, known some Christians who did believe that the second coming was imminent. I knew a person who frightened his congregation terribly by telling them that the second coming was very imminent indeed, but they were much consoled when they found that he was planting trees in his garden. The early Christians did really believe it, and they did abstain from such things as planting trees in their gardens, because they did accept from Christ the belief that the second coming was imminent. In that respect, clearly He was not so wise as some other people have been, and He was certainly not superlatively wise.

THE MORAL PROBLEM

Then you come to moral questions. There is one very serious defect to my mind in Christ's moral character, and that is that He believed in hell. I do not myself feel that any person who is really profoundly humane can believe in everlasting punishment. Christ certainly as depicted in the Gospels did believe in everlasting punishment, and one does find repeatedly a vindictive fury against those people who would not listen to His preaching—an attitude which is not uncommon with preachers, but which does somewhat detract from superlative excellence. You do not, for instance, find that attitude in Socrates. You find him quite bland and urbane toward the people who would not listen to him; and it is, to my mind, far more worthy of a sage to take that line than to take the line of indignation. You probably all remember the sort of things that Socrates was saying when he was dying, and the sort of things that he generally did say to people who did not agree with him.

You will find that in the Gospels Christ said, "Ye serpents, ye generation of vipers, how can ye escape the damnation of hell." That was said to people who did not like His preaching. It is not really to my mind quite the best tone, and there are a great many of these things about hell. There is, of course, the familiar text about the sin against the Holy Ghost: "Whosoever speaketh against the Holy Ghost it shall not be forgiven him neither in this World nor in the world to come." That text has caused an unspeakable amount of misery in the world, for all sorts of people have imagined that they have committed the sin against the Holy Ghost, and thought that it would not be forgiven them either in this world or in the world to come. I really do not think that a person with a proper degree of kindliness in his nature would have put fears and terrors of that sort in the world.

Then Christ says, "The Son of Man shall send forth His angels, and they shall gather out of His kingdom all things that offend, and them which do iniquity, and shall cast them into a furnace of fire; there shall be wailing and gnashing of teeth"; and He goes on about the wailing and gnashing of teeth. It comes in one verse after another, and it is quite manifest to the reader that there is a certain pleasure in contemplating wailing and gnashing

of teeth, or else it would not occur so often. Then you all, of course, remember about the sheep and the goats; how at the second coming He is going to divide the sheep from the goats, and He is going to say to the goats, "Depart from me, ye cursed, into everlasting fire." He continues, "And these shall go away into everlasting fire." Then He says again, "If thy hand offend thee, cut it off; it is better for thee to enter into life maimed, than having two hands to go into hell, into the fire that never shall be quenched; where the worm dieth not and the fire is not quenched." He repeats that again and again also. I must say that I think all this doctrine, that hell-fire is a punishment for sin, is a doctrine of cruelty. It is a doctrine that put cruelty into the world and gave the world generations of cruel torture: and the Christ of the Gospels, if you could take Him as His chroniclers represent Him, would certainly have to be considered partly responsible for that.

There are other things of less importance. There is the instance of the Gadarene swine, where it certainly was not very kind to the pigs to put devils into them and make them rush down the hill to the sea. You must remember that He was omnipotent, and He could have made the devils simply go away; but He chose to send them into the pigs. Then there is the curious story of the fig tree, which always rather puzzled me. You remember what happened about the fig tree. "He was hungry; and seeing a fig tree afar off having leaves, He came if haply He might find anything thereon; and when He came to it He found nothing but leaves, for the time of figs was not yet. And Jesus answered and said unto it: 'No man eat fruit of thee hereafter for ever' . . . and Peter . . . saith unto Him: 'Master, behold the fig tree which thou cursedst is withered away.'" This is a very curious story, because it was not the right time of year for figs, and you really could not blame the tree. I cannot myself feel that either in the matter of wisdom or in the matter of virtue Christ stands quite as high as some other people known to history. I think I should put Buddha and Socrates above Him in those respects.

THE EMOTIONAL FACTOR

As I said before, I do not think that the real reason why people accept religion has anything to do with argumentation. They accept religion on emotional grounds. One is often told that it is a very wrong thing to attack religion, because religion makes men virtuous. So I am told; I have not noticed it. You know, of course, the parody of that argument in Samuel Butler's book, *Erewhon Revisited*. You will remember that in *Erewhon* there is a certain Higgs who arrives in a remote country, and after spending some time there he escapes from that country in a balloon. Twenty years later he comes back to that country and finds a new religion in which he is worshiped under the name of the "Sun Child," and it is said that he ascended into heaven. He finds that the Feast of the Ascension is about to be celebrated, and he hears Professors Hanky and Panky say to each other that they never set eyes on the man Higgs, and they hope they never will; but they are the high priests of the religion of the Sun Child. He is very indignant, and he comes up to them, and he says, "I am going to expose all this humbug and tell the people of Erewhon that it was only I, the man Higgs, and I went up in a balloon." He was told, "You must not do that, because all the morals of this country are bound round this myth, and if they once know that you did not ascend into heaven they will all become wicked"; and so he is persuaded of that and he goes quietly away.

That is the idea—that we should all be wicked if we did not hold to the Christian religion. It seems to me that the people who have held to it have been for the most part extremely wicked. You find this curious fact, that the more intense has been the religion of any period and the more profound has been the dogmatic belief, the greater has been the cruelty and the worse has been the state of affairs. In the so-called ages of faith, when men really did believe the Christian religion in all its completeness, there was the Inquisition, with its tortures; there were millions of unfortunate women burned as witches; and there was every kind of cruelty practiced upon all sorts of people in the name of religion.

You find as you look around the world that every single bit of progress in humane feeling, every improvement in the criminal law, every step toward the diminution of war, every step toward better treatment of the colored races, or every mitigation of slavery, every moral progress that there has been in the world, has been consistently opposed by the organized churches of the world. I say quite deliberately that the Christian religion, as organized in its churches, has been and still is the principal enemy of moral progress in the world.

HOW THE CHURCHES HAVE RETARDED PROGRESS

You may think that I am going too far when I say that that is still so. I do not think that I am. Take one fact. You will bear with me if I mention it. It is not a pleasant fact, but the churches compel one to mention facts that are not pleasant. Supposing that in this world that we live in today an inexperienced girl is married to a syphilitic man; in that case the Catholic Church says, "This is an indissoluble sacrament. You must endure celibacy or stay together. And if you stay together, you must not use birth control to prevent the birth of syphilitic children." Nobody whose natural sympathies have not been warped by dogma, or whose moral nature was not absolutely dead to all sense of suffering, could maintain that it is right and proper that that state of things should continue.

That is only an example. There are a great many ways in which, at the present moment, the church, by its insistence upon what it chooses to call morality, inflicts upon all sorts of people undeserved and unnecessary suffering. And of course, as we know, it is in its major part an opponent still of progress and of improvement in all the ways that diminish suffering in the world, because it has chosen to label as morality a certain narrow set of rules of conduct which have nothing to do with human happiness; and when you say that this or that ought to be done because it would make for human happiness, they think that has nothing to do with the matter at all. "What has human happiness to do with morals? The object of morals is not to make people happy."

FEAR, THE FOUNDATION OF RELIGION

Religion is based, I think, primarily and mainly upon fear. It is partly the terror of the unknown and partly, as I have said, the wish to feel that you have a kind of elder brother who will stand by you in all your troubles and disputes. Fear is the basis of the whole thing—fear of the mysterious, fear of defeat, fear of death. Fear is the parent of cruelty, and therefore it is no wonder if cruelty and religion have gone hand in hand. It is because fear is the basis of those two things. In this world we can now begin a little to understand things, and a little to master them by help of science, which has forced its way step by step against the Christian religion, against the churches, and against the opposition of all the old precepts. Science can help us to get over this craven fear in which mankind has lived for so many generations. Science can teach us, and I think our own hearts can teach us, no longer to look around for imaginary supports, no longer to invent allies in the sky, but rather to look to our own efforts here below

to make this world a fit place to live in, instead of the sort of place that the churches in all these centuries have made it.

WHAT WE MUST DO

We want to stand upon our own feet and look fair and square at the world—its good facts, its bad facts, its beauties, and its ugliness; see the world as it is and be not afraid of it. Conquer the world by intelligence and not merely by being slavishly subdued by the terror that comes from it. The whole conception of God is a conception derived from the ancient Oriental despotisms. It is a conception quite unworthy of free men. When you hear people in church debasing themselves and saying that they are miserable sinners, and all the rest of it, it seems contemptible and not worthy of self-respecting human beings. We ought to stand up and look the world frankly in the face. We ought to make the best we can of the world, and if it is not so good as we wish, after all it will still be better than what these others have made it in all these ages. A good world needs knowledge, kindliness, and courage; it does not need a regretful hankering after the past or fettering of the free intelligence by the words uttered long ago by ignorant men. It needs a fearless outlook and a free intelligence. It needs hope for the future, not looking back all the time toward a past that is dead, which we trust will be far surpassed by the future that our intelligence can create.

The Future of an Illusion

Sigmund Freud

Sigmund Freud was among the towering thinkers of the nineteenth century. He is credited with developing psychoanalysis and was perhaps the most important theorist of the unconscious. In his book *The Future of an Illusion,* Freud situates religion in the context of human psychology and history. His main concern is to understand religion's role in human life and whether its continuation is justified. Civilization, he argues, has allowed human beings to rise above animals by providing us with the knowledge needed to control an often cruel and always indifferent nature and with regulations governing human relationships. People are by nature ruled by passions and are often selfish and inclined to violence. These instincts must be controlled if civilization is to progress, which means people must largely "internalize" a whole variety of self-controls. Living in a civilized society is therefore frustrating to our natural instincts, yet it is also essential if we are to be protected from the ravages of nature and our fellow humans. Religion aids in this by exorcising the terrors of nature such as diseases and natural disasters, reconciling people to their fate (and death), and compensating for the frustrations imposed by civilization. Religion accomplishes this in many ways, including teaching that the laws of nature are in reality divine laws and that we will be rewarded in heaven even if we suffer and die on earth and reinforcing morality with divine authority. But religion is an "illusion": it cannot be proved true or false (only science is capable of that), and its origin is in human wishes and desires.

> *As you read through this essay, consider the following:*
>
> 1. What is Freud's picture of human nature and of the human condition and its problems?
> 2. What is civilization, and how does it help in addressing the problems humans face?
> 3. How does religion figure in Freud's conception of the role of civilization?
> 4. Is this a critique of religion, or a defense of it?

We have spoken of the hostility to civilization which is produced by the pressure that civilization exercises, the renunciations of instinct which it demands. If one imagines its prohibitions lifted—if, then, one may take any woman one pleases as a sexual object, if one may without hesitation kill one's rival for her love or anyone else who stands in one's way, if, too, one can carry off any of the other man's belongings without asking leave—how splendid, what a string of satisfactions one's life would be! True, one soon comes across the first difficulty: everyone else has exactly the same wishes as I have and will treat me with no more consideration than I treat him. And so in reality only one person could be made unrestrictedly happy by such a removal of the restrictions of civilization, and he would be a tyrant, a dictator, who had seized all the means to power. And even he would have every reason to wish that the others would observe at least one cultural commandment: 'thou shalt not kill'.

But how ungrateful, how short-sighted after all, to strive for the abolition of civilization! What would then remain would be a state of nature, and that would be far harder to bear. It is true that nature would not demand any restrictions of instinct from us,

From Sigmund Freud, *The Future of an Illusion,* tr. William Robson-Scott (1928).

she would let us do as we liked; but she has her own particularly effective method of restricting us. She destroys us—coldly, cruelly, relentlessly, as it seems to us, and possibly through the very things that occasioned our satisfaction. It was precisely because of these dangers with which nature threatens us that we came together and created civilization, which is also, among other things, intended to make our communal life possible. For the principal task of civilization, its actual *raison d'etre* is to defend us against nature.

We all know that in many ways civilization does this fairly well already, and clearly as time goes on it will do it much better. But no one is under the illusion that nature has already been vanquished; and few dare hope that she will ever be entirely subjected to man. There are the elements, which seem to mock at all human control: the earth, which quakes and is torn apart and buries all human life and its works; water, which deluges and drowns everything in a turmoil; storms which blow everything before them; there are diseases, which we have only recently recognized as attacks by other organisms; and, finally there is the painful riddle of death, against which no medicine has yet been found, nor probably will be. With these forces nature rises up against us, majestic, cruel and inexorable; she brings to our mind once more our weakness and helplessness, which we thought to escape through the work of civilization. One of the few gratifying and exalting impressions which mankind can offer is when, in the face of an elemental catastrophe, it forgets the discordancies of its civilization and all its internal difficulties and animosities, and recalls the great common task of preserving itself against the superior power of nature.

For the individual, too, life is hard to bear, just as it is for mankind in general. The civilization in which he participates imposes some amount of privation on him, and other men bring him a measure of suffering, either in spite of the precepts of his civilization or because of its imperfections. To this are added the injuries which untamed nature—he calls it Fate—inflicts on him. One might suppose that this condition of things would result in a permanent state of anxious expectation in him and a severe injury to his natural narcissism. We know already how the individual reacts to the injuries which civilization and other men inflict on him: he develops a corresponding degree of resistance to the regulations of civilization and of hostility to it. But how does he defend himself against the superior powers of nature, of Fate, which threaten him as they threaten all the rest?

Civilization relieves him of this task, it performs it in the same way for all alike; and it is noteworthy that in this almost all civilizations act alike. Civilization does not call a halt in the task of defending man against nature, it merely pursues it by other means. The task is a manifold one. Man's self-regard, seriously menaced, calls for consolation; life and the universe must be robbed of their terrors; moreover his curiosity, moved, it is true, by the strongest practical interest, demands an answer.

A great deal is already gained with the first step: the humanization of nature. Impersonal forces and destinies cannot be approached; they remain eternally remote. But if the elements have passions that rage as they do in our own souls, if death itself is not something spontaneous but the violent act of an evil Will, if everywhere in nature there are Beings around us of a kind that we know in our own society, then we can breathe freely, can feel at home in the uncanny and can deal by psychical means with our senseless anxiety. We are still defenceless perhaps, but we are no longer helplessly paralyzed; we can at least react. Perhaps, indeed, we are not even defenceless. We can apply the same methods against these violent supermen outside that we employ in our own society; we can try to adjure them, to appease them, to bribe them, and, by so influencing them, we may rob them of a part of their power. A replacement like this of natural science by psychology not only provides immediate relief, but also points the way to a further mastering of the situation.

For this situation is nothing new. It has an infantile prototype, of which it is in fact only the continuation. For once before one has found oneself in a similar state of helplessness: as a small child, in relation to one's parents. One had reason to fear them, and especially one's father, and yet one was sure of his protection against the dangers one knew. Thus it was natural to assimilate the two situations. Here, too, wishing played its part, as it does in dream-life. The sleeper may be seized with a presentiment of death, which threatens to place him in the grave. But the dream-work knows how to select a condition that will turn even that dreaded event into a wish-fulfillment. . . . In the same way, a man makes the forces of nature not simply into persons with whom he can associate as he would with his equals—that would not do justice to the overpowering impression which those forces make on him—but he gives them the character of a father. He turns them into gods, following in this, as I have tried to show, not only an infantile prototype but a phylogenetic one.

In the course of time the first observations were made of regularity and conformity to law in natural phenomena, and with this the forces of nature lost their human traits. But man's helplessness remains and along with it his longing for his father, and the gods. The gods retain their threefold task: they must exorcise the terrors of nature, they must reconcile men to the cruelty of Fate, particularly as it is shown in death, and they must compensate them for the sufferings and privations which a civilized life in common has imposed on them.

But within these functions there is a gradual displacement of accent. It was observed that the phenomena of nature developed automatically according to internal necessities. Without doubt the gods were the lords of nature; they had arranged it to be as it was and now they could leave it to itself. Only occasionally, in what are known as miracles, did they intervene in its course, as though to make it plain that they had relinquished nothing of their original sphere of power. As regards the apportioning of destinies, an unpleasant suspicion persisted that the perplexity and helplessness of the human

race could not be remedied. It was here that the gods were most apt to fail. If they themselves created Fate, then their counsels must be deemed inscrutable. The notion dawned on the most gifted people of antiquity that Moira (Fate) stood above the gods and that the gods themselves had their own destinies. And the more autonomous nature became and the more the gods withdrew from it, the more earnestly were all expectations directed to the third function of the gods—the more did morality become their true domain. It now became the task of the gods to even out the defects and evils of civilization, to attend to the sufferings which men inflict on one another in their life together and to watch over the fulfillment of the precepts of civilization, which men obey so imperfectly. Those precepts themselves were credited with a divine origin; they were elevated beyond human society and were extended to nature and the universe.

And thus a store of ideas is created, born from man's need to make his helplessness tolerable and built up from the material of memories of the helplessness of his own childhood and the childhood of the human race. It can clearly be seen that the possession of these ideas protects him in two directions—against the dangers of nature and Fate, and against the injuries that threaten him from human society itself. Here is the gist of the matter. Life in this world serves a higher purpose; no doubt it is not easy to guess what that purpose is, but it certainly signifies a perfecting of man's nature. It is probably the spiritual part of man, the soul, which in the course of time has so slowly and unwillingly detached itself from the body, that is the object of this elevation and exaltation. Everything that happens in this world is an expression of the intentions of an intelligence superior to us, which in the end, though its ways and byways are difficult to follow, orders everything for the best—that is, to make it enjoyable for us. Over each one of us there watches a benevolent Providence which is only seemingly stern and which will not suffer us to become a plaything of the over-mighty and pitiless forces of nature. Death itself is not extinction, is not a return to inorganic lifelessness, but the beginning of a new kind of existence which lies on the path of development to something higher. And, looking in the other direction, this view announces that the same moral laws which our civilizations have set up govern the whole universe as well, except that they are maintained by a supreme court of justice with incomparably more power and consistency. In the end all good is rewarded and all evil punished, if not actually in this form of life then in the later existences that begin after death. In this way all the terrors, the sufferings and the hardships of life are destined to be obliterated. Life after death, which continues life on earth just as the invisible part of the spectrum joins on to the visible part, brings us all the perfection that we may perhaps have missed here. And the superior wisdom which directs this course of things, the infinite goodness that expresses itself in it, the justice that achieves its aim in it—these are the attributes of the divine beings who also created us and the world as a whole, or rather, of the one divine being into which, in our civilization, all the gods of antiquity have been condensed. . . .

Section 23

Religion and Education

Should Creationism Be Taught in Public Schools?

Robert T. Pennock

Given wide differences of opinion about religion, along with the importance of religious education to parents, it is not at all surprising that controversy abounds when educational and religious issues are mixed. Some religious people have no trouble accepting evolutionary theory, believing that God created humans through the biological processes of natural selection. Others disagree with teaching evolutionary theory, arguing that evolution is only a "theory" and that "creation science" should be taught side by side with evolution. In this essay, Robert T. Pennock discusses various aspects of this topic, including the core claims of creationists, how the courts have handled the issues, the central issues about the truth of creationism versus evolutionary theory, the charge that excluding creationism is a form of discrimination, and, finally, the aims of science education. Robert T. Pennock is professor of philosophy at Michigan State University.

As you read through this essay, consider the following:

1. How does Pennock describe creationism?
2. How has the law dealt with the creationism controversy?
3. What is the argument that teaching evolution is unfair because such teaching is "viewpoint discrimination"? How does Pennock answer that charge?
4. Some have argued that evolution is merely one theory among many. What is Pennock's response to this "epistemological" argument?
5. How does Pennock understand the aims of education, and how is that relevant to his position?

I. THE QUESTION

Should creationism be taught in the public schools? The full range of issues for educational philosophy and policy that are the subject of debate in the creation/evolution controversy are too numerous to be covered in any one article, so in this first section I begin by analyzing the question so that we might better focus our discussion. I will use this opportunity to point out related questions that have so far not been considered in the debate, but that deserve the attention of philosophers of education. In subsequent sections I will discuss, in turn, a variety of legal arguments, creationists' extralegal arguments, epistemological arguments, religious protection arguments and arguments from educational philosophy and justice that are relevant to our specific question. Because creationism is primarily an American phenomenon, some of the considerations will be specific to the circumstances in the United States, but many of the arguments are generally applicable.

A. The Public Schools

The controversies about educational policies concerning creationism have almost exclusively involved the teaching of evolution in the public schools, so this is a natural locus from which to consider the problem. However, several key elements of the controversy would be quite different if we looked at the issue in other educational settings, such as private and parochial schools, home schooling, and in higher education.

There has been very little consideration of the issues for private rather than public schools, no doubt because the governance of the former is not subject to public control and review in the same way. However, there is still a measure of external oversight in that private

schools must meet certain standards in order to get and maintain accreditation. It is a reasonable question to ask whether a school deserves to be accredited if it teaches creationism rather than evolution in its science classes. Given that accreditation implies that a school meets professional standards in the appropriate subject matter, a school that teaches creationism in science classes does not meet the standard, since evolution is at the core of basic scientific knowledge. Moreover, as we shall see, creationism rejects not only evolution, but other well-established scientific facts from across the sciences. In general, however, we tend to take for granted that private schools, if they do not receive public funds or certification, are not subject to public standards and may teach whatever private, esoteric doctrines they choose.

For parochial schools, we fully expect that religious views will be taught. This is the most natural setting for creationist views, and it is primarily here that we find creationism taught in science classes. This is not to say, of course, that all or even most parochial schools teach creationism. For instance, based on an informal assessment of my undergraduate students, those who studied at Catholic high schools typically have had the best education on evolution, often better than their public school counterparts. Fundamentalist and evangelical "Bible schools," on the other hand, often cite the creationist orientation of their science curriculum as a major selling point to their clientele. As they see it, all true knowledge has a biblical basis. . . .

Unless the government begins to significantly fund parochial schools with tax dollars, such as through a voucher program or through religious charter schools, parochial schools can probably expect to remain free to teach creationism or whatever religious doctrines they choose. Moreover, fundamentalist and evangelical schools often choose to forgo secular educational accreditation, and may be accredited only within their own independent system. Nevertheless, I would still argue that there are serious issues of educational philosophy to consider even in this setting. Is it

From Robert T. Pennock, "Should Creationism Be Taught in the Public Schools?" *Science and Education*, Vol. 10, No. 3, 2001. Reprinted with kind permission from Kluver Academic Publishers.

right to teach children that something that is known to be true is false? Is it not bad faith to misrepresent the findings of science in what is purported to be a science class? If the basis for knowledge is taken to be biblical revelation, is it not intellectually dishonest to put such revelations forward as science? Important moral questions are at issue here; religious schools that teach creationism as science are violating basic norms of honesty.

Most of these same considerations apply if we move to consideration of home schooling. There have always been parents who, for one reason or other, chose to teach their own children at home rather than send them to school, but currently the vast majority of home schoolers consists of religious conservatives who do not want their children to be exposed to what they take to be the evils of the public schools, be it sex education or evolution. Home schooling raises some unique policy issues, since basic education is compulsory and parents must demonstrate that they are providing their children with an education that meets state standards. Oversight of parents who teach their own children is inconsistent, and it seems to be fairly common that fundamentalist home schoolers teach the bare minimum of what they have to of subjects they object to, and then regularly supplement the required curriculum with the religious education—in Bible study, creationism, and so on—that they desire. Are parents doing an educational disservice to their children in teaching them creationism on the sly? One might ask whether stricter oversight is necessary in such cases.

Examining the issue in the setting of higher education overlaps some of the previous considerations, but with some relevant differences. One of the most important is the age and maturity of the students. Most undergraduates are at a more advanced developmental stage than they were in high school, so some new educational goals begin to apply. Certainly one of the most significant is that we expect undergraduates to begin to hone their critical and evaluative thinking skills, and to develop disciplined independence of mind. At this stage, it can be quite appropriate and instructive to discuss creationist views, so that students can learn to see what is wrong with them. Of course, there are any number of other topics that could also serve the same end, but a professor might legitimately choose to dissect creationism in the same way that one might choose to have students dissect a snake rather than a frog in anatomy class. One question we will have to address is whether this might not be a reasonable educational goal in secondary school public education as well.

For the most part, we will leave consideration of these other venues aside, and focus on the public schools, which historically have been (and for the most part remain) the central locus of the controversy. . . .

B. Kinds of Creationism

The next element of the question before us that we need to examine is the notion of creationism itself. If creationism were to be taught, what would that include? In general, creationism is the rejection of evolution in favor of special creation of some form, but we must recognize that there are a wide variety of different, competing views that fall under this concept.

The most common form of "creation-science" is what is known as "young-earth creationism" (YEC). In the law they got passed in 1982 in Arkansas, creationists proposed the following outline of what they wanted to have taught.

(1) Sudden creation of the universe, energy, and life from nothing; (2) The insufficiency of mutation and natural selection in bringing about the development of all living kinds from a single organism; (3) Changes only within fixed limits of originally created kinds of plants and animals; (4) Separate ancestry of humans and apes; (5) Explanation of the earth's geology by catastrophism, including the occurrence of a worldwide flood; and (6) A relatively recent inception of the earth and living kinds. (La Follette 1983, p. 16)

A more complete outline of the young-earth "Creation-model" may be found in (Aubrey 1998 (1980)). It is also important to understand that creationism does not end with its rejection of biological evolution, though this is the main thesis that so far has been at issue in the public controversy. As we see in the list above, and as I have shown in detail elsewhere (Pennock 1999, Ch. 1), creationism also rejects scientific conclusions of anthropology, archeology, astronomy, chemistry, geology, linguistics, physics, psychology, optics, and so on. For instance, when creationists on the Kansas State Board of Education removed references to evolution from the state's science curriculum standards in 1999, they also took out plate tectonics, the geological chronology, Big Bang cosmology, and any mention of the ancient age of the earth.

We must also be aware that there is now considerable factionalism among creationists. Disagreements about the details of Christian theology, partial acceptance of scientific views, and different political strategies have given rise to splinter groups that question one or another of the standard views. Old-earth creationists, for example, do not insist that the world is only six to ten thousand years old and accept something closer to the scientific chronology. A few creationists doubt that there was a single, catastrophic worldwide flood, and hold that the Noachian Deluge may have been local to the Mediterranean, or, if global, then "tranquil" rather than catastrophic. Adherents of the YEC view far outnumber members of other factions, but it is important that we recognize that creationism is not a monolithic view and is split by deep divisions.

Though the traditional creationists remain the most active in their political and educational work, there was a significant evolution of creationism in the 1990s, beginning with the publication of *Darwin on Trial*, by Berkeley law professor Phillip Johnson. Johnson neither endorses nor denies the young-earth view, and argues that we should understand creationism as belief in the process of creation in a more general sense. People are creationists, according to Johnson's definition, "if they believe that a supernatural Creator not only initiated this process but in

some meaningful sense *controls* it in furtherance of a purpose" (Johnson 1991, p. 4). Rather than speaking of "creation-science," Johnson and others among these new creationists, call their view "intelligent-design theory" and advocate a "theistic science." Intelligent-design creationists include both young-earth and old-earth creationists, but for the most part they keep their specific commitments hidden and speak only of the generic thesis of "mere creation." As do other creationists, they oppose accommodation to evolution and take it to be fundamentally incompatible with Christian theism. In another way, however, they go further than creation-science does; they reject scientific methodology itself, arguing that scientific naturalism itself must be tossed out and replaced by their theistic science (though they are never clear about what its distinctive methods might be).

Although it has been fundamentalist and evangelical Christian creationists, especially the YECs, who have been the most active in opposing the teaching of evolution in the schools and pressing for inclusion of their view of Creation, we cannot fairly evaluate the question without also taking into account non-Christian creationist views. For the most part, adherents of these views have not been as politically active in the United States so these have not reached the public attention to the same degree. It is impossible to even begin to canvas these numerous views, but I will mention by way of example, [one] recent case that [has] made the news.

In Kennewick, Washington, the 1996 discovery of a fossil human skeleton led to a very public legal battle between science and religion. The nine thousand–plus year old bones were claimed by a coalition of Northwest Indians who wanted to immediately bury them. However, features of the skull seemed to be more Caucasian than Indian, and scientists questioned whether it was really a tribal ancestor and suggested that further analysis could help reveal something of early human history in the area. Armand Minthorn, of Oregon's Umatilla Tribe, said his people were not interested in the scientist's views: "We already know our history. It is passed on to us through our elders and through our religious practices." Their history says that their God created them first in that place. Many Amerindian tribes have origin stories that, on their face, are antithetical to evolutionary theory and other scientific findings. (In parts of northern Canada, an alliance of Native Indians and Christian creationists has formed to oppose teaching evolution in the schools. It is an uneasy union, of course, because the groups differ sharply in what story of Creation they would put in its stead.) The controversy over the Kennewick skeleton also involves another religious group, the Asatru Folk Assembly, an Old Norse pagan group. The members of this pre-Christian faith revere Viking-era Scandinavian gods and goddesses, and believe that their ancestors were the first inhabitants of the region. They expect that scientific study of the skull would support their claim of priority, though their other religious beliefs would certainly put them at odds with other aspects of the scientific picture.

Another religious anti-evolutionary view became newsworthy in 1995, when NBC broadcast a program entitled *Mysterious Origins of Man*, that purported to reveal scientific evidence that human beings had lived tens of millions of years ago. Creationists were at first elated by this prime-time repudiation of evolution, but quickly withdrew their endorsement when they learned that the program was based on the 1993 book *Forbidden Archeology* (Cremo and Thompson 1993), which advances purportedly scientific evidence for a position that mirrors a Hindu view of creation and reincarnation.

Finally, let me mention one more type of view that is relevant to the controversy. The Raëlian Movement, which had its start in France in the 1970s, calls itself a "scientific religion." Raëlians reject evolution and believe that life on earth is the result of purposeful, intelligent design, but they also reject creationism, in the sense that they believe that the creator was not supernatural. Instead, they believe that life on earth was genetically engineered from scratch by extraterrestrials. The founder of the Raëlian Movement, Claude Vorilhon, claims that he knows this because the truth was revealed to him by an extraterrestrial, who anointed him as the Guide of Guides for our age. Some 70,000 adherents worldwide, many in the U.S. and Canada, share this faith.

In considering whether creationism should be taught in the public schools, we must always keep in mind that . . . antievolutionary views would have to be included as "alternative theories" to the scientific conclusions.

C. Taught How?

The third element of the question that requires preliminary discussion involves the *kind* of academic course in which, and the *way* in which creationism might be taught.

The issues change dramatically, for instance, if the different forms of creationism were to be taught in a comparative religion class. The Constitution is not taken to bar discussion of religion in a course of this sort. One could imagine a course that surveyed the splendid variety of views of creation of different religions, and could make a good case that such a course might serve a useful educational purpose in fostering an appreciation of American and global cultural diversity. Many opponents of teaching creationism in the schools would be willing to compromise if the topic were to be introduced in such a course. The controversy arises mostly because creationists insist that their view be included as part of the science curriculum, and that it replace or be given equal weight to evolution.

Moreover, creationists want evolution to be revealed as a false model. Creationist textbooks that are used in fundamentalist schools often go further and teach that it is an evil view as well, promoted by atheist scientists who want to lure people away from God. Textbooks that they have promoted for use in public schools, however, keep the sermonizing about evolutionary evils to a minimum. The most common creationist proposals have followed what is known as the "dual model" approach, whereby "the two theories" are presented and contrasted. The Arkansas "Balanced Treatment" Act specified that the schools should give equal consideration to "creation-science" and "evolution-science." Since all such legislation has been found unconstitutional, creationists now try to argue that science classes should simply present "alternative theories" besides the scientific view. In practice, however, the proposals are essentially unchanged. For example, the textbook *Of Pandas and People* (Davis and Kenyon 1993), which presents intelligent-design creationism and is by far the most carefully crafted creationist offering to date, follows the same misleading framework of presenting the views of those who hold "the two" theories of biological origins, natural evolution and intelligent design, neglecting the variety of other views. The terms may have changed, but the dubious strategy it adopts is the same: Evolutionary theory is claimed to be riddled with holes, with creationism left as the only alternative. Students are told that the textbook will allow them to do what no other does, namely, let them decide for themselves which theory is true. Of course, the deck is stacked so that evolution appears to lose on every point. . . .

Finally, let me suggest one further way that creationism might be taught that has not been considered in the literature: Creationist views could be taught as illustrations of how *not* to do science. Specific creationist tenets could be presented and then the evidence reviewed, showing how scientists came to see that they were false. If not carried to extremes, this might turn out to be a useful educational exercise, in that examination of some of the many errors of so-called "creation-science" or "intelligent design" could help teach students how real science is done. . . .

I will return to some of these issues shortly, but having delimited the focus of our discussion, let me now turn to the relevant arguments, beginning with a brief review of the legal reasoning that has excluded creationism from the public schools.

II. LEGAL ARGUMENTS

Because our focus is upon the public schools in the United States, the legal arguments involving the teaching of creationism have been and continue to be the most significant politically and practically. Both sides in the legal debate have argued that this is primarily a Constitutional question, with some proponents of teaching creationism claiming that it should actually be protected by the First Amendment, under the free exercise of religion clause. Opponents respond that creationists are not being prevented from exercising their beliefs in their churches, homes or private schools, but that teaching Creation in the public schools would violate the First Amendment's establishment clause. In a long series of cases, the courts have consistently ruled against the antievolutionists' arguments.

Antievolution laws were struck down by the U.S. Supreme Court in the 1968 *Epperson v. Arkansas* case, on the grounds that the Constitution does not permit a state to tailor its requirements for teaching and learning to the principles or prohibitions of any particular religious sect or doctrine. Subsequent rulings have helped define the boundaries of this ruling. In a 1981 case, a parent sued in California, claiming that classes in which evolution was taught prohibited his and his children's free exercise of religion. The Sacramento Superior Court ruled (*Segraves v. California*) that teaching evolution did not infringe on religious freedom, and that a 1972 antidogmatism policy of the School Board—which said that statements about origins should be presented nondogmatically, and that class discussions on the topic should emphasize that scientific explanations focus on how things occur, not on ultimate causes—was an appropriate compromise between state science teaching and individual religious beliefs.

Creationists next tried to argue that their view should *not* be excluded on grounds of separation of Church and State, because it was not religion but science. The Arkansas legislature passed a bill requiring "balanced treatment" of what they called "creation-science" and "evolution-science." The court struck down the law in the 1982 *McLean v. Arkansas* case, finding that creation-science was not a science but a religious view. The U.S. Supreme Court came to the same conclusion in the 1987 *Edwards v. Aguillard* case, striking down Louisiana's "Creationism Act," which required the teaching of creationism whenever evolution was taught. The court found that, by advancing the religious belief that a supernatural being created humankind, the act impermissibly legislated the teaching of religion, and that a comprehensive science education is undermined when it is forbidden to teach evolution except when creation science is also taught.

The court has also ruled, as in the 1994 *Peloza v. Capistrano School District* case, that a teacher's First Amendment right to free exercise of religion is not violated by a school district's requirement that evolution be taught in biology classes, rejecting creationists' contention that "evolutionism" is a religion. In another recent case, in Louisiana, the 1997 *Freiler v. Tangipahoa Parish Board of Education* case, the court overturned a policy that would require teachers to read aloud a disclaimer whenever they taught about evolution, and also found that making curriculum proposals in terms of "intelligent-design" is no different from the legal standpoint than earlier proposals for teaching "creation-science."

When considering questions about what we ought or ought not do, however, we may never be content with answers that stop with the law, if only because we may have ethical duties that require more of us than the law does. Moreover, we must always consider the possibility that current law is itself unjust or unwise. In the sections that follow, I will examine several other sorts of arguments that address these points.

III. CREATIONIST EXTRALEGAL ARGUMENTS

. . . By far the most common argument creationists make is to say that it is *unfair* for the law to exclude their view from the public school science classroom. Isn't it biased and one-sided, they challenge, to teach evolution to the exclusion of creationism? [Creationist lawyer Wendell] Bird argues that "The only fair approach is to let the children hear all the scientific information and make up their own minds." Phillip Johnson makes the argument in stronger terms, claiming that excluding creationism amounts to "viewpoint discrimination" (Johnson 1995, pp. 33–34). Bird tries to bolster the argument by appealing to *majority rule*, saying "The fact is that, contrary to all of the smoke, the great majority of the American public feels that it is unfair to teach just the theory of evolution." He cites polls indicating that a large percentage of Americans believe that "the scientific theory of Creation" should be taught alongside evolution in the schools.[1] . . .

Creationists also appeal to what is properly taken to be a prime educational value, *academic freedom*. Bird says:

> To me the basic issue is academic freedom, because no one is trying to exclude evolution from public schools while teaching a theory of creation. Instead, the evolutionists are trying to exclude alternatives, while, in general, defending the exclusive teaching of evolutionism.

. . . Science educators do now usually defend the exclusive teaching of the scientific view, and this leads to his final objection. Mentioning organizations that oppose teaching creationism, he concludes that what they are doing amounts to *censorship*:

> They have a very specific desire to preserve the exclusive teaching of evolution and to exclude any teaching of a scientific theory of creation or a scientific theory of abrupt appearance. That's censorship in my view.

We should agree that, at first glance at least, some of these charges exert a powerful emotional pull upon us. No one wants to be seen as engaging in censorship or in unfair, discriminatory exclusion of a popular viewpoint. It is certainly incumbent upon professionals to take such charges seriously, and to examine them carefully to see whether they have merit. When we do this, however, we find that the charges do not apply or are irrelevant to the issue before us.

The notion of parental rights to determine what one's children are to be taught may sound attractive at first, but parents typically have no special expertise about specific subject matter, and they certainly do not have a right to demand that teachers teach what is demonstrably false. A recent poll showed that 44 percent believe the creationist view that "Humans were created pretty much in their present form about ten thousand years ago," but it is not relevant that a large number of Americans reject the scientific findings and do not believe that evolution occurred. It does not matter what the poll figures are because matters of empirical fact are not appropriately decided by majority rule. Nor is it "unfair" to teach what is true even though many people don't want to hear it. Neither are the schools "censoring" creationism; they are simply and properly leaving out what does not belong in the curriculum.

The charge that such a policy violates academic freedom is not so easily dismissed. One might reasonably dispute about whether academic freedom applies in the public elementary and secondary schools in the same *way* that it does in higher education, but prima facie there seems to be no good reason to think that this important protection should be afforded to university professors and not to others of the teaching profession who serve in other educational settings. However, aca-demic freedom is not a license to teach whatever one wants. Along with that professional freedom comes special professional responsibilities, especially of objectivity and intellectual honesty. Neither "creation-science" nor "intelligent-design" (nor any of the latest euphemisms) is an actual or viable competitor in the scientific field, and it would be irresponsible and intellectually dishonest to teach them as though they were. (It should be obvious, but let me nevertheless state explicitly that in making these arguments I am taking it for granted that evolutionary

theory is true. I mean this, of course, in the standard scientific sense of approximate, revisable truth; no one thinks that evolutionary theory is complete or that one or another of its specific elements might not have to be modified should new, countervailing evidence be found. Creationism is false in the basic sense that, whatever its specific positive commitments, it by definition rejects evolution. Most of creationists' specific claims about the processes of the origins of cosmological, geological, and biological phenomena (among others) have been shown to be false as well, provided that we are able to judge these by ordinary scientific means and standards. Note, however, that I do not assume that this means that God does not exist; the larger question of whether a supernatural designer created the world is not answerable simply by appeal to scientific methods. I have discussed some of the evidence for these conclusions elsewhere (Pennock 1999, Ch. 2–3), and will not review them here.)

In the previous century, the situation in science with regard to the question of the origin of species was quite different, but it cannot now be fairly said that the basic theses of evolution are scientifically controversial. There are currently no "alternative theories" to evolution that scientists take seriously, since the evidence has gone against previous contenders (including the forms of creationism held by nineteenth-century scientists) and continues to accrue in favor of evolutionary theory. Evolution is in no sense "a theory in crisis," as creationists purport. This is not to say that there are not interesting problems that remain to be solved, but that is true of every science, and such issues are of sufficient complexity that they are properly reserved for consideration at professional meetings, in the primary literature, and in graduate programs. Unresolved issues at the cutting-edge of science are well above the level that would be likely to be included in secondary school textbooks. What is included at the lower levels that concern us here is well confirmed and scientifically uncontroversial.

IV. EPISTEMOLOGICAL ARGUMENTS

Creationists of course refuse to accept the evidence that supports the various hypotheses of evolutionary theory. As they see it, one must look to revelation to determine what is absolutely true, rather than believing the "mere theories" of science. The basic issue, as they see it, is whose truths are to be taught. God help us, they say, if we fail to teach our children God's Truth. Phillip Johnson has outlined a new legal strategy for reintroducing creationism into the public schools, arguing that excluding the religious perspective amounts to "viewpoint discrimination." Citing the 1993 *Lamb's Chapel* case, in which the court found that a school could not bar an evangelical Christian perspective in a class that discussed the subject of family relationships, Johnson claims that it is similarly improper to bar consideration of intelligent design when the topic of biological origins is discussed in science class.

One major problematic assumption behind this kind of argument is thinking that questions about empirical fact are simply a matter of one's peculiar point of view, so that excluding one or another is "discrimination," in the sense of subjective prejudice rather than the sense of objective assessment of differences. But there is a real difference between what is true and what is false, what is well-confirmed and what is disconfirmed, and surely it is a good thing for science to discriminate the true empirical hypotheses from the false by empirical tests that can tell which is which. Creationists also are interested in truth, but they believe that they already know what the truths are—indeed, as Johnson puts it, with what the truths "with a capital 'T'" are. However, one cannot ascertain truths except by appropriate methods, and creationists are typically unwilling to say even what their special methods are, let alone show that they are reliable.

A second major questionable assumption is that it makes sense to talk about "the religious" or even "the creationist" viewpoint.

Professor Plantinga recognizes that truths must be ascertained by a justifiable method, but he argues that different epistemological assumptions may be taken to be properly basic. On that ground, he argues for what he calls an "Augustinian science," in which scientists pursue their research along parallel epistemological tracks. Christians, he tells us, should do their science starting with "what Christians know" (Plantinga 1997). The problem with this is that there is little that Christians can say univocally that they know.

Christians disagree, sometimes violently, about what it is they supposedly know. With the exception perhaps of Roman Catholicism, fundamentalist Christianity actually provides perhaps the broadest general consensus to be found, since it traces its roots to a series of publications at the beginning of the twentieth century the explicit purpose of which was to try to distill just "the fundamentals" of the faith. But even our brief view of the factions among creationists reveals the splinters that nevertheless form among even fundamentalists over disagreements about the smallest points of theology. (Intelligent-design creationists try to paper over this problem by remaining silent about the details and promoting the minimal positive thesis that God creates for a purpose. Though even this vaguely stated view may resonate with religious meaning, it is devoid of empirical content—it certainly neither opposes nor supports any particular view about the truth of evolutionary theory—and provides no method of investigation.) The problems increase exponentially once we look beyond Christianity, and bring Hindu, Pagan, Amerindian and other creationist viewpoints into the classroom, taking into account what these other religions take to be properly basic beliefs. If these theologically perspectival epistemologies are taken to stand on a par with ordinary natural science, then what we will be left with is a balkanized science where specific private revelations that one or another group professes to "know" and take as given will vie with one another with no hope of public resolution.

The knowledge that we should impart in public schools is not this private esoteric "knowledge," but rather public knowledge—knowledge that we acquire by customary, natural means. The methodological constraints that science puts upon itself serve to provide just this sort of knowledge, and thus it is scientific knowledge that is appropriate to teach in the public schools.

V. RELIGIOUS PROTECTION ARGUMENTS

It is in part because the esoteric knowledge claims of religions are of a different sort than the conclusions of scientific investigation, that we need the special Constitutional protection of freedom of religion. This leads to several additional arguments for excluding creationism from the public schools.

The main reason typically offered against the teaching of creationism is that it improperly promotes one religious view over others. We need not dig into the theological soils in which creationism is rooted to see that this is so. In their literature, creationists write as though they are defending the Christian faith and that the enemy consists solely of godless evolutionists, but in reality it is the religious who are more often in the forefront of the opposition to seeing creationism taught in the schools. The plaintiffs opposing the "Balanced Treatment" Act in the Arkansas case included Episcopal, Methodist, A.M.E., Presbyterian, Roman Catholic, and Southern Baptist officials, and national Jewish organizations. Though creationists attempt to portray their views as purely scientific and nonsectarian, other religious groups are not taken in by the disguise, and quite understandably argue that to sanction the teaching of creationism would indeed be to privilege one religious viewpoint over others.

One might argue that this unfair singling out of one view could be avoided by allowing *all* religious views into the science class. So should we then, following the creationists' pedagogic philosophy, teach them all and let the children decide which is the true one? This is hardly a wise course of action, in that it would make the classroom a theological battleground where different religions were inevitably pitted against one another.

Creationists and other conservative Christians often take issue with the Court's interpretation of the Constitution that set up the "wall of separation" between Church and State in the 1947 *Everson v. Board of Education* case. However, the idea of tossing all religions into the science classroom to see which wins, would violate what some take to be the original intent of the establishment clause of the First Amendment. The influential nineteenth-century Supreme Court Justice, Joseph Story, wrote that its main object was not just to prevent the exclusive patronage of some particular religion that would result from any national ecclesiastical establishment, but also "to exclude all rivalry among Christian sects . . ." (Larson 1989, p. 93). Religious rivalry and outright persecution were all too common in the American colonies when theocracy was the norm, and it seems reasonable to thank the secularization of the government and the Constitutional policy of religious neutrality in large measure for the fact that the United States has been relatively free of the sectarian violence that continues in other parts of the world. In a comparative religion class, religious differences could be respectfully described and studied, but in the setting of a science class, where the point is to seek the truth by submitting differences to the rigors of crucial tests, it is hard to see how conflict could be avoided. . . .

VI. EDUCATIONAL ARGUMENTS

In this section, let us set the above considerations aside and simply ask whether it would be a good educational policy to teach creationism if there were no other factors to consider. To answer the question put this way we must turn our attention to philosophy of education more generally.

The choice of what to teach in the public schools must be made in light of the goals of public education. I take it for granted that one of the basic goals of education is to provide students a realistic picture of the natural world we share. Another is to develop the skills and instill the civic virtues that they will require to function in society in harmony. While there are several common purposes of this kind towards which all public education aims, the more specific goals, of course, will vary depending upon, among other things, the age of the student. It makes little sense, for example, to confront students with material that is beyond their developmental level. We also need to ask what is to be included when one teaches a discipline. What should be taught under the particular subject heading of *Science*? In particular, does creationism belong within that subject area?

If we think of science in terms of its set of conclusions, then it is clear that creationism does not belong. That creationism and science both have things to say about "the subject of origins" is not sufficient to say that the views of the former are a part of the subject matter we ought to teach. The specific hypotheses of creation-science have been rejected by science as the evidence accumulated against them, and the general thesis that "God creates" is not a hypothesis that science considers or can treat at all. Some scientists do discuss their theological musings—some theistic, some atheistic—in their popular writings, but research on the questions of the existence, or possible activities and purposes of a Creator simply is not to be found in the primary scientific literature. The only proper way to treat the specific empirical claims of creation-science in a science textbook is, thus, as an interesting historical footnote about hypotheses that have been long overturned.

But now let me return to [John] Dewey's important contention that to teach science properly is to teach not a collection of facts but a way of thought. Science education that focuses only on scientific conclusions, and omits teaching scientific methods, misrepresents the nature of scientific inquiry and fails in its basic mission of preparing students with the best skills to function in the natural world. "Theistic science," despite its name, rejects science's methodology and therefore does not belong within the subject. "Creation-science," "abrupt appearance theory," "intelligent-design theory" and so on are the creationists' cuckoo eggs that they hope will pass unnoticed, enabling them to garner the resources (and cultural prestige) of science and the forum of the science classroom for their own religious ends.

We should not haggle over mere terminology, but it remains the case that neither the conclusions nor the methods of creationism are properly described as "science." Disciplinary boundaries may not be sharply defined, nor should we expect them to be, but they are generally distinguished by a characteristic order. It is because practitioners must adhere to constraints—be they the precedents of (tentatively) accepted conclusions or the procedures of inquiry themselves—that the notion of a "discipline" makes sense at all. . . .

Consider what the effect would be if we were to buy into the curricular framework that creationists propose; it would not be only evolutionary biology that would have to be put under critical scrutiny. Take, for instance, the subject of world history. There are any number of advocacy groups that, for religious, political or other ideological reasons, advance some idiosyncratic version of history that is at odds with the findings of historians. If we accept the creationists' proposals regarding evolution, we should also be sure to present alternative theories, attach disclaimers to the standard accounts, and give equal time to the "evidence against" the conclusions of historical research so that the students can judge for themselves. In studying the assassination of President Kennedy, for example, we might begin by screening Oliver Stone's movie *JFK*, and then go on to consider the other theories, such as that Vice President Johnson masterminded his death, or that the CIA was behind it, or the Mafia. When studying the landing of American astronauts on the moon, we should probably issue a disclaimer and respectfully consider the views of those who believe that the whole event was filmed by the government in a secret Hollywood studio as part of an elaborate charade. When teaching about World War II we would need to give balanced treatment to those who hold that the Holocaust never happened and was just a Zionist propaganda ploy to gain sympathy for Jews. But such a notion of "fairness" and "balance" is absurd. It is certainly not sound educational philosophy.

We should be no less diligent in teaching the results of careful investigation of the history of life on earth as we are in teaching the history of our nation and the other nations of the world. Critical thinking does not mean indiscriminate thinking, but thinking governed by the rules of reason and evidence. . . .

VII. THE ANSWER

In reviewing the arguments, we find many good reasons for excluding creationism from the schools, and few good reasons for not doing so. On balance, it seems clear that the wiser course is not to allow the conflict into the classroom. Should creationism be taught in the public schools? The answer is that it should not.

Notes

1. Such a poll question is misleading and biased, however, in that it assumes what is false, namely, that there is just *one* theory of creation, and that it is a science.

References

Aubrey, Frank. 1998 (1980). Yes, Virginia, There Is a Creation Model. *Reports of the National Center for Science Education* **18** (1):6.

Cremo, Michael A., and Richard L. Thompson. 1993. *Forbidden Archeology: The Hidden History of the Human Race.* Alachua, FL: Govardhan Hill Publishing.

Davis, Percival, and Dean H. Kenyon. 1993. *Of Pandas and People.* Dallas, TX: Haughton Publishing Co.

Dewey, John. 1964 (1938). The Relation of Science and Philosophy as a Basis of Education. In *John Dewey on Education: Selected Writings*, edited by R. D. Archambault. Chicago: University of Chicago Press.

Johnson, Phillip E. 1991. *Darwin on Trial*, 1st ed. Washington, D.C.: Regnery Gateway.

———. 1995. *Reason in the Balance: The Case Against Naturalism in Science, Law & Education.* Downers Grove, IL: InterVarsity Press.

La Follette, Marcel Chotkowski, ed. 1983. *Creationism, Science, and the Law: The Arkansas Case.* Cambridge, MA: The MIT Press.

Larson, Edward J. 1989. *Trial and Error: The American Controversy over Creation and Evolution*, updated ed. New York and Oxford: Oxford University Press.

Pennock, Robert T. 1999. *Tower of Babel: The Evidence against the New Creationism.* Cambridge, MA: MIT Press.

Plantinga, Alvin. 1997. Methodological Naturalism? *Perspectives on Science and Christian Faith* **49** (3):143–154.

Secular Humanism as Official Religion?

Smith v. Board of Education of Mobile, Alabama

The First Amendment guarantees citizens the right to exercise their religion and prevents government from "establishing" an official religion. But if religion is broadly enough defined, then it is possible to argue that by teaching "secular humanism" schools establish secular humanism as a religion. U.S. District Court Judge Brevard Hand makes that argument in the case below, *Smith v. Board of Education of Mobile.* The impetus for the case came in 1982 when the Supreme Court overruled an earlier decision by Judge Hand in which he had argued that a one-minute period of silent prayer in schools was not a violation of the establishment clause. Having lost that argument, Judge Hand did not let the issue die, suggesting in his opinion that should he be overruled (as he later was), he would then be willing to consider arguments that the school board had established another religion—secular humanism—in violation of the establishment clause. A group of religious conservatives took up the judge's offer and filed this case, *Smith v. Board of Education of Mobile*. After the trial, which included many expert witnesses on both sides, Judge Hand wrote a lengthy opinion contending that secular humanism is a religion and that the Mobile school board "established" it by requiring students to read certain textbooks. Although this decision was later overturned as well, Judge Hand's opinion in *Smith* raises important and difficult issues concerning the extent to which school texts that have the effect of undermining the values and religious beliefs of a community can be required.

As you read through this essay, consider the following:

1. What is the legal issue in this case?
2. How does Judge Hand define religion?
3. Why does Hand think humanism is a religion?
4. What was it in the textbooks that led Hand to conclude they "establish" religion?
5. How might Robert Pennock respond to this decision? Is he right? Why or why not?

I. A FIRST AMENDMENT DEFINITION OF RELIGION

The Supreme Court has never stated an absolute definition of religion under the first amendment. . . .

The application of these principles to the question of what constitutes a religion under the first amendment indicates that the state may not decide the question by reference to the validity of the beliefs or practices involved. . . . The state must instead look to factors common to all religious movements to decide how to distinguish those ideologies worthy of the protection of the religious clauses from those which must seek refuge under other constitutional provisions.

Any definition of religion must not be limited, therefore, to traditional religions, but must encompass systems of belief that are equivalent to them for the believer. . . . The Supreme Court has focused on such factors as a person's "ultimate concern," organization and social structure, and on equivalency to belief in a Supreme Deity. All of these are evidence of the type of belief a person holds. But all religious beliefs may be classified by the questions they raise and issues they address. Some of these matters over-

lap with non-religious governmental concerns. A religion, however, approaches them on the basis of certain fundamental assumptions with which governments are unconcerned. These assumptions may be grouped as about: (1) the existence of supernatural and/or transcendent reality; (2) the nature of man; (3) the ultimate end, or goal or purpose of man's existence, both individually and collectively; (4) the purpose and nature of the universe. . . .

Whenever a belief system deals with fundamental questions of the nature of reality and man's relationship to reality, it deals with essentially religious questions. A religion need not posit a belief *in* a deity, or a belief *in* supernatural existence. A religious person adheres to some position on whether supernatural and/or transcendent reality exists at all, and if so, how, and if not, why. A mere "comprehensive world-view" or "way of life" is not by itself enough to identify a belief system as religious. A world-view may be merely economic, or sociological, and a person might choose to follow a "way of life" that ignores ultimate issues addressed by religions. . . .

There are also a number of characteristics exhibited by most known religious groups to which courts can look when trying to determine if a set of theories or system of ideas is religious in nature. First would be the sincerity of the adherents' claims. . . . Another

655 F. Supp. 939 (S.D. Ala. 1987).

factor is group organization and hierarchical structure, which evidence the social characteristics of a movement, and show that the adherents sincerely follow a theory of human relationship. Literary manifestations of a movement may also be important, particularly if they take the form of an authoritative text. Ritual and worship also would be significant because they would be evidence of the religion's belief about supernatural or transcendent reality. . . .

II. HUMANISM A RELIGION?

In the present case, the plaintiffs contend that a particular belief system fits within the first amendment definition of religion. . . . All of the experts, and the class representatives, agreed that this belief system [humanism] is a religion which: "makes a statement about supernatural existence a central pillar of its logic; defines the nature of man; and sets forth a goal or purpose for individual and collective human existence; and defines the nature of the universe, and thereby delimits its purpose."

It purports to establish a closed definition of reality; not closed in that adherents know everything, but in that everything is knowable: can be recognized by human intellect aided only by the devices of that intellect's own creation or discovery. The most important belief of this religion is its denial of the transcendent and/or supernatural: there is no God, no creator, no divinity. By force of logic the universe is thus self-existing, completely physical and hence, essentially knowable. Man is the product of evolutionary, physical forces. He is purely biological and has no supernatural or transcendent spiritual component or quality. Man's individual purpose is to seek and obtain personal fulfillment by freely developing every talent and ability, especially his rational intellect, to the highest level. Man's collective purpose is to seek the good life by the increase of every person's freedom and potential for personal development.

In addition, humanism, as a belief system, erects a moral code and identifies the source of morality. This source is claimed to exist in humans and the social relationships of humans. Again, there is no spiritual or supernatural origin for morals: man is merely physical, and morals, the rules governing his private and social conduct, are founded only on man's actions, situation and environment. In addition to a moral code, certain attitudes and conduct are proscribed since they interfere with personal freedom and fulfillment. In particular any belief in a deity or adherence to a religious system that is theistic in any way is discouraged.

Secular humanism, or humanism in the sense of a religious belief system, (as opposed to humanism as just an interest in the humanities), has organizational characteristics. . . .

These organizations publish magazines, newsletters and other periodicals, including *Free Inquiry*, *The Humanist* and *Progressive World*. The entire body of thought has three key documents that furnish the text upon which the belief system rests as on a platform: *Humanist Manifesto I*, *Humanist Manifesto II* and the *Secular Humanist Declaration*. . . .

To say that science is only concerned with data collected by the five senses as enhanced by technological devices of man's creation is to define science's limits. These are the parameters within which scientists function. However, to claim that there is nothing real beyond observable data is to make an assumption based not on science, but on faith, faith that observable data is all that is real. A statement that there is no transcendent or supernatural reality is a *religious* statement. . . .

This Court is holding that the promotion and advancement of a religious system occurs when one faith-theory is taught to the exclusion of others and this is prohibited by the first amendment religion clauses.

For purposes of the first amendment, secular humanism is a religious belief system, entitled to the protections of, and subject to the prohibitions of, the religion clauses. It is not a mere scientific methodology that may be promoted and advanced in the public schools.

III. RELIGIOUS PROMOTION IN TEXTBOOKS?

. . . [T]he Supreme Court has declared that teaching religious tenets in such a way as to promote or encourage a religion violates the religion clauses. This prohibition is not implicated by mere coincidence of ideas with religious tenets. Rather, there must be systematic, whether explicit or implicit, promotion of a belief system as a whole. The facts showed that the State of Alabama has on its state textbook list certain volumes that are being used by school systems in this state, which engage in such promotion. . . .

The virtually unanimous conclusion of the numerous witnesses, both expert and lay, party and non-party, was that textbooks in the fields examined were poor from an educational perspective. Mere rotten and inadequate textbooks, however, have not yet been determined to violate any constitutional provision, much less the religion clauses. . . . Their expert opinion was that religion was so deliberately underemphasized and ignored that theistic religions were effectively discriminated against and made to seem irrelevant and unimportant within the context of American history. . . . The religious influence on the abolitionist, woman's suffrage, temperance, modern civil rights and peace movements is ignored or diminished to insignificance. The role of religion in the lives of immigrants and minorities, especially southern blacks, is rarely mentioned. After the Civil War, religion is given almost no play. . . .

In addition to omitting particular historical events with religious significance, these books uniformly ignore the religious aspect of most American culture. The vast majority of Americans, for most of our history, have lived in a society in which religion was a part of daily life. . . . For many people, religion is still this important. One would never know it by reading these books. Religion, where treated at all, is generally represented as a private matter, only influencing American public life at some extraordinary moments. This view of religion is one humanists have been

seeking to instill for fifty years. These books assist that effort by perpetuating an inaccurate historical picture. . . .

According to humanistic psychology, as with humanism generally, man is the center of the universe and all existence. Morals are a matter of taste, dependent upon whether the consequences of actions satisfy human "needs." These needs are always defined as purely temporal and nonsupernatural. . . .

The [social studies] books do not state that this is a *theory* of the way humans make choices, they teach the student that things *are* this way. . . . The books teach that the student must determine right and wrong based only on his own experience, feelings and "values." These "values" are described as originating from within. A description of the origin of morals must be based on a faith assumption: a religious dogma. The books are not simply claiming that a moral rule must be internally accepted before it becomes meaningful, because this is true of *all* facts *and* beliefs. . . . The books repeat, over and over, that the decision is "yours alone," or is "purely personal" or that "only you can decide." The emphasis and overall approach implies, and would cause any reasonable, thinking student to infer, that the book is teaching that moral choices are just a matter of preference, because, as the books say, "you are the most important person in your life." . . . This faith assumes that self-actualization is the goal of every human being, that man has no supernatural attributes or component, that there are only temporal and physical consequences for man's actions, and that these results, alone, determine the morality of an action. This belief strikes at the heart of many theistic religions' beliefs that certain actions are in and of themselves immoral, *whatever the consequences*, and that, in addition, actions will have extratemporal consequences. The Court is not holding that high school . . . books must not discuss various theories of human psychology. But it must not present faith based systems to the exclusion of other faith based systems, it must not present one as true and the other as false, and it *must* use a comparative approach to withstand constitutional scrutiny. . . .

With these [history and social studies] books, the State of Alabama has overstepped its mark, and must withdraw to perform its proper nonreligious functions. . . . The Court will enter an order to prohibit further use of the books.

Who Controls a Child's Education?

Wisconsin v. Yoder

This well-known case arose in response to a Wisconsin law requiring all children to be sent to school until the age of sixteen. The Amish parents of two children, ages fourteen and fifteen, refused to comply, arguing that compulsory school attendance beyond eighth grade violated their constitutional right of "free exercise" of religion protected by the First Amendment to the U.S. Constitution. The case went all the way to the Supreme Court, and the Court overturned the law, upholding the right of the Amish parents to guide the religious future and education of their children. In his dissenting opinion, Justice William O. Douglas discusses problems associated with allowing parents to impose their religious notions on children as well as the possible effects of the Court's ruling on the children's educational development.

As you read through this essay, consider the following:

1. What is the legal issue in this case?
2. Does Justice Warren Burger seem to rely more on religious freedom or the rights of parents to make decisions for children?
3. On what basis does Justice Douglas dissent?
4. Does Justice Burger think the Constitution should be "neutral" among different religions? Why?
5. Children will eventually have the right to make decisions for themselves in many areas, independent of what government or others may think. Can parents sometimes damage their children's future right to self-determination? Explain, giving examples.
6. Is this opinion consistent with *Smith v. Board of Education?* Why?

MR. CHIEF JUSTICE BURGER

On complaint of the school district administrator for the public schools, respondents [Mr. and Mrs. Yoder] were charged, tried, and convicted of violating the compulsory-attendance law in Green County Court and were fined the sum of $5 each. Respondents defended on the ground that the application of the compulsory-attendance law violated their rights under the First and Fourteenth Amendments. The trial testimony showed that respondents believed, in accordance with the tenets of Old Order Amish communities generally, that their children's attendance at high school, public or private, was contrary to the Amish religion and way of life. . . . The State stipulated that respondents' religious beliefs were sincere.

In support of their position, respondents presented as expert witnesses scholars on religion and education whose testimony is uncontradicted. They expressed their opinions on the relationship of the Amish belief concerning school attendance to the more general tenets of their religion, and described the impact that compulsory high school attendance could have on the continued survival of Amish communities as they exist in the United States today. . . .

Amish beliefs require members of the community to make their living by farming or closely related activities. Broadly speaking, the Old Order Amish religion pervades and determines the entire mode of life of its adherents. . . .

Amish objection to formal education beyond the eight grade is firmly grounded in these central religious concepts. They object to the high school, and higher education generally, because the values they teach are in marked variance with Amish values and the Amish way of life; they view secondary school education as an impermissible exposure of their children to a "worldly" influence in conflict with their beliefs. The high school tends to emphasize intellectual and scientific accomplishments, self-distinction, competitiveness, worldly success, and social life with other students. Amish society emphasizes informal learning-through-doing; a life of "goodness," rather than a life of intellect; wisdom, rather than technical knowledge; community welfare, rather than competition; and separation from, rather than integration with, contemporary worldly society.

Formal high school education takes [Amish children] away from their community, physically and emotionally, during the crucial and formative adolescent period of life. During this period, the children must acquire Amish attitudes favoring manual work and self-reliance and the specific skills needed to perform the adult role of an Amish farmer or housewife. They must learn to enjoy physical labor. . . . And, at this time in life, the Amish child must also grow in his faith and his relationship to the Amish community if he is to be prepared to accept the heavy obligations imposed by adult baptism. . . .

The Amish do not object to elementary education through the first eight grades as a general proposition because they agree that their children must have basic skills in the "three Rs" in order to read the Bible, to be good farmers and citizens, and to be able to deal with non-Amish people when necessary in the course of daily affairs. They view such a basic education as acceptable because it does not significantly expose their children to worldly values or interfere with their development in the Amish community during the crucial adolescent period. . . .

On the basis of such considerations, [an expert] testified that compulsory high school attendance could not only result in great psychological harm to Amish children, because of the conflicts it would produce, but would also, in his opinion, ultimately result in the destruction of the Old Order Amish church community as it exists in the United States today. . . .

In order for Wisconsin to compel school attendance beyond the eighth grade against a claim that such attendance interferes with the practice of a legitimate religious belief, it must appear either that the State does not deny the free exercise of religious belief by its requirement, or that there is a state interest of sufficient magnitude to override the interest claiming protection under the Free Exercise Clause. . . .

A way of life, however virtuous and admirable, may not be interposed as a barrier to reasonable state regulation of education if it is based on purely secular considerations; to have the protection of the Religion Clauses, the claims must be rooted in religious belief. Although a determination of what is a "religious" belief or practice entitled to constitutional protection may present a most delicate question, the very concept of ordered liberty precludes allowing every person to make his own standards on matters of conduct in which society as a whole has important interests. Thus, if the Amish asserted their claims because of their subjective evaluation and rejection of the contemporary secular values accepted by the majority, much as Thoreau

---

406 U.S. 205 (1972).

rejected the social values of his time and isolated himself at Walden Pond, their claims would not rest on a religious basis. Thoreau's choice was philosophical and personal rather than religious, and such belief does not rise to the demands of the Religion Clauses.

Giving no weight to such secular considerations, however, we see that the record in this case abundantly supports the claim that the traditional way of life of the Amish is not merely a matter of personal preference, but one of deep religious conviction, shared by an organized group, and intimately related to daily living. That the Old Order Amish daily life and religious practice stem from their faith is shown by the fact that it is in response to their literal interpretation of the Biblical injunction from the Epistle of Paul to the Romans, "be not conformed to this world. . . ."

Their way of life in a church-oriented community, separated from the outside world and "worldly" influences, their attachment to nature and the soil, is a way inherently simple and uncomplicated, albeit difficult to preserve against the pressure to conform. Their rejection of telephones, automobiles, radios, and television, their mode of dress, of speech, their habits of manual work do indeed set them apart from much of contemporary society; these customs are both symbolic and practical. . . .

The State advances two primary arguments in support of its system of compulsory education. It notes, as Thomas Jefferson pointed out early in our history, that some degree of education is necessary to prepare citizens to participate effectively and intelligently in our open political system if we are to preserve freedom and independence. Further, education prepares individuals to be self-reliant and self-sufficient participants in society. We accept these propositions.

However, the evidence adduced by the Amish in this case is persuasively to the effect that an additional one or two years of formal high school for Amish children in place of their long-established program of informal vocational education would do little to serve those interests. . . . It is one thing to say that compulsory education for a year or two beyond the eighth grade may be necessary when its goal is the preparation of the child for life in modern society as the majority live, but it is quite another if the goal of education be viewed as the preparation of the child for life in the separated agrarian community that is the keystone of the Amish faith. . . .

Whatever their idiosyncrasies as seen by the majority, the Amish community has been a highly successful social unit within our society, even if apart from the conventional "mainstream." Its members are productive and very law-abiding members of society; they reject public welfare in any of its usual modern forms. . . .

This case involves the fundamental interest of parents, as contrasted with that of the State, to guide the religious future and education of their children. The history and culture of Western civilization reflect a strong tradition of parental concern for the nurture and upbringing of their children. This primary role of the parents in the upbringing of their children is now established beyond debate as an enduring American tradition. . . .

To be sure, the power of the parent, even when linked to a free exercise claim, may be subject to limitation if it appears that parental decisions will jeopardize the health or safety of the child, or have a potential for significant social burdens. But in this case, the Amish have introduced persuasive evidence undermining the arguments the State has advanced to support its claims in terms of the welfare of the child and society as a whole.

MR. JUSTICE DOUGLAS, DISSENTING IN PART

The Court's analysis assumes that the only interests at stake in the case are those of the Amish parents on the one hand, and those of the State on the other. The difficulty with this approach is that, despite the Court's claim, the parents are seeking to vindicate not only their own free exercise claims, but also those of their high-school-age children. . . .

No analysis of religious-liberty claims can take place in a vacuum. If the parents in this case are allowed a religious exemption, the inevitable effect is to impose the parents' notions of religious duty upon their children. Where the child is mature enough to express potentially conflicting desires, it would be an invasion of the child's rights to permit such an imposition without canvassing his views. . . . As the child has no other effective forum, it is in this litigation that his rights should be considered. And, if an Amish child desires to attend high school, and is mature enough to have that desire respected, the State may well be able to override the parents' religiously motivated objections.

This issue has never been squarely presented before today. Our opinions are full of talk about the power of the parents over the child's education. . . . And we have in the past analyzed similar conflicts between parent and State with little regard for the views of the child. . . . Recent cases, however, have clearly held that the children themselves have constitutionally protectible interests.

These children are "persons" within the meaning of the Bill of Rights. . . . While the parents, absent dissent, normally speak for the entire family, the education of the child is a matter on which the child will often have decided views. He may want to be a pianist or an astronaut or an oceanographer. To do so he will have to break from the Amish tradition. . . .

If a parent keeps his child out of school beyond the grade school, then the child will be forever barred from entry into the new and amazing world of diversity that we have today. . . .

[In the cases in which the Court held antipolygamy laws constitutional,] action which the Court deemed to be antisocial could be punished even though it was grounded on deeply held and sincere religious convictions. What we do today, at least in this respect, opens the way to give organized religion a broader base than it has ever enjoyed.

In another way, however, the Court retreats when in reference to Henry Thoreau it says his "choice was philosophical and personal rather than religious, and such belief does not rise to the demands of the Religion Clauses." That is contrary to what we held in *United States v. Seeger,* where we were concerned with the meaning of the words "religious training and belief" in the Selective Service Act, which were the basis of many conscientious objector claims. We said: "Within that phrase would come all sincere religious beliefs which are based upon a power or being, or upon a faith, to which all else is subordinate or upon which all else is ultimately dependent. The test might be stated in these words: A sincere and meaningful belief which occupies in the life of its possessor a place parallel to that filled by the God of those admittedly qualifying for the exemption comes within the statutory definition. This construction avoids imputing to Congress an intent to classify different religious beliefs, exempting some and excluding others, and is in accord with the well-established congressional policy of equal treatment for those whose opposition to service is grounded in their religious tenets."

Section 24

Religion and Politics

A Letter Concerning Toleration

John Locke

Religious conflict has been and in many cases continues to be a source of political strife, blood-shed, and death. Central to the concerns of the framers of the U.S. Constitution was how the government should handle religious conflict and protect the rights of various religious groups. But religious freedoms are of course only one of many liberties governments are required to protect. So while the readings in this section use religion as a focus of discussion, the issues extend far beyond religious rights to the legitimacy of state power and the ideal of justice itself. The discussion begins with a classic statement of the principles of religious freedom.

Born in 1632, John Locke was an important figure in both British and American politics; indeed, there are few, if any, philosophers who were more influential in the development of American political institutions and beliefs than John Locke. Locke's father was a politically influential lawyer who supported Oliver Cromwell and the British Parliament against King Charles I. John Locke was sent to Oxford at fifteen, where he became friendly with noted chemist Robert Boyle as well as other scientists, all of whom exerted an important influence on young John. After graduation, Locke worked as a tutor in Greek. Then, after serving a period as a diplomat, he returned to Oxford to study medicine. Locke was active throughout his life in political and public affairs. At one point he was forced into exile by the king, but he returned to England after the Glorious Revolution in 1688. He died in 1704 at the age of seventy-two.

In *A Letter Concerning Toleration*, which was widely read by the framers of the U.S. Constitution, Locke begins with a brief indication of his general theory of the powers of government. Legitimate government, he thinks, derives its powers from the consent of the governed. Consent can best be understood by first imagining people in a prepolitical state of nature. There, Locke thinks, people would give up their natural right to life and property in order to gain greater protection of those rights by the state. The powers of the state, however, are limited by the original reasons that would motivate people to join and accept its authority. States have no right, therefore, to violate the rights of their citizens, and if they do so the citizens may reject the government in favor of another. With this as background, Locke considers freedom of religion and conscience. No government, he argues, should exercise force to promote or prohibit religious beliefs and practices. He develops his argument by considering the nature of religious faith and the limits and authority of government.

As you read through this essay, consider the following:

1. What is the justification of the use of governmental power, according to Locke?
2. What are the three reasons why Locke thinks that the state must leave religious matters to the individual?
3. How does Locke understand religion, and how is that relevant to his discussion?
4. Why does Locke think that atheists need not be tolerated? Is that related in some way to his view on the nature and legitimacy of government?
5. Do you agree with Locke's claim that "nobody is born a member of a church"? What do you think he means by it?

Honored sir, . . . I esteem it above all things necessary to distinguish exactly the business of civil government from that of religion, and to settle the just bound that lie between the one and the other. If this be not done, there can be no end put to the controversies that will be always arising between those that have, or at least pretend to have, on the one side, a concernment for the interest of men's souls, and, on the other side, a care of the commonwealth.

The commonwealth seems to me to be a society of men constituted only for the procuring, preserving, and advancing their own civil interests.

Civil interests I call life, liberty, health, and indolency of body; and the possession of outward things, such as money, lands, houses, furniture, and the like.

It is the duty of the civil magistrate, by the impartial execution of equal laws, to

secure unto all the people in general, and to every one of his subjects in particular, the just possession of these things belonging to this life. If any one presume to violate the laws of public justice and equity, established for the preservation of those things, his presumption is to be checked by the fear of punishment, consisting of the deprivation or iminution of those civil interests, or goods, which otherwise he might and ought to enjoy. But seeing no man does willingly suffer himself to be punished by the deprivation of any part of his goods, and much less of his liberty or life, therefore is the magistrate armed with the force and strength of all his subjects, in order to the punishment of those that violate any other man's rights.

Now that the whole jurisdiction of the magistrate reaches only to these civil concernments, and that all civil power, right, and dominion, is bounded and confined to the only care of promoting these things; and that it neither can nor ought in any manner to be

From John Locke, *A Letter Concerning Toleration* (1689).

extended to the salvation of souls, these following considerations seem unto me abundantly to demonstrate.

First, because the care of souls is not committed to the civil magistrate, any more than to other men. It is not committed unto him, I say, by God: because it appears not that God has ever given any such authority to one man over another, as to compel any one to his religion. Nor can any such power be vested in the magistrate by the consent of the people, because no man can so far abandon the care of his own salvation as blindly to leave to the choice of any other, whether prince or subject, to prescribe to him what faith or worship he shall embrace. For no man can, if he would, conform his faith to the dictates of another. All the life and power of true religion consist in the inward and full persuasion of the mind; and faith is not faith without believing. Whatever profession we make, to whatever outward worship we conform, if we are not fully satisfied in our own mind that the one is true, and the other well pleasing unto God, such profession and such practice, far from being any furtherance, are indeed great obstacles to our salvation. For in this manner, instead of expiating other sins by the exercise of religion, I say, in offering thus unto God Almighty such a worship as we esteem to be displeasing unto him, we add unto the number of our other sins those also of hypocrisy, and contempt of his Divine Majesty.

In the second place, the care of souls cannot belong to the civil magistrate, because his power consists only in outward force; but true and saving religion consists in the inward persuasion of the mind, without which nothing can be acceptable to God. And such is the nature of the understanding, that it cannot be compelled to the belief of anything by outward force. Confiscation of estate, imprisonment, torments, nothing of that nature can have any such efficacy as to make men change the inward judgment that they have framed of things.

It may indeed be alleged that the magistrate may make use of arguments, and thereby draw the heterodox into the way of truth, and procure their salvation. I grant it;

but this is common to him with other men. In teaching, instructing, and redressing the erroneous by reason, he may certainly do what becomes any good man to do. Magistracy does not oblige him to put off either humanity or Christianity; but it is one thing to persuade, another to command; one thing to press with arguments, another with penalties. This civil power alone has a right to do; to the other good-will is authority enough. Every man has commission to admonish, exhort, convince another of error, and, by reasoning, to draw him into truth; but to give laws, receive obedience, and compel with the sword, belongs to none but the magistrate. And upon this ground, I affirm that the magistrate's power extends not to the establishing of any articles of faith, or forms of worship, by the force of his laws. For laws are of no force at all without penalties, and penalties in this case are absolutely impertinent, because they are not proper to convince the mind. Neither the profession of any articles of faith, nor the conformity to any outward form of worship (as has been already said), can be available to the salvation of souls, unless the truth of the one, and the acceptableness of the other unto God, be thoroughly believed by those that so profess and practise. But penalties are no way capable to produce such belief. It is only light and evidence that can work a change in men's opinions; which light can in no manner proceed from corporal sufferings, or any other outward penalties.

In the third place, the care of the salvation of men's souls cannot belong to the magistrate; because, though the rigour of laws and the force of penalties were capable to convince and change men's minds, yet would not that help at all to the salvation of their souls. For there being but one truth, one way to heaven, what hope is there that more men would be led into it if they had no rule but the religion of the court, and were put under the necessity to quit the light of their own reason, and oppose the dictates of their own consciences, and blindly to resign themselves up to the will of their governors, and to the religion which either ignorance, ambition, or superstition had chanced to establish in the countries where they were born? In the variety and contradiction of opinions in religion, wherein the princes of the world are as much divided as in their secular interests, the narrow way would be much straitened; one country alone would be in the right, and all the rest of the world put under an obligation of following their princes in the ways that lead to destruction; and that which heightens the absurdity, and very ill suits the notion of a Deity, men would owe their eternal happiness or misery to the places of their nativity.

These considerations, to omit many others that might have been urged to the same purpose, seem unto me sufficient to conclude that all the power of civil government relates only to men's civil interests, is confined to the care of the things of this world, and hath nothing to do with the world to come.

Let us now consider what a church is. A church, then, I take to be a voluntary society of men, joining themselves together of their own accord in order to the public worshipping of God in such manner as they judge acceptable to him, and effectual to the salvation of their souls.

I say it is a free and voluntary society. Nobody is born a member of any church; otherwise the religion of parents would descend unto children by the same right of inheritance as their temporal estates, and every one would hold his faith by the same tenure he does his lands, than which nothing can be imagined more absurd. Thus, therefore, that matter stands. No man by nature is bound unto any particular church or sect, but every one joins himself voluntarily to that society in which he believes he has found that profession and worship which is truly acceptable to God. The hope of salvation, as it was the only cause of his entrance into that communion, so it can be the only reason of his stay there. For if afterwards he discover anything either erroneous in the doctrine or incongruous in the worship of that society to which he has joined himself, why should it not be as free for him to go out as it was to enter? No member of a religious society can be tied with any other bonds but

what proceed from the certain expectation of eternal life. A church, then, is a society of members voluntarily uniting to that end.

It follows now that we consider what is the power of this church, and unto what laws it is subject.

Forasmuch as no society, how free soever, or upon whatsoever slight occasion instituted, whether of philosophers for learning, of merchants for commerce, or of men of leisure for mutual conversation and discourse, no church or company, I say, can in the least subsist and hold together, but will presently dissolve and break in pieces, unless it be regulated by some laws, and the members all consent to observe some order. Place and time of meeting must be agreed on; rules for admitting and excluding members must be established; distinction of officers, and putting things into a regular course, and such-like, cannot be omitted. But since the joining together of several members into this church-society, as has already been demonstrated, is absolutely free and spontaneous, it necessarily follows that the right of making its laws can belong to none but the society itself; or, at least (which is the same thing), to those whom the society by common consent has authorised thereunto. . . .

The end of a religious society (as has already been said) is the public worship of God, and, by means thereof, the acquisition of eternal life. All discipline ought therefore to tend to that end, and all ecclesiastical laws to be thereunto confined. Nothing ought nor can be transacted in this society relating to the possession of civil and worldly goods. No force is here to be made use of upon any occasion whatsoever. For force belongs wholly to the civil magistrate, and the possession of all outward goods is subject to his jurisdiction.

But, it may be asked, by what means then shall ecclesiastical laws be established, if they must be thus destitute of all compulsive power? I answer: They must be established by means suitable to the nature of such things, whereof the external profession and observation—if not proceeding from a thorough conviction and approbation of the mind—is altogether useless and unprofitable. The arms by which the members of this society are to be kept within their duty are exhortations, admonitions, and advices. If by these means the offenders will not be reclaimed, and the erroneous convinced, there remains nothing further to be done but that such stubborn and obstinate persons, who give no ground to hope for their reformation, should be cast out and separated from the society. This is the last and utmost force of ecclesiastical authority. No other punishment can thereby be inflicted than that, the relation ceasing between the body and the member which is cut off. The person so condemned ceases to be a part of that church.

These things being thus determined, let us inquire, in the next place: How far the duty of toleration extends, and what is required from every one by it?

And, first, I hold that no church is bound, by the duty of toleration, to retain any such person in her bosom as, after admonition, continues obstinately to offend against the laws of the society. For these being the condition of communion and the bond of the society, if the breach of them were permitted without any animadversion the society would immediately be thereby dissolved. . . .

Secondly, no private person has any right in any manner to prejudice another person in his civil enjoyments because he is of another church or religion. All the rights and franchises that belong to him as a man, or as a denizen, are inviolably to be preserved to him. These are not the business of religion. No violence nor injury is to be offered him, whether he be Christian or Pagan. Nay, we must not content ourselves with the narrow measures of bare justice; charity, bounty, and liberality must be added to it. This the Gospel enjoins, this reason directs, and this that natural fellowship we are born into requires of us. If any man err from the right way, it is his own misfortune, no injury to thee; nor therefore art thou to punish him in the things of this life because thou supposest he will be miserable in that which is to come.

What I say concerning the mutual toleration of private persons differing from one another in religion, I understand also of particular churches which stand, as it were, in the same relation to each other as private persons among themselves; nor has any one of them any manner of jurisdiction over any other; no, not even when the civil magistrate (as it sometimes happens) comes to be of this or the other communion. For the civil government can give no new right to the church, nor the church to the civil government. So that whether the magistrate join himself to any church, or separate from it, the church remains always as it was before—a free and voluntary society. It neither requires the power of the sword by the magistrate's coming to it, nor does it lose the right of instruction and excommunication by his going from it. This is the fundamental and immutable right of a spontaneous society—that it has power to remove any of its members who transgress the rules of its institution; but it cannot, by the accession of any new members, acquire any right of jurisdiction over those that are not joined with it. And therefore peace, equity, and friendship are always mutually to be observed by particular churches, in the same manner as by private persons, without any pretence of superiority or jurisdiction over one another.

. . . No peace and security, no, not so much as common friendship, can ever be established or preserved amongst men so long as this opinion prevails, that dominion is founded in grace and that religion is to be propagated by force of arms. . . .

Lastly, those are not at all to be tolerated who deny the being of God. Promises, covenants, and oaths, which are the bonds of human society, can have no hold upon an atheist. The taking away of God, though but even in thought, dissolves all. Besides also, those that by their atheism undermine and destroy all religion, can have no pretense of religion whereupon to challenge the priviledge of a toleration.

Justice and Religious Freedom

John Rawls

Political philosophy has experienced a renaissance in recent years, in large part because of the work of John Rawls. His book *A Theory of Justice* has been translated into Japanese, Chinese, and Korean, as well as every major European language. In it, Rawls revives the social contract tradition. The focus of social justice is what he terms society's basic structure, by which he means its constitution and its economic system, not the justice or injustice of individual acts. Rawls's social contract is hypothetical rather than historical: Correct principles of justice are ones that would be chosen in a fair position of equality. That, in turn, requires us to imagine ourselves in an "original position" behind a "veil of ignorance" that prevents us from relying on such morally irrelevant factors as race, gender, religion, class, or even our particular talents. By forcing ourselves to choose under fair circumstances, he argues, justice is assured. Situated in such a position, he then argues, people would choose to construct their government according to principles that (1) respect basic liberties and (2) allow social and economic inequalities only if they benefit everybody, in particular society's least advantaged, and assure that everyone is given genuine (fair) equality of opportunity to seek various positions. The selection concludes with a discussion of religious freedom: the ways religious freedom is important, why it is a basic right chosen in the original position, and how a just society would want to limit religious freedom in accord with public standards acceptable and defensible to all. John Rawls is professor emeritus of philosophy at Harvard University.

As you read through this essay, consider the following:

1. What does Rawls mean by the "basic structure" of society?
2. How does he describe the original position: Behind the veil of ignorance, what do people know, and what do they not know?
3. What are "social primary goods"? What role do they play in Rawls's theory?
4. In what sense are the social contractors equal? How does Rawls's theory express the idea that all persons are "created equal"?
5. Why does Rawls term his theory "justice as fairness"? What reasons does Rawls give for using this hypothetical thought experiment of a veil of ignorance?
6. Why does Rawls think religious liberties would be protected by people behind the veil of ignorance?
7. On what basis and in what way is religious freedom limited?
8. It is sometimes said that Rawls unreasonably assumes people can "forget" their social class, natural talents, and conception of the good when, in fact, they cannot do so. How would Rawls respond to that objection? Describe other circumstances in which we expect people to ignore what they know in making a decision.

1. THE MAIN IDEA OF THE THEORY OF JUSTICE

My aim is to present a conception of justice which generalizes and carries to a higher

level of abstraction the familiar theory of the social contract as found, say, in Locke, Rousseau, and Kant. In order to do this we are not to think of the original contract as one to enter a particular society or to set up a particular form of government. Rather, the guiding idea is that the principles of justice for the basic structure of society are the object of the original agreement. They are the principles that free and rational persons concerned to further their own interests would accept in an initial position of equality as defining the fundamental terms of their association. These principles are to regulate all further agreements; they specify the kinds of social cooperation that can be entered into and the forms of government that can be established. This way of regarding the principles of justice I shall call justice as fairness.

Thus we are to imagine that those who engage in social cooperation choose together, in one joint act, the principles which are to assign basic rights and duties and to determine the division of social benefits. Men are to decide in advance how they are to regulate their claims against one another and what is to be the foundation charter of their society. Just as each person must decide by rational reflection what constitutes his good, that is, the system of ends which it is rational for him to pursue, so a group of persons must decide once and for all what is to count among them as just and unjust. The choice which rational men would make in this hypothetical situation of equal liberty, assuming for the present that this choice problem has a solution, determines the principles of justice.

In justice as fairness the original position of equality corresponds to the state of nature in the traditional theory of the social contract. This original position is not, of course, thought of as an actual historical state of affairs, much less as a primitive condition of culture. It is understood as a purely hypothetical situation characterized so as to lead to a certain conception of justice. Among the essential features of this situation is that no one knows his place in society, his class position or social status, nor does any one know his fortune in the distribution of natural assets and abilities, his intelligence, strength, and the like. I shall even assume that the parties do not know their conceptions of the good or their special psychological propensities. The principles of justice are chosen behind a veil of ignorance. This ensures that no one is advantaged or disadvantaged in the choice of principles by the outcome of natural chance or the contingency of social circum-

stances. Since all are similarly situated and no one is able to design principles to favor his particular condition, the principles of justice are the result of a fair agreement or bargain. For given the circumstances of the original position, the symmetry of everyone's relations to each other, this initial situation is fair between individuals as moral persons, that is, as rational beings with their own ends and capable, I shall assume, of a sense of justice. The original position is, one might say, the appropriate initial status quo, and thus the fundamental agreements reached in it are fair. This explains the propriety of the name "justice as fairness": it conveys the idea that the principles of justice are agreed to in an initial situation that is fair. The name does not mean that the concepts of justice and fairness are the same, any more than the phrase "poetry as metaphor" means that the concepts of poetry and metaphor are the same.

Justice as fairness begins, as I have said, with one of the most general of all choices which persons might make together, namely, with the choice of the first principles of a conception of justice which is to regulate all subsequent criticism and reform of institutions. Then, having chosen a conception of justice, we can suppose that they are to choose a constitution and a legislature to enact laws, and so on, all in accordance with the principles of justice initially agreed upon. Our social situation is just if it is such that by this sequence of hypothetical agreements we would have contracted into the general system of rules which defines it. Moreover, assuming that the original position does determine a set of principles (that is, that a particular conception of justice would be chosen), it will then be true that whenever social institutions satisfy these principles those engaged in them can say to one another that they are cooperating on terms to which they would agree if they were free and equal persons whose relations with respect to one another were fair. They could all view their arrangements as meeting the stipulations which they would acknowledge in an initial situation that embodies widely accepted and reasonable constraints on the choice of principles. The general recognition of this fact would provide the basis for a public acceptance of the corresponding principles of justice. No society can, of course, be a scheme of cooperation which men enter voluntarily in a literal sense; each person finds himself placed at birth in some particular position in some particular society, and the nature of this position materially affects his life prospects. Yet a society satisfying the principles of justice as fairness comes as close as a society can to being a voluntary scheme, for it meets the principles which free and equal persons would assent to under circumstances that are fair. In this sense its members are autonomous and the obligations they recognize self-imposed.

One feature of justice as fairness is to think of the parties in the initial situation as rational and mutually disinterested. This does not mean that the parties are egoists, that is, individuals with only certain kinds of interests, say in wealth, prestige, and domination. But they are conceived as not taking an interest in one another's interests. They are to presume that even their spiritual aims may be opposed, in the way that the aims of those of different religions may be opposed. Moreover, the concept of rationality must be interpreted as far as possible in the narrow sense, standard in economic theory, of taking the most effective means to given ends. . . . [O]ne must try to avoid introducing into it any controversial ethical elements. The initial situation must be characterized by stipulations that are widely accepted.

In working out the conception of justice as fairness one main task clearly is to determine which principles of justice would be chosen in the original position. To do this we must describe this situation in some detail and formulate with care the problem of choice which it presents. . . . It may be observed, however, that once the principles of justice are thought of as arising from an original agreement in a situation of equality, it is an open question whether the principle of utility would be acknowledged. Offhand it hardly seems likely that persons who view themselves as equals, entitled to press their claims upon one another, would agree to a principle which may require lesser life prospects for some simply for the sake of a greater sum of advantages enjoyed by others. Since each desires to protect his interests, his capacity to advance his conception of the good, no one has a reason to acquiesce in an enduring loss for himself in order to bring about a greater net balance of satisfaction. In the absence of strong and lasting benevolent impulses, a rational man would not accept a basic structure merely because it maximized the algebraic sum of advantages irrespective of its permanent effects on his own basic rights and interests. Thus it seems that the principle of utility is incompatible with the conception of social cooperation among equals for mutual advantage. It appears to be inconsistent with the idea of reciprocity implicit in the notion of a well-ordered society. Or, at any rate, so I shall argue.

I shall maintain instead that the persons in the initial situation would choose two rather different principles: the first requires equality in the assignment to basic rights and duties, while the second holds that social and economic inequalities, for example inequalities of wealth and authority, are just only if they result in compensating benefits for everyone, and in particular for the least advantaged members of society. These principles rule out justifying institutions on the grounds that the hardships of some are offset by a greater good in the aggregate. It may be expedient but it is not just that some should have less in order that others may prosper. But there is no injustice in the greater benefits earned by a few provided that the situation of persons not so fortunate is thereby improved. The intuitive idea is that since everyone's well-being depends upon a scheme of cooperation without which no one could have a satisfactory life, the division of advantages should be such as to draw forth the willing cooperation of everyone taking part in it, including those less well situated. Yet this can be expected only if reasonable terms are proposed. The two principles mentioned seem to be a fair agreement on the basis of which those better endowed, or more fortunate in their social position, neither of which we can be said to deserve, could expect the willing cooperation of others when some workable scheme is a necessary condition of the welfare of all. Once we decide to look for a conception of justice that nullifies the accidents of natural endowment and the contingencies of social circumstance as counters in quest for political and economic advantage, we are led to these principles. They express the result of leaving aside those aspects of the social world that seem arbitrary from a moral point of view. . . .

2. THE ORIGINAL POSITION AND JUSTIFICATION

I have said that the original position is the appropriate initial status quo which insures that the fundamental agreements reached in it are fair. This fact yields the name "justice as fairness." It is clear, then, that I want to say that one conception of justice is more reasonable than another, or justifiable with respect to it, if rational persons in the initial situation would choose its principles over those of the other for the role of justice. Conceptions of justice are to be ranked by their acceptability to persons so circumstanced. Understood in this way the question of justification is settled by working out a problem of deliberation: we have to ascertain which principles it would be rational to adopt given the contractual situation. This connects the theory of justice with the theory of rational choice.

If this review of the problem of justification is to succeed, we must, of course, describe in some detail the nature of this choice problem. A problem of rational decision has a definite answer only if we know the beliefs and interests of the parties, their relations with respect to one another, the alternatives between which they are to choose, the procedure whereby they make up their minds, and so on. . . . The concept of the original position, as I shall refer to it, is that

of the most philosophically favored interpretation of this initial choice situation for purposes of a theory of justice.

But how are we to decide on the most favored interpretation? . . . To justify a particular description of the initial situation one shows that it incorporates these commonly held presumptions. One argues from widely accepted but weak premises to more specific conclusions. Each of the presumptions should by itself be natural and plausible; some of them may seem innocuous or even trivial. The aim of the contract approach is to establish that taken together they impose significant bounds on acceptable principles of justice. . . .

One should not be misled, then, by the somewhat unusual conditions which characterize the original position. The idea here is simply to make vivid to ourselves the restrictions that it seems reasonable to impose on arguments for principles of justice, and therefore on these principles themselves. Thus it seems reasonable and generally acceptable that no one should be advantaged or disadvantaged by natural fortune or social circumstances in the choice of principles. [*Rawls thus argues in a later section that it is reasonable in the original position to exclude knowledge of "natural talents" such as intelligence as well as inherited wealth and social class, race, and gender, because all of these are "morally arbitrary." Social class and natural talents are not "deserved," and one's "character" also "depends in large part on fortunate family and social circumstances."—Eds.*] It also seems widely agreed that it should be impossible to tailor principles to the circumstances of one's own case. We should insure further that particular inclinations and aspirations, and persons' conceptions of their good do not affect the principles adopted. The aim is to rule out those principles that it would be rational to propose for acceptance, however little the chance of success, only if one knew certain things that are irrelevant from the standpoint of justice. For example, if a man knew that he was wealthy, he might find it rational to advance the principle that various taxes for welfare measures be counted unjust;

if he knew that he was poor, he would most likely propose the contrary principle. To represent the desired restrictions one imagines a situation in which everyone is deprived of this sort of information. One excludes the knowledge of those contingencies which sets men at odds and allows them to be guided by their prejudices. In this manner the veil of ignorance is arrived at in a natural way. This concept should cause no difficulty if we keep in mind the constraints on arguments that it is meant to express. At any time we can enter the original position, so to speak, simply by following a certain procedure, namely, by arguing for principles of justice in accordance with these restrictions.

It seems reasonable to suppose that the parties in the original position are equal. That is, all have the same rights in the procedure for choosing principles; each can make proposals, submit reasons for their acceptance, and so on. Obviously the purpose of these conditions is to represent equality between human beings as moral persons, as creatures having a conception of their good and capable of a sense of justice. The basis of equality is taken to be similarity in these two respects. Systems of ends are not ranked in value; and each man is presumed to have the requisite ability to understand and to act upon whatever principles are adopted. Together with the veil of ignorance, these conditions define the principles of justice as those which rational persons concerned to advance their interests would consent to as equals when none are known to be advantaged or disadvantaged by social and natural contingencies.

There is, however, another side to justifying a particular description of the original position. This is to see if the principles which would be chosen match our considered convictions of justice or extend them in an acceptable way. We can note whether applying these principles would lead us to make the same judgments about the basic structure of society which we now make intuitively and in which we have the greatest confidence; or whether, in cases where our present judg-

ments are in doubt and given with hesitation, these principles offer a resolution which we can affirm on reflection. There are questions which we feel sure must be answered in a certain way. For example, we are confident that religious intolerance and racial discrimination are unjust. We think that we have examined these things with care and have reached what we believe is an impartial judgment not likely to be distorted by an excessive attention to our own interests. These convictions are provisional fixed points which we presume any conception of justice must fit. But we have much less assurance as to what is the correct distribution of wealth and authority. Here we may be looking for a way to remove our doubts. We can check an interpretation of the initial situation, then, by the capacity of its principles to accommodate our firmest convictions and to provide guidance where guidance is needed. . . .

3. TWO PRINCIPLES OF JUSTICE

I shall now state in a provisional form the two principles of justice that I believe would be agreed to in the original position. The first formulation of these principles is tentative. As we go on I shall consider several formulations and approximate step by step the final statement to be given much later. I believe that doing this allows the exposition to proceed in a natural way.

The first statement of the two principles reads as follows.

> First: each person is to have an equal right to the most extensive scheme of equal basic liberties compatible with a similar scheme of liberties for others.
> Second: social and economic inequalities are to be arranged so that they are both (a) reasonably expected to be to everyone's advantage, and (b) attached to positions and offices open to all. . . .

These principles primarily apply, as I have said, to the basic structure of society and govern the assignment of rights and duties and regulate the distribution of social and economic advantages. Their formulation presupposes that, for the purposes of a theory of justice, the social structure may be viewed as having two more or less distinct parts, the first principle applying to the one, the second principle to the other. Thus we distinguish between the aspects of the social system that define and secure the equal basic liberties and the aspects that specify and establish social and economic inequalities. Now it is essential to observe that the basic liberties are given by a list of such liberties. Important among these are political liberty (the right to vote and to hold public office) and freedom of speech and assembly; liberty of conscience and freedom of thought; freedom of the person, which includes freedom from psychological oppression and physical assault and dismemberment (integrity of the person); the right to hold personal property and freedom from arbitrary arrest and seizure as defined by the concept of the rule of law. These liberties are to be equal by the first principle.

The second principle applies, in the first approximation, to the distribution of income and wealth and to the design of organizations that make use of differences in authority and responsibility. While the distribution of wealth and income need not be equal, it must be to everyone's advantage, and at the same time, positions of authority and responsibility must be accessible to all. One applies the second principle by holding positions open, and then, subject to this constraint, arranges social and economic inequalities so that everyone benefits.

. . . Since they may be limited when they clash with one another, none of these liberties is absolute; but however they are adjusted to form one system, this system is to be the same for all. It is difficult, and perhaps impossible, to give a complete specification of these liberties independently from the particular circumstances—social, economic, and technological—of a given society. The hypothesis is that the general form of such a list could be devised with sufficient exactness to sustain this conception of justice. Of course, liberties not on the list, for example, the right to own certain kinds of property (e.g., means of production) and freedom of contract as understood by the doctrine of laissez-faire are not basic; and so they are not protected by the priority of the first principle. Finally, in regard to the second principle, the distribution of wealth and income, and positions of authority and responsibility, are to be consistent with both the basic liberties and equality of opportunity.

The two principles are rather specific in their content, and their acceptance rests on certain assumptions that I must eventually try to explain and justify. For the present, it should be observed that these principles are a special case of a more general conception of justice that can be expressed as follows.

All social values—liberty and opportunity, income and wealth, and the social bases of self-respect—are to be distributed equally unless an unequal distribution of any, or all, of these values is to everyone's advantage.

Injustice, then, is simply inequalities that are not to the benefit of all. Of course, this conception is extremely vague and requires interpretation.

As a first step, suppose that the basic structure of society distributes certain primary goods, that is, things that every rational man is presumed to want. These goods normally have a use whatever a person's rational plan of life. For simplicity, assume that the chief primary goods at the disposition of society are rights, liberties, and opportunities, and income and wealth. . . . These are the social primary goods. Other primary goods such as health and vigor, intelligence and imagination, are natural goods; although their possession is influenced by the basic structure, they are not so directly under its control. Imagine, then, a hypothetical initial arrangement in which all the social primary goods are equally distributed: everyone has similar rights and duties, and income and wealth are evenly shared. This state of affairs provides a benchmark for judging improvements. If certain inequalities of wealth and differences in authority would make everyone better off than in this hypothetical starting situation, then they accord with the general conception.

Now it is possible, at least theoretically, that by giving up some of their fundamental liberties men are sufficiently compensated by the resulting social and economic gains. The general conception of justice imposes no restrictions on what sort of inequalities are permissible; it only requires that everyone's position be improved. We need not suppose anything so drastic as consenting to a condition of slavery. Imagine instead that people seem willing to forego certain political rights when the economic returns are significant. It is this kind of exchange which the two principles rule out; being arranged in serial order they do not permit exchanges between basic liberties and economic and social gains except under extenuating circumstances. . . .

The fact that the two principles apply to institutions has certain consequences. First of all, the rights and basic liberties referred to by these principles are those which are defined by the public rules of the basic structure. Whether men are free is determined by the rights and duties established by the major institutions of society. Liberty is a certain pattern of social forms. The first principle simply requires that certain sorts of rules, those defining basic liberties, apply to everyone equally and that they allow the most extensive liberty compatible with a like liberty for all. The only reason for circumscribing basic liberties and making them less extensive is that otherwise they would interfere with one another.

Further, when principles mention persons, or require that everyone gain from an inequality, the reference is to representative persons holding the various social positions, or offices established by the basic structure. Thus in applying the second principle I assume that it is possible to assign an expectation of well-being to representative individuals holding these positions. This expectation indicates their life prospects as viewed from their social station. . . .

4. EQUAL LIBERTY OF CONSCIENCE

. . . Turning then to liberty of conscience, it seems evident that the parties must choose principles that secure the integrity of their religious and moral freedom. They do not know, of course, what their religious or moral convictions are, or what is the particular content of their moral or religious obligations as they interpret them. Indeed, they do not know that they think of themselves as having such obligations. The possibility that they do suffices for the argument, although I shall make the stronger assumption. Further, the parties do not know how their religious or moral view fares in their society, whether, for example, it is in the majority or the minority. All they know is that they have obligations which they interpret in this way. The question they are to decide is which principle they should adopt to regulate the liberties of citizens in regard to their fundamental religious, moral, and philosophical interests.

Now it seems that equal liberty of conscience is the only principle that the persons in the original position can acknowledge. They cannot take chances with their liberty by permitting the dominant religious or moral doctrine to persecute or to suppress others if it wishes. Even granting (what may be questioned) that it is more probable than not that one will turn out to belong to the majority (if a majority exists), to gamble in this way would show that one did not take one's religious or moral convictions seriously, or highly value the liberty to examine one's beliefs. Nor on the other hand, could the parties consent to the principle of utility. In this case their freedom would be subject to the calculus of social interests and they would be authorizing its restriction if this would lead to a greater net balance of satisfaction. Of course, as we have seen, a utilitarian may try to argue from the general facts of social life that when properly carried out the computation of advantages never justifies such limitations, at least under reasonably favorable conditions of culture. But even if the parties were persuaded of this, they might as well guarantee their freedom straightway by adopting the principle of equal liberty. There is nothing gained by not doing so, and to the extent that the outcome of the actuarial calculation is unclear a great deal may be lost. Indeed, if we give a realistic interpretation to the general knowledge available to the parties . . . they are forced to reject the utilitarian principle. These considerations have all the more force in view of the complexity and vagueness of these calculations (if we can so describe them) as they are bound to be made in practice.

Moreover, the initial agreement on the principle of equal liberty is final. An individual recognizing religious and moral obligations regards them as binding absolutely in the sense that he cannot qualify his fulfillment of them for the sake of greater means for promoting his other interests. Greater economic and social benefits are not a sufficient reason for accepting less than an equal liberty. It seems possible to consent to an unequal liberty only if there is a threat of coercion which it is unwise to resist from the standpoint of liberty itself. For example, the situation may be one in which a person's religion or his moral view will be tolerated provided that he does not protest, whereas claiming an equal liberty will bring greater repression that cannot be effectively opposed. But from the perspective of the original position there is no way of ascertaining the relative strength of various doctrines and so these considerations do not arise. The veil of ignorance leads to an agreement on the principle of equal liberty; and the strength of religious and moral obligations as men interpret them seems to require that the two principles be put in serial order, at least when applied to freedom of conscience.

It may be said against the principle of equal liberty that religious sects, say, cannot acknowledge any principle at all for limiting their claims on one another. The duty to religious and divine law being absolute, no understanding among persons of different faiths is permissible from a religious point of view. Certainly men have often acted as if they held this doctrine. It is unnecessary, however, to argue against it. It suffices that if any principle can be agreed to, it must be that of equal liberty. A person may indeed think that others ought to recognize the same beliefs and first principles that he does, and that by not doing so they are grievously in error and miss the way to their salvation. But an understanding of religious obligation and of philosophical and moral first principles shows that we cannot expect others to acquiesce in an inferior liberty. Much less can we ask them to recognize us as the proper interpreter of their religious duties or moral obligations.

We should now observe that these reasons for the first principle receive further support once the parties' concern for the next generation is taken into account. Since they have a desire to obtain similar liberties for their descendants, and these liberties are also secured by the principle of equal liberty, there is no conflict of interests between generations. . . . We can express this by noting that were a father, for example, to assert that he would accept the principle of equal liberty, a son could not object that were he (the father) to do so he would be neglecting his (the son's) interests. The advantages of the other principles are not this great and appear in fact uncertain and conjectural. The father could reply that when the choice of principles affects the liberty of others, the decision must, if possible, seem reasonable and responsible to them once they come of age. Those who care for others must choose for them in the light of what they will want whatever else they want once they reach maturity. Therefore following the account of primary goods, the parties presume that their descendants will want their liberty protected.

At this point we touch upon the principle of paternalism that is to guide decisions taken on behalf of others. . . . We must choose for others as we have reason to believe they would choose for themselves if they were at the age of reason and deciding rationally. Trustees, guardians, and benefactors are to act in this way, but since they usually know the situation and interests of their wards and beneficiaries, they can often make accurate estimates as to what is or will be wanted. The persons in the original position, however, are prevented from knowing any more about their descendants than they do about themselves, and so in this case too they must rely upon the theory of primary goods. Thus the father can say that he would be irresponsible if he were not to guarantee the rights of his descendants by adopting the principle of equal liberty. From the perspective of the original position, he must assume that this is what they will come to recognize as for their good. . . .

5. TOLERATION AND THE COMMON INTEREST

Justice as fairness provides, as we have now seen, strong arguments for an equal liberty of conscience. I shall assume that these arguments can be generalized in suitable ways to support the principle of equal liberty. Therefore the parties have good grounds for adopting this principle. It is obvious that these considerations are also important in making the case for the priority of liberty. From the perspective of the constitutional convention these arguments lead to the choice of a regime guaranteeing moral liberty and freedom of thought and belief, and of religious practice, although these may be regulated as always by the state's interest in public order and security. The state can favor no particular religion and no penalties or disabilities may be attached to any religious affiliation or lack thereof. The notion of a confessional state is rejected. Instead, particular associations may be freely organized as their members wish, and they may have their own internal life and discipline subject to the restriction that their members have a real choice of whether to continue their affiliation. The law protects the right of sanctuary in the sense that apostasy is not recognized, much less penalized, as a legal offense, any more than is having no religion at all. In these ways the state upholds moral and religious liberty.

Liberty of conscience is limited, everyone agrees, by the common interest in public order and security. This limitation itself is readily derivable from the contract point of view. First of all, acceptance of this limitation does not imply that public interests are in any sense superior to moral and religious interests; nor does it require that government view religious matters as things indifferent or claim the right to suppress philosophical beliefs whenever they conflict with affairs of state. The government has no authority to render associations either legitimate or illegitimate any more than it has this authority in regard to art and science. These matters are simply not within its competence as defined by a just constitution. Rather, given the principles of justice, the state must be understood as the association consisting of equal citizens. It does not concern itself with philosophical and religious doctrine but regulates individuals' pursuit of their moral and spiritual interests in accordance with principles to which they themselves would agree in an initial situation of equality. By exercising its powers in this way the government acts as the citizens' agent and satisfies the demands of their public conception of justice. . . .

Granting all this, it now seems evident that, in limiting liberty by reference to the common interest in public order and security, the government acts on a principle that would be chosen in the original position. For in this position each recognizes that the disruption of these conditions is a danger for the liberty of all. This follows once the maintenance of public order is understood as a necessary condition for everyone's achieving his ends whatever they are (provided they lie within certain limits) and for his fulfilling his interpretation of his moral and religious obligations. . . .

Furthermore, liberty of conscience is to be limited only when there is a reasonable expectation that not doing so will damage the public order which the government should maintain. This expectation must be based on evidence and ways of reasoning acceptable to all. It must be supported by ordinary observation and modes of thought (including the methods of rational scientific inquiry where these are not controversial) which are generally recognized as correct. Now this reliance on what can be established and known by everyone is itself founded on the principles of justice. It implies no particular metaphysical doctrine or theory of knowledge. For this criterion appeals to what everyone can accept. It represents an agreement to limit liberty only by reference to a common knowledge and understanding of the world. Adopting this standard does not infringe upon anyone's equal freedom. On the other hand, a departure from generally recognized ways of reasoning would involve a privileged place for the views of some over others, and a principle which permitted this could not be agreed to in the original position.

Religion and the Liberal State: A Communitarian Critique

Michael J. Sandel

In this selection, Michael J. Sandel argues that the "unencumbered" understanding of the self that underlies the dominant, liberal public philosophy of our day is deeply defective. He uses as an example the law's treatment of religious freedom. Tracing the liberal self to Locke, Kant, and Rawls, Sandel contrasts it with the traditional, "encumbered" understanding that sees the self as tied to its past. Ultimately, Sandel claims, the unencumbered self is neither an accurate portrayal of human nature nor a sound basis on which to build successful democratic institutions. This is especially clear, he argues, when looking at the U.S. Supreme Court's approach to religious freedom, which has not been well served by its liberal assumptions about the nature of the self and about religious faith. Michael J. Sandel is professor of government at Harvard University.

As you read through this essay, consider the following:

1. What is the liberal ideal of neutrality? Why does Sandel think it cannot be defended by moral relativism?
2. What distinguishes liberal from republican freedom?
3. What are the two sources of liberalism's appeal?
4. What are the reasons Sandel gives for rejecting Kantian liberalism?
5. Sandel describes the Supreme Court's attempt to enforce neutrality as justified in two different ways. What are they?
6. What is the difference between the voluntarist conception of religious liberty and the traditional conception?
7. Why does Sandel think that the liberal, neutral approach to religious freedom is a failure?

THE PUBLIC PHILOSOPHY OF CONTEMPORARY LIBERALISM

The Aspiration to Neutrality

The idea that government should be neutral on the question of the good life is distinctive to modern political thought. Ancient political theory held that the purpose of politics was to cultivate the virtue, or moral excellence, of citizens. All associations aim at some good, Aristotle wrote, and the polis, or political association, aims at the highest, most comprehensive good: "any polis which is truly so called, and is not merely one in name, must devote itself to the end of encouraging goodness. Otherwise, a political association sinks into a mere alliance, which only differs in space from other forms of alliance where the members live at a distance from one another. Otherwise, too, law becomes a mere covenant—or (in the phrase of the Sophist Lycophron) 'a guarantor of men's rights against one another'—instead of being, as it should be, a rule of life such as will make the members of a polis good and just."[1]

According to Aristotle, political community is more than "an association for residence on a common site, or for the sake of preventing mutual injustice and easing exchange." Although these are necessary conditions for political community, they are not its purpose or ultimate justification. "The end and purpose of a polis is the good life, and the institutions of social life are means to that end." It is only as participants in political association that we can realize our nature and fulfill our highest ends.[2]

Unlike the ancient conception, liberal political theory does not see political life as concerned with the highest human ends or with the moral excellence of its citizens. Rather than promote a particular conception of the good life, liberal political theory insists on toleration, fair procedures, and respect for individual rights—values that respect people's freedom to choose their own values. But this raises a difficult question. If liberal ideals cannot be defended in the name of the highest human good, then in what does their moral basis consist?

It is sometimes thought that liberal principles can be justified by a simple version of moral relativism. Government should not "legislate morality," because all morality is merely subjective, a matter of personal preference not open to argument or rational debate. "Who is to say what is literature and what is filth? That is a value judgment, and whose values should decide?" Relativism usually appears less as a claim than as a question:

"Who is to judge?" But the same question can be asked of the values that liberals defend. Toleration and freedom and fairness are values too, and they can hardly be defended by the claim that no values can be defended. So it is a mistake to affirm liberal values by arguing that all values are merely subjective. The relativist defense of liberalism is no defense at all.

Utilitarianism versus Kantian Liberalism

What, then, is the case for the neutrality the liberal invokes? Recent political philosophy has offered two main alternatives—one utilitarian, the other Kantian. The utilitarian view, following John Stuart Mill, defends liberal principles in the name of maximizing the general welfare. The state should not impose on its citizens a preferred way of life, even for their own good, because doing so will reduce the sum of human happiness, at least in the long run. It is better that people choose for themselves, even if, on occasion, they get it wrong.

"The only freedom which deserves the name," writes Mill in *On Liberty*, "is that of pursuing our own good in our own way, so long as we do not attempt to deprive others of theirs, or impede their efforts to obtain it." He adds that his argument does not depend on any notion of abstract right, only on the principle of the greatest good for the greatest number. . . .

[Sandel goes on to explain why Kantian liberals such as John Rawls reject utilitarianism. First, he points out that it is possible for utilitarians to justify gross violations of rights if enough people get enough pleasure from doing so. More important, according to Kantians, utilitarianism does not respect the dignity of persons because it ignores the individual in favor of whatever will most likely produce the greatest total happiness. Utilitarianism does not take differences between people seriously; it treats the many individual desires of persons as a single system of desires.—Eds.]

. . . For Kantian liberals, it is precisely because we are freely choosing, independent selves that we need a neutral framework, a framework of rights that refuses to choose among competing values and ends. For the liberal self, what matters above all, what is most essential to our personhood, is not the ends we choose but our capacity to choose them. "It is not our aims that primarily reveal our nature," but rather the framework of rights we would agree to if we could abstract from our aims. "For the self is prior to the ends which are affirmed by it; even a dominant end must be chosen from among numerous possibilities."[3]

The liberal ethic derives much of its moral force from the appeal of the self-image that animates it. This appeal has at least two sources. First, the image of the self as free and independent, unencumbered by aims and attachments it does not choose for itself, offers a powerful liberating vision. Freed from the sanctions of custom and tradition and inherited status, unbound by moral ties antecedent to choice, the liberal self is installed as sovereign, cast as the author of the only obligations that constrain. More than the simple sum of circumstance, we become capable of the dignity that consists in being persons of our "own creating, making, choosing."[4] We are agents and not just instruments of the purposes we pursue. We are "self-originating sources of valid claims."[5]

A second appeal of the liberal self-image consists in the case it implies for equal respect. The idea that there is more to a person than the roles he plays or the customs she keeps or the faith he affirms suggests a basis for respect independent of life's contingencies. Liberal justice is blind to such differences between persons as race, religion, ethnicity, and gender, for in the liberal self-image, these features do not really define our identity in the first place. They are not constituents but merely attributes of the self, the sort of things the state should look beyond. "Our social position and class, our sex and race should not influence deliberations made from a moral point of view."[6] Once these contingencies are seen as products of our situation rather than as aspects of our person, they cease to supply the familiar grounds for prejudice and discrimination.

Nor does it matter, from the standpoint of liberal justice, what virtues we display or what values we espouse. "That we have one conception of the good rather than another is not relevant from a moral standpoint. In acquiring it we are influenced by the same sort of contingencies that lead us to rule out a knowledge of our sex and class."[7] Despite their many differences, libertarian and egalitarian liberals agree that people's entitlements should not be based on their merit or virtue or moral desert, for the qualities that make people virtuous or morally deserving depend on factors "arbitrary from a moral point of view."[8] The liberal state therefore does not discriminate; none of its policies or laws may presuppose that any person or way of life is intrinsically more virtuous than any other. It respects persons as persons, and secures their equal right to live the lives they choose.

Critique of Kantian Liberalism

Kantian liberals thus avoid affirming a conception of the good by affirming instead the priority of the right, which depends in turn on a picture of the self given prior to its ends. But how plausible is this self-conception? Despite its powerful appeal, the image of the unencumbered self is flawed. It cannot make sense of our moral experience, because it cannot account for certain moral and political obligations that we commonly recognize, even prize. These include obligations of solidarity, religious duties, and other moral ties that may claim us for reasons unrelated to a choice. Such obligations are difficult to account for if we understand ourselves as free and independent selves, unbound by moral ties we have not chosen. Unless we think of ourselves as encumbered selves, already claimed by certain projects and commitments, we cannot make sense of these indispensable aspects of our moral and political experience.

Consider the limited scope of obligation on the liberal view. According to Rawls, obligations can arise in only one of two ways, as "natural duties" we owe to human beings as such or as voluntary obligations we incur by consent. The natural duties are those we owe persons *qua* persons—to do justice, to avoid cruelty, and so on. All other obligations, the ones we owe to particular others, are founded in consent and arise only in virtue of agreements we make, be they tacit or explicit.[9]

Conceived as unencumbered selves, we must respect the dignity of all persons, but beyond this, we owe only what we agree to owe. Liberal justice requires that we respect people's rights (as defined by the neutral framework), not that we advance their good. Whether we must concern ourselves with other people's good depends on whether, and with whom, and on what terms, we have agreed to do so.

One striking consequence of this view is that "there is no political obligation, strictly speaking, for citizens generally." Although those who run for office voluntarily incur a political obligation (that is, to serve their country if elected), the ordinary citizen does not. "It is not clear what is the requisite binding action or who has performed it."[10] The average citizen is therefore without any special obligations to his or her fellow citizens, apart from the universal, natural duty not to commit injustice.

The liberal attempt to construe all obligation in terms of duties universally owed or obligations voluntarily incurred makes it difficult to account for civic obligations and other moral and political ties that we commonly recognize. It fails to capture those loyalties and responsibilities whose moral force consists partly in the fact that living by them is inseparable from understanding ourselves as the particular persons we are—as members of this family or city or nation or people, as bearers of that history, as citizens of this republic. Loyalties such as these can be more than values I happen to have, and to hold, at a certain distance. The moral responsibilities they entail may go beyond the obligations I voluntarily incur and the "natural duties" I owe to human beings as such.

Some of the special responsibilities that flow from the particular communities I inhabit I may owe to fellow members, such as obligations of solidarity. Others I may owe to members of those communities with which my own community has some morally relevant history, such as the morally burdened relations of Germans to Jews, of American whites to American blacks, or of England and France to their former colonies. Whether they look inward or outward, obligations of membership presuppose that we are capable of moral ties antecedent to choice. To the extent that we are, the meaning of our membership resists redescription in contractarian terms.

It is sometimes argued, in defense of the liberal view, that loyalties and allegiances not grounded in consent, however psychologically compelling, are matters of sentiment, not of morality, and so do not suggest an obligation unavailable to unencumbered selves. But it is difficult to make sense of certain familiar moral and political dilemmas without acknowledging obligations of solidarity and the thickly constituted, encumbered selves that they imply.

Consider the case of Robert E. Lee on the eve of the Civil War. Lee, then an officer in the Union army, opposed secession, in fact regarded it as treason. And yet when war loomed, Lee concluded that his obligation to Virginia outweighed his obligation to the Union and also his reported opposition to slavery. "With all my devotion to the Union," he wrote, "I have not been able to make up my mind to raise my hand against my relatives, my children, my home. . . . If the Union is dissolved, and the Government disrupted, I shall return to my native State and share the miseries of my people. Save in her defense, I will draw my sword no more."[11]

One can appreciate the poignance of Lee's predicament without necessarily approving of the choice he made. But one cannot make sense of his dilemma as a *moral* dilemma without acknowledging that the call to stand with his people, even to lead them in a cause he opposed, was a claim of moral and not merely sentimental import, capable at least of weighing in the balance against other duties and obligations. Otherwise, Lee's predicament was not really a moral dilemma at all, but simply a conflict between morality on the one hand and mere sentiment or prejudice on the other.

A merely psychological reading of Lee's predicament misses the fact that we not only sympathize with people such as Lee but often admire them. . . .

RELIGIOUS LIBERTY

After World War II, the Supreme Court assumed as its primary role the protection of individual rights against government infringement. Increasingly, it defined these rights according to the requirement that government be neutral on the question of the good life, and defended neutrality as essential to respecting persons as free and independent selves, unencumbered by moral ties antecedent to choice. The modern Supreme Court thus gives clear expression to the public philosophy of the procedural republic. In its hands, American constitutional law has come to embody the priority of the right over the good. . . .

Seeking Neutrality Toward Religion

The principle of government neutrality found its first sustained application in cases involving religion. Time and again the Supreme Court has held that "in the relationship between man and religion, the State is firmly committed to a position of neutrality."[12] "Government in our democracy, state and national, must be neutral in matters of religious theory, doctrine, and practice. . . . The First Amendment mandates governmental neutrality between religion and religion, and between religion and nonreligion."[13] Whether described as "a strict and lofty neutrality,"[14] a "wholesome neutrality,"[15] or a "benevolent neutrality,"[16] the principle "that the Government must pursue a course of complete neutrality toward religion"[17] is well established in American constitutional law.

In liberal political thought, religion offers the paradigmatic case for bracketing controversial conceptions of the good.[18] The Supreme Court has conveyed its insistence on bracketing religion by invoking Jefferson's metaphor of a "wall of separation between church and state."[19] While some have complained that "a rule of law should not be drawn from a figure of speech,"[20] most see the wall as a symbol of resolve to keep religion from bursting the constitutional brackets that contain it. Since "the breach of neutrality that is today a trickling stream may all too soon become a raging torrent,"[21] the "wall between Church and State . . . must be kept high and impregnable."[22]

For all its familiarity, the requirement that government be neutral on matters of religion is not a long-standing principle of constitutional law, but a development of the last fifty years. Not until 1947 did the Supreme Court hold that government must be neutral toward religion.[23] The American tradition of religious liberty goes back further, of course. The Constitution forbids religious tests for federal office (Article VI), and the first words of the First Amendment declare that "Congress shall make no law respecting an establishment of religion, or prohibiting the free exercise thereof." But the Bill of Rights did not apply to the states, and at the time of its adoption, six of the thirteen states maintained religious establishments. Far from prohibiting these arrangements, the First Amendment was enacted in part to protect state religious establishments from federal interference. . . .

Not until the 1940s did the Court apply the First Amendment's religion clauses to the states and declare the separation of church and state a principle of constitutional law. In *Cantwell v. Connecticut* (1940), the Court held that the Fourteenth Amendment incorporated both the establishment and free exercise clauses of the Bill of Rights and "rendered the legislatures of the states as incompetent as Congress to enact such laws."[24] In *Everson v. Board of Education of Ewing Township* (1947), the Court gave the establishment clause a broad interpretation and enforced, for the first time, Jefferson's "wall of separation between church and state."[25]

Writing for the Court, Justice Black gave forceful expression to the principle of government neutrality. "Neither a state nor the Federal Government can set up a church. Neither can pass laws which aid one religion, aid all religions, or prefer one religion over another. . . . No tax in any amount, large or small, can be levied to support any religious activities or institutions." The First Amendment "requires the state to be a neutral in its relations with groups of religious believers and non-believers."[26]

Since *Everson*, religion has generated much constitutional controversy, but the principle that government must be neutral toward religion has rarely been questioned.[27] For the most part, the justices have cast their disagreements as arguments about the proper application of neutrality, not about the principle itself. In fact Black's landmark opinion in *Everson* came in the course of upholding a state subsidy for bus transportation of parochial school students. The dissenters applauded the Court's insistence on "complete and uncompromising separation" but found it "utterly discordant" with the result in the case.[28]

In 1963 the Court ruled that Bible reading in the public schools was a religious exercise at odds with the requirement "that the Government maintain strict neutrality, neither aiding nor opposing religion." Justice Potter Stewart dissented, but in the name of neutrality. Permission of religious exercises is necessary, he argued, "if the schools are truly to be neutral in the matter of religion. A refusal to permit religious exercises thus is seen, not as the realization of state neutrality, but rather as the establishment of a religion of secularism, or at the least, as government support of the beliefs of those who think that religious exercises should be conducted only in private."[29]

In 1968 the Court struck down an Arkansas law that banned the teaching of evolution. "Government must be neutral in matters of religious theory, doctrine, and practice," wrote Justice Abe Fortas. "It may not be hostile to any religion." In a concurring opinion, Justice Black agreed with the result but doubted that the principle of neutrality supported it. If Darwinism contradicts some people's religious convictions, then it is hardly neutral to teach it in the public schools: "If the theory is considered anti-religious, how can the State be bound by the Federal Constitution to permit its teachers to advocate such an 'anti-religious' doctrine to schoolchildren?"[30]

Black pointed out that the Court might simply take the view that fundamentalists who regard evolution as antireligious are wrong. But that would be taking sides in the controversy the Court purports to bracket. "Unless this Court is prepared simply to write off as pure nonsense the views of those who consider evolution an anti-religious doctrine," Black argued, the issue was more difficult than the Court acknowledged. A better way to bracket, he suggested, might be to remove the controversial subject from the schools altogether, as Arkansas arguably did. So long as the biblical account of creation was not taught instead, "does not the removal of the subject of evolution leave the State in a neutral position toward these supposedly competing religious and anti-religious doctrines?"[31]

The contest for the mantle of neutrality continued in 1985, when the Court struck down a moment-of-silence statute permitting voluntary prayer in Alabama schools. The Court held that since the purpose of the law was to restore prayer to the schools, it violated "the established principle that the Government must pursue a course of complete neutrality toward religion." Chief Justice Warren Burger dissented, arguing that the prohibition "manifests not neutrality but hostility toward religion."[32]

Even in cases in which the Supreme Court has upheld government involvement in arguably religious practices, it has taken pains to maintain that the religious aspect is only incidental, that the involvement does not endorse or advance or prefer religion. In

McGowan v. Maryland (1961), the Court upheld Sunday closing laws on the grounds that they no longer retained their religious character. Notwithstanding their religious origins, wrote Chief Justice Warren, laws prohibiting business and commercial activity on Sundays now served the secular purpose of "providing a Sunday atmosphere of recreation, cheerfulness, repose and enjoyment. . . . The air of the day is one of relaxation rather than one of religion."[33]

In 1984 the Burger Court upheld on similar grounds a city-sponsored Christmas display including a creche, or nativity scene. The purpose of the display was to celebrate the holiday and to depict its origins, the Court held. "These are legitimate secular purposes." Any benefit it brought to religion was "indirect, remote and incidental." Display of the creche was no more an advancement or endorsement of religion than the exhibition of religious paintings in governmentally supported museums.[34]

In both cases, dissenters criticized the Court for failing to take seriously the religious character of the practices they upheld. "No matter what is said, the parentage of [the Sunday closing] laws is the Fourth Commandment," wrote Justice William O. Douglas. "They serve and satisfy the religious predispositions of our Christian communities."[35] Dissenting in the creche case, Justice Harry A. Blackmun complained that the majority had done "an injustice to the creche and the message it manifests." In the hands of the Court, "The creche has been relegated to the role of a neutral harbinger of the holiday season, useful for commercial purposes, but devoid of any inherent meaning and incapable of enhancing the religious tenor of a display of which it is an integral part. . . . Surely, this is a misuse of a sacred symbol."[36]

Justifying Neutrality Toward Religion

In order to assess the Court's conflicting applications of neutrality, it is necessary to consider the reasons for neutrality. What counts as neutrality depends partly on what justifies neutrality, and the Court has offered two different sorts of justification for insisting that government be neutral toward religion. The first has to do with protecting the interests of religion on the one hand and those of the state on the other. "The First Amendment rests on the premise that both religion and government can best work to achieve their lofty aims if each is left free from the other within its respective sphere."[37] "We have staked the very existence of our country on the fact that complete separation between the state and religion is best for the state and best for religion."[38] "In the long view the independence of both church and state in their respective spheres will be better served by close adherence to the neutrality principle."[39]

The religious interest served by separation is in avoiding the corruption that comes with dependence on civil authority. A century and a half before Jefferson stated the secular case for a "wall of separation" between church and state, Roger Williams gave the metaphor a theological meaning. "When they have opened a gap in the hedge or wall of separation between the garden of the church and the wilderness of the world," he wrote, "God hath ever broke down the wall itself, removed the candlestick, and made His garden a wilderness, as at this day."[40] . . .

Existing alongside the argument that neutrality is best for both religion and the state is an argument in the name of individual freedom. On this justification, the state must be neutral not only to avoid compromising religion and provoking sectarian strife, but also to avoid the danger of coercion. This argument goes back to the eighteenth-century concern for freedom of conscience, and in its modern form emphasizes respect for persons' freedom to choose their religious convictions for themselves. It thus connects the case for neutrality with the liberal conception of the person.

In its modern, or voluntarist, version, this argument for religious liberty first appears in *Cantwell*, the case that announced the incorporation of the religion clauses. "Freedom of conscience and freedom to adhere to such religious organization or form of worship as the individual may choose cannot be restricted by law." The First Amendment "safeguards the free exercise of the chosen form of religion."[41] In banning Bible reading in the public schools, the Court found justification for neutrality in "the right of every person to freely choose his own course" with reference to religion, "free of any compulsion from the state." Justice Stewart dissented from the result but endorsed the view that neutrality is required for the sake of the result for individual choice, "a refusal on the part of the state to weight the scales of private choice."[42]

Contemporary commentators have identified the voluntarist argument for neutrality as the primary justification for the separation of church and state. "[T]he fundamental principle underlying both religion clauses is the protection of individual choice in matters of religion—whether pro or con."[43] "[S]ince freedom of religious choice, not neutrality per se, is the fundamental establishment value, the neutrality tool is useful only insofar as it promotes that choice."[44] "[T]he moral basis of the antiestablishment clause is . . . equal respect," not for religious beliefs themselves, but "for the processes of forming and changing such conceptions."[45]

By the 1980s and 1990s, the freedom of choice assumed to be at stake in religion cases was not only the right to choose a form of worship that expresses one's religious beliefs but also the right to choose the beliefs themselves. In a case involving a city-sponsored display of a menorah alongside a Christmas tree, Justice Sandra Day O'Connor approved the arrangement on the grounds that it did not endorse religion but conveyed "a message of pluralism and freedom to choose one's own beliefs."[46] Concurring in a case that banned prayers led by clergy at public school graduation ceremonies, Justice Blackmun wrote: "Even subtle pressure diminishes the right of each individual to choose voluntarily what to believe."[47]

Perhaps the most explicit statement of the voluntarist conception of religious liberty is the one that appears in Justice John Paul Stevens' opinion for the Court in a 1985 case striking down Alabama's moment of silence for voluntary prayer in public schools. "[T]he individual's freedom to choose his own creed is the counterpart of his right to refrain from accepting the creed established by the majority," Stevens wrote; "the Court has unambiguously concluded that the individual freedom of conscience protected by the First Amendment embraces the right to select any religious faith or none at all. This conclusion derives support not only from the interest in respecting the individual's freedom of conscience, but also from the conviction that *religious beliefs worthy of respect are the product of free and voluntary choice* by the faithful."[48]

Stevens' opinion illustrates the connection between the voluntarist justification of neutrality and the liberal conception of the person. It holds that government should be neutral toward religion in order to respect persons as free and independent selves, capable of choosing their religious convictions for themselves. The respect this neutrality commands is not, strictly speaking, respect for religion, but respect for the self whose religion it is, ore respect for the dignity that consists in the capacity to choose one's religion freely. Religious beliefs are "worthy of respect," not in virtue of what they are beliefs *in*, but rather in virtue of being "the product of free and voluntary choice," in virtue of being beliefs of a self unencumbered by convictions antecedent to choice.

By invoking the voluntarist conception of neutrality, the Court gives constitutional expression to the version of liberalism that conceives the right as prior to the good and the self as prior to its ends, at least where religion is concerned. We are now in a position to see how both the promise and the problems of the theory make themselves felt in the practice the theory informs.

The voluntarist case for neutrality, insisting as it does on respect for persons, seems to secure for religious liberty a firm foundation. Unlike Roger Williams' case for separation of church and state, it does not depend on any particular religious doctrine. And unlike the political case for separation, it does not leave religious liberty hostage to uncertain calculations about how best to avoid civil strife. Under present conditions, such calculations may or may not support the separation of church and state. As Justice Lewis Powell has observed, the risk "of deep political divisions along religious lines" is by now "remote."[49] We do not live on the brink of the wars of religion that made the case for separation so pressing. Even granting the importance of avoiding sectarian strife, a strict separation of church and state may at times provoke more strife than it prevents. The school prayer decisions of the early 1960s, for example, set off a storm of political controversy that has persisted over three decades. A Court concerned above all to avoid social discord might reasonably have decided those cases the other way.

The voluntarist case for neutrality, by contrast, does not tie religious liberty to such contingencies. In affirming a notion of respect for persons, it recalls the ideal of freedom of conscience. By emphasizing the individual's right to choose his or her beliefs, it points beyond religion to "the broader perspective" of autonomy rights in general, including "the rights of privacy and personhood."[50] It thus casts religious liberty as a particular case of the liberal claim for the priority of the right over the good and the self-image that attends it. Respecting persons as selves defined prior to the religious convictions they affirm becomes a particular case of the general principle of respect for selves defined prior to their aims and attachments.

But as we have seen, the image of the unencumbered self, despite its appeal, is inadequate to the liberty it promises. In the case of religion, the liberal conception of the person ill equips the Court to secure religious liberty for those who regard themselves as claimed by religious commitments they have not chosen. Not all religious beliefs can be redescribed without loss as "the product of free and voluntary choice by the faithful."

Freedom of Conscience versus Freedom of Choice

This difficulty can be seen by contrasting the voluntarist account of religious liberty with freedom of conscience as traditionally conceived. For Madison and Jefferson, freedom of conscience meant the freedom to exercise religious liberty—to worship or not, to support a church or not, to profess belief or disbelief—without suffering civil penalties or incapacities. It had nothing to do with a right to choose one's beliefs. Madison's *Memorial and Remonstrance* consists of fifteen arguments for the separation of church and state, and not one makes any mention of "autonomy" or "choice." The only choice referred to in Jefferson's "Bill for Establishing Religious Freedom" is attributed to God, not man.

Madison and Jefferson understood religious liberty as the right to exercise religious duties according to the dictates of conscience, not the right to choose religious beliefs. In fact their argument for religious liberty relies heavily on the assumption that beliefs are not a matter of choice. The first sentence of Jefferson's Bill states this assumption clearly: "the opinions and beliefs of men depend not on their own will, but follow involuntarily the evidence proposed to their own minds." Since I can believe only what I am persuaded is true, belief is not the sort of thing that coercion can compel. Coercion can produce hypocrisy but not conviction. In this assumption Jefferson echoed the view of John Locke, who wrote in *A Letter Concerning Toleration* (1689), "it is absurd that things should be enjoined by laws which are not in men's power to perform. And to believe this or that to be true, does not depend upon our will."[51]

It is precisely because belief is not governed by the will that freedom of conscience is inalienable. Even if he would, a person could not give it up. . . .

To question the voluntarist justification of religious liberty is not necessarily to agree with Locke that people never choose their religious beliefs. It is simply to dispute what the voluntarist view asserts, that religious beliefs worthy of respect are the products of free and voluntary choice. What makes a religious belief worthy of respect is not its mode of acquisition—whether by choice, revelation, persuasion, or habituation—but its place in a good life or, from a political point of view, its tendency to promote the habits and dispositions that make good citizens. Insofar as the case for religious liberty rests on respect for religion, it must assume that, generally speaking, religious beliefs and practices are of sufficient moral or civic importance to warrant special constitutional protection.

For procedural liberalism, however, the case for religious liberty derives not from the moral importance of religion but from the need to protect individual autonomy; government should be neutral toward religion for the same reason it should be neutral toward competing conceptions of the good life generally—to respect people's capacity to choose their own values and ends. But despite its liberating promise, or perhaps because of it, this broader mission depreciates the claims of those for whom religion is not an expression of autonomy but a matter of conviction unrelated to a choice. Protecting religion as a life-style, as one among the values that an independent self may have, may miss the role that religion plays in the lives of those for whom the observance of religious duties is a constitutive end, essential to their good and indispensable to their identity. Treating persons as "self-originating sources of valid claims"[52] may thus fail to respect persons bound by duties derived from sources other than themselves.

The case of *Thornton v. Caldor, Inc.* (1985) shows how voluntarist assumptions can crowd out religious liberty for encumbered selves. In an eight-to-one decision, the Supreme Court struck down a Connecticut statute guaranteeing sabbath observers a right not to work on their sabbath.[53] Although the law gave all workers the right to one day off each week, it gave to sabbath observers alone the right to designate their day. In this lack of neutrality the Court found constitutional infirmity.

Chief Justice Burger, writing for the Court, noted that sabbath observers would typically take a weekend day, "widely prized as a day off." But "other employees who have strong and legitimate, but non-religious reasons for wanting a weekend day off have no rights under the statute." They "must take a back seat to the Sabbath observers." Justice O'Connor echoed this worry in a concurring opinion: "All employees, regardless of their religious orientation, would value the benefit which the statute bestows on Sabbath observers—the right to select the day of the week in which to refrain from labor.[54]

But this objection confuses the right to perform a duty with the right to make a choice. Sabbath observers, by definition, do not *select* the day of the week they rest; they rest on the day their religion requires. The benefit the statute confers is not the right to choose a day of rest, but the right to perform the duty of sabbath observance on the only day it can be carried out.

Considered together with earlier decisions upholding Sunday closing laws, *Thornton v. Caldor* yields a curious constitutional conclusion: A state may require everyone to rest on Sunday, the day of the Christian sabbath, so long as the aim is not to accommodate observance of the sabbath. But it may not give sabbath observers the right to rest on the day of the week their religion requires. Perverse though this result may seem from the standpoint of respecting religious liberty, it aptly reflects the constitutional consequences of seeing ourselves as unencumbered selves. . . .

. . . Captain Simcha Goldman was an Orthodox Jew whom the Air Force prohibited from wearing a yarmulke while on duty in the health clinic where he served. Justice William H. Rehnquist, writing for the Court, held for the Air Force on grounds of judicial deference to the "professional judgment of military authorities" on the importance of uniform dress. Of the precedents he cited in support of deference to the military, all involved interests other than religious duties or conscientious imperatives. "The essence of military service 'is the subordination of the desires and interests of the individual to the needs of the service.'" Standardized uniforms encourage "the subordination of personal preferences and identities in favor of the overall mission." Having compared the wearing of a yarmulke to "desires," "interests," and "personal preferences" unrelated to religion, Rehnquist did not require the Air Force to show that an exception for yarmulkes would impair its disciplinary objectives. Nor even did he acknowledge that a religious duty was at stake, allowing only that, given the dress code, "military life may be more objectionable for petitioner."[55]

The Court's lack of concern for persons encumbered by religious convictions found its most decisive expression in a 1990 case that involved the sacramental use of the drug peyote by members of the Native American Church. Two members of the church were fired from their jobs at a private drug rehabilitation center because they ingested peyote, a drug prohibited by state law, as part of a religious ceremony. The workers were denied unemployment compensation on the grounds that they had been dismissed for violating a law. The Supreme Court upheld the denial. Writing for the Court, Justice Antonin Scalia maintained that the right of free exercise protects persons only from laws directed against their religion, not from neutral laws of general applicability that happen to burden their religious practice. Provided it did not target a particular religion, a state could pass laws that burdened certain religious practices even without having to show a "compelling state interest," or special justification.[56]

It might seem that Court rulings refusing special protection for sacramental peyote, the wearing of yarmulkes, or the accommodation of sabbath observance are decisions that depart from liberal principles; since they fail to vindicate the rights of individuals against the prerogatives of the majority, such decisions might seem at odds with the liberalism that asserts the priority of the right over the good. But these cases illustrate two features of procedural liberalism that, ironically, lead to illiberal consequences where religion is concerned. First, the conception of persons as freely choosing selves, unencumbered by antecedent moral ties, supports the notion that religious beliefs should be regarded, for constitutional purposes at least, as products of "free and voluntary choice." If all religious beliefs are matters of choice, however, it is difficult to distinguish between claims of conscience on the one hand and personal preferences and desires on the other. Once this distinction is lost, the right to demand of the state a special justification for laws that burden religious beliefs is bound to appear as nothing more than "a private right to ignore generally applicable laws." So indiscriminate a right would allow each person "to become a law unto himself" and create a society "courting anarchy."[57]

Second, the procedural liberal's insistence on neutrality fits uneasily with the notion that the Constitution singles out religion for special protection. If religious beliefs must be accorded constitutional protection that other interests do not enjoy, then judges must discriminate, at least to the extent of assessing the moral weight of the governmental interest at stake and the nature of the burden that interest may impose on certain religious practices. The attempt to avoid substantive moral judgments of this kind leads some to insist on neutrality even at the cost of leaving religious liberty subject to the vagaries of democratic politics. For example, Scalia concedes that leaving religious accommodation to the political process will place religious minorities at a disadvantage, but he maintains that this "unavoidable consequence of democratic government must be preferred to a system in which each conscience is a law unto itself or in which judges weigh the social importance of all laws against the centrality of all religious beliefs."[58]

Outrage from religious organizations and civil liberties groups at the weakening of religious liberty in the peyote case prompted Congress to enact the Religious Freedom Restoration Act (1993), a statute barring government from substantially burdening the exercise of religion without demonstrating a compelling governmental interest. But the way the constitutional law of religion has unfolded over the past half-century sheds light on the liberal political theory it came to express. The Court's tendency to assimilate religious liberty to liberty in general reflects the aspiration to neutrality; people should be free to pursue their own interests and ends, whatever they are, consistent with a similar liberty for others. But this generalizing tendency does not always serve religious liberty well. It confuses the pursuit of preferences with the exercise of duties, and so forgets the special concern of religious liberty with the claims of conscientiously encumbered selves.

This confusion has led the Court to restrict religious practices it should permit, such as yarmulkes in the military, and also to permit practices it should probably restrict, such as nativity scenes in the public square. In different ways, both decisions fail to take religion seriously. Permitting Pawtucket's creche might seem to be a ruling sympathetic to religion. But as Justice Blackmun rightly protested, the Court's permission came at the price of denying the sacred meaning of the symbol it protected.

Notes

1. Aristotle, *The Politics*, trans. Ernest Barker, book 3, chap. 9 (London: Oxford University Press, 1946), p. 119.

2. Ibid., pp. 119–120.

3. John Rawls, *A Theory of Justice* (Cambridge, Mass.: Harvard University Press, 1971), p. 560.

4. George Kateb, "Democratic Individuality and the Claims of Politics," *Political Theory*, 12 (August 1984), 343.

5. John Rawls, "Kantian Constructivism in Moral Theory," *Journal of Philosophy*, 77 (Summer 1980), 543.

6. John Rawls, "Fairness to Goodness," *Philosophical Review*, 84 (October 1985), 537.

7. Ibid.

8. Rawls, *A Theory of Justice*, p. 312, and, generally, pp. 310–315. See also Friedrich A. Hayek, *The Constitution of Liberty* (Chicago: University of Chicago Press, 1960), chap. 7; and Robert Nozick, *Anarchy, State, and Utopia*, (New York: Basic Books, 1977), pp. 155–160.

9. Rawls, *A Theory of Justice*, pp. 108–117.

10. Ibid., p. 114.

11. Lee quoted in Douglas Southall Freeman, *R. E. Lee* (New York: Charles Scribner's Sons, 1934), pp. 443, 421. See also the discussions of Lee in Morton Grodzins, *The Loyal and the Disloyal* (Chicago: University of Chicago Press, 1965), pp. 142–143; and Judith Shklar, *Ordinary Vices* (Cambridge, Mass.: Harvard University Press, 1984), p. 160.

12. *Abington Township School District v. Schempp*, 374 U.S. 203, 226 (1963).

13. *Epperson v. Arkansas*, 393 U.S. 97, 104–104 (1968).

14. *Everson v. Board of Education of Ewing Township*, 330 U.S. 1, 24 (1947), Justice Jackson dissenting.

15. *Abington*, 374 U.S. at 221.

16. *Walz v. Tax Commission of the City of New York*, 397 U.S. 664, 669 (1970).

17. *Wallace v. Jaffree*, 472 U.S. 38, 60 (1985).

18. See, for example, John Locke, *A Letter Concerning Toleration* (1689), ed. James H. Tully (Indianapolis: Hackett, 1983); and John Rawls, "Justice as Fairness: Political not Metaphysical," *Philosophy & Public Affairs*, 14 (Summer 1985), 249.

19. *Everson*, 330 U.S. at 16. The quotation is from Jefferson's letter to the Baptists of Danbury, Connecticut, January 1, 1802, in *Jefferson Writings*, ed. Merrill D. Peterson (New York: Library of America, 1984), p. 510.

20. *McCollum v. Board of Education*, 333 U.S. 203, 247 (1948), Justice Reed dissenting.

21. *Abington*, 374 U.S. at 203.

22. *McCollum*, 333 U.S. at 203.

23. In *Everson*, 330 U.S.

24. *Cantwell v. Connecticut*, 310 U.S. 296, 303 (1940).

25. *Everson*, 330 U.S. at 16.

26. Ibid. at 15–16.

27. A recent exception is Justice Rehnquist's dissent in *Wallace*, 472 U.S. at 91.

28. *Everson*, 330 U.S. at 19.

29. *Abington*, 374 U.S. at 225, 313. In *Engel v. Vitale*, 370 U.S. 421 (1962), by contrast, Stewart had defended school prayer by appealing not to neutrality but to "the history of the religious traditions of our people" and "the deeply entrenched and highly cherished spiritual traditions of our Nation."

30. *Epperson*, 393 U.S. at 113.

31. Ibid. The dispute over the proper interpretation of neutrality also arose in *Edwards v. Aguillard*, 482 U.S. 578 (1987), a case involving a Louisiana law mandating "balanced treatment" of creationism and evolution in the public schools.

32. *Wallace*, 472 U.S. at 60, 85. In a separate dissent, Justice Rehnquist challenged the assumption, accepted since *Everson*, that the establishment clause requires government to be neutral between religion and irreligion; ibid. at 99.

33. *McGowan v. Maryland*, 366 U.S. 420, 448 (1961).

34. *Lynch v. Donnelly*, 465 U.S. 668, 681, 683 (1984). In *Marsh v. Chambers*, 463 U.S. 783 (1983), the Court upheld the Nebraska legislature's practice of opening each day with a prayer by a chaplain paid by the

state, citing the long history of the practice. Writing in dissent, Justice Brennan construed the decision as carving out a narrow exception to establishment clause doctrine.

35. *McGowan*, 366 U.S. at 572–573.

36. *Lynch*, 465 U.S. at 727.

37. *McCollum*, 333 U.S. at 212.

38. *Everson*, 330 U.S. at 59, Justice Rutledge dissenting.

39. *Abington*, 374 U.S. at 245, Justice Brennan concurring.

40. Roger Williams quoted in Mark de Wolfe Howe, *The Garden and the Wilderness*, (Chicago: University of Chicago Press, 1965), pp. 6–7.

41. *Cantwell*, 310 U.S. at 303.

42. *Abington*, 374 U.S. at 222, 317, Justice Clark for the Court, Justice Stewart in dissent.

43. Gail Merel, "The Protection of Individual Choice: A Consistent Understanding of Religion under the First Amendment," *University of Chicago Law Review*, 45 (1978), 806.

44. Alan Schwarz, "No Imposition of Religion: The Establishment Clause Value, *Yale Law Journal*, 77 (1968), 728.

45. David A. J. Richards, *Toleration and the Constitution* (New York: Oxford University Press, 1986), p. 140.

46. *Allegheny County v. ACLU*, 492 U.S. 573, 634 (1989).

47. *Lee v. Weisman*, 112 S.Ct. 2649, 2665 (1992).

48. *Wallace*, 472 U.S. at 52–53; emphasis added.

49. *Wolman v. Walter*, 433 U.S. 229, 263 (1977), Justice Powell concurring and dissenting. See also Chief Justice Burger's dissent in *Meek v. Pittenger*, 421 U.S. 349 (1975).

50. Laurence Tribe, *American Constitutional Law* (Mineola, N.Y.: Foundation Press, 1978), p. 885.

51. Locke, *Letter Concerning Toleration*, p. 46.

52. The phrase is from John Rawls, "Kantian Constructivism in Moral Theory," *Journal of Philosophy*, 77 (September 1980), 543.

53. *Thornton v. Caldor, Inc.*, 474 U.S. 703 (1985).

54. Ibid., Burger at 710, O'Connor at 711.

55. *Goldman v. Weinberger*, 475 U.S. 503, 507–509 (1986).

56. *Employment Division v. Smith*, 494 U.S. 872, 879, 885 (1990).

57. Ibid. at 886, 885, 888.

58. Ibid. at 890.

Essay and Paper Topics for "Religious Practice and Culture"

1. Discuss the historical and social impact of religious institutions and practices. In doing so, consider the essays by Johnson, Russell, and Freud, along with any other material you think relevant.

2. Using the *Smith v. Board of Education of Mobile, Alabama* case as a starting point, write an essay in which you defend teaching creationism against the arguments offered by Pennock.

3. Both Locke and Rawls believe in the social contract and in freedom of religion. Write an essay comparing and contrasting their views on these two issues.

4. Compare John Stuart Mill's defense of liberty with the defense offered by Rawls. Which position do you find most attractive and why? Is it possible to hold both positions? Why or why not?

5. Critically assess the argument Sandel makes against liberalism, indicating how Rawls and/or Locke might respond. Which position is the strongest on this issue? Why?

6. Suppose you are Sandel. Write an essay in which you discuss the legal issues presented in *Smith v. Board of Education* and *Wisconsin v. Yoder* and in Pennock's critique of teaching creationism in schools from Sandel's perspective. In conclusion, discuss whether you agree with Sandel's position or not, and why.

Part X

Religious Practice and Reason

Evidence for the Existence of God

The Design Argument: Pro and Con

William Paley and David Hume

As we will see in later readings, some philosophers and theologians have maintained that it is neither possible nor necessary to justify belief in God. Faith, it is said, is perfectly reasonable even in the absence of good evidence. But there is another tradition that maintains that it *is* possible for the human mind, aided by reason and observation, to come to an understanding that there is a God. The argument from design is among the most influential of these arguments, in part no doubt because it begins by observing the world and appreciating the success of science in discovering the order inherent in it. William Paley offered a clear and lively defense of the design argument. Paley (1743–1805) was an English theologian and philosopher who lectured at Cambridge. He also served as archdeacon of the diocese as well as chancellor. One of his books, *Horae Paulinae* (1790), argued that the New Testament is not a "cunningly devised fable." David Hume, on the other hand, was deeply skeptical about the possibility of demonstrating through reason that God exists. The reading following Paley is from Hume's famous *Dialogues Concerning Natural Religion*. (Before his death, Hume left instructions that they be published posthumously.) These dialogues have three main characters: Cleanthes represents those who defend natural theology and our ability to know God exists through our powers of observation and reason; Philo is the skeptic who doubts the existence of God and questions the evidence; a third character, Demea, appears in a later reading. For biographical information about Hume, see his essay on morality and feeling reprinted above.

As you read through these essays, consider the following:

1. The argument from design as presented by Paley depends on an analogy between the universe and a watch. What is Paley's argument?
2. Paley anwers those who would try to invalidate his conclusion. How does he do that?
3. How does Cleanthes's version of the design argument compare with Paley's?
4. What consequences does Philo think would follow from the adoption of the argument about the nature of God?
5. How does Philo suggest that the order of the universe might be explained if not by an intelligent creator?

William Paley: Defense of the Design Argument

In crossing a heath, suppose I pitched my foot against a *stone*, and were asked how the stone came to be there; I might possibly answer, that, for any thing I knew to the contrary, it had lain there for ever; nor would it perhaps be very easy to shew the absurdity of this answer. But suppose I had found a *watch* upon the ground, and it should be enquired how the watch happened to be in that place; I should hardly think of the answer which I had before given, that, for anything I knew, the watch might have always been there. Yet why should not this answer serve for the watch as well as for the stone? why is it not as admissible in the second case, as in the first? For this reason, and for no other, viz. that, when we come to inspect the watch, we perceive (what we could not discover in the stone) that its several parts are framed and put together for a purpose, *e.g.* that they are so formed and adjusted as to produce motion, and that motion so regulated as to point out the hour of the day; that, if the several parts had been differently shaped from what they are, of a different size from what they are, or placed after any other manner, or in any other order, than that in which they are placed, either no motion at all would have been carried on in the machine, or none which would have answered the use that is now served by it. To reckon up a few of the plainest of these parts, and of their offices, all tending to one result:—We see a cylindrical box containing a

From William Paley, *Natural Theology* (1802).

coiled, elastic spring, which, by its endeavour to relax itself, turns round the box. We next observe a flexible chain (artificially wrought for the sake of flexure) communicating the action of the spring from the box to the fusee. We then find a series of wheels, the teeth of which catch in, and apply to, each other, conducting the motion from the fusee to the balance, and from the balance to the pointer; and at the same time, by the size and shape of those wheels, so regulating that motion, as to terminate in causing an index, by an equable and measured progression, to pass over a given space in a given time. We take notice, that the wheels are made of brass, in order to keep them from rust; the springs of steel, no other metal being so elastic; that over the face of the watch there is placed a glass, a material employed in no other part of the work, but in the room of which, if there had been any other than a transparent substance, the hour could not be seen without opening the case. This mechanism being observed (it requires indeed an examination of the instrument, and perhaps some previous knowledge of the subject, to perceive and understand it; but being once, as we have said, observed and understood), the inference, we think, is inevitable, that the watch must have had a maker: that there must have existed, at some time, and at some place or other, an artificer or artificers who formed it for the purpose which we find it actually to answer; who comprehended its construction, and designed its use.

Nor would it, I apprehend, weaken the conclusion, that we had never seen a watch made; that we had never known an artist capable of making one; that we were altogether incapable of executing such a piece of workmanship ourselves, or of understanding in what manner it was performed; all this being no more than what is true of some exquisite remains of ancient art, of some lost arts, and, to the generality of mankind, of the more curious productions of modern manufacture. Does one man in a million know how oval frames are turned? Ignorance of this kind exalts our opinion of the unseen and unknown artist's skill, if he be unseen and unknown, but raises no doubt in our minds of the existence and agency of such an artist, at some former time, and in some place or other. Nor can I perceive that it varies at all the inference, whether the question arise concerning a human agent, or concerning an agent of a different species, or an agent possessing, in some respects, a different nature.

Neither, secondly, would it invalidate our conclusion, that the watch sometimes went wrong, or that it seldom went exactly right. The purpose of the machinery, the design, and the designer, might be evident, and in the case supposed would be evident, in whatever way we accounted for the irregularity of the movement, or whether we could account for it or not. It is not necessary that a machine be perfect, in order to shew with what design it was made: still less necessary, where the only question is, whether it were made with any design at all.

Nor, thirdly, would it bring any uncertainty into the argument, if there were a few parts of the watch, concerning which we could not discover, or had not yet discovered, in what manner they conduced to the general effect; or even some parts, concerning which we could not ascertain, whether they conduced to that effect in any manner whatever. For, as to the first branch of the case; if by the loss, or disorder, or decay of the parts in question, the movement of the watch were found in fact to be stopped, or disturbed, or retarded, no doubt would remain in our minds as to the utility or intention of these parts, although we should be unable to investigate the manner according to which, or the connection by which, the ultimate effect depended upon their action or assistance; and the more complex is the machine, the more likely is this obscurity to arise. Then, as to the second thing supposed, namely, that there were parts which might be spared, without prejudice to the movement of the watch, and that we had proved this by experiment,— these superfluous parts, even if we were completely assured that they were such, would not vacate the reasoning which we had instituted concerning other parts. The indication of contrivance remained, with respect to them, nearly as it was before.

Nor, fourthly, would any man in his senses think the existence of the watch, with its various machinery, accounted for, by being told that it was one out of possible combinations of material forms; that whatever he had found in the place where he found the watch, must have contained some internal configuration or other; and that this configuration might be the structure now exhibited, viz. of the works of a watch, as well as a different structure.

Nor, fifthly, would it yield his enquiry more satisfaction to be answered, that there existed in things a principle of order, which had disposed the parts of the watch into their present form and situation. He never knew a watch made by the principle of order; nor can he even form to himself an idea of what is meant by a principle of order, distinct from the intelligence of the watch-maker.

Sixthly, he would be surprised to hear, that the mechanism of the watch was no proof of contrivance, only a motive to induce the mind to think so:

And not less surprised to be informed, that the watch in his hand was nothing more than the result of the laws of *metallic* nature.— It is a perversion of language to assign any law, as the efficient, operative cause of any thing. A law presupposes an agent; for it is only the mode, according to which an agent proceeds: it implies a power; for it is the order, according to which that power acts. Without this agent, without this power, which are both distinct from itself, the *law* does nothing; is nothing. The expression, "the law of metallic nature," may sound strange and harsh to a philosophic ear; but it seems quite as justifiable as some others which are more familiar to him, such as "the law of vegetable nature,"— "the law of animal nature," or indeed as "the law of nature" in general, when assigned as the cause of phænomena, in exclusion of agency and power; or when it is substituted into the place of these.

Neither, lastly, would our observer be driven out of his conclusion, or from his confidence in its truth, by being told that he knew nothing at all about the matter. He knows enough for his argument: he knows the utility of the end: he knows the subserviency and adaptation of the means to the end. These points being known, his ignorance of other points, his doubts concerning other points, affect not the certainty of his reasoning. The consciousness of knowing little, need not beget a distrust of that which he does know.

David Hume: Critique of the Design Argument

I shall briefly explain how I conceive this matter [said Cleanthes]. Look round the world, contemplate the whole and every part of it: you will find it to be nothing but one great machine, subdivided into an infinite number of lesser machines, which again admit of subdivisions to a degree beyond what human senses and faculties can trace and explain. All these various machines, and even their most minute parts, are adjusted to each other with an accuracy which ravishes into admiration all men who have ever contemplated them. The curious adapting of means to ends, throughout all nature, resembles exactly though it much exceeds the productions of human contrivance, of human designing, thought, wisdom and intelligence. Since therefore the effects resemble each other, we are led to infer by all the rules of analogy, that the

causes also resemble, and that the Author of Nature is somewhat similar to the mind of man, though possessed of much larger faculties, proportioned to the grandeur of the work which he has executed. By this argument *a posteriori* [following observations], and by this alone, do we prove at once the existence of a Deity and his similarity to human mind and intelligence. . . .

Now, Cleanthes, said Philo, with an air of alacrity and triumph, mark the consequences. *First*, by this method of reasoning you renounce all claim to infinity in any of the attributes of the Deity. For, as the cause ought only to be proportioned to the effect, and the effect, so far as it falls under our cognizance, is not infinite, what pretensions have we, upon your suppositions, to ascribe that attribute to the divine Being? You will still insist that, by removing him so much from all similarity to human creatures, we give in to the most arbitrary hypothesis, and at the same time weaken all proofs of his existence.

Secondly, you have no reason, on your theory, for ascribing perfection to the Deity, even in his finite capacity; or for supposing him free from every error, mistake, or incoherence, in his undertakings. There are many inexplicable difficulties in the works of nature which, if we allow a perfect author to be proved *a priori*, are easily solved, and become only seeming difficulties from the narrow capacity of man, who cannot trace infinite relations. But according to your method of reasoning, these difficulties become all real; and, perhaps, will be insisted on as new instances of likeness to human art and contrivance. At least, you must acknowledge that it is impossible for us to tell, from our limited views, whether this system contains any great faults or deserves any considerable praise if compared to other possible and even real systems. Could a peasant, if the *Aeneid* were read to him, pronounce that poem to be absolutely faultless, or even assign to it its proper rank among the productions of human wit, he who had never seen any other production?

But were this world ever so perfect a production, it must still remain uncertain

David Hume, *Dialogues Concerning Natural Religion* (1779).

whether all the excellences of the work can justly be ascribed to the workman. If we survey a ship, what an exalted idea must we form of the ingenuity of the carpenter who framed so complicated, useful, and beautiful a machine? And what surprise must we feel when we find him a stupid mechanic who imitated others, and copied an art which, through a long succession of ages, after multiplied trials, mistakes, corrections, deliberations, and controversies, had been gradually improving? Many worlds might have been botched and bungled, throughout an eternity, ere this system was struck out; much labour lost; many fruitless trials made; and a slow but continued improvement carried on during infinite ages in the art of world-making. In such subjects, who can determine where the truth, nay, who can conjecture where the probability lies, amidst a great number of hypotheses which may be proposed, and a still greater which may be imagined?

And what shadow of an argument, continued Philo, can you produce from your hypothesis to prove the unity of the Deity? A great number of men join in building a house or ship, in rearing a city, in framing a commonwealth; why may not several deities combine in contriving and framing a world? This is only so much greater similarity to human affairs. By sharing the work among several, we may so much further limit the attributes of each, and get rid of that extensive power and knowledge which must be supposed in one deity, and which, according to you, can only serve to weaken the proof of his existence. And if such foolish, such vicious creatures as man can yet often unite in framing and executing one plan, how much more those deities or demons, whom we may suppose several degrees more perfect?

To multiply causes without necessity is indeed contrary to true philosophy, but this principle applies not to the present case. Were one deity antecedently proved by your theory who were possessed of every attribute requisite to the production of the universe, it would be needless, I own (though not absurd), to suppose any other deity existent.

But while it is still a question whether all these attributes are united in one subject or dispersed among several independent beings; by what phenomena in nature can we pretend to decide the controversy? Where we see a body raised in a scale, we are sure that there is in the opposite scale, however concealed from sight, some counterpoising weight equal to it; but it is still allowed to doubt whether that weight be an aggregate of several distinct bodies or one uniform united mass. And if the weight requisite very much exceeds anything which we have ever seen conjoined in any single body, the former supposition becomes still more probable and natural. An intelligent being of such vast power and capacity as is necessary to produce the universe—or, to speak in the language of ancient philosophy, so prodigious an animal—exceeds all analogy and even comprehension.

But further, Cleanthes, men are mortal, and renew their species by generation; and this is common to all living creatures. The two great sexes of male and female, says Milton, animate the world. Why must this circumstance, so universal, so essential, be excluded from those numerous and limited deities? Behold, then, the theogeny of ancient times brought back upon us.

And why not become a perfect anthropomorphite? Why not assert the deity of deities to be corporeal, and to have eyes, a nose, mouth, ears, etc.? Epicurus maintained that no man had ever seen reason but in a human figure; therefore, the gods must have a human figure. And this argument, which is deservedly so much ridiculed by Cicero, becomes, according to you, solid and philosophical.

In a word, Cleanthes, a man who follows your hypothesis is able, perhaps, to assert or conjecture that the universe sometime arose from something like design; but beyond that position he cannot ascertain one single circumstance, and is left afterwards to fix every point of his theology by the utmost license of fancy and hypothesis. This world, for aught he knows, is very faulty and imperfect, compared to a superior standard; and was only the first rude essay of some infant deity who afterwards abandoned it, ashamed of his lame performance; it is the work only of some dependent, inferior deity, and is the object of derision to his superiors; it is the production of old age and dotage in some superannuated deity; and ever since his death has run on at adventures, from the first impulse and active force which it received from him. You justly give signs of horror, Demea, at these strange suppositions; but these, and a thousand more of the same kind, are Cleanthes' suppositions, not mine. From the moment the attributes of the Deity are supposed finite, all these have place. And I cannot, for my part, think that so wild and unsettled a system of theology is, in any respect, preferable to none at all.

These suppositions I absolutely disown, cried Cleanthes; they strike me, however, with no horror, especially when proposed in that rambling way in which they drop from you. On the contrary, they give me pleasure when I see that, by the utmost indulgence of your imagination, you never get rid of the hypothesis of design in the universe, but are obliged at every turn to have recourse to it. To this concession I adhere steadily; and this I regard as a sufficient foundation for religion. . . .

That a stone will fall [said Philo], that fire will burn, that the earth has solidity, we have observed a thousand and a thousand times; and when any new instance of this nature is presented, we draw without hesitation the accustomed inference. The exact similarity of the cases gives us a perfect assurance of a similar event and a stronger evidence is never desired nor sought after. But wherever you depart, in the least, from the similarity of the cases, you diminish proportionately the evidence and may at last bring it to a very *weak analogy* which is confessedly liable to error and uncertainty. After having observed the circulation of the blood in human creatures, we make no doubt that it takes place in Titius and Maevius; but from its circulation in frogs and fishes it is only a presumption, though a strong one, from analogy that it takes place in men and other animals. The analogical reasoning is much weaker when we infer the circulation of the sap in vegetables from our experience that the blood circulates in animals; and those who hastily followed that imperfect analogy are found, by more accurate experiments, to have been mistaken.

If we see a house, Cleanthes, we conclude, with the greatest certainty, that it had an architect or builder; because this is precisely that species of effect which we have experienced to proceed from that species of cause. But surely you will not affirm, that the universe bears such a resemblance to a house, that we can with the same certainty infer a similar cause, or that the analogy is here entire and perfect. The dissimilitude is so striking, that the utmost you can here pretend to is a guess, a conjecture, a presumption concerning a similar cause; and how that pretension will be received in the world, I leave you to consider.

It would surely be very ill received, replied Cleanthes, and I should be deservedly blamed and detested, did I allow that the proofs of a Deity amounted to no more than a guess or conjecture. But is the whole adjustment of means to ends in a house and in the universe so slight a resemblance? The economy of final causes? The order, proportion and arrangement of every part? Steps of a stair are plainly contrived that human legs may use them in mounting; and this inference is certain and infallible. Human legs are also contrived for walking and mounting, and this inference, I allow is not altogether so certain, because of the similarity which you remark, but does it therefore deserve the name only of presumption or conjecture?. . .

Were a man to abstract from everything which he knows or has seen [said Philo], he would be altogether incapable, merely from his own ideas, to determine what kind of scene the universe must be, or to give the preference to one state or situation of things above another. For as nothing which he clearly conceives could be esteemed impossible or implying a contradiction, every chimera of his fancy would be upon an equal footing; nor could he assign any just reason why he adheres to one idea or system, and rejects the others which are equally possible.

Again; after he opens his eyes, and contemplates the world as it really is, it would be impossible for him at first to assign the cause of any one event, much less of the whole of things, or of the universe. He might set his fancy a rambling; and she might bring him in an infinite variety of reports and representations. These would all be possible; but being all equally possible, he would never of himself give a satisfactory account for his preferring one of them to the rest. Experience alone can point out to him the true cause of any phenomenon.

. . . For aught we can know *a priori*, matter may contain the source or spring of order originally within itself, as well as mind does; and there is no more difficulty in conceiving that the several elements, from an internal unknown cause, may fall into the most exquisite arrangement, than to conceive that their ideas, in the great universal mind, from a like internal unknown cause, fall into that arrangement. The equal possibility of both these suppositions is allowed.

The Cosmological Argument: Pro and Con

Samuel Clarke and David Hume

Like William Paley, Samuel Clarke (1675–1729) was an English philosopher and theologian. He was a strong supporter of Isaac Newton and had an ongoing dispute with Gottfried Leibniz about the nature of space. He also maintained that moral law was as certain as mathematics. In this selection, Clarke presents what has come to be known as the cosmological argument, another of the important attempts to justify belief in God with the use of reason. The article is criticized by Hume in a selection from his *Dialogues Concerning Natural Religion* (see the preceding reading). In Hume's dialogue, the argument is presented by Demea, with Cleanthes and Philo raising questions.

As you read through these essays, consider the following:

1. Clarke's argument does not rest on the orderliness of the universe. On what fact does it depend?
2. How does Clarke think the universe's existence proves the existence of an independent being?
3. Is there any important difference between Demea's description of the argument and Clarke's?
4. Why does Cleanthes reject the argument? What is the metaphysical issue or issues that divide him from Demea?
5. What does Philo add to the argument?
6. What does Philo suggest is the source of religious faith?

Samuel Clarke: Defense of the Cosmological Argument

There has existed from eternity some one unchangeable and independent being. For since something must needs have been from eter-

From Samuel Clarke, *A Demonstration of the Being and Attributes of God* (1705), Part II.

nity; as hath been already proved, and is granted on all hands: either there has always existed one unchangeable and *independent* Being, from which all other beings that are or ever were in the universe, have received their original; or else there has been an infinite succession of changeable and *dependent* beings, produced one from another in an endless progression, without any original cause at all: which latter supposition is so very absurd, that tho' all atheism must in its account of most things (as shall be shown hereafter) terminate in it, yet I think very few atheists ever were so weak as openly and directly to defend it. For it is plainly impossible and contradictory to itself. I shall not argue against it from the supposed impossibility of infinite succession, *barely and absolutely considered in itself*; for a reason which shall be mentioned hereafter: but, if we consider such an infinite progression, as *one* entire endless *series* of *dependent* beings; 'tis plain this whole *series* of beings can have no cause *from without*, of its existence; because in it are supposed to be included *all things* that are or ever were in the universe: and 'tis plain it can have no reason *within itself*, of its existence; because no one being in this infinite succession is supposed to be self-existent or *necessary* (which is the only ground or reason of existence of any thing, that can be imagined *within the thing itself*, as will presently more fully appear), but every one *dependent* on the foregoing: and where *no part* is necessary, 'tis manifest *the whole* cannot be necessary; absolute necessity of existence, not being an outward, relative, and accidental determination; but an inward and essential property of the nature of the thing which so exists. An infinite succession therefore of merely *dependent* beings, without any original independent cause; is a *series* of beings, that has neither necessity nor cause, nor any reason *at all* of its existence, neither *within itself* nor *from without*: that is, 'tis an express contradiction and impossibility; 'tis a supposing *something* to be *caused* (because it's granted in every one of its stages of succession, not to be necessary and from itself); and yet that in the whole it is caused *absolutely by nothing*: Which every man knows is a contradiction to be done *in time*; and because duration in this case makes no difference, 'tis equally a contradiction to suppose it done from eternity: And consequently there must *on the contrary*, of necessity have existed from eternity, *some one* immutable and *independent* Being. . . .

David Hume: A Critique
of the Cosmological Argument

[Cleanthes said] It is first proper, in my opinion, to determine what argument of this nature you choose to insist on; and we shall afterwards, from itself, better than from its *useful* consequences, endeavor to determine what value we ought to put upon it.

The argument, replied Demea, which I would insist on is the common one. Whatever exists must have a cause or reason of its existence, it being absolutely impossible for anything to produce itself or be the cause of its own existence. In mounting up, therefore, from effects to causes, we must either go on in tracing an infinite succession, without any ultimate cause at all, or must at last have recourse to some ultimate cause that is *necessarily* existent. Now, that the first supposition is absurd may be thus proved. In the infinite chain or succession of causes and effects, each single effect is determined to exist by the power and efficacy of that cause which immediately preceded; but the whole eternal chain or succession, taken together, is not determined or caused by anything; and yet it is evident that it requires a cause or reason, as much as any particular object which begins to exist in time. The question is still reasonable why this particular succession of causes existed from eternity, and not any other succession or no succession at all. If there be no necessarily existent being, any supposition which can be formed is equally possible; nor is there any more absurdity in nothing's having existed from eternity than there is in that succession of causes which constitutes the universe. What was it, then, which determined something to exist rather than nothing, and bestowed being on a particular possibility, exclusive of the rest? *External causes*, there are supposed to be none. *Chance* is a word without a meaning. Was it *nothing*? But that can never produce anything. We must, therefore, have recourse to a necessarily existent Being who carries the *reason* of his existence in himself; and who cannot be supposed not to exist, without an express contradiction. There is, consequently, such a Being—that is, there is a Deity.

I shall not leave it to Philo, said Cleanthes (though I know that the starting objections is his chief delight), to point out the weakness of this metaphysical reasoning. It seems to me so obviously ill-grounded, and at the same time of so little consequence to the cause of true piety and religion, that I shall myself venture to show the fallacy of it.

I shall begin with observing that there is an evident absurdity in pretending to demonstrate a matter of fact, or to prove it by any arguments *a priori*. Nothing is demonstrable unless the contrary implies a contradiction. Nothing that is distinctly conceivable implies a contradiction. Whatever we conceive as existent, we can also conceive as non-existent. There is no being, therefore, whose non-existence implies a contradiction. Consequently there is no being whose existence is demonstrable. I propose this argument as entirely decisive, and am willing to rest the whole controversy upon it.

It is pretended that the Deity is a necessarily existent being; and this necessity of his existence is attempted to be explained by asserting that, if we knew his whole essence or nature, we should perceive it to be as impossible for him not to exist, as for twice two not to be four. But it is evident that this can never happen, while our faculties remain the same as at present. It will still be possible for us, at any time, to conceive the non-existence of what we formerly conceived to exist; nor can the mind ever lie under a necessity of supposing any object to remain always in being; in the same manner as we lie under a necessity of always conceiving twice two to be four. The words, therefore, *necessary existence* have no meaning; or, which is the same thing, none that is consistent.

But further, why may not the material universe be the necessarily existent Being, according to this pretended explication of necessity? We dare not affirm that we know all the qualities of matter; and, for aught we can determine, it may contain some qualities which, were they known, would make its nonexistence appear as great a contradiction as that twice two is five. I find only one argument employed to prove that the material world is not the necessarily existent Being; and this argument is derived from the contingency both of the matter and the form of the world. "Any particle of matter," it is said, "may be *conceived* to be annihilated, and any form may be *conceived* to be altered. Such an annihilation or alteration, therefore, is not impossible." [Dr. Samuel Clarke] But it seems a great partiality not to perceive that the same argument extends equally to the Deity, so far as we have any conception of him; and that the mind can at least imagine him to be nonexistent, or his attributes to be altered. It must be some unknown, inconceivable qualities which can make his non-existence appear impossible or his attributes unalterable: And no reason can be assigned why these qualities may not belong to matter. As they are altogether unknown and inconceivable, they can never be proved incompatible with it.

Add to this that in tracing an eternal succession of objects it seems absurd to inquire for a general cause or first author. How can anything that exists from eternity have a cause, since that relation implies a priority in time and a beginning of existence?

In such a chain, too, or succession of objects, each part is caused by that which preceded it, and causes that which succeeds it. Where then is the difficulty? But the *whole*, you say, wants a cause. I answer that the uniting of these parts into a whole, like the uniting of several distinct countries into one kingdom, or several distinct members into one body, is performed merely by an arbitrary act of the mind, and has no influence on the nature of things. Did I show you the particular causes of each individual in a collection of twenty particles of matter, I should think it very unreasonable should you afterwards ask me what was the cause of the whole twenty. This is sufficiently explained in explaining the cause of the parts.

Though the reasonings which you have urged, Cleanthes, may well excuse me, said Philo, from starting any further difficulties; yet I cannot forebear insisting still upon another topic. It is observed by arithmeticians that the products of 9 compose always either 9 or some lesser product of 9 if you add together all the characters of which any of the former products is composed. Thus, of 18, 27, 36, which are products of 9, you make 9 by adding 1 to 8, 2 to 7, 3 to 6. Thus 369 is a product also of 9; and if you add 3, 6, and 9, you make 18, a lesser product of 9. To a superficial observer so wonderful a regularity may be admired as the effect either of chance or design; but a skillful algebraist immediately concludes it to be the work of necessity, and demonstrates that it must forever result from the nature of these numbers. Is it not probable, I ask, that the whole economy of the universe is conducted by a like necessity, though no human algebra can furnish a key which solves the difficulty? And instead of admiring the order of natural beings, may it not happen that, could we penetrate into the intimate nature of bodies, we should clearly see why it was absolutely impossible they could ever admit of any other disposition? So dangerous is it to introduce this idea of necessity into the present question! and so naturally does it afford an inference directly opposite to the religious hypothesis!

But dropping all these abstractions, continued Philo, and confining ourselves to more familiar topics, I shall venture to add an observation that the argument *a priori* has seldom been found very convincing, except to people of a metaphysical head who have accustomed themselves to abstract reasoning, and who, finding from mathematics that the understanding frequently leads to truth through obscurity, and contrary to first appearances, have transferred the same habit of thinking to subjects where it ought not to have place. Other people, even of good sense and the best inclined to religion, feel always some deficiency in such arguments, though they are not perhaps able to explain distinctly where it lies—a certain proof that men ever did and ever will derive their religion from other sources than from this species of reasoning.

The Ontological Argument: Pro and Con

St. Anselm and Immanuel Kant

This argument is a favorite among many philosophers, though it is less widely known among religious people in general. Termed the "ontological" argument because of its focus on the nature of God's being or existence, it is distinct from the others in that it relies on neither the characteristics of the known world nor on the fact that the universe exists and is in need of explanation. It is an entirely a priori argument, based on the concept of God itself. St. Anselm (1033?–1109) was an English monk and religious reformer who sought to reduce the abuses and corruption of the Catholic Church. Anselm believed that revelation and reason were in strict harmony and that human beings' God-given reason was adequate to understand the existence and the nature of God. Immanuel Kant famously attacked the ontological argument, claiming that it rests on a logical error. For biographical information about Kant, see the selection from his moral philosophy reprinted earlier.

As you read through these essays, consider the following:

1. What is the concept of God, according to Anselm?
2. Why does Anselm think that God cannot be thought not to exist?
3. One way to read Anselm is to say he first assumes the opposite of what he wants to show (that is,

he assumes God does not exist), but that he then shows how this assumption cannot be accepted because it leads to an absurd contradiction. Does that capture the key idea here?

4. Why can the fool say what he cannot think?

5. On what basis does Kant dispute this argument?

St. Anselm: A Defense of the Ontological Argument

CHAPTER I.

Exhortation of the mind to the contemplation of God.

Up now, slight man! flee, for a little while, thy occupations; hide thyself, for a time, from thy disturbing thoughts. Cast aside, now, thy burdensome cares, and put away thy toilsome business. Yield room for some little time to God; and rest for a little time in him. Enter the inner chamber of thy mind; shut out all thoughts save that of God, and such as can aid thee in seeking him; close thy door and seek him. Speak now, my whole heart! speak now to God, saying, I seek thy face; thy face, Lord, will I seek (Psalms xxvii. 8). And come thou now, O lord my God, teach my heart where and how it may seek thee, where and how it may find thee.

Lord, if thou art not here, where shall I seek thee, being absent? But if thou art everywhere, why do I not see thee present? Truly thou dwellest in unapproachable light. But where is unapproachable light, or how shall I come to it? Or who shall lead me to that light and into it, that I may see thee in it? Again, by what marks, under what form, shall I seek thee? I have never seen thee, O Lord, my God; I do not know thy form. What, O most high Lord, shall this man do, an exile far from thee? What shall thy servant do, anxious in his love of thee, and cast out afar from thy face? He pants to see thee, and thy face is too far from him. He longs to come to thee, and thy dwelling-place is inaccessible. He is eager to find thee, and knows not thy place. He desires to seek thee, and does not know thy face. Lord, thou art my God, and thou art my Lord, and never have I seen thee. It

From *St. Anselm: Basic Writings*, translated by S. N. Deane (1903).

is thou that hast made me, and hast made me anew, and hast bestowed upon me all the blessings I enjoy; and not yet do I know thee. Finally, I was created to see thee, and not yet have I done that for which I was made. . . .

. . . How long, O Lord, dost thou forget us; how long dost thou turn thy face from us? When wilt thou look upon us, and hear us? When wilt thou enlighten our eyes, and show us thy face? When wilt thou restore thyself to us? Look upon us, Lord; hear us, enlighten us, reveal thyself to us. Restore thyself to us, that it may be well with us,—thyself, without whom it is so ill with us. Pity our toilings and strivings toward thee, since we can do nothing without thee. Thou dost invite us; do thou help us. . . .

. . . Teach me to seek thee, and reveal thyself to me, when I seek thee, for I cannot seek thee, except thou teach me, nor find thee, except thou reveal thyself. Let me seek thee in longing, let me long for thee in seeking; let me find thee in love, and love thee in finding. Lord, I acknowledge and I thank thee that thou hast created me in this thine image, in order that I may be mindful of thee, may conceive of thee, and love thee; but that image has been so consumed and wasted away by vices, and obscured by the smoke of wrong-doing, that it cannot achieve that for which it was made, except thou renew it, and create it anew. I do not endeavor, O Lord, to penetrate thy sublimity, for in no wise do I compare my understanding with that; but I long to understand in some degree thy truth, which my heart believes and loves. For I do not seek to understand that I may believe, but I believe in order to understand. For this also I believe,—that unless I believed, I should not understand.

CHAPTER II.

Truly there is a God, although the fool hath said in his heart, There is no God.

And so, Lord, do thou, who dost give understanding to faith, give me, so far as thou knowest it to be profitable, to understand that thou art as we believe; and that thou art that which we believe. And, indeed, we believe that thou art a being than which nothing greater can be conceived. Or is there no such nature, since the fool hath said in his heart, there is no God? (Psalms xiv. 1). But, at any rate, this very fool, when he hears of this being of which I speak—a being than which nothing greater can be conceived—understands what he hears, and what he understands is in his understanding; although he does not understand it to exist.

For, it is one thing for an object to be in the understanding, and another to understand that the object exists. When a painter first conceives of what he will afterwards perform, he has it in his understanding, but he does not yet understand it to be, because he has not yet performed it. But after he has made the painting, he both has it in his understanding, and he understands that it exists, because he has made it.

Hence, even the fool is convinced that something exists in the understanding, at least, than which nothing greater can be conceived. For, when he hears of this, he understands it. And whatever is understood, exists in the understanding. And assuredly that, than which nothing greater can be conceived, cannot exist in the understanding alone. For, suppose it exists in the understanding alone: then it can be conceived to exist in reality; which is greater.

Therefore, if that, than which nothing greater can be conceived, exists in the understanding alone, the very being, than which nothing greater can be conceived, is one, than which a greater can be conceived. But obviously this is impossible. Hence, there is no doubt that there exists a being, than which nothing greater can be conceived, and it exists both in the understanding and in reality.

CHAPTER III.

God cannot be conceived not to exist.—God is that, than which nothing greater can be conceived.—That which can be conceived not to exist is not God.

And it assuredly exists so truly, that it cannot be conceived not to exist. For, it is possible to conceive of a being which cannot be conceived not to exist; and this is greater than one which can be conceived not to exist. Hence, if that, than which nothing greater can be conceived, can be conceived not to exist, it is not that, than which nothing greater can be conceived. But this is an irreconcilable contradiction. There is, then, so truly a being than which nothing greater can be conceived to exist, that it cannot even be conceived not to exist; and this being thou art, O Lord, our God.

So truly, therefore, dost thou exist, O Lord, my God, that thou canst not be conceived not to exist; and rightly. For, if a mind could conceive of a being better than thee, the creature would rise above the Creator; and this is most absurd. And, indeed, whatever else there is, except thee alone, can be conceived not to exist. To thee alone, therefore, it belongs to exist more truly than all other beings, and hence in a higher degree than all others. For, whatever else exists does not exist so truly, and hence in a less degree it belongs to it to exist. Why, then, has the fool said in his heart, there is no God (Psalms xiv. 1), since it is so evident, to a rational mind, that thou dost exist in the highest degree of all? Why, except that he is dull and a fool?

CHAPTER IV.

How the fool has said in his heart what cannot be conceived.

But how has the fool said in his heart what he could not conceive; or how is it that he could not conceive what he said in his heart? since it is the same to say in the heart, and to conceive.

But, if really, nay, since really, he both conceived, because he said in his heart; and did not say in his heart, because he could not conceive; there is more than one way in which a thing is said in the heart or conceived. For, in one sense, an object is conceived, when the word signifying it is conceived; and in another, when the very entity, which the object is, is understood.

In the former sense, then, God can be conceived not to exist; but in the latter, not at all. For no one who understands what fire and water are can conceive fire to be water, in accordance with the nature of the facts themselves, although this is possible according to the words. So, then, no one who understands what God is can conceive that God does not exist; although he says these words in his heart, either without any, or with some foreign, signification. For, God is that than which a greater cannot be conceived. And he who thoroughly understands this, assuredly understands that this being so truly exists, that not even in concept can it be non-existent. Therefore, he who understands that God so exists, cannot conceive that he does not exist.

I thank thee, gracious Lord, I thank thee; because what I formerly believed by thy bounty, I now so understand by thine illumination, that if I were unwilling to believe that thou dost exist, I should not be able not to understand this to be true.

CHAPTER V.

God is whatever it is better to be than not to be; and he, as the only self-existent being, creates all things from nothing.

What art thou, then, Lord God, than whom nothing greater can be conceived? But what art thou, except that which, as the highest of all beings, alone exists through itself, and creates all other things from nothing? For, whatever is not this is less than a thing which can be conceived of. But this cannot be conceived of thee. What good, therefore, does the supreme Good lack, through which every good is? Therefore, thou art just, truthful, blessed, and whatever it is better to be than not to be. For it is better to be just than not just; better to be blessed than not blessed.

Immanuel Kant: A Critique of the Ontological Argument

It is evident from what has been said, that the conception of an absolutely necessary being is a mere idea, the objective reality of which is far from being established by the mere fact that it is a need of reason. On the contrary, this idea serves merely to indicate a certain unattainable perfection, and rather limits the operations than, by the presentation of new objects, extends the sphere of the understanding. But a strange anomaly meets us at the very threshold; for the inference from a given existence in general to an absolutely necessary existence, seems to be correct and unavoidable, while the conditions of the *understanding* refuse to aid us in forming any conception of such a being.

Philosophers have always talked of an *absolutely necessary* being, and have nevertheless declined to take the trouble of conceiving, whether—and how—a being of this nature is even cogitable, not to mention that its existence is actually demonstrable. A verbal definition of the conception is certainly easy enough; it is something, the non-existence of which is impossible. But does this definition throw any light upon the conditions which render it impossible to cogitate the non-existence of a thing—conditions which we wish to ascertain, that we may discover whether we think anything in the conception of such a being or not? For the mere fact that I throw away, by means of the word *Unconditioned*, all the conditions which the understanding habitually requires in order to regard anything as necessary, is very far from making clear whether by means of the conception of the unconditionally necessary I think of something, or really of nothing at all.

Nay, more, this chance-conception, now become so current, many have endeavored to explain by examples, which seemed to render any inquiries regarding its intelligibility quite needless. Every geometrical proposition—a triangle has three angles—it was said, is

From Immanuel Kant, *Critique of Pure Reason* (1787).

absolutely necessary; and thus people talked of an object which lay out of the sphere of our understanding as if it were perfectly plain what the conception of such a being meant.

All the examples adduced have been drawn, without exception, from *judgments*, and not from *things*. But the unconditioned necessity of a judgment does not form the absolute necessity of a thing. On the contrary, the absolute necessity of a judgment is only a conditioned necessity of a thing, or of the predicate in a judgment. The proposition above-mentioned, does not enounce that three angles necessarily exist, but, upon condition that a triangle exists, three angles must necessarily exist—in it. And thus this logical necessity has been the source of the greatest delusions. Having formed an *à priori* conception of a thing, the content of which was made to embrace existence, we believed ourselves safe in concluding that, because existence belongs necessarily to the object of the conception (that is, under the condition of my positing this thing as given), the existence of the thing is also posited necessarily, and that it is therefore absolutely necessary—merely because its existence has been cogitated in the conception.

If, in an identical judgment, I annihilate the predicate in thought, and retain the subject, a contradiction is the result; and hence I say, the former belongs necessarily to the latter. But if I suppress both subject and predicate in thought, no contradiction arises; for there *is nothing* at all, and therefore no means of forming a contradiction. To suppose the existence of a triangle and not that of its three angles, is self-contradictory; but to suppose the non-existence of both triangle and angles is perfectly admissible. And so is it with the conception of an absolutely necessary being. Annihilate its existence in thought, and you annihilate the thing itself with all its predicates; how then can there be any room for contradiction? Externally, there is nothing to give rise to a contradiction, for a thing cannot be necessary externally; nor internally, for, by the annihilation or suppression of the thing itself, its internal properties are also annihilated. God is omnipotent—that is a necessary judgment. His omnipotence cannot be denied, if the

existence of a Deity is posited—the existence, that is, of an infinite being, the two conceptions being identical. But when you say, *God does not exist*, neither omnipotence nor any other predicate is affirmed; they must all disappear with the subject, and in this judgment there cannot exist the least self-contradiction. . . .

It is absurd to introduce—under whatever term disguised—into the conception of a thing, which is to be cogitated solely in reference to its possibility, the conception of its existence. . . .

Being is evidently not a real predicate, that is, a conception of something which is added to the conception of some other thing. It is merely the positing of a thing, or of certain determinations in it. Logically, it is merely the copula of a judgment. The proposition, *God is omnipotent*, contains two conceptions, which have a certain object or content; the word *is*, is no additional predicate—it merely indicates the relation of the predicate to the subject. Now, if I take the subject (God) with all its predicates (omnipotence being one), and say, *God is*, or, *There is a God*, I add no new predicate to the conception of God, I merely posit or affirm the existence of the subject with all its predicates—I posit the *object* in relation to my *conception*. The content of both is the same; and there is no addition made to the conception, which expresses merely the possibility of the object, by my cogitating the object—in the expression, it *is*—as absolutely given or existing. Thus the real contains no more than the possible. A hundred real dollars contain no more than a hundred possible dollars. For, as the latter indicate the conception, and the former the object, on the supposition that the content of the former was greater than that of the latter, my conception would not be an expression of the whole object, and would consequently be an inadequate conception of it. But in reckoning my wealth there may be said to be more in a hundred real dollars, than in a hundred possible dollars—that is, in the mere conception of them. . . .

By whatever and by whatever number of predicates—even to the complete determination of it—I may cogitate a thing I do not in

the least augment the object of my conception by the addition of the statement, this
thing exists. Otherwise, not exactly the same,
but something more than what was cogitated
in my conception, would exist, and I could
not affirm that the exact object of my conception had real existence. . . . If the question
regarded an object of sense merely, it would
be impossible for me to confound the conception with the existence of a thing. For the
conception merely enables me to cogitate an
object as according with the general conditions of experience; while the existence of the
object permits me to cogitate it as contained
in the sphere of actual experience. At the
same time, this connection with the world of
experience does not in the least augment the
conception, although a possible perception
has been added to the experience of the mind.
But if we cogitate existence by the pure category alone, it is not to be wondered at, that
we should find ourselves unable to present
any criterion sufficient to distinguish it from
mere possibility.

Whatever be the content of our conception of an object, it is necessary to go beyond
it, if we wish to predicate existence of the
object. In the case of sensuous objects, this is
attained by their connection according to
empirical laws with some one of my perceptions; but there is no means of cognizing the
existence of objects of pure thought, because
it must be cognized completely *à priori*. But
all our knowledge of existence (be it immediately by perception, or by inferences connecting some object with a perception) belongs
entirely to the sphere of experience—which is
in perfect unity with itself—and although an
existence out of this sphere cannot be
absolutely declared to be impossible, it is a
hypothesis the truth of which we have no
means of ascertaining.

Evidence There Is No God

Evil and Suffering Prove Atheism Is True

B. C. Johnson

Just as it has often been thought that we can know of God's existence and even characteristics by careful study of the world and how it works, so too has it been argued that we can know the opposite. The pervasiveness of evil and suffering in the world, it is claimed, show clearly that the just, loving, all-powerful God of many religions cannot possibly exist. As a character in Dostoevsky's *The Brothers Karamazov* put it: "The only excuse for God is that He does not exist." In this essay, B. C. Johnson (the pen name of a writer who wishes to remain anonymous) presents the atheist's case.

As you read through this essay, consider the following:

1. Johnson begins with an analogy. What is it?
2. How does Johnson answer each of the suggested excuses for God's failure to intervene in disasters?
3. Why does the need to create the possibility of virtuous behavior not answer the atheist?
4. Is evil necessary as a contrast to good? Why or why not?
5. Why does Johnson reject the idea that God has a "higher morality"?
6. Is there a response that might solve the problem by rethinking the concept of God? What is it?

Here is a common situation: a house catches on fire and a six-month-old baby is painfully burned to death. Could we possibly describe as "good" any person who had the power to save this child and yet refused to do so? God undoubtedly has this power and yet in many cases of this sort he has refused to help. Can we call God "good"? Are there adequate excuses for his behavior?

First, it will not do to claim that the baby will go to heaven. It was either necessary for the baby to suffer or it was not. If it was not, then it was wrong to allow it. The child's ascent to heaven does not change this fact. If it was necessary, the fact that the baby will go to heaven does not explain why it was necessary, and we are still left without an excuse for God's inaction.

It is not enough to say that the baby's painful death would in the long run have good results and therefore should have happened, otherwise God would not have permitted it. For if we know this to be true, then we know—just as God knows—that every action successfully performed must in the end be good and therefore the right thing to do, otherwise God would not have allowed it to happen. We could deliberately set houses ablaze to kill innocent people and if successful we would then know we had a duty to do it. A defense of God's goodness which takes as its foundation duties known only after the fact would result in a morality unworthy of the name. Furthermore, this argument does not explain why God allowed the child to burn to death. It merely claims that there is some reason discoverable in the long run. But the belief that such a reason is within our grasp must rest upon the additional belief that God is good. This is just to counter evidence against such a belief by assuming the belief to be true. It is not unlike a lawyer defending his client by claiming that the client is innocent and therefore the evidence against him must

From *The Atheist Debater's Handbook* by B. C. Johnson (Buffalo, N.Y.: Prometheus Books, 1981). Copyright © 1981 by B. C. Johnson. Reprinted by permission of the publisher.

be misleading—that proof vindicating the defendant will be found in the long run. No jury of reasonable men and women would accept such a defense and the theist cannot expect a more favorable outcome.

The theist often claims that man has been given free will so that if he accidentally or purposefully cause fires, killing small children, it is his fault alone. Consider a bystander who had nothing to do with starting the fire but who refused to help even though he could have saved the child with no harm to himself. Could such a bystander be called good? Certainly not. If we could not consider a mortal human being good under these circumstances, what grounds could we possibly have for continuing to assert the goodness of an all-powerful God?

The suggestion is sometimes made that it is best for us to face disasters without assistance, otherwise we would become dependent on an outside power for aid. Should we then abolish modern medical care or do away with efficient fire departments? Are we not dependent on their help? Is it not the case that their presence transforms us into soft, dependent creatures? The vast majority are not physicians or firemen. These people help in their capacity as professional outside sources of aid in much the same way that we would expect God to be helpful. Theists refer to aid from firemen and physicians as cases of man helping himself. In reality, it is a tiny minority of men helping a great many. We can become just as dependent on them as we can on God. Now the existence of this kind of outside help is either wrong or right. If it is right, then God should assist those areas of the world which do not have this kind of help. In fact, throughout history, such help has not been available. If aid ought to have been provided, then God should have provided it. On the other hand, if it is wrong to provide this kind of assistance, then we should abolish the aid altogether. But we obviously do not believe it is wrong.

Similar considerations apply to the claim that if God interferes in disasters, he would destroy a considerable amount of moral urgency to make things right. Once again, note that such institutions as modern medicine and fire departments are relatively recent. They function irrespective of whether we as individuals feel any moral urgency to support them. To the extent that they help others, opportunities to feel moral urgency are destroyed because they reduce the number of cases which appeal to us for help. Since we have not always had such institutions, there must have been a time when there was greater moral urgency than there is now. If such a situation is morally desirable, then we should abolish modern medical care and fire departments. If the situation is not morally desirable, then God should have remedied it.

Besides this point, we should note that God is represented as one who tolerates disasters, such as infants burning to death, in order to create moral urgency. It follows that God approves of these disasters as a means to encourage the creation of moral urgency. Furthermore, if there were no such disasters occurring, God would have to see to it that they occur. If it so happened that we lived in a world in which babies never perished in burning houses, God would be morally obliged to take an active hand in setting fire to houses with infants in them. In fact, if the frequency of infant mortality due to fire should happen to fall below a level necessary for the creation of maximum moral urgency in our real world, God would be justified in setting a few fires of his own. This may well be happening right now, for there is no guarantee that the maximum number of infant deaths necessary for moral urgency are occurring.

All of this is of course absurd. If I see an opportunity to create otherwise nonexistent opportunities for moral urgency by burning an infant or two, then I should *not* do so. But if it is good to maximize moral urgency, then I *should* do so. Therefore, it is not good to maximize moral urgency. Plainly we do not in general believe that it is a good thing to maximize moral urgency. The fact that we approve of modern medical care and applaud medical advances is proof enough of this.

The theist may point out that in a world without suffering there would be no occasion

for the production of such virtues as courage, sympathy, and the like. This may be true, but the atheist need not demand a world without suffering. He need only claim that there is suffering which is in excess of that needed for the production of various virtues. For example, God's active attempts to save six-month-old infants from fires would not in itself create a world without suffering. But no one could sincerely doubt that it would improve the world.

The two arguments against the previous theistic excuse apply here also. "Moral urgency" and "building virtue" are susceptible to the same criticisms. It is worthwhile to emphasize, however, that we encourage efforts to eliminate evils; we approve of efforts to promote peace, prevent famine, and wipe out disease. In other words, we do value a world with fewer or (if possible) no opportunities for the development of virtue (when "virtue" is understood to mean the reduction of suffering). If we produce such a world for succeeding generations, how will they develop virtues? Without war, disease, and famine, they will not be virtuous. Should we then cease our attempts to wipe out war, disease, and famine? If we do not believe that it is right to cease attempts at improving the world, then by implication we admit that virtue-building is not an excuse for God to permit disasters. For we admit that the development of virtue is no excuse for permitting disasters.

It might be said that God allows innocent people to suffer in order to deflate man's ego so that the latter will not be proud of his apparently deserved good fortune. But this excuse succumbs to the arguments used against the preceding excuses and we need discuss them no further.

Theists may claim that evil is a necessary by-product of the laws of nature and therefore it is irrational for God to interfere every time a disaster happens. Such a state of affairs would alter the whole causal order and we would then find it impossible to predict anything. But the death of a child caused by an electrical fire could have been prevented by a miracle and no one would ever have known.

Only a minor alteration in electrical equipment would have been necessary. A very large disaster could have been avoided simply by producing in Hitler a miraculous heart attack—and no one would have known it was a miracle. To argue that continued miraculous intervention by God would be wrong is like insisting that one should never use salt because ingesting five pounds of it would be fatal. No one is requesting that God interfere all of the time. He should, however, intervene to prevent especially horrible disasters. Of course, the question arises: where does one draw the line? Well, certainly the line should be drawn somewhere this side of infants burning to death. To argue that we do not know where the line should be drawn is no excuse for failing to interfere in those instances that would be called clear cases of evil.

It will not do to claim that evil exists as a necessary contrast to good so that we might know what good is. A very small amount of evil, such as a toothache, would allow that. It is not necessary to destroy innocent human beings.

The claim could be made that God has a "higher morality" by which his actions are to be judged. But it is a strange "higher morality" which claims that what we call "bad" is good and what we call "good" is bad. Such a morality can have no meaning to us. It would be like calling black "white" and white "black." In reply the theist may say that God is the wise Father and we are ignorant children. How can we judge God any more than a child is able to judge his parent? It is true that a child may be puzzled by his parents' conduct, but his basis for deciding that their conduct is nevertheless good would be the many instances of good behavior he has observed. Even so, this could be misleading. Hitler, by all accounts, loved animals and children of the proper race; but if Hitler had had a child, this offspring would hardly have been justified in arguing that his father was a good man. At any rate, God's "higher morality," being the opposite of ours, cannot offer any grounds for deciding that he is somehow good.

Perhaps the main problem with the solutions to the problem of evil we have thus far considered is that no matter how convincing they may be in the abstract, they are implausible in certain particular cases. Picture an infant dying in a burning house and then imagine God simply observing from afar. Perhaps God is reciting excuses in his own behalf. As the child succumbs to the smoke and flames, God may be pictured as saying: "Sorry, but if I helped you I would have considerable trouble deflating the ego of your parents. And don't forget I have to keep those laws of nature consistent. And anyway if you weren't dying in that fire, a lot of moral urgency would just go down the drain. Besides, I didn't start this fire, so you can't blame *me*."

It does no good to assert that God may not be all-powerful and thus not able to prevent evil. He can create a universe and yet is conveniently unable to do what the fire department can do—rescue a baby from a burning building. God should at least be as powerful as a man. A man, if he had been at the right place and time, could have killed Hitler. Was this beyond God's abilities? If God knew in 1910 how to produce polio vaccine and if he was able to communicate with somebody, he should have communicated this knowledge. He must be incredibly limited if he could not have managed this modest accomplishment. Such a God if not dead, is the next thing to it. And a person who believes in such a ghost of a God is practically an atheist. To call such a thing a god would be to strain the meaning of the word.

The theist, as usual, may retreat to faith. He may say that he has faith in God's goodness and therefore the Christian Deity's existence has not been disproved. "Faith" is here understood as being much like confidence in a friend's innocence despite the evidence against him. Now in order to have confidence in a friend one must know him well enough to justify faith in his goodness. We cannot have justifiable faith in the supreme goodness of strangers. Moreover, such confidence must come not just from a speaking acquaintance.

The friend may continually assure us with his words that he is good but if he does not act like a good person, we would have no reason to trust him. A person who says he has faith in God's goodness is speaking as if he had known God for a long time and during that time had never seen Him do any serious evil. But we know that throughout history God has allowed numerous atrocities to occur. No one can have justifiable faith in the goodness of such a God. This faith would have to be based on a close friendship wherein God was never found to do anything wrong. But a person would have to be blind and deaf to have had such a relationship with God. Suppose a friend of yours had always claimed to be good yet refused to help people when he was in a position to render aid. Could you have justifiable faith in his goodness?

You can of course say that you trust God anyway—that no arguments can undermine your faith. But this is just a statement describing how stubborn you are; it has no bearing whatsoever on the question of God's goodness.

The various excuses theists offer for why God has allowed evil to exist have been demonstrated to be inadequate. However, the conclusive objection to these excuses does not depend on their inadequacy.

First, we should note that every possible excuse making the actual world consistent with the existence of a good God could be used in reverse to make that same world consistent with an evil God. For example, we could say that God is evil and that he allows free will so that we can freely do evil things, which would make us more truly evil than we would be if forced to perform evil acts. Or we could say that natural disasters occur in order to make people more selfish and bitter, for most people tend to have a "me-first" attitude in a disaster (note, for example, stampedes to leave burning buildings). Even though some people achieve virtue from disasters, this outcome is necessary if persons are to react freely to disaster—necessary if the development of moral degeneracy is to continue freely. But, enough; the point is

made. Every excuse we could provide to make the world consistent with a good God can be paralleled by an excuse to make the world consistent with an evil God. This is so because the world is a mixture of both good and bad.

Now there are only three possibilities concerning God's moral character. Considering the world as it actually is, we may believe: (*a*) that God is more likely to be all evil than he is to be all good; (*b*) that God is less likely to be all evil than he is to be all good; or (*c*) that God is equally as likely to be all evil as he is to be all good. In case (*a*) it would be admitted that God is unlikely to be all good. Case (*b*) cannot be true at all, since—as we have seen—the belief that God is all evil can be justified to precisely the same extent as the belief that God is all good. Case (*c*) leaves us with no reasonable excuses for a good God to permit evil. The reason is as follows: if an excuse is to be a reasonable excuse, the circumstances it identifies as excusing conditions must be actual. For example, if I run over a pedestrian and my excuse is that the brakes failed because someone tampered with them, then the facts had better bear this out. Otherwise the excuse will not hold. Now if case (*c*) is correct and, given the facts of the actual world, God is as likely to be all evil as he is to be all good, then these facts do not support the excuses which could be made for a good God permitting evil. Consider an analogous example. If my excuse for running over the pedestrian is that my brakes were tampered with, and if the actual facts lead us to believe that it is no more likely that they were tampered with than that they were not, the excuse is no longer reasonable. To make good my excuse, I must show that it is a fact or at least highly probable that my brakes were tampered with—not that it is just a possibility. The same point holds for God. His excuse must not be a possible excuse, but an actual one. But case (*c*), in maintaining that it is just as likely that God is all evil as that he is all good, rules this out. For if case

(c) is true, then the facts of the actual world do not make it any more likely that God is all good than that he is all evil. Therefore, they do not make it any more likely that his excuses are good than that they are not. But, as we have seen, good excuses have a higher probability of being true.

Cases (*a*) and (*c*) conclude that it is unlikely that God is all good, and case (*b*) cannot be true. Since these are the only possible cases, there is no escape from the conclusion that it is unlikely that God is all good. Thus the problem of evil triumphs over the traditional theism.

The Problem of Evil and Suffering: A Response

John Hick

In this essay, John Hick undertakes to answer the atheist's claim that the existence of evil and suffering in the world proves there is no God. After first discussing solutions such as the ideas that there really is no evil or that God does the best s/he can, Hick turns to the related problems of the moral evil caused by humans and the suffering caused by nature. Neither, he concludes, provides conclusive evidence that an all-powerful, all-knowing, and just creator does not exist. For biographical information about John Hick, see his contribution in an earlier reading.

As you read through this essay, consider the following:

1. Why does Hick reject the Christian Science and Personalist solutions?
2. How is freedom of the will a defense against the problem of evil?
3. Why does Hick think that our world and one in which the finest sorts of moral character is developed are substantially similar?
4. What sort of limitation does Hick envision on the power of God to create value?

To many, the most powerful positive objection to belief in God is the fact of evil. Probably for most agnostics it is the appalling depth and extent of human suffering, more than anything else, that makes the idea of a loving Creator seem so implausible and disposes them toward one or another of the various naturalistic theories of religion.

As a challenge to theism, the problem of evil has traditionally been posed in the form of

From John Hick, *Philosophy of Religion*, 1st ed. Reprinted by permission of Prentice-Hall, Inc., Upper Saddle River, NJ.

a dilemma: if God is perfectly loving, he must wish to abolish evil; and if he is all-powerful, he must be able to abolish evil. But evil exists; therefore God cannot be both omnipotent and perfectly loving.

Certain solutions, which at once suggest themselves, have to be ruled out so far as the Judaic-Christian faith is concerned.

To say, for example (with contemporary Christian Science), that evil is an illusion of the human mind, is impossible within a religion based upon the stark realism of the Bible. Its pages faithfully reflect the characteristic mixture of good and evil in human experience. They record every kind of sorrow and suffering, every mode of man's inhumanity to man and of his painfully insecure existence in the world. There is no attempt to regard evil as anything but dark, menacingly ugly, heart-rending, and crushing. In the Christian scriptures, the climax of this history of evil is the crucifixion of Jesus, which is presented not only as a case of utterly unjust suffering, but as the violent and murderous rejection of God's Messiah. There can be no doubt, then, that for biblical faith, evil is unambiguously evil, and stands in direct opposition to God's will.

Again, to solve the problem of evil by means of the theory (sponsored, for example, by the Boston "Personalist" School)[1] of a finite deity who does the best he can with a material, intractable and co-eternal with himself, is to have abandoned the basic premise of Hebrew-Christian monotheism; for the theory amounts to rejecting belief in the infinity and sovereignty of God.

Indeed, any theory which would avoid the problem of the origin of evil by depicting it as an ultimate constituent of the universe, coordinate with good, has been repudiated in advance by the classic Christian teaching, first developed by Augustine, that evil represents the going wrong of something which in itself is good.[2] Augustine holds firmly to the Hebrew-Christian conviction that the universe is *good*—that is to say, it is the creation of a good God for a good purpose. He completely rejects the ancient prejudice, widespread in his day, that matter is evil. There are, according to Augustine, higher and lower, greater and lesser goods in immense abundance and variety; but everything which has being is good in its own way and degree, except in so far as it may have become spoiled or corrupted. Evil—whether it be an evil will, an instance of pain, or some disorder or decay in nature—has not been set there by God, but represents the distortion of something that is inherently valuable. Whatever exists is, as such, and in its proper place, good; evil is essentially parasitic upon good, being disorder and perversion in a fundamentally good

creation. This understanding of evil as something negative means that it is not willed and created by God; but it does not mean (as some have supposed) that evil is unreal and can be disregarded. Clearly, the first effect of this doctrine is to accentuate even more the question of the origin of evil.

Theodicy,[3] as many modern Christian thinkers see it, is a modest enterprise, negative rather than positive in its conclusions. It does not claim to explain, nor to explain away, every instance of evil in human experience, but only to point to certain considerations which prevent the fact of evil (largely incomprehensible though it remains) from constituting a final and insuperable bar to rational belief in God.

In indicating these considerations it will be useful to follow the traditional division of the subject. There is the problem of *moral evil* or wickedness: why does an all-good and all-powerful God permit this? And there is the problem of the *non-moral evil* of suffering or pain, both physical and mental: why has an all-good and all-powerful God created a world in which this occurs?

Christian thought has always considered moral evil in its relation to human freedom and responsibility. To be a person is to be a finite center of freedom, a (relatively) free and self-directing agent responsible for one's own decisions. This involves being free to act wrongly as well as to act rightly. The idea of a person who can be infallibly guaranteed always to act rightly is self-contradictory. There can be no guarantee in advance that a genuinely free moral agent will never choose amiss. Consequently, the possibility of wrongdoing or sin is logically inseparable from the creation of finite persons, and to say that God should not have created beings who might sin amounts to saying that he should not have created people.

This thesis has been challenged in some recent philosophical discussions of the problem of evil, in which it is claimed that no contradiction is involved in saying that God might have made people who would be genuinely free and who could yet be guaranteed always to act rightly. A quotation from one of these discussions follows:

> If there is no logical impossibility in a man's freely choosing the good on one, or on several occasions, there cannot be a logical impossibility in his freely choosing the good on every occasion. God was not, then, faced with a choice between making innocent automata and making beings who, in acting freely, would sometimes go wrong: there was open to him the obviously better possibility of making beings who would act freely but always go right. Clearly, his failure to avail himself of this possibility is inconsistent with his being both omnipotent and wholly good.[4]

A reply to this argument is suggested in another recent contribution to the discussion.[5] If by a free action we mean an action which is not externally compelled but which flows from the nature of the agent as he reacts to the circumstances in which he finds himself, there is, indeed, no contradiction between our being free and our actions being "caused" (by our own nature) and therefore being in principle predictable. There is a contradiction, however, in saying that God is the cause of our acting as we do but that we are free beings in relation to God. There is, in other words, a contradiction in saying that God has made us so that we shall of necessity act in a certain way, and that we are genuinely independent persons in relation to him. If all our thoughts and actions are divinely predestined, however free and morally responsible we may seem to be to ourselves, we cannot be free and morally responsible in the sight of God, but must instead be his helpless puppets. Such "freedom" is like that of a patient acting out a series of posthypnotic suggestions: he appears, even to himself, to be free, but his volitions have actually been predetermined by another will, that of the hypnotist, in relation to whom the patient is not a free agent.

A different objector might raise the question of whether or not we deny God's omnipotence if we admit that he is unable to create persons who are free from the risks inherent in personal freedom. The answer that has always been given is that to create such beings is logically impossible. It is no limitation upon God's power that he cannot accomplish the logically impossible, since there is nothing here to accomplish, but only a meaningless conjunction of words[6]—in this case "person who is not a person." God is able to create beings of any and every conceivable kind; but creatures who lack moral freedom, however superior they might be to human beings in other respects, would not be what we mean by persons. They would constitute a different form of life which God might have brought into existence instead of persons. When we ask why God did not create such beings in place of persons, the traditional answer is that only persons could, in any meaningful sense, become "children of God," capable of entering into a personal relationship with their Creator by a free and uncompelled response to his love.

When we turn from the possibility of moral evil as a correlate of man's personal freedom to its actuality, we face something which must remain inexplicable even when it can be seen to be possible. For we can never provide a complete causal explanation of a free act; if we could, it would not be a free act. The origin of moral evil lies forever concealed within the mystery of human freedom.

The necessary connection between moral freedom and the possibility, now actualized, of sin throws light upon a great deal of the suffering which afflicts mankind. For an enormous amount of human pain arises either from the inhumanity or the culpable incompetence of mankind. This includes such major scourges as poverty, oppression and persecution, war, and all the injustice, indignity, and inequity which occur even in the most advanced societies. These evils are manifestations of human sin. Even disease is fostered to an extent, the limits of which have not yet been determined by psychosomatic medicine, by moral and emotional factors seated both in the individual and in his social environment. To the extent that all of these evils stem from human failures and wrong decisions, their possibility is inherent in the creation of free persons inhabiting a world which presents them with real choices which are followed by real consequences.

We may now turn more directly to the problem of suffering. Even though the major bulk of actual human pain is traceable to man's misused freedom as a sole or part cause, there remain other sources of pain which are entirely independent of the human will, for example, earthquake, hurricane, storm, flood, drought, and blight. In practice, it is often impossible to trace a boundary between the suffering which results from human wickedness and folly and that which falls upon mankind from without. Both kinds of suffering are inextricably mingled together in human experience. For our present purpose, however, it is important to note that the latter category does exist and that it seems to be built into the very structure of our world. In response to it, theodicy, if it is wisely conducted, follows a negative path. It is not possible to show positively that each item of human pain serves the divine purpose of good; but, on the other hand, it does seem possible to show that the divine purpose as it is understood in Judaism and Christianity could not be forwarded in a world which was designed as a permanent hedonistic paradise.

An essential premise of this argument concerns the nature of the divine purpose in creating the world. The skeptic's assumption is that man is to be viewed as a completed creation and that God's purpose in making the world was to provide a suitable dwelling-place for this fully-formed creature. Since God is good and loving, the environment which he has created for human life to inhabit is naturally as pleasant and comfortable as possible. The problem is essentially similar to that of a man who builds a cage for some pet animal. Since our world, in fact, contains sources of hardship, inconvenience, and danger of innumerable kinds, the conclusion follows that this world cannot have been created by a perfectly benevolent and all-powerful deity.[7]

Christianity, however, has never supposed that God's purpose in the creation of the world was to construct a paradise whose inhabitants would experience a maximum of pleasure and a minimum of pain. The world is seen, instead, as a place of "soul-making" in which free beings grappling with the tasks and challenges of their existence in a common environment, may become "children of God" and "heirs of eternal life." A way of thinking theologically of God's continuing creative purpose for man was suggested by some of the early Hellenistic Fathers of the Christian Church, especially Irenaeus. Following hints from St. Paul, Irenaeus taught that man has been made as a person in the image of God but has not yet been brought as a free and responsible agent into the finite likeness of God, which is revealed in Christ.[8] Our world, with all its rough edges, is the sphere in which this second and harder stage of the creative process is taking place.

This conception of the world (whether or not set in Irenaeus' theological framework) can be supported by the method of negative theodicy. Suppose, contrary to fact, that this world were a paradise from which all possibility of pain and suffering were excluded. The consequences would be very far-reaching. For example, no one could ever injure anyone else: the murderer's knife would turn to paper or his bullets to thin air; the bank safe, robbed of a million dollars, would miraculously become filled with another million dollars (without this device, on however large a scale, proving inflationary); fraud, deceit, conspiracy, and treason would somehow always leave the fabric of society undamaged. Again, no one would ever be injured by accident: the mountain-climber, steeplejack, or playing child falling from a height would float unharmed to the ground; the reckless driver would never meet with disaster. There would be no need to work, since no harm could result from avoiding work; there would be no call to be concerned for others in time of need or danger, for in such a world there could be no real needs or dangers.

To make possible this continual series of individual adjustments, nature would have to work by "special providences" instead of running according to general laws which men must learn to respect on penalty of pain or death. The laws of nature would have to be extremely flexible: sometimes gravity would operate, sometimes not; sometimes an object would be hard and solid, sometimes soft. There could be no sciences, for there would be no enduring world structure to investigate. In eliminating the problems and hardships of an objective environment, with its own laws, life would become like a dream in which, delightfully but aimlessly, we would float and drift at ease.

One can at least begin to imagine such a world. It is evident that our present ethical concepts would have no meaning in it. If, for example, the notion of harming someone is an essential element in the concept of a wrong action, in our hedonistic paradise there could be no wrong actions—nor any right actions in distinction from wrong. Courage and fortitude would have no point in an environment in which there is, by definition, no danger or difficulty. Generosity, kindness, the *agape* aspect of love, prudence, unselfishness, and all other ethical notions which presuppose life in a stable environment, could not even be formed. Consequently, such a world, however well it might promote pleasure, would be very ill adapted for the development of the moral qualities of human personality. In relation to this purpose it would be the worst of all possible worlds.

It would seem, then, that an environment intended to make possible the growth in free beings of the finest characteristics of personal life, must have a good deal in common with our present world. It must operate according to general and dependable laws; and it must involve real dangers, difficulties, problems, obstacles, and possibilities of pain, failure, sorrow, frustration, and defeat. If it did not contain the particular trials and perils which—subtracting man's own very considerable contribution—our world contains, it would have to contain others instead.

To realize this is not, by any means, to be in possession of a detailed theodicy. It is to understand that this world, with all its "heartaches and the thousand natural shocks that flesh is heir to," an environment so manifestly not designed for the maximization of human pleasure and the minimization of human pain, may be rather well adapted to the quite different purpose of "soul-making."

Notes

1. Edgar Brightman's *A Philosophy of Religion* (Englewood Cliffs, N.J.: Prentice-Hall, Inc., 1940), Chaps. 8–10, is a classic exposition of one form of this view.

2. See Augustine's *Confessions*, Book VII, Chap. 12; *City of God*, Book XII, Chap. 3; *Enchiridion*, Chap. 4.

3. The word "theodicy" from the Greek *theos* (God) and *dike* (righteous) means the justification of God's goodness in face of the fact of evil.

4. J. L. Mackie, "Evil and Omnipotence," *Mind* (April, 1955), p. 209. A similar point is made by Antony Flew in "Divine Omnipotence and Human Freedom," *New Essays in Philosophical Theology*. An important critical comment on these arguments is offered by Ninian Smart in "Omnipotence, Evil and Supermen," *Philosophy* (April, 1961), with replies by Flew (January, 1962) and Mackie (April, 1962).

5. Flew, in *New Essays in Philosophical Theology*.

6. As Aquinas said, "... nothing that implies a contradiction falls under the scope of God's omnipotence." *Summa Theologica*, Part 1, Question 25, article 4.

7. This is the nature of David Hume's argument in his discussion of the problem of evil in his *Dialogues*, Part XI.

8. See Irenaeus' *Against Heresies*, Book IV, Chaps. 37 and 38.

Faith and Reason

The Ethics of Belief

W. K. Clifford

People have differed throughout history about whether or not there is good evidence to believe there is a God, to believe there is no God, or to believe neither. Suppose we set that issue aside, then, and look at matters from a different perspective. For surely, it may be suggested, religion is a matter of faith more than reason. If that widely held belief is true, then it raises another set of questions about whether or not people should believe in and practice religion without adequate evidence and, additionally, about the nature of faith itself.

In this well-known essay W. K. Clifford attacks those who take the position that people are entitled, morally, to believe on insufficient evidence. Clifford (1845–1879) was an English philosopher and mathematician.

As you read through this essay, consider the following:

1. What is the analogy Clifford uses to make his case?
2. What does Clifford mean when he suggests it is not the belief but the action that is wrong? How does he respond to that claim?
3. What is the principle that Clifford thinks captures our duty with respect to the ethics of belief?
4. In what sense does Clifford think the principle is a "hard" one?
5. Which, if any, of our nonreligious, commonsense beliefs would pass Clifford's test?

A shipowner was about to send to sea an emigrant-ship. He knew that she was old, and not over-well built at the first; that she had seen many seas and climes, and often had needed repairs. Doubts had been suggested to him that possibly she was not seaworthy. These doubts preyed upon his mind, and made him unhappy; he thought that perhaps he ought to have her thoroughly overhauled and refitted, even though this should put him to great expense. Before the ship sailed, however, he succeeded in overcoming these melancholy reflections. He said to himself that she had gone safely through so many voyages and weathered so many storms that it was idle to suppose she would not come safely home from this trip also. He would put his trust in Providence, which could hardly fail to protect all these unhappy families that were leaving their fatherland to seek for better times elsewhere. He would dismiss from his mind all ungenerous suspicions about the honesty of builders and contractors. In such ways he acquired a sincere and comfortable conviction that his vessel was thoroughly safe and seaworthy; he watched her departure with a light heart, and benevolent wishes for the success of the exiles in their strange new home that was to be; and he got his insurance-money when she went down in mid-ocean and told no tales.

What shall we say of him? Surely this, that he was verily guilty of the death of those men. It is admitted that he did sincerely believe in the soundness of his ship; but the sincerity of his conviction can in no wise help him, because *he had no right to believe on such evidence as was before him*. He had acquired his belief not by honestly earning it in patient investigation, but by stifling his doubts. And although in the end he may have felt so sure about it that he could not think otherwise, yet inasmuch as he had knowingly and willingly worked himself into that frame of mind, he must be held responsible for it.

Let us alter the case a little, and suppose that the ship was not unsound after all; that

she made her voyage safely, and many others after it. Will that diminish the guilt of her owner? Not one jot. When an action is once done, it is right or wrong for ever; no accidental failure of its good or evil fruits can possibly alter that. The man would not have been innocent, he would only have been not found out. The question of right or wrong has to do with the origin of his belief, not the matter of it; not what it was, but how he got it; not whether it turned out to be true or false, but whether he had a right to believe on such evidence as was before him.

There was once an island in which some of the inhabitants professed a religion teaching neither the doctrine of original sin nor that of eternal punishment. A suspicion got abroad that the professors of this religion had made use of unfair means to get their doctrines taught to children. They were accused of wresting the laws of their country in such a way as to remove children from the care of their natural and legal guardians; and even of stealing them away and keeping them concealed from their friends and relations. A certain number of men formed themselves into a society for the purpose of agitating the public about this matter. They published grave accusations against individual citizens of the highest position and character, and did all in their power to injure these citizens in the exercise of their professions. So great was the noise they made, that a Commission was appointed to investigate the facts; but after the Commission had carefully inquired into all the evidence that could be got, it appeared that the accused were innocent. Not only had they been accused on insufficient evidence, but the evidence of their innocence was such as the agitators might easily have obtained, if they had attempted a fair inquiry. After these disclosures the inhabitants of that country looked upon the members of the agitating society, not only as persons whose judgment was to be distrusted, but also as no longer to be counted honourable men. For although they had sincerely and conscientiously believed in the charges they had made, yet *they had no right to believe on such evidence as was before them*. Their

From W. K. Clifford, *Lectures and Essays* (London: Macmillan Co. 1879).

sincere convictions, instead of being honestly earned by patient inquiring, were stolen by listening to the voice of prejudice and passion.

Let us vary this case also, and suppose, other things remaining as before, that a still more accurate investigation proved the accused to have been really guilty. Would this make any difference in the guilt of the accusers? Clearly not; the question is not whether their belief was true or false, but whether they entertained it on wrong grounds. They would no doubt say, "Now you see that we were right after all; next time perhaps you will believe us." And they might be believed, but they would not thereby become honourable men. They would not be innocent, they would only be not found out. Every one of them, if he chose to examine himself *in foro conscientiæ*, would know that he had acquired and nourished a belief, when he had no right to believe on such evidence as was before him; and therein he would know that he had done a wrong thing.

It may be said, however, that in both of these supposed cases it is not the belief which is judged to be wrong, but the action following upon it. The shipowner might say, "I am perfectly certain that my ship is sound, but still I feel it my duty to have her examined, before trusting the lives of so many people to her." And it might be said to the agitator, "However convinced you were of the justice of your cause and the truth of your convictions, you ought not to have made a public attack upon any man's character until you had examined the evidence on both sides with the utmost patience and care."

In the first place, let us admit that, so far as it goes, this view of the case is right and necessary; right, because even when a man's belief is so fixed that he cannot think otherwise, he still has a choice in regard to the action suggested by it, and so cannot escape the duty of investigating on the ground of the strength of his convictions; and necessary, because those who are not yet capable of controlling their feelings and thoughts must have a plain rule dealing with overt acts.

But this being premised as necessary, it becomes clear that it is not sufficient, and that our previous judgment is required to supple-

ment it. For it is not possible so to sever the belief from the action it suggests as to condemn the one without condemning the other. No man holding a strong belief on one side of a question, or even wishing to hold a belief on one side, can investigate it with such fairness and completeness as if he were really in doubt and unbiased; so that the existence of a belief not founded on fair inquiry unfits a man for the performance of this necessary duty.

Nor is that truly a belief at all which has not some influence upon the actions of him who holds it. He who truly believes that which prompts him to an action has looked upon the action to lust after it, he has committed it already in his heart. If a belief is not realized immediately in open deeds, it is stored up for the guidance of the future. It goes to make a part of that aggregate of beliefs which is the link between sensation and action at every moment of all our lives, and which is so organized and compacted together that no part of it can be isolated from the rest, but every new addition modifies the structure of the whole. No real belief, however trifling and fragmentary it may seem, is ever truly insignificant; it prepares us to receive more of its like, confirms those which resembled it before, and weakens others; and so gradually it lays a stealthy train in our inmost thoughts, which may some day explode into overt action, and leave its stamp upon our character forever.

And no one man's belief is in any case a private matter which concerns himself alone. Our lives are guided by that general conception of the course of things which has been created by society for social purposes. Our words, our phrases, our forms and processes and modes of thought, are common property, fashioned and perfected from age to age; an heirloom which every succeeding generation inherits as a precious deposit and a sacred trust to be handed on to the next one, not unchanged but enlarged and purified, with some clear marks of its proper handiwork. Into this, for good or ill, is woven every belief of every man who has speech of his fellows. An awful privilege, and an awful responsibility, that we should help to create the world in which posterity will live.

In the two supposed cases which have been considered, it has been judged wrong to believe on insufficient evidence, or to nourish belief by suppressing doubts and avoiding investigation. The reason of this judgment is not far to seek; it is that in both these cases the belief held by one man was of great importance to other men. But for as much as no belief held by one man, however seemingly trivial the belief, and however obscure the believer, is ever actually insignificant or without its effect on the fate of mankind, we have no choice but to extend our judgment to all cases of belief whatever. Belief, that sacred faculty which prompts the decisions of our will, and knits into harmonious working all the compacted energies of our being, is ours not for ourselves, but for humanity. It is rightly used on truths which have been established by long experience and waiting toil, and which have stood in the fierce light of free and fearless questioning. Then it helps to bind men together, and to strengthen and direct their common action. It is desecrated when given to unproved and unquestioned statements, for the solace and private pleasure of the believer; to add a tinsel splendor to the plain straight road of our life and display a bright mirage beyond it; or even to drown the common sorrows of our kind by a self-deception which allows them not only to cast down, but also to degrade us. Whoso would deserve well of his fellows in this matter will guard the purity of his belief with a very fanaticism of jealous care, lest at any time it should rest on an unworthy object, and catch a stain which can never be wiped away.

It is not only the leader of men, statesman, philosopher, or poet, that owes this bounden duty to mankind. Every rustic who delivers in the village alehouse his slow, infrequent sentences, may help to kill or keep alive the fatal superstitions which clog his race. Every hard-worked wife of an artisan may transmit to her children beliefs which shall knit society together, or rend it in pieces. No simplicity of mind, no obscurity of station, can escape the universal duty of questioning all that we believe.

It is true that this duty is a hard one, and the doubt which comes out of it is often a very bitter thing. It leaves us bare and powerless where we thought that we were safe and strong. To know all about anything is to know how to deal with it under all circumstances. We feel much happier and more secure when we think we know precisely what to do, no matter what happens, than when we have lost our way and do not know where to turn. And if we have supposed ourselves to know all about anything, and to be capable of doing what is fit in regard to it, we naturally do not like to find that we are really ignorant and powerless, that we have to begin again at the beginning and try to learn what the thing is and how it is to be dealt with—if indeed anything can be learned about it. It is the sense of power attached to a sense of knowledge that makes men desirous of believing, and afraid of doubting.

This sense of power is the highest and best of pleasures when the belief on which it is founded is a true belief, and has been fairly earned by investigation. For then we may justly feel that it is common property, and holds good for others as well as ourselves. Then we may be glad, not that *I* have learned secrets by which I am safer and stronger, but that *we men* have got mastery over more of the world; and we shall be strong, not for ourselves, but in the name of Man and in his strength. But if the belief has been accepted on insufficient evidence, the pleasure is a stolen one. Not only does it deceive ourselves by giving us a sense of power which we do not really possess, but it is sinful, because it is stolen in defiance of our duty to mankind. That duty is to guard ourselves from such beliefs as from a pestilence, which may shortly master our own body and then spread to the rest of the town. What would be thought of one who, for the sake of a sweet fruit, should deliberately run the risk of bringing a plague upon his family and his neighbors?

And, as in other such cases, it is not the risk only which has to be considered; for a bad action is always bad at the time when it is done, no matter what happens afterwards. Every time we let ourselves believe for unworthy reasons, we weaken our power of self-control, of doubting, of judicially and fairly weighing evidence. We all suffer severely enough from the maintenance and support of false beliefs and the fatally wrong actions which they lead to, and the evil born when one such belief is entertained is great and wide. But a greater and wider evil arises when the credulous character is maintained and supported, when a habit of believing for unworthy reasons is fostered and made permanent. If I steal money from any person, there may be no harm done by the mere transfer of possession; he may not feel the loss, or it may prevent him from using the money badly. But I cannot help doing this great wrong towards Man, that I make myself dishonest. What hurts society is not that it should lose its property, but that it should become a den of thieves; for then it must cease to be society. This is why we ought not to do evil that good may come; for at any rate this great evil has come, that we have done evil and are made wicked thereby. In like manner, if I let myself believe anything on insufficient evidence, there may be no great harm done by the mere belief; it may be true after all, or I may never have occasion to exhibit it in outward acts. But I cannot help doing this great wrong toward Man, that I make myself credulous. The danger to society is not merely that it should believe wrong things, though that is great enough; but that it should become credulous, and lose the habit of testing things and inquiring into them; for then it must sink back into savagery.

The harm which is done by credulity in a man is not confined to the fostering of a credulous character in others, and consequent support of false beliefs. Habitual want of care about what I believe leads to habitual want of care in others about the truth of what is told to me. Men speak the truth to one another when each reveres the truth in his own mind and in the other's mind; but how shall my friend revere the truth in my mind when I myself am careless about it, when I believe things because I want to believe them, and because they are comforting and pleasant? Will he not learn to cry, "Peace," to me, when there is no peace? By such a course I shall surround myself with a thick atmosphere of falsehood and fraud, and in that I must live. It may matter little to me, in my cloud-castle of sweet illusions and darling lies; but it matters much to Man that I have made my neighbors ready to deceive. The credulous man is father to the liar and the cheat; he lives in the bosom of this his family, and it is no marvel if he should become even as they are. So closely are our duties knit together, that whoso shall keep the whole law, and yet offend in one point, he is guilty of all.

To sum up: it is wrong always, everywhere, and for anyone, to believe anything upon insufficient evidence.

If a man, holding a belief which he was taught in childhood or persuaded of afterwards, keeps down and pushes away any doubts which arise about it in his mind, purposely avoids the reading of books and the company of men that call in question or discuss it, and regards as impious those questions which cannot easily be asked without disturbing it—the life of that man is one long sin against mankind.

If this judgment seems harsh when applied to those simple souls who have never known better, who have been brought up from the cradle with a horror of doubt, and taught that their eternal welfare depends on what they believe, then it leads to the very serious question. Who hath made Israel to sin? . . .

Inquiry into the evidence of a doctrine is not to be made once for all, and then taken as finally settled. It is never lawful to stifle a doubt; for either it can be honestly answered by means of the inquiry already made, or else it proves that the inquiry was not complete.

"But," says one, "I am a busy man; I have no time for the long course of study which would be necessary to make me in any degree a competent judge of certain questions, or even able to understand the nature of the arguments." Then he should have no time to believe.

The Will to Believe

William James

This essay is not just the most famous written by William James, though it is probably that, but it is among the most widely read essays by any American philosopher. One of the founders of philosophical pragmatism, James is concerned here to respond to those who argue that people ought to believe only what they have already acquired evidence for and only to the degree that the evidence warrants. Thus, it might be said that if you have evidence it is very probably raining in New York, you should believe it strongly; if you have no evidence one way or another, however, you should withhold belief altogether. James disputes that apparently commonsense claim, arguing instead that it would be foolish to follow such a principle. For biographical information about William James, see his essay in Section 20.

As you read through this essay, consider the following:

1. What is the difference between a living and a dead option? a forced or avoidable option? a momentous or trivial option?
2. How does James answer those who say that we cannot choose what to believe? What can people do to make themselves believe?
3. When an option is momentous, James thinks it is often wise to reject those who, like Clifford, would counsel avoiding erroneous beliefs. Why does he think that?
4. What does James think might be lost if we take the wrong path with respect to religious belief?

I have long defended to my own students the lawfulness of voluntarily adopted faith; but as soon as they have got well imbued with the logical spirit, they have as a rule refused to admit my contention to be lawful philosophically, even though in point of fact they were personally all the time chock-full of some faith or other themselves. I am all the while, however, so profoundly convinced that my own position is correct, that your invitation has seemed to me a good occasion to make my statements more clear. Perhaps your minds will be more open than those with which I have hitherto had to deal. I will be as little technical as I can, though I must begin by setting up some technical distinctions that will help us in the end.

This essay, originally an address delivered before the Philosophical Clubs of Yale and Brown Universities, was first published in 1896.

I

Let us give the name of hypothesis to anything that may be proposed to our belief; and just as the electricians speak of live and dead wires, let us speak of any hypothesis as either *live* or *dead*. A live hypothesis is one which appeals as a real possibility to him to whom it is proposed. If I ask you to believe in the Mahdi, the notion makes no electric connection with your nature—it refuses to scintillate with any credibility at all. As an hypothesis it is completely dead. To an Arab, however (even if he be not one of the Mahdi's followers), the hypothesis is among the mind's possibilities: It is alive. This shows that deadness and liveness in an hypothesis are not intrinsic properties, but relations to the individual thinker. They are measured by his willingness to act. The maximum of liveness in an hypothesis means willingness to act irrevocably. Practically, that means belief; but there is some believing tendency wherever there is willingness to act at all.

Next, let us call the decision between two hypotheses an *option*. Options may be of several kinds. They may be first, *living* or *dead*; secondly, *forced* or *avoidable*; thirdly, *momentous* or *trivial*; and for our purposes we may call an option a *genuine* option when it is of the forced, living, and momentous kind.

1. A living option is one in which both hypotheses are live ones. If I say to you: "Be a theosophist or be a Mohammedan," it is probably a dead option, because for you neither hypothesis is likely to be alive. But if I say: "Be an agnostic or be a Christian," it is otherwise: trained as you are, each hypothesis makes some appeal, however small, to your belief.

2. Next, if I say to you: "Choose between going out with your umbrella or without," I do not offer you a genuine option, for it is not forced. You can easily avoid it by not going out at all. Similarly, if I say, "Either love me or hate me," "Either call my theory true or call it false," your option is avoidable. You may remain indifferent to me, neither loving nor hating, and you may decline to offer any judgment as to my theory. But if I say, "Either accept this truth or go without it," I put on you a forced option, for there is no standing place outside of the alternative. Every dilemma based on a complete logical disjunction, with no possibility of not choosing, is an option of this forced kind.

3. Finally, if I were Dr. Nansen and proposed to you to join my North Pole expedition, your option would be momentous; for this would probably be your only similar opportunity, and your choice now would either exclude you from the North Pole sort of immortality altogether or put at least the chance of it into your hands. He who refuses to embrace a unique opportunity loses the prize as surely as if he tried and failed. *Per contra*, the option is trivial when the opportunity is not unique, when the stake is insignificant, or when the

decision is reversible if it later prove unwise. Such trivial options abound in the scientific life. A chemist finds an hypothesis live enough to spend a year in its verification: he believes in it to that extent. But if his experiments prove inconclusive either way, he is quit for his loss of time, no vital harm being done.

It will facilitate our discussion if we keep all these distinctions well in mind.

II

The next matter to consider is the actual psychology of human opinion. When we look at certain facts, it seems as if our passional and volitional nature lay at the root of all our convictions. When we look at others, it seems as if they could do nothing when the intellect had once said its say. Let us take the latter facts up first.

Does it not seem preposterous on the very face of it to talk of our opinions being modifiable at will? Can our will either help or hinder our intellect in its perceptions of truth? Can we, by just willing it, believe that Abraham Lincoln's existence is a myth, and that the portraits of him in *McClure's Magazine* are all of some one else? . . .

The talk of believing by our volition seems, then, from one point of view, simply silly. From another point of view it is worse than silly, it is vile. When one turns to the magnificent edifice of the physical sciences, and sees how it was reared; what thousands of disinterested moral lives of men lie buried in its mere foundations; what patience and postponement, what choking down of preference, what submission to the icy laws of outer fact are wrought into its very stones and mortar; how absolutely impersonal it stands in its vast augustness—then how besotted and contemptible seems every little sentimentalist who comes blowing his voluntary smoke-wreaths, and pretending to decide things from out of his private dream! . . . Huxley exclaims: "My only consolation lies in the reflection that, however bad our posterity may become, so far as they hold by the plain rule of not pretending to believe what they have no reason to believe, because it may be to their advantage so to pretend [the word 'pretend' is surely here redundant], they will not have reached the lowest depth of immorality." And that delicious *enfant terrible* Clifford writes: "Belief is desecrated when given to unproved and unquestioned statements for the solace and private pleasure of the believer. . . . Whoso would deserve well of his fellows in this matter will guard the purity of his belief with a very fanaticism of jealous care, lest at any time it should rest on an unworthy object, and catch a stain which can never be wiped away. . . . If [a] belief has been accepted on insufficient evidence [even though the belief be true, as Clifford on the same page explains] the pleasure is a stolen one. . . . It is sinful because it is stolen in defiance of our duty to mankind. That duty is to guard ourselves from such beliefs as from a pestilence which may shortly master our own body and then spread to the rest of the town. . . . It is wrong always, everywhere, and for every one, to believe anything upon insufficient evidence."

III

All this strikes one as healthy, even when expressed, as by Clifford, with somewhat too much of robustious pathos in the voice. Free will and simple wishing do seem, in the matter of our credences, to be only fifth wheels to the coach. Yet if any one should thereupon assume that intellectual insight is what remains after wish and will and sentimental preference have taken wing, or that pure reason is what then settles our opinions, he would fly quite as directly in the teeth of the facts.

It is only our already dead hypotheses that our willing nature is unable to bring to life again. But what has made them dead for us is for the most part a previous action of our willing nature of an antagonistic kind. When I say "willing nature," I do not mean only such deliberate volitions as may have set up habits of belief that we cannot now escape from—I mean all such factors of belief as fear and hope, prejudice and passion, imitation and

partisanship, the circumpressure of our caste and set. As a matter of fact we find ourselves believing, we hardly know how or why. . . .

Evidently, then, our non-intellectual nature does influence our convictions. There are passional tendencies and volitions which run before and others which come after belief, and it is only the latter that are too late for the fair; and they are not too late when the previous passional work has been already in their own direction. . . .

IV

Our next duty, having recognized this mixed-up state of affairs, is to ask whether it be simply reprehensible and pathological, or whether, on the contrary, we must treat it as a normal element in making up our minds. The thesis I defend is, briefly stated, this: *Our passional nature not only lawfully may, but must, decide an option between propositions, whenever it is a genuine option that cannot by its nature be decided on intellectual grounds; for to say, under such circumstances, "Do not decide, but leave the question open," is itself a passional decision—just like deciding yes or no—and is attended with the same risk of losing the truth. . . .*

VII

One more point, small but important, and our preliminaries are done. There are two ways of looking at our duty in the matter of opinion—ways entirely different, and yet ways about whose difference the theory of knowledge seems hitherto to have shown very little concern. *We must know the truth*; and *we must avoid error*—these are our first and great commandments as would-be knowers; but they are not two ways of stating an identical commandment, they are two separable laws. . . .

Believe truth! Shun error!—these, we see, are two materially different laws; and by choosing between them we may end by coloring differently our whole intellectual life. We may regard the chase for truth as paramount, and the avoidance of error as secondary; or we may, on the other hand, treat the avoidance of error as more imperative, and let truth take its chance. Clifford, in the instructive passage which I have quoted, exhorts us to the latter course. Believe nothing, he tells us, keep your mind in suspense forever, rather than by closing it on insufficient evidence incur the awful risk of believing lies. You, on the other hand, may think that the risk of being in error is a very small matter when compared with the blessings of real knowledge, and be ready to be duped many times in your investigation rather than postpone indefinitely the chance of guessing true. I myself find it impossible to go with Clifford. . . .

VIII

. . . Wherever the option between losing truth and gaining it is not momentous, we can throw the chance of *gaining truth* away, and at any rate save ourselves from any chance of *believing falsehood*, by not making up our minds at all till objective evidence has come. In scientific questions, this is almost always the case; and even in human affairs in general, the need of acting is seldom so urgent that a false belief to act on is better than no belief at all. . . . What difference, indeed, does it make to most of us whether we have or have not a theory of the Röntgen rays, whether we believe or not in mind-stuff, or have a conviction about the causality of conscious states? It makes no difference. Such options are not forced on us. On every account it is better not to make them, but still keep weighing reasons *pro et contra* with an indifferent hand.

I speak, of course, here of the purely judging mind. For purposes of discovery such indifference is to be less highly recommended, and science would be far less advanced than she is if the passionate desires of individuals to get their own faiths confirmed had been kept out of the game. . . . The most useful investigator, because the most sensitive observer, is always he whose eager interest in one side of the question is balanced by an equally keen nervousness lest he become deceived. . . . Let us agree, however, that wherever there is no forced option, the dispassionately judicial intellect with no pet hypothesis, saving us, as it does, from dupery at any rate, ought to be our ideal.

The question next arises: Are there not somewhere forced options in our speculative questions, and can we (as men who may be interested at least as much in positively gaining truth as in merely escaping dupery) always wait with impunity till the coercive evidence shall have arrived? . . .

IX

Moral questions immediately present themselves as questions whose solution cannot wait for sensible proof. A moral question is a question not of what sensibly exists, but of what is good, or would be good if it did exist. Science can tell us what exists; but to compare the *worths*, both of what exists and of what does not exist, we must consult not science, but what Pascal calls our heart. . . .

Turn now from these wide questions of good to a certain class of questions of fact, questions concerning personal relations, states of mind between one man and another. *Do you like me or not?*—for example. Whether you do or not depends, in countless instances, on whether I meet you halfway, am willing to assume that you must like me, and show you trust and expectation. The previous faith on my part in your liking's existence is in such cases what makes your liking come. But if I stand aloof, and refuse to budge an inch until I have objective evidence, until you shall have done something apt, as the absolutists say, *ad extorquendum assensum meum*, ten to one your liking never comes. How many women's hearts are vanquished by the mere sanguine insistence of some man that they *must* love him! He will not consent to the hypothesis that they cannot. The desire for a certain kind of truth here brings about that special truth's existence; and so it is in innumerable cases of other sorts. . . . *And where faith in a fact can help create the fact*, that would be an insane logic which should say that faith running ahead of scientific evidence is the "lowest kind of immorality" into which a thinking being can fall. Yet such is the logic by which our scientific absolutists pretend to regulate our lives!

X

In truths dependent on our personal action, then, faith based on desire is certainly a lawful and possibly an indispensable thing.

But now, it will be said, these are all childish human cases, and have nothing to do with great cosmical matters, like the question of religious faith. Let us then pass on to that. Religions differ so much in their accidents that in discussing the religious question we must make it very generic and broad. What then do we now mean by the religious hypothesis? Science says things are; morality says some things are better than other things; and religion says essentially two things.

First, she says that the best things are the more eternal things, the overlapping things, the things in the universe that throw the last stone, so to speak, and say the final word. "Perfection is eternal"—this phrase of Charles Secrétan seems a good way of putting this first affirmation of religion, an affirmation which obviously cannot yet be verified scientifically at all.

The second affirmation of religion is that we are better off even now if we believe her first affirmation to be true.

Now, let us consider what the logical elements of this situation are *in case the religious hypothesis in both its branches be really true*. (Of course, we must admit that possibility at the outset. If we are to discuss the question at all, it must involve a living option. If for any of you religion be a hypothesis that cannot, by any living possibility, be true, then you need go no farther. I speak to the "saving remnant" alone.) So proceeding, we see, first, that religion offers itself as a *momentous* option. We are supposed to gain, even now, by our belief, and to lose by our non-belief, a certain vital good. Secondly, religion is a *forced* option, so far as that good

goes. We cannot escape the issue by remaining sceptical and waiting for more light, because, although we do avoid error in that way *if religion be untrue*, we lose the good, *if it be true*, just as certainly as if we positively chose to disbelieve. It is as if a man should hesitate indefinitely to ask a certain woman to marry him because he was not perfectly sure that she would prove an angel after he brought her home. Would he not cut himself off from that particular angel-possibility as decisively as if he went and married some one else? Scepticism, then, is not avoidance of option; it is option of a certain particular kind of risk. *Better risk loss of truth than chance of error*—that is your faith-vetoer's exact position. He is actively playing his stake as much as the believer is; he is backing the field against the religious hypothesis, just as the believer is backing the religious hypothesis against the field. To preach scepticism to us as a duty until "sufficient evidence" for religion be found, is tantamount therefore to telling us, when in presence of the religious hypothesis, that to yield to our fear of its being error is wiser and better than to yield to our hope that it may be true. It is not intellect against all passions, then; it is only intellect with one passion laying down its law. And by what, forsooth, is the supreme wisdom of this passion warranted? Dupery for dupery, what proof is there that dupery through hope is so much worse than dupery through fear? I, for one, can see no proof; and I simply refuse obedience to the scientist's command to imitate his kind of option, in a case where my own stake is important enough to give me the right to choose my own form of risk. If religion be true and the evidence for it be still insufficient, I do not wish, by putting your extinguisher upon my nature (which feels to me as if it had after all some business in this matter), to forfeit my sole chance in life of getting upon the winning side—that chance depending, of course, on my willingness to run the risk of acting as if my passional need of taking the world religiously might be prophetic and right.

All this is on the supposition that it really may be prophetic and right, and that, even to us who are discussing the matter, religion is a live hypothesis which may be true. Now, to most of us religion comes in a still further way that makes a veto on our active faith even more illogical. The more perfect and more eternal aspect of the universe is represented in our religions as having personal form. The universe is no longer a mere *It* to us, but a *Thou*, if we are religious; and any relation that may be possible from person to person might be possible here. For instance, although in one sense we are passive portions of the universe, in another we show a curious autonomy, as if we were small active centers on our own account. We feel, too, as if the appeal of religion to us were made to our own active goodwill, as if evidence might be forever withheld from us unless we met the hypothesis halfway to take a trivial illustration: just as a man who in a company of gentlemen made no advances, asked a warrant for every concession, and believed no one's word without proof, would cut himself off by such churlishness from all the social rewards that a more trusting spirit would earn—so here, one who should shut himself up in snarling logicality and try to make the gods extort his recognition willy-nilly, or not get it at all, might cut himself off forever from his only opportunity of making the gods' acquaintance. This feeling, forced on us we know not whence that by obstinately believing that there are gods (although not to do so would be so easy both for our logic and our life) we are doing the universe the deepest service we can, seems part of the living essence of the religious hypothesis. If the hypothesis *were* true in all its parts, including this one, then pure intellectualism, with its veto on our making willing advances, would be an absurdity; and some participation of our sympathetic nature would be logically required. I therefore, for one, cannot see my way to accepting the agnostic rules for truth-seeking, or willfully agree to keep my willing nature out of the game. I cannot do so for this plain reason, that *a rule of thinking which would absolutely prevent me from acknowledging certain kinds of truth if those kinds of truth were really there, would be an irrational rule.* That for me is the long and short of the formal logic of the situation, no matter what the kinds of truth might materially be.

I confess I do not see how this logic can be escaped. But sad experience makes me fear that some of you may still shrink from radically saying with me, *in abstracto*, that we have the right to believe at our own risk any hypothesis that is live enough to tempt our will. I suspect, however, that if this is so, it is because you have got away from the abstract logical point of view altogether, and are thinking (perhaps without realizing it) of some particular religious hypothesis which for you is dead. The freedom to "believe what we will" you apply to the case of some patent superstition; and the faith you think of is the faith defined by the schoolboy when he said, "Faith is when you believe something that you know ain't true." I can only repeat that this is misapprehension. *In concreto*, the freedom to believe can only cover living options which the intellect of the individual cannot by itself resolve; and living options never seem absurdities to him who has them to consider. When I look at the religious question as it really puts itself to concrete men, and when I think of all the possibilities which both practically and theoretically it involves, then this command that we shall put a stopper on our heart, instincts, and courage, and *wait*—acting of course meanwhile more or less as if religion were *not* true—till doomsday, or till such time as our intellect and senses working together may have raked in evidence enough—this command, I say, seems to me the queerest idol ever manufactured in the philosophic cave. Were we scholastic absolutists, there might be more excuse. If we had an infallible intellect with its objective certitudes, we might feel ourselves disloyal to such a perfect organ of knowledge in not trusting to it exclusively, in not waiting for its releasing word. But if we are empiricists, if we believe that no bell in us tolls to let us know for certain when truth is in our grasp, then it seems a piece of idle fantasticality to preach so solemnly our duty of waiting for the bell. Indeed we *may* wait if we will—I hope you do not think that I am denying that—but if we do so, we do so at our peril as much as if we believed. In either case we *act*, taking our life in our hands. No one of us ought to issue vetoes to the other, nor should we bandy words of abuse. We ought, on the contrary, delicately and profoundly to respect one another's mental freedom: then only shall we bring about the intellectual republic; then only shall we have that spirit of inner tolerance without which all our outer tolerance is soulless, and which is empiricism's glory; then only shall we live and let live, in speculative as well as in practical things.

What Is Faith?: The Parable of the Gardener

Antony Flew, R. M. Hare, and Raeburne S. Heimbeck

In the first of these three short discussions, the stage is set by Antony Flew. He offers a parable involving an invisible gardener as a way to explore the nature of religious belief. What starts out as an apparently clear case of a belief may, he argues, turn out to be, in effect, qualified out of existence so that it is not really a belief at all. Offering his own parable, R. M. Hare inquires further into the nature of faith by introducing the notion of a *blik* and its role in human life. Raeburne S. Heimbeck also disputes the appropriateness of Flew's parable, arguing that religious beliefs are neither confirmable by empirical observation nor vacuous, as Flew suggests. Neither, argues Heimbeck, is religious belief part of the empirical universe of discourse, which means Flew's objections do not pose a problem for religious believers. Antony Flew taught philosophy at the University of Keele in England and wrote many books, including *Hume's Philosophy of Belief*. R. M. Hare has taught philosophy at Oxford and at the University of Florida. His major works include *Freedom and Reason* (1963) and *Moral Thinking* (1981). Raeburne S. Heimbeck is professor of philosophy at Central Washington University and the author of *Theology and Meaning* (1969).

As you read through these essays, consider the following:

1. What is the gardener parable and what point does Flew make with it?
2. Hare thinks Flew wins on his own terms, but he offers another parable. What is that parable? When Hare says that it is important to have a sane *blik*, what does he mean?
3. Explain why Heimbeck rejects Flew's claim that religious beliefs are often not beliefs at all because they have died the death of a thousand qualifications?
4. How might Flew respond to Heimbeck? To Hare?

Antony Flew

Let us begin with a parable. It is a parable developed from a tale told by John Wisdom in his haunting and revelatory article "Gods [reprinted in Section 28]." Once upon a time two explorers came upon a clearing in the jungle. In the clearing were growing many flowers and many weeds. One explorer says, "Some gardener must tend this plot." The other disagrees, "There is no gardener." So they pitch their tents and set a watch. No gardener is ever seen. "But perhaps he is an invisible gardener." So they set up a barbed-wire fence. They electrify it. They patrol with bloodhounds. (For they remember how H. G. Wells's *The Invisible Man* could be both smelt and touched though he could not be seen.) But no shrieks ever suggest that some intruder has received a shock. No movements of the wire ever betray an invisible climber. The bloodhounds never give cry. Yet still the Believer is not convinced. "But there is a gardener, invisible, intangible, insensible to electric shocks, a gardener who has no scent and makes no sound, a gardener who comes secretly to look after the garden which he loves." At last the Skeptic despairs, "But what remains of your original assertion? Just how does what you call an invisible, intangible, eternally elusive gardener differ from an imaginary gardener or even from no gardener at all?"

In this parable we can see how what starts as an assertion, that something exists or that there is some analogy between certain complexes of phenomena, may be reduced step by step to an altogether different status, to an expression perhaps of a "picture preference."[1] The Skeptic says there is no gardener. The Believer says there is a gardener (but invisible, etc.). One man talks about sexual behaviour. Another man prefers to talk of Aphrodite (but knows that there is not really a superhuman person additional to, and somehow responsible for, all sexual phenomena). The process of qualification may be checked at any point before the original assertion is completely withdrawn and something of that first assertion will remain (tautology). Mr. Wells's invisible man could not, admittedly, be seen, but in all other respects he was a man like the rest of us. But though the process of qualification may be, and of course usually is, checked in time, it is not always judiciously so halted. Someone may dissipate his assertion completely without noticing that he has done so.

A fine brash hypothesis may thus be killed by inches, the death by a thousand qualifications.

And in this, it seems to me, lies the peculiar danger, the endemic evil, of theological utterance. Take such utterances as "God has a plan," "God created the world," "God loves us as a father loves his children." They look at first sight very much like assertions, vast cosmological assertions. Of course, this is no sure sign that they either are, or are intended to be, assertions. But let us confine ourselves to the cases where those who utter such sentences intend them to express assertions. (Merely remarking parenthetically that those who intend or interpret such utterances as crypto-commands, expressions of wishes, disguised ejaculations, concealed ethics, or as anything else but assertions are unlikely to succeed in making them either properly orthodox or practically effective.)

Now to assert that such and such is the case is necessarily equivalent to denying that such and such is not the case. Suppose then that we are in doubt as to what someone who gives vent to an utterance is asserting, or suppose that, more radically, we are skeptical as to whether he is really asserting anything at all, one way of trying to understand (or perhaps it will be to expose) his utterance is to attempt to find what he would regard as counting against, or as being incompatible with, its truth. For if the utterance is indeed an assertion, it will necessarily be equivalent to a denial of the negation of that assertion. And anything which would count against the assertion, or which would induce the speaker to withdraw it and to admit that it had been mistaken, must be part of (or the whole of) the meaning of the negation of that assertion. And to know the meaning of the negation of an assertion is as near as makes no matter to know the meaning of that assertion. And if there is nothing which a putative assertion denies then there is nothing which it asserts either: and so it is not really an assertion. When the Skeptic in the parable asked the Believer, "Just how does what you call an invisible, intangible, eternally elusive gardener differ from an imaginary gardener or even from no gardener at all?" he was suggesting that the Believer's earlier statement had been so eroded by qualification that it was no longer an assertion at all.

Now it often seems to people who are not religious as if there was no conceivable event or series of events the occurrence of which would be admitted by sophisticated religious people to be a sufficient reason for conceding "There wasn't a God after all" or "God does not really love us then." Someone tells us that God loves us as a father loves his children. We are reassured. But then we see a child dying of inoperable cancer of the throat. His earthly father is driven frantic in his efforts to help, but his Heavenly Father reveals no obvious sign of concern. Some qualification is made—God's love is "not a merely human love" or it is "an inscrutable love," perhaps—and we realize that such sufferings are quite compatible with the truth of the assertion that "God loves us as a father (but, of course, . . .)." We are reassured again. But then perhaps we ask: what is this assurance of God's (appropriately qualified) love worth, what is this apparent guarantee really a guarantee against? Just what would have to happen not merely (morally and wrongly) to tempt but also (logically and rightly) to entitle us to say "God does not love us" or even "God does not exist"? I therefore put to the succeeding symposiasts the simple central questions, "What would have to occur or to have occurred to constitute for you a disproof of the love of, or of the existence of, God?"

Notes

1. Cf. J. Wisdom, "Other Minds," *Mind* (1940).

R. M. Hare

I wish to make it clear that I shall not try to defend Christianity in particular, but religion in general—not because I do not believe in Christianity, but because you cannot understand what Christianity is, until you have understood what religion is.

I must begin by confessing that, on the ground marked out by Flew, he seems to me

to be completely victorious. I therefore shift my ground by relating another parable. A certain lunatic is convinced that all dons want to murder him. His friends introduce him to all the mildest and most respectable dons that they can find, and after each of them has retired, they say, "You see, he doesn't really want to murder you; he spoke to you in a most cordial manner; surely you are convinced now?" But the lunatic replies "Yes, but that was only his diabolical cunning; he's really plotting against me the whole time, like the rest of them; I know it I tell you." However many kindly dons are produced, the reaction is still the same.

Now we say that such a person is deluded. But what is he deluded about? About the truth or falsity of an assertion? Let us apply Flew's test to him. There is no behaviour of dons that can be enacted which he will accept as counting against his theory; and therefore his theory, on this test, asserts nothing. But it does not follow that there is no difference between what he thinks about dons and what most of us think about them—otherwise we should not call him a lunatic and ourselves sane, and dons would have no reason to feel uneasy about his presence in Oxford.

Let us call that in which we differ from this lunatic, our respective *bliks*. He has an insane *blik* about dons; we have a sane one. It is important to realize that we have a sane one, not no *blik* at all; for there must be two sides to any argument—if he has a wrong *blik*, then those who are right about dons must have a right one. Flew has shown that a *blik* does not consist in an assertion or system of them; but nevertheless it is very important to have the right *blik*.

Let us try to imagine what it would be like to have different *bliks* about other things than dons. When I am driving my car, it sometimes occurs to me to wonder whether my movements of the steering-wheel will always continue to be followed by corresponding alterations in the direction of the car. I have never had a steering failure, though I have had skids, which must be similar. Moreover, I know enough about how the steering of my car is made to know the sort of thing that would have to go wrong for the steering to fail—steel joints would have to part, or steel rods break, or something—but how do I know that this won't happen? The truth is, I don't know; I just have a *blik* about steel and its properties, so that normally I trust the steering of my car; but I find it not at all difficult to imagine what it would be like to lose this *blik* and acquire the opposite one. People would say I was silly about steel; but there would be no mistaking the reality of the difference between our respective *bliks*—for example, I should never go in a motor-car. Yet I should hesitate to say that the difference between us was the difference between contradictory assertions. No amount of safe arrivals or bench-tests will remove my *blik* and restore the normal one; for my *blik* is compatible with any finite number of such tests.

It was Hume who taught us that our whole commerce with the world depends upon our *blik* about the world; and that differences between *bliks* about the world cannot be settled by observation of what happens in the world. That was why, having performed the interesting experiment of doubting the ordinary man's *blik* about the world, and showing that no proof could be given to make us adopt one *blik* rather than another, he turned to backgammon to take his mind off the problem. It seems, indeed, to be impossible even to formulate as an assertion the normal *blik* about the world which makes me put my confidence in the future reliability of steel joints, in the continued ability of the road to support my car, and not gape beneath it revealing nothing below; in the general non-homicidal tendencies of dons; in my own continued well-being (in some sense of that word that I may not now fully understand) if I continue to do what is right according to my lights; in the general likelihood of people like Hitler coming to a bad end. But perhaps a formulation less inadequate than most is to be found in the Psalms: "The earth is weak and all the inhabiters thereof: I bear up the pillars of it."

The mistake of the position which Flew selects for attack is to regard this kind of talk as some sort of *explanation*, as scientists are accustomed to use the word. As such, it would obviously be ludicrous. We no longer believe in God as an Atlas—*nous n'avons pas besoin de cette hypothèse*. But it is nevertheless true to say that, as Hume saw, without a *blik* there can be no explanation; for it is by our *bliks* that we decide what is and what is not an explanation. Suppose we believed that everything that happened, happened by pure chance. This would not of course be an assertion; for it is compatible with anything happening or not happening, and so, incidentally, is its contradictory. But if we had this belief, we should not be able to explain or predict or plan anything. Thus, although we should not be *asserting* anything different from those of a more normal belief, there would be a great difference between us; and this is the sort of difference that there is between those who really believe in God and those who really disbelieve in him.

The word "really" is important, and may excite suspicion. I put it in, because when people have had a good Christian upbringing, as have most of those who now profess not to believe in any sort of religion, it is very hard to discover what they really believe. The reason why they find it so easy to think that they are not religious is that they have never got into the frame of mind of one who suffers from the doubts to which religion is the answer. Not for them the terrors of the primitive jungle. Having abandoned some of the more picturesque fringes of religion, they think that they have abandoned the whole thing—whereas in fact they still have got, and could not live without, a religion of a comfortably substantial, albeit highly sophisticated, kind, which differs from that of many "religious people" in little more than this, that "religious people" like to sing Psalms about theirs—a very natural and proper thing to do. But nevertheless there may be a big difference lying behind—the difference between two people who, though side by side, are walking in different directions. I do not know in what direction Flew is walking; perhaps he does not know either. But we have had some examples recently of various ways in which one can walk away from Christianity, and there are any number of possibilities. After all, man has not changed biologically since primitive times; it is his religion that has changed, and it can easily change again. And if you do not think that such changes make a difference, get acquainted with some Sikhs and some Mussulmans of the same Punjabi stock; you will find them quite different sorts of people.

There is an important difference between Flew's parable and my own which we have not yet noticed. The explorers do not *mind* about their garden; they discuss it with interest, but not with concern. But my lunatic, poor fellow, minds about dons; and I mind about the steering of my car; it often has people in it that I care for. It is because I mind very much about what goes on in the garden in which I find myself, that I am unable to share the explorers' detachment.

Raeburne S. Heimbeck

Flew . . . asks what in principle would have to occur or to have occurred to constitute a disproof of the existence of God. It is relatively simple to outline what would have to happen or to have happened in order to constitute a proof, rather than a disproof, of the existence of God. . . .

In establishing a checking procedure for the statement made by "God exists," the first step that must be accomplished is the rejection of any untoward strictures on "exists." Keeping the full range of actual applications of "exists" in mind, we must oppose the demand that "exists" be limited in application to what is empirical or to logical constructions out of empiricals. For it surely makes sense to assert that there exists a prime number between 1 and 5. Yet the prime number 3 is not empirical, nor is talk about it reducible to talk about numerals, which are empirical. And, again, it surely makes sense to say that the state exists for the benefit of its citizens.

The state, however, is not empirical, and talk about the state is not logically equivalent to talk about the citizens who comprise the state. Within their proper universes of discourse, we may meaningfully speak of Huckleberry Finn existing (in the world of fiction), of fairies and elves existing (in the world of make-believe, which is like the world of fiction in some respects but different in other respects), of motives and wishes and even suppressed or unconscious desires existing (in the world of the mind), of tautologies and hence also of self-contradictions existing (in the world of statements, not to be confused with the world of sentences), and even of nothingness existing (cf. a void in memory, a vacuum in space, a silence that deafens, the null class, oblivion that the mystic experiences, anti-matter—all these negatives are subjects of true and hence genuine assertions and therefore must exist).

. . . [The idea is that] God has an existence-status quite different from that of empirical objects, and that if we are to think and speak properly of God we must disobjectify our thought and speech about God, i.e. free them from the forms, associations, and demands which control thought and speech about empirical or physical objects. It does not follow from the above observation that "God"-talk is ruled out as meaningless discourse or that the assertion of God's existence understood disobjectifyingly is some sort of logical monstrosity. Granted, if God is meaningfully to be said to exist disobjectifyingly (with an existence-status other than that of empirical objects), then it must be possible to say clearly what this disobjectified existence-status is like and in what sense of "exists" God exists. But this is merely an invitation to characterize the universe of discourse to which the numinous strand of "God"-talk belongs by stating what sort of existent God is, what the key properties are which single out, distinguish, and identify God uniquely in thought.

The metatheological problem of identification is bound to arise—so dominated are we by empirical forms of thinking and speaking—wherever it is acknowledged (as it certainly is in classical Christian theism) that God is not empirically indictable and talk about God not reducible to expressions denoting only empiricals. That certain metatheological sceptics find the problem intractable derives partially from general empiricist predilections and partially from a confusion—the confusion of the problem of identifying God *in experience* with the problem of identifying God *in thought*. It is the former problem which they end up discussing, whereas it is the latter alone which has pertinence to the investigation of the cognitive significance of "G"-sentences.

Section 28

Rethinking Religious Practice

Religious Belief and Practice

Dewi Z. Phillips

What, precisely, is it that religious people believe when they say they believe in God or have been saved by Christ? Dewi Z. Phillips suggests that such claims are best understood not as coming from outside religious practice but rather from within the religion itself. Philosophers have often overlooked that, he thinks, and have treated such claims as "God exists" as though they were being offered as evidence for the truth of religion. But religious people, and religious practice, do not depend on philosophical proofs of God derived from outside religious practice, says Phillips. The God of religion is not a being, like a plant, which exists along with other entities and whose existence can be a matter of indifference to religious believers. The philosophers' God is thus not the God of religious people, but rather is a different sort of entity—an "anthropomorphic" fiction of philosophers. Dewi Z. Phillips teaches philosophy at the University of Wales.

As you read through this essay, consider the following:

1. How would you describe the difference between the philosopher's understanding and the believer's understanding of what it is to be religious?
2. What does Phillips mean when he says that the philosophers' conception of God is different from the religious person's?

3. How does Phillips think a philosopher interested in religion should investigate the subject of religion, if not by looking at the evidence for and against God's existence?
4. What does Phillips mean when he says that there are different senses of "rationality" and of "existence" that philosophers of religion should not overlook?

The relation between religion and philosophical reflection needs to be reconsidered. For the most part, in recent philosophy of religion, philosophers, believers, and non-believers alike, have been concerned with discovering *the grounds* of religious belief. Philosophy, they claim, is concerned with reasons; it considers what is to count as good evidence for a belief. In the case of religious beliefs, the philosopher ought to enquire into the reasons anyone could have for believing in the existence of God, for believing that life is a gift from God, or for believing that an action is the will of God. Where can such reasons be found? One class of reasons comes readily to mind. Religious believers, when asked why they believe in God, may reply in a variety of ways. They may say, 'I have had an experience of the living God', 'I believe on the Lord Jesus Christ', 'God saved me while I was a sinner', or, 'I just can't help believing'. Philosophers have not given such reasons very much attention. The so-called trouble is not so much with the content of the replies as with the fact that the replies are made by believers. The answers come from *within* religion, they presuppose the framework of Faith, and therefore cannot be treated as *evidence* for religious belief. Many philosophers who argue in this way seem to be searching for evidence or reasons for religious beliefs *external* to belief itself. It is assumed that such evidence and reasons would, if found, constitute the grounds of religious belief.

The philosophical assumption behind the ignoring of religious testimony as begging the question, and the search for external reasons for believing in God, is that one could settle the question of whether there is a God or not without referring to the form of life of which belief in God is a fundamental part.

From *Faith and Philosophical Enquiry* (London: Routledge, 1970). Reprinted by permission of Taylor & Francis.

What would it be like for a philosopher to settle the question of the existence of God? Could a philosopher say that he believed that God exists and yet never pray to Him, rebel against Him, lament the fact that he could no longer pray, aspire to deepen his devotion, seek His will, try to hide from Him, or fear and tremble before Him? In short, could a man believe that God exists without his life being touched *at all* by the belief? Norman Malcolm asks with good reason, 'Would a belief that he exists, if it were completely non-affective, really be a belief that he exists? Would it be anything at all? What is "the form of life" into which it would enter? What difference would it make whether anyone did or did not have this belief?'

Yet many philosophers who search for the grounds of religious belief, claim, to their own satisfaction at least, to understand what a purely theoretical belief in the existence of God would be. But the accounts these philosophers give of what religious believers seem to be saying are often at variance with what many believers say, at least, when *they* are not philosophizing. Every student of the philosophy of religion will have been struck by the amount of talking at cross purposes within the subject. A philosopher may say that there is no God, but a believer may reply, 'You are creating and then attacking a fiction. The god whose existence you deny is not the God I believe in.' Another philosopher may say that religion is meaningless, but another believer may reply, 'You say that when applied to God, words such as "exists", "love", "will", etc., do not mean what they signify in certain non-religious contexts. I agree. You conclude from this that religion is meaningless, whereas the truth is that you are failing to grasp the meaning religion has.' Why is there this lack of contact between many philosophers and religious believers? One reason is that many philosophers who do not believe that God exists assume that they know what it means to say that there is a God. Norman Kemp Smith made a penetrating analysis of this fact when commenting on the widespread belief among American philosophers in his day of the uselessness of philosophy of religion.

> ... those who are of this way of thinking, however they may have thrown over the religious beliefs of the communities in which they have been nurtured, still continue to be influenced by the phraseology of religious devotion—a phraseology which, in its endeavour to be concrete and universally intelligible, is at little pains to guard against the misunderstandings to which it may so easily give rise. As they insist upon, and even exaggerate, the merely literal meaning of this phraseology, the God in whom they have ceased to believe is a Being whom they picture in an utterly anthropomorphic fashion. ...

The distinction between religious believers and atheistical philosophers is not, of course, as clear-cut as I have suggested. It is all too evident in contemporary philosophy of religion that many philosophers who *do* believe in God philosophize about religion in the way which Kemp Smith found to be true of philosophical non-believers. Here, one can say either that their philosophy reflects their belief, in which case they believe in superstition but not in God, or, taking the more charitable view, that they are failing to give a good philosophical account of what they really believe.

Insufficient attention has been paid to the question of what kind of philosophical enquiry the concept of divine reality calls for. Many philosophers assume that everyone knows *what* it means to say that there is a God, and that the only outstanding question is *whether* there is a God. Similarly, it might be thought, everyone knows what it means to say that there are unicorns, although people may disagree over whether in fact there are any unicorns. If there were an analogy between the existence of God and the existence of unicorns, then coming to see that there is a God would be like coming to see that an additional being exists. 'I know what people are doing when they worship,' a philosopher might say. 'They praise, they confess, they thank, and they ask for things. The only difference between myself and religious believers is that I do not believe that there is a being who receives their worship.' The assumption, here, is that the meaning of worship is contingently related to the question whether there is a God or not. The assumption might be justified by saying that there need be no consequences of existential beliefs. Just as one can say, 'There is a planet Mars, but I couldn't care less,' so one can say, 'There is a God, but I couldn't care less.' But what is one *saying* here when one says that there is a God? Despite the fact that one need take no interest in the existence of a planet, an account could be given of the kind of difference the existence of the planet makes, and of how one could find out whether the planet exists or not. But all this is foreign to the question where there is a God. That is not something anyone could *find out*. It has been far too readily assumed that the dispute between the believer and the unbeliever is over a *matter of fact*. Philosophical reflection on the reality of God then becomes the philosophical reflection appropriate to an assertion of a matter of fact. I have tried to show that this is a misrepresentation of the religious concept, and that philosophy can claim justifiably to show what is meaningful in religion only if it is prepared to examine religious concepts in the contexts from which they derive their meaning.

A failure to take account of the above context has led some philosophers to ask religious language to satisfy criteria of meaningfulness alien to it. They say that religion must be rational if it is to be intelligible. Certainly, the distinction between the rational and the irrational must be central in any account one gives of meaning. But this is not to say that there is a paradigm of rationality to which all modes of discourse conform. A necessary prolegomenon to the philosophy of religion, then, is to show the diversity of criteria of rationality; to show that the distinction between the real and the unreal does not come to the same thing in every context. If this were observed, one would no longer wish to construe God's reality as being that of an existent among existents, an object among objects.

Coming to see that there is a God is not like coming to see that an additional being exists. If it were, there would be an extension of one's knowledge of facts, but no extension of one's understanding. Coming to see that there is a God involves seeing a new meaning in one's life, and being given a new understanding. The Hebrew-Christian conception of God is not a conception of a being among beings. Kierkegaard emphasized the point when he said bluntly, 'God does not exist. He is eternal.'

Religion Without God

Steven M. Cahn

Many people assume that religious faith and practice depend on belief in God. If God does not exist, it is thought that religion itself is pointless at best. Steven M. Cahn disputes that claim, arguing that neither ritual nor prayer depends on a supernaturalistic rather than an entirely naturalistic conception of the universe. Steven Cahn is professor of philosophy at the City University of New York.

As you read through this essay, consider the following:

1. What is the role of ritual in a naturalistic religion?
2. Why does Cahn think it is reasonable to pray even if one does not believe in God?
3. What sort of metaphysical view or system is "naturalistic"? How does that differ from a super-naturalistic metaphysical view?

Most of us suppose that all religions are akin to the one we happen to know best. But this assumption can be misleading. For example, many Christians believe that all religions place heavy emphasis on an afterlife, although the central concern of Judaism is life in this world, not the next. Similarly, many Christians and Jews are convinced that a person who is religious must affirm the existence of a supernatural God. They are surprised to learn that religions such as Jainism or Theravada Buddhism deny the existence of a Supreme Creator of the world.

How can there be a nonsupernatural religion? To numerous theists as well as atheists, the concept appears contradictory. I propose to show, however, that nothing in the theory or practice of religion—not ritual, not prayer, not metaphysical belief . . . —necessitates a commitment to traditional theism. In other words, one may be religious while rejecting supernaturalism.

Let us begin with the concept of ritual. A ritual is a prescribed symbolic action. In the case of religion, the ritual is prescribed by the religious organization, and the act symbolizes some aspect of religious belief. Those who find the beliefs of supernaturalistic religion unreasonable or the activities of the organization unacceptable may come to consider any ritual irrational. Yet although particular rituals may be based on irrational beliefs, nothing is inherently irrational about ritual.

Consider the simple act of two people shaking hands when they meet. This act is a ritual, prescribed by our society and symbolic of the individuals' mutual respect. The act is in no way irrational. Of course, if people shook hands in order to ward off evil demons, then shaking hands would be irrational. But that is not the reason people shake hands. The ritual has no connection with God or demons but indicates the attitude one person has toward another.

It might be assumed that the ritual of handshaking escapes irrationality only because the ritual is not prescribed by any specific organization and is not part of an elaborate ceremony. To see that this assumption is false, consider the graduation ceremony at a college. The graduates and faculty all wear peculiar hats and robes, and the participants stand and sit at appropriate times. However, the ceremony is not at all irrational. Indeed, the rites of graduation day, far from being irrational, are symbolic of commitment to the process of education and the life of reason.

At first glance, rituals may seem a comparatively insignificant feature of life; yet they are a pervasive and treasured aspect of human experience. Who would want to eliminate the festivities associated with holidays such as Independence Day or Thanksgiving? What would college football be without songs, cheers, flags, and the innumerable other symbolic features surrounding the game? Those who disdain popular rituals typically proceed to establish their own distinctive ones, ranging from characteristic habits of dress to the use of drugs, symbolizing a rejection of traditional mores.

Religious persons, like all others, search for an appropriate means of emphasizing their commitment to a group or its values. Rituals provide such a means. Granted, supernaturalistic religion has often infused its rituals with superstition, but nonreligious rituals can be equally as superstitious as religious ones. For instance, most Americans view the Fourth of July as an occasion on which they can express pride in their country's heritage. With this purpose in mind, the holiday is one of great significance. However, if the singing of the fourth verse of "The Star Spangled Banner" four times on the Fourth of July were thought to protect our country against future disasters, then the original meaning of the holiday would soon be lost in a maze of superstition.

A naturalistic (i.e., nonsupernaturalistic) religion need not utilize ritual in a superstitious manner, for such a religion does not employ rituals in order to please a benevolent deity or to appease an angry one. Rather, naturalistic religion views rituals, as one of its exponents has put it, as "the enhancement of life through the dramatization of great ideals."[1] If a group places great stress on justice or freedom, why should it not utilize ritual in order to emphasize these goals? Such a use of ritual serves to solidify the group and to strengthen its devotion to its expressed purposes. These are strengthened all the more if the ritual in question has the force of tradition, having been performed by many generations who have belonged to the same group and have struggled to achieve the same goals. Ritual so conceived is not a form of superstition; rather, it is a reasonable means of strengthening religious commitment and is as useful to naturalistic religion as it is to supernaturalistic religion.

Having considered the role of ritual in a naturalistic religion, let us next turn to the concept of prayer. It might be thought that naturalistic religion could have no use for prayer, since prayer is supposedly addressed to a supernatural being, and proponents of naturalistic religion do not believe in the existence of such a being. But this objection oversimplifies the concept of prayer, focusing attention on one type while neglecting an equally important but different sort.

Supernaturalistic religion makes extensive use of petitionary prayer, prayer that petitions a supernatural being for various favors. These may range all the way from the personal happiness of the petitioner to the general welfare of all society. Since petitionary prayer rests on the assumption that a supernatural being exists, such prayer clearly has no place in a naturalistic religion.

However, not all prayers are prayers of petition. Some prayers are prayers of meditation. These are not directed to any supernatural being and are not requests for the granting of favors. Rather, these prayers provide the opportunity for persons to rethink their ultimate commitments and rededicate themselves to live up to their ideals. Such prayers may take the form of silent devotion or may involve oral repetition of certain central tests. Just as Americans repeat the Pledge of Allegiance and reread the Gettysburg Address, so adherents of naturalistic religion repeat the statements of their ideals and reread the documents that embody their traditional beliefs.

It is true that supernaturalistic religions, to the extent that they utilize prayers of meditation, tend to treat these prayers irrationally, by supposing that if the prayers are not uttered a precise number of times under certain specified conditions, then the prayers lose all value. Yet prayer need not be viewed in this way. Rather, as the British biologist Julian Huxley wrote, prayer "permits the bringing before the mind of a world of thought which in most people must inevitably be absent during the occupations of ordinary life: . . . it is the means by which the mind may fix itself upon this or that noble or beautiful or awe-inspiring idea, and so grow to it and come to realize it more fully."[2]

Such a use of prayer may be enhanced by song, instrumental music, and various types of symbolism. These elements, fused together, provide the means for adherents of naturalistic religion to engage in religious services akin to those engaged in by adherents of supernaturalistic religion. The difference between the two services is that those who attend the latter come to relate themselves to God, while those who attend the former come to relate themselves to their fellow human beings and to the world in which we live.

We have so far discussed how ritual and prayer can be utilized in naturalistic religion, but to adopt a religious perspective also involves metaphysical beliefs and moral commitments. Can these be maintained without recourse to supernaturalism?

If we use the term "metaphysics" in its usual sense, referring to the systematic study of the most basic features of existence, then a metaphysical system may be either supernaturalistic or naturalistic. The views of Plato, Descartes, and Leibniz are representative of a supernaturalistic theory; the views of Aristotle, Spinoza, and Dewey are representative of a naturalistic theory.

Spinoza's *Ethics*, for example, one of the greatest metaphysical works ever written, explicitly rejects the view that any being exists apart from Nature itself. Spinoza identifies God with Nature as a whole and urges that the good life consists in coming to understand Nature. In his words, "our salvation, or blessedness, or freedom consists in a constant and eternal love toward God."[3] Spinoza's concept of God, however, is explicitly not the supernaturalistic concept of God, and Spinoza's metaphysical system thus exemplifies not only a naturalistic metaphysics, but also the possibility of reinterpreting the concept of God within a naturalistic framework. . . .

We have now seen that naturalistic religion is a genuine possibility, since reasonable individuals may perform rituals, utter prayers [and] accept metaphysical beliefs . . . without believing in supernaturalism. Indeed, one can even do so while maintaining allegiance to Christianity or Judaism. Consider, for example, those Christians who accept the "Death of God"[4] or those Jews who adhere to Reconstructionist Judaism.[5]

Such options are philosophically respectable. Whether to choose any of them is for each reader to decide.

Notes

1. Jack Cohen, *The Case for Religious Naturalism* (New York: Reconstructionist Press, 1958), p. 150.

2. Julian Huxley, *Religion Without Revelation* (New York: New American Library, 1957), p. 141.

3. Spinoza, *Ethics*, ed. James Gutmann (New York: Hafner, 1957), pt 5, prop. 36, note.

4. See John H. T. Robinson, *Honest to God* (Philadelphia: Westminster, 1963).

5. See Mordecai M. Kaplan, *Judaism as a Civilization* (New York: Schocken, 1967).

Religious Practice and Make-Believe

Robin Le Poidevin

This essay begins with a description of the doubt that another philosopher had, a doubt that led him to leave the priesthood. It concerned whether it is possible for a theistic agnostic to affirm the existence of God, as is done when saying a creed. Using fictional literature as an example, Robin Le Poidevin argues that in fact one can be an atheistic naturalist and not only participate in prayer and ritual but also affirm belief in God by saying a creed. Robin Le Poidevin teaches philosophy at Leeds University in England.

As you read through this essay, consider the following:

1. What is the distinction between a naturalist and a supernaturalist?
2. Why might a naturalistically minded person nonetheless affirm belief in God?
3. How does Le Poidevin respond to someone who thinks that understanding religious statements as fictional is less powerful than understanding them as true?

In *A Path from Rome*, Anthony Kenny describes the doubts and conflicts which eventually led to his leaving the Catholic priesthood. He also tells us that, in spite of his agnosticism, he continued to attend church regularly, though never receiving Communion or reciting the Creed. He did this, not to pretend to a faith which he no longer had, but because of the important role that certain religious practices, including prayer, can continue to have even in the life of someone who has given up firm belief in theism. In an earlier book, *The God of the Philosophers*, he compares the agnostic at prayer to someone "adrift in the ocean, trapped in a cave, or stranded on a mountainside, who cries for help though he may never be heard or fires a signal which may never be seen." Just as there is nothing unreasonable in this latter activity, the implication is, so there is nothing unreasonable in the former: the agnostic does not know whether there is anyone listening to his prayer, but there is a chance that there is, and that the prayer will be answered.

What, for Kenny, justifies prayer does not extend to saying the Creed. Kenny's position is clearly a [supernatural] one, which implies that when one says "I believe in God, the father Almighty, maker of heaven and earth . . ." one is stating what one intends to be the literal truth. An agnostic cannot utter these words without either hypocrisy or self-deception. This defence of a rather limited range of religious practices—just those which do not definitely commit one to any theistic doctrine—would not be accepted by the theological [naturalist]. If religion has a point, it is not, for the [naturalist], because it *might*, for all we know, be true. It is neither true nor false. What is needed, for [naturalism] to be a viable theological position, is a defence of religious practice which allows an atheist, someone who believes that, realistically construed, theism is false, to engage in worship and prayer. I suggest that such a defence can be found in comparing the effects of religion to the beneficial effects of fiction. . . .

To engage in religious practice, on this account, is to engage in a game of make-believe. We make-believe that there is a God, by reciting, in the context of the game, a statement of belief. We listen to what make-believedly are accounts of the activities of God and his people,

From Robin Le Poidevin, *Arguing for Atheism* (London: Routledge, 1996). Reprinted by permission of Taylor & Francis. (Some of the terminology was changed to make it consistent with the Flew and Hare essays.)

and we pretend to worship and address prayers to that God. . . . We locate ourselves in that fictional world, and in so doing we allow ourselves to become emotionally involved, to the extent that a religious service is capable of being an intense experience. The immediate object of our emotions is the fictional God, but there is a wider object, and that is the collection of real individuals in our lives. In the game of make-believe (for example, the Christian one), we are presented with a series of dramatic images: an all-powerful creator, who is able to judge our moral worth, to forgive us or to condemn, who appears on Earth in human form and who willingly allows himself to be put to death. What remains, when the game of make-believe is over, is an awareness of our responsibilities for ourselves and others, of the need to pursue spiritual goals, and so on.

How adequate is this account? [It could be argued that] this justification of religious practice seems far less powerful than the one which is available to the [supernaturalist], for whom prayer and worship really is God-directed, and for whom the emotions thus evoked are real, capable of having a direct effect on one's life. The [naturalist], in contrast, has to make do with . . . quasi-emotions: a make-believe imitation of the real thing. Is such a watered-down version of religious practice worth preserving? . . .

The [naturalist] can answer . . . by pointing out that . . . [if supernaturalism] is itself a highly problematic position, it can hardly provide an adequate justification of any practice based on it. The [naturalist] justification of religious practice is superior, simply because it is not based on dubious metaphysical assumptions. But there is still the point about emotions. Against the [naturalist] is the consideration that someone who believes in the literal truth of what is said in a religious ritual will, surely, experience genuine emotions which, because they are genuine, are far more likely to have an impact on their life than the quasi-emotions generated in a game of religious make-believe. What can be said about this? The true (i.e. in this context, the [supernaturalist]) believer will be motivated not just by the emotions caused by religious ritual but also by his beliefs. Now, if the [naturalist] is right, some of those beliefs, namely those concerning the literal truth of religious doctrines, are false, and therefore give rise to a degenerate kind of spiritual life. The effect of a literal faith on one's life may actually be (in part) a negative one.

Gods

John Wisdom

Like other writers we have discussed, John Wisdom wants to shift the discussion of religion away from the truth or justification of the religious beliefs and toward the effect that the beliefs have on the life of those who participate in the practice. Rather than disagreeing over something that might be proven or disproven by empirical or mathmatical means, Wisdom uses his famous gardener parable along with other examples to try to explore what is really at stake between the religious person and the nonreligious person. Unlike some, he does not think that the difference is solely about how the two feel toward the garden; religion is not simply an expression of a certain attitude or feeling. A better analogy, he suggests, is disagreement over whether or not a painting is beautiful, or disagreement with a person who believes it "appropriate" to treat flowers gently or to continue to love another person. Reasoning has a different role here than in other areas of life, according to Wisdom. John

Wisdom (1904–1993) was professor of philosophy at Cambridge University. He wrote mainly in the philosophy of language and was concerned with problems of meaning as well as with the purpose of philosophy and philosophical language itself.

As you read through this essay, consider the following:

1. What does Wisdom mean when he says the existence of God is not an "experimental issue" as it once was?
2. What point does Wisdom make using the gardener parable?
3. Explain whether or not Wisdom thinks that if the issue between a religious person and a nonreligious person is not an experimental one then there can be no right or wrong or better or worse answer to the dispute.
4. What does Wisdom mean by the "connection technique"?
5. What is the point Wisdom makes about human beings and the "propriety" of belief in the Gods? about the Gods always being within us as well as without?

The existence of God is not an experimental issue in the way it was. An atheist or agnostic might say to a theist "You still think there are spirits in the trees, nymphs in the streams, a God of the world." He might say this because he noticed the theist in time of drought pray for rain and make a sacrifice and in the morning look for rain. But disagreement about whether there are gods is now less of this experimental or betting sort than it used to be. This is due in part, if not wholly, to our better knowledge of why things happen as they do. . . .

What are [the] differences [between theists and atheists]? And is it that theists are superstitious or that atheists are blind? A child may wish to sit a while with his father and he may, when he has done what his father dislikes, fear punishment and feel distress at causing vexation, and while his father is alive he may feel sure of help when danger threatens and feel that there is sympathy for him when disaster has come. When his father is dead he will no longer expect punishment or help. Maybe for a moment an old fear will come or a cry to help escape him, but he will at once remember that this is no good now. He may feel that his father is no more until perhaps someone

From John Wisdom, "Gods," *Proceedings of the Aristotelian Society*. Reprinted by courtesy of the Editor of the Aristotelian Society. Copyright © 1944–45.

says to him that his father is still alive though he lives now in another world and one so far away that there is no hope of seeing him or hearing his voice again. The child may be told that nevertheless his father can see him and hear all he says. When he has been told this the child will still fear no punishment nor expect any sign of his father, but now, even more than he did when his father was alive, he will feel that his father sees him all the time and will dread distressing him and when he has done something wrong he will feel separated from his father until he has felt sorry for what he has done. Maybe when he himself comes to die he will be like a man who expects to find a friend in the strange country where he is going, but even when this is so, it is by no means all of what makes the difference between a child who believes that his father lives still in another world and one who does not.

Likewise one who believes in God may face death differently from one who does not, but there is another difference between them besides this. This other difference may still be described as belief in another world, only this belief is not a matter of expecting one thing rather than another here or hereafter, it is not a matter of a world to come but of a world that now is thought beyond our senses.

We are at once reminded of those other unseen worlds which some philosophers "believe in" and others "deny," while non-philosophers unconsciously "accept" them by using them as models with which to "get the hang of" the patterns in the flux of experience. We recall the timeless entities whose changeless connections we seek to represent in symbols, and the values which stand firm amidst our flickering satisfaction and remorse, and the physical things which, though not beyond the corruption of moth and rust, are yet more permanent than the shadows they throw upon the screen before our minds. We recall, too, our talk of souls and of what lies in their depths and is manifested to us partially and intermittently in our own feelings and the behaviour of others. The hypothesis of mind, of other human minds and of animal minds, is reasonable because it explains for each of us why certain things behave so cunningly all by themselves unlike even the most ingenious machines. Is the hypothesis of minds in flowers and trees reasonable for like reasons? Is the hypothesis of a world mind reasonable for like reasons—someone who adjusts the blossom to the bees, someone whose presence may at times be felt—in a garden in high summer, in the hills when clouds are gathering, but not, perhaps, in a cholera epidemic? . . .

Let us now approach these same points by a different road. How it is that an explanatory hypothesis, such as the existence of God, may start by being experimental and gradually become something quite different can be seen from the following story:

Two people return to their long-neglected garden and find among the weeds a few of the old plants surprisingly vigorous. One says to the other "It must be that a gardener has been coming and doing something about these plants." Upon inquiry they find that no neighbour has ever seen anyone at work in their garden. The first man says to the other "He must have worked while people slept." The other says "No, someone would have heard him and besides, anybody who cared about the plants would have kept down these weeds." The first man says "Look at the way these are arranged. There is purpose and a feeling for beauty here. I believe

that someone comes, someone invisible to mortal eyes. I believe that the more carefully we look the more we shall find confirmation of this." They examine the garden ever so carefully and sometimes they come on new things suggesting that a gardener comes and sometimes they come on new things suggesting the contrary and even that a malicious person has been at work. Besides examining the garden carefully they also study what happens to gardens left without attention. Each learns all the other learns about this and about the garden. Consequently, when after all this, one says "I still believe a gardener comes" while the other says "I don't," their different words now reflect no difference as to what they have found in the garden, no difference as to what they would find in the garden if they looked further and no difference about how fast untended gardens fall into disorder. At this stage, in this context, the gardener hypothesis has ceased to be experimental, the difference between one who accepts and one who rejects it is now not a matter of the one expecting something the other does not expect. What is the difference between them? The one says "A gardener comes unseen and unheard. He is manifested only in his works with which we are all familiar," the other says "There is no gardener," and with this difference in what they say about the gardener goes a difference in how they feel towards the garden, in spite of the fact that neither expects anything of it which the other does not expect.

But is this the whole difference between them—that the one calls the garden by one name and feels one way towards it, while the other calls it by another name and feels in another way towards it? And if this is what the difference has become then is it any longer appropriate to ask "Which is right?" or "Which is reasonable?"

And yet surely such questions *are* appropriate when one person says to another "You still think the world's a garden and not a wilderness, and that the gardener has not forsaken it" or "You still think there are nymphs of the streams, a presence in the hills, a spirit of the world." Perhaps when a man sings "God's in His heaven" we need not take this as more than an expression of how he feels. But when Bishop Gore or Dr. Joad write about belief in God and young men read them in order to settle their religious doubts the impression is not simply that of persons choosing exclamations with which to face nature and the "changes and chances of this mortal life." The disputants speak as if they are concerned with a matter of scientific fact, or of trans-sensual, trans-scientific and meta-physical fact, but still of fact and still a matter about which reasons for and against may be offered, although no scientific reasons in the sense of field surveys for fossils or experiments on delinquents are to the point . . .

Suppose two people are looking at a picture or natural scene. One says "Excellent" or "Beautiful" or "Divine," the other says "I don't see it." He means he doesn't see the beauty. And this reminds us of how we felt the theist accuse the atheist of blindness and the atheist accuse the theist of seeing what isn't there. And yet surely each sees what the other sees. It isn't that one can see part of the picture which the other can't see. So the difference is in a sense not one as to the facts. And so it cannot be removed by the one disputant discovering to the other what so far he hasn't seen. It isn't that the one sees the picture in a different light and so, as we might say, sees a different picture. Consequently the difference between them cannot be resolved by putting the picture in a different light. And yet surely this is just what can be done in such a case—not by moving the picture but by talk perhaps. To settle a dispute as to whether a piece of music is good or better than another we listen again, with a picture we look again. Someone perhaps points to emphasize certain features and we see it in a different light. Shall we call this "field work" and "the last of observation" or shall we call it "reviewing the premises" and "the beginning of deduction . . ."?

And if we say as we did at the beginning that when a difference as to the existence of a God is not *one as to future happenings then it is not experimental and therefore not as to the facts, we must not forthwith assume that there is no right and wrong about it*, no rationality or irrationality, no appropriateness or inappropriateness, no procedure which tends to settle it, *nor even that this procedure is in no sense a discovery of new facts.* After all even in science this is not so. Our two gardeners even when they had reached the stage when neither expected any experimental result which the other did not, might yet have continued the dispute, each presenting and representing the features of the garden favouring his hypothesis, that is, fitting his model for describing the accepted fact; each emphasizing the pattern he wishes to emphasize. True, in science, there is seldom or never a pure instance of this sort of dispute, for nearly always with difference of hypothesis goes some difference of expectation as to the facts. But scientists argue about rival hypotheses with a vigour which is not exactly proportioned to difference in expectations of experimental results.

The difference as to whether a God exists involves our feelings more than most scientific disputes and in this respect is more like a difference as to whether there is beauty in a thing.

The Connecting Technique. Let us consider again the technique used in revealing or proving beauty, in removing a blindness, in inducing an attitude which is lacking, in reducing a reaction that is inappropriate . . . Imagine that a man picks up some flowers that lie half withered on a table and gently puts them in water. Another man says to him "You believe flowers feel." He says this although he knows that the man who helps the flowers doesn't expect anything of them which he himself doesn't expect; for he himself expects the flowers to be "refreshed" and to be easily hurt, injured, I mean, by rough handling, while the man who puts them in water does not expect them to whisper "Thank you." The Sceptic says "You believe flowers feel" because something about the way the other man lifts the flowers and puts them in water suggests an attitude to the flowers which he feels inappropriate although perhaps he would not feel it inappropriate to butterflies. He feels that this attitude to flowers is somewhat crazy *just as it is sometimes felt that a lover's attitude is somewhat crazy even when this is not a matter of his having false hopes about how the person he is in love with will act.* It is often said in such cases that reasoning is useless. But the very person who says this feels that the lover's attitude is crazy, is inappropriate like some dreads and hatreds, such as some horrors of enclosed places. And often one who says "It is useless to reason" proceeds at once to reason with the lover, nor is this reasoning always quite without effect. We may draw the lover's attention to certain things done by her he is in love with and trace for him a path to these from things done by others at other times which have disgusted and infuriated him. And by this means we may weaken his admiration and confidence, make him feel it unjustified and arouse his suspicion and contempt and make him feel our suspicion and contempt reasonable. It is possible, of course, that he has already noticed the analogies, the connections, we point out and that he has accepted them—that is, he has not denied them nor passed them off. He has recognized them and they have altered his attitude, altered his love, but he still loves. We then feel that perhaps it is we who are blind and cannot see what he can see.

What happens, what should happen, when we inquire in this way into the reasonableness, the propriety of belief in the Gods? . . . What are the stories of the gods? What are our feelings when we believe in God? They are feelings of awe before power, dread of the thunderbolts of Zeus, confidence in the everlasting arms, unease beneath the all-seeing eye. They are feelings of guilt and inescapable vengeance, of smothered hate and of a security we can hardly do without. We have only to remind ourselves of these feelings and the stories of the gods and goddesses and heroes in which these feelings find expression, to be reminded of how we felt as children to our parents and the big people of our childhood. Writing of a first telephone call from his grandmother, Proust says: ". . . it was rather that this isolation of the voice was like a symbol, a presentation, a direct consequence of another isolation, that of my grandmother, separated for the first time in my life, from myself. The orders or prohibitions which she addressed to me at every moment in the ordinary course of my life, the tedium of obedience or the fire of rebellion which neutralized the affection that I felt for her were at this moment eliminated . . . 'Granny!' I cried to her . . . but I had beside me only that voice, a phantom, as unpalpable as that which would come to revisit me when my grandmother was dead. 'Speak to me!' but then it happened that, left more solitary still, I ceased to catch the sound of her voice. My grandmother could no longer hear me . . . I continued to call her, sounding the empty night, in which I felt that her appeals also must be straying. I was shaken by the same anguish which, in the distant past, I had felt once before, one day when, a little child, in a crowd, I had lost her." . . .

When a man's father fails him by death or weakness, how much he needs another father, one in the heavens with whom is "no variableness nor shadow of turning". . . . Freud says: "The ordinary man cannot imagine this Providence in any other form but that of a greatly exalted father, for only such a one could understand the needs of the sons of men, or be softened by their prayers and be placated by the signs of their remorse. The whole thing is so patently infantile, so incongruous with reality . . ." "So incongruous with reality!" It cannot be denied.

But here a new aspect of the matter may strike us. For the very facts which make us feel that now we can recognize systems of superhuman, subhuman, elusive, beings for what they are—the persistent projections of infantile phantasies—include facts which make these systems less fantastic. What are these facts? They are patterns in human reactions which are well described by saying that we are as if there were hidden within us powers, persons, not ourselves and stronger than ourselves. That this is so may perhaps be said to have been common knowledge yielded by ordinary observation of people, but we did not know the degree in which this is so until recent study of extraordinary cases in extraordinary conditions had revealed it. I refer, of course, to the study of multiple personalities and the wider studies of psycho-analysts. Even when the results of this work are reported to us, that is not the same as tracing the patterns in the details of the cases on which the results are based; and even that is not the same as taking part in the studies oneself. One thing not sufficiently realized is that some of the things shut within us are not bad but good.

Now the gods, good and evil and mixed, have always been mysterious powers outside us rather than within. But they have also been within. It is not a modern theory but an old saying that in each of us a devil sleeps. Eve said: "The serpent beguiled me." . . . Elijah found that God was not in the wind, nor in the thunder, but in a still small voice. The kingdom of Heaven is within us, Christ insisted, though usually about the size of a grain of mustard seed, and he prayed that we should become one with the Father in Heaven.

New knowledge made it necessary either to give up saying "The sun is sinking" or to give the words a new meaning. In many contexts we preferred to stick to the old words and give them a new meaning which was not entirely new, but, on the contrary, *practically* the same as the old. The Greeks did not speak of the dangers of repressing instincts, but they did speak of the dangers of thwarting Dionysos, of neglecting Cypris for Diana, of forgetting Poseidon for Athena. We have eaten of the fruit of a garden we cannot forget, though we were never there, a garden we still look for though we can never find it . . .

Essay and Paper Topics for "Religious Practice and Reason"

1. Kant said that the three arguments for the existence of God—design, cosmological, and ontological—lead naturally from one to the other. Discuss each one, indicating whether or not you see any sort of logical progression.

2. Discuss whether or not you think Hick has answered Johnson's arguments that evil and suffering show there is no God.

3. Describe how Clifford and James each understand the duty people have with respect to what they believe. Which position seems the most reasonable? Why?

4. Compare what James says about the sources of belief with Hume's position in his essay on emotion and reason in ethics in Section 8.

5. Explain the position of those who think religious practice does not necessarily depend on the existence of God to be meaningful and rational.

6. Compare the views of James and Wisdom on religious faith.

7. Discuss what is meant by "God exists" and whether it is true, false, neither, or irrelevant.